E/MJ Operating Handbook of Mineral Surface Mining and Exploration

**Edited by
RICHARD HOPPE**

SENIOR EDITOR, Engineering and Mining Journal

Vol. 2-E/MJ Library of Operating Handbooks

E/MJ MINING INFORMATIONAL SERVICES
McGraw-Hill, Inc.
1221 Avenue of the Americas, New York, N.Y. 10020 U.S.A.

E/MJ OPERATING HANDBOOK OF SURFACE MINING

Copyright © 1978 by McGraw-Hill, Inc., New York, N. Y. All Rights Reserved. Printed in the United States of America. No part of this publication may be reproduced, stored in a retrieval system, or transmitted, in any form or by any means, electronic, mechanical, photocopying, recording, or otherwise, without the prior written permission of the publisher.

Library of Congress Catalog Card Number 78-4501.

07-019518-8

Foreword

For several decades to come, surface mining will continue to play a major role as the main source of much of the world's mineral wealth. Billions of tons of metallic ores, fertilizers, and associated waste products are mined from surface deposits each year around the world. This handbook was organized to provide the reader engaged in the search, design, and operation of such surface mines, with current, useful information of practical application. The articles were gleaned and edited from recent issues of *Engineering and Mining Journal*.

The latter half of the handbook deals exclusively with practices at dozens of operating mines—for a multitude of minerals, over most of the world's surface. Hopefully, it will provide the reader with a good picture of the state of the art. The range of practices described herein should be sufficiently wide for most readers to identify some problems, tools, and solutions applicable to their own areas of interest.

Serious problems currently afflict surface mining. These include: declining ore grades, increased waste removal, deeper excavations, skyrocketing fuel costs, inflation, expanded financing requirements, land withdrawals, excessive government intervention, expropriations, costly, mounting and wasteful paper work, and overriding concerns about the industry's effects on the environment.

The industry continues to cope—using brains, energy, organization and new tools.

E/MJ believes information is one of the industry's most important tools. Therefore, besides the monthly magazine, the *E/MJ Operating Handbook of Surface Mining* is the second of a series of planned publications covering such elements of the minerals industry as underground mining, mineral processing, labor and management, and the like.

E/MJ welcomes all comments and suggestions for improving future volumes and hopes you will find this information of value.

Richard Hoppe

Contents

Foreword	iii
Chapter 1—Surface Mining, Overview	**1**
Surface mining: the largest source of minerals for the US economy	2
Guide to understanding resources: the mining man's perspective	10
Major open-pit metal and non-metallic mines of the Free World	12
Chapter 2—Prospecting and Exploration	**17**
Discovery rate and exploration methods for metallic mineral deposits in US, 1940-1976	18
USGS Denver R&D group seeks practical uses for emerging prospecting technology	21
Remote sensing continues to open new horizons for ore seekers	25
Looking for minerals via satellite: a far-out approach to exploration	32
Rock geochemistry: a mixed bag of analytical techniques	40
Data storage and retrieval buy time for geologists	43
Aeromagnetic studies are versatile search tools	44
Hydrogeochemistry aids search for uranium, base metals	46
Geobotany, biogeochemistry target potential orebodies	47
New technique traces buried ancient stream channels in search of uranium	49
Induced polarization: a versatile tool	51
EM proves useful reconnaissance tool	52
Radiometry: refinements in uranium search soften energy crisis	55
Copper exploration restrained by resource nationalism and low metal prices	58
Project Radam maps the unknown in Brazil	62
CPRM: a catalyst in Brazilian exploration programs	66
Docegeo diversifies CVRD horizon with new discoveries	69
Appraising large-diameter core and percussion drilling for bulk samples	72
Nuclear logging system obtains 'bulk samples' from small boreholes	75
New technique enhances the art of bulk sampling placer deposits	78
Chapter 3—Finance, Engineering, and Reclamation	**81**
How to value a mineral property	82
Delaying debt during early development: a new approach to mine financing	86
How to cut risk of slope failure in designing optimum pit slopes	92
Pit slope displacement monitoring: an aid to open-pit mine operations	99
Select berm width to contain local failures	103
Open-pit engineering takes quantum leap	107
Choose the right vertical wet pit sump pump	110
High efficiency motors cut energy costs	119
Nomographs simplify cable tramway design	120
New survey instrument displays readings on both sides	123
Nomograph for in-situ uranium leaching	124
Water slurry properties	125
Environmental impacts focus on waste handling	126
Copper mine waters: good potential as medium for growing livestock forage	128
Georgia kaolin producers are reclaiming an acre of land for each acre mined	130
Homestake nears completion of project to impound tailings and recycle water	133

Chapter 4—Drilling and Blasting — 137

- Blasthole drilling economics: a look at the costs behind the costs — 138
- Tank-mounted rock drill — 141
- International mining exhibition — 142
- Rotary drills dominate in open pits — 143
- Drilling trends: improved accuracy and mobility — 147
- New bit concepts get tryouts at Sandia Labs — 149
- Joy demonstrates 'maxi' and 'mini' high-energy impactors — 151
- Explosives: their classification and characteristics — 152
- The chemistry and physics of explosives — 157
- Explosives: the mechanics of detonation — 167
- Commercial applications of explosives — 169
- How to select an explosive or blasting agent for a specific job — 172
- Aluminum additives impart energy and sensitivity to many explosives — 184
- Keeping the lid on flyrock in open pit blasting — 187

Chapter 5—Materials Handling and Transport — 193

- Ongoing evolution in dredge design pays off for world's placer miners — 194
- Many improvements in shovels and draglines — 202
- How to maximize efficiency of excavators in high altitude environment — 207
- Cat rolls out world's largest crawler tractor — 212
- New conveyor drive with feedback circuit: soft starts for loaded mine belts — 213
- Pena Colorada development includes 30-mi slurry pipeline — 215
- Polybutylene: for piping corrosive slurries — 216
- Trucks are key transport at most open pit mines — 216
- Open pit conveyors offer potential savings — 221
- Marconaflo strips silt and pumps new life into Caland — 222
- New rail corridor developed for Minas Gerais iron ore — 225
- Iron ore transport—Great Lakes are major artery for North American trade — 226

Chapter 6—Maintenance — 229

- Open pit maintenance backstops rising production demands — 230
- Troubleshooting the rotary compressor — 236
- Pointers on selection, use, and maintenance of hose — 240
- Reuseable pipe insulation saves energy and speeds up installation and maintenance — 242
- New anaerobic adhesive technology helps keep mine and plant equipment running — 244
- The dollars and sense of selecting wear materials — 248
- Diverse uses win an expanding market for rubber in mining — 254
- Rebuilding worn mine car wheels — 259
- New load sensing system keeps ore trucks well filled — 260
- Wire rope fittings — 260
- New choker hitch adjustment table for wire rope slings — 263
- Simulator helps train fire fighters — 264
- New device protects mine vehicles from fire — 265
- Wet suppression system controls dust problems at Inspiration — 266

Chapter 7—Copper Ore — 267

- Copper: the birth of modern mass mining of low grade ore — 268
- Open-pit copper mining in Arizona — 272
- Pinto Valley's deep, low-grade pit: success through good planning — 284
- Montana's giant Berkeley pit girds for another 22 years — 287
- Construction is well along at Aznalcollar — 290
- Rio Tinto Patino mines in northwest Spain — 292
- Panama: A major mine takes shape at Cerro Colorado — 294

Chapter 8—Iron Ore — 299
Iron ore: how producers tailor a product for iron making — 300
Hibbing Taconite starts up phase 1 with notable mining and milling features — 307
Minntac expanding to 18.5 million ltpy — 308
Hanna's Whitney mine — 310
Erie at Hoyt Lakes—a taconite pioneer — 311
Reserve — 312
Butler — 313
National — 314
Eagle Mountain moves 170,000 tpd of ore and waste — 314
Utah's Iron Springs district is a major western resource — 315
McKinley — 316
Republic transfers primary crusher to pit — 317
Lind-Greenway—mining two western Mesabi pits — 318
Tilden — 318
Empire expansion is second in decade — 320
Inland profits by proximity to Jackson County Iron — 321
Cliffs in Minnesota—Canisteo natural ores — 321
MacIntyre mines ilmenite-magnetite ores — 322
IOC—a study of logistics, based on varied resources — 322
Steep Rock has the deepest open pits in Canada — 324
Scully mine — 325
Caland — 326
Aguas Claras: programmed growth to 25 million tons of ore — 328
Samarco: major new materials handling concepts for iron ore — 332

Chapter 9—Bauxite — 335
Sangaredi pit in Guinea carves up a rich deposit of solid bauxite — 336
Sangaredi—an African plateau of bauxite — 339
Surinam: 62 years of bauxite development — 347
Guybau and Bermine: Digging deep for ore — 359
Jamaica: government partnership and recent declines shape industry's profile — 362
Trombetas: major bauxite reserves in search of a future — 374
Reynolds is Haiti's only bauxite producer — 377
Alcoa's Dominican bauxite mine uses solar drying — 378

Chapter 10—Phosphates — 381
Phosphates are vital to agriculture—and Florida mines for one-third the world — 382
Lee Creek may share link with Kidd Creek as the two Texasgulf
  units gear for expansions — 393

Chapter 11—Uranium — 395
Rapid building program puts RMEC into production of U_3O_8
  in Powder River Basin — 396
Wyoming uranium miners set sights on higher production — 400
In-situ leaching opens new uranium reserves in Texas — 405
Developers eye Texas potential for in-situ leaching — 413

Chapter 12—Other Surface Mines — 415
Placer mining's dwindling experts review vanishing technology — 416
How Cortez Gold Mines heap leached low grade gold ores
  at two Nevada properties — 419
Heap leaching will produce 85,000 oz/year of dore bullion
  for Smoky Mountain Mining — 424
Mining the beach for diamonds at CDM — 427
Kerr-McGee expands soda ash output nine-fold from Searls Lake brines — 434
Brines are source for iodine, bromine, and other minerals — 439
Petrosix: a Brazilian answer to oil shale technology — 439
New McDermitt mine joint venture emerges as dominant
  force in US mercury production — 442
Nevada barite output up sharply in '70s — 444

Index — 446

Chapter 1
Surface Mining, Overview

Surface mining: the largest source of minerals for the US economy 2
Guide to understanding resources: the mining man's perspective 10
Major open-pit metal and non-metallic mines of the Free World 12

Now at the midpoint of its productive life, Anaconda's Berkeley copper pit in Butte, Mont., recently passed the 1-billion-ton mark for material moved since 1955. Berkeley was once the largest US open-pit operation using truck haulage.

Surface mining: the largest source of minerals for the US economy

THE IMPORTANCE of open-pit mine production to modern industrial economies can hardly be overstated. In fact, development of mass production manufacturing techniques during the past 100 years or so, supplying a broad range of goods to US consumers, could not have proceeded at such a rapid pace had there not been a parallel development of large open-pit iron mines in northern Minnesota and on Michigan's Upper Peninsula and of open-pit copper mines in the southwestern US to supply manufacturers with low cost raw materials.

In 1975, US surface mines, excluding the categories of coal, sand and gravel, and stone, produced 786 million tons of crude ore—86% of the national total—while underground mines produced 123 million tons. Overburden removed at surface mines totaled 1.55 billion tons, very nearly double the crude ore tonnage, and the total materials handled reached 2.33 billion tons.

Minnesota, Arizona, and Florida (where phosphate rock mining accounts for the bulk of the surface-mined tonnage) were the three largest producers of crude ore from surface mines. The respective totals for these states during 1975 were 171 million, 159 million, and 156 million tons. In fourth place, far below the top three, was Utah, where the bulk of the 41 million tons of crude ore mined was produced at Kennecott's Bingham Canyon mine, the world's largest open pit.

When waste tonnages are added to crude ore totals, Arizona moves into first place in open-pit mining, at 606 million tons. Florida is second at 325 million tons, Minnesota third at 317 million tons, and Utah fourth at 159 million tons.

Outside the US, surface mining also contributes the major portion of the world's mineral supply, although the percentage of the total is not so large as in the US. A recent estimate places the world tonnage of surface-mined metallic ore at 1.2 billion tons, 57% of the total 2.1 billion tons. (In comparison with the US, the larger share contributed to world production by underground mines is attributable primarily to iron and copper operations.) For nonmetallic ores outside the US, surface

The new Metcalf pit of Phelps Dodge, 2 mi north of Morenci, was opened in 1975 and now mines nearly 110,000 tons of ore and waste daily. The orebody location is favorable, permitting both side-hill cuts and downhill haulage of ore.

Railroad mining at Morenci has been a successful operation since startup of the pit during World War II. The orebody has been mined since shortly after the Civil War, at first by underground methods. Reserves are still extensive.

Hibbing Taconite Co. came on stream in late 1976 with some of the largest surface mining equipment in use on Minnesota's Mesabi Range. In the pit, taconite is loaded into 170-ton haulage trucks by electric shovels equipped with 16-cu-yd dippers.

Material handled at US surface mines, 1975*

(000 short tons)

State	Crude ore	Waste	Total	State	Crude ore	Waste	Total
Alabama	3,690	5,860	9,550	Nebraska	145	—	145
Alaska	3,440	235	3,670	Nevada	25,900	63,400	89,300
Arizona	159,000	447,000	606,000	New Hampshire	W	—	W
Arkansas	4,210	8,640	12,800	New Jersey	11,200	2,070	13,300
California	20,800	71,300	92,100	New Mexico	31,500	122,000	153,000
Colorado	3,580	4,300	7,870	New York	6,600	6,880	13,500
Connecticut	277	5	282	North Carolina	10,800	23,300	34,100
Delaware	W	—	W	North Dakota	79	—	79
Florida	156,000	169,000	325,000	Ohio	3,500	—	3,500
Georgia	10,600	2,740	13,300	Oklahoma	2,290	11,400	13,700
Hawaii	388	5	393	Oregon	3,570	601	4,170
Idaho	6,680	36,000	42,700	Pennsylvania	2,390	11	2,400
Illinois	1,680	41	1,720	Rhode Island	—	—	—
Indiana	893	—	893	South Carolina	2,400	744	3,150
Iowa	1,850	2,410	4,270	South Dakota	381	6	387
Kansas	1,190	—	1,190	Tennessee	5,840	9,930	15,800
Kentucky	1,030	—	1,030	Texas	10,700	29,000	39,600
Louisiana	1,170	—	1,170	Utah	41,300	118,000	159,000
Maine	146	—	146	Vermont	W	W	W
Maryland	832	—	832	Virginia	2,250	11	2,260
Massachusetts	218	—	218	Washington	500	863	1,360
Michigan	30,500	33,000	63,500	West Virginia	339	—	339
Minnesota	171,000	145,000	317,000	Wisconsin	W	W	W
Mississippi	2,010	—	2,010	Wyoming	10,000	109,000	119,000
Missouri	2,390	1,740	4,130	Undistributed	3,890	51,300	55,200
Montana	26,500	69,100	95,600	**Totals**	**786,000**	**1,550,000**	**2,330,000**

Source: US Bureau of Mines. *Excludes coal, sand and gravel, stone, wells, ponds, and pumping operations. W—Withheld to avoid disclosing individual company confidential data; included in "Undistributed."

The Sangaredi open pit in Guinea, west Africa, is the single largest deposit of high grade bauxite in the world. Production started in 1973 and now exceeds 7 million mtpy, all mined by single-level railroad with no waste removal.

mines also supply the lion's share of the tonnage—1.2 billion of an estimated 1.5 billion mined, or 80% of the total.

Iron ore, the key metallic raw material for modern industry, is mined in large tonnages from surface operations in such diverse nations as Australia, India, Canada, Venezuela, Brazil, Liberia, Mauritania, Peru, and South Africa, among others. World bauxite supplies originate primarily at surface mines, with major producers including Jamaica, Guinea, Australia, the Dominican Republic, Surinam, Greece, and Yugoslavia. Open-pit copper mines are found in Chile, Peru, Zambia, Zaire, the Philippines, Papua New Guinea, Spain, South Africa, Mexico, Ireland, and a number of other nations. Many other commodities also move to world markets from surface mining operations—lead, zinc, manganese, nickel, fluorspar, and diamonds among them. This issue of E/MJ describes a number of surface mines in the US and elsewhere, offering insights into surface mining practice as it stands in mid-1977.

Equipment continues quiet evolution

The evolutionary development of materials handling equipment has been a key force in modern open-pit mining practice, and manufacturers continue to supply mine operators with ever-improving explosives and larger and more efficient drilling, loading, and hauling equipment. The volume and type of overburden to be removed and the degree of ore control required strongly influence deliberations on equipment selection, along with planned daily production rate, anticipated life of the property, overburden-to-ore ratio, pit parameters, capital availability, and climate.

Shovel-and-truck loading and haulage equipment have become the predominant means for moving ore out of the pit at most large metallic ore mines, but some operators also make extensive use of front-end wheel loaders and a few move ore by rail haulage or on conveyor systems. At nonmetallic mines, such as the Florida phosphate operations and the Georgia kaolin mines, the softer nature of overburden and ore permits excavation with draglines or scrapers, and ore may be slurried for pipeline transport to processing plants.

Rotary drills now predominate for blasthole drilling at large open-pit mines. In taconites, holes up to 17-in. diameter are drilled to 65 ft in a single pass, and drills with pull-down forces of 130,000 lb and automated control of major functions are common. Such rigs can penetrate even the hardest formations at 30 to 50 ft per

Overburden removal is under way in preparation for mining the Aznalcollar orebody of Andaluza de Piritas in southwest Spain. The pit will be Europe's largest surface metal mine and will eventually reach a depth of 300 m below the surface.

hr. Drill manufacturers feel that recently introduced automation reduces maintenance and repair costs and increases availability, thus cutting down on overall costs per ton of material drilled.

Another improvement in drilling technology (discussed in greater detail in the June 1976 issue of E/MJ, p 187) is improved bit design. Rotary blasthole bits can now attack quartzites and taconites—once the province of down-the-hole drilling and jet piercing. Bit improvements include changes in the metallurgy of tungsten-carbide buttons, use of larger numbers of smaller inserts, specially shaped inserts, two-tier bits, larger bit bearings, and solid lubricants for bearing thrust faces. Another development is the use of stabilizers on the bit to maintain alignment during collaring, for improved back-reaming and better bearing and cutter structure loading during drilling.

Electric shovels having dipper capacities in the 12-yd to 25-yd capacity range are the most important advance in loading equipment during the past 10 years. These massive units provide exceptional availability around the clock through many years of service.

Selection of the largest possible shovel size for a given operation usually yields advantages in lower operating costs per ton moved, lower capital and labor costs, and fewer operating faces. However, the capability of blending ore and controlling grade diminishes as shovel size increases.

Haulage trucks have been scaled up to meet demands for moving ever-larger tonnages of ore and waste, with the prototype 350-ton-capacity Terex Model 33-19 being the largest yet built. Terex put the 33-19 through two years of testing at the Eagle Mountain mine of Kaiser Steel Corp. in California and expects to build more of these units soon. The availability of this truck and the 200-ton-capacity haulers offered by a number of manufacturers will influence future open-pit design. However, for the present, trucks of 170-ton capacity or smaller are in more widespread use.

At the Lonesome mine of Brewster Phosphates in Hillsborough County, Florida, a 2¾-mi belt conveyor system moves deslimed phosphate matrix to the plant on the top belt, and flotation plant sand tailings to reclamation areas on the return side. The 54-in. belt, which travels 885 ft per min, is driven by steel-belted radial tires in drive modules spaced an average of 1,200 ft apart. The system, designed and built by Continental Conveyor and Equipment Co. and B. F. Goodrich Co., has 11 drive modules. It is reported to offer lower operating and maintenance costs than the slurry pipeline

An elevating scraper (above) takes on a load of overburden at American Industrial Clay's kaolin mine near Deepstep, Ga., while a 1-yd dragline (below) loads raw kaolin into a portable blunger, for slurrying and pipeline transport to processing plant.

A 6-yd B-E dragline mines and stockpiles kaolin at Thiele Kaolin's Avant mine. Front end-loaders load the material into trucks for transport to a stationary blunger outside the pit.

systems in use at most Florida phosphate mines. A conveyor system to move ore and waste out of Duval's Sierrita open-pit copper mine in Arizona is described in detail in this issue.

While equipment for surface mining has been growing in size and sophistication, such improvements have not been sufficient to keep annual increases in output per man-hour in surface mining on a par with productivity of other manufacturing industries—in the US and elsewhere in the world—during the past 10 years. Labor productivity in the US copper industry, for example, has been increasing at the rate of 3.2% per year. In Japan, the productivity growth rate for all manufacturing has been 12.9% per year; in West Germany, 5.8%; in Canada, 4.7%; and in the US, 3.4%.

S. D. Michaelson, chief engineer of the Metal Mining Div. of Kennecott Copper Corp., has suggested that to counter this trend, R&D should be undertaken on a scale large enough to develop wholly new technologies, in contrast to the current approach of simply increasing equipment size in a framework of conventional open-pit layouts and practices, which offers only relatively small improvements in productivity.

The impact of environmental regulations

Since Jan. 1, 1970, when the National Environmental Policy Act was signed, a flood of environmental legislation has been enacted that in one way or another affects mine operations. An article by James R. Walpole,[1] assistant general counsel for the American Mining Congress, singled out the following federal enactments: The Clean Air Act, The Noise Control Act of 1972, The Coastal Zone Management Act of 1972, The Ocean Dumping Act, The Marine Protection, Research and Sanctuaries Act of 1972, The Endangered Species Act of 1973, The Federal Insecticide, Fungicide and Rodenticide Act, The Energy Supply and Environmental Coordination Act of 1974, The Federal Water Pollution Control Act, The Safe Drinking Water Act, The Toxic Substances Control Act, and The Resources Conservation and Recovery Act of 1976.

"Statutes, some of which are listed above, provide the authority for a federal agency or department to develop and promulgate rules and regulations to implement and enforce regulatory programs," Walpole noted. "Keeping in mind the total number of statutes, and recognizing the broad and general scope of many of them, it is not surprising that the rules and regulations, generated by agency and department personnel, appear to be endless.

"Normally, regulatory programs are designed to accommodate one statute, or very often, one portion of one statute. The personnel developing one set of regulations oftentimes have no knowledge or understanding of related work being done on regulations for another statute or another portion of the same statute. In many instances, the regulatory programs designed to control or eliminate a 'pollution' situation cause another 'pollution' problem. For example, in resolving certain water pollution problems, waste materials must be disposed of

The Greystone barite mine of Dresser Minerals produces 250,000 tpy of barite, making it the largest source of barite used for drilling mud in the US and one of the largest in the world. The mine is south of Battle Mountain, Nev.

through processes which may cause air pollution, or the seepage of waste material into drinking water supplies, or create solid waste problems."

Walpole added: "An example of how a regulation can have serious detrimental effects can be seen in the Environmental Protection Agency proposed regulations to control state underground injection control programs (pursuant to the Safe Drinking Water Act). The proposed regulations were designed to protect existing and potential drinking water supplies. However, they could prohibit or seriously affect various types of solution mining in the US, and solution mining can be one of the more environmentally sound methods of extracting mineral material from the ground."

Of immediate concern to surface mine operators are legislative proposals now in the hopper. A surface mining act regulating coal mine operations will probably be passed during 1977 and signed into law by President Carter. Open-pit hardrock mine operators find cause for concern in the suggestions by some environmentalists and legislators that strip mine reclamation imposed on the coal industry be used as a model for open-pit regulations for western copper mines and Minnesota and Michigan iron mines or that open-pit mines be "returned to their original contour."

Mine operators have invested heavily in reclamation programs when reclamation is possible. Kaolin producers in Georgia, working shallow, nearly flat-lying beds, are compiling a noteworthy record in restoring an acre of ground for each acre mined. However, there is no practical way to restore deep copper and iron ore pits, and any legislation affecting such mines must be tailored to their economic and operating realities. Such legislation will have special importance in the extent to which it affects future mine development. If future regulations are too demanding, potential surface mines will remain undeveloped, and radical adjustments will have to be made in the sources of US minerals supply—adjustments that are obvious in light of the statistics cited at the beginning of this report.

Some critics, lacking the wit to understand or the courage to acknowledge the extent to which their own well-being depends on surface-mined products, view surface mining as nothing more than gutting the earth. Such sentiment is largely responsible for the wave of environmental and land withdrawal legislation that has swept across the mining industry during the past 10 years. Perhaps, having corrected the excesses characteristic of some surface mine operations in the past, public sentiment may eventually reacquaint itself with the key role played by mined products in modern economic life.

Withdrawals also curtail development

Environmental regulations for operating mines are

How Alaska Native Claims Settlement Act affects mineral withdrawals

Mining Law (metalliferous)
Total US lands owned in Alaska	353,383,000
Reserve acreage prior to ANCSA, including open National Forest lands	72,919,000
Acquired lands	17,000
State selected lands, patents, tentative approval of patents (unperfected entries)	25,500,000
Net public domain open to location prior to ANCSA	254,947,000
Acres withdrawn from metalliferous location (utility corridor)	2,898,000
Lands open to metalliferous location after ANCSA	46,000,000
Net lands withdrawn from metalliferous and nonmetalliferous location by ANCSA	**206,049,000**

Mining Law (nonmetalliferous only)
Net public domain open to location prior to ANCSA	254,947,000
Withdrawn for utility corridor	5,343,000
Withdrawn from metalliferous and nonmetalliferous by ANCSA	206,049,000
Net withdrawn from nonmetalliferous only by ANCSA	**43,555,000**

Leasing laws
Total US lands owned in Alaska	353,383,000
Reserved acreage prior to ANCSA, including open national forest lands	72,919,000
Lands selected by states, patents, and tentative approval of patents (unperfected entries)	25,500,000
Area withdrawn for the utility corridor	5,343,000
Area withdrawn from leasing by ANCSA	**249,621,000**

Source: Bennethum and Lee.

---

only one of the limitations government has placed on future US mine development—and perhaps not the most important one. Over the past decade, large blocks of public lands have been withdrawn from mineral exploration and development, and these withdrawals will surely keep some potential mines out of production.

A widely quoted study by Bennethum and Lee[2] makes these observations: "History has shown that after lands have been withdrawn for certain uses, only rarely are they reopened by a revocation of the withdrawal specifically to allow mineral exploration and development to again occur. Realistically, nothing short of a national emergency will provide the incentive for reopening many of these withdrawn lands to mineral development."

Because withdrawals prohibit even mineral exploration, they restrict both surface and underground mining alike.

Mining on public lands is governed by the Mining Law of 1872 and the Mineral Leasing Act of 1920. The Mining Law applies to all minerals except oil, gas, coal, phosphate, sodium, oil shale, sulphur, potash, and certain other hydrocarbons and nonmetallics that are provided for under the Mineral Leasing Act. As of 1974, 742 million acres of land were subject to the Mining Law and 824 were subject to the Leasing Act, according to Bennethum and Lee. Of the 742 million acres subject to the Mining Law, 53% were withdrawn from mineral entry and another 14% were classified as de facto withdrawals. These figures had risen from a combined total of about 17% in 1968, when the current wave of withdrawals was ushered in. Under the Leasing Act, withdrawn lands increased from 17% to 64% of the available total during the years from 1968 to 1974, while de facto withdrawals rose from 7% to 9%. Much of the recently withdrawn land is located in Alaska. (See table.)

"The mining industry everywhere faces skirmishes and fire fights over withdrawal of public land from mineral activity," commented H. Stanley Dempsey,[3] general attorney, western area, Amax Inc. "It is not merely a fire fight which is being waged by the champions of withdrawal in Alaska, however. Large percentages of our remaining public domain are at stake there."

What has happened in Alaska cannot be called land use planning, Dempsey charges, but at best represents a negative land use policy that precludes wise use of resources: "So far as knowledge of mineral resources in Alaska is concerned, few of the facts are in. We have barely scratched the surface. We simply do not know how extensive Alaska's mineral resources are, and we do not know where they are. The Bureau of Mines has been given $600,000 for purposes of evaluating the 80 million acres withdrawn for (d)(2) selection [for inclusion in the National Parks, National Forests, Wildlife Refuges, or Wild and Scenic Rivers systems]. It is doubtful that the results of their studies will contribute in any measurable way to our appreciation of the mineral potential of these vast areas. Certainly it would seem unwise to withdraw these large areas irrevocably from mineral activities after such a cursory glance at their potential. Nevertheless, this is happening." □

Protected by a man-made sea wall, CDM mines diamondiferous beach gravels using this BWE to strip overlying sands.

References

1) Walpole, J. R., "An Environmental Sketch of 1976," MINING CONGRESS JOURNAL, February 1977.
2) Bennethum, G., and L. C. Lee, "Is Our Account Overdrawn?," MINING CONGRESS JOURNAL, September 1975.
3) Dempsey, H. S., "Mining in Alaska—the Effects of Withdrawals," MINING CONGRESS JOURNAL, December 1976.

Guide to understanding resources: the mining man's perspective

A HIGHLY ORGANIZED SUMMARY of world mineral resources, their importance to society, and their abundance and nature was recently published by the American Institute of Professional Geologists. Titled "Guide: Understanding Mineral Resources," by Dr. James R. Dunn of Dunn Geoscience, the 30-page document is marked "tentative" because it is undergoing continuous review and update. Its primary purpose is to give geologists a data base for explaining to the general public the significance of the mining industry. The document summarizes the abundance and distribution of both resources and reserves; describes briefly some interrelationships of minerals and other natural resources, and discusses some of the economic, political, technical, and social factors that influence development and production of mineral resources.

The importance of mineral resources

The document begins by citing historical and economic examples of the importance of mineral resources to society. Historically, civilizations have been identified by their ability to utilize minerals (Stone Age, Bronze Age, Iron Age, Atomic Age). Today, a nation's standard of living, livelihood, and national security are dependent upon the availability and continuing flow of minerals and fuels, the guide says. Although their direct contribution to the GNP is not large (about 1% in the US), mineral resources are vitally important to the national wellbeing, quality of life, and survival as a world power.

The value of mineral materials to societies of the world is evident in virtually every aspect of living. Shelter and transportation are two necessities that draw heavily on the mineral industry for raw materials. Most basic raw materials used by the people of the world are, in fact, obtained from only four industries: mining, drilling (including oil, gas, water, and geothermal steam), agriculture, and forestry.

The document also notes that there is frequently a correlation between the ability of countries to develop and utilize mineral resources and their economic and political stability. The least stable countries tend to have the least broadly based mineral development.

The minerals industry is not only directly essential to all elements of civilization but for the US, it also has indirectly increased the size of forests, recreational resources, ground water resources, and crop yields, according to the guide. Readily available mineral materials are thus not only critical to civilization, but are critically important to conservation of other earth resources.

Abundance and distribution of resources

For the benefit of non-geologists, this section of the guide starts out with basic definitions of minerals, rocks, ores, and concentrates, then graduates to the distinction between resources ("potential" sources) and reserves (well defined, economically workable deposits), and finally arrives at the subtler distinctions between hypothetical, speculative, and identified subeconomic resources.

In discussing resource quantities, the document makes it clear that the earth's non-fuel mineral resources are enormous—in fact, virtually inexhaustible. Table 1 summarizes the quantity and gross value of several mineral materials occurring in an average cubic mile of the earth's crust. (Bear in mind that the wildest projections of technology and economic viability will not make all the minerals in that cubic mile recoverable.) The document draws on the data of mineral economists Brooks and Andrews (1974), who stated: "The literal notion of running out of mineral supplies is ridiculous," although the point at which mineral *recovery* becomes economic (or uneconomic) is exceedingly complex and varies from commodity to commodity.

Whereas the quantities of minerals appear almost limitless, their distribution is such that in any defined small area, the number of potentially important materials is limited. "To qualify as ore, the mineral concentration must usually be higher than that found in the average crust," according to the guide. Table 2 shows the concentration needed to qualify some common mineral materials as ore.

A natural observation in the history of mineral production is that as time passes, lower and lower grades of ore are mined, primarily because of depletion of higher grade minerals. Fortunately, technological innovations have managed to keep most mineral prices low (when measured in constant dollars).

The document outlines several other "rules regarding mineral resource abundance and use," to help define "a useful view of mineral resources":

1) The elements (and their compounds) in the earth's crust are used by mankind roughly in the order of their abundance (i.e., the most abundant are used most). The eight most abundant elements in the earth's crust, in order of decreasing abundance, are oxygen, silicon, aluminum, iron, calcium, sodium, potassium, and magnesium.

Table 1—Quantity and value of selected materials occurring in 1 cu mi of earth's crust

Material	Quantity[1] (000 st)	Average 1974 price[2] (per ton)	Gross value ($ million)	Total years of 'reserves' at present consumption rate
Aluminum	898,000	$ 682	$612,000	64
Potash (K_2O)	342,000	46	15,700	589
Iron	546,000	122	66,700	0.41
Magnesium	228,000	1,160	264,000	1,640
Manganese	10,090	1,750	175,000	0.94
Zinc	1,420	718	1,020	0.43
Copper	765	1,540	1,180	0.14
Nickel	871	3,380	2,940	1.13

1) Modified from Mason (1966). 2) Sources: USBM and USGS.
Note: This table is not to be construed as indicating that the average of the earth's crust can or will ever be ore. The forms that elements and their compounds take, and the concentration of mineral materials, are critical to what is definable as ore. What is clearly shown in the table is that the total quantity of the elements is enormously large.

2) Any rock or mineral material has potential value under some set of technical, cultural, or economic conditions. It follows that the whole of the earth's accessible crust (57,506,000 sq mi of continental crust to an unknown depth plus unmeasured oceanic crust) is potentially valuable. Also, the parameters that determine a mineral "reserve" are time-sensitive and culture-sensitive, and are dependent upon economics, need, and technology. Mineral reserves "come and go," so to speak.

3) Any large, accessible, high concentration of virtually any mineral substance is likely to have great value.

4) The minerals that are recoverable from reserves under any one set of engineering, economic, and sociologic conditions are always finite. Reserves are a manmade concept, and proving (measuring) reserves is rarely economic beyond the number of years needed to amortize the original mining investment (about 20 years in most cases).

5) The mineral quantity recoverable from the world's measurable ore reserves of any commodity at any given time is only a trivial fraction of the total quantity of that mineral in the crust. This is true because the total quantity of a given mineral in the crust is virtually limitless.

6) The total amount of metals recoverable increases enormously as the grade of the ore considered workable at any given time decreases. At one extreme is exceptionally high grade ore—extremely limited in quantity. On the other hand, if rock containing the average copper content of the continental crust were ever to become economic, the quantity of copper "ore" available in only the top mile of half the crust would be about 4 million times the world's current annual consumption.

7) In a freely-operating world market system, the quantity of mineral materials present in reserves tends to be directly proportional to demand. This is, of course, the classic economic law of supply and demand. For a mineral for which there is no demand, reserves are not likely to have been tested. For example, there were almost no reserves of uranium until the 1940s, when uranium became valuable.

8) In a free market system, reserves of most mineral commodities rise with rising price, and the price falls when supply catches up with demand. Another classic rule of economics, this often presents a devastating problem for the mineral industry, since price fluctuations can cause considerable hardship.

9) The total mineral resources available are roughly proportional to the amount of land on which mineral operations are possible. In other words, a 50% reduction in the land on which mineral developments are possible can result in a 50% reduction of the mineral resource base. The document argues: "Society does not run out of many of its mineral resources, but it may run out of places where they can be developed."

According to the document, the major cause of reduction of the world's mineral resources base is the prevention of mining by various forms of "cultural nullification"—largely the result of adverse zoning restrictions and construction atop mineral deposits. Adverse zoning and other forms of nullification related to urbanization alone may have reduced the effective total mineral supply by as much as 20% in the US, the guide estimates.

Resources management and mismanagement

A substantial portion of the document is given over to summarizing problems in mineral resource management and suggesting methods of bringing that management more in line with public interest. Among the suggestions:

- Minimize conditions that encourage "high-grading"

Table 2—Concentrations required to classify selected metals as 'ores'[1]

Metal	% weight in earth's crust	Minimum % for profitable extraction[2]	Concentration multiple needed for an orebody
Al	8.13	30	4
Fe	5.00	30	6
Mn	0.10	35	350
Cr	0.02	30	1,500
Cu	0.007	1	140
Ni	0.008	1.5	175
Zn	0.013	4	300
Sn	0.004	1	250
Pb	0.0016	4	2,500
U	0.0002	0.1	500

1) Modified from Mason (1966).
2) The current (1975) percentages needed for profitable extraction are significantly lower for some metals than those listed here.

practices (removing the best ore first).

- Make mineral lands more readily available (see rule 9).
- Show the value of minerals to society.
- Reduce the financial exposure of exploration through risk-sharing between companies, increased tax write-offs, etc.
- Reduce the lead time from exploration to mining, thus avoiding tying up large amounts of capital for long periods.
- Improve the education of technical personnel, a step that also reduces exploration risks.
- Measure and define reserves and identify potential resource areas (where realistic). Such inventories aid in planning for mineral development.
- Realize the significant differences between high-bulk, low-value, "transport-sensitive" minerals and high-value minerals.
- Maintain a vigorous domestic mineral industry, to achieve immediate economic benefits, a stronger negotiating position in foreign mineral trade, and a stronger national defense position.
- Maintain stockpiles of minerals, including petroleum products, both for defense and for bargaining strength in international markets.
- Plan for sequential, multiple uses for mineral land wherever possible, to enhance long term values. Space created by mining can be exceedingly valuable—as demonstrated by the underground warehouses in the Kansas City area.
- Encourage the sharing of exploration data among companies, to reduce immediate exploration costs and to increase the probability of success. Certainly, data should not be shared until the exploring entity has gained the appropriate benefits.
- Assure that product specifications aim at both quality and conservation. It should be remembered that mineral product specifications have an influence on potential reserves.

Because of the extreme complexity of the subject covered by this guide, a large number of reviewers from government, industry, and education were consulted prior to the final draft, to obtain the broadest base of agreement possible. The document (in loose-leaf form) is available at $3 per copy for AIPG members and $6 for non-members. Write to: American Institute of Professional Geologists, PO Box 957, Golden, Colo. 80401. □

Two Arizona copper mines: the Cyprus Pima pit at lower left and the Mission pit of Asarco at upper right.

Major open-pit metal and nonmetallic mines of the Free World

(production greater than 500,000 tpy of ore)

Company	Mine or location	Ore produced	Tonnage size	Mill capacity (tpd)	Company	Mine or location	Ore produced	Tonnage size	Mill capacity (tpd)
				UNITED	STATES				
ARIZONA					**ARKANSAS**				
Anamax Mining Co.	Twin Buttes	Copper	2	40,000					
Asarco Inc.	Mission	Cu, Ag, Mo	2	22,500	Aluminum Co. of America	Bauxite	Bauxite	3	
	Silver Bell	Cu, Mo, Ag	2	11,000	Reynolds Mining Corp.	Arkansas Mines	Bauxite	3	
	Sacaton	Copper	2	9,000					
	San Xavier	Copper	2	4,000	**CALIFORNIA**				
Cities Service Co.	Miami	Copper	2	14,000					
	Pinto Valley	Cu, Mo	1	40,000	H. M. Holloway Inc.	Lost Hills	Gypsum	3	3,000
Cyprus Johnson Copper Co.	Benson	Copper	2		Johns-Manville Products Corp.	Lompoc	Nonmetallic	3	1,100
Cyprus Mines Corp.	Bagdad	Cu, Mo, Ag	2	6,000	Kaiser Aluminum & Chemical Corp.	Salinas	Dolomite	3	2,400
Cyprus Pima Mining Co.	Pima	Cu, Ag, Mo	1	53,500	Kaiser Steel Corp.	Eagle Mountain	Iron	2	50,000
Duval Corp.	Mineral Park	Cu, Mo, Ag	2	17,000	Pfizer Inc.	Lucerne Valley	Limestone	3	NA
	Esperanza	Cu, Mo, Ag	2	19,000	Standard Slag Co.	Beck Iron	Magnetite	3	2,000
Duval Sierrita Corp.	Sierrita	Cu, Mo, Ag	1	85,000	Superior Gypsum Co.	Superior	Gypsum	3	
Inspiration Cons. Copper Co.	Inspiration	Cu, Ag, Au	2	20,000	U.S. Borax & Chem. Corp.	Boron	Boron	2	
	Christmas	Copper	2	6,000					
	Ox Hide	Copper	2		**FLORIDA**				
Kennecott Copper Corp.	Ray	Copper	1	25,400					
Phelps Dodge Corp.	Morenci	Copper	1	60,000	Agrico Chemical Co.	Pierce	Phosphate	2	NA
	New Cornelia	Copper	2	34,000	American Cyanamid Co.	Bradley	Phosphate	2	24,000
Ranchers Explor. & Devel. Corp.	Bluebird	Copper	2		Borden Inc.	Tenoroc	Phosphate	3	NA

Editor's note: The source for this table is the Master Data Bank of the E/MJ International Directory of Mining and Mineral Processing Operations, which also offers information on underground mines and on a substantial number of open-pit mines producing less than 500,000 tpy of ore.

Tonnage size ranges, annual ore production:
1—Over 10 million tpy.
2—1 to 10 million tpy.
3—500,000 to 1 million tpy.
NA—Tonnage capacity not available.
∗ —Tonnage reflects combined open-pit and underground operations
(U)—Under development.

Company	Mine or location	Ore produced	Tonnage size	Mill capacity (tpd)
Brewster Phosphates	Haynsworth	Phosphate	1	28,800
	Lonesome	Phosphate	NA(U)	
E. I. du Pont de Nemours	Highland	Ti, Zr, Cu	2	24,000
	Trail Ridge	Ti, Zr, Al	2	24,000
Freeport Chemical Co.	Rockland	Phosphate	2	21,600
W. R. Grace & Co.	Bartow	Phosphate	2	20,000
International Minerals & Chem. Corp.	Bartow	Phosphate	2	33,000
	Clear Springs	Phosphate	2	
	Kingsford	Phosphate	2	
	Noralyn	Phosphate	2	
Mobil Chemical Co.	Nichols	Phosphate	2	NA
	Fort Meade	Phosphate	2	NA
Occidental Chemical Co.	Suwannee River	Phosphate	2	36,000
Swift Agricultural Chem. Div.	Silver City	Phosphate	2	4,500
	Watson	Phosphate	2	10,000
USS Agri-Chemicals	Fort Meade	Phosphate	NA	NA

GEORGIA

Company	Mine or location	Ore produced	Tonnage size	Mill capacity (tpd)
Engelhard Minerals & Chem. Corp.	Edgar	Kaolin	2	3,600

IDAHO

Company	Mine or location	Ore produced	Tonnage size	Mill capacity (tpd)
Monsanto Industrial Chemicals Co.	Soda Springs	Phosphate	2	
J. R. Simplot Co.	Gay	Phosphate	2	
	Conda	Phosphate	3	2,900
	Centennial	Phosphate	NA	

MASSACHUSETTS

Company	Mine or location	Ore produced	Tonnage size	Mill capacity (tpd)
Pfizer Inc.	Adams	Limestone	3	NA

MICHIGAN

Company	Mine or location	Ore produced	Tonnage size	Mill capacity (tpd)
Empire Iron Mining Co.	Ishpeming	Iron	1	31,000
Hanna Mining Co.	Groveland	Iron	2	14,300
Marquette Iron Mining Co.	Republic	Iron	2	23,500
Tilden Mining Co.	Cleveland	Iron	2	NA
United States Gypsum Co.	Alabaster	Gypsum	3	

MINNESOTA

Company	Mine or location	Ore produced	Tonnage size	Mill capacity (tpd)
Cleveland-Cliffs Iron Co.	Canisteo	Iron	2*	30,000
Erie Mining Co.	Hoyt Lake	Taconite	1	NA
Eveleth Taconite Co.	Thunderbird	Taconite	2	
Hanna Mining Co.	National Steel	Iron	2	24,000
	Butler	Iron	2	22,300
	Whitney	Iron	2	24,000
Hibbing Taconite Co.	Hibbing	Taconite		
Jones & Laughlin Steel Corp.	Hill Annex	Iron	2	
	Lind & Greenway	Iron	2	NA
	McKinley	Iron	2	NA
Pittsburgh Pacific Co.	Mesabi	Iron	3	
	Neville	Iron	3	8,400
	Cuyuna	Iron	NA	
Reserve Mining Co.	Babbitt	Taconite	1	
Rhude & Fryberger Inc.	Rand	Iron	2	
United States Steel Corp.	Arcturus	Iron	NA	NA
	Plummer	Iron	2	NA
	Stephens	Iron	2	
	Sherman	Iron	2	NA
	Minntac	Iron	1	NA
	Rouchleau	Iron	3	NA

MONTANA

Company	Mine or location	Ore produced	Tonnage size	Mill capacity (tpd)
Anaconda Co.	Butte	Cu, Ag, Au	1*	50,000
W. R. Grace & Co.	Libby	Vermiculite	2	3,600

NEVADA

Company	Mine or location	Ore produced	Tonnage size	Mill capacity (tpd)
Anaconda Co.	Yerington	Copper	1	30,700
Basic Inc.	Gabbs	Magnesite, clay	3	
Carlin Gold Mining Co.	Carlin	Gold, mercury	2	2,500
Cortez Gold Mines	Cortez	Gold	3	2,200
Duval Corp.	Battle Mountain	Cu, Au, Ag	2	4,600
Kennecott Copper Corp.	McGill	Copper	2	21,500

NEW JERSEY

Company	Mine or location	Ore produced	Tonnage size	Mill capacity (tpd)
SCM Corp.	Lakehurst	Ilmenite, silica	2	8,000

NEW MEXICO

Company	Mine or location	Ore produced	Tonnage size	Mill capacity (tpd)
Anaconda Co.	Jackpile-Paguate	Uranium	2	2,300
Kennecott Copper Corp.	Chino	Cu, Mo	2	22,000
Molycorp Inc.	Questa	Molybdenum	2	16,500
Phelps Dodge Corp.	Tyrone	Cu, Au, Ag	1	50,000
USNR Mining & Minerals Inc.	Silver City	Copper	3	
U. V. Industries Inc.	Continental	Copper, zinc	3*	5,000

NEW YORK

Company	Mine or location	Ore produced	Tonnage size	Mill capacity (tpd)
Jones & Laughlin Steel Corp.	Benson	Iron	2	17,000

NORTH CAROLINA

Company	Mine or location	Ore produced	Tonnage size	Mill capacity (tpd)
Foote Mineral Co.	Kings Mountain	Feldspar, silica, mica	3	NA
Powhatan Mining Co.	Bakersville	Asbestos	3	
Texasgulf Inc.	Lee Creek	Phosphate	2	25,000

OHIO

Company	Mine or location	Ore produced	Tonnage size	Mill capacity (tpd)
Basic Inc.	Fostoria	Dolomite	2	
Pfizer Inc.	Gibsonburg	Dolomite	3	NA

OREGON

Company	Mine or location	Ore produced	Tonnage size	Mill capacity (tpd)
Earth Resources Co.	DeLamar	Gold, silver	3	1,700(U)
Hanna Mining Co.	Nickel Mountain	Nickel	2	

TENNESSEE

Company	Mine or location	Ore produced	Tonnage size	Mill capacity (tpd)
Monsanto Industrial Chem. Co.	Columbia	Phosphate	2	10,000
Stauffer Chemical Co.	Globe	Phosphate	4	2,000
M. C. West Inc.	Columbia	Phosphate	2	

TEXAS

Company	Mine or location	Ore produced	Tonnage size	Mill capacity (tpd)
Dresser Minerals	Kosse	Silica, kaolin	3	2,000
Lone Star Steel Co.	Lone Star	Iron	2	31,920

UTAH

Company	Mine or location	Ore produced	Tonnage size	Mill capacity (tpd)
CF&I Steel Corp.	Comstock	Iron	3	
Kennecott Copper Corp.	Utah Copper	Cu, Mo, Au, Ag, Pt	1	108,500
Stauffer Chemical Co.	Vernal-Phoston	Phosphate	3	2,000

VERMONT

Company	Mine or location	Ore produced	Tonnage size	Mill capacity (tpd)
Vermont Asbestos Group Inc.	Hyde Park	Asbestos	3	3,500

VIRGINIA

Company	Mine or location	Ore produced	Tonnage size	Mill capacity (tpd)
Engelhard Minerals & Chem. Corp.	Chemstone	Limestone	3	1,750

WISCONSIN

Company	Mine or location	Ore produced	Tonnage size	Mill capacity (tpd)
Jackson County Iron Co.	Black River Falls	Iron	3	NA

WYOMING

Company	Mine or location	Ore produced	Tonnage size	Mill capacity (tpd)
Exxon Co.	Highland	Uranium	3	2,000
United States Steel Corp.	Atlantic City	Taconite	2	NA

CANADA

BRITISH COLUMBIA

Company	Mine or location	Ore produced	Tonnage size	Mill capacity (tpd)
Bethlehem Copper Corp.	Ashcroft	Cu, Ag, Au	2	17,700
Brenda Mines Ltd.	Brenda	Cu, Mo	1	24,000
Canex Placer Ltd.	Endako	Molybdenum	2	28,000
Cassiar Asbestos Corp. Ltd.	Cassiar	Asbestos	3	4,200
Gibraltar Mines Ltd.	Gibraltar	Copper	1	41,000
Granby Mining Corp.	Phoenix	Cu, Au, Ag	4	2,750
Granisle Copper Ltd.	Granisle	Cu, Au, Ag	2	14,000
Highmont Mining Corp. Ltd.	Highmont	Cu, Mo	2	25,000
Lornex Mining Corp. Ltd.	Logan Lake	Cu, Mo	1	45,000
Noranda Mines Ltd.	Bell Copper	Copper	2	11,500
Red Mountain Mines Ltd.	Rossland		4	700
Similkameen Mining Co. Ltd.	Ingerbelle	Cu, Au, Ag	2	15,000
Texada Mines Ltd.	Texada	Magnetite, copper	2	3,400
Utah Mines Ltd.	Island Copper	Cu, Au, Mo	1	38,000
Wesfrob Mines Ltd.	Tasu	Iron, copper	2*	NA

MANITOBA

Company	Mine or location	Ore produced	Tonnage size	Mill capacity (tpd)
Inco Ltd.	Pipe	Nickel	2	
Sherritt Gordon Mines Ltd.	Ruttan	Copper, zinc	2	10,000

E/MJ OPERATING HANDBOOK OF SURFACE MINING

Company	Mine or location	Ore produced	Tonnage size	Mill capacity (tpd)
NEWFOUNDLAND & LABRADOR				
Advocate Mines Ltd.	Baie Verte, Nfld.	Asbestos	2	5,000
Iron Ore Co. of Canada	Carol Lake, Nfld.	Iron	1	NA
Wabush Mines	Scully, Labrador	Hematite	1	50,000
NEW BRUNSWICK				
Brunswick Mining & Smelting Corp. Ltd.	Bathurst	Zn, Pb, Cu, Ag	2*	9,850
NOVA SCOTIA				
Fundy Gypsum Co. Ltd.	Millers Creek/Wentworth	Gypsum	2	
National Gypsum (Canada) Ltd.	Dartmouth	Gypsum	2	
ONTARIO				
Caland Ore Co. Ltd.	Atikokan	Iron	2	
Can. Johns-Manville Co. Ltd.	Reeves	Asbestos	2	4,000
Dominion Foundries & Steel Ltd.	Adams	Iron	2	3,500
	Sherman	Iron	2	3,000
The Griffith Mine	Red Lake	Magnetite	2	16,500
Inco Ltd.	Clarabelle	Nickel, copper	2	
Indusmin Ltd.	Badgeley Island	Silica	2	4,000
Marmoraton Mng. Co.	Marmora	Iron	2	NA
National Steel Corp. of Canada Ltd.	Moose Mountain	Magnetite	2	4,368
Sherman Mine Joint Venture	Timagami	Iron	1	9,000
Steep Rock Iron Mines Ltd.	Atikokan	Hematite	2	7,200
United Asbestos Inc.	Midlothian Twp.	Asbestos	2	4,000
QUEBEC				
Asbestos Corp. Ltd.	British Canadian	Asbestos	2	13,380
	Normandie	Asbestos	2*	7,600
	Asbestos Hill	Asbestos	2	6,000
Can. Johns-Manville Co. Ltd.	Jeffrey	Asbestos	2	NA
Carey-Canadian Mines Ltd.	East Broughton	Asbestos	2	6,000
Dominion Foundries and Steel Ltd.	Wabush	Iron	2	2,700
Gaspe Copper Mines Ltd. (N.P.L.)	Copper Mountain	Copper	2	29,500
	Needle Mountain	Cu, Mo	2*	4,000
Hilton Mines Ltd.	Shawville	Magnetite	2	NA
Iron Ore Co. of Canada	Schefferville	Iron	1	
Lake Asbestos of Quebec Ltd.	Black Lake	Asbestos	2	6,000
	National	Asbestos	3	3,500
Noranda Mines Ltd.	Horne	Cu, Au, Pyrites, Ag	3*	2,000
Quebec Cartier Mining Co.	Lac Jeannine	Hematite	2	NA
Quebec Iron and Titanium Corp.	Havre St. Pierre	Ilmenite	2	
YUKON & NORTHWEST TERRITORIES				
Cassiar Asbestos Corp. Ltd.	Clinton, Yukon	Asbestos	2	4,500
Cyprus Anvil Mining Corp.	Faro, Yukon	Pb, Zn, Ag	2	10,000
Pine Point Mines Ltd.	Pine Point, NWT	Zinc, lead	2*	11,000

INTERNATIONAL

Company	Mine or location	Ore produced	Tonnage size	Mill capacity (tpd)
ALGERIA				
Sonarem	Ovenza	Iron	2	NA
ANGOLA				
Angola Diamond Co.	Dundo	Diamonds	2	NA
Cia. Mineira Do Lobito	Cassinga	Iron	2	NA
AUSTRALIA				
Alcoa Of Australia (W.A.) Ltd.	Jarrahdale	Bauxite	2	
	Del Park	Bauxite	2	
Associated Minerals Cons. Ltd.	Diamond Head	Ti, Zr, ilmenite	2	NA
	Jerusalem Creek	Ti, Zr, ilmenite	2	
	Wyong	Ti, Zr, ilmenite	1	NA
Broken Hill Pty. Ltd.	Middleback Ranges	Iron	2	5,400
Cliffs Robe River Iron Associates	Robe River	Iron	1	
Commonwealth Aluminium Corp. Ltd.	Weipa	Bauxite	2	20,000
Consolidated Rutile Ltd.	Brisbane	Ti, Zr, ilmenite	1	40,320
Dampier Mining Co. Ltd.	Koolyanobbing	Iron	2	
	Yampi Sound	Iron	2	
Goldsworthy Mining Ltd.	Mount Goldsworthy	Iron	2	
	Shaygap/Sunrise Hill	Iron	2	
Greenbushes Tin NL	Greenbushes	Sn, Ta, kaolin	2	NA
Hamersley Iron Pty. Ltd.	Mt. Tom Price	Iron	1	
Kanmantoo Mines Ltd.	Nairne	Copper	3	3,300
Mount Isa Mines Ltd.	Mount Isa	Cu, Pb, Ag, Zn	2*	22,000
Mount Lyell Mining & Railway Co. Ltd.	Queenstown	Cu, Au, Ag, pyrites	2*	7,150
Mt. Newman Mining Co. Pty. Ltd.	Newman	Iron ore	1	NA
Nabalco Pty. Ltd.	Gove	Alumina, bauxite	2	
Pilbara Tin Pty. Ltd.	Perth	Tin, tantalum	2	24,000
Queensland Nickel Pty. Ltd.	Greenvale	Nickel, cobalt	2	
Savage River Mines	Savage River	Magnetite	2	NA
Warman International Ltd.	Mount Morgan	Cu, Au, pyrites	2	3,000
Western Mineral Sands Pty. Ltd.	Capel	Ilmenite	2	3,500
Westralian Sands Ltd.	Capel	Ti, Zr, rare earth	2	5,000
AUSTRIA				
Voest Alpine AG	Erzberg	Iron	2	NA
BOTSWANA				
Bamangwato Concessions Ltd.	Selebi-Pikwe	Nickel, copper	2*	5,714
De Beers Botswana Mining Co. Ltd.	Orapa	Diamonds	2	NA
BRAZIL				
Cia. Siderurgica Nacional	Casa de Pedra	Iron	2	NA
Cia. Vale Do Rio Doce	Itabira	Hematite	2	
Ferteco Mineracao SA	Brumadinho	Iron	2	7,000
	Congonhas do Campo	Iron	2	NA
Industria e Comercio de Minerios SA	Serra do Navio	Manganese	2	3,220
Mannesmann Mineracao SA	Mutuca	Hematite	3	
Mineracoes Brasileiras Reunidas	Novalimense	Iron	2	NA
	Aguas Claras	Iron	1	NA
S/A Mineracao Da Trindade	Alegria	Hematite, ferroalloys	2	
	Morro Agudo	Iron	2	
	Andrade	Iron	3	
CHILE				
Cia. De Acero Del Pacifico SA	El Algarrobo	Iron	2	
	El Romeral	Iron	2	
	Santa Fe	Iron	2	
Corp. National Del Cobre	Chuquicamata	Cu, Mo	1	100,000
	Exotica	Copper	2	NA
Cia. Minera Disputada De Las Condes SA	Grupo Disputada	Copper	2*	7,200
Cia. Minera Santa Barbara SA	Copiapo	Iron ore	2	7,500
	Vallenar	Iron ore	2*	13,500
Emp. Minera De Mantos Blancos SA	Mantos Blancos	Copper	2*	
Soc. Quimica y Minera de Chile	Maria Elena	Na-K comp.	2	23,500
	Pedro de Valdivia	Na comp.	2	36,000
	Victoria	Na comp.	2	7,000
CHRISTMAS IS.				
British Phosphate Commissioners	South Point	Phosphate	2	4,800
CUBA				
Cubaniguel	Moa Bay	Nickel	2	NA
	Nicaro	Nickel	2	NA
CYPRUS				
Cyprus Mines Corp.	Skouriotissa	Copper	2	NA

Company	Mine or location	Ore produced	Tonnage size	Mill capacity (tpd)
Cyprus Asbestos Mines Ltd.	Amiandos	Asbestos	2	7,000
DOMINICAN REPUBLIC				
Alcoa Exploration Co.	Cabo Rojo	Bauxite, limestone	3	
Falconbridge Dominicana	Bonao	Nickel	2	
Rosario Dominicana	Pueblo Viejo	Gold, silver	2	7,260
EGYPT				
Egyptian Iron & Steel Organization	Aswan	Hematite	3*	
EIRE				
Avoca Mines Ltd.	Avoca	Copper, pyrites	3*	3,000
Irish Base Metals Ltd.	Tynagh	Pb, Zn, Ag, Cu	3*	2,400
ENGLAND				
British Steel Corp.	Corby	Iron	2	
	Scunthorpe	Iron	2*	
FINLAND				
Outokumpu Oy	Vuonos	Cu, Ni, Zn, Co	2*	5,000
	Kemi	Chromite	3	1,500
Rautaruukki Oy	Mustavaara	Vanadium	2	5,000
FRANCE				
Aluminum Pechiney	Var	Bauxite	2	
ARBED	Audun le Tiche	Iron	2*	
Soc. des Mines de Fer de Saint-Pierremont	Saint-Pierremont	Iron	2*	
GABON				
Cie. des Mines d'Uranium de Franceville	Mounana	Uranium	4*	
Cie. Miniers de L'Ogooue	Moanda	Manganese	2	NA
GHANA				
Ghana Bauxite Co. Ltd.	Awaso	Bauxite	3	NA
Ghana Consolidated Diamond Ltd.	Akwatia	Diamonds	2	NA
GREECE				
Bauxites Parnasse Mining Co.	Athens	Bauxite	2*	3,000
Eleusis Bauxite Mines	Eleusis	Bauxite	3	
	Itea	Bauxite	3	
	Lamia	Bauxite	3	
GUINEA				
Cie. des Bauxites de Guinee	Boke	Bauxite	2	
Fria, Cie. Intern. pour la Prod. de L'Alumine	Conakry	Bauxite, alumina	2	
GUYANA				
Berbice Mining Enterprise	Georgetown	Bauxite	2	
The Guyana Bauxite Co. Ltd.	Georgetown	Bauxite, alumina	3	
HAITI				
Reynolds Haitian Mines Inc.	Port-au-Prince	Bauxite	3	2,000
INDIA				
Bolani Ores Ltd.	Keonjhar	Fe, Mn	3	
Chowgule & Co. Ltd.	Sirigao	Fe, Mn	4	3,000
	Pale	Iron	2	3,000
National Mineral Development Corp. Ltd.	Bailadila	Iron	2	
	Kudremukh	Iron	1	NA
New India Mining Corp. Ltd.	Redi	Iron	3	
Orissa Minerals Development Co. Inc.	Keonjaar	Fe, Mn	3	
Sesa Goa Ltd.	Sonshi	Iron	3	
	Sanquelim	Iron	2	
	Orasso Dongor	Iron	3	
Soc. de Fomento Industrial Ltd.	Cuddegal	Iron	3	
Tata Iron & Steel Corp.	Joda	Iron	2	NA
	Noamundi	Iron	2	NA
INDONESIA				
Freeport Indonesia Inc.	Irian Jaya	Copper	2	7,500
P. T. Aneka Tambang	Kijang	Bauxite	3	
	Ujung Pandang	Nickel	3	
ISRAEL				
Negev Phosphate Co. Ltd.	Ein Yahar	Phosphate	3	NA
	Oron	Phosphate	2	NA
Timna Copper Mines Ltd.	Timna	Copper	3*	700
ITALY				
Amiantifera di Balangero	Belangero	Asbestos	2	NA
NL Industries Inc. (Baroid Div.)	Nuxis	Barite, bentonite	NA	
JAMAICA				
Alcan Jamaica Ltd.	Ewarton	Bauxite, alumina	2	
	Kirkvine	Bauxite, alumina	2	
Alcoa Minerals of Jamaica Inc.	Mocho	Bauxite, alumina	2	
Kaiser Bauxite Co.	Discovery Bay	Bauxite	2	
Reynolds Jamaica Mines Ltd.	St. Ann	Bauxite	2	
JAPAN				
Nittetsu Mining Co. Ltd.	Kamaishi	Cu, Fe, W	2*	7,000
JORDAN				
Jordan Phosphate Mines Co. Ltd.	El-Hassa	Phosphate	2	20,580
	Ruseifa	Phosphate	2	9,120
LIBERIA				
Bong Mining Co. Inc.	Monrovia	Hematite	1	35,000
Lamco Joint Venture	Mt. Nimba	Iron	1	NA
Liberia Mining Co. Ltd.	Monrovia	Iron	2	
National Iron Ore Co. Inc.	Mano River	Iron	2	NA
LUXEMBOURG				
ARBED	Esch/Alzette	Iron	2*	NA
MALAYSIA				
Ayer Hitam Tin Dredging Ltd.	Ulu Langat	Tin	1	NA
Berjuntai Tin Dredging	Selangor	Tin	1	NA
Eastern Mining & Metals Co.	Bukit Besa	Iron	2	NA
	Bukit Ibam	Iron	2	NA
Johore Mining & Stevedoring Co. Ltd.	Pengerang	Bauxite	3	
Killinghall Tin Ltd.	Kuala Lumpur	Tin	2	NA
Kinta Kellas Tin Dredging Co. Ltd.	Kinta Valley	Tin	2	NA
Malayan Tin Dredging Ltd.	Selangor	Tin	1	NA
Southern Malayan Tin Dredging Ltd.	Selangor	Tin	2	NA
Sungei Besi Mines Ltd.	Kuala Lumpur	Tin	2	NA
MAURITANIA				
SA des Mines de Fer de Mauritanie	F'Derik	Iron	2	
	F'Derik-Eboulis	Iron	3	
	Rouessa	Iron	2	
	Tazadit	Iron	2	
Soc. Miniere de Mauritanie	Akjoujt	Cu, Au, Ag	2	3,600
MEXICO				
Cerro de Mercado SA	Durango	Iron	2	
Cia. Minera de Cananea SA	Cananea	Cu, Ag, Au	2	NA
La Perla Minas De Fierro SA	La Perla	Iron	2	
Yeso Mexicano SA	La Borreguita	Gypsum	2	
MOROCCO				
Cherifien des Phosphates	Khouribdga	Phosphate	2*	NA
	Youssoufia	Phosphate	2*	NA
NAURU				
Nauru Phosphate Corp.	Aiwo	Phosphate	2	12,000
NEW CALEDONIA				
Le Nickel	Noumea	Nickel	2	

Company	Mine or location	Ore produced	Tonnage size	Mill capacity (tpd)
NEW ZEALAND				
New Zealand Steel Ltd.	Gleenbrook	Iron	2	
Waipipi Iron Sands Ltd.	North Is.	Iron	2	
NICARAGUA				
Rosario Mining of Nicaragua Inc.	Rosita	Cu, Au, Ag	3*	2,360
NIGERIA				
Amalgamated Tin Mines of Nigeria Ltd.	Benue	Sn, Cb	2	NA
Ex-Lands Nigeria Ltd.	Benue	Tin	2	NA
Gold & Base Metal Mines of Nigeria Ltd.	Benue	Sn, Cb	2	NA
NORWAY				
A/S Norsk Jernerk	Mo	Iron	2	12,000
AS Sydvaranger	Kirkenes	Magnetite	1	16,000
NL Industries Inc. (Titania A/S)	Hauge-Dalane	Ilmenite, magnetite	2	4,500
PAPUA NEW GUINEA				
Bougainville Copper Ltd.	Panguna	Cu, Au, Ag	1	86,500
PERU				
Emp. Minera del Centro del Peru	Cerro de Pasco	Ag, Pb, Zn	2*	5,500
	San Cristobal	Zn, Ag, Pb, W	3*	
Marcona Mining Co.	Marcona Plateau	Iron	1	45,000
Southern Peru Copper Corp.	Toquepala-Ilo	Cu, Mo	1	40,000
PHILIPPINES				
Apex Exploration & Mining Co. Inc.	Wagas Mapula	Copper, Gold	2	NA
Atlas Consolidated Mining and Development Corp.	Toledo	Cu, Fe, Au, Ag	1*	74,000
Baguio Gold Mining Co.	Sto. Nino	Cu, Au, Ag	2*	3,200
Benguet Consolidated Inc.	Dizon	Copper	2	20,000(U)
	CMI Chrome	Chromite	2*	3,000
CDCP Mining Corp.	Basay	Cu, Mo, Au, Ag	2	NA
Consolidated Mines Inc.	Makati	Chromite	3*	1,200
	Isao-Pili	Fe, Cu	3	1,250
Inco Mining Corp.	Makati	Magnetite	3	
Marcopper Mining Corp.	Tapian	Cu, Au, Ag	1	18,000
Marinduque Mining and Industrial Corp.	Sipalay	Cu, Mo	2	14,500
	Surigao	Ni, Co, Fe	2	
Philippine Iron Mines Inc.	Larap	Fe, Cu	3*	6,000
RHODESIA				
M.T.D. (Mangula) Ltd.	Mangula	Copper	2*	2,700
Pangani Asbestos Ltd.	Vanguard	Asbestos	3	NA
	Pangani	Asbestos	2	NA
SENEGAL				
Cie. Senegalaise des Phosphates	Taipa	Phosphate	2	NA
SIERRA LEONE				
National Diamond Mining Co.	Yengema	Diamonds	2	5,000
Sierra Leone Develop. Co. Ltd.	Marampa	Iron	2	NA
Sierra Leone Ores & Metals Co.	Mayamba	Bauxite	3	NA
SOUTH AFRICA				
African Chrysotile Asbestos Ltd.	Chrysbestos	Asbestos	3*	1,400
Associated Manganese Mines of S. Africa Ltd.	Postmasburg	Mn, Fe	2	
De Beers Consolidated Mines Ltd.	Koffiefontein	Diamonds	2*	NA
	Namaqualand	Diamonds	2	NA
Finsch Diamonds (Pty) Ltd.	Finsch	Diamonds	2*	NA
Highveld Steel and Vanadflum Corp. Ltd.	Mapochs	Iron	3	
Palabora Mining Co. Ltd.	Palabora	Cu, Fe, U, Zr, vermiculite	1	58,000
	Vermiculite	Vermiculite, nonmetallics	2	3,500
South African Iron and Steel Industrial Corp.	Sishen	Iron	2	35,000
	Thabazimbi	Iron	2*	9,900
S.A. Manganese	Hotazel	Manganese	3*	
Amcor Ltd.	Mamatwan	Manganese	3	
SOUTH WEST AFRICA				
Consolidated Diamond Mines of South West Africa	Oranjemund	Diamonds	1	NA
South African Iron and Steel Industrial Corp.	Uis	Tin	3	2,400
South West Africa Co. Ltd.	Brandberg	Tin, tungsten	2	310
SPAIN				
Agrupacion Minera SA	Agruminsa	Iron	3	
Cia. Andaluza De Minas	Marquesada	Iron	2	4,000
Espanola del Zinc SA	El Hondon Torreciega	Zinc, sulphur	2*	
Penarroya Espagne SA	Cartagena	Lead, zinc	2	6,000
Rio Tinto Patino SA	Cerro Colorado	Cu, Au, Ag	2	9,000
	Santiago	Copper	2	4,000
Tharsis Sulphur & Copper Co. Ltd.	Tharsis	Fe, Cu	3	NA
Union Explosivos Rio Tinto SA	Riotinto	Fe, Cu	2*	NA
Fosfatos Bu Craa SA	Bu Craa	Phosphate	2	NA
SURINAME				
Suriname Aluminum Co.	Moengo	Bauxite	2	
SWAZILAND				
Swaziland Iron Ore Development Co. Ltd.	Ngwengya	Iron	2	
SWEDEN				
Boliden AB	Aitik	Copper	2	22,000
Luossavaara-Kiirunavaara AB	Kiruna and Svappavaara	Magnetite	1*	18,500
Norbergs Grufforvaltning	Forening	Iron	2*	3,500
TOGA				
Cie. Togolaise des Mines du Benin	Benin	Phosphate	2	NA
TUNISIA				
Cie. des Phosphates et du Chemin de Fer de Gafsa	Redeyef	Phosphate	3*	3,000
Cie. Nouvelle des Phosphates de Djebel Mdilla	Tunis	Phosphate	3*	2,300
Soc. du Djebel Djerissa	Djerissa	Hematite	3*	
TURKEY				
Divrigi Iron Mines	Divrigi	Iron	2	
Etibank Genel Mudurlugu	Maden-Elazig	Copper	3	1,700
VENEZUELA				
CVG Ferrominera Orinoco	El Pao	Hematite	2	
	Puerto Ordaz	Iron	1	
ZAIRE				
La Generale des Carrieres et des Mines du Zaire	Kolwezi	Copper, cobalt	2	
	Kakanda	Copper, cobalt	3	2,200
	M'sesa	Copper, cobalt	2	NA
	Mutoshi	Copper, cobalt	2	NA
Soc. Miniere de Bakwanga	Bakwanga	Diamonds	2	NA
Symetain	Kalima	Tin	2	NA
Zairetain	Manono	Tin, tantalum	2	8,600
ZAMBIA				
Miniera Di Fragne	Mkushi Bona	Copper	2	3,000
Nchanga Consolidated Copper Mines Ltd.	Chingola	Copper	2*	27,500
	Rokana	Copper, cobalt	2*	18,000
	Buoana Mkubwa	Copper	2	2,300
Roan Consolidated Mines Ltd.	Chambishi	Copper	2*	6,000

Chapter 2
Prospecting and Exploration

Discovery rate and exploration methods for metallic mineral deposits in US, 1940-1976	18
USGS Denver R&D group seeks practical uses for emerging prospecting technology	21
Remote sensing continues to open new horizons for ore seekers	25
Looking for minerals via satellite: a far-out approach to exploration	32
Rock geochemistry: a mixed bag of analytical techniques	40
Data storage and retrieval buy time for geologists	43
Aeromagnetic studies are versatile search tools	44
Hydrogeochemistry aids search for uranium, base metals	46
Geobotany, biogeochemistry target potential orebodies	47
New technique traces buried ancient stream channels in search of uranium	49
Induced polarization: a versatile tool	51
EM proves useful reconnaissance tool	52
Radiometry: refinements in uranium search soften energy crisis	55
Copper exploration restrained by resource nationalism and low metal prices	58
Project Radam maps the unknown in Brazil	62
CPRM: a catalyst in Brazilian exploration programs	66
Docegeo diversifies CVRD horizon with new discoveries	69
Appraising large-diameter core and percussion drilling for bulk samples	72
Nuclear logging system obtains 'bulk samples' from small boreholes	75
New technique enhances the art of bulk sampling placer deposits	78

Discovery rate and exploration methods for metallic mineral deposits in the US, 1940-76

John P. Albers, geologist, US Geological Survey

IN 1967, A. H. LANG of the Geological Survey of Canada published a report[1] on discovery methods for mines that began production in Canada after 1955, and in 1970, Duncan R. Derry of Toronto contributed a paper[2] on the rate of new mineral discoveries in Canada, the methods used, and the annual exploration expenditures from 1950 to 1969. The report here presents some of the same type of information for the US during the interval 1940-1976. However, only mines having an annual production of 150,000 tpy or more are included here, and there is no detailed information on annual company exploration expenditures in the US.

The basic data in the report were derived from four principal sources: 1) published literature, 2) US Geological Survey commodity geologists, 3) state geologists, and 4) officials of mining companies. Although the data are thought to be generally reliable, there is a strong likelihood that they are incomplete. There is also a possibility of error because, for some of the mines listed, the discovery date and/or principal exploration method that led to discovery are based on the recollection of an individual having intimate knowledge of a property, rather than on published documentation. Nevertheless, the report gives a reasonably accurate summary that will be useful for educational purposes and possibly also as an aid in planning research and exploration programs by government organizations, companies, or private individuals.

Of the 65 mining properties listed in Table 1, 50 were producing in 1976. Fifteen deposits, mostly large porphyry copper, had not yet been brought into production at the end of 1975. An additional unknown, but small, number of deposits had been discovered by the end of 1975 but were not yet in production. Data are insufficient to permit including this last category of deposits in the discussion.

Of the 50 mines in Table 1 known to be producing in mid-1976, each has a capacity of at least 150,000 tpy of ore. Important deposits such as Ajo, Bingham, Anaconda Vein, and Morenci are not included because they were discovered prior to 1940. The 65 properties listed are chiefly base metal deposits, but they include also major uranium deposits, precious metals, and a few other types. Phosphate, potash, and most iron and titanium deposits are not included because the basis for their exploration and discovery generally depends on technological and economic factors different from those controlling the discovery of concealed base metal and precious metal deposits.

Some discoveries are rediscoveries

Because the minerals search has in the recent past concentrated to an ever-increasing degree on finding concealed orebodies, only mines discovered since 1940 have been listed. However, data were compiled for active mines back to the mid-19th century.

The older data show a period of intense prospecting from the Civil War to around 1890, during which such famous deposits and districts as Butte, Bingham, Homestake, Coeur d'Alene, and Ajo were discovered. Many other deposits also were found during this period by prospectors, who worked the rich surficial oxides for precious metals, only to abandon the deposits when primary sulphide base metal ores were uncovered.

Many of these old, partially worked deposits have in recent years become targets for sophisticated exploration by mining companies, and some have proven to be the surface manifestations of economically important porphyry copper or other types of deposits. Consequently, some of the discovery dates shown in Tables 1 and 2 are, in a sense, "rediscovery" dates for some deposits, rather than the date of original discovery by the prospector of earlier days. However, the interval between discovery and first production for such new mines can be determined meaningfully only if the rediscovery dates are considered to be the time of discovery.

Four methods of discovery are identified in the tables: conventional prospecting, geological inference, geophysical anomaly, and geochemical anomaly. Of the 65 discoveries in Table 1, 46 were made by geologic inference, seven by geophysical anomaly, two by geochemical anomaly, four by conventional prospecting, and six by a combination of methods in which each method played a role of equal importance in discovery.

As Derry points out, identifying the principal method of discovery is often difficult because few ore deposits are found now by only one method or by only one person. Obviously, geologic inference must be a factor in a very high percentage of discoveries. But if credit is given to every method involved in a discovery, there is no basis for classification. Therefore, the method that played the most important part in the discovery, according to the best advice available, is the one listed in the tables.

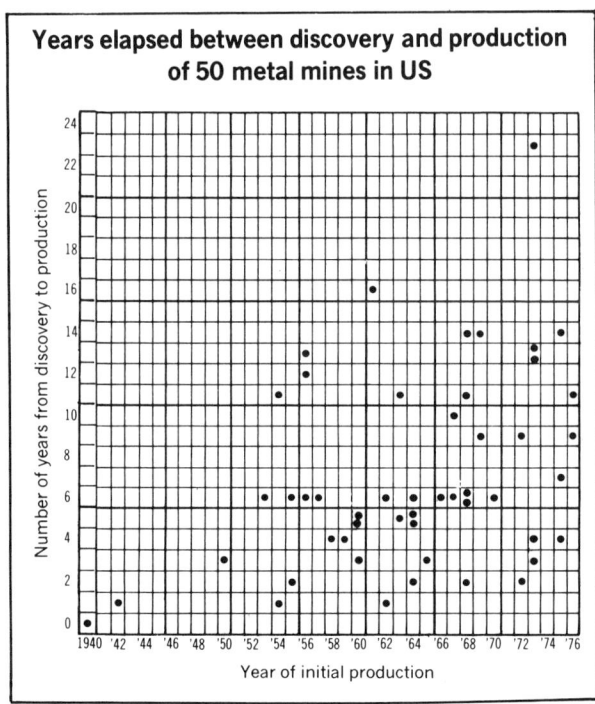

Years elapsed between discovery and production of 50 metal mines in US

Table 1—Discovery and production data for 50 US metal mines, 1940 through 1976[1]

Property	Metal(s) or mineral(s) produced	Date of discovery or rediscovery[2]	Date of first production	Method of discovery*	Years between discovery and first production	Type of operation[3]	Size of operation[4]
Carlin, Nevada	Au	1962	1965	O	3	P	C
Cortez, Nevada	Au	1966	1968	■	2	P	B
Battle Mountain, Nevada	Cu, Ag	1961	1967	O §	6	P	B
Creta, Oklahoma	Cu	1962	1964	O	2	P	E
Lakeshore, Arizona	Cu	1968	1975	O	7	U	A
Mineral Park, Arizona	Cu	1959	1964	■	5	P	A
Nacimiento, New Mexico	Cu	1970	1972	O	2	P	B
Pima, Arizona (Mission)?	Cu, Ag	1951	1957	O	6	P	A
Pinto Valley, Arizona	Cu	1971	1975	O	4	P	B
Twin Buttes, Arizona	Cu, Ag	1957	1968	O	11	P	A
Tyrone, New Mexico	Cu, Ag	1950	1973	O	23	P	A
Lower OxHide, Arizona	Cu	1967	1976	O	9	P	A
San Xavier, Arizona	Cu	1955	1969	O §	14	P	C
Yerington, Nevada	Cu	1945	1961	O	16	P	A
Questa, New Mexico	Mo	1960	1966	O	6	P	A
Henderson, Colorado	Mo	1965	1976	O	11	U	A
Continental, New Mexico	Cu, Zn, Ag	1970	1973	O	3	U	B
Esperanza, Arizona	Cu, Mo	1955	1959	O	4	P	A
San Manuel, Arizona	Cu, Mo, Zn, Ag	1943	1956	O	13	U	A
Sierrita, Arizona	Cu, Mo	1960	1973	X	13	P	A
Copper Cities, Arizona	Cu	1943	1954	O ■	11	P	A
Sacaton, Arizona	Cu	1961	1975	O	14	P	B
Lucky Friday, Idaho	Pb, Zn, Ag	1940	1940	X	0	U	E
Blue Hill, Maine	Pb, Zn, Cu	1963	1972	O §	9	U	E
Viburnum, Missouri	Pb, Zn, Cu, Ag	1955	1960	O	5	U	B
Brushy Creek, Missouri	Pb, Zn	1960	1973	O	13	U	B
Buick, Missouri	Pb, Zn, Ag	1960	1969	O	9	U	B
Fletcher, Missouri	Pb, Zn	1958	1964	O	6	U	B
Indian Creek Mines, Missouri	Pb, Zn, Ag	1947	1953	O	6	U	C
Bergen, Utah	Pb, Zn	1950	1963	O	13	U	E
Ozark, Missouri	Pb, Zn, Ag	1962	1968	O	6	U	B
Friedensville, Pennsylvania	Zn	1954	1958	O	4	U	D
Immel, Tennessee	Zn	1954	1968	O	14	U	E
Jefferson City, Tennessee	Zn	1950	1956	O	6	U	D
New Market, Tennessee	Zn	1952	1963	O	11	U	C
Young, Tennessee	Zn	1959	1964	O	5	U	E
Magmont, Missouri	Zn, Pb, Cu, Ag	1962	1968	O	6	U	C
Schullsburg, Wisconsin	Zn, Pb	1947	1950	O	3	U	D
Sunnyside, Colorado	Zn, Pb, Au, Ag	1961	1962	O	1	U	E
McIntyre, New York	Ti	1941	1942	X	1	A	D
Dave Group, Sec. 10, Wyoming	U_3O_8	1955	1960	§	5	P	C
F Group, Wyoming	U_3O_8	1957	1960	O	3	P	B
Highland, Wyoming	U_3O_8	1969	1973	§	4	P	B
Humeca, Utah	U_3O_8	1964	1970	O	6	U	B
Lucky Mc, Wyoming	U_3O_8	1953	1954	§	1	P	B
Paguate, New Mexico	U_3O_8	1956	1962	O	6	P	A
Pay-Aljob, Wyoming	U_3O_8	1953	1955	§ X	2	P	C
Schwartzwalder, Colorado	U_3O_8	1949	1955	X	6	U	B
Sec. 1, T. 13N., R. 9W., New Mexico	U_3O_8	1957	1967	O	10	U	C
Walker Lease, Wyoming	U_3O_8	1958	1963	§	5	P	C

Partial list of new deposits discovered but not yet in production

Property	Metal(s) or mineral(s) produced	Date of discovery or rediscovery[2]	Date of first production	Method of discovery*
Golden Sunlight, Montana	Au	1946?	—	O
Copper Creek, Arizona	Cu	1966	—	O
Heddleston, Montana	Cu	1966	—	O
Helvetia, Arizona	Cu	1970	—	O §
Hillsborough, New Mexico	Cu	1975	—	O
Flambeau, Wisconsin	Cu	1968	—	§
Kalamazoo, Arizona	Cu	1965	—	O
Poston Butte, Arizona	Cu	1970	—	O
Red Mountain, Arizona	Cu	1970	—	O
Safford (Kennecott), Arizona	Cu	1955	—	O
Safford (Phelps Dodge), Arizona	Cu	1957	—	O
Vekol, Arizona	Cu	1965	—	§
Yerington Largo (Phelps Dodge), Nevada	Cu	1970	—	O
Spar Lake, Montana	Cu, Zn	1962	—	O
Punkin Hollow, Nevada	Fe	1961	—	§

*Legend for method of discovery:
O—Geologic inference
X—Conventional prospecting
§—Geophysical anomaly
■—Geochemical anomaly
O§—Combination of geologic inference and other anomaly(ies)

1) List of mines and their sizes is adapted in part from MINING MAGAZINE, September 1975, pp 188-189, supplemented by additional information from other sources. List includes concealed deposits and deposits whose surficial exposures are of no commercial value. 2) See text for explanation. 3) P—open pit; U—underground; A—alluvial. 4) Legend: A—over 3 million tpy (average 7 million tpy); B—1 million to 3 million tpy; C—500,000 to 1 million tpy; D—300,000 to 500,000 tpy; E—150,000 to 300,000 tpy. (Operations of less than 150,000 tpy are excluded.)

Data indicate reduced discovery rate since 1971

As Table 1 shows, of the 65 deposits considered in this review, 15* have not yet begun operations and are still in our mineral resource bank. While these undeveloped deposits provide a limited cushion of reserves (principally for the copper industry) for the short term, new discoveries must be made at a substantial rate if the cushion is to be maintained.

Data in Tables 1 and 2 suggest that the number of discoveries has dropped markedly since 1971. However, not all reported discoveries have been listed, because of inadequate or conflicting information on dates, and some discoveries have probably not been reported. Furthermore, the lower number of discoveries in the early 1970s could prove to be only a brief aberration in the long term picture. Any one of these factors or a combination of them might explain the apparent dearth of new discoveries. On the other hand, the phenomenon might result from a sharp cutback in exploration activity or from increasing scarcity of geologically favorable prospecting ground, with a consequent increase in the difficulty of finding additional deposits.

Brown[3] observes that statistics compiled by the Canadian Diamond Driller's Association show that exploratory drilling for new metal mines in Canada dropped from 6.2 million ft in 1970 to 4.4 million ft in 1974—a very substantial decline. According to Brown, this and other indications show that, under present conditions, the Canadian mining industry is not spending enough to achieve the discovery and development of the new resources that are necessary to maintain the relative importance of Canadian mineral production beyond the mid-1980s.

Data on annual exploratory drilling for mineral resources and on total annual exploration expenditures are not available for the US. However, if the downward trend observed by Brown for Canada is also applicable to the US, the indicated decline in new domestic discoveries could be the beginning of a long term trend, with unfavorable implications for the US in its ability to satisfy the ever-increasing need for mineral raw materials.

The interval between discovery and first production

The average time between discovery and first production for the 50 mines listed is about seven years. The accompanying graph shows that the time between discovery and production ranges up to 23 years.

Technological factors, economic factors, or a combination of these may affect the discovery-to-production time span for a particular deposit. Economic factors noted by Cranstone and Martin[4] include the following:

■ The owners of the deposit may have deposits of higher grade or greater profitability that can supply all the ore they can possibly sell.

■ The owners may not be able to raise capital or to afford the financial risk of bringing a new mine into production.

■ The markets are not currently available.

■ The owners prefer to await higher prices.

Some of the 15 deposits still not in production (Table 1) are in the category of nonproducers simply because they have been discovered too recently to have permitted development. At least five of the deposits have been discovered since 1970, and all but three of the remaining 10 were discovered during the 1960s. Whatever the reason that these properties have not yet been brought into production, the third column in Table 2 indicates that production starts have, in general, fluctuated in a fairly regular manner since the mid-1950s. □

References

1) Lang, A. H., "Discovery methods of post-1955 new producers," CANADIAN MINING JOURNAL, Vol. 88 (1967), No. 1, pp 47-50.
2) Derry, D. R., "Exploration expenditure, discovery rate, and methods," CIM BULLETIN, Vol. 63 (1970), No. 695, pp 362-366.
3) Brown, R. D., "Taxation and our future resources," CIM BULLETIN, Vol. 69 (1976), No. 769, pp 124-126.
4) Cranstone, D. A., and H. L. Martin, "Are discovery costs increasing?," CANADIAN MINING JOURNAL, April 1973.
5) MINING MAGAZINE, "International mining survey," Vol. 133 (1975), No. 3, pp 185-221.

Table 2—Number of discoveries and production starts each year, 1940-1976

Year	Number of discoveries, by method*	Production starts
1940	X	1
1941	X	—
1942	—	—
1943	O ★	—
1944	—	—
1945	O	—
1946	O	—
1947	OO	—
1948	—	—
1949	X	—
1950	OOO	—
1951	O	—
1952	O	—
1953	§ ★	1
1954	OO	2
1955	★ OO § O	2
1956	O	2
1957	OOOO	1
1958	O §	1
1959	■ O	1
1960	OXOO	3
1961	★ OO §	1
1962	OOOOO	2
1963	★	3
1964	O	4
1965	OO §	1
1966	■ OO	1
1967	O	2
1968	O §	5
1969	§	2
1970	OO ★ OOO	1
1971	O	—
1972	—	2
1973	—	5
1974	—	—
1975	O	3
1976	—	2

*Legend:
O — Geologic inference
X — Conventional prospecting
§ — Geophysical anomaly
■ — Geochemical anomaly
★ — Combination of geologic inference and some type(s) of geophysical and/or geochemical anomaly

*This is a minimal number, at least for porphyry copper deposits discovered since 1940 but not yet in production.

Fire assay unit, a backup to field studies, is used to concentrate a sample for spectrographic determination of Pt, Pd, Ir, Rb, and Ru.

USGS Denver R&D group seeks practical uses for emerging prospecting technology

Robert Sisselman, Associate editor

CHANGING PRIORITIES within the Department of the Interior in the last few years are causing the department's US Geological Survey to shift from a research orientation to an emphasis on applications of technology. An example of that metamorphosis is the USGS Denver, Colo., Exploration Research Branch, where scientists are redirecting their efforts from research in ore-finding methods to application of available technology for rapid evaluation of mineral resources on Federal lands. Nevertheless, USGS scientists still manage to pursue a wide array of research activities.

Some of the studies under way, from Maine to Alaska, are using:

■ Soil gas, including mercury and the halogens, to detect concealed mineralization.

■ Geochemical dispersion patterns, to extend known lead-silver resources and to identify potential resources in the Coeur d'Alene mining district of Idaho.

■ Plants growing in stream channels, to sample ground water inexpensively.

■ Satellite and fixed-wing aircraft surveys over vegetated terrain, to target geochemically stressed plants.

Soil gas studies are expanding

One of the main research efforts under way at the Denver branch is the use of mercury vapor to indicate the presence of sulphide mineralization. Although such studies have been conducted in the Soviet Union since 1946, mercury detection, or 'sniffing,' is relatively new to the US. The USGS instituted testing in 1963. Since then, US mining companies have established their own research programs in mercury detection.

J. Howard McCarthy, who heads up the Denver group's work on soil gas detection of anomalies, thinks many buried deposits remain to be found: "Our job is to develop techniques that will aid in defining those concealed deposits, and gas analysis is one way of doing it."

In addition to mercury as a gaseous indicator, researchers are looking also at such gases as helium and the halogens. McCarthy believes that if current theory on ore forming solutions is correct, the volatility of brine solutions containing bromine, iodine, and fluorine, and the halogens in the free state, should be detectable at the surface. Detectability would depend on the permeability and porosity of the rock. Glacial clays, shales, and caliche are problems, he said. However, such types of rock are often fractured, and even glacial till may permit gas flow, as permafrost does under certain conditions.

One of the problems facing scientists is a lack of knowledge of the specific gases that are given off by each type of deposit. They still don't know whether gases emanate directly from deposits themselves, nor have they determined the parameters that control the escape of such vapors. One of the projects soon to get under way will be to crush a wide variety of mineral samples and to observe what gases, if any, are emitted.

However, researchers are not totally in the dark on the subject of gas-mineralization links. They believe that fluorine, for instance, is commonly associated with pneumatolytic deposits of molybdenum and tungsten. Fluorine is also present as a gangue material in the lead-zinc deposits of the mid-Continent and may some day provide indication of similar, unknown deposits. Halogen salts, commonly found in semiarid and desert regions of the Basin and Range province in the US, appear to be associated with silver chloride bonanza-type deposits. Bromine and iodine also are linked with silver occurrences.

Many parameters affect the liberation of soil gases. For example, researchers working with mercury established that barometric pressure has a substantial effect on the release of gases. "One gets maximum mercury when there is maximum low pressure," said McCarthy, "and that is very logical if one thinks of an earth-atmosphere interface as a breathing process."

Some gases are suitable as indicators for certain types of deposits and unsuitable for others. Mercury has not been very useful in detecting porphyry copper deposits, for example. Other gases, however, may pick up the slack. Bromine gas, for instance, has been measured over porphyry copper deposits.

Other elements, including selenium and tellurium, have been found to be associated with copper porphyries, but only as solids in the rock. However, some oxidizing copper sulphide dumps emit gaseous odors other than sulphur dioxide and it is believed that selenium may be among the emissions. "This could mean that such elements could eventually be measured at surface," McCarthy noted.

To detect gases and correlate their occurrence with specific mineralization, both basic and highly sophisticated instruments are required. Aside from the mercury detector developed by the USGS in 1963—a flameless atomic absorption unit used to detect mercury in rock, soils, and stream sediments—McCarthy's group will shortly acquire a portable quadrapole mass spectrometer having a range of 0 to 300 atomic mass units, which will permit coverage of a wide range of inorganic gases of primary interest.

Coeur d'Alene: piecing a puzzle back together

One of the more recent developments that has captured mining companies' attention is the work of the Denver USGS group in the Coeur d'Alene mining district of Idaho, one of the world's richest lead-silver belts. Mining companies operating in the lead-silver district, and outsiders as well, are virtually "waiting at the door for anything we publish," said one USGS spokesman. The reason: USGS scientists have used geochemistry to reconstruct the Coeur d'Alene as it existed before faulting and intrusions, and to target for exploration certain areas that were previously not of interest.

Garland Gott and John Cathrall, scientists on the USGS staff in Denver, have worked in the Coeur d'Alene for a number of years, and the approach they took in modeling the geology of the mining district may significantly extend its life.

Cathrall explains: "Almost everybody tried to put the geology back together principally from looking at the structural and stratigraphic sequences. But we asked ourselves: 'Could we piece the district back together prior to all the faulting and intrusions using geochemical patterns?'" The answer was yes, and geochemical patterns in fact confirmed the known lateral displacement on the two principal faults in the district—the Osborn and Dobson Pass.

In one area of the district, some of the known mineral belts and associated geochemical dispersion patterns were found to have been intruded by monzonite stocks, destroyed to a certain extent, remobilized, and then dispersed in a halo pattern. "As a result," says Cathrall, "it looks like about 85% of the Coeur d'Alene ores have been derived from the area encompassed by the geochemical halos. Only about one-half the area within the halo has been prospected, leaving large unexplored target areas."

Biogeochemical guides in arid environments

Developing and modifying new and established methods of exploration using plants in arid environments is one of the interests of geologist Maurice Chaffee. Chaffee observed the surface expression of several partially exposed copper porphyry deposits in Arizona. In doing so, he sampled rock, residual soils, stream sediments, and both riparian and nonriparian plants. (Riparian plants are those that grow in stream channels, generally relying on near-surface ground water. Nonriparian plants grow on hillsides and are not necessarily related to drainage channels.)

Generally, Chaffee believes, there is no real advantage in sampling nonriparian species if residual soil is accessible. However, he states, "A thin cover of 10 ft or so of postmineralization alluvium or the presence of a significant amount of aeolean or windborne contamination in the area may make nonriparian plants advantageous."

Chaffee believes that riparian plants do offer "some real advantages" because the chemistry of these plants may re-

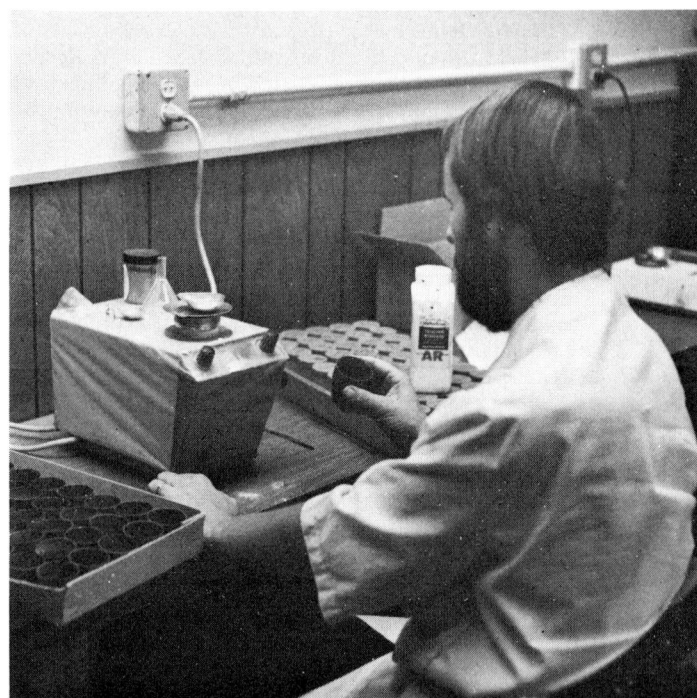

Chemist at USGS laboratories weighs sample into nickel crucibles for specific ion fluoride analysis.

Campers outfitted for sample preparation are used in conjunction with field investigations.

flect the chemistry of the ground water, especially in arid or semiarid regions, where there is virtually no exposed water to be contaminated from external sources.

Most riparian plants are phreatophytes (deep-rooted). They have been known to penetrate as deep as 175 ft but usually go no deeper than 50 to 100 ft. Since examination of riparian plants doesn't require drilling a water well or an exploration drillhole to sample ground water at depth, it is a relatively inexpensive means of exploration, Chaffee maintains. Although the plants do not penetrate deeper than about 150 ft, Chaffee pointed out that large tracts of gravel or alluvium in Arizona's copper belt may not be deeper than that.

Evaluating the potential resources of Alaska

Many of the efforts under way at USGS offices around the US are aimed at assessing the resource potential of Alaska, as well as of Wilderness areas. Gary Curtin, of the Denver branch of USGS, heads one group that is conducting reconnaissance geochemical studies as part of the Federally funded Alaska Mineral Resource Assessment Program. The program, which started on July 1, 1974, has a dual purpose: 1) to assess the mineral resources of some 80 million acres of national interest lands pursuant to the Native Claims Settlement Act of 1971, and 2) to produce an inventory of Alaska's minerals as soon as possible. Phase one of the program will be completed in 1978; phase two is to be completed several years thereafter.

The USGS team also hopes to be able to find definitive sampling media for the various physiographic areas of the state that will aid in the search for potential mineral deposits.

In Alaska, investigators have found that separate geochemical studies must be made to define effectively mineral targets in at least two kinds of terrain: rugged mountainous areas (such as the Alaska Range) and areas of low relief (muskeg and marshes). Curtin's group found that in areas of low relief, where chemical weathering plays an important role, several types of sample analyses seem to be more effective when used in combination. Such samples include: secondary iron-manganese oxides that have been leached from stream sediments using oxalic acid, stream bank sod (a mixture of organic material, silt, and sand), moss growing in streams, and vegetation. In the mountains, however, where the primary weathering process is mechanical and where the geology is more visible, stream sediments and heavy mineral concentrations such as gold provide geochemists with all the information they need to define target areas. Geologists also collect samples of various rock units to provide information on regional background values.

There have been some payouts as a direct result of USGS investigations. Curtin states that porphyry copper mineralization has been reported in the Yukon-Tanana Upland in eastern Alaska and, based on preliminary data, possible new metal occurrences are indicated in the central Alaska range. In addition, USGS teams have more accurately defined potential porphyry copper deposits in the eastern Alaska range.

Satellite studies: no 'glowing bullseyes' . . . yet

In many parts of the world, especially such inaccessible areas as tropical rain forests, ground sampling techniques may be successful—but they are also very expensive. Hoping to bypass at least some of these costly mineral evaluation efforts, the USGS in the 1960s began to mesh botanical prospecting methods with sophisticated remote sensing techniques such as multiband photography, multispectral line scanning surveys and later, in the 1970s, satellite imaging.

The main discovery made from the initial ground studies using spectrophotometers, according to geologist Frank Canney, was that trees growing in anomalous areas have identifiable spectral reflectance characteristics in the visible and infrared spectra. It has long been known, of course, that trees growing in anomalous areas sometimes show visible differences in color, growth rate, and other morphological characteristics.

The possibilities of finding anomalous mineralized areas through vegetation differentiation using remote sensors excited scientists such as Canney, who heads the project that applies remote sensing to mineral exploration.

Much of the earlier development work performed by Canney and associates was supported by the National Aeronautics and Space Administration (NASA) and the EROS program of the US Department of Interior. This research was given further impetus through funding arranged for the USGS by the State Department's Agency for International Development. The later work was funded to determine the reflectance characteristics of the dense tropical rain forests that are native to many of the underdeveloped countries. Programs were started in the Philippines, Thailand, and Brazil, as well as at several sites in the US.

Unfortunately, the "glowing bullseyes"—as Canney calls the patterns related to vegetative anomalies that are sought in multiband photography and multispectral scanner imagery—were not observed. However, Canney's group did learn from these studies.

"The reason we didn't get concrete visuals or anomalies from overflights," he said, "is because we underestimated the complexity of light reflectance from vegetation. Light reflectance from vegetative sources is a dynamic variable in time and space and is a function of many things: number, type, and density of trees in an area; the fullness of the tree canopy; and the position and angle of the sun, among others. In addition, no narrow band 'spectral spikes' that would identify specific metals have been observed in the spectral reflectance curves." However, he suggested, "this may be the result of the coarse resolution of the radiometers used in the early research."

Some of the more recent flights, made in 1976, used an experimental 500-channel spectrometer developed under NASA auspices by the Goddard Institute for Space Studies. With the "tremendous resolution" available from this unit, Canney hopes to see whether spectral spikes do in fact exist, indicating the presence of, perhaps, copper or molybdenum in a plant system.

Space fast emerging the final frontier

In the 1970s, the USGS discovered the advantages of satellites over fixed-wing aircraft. For instance, data were made readily available in digital format, to be analyzed and manipulated by computers. In addition, many of the variables that plague aircraft data (sun angle, azimuth, and topographic effects) are held relatively constant or minimized with satellites because the "look angle" of the space scanner varies only about ±5° from the vertical. Coverage of an area is also quick. A surface of 100 mi x 100 mi, for instance, might be imaged in 25 sec.

Disadvantages of satellite surveys include the relatively coarse resolution of the scanner, which is about 80 m—offering little hope of detecting vegetative anomalies associated with smaller deposits. However, says Canney, there is little question that anomalies related to copper-molybdenum porphyry deposits are usually of sufficient size to be theoretically detectable.

Canney and associates will also try some techniques similar to those developed by Lawrence Rowan of the USGS to discriminate hydrothermally altered rock types in exposed terrain. (See E/MJ, May 1975, pp 87-94.) However, Canney will focus on vegetated areas. Rowan's group developed some interesting methods using computer ratioing of spectral bands to highlight surface features and chemistry as possible indications of subsurface mineralization.

Another approach to be used by Denver-based scientists is temporal analysis—the comparison of a vegetated area on two separate occasions (e.g., the start and the end of the dry season) to detect physical changes. The premise here, says Canney, is that geochemically stressed trees will give a more pronounced reaction to changes in other environmental factors. One of the biggest problems in temporal analysis, he reports, is that vegetation reacts similarly to a variety of stresses—one of which might or might not be caused by a nearby geochemical anomaly.

'Feverish' trees attract USGS investigators

Another idea to be exploited by the Denver USGS group is based on the premise that sick trees have abnormally high temperatures. When the Department of Agriculture studied the problem of bark beetle infestation in the pine forests of South Dakota, numerous trees were wired up, and it was found that the temperature of a tree under stress from beetle attack was as much as 5°C higher than that of a healthy tree. Reading about these experiments, USGS scientists questioned whether a tree growing in a geochemically stressed area might react similarly. Perhaps metallic concentrations in a tree or its supporting soil will make it more difficult for that tree to transpire water, thus keeping the tree warmer than normal.

Experiments on the subject, using both airborne and ground-based thermal scanners, have yielded contradictory results so far, but they suggest the desirability of more work. □

Interior of mobile spectrographic unit. Visual comparator is situated in the adjoining room, behind the doors.

Radar image, taken from Caravelle jet at 40,000 ft, shows volcanic formation on Flores Island, Indonesia. (Credit: Aero Service Corp.)

Remote sensing continues to open new horizons for ore seekers

Thomas E. Wayland, chief geologist, Mountain States Development Corp.

THE VAST POTENTIAL FOR MINERAL DISCOVERY inherent in the space age technology of remote sensing has opened new doors through which the earth sciences and other disciplines will move—separately in some cases, interdependently in others. The practical applications of remote sensing to minerals search offer striking advantages for large and small exploration companies.

Cameras, scanners, and radar are neatly packaged

One primary objective of remote sensing is to detect and record energy in a selected portion of the electromagnetic (EM) spectrum. In order to deal intelligently with such data, explorationists should have a basic understanding of illumination (optical physics), atmospheric effects, and other pertinent fields of earth science.

Emphasis in remote sensing has been placed on the modern sensor system,[8] which generally records data in the form of images (photographs). Such a sensor detects light being reflected by, and heat radiating from, the earth's surface. The main imaging devices now in use are aerial cameras, multispectral scanners (MSS), and side-looking airborne radar (SLAR).

The essential function of an aerial camera is to produce pictures of the earth by focusing reflected light onto either black-and-white or color film. Aerial cameras are very versatile in being able to take photographs using either visible light (red, green, and blue) or invisible infrared light. Because of the variety of ways that many earth materials reflect infrared light, unusual colors can be recorded by infrared photography. Such colors can be used to detect areas of stressed vegetation, anomalous soil and water conditions, and the surface traces of fault systems.

The capability of recording a great variety of wavelengths (frequencies) distinguishes the multispectral scanner from other systems. The MSS typically detects and records heat radiated by the earth's surface in the form of long-wavelength infrared rays. Multispectral scanner imagery shows earth reflectance in four separate wavelengths: green, red, and two infrared bands. Black and white scanner images can be observed separately, or as a composite formed by combining the green, red, and infrared images. Reflectance data from orbital imagery are recorded on magnetic tapes for analysis by digital computers. The multispectral signal can also be reconstituted to pictorial form and analyzed manually.

The SLAR systems have unique functions; they artificially illuminate the earth's surface with extremely long, invisible radar waves, and they record the reflected waves in picture form. Unusual features of the SLAR systems in-

EROS Data Center in Sioux Falls, S. Dak., supplies satellite imagery and related data at nominal cost to anyone in the world.

clude the capability to produce imagery in darkness or through a dense cloud cover.

Various process adjustments are made to improve orbital imagery. Because of the ultrasophisticated nature and high costs of some of these methods, a detailed discussion is beyond the scope of this paper. However, the end result of such enhancement has great potential—particularly in the study of lineaments. The imagery can be sharpened by restoration of its high frequency components—thereby emphasizing certain preferred edges (or all edges) as an aid to interpretation. Other computer-processed adjustments include:

- Destriping and dropout removal—accomplished by filtering techniques.
- Geometric corrections—designed to compensate for earth rotation and other effects that cause the area scanned to be a parallelogram, rather than a square.
- Range stretch and haze removal—performed to increase the contrast and equalize the average brightness of individual spectral components.
- Ratioing—a type of enhancement that minimizes topographically related differences in brightness. This process can be of help in detecting geochemical anomalies in heavily forested areas.

How satellites have closed the gap between geology and geophysics

Definitions of remote sensing range from the ridiculous to the sublime. A couple of awkward examples:

Acquiring information about a phenomenon while still at some distance from it.

Sensing an object or phenomenon without having the sensor in direct contact with the object being sensed.

Those who prefer a more comprehensive definition will appreciate this one: "The science involved with the gathering of data about the earth's surface or near-surface environment, through the use of a variety of sensor systems that are usually borne by aircraft or spacecraft, and the processing of these data into information useful for the understanding and managing of man's environment."[1]

The author himself is partial to his employer's appraisal of remote sensing: "Something geophysicists and girlwatchers have been engaged in for a long time."[2]

Reduced to bare essentials, the most practical definition of remote sensing appears to be: "The instrumental measurement and perception of distant objects." This brief description neither lessens the mystique of the term nor softens its foundations in both the pure and applied arts and sciences.

The value of aerial photography

The many facets of the remote sensing discipline were brought into sharp focus in 1960 by geographer Evelyn Pruitt, who is credited with being the first to use the term remote sensing.[3] The term was adopted more than 100 years after the first crude aerial photographs of the earth's surface were taken, during a balloon flight in 1848. Subsequent aerial photographic techniques included use of additional balloons, kites, pigeons, rockets, and finally airplanes in 1909.

For several years following this period, the major application of aerial photography was in gathering military intelligence data. Recognition of the practicality of aerial photography for mapping purposes came slowly. Topographic mapping began in the mid-1920s, and a formal program to map the US was adopted in 1930. The value of aerial photos in geologic mapping soon became apparent, and extensive application of such photos for this purpose began in the mid-1930s.

Meanwhile, ground-based geophysical instrumentation became airborne, adding a new "remote" dimension to geophysics and greatly increasing its practical value through increased mobility. The paths of geology and geophysics have, in fact, been drawn even more closely together with the advent of satellite imagery.

From Sputnik to satellite snapshots

Major advances have been made in remote sensing

Experience, deductive reasoning lead to clues

The interpretation and analysis of orbital imagery has been called an exercise in pattern recognition. As in conventional photogeology, geologic interpretation of orbital imagery follows orderly, logical steps. Keen observation in the study of most surface features will lead to their recognition through an awareness of the presence or absence of definite shapes, sizes, textures, associations, and other criteria. This step can lead, through deduction, to the positive identification of very subtle features in orderly succession.[9]

Lineaments may be clearly indicated by differences in topography, vegetation, soil color, and land use. Straight segments of streams, unusually long, straight valleys, a linear arrangement of topographic forms, and the alignment of volcanoes may all be indications of structural control. In addition to the other, more easily recognized linear features, possible faults may be indicated by subtle differences in tone. Recognition of edges and boundaries has universal importance. The random trends of multiple joints or joint sets may form distinctive textural patterns which can aid in the recognition of intrusive rocks. However, ground truth determinations are needed to follow up remote sensing interpretations because nongeologic lineaments may be emphasized under some natural conditions and in imagery recorded by certain sophisticated and ultrasophisticated sensors.

Although there are obvious benefits in concentrating on linear features, the explorationist should not overlook other geometrical "shapes" in his attempts to identify and interpret structure in terms of possible mineral indicators. Under certain conditions, misalignments (offsets) of drainage, land forms, and radial, circular, ellipsoidal, or other multidirectional features can be equally important in the analysis of a given region.

Differences in topographic expression should be used with caution in orbital imagery interpretation to be certain that these differences are not more apparent than real. However, with the expected steady improvement in resolution, confidence and proficiency of the interpreter should increase: scarps and fault lines will be easier to identify; drainage discordance, including the meanders of some large streams, may be discernible; the broad curve of a major stream lying generally parallel to smaller streams could indicate underlying structure such as the end of a pitching fold.

Aside from its more obvious advantages, the greatest benefits of orbital imagery in geologic interpretation will probably be realized in:

- Correlation or comparison of data available in existing maps.
- Matching with data from similar but distant areas.
- Application to geologic problems of regional scope.

Considering only the mechanics of interpretation and analysis, imagery can be used conveniently as a base map on which to superimpose interpretations of geologic structure, lithology, geochemistry, geophysical results, unidentified lineament patterns, and any other features of probable significance.

The advantages of satellites in ore search

Some of the pros and cons of using orbital imagery interpretation and analysis in geological exploration are summarized below. Used knowledgeably and within reasonable financial restrictions, the advantages of this technology greatly outweigh the disadvantages.

Synoptic view. Regional coverage by satellites affords a broad perspective, or synoptic view, wherein features having no apparent importance when viewed in a more limited perspective may "complete the picture." Geochemical anomalies, complete structures, or structural systems and their relationships to adjacent areas may be visible on a single image; in addition, the extensive view (more than 13,000 sq mi) allows discontinuous features to be detected, traced, and related with more ease and confidence. The probability of misinterpretation as a result of observations made of more restricted areas (such as those shown by conventional aerial photographs) is reduced.

Repetitive coverage. Subtle differences are detectable from one period to another (time of day, seasons, etc.) through the effects of different sun angles and changes in vegetation.

Reliable, responsive, versatile instrumentation. Lighting and imagery exposure are constant and uniform, and the field of view is instantaneous and near-vertical; output is digital; and a repeated sequence of images is delivered from defined geographic areas.

Favorable economics. Orbital imagery and related data can be purchased at nominal cost by anyone, worldwide, from the EROS Data Center in Sioux Falls, S. Dak. Total exploration cost savings ranging from 20% to 50% have been reported.[10] A mosaic of the US required only 595 satellite images and three months' time to composite.[11] This accomplishment contrasts greatly with the years and the excessive number of individual photographs that would be needed to do the job by U2 flights (50,000-plus photos), or by conventional aerial photographs (approximately 1,760,000).

But there are also drawbacks in the use of orbital imagery:

---

technology in the US during the period from the Explorer satellite in 1958 to the present-day crop of space vehicles circling and soon to circle the earth. Following are milestones in the history of orbital imagery:

1958: Explorer launched, following the successful launching of the unmanned Soviet satellite Sputnik in 1957.

1959: Discoverer launched.

1960: Tiros weather satellite launched; utilized television and infrared imagery.

1961: Mercury sent up—first manned spacecraft; followed by Gemini and Apollo launchings.

1964: Nimbus launched; used high-resolution infrared system.

1965: Handheld cameras (70 mm) used by Gemini astronauts to record images of interest in large-scale geologic and other applications.

1970: Some cameras still handheld, but new data recorded by mounted instruments sensing in several parts of the electromagnetic spectrum.

1972: ERTS-1 (now called Landsat-1) launched into a sun-synchronous polar orbit, with instrumentation capable of recording imagery in three and four bands (multispectral).

1973: Skylab and ERTS-2 (Landsat-2) launched.

1977 and beyond: Landsat-3 launching will bring further advances in orbital imagery through new techniques and instrumentation to improve resolution and measure heat capacity.[6] Plans on the drawing board include a possible geoscientific observatory and laboratory (shuttle space lab) and some proposed new instruments, such as the Landsat-D Thematic Mapper.[7]

Navy YE 3A reconnaissance aircraft equipped with Westinghouse AN/APQ97 radar system. Antenna is visible on bottom of jet.

Low resolution. Generally, images smaller than about 8 acres are not recorded; however, major linears and other important features are usually discernible at low resolutions.

Small scales. Orbital imagery in standard use is largely confined to scales of:

1) 1:1,000,000 (approximately 1 in. to 16 mi).
2) 1:500,000 (approximately 1 in. to 8 mi).
3) 1:250,000 (approximately 1 in. to 4 mi).

Interpretation restrictions. Assuming reasonable skill on the part of an observer, the following represent problems in interpretation:

- Nongeologic linears may be shown as well as, or better than, geologic linears, and some linears may be polygenetic.
- Diagnostic features may not be recognized because of the time at which the imagery was recorded (daytime vs. night, morning vs. afternoon, spring vs. fall, etc.).
- Similar reflectance values may be recorded for both significant and unrelated features.
- Standard imagery is orthographic, precluding the determination of relative differences in elevation and use in topographic mapping.

Some of these problems may be minimized through sophisticated and ultrasophisticated processing methods and techniques (such as thermal infrared imagery), but the unit costs of such processing are relatively high. As in most other mineral exploration projects, however, it is necessary to determine whether the potential for success is worth the expense. The expense involved should be evaluated in terms of the beneficial end results.

Getting some practical feedback

More than 50 nations, including several of the developing countries, are participating to some degree in the programs and services available from the National Aeronautics and Space Administration (NASA) of the US. Eighteen international seminars and workshops on the subject of remote sensing have been held, and additional meetings are planned. At the EROS Data Center in South Dakota, training courses of international scope are offered regularly.[12] Following are some examples of worldwide progress in the application of orbital imagery and associated remote sensing technologies to mineral resources.

In the Soviet Union, three diamond pipes have been discovered as a result of exploration guidelines established by orbital imagery studies. Subtle contrasts in vegetation were observed, indicating a gross target for ground-based exploration. Ultimate success in the project was achieved in the final target area, which was underlain by residual kimberlite soils whose richness encouraged a more luxuriant plant growth.

In Pakistan, the government is determining the feasibility of several copper prospects discovered during an exploration program that was guided by the application of some ultrasophisticated remote sensing techniques. Following calibration on a known deposit of porphyry copper, 23 possible copper-bearing sites were detected. A ground truth investigation resulted in the selection of five sites for more detailed examination.[13]

In Mexico, multidirectional structures interpreted from orbital imagery have given government authorities new insight into the regional structural control of some older mining districts. The new data are expected to reveal more of the details of pluton emplacement and perhaps shed some light on the metallogenic process.[14]

In Kenya, a study of orbital imagery has resulted in the recognition of lineaments and basin boundaries in a flat, relatively featureless area. This information has been confirmed by the position and geometry of both magnetometer and gravity anomalies. The substantial savings of time and money by the recognition of these features through orbital imagery interpretation is obvious.[15]

In the US, Project Birddog, sponsored by the US Geological Survey, is searching for surface manifestations of deeply buried hydrocarbons escaping slowly to the surface through the imperfect rock seals that cap some oil and gas deposits. These data were obtained during calibration of the method over known production areas. Their value as an exploration tool has not been determined.[16]

Known precious and base metal deposits in southern Nevada, northwestern Arizona, and eastern California apparently have spatial relationships with generally east-west structural trends. Orbital imagery data point to pre-

A glossary of terms used in remote sensing

Aberration. A defect in an optical image. (All lens systems have some aberration.)

Absorption. A process of attenuation which an electromagnetic emanation undergoes as it passes through the atmosphere or other medium or as it strikes an object.

Absorption spectroscope. An instrument used to determine (by means of spectral analysis) the amount of absorption that occurs when energy is directed through a specific type of surface or material.

Active system. A remote sensing system which transmits its own electromagnetic emanations at an object(s) and then records the energy reflected or refracted back to the sensor.

Angstrom (Å). A unit of measurement equal to one ten-millionth of a millimeter.

Band. A set of adjacent wavelengths in the electromagnetic spectrum with a common characteristic, such as the visible band.

Cathode ray tube. A vacuum tube generating a focused beam of electrons which can be deflected by electronic and magnetic fields. The terminus of the beam is visible as a spot or line of luminescence on a sensitized screen at one end of the tube.

Classification. 1) An administrative system wherein information, equipment, or processes are categorized according to their importance in national security. 2) A systematic arrangement of objects (which have been imaged) into a logical structure or hierarchy.

Detector. A device or substance capable of receiving, transforming, and/or recording directly energy emitted and/or reflected from objects.

Electromagnetic (EM) spectrum. An array of all electromagnetic radiation that moves with the constant velocity of light in a harmonic wave characterized by wavelength, frequency, or amplitude.

Emission. Electromagnetic energy given off from an object, created by the molecular oscillations of the body itself.

Emissivity. A ratio relating the amount of energy given off by an object to the amount given off by a "black body" at the same temperature; normally expressed as a real positive number between 0 and 1.

Emulsion. A suspension of a light-sensitive silver halide (usually silver chloride or silver bromide) in a colloidal medium (usually gelatin) used for coating photographic films, plates, and papers.

Enhancement. Various processes and techniques designed to render optical densities on imagery more susceptible to interpretation.

Gamma. A numerical measure of the degree of difference between the contrast of a subject matter on a photographic negative and the actual contrast of the subject photographed. A gamma of 1.0 indicates unity of contrast; a gamma of 1.1 indicates that the negative has more contrast than the subject.

Ground truth. Information concerning the actual state of the environment at the time of a remote sensing overflight.

Hardware. Physical equipment used for data collection and handling, including such objects as remote sensing equipment and computers.

Illumination. The "light" or energy impinging upon a given area or object. Usually this light consists of direct sunlight plus skylight.

Image motion compensation (IMC). A process wherein film is moved backward through a camera during exposure to compensate for the forward motion of the aircraft along the flight path; this prevents image blurring.

Imagery. The visual representation of energy recorded by remote sensing instruments.

Line scanning. The use of a facsimile device, such as an intensity-modulated cathode ray tube, which produces an image by viewing and recording a scene one line at a time.

Low-light-level television system. A system in which incident light is intensified by utilizing a photoemissive cathode, focusing electronic optics and a screen; can be used to provide effective night capability in the visible and near-visible spectral range.

Micrometer (u). A unit of measurement equal to one-millionth of a meter or one-thousandth of a millimeter.

Micron. The equivalent of micrometer.

Microwave. Energy transmitted at a wavelength between 10^2 and 10^{-1} cm.

Modulation transfer function (MTF). An optical analogue to general systems theory whereby the total resolution of the components of an optical system can be measured in terms of brightness as a linear function.

Multiband. The use of one or more sensors to obtain imagery from different portions of the reflectance portion of the electromagnetic spectrum (most commonly used in connection with black-and-white photography).

Multispectral. The use of one or more sensors to obtain imagery from different portions of the electromagnetic spectrum.

Multispectral scanner (MSS). A line scanning device which employs an oscillatory mirror to continuously scan perpendicular to a platform's velocity. Optical energy is sensed simultaneously by an array of detectors in visible bands from 0.5 to 1.1 u. Platform motion provides the along-track progression of the scan lines.

Nanometer (um). A unit of measurement equal to one millimicron or one-millionth of a millimeter.

Near-infrared (black-and-white, color). That portion of the electromagnetic spectrum between visible light and thermal infrared with wavelengths from 0.7 to 1 u. Black-and-white infrared versus color infrared refers to the film type which is used to image in the portion of the spectrum from 0.7 to 0.9 u.

Noise. An unwanted disturbance recorded by a remote sensing device which makes recognition more difficult.

Optical density. The transparency of an object or the degree to which it prevents light from passing through it. It equals $\log_{10}$[intensity of incident light ÷ intensity of transmitted light].

Optical-mechanical scanner. A system utilizing a rotating mirror and a detector in conjunction with lenses and prisms to record reflected and/or emitted electromagnetic energy in a scanning mode along the flight path.

Optical system. A system whose basic function is the recording of a scene by the use of lenses and/or prisms.

Passive system. A remote sensing system which images energy emitted or reflected as radiation from a given scene. The system produces, transmits, and records no energy of its own.

Phonon. A quantum of sound energy analogous to the photon of electromagnetic energy. It is a function of a constant and the vibration of a sound wave.

Photographic system. A remote sensing system which produces an image directly on a film emulsion from reflected electromagnetic radiation of wavelengths in the visible and near-infrared portions of the EM spectrum.

Photon. The minimum energy unit in electromagnetic radiation; an indivisible quantity of electromagnetic energy. Intensity of radiation depends upon the number of photons for a unit area over a certain amount of time. Its magnitude is directly proportional to the frequency of the wavelengths.

Platform. The object, structure, vehicle, or base upon which a remote sensor is mounted.

Polarization. The act or process of filtering energy in such a way that the vibrations are restricted to a single plane. Unpolarized energy vibrates in all directions perpendicular to the propagating source.

Continued

Glossary (continued)

Quanta. The equivalent of photon.

Radar. A sensor that directs energy from its own source at an object and then records the echo return of the transmitted beam in the radio frequency range.

    Synthetic aperture. Systems which use a physically small antenna to simulate an antenna of greater length, by transmitting and receiving a series of pulses which are then integrated into a single pulse for display.

    Brute force. Systems using a physically fixed antenna to transmit and receive single pulses, which are then displayed directly.

Radiometer. An instrument for measuring radiant energy.

Reflectance. A measure of the ability of a body to reflect light or sound. The reflectance of a surface depends on the type of surface, the wavelength of the illumination, and the illumination and viewing angles.

Reflectance infrared. Radiation in the spectral region from 0.7 to 3.0 u which is reflected as a result of illumination from natural sources. The portion of the infrared region which is imaged on infrared sensitive films (up to $\simeq$ 1.5 u).

Resolution. The ability of a remote sensing system to distinguish signals that are close to each other spatially, temporally, or spectrally.

    Ground resolution. The minimum distance between two or more adjacent features or the minimum size of a feature which can be detected; usually measured in conventional distance units (e.g., feet or inches).

    Image resolution. Resolution expressed in terms of lines per millimeter for a given photographic emulsion under given situations.

    Thermal resolution. Image resolution expressed as a function of the minimum temperature difference between two objects or phenomena.

Return. Emitted or reflected energy received by a sensor from a source.

Scattering. The deflection or absorption and re-emission of electromagnetic energy as it passes through a medium (usually the earth's atmosphere).

    Rayleigh scattering. The circumference of the particles is less than about one-tenth of the wavelength of the incident radiation; thus, the scattering coefficient is inversely proportional to the fourth power of the wavelength.

    Mie scattering. Produced by spherical particles whose diameter is comparable with the wavelength of the energy scattered.

    Nonselective scattering. The size of the scattering particles becomes several times larger than the wavelength of the light energy, causing all colors to scatter equally. This accounts for the white appearance of clouds.

    Raman scattering. (Much less common than the other types.) Caused when a photon has a partially elastic collision with a molecule. The wavelength is altered by an amount equivalent to the amount of energy given up or received by the photon.

Sensor. An instrument used to detect and/or record electromagnetic energy associated with an environmental phenomenon(a).

Signal. A pulse or unit wave of electromagnetic energy transmitted or received by a sensor.

Signature. The unique spectral reflectance or emission response from a particular object or environmental association.

Software. Methods, techniques, and systems of interpretation of imagery; examples: photointerpretation keys and computer programs.

Spectrophotometer. An optical instrument used to compare the intensities of the corresponding colors of two spectra.

Specular reflection. The reflection of electromagnetic energy without scattering or diffusion.

Surrogate (proxy). An indicator of the presence of some object or condition of interest which, although not visible, is functionally related to phenomena identifiable on the imagery.

Synoptic. Providing a summary of information about a whole characterized by comprehensiveness or breadth of view; i.e., the general overall view of a large portion of the earth's surface afforded by imagery obtained from high-altitude platforms such as satellites.

Target. The object or objects imaged by remote sensors; also, a planned array of objects used to calibrate one or more remote sensing instruments.

Thermal infrared. Electromagnetic energy between wavelengths of approximately 3 um and 1,000 um. The intensity of emissions is dependent upon temperature and emissivity of the object being sensed.

Thermography. Word proposed to replace the phrase "thermal infrared imagery." Thermography would be a record of emitted thermal energy in the same context as photography is a record of reflected energy. A thermogram would then be a quantitative thermal infrared image.

Transmission. The passage or propagation of energy through a medium.

Ultraviolet. Electromagnetic energy that is shorter than visible light but longer than X-rays, located between 10 and 400 millimicrons.

Vidicon. A camera system in which a light pattern is stored on the surface of a photoconductor, which is then scanned by an electron beam.

Visible. That portion of the electromagnetic spectrum between wavelengths of 400 to 700 millimicrons, which corresponds to the spectral response of the human eye.

Wavelength. The distance between two successive crests or troughs of a wave at uniform frequency and oscillation, measured in the direction of the propagation of the wave. Wavelength equals velocity divided by frequency.

Window. A band of the electromagnetic spectrum which offers maximum transmission and minimal attenuation through a particular medium with the use of a specific sensor.

---

viously unrecognized elements of the north-south structural grain typical of the Basin and Range Province. Field reconnaissance confirmed both spatial and temporal associations. Such systematic analysis provides the basis for selecting additional exploration targets for ground-based reconnaissance, assuming the genetic relationship between mineralization and structure is definite.[17]

Other studies show the concentration of several major mining districts along major lineaments in Nevada.[18]

Worthington[19] reports the coincidence of known ore deposits and linears in two separate regions (Colorado and Kentucky-Illinois). Similar associations have been found in the Michigan-Illinois Basins, where the prominent shear zones associated with carbonate breccia petroleum reservoirs have been detected in orbital imagery from ERTS.

Working with space imagery of the Colorado Plateau as a base, Davis[20] concludes: "As loci of major fracturing, folding, and 'rapid' facies changes, the inferred fracture zones may have exerted some control on the entrapment of oil and gas." Work now in progress on the Colorado Plateau suggests that uranium distribution here may also be systematically disposed with respect to the major fracture zones.

The measurement of luminescence of geochemically stressed trees and other materials has been discussed by Hemphill et al. Differences were detected in the luminescence of trees growing in soils containing geochemically anomalous concentrations of copper (near Denver, Colo.) and molybdenum (near Reno, Nev.).[21]

Recent work in Alaska indicates that locations of known mineral deposits and altered zones correlate well with linears. Numerous areas of anomalous light reflectance were detected; most are associated with known mineral deposits and altered zones, whereas others are not and

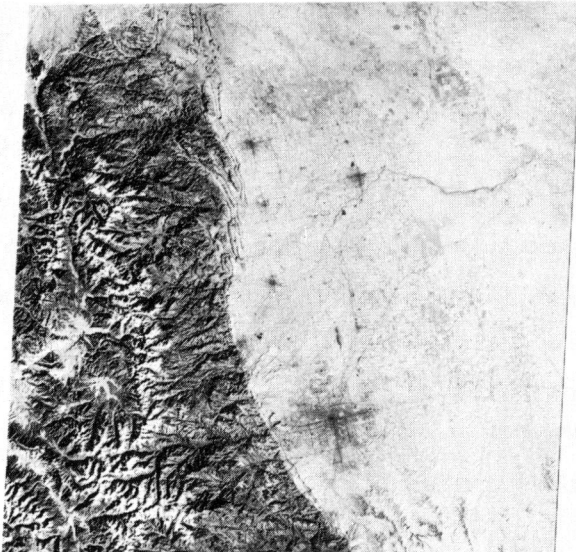

Landsat image of Rocky Mountains, Denver, and Fort Collins, taken in Band 7—the visible or near-infrared.

Landsat Band 7 image of part of Colorado. Oblong, lower left center, is West Elk Mountains, with San Juan range to the south.

may represent unexplored areas with mineral potential.[22]

A tentative (and highly suppositional) prediction of the potential of remote sensing, is offered by Hodgson: "It may become possible to develop a valid genetic theory for predicting in advance the location of environments specifically favorable for mineral deposits."[23] □

References

1) Hoffer, R. M., "The Importance of 'Ground Truth' Data in Remote Sensing," LARS Print 120371, Laboratory for Applications of Remote Sensing, Purdue University, West Lafayette, Ind., 1971.
2) Pierce, J. C., "Mineral Development," MINING MATTERS, Mountain States Mineral Enterprises, Tucson, Ariz., 1975.
3) Estes, John E., and Senger, Leslie W., *Remote Sensing Techniques for Environmental Analysis*, Hamilton Publishing Co., Santa Barbara, Calif., 1974.
4) Bidwell, Timothy C., "College and University Sources of Remote Sensing Information," PHOTOGRAMMETRIC ENGINEERING AND REMOTE SENSING, Vol. 41, No. 10, October 1975.
5) Alexander, Larry, et al, "Remote Sensing—Environmental Geotechnical Applications," Engineering Bulletin 45, Dames & Moore, August 1974.
6) Nordberg, W., "NASA Plans for Future Earth Resources Missions," First Annual William T. Pecora Memorial Symposium, Sioux Falls, S. Dak., October 1975.
7) Maxwell, Marvin S., "Future Sensor Technology for Geologic and Related Missions," ibid.
8) Woodring, S. M., "Remote Sensing—Studying West Virginia from the Air," NEWSLETTER, West Virginia Geological Survey, Issue 18, Morgantown, W. Va., December 1974.
9) Ray, Richard G., "Aerial Photographs in Geologic Interpretation and Mapping," US Geological Survey Professional Paper 373, 1960.
10) "Geologic Exploration by Remote Sensing from Space," SKILLINGS MINING REVIEW, November 8, 1975.
11) Anderson, Arthur T., "First ERTS-1 Mosaic of the U.S.," PHOTOGRAMMETRIC ENGINEERING AND REMOTE SENSING, Vol. 41, No. 10, October 1975.
12) Reinemund, John A., "International Implications of LANDSAT Data From A Geological Viewpoint," William T. Pecora Memorial Symposium.
13) Schmidt, R. G., and Bernstein, Ralph, "Evaluation of Improved Digital Processing Techniques of LANDSAT Data for Sulfide Mineral Prospecting," ibid.
14) Salas, G. P., "Relationship of Mineral Resources to Linear Features In Mexico As Determined From LANDSAT (ERTS) Data," ibid.
15) Miller, John B., "LANDSAT Images As Applied to Petroleum Exploration in Kenya," ibid.
16) Donovan, T. J., "LANDSAT Data Contributions To Project Birddog," ibid.
17) Liggett, M. A., and Childs, John F., "An Application of Satellite Imagery to Mineral Exploration," ibid.
18) Levandowski, D. W., et al, "Applications of ERTS-1 Imagery to Mapping of Lineaments Favorable to the Localization of Ore Deposits in Central Nevada," LARS Information Note 101073, Laboratory For Applications of Remote Sensing, 1973.
19) Worthington, R. W., "Exploration By Petroleum Independents Using Imagery and Photos From EROS and Manned Space Surveys," William T. Pecora Memorial Symposium.
20) Davis, George H., "Tectonic Analysis of Folds in the Colorado Plateau of Arizona," OALS Bulletin 9, Office of Arid Land Studies, University of Arizona, Tucson, 1975.
21) Hemphill, W. R., et al, "Measurement of Luminescence of Geochemically Stressed Trees and Other Materials," William T. Pecora Memorial Symposium.
22) Nairn, R. D. A., and Chavez, P. S. Jr., "Computer Enhanced LANDSAT Imagery as a Tool for Mineral Exploration in Alaska," ibid.
23) Hodgson, R. A., "Regional Linear Analysis as a Guide to Mineral Resources Exploration—Using LANDSAT (ERTS) Data," ibid.

Pre-dawn satellite flight provided this thermal infrared image of Superstition Hills fault and anticline (center) in Arizona.

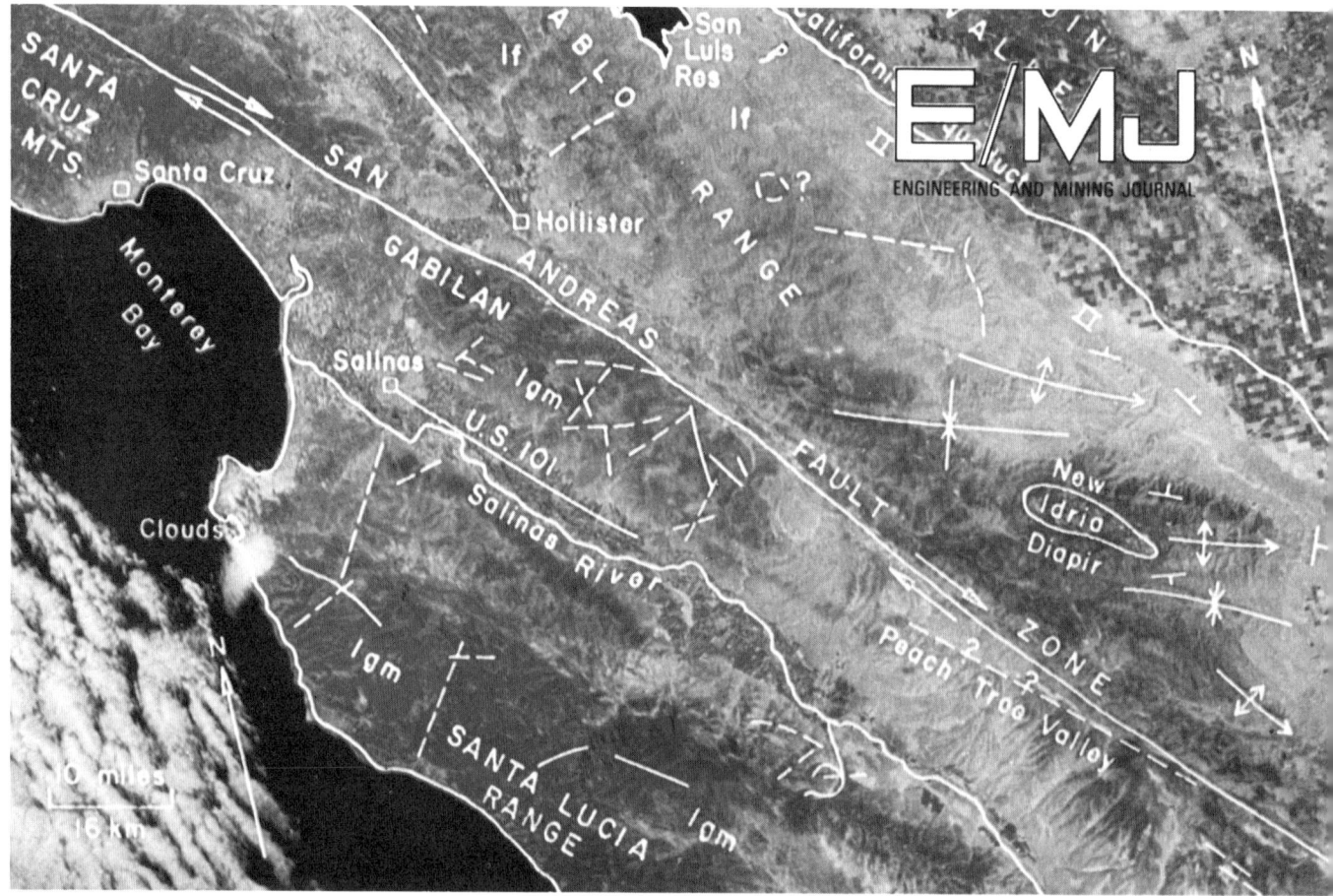

Color composite of Landsat-1 images of California. The imagery was used in work by Abdel-Gawad and Silverstein to demonstrate link between six mercury mining districts (including New Idria) and transverse faults in the southern Coast Ranges.

Looking for minerals via satellite: a far-out approach to exploration

Satellite imagery—interpreted through conventional photogeologic techniques and innovative computer processing—can zero in on metallic ore deposits, providing a useful new supplement to ground studies

Robert Sisselman, Associate editor

PINPOINTING MINERAL DEPOSITS from observation of satellite images—fast becoming a reality—will require both the perfection and possible combined application of two techniques: analysis of lineaments and crustal fractures, and the use of computer-processed satellite images to locate patches of hydrothermally altered surfaces of the earth.

The ability to recognize linears—and particularly systems—is expected to increase the probability of finding mineralization. This expectation is based on the theory that such linears (when confirmed as fractures) may provide a local control for the introduction of mineral solutions. In fact, research conducted by public and private organizations in locations including Colorado, Alaska, Mexico, and Maine has tended to support the contention that fractures spotted from space do point the way toward orebodies.

The belief that surface alteration or secondary enrichment of surface rock and soil may be a manifestation of a shallow orebody has prompted one government spokesman to speculate that satellite interpretation, "if it bears up under further testing, now stands as a major breakthrough in mineral prospecting."

Recent events have lent some support to this claim. Two experiments conducted by scientists of the US Geological Survey have shown that computer-processed satellite images of the earth's surface, principally from the Landsat-1 earth resources survey satellite, can be used to find buried metallic mineral deposits in arid regions. (Landsat-1 was formerly called ERTS-1.)

In one such experiment, five copper-bearing deposits were located in a remote part of Pakistan. In the other ex-

Standard color composite of Lake Mead, Nev., and California and Arizona, made by taking images of Landsat MSS bands 4, 5, and 7, assigning color filters to each, and sandwiching images to make a color rendition. (Image courtesy of Argus Exploration.)

periment, "signatures" (light reflectance characteristics of the earth's surface recorded by computer) were arrived at for known mineral deposits in Nevada in the US, demonstrating that such distinctive signatures on space images of other areas can be used to discover new orebodies.

Both experiments relied on the fact that different rocks, soils, and other materials on the earth's surface reflect varying amounts of light. These variations in reflectance are recorded on images taken by a multispectral line scanner (MSS) aboard the Landsat-1 satellite orbiting the earth. (Landsat-1, launched July 23, 1972, was joined in orbit January 22, 1975, by Landsat-2.)

Critics of Landsat's potential take issue with the ballyhoo that has accompanied these more esoteric approaches to minerals exploration. As one corporate exploration specialist stated: "We use Landsat photographs quite a lot. But they are more useful overseas. Even then, their immediate value to us depends on the extent to which existing geological maps in a given region are available."

Still others in the industry, described by one Landsat investigator as "hardcore crusty management types," have charged that the "Landsat-1 boondoggle" was not worth anywhere near the $60 million required to launch and operate the satellite.

There seems to be little question in the minds of some researchers that remote identification of ore deposits would yield significant economic benefits in the long run. According to one source, remote sensing of alteration zones and other rock units on the earth's surface might result in a 20% savings in the costs of geologic mapping, a critical part of mining exploration.

While some exploration specialists take a skeptical view, many are pursuing a positive but cautious, middle-of-the-road course, doubtless due to the speculative nature of satellite interpretation of potential orebodies.

One corporate vice president in charge of exploration recently told E/MJ that his company "has, in fact, established a photogeologic department which advises our other people on the present and future value of these [Landsat] images."

Aside from the government and private industry, other interested parties, including consulting groups such as Dames & Moore, are taking advantage of the relatively inexpensive methods of Landsat imagery interpretation. D&M is offering its services to industry clients interested in the practical application of Landsat or other remote sensors to help define potential mineral targets. Such specialized interpretive servicing is expanding.

Photo linears linked to mineralization

One of the pioneering Landsat-1 studies, conducted from June through November 1973, successfully correlated the identification of photo-linear structures with the known location and distribution of metallic mineral deposits in the Colorado mineral belt in the western US.[1]

Working on Landsat image No. E1172-17141 was a joint team of scientists and graduate students from the Planetary Geology Laboratory at Martin Marietta Corp. in Denver, Colo., and the Department of Geology of the Col-

False color ratio image of Lake Mead area, produced by ratioing MSS bands, "stretching" them for contrast to enhance spectral differences, and further enhancing them by preparing color composites of two or more stretched ratio images.

orado School of Mines in Golden, Colo. The sequence of events leading up to the location of mineral targets using Landsat-1 imagery dramatizes the potential benefits that may accrue from other remote sensing experiments that must be verified or "controlled" in terms of ground truth (i.e., corroborated via ground studies).

Image E1172-17141 covered a portion of the Colorado mineral belt, including Leadville-Climax-Alma, Breckenridge, Tomichi, Bonanza, and Cripple Creek. Using the image as a base map, all lineaments perceived by researchers were plotted on a transparent overlay. No attempt was made to differentiate between fractures, contacts, old pipelines, or other natural or man-made linear features on the earth's surface.

The image, recorded on January 11, 1973, was examined at a scale of about 1:1,000,000, using both stereoscopic and monoscopic modes. The 9.5 x 9.5-in. positive transparencies were viewed in all multispectral bands.

The Landsat-1 multispectral line scanner simultaneously records four images—two in the visible part of the spectrum and two in the infrared—each covering the same 115 x 115-mi area. Band 4 is green (0.5-0.6 micrometers), Band 5 is red (0.6-0.7 micrometers), Band 6 is near infrared (0.7-0.8 micrometers), and Band 7 is near infrared (0.8-1.1 micrometers).

Most of the information pertinent to the Colorado experiment was gleaned from Band 7, which permitted the clearest visualization of linear features. Band 7 is normally used as the basic medium for this type of interpretation because, being in the near-infrared range of the spectrum, it is sensitive to differences in moisture content. Water absorbs infrared energy, and since it has a tendency to collect in and move through faults and fractures, these features generally are more easily recognized in Band 7. Both straight and curvilinear or circular features were traced on the overlay. Areas were pinpointed for further investigation based on the assumption that an intersection of two or more faults or fractures (if the linears are, in fact, faults) may constitute the weakest segment of the earth's crust at that point—hence, the most likely location for intrusion of mineral solutions.

The 10 best targets in the study were selected, each corresponding to an area on the ground of about 9 mi in diameter (represented by an approximately 0.5-in.-dia circle on the 1:1,000,000 scale image). The most promising of these areas was judged to house a complex mixture of intersections, of both rectilinear and circular features. Five of these 10 target areas were found to coincide with the known mineral districts. The others are considered high priority exploration sites.

This pioneering effort helped trigger the ongoing evolution of technology employed in the interpretation of Landsat imagery, with the eventual goal of providing a reliable supplementary aid in the detection of mineral deposits. Interpretation of that imagery presently ranges from techniques as basic and time-proven as stereoscopic viewing to the more sophisticated digital computer interactive displays.

Many mining companies are proceeding under their own steam with Landsat interpretation, taking advantage

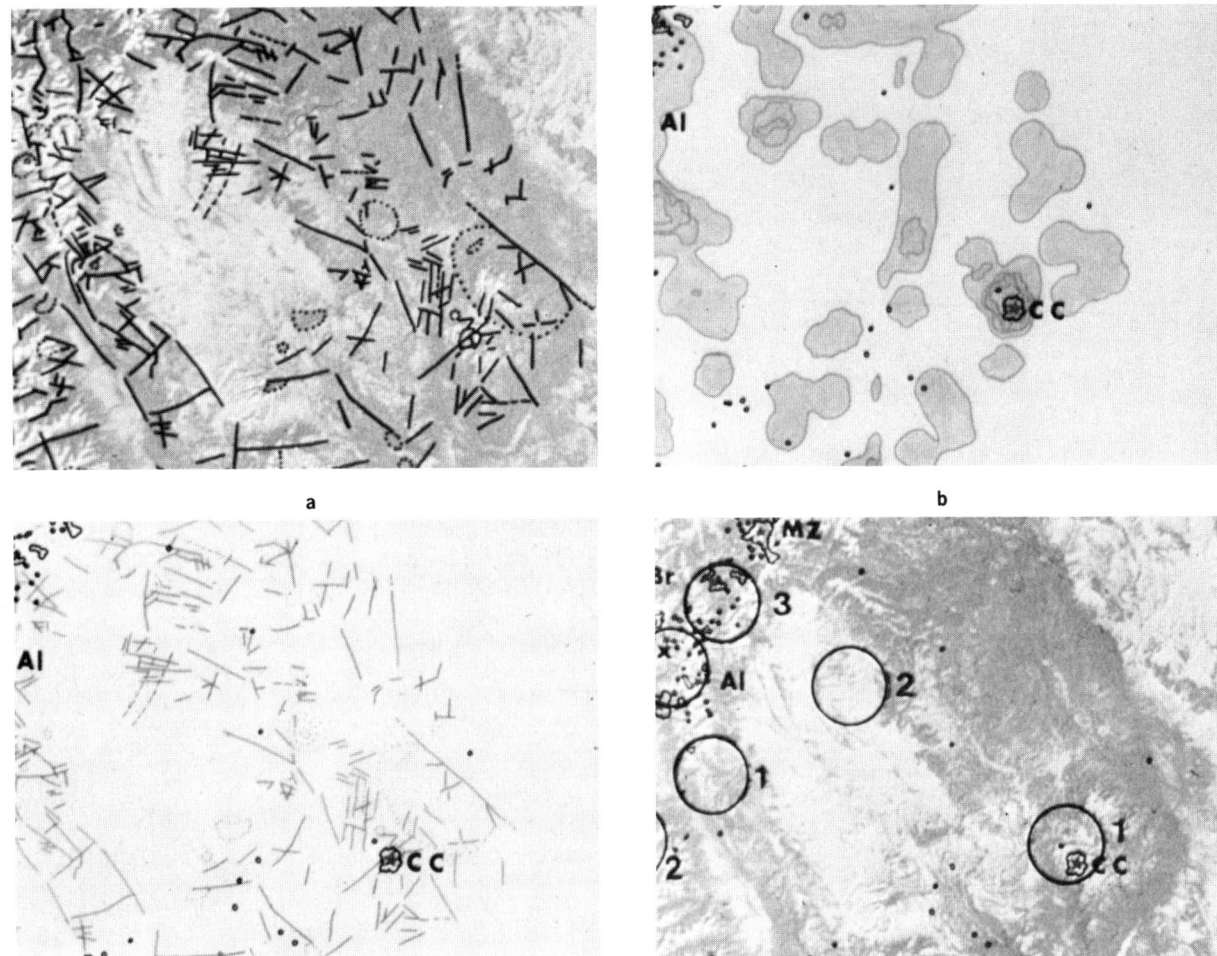

Overlay map of linears in a portion of Colorado mineral belt (a) from Cripple Creek (CC) to Alma (A1) shows identified linears as solid lines, possible linears as dotted lines. Contours of relative density of linear intersections are shown (b). Locations of present and past mining operations are indicated by red stars (c). Study indicated areas with potential for exploration (d), numbered (in order of priority) 1, 2, and 3. (Photos courtesy of Colorado School of Mines and Martin Marietta Corp.)

of custom-produced transparencies available from such sources as the Landsat Data Center in Sioux Falls, N. Dak., and General Electric's photoengineering laboratory in Beltsville, Md. Still other mining companies are employing the services of consultants, who appear concerned not only with satellite interpretation itself, but also with followup confirmation of those findings on the ground.

The application of remote sensing techniques to mineral exploration is illustrated by a Dames & Moore Landsat study conducted for the International Paper Co. in northwestern Maine. Because the area is isolated, heavily timbered, and estimated to contain less than 5% rock outcrop, little geological information is obtainable. An analysis and interpretation of roughly 10,000 sq mi located more than 700 lineaments ranging from 2 mi to over 200 mi long, of which fewer than 10% were previously known or recorded. In addition, the analysis identified more than 25 monadnocks (erosional remnants), possibly of igneous origin, which had not previously been recognized. Based upon existing geological information and the Landsat study, a number of areas were believed to warrant further detailed reconnaissance. It was subsequently learned that two of the more interesting areas defined were "coincident with soil geochemical anomalies."

Similar studies have also been conducted in other, diverse regions of the US and Mexico, with equally interesting results. It must be stressed, however, that Landsat-1 imagery is at this time essentially a means of performing a regional reconnaissance quickly and cheaply. Its use in conjunction with *other* exploration tools, such as aeromagnetics and gravimetrics, will increase its value and provide significant additional information.

The usefulness of combined techniques was demonstrated in a recent publication from Dames & Moore, "Engineering Bulletin 45," covering southeastern Arizona. Limited to geological structures, the study combined available aeromagnetic, gravimetric, geologic, and mineral occurrence maps with Landsat-1 coverage of the area. Interpretations were made of the Landsat imagery and the aeromagnetic and gravimetric maps. All of the accumulated information was compiled on four clear overlays. A fifth overlay showed the coincidence and intersection of aeromagnetic and/or gravity lineaments with Landsat-1 lineaments. The results are believed to contribute substantially to an understanding of the regional structural geology and may well assist in minerals exploration of the area.

Hypothetically, the conducting of an exploration program using Landsat information by a group such as D&M might follow a more or less prescribed sequence, beginning with a literature search to produce a single map that

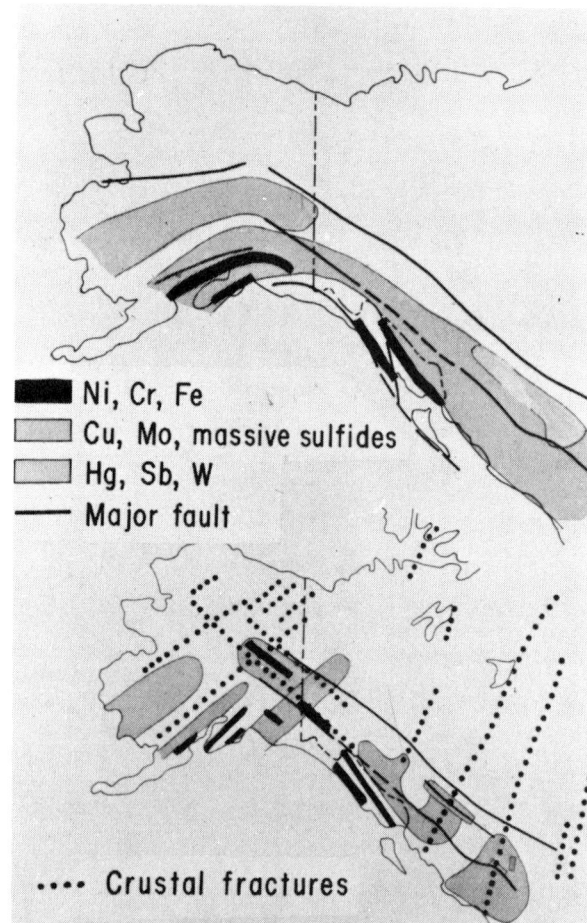

Tectonic and metallogenic-province model of southern Alaska is based partly on analysis of imagery from Landsat-1 satellite.

would serve as a framework for ground truth (i.e., confirming data received from remote sensing sources through field studies on the ground). This would be followed by interpretation and analysis, by different scientists, of whatever remote sensor records were available (including satellite images). Following the comparison of these interpretations, a transfer scope would be used to plot all of the delineated features of structure and lithology at a common scale and format on separate transparent overlays, which would be registered to a common base map—the map compiled during the literature search. A synthesized overlay would then be prepared, combining all of the geological features of the separate overlays. From this, a metallogenic map would be prepared, based on geological inference and known occurrences of minerals in the area as they correlate with lithology and structure.

Alaskan linears define metallogenic relationships

The most promising structural correlations with known mineral deposits were shown by Ernest H. Lathram[2] in Alaska, where a revision of theories on faulting sequences and identification of new structures has led to the discovery of six porphyry copper deposits by one mining company.

Ideally suited to remote sensing—since transportation is limited, terrain is rugged, and the geology is complex—the 49th state is being mapped with the aid of Landsat technology.

Close inspection of a Nimbus weather satellite image by Lathram revealed numerous dark, linear features extending great distances across the image in northeast and northwest trends. Many of these presumably structural features had not been previously known nor correlated and recognized as continuous structures in the earth's crust. Their great length led Lathram and his associates to conclude that the linears were probably of a fundamental, crustal nature and were thus important in reaching an understanding of metallogenic relationships throughout Alaska.

Comparison of the northeast- and northwest-trending sets of possible crustal faults or fractures revealed by the Nimbus photo, along with the distribution of known Alaskan mineral deposits, suggested a cause and effect relationship. Specifically, massive sulphide mineralizations in Prince William Sound and in the upper Copper River areas, along with porphyry coppers in the Nabesna area, form a broad northeast-trending belt that may be related to the Minto Arch on the Canadian Shield. The mineral belt in the western Alaska Range follows a comparable northeast trend.

Furthermore, mercury deposits, suggested by geologists to be fault-controlled, together with most tin and tungsten deposits, occupy a northeast-trending belt between the Bristol Bay-Mackenzie Bay lineament, as extensions of a lineament along the lower Yukon River. This belt intersects the northwest-trending Canadian belt of similar deposits in the Fairbanks area.

Faulting in California traces mercury deposits

Using Landsat imagery, Monem Abdel-Gawad and Joel Silverstein[3] observed an apparent correlation between the distribution of mercury deposits in the California Coast Ranges and transverse fault zones trending west-northwest, oblique to the trend of the San Andreas fault system. It appears to be economically important that these transverse faults are a distinct part of the deformation history of the Pacific mountain system of California.

The most striking correlation seen in northern California is in the Clear Lake and the Great Western mercury districts. Plotting an overlay map of this area has shown known faults as well as others inferred from Landsat imagery. The collection of mercury mines in the Great Western, Aetna, Mirabel, and Oat Hill districts is most striking—forming a distinct belt trending west-northwest and coinciding with a zone of transverse faults.

Abdel-Gawad and Silverstein have plotted known mercury occurrences together with transverse fault zones inferred from Landsat-1. In this area of the Coast Ranges, there are six mercury mining districts, including the New Almaden—one of the two most productive mercury mines in California since 1846.

Landsat imagery put to the test in Mexico

In a more practical context, Landsat imagery was put to the test in the complex porphyry copper province of northwestern Sonora, Mexico, by a team composed of Richard Pascucci, Andrew Stanicoff, and George Rabchevsky.[4] Using Landsat-derived data in combination with a variety of other data sources, a number of exploration targets were pinpointed. These targets, reported the authors, "should serve as a relatively good guide to a reconnaissance exploration program."

In the study, good quality Landsat imagery enabled the investigators to establish major geomorphic, structural and lithologic relationships of the Sonoran Sierra Madre Occi-

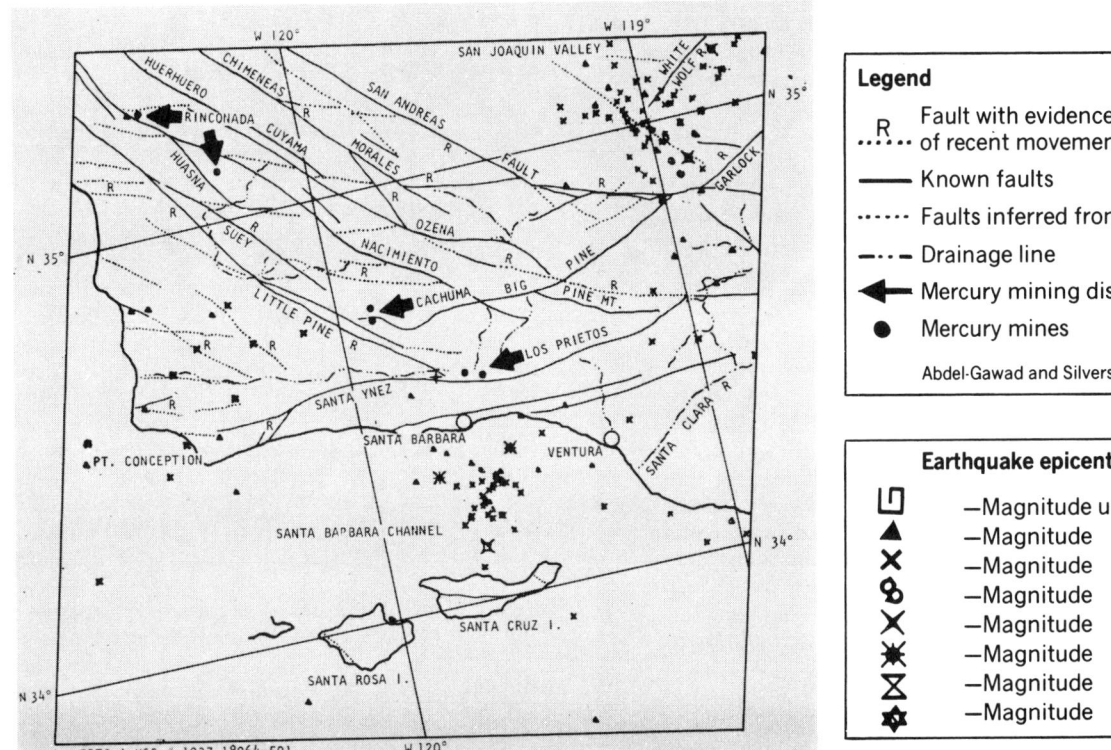

Many fault lineaments inferred from Landsat-1 imagery, which were either not previously mapped or shown on maps incorporated with other faults. Three mercury districts—Rinconada, Cachuma, and Los Prietos—are related to transverse faults.

dental and to relate these features to the well known geology of Arizona and to the structurally active zones in the Gulf of California. The environment for porphyry copper occurrences as established in the southwestern US was noted to be similar to that in the Sonora area, and Landsat imagery provided a means of utilizing these similarities to define exploration targets.

A mosaic of a 10,000-sq-mi area in northwest Sonora was constructed at a scale of 1:250,000, using three frames from two orbits of an August 1972 Landsat overflight; channel 5 imagery was employed. Lithologic, structural, and other interpretive efforts were conducted using the black and white mosaic at a scale of 1:250,000 and two types of color composite transparencies at a scale of 1:1,000,000. These interpretations were then plotted on transparent overlays and, based on this information, 14 specific target areas were proposed for a porphyry copper exploration program.

Of the targets chosen in the initial interpretation, only one was visible on the ground. This target was located at the intersection of at least three faults. A large quartz monzonite porphyry intrusive associated with extrusive volcanics was found to contain brecciated zones and veins in which copper mineralization was present. It was subsequently disclosed that a mining group in Tucson, Ariz., had taken out exploration permits over the area after having conducted a geochemical survey.

It was found that one obvious advantage of Landsat interpretation is the identification of a certain limited amount of lithology. Extrusives, for instance, were easily mapped on the basis of overall flow structures and drainage patterns; loci of volcanic areas were postulated; granitic rocks could be identified where rectangular drainage was well developed; and sediments were easily distinguished on the basis of tone and drainage. Resolution of Landsat imagery was also judged good enough to allow differentiation of rock units to a degree that produced a "crowded map."

On the debit side, however, the authors concluded after completion of the Mexican study that they should have made initial structural interpretation on 9 x 9-in. color composite imagery; should have considered mapping structure on three separate overlays (mapping each of three directional systems separately); and should have enlarged four to six adjacent images, which would have been of great assistance in regional analysis.

They also concluded that a much better result would have been achieved with the following approach:

■ Later-date imagery should have been used.
■ Two to three cross sections should have been produced using United Nations maps for comparison.
■ Thrust fault margins should have been located with great care, and fault block relationships established.
■ A series of overlays should have been prepared on which favorable criteria could have been independently designated by use of Zipatone patterns on a different overlay. By compilation of these overlays, target areas would automatically appear as the darkest areas. This would have provided a much more objective method for choosing targets.

Genetic link between linears and orebodies

Structural analysis of Nevada by Lawrence Rowan and Pamela Wetlaufer[5] using Landsat-1 images shows several previously unrecognized lineaments that may be the surface manifestation of major fault or fracture zones. Principal trends are NE, NW, NNE-NNW, ENE. Two lineament zones, the Walker Lane and Midas Trench lineament system, cut across the predominantly NNE-NNW trending mountain ranges for more than 500 km; 50 circular features have also been delineated. Comparison with known Tertiary volcanic centers and reference to geologic maps suggest eight new volcanic centers.

The distribution of mines and Tertiary volcanic centers along some of the major lineaments suggests a genetic relationship. The intersection of three previously unmapped lineaments in northwestern Nevada is the location of a highly productive metallogenic district. In the Walker Lane, ENE-trending lineaments appear to be related to the occurrence of productive ore deposits.

Although the authors believe that structural significance of the lineaments mapped here is not clear, they do believe that a genetic relationship is implied by the coincidence of productive orebodies and some major lineaments.

They found that the distribution of active silver, gold, copper, lead, and zinc mining appears to be almost random, except perhaps for a concentration along the Walker Lane. However, comparison of major lineaments delineated on Landsat images with mining districts shows that several important districts are located at lineament intersections.

Productive districts occur mostly along the northeastern part of the Midas Trench lineament zone, and a number of highly productive areas are concentrated there. (See accompanying image mosaic.)

The results of the Rowan-Wetlaufer study, although unsubstantiated, point toward the potential of Landsat images for regional structural analysis. Most of the major lineaments mapped in this study were either previously unrecognized or known only locally. Concentration of known orebodies along some of the lineaments and at intersections strongly suggests a genetic relationship. Tertiary volcanic centers are aligned similarly but seem to be less important in the segregation of these metallic ore deposits.

Computer processing scouts out surface alteration

Aside from the structural interpretation of Landsat imagery, another potentially valuable application is the identification of surface-altered materials, to provide clues to the location of shallow mineral deposits. The assumption here is that such alterations are manifestations of shallow mineralization.

The means for identifying hydrothermally altered areas of the earth's surface originate from the Landsat multispectral line scanner, which records images of the earth's surface electronically in digital form. The smallest image or area distinguished by the MSS is called a picture element ("pixel"). Each pixel covers about 1 acre of the earth's surface, with approximately 7.5 million pixels comprising each Landsat image of an area 115 x 115 mi. The size of the number recorded for each pixel in the digital format—from 1 to 255—represents the amount of light reflected by the corresponding acre on the earth's surface.

Computers and other processing equipment at NASA's Goddard Space Flight Center in Greenbelt, Md., convert the series of numbers for each scene to a picture format.

Identification and classification of hydrothermally altered rocks from Landsat data by means of rock coloration and relative reflectance is not always dependable. However, Robert Vincent[6], in work performed on the iron-bearing rocks of the Wind River Range in Wyoming, developed an interesting approach. Vincent was able to take pairs of MSS bands, ratio them, and reproduce images or computer printouts from the ratio signals. This work indicates that iron-bearing rocks can be successfully segregated from other lithologic units via selective ratioing of MSS bands.

Landsat is also capable of singling out patches of hydrothermally altered terrain by means of a special film pro-

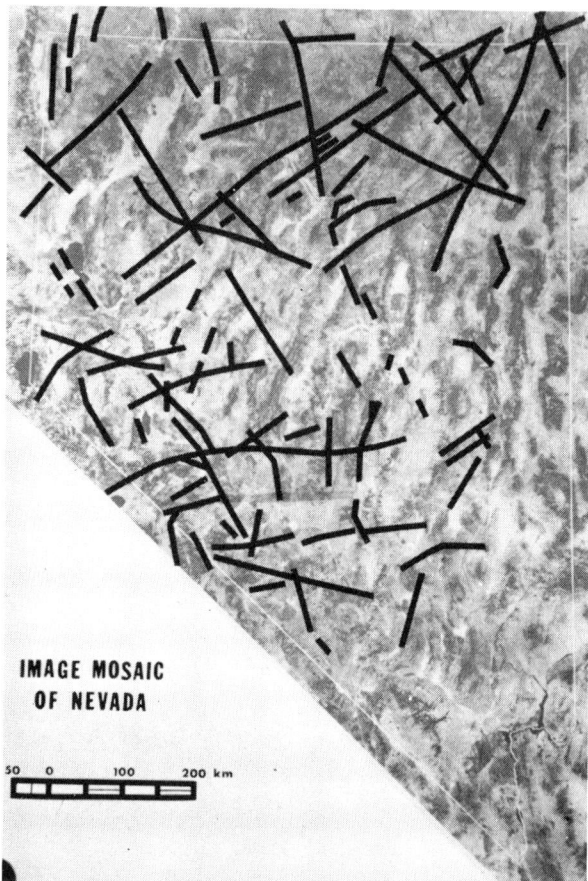

Image of northern Nevada's northeast–trending linear, Midas Trench system, and northwest-trending Walker Lane zone.

cessing technique developed by A. F. H. Goetz.[7] The Goetz technique employs MSS band ratioed images similar to Vincent's approach. However, after these enhanced black and white images (representing several selected ratios) are obtained, they are passed through an optical processor equipped with color filters, resulting in the production of color composites. Variations of these ratio-derived color composites can be made, depending upon the band ratios and enhancement chosen, and the varieties of color combination tried.

One of the areas examined by Goetz, situated in north-central Arizona, extends about 70 mi north-south and is 50 mi wide, including portions of the Colorado Plateau and the mountainous region to the south. The area is centered in the Verde Valley and, on the west, includes part of the Chino Valley.

Bulk and computer-enhanced frames of the Verde Valley region of central Arizona—an area that has been well mapped—have been analyzed for structural information and rock unit identification. Most major rock units with sparse ground cover are identifiable on enhanced "false-color" composites. Regional structural patterns are highly visible on the Landsat images.

During the mid-Tertiary, the area studied was the site of plutonism and genetically related volcanism fed by fissure systems now exposed as dike swarms. Dikes, elongate plutons, and coeval normal faults trend generally northward and are believed to have resulted from east-west crustal extension. In the extensional province, gold and silver mineralization is closely related to Tertiary igneous activity. Goetz deduced that similarities in ore, structural setting, and rock types define a metallogenic district with high potential for exploration.

Computer indicates possible Pakistani copper

Most experiments conducted to date using Landsat data have been based on black and white images with each of the four MSS bands, or on "false color" composites made by combining two or more of the spectral bands.

In a different approach, Robert Schmidt, a geologist with the US Geological survey in Reston, Va., made use of a computer printout of the original digital data to help outline five potential copper deposits in Pakistan.

With known copper deposits near Saindak (near the borders of Iran and Afghanistan) as a control area, Schmidt used a computer to determine "signatures" (distinctive ranges of digital numbers) of pixels representing the known copper-bearing zones. Wherever these same signatures showed up elsewhere on Landsat images used in the experiment, distinctive symbols appeared on the computer printouts, giving Schmidt a digital "map" that he matched up with the corresponding area on the ground.

These signatures showed up for 50 other sites in an 800-sq-mi area of the Chagai region. Schmidt eliminated 20 sites because they were known to include sand deposits or hot springs that had signatures similar to the copper zones. Examination of aerial photographs eliminated another seven sites, also sand deposits.

Schmidt made ground inspections of 19 of the remaining 23 sites, eliminating 14 as unlikely copper zones and leaving five he believed should be explored in more detail. As a result of his study, the Pakistani government plans to conduct additional prospecting to determine whether the sites have copper deposits worth exploiting. The five sites appeared promising because the rocks and rock alterations fit known patterns for major copper-bearing deposits.

Nevada 'signatures' show exploration potential

In what has been described as a more complex and sophisticated procedure, another group led by Lawrence Rowan[8] of the USGS used the digital values in intermediate steps, leading to computer enhancement of subtle tonal differences on Landsat pictures of the Goldfield mining district of south-central Nevada. The enhancement increased the contrast of the pictures to help delineate mineralized zones that were not evident to the human eye on the original images. Hydrothermally altered zones show up differently on Landsat images than other areas, although the tonal differences on unenhanced pictures are usually too faint to be seen by the human eye.

In the Nevada experiment, Rowan and his associates used a more complicated three-step procedure: ratioing of MSS bands, contrast "stretching," and production of false color composites. First they determined ratio values between the amount of reflected light recorded in the four light bands for each pixel in a Landsat image, and used these values as the basis for producing new images. However, since these ratio value differences were usually small, the researchers first selected only part of the range of ratio values and "stretched" it to cover a wider range of dark to light tones, thus increasing the contrast. Further enhancement was achieved by superimposing two or more of these ratioed and stretched images and using a different color filter for each image to produce "false color" composites that further accentuated tonal differences.

In Rowan's study, major lineaments (greater than 10 cm) seen on a Landsat image mosaic of Nevada at a scale of 1:1,000,000 were digitized using a grid base. Such values

> Data on imagery or photography may be obtained from the EROS Data Center, Data Management Center, Sioux Falls, S. Dak. 57198. (Telephone 605-399-2270.) A price list is available on request.
> Imagery is also available from General Electric Co. Write to Ralph Baker, Earth Resources Analyst, General Electric Photographic Engineering Laboratory, 5030 Herzel Place, Beltsville, Md. 20705. (Telephone: 301-345-6000.)

as mean length and dominant trend directions were determined via computer analysis.

Spectra for two basalts, a limonitic area, and a playa were determined by Rowan from ratioing the MSS values. In this procedure, the bands are ratioed. The spectral reflectance measured in one band is divided by the spectral reflectance in another—usually an adjacent band, although any one of four MSS bands can be used.

Rowan reported the following significant results:

Most major rock units and unaltered and altered areas in the study area can be discriminated on the basis of visible and near-infrared spectral reflectivity differences recorded from satellite altitude. These subtle spectral differences are not detectable through conventional optical methods of analysis. Digital ratioing of the MSS bands and subsequent stretching to increase the contrast are necessary to enhance spectral differences, which are manifested as slight variations in the slope of the spectra. Although the basic spectral differences are contained in the stretched ratio images, color ratio composites—especially combinations of three ratio images—appear to be the best means of display for geologic interpretation. The optimum combinations of ratios and colors appear to be MSS 4/5 (blue), MSS 5/6 (yellow), and MSS 6/7 (magenta).

Hydrothermally altered areas appear as anomalous color patches within the volcanic rock areas on the composites and may be due either to mineralization or surface manifestation of geothermal areas.

Ultimately, through the use of surface standards, Rowan believes it should be possible to derive relative reflectance spectra for the surface rock units that would provide a means of placing bounds on mineral composition. In the meantime, simple discrimination of regional or major rock units and altered and unaltered areas is possible using computer-enhanced MSS data. □

References

1) "Geologic and Mineral and Water Resources Investigations in Western Colorado Using ERTS-1 Data: Progress Report IX," Department of Geology, Colorado School of Mines, December 1973.
2) Lathram, Ernest H., Tailleur, Irvin L., Patton, William W. Jr., and Fischer, William A., "Preliminary Geologic Application of ERTS-1 Imagery in Alaska," ERTS symposium.*
3) Abdel-Gawad, Monem, and Silverstein, Joel, "ERTS Applications in Earthquake Research and Mineral Exploration in California," ERTS symposium.*
4) Stanicoff, Andrew, Pascucci, Richard, and Rabchevsky, George, "Application of Satellite Photography to Mineral Exploration in Sonora, Mexico," Symposium of the American Society of Photogrammetry, October 1973.
5) Rowan, Lawrence C., and Wetlaufer, Pamela H., "Structural Geologic Analysis of Nevada Using ERTS-1 Images: A Preliminary Report," ERTS symposium.*
6) Vincent, Robert K., "Ratio Maps of Iron Ore Deposits Atlantic City District, Wyoming," ERTS symposium.*
7) Goetz, Alexander F. H. et al, "Preliminary Geologic Investigations in the Colorado Plateau Using Enhanced ERTS Images," ERTS symposium.*
8) Rowan, Lawrence C., "Iron-absorption Band Analysis for the Discrimination of Iron-Rich Zones," Type 11 Progress Report, USGS, January 30, 1974.

*NASA-sponsored Symposium on Significant Results Obtained from Earth Resources Technology Satellite-1, March 5-9, 1973.

Rock geochemistry: a mixed bag of analytical techniques

CHEMICAL ANALYSIS OF WHOLE ROCK SAMPLES is employed in both regional and local prospecting for base metals. At one time, rock geochemistry was primarily concerned with the concentrations in bare rock of target metals, including copper, molybdenum, zinc, and gold. Recently, however, attention has focused on elements whose distribution near mineral deposits may be useful because they create halos more easily recognizable than those of the metals being sought. Barium and strontium, among other elements, are relatively abundant and can be determined in most rocks.[1] Exploration techniques used in the analysis of rocks include dispersion patterns, mineral zonation, fluid-inclusion studies, pathfinder elements, and isotopic studies.

Primary dispersion patterns and halos

Many mineral deposits of igneous or hydrothermal origin are characterized by a central zone, such as a vein, in which the important elements or minerals may be concentrated sufficiently to warrant mining. In most instances, there is a steady decline in the quantity of the valuable element in the deposit until the content equals that of the enclosing rock (background value). The zone within which the content of valuable elements drops to background values is called the *primary halo* or *aureole*. Halos represent the distribution patterns of elements that formed as a result of *primary dispersion*.[2]

Dispersion patterns may be classified as primary or secondary, depending on whether they were formed at depth by igneous or metamorphic processes, or at the surface by agents of weathering, erosion, and surface transportation.[3]

The recognition and interpretation of primary halos is one of the main goals of geochemical rock surveys. Primary halos are subdivided into three types: 1) those that cover wide areas, resulting from massive injection of rock by hydrothermal solutions or other fluids percolating from depth; 2) those that are manifested in leakage patterns possessing well-defined channelways for the dispersement of fluids; 3) those that form wall rock patterns, where the rock adjacent to these solution channelways has been hydrothermally altered.

Leakage halos vary in dimension, but they are particularly valuable in the search for several types of hidden ore deposits.

Gaseous leakage halos are even more important in exploration for deep ore deposits because gases such as mercury, iodine, and bromine move easily through rock and soil pores and fractures.[2]

Fluid-inclusion studies

Fluid-inclusion studies—particularly qualitative microscopic studies—remain the most direct method of sampling hydrothermal fluids. During the crystallization of minerals or during recrystallization after fracturing, small portions of the fluids present may become trapped within the mineral grains. Most of these fluid inclusions are small (0.001 to 0.01 mm in diameter), and they frequently contain a small gaseous bubble in addition to the liquid.

Results of a fluid-inclusion study in Puerto Rico may help solve problems in porphyry copper exploration. Researchers demonstrated that the halite content of fluid inclusions in quartz correlates directly with the copper content of the rock and that the inclusions are probably unaffected during weathering and formation of soils. The researchers further suggest that, as a simple addition to soil geochemical exploration programs, study of fluid inclusions in residual quartz grains might be of value. This is particularly true in tropical latitudes where intense leaching may remove most of the copper from the soils above an orebody.[4]

In another study conducted at Bagdad, Ariz., quartz in chalcopyrite- and molybdenite-bearing veins was found to

Examples of pathfinder elements used to detect mineralization

Pathfinder elements	Type of deposit
As	Au, Ag; vein-type
As	Au-Ag-Cu-Co-Zn; complex sulphide ores
B	W-Be-Zn-Mo-Cu-Pb; skarns
B	Sn-W-Be; veins or greisens
Hg	Pb-Zn-Ag; complex sulphide deposits
Mo	W-Sn; contact metamorphic deposits
Mn	Ba-Ag; vein deposits; porphyry copper
Se, V, Mo	U; sandstone-type
Cu, Bi, As, Co, Mo, Ni	U; vein-type
Mo, Te, Au	Porphyry copper
Pd, Cr, Cu, Ni, Co	Platinum in ultramafic rocks
Zn	Ag-Pb-Zn; sulphide deposits in general
Zn, Cu	Cu-Pb-Zn; sulphide deposits in general
Rn	U; all types of occurrences
SO_4	Sulphide deposits of all types

Note: In most cases, several types of material (e.g., rock, soil, sediment, water and vegetation) can be sampled. In some cases, such as radon, only water and soil gas are practical. In the case of sulphate, only water is practical
Source: A. A. Levinson, *Introduction to Exploration Geochemistry*, 1974.

contain two predominant types of fluid inclusions: one having moderate salinity (about 8%) and filling temperatures from 320° to 373°C, and the other having high salinity (30-35%) and filling temperatures of 223° to 310°C. Sparse gas-rich inclusions indicate brief periods of boiling. Temperatures and salinities of ore fluids at Bagdad were found to be significantly lower than in other porphyry copper deposits studied, indicating that chemically and physically diverse fluids affect mineralization in these deposits.[5]

In Canada, the recently discovered Polaris lead-zinc deposit (Little Cornwallis Island, NWT) was found to be comparable to the Pine Point, NWT, deposit in mineralogy, texture, and environment. The freezing stage results and the homogenization temperatures of the fluid inclusions in sphalerite show that the ore was precipitated from clean, probably highly saline, dense brines at temperatures of 52° to 105°C. The calcite probably formed at a lower temperature. These factors preclude a syngenetic origin and favor epigenetic precipitation from heated basinal brines that could have been mixed with surface waters.[6]

Pathfinders are especially valuable

Pathfinder elements or minerals are good clues in the search for hidden orebodies because they generally form large halos. Pathfinders, used in both primary and secondary environments, are defined as relatively mobile elements (or gases) closely associated with the element being sought, but more easily located—either because they form a broader halo, or because they are easier to detect by current analytical procedures.[2]

Halogen geochemistry raises questions

The analytical potential of water and halogen abundances in the formation of magmatic-hydrothermal ore deposits is well known. Most recent evaluations of halogen and water abundances for mineral exploration have focused on analysis of biotite from mineralized and barren intrusive rocks. Results have been conflicting. However, evidence suggests that the variation of whole rock halogen abundances in single intrusions can provide guides to mineralization.[7]

During recent years, numerous studies of the geochemistry of biotite have stressed factors related to mineral exploration, particularly for porphyry-type copper deposits. Trace element data obtained from plutonic biotite has been used to distill information about the parent magma and the hydrothermal system, which together generate porphyry copper deposits.

One recent study concluded that use of copper in biotite as a prospecting tool is prone to extraneous complications, which can lead to serious errors in interpretation. These complications include superfluous or false anomalies created by minor sources of oxidizing copper; variation in vermiculite content which, if too small or absent, could negate anomalous copper assays even if copper is present; contamination of biotite samples by trace amounts of copper-bearing iron oxides; and the occurrence of porphyry copper deposits which have not dispersed hypogene copper outward by significant distances into unaltered rocks.[8]

Studies also indicate that easily distinguishable anomalous fluoride values for water leach and total fluoride in rocks are associated with areas of tin mineralization.[9]

Analyses of fluorine in ground water (see hydrogeochemistry section) deserve careful consideration as a method of geochemical exploration for lead-zinc-barium-fluorine mineralization in the flat-lying carbonate rocks of mid-continent North America.[10]

Use of an iodide-ion-selective electrode has been found to permit rapid and fairly accurate determination of iodine (as iodide) in rocks and soils, in concentrations as low as 0.5 ppm. When bromine concentration exceeds 5 ppm, the same method can be used for bromine determination. This procedure merits further investigation.[11]

The future for pyrite geochemistry

In some instances, pyrite geochemistry shows potential in helping to define targets for detailed exploration. In one study, 111 pyrite samples from three porphyry-type copper deposits in the Canadian cordillera were analyzed by atomic absorption spectrophotometry for cobalt, nickel, copper, lead, zinc, and manganese. Cobalt and nickel show zonal patterns that relate generally to mineralogical zones in the porphyry systems, particularly if contoured as the cobalt/nickel ratio. High copper values in pyrites also correlate with copper-rich mineral zones. Other elements studied appear less regular in their distribution patterns, although zinc highs in pyrite seem to occur sporadically near the margins of porphyry systems.[12]

Roll-type uranium deposits contain both ore-stage pyrite and pre-ore or diagenetic pyrite that was present in the host rock before the deposits began to form. Ore-stage pyrite is formed by redistribution and accretion from the pre-ore pyrite. Accretion of the ore-stage pyrite seems to be governed by natural laws that limit its concentration to only a few times the concentration of the pre-ore pyrite. Accumulations of ore-stage pyrite build up along the leading edge of a supergene oxidation zone which spreads through the host rocks, literally pushing the ore deposits ahead of it.[13]

Arsenic one of most common pathfinders

Arsenic is an indicator element in geochemical prospecting, being a widespread constituent of many types of mineral deposits, particularly those containing sulphides and sulpho-salts. In these and other deposits, arsenic commonly accompanies copper, gold, silver, zinc, molybdenum, cadmium, mercury, uranium, tin, lead, tungsten, phosphorus, antimony, bismuth, selenium, tellurium, iron, nickel, cobalt, and platinum metals.

Under most conditions, arsenic is a suitable indicator of deposits of these elements, being especially useful in geochemical surveys utilizing primary halos in rocks, and secondary halos and trains in soils and glacial materials, stream and lake sediments, natural waters, and vegetation. Some natural arsenic compounds are volatile, but techniques to use gaseous arsenic halos for geochemical prospecting have not yet been developed.[14]

Some potential pathfinder elements have yet to be exploited, mainly because present analytical methods are not sufficiently sensitive to detect them at the extremely low levels in which they occur. Rhenium is such a potential indicator for porphyry copper deposits. Rhenium occurs in small amounts (less than 2,000 ppm) with molybdenite, which occurs in association with porphyry copper deposits and is very soluble in water. The solubility permits rhenium to form extensive, but as yet undetectable, halos in the secondary or surface environment.[2,15]

Lead isotopes as an ore indicator

Lead isotope analysis of regional samples of lead in surface gossans and ore minerals may indicate a mineral deposit and the probable point of origin of the mineralization.[16] Interpretation depends on the recognition of

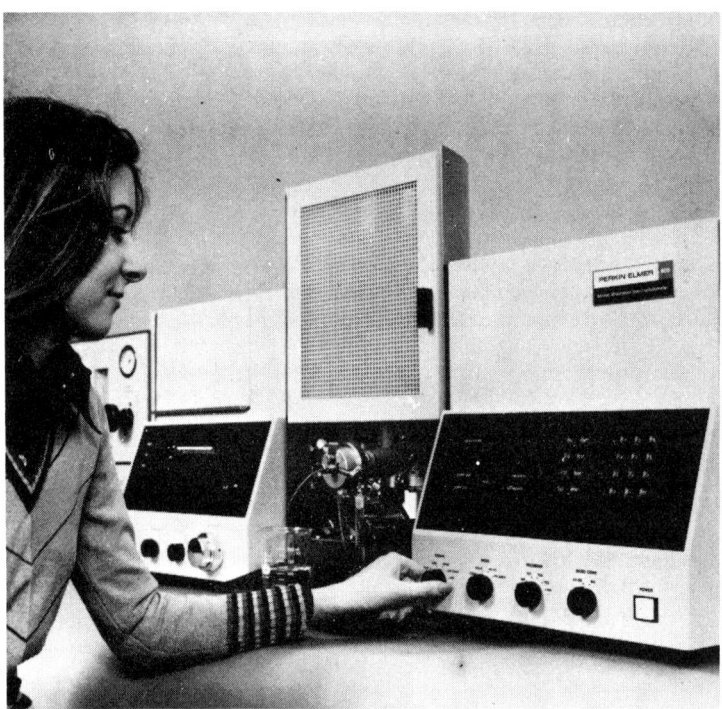

Used in rock analysis, new Perkin-Elmer Model 603 atomic absorption spectrophotometer combines microcomputer electronics and double-beam optics for high resolution.

A lead isotope survey is likely to be most successful on a regional rather than a local scale, although detailed sampling may be justified in some areas.

Based on accumulated statistics from known ore deposits, the following criteria are recommended as guides to major mineral deposits: uniformity of lead isotopic composition, low radiogenic lead content relative to other genetically related samples in the same district, and isotopic ratios that plot close to the ore-lead growth curve.[16]

Variations in barium and strontium concentrations occur in granitic host rocks of the Highland Valley porphyry copper deposits. At Valley Copper and a large part of Lornex Mining in British Columbia, barium concentrations decrease progressively from the outer margins to central zones of intense argillic/phyllic alteration and mineralization. In contrast, at Bethlehem JA and part of Lornex, where potassic alteration is dominant, enhanced values are encountered. Strontium levels consistently decrease from the periphery to inner zones of alteration and mineralization. Ba:Sr ratios exceeding 1 define mineralized zones. On the basis of these results, absolute and relative concentrations of barium and strontium could be a useful geochemical tool in exploration for porphyry copper deposits in the Highland Valley.[1]

Relative and absolute concentrations of barium and strontium in country rock may also prove useful in searching for mineral deposit extensions at two other well known British Columbia properties: the Dusty Mac, a silver occurrence in the southern Okanogan, and the Island Copper mine on northern Vancouver Island. □

ordinary and *anomalous* leads, their genetic relationship, and their spatial distribution.

In studying ore genesis, the major applications of geochemistry are in defining the source material of the lead in the ores and in estimating the age of mineralization. Isotopic leads have shown that: 1) the lead in the Phanerozoic galena ores of southwest Missouri originated mainly from a Cambrian sandstone aquifer unit, and perhaps partly from the Precambrian basement and Paleozoic carbonate host rock units; and 2) the age of the bulk ores in the Coeur d'Alene district in Idaho is probably Precambrian, rather than Cenozoic as previously thought.[17]

Lead uniquely possesses three radiogenic isotopes, which cause natural variations in the isotopic composition, high atomic mass (making it insensitive to natural mass-dependent fractionation processes), and a natural affinity for sulphide minerals. These properties make lead a sensitive indicator of the magnitude of natural ore-forming processes.[18]

Most major base metal deposits of the world have characteristic lead isotope ratios and many appear to have lead isotope compositions that evolved under nearly single-stage conditions (i.e., maintaining chemical homogeneity over the duration of time). Under such conditions, no changes have occurred in uranium-to-lead and thorium-to-lead ratios in the source of the ores since the formation of the earth, except for those resulting from radioactive decay of uranium and thorium. Numerous minor deposits seem not to have evolved under these conditions.

In one application of lead isotopes, the lead distribution of a specific prospect is compared with that of an adjacent producing deposit, because different producing deposits within a district frequently possess parallel lead isotope compositions. This application extends the use of lead isotopes for evaluation of potential deposits to major orebodies that contain anomalous lead values, such as those of the Mississippi Valley of the US.

References

1) Warren, H. V., Church, B. N., and Northcote, K. E., "Barium-Strontium Relationships Possible Geochemical Tool in Search for Orebodies," WESTERN MINER, April 1974, pp 107-111.
2) Levinson, A. A., *Introduction to Exploration Geochemistry* Applied Publishing Ltd., Maywood, Ill., 1974.
3) Hawkes, H. E., "Principles of Geochemical Prospecting," US Geological Survey Bulletin 1000-F, 1957.
4) Cox, D. P., Gonzalez, I. P., and Nash, J. T., "Geology, Geochemistry, and Fluid-Inclusion Petrography of the Sapo Alegre Porphyry Copper Prospect and its Metavolcanic Wallrocks, West-Central Puerto Rico," JOUR. RESEARCH, US Geological Survey, Vol. 3, No. 3, May-June 1975, pp 313-327.
5) Nash, J. T., and Cunningham, C. G. Jr., "Fluid-Inclusion Studies of the Porphyry Copper Deposit at Bagdad, Arizona," ibid., Vol. 2, No. 1, January-February 1974, pp 31-34.
6) Jowett, E. C., "Nature of the Ore-Forming Fluids of the Polaris Lead-Zinc Deposit, Little Cornwallis Island, N. W. T., From Fluid-Inclusion Studies," CIM BULLETIN, March 1975, pp 124-129.
7) Kesler, S. E., Issigonis, M. J., and Van Loon, J. C., "An Evaluation of the Use of Halkcen and Water Abundances in Efforts to Distinguish Mineralized and Barren Intrusive Rocks," JOUR. GEOCHEMICAL EXPLORATION, Elsevier Scientific Publishing Co., Vol. 4, 1975, pp 235-245.
8) Rehrig, W. A., and McKinney, C. N., "The Distribution and Origin of Anomalous Copper in Biotite," Annual Meeting, AIME, Las Vegas, Nev., February 1976.
9) Kesler, J. E., Van Loon, J. C., and Bateson, J. H., "Analysis of Fluoride in Rocks and an Application to Exploration," JOUR. GEOCHEMICAL EXPLORATION, Vol. 2, 1973, pp 11-17.
10) "Fluorine in Groundwater as a Guide to Pb-Zn-Ba-F Mineralization," ECONOMIC GEOLOGY, Vol. 70, No. 2, March-April 1975, pp 396-398.
11) Ficklin, W. H., "Ion-Selective Electrode Determination of Iodine in Rocks and Soils," JOUR. RESEARCH, US Geological Survey, Vol. 3, No. 6, November-December 1975, pp 753-755.
12) Sinclair, A. J., et al, "Minor Elements in Pyrites from Some Porphyry-Type Deposits, British Columbia," Annual Meeting, AIME, Las Vegas, Nev., February 1976.
13) Warren, C. G., and Granger, H. C., "The Concept of Growth and Maturity of Ore-Stage Pyrite in Roll-Type Uranium Deposits," JOUR. RESEARCH, US Geological Survey, Vol. 1, No. 2, March-April 1973, pp 151-155.
14) Boyle, R. W., and Jonasson, I. R., "The Geochemistry of Arsenic and Its Use as an Indicator Element in Geochemical Prospecting," JOUR. GEOCHEMICAL EXPLORATION, Vol. 2, 1973, pp 251-296.
15) Coope, J. A., "Geochemical Prospecting for Porphyry Copper-Type Mineralization—A Review," ibid., pp 81-102.
16) Loveless, A. J., "Lead Isotopes—A Guide to Major Mineral Deposits," GEOEXPLORATION, Elsevier Scientific Publishing Co., Amsterdam, Vol. 13, 1975, pp 13-27.
17) Hedge, Carl E., "Strontium Isotopes in Economic Geology," ECONOMIC GEOLOGY, Vol. 69, 1974, pp 823-825.
18) Doe, B. R., and Stacey, J. S., "The Application of Lead Isotopes to the Problems of Ore Genesis and Ore Prospect Evaluation: A Review," ibid., pp 757-776.

Data storage and retrieval buy time for geologists

THE MAGNITUDE OF INFORMATION obtained from drill cores and boreholes is overwhelming. To analyze such information, there has been a rapid increase—especially in the last 10 years—in utilization of geological data storage and retrieval systems. Computer systems save time and money and facilitate the logical collection of information that often aids in the discovery of orebodies.

In the US, the recently established Computerized Resources Information Bank (CRIB) is expected to play an increasingly important role in the study of US mineral resources. The CRIB data bank, established by the USGS in mid-1972, already contains over 15,000 sets of records on the mineral deposits and commodities of the US and other regions of the world. The system provides the USGS and other users with a means of organizing, analyzing, and summarizing mineral resources information and for presenting the results in reports, tables, and maps.

COREMAP[1] is a data system for recording and processing information from drill cores, boreholes, tunnels, and adits. This stored information, say its Swedish developers, will serve as a valuable tool in prospecting and geological mapping. COREMAP makes it possible to record general, geological, chemical, joint, and borehole deviation data in standard formats, but the system may also be extended to other types of data.

COREMAP produces decoded lists, lists of any specified parameter(s), and a simplified description of cores on a line-printer. The system plots borehole deviation, data location on chosen levels, and vertical sections parallel to the x- or y-axes. It also plots the length of each analyzed interval, together with one optional chemical element. All boreholes running through a defined slice of rock are projected as a plane. The scale of the plot is determined by the user, and strike and dip may be corrected during projection.

GEOMAP,[2] tested and developed in Scandinavia, is a computer system for processing field data on hard rocks. Records on field data sheets are transcribed onto punch cards and later onto tapes for ultimate storage, retrieval, and automatic processing in a geological data bank.

The processing routines of GEOMAP include a complete list of observations from each outcrop. Special parameters are set up in a tabular format. Plotted maps of outcrops, rock types, and all combinations of tectonic data are generated. There are also subroutines for fabric analyses and geostatistics.

Finland's Geological Survey[3] has installed a "minicomputer system" to aid exploration in that country. In addition to data obtained from field prospecting, the computer, a Hewlett-Packard 3000, processes a great deal of geophysical, geochemical, and hydrologic information. The unit reportedly permits simultaneous access by several users.

MINDEP,[4] another application of computers, is a research project to gather and study data on more than 8,000 mineral deposits in British Columbia. Knowledge of the distribution and geologic setting of these deposits can be a very useful aid to exploration. In addition, since these deposits represent only a portion of British Columbia's mineral resources, they provide a means for estimating resource potential.

GEOLOG,[5] also developed at the University of British Columbia, is a computer-oriented method of recording and interpreting geological field data, mainly from drillholes, in porphyry-type and other mineral deposits. According to its creators, time and effort expended in collecting drill core information for the GEOLOG system are comparable to common logging procedures.

During the past six years, several experimental, computer-based data banks have been developed at the Geological Survey of Canada[6] for predicting mineral potential over large areas. One such data bank covers the Superior Province of the Canadian Shield. Data can be extracted selectively from this bank to provide summary statistics, histograms, maps for areal distribution patterns of single parameters, or secondary files for specific geomathematical studies.

CANMINDEX[7] is a proposed computerized index file of all reported mineral occurrences in Canada. The project is a joint effort of two organizations within the Department of Energy, Mines & Resources: the Geological Survey of Canada and the Mineral Development Sector.

In Great Britain, a new geological computer reference system known as Geoarchives[8] was recently unveiled. The system, demonstrated on a Sperry Univac 500 terminal and linked to a Sperry Univac 1108, has been written at Geosystems Ltd. There are presently more than 500,000 literature references on file, a figure that is growing. These references cover all fields of geology, including geophysics.

Geostatistics fast emerging as ore evaluator

Geostatistics has evolved to the stage of being not only a credible means of evaluating ore deposits, but also sufficiently better than conventional methods to justify the higher level of mathematical education necessary for its proper utilization.[9]

A number of major advances in geostatistics have been made recently. One of the most important achievements is the establishment of methods that accurately predict cutoff grade-tonnage curves and average grade of ore-tonnage curves for deposits in which ore and waste are present together. The problem of underestimating ore grade and overestimating tonnage by means of grade-tonnage curves based on widely spaced exploration data has been solved by calculating the conditional probability distributions for the unknown grade of a block.

Another advance has been made in the area of geostatistical estimation for deposits in which a trend is present. Previously, a method called Universal Kriging was employed. This method involves a good deal of subjective judgment. A new method—generalized increments—permits computers to estimate such deposits. Simplified algorithms to save computer costs have been found for numerous geostatistical methods. □

References

1) Ekstrom, T. K., Wirstam, A., and Larsson, L., "COREMAP–A Data System for Drill Cores and Boreholes," ECONOMIC GEOLOGY, Vol. 70, 1975, pp 359-368.
2) Berner, H., et al, "GEOMAP–A Data System for Geological Mapping," 24th International Geological Congress, 1972, Section 16, pp 3-11.
3) "Prospecting with Minicomputer," WORLD MINING, August 1975, p 53.
4) Wynne-Edwards, H. R., and Sinclair, A. J., "MINDEP–Computer-Processable Files of Mineral Deposit Information," WESTERN MINER, February 1976.
5) Blanchet, P. H., and Godwin, C. I., " 'Geolog System' for Computer and Manual Analysis of Geologic Data from Porphyry and Other Deposits," ECONOMIC GEOLOGY, Vol. 67, 1972, pp 796-813.
6) Fabbri, A. G., "Design and Structure of Geological Data Banks for Regional Mineral Potential Evaluation," CIM BULLETIN, August 1975, pp 91-97.
7) Goddard, J. P., and Hutchison, W. W., "CANMINDEX," Prospectors and Developers Association, Annual Meeting, Toronto, Ont., March 1976.
8) "Geoarchive Retrieval System," MINING JOURNAL, October 31, 1975, p 330.
9) Parker, H. M., and Sandefur, R. L., "A Review of Recent Developments in Geostatistics," 105th Annual AIME Meeting, February 1976, Las Vegas, Nev.

Aeromagnetic studies are versatile search tools

GRAVITY AND MAGNETICS ARE IMPORTANT TOOLS in the search for orebodies. In mineral exploration, there are two main applications of gravity-measuring instrumentation: in regional studies that yield a gravity map of an entire country and reveal something of the geological framework, and in gravity surveys on properties where graphite is present.

Gravity and airborne electromagnetic studies pinpoint drilling targets, with airborne EM usually performed over reasonably large areas. Followup gravity studies are then made on the ground. (The cost of ground surveys employing gravimetry is high—up to 10 times the cost of an airborne EM survey.)

Equipment utilized in airborne gravimetry includes La Coste and Romberg gravimeters.[1] Recent advances in gravimetry have emphasized interpretation of gravity and magnetic results, rather than the development of radically different instrumentation.

Several computer techniques are used for rapid interpretation of gravity anomalies in two dimensions. For three dimensional curves, various diagrams and nomograms are not uncommon. Elliott Geophysical Co. of Tucson, Ariz., has continued development of computer programs to reduce, correct, and interpret gravity data. The company currently offers a commercial system. A good deal of interest has reportedly been shown in gravity surveys in mountainous terrain, such as the western US and Canada.

Proton magnetometers are most widely used

The proton magnetometer developed by Varian Associates operates on the principle of nuclear magnetic resonance to produce a measurement of the earth's total magnetic field intensity. In a proton magnetic sensor—whether airborne, marine, or portable—a uniform magnetic field is created by passing a few amperes of current through a coil surrounded by water or kerosene, which provides a source of protons. Spinning protons act as small magnetic dipoles and align themselves with the applied field. When the current is removed, the spin of the protons causes them to *precess* in phase about the direction of the earth's magnetic field, much as a spinning top precesses about the gravity field.[1] The precessing protons then generate a small signal in the coil used to polarize them; the frequency of the signal is precisely proportional to the total magnetic field intensity and is independent of the orientation of the coil (i.e., sensor of the magnetometer). The proportionality constant that relates frequency to field intensity is a well known atomic constant: the gyromagnetic ratio of the proton. This constant is 23.4875 gamma per Hz.

The precessing signal is actually induced by the motion of the precessing protons in the coil used for polarizing the sample. The frequency of the precession signal, as determined by the gyromagnetic ratio, is about 0.04 Hz per gamma, or between 1,000 and 4,000 Hz, corresponding to a range of 25,000 to 100,000 gammas in the earth's magnetic field.

The main advantage of the proton magnetometer is that the gyromagnetic ratio, or the atomic constant, is the basis for its accuracy. Because of the constant, the unit is not affected by temperature, rotation or orientation of the earth's magnetic field, or by gravity. The instrument can be carried aboard ship or flown in an aircraft without the need to balance, level, or calibrate it.

Flux-gate magnetometer used for local studies

Older magnetometers, such as the flux gate or the cesium-rubidium units, use a physical measuring system. The flux gate must be leveled before a measurement is taken. The cesium-rubidium magnetometer does not require much leveling, but it does require very careful handling because it is highly sensitive. Both these units measure only the vertical component of the magnetic field, not the horizontal. The proton magnetometer measures the total field, both vertical and horizontal, yielding more information on the magnetic field.

The flux-gate magnetometer is operated from a towed bird or attached to the lower portion of the tail section of an aircraft. Developed in the early 1940s by Gulf Research, the unit was first flown by the US Geological Survey in 1945.

The flux gate is employed for detailed studies of localized magnetic fields. The instrument consists of two highly permeable, identical, saturable (in magnetism) cores, oppositely wound with identical coils. An alternating current in these coils magnetizes them first with one polarity, then the reverse. If an additional field is present, such as the earth's magnetic field, that field will add to the flux in one coil while decreasing the field in the other. As a result, the voltage drop across the two coils will differ. The degree of this difference is proportional to the unvarying field, which can therefore be measured by noting the average voltage difference between the two halves of the flux gate. Accuracy is ±1 gamma.

In airborne use, the flux-gate magnetometer is kept aligned with the magnetic field through the use of two additional flux gates. When these are at right angles to the earth's field, they generate no voltage, but if they depart from this position, they can be made to generate voltages that operate motors to return them to proper alignment. In

Navajo aircraft owned by GeoMetrics is used for detailed exploration. Magnetometer "tail stinger" sensor is made from fiberglass with ventilation scoops and auxiliary lifts.

Portable proton magnetometer, the Model G-816 from GeoMetrics, has 1-gamma sensitivity and repeatability, weighs 12 lb.

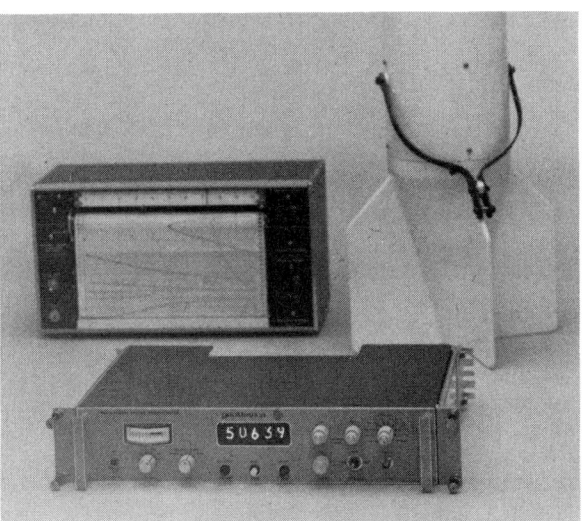

Typical airborne magnetometer from GeoMetrics, equipped with "bird" sensor and dual channel HP strip chart recorder.

this manner, the recording element is always held parallel to the total field.

Optically pumped magnetometers: very sensitive

Another type of magnetometer, pioneered by Varian Associates in the late 1950s, is the optically pumped magnetometer. This unit depends on what is known as the Zeeman effect, which involves splitting the energy states of an atom into substates in the presence of a magnetic field. The energy differences between the various sublevels are proportional to the strength of the magnetic field and therefore give a means of measuring the magnetic field. Light of a particular wavelength raises the atoms to an exited state—the basis for the term "optical pumping."[2]

This instrument, however, is somewhat more sensitive than proton magnetometers to orientation, and is thus not as well suited to mobile applications.

The development of optically pumped devices has allowed greater resolution in geomagnetic measurements for exploration purposes. Alkali metals, principally rubidium and cesium, have been used as active elements to obtain the magnetic-field-dependent Larmor frequency (protons precessing about the direction of the earth's field at a rate proportional to the total magnetic intensity).

Gradiometers sport some unique advantages

Exploration specialists have also shown interest in measuring various magnetic gradients, particularly the vertical gradient utilizing ground and airborne magnetometers. One of the unique advantages is that gradient anomalies tend to resolve composite or complex anomalies into their individual components. The gradients can also be used in determining depth of anomaly, magnetic moment, shape, and location.[3]

Recent tests of an airborne gradiometer system were conducted aboard a Beechcraft B80 Queenair by Canada's Geological Survey.[4] The vertical gradiometer is designed to map vertical contacts between large near-surface rock formations having a minimum effective susceptibility contrast of about 500×10^{-6} emu/cc, which is typical for much of Canada's Precambrian Shield.

The results obtained to date have demonstrated conclusively that a vertical aeromagnetic gradiometer is a better geological mapping tool than a single-sensor magnetometer. However, the study concluded, the gradiometer application is more suited for detailed geologic mapping programs at a scale of 1:50,000 or smaller. The standard-sensitivity aeromagnetic survey program being conducted by the Canadian Geological Survey remains ideally suited for reconnaissance mapping at the 1:250,000 scale.

The main advantages of the gradiometer over the single-sensor magnetometer as a geological mapping tool were summarized in the study:

- Direct delineation of vertical contacts by the zero-gradient contour value (i.e., vertical contact mapper).
- Superior resolution of anomalies produced by closely spaced geological formations.
- Emphasizing of anomalies produced by near-surface features over those resulting from more deeply buried rock formations.
- Automatic removal of the regional gradient of the earth's magnetic field.

Superconducting gradiometers offer potential

The superconducting gradiometer, conceived by Superconducting Technology of Mountain View, Calif., is also very useful for geophysical exploration, although it has not been as widely used as the magnetometer. The unit has been employed to determine the magnetic signature of various objects moving relative to the gradiometer.

The company recently delivered a three-axis gradiometer to a Navy group for use in airborne surveys. This instrument will be mounted in a fiberglass aerodynamic enclosure and towed behind a Navy plane for field gradient mapping. According to the company, this type of system would be useful for geophysical exploration.

Several other superconducting magnetometer systems are made by the company, including the C 300 series multiaxis magnetometer—a lightweight, highly sensitive magnetometer used in magnetotelluric and magnetic sounding exploration studies. ☐

References

1) "Aerial Gravimetry Experiments Could Mean a New Approach to Gravity Surveying," CIM BULLETIN, June 1975, p 127.
2) Richards, D. J., and Walraven, F., "Airborne Geophysics and ERTS Imagery," MINERALS SCI. ENG., Vol. 7, No. 3, July 1975, pp 234-278.
3) Breiner, S., "Applications Manual for Portable Magnetometers," GeoMetrics, Sunnyvale, Calif., 1973.
4) Kornik, L. J., McGrath, P. H., and Hood, P., "Geological Interpretation of Aeromagnetic Gradiometer Survey," 78th Annual Meeting, Canad. Instit. of Mining and Metallurgy, Quebec, April 1976.

Hydrogeochemistry aids search for uranium, base metals

MOST HYDROGEOCHEMICAL EXPLORATION has focused on lake waters. However, hot and cold spring waters and their precipitates, streams, seeps, wells, and the sea have also been sampled, in addition to ice and snow. Trace metals have also been found in organic gels, waterborne microorganisms, and in colloidal matter of finely dispersed sediment.[1]

Rapid analysis of the water in streams and other surface drainage may eliminate certain areas from further consideration for exploration. By eliminating tributaries of low metallic ion concentrations and following those of high content, a prospector can locate a mineralized body. In such instances, soil geochemistry, biogeochemistry, and geobotanical techniques may serve to define the mineralized zone.[2]

Primary metallic ore minerals are stable and are relatively insoluble in water. However, under the physical and chemical conditions present in an outcrop zone, most primary minerals are altered to secondary minerals that are more soluble in water.

Secondary minerals form sulphurous and sulphuric acids. In acid solutions, copper, a prime example, tends to be highly soluble in water. Molybdenum is soluble over a much wider range of pH—as molybdate or in inorganic complexes in alkaline environments, and as less complex cations when the pH is low.

In Arizona's Pima copper district, anomalous amounts of molybdenum in alkaline ground waters have been found up to 8 mi from the sources. Copper in ground water is less mobile. However, other natural factors, including bacteria, also affect the mobility of copper and molybdenum in ground waters.

The distribution of molybdenum in ground water of the Pima district indicates the potential of hydrogeochemistry as a regional reconnaissance tool for porphyry copper mineralization in areas of transported soil and hidden outcrops. Measurements in other areas indicate that in the alkaline environments of the southwestern US, copper occurs in very small amounts in alkaline waters in the vicinity of mineralization.[3]

Geochemical processes in neutral waters

The migration of microcomponents in neutral or near-neutral waters is of major interest to exploration geochemists. Only recently, it appeared that two opposing poles—acid waters and alkaline waters—existed in the supergene zone. Neutral waters, which occupy an intermediate position, are least favorable for migration of the majority of microcomponents, which in these conditions are subject to hydrolysis. However, a number of geochemical processes in the supergene zone do, in fact, take place in media that are close to neutral.[4]

Pinpointing deep uranium mineralization

Hydrogeochemical exploration for uranium deposits primarily traces uranium, radium, and radon in natural waters. Under favorable conditions, hydrogeochemistry can locate uranium mineralization at considerable depth. In mountainous terrain, hydrogeochemical exploration can locate deposits buried 300 to 400 m and in foothill regions, 50 to 70 m.

Of great importance in such prospecting is the regional background concentration of the elements. In northern climates and mountainous terrain, a uranium concentration of 10^{-6} gpl may be anomalous. However, in arid environments, evaporation of water will give backgrounds as great as 10^{-4} gpl.

In environments of intensive oxidation, uranium is leached from rocks. In reducing environments, uranium is precipitated from solution. Water from acidic rocks enriched in uranium is more radioactive than water circulating in basic rocks.

The radioactive equilibrium between uranium, radium, and radon is a useful guide to ore potential.[5]

The value of natural water samples for uranium exploration lies partly in the simplicity and detection limits of the method used for analyses. The uranium concentration of natural water is typically in the ppb range, which is easily detectable by the fission track technique.

Fission track method analyzes for uranium

Fission track, which is based on the neutron-induced fission of uranium-235, is a versatile technique for routine analysis of uranium in liquid samples of natural water. A polycarbonate plastic sheet, muscovite mica, or silica glass detector is immersed in the sample and both are irradiated. The fission track density observed in the detector is directly proportional to uranium concentration.

The specific advantages of this method are: 1) only a small quantity of sample, typically 0.1 to 1.0 ml, is needed;

Technician samples bottom-dwelling organisms from stream to determine possible changes in water quality. (Photo: Amax.)

2) no sample concentration is necessary; 3) it is capable of providing analyses with a lower reporting limit of 1 microgram per liter; and 4) actual time spent on an analysis may be only a few minutes.[6]

NURE program evaluates US uranium resources

In the spring of 1973, the National Uranium Resource Evaluation project (NURE) was announced by the US Atomic Energy Commission (since reorganized to form ERDA). The goal of the program is to evaluate domestic uranium resources and to identify areas favorable for uranium exploration.

The NURE program emphasizes the systematic collection of data from which a more complete resource assessment can be made. NURE subprograms include hydrogeochemical and stream sediment reconnaissance. The goal of these two subprograms is to complete by 1980 a systematic survey of the nation's surface waters, ground waters, and stream sediments to determine the role played by variations in uranium and its pathfinder elements as guides for uranium search.

Plans call for sampling at a scale of approximately 1 sample per 10 sq km of uranium distributed in the near-surface hydrologic system.[7] The sampling system includes stream and lake waters, river and lake sediments, dry alluvium, and ground water. The NURE program is administered and coordinated by the Grand Junction, Colo., office of ERDA. □

References

1) Chaffee, Maurice A., "Geochemical Exploration Techniques Applicable in the Search for Copper Deposits," US Geological Survey, Professional Paper 907-B, 1975.
2) Masson, Donald L., "Prospecting by Water Analysis: Hydrogeochemical Prospecting," Washington State Institute of Technology, Circular No. 6, 1963.
3) Coope, J. Alan, "Geochemical Prospecting for Porphyry Copper-Type Mineralization—A Review," JOUR. OF GEOCHEMICAL EXPLORATION, Elsevier Scientific Publishing Co., Amsterdam, Vol. 2, 1973, pp 81-102.
4) Shvartsev, S. L., Udodov, P. A., and Rasskazov, N. M., "Some Features of the Migration of Microcomponents in Neutral Waters of the Supergene Zone," JOUR. OF GEOCHEMICAL EXPLORATION, Vol. 4, 1975, pp 433-439.
5) Dyck, Willy, "Geochemistry Applied to Uranium Exploration," Prospectors & Developers Association Meeting, Toronto, Ont., March 1975.
6) Reimer, G. M., "Uranium Determination in Natural Water by the Fission-Track Technique," JOUR. OF GEOCHEMICAL EXPLORATION, Vol. 4, 1975, pp 425-431.
7) Dahlem, David H., "A National Hydrogeochemical Sampling Program for Uranium," Annual Meeting, AIME, Las Vegas, Nev., February 1976.

Geobotany, biogeochemistry target potential orebodies

BOTH GEOBOTANY AND BIOGEOCHEMISTRY are gaining acceptance as prime techniques in the search for ore deposits. Geobotany uses the siting of individual plant types or plant communities as a guide to subsurface mineralization. It is a well established discipline, and earth scientists have for some time used geobotany as an aid in mapping geological formations and in locating fresh water, saline aquifers, and mineral deposits.

As a practical science, geobotany requires:
- An understanding of the nature and the distribution of plant communities and indicator plants.
- Recognition of the morphological (form and structural) changes in such plants.
- Application of this knowledge to botanical information collected through remote sensing (aerial photography).

The presence of *indicator plants* signals the existence of a particular element in the soil in which they grow. Indicator plants are considered better than plant communities as geobotanical tools because they are likely to pinpoint mineralization more precisely. Those plants that consistently point to the presence of a specific element are called *universal indicators*. Those plants used to locate mineralization only within a specified district are known as *local indicators*.

Indicator communities do not always directly indicate mineralization, but they permit the characterization of regions in which mineralization may occur.

Most indicators are herbaceous (no woody stem). However, certain indicator trees are well known. In British Columbia, important indicators include the silver birch for zinc, hemlock for manganese, and balsam for molybdenum. Another characteristic of all indicator plants is that the metallic content of their ash is high.

Plants spotted from sky

Remote sensing from aircraft and satellites is now being vigorously applied in the geobotanical study of vegetation. Metal-rich soil and associated vegetation can be found by remote sensing, generally using multispectral techniques.[1]

One such investigation used visual interpretation of multiband photography to detect changes in vegetation caused by abnormal concentrations of metals in the soil. Cooperative studies have been initiated to test this technique in selected mineral districts in Brazil, the Philippines, and Thailand, and experimental work has been done in a variety of districts in the US.[2]

Recent research has found that measurements of the

Indicator plants used in the US

Element	Species*	Common name	Location
Copper	Eschscholtzia mexicana (L)	California poppy	Arizona
	Mielichhoferia macrocarpa (U)	Copper moss	Alaska
	Mielichhoferia mielichhoferi (U)	Copper moss	North America
	Merceya ligulata (U)	Copper moss	North America
Lead	Baptisia bracteata (L)	Wild indigo	Wisconsin
	Erianthus giganteus (L)	Beardgrass	Tennessee
Selenium (and uranium)	Aster venusta (U)	Woody aster	Western US
	Astragalus spp. (U)	Poison vetch	Western US
	Oonopsis spp. (U)	Goldenweed	Western US
	Stanleya spp. (U)	Princesplume	Western US
Silver	Eriogonum ovalifolium (L)	Buckwheat	Montana
Vanadium	Astragalus bisulcatus (U)	Poison vetch	Western US
Zinc	Philadelphus spp. (L)	Mock orange	US

* U = Universal indicator; L = Local indicator.
Source: A. A. Levinson, *Introduction to Exploration Geochemistry*, 1974.

Some species of locoweed are useful in geobotanical exploration for uranium in western US. (Photo: M. Chaffee, USGS.)

Mesquite is commonly used in biogeochemical exploration surveys in Arizona and New Mexico. (Photo: M. Chaffee, USGS.)

Fraunhofer line of solar radiation conducted from light aircraft allow detection of soils rich in phosphate and gypsum. Further, in the Pine Nut district of Nevada, the luminescence of juniper trees correlates well with the molybdenum content of the tree ash.[3]

In the porphyry copper region of the southwestern US, studies have shown that abundant populations of the California poppy (*Eschscholtzia mexicana*) grow in close association with copper-rich soils near many porphyry deposits. Unfortunately, researchers discovered, the poppies are not found growing over all copper-bearing soils of the region, nor are all wild poppy populations associated with copper-bearing soils.[4]

Biogeochemistry analyzes plants

Chemical analyses of plants or plant parts can be used as a prospecting technique when the chemical content of the vegetation sampled bears a direct relationship to the chemical content of the soil or bedrock, or to the ground water passing through the soil or bedrock.

Biogeochemical sampling should be an improvement over soil or rock sampling in regions of widespread but relatively thin post-mineralization-age overburden because biogeochemical sampling is based, when possible, on deeply rooted plants (some as much as 200 ft deep).

Plant material is sampled and analyzed periodically to minimize the effects of variations in precipitation, temperature, soil Eh and pH, soil type and texture, and plant physiology.

Airtrace holds promise in overburden areas

One of the more recent advances in airborne biogeochemistry applied to mineral exploration is the Airtrace system, developed by Barringer Research Ltd. Airtrace is based on the fact that an atmospheric sample can be shown to be closely related to the geochemistry of the subsurface.

Biological interaction of metals in the ground with the rich organic topsoil has been found to occur. Metals complexed or bound to organic soil materials migrate upward from the soil into the air in minute but detectable quantities. The Airtrace system collects air samples, from which metals are extracted.

Airtrace surveys, at altitudes greater than 200 ft, reportedly show great promise for exploration in areas of transported overburden. Barringer says that the system can operate effectively in both semiarid and tropical environments. Metals detected directly by the Barringer system include mercury, copper, lead, zinc, and silver. The equipment can be mounted in a helicopter as well as in fixed-wing aircraft.[5]

Elemental contents in the ash of some indicator plants

Element	Species	Normal content (ppm)	Maximum content (ppm)	Location
Cobalt	Crotalaria cobalticola	9	18,000	Katanga
Copper	Becium homblei	183	2,500	Zambia
Copper	Gypsophila patrini	183	500	USSR
Manganese	Fucus vesiculosus	4,815	90,000	USSR
Nickel	Alyssum bertolonii	65	100,000	Italy
Zinc	Thlaspi calaminare	1,400	10,000	Germany

Source: A. A. Levinson, *Introduction to Exploration Geochemistry*, 1974.

References

1) Levinson, A. A., *Introduction to Exploration Geochemistry*, Applied Publishing Ltd., Maywood, Ill., 1974, pp 392-399.
2) Canney, Frank C., "Development and Application of Remote-Sensing Techniques in the Search for Deposits of Copper and Other Metals in Heavily Vegetated Areas," US Dept. of Commerce, National Technical Information Service Report PB-246 284, 1975.
3) Weaver, Richard R., "Geochemistry," MINING ENGINEERING, February 1976, p 43.
4) Chaffee, Maurice A., "Geochemical Exploration Techniques Applicable in the Search for Copper Deposits," US Geological Survey Professional Paper 907-B, 1975, p B14.
5) "Airborne Biogeochemistry to Detect Minerals," WESTERN MINER, Vol. 47, No. 1, January 1974, p 17.

New technique traces buried ancient stream channels in search of uranium

Based on results of past projects, scientists of Hydrotechnics believe that the Thermonic Channel-Trace method may develop into a useful technique in exploration for ancient channel sands; each case, however, must be evaluated separately.

William M. Turner consulting geologists, Hydrotechnics

THE ASSOCIATION OF URANIUM MINERALIZATION with paleo-stream channels is well documented. In many instances, the paleo-stream channel deposits have been buried by younger marine sediments, and the courses of the paleo channels are not easily traceable from the surface. In areas where subsurface data are sparse, considerable time and money may be spent in the search for the buried channels and associated uranium mineralization.

The Thermonic Channel-Trace method, developed initially by Hydrotechnics, can quickly and inexpensively trace the sources of buried channels, enabling exploration companies to focus on likely targets more rapidly and increasing the likelihood of success in finding targets. Thermonics is a method of groundwater flow system analysis based upon the redistribution of geothermal heat by moving groundwater. Developed initially as a tool for groundwater exploration, well site selection, quantitative analysis of groundwater flow systems, and monitoring of in-situ leaching operations, Thermonics has been found useful in mapping buried channel systems that are presently saturated with groundwater. This application of the system has been labeled Channel-Trace.

The basic principle in the application of the Thermonic Channel-Trace method is that the clastic deposits in the channels continue to serve as conduits for groundwater flow, and that the rate of groundwater flow is greatest at the center of the channel, where the clastics are cleaner and more permeable. The Thermonic Channel-Trace method seeks out the zone of maximum groundwater flow, which is assumed to correspond with the buried channel. Experience indicates that this is the case.

Two case studies illustrate the application of the Channel-Trace method.

Case study 1. In the vicinity of the village of Chapucal in the Santa Elena Peninsula of Ecuador, Quaternary continental and marine clastic deposits of the Tablazo Formation have been deposited above an irregular surface of truncated Tertiary sediments. Groundwater occurs under

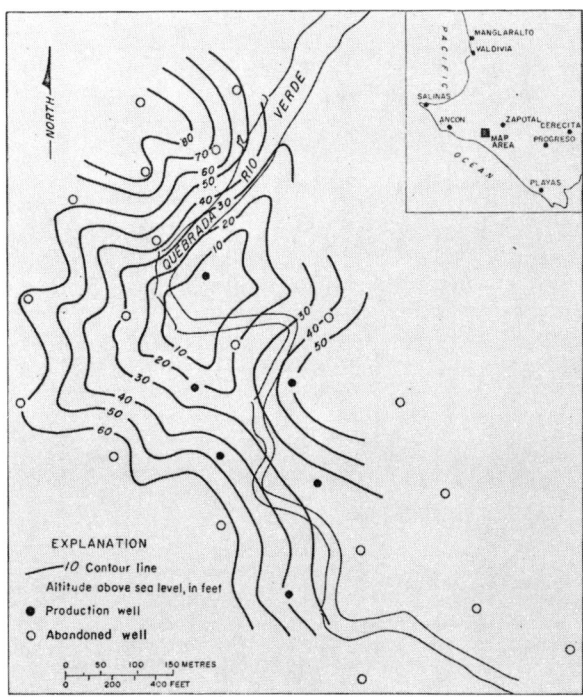

Fig. 1—Subcrop topography beneath the Quaternary Tablazo deposits in the Chapucal water well field area of Ecuador.

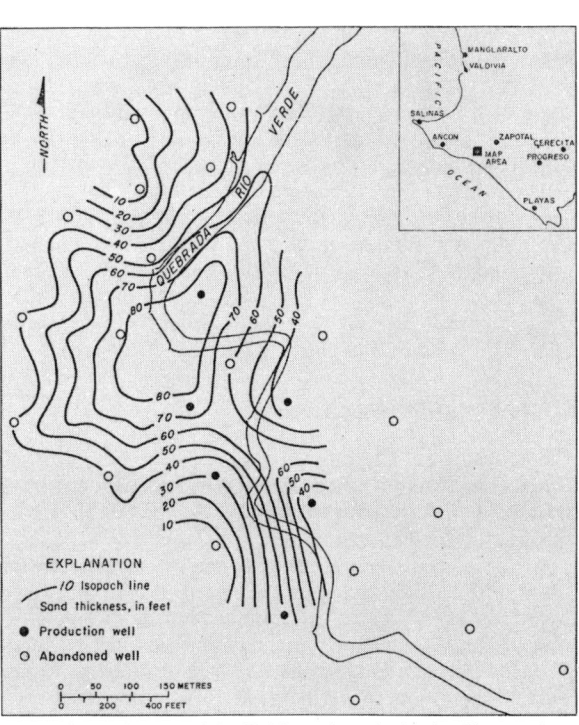

Fig. 2—Isopach map of the Tablazo deposits in the Chapucal water well field area.

Acknowledgement

The authors wish to thank Sohio Petroleum Co. for permission to publish the results of Thermonic studies conducted on its property, and Buck, Seifert & Jost, consulting engineers, and Empresa Municipal de Agua Potable de Guayaquil, Ecuador, for permission to publish data from the Chapucal well field.

phreatic conditions in the Tablazo. Figs. 1 and 2, prepared by petroleum geologists in Ecuador, show the subcrop topography beneath the Tablazo and the thickness of the Tablazo in the Chapucal area, respectively.

A Thermonic Channel-Trace study of the Chapucal well field was conducted to locate the zone of highest aquifer transmissivity, indicating the location of the buried channel. Thermonic data were obtained from each of the existing water wells, corrected for errors caused by differing thermal diffusivities of the soils in the area, and contoured. (See Fig. 3.) Interpretation of the Thermonic data indicates that a zone of high aquifer transmissivity extends from north-northwest to south-southeast. This zone is interpreted to correspond to the location of the buried channel, and its location is in good agreement with the subcrop valley and the zone of greatest Tablazo thickness. Near the northern margin of Fig. 3, Thermonic data indicate that the buried channel is wider and not well defined, which corresponds well with data from the isopach and subcrop maps.

Case study 2. The Jackpile sandstone of Late Jurassic age, a burial fluvial system, is mined for its contained uranium at several localities north of Laguna, N. Mex. The object of the study was to determine whether Thermonic Channel-Trace methods could trace the Jackpile channel. Thermonic measurements were made over a blocked-out uranium deposit which occurs in the Jackpile channel and which is overlain by 600 to 1,500 ft of marine Mancos shale of Cretaceous age. Thermonic measurements were made in both the saturated and unsaturated parts of more than 90 boreholes in the area of interest.

The result of the Thermonic Channel-Trace survey (Fig. 4) is based on data collected from a depth of 100 ft beneath the land surface, or more than 500 ft above the Jackpile channel. The map shows that the sand in the main Jackpile channel and its tributaries is the major conduit for groundwater flow. The result of the survey is confirmed by the Jackpile sand isopach map of the area.

Limitations of the technique

The results of Thermonic Channel-Trace programs carried out to date have been verified by independent methods. As with any indirect method, however, Thermonic Channel-Trace has its limitations:
- The buried channel deposits may occur beneath major aquifers, which can mask the effects of heat transfer by water moving in the buried channel deposits.
- Faults or other fractures may cut the buried channel deposits and act as conduits for groundwater movement themselves. Flow of groundwater up these faults can create thermal patterns that may obscure thermal patterns caused by groundwater flow in the channel deposits. □

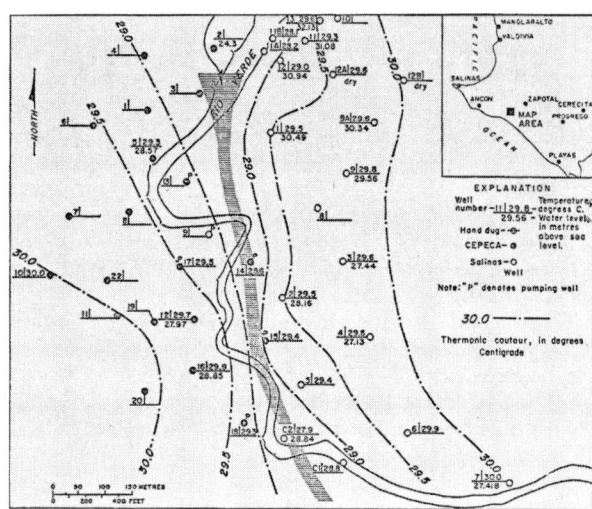

Fig. 3—Thermonic data from Chapucal water well field area.

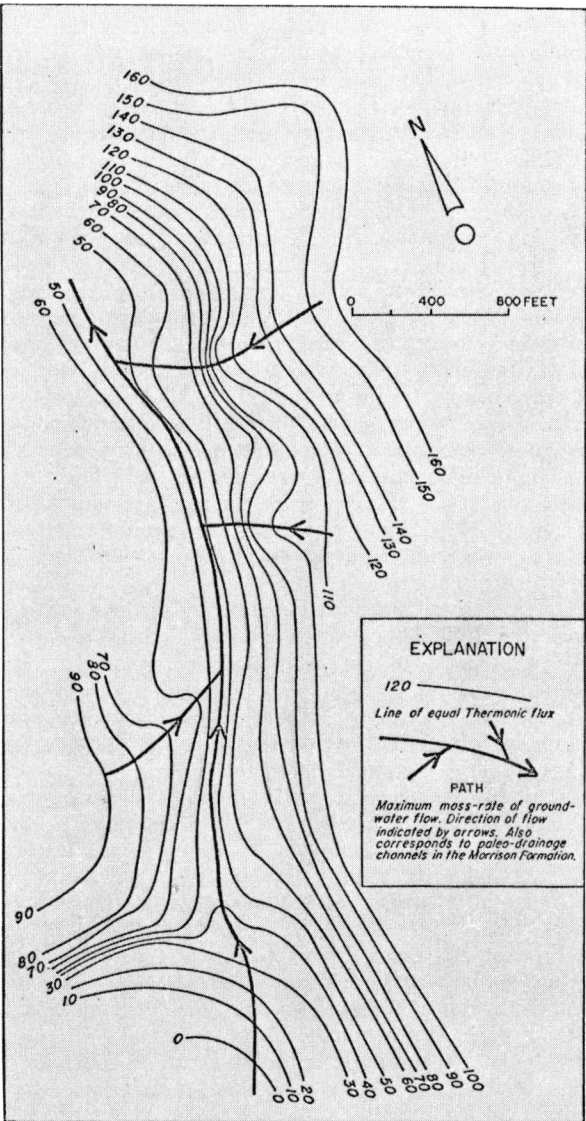

Fig. 4—Thermonic data from L-Bar property in New Mexico.

Induced polarization: a versatile exploration tool

WHEN AN ELECTRIC CURRENT PASSING INTO THE EARTH through ground electrodes is suddenly interrupted, a potential can be measured between these and nearby electrodes for some time after the current stops. This potential decays exponentially with time. The effect was observed as early as 1912 by Schlumberger, who ascribed it to polarization of earth material by the current. Known as induced polarization (IP), this effect is associated with electrochemical reactions in the earth.

Since the early 1950s, induced polarization has played an important role in mineral discoveries. Its ability to detect and define large, low grade sulphide deposits where other systems have proven inadequate has led to the discovery of enormous ore reserves. Induced polarization can also detect and define vein-type deposits buried under thin cover, making it perhaps the most versatile prospecting tool on the market. A great deal of expensive drilling can be avoided by conducting an adequate IP survey to define likely target areas and to eliminate those of less promise.

New IP equipment on the market brings this prospecting system well within the technical and financial reach of smaller companies and individual prospectors.

In its simplest form, the IP principle may be described as an RC (resistance capacitor) circuit, in which the ground becomes the resistor and the metal sulphide particles become the capacitor. When a current is passed through a porous rock mass containing mineral salts in a solution, current flows from one electrode to the other in ionic fashion. Nearly all rocks contain at least 2% water.

When a metallic sulphide is present in the rock, the mode of conduction changes from ionic to electronic. At the point of contact with the metallic conductor, the free electrons pass through and a cloud of ions form on the metallic particles. After the current is turned off, the electrons and ions seek their natural equilibrium and this effect appears at the surface of the ground as a small *decaying* voltage, which can be measured by sensitive equipment.

Some investigators have shown that the IP decay curve cannot be described by a single exponential function. Taking this a step further, decomposition of the decay curve into a series of exponentials will provide additional information.

Nearly all orebodies contain metallic sulphide particles below the water table—that is, below the point where there is enough free oxygen in the mass to oxidize most sulphide ores.

Sulphide minerals are normally formed by the introduction of sulphur either from magmatic water solutions, hot gases, or by sulphur contained in ground water. These particles, which are usually much better conductors than the surrounding rock, include almost every kind of metallic sulphide. Elements such as gold, silver, platinum, and tellurides are detectable if present in substantial amounts.

All known metallic sulphides and some oxides such as magnetite and pyrolusite give rise to IP responses and can be detected readily if their content in the rock is at least 0.25% of the total volume of rock encompassed by a given electrode array. Other conductors such as graphite and certain clay minerals also give IP responses, but are much less pervasive than metallic sulphides, especially in mineralized areas.

The system also works well on vein-type deposits buried under thin overburden or, if sufficient power is available, it can detect large, low grade commercial deposits a mile or two beneath the surface. To increase search depth, it is only necessary to expand the electrode array and introduce additional electrical power into the ground.

From the IP response at different arrays on a grid pattern, exploration crews can determine with reasonable accuracy the strike and dip of an orebody, its horizontal dimensions, and the approximate metallic sulphide content. Drillholes may also be located with a high degree of accuracy.

The IP concept is applicable to almost any prospecting problem. It is especially useful in areas where deep oxidation or thick alluvial cover make detection impossible by any other method.

In the initial applications of the IP method, all measurements were made using the time domain technique; a direct current was applied to the ground and suddenly cut off. The induced polarization present gave rise to a pulse transient, the decay of which was measured. The parameter was the apparent chargeability (m_a), a dimensionless factor equivalent to the frequency effect.

The widespread use at present of the variable frequency technique rather than the time domain method is the result of a number of practical considerations. The same electrode configuration is used for both methods, but while the pulse transient technique requires a transmitter with an output of several thousand watts of power, the variable frequency method requires only several hundred watts. This advantage, coupled with the relative ease of measurement, made the latter method more popular.

Since 1960, Canadians have also used IP in exploring for strata-bound lead-zinc mineralization in Paleozoic limestones.[1] IP came into widespread use when it became clear that the EM method, even at high frequencies, could not always detect this type of deposit. Several orebodies at shallow depth, of considerable lateral extent, and containing appreciable iron sulphide could not be detected by EM surveys. In some of these programs—in Ireland, for instance—the IP method was used in a semireconnaissance mode.

The use of IP has also been well accepted for porphyry copper exploration in the Canadian Cordillera.

Portable power packs from Geo-Western are one of major refinements in induced polarization. This unit weighs less than 1,000 lb and may be mounted in a ¾-ton vehicle.

The IP method is, however, more ponderous and costly than EM and magnetic methods. There are also problems of making electrical contact with the ground in dry, sandy, or frozen areas, and of masking in areas with conducting overburden. These disadvantages will be overcome if the magnetic induced polarization method (MIP) now being tested becomes successful. Its potential as a reconnaissance tool has been called "tremendous."

The Scintrex MIP method,[2] which detects induced polarization effects through measurements of the magnetic fields associated with polarization currents, is now used in South Africa and Australia. Scintrex reports that the method is proving especially useful in areas of highly conductive or highly resistive surface materials—conditions that are common in semiarid countries. The MIP system is being applied in the search for a variety of base metal deposits and even for heavy minerals in beach sands. MIP is also well suited, says Scintrex, to explore for bedded lead-zinc deposits, which are often overlain by a sequence of conducting and resistive horizons.

Suppliers offer portable IP power packs

One of the major refinements of IP is not a modification of the system itself, but the development of portable power packs. Geo-Western of Salt Lake City, Utah, developed recently a series of large, rechargeable, lightweight power supplies for its line of IP units. The power unit weighs less than 1,000 lb and can be mounted in any vehicle with a ¾-ton rating.

In the past, a large generator and two or three trucks were required to handle the necessary IP equipment. The Geo-Western power prototype and two other units on the market have reportedly been used with success in deep level mineral and geothermal exploration. One of the major advantages of this type of power unit is the clean, smooth current flow produced by the batteries. The unit is more reliable than generators and requires considerably less maintenance.

Several other companies are also using smaller power packs for their IP units. □

References

1) Hallof, Philip G., "Induced Polarization Method a Feasible Reconnaissance Technique," NORTHERN MINER, March 4, 1976, p B23.
2) Hood, Peter, "Mineral Exploration Trends and Developments in 1975," CANADIAN MINING JOURNAL, February 1976, p 186.

EM proves useful reconnaissance tool

AIRBORNE ELECTROMAGNETICS (EM) is a relatively inexpensive means of mapping variations in the electrical conductivity of the upper 350 ft or so of the earth's crust. The general principle is very similar to that of a mine detector.[1] In EM, an alternating current passing through the transmitter coil generates an alternating electromagnetic field. If this field impinges on an electrical conductor—a metallic sulphide orebody, for example—eddy currents are induced in the conductor. The eddy currents in turn generate an alternating electromagnetic field that is picked up by a detector coil and recorded.

Radar to detect objects below land, water, or ice is offered by Geophysical Survey Systems for electromagnetic profiles.

One or more frequencies (usually in the range of 100 to 4,000 Hz) may be employed, and the transmitted signals may be continuous or pulsed. If the exciting signal is transmitted continuously, the induced field is normally measured continuously, while those parts of the induced field that are in phase and out of phase with the transmitted field are measured separately. (Out-of-phase parts of the induced field are "at *quadrature*.") Such measurements are said to have been made in the *frequency domain*. (Early quadrature systems have largely disappeared since the mid-1960s, although McPhar is using a variation that it believes to be extremely useful and in some ways advantageous over other EM systems.)

If the transmitted signal is pulsed, then the decay of the signal can be observed between pulses. The better the conductor, the longer the signal takes to decay. This technique makes use of measurements in the *time domain* and is chiefly represented by Barringer Research's INPUT system[2] and Crone Geophysics' ground pulse system.[3] The other systems available are continuous wave systems, in which an alternating (ac) field is transmitted continuously and the secondary field is measured in the presence of the transmitted field.

Most EM systems, airborne or ground, incorporate a separate transmitter, produce an electromagnetic field, and measure distortions in that field. However, a few systems are only receivers of naturally transmitted fields or of some distant transmitter such as a radio station. Systems that are receivers-only include AFMAG (audio frequency magnetometer) and VLF-EM (very low frequency). These are continuous wave systems, but they are receiver-only systems too. They do not offer the same degree of resolution as other systems, nor are they able to distinguish different types of conductors. They tend, therefore, to be used only in rough applications. For example, both AFMAG and VLF are adept at mapping faults; features of major proportions will concentrate or distort these very widespread fields, and anomalies will be spotted along faults or large graphite horizons.

In a recent comparative study[3] of the effectiveness of certain exploration methods in the search for mineralized faults, it was found that the VLF-EM method provides a rapid means of locating target areas. One of the greatest advantages is that VLF survey work can be done by a single operator.

The main disadvantage of the VLF method, the study found, is that metal conductors, such as fences, frequently give rise to prominent anomalies, although the effect is not consistent. Another disadvantage is that the depth of VLF penetration is severely limited in conductive ground. Anomalies generated by conductivity changes within the overburden or at the overburden-rock interface may be difficult to distinguish from anomalies caused by conductivity changes within the rock. However, the conductivity contrast associated with sheared, brecciated, or mineralized faults normally produces VLF anomalies, so the method is useful for geological mapping, and in particular for locating narrow fault zones.

None of the EM systems penetrates very deeply. The maximum depth is perhaps 500 to 600 ft, but the range may be from 100 to 600 ft. Penetration, therefore, is one major variable. The other is interpretability, which is a function of: the number of frequencies measured; orientation of the coils with respect to one another; distance of separation of coils; signal-to-noise ratio; and the influence of the airplane itself on the instrumentation.

Airborne AFMAG

The AFMAG EM system, in simplified terms, consists solely of an extremely sensitive receiver that is capable of measuring the spatial variations in an electromagnetic field. In an airborne AFMAG instrument, the tilt of the plane of polarization of a natural magnetic field is recorded simultaneously at two different frequencies.

The main advantage of the system over conventional inductive EM methods is claimed to be much greater depth of penetration. Because the transmitter is theoretically at infinity, it is capable of a greater inherent depth of penetration.

The dip angle, or inclination, of the plane of polarization is measured by a receiver towed in a bird about 200 to 300 ft from the aircraft. The dip angle is recorded by two orthogonally placed coils, both of whose planes lie at 45° to the direction of flight. In a perfect, horizontally plane-polarized field, the output from both coils will be equal. Any change in the polarization from the horizontal will cause a difference in the compared outputs from these two coils.

One of the main disadvantages of the AFMAG is its reliance on natural EM fields, which vary daily as well as seasonally. In northern latitudes, the strength of the earth's natural electromagnetic fields at the recorded frequencies is high enough for surveying purposes only during the summer months of June, July, August, and occasionally during part of September. In the southern latitudes, fields are at their highest strengths during December, January, and February. The strengths of natural fields are also characterized by a diurnal pattern, being highest in the early morning and late afternoon, and at a low point about midday.

In-phase, out-of-phase and quadrature airborne EM

Another EM category consists of primarily airborne systems within the continuous wave systems. These units are of two types: one measures in-phase and out-of-phase at one or more frequencies; the second measures quadrature only, at two or more frequencies.

The objective of measuring these components is to determine the conductivity of the material that is being overflown. The ratio of in-phase to out-of-phase varies according to the conductivity of the source. The ratio of quadrature at two different frequencies varies in similar fashion. Therefore, using at least two channels and comparing ratios gives an indication of the order of conductivity of the material.

According to Barringer Research, the trend is to add additional frequencies to improve interpretability of the results. Knowledgeable sources say there is no question that the use of multiple frequencies allows increased resolution of conductivity parameters in the terrain. However, Barringer's opinion is that the main objective of development should be to improve the separation of overburden conductivity effects from underlying conductors, rather than the more precise determination of electrical factors such as the conductivity-width product of anomalies.

Dighem: a helicopter system

The Dighem I system is a relatively recent innovation in aerial EM exploration. It is a multicoil, helicopter-towed system with three mutually orthogonal receiver coils at one end of a 30-ft bird. The vertical transmitter coil at the other end, with its axis parallel to the flight direction, transmits at 918 Hz. Geological noise is said to be small,

Stream sediment samples are collected by US Geological Survey geologist. (Photo credit: K. Robinson, USGS.)

Ground-pulse EM system similar in design to Barringer's INPUT system has been developed by Crone Geophysics Ltd.

and broad-scale conductive features are not emphasized relative to smaller discrete massive sulphide orebodies. The three-dimensional recording of anomalies provides diagnostic geometric information on conductors that is said not to be available with other systems.

A Geometrics G-704 data acquisition system records the geophysical data in digital form. A computer produces electromagnetic maps with all anomalies interpreted according to conductance and depth of burial; contoured total field magnetic maps; and contoured enhanced maps.

Dighem Ltd. has also developed a new airborne EM system, Dighem II. It incorporates a Dighem I system with an additional transmitter coil. The system provides excellent coupling to conductors of virtually any attitude. In test flights with Dighem II, the noise levels have been as low as with Dighem I. The first Dighem II system was sold to the West German government for delivery this spring. The second system will begin commercial surveying in North America in the summer of 1976.

Barringer's INPUT dominates EM exploration

The Barringer INPUT system dominates the scene in airborne EM exploration. The reason is its top rating in terms of penetration and interpretability. According to one industry source, Barringer's INPUT system is used in more than 50% of Canada's airborne EM studies, while 80% of foreign airborne EM uses its pulse EM system.

Developed by Barringer in 1962, INPUT is generally used for detecting electrically conductive orebodies. This system has opened up a new approach to exploration in regions characterized by deep overburden or high surface conductivity, such as numerous clay belts and semiarid regions. Developed by Barringer with the sponsorship of Selco Exploration Co. Ltd., the system is loosely analogous to radar in that it depends on the generation of high powered electromagnetic pulses and the reception of signals following the termination of such pulses. The electromagnetic pulses are formed by pulses of current of 1.4 millisec duration circulated in a loop surrounding the survey aircraft. The pulses generate eddy currents in any conductive bodies lying within range of the system, which in turn creates secondary electromagnetic fields. The secondary fields take a finite time to collapse following the abrupt termination of the primary pulse. During this decay, or transient, period INPUT receiving equipment records the strength. The conductivity of the body controls the rate of collapse of the secondary field, and careful analysis of the rate of decay can determine conductivity of a sulphide mass or other natural conductor.

The system employs a horizontal transmitting loop and a vertical receiving coil axis in line with the flight direction. The receiving coil is towed in a bird on 500 ft of cable and flies about 225 ft below the aircraft. Normal survey height is 400 ft. The rate of decay of the transient responses is measured by sampling the decay curve at four different delay positions following the termination of the primary pulse; the average value of these samples is smoothed over a period of a few seconds and recorded as four separate and continuous profiles on a paper recorder. The decay characteristics of a conductive anomaly are determined by calculating the ratios between the peak values obtained on each trace.

Crone markets ground-pulse system

A ground-pulse EM system similar in design to Barringer's INPUT system has been developed by Crone Geophysics Ltd. in cooperation with Newmont Exploration Ltd.—the first unit in a planned integrated system of surface and borehole pulse EM equipment. Newmont had previously developed an operational pulse EM unit for use in areas of very high surface conductivity. The Newmont equipment was a large, heavy apparatus that required motorized transport and operated in the equivalent frequency spectrum of 10 Hz to 2.5 Hz.

Crone's basic intent was to design a pulse EM system more portable than Newmont's that could be operated in all field conditions, including heavily wooded and mountainous terrain. The company also sought to record the higher-frequency data that is contained in the pulse EM waveform.

High frequency information is needed for various reasons:

- Field tests conducted over massive sulphide bodies in the Arizona desert indicated that the desert weathering process tended to break down the electrical contact between sulphide crystals. The net effect is to reduce the conductivity of a massive sulphide body, particularly narrow bodies or highly fractured sulphide zones.
- It is important to be able to detect occurrences as low as 5% of sulphides, which are usually poor to moderate conductors.

■ There is a need to determine the presence and extent of surficial conductive formations and clay deposits, since many airborne EM anomalies are caused by such bodies.

The first equipment designed by Crone consists of a moving coil system that is primarily used with a horizontal loop configuration. The transmitter is a small loop 3 to 5 m in diameter that is laid out horizontally on the ground. The loop is energized by a pulse of current of approximately 20 amps obtained from two 12-v batteries. The current is turned off by a special ramp circuit. The on-off time is 10.8 millisec. The receiver coil is generally spaced 50 to 100 m from the transmit loop, and the signal on the receiver coil is sampled, averaged, and then stored during the reading interval. One sample is taken of the primary pulse and eight samples are taken of the secondary field during the "off" time. Time synchronization is by radio link or cable. The reading point is located midway between the transmitter and receiver.

Both coils are moved along the survey line, together or in leapfrog fashion. Reading time per station other than moving is 30 sec, with the number of stations read per day depending upon terrain but usually varying between 75 and 150. The transmitter weight including batteries is 40 kilos and the receiver weight is 11 kilos. □

References

1) Richards, D. J., and Walraven, F., "Airborne Geophysics and ERTS Imagery," MINERALS SCI. ENG., Vol. 7, No. 3, July 1975, pp 234-278.
2) Barringer, A. R., "Recent Developments in the INPUT Airborne Electrical Pulse Prospecting System," American Mining Congress, San Francisco, Calif., September 1962.
3) Phillips, W. J., and Richards, W. E., "A Study of the Effectiveness of the VLF Method for the Location of Narrow Mineralized Fault Zones," GEOEXPLORATION, Elsevier Scientific Publishing Co., Vol. 13, 1975, pp 215-226.

Radiometry: refinements in uranium search soften energy crisis

MAJOR STRIDES HAVE BEEN MADE over the last 10 years in the development of new and refined methods for finding radioactive materials—uranium in particular. These changes have doubtless contributed to an acceleration in the rate of discoveries, which are sorely needed to alleviate well-publicized energy shortages.

Although the initial expenditure is substantial, airborne prospecting for radioactive resources over large areas is actually less costly per unit area surveyed than an equivalent ground search. Furthermore, while airborne reconnaissance surveys do not equal the degree of resolution of ground techniques, they *are* the quickest method for locating specific promising sites. Such sites can then be more closely scrutinized by ground studies.[1]

Generally speaking, gamma-ray spectrometry is the most effective airborne tool for uranium exploration. Airborne prospecting requires very efficient gamma spectrometers capable of recording separately the total intensity and the specific intensities of potassium, uranium, and thorium. Gamma radiation is the only significant variable in airborne radioactivity prospecting, since it is the only one of the three types of radiation (gamma, beta, alpha) that can be detected many feet from the source.[2]

Potassium, thorium, and uranium, the three most significant sources of natural radioactivity, occur together in most common rock types, and their relative proportions vary only within very narrow limits throughout a wide range of rocks. Thus, in granite with a high potassium content, the uranium and thorium contents are also high. In diabase, where potassium content is low, uranium and thorium are also proportionately low. The occurrence of uranium as ore changes these ratios, and the ratios of uranium to potassium and uranium to thorium immediately become anomalous.[3]

Because gamma radiation is to some extent absorbed and scattered by air and overburden, very sensitive equipment is needed. One researcher found that there is an optimum relationship between aircraft velocity, spectrometer sampling time, altitude, and upper limit of anomaly wavelength resolution. Improving counting statistics by flying at lower than optimum altitude is done at the expense of aliasing shorter wavelength components.[4]

Airborne gamma-ray spectrometry is also a regional geochemical exploration tool, the only difference being that chemical contents are determined remotely by a physical means, rather than by chemical analysis of a collected sample.[5]

In all exploration, the configuration of the source relative to the detecting crystal is an important factor. Most modern ground devices designed to detect natural radioactivity utilize a sodium iodide crystal enriched with thallium [NaI(Tl)]. This is the most efficient and accurate method of detecting and measuring gamma radiation for field instrumentation. A gamma ray that passes into and interacts with the crystal is changed into energetic elec-

New gamma-ray spectrometer—GAD-4 from Scintrex—said to be first portable to automatically read Compton Stripped values.

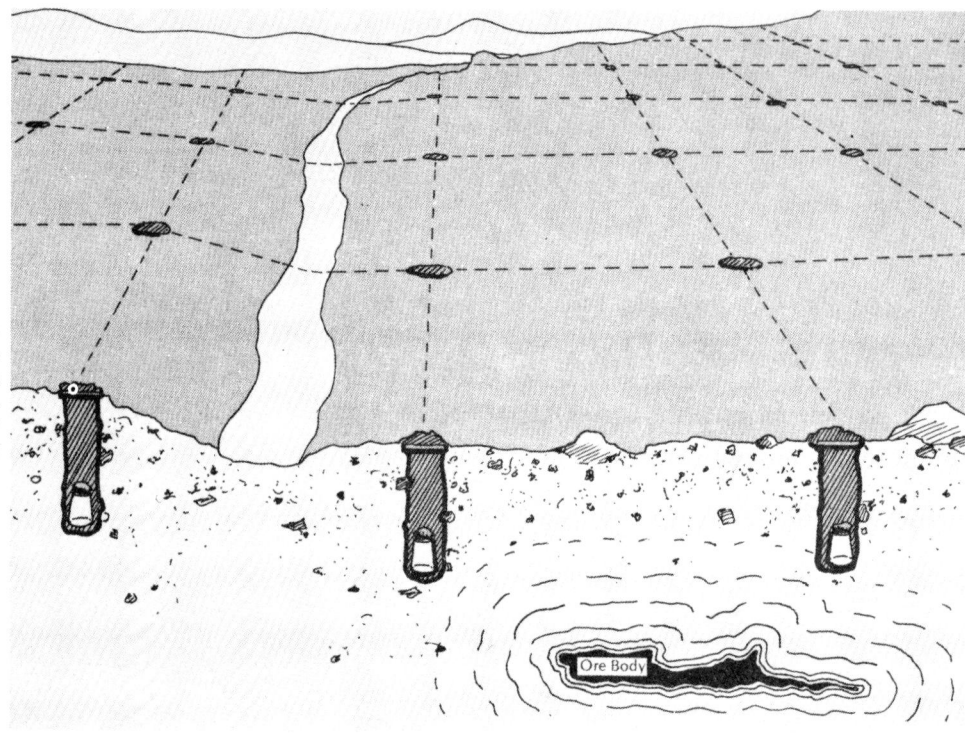

'Track Etch' sampling system, developed by Terradex, is said to eliminate 30% to 90% of the exploration drilling usually needed in any uranium search program.

trons, which then give up their energy by causing the crystal to scintillate (produce visible pulses of light). The total light flux is proportional to the energy deposited by the gamma ray in the crystal. A photomultiplier tube, optically coupled to the crystal, changes these light scintillations into small electronic pulses, which are amplified. The amplified pulse heights are then proportional to the energy of the individual gamma rays that have been detected.[6]

There have been no recent major developments in instrumentation for measuring radioactivity, although improvements in design detail and reliability and stability are to be expected. A proprietary development of a polycrystalline detector may permit building a more efficient economic unit. There is also a possibility of photodiodes replacing photomultipliers, which would make instrumentation smaller.[2]

Ground studies use portable spectrometers

A number of devices are marketed for ground exploration or adjunct studies to airborne gamma-ray surveys. The cheapest—though somewhat insensitive—unit is the Geiger-Muller type scintillometer, which is capable of detecting gamma radiation using a vacuum tube instead of a thallium-enriched sodium iodide crystal.

Scintillometers are commonly mounted on trucks. Whenever possible, a ground area is surveyed on a grid system and the results are plotted on an anomaly map as isograd contour lines. This map, when compared with airborne radiometric mapping, provides accurate data on the areal extent of a mineralized zone.

Ground radiometric surveys can be laborious and time consuming. Tackling this problem, South Africa's Atomic Energy Board developed a continuous recording instrument attached to a scintillometer which, in turn, is mounted on a cyclometer. One advantage of this instrument—which can be used only in flat terrain—is a continuous recording device that permanently records the ground traverse and allows unskilled labor to be used for leg work.[1]

In situations where airborne surveys may confuse uranium with thorium mineralization, it might prove useful to perform ground studies with a portable field gamma-ray spectrometer.

Where "disequilibrium" is a serious problem, as in many of the uranium deposits of Wyoming, a portable X-ray fluorescence analyzer is a reliable alternative to the conventional geiger or scintillation counter. X-ray fluorescence (XRF) analysis is being employed more frequently in exploration. For certain elements—thorium, tantalum, and niobium, for example—XRF is reportedly faster and simpler than atomic absorption, emission spectroscopy, and other analytical methods in most situations where detection limits of 50 ppm are acceptable. In other cases, as in the analysis of uranium, vanadium, or titanium, XRF is thought to be at least competitive in many circumstances.

Borehole logging still prominent in uranium search

The gamma-ray log, introduced back in 1939, was one of the first nuclear techniques for correlation of rock types. Originally of interest only to the oil industry, the gamma log evolved into one of the prime exploration tools for uranium deposits of the type found in the southwestern US. The search for uranium in hardrock environments and the decrease in the cutoff grade for ore have led to the requirement for gamma-ray spectrometric logging. Digital recording has been introduced, and several logging service companies have digital systems in the field.

In addition to applications in uranium and potash exploration, gamma logging appears to have some potential for base metal exploration because significant changes in potassium, uranium, and thorium distributions may occur as halos around certain types of mineral deposits.[7]

Gamma-ray logging can assist in defining certain rock types and stratigraphic units for detailed correlation. In the US, borehole techniques have achieved a degree of sophistication that allows logging to be applied to the evaluation of ore reserves.

One practical problem in the past has been the limited availability of probes that would fit inside the small diameter exploration holes commonly used in mineral exploration.

Radon exploration offers better penetration

The radon method of uranium exploration offers greater depth penetration than gamma-ray spectrometry. The only gaseous isotope in the uranium decay series, radon alone can travel over greater ranges than gamma rays in solid rock. Therefore, it can be used to detect potential uranium orebodies under heavy cover—10 to 50 ft of overburden. Gamma radiation can penetrate only several inches.

Virtually all available radon instrumentation detects radon gas by measuring emissions of alpha particles. Alpha detection devices consist essentially of a probe for insertion in the soil; a mechanism for transferring the soil air from the soil to an alpha detector; and the alpha detector itself—either a photomultiplier coupled to a zinc sulphide-coated detecting element or, less commonly, an ionization chamber.

'Track Etch' simplifies radon measurement

The "Track Etch" system is a relatively new technique for uranium exploration based on the detection of radon gas anomalies. Track Etch uses small, solid-state alpha track detectors to measure radon in the near-surface soil gas. Because the Track Etch technique measures a long term sample of soil gas, it eliminates the major problems in using radon measurements as guides to subsurface uranium mineralization. Track Etch is said to be simpler, more reliable, and more sensitive than the emanometer methods for radon detection.

In sampling radon with emanometers (or "sniffers"), the procedure is to measure the alpha radiation emitted by a small sample of soil gas pumped from near-surface soil. The detector is either an alpha-sensitive, phosphor-coated chamber coupled to a photomultiplier or an alpha-sensitive ionization chamber. The gas sampling period is usually several seconds or minutes.

Emanometers are relatively complex, both electronically and mechanically, and the phosphor-coated sample chamber is subject to surface contamination from radon daughter products, particularly when high radon levels are measured. The most significant problem, however, appears to be that emanometers measure only a short term soil gas sample, which is usually not indicative of the average radon concentration in the immediate area. To obtain more meaningful radon data, officials of Terradex Corp. say that integrated readings must be obtained over a period of time, which is readily accomplished with the Track Etch system.

Track Etch uses small radiation-sensitive solid-state plastic detectors. The detectors are attached to the inside bottom surfaces of small sampling cups that are placed in shallow holes, where they measure radon concentrations in soil gas. The Track Etch detectors are then processed in a special etching solution where they produce visible track-like images of the alpha particles that have impinged upon the detectors.

In a typical uranium exploration program,[8] sampling cups containing Track Etch detectors are placed in holes about 75 cm deep over the area being explored. The sample holes are normally located in a grid pattern, 30 and 1,000 m apart, depending on the size of the area, the dimensions of the expected orebodies, the local structural trends, and other factors. After the cups are in place, the holes are covered and the cups are left undisturbed for three to four weeks or longer to continuously accumulate the readings produced by the varying radon soil gas concentrations. The cups are recovered and the detectors processed and read to determine the number of alpha tracks recorded and hence the average radon level at the sample location. The data are usually presented in the form of radon contour maps or graphs.

Alphameter may replace current techniques

It has recently become possible to detect and count alpha rays directly in situ in the overburden by semiconductor crystals, notably using an instrument built by Alpha Nuclear Corp.[9] Field tests performed by Soquem, of Quebec, and others show that the instrument, called an alphameter, permits a direct reading in the field after 1 hr of radon in quasi-equilibrium in the soil. The unit permits rapid coverage of large areas to detail anomalies for drilling.

Instruments of this type, according to Soquem, seem to fill an important, intermediate role between Track Etch and emanometer surveys, and alphameters may supplant these two radiometric methods.

The alphameter consists of a tube 1½ to 2 in. in diameter and 14 in. long. A silicium detector is located at one end of the tube, recessed 2 in. The tube is inserted into a hole in the ground made with a steel rod. The soil gas equilibrium, barely disturbed, is rapidly re-established. Alpha rays of an energy greater than 1 MeV, coming from radon in the cavity of the tube, strike the silicium detector and are counted and stored in an electronic memory. After one hour, one day, or one week, the counter is read, and the instrument is retrieved and inserted in another location.

Other researchers have described a soil radium method of uranium exploration.[10] Radium in soil samples is measured by immersing the samples in water for a fixed period and then analyzing for radon emanated into the water. The method can penetrate at least several feet deeper than radiometric equipment. Field samples are cited in the study, which compares soil radium, scintillometer, and emanometer results over specific uranium occurrences near Uranium City, Sask. Among the other advantages of the soil radium method: results can be obtained at the site of the survey, equipment is simple, and results are reproducible. □

References

1) Toens, P. D., "Geochemical Behavior Points the Way to Uranium Concentration," S. AFRICAN CHAMBER OF MINES JOURNAL, January 1976, pp 34-37.
2) Hartman, Ronald R., "Airborne Gamma Ray Spectrometry," Aero Service Corp., Philadelphia, Pa., 1967.
3) Darnley, A. G., "Geophysics in Uranium Exploration," Annual Meeting, Prospectors & Developers Association, Toronto, Ont., March 1975.
4) Killeen, P. G., Carson, J. M., and Hunter, J. A., "Optimizing Some Parameters for Airborne Gamma Ray Spectrometric Surveying," GEOEXPLORATION, Elsevier Scientific Publishing Co., Amsterdam, Vol. 13, 1975, pp 1-12.
5) Garrett, R. G., and Darnley, A. G., "Regional Geochemistry—Its Philosophy and Use," NORTHERN MINER, November 28, 1974, p 64.
6) Baird, Jon G., "Portable Gamma-Ray Spectrometers Will Help," NORTHERN MINER, March 4, 1976.
7) Killeen, P. G., "Trends in Gamma-Ray Logging of Mineral Exploration Boreholes," 78th Annual General Meeting, Canad. Instit. of Mining and Metallurgy, April 1976.
8) Gingrich, James E., and Fisher, James C., "Uranium Exploration Using the Track Etch Method," International Symposium on Exploration of Uranium Ore Deposits, Vienna, Austria, March 29-April 2, 1976.
9) Gaucher, Edwin, "Uranium Prospecting by Detecting Radon with Alphameters: The Newest Development in the Oldest Radiometric Method of Prospecting," Annual Meeting, Prospectors & Developers Association, Toronto, Ont., March 1976.
10) Sutton, W. R., and Soonawala, N. M., "A Soil Radium Method for Uranium Prospecting," CIM Bulletin, May 1975, pp 51-56.

Copper exploration restrained by resource nationalism and low metal prices

Michael Chender, Copper Studies Inc.

DESPITE THE CURRENT RECORD-HIGH LEVEL of LME copper stocks, and the likelihood of a slower growth in consumption over the next decade, many in the industry are warning of a period of severe copper shortages sometime in the 1980s. The origin of these shortages is anticipated to lie not in a sudden spurt in consumption or in the usual cyclical pattern of the copper industry, but rather in current constraints on exploration and development that are severely curtailing the growth of future supply.

Little development activity now under way

The emergence of "resource nationalism," with attendant changes in investment ground rules in mineral areas, combined with sharply rising exploration and development costs, is causing problems for much potential mine development.

There is no disputing the fact that several years ago known reserves around the world were substantial enough to fulfill projected copper needs well into the 21st century. However, both economic and political developments since then have made questionable the ultimate development of a large portion of these deposits. As "reserves" are defined by economic conditions, it is accurate to say that in certain cases reserves have shrunk. The economic problems—low copper prices and high development costs—might be expected to correct themselves over time. More worrisome to the industry are certain political developments in many countries: the reality or threat of direct government intervention, or the imposition of royalty and tax schedules that make mineral development unprofitable.

At present, few major copper mines are under development. La Caridad in Mexico and Tenke-Fungurume (currently idled in Zaire) fall into this category, as do the Glogow area mines in Poland. The Texasgulf expansion to underground mining at Kidd Creek in Canada can also be included. Cuajone (Peru) and Sar Chesmeh (Iran) are nearly completed. Given the current lead times for mine development, we can expect that, on the average, not more than one major copper mine will come onstream yearly over the next four years.

This outlook contrasts sharply with the situation four or five years ago, when several major copper mines were coming onstream each year. The problem is acute because of the necessity to develop new reserves constantly to ensure longer-term availability.

Given the current difficulties facing mineral exploration, one must wonder what incentives will be found to encourage development of supply sufficient to meet demand projections. In the absence of adequate incentives, will government participation be required to an even greater extent to keep the copper industry healthy? Will copper be pushed through increasingly violent price cycles because of the lack of adequate planning? Or will the copper price move to new plateaus, encouraging substitution in the face of a supply shortfall?

Recent developments in exploration

In this article, the term "exploration" refers to prospecting for and testing of potential deposits up to the stage where a decision is made to develop a producing mine. The investment possibilities in specific areas and the future price outlook for specific metals will play a large part in determining where and how intensely to explore. In its early stages, copper exploration is often inseparable from exploration for all base metals; it becomes identifiable as such only when copper indications are being followed up.

The most notable feature of base metal exploration in the past several years has been the geographical redistribution of activities, accompanied by a slowdown in spending in late 1974 and 1975.

The drop in expenditures was largely a function of low metal prices. For mineral producing companies, exploration expenditures (within the parameters of specific corporate objectives) will be closely linked to available funds in most cases. These funds are, in turn, largely a function of price. Small exploration companies, such as those in Canada and Australia, are not so directly linked to current prices as a source of income, but their financing possibilities fluctuate with the changing metal market pictures. For companies that are not base metal producers but want to diversify (e.g., oil companies), the level of expenditures will be determined primarily by the corporate view on the desirability of becoming a metals producer. Current metals prices will not have a direct effect in these cases.

Base metal exploration activity worldwide surged in the late 1960s, and then fell back somewhat with the depressed market of 1971-72. Another boom period seemed to be shaping up in 1973-74 as soaring metals markets and the general psychology of shortages indicated a strong long term outlook for metals.

This market climate, however, sparked a reaction in the mineral-rich countries. The trend toward increasing government involvement in existing copper industries had already been clearly established, starting in the 1960s in such places as Mexico, Chile, and Peru. However, the 1973-74 period of high prices brought increased awareness of the value of mineral resources. Governments in previously "safe" investment areas such as British Columbia and Australia clamped down with tax, royalty, and investment regulations on what they considered to be "excessive profits" taken by mining companies.

These moves caused some dramatic geographical redistributions of exploration spending, while the crash in prices of most metals in 1974-75 led to a cutback in spending levels. In Canada, exploration activity in 1974 dropped by 30% in British Columbia (a prime area for copper), but nearly doubled in the Yukon and Northwest Territories, which do not have provincial tax systems. This pattern continued through 1975, with much of the drop in British Columbia activity being picked up in Alaska, the continental US, Quebec, Ontario, and the Canadian Maritime Provinces, all of which have relatively favorable tax structures.

Activity in Australia likewise began to drop sharply in 1973-74, after the return to power of the Labor government. The Philippines benefited from a shifting of some companies' activities. Many US companies previously active in Canada and Australia reined in some of their overseas interests and concentrated their exploration efforts domestically. Southern Africa continued to be one of the few areas in the world still considered "safe" for mining investment, and both South Africa and Namibia saw a great deal of interest.

More recently, interest in Namibia dropped off considerably following various troubles in that part of Africa. However, exploration continues at a high pitch in South Africa, which is still viewed favorably by mining companies despite its neighbor's problems.

The emergence of resource nationalism

The view that natural resources represent a country's patrimony and should yield a profit to the state was originally seen by mining companies as an expression of hostility on the part of the local governments. However, in recent years, this view has been almost universally endorsed by developed-country groups such as the EEC, as well as by developing nations. The practical manifestations of this view range from the 51% domestic ownership requirement existing in many countries to the apparent willingness of some governments to leave known resources in the ground until their stringent development terms are met. Service contracts, under which the operating company has little or no equity, are now being more seriously regarded in the industry as vehicles for mine development in the future.

At the exploration level in particular, there is little fear of excessive government action. It is in any country's best interest for its resources to be defined and quantified. Therefore, at the exploration stage, resource nationalism is expressed in the trend toward setting time limits and minimum work schedules for exploration licenses. This trend is aimed at eliminating the proliferation of "dead ground"—areas licensed exclusively to a company conducting little (according to government criteria) or no exploration.

Until recently, exploration licenses in most countries carried options on later mining rights as an incentive to prospecting companies. In the past few years, some governments have attempted to move away from this practice, while others have simply canceled the development option in a company's contract after an orebody has been proven, and then presented the orebody for competitive bidding.

The logical outgrowth of this approach would be the use of an exploration contract, under which the costs of exploration would be covered by the host country, and participation in the work would carry no binding rights to subsequent exploration. Although this type of contract has been employed by the Middle East oil-producing countries, mineral-rich nations have been slow to make use of such contracts, usually because they lack the requisite financing. Mining companies naturally find such approaches unattractive, feeling that their skills are better employed in situations that promise potentially greater returns.

The positive forces in exploration

So far, we have drawn a gloomy picture, with which industry is quite familiar. Exploration and development of new mines is becoming increasingly uncertain, not only because of high costs and low copper prices, but also because of lack of investment incentives around the world. However, on the positive side, several factors are contributing to the continuation of exploration and development:

- Most dramatically, a new maturity in resource politics is becoming apparent, as governments of mineral-rich countries learn that the realities of developing and financing new sources of production may not be compatible with their investment policies. Burma and Bolivia are examples of mineral-rich countries that were among the first to nationalize domestic mining interests and effectively discourage foreign investment. After many years of frustration in developing domestic mining, both countries within the past two years implemented plans to attract foreign participation once again. British Columbia and Australia, heavily involved in mining, in the past few years initiated prohibitive tax and royalty restrictions on private mining development. The maturation process here took place much quicker—in both cases the governments involved were removed from power after two to three years, and levies on mining have been eased dramatically. Chile can also be included in this category; it is now wooing foreign investment after a frustrating lack of ability to finance its industry under the Allende regime.
- At the same time that some governments are loosening investment guidelines, companies are adjusting their expectations to the new rules of the game.
- Organizations other than traditional metal producers, namely oil companies and government agencies, are increasing their efforts in base metals exploration.
- On the corporate level, the same factors that are leading to a diminishing effort by some companies are encouraging others. Visions of future copper supply problems also imply relatively high prices for the available output.

Political cyclicality in minerals development

The development histories of the areas mentioned—Bolivia, Burma, Chile, British Columbia, and Australia—all point to some degree of political cyclicality in minerals development. In other words, while mining companies and governments around the world continue to battle publicly over "fair" development provisions, the pendulum is quietly swinging back to a position of workable compromise in many situations. This is a predictable outgrowth of the experience of government and industry over the last few years.

A country must have two additional resources with which to develop its mineral wealth: technical expertise and finances. Unless both are present domestically in sufficient quantity and unless they are under the control of the state (which is rarely the case), they must be secured by offering an attractive return. In some cases, a country will be able to attract both technical and financial aid under government-to-government programs, avoiding a compromise on stringent investment criteria. In the great majority of cases, however, development is stagnated by the need for money and expertise, coupled with contract terms that promise to yield little or no benefit to their supplier.

Such stagnation has already been experienced by many countries. The extent to which a country can tolerate such an impasse is related to the degree of dependence on minerals as a source of wealth. Thus, an area like Puerto Rico, where a copper deposit has been waiting in the wings for well over 10 years due to an inability to decide on development terms, can wait for years if it likes, until its terms are met. On the other hand, the economies of other countries, such as Chile, are closely linked to mineral production, and they cannot afford such a rigid stance.

Regarding the maturation process, the most noteworthy developments in recent months are the more lenient criteria governing the mining industry adopted by the new governments in Australia and British Columbia. The latter, with many known but undeveloped porphyry deposits, has recently repealed the infamous Mineral Royalties Act and returned to a profits-based tax. Australia is now allowing companies to go ahead with mine development even though their "best efforts" at attracting the required 50% Australia capital are unsuccessful. Mining companies are enthusiastic about these developments, and a period of higher base metals prices can be expected to spark a dramatic pickup in exploration activity in both British Columbia and Australia.

Companies are revising their criteria

As it becomes clear that there is no longer an abundance of "safe" areas, where a mining company can own the majority of its minerals find and expect government investment, some companies are revising their criteria for entering a country instead of cutting back on exploration activities.

Mexico provides an interesting case history of changing criteria for company investment. The country was long shunned by overseas mining companies after it instituted a 51% domestic ownership requirement under the Mexicanization program, which started in 1961. A decade later, as similar requirements were increasingly adopted elsewhere, Mexico began to be viewed in a more favorable light by some companies. The stability of Mexico's investment regulations, rather than their content alone, became a salient factor. Mining companies could plan their budgets in Mexico with reasonable certainty, whereas in areas with rapidly changing or unformed investment and tax policies, it was impossible to properly evaluate future projects.

With its great copper potential, Mexico attracted increasing interest, and in recent years it was regarded by many as one of the more stable sites for mine exploration and development. Recently, the attitude of mining companies has again become more cautious as they await implementation of the new mining law and the installation of the next administration.

To illustrate an individual company's approach, let's look at the exploration and development record of Noranda. Noranda's activities cover a wide range, reflecting many of the issues discussed in this article. (Canadian mining companies in general are willing to explore in areas that most US and European companies shy away from, possibly because the Canadians were never directly hurt by nationalization of overseas properties, as many US and European concerns have been.)

Noranda's exploration was traditionally highly concentrated in Canada. The changing taxation system in Canada provided the major impetus to create a strong overseas program, and the company substantially increased its exploration expenditures in 1970. Outlays in that year totaled $8.7 million, compared with $5.5 million the year before. Canadian mineral exploration accounted for 54% of total costs. The company's 1970 programs also included exploration in the US, Mexico, Australia, Great Britain, Ireland, Spain, Argentina, the Philippines, and the Dominican Republic. During the following year, search projects were started in Greece, Sardinia, Portugal, South Africa, and Brazil, and exploration was concluded in the Philippines and the Dominican Republic. Canadian expenditures fell to 45% of the total, while Australia's share was 28%, the US 13%, and other countries 14%.

By 1974, exploration spending had risen to $17.9 million. The Canadian share was still 45%, but the Australian share had dropped to 8% while US expenditures had risen to 26%. Other areas in Europe, Asia, Africa, and South America accounted for the remaining 21%. In 1975, total expenditures rose again, to $20.6 million. The Canadian share was 48%, the US portion was up to 31%, and the Australian share had dropped to 4%. Ocean mining accounted for 6%, and the remaining interests 11%. (Noranda has a 10% interest in the undersea mining consortium that also includes Rio Tinto-Zinc, Consolidated Gold Fields, Kennecott, and Mitsubishi.) Brazil, where the company is involved in a number of joint ventures, accounted for a significant portion of the "remaining interest" category.

Although the Canadian share of exploration expendi-

Minerals exploration expenditures for selected major companies
(millions of dollars)

	1972	1973	1974	1975
Asarco	NA	6.7	6.6	7.1
Amax	12.0	24.7	19.5	14.8
Cominco	NA	2.5	6.8	7.0
Conzinc Rio Tinto	7.4	10.1	14.6	NA
Cyprus Mines	3.8	4.1	5.5	6.1
Hudson Bay	2.8	2.9	4.2	3.2
Inco*	18.7	17.8	19.9	30.1
Newmont	8.9	15.9	15.0	11.2
Noranda	8.8	11.4	17.9	20.6
Phelps Dodge	7.0	8.8	8.9	9.6
Union Miniere**	2.8	3.8	4.6	NA

NA—Not available.
*Oil and gas exploration included; 1975 increases attributable primarily to this sector.
**Converted from Belgium francs based on the year's average rate as published by US Federal Reserve Board.
Source: Annual reports.

tures has remained roughly the same, Noranda's efforts in its home country have increased considerably in the Yukon and Northwest Territories, which are under Federal control and thus free of provincial taxation problems. The company is now conducting a feasibility study on a small US copper-zinc property in Wisconsin; a production decision would result in the only US copper mine wholly owned by a foreign company.

One of the interesting features of the present exploration program is Noranda's entrance into Zambia in 1974, where it is one of the very few foreign companies now active. Mindeco-Noranda Ltd. is exploring several properties, with Noranda supplying 49% of the funds and managing the program. Noranda pulled out of South Africa (where it had been exploring for over two years) at the end of 1973, prior to its agreement with the Zambians. The direction of these maneuvers is opposite to that of the industry mainstream.

Earlier this year, Noranda secured the third major exploration concession granted in Saudi Arabia to look primarily for copper. US Steel and the French state company BRGM are the other two concession holders.

While Noranda is active in exploration, its expansion philosophy is based primarily on providing development capital after another company has discovered an orebody. This is how it gained equity interests in so many Canadian companies. As the major custom smelter in Canada, Noranda has been well placed over the years to supply capital and development/management expertise to some of the smaller local exploration companies. This service orientation fits in well with the emerging pattern worldwide. Noranda bid to play a similar role in Panama, as manager and minor equity partner in Cerro Colorado, but it lost out last year to Texasgulf. At the beginning of 1976, Noranda won rights to a 49% share in developing the Andocollo deposits in cooperation with the Chilean government.

Oil companies seek role in minerals

The third factor bolstering exploration activity is the growing role in recent years of interests outside the minerals-producing sector. Almost all major oil companies now conduct metals exploration programs. Among the major companies with subsidiaries examining copper indications are Atlantic Richfield, British Petroleum, Continental Oil, Exxon, Getty Oil, Gulf Oil, Occidental, Shell, Standard Oil of California (Chevron), and Standard Oil of Indiana (Amoco Minerals).

Many oil companies have expanded into mineral exploration and development over the past decade; this trend gained impetus from the recent period of high metals prices and the fear of future shortages. Other reasons include the loss of substantial foreign oil holdings, a strong cash position resulting from super-profitable years, and government pressure to diversify.

Many oil producers see minerals exploration as a natural step, believing that they possess the geological sophistication to compete with existing mining companies. Although this is debatable (because of the different types of geology), the fact that minerals exploration is conducted at a fraction of the cost of oil exploration is undoubtedly a selling point for the large oil producers. Annual budgets for oil exploration by the largest companies run into hundreds of millions of dollars—close to $1 billion in some cases—while the most active mineral company exploration programs are in the $15 million to $30 million range. It is quite possible that Exxon has spent more in the past few years on mineral exploration than any mineral producer.

The attraction of the metals industry for oil interests is also evidenced by recent purchases—of Billiton by Shell, of a share in Anaconda by Atlantic Richfield, of a partnership in the Le Nickel-Penarroya group by Ste. National des Petroles d'Aquitaine (the French national oil company), and of a percentage of Amax by Standard Oil of Caiforni. In the US, Cities Service and Pennzoil (through Duval) already have producing copper mines. El Paso Natural Gas is a partner in the Lakeshore mine and Union Oil owns a part of the Pima mine. Continental Oil has a copper prospect in Arizona that it is seriously evaluating for production.

The involvement of oil companies in minerals exploration tends to bring into the field substantial new funds not so closely linked to the current fortunes of metals markets. The oil companies' financial muscle naturally irks many mining executives, who claim that some oil companies "ruin" the business by freely bidding up the price of leases they want.

While oil companies bring more money into copper exploration, they use the same general investment criteria as mining companies in deciding how to employ the funds. Government agencies, however, use completely different criteria.

Government agencies get into the action

Government or government-sponsored agencies are likely to play a bigger role in copper exploration in the future, for two reasons. One is that the politicization of resource development in the past several years, along with wild fluctuations of commodity markets, have opened the eyes of governments in major consuming countries to the wisdom of securing long range raw materials supplies. As exemplified by the Japanese, one way to attain such security is by helping to finance and participating in the development of supplies abroad, in return for payment in copper and/or favorable purchase commitments.

Aside from companies owned or financed by the Japanese government, the French Bureau de Recherches et des Participations Minieres is the most active government agency in minerals exploration and development. Countries in which BRGM is active in copper development include Bolivia, Zaire, Jordan, and Saudi Arabia.

The Rumanian state-owned company Geomin is also quite active in exploration and mining projects abroad. Its motives are different—Geomin is primarily interested in creating markets for its machinery and technology. The Canadian International Development Agency has been greatly increasing its visibility in recent years, using Canadian expertise in exploration and development projects around the world.

The second key factor in the growing role of government agencies is that they can afford to take more risks in developing countries than private companies can, because return on investment from a potential project is only a secondary concern for governments.

The big question

The exploration scene today is quite confused. Various points discussed here shed some light on an otherwise murky picture; nevertheless, even where exploration can proceed under seemingly "reasonable" conditions, questions still remain. Once projections of copper supply, demand, and price have been sorted out, the chief question is whether exploration can be economically justifiable without the possibilities of great profits to offset the inevitable cash outflows. To this question, every company must attempt to write its own answer. □

Project Radam maps the unknown in Brazil

Areas mapped by side-look radar

AS DOCEGEO EXPLORATION GEOLOGIST Garret McCandless once said, "Man may know more about the surface of the moon than the surface of the Amazon Basin." McCandless knows what he is talking about. For several years he has canoed, flown over, and slashed his way through the jungle while serving as a top technical advisor to Breno A. Dos Santos, one of the first men to set foot on Carajas. Dos Santos now directs Docegeo's Amazon exploration effort. The drainage basin of this river accounts for about 60% of the surface area of Brazil.

The Amazon, however, is being put into perspective by Project Radam, which had its origin in an aerial resources survey using side-look radar (SLAR) imaging, as well as a multispectral camera and a conventional mapping camera. This portion of the project was carried out jointly by Aero Service Div. of Litton Industries, Goodyear Aerospace Corp. (both of the US), and Brazilian-based Laza, South America's leading aerial survey company.

Project Radam started in 1971 as a mapping campaign covering 1.5 million sq km of the Amazon Basin. Since this region is almost always blanketed by a dense cloud cover, side-look radar was used as the primary scanning system because it can image the earth at night, through clouds, and during almost all climatic disturbances except extremely severe torrential thunderstorm cells.

The initial program produced such tantalizing results that the project was broadened to cover the entire Amazon region—an area amounting to about 4.26 million sq km. Because the 1:250,000 photomosaics pieced together from the imagery are revealing features that would never be detected by conventional systems, Project Radam has now been enlarged to cover the entire surface area of Brazil. This tremendous mapping program will involve an additional 3.6 million sq km of aerial surveying by SLAR and associated systems.

Side-look radar records in great detail the hydrology, geology, soil, and vegetation conditions of an area, and yields other essential data. The flights over the Amazon region were completed in 1972. Those over the rest of the nation started in October of this year and should be completed in April 1976. The photomosaic sheets produced from SLAR have a map-like dimensional quality.

The output: an inventory of potential resources

In the Amazon region, Project Radam can be viewed as a three-pronged program. First is the aerial survey. Next comes the job of map compilation and interpretation. The third step is ground investigations at sites selected from interesting features revealed on the maps. The output of Radam is building a skeletal blueprint for land-use classification and planning. Paradoxically, this vast unknown region of the world is being inventoried and recorded by a highly sophisticated system. Brazil is thus leading the world in land-use planning and doing so in its most remote area.

Mining will reap important side benefits of the program. Mineral occurrences and indications are being revealed at a rate never before possible. Furthermore, exploration geologists are slowly beginning to get a much better understanding of the geologic environment. But perhaps the most important benefit is that accurate maps on a 1:250,000 scale are being made available to help guide government and private field crews in the dense tropical forest. The only maps previously available were crude and sometimes greatly erroneous. As a result of Radam, an unknown 757-km river has been found. It was once commonly believed—except by a few pioneers and geologists—that the Amazon Basin was a flat lowland of limited relief. In reality, it contains a number of substantial mountain ranges.

The Radam program in the Amazon is a $30 million adventure in the unknown. The estimated budget covers flight expenses, production of photomosaics, follow-up field missions, sampling and analyses, and publication of findings. The Amazon field missions are scheduled to be completed in mid-1976, and the ongoing publication of a 21-volume summary of interpretations should begin to wind down in 1977.

Project Radam is administered through the Ministry of Mines and Energy's Department of National Mineral Production. Many personnel in the program, particularly the field crews, are in the process of working themselves out of a job. Nevertheless there is surprisingly little turnover among technical personnel because most are challenged by the pioneering aspects of the program.

The hardware involved in the flights

The SLAR system used in the Brazilian survey was developed by Goodyear Aerospace for the US Air Force and declassified about the time the Amazon mapping project was about to be launched. The instrumentation is carried

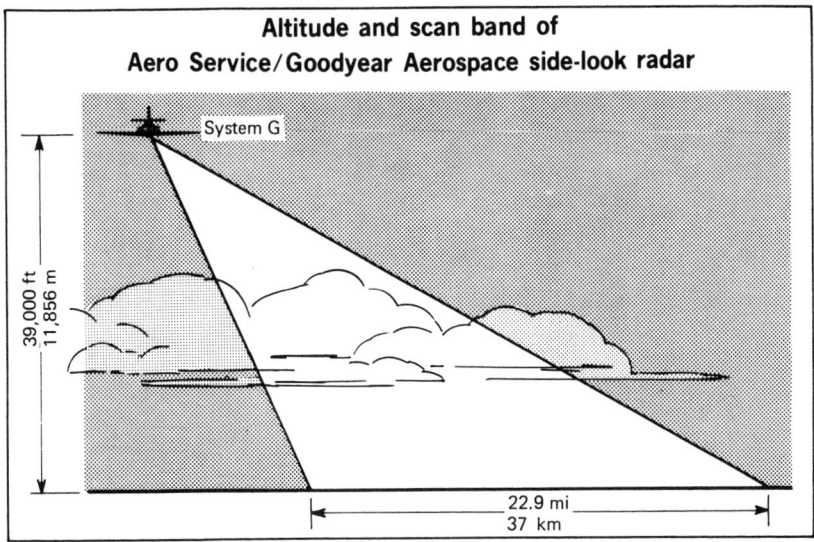

Altitude and scan band of Aero Service/Goodyear Aerospace side-look radar

aboard an Aero Service Caravelle jet. Both firms normally operate as technical partners in a survey. Goodyear Aerospace is responsible for installing and operating the radar equipment that produces the images from which the maps are made. Aero Service supplies the aircraft, handles the marketing, and compiles the maps. For Project Radam, however, map compilation was handled by Laza.

The first procedure in the Amazon Basin was to establish ground stations of known position for navigational guidance of the Caravelle. This was done through the use of a transit satellite system. A radio receiver, designed for this purpose, can be set up at a given station. After 18 hr of observation of the satellite signals, the latitude, longitude, and altitude of the station can be determined within 10 m.

The survey team fixed the position of 30 stations in the Amazon, mostly at small airports slashed out of the jungle. At these stations, SHORAN transmitters were placed. This radio system provides a fix for a moving aircraft with an accuracy of 20 m or so when the receiver in the aircraft homes in on two SHORAN stations. To keep deviations to a minimum, the whole aerial survey system is designed to fly under the utmost discipline. Aero Service vice president, Homer Jensen, says there are advantages to using a fast aircraft because all error factors affect the system more at a slow speed.

Flights took place at 39,000 ft (about 12.5 km) under the control of a Litton inertial navigator, which drives the jet along a south-north course line. The SLAR system scans a band from minus 10° to minus 45° below a horizontal plane. This provides coverage of a 37-km band (20 nautical mi) of terrain at the flight altitude. Depending on the amount of overlap desired in the scanning, the jet undergoes a pilot maneuver at the end of a survey line and returns on a north-south offset course. The Radam survey was flown at intervals of 15 nautical mi. This pattern corresponds to 15 min of longitude at the equator, providing a 5-nautical-mi overlap. The flight lines on the Radam project were up to 1,000 km long.

It takes about an hour to reach the 39,000-ft altitude. After 5 hr of flying time, the jet returns to an air base. The flights can cover from 10,000 to 20,000 sq mi a day. The multispectral camera and a conventional mapping unit loaded with false color infrared film were carried in the back of the jet outside the pressurized area. The cameras were filming all the time "just to keep us honest," said Homer Jensen. Surprisingly, about 60% of the area was filmed by multispectral coverage.

The jet lands with radar signals stored on 750-ft rolls of film exposed at a rate of about 1 ft per mi. The data film is chemically and optically processed to produce the final image. Since the data film is relatively unaffected by handling, the process can be repeated to form as many original negatives as desired.

The capability to produce multiple original negatives has several attractive features. After the first correlation in the Goodyear Aerospace processing equipment, any small residual overall scale discrepancies may be measured and corrected to the accuracy desired. Each critical user may have an original negative for interpretation if desired. Also, processing variables may be optimized for different applications.

The final product of the correlator is a photographic image produced to a scale of 1:400,000 with an accuracy of better than 1%. From these images, map mosaics are matched and pieced together at a scale of 1:250,000.

Field operations: a blitz-like reconnaissance

On-site examination by Radam personnel is a fantastic operation serviced by Air Force helicopters from a base camp. Radam's Amazon exploration mobilizes a 60- to 70-man field crew of civilians, among which there is usually a pair of geologists, two agronomists, and two forestry engineers, or personnel in other technical disciplines required for specfic projects. The field force is supported by a central staff of engineers and administrators, headquartered in Belem, and a fleet of 12 slow-flying, six-seat aircraft for short range shuttling of personnel and supplies. In all, about 100 technicians are involved in the Radam program.

Sites are selected for regional reconnaissance after study and interpretation of potential features of interest from the maps produced by side-look radar imaging. The sites selected cover a little over 490 sq km in a circular pattern. This area corresponds to a 150-km radius ring about the base camp—a distance equivalent to the maximum round-trip fuel supply of a Brazilian Air Force Bell UH1A helicopter, with a 1-hr reserve of flying time in the unfortunate event that pilot and crew get lost.

The base camp reconnaissance routine is supported by a complement of Brazilian Air Force personnel. The Air Force supplies four helicopters, the pilots, and flight crews, as well as maintenance specialists to the field camp. Project Radam in turn pays the Air Force a fee based on actual

How the Aero Service/Goodyear Aerospace Caravelle is equipped

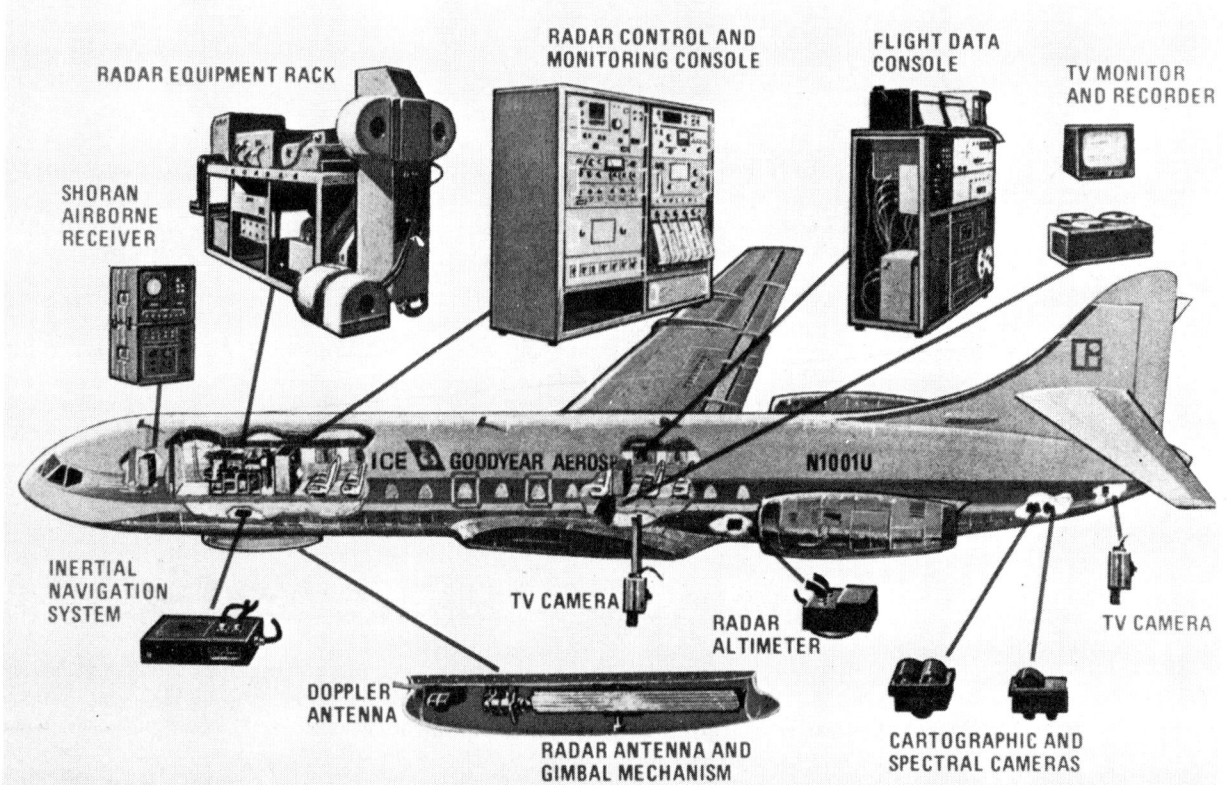

flying time and pays a per diem rate for the Air Force personnel.

Radam and Air Force personnel share a rustic mess facility in a primitive setting—a tent city hacked out of the wilderness and populated by up to 25 Air Force members and 60 or 70 Radam personnel. The Radam crew is split into logistic teams for on-site investigations.

It was E/MJ's privilege to visit a base camp at Igarape Preto—roughly 300 km east of Porto Velho. Compared with most base camps locations, it was probably a spa. Already equipped with a landing strip leveled by a tin mining company, Igarape Preto was on its way toward semicivilization as a result of the nearby tin dredging operations. From this base camp, 80 site visits had been scheduled—all circled on a Radam map at a command control headquarters tent where radio communication is established with Belem.

The day starts before 6 a.m., taking care of human necessities. Before 7 a.m., the first of the day's nine logistic teams of four members is in the air en route to a targeted examination site. Loaded with chain saws, block and tackle, machetes, axes, knives, and survival packs, an Air Force-piloted helicopter hovers just over treetop level and lowers the work crew by winches and slings some 150 ft or more to the floor of the jungle. In a seasoned burst of activity, the work crew levels an area of 0.25 to 0.5 acres and lays a crude landing mat for a helicopter in a matter of 4 or 5 hr.

In the afternoon, technical personnel are landed in the clearing by helicopter and they begin a short reconnaissance, taking samples of flora, noting fauna, and collecting rock samples, geochemical samples, and other specimens of the area. Outcrop structures and trends are noted for later mapping. The physical day ends at dusk, and dinner is after dark. Practically nothing on the menu comes out of a can. Most of the food is fresh meat and produce—up to 2,000 kilos a month.

Camp life is lively after a shower supplied from a set of solar-heated canvas water bags, and the day cools off. Then a meeting starts at roughly 8:30 p.m. The agenda includes a briefing of plans and logistics for the following day, as well as heated discussions of alternative objectives and the findings of the day's missions. In the meantime, samples are collected, tagged, and readied for air transport from the base camp. After delivery, they head straight into a weak spot of Project Radam—the lack of analytical facilities. Radam is dependent upon commercial and university laboratories, and the waiting time for analyses can range up to six months. There are few commercial analytical laboratories in Brazil.

The crew at Igarape Preto retires by 10 p.m. in a physically and mentally exhausted state to rest up before risking their lives on the following day's mission. The on-site crews spend 30 days in the field and seven days at Belem or Manaus.

The inputs for planning

Back at headquarters, field examinations are synthesized and evaluated against a set of standards to establish a natural land-use map. In oversimplified terms, the geology, soil, natural vegetation, and the geomorphology are considered in the evaluation, as are the climate and topography. Also included are any restraining factors that might come to light during the field observations. Ore mineral data are recorded, along with possible judgments of the mineral-finding potential.

These and many other factors are rated on a scale of one to 10 to develop a set of ranking averages for the best

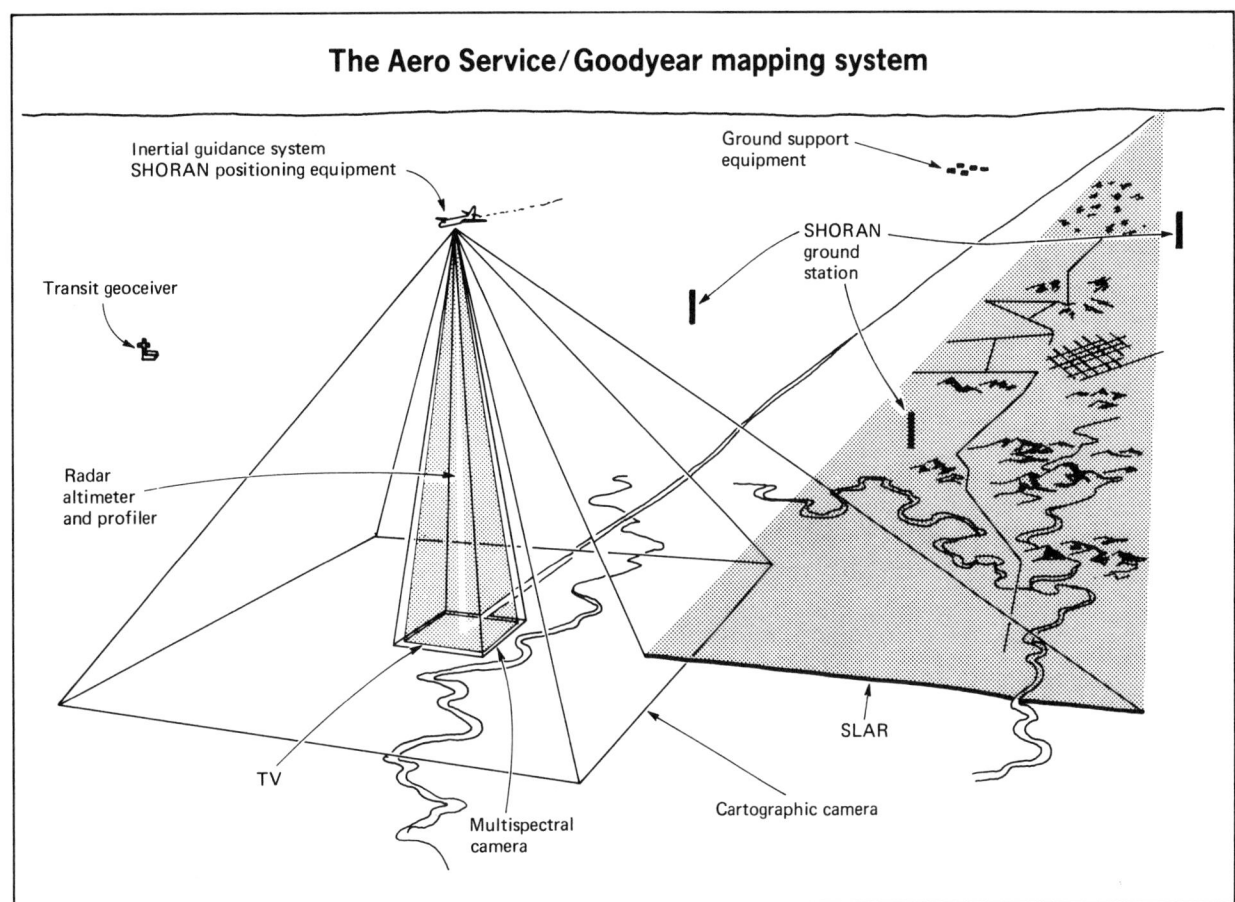

The Aero Service/Goodyear mapping system

land-use potential. Radam personnel say they do not consider economic factors in arriving at the natural land-use map.

Land uses are then grouped in five categories: 1) areas containing good timber; 2) regions suitable for agriculture or pasture land (a surprisingly small amount of land in the Amazon has good soil conditions for agriculture); 3) regions where the natural vegetation yields extractable products such as rubber or vegetable oils; 4) areas where ranching can be carried on; and 5) an ecological category. The last classification includes tracts that should be reserved for national parks or forests and where wild life should be protected by law.

About the mineral potential of the Amazon

It is all but impossible to offer more than a general idea of what may be revealed by further exploration in the Amazon, but many interesting showings have been found as a result of the spot checks conducted by Radam geologists. While they are generally announced as they are discovered, such showings require an extensive amount of more detailed exploration.

Occurrences of iron, manganese, tin, bauxite, and coal have been noted. In Roraima a number of radioactive anomalies have been detected.

At mid-1975, Radam geologists had finished an examination of a northern sector of the Amazon basin. Here, a large craton exists, bordered on the east by the Atlantic, on the west by the Orinoco River, and on the south by the Amazon River. Some of the rocks in this system have been dated at 3.6 billion years.

The shield area shows some similarities to formations of like type in Africa, Russia, and elsewhere. There are many basic granites and large events of volcanism with the formation of acid granitic rocks. The alkaline rocks, said to be similar to those of Nigeria, are considered likely exploration targets for tin, tungsten, nickel, and uranium.

Several carbonatites have been located, but none have yet revealed any copper mineralization. Samples grading 4.1% nickel have been cut from a laterite that overlies one carbonatite. The carbonatites, however, are similar in chemical analysis to Palabora in South Africa and are thus candidates for phosphate and rare earth mineralization. Of two carbonatites, one carries a high titanium content in a mass estimated at 5 billion tons, and another contains 0.5% to 1% vanadium in a magnetite complex.

Radam personnel recommend conglomeritic zones overlying portions of the shield as likely prospecting targets for gold and radioactive minerals.

Kimberlite pipes have been found in relation with nepheline syenites in Roraima. The diamond-bearing kimberlites of Africa are always related to syenites.

The probabilities of finding copper in the volcanics of the craton are not rated highly. Most of these rocks are 1.8 billion years old, and no known major copper districts of the world are in rocks of this age. Since the volcanics are continental and not orogenic, there is a strong suggestion that copper would not occur in the volcanics. Elsewhere, in the northern region, tin, columbium, tantalum, zirconium, and gold concentrations have been found in placer deposits.

Whatever the future of the Amazon Basin, the vast amount of terrain to be prospected raises intriguing possibilities, although exploration campaigns are difficult and expensive. □

CPRM: a catalyst in Brazilian exploration programs

USUALLY REFERRED TO as the government's exploration company, CPRM* has a much broader mandate than prospecting. Created in 1969 by Presidential Decree, CPRM functions under the Ministry of Mines and Energy. Today it employs more than 500 geologists, mining engineers, and chemists.

CPRM's purpose is three-fold: 1) to improve basic geologic knowledge of the nation, 2) to provide financial assistance to other companies for exploration and mine development, and 3) to sponsor and develop the technology base for a Brazilian minerals industry.

CPRM operates in three ways. First, it can be considered a service company, working under contract to DNPM** and other agencies of the Ministry of Mines and Energy, as well as private companies. In this capacity, CPRM performs geological mapping, geophysical studies, geochemical work, drilling, and mineral testing. In 1974 CPRM executed 160 such projects, which brought it an income of $37 million.

Although the results of work done by CPRM under contract belong to the clients, government agencies that are clients can make the information available to interested companies and geologists. There are a few exceptions to this rule, notably certain strategic minerals.

Another way in which CPRM functions is as an exploration company seeking new mineral deposits for its own account. As of June 1975 CPRM was working on 13 such projects and had completed work on 27 others. At that time, it was awaiting a decision from DNPM on 23 additional programs.

In searching out its own mineral deposits, CPRM carries on all necessary investigations, estimates reserves, and calls for public bids for development of mines. The company has already completed this cycle for two projects—potash in Sergipe and kaolin in Para. In mid-1975, it was scheduled to close the cycle on two others—a nickel property in Goias and a gypsum deposit in Para. CPRM also recently announced that it may undertake mining of an important phosphate zone in Minas Gerais. It is in the process of building a pilot phosphate beneficiation plant.

Seed money for exploration and mining

In its third mode of operation, CPRM can be viewed as a finance company. Under certain circumstances, CPRM will advance up to 80% of the funds required for an approved exploration program. Money is obtained under two sets of conditions: 1) loans with risk clauses, in which the financing agency assumes the risk; and 2) loans without risk clauses. In both cases, an applicant must have a zone with indications of mineralization and must present an exploration program, including estimated costs.

Loans with risk clauses need not be repaid if the exploration results are negative. If, however, a mine is developed, the loan is repaid but the principal is increased by a risk quota derived from a risk coefficient table. For example, for a copper deposit discovered in the northeast region, the risk quota was 1.5. This means that 1.5 times the loan amount must be repaid. In the case of an alluvial gold deposit in the south, the quota would amount to three times the loan principal.

Loans made without risk clauses are more conventional. The recipient must repay all funds advanced by CPRM regardless of the outcome of the exploration program. The loan is repaid at a 5% interest rate. There is now no maximum monetary limit on loans, but the borrower may be requested to put up 20% of the total investment. A summary of CPRM's financing activities is shown in Table 1.

Mapping a nation of many unknowns

A most important objective of CPRM is to map Brazil and carry out basic geological surveys. Photogeologic surveys and geologic reconnaissance mapping at a scale of 1:500,000 represent a large portion of the basic geologic work. However, more detailed mapping has been undertaken in certain areas at scales of 1:250,000 and 1:50,000, and these projects have been complemented by geochemical reconnaissance to improve the qualities of the surveys.

Over 300,000 sq km has been mapped at a scale of 1:500,000, and about 70,000 sq km is being mapped at scales from 1:50,000 to 1:100,000. Since the birth of CPRM, more than 2 million sq km of Brazil has been described from aerial photogeologic interpretation at a scale of 1:250,000—an amount equivalent to about 25% of the surface of the country. The objective of the basic surveys is to pull together a panoramic view of the subsoil related to mineral resources by the end of 1975. More specific surveys will then be organized in selected areas.

Some specific areas have already been identified for de-

Table 1—Mineral exploration projects financed by CPRM

Year	Number of projects		Financing (000 Cr $)	
	Received	Approved	Requested	Approved
1971	12	2	45,000	6,000
1972	14	9	53,000	27,000
1973	21	9	58,000	29,000
1974	14	13	68,000	43,000

Table 2—Summary statistics of CPRM activities
(July 1970 to March 1975)

Geologic mapping, sq km	2,089,279
Geologic reconnaissance mapping, sq km	1,190,019
Radiogeologic reconnaissance, sq km	901,270
Photointerpretation, sq km	4,505,413
Geochemical prospecting (samples)	74,483
Mineral deposits examined	6,335
Petrographic analyses	14,739
Mineralogic analyses	9,576
Chemical analyses	18,460
Geochemical analyses	67,139
Geophysical prospecting and reconnaissance	
Aeromagnetometry, km	689,963
Aeroscintillometry, km	476,802
General geophysics, km	2,969
Drilling, m	617,412
Well-logging, m	409,709
Concluded projects	173
Non-concluded projects	119

---

*CPRM is an acronym for Cia. de Pesquisas de Recursos Minerais (translated as Mineral Resources Research Co.).
**DNPM is an acronym for Departamento Nacional de Producao Mineral, an agency of the Ministry of Mines and Energy.

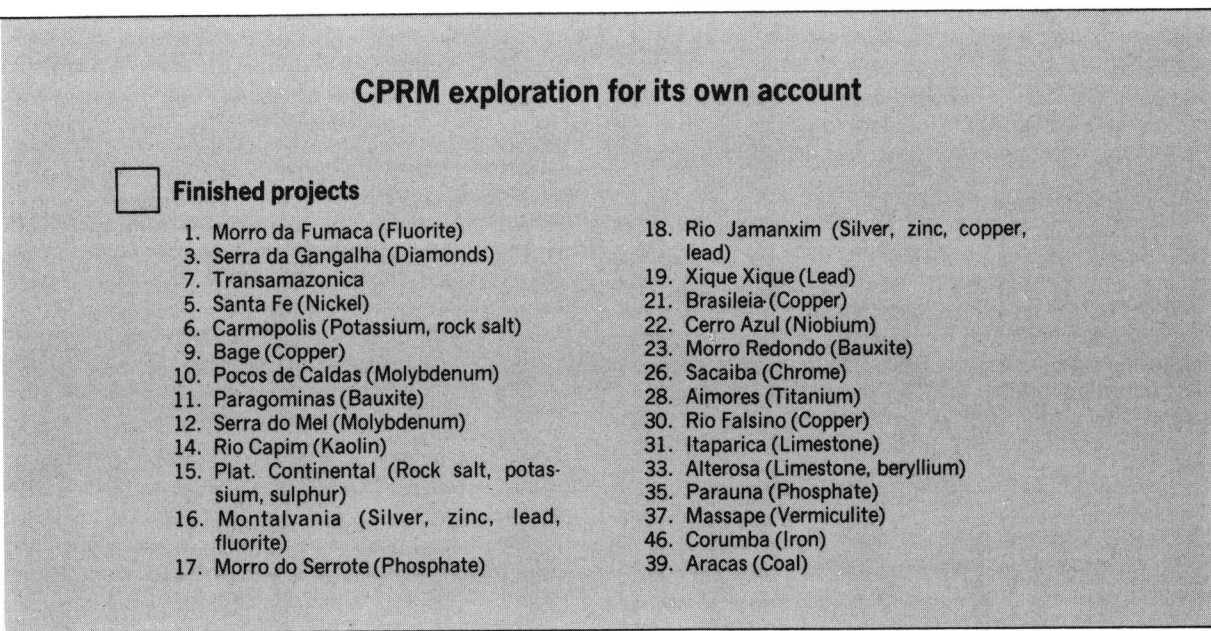

CPRM exploration for its own account

☐ **Finished projects**

1. Morro da Fumaca (Fluorite)
3. Serra da Gangalha (Diamonds)
7. Transamazonica
5. Santa Fe (Nickel)
6. Carmopolis (Potassium, rock salt)
9. Bage (Copper)
10. Pocos de Caldas (Molybdenum)
11. Paragominas (Bauxite)
12. Serra do Mel (Molybdenum)
14. Rio Capim (Kaolin)
15. Plat. Continental (Rock salt, potassium, sulphur)
16. Montalvania (Silver, zinc, lead, fluorite)
17. Morro do Serrote (Phosphate)
18. Rio Jamanxim (Silver, zinc, copper, lead)
19. Xique Xique (Lead)
21. Brasileia (Copper)
22. Cerro Azul (Niobium)
23. Morro Redondo (Bauxite)
26. Sacaiba (Chrome)
28. Aimores (Titanium)
30. Rio Falsino (Copper)
31. Itaparica (Limestone)
33. Alterosa (Limestone, beryllium)
35. Parauna (Phosphate)
37. Massape (Vermiculite)
46. Corumba (Iron)
39. Aracas (Coal)

Projects under way

2. Morro do Engenho (Nickel)
13. Andorinha (Chrome)
24. Arapoema (Nickel, copper)
25. Sao Felix do Xingu (Lead)
29. Catalao (Chrome)
32. Chamines Alcalinas (Phosphate, diamonds, titanium, niobium)
34. Januaria-Itacarambi (Vanadium, silver, lead)
36. Curaca (Copper)
38. Aprazivel (Copper)
40. Itamaguari (Gypsum)
42. Canada (Copper)
44. Gradaus (Iron)
48. Patos de Minas (Phosphate)

Projects awaiting a decision from DNPM

27. Orleaes (Coal)
41. Ararangua (Coal)
43. Tombador (Syenite)
45. Santa Barbara (Copper, chrome)
49. Bom Jardim (Lead, zinc)
50. Ita (Silver)
51. Ipira (Chrome)
52. Pimenteiras (Phosphate)
53. Candiota (Coal)
54. Coite (Copper)
55. Tres Ranchos (Niobium)
56. Ouvidor (Niobium)
57. Rio Jutai (Lignite, peat, saprolite)
58. Ilheus (Phosphate)
59. Barra do Mendes (Nickel)
60. Aveiro (Limestone)
61. Dianopolis (Zinc)
62. Irui-Butia (Lignite)
63. Presidente Hermes (Iron)
64. Sao Cristovao (Phosphate, limestone, gypsum)
65. Propria (Phosphate)
66. Uaupes (Titanium)
67. Tapuruquara (Titanium)

1975 projects financed through CPRM

68. Mineracao Angelim SA (Cassiterite)
69. Concisa—Construcao Civil e Industrial Ltda. (Cassiterite)
70. Progresso da Rondonia Mineracao (Cassiterite)
71. Tin Brasil Mineracao Ltda. (Cassiterite)
72. Mineracao Aracazeiros Ltda. (Cassiterite)
73. Mineracao Rio das Garcas Ltda. (Cassiterite)
74. Mineracao Amarante (Scheelite)
75. Mineracao Tijuca Ltda. (Scheelite)
76. Mineracao Acquarius (Scheelite)
77. Zangarelhas Mineracao Ltda. (Scheelite)
78. Mineracao Nordeste do Brasil Ltda. (Scheelite)
79. Camita SA (Rock salt)
80. Serrasa—Serra do Ramalho Mineracao Ltda. (Fluorite)
81. Operadora de Equipamentos SA (Chromite)
82. Emp. Min. Imarui e Salomao Mineracao Ltda. (Fluorite)
83. Leprevost e Cia. (Gold)
84. Mineracao Morretes (Gold)
85. Minas Del Rei D. Pedro SA (Gold)
86. Mineracao Morro Velho SA (Gold)
87. Eneel (Nickel)
88. C. R. Almeida SA (Ilmenite)
89. Somicol SA (Manganese)
90. Cia. Bozano Simonsen (Iron)

tailed evaluation of mineral resources and are now under survey (see map). The specific area program has led to more than 600,000 m of drilling—mostly for priority minerals, which include copper, lead, zinc, nickel, coal, manganese, phosphate, potash, sulphur, and uranium, although the latter is the responsibility of Brazil's Nuclebras.

There has been a dramatic increase in the use of airborne and ground geophysical surveys to pinpoint mineral targets in Brazil. This trend has developed because members of the German Geological Survey are assisting CPRM project teams under an agreement between the two governments. To service programs requested by DNPM and CNEN, it has been necessary for CPRM to enter into agreements with specialized Brazilian firms to provide both aeromagnetic and aeroscintillometric surveys.

Building technology

The need to develop a mineral refining industry has generated problems that Brazilians had never thought about before. Thus CPRM and DNPM are jointly building a Mineral Technological Center (Cetem) at University City in Rio de Janeiro State. This center will engage in ore dressing and mineral recovery projects. In addition, a Mineral Analysis Laboratory (Lamin) has been established to enable CPRM to carry out its various commitments and assist other government agencies or private companies in prospecting activities.

Cetem and Lamin, as well as many specific areas of economic geology, remote sensing, geophysics, and geochemical exploration, have benefited directly from the technical guidance, financial assistance, and academic facilities of the US. Such assistance evolved through the US AID program and the US Geological Survey in an agreement with the Ministry of Mines and Energy.

In cooperation with several government agencies, CPRM has also undertaken studies of the natural resource potential of the continental shelf. By the end of the current year, preliminary information will be presented on prospecting conditions of the shelf area.

CPRM has also compiled 1,700 photomosaics at a scale of 1:100,000 from the radar images produced by Project Radam.

Beyond administrative headquarters, the work of CPRM is supported through nine regional offices located at Porto Velho, Manaus, Belem, Recife, Salvador, Belo Horizonte, Goiania, Sao Paulo, and Porto Alegre.

A summary of work performed by CPRM is presented in Table 2. This remarkable agency, functioning in a catch-up set of circumstances, is surely headed in the right direction. ☐

Docegeo diversifies CVRD horizon with new discoveries

LEADING THE EXPLORATION PACK in Brazil is Docegeo,* a subsidiary of the government-owned CVRD, with a budgeted 1975 program of just over $16 million—up 70% over the 1974 level but significantly under the $19 million spending pattern anticipated in 1976.

Created in July 1971, Docegeo's objectives are exploration and development of nonferrous and nonmetallic mineral resources. When Docegeo was set up, the technical-administrative structure was established for its first three-year plan. Regional exploration offices were opened in Belem, Goiania, Belo Horizonte, and Salvador. These offices are administered from Rio de Janeiro, where the company has assembled top-flight personnel for planning, coordinating, and supervising Docegeo activities. Docegeo also maintains offices at Araxa in Minas Gerais State and at Cachoeiro do Itapemirim in Espirito Santo State.

The regional offices are headquarters for the four exploration districts (see table accompanying the map). Docegeo now employs 831 people, of which 108 are professionals in geology, geophysics, geochemistry, or mineral economics.

The entire operation comes close to an exploration man's ideal. For instance, a nation-wide radio system has been established for rapid communication with district offices and field crews. In all, this network incorporates 56 fixed and portable units. Docegeo owns two twin-turbine Bolkow helicopters, used mainly to assist exploration in the Amazon region. These also are radio-equipped and tuned in to the central network frequency.

Laboratory support (chemical, geochemical, petrographic, spectrographic, metallurgical, and analytical) is provided mainly by CVRD's central research center—an outstandingly well-equipped unit in a campus-like setting on the outskirts of Belo Horizonte. The Belem office is equipped for both chemical and geochemical analysis and the Bahia office at Salvador contains a chemical laboratory.

Docegeo's activities fall into three general groups: exploration, specific projects, and special projects. Exploration projects encompass the evaluation of any mineral occurrence or geologic environment, on both regional and local scales. Specific projects are those that establish the economic viability of a deposit delineated by internal exploration or brought to the company's attention by outsiders. Special projects involve evaluation of mineralized zones for other parties.

Because a large portion of Brazil has never been covered by adequate geologic mapping, many of the exploration projects during the first three years of Docegeo's existence were regional reconnaissance programs.

Output of Docegeo is impressive

Five important mineralized districts have been well delineated and now are in a feasibility stage. A number of promising prospects are at a point where they may enter

*Docegeo is an acronym for Rio Doce Geologia e Mineracao.

How personnel are distributed

Personnel	Rio	Amazonia	Central West	Central East	East	Totals
Brazilian professionals	14	21	19	18	21	93
Foreign professionals	8	2	1	3	1	15
Technicians, clerks	47	251	30	112	70	510
Administration	85	43	17	44	24	213
Subtotals	154	317	67	177	116	
Totals	154	———677———				831

Expenditures on mineral exploration
(million $US)

Program	Disbursement				1975	Estimated		
	1971	1972	1973	1974		1976	1977	1978
First three-year plan of geologic exploration	$0.42	$4.01	$7.08	$7.14	$1.21	–	–	–
Specific projects, CVRD	0.04	0.37	0.56	1.10	1.56	$0.39	–	–
Specific projects, CRVD/BNDE	–	–	–	1.16	4.43	5.21	$5.21	$5.21
Second three-year plan of geologic exploration	–	–	–	–	6.60	7.81	7.81	7.81
Special projects	–	–	–	–	2.21	6.12	2.60	2.60
Totals	$0.46	$4.38	$7.64	$9.40	$16.01	$19.53	$15.62	$15.62

$US1 = Cr$7.684 (average first-half 1975).

Exploration budget for 1975
(million $US)

Districts	Triannual plan of geologic prospecting	Specific projects	Special projects	Totals	%
Amazonia	$2.78	$1.50	–	$4.28	26.7
Central west	1.02	0.73	0.78	2.53	15.8
Central east	1.56	1.88	–	3.44	21.5
East	0.94	0.70	1.26	2.90	18.1
Central office operations division	Sectors: geophysics, geochemistry, petrography, claim analysis, communications, operation superintendents, planning and evaluation, mineral economics			1.73	10.8
Administration	–			1.13	7.1
Totals				$16.01	100.0

Docegeo's mineral exploration activities

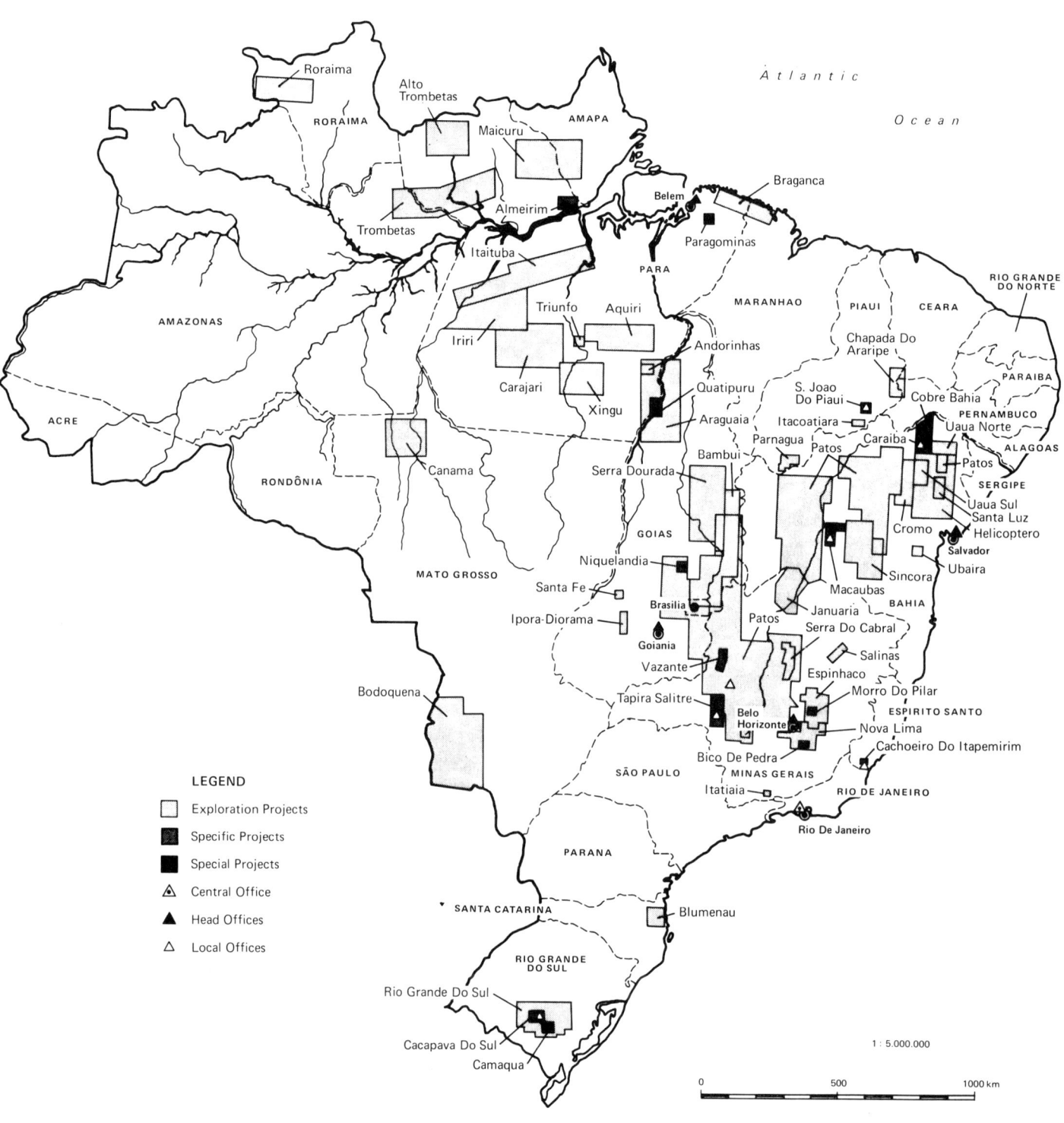

Docegeo Amazon crews are well administered and explore at a cost of $50 per sq km, about half a UN estimate for same area.

evaluation for commercial production. The five important zones under consideration for development are as follows:

- Refractory and metallurgical grade bauxite deposits and kaolin in the Jabuti and Futuro sectors of the Paragominas (specific project in Para). Reserves updated to mid-1975 are: Jabuti—230 million mt of metallurgical grade bauxite; Futuro—150 million mt of refractory and metallurgical grade bauxite. The kaolin reserves have not been calculated.

- A refractory and metallurgical grade bauxite deposit and kaolin near Almeirim, Para. Prospecting carried out as specific project PE-6 has established an estimated 20 million mt of refractory grade bauxite.

- A nickel deposit at Sao Joao do Piaui (specific project PE-4). The first estimate was 9 million mt of ore containing 1.9% Ni; however, further prospecting in 1974 established measured reserves of 20 million mt of 1.58% Ni.

- Limestone deposits in the region of Cachoeiro do Itapemirim, Espirito Santo. Proven reserves are 143 million mt of mineable limestone, dolomitic limestone, and dolomites. About 70.8 million mt of this reserve have the appropriate physical and chemical characteristics for use in CVRD iron pelletizing plants.

- Phosphate and titanium deposits associated with alkaline intrusions of Tapira and Salitre, Minas Gerais. Proven reserves are 184 million mt of 7.9% P_2O_5 in one part of the Tapira area. The total potential of this intrusion is estimated at 500 million mt of 8.0% P_2O_5. In addition, there are inferred reserves of 130 million mt of similar phosphate ore at Salitre. Proven reserves of titanium (occurring as anatase) in portions of the Tapira and Salitre concessions are 125 million mt of 23% TiO_2.

Other targets with a promising potential

There are several other bright spots on the Docegeo horizon. Based on preliminary results, Docegeo considers the following discoveries to be most important.

Strong lead and zinc geochemical anomalies near Vazante, Minas Gerais State, were found in rocks of an age equivalent to those bearing zinc mineralization at the mines of Cia. Mineira de Metais and Cia. Industrial e Mercantil Inga, as well as the lead-zinc orebody of Morro Agudo.

Chromium geochemical anomalies were discovered in ultrabasic rocks of Serra do Espinhaco at Morro do Pilar in Minas Gerais State. Copper, lead, and zinc geochemical anomalies in acid to intermediate volcanic rocks are being further investigated in the Triunfo area of the Xingu River.

Docegeo has claimed some of the best copper occurrences in the Andrade-Primavera belt in Cacapava do Sul, Rio Grande do Sul State. In a small area located among the Docegeo holdings, Cia. Riograndense de Mineracao has blocked out 2.8 million tons of ore grading 0.8% Cu. The Docegeo holdings are being explored as a specific project.

Docegeo holds exploration rights for a number of areas adjacent to the Caraiba copper deposits, and for nearby areas north of the Caraiba where strong geochemical and geophysical anomalies were discovered by a joint DNPM/CPRM copper exploration program. Caraiba contains Brazil's largest known copper reserve (about 45 million mt of 1.3% Cu). Docegeo has launched a specific project—Cobre Bahia—to carry on a detailed exploration program in these areas.

Nickel silicate deposits have been discovered in the Quatipuru ultrabasic complex in Para, and preliminary evaluation indicates the possibility of 30 million mt of nickel silicate ore. Occurrences of copper-nickel sulphide were also recently discovered in this area.

A cassiterite deposit in the Serra da Pedra Branca area, Nova Roma district, Goias, is getting careful attention. This is within the Serra Dourada Project area.

Copper-nickel sulphides and chrysotile have been found in the Niquelandia basic-ultrabasic complex of Goias. The area is now being drilled, and the program has reached specific project status (PE-11), which means that preliminary feasibility work is under way.

Significant geochemical and geophysical anomalies discovered by regional exploration in a number of areas have been isolated as specific projects for more intensive detailed investigation. □

Appraising large diameter core and percussion drilling for bulk samples

James V. Thompson, manager, Department of Mineral Economy and Technology, and **David L. Watson,** project engineer, Minerals Div., Kaiser Engineers

Table 1—Large diameter core drilling

Starting date	April 11, 1975
Completion date	July 23, 1975
Elapsed days	104
Drilling days	65
Rig hours paid @ $55.00/hr	617
Feet of core per paid hour	1.81
Feet of core per actual drilling hour (502 hr)	2.23
Holes collared	6*
Holes completed	5
Total feet	1,118
Scheduled depth per hole (ft)	200**
Length of core barrel (ft)	10

Cost

Snowplowing and access	$ 1,400
Contract drilling @ 1,118 ft	39,900
Large diameter pits, 6 in.	7,900
Boxes, materials, core storage, and misc. supplies	4,300
Trucking core to Golden, Colo.	1,400
Field geological supervision	4,000
Supervisor's FWD pickup	2,400
Supervisor's subsistence	2,400
Logging, assaying, and photographing core at Hazen Research	9,000
Total cost	**$72,700**

Cost per foot = $65.027.

*One hole was aborted at 103 ft because of highly weathered and altered very low grade ore.
**Completed holes were actually drilled to 203 ft.

A 6-in. bit on a 10-in. barrel was used for core drilling.

A PROGRAM of large diameter core drilling to obtain representative bulk samples for metallurgical tests on a bench scale and in a small pilot plant has been completed by Buttes Gas & Oil Co. of Oakland, Calif., on its titanium ore prospect in Gunnison County, Colo. Five 6-in.-dia core holes were economically and satisfactorily drilled. The costs and drilling statistics for these holes are indicated in Table 1.

Buttes' titanium property consists of a random mixture of coarse segregations of magnetite, augite, biotite, mica, and perovskite. All mineral species are titaniferous, but the perovskite, especially, is being studied by Buttes as a potential titaniferous raw material. Ore occurs as fine grained perovskite ($CaTiO_3$) encapsulated in titaniferous magnetite, massive perovskite often several feet thick and containing little or no magnetite, and minimal amounts of fine grained perovskite in augite with very little attendant magnetite. Biotite also contains minor amounts of both perovskite and magnetite. Only the perovskite in magnetite has survived at the surface. Perovskite in massive form and unprotected by magnetite weathers to leucoxene and is carried off by erosion.

After the occurrence of massive perovskite was noted in small diameter diamond drillholes, more massive perovskite was observed near the surface in bulldozer cuts. The massive form of perovskite had been overlooked by investigators in the belief that it occurred only as fine grained crystals in magnetite.

The orebody has been drilled to the extent of more than 16,000 ft of small diameter core holes, and more than 1,600 assays for titanium have been made. Based on this information, a computer analysis of ore reserves was made early in 1976 by Kaiser Engineers. The results: 97 million tons of measured ore assaying about 12% TiO_2 at a 9% cutoff grade; 227 million tons of indicated ore of approximately equal grade and cutoff; and 419 million tons of inferred ore at 11.6% TiO_2 and 9% cutoff.

Metallurgical samples could not be obtained from the surface or from even the deepest bulldozer cuts. Core recovery was always poor to depths of about 40 ft because of deeply weathered material containing little or highly-altered perovskite. Below 40 ft, core recovery was almost 100%, and coarse crystals and wide segregations of massive perovskite were found to be common.

Representative ore samples for metallurgical test work were obtainable in any one of three ways: driving an adit, sinking a shaft, or drilling large diameter holes. Shafts and adits presented certain disadvantages:

- Difficulty in finding contractors to handle the work and attracting labor for hand mucking in a small shaft.

- Extensive collar and portal timbering.
- Safety hazards and potential owner liability for injury.
- Over-production of ore to be handled by an automatic sampler at the portal.
- Possibility of unauthorized entry.
- Costly sampling at five different locations in 3½ months, requiring five shafts and/or adits to be driven simultaneously. A 200-ft shaft might be sunk for $350 per ft and a 200-ft adit driven for $150 per ft. Shafts would have been 4 x 6 ft and adits 5 x 7 ft, with much collar and portal timber.

For these reasons, a large diameter core drilling program was undertaken. Its advantages:
- Reliable, fully insured drilling contractors were available for the work.
- Costs were predicted even though the contractor was working by the rig hour, plus bits and water haulage.
- Risk of personal injury was minimized.
- Cores recovered produced the proper amount of sample—19 tons—for the test program.
- Cores were believed representative, producing a good statistical sample of several grades of ore.
- Cost of drilling was less than that for one shaft.

The program called for drilling five holes to a depth of 200 ft—the equivalent of at least five benches in any future open-pit mine. Below 200 ft, the drilling would have become too costly, since the large 10-ft core barrel was not operated with a wire line. From the highest collar elevations to the bottom of the hole having the lowest collar elevation, the total ore column amounted to 462 ft, equal in height to at least 11 benches.

Each hole was offset 10 ft from a small diameter core hole of known log and assay. The pilot holes were selected to have TiO_2 assay ranges of 9-11%; 11-13%; 13-15%; and over 15%. One of the five holes was drilled in highly altered ore. A sixth hole was aborted at a depth of about 100 ft.

Core recovery was 100% below the first 13 ft of drilling. Wooden boxes with hinged tops were constructed for each 5-ft section of core. The boxes offered the unexpected advantage of being excellent storage containers for the cores after crushing to minus 1 in. for head sampling at Hazen Research Inc., in Golden, Colo. All core was logged and photographed before being crushed.

Because of the completely random nature of the orebody, results from the large diameter holes did not match the pilot holes very well, averaging somewhat higher in grade than expected. However, with 200 boxes, each containing a 5-ft length of core, it was possible to make a composite of any grade or type or ore required for test work.

Large diameter percussion drilling

The large diameter core drilling program was started in the hope that a mineral beneficiation scheme could be devised to reject coarse tailings at sizes up to 1 in. The

Setting up the rig to core drill for massive perovskite.

Rig and flatbed water truck are prepared for drilling.

Six-in.-dia core fits snugly into 5-ft-long wooden box.

Mounting a down-the-hole hammer for percussion drilling.

Table 2—Large diameter percussion drilling

Starting date	Oct. 14, 1976
Completion date	Oct. 24, 1976
Elapsed days	11
Drilling days	11
Rig hours paid	120
Feet of hole drilled per paid hour	35.7
Total feet drilled	4,050
Average depth per hole (ft)	225

Cost

Contract drilling	$17,400
Supervision and sampling labor	11,700
Travel and subsistence	1,600
Supplies	2,500
Freight	1,100
Field transportation	1,300
Assaying	4,000
Total cost	**$39,600**

Cost per foot = $9.78.

---

metallurgical test work, however, indicated that satisfactory recoveries would require grinding ore to minus 35 mesh. When larger samples were required, percussion drilling was investigated. When the percussion drill cuttings were screened on 35 mesh and the oversize reground, the combined product had a screen analysis similar to grind achieved with run-of-mine lump ore.

A percussion drilling and sampling campaign was launched by Kaiser Engineers in October 1976 as a followup to the core drilling program. The purpose was to obtain samples suitable for metallurgical testing by dry drilling with air from three different areas of the orebody.

Drillholes were positioned to correlate results with previous small diamond drillholes. Eighteen percussion holes ranging from 80 to 360 ft deep were drilled in an 11-day period. Holes that encountered excessive water inflows were abandoned in favor of obtaining dry samples and avoiding the costs of sampling wet sludge.

The drill rig used was a truck-mounted unit equipped with a down-the-hole hammer. Holes were drilled at 8-in. diameter for the first 20 ft, casing was set, and the remainder of the holes were drilled at 6-in. diameter. Both cross-bits and button bits were used, but only two holes were drilled with the cross-bit because screening tests in the field showed that coarser material was produced with the button bit. Air pressure was maintained at approximately 150 psi and down pressure was varied by the operator according to the material being drilled.

Drill samples were obtained by shoveling cuttings from plywood boards placed around the drill pipe into 30-gal steel barrels accommodating 400 to 500 lb of cuttings. Each barrel held a volume of sample representative of a mining bench, and when necessary the sample was split before going into the barrel. During sampling, the barrel was placed on a Heil lift mounted on a flatbed truck to facilitate barrel movement. Grab samples of material shoveled into the barrels were taken every 10 ft for control purposes. In addition, screen analyses were made on composite grab samples from selected holes.

Percussion drilling: the findings

The entire sample, consisting of 160 barrels totaling 35 tons, was shipped by motor freight to Denver, Colo., for test work. Costs and other statistics are shown in Table 2. Although metallurgical work is still under way, certain aspects of the percussion drilling program have been evaluated.

- Comparison of the 10-ft grab samples obtained from percussion drilling with the assays obtained from core drilling showed the overall TiO_2 averages to be remarkably close. The diamond drillholes averaged 12.0% TiO_2, and percussion drillholes 12.2% TiO_2.
- Size distribution of the percussion cuttings was coarse enough so that pilot plant grind from these cuttings was very similar to the grind expected from a proposed commercial-scale milling operation.
- Percussion drilling will apparently yield suitable results in comparison with core drilling, provided the values in the orebody assay high enough to preclude significant salting from side wall contamination. Such contamination would obviously distort the results when drilling ores assaying only a few tenths of a percent. □

Acknowledgement

The authors wish to thank Buttes Gas Oil Co. for permission to publish this report and Robert Norman of Buttes Gas & Oil for his assistance. Boyles Bros. Drilling Co., Storm Drilling Co., Humphreys Engineering Co., and Hazen Research Inc. also made contributions.

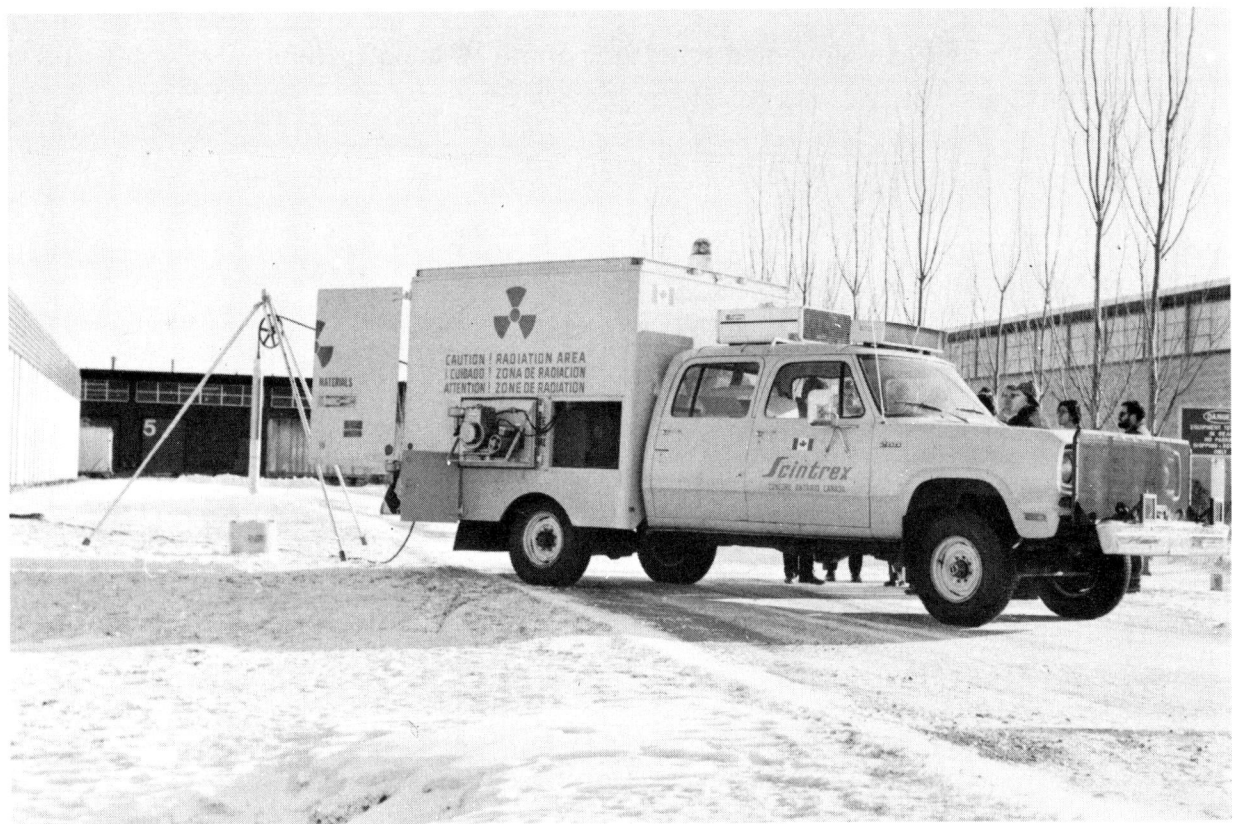

The prototype Metalog field truck houses all equipment necessary to analyze data from the gamma-sensing sonde (left).

Nuclear logging system obtains 'bulk samples' from small boreholes

Dr. H. O. Seigel, president, and **Dr. S. S. Nargolwalla,** nuclear chemist, Scintrex Ltd.

THE DETERMINATION OF A MINERAL GRADE through sampling of a given volume of rock is a compromise between cost and accuracy. Obviously, including more rock in a sample will make the results more accurate—and increase the cost of sampling. A new nuclear logging technique, the "Metalog" system, now makes bulk sampling possible using inexpensive, 6-in.-dia boreholes. Assays obtained with this system are representative of a cylinder of rock about 36 in. in diameter, centered on the hole.

The Metalog system effectively measures the grade of a bulk sample around the hole with an accuracy adequate for most purposes, at costs comparable to those of present sampling and analytical techniques. In some instances, the logging system obviates the need for core drilling in the development stage of mineral exploitation, since it may be coupled with non-coring techniques to increase the accuracy of assays. In addition, the system makes grade information available as soon as each hole is logged, allowing planning decisions to be made quickly. The prompt availability of grade information may itself result in significant cost savings.

Scintrex Ltd. developed the Metalog system during almost five years of continuous research and testing. Scintrex credits the Canadian government for its assistance in the form of research and development grants.

Among the metals responding well to the Metalog system are copper, nickel, iron, chromium, tungsten, and silicon. Several of these metals may be assayed simultaneously. Typical accuracies of grade achieved are ±0.075% in a copper grade of 0.5% and ±0.05% in a nickel grade of 1.0%.

The basic technique employed in the system is the "neutron capture-prompt gamma" process. This entails a source of neutrons which, after thermalizing, are captured by the nuclei of elements around the sample hole. The resulting compound nuclei instantaneously emit gamma rays of intermediate and high energy, on the order of 2 to 10 million electron volts. Many base metals, such as copper, iron, nickel, and chromium, produce *very* high energy gamma rays (greater than 7 Mev), making it possible to analyze for these elements in the presence of major rock constituents of lower atomic weight. Moreover, at these high energies, gamma rays can pass through a foot or more of rock.

The accuracy of the Metalog grade determinations is the result of careful normalization of the nuclear data for a number of significant fluctuations in rock matrix and borehole conditions. The basic mechanism of the system is shown in Fig. 1.

The age-old sampling problem

Since truly homogeneous ore deposits are very rare in nature, sampling a deposit is an imperfect process. Extra-

Fig. 1—Simplified schematic of the Metalog system

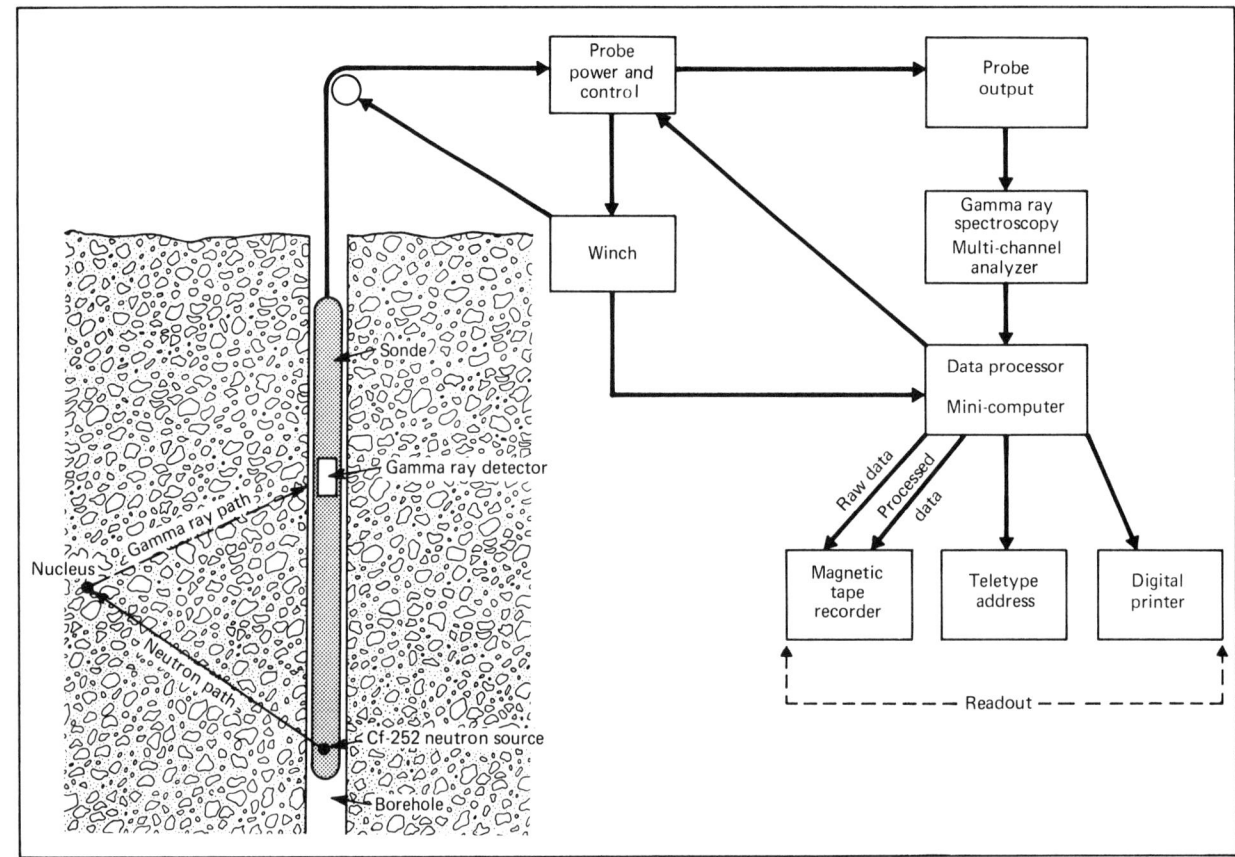

polations to a ridiculous degree are often made to estimate the grade of a large volume of rock. For example, in the development drilling of a large porphyry copper deposit, using holes at 200-ft centers, the extrapolation ratio is approximately 10^7—not surprising when one considers the relationship between the volume of material taken from the sample hole and the volume of the ore block that the sample is supposed to represent.

The extrapolation ratio is actually even larger because only a few grams of material from each section of the core are actually chemically analyzed. Extrapolation ratios of up to 10^{10} are often employed without much consideration of the statistical factors and the size of the error margin involved. Grade determination from blastholes in open-pit operations is especially open to error since it is based on the analysis of a small sample of chips, often gathered at ramdom from the cuttings at the collar of the hole.

It is generally accepted that mine planning and production would be improved by greater accuracy in sampling. It is also accepted that larger assay volumes increase sampling accuracy—no one would dispute that analyzing the material from a 36-in.-bulk sampling hole would give a better extrapolation than the material from a 6-in.-dia (or worse still, a 1.5-in.-dia) hole. However, bulk sampling holes are usually not drilled for development data on open-pit deposits because the cost of the larger holes is too high.

Lab and field tests prove successful

Near the outset of the R&D program that resulted in successful development of the Metalog, a computer study was made to obtain information on the behavior of the system as a function of many independent variables. These variables included borehole diameter, density and moisture content of the bulk matrix, separation between the neutron source and the gamma detector, and the effect of various interfering elements. A special laboratory was established to simulate field borehole conditions, and the predictions of the computer study were tested and refined by experiment in these facilities. Multiple tons of both natural and reconstituted ores were used to simulate actual geological environments. Two specific cases of economic significance have been investigated in the laboratory thus far: copper in porphyry copper deposits and nickel in lateritic nickel deposits.

On the basis of favorable results in both theoretical and experimental investigations, a field test on a lateritic nickel deposit was made in early 1974 in close collaboration with a major Canadian mining company. Metalog, core, and bulk assays were compared in an attempt to prove the merits of the Metalog system. After employing Metalog and core assay techniques, 4-ft-dia shafts were sunk on the test holes and samples weighing about 1,500 lb each were extracted. These bulk samples were taken as accurate bases against which the Metalog and core assays were compared. Data were assayed for nickel, iron, and silicon.

The correlation between the Metalog and the bulk sample assays for nickel is shown in Fig. 2. The probable error of the Metalog assays was found to be less than 5% of the actual nickel grade over the total range of values encountered in these holes. The probable error of core assay samples was found to be almost twice as large.

After successful completion of the field tests, a produc-

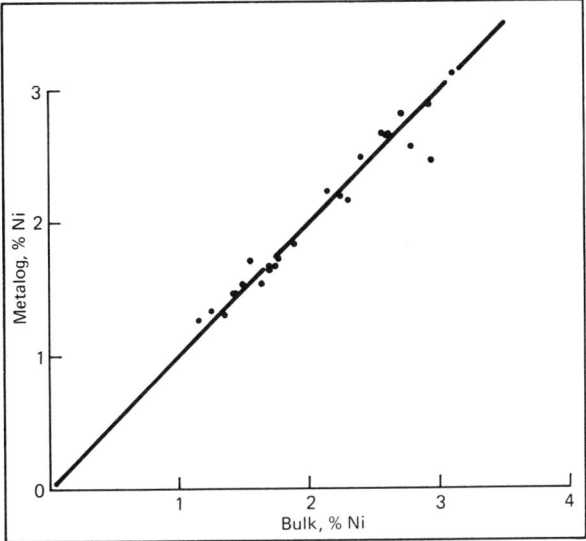

Fig. 2—Comparison plot of Metalog and bulk assays

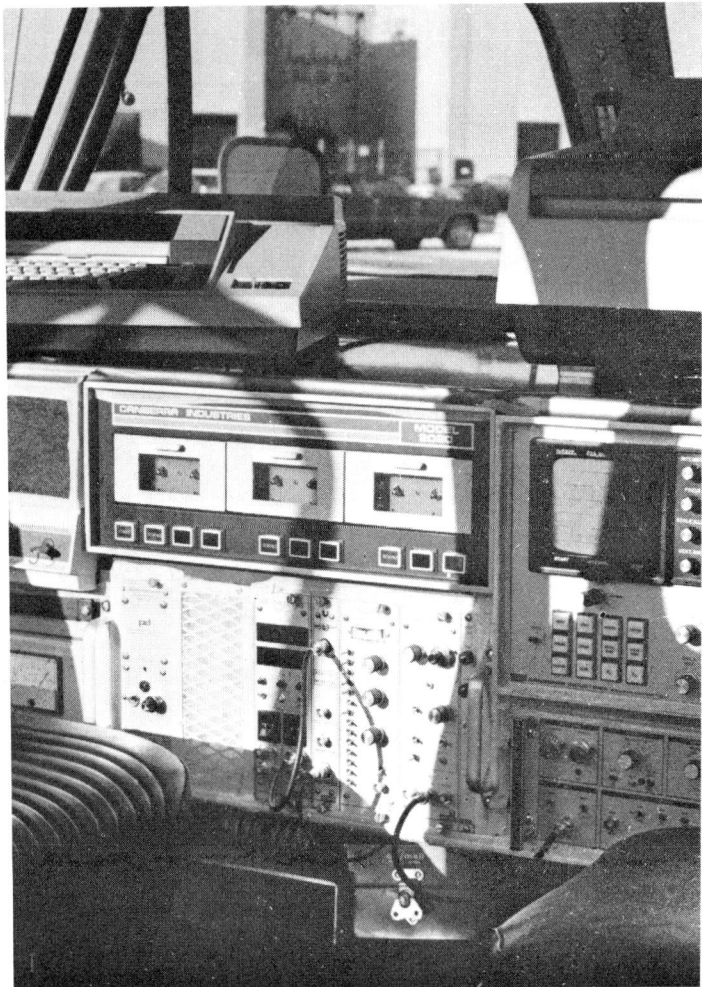

Instruments in the truck's cab include multi-channel analyzer, computer, analog converter, and line printer.

tion prototype of a Metalog field truck was assembled and employed in further logging programs. The basic vehicle is a four-wheel-drive Dodge Power Wagon with a crew cab. The sonde that is inserted into the borehole is 4 in. in diameter and includes Californium-252 (a USAEC-produced artificial isotope) as a neutron source. A high-resolution sodium iodide crystal acts as a gamma ray detector that feeds advance-pulse handling circuitry, providing the high degree of sensitivity and stability necessary for the required accuracy of the system. The pulses are processed by instrumentation mounted in the cab of the truck. Instrumentation includes a multi-channel analyzer, analog-to-digital converter, mini-computer, mass storage system, line printer, and digital depth meter.

For each assay, the depth and grades for selected elements are printed out on a teletype printer, as well as being stored in digital form on magnetic tape. The tape storage lends itself to rapid treatment by the computer, which may then perform grade, tonnage, feasibility, and mine planning studies. The computer calculation of grade and the teleprinter output take place while the next accumulation of gamma ray counts is being made. Thus, grade information may be inspected with practically no delay while a new hole is being logged.

The economics of specific applications

As with any sampling system, Metalog's costs per foot of hole depend on the assay interval selected for the hole and on the required accuracy of the grade determination. Statistical accuracy of the Metalog system is improved by longer gamma counting times, i.e. by slower logging speeds.

Logging rates vary directly with the desired assay interval for a given constant accuracy. In porphyry copper logging, with assays averaged over 10-ft intervals, rates of 60 fph are currently feasible for ±0.075% Cu accuracy. For lateritic nickel deposits, rates of 20 to 30 fph are being employed for accuracies of ±0.05% Ni, averaged over 3- to 5-ft intervals. If only a single average assay is required per hole (for grade control during actual mining production phase), data may be obtained in 10-15 min per hole with the above stated grade accuracy.

A comparison of the relative costs of the Metalog system and other sampling procedures must include in the latter the total cost of sample collection plus transportation and analysis. When these factors are weighed in, Metalog costs on a full production basis are comparable to those of other sampling techniques.

In some deposits, where expensive, slow core drilling is being used to get assays of adequate accuracy, it is now possible to use relatively inexpensive and faster non-coring techniques coupled with Metalog for assaying. The resultant reduction in drilling costs can be substantial, often on the order of $5-7 per ft.

The bulk sampling capability of the Metalog system means that it can produce far more meaningful data than core or chip samples in deposits that are *highly* heterogeneous. In addition, the prompt availability of Metalog assays may enable a large scale development program to proceed rapidly and economically, with few wasted holes. The speed factor makes the system a valuable tool for grade control, particularly in large tonnage, low grade open-pit deposits. The system is also well suited to the sampling of dumps, often a very difficult task using other techniques.

In summary, the Metalog system provides accurate, rapid, large-volume grade information at a reasonable cost from small-diameter holes. This type of logging will be of considerable service to the mining industry in years to come. □

New technique enhances the art of bulk sampling placer deposits

R. A. Hildebrand, president, Polaris Resources Inc.

A NEW BULK SAMPLING TECHNIQUE, introduced in North America on a Nevada placer project, has enhanced the art of sampling over previously used methods. Brought to this country by Polaris Resources Inc., of Lakewood, Colo., the Hochstrasser-Weise caisson method is a German technique that has been patented worldwide. The primary application has been in sinking cased shafts for foundation piers for industrial and large commercial buildings. The technique can be used to sink cased holes up to 6 ft in diameter through rock/soil mixtures. Common depths of foundation piers range from 20 to 100 ft.

Polaris' first exposure to the H-W caisson drill was on a construction site in West Germany, where Polaris representatives observed the sinking of 36-in.-dia shafts through a gravel bed to install building foundation piers. Although the operators were not interested in the gravel excavated, it was apparent to Polaris that the technique could be modified to obtain an excellent bulk sample from placers, mine dumps, stockpiles, and coal deposits.

Before describing the Nevada case history, a review of some of the problems encountered in conventional drill sampling is in order.

The drawbacks of conventional bulk sampling

Several problems are encountered in standard driven pipe sampling methods (Fig. 1). High resistance to penetration limits this method to relatively small diameter holes (a common size casing shoe might be 7½ in.). As Fig. 1 illustrates, sample distortion occurs when the cutting edge of the casing shoe encounters a boulder partially outside of the sample area and small enough to rise in the pipe. The boulder either enters the pipe or is crowded out, but in either case the sample is distorted because the boulder adds to or detracts from the sample volume.

Long experience with the 7½-in. Keystone drill indicates that the sample recovery is only 88% of the theoretical volume. This percentage, or its complementary 12%, is known as the Radford or Keystone Factor. The crowding effect is dependent on the outside diameter of the drive tube and is a function of the ratio of the area of the cutting shoe edge to the entire cross-sectional area of the shoe. For a 7½-in. pipe, this ratio is approximately 25%, while for a 40-in. hole, it is 9½% (a 68% reduction of the crowding effect).

Item B of Fig. 1 illustrates another common problem encountered in drilling placers or stockpiles. A boulder that is too large to enter the drill shoe blocks pipe penetration or, in relatively unconsolidated material, it is pushed down, displacing the material to be sampled. The obvious way to obtain a true sample in this type of material is to drill larger holes.

A third problem encountered when using driven pipe sampling involves hydrostatic pressure in wet ground (Item C, Fig. 1). Such pressure may cause run-ins, resulting in sample contamination. One solution is to pressurize

Editor's note: This paper was originally presented at the National Western Mining Conference and Exhibition, Denver, Colo., February 2-4, 1976.

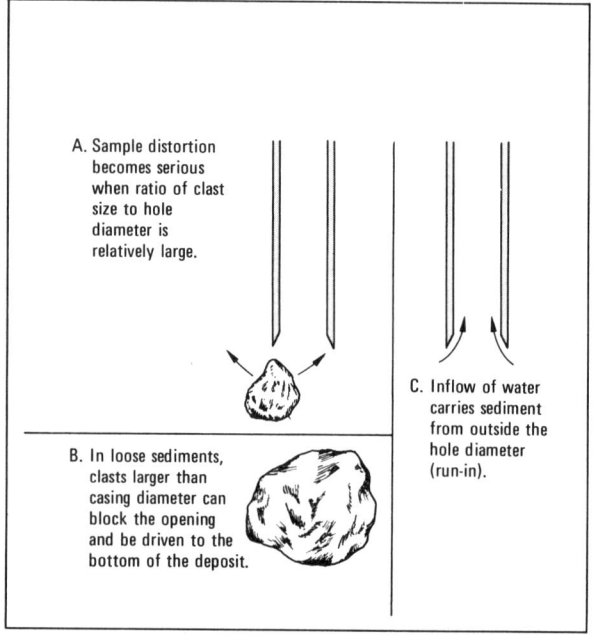

A. Sample distortion becomes serious when ratio of clast size to hole diameter is relatively large.

B. In loose sediments, clasts larger than casing diameter can block the opening and be driven to the bottom of the deposit.

C. Inflow of water carries sediment from outside the hole diameter (run-in).

the pipe and drive it like a true caisson. A large diameter pipe has a better chance of avoiding run-in because the larger sample plug can resist water inflow.

In an attempt to avoid the difficulties encountered when driving large diameter pipes, operators have resorted to sampling from open uncased holes, only to encounter a new set of problems. Fig. 2 shows a drill section through a permeable water-bearing sand. If the sand bed is friable enough, it may slough and mingle with the sample taken from the bottom. If the permeable bed is relatively higher or lower in values than the rest of the section, serious salting or contamination may result. Other sources of contamination are introduced by hole wall cavings caused by the drill string and drilling fluid.

A few examples will help to clarify the dimensions of the sampling problems. Today's commercial gold placer contains ½ to 1 ppm of gold to waste. The sampling of such a deposit is equivalent to obtaining a representative sample out of a 55-gal drum of sand containing one BB shot.

In sampling coal, sand contamination reports directly to ash in a proximate analysis. A 5% variance in ash can easily render a coal deposit unprofitable to mine. This problem is amplified by the substantially higher density of sand compared with coal. The addition of a given volume of sand results in a weight-basis dilution 1.4 times larger than the volumetric dilution.

A dilution problem also results from gravity separation in fluidized systems (Fig. 3). Sorting occurs in the fluid column because of the different densities of the recovered minerals and the waste matrix. In the case of gold, which in water is 11 times the weight of sand, particles tend to lag in the sample recovery (heavy minerals lag in a low-velocity zone). Lost circulation can significantly affect the velocity of the air stream or water base fluid, which in turn re-

The basic elements of the H-W system are the specially designed 3-cu-ft capacity digging clam (left) and the 12-ton swinghead mounted on top of the 40-in.-dia caisson.

Before placing the swinghead-caisson assembly into position for drilling, a 9-ft-deep pilot hole is excavated by the clam and a 50-ton crane. A guide pipe is then swung into place.

duces the carrying capacity of the drilling medium.

In an open hole, an irregular hole diameter also affects the velocity of the drilling medium, causing sample distortion. In addition, the density of the fluid column may cause gravity separation of the sample. Fluid density increases or decreases, depending on the lithology of the hole bottom.

Dry excavation from larger-diameter cased holes will overcome the problems described in Figs. 1-3. In the old days, hand-dug cribbed shafts provided placer engineers with excellent samples. However, the high labor requirement of this method makes it uneconomical now, and attempts to use large diameter augers generally have been unsuccessful because of their inability to excavate boulders and handle casing.

A clam-drill system, used in various operations, has had considerable success in obtaining reliable placer samples. However, this system has run into problems in driving and extracting casing from wet or squeezing ground.

Nevada caisson tests succeed

Last summer, Polaris Resources used the Hochstrasser-Weise caisson method on a gold placer deposit in Nevada. The method succeeded in drilling 40-in.-dia cased holes to depths of 40 ft through gravel and broken rock, and in recovering representative samples with a specially designed digging clam. Drilling costs totaled $900 per day, including contract rental of equipment and labor. In addition, a license fee of $5 per ft was required. A production rate of 40 ft per day was achieved.

The components of the H-W system include a 50-ton truck-mounted crane with a 90-ft boom, 600-cfm air compressor, sample bins, and a 12-ton swinghead mounted on top of a 40-in.-dia caisson.

The weighted swinghead, linked to the top of the cais-

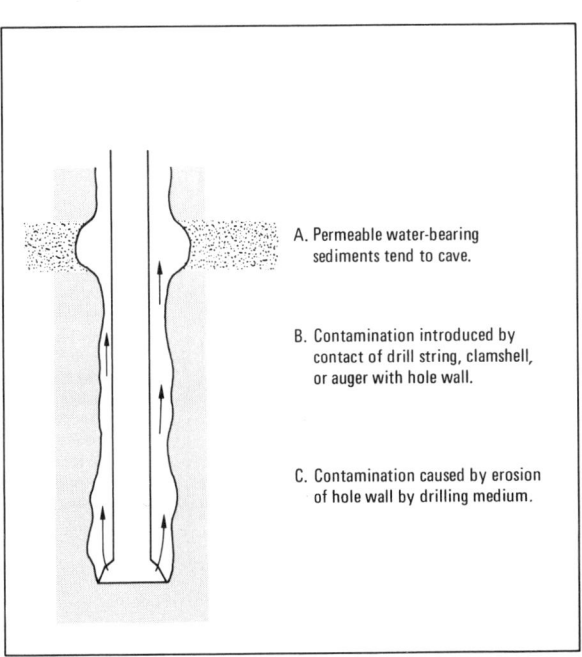

A. Permeable water-bearing sediments tend to cave.

B. Contamination introduced by contact of drill string, clamshell, or auger with hole wall.

C. Contamination caused by erosion of hole wall by drilling medium.

The top of the swinghead-caisson assembly has a guide cone, which projects above the surface of the swinghead. The cone facilitates the clam's entry into the casing.

Conventional clean-up and recovery of gold is from 18-in.-long individual riffle sections. Hungarian-type riffles (not shown) collect the washed, screened undersize material.

son by a casing drivehead, rotates horizontally through a limited arc. Compressed-air cylinders initiate the rotation. The swinghead engages a set of latches fixed to the top of the casing, and stops at the end of a 40° swing. Upon impact, the angular momentum of the swinghead is transferred to the casing, causing it to twist in the direction of the original swing of the head. At this point, the compressed air is diverted through a valve arrangement to the compressed air cylinders, initiating rotation in the reverse direction.

Each impact delivers a torque of 430,000 ft-lb. The cycle is repeated 30 times per min, moving the casing 1 to 5 in. in either direction. The caisson's movement serves to break skin friction along the walls.

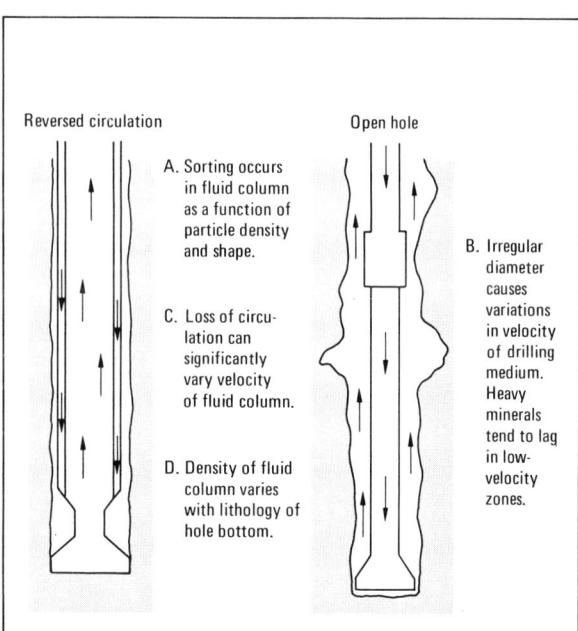

Reversed circulation   Open hole

A. Sorting occurs in fluid column as a function of particle density and shape.

C. Loss of circulation can significantly vary velocity of fluid column.

D. Density of fluid column varies with lithology of hole bottom.

B. Irregular diameter causes variations in velocity of drilling medium. Heavy minerals tend to lag in low-velocity zones.

The drill sequence begins by excavating a 9-ft-deep pilot hole with the clam to accept a guide pipe. The swinghead-caisson assembly is inserted into the guide pipe. At this stage in the cycle, the swinghead begins oscillating, and the crane prepares to drop the digging clam through the opening in the swinghead and down into the casing.

The clam used on this project weighs 5,000 lb and has a cycle time of approximately 45 sec. Combined weights of the swinghead and caisson, and the continuous twisting action, enable the cutting shoe of the drill pipe to sink steadily below the leading edge of the digging clam.

After reaching target depth, the bottom of the hole can be inspected by a geologist, who is lowered by the crane in a bosun's chair. The ability of the crane to reach otherwise inaccessible places, such as the hillside location at the test site, minimizes environmental damage.

Casing is recovered from the hole by lifting the entire assembly with the crane, while the swinghead oscillates to break skin friction. Recovery is facilitated by closing the opening in the swinghead and pressurizing the caisson with compressed air, adding upward thrust. One of the main advantages of the H-W system is the ease with which casing can be removed.

Wash plant processes high-volume samples

At a penetration rate of 40 ft per shift, the volume of sample amounted to 350 cu ft, or 13 cu yd, per day. Available standard equipment lacked capacity to process this volume of sample. Consequently, a custom plant having a capacity of 3-5 cu yd per hr was designed and built for this project. In the system, the sample is washed in a 3-ft-dia x 6-ft-long trommel. Undersized washed, screened material reports to a 14-ft-long Hungarian-type riffle. Conventional clean-up and recovery of the gold was from 18-in.-long individual riffle sections.

As a final comment, the outcome of the first H-W sampling program in North America produced no unusual results: gold values were far less than the property owner had represented. □

Chapter 3
Finance, Engineering and Reclamation

How to value a mineral property	82
Delaying debt during early development: a new approach to mine financing	86
How to cut risk of slope failure in designing optimum pit slopes	92
Pit slope displacement monitoring: an aid to open-pit mine operations	99
Select berm width to contain local failures	103
Open-pit engineering takes quantum leap	107
Choose the right vertical wet pit sump pump	110
High efficiency motors cut energy costs	119
Nomographs simplify cable tramway design	120
New survey instrument displays readings on both sides	123
Nomograph for in-situ uranium leaching	124
Water slurry properties	125
Environmental impacts focus on waste handling	126
Copper mine waters: good potential as medium for growing livestock forage	128
Georgia kaolin producers are reclaiming an acre of land for each acre mined	130
Homestake nears completion of project to impound tailings and recycle water	133

How to value a mineral property

James E. Castle, consulting mining engineer

A VALUATION of a mineral property requires data on geology, mining, metallurgy, marketing, pricing, and financing, and no single factor plays a determinative role.

The quantitative data needed to perform a sound mineral valuation include:

- Size and tenor of an orebody to feed an operation for the number of years prescribed in the valuation.
- Mining and processing methods.
- Survey of the product market and selling price.
- Mine and plant design.
- Estimates of capital requirements and operating costs, including direct costs and depreciation.
- Profit calculations, including depletion allowances.
- Cash flow calculations, including profits, depreciation, new capital investment, a sinking fund to extinguish debt, and cash flow discounted at 12% interest.

Points sometimes overlooked in making such quantitative studies:

- Estimates of labor costs should be reasonably close to the average prevailing in the area of proposed operations. The average is a variable that must be verified in each case. Estimates should include realistic provisions for the cost of fringe benefits.
- Operating costs should include reasonable provisions for environmental protection, including appropriations to a fund for environmental restoration at the end of mine life.
- Capital requirements should include reasonable sums to finance product inventories, operating supplies, and accounts receivable. Significant amounts are invested in these categories and are not recovered and placed in the cash flow until the last year of operations.
- Additional capital investment to increase productive capacity in later years must be deducted from the cash flow through the depreciation account.

What to expect when operating a business

The data presented in Table 1 provide reasonable indications of what might occur when operating an industrial mineral business (based on the hypothetical mineral "montelisite") over a 26-year period. The current value of the montelisite mineral deposit is given by the index number 240.149, the bottom figure in the last column.

Table 1 demonstrates a method of calculating the current value of the montelisite deposit using a discounted cash flow (DCF). In a given year of mine life, cash flow equals profit plus depreciation less additional capital investment and yearly appropriations to a sinking fund to extinguish long term indebtedness. For each year of mine life, the cash flow is discounted at 12% to arrive at that year's contribution to the current value of the mineral property.

Prior to Year 1, all the appropriate technical, economic, engineering, and financial data are collected. The decision is made to exploit the deposit. Mining and beneficiation plants are designed. Arrangements are made for financing the venture. The cost of these moves is carried by the organizers and promoters of the new mining company.

Year 1 itself is a time of plant construction, with the newly organized mining company incurring no profits or losses, since all expenditures are on capital account.

The tonnage index figures in Table 1 are based on a statistical study of the montelisite market for 25 years and a projection of the development of this market over the life of the new mine. In this case, the market is projected to rise annually at 5.2%, a figure not uncommon for industrial minerals.

The sales index figures include not only the tonnage index figures but also expected price increases. In this case, selling prices are projected to increase annually at 3.7%. This figure results from a statistical study of montelisite price movements and a reasonable projection for the future. The selection of initial plant capacity is based not only on the extent of ore reserves, but also, more important, on a practical consideration of the percentage of a growing montelisite market that could be taken over by a new producer. Also important is the question of potential customer reactions to a new producer, as determined by a customer survey.

The cost figures result from rigorous engineering analysis. To be reliable and credible, cost figures must bear reasonable resemblance to those of other mineral businesses, in terms of tonnages, selling prices, technical efficiency, and markets.

Profits are estimated to increase at an annual rate of 9.7% after Year 5, the first year in which the initially designed sales tonnage is achieved. The 9.7% annual increase in profit reflects the annual 5.2% increase in tons of product sold, an annual 3.7% price increase, and a yearly 2% increase in productivity.

The productivity increase of 2% is practical. During the life of a mine, a gradual shift from 10-ton quarry trucks initially to 20-ton trucks at maturity is not unusual. Productivity also relates to the skill and enthusiasm of an operating crew at Year 9, vs. an inexperienced, relatively ineffective crew at Year 2. Improved

Table 1—Current value of a hypothetical mining business
(expressed in index numbers)

Year	Tons of product sold	Value of sales	Costs (including tax)	Cash flow Net profit	Depre- ciation	Sinking fund	Total cash flow	Current value of cash flow discounted at 12% Year	Running total
1	0	0	0	0	0	0	0	0	0
2	50.00	45.098	49.637	(4.539)	5.047	0	0.508	0.454	0.454
3	63.00	58.812	58.812	0	5.047	(1.468)	3.579	2.853	3.307
4	80.00	77.298	64.848	12.450	5.047	(1.468)	16.029	11.409	14.716
5	100.00	100.00	81.167	18.833	5.047	(1.468)	22.412	14.243	28.959
6	104.20	107.700	87.040	20.660	5.047	(1.468)	24.239	13.753	42.712
7	108.55	115.993	93.330	22.663	5.047	(1.468)	26.242	13.294	56.006
8	113.14	124.924	100.062	24.862	5.047	(1.468)	28.441	12.864	68.870
9	117.89	134.544	107.270	27.274	5.047	(1.468)	30.853	12.462	81.332
10	122.54	144.903	114.984	29.919	—	(1.468)	28.451	10.259	91.591
11	128.00	156.061	123.239	32.822	—	(1.468)	31.354	10.095	101.686
12	133.37	168.078	132.073	36.005	—	(1.468)	34.537	9.929	111.615
13	138.98	181.020	141.522	39.498	—	(1.468)	38.030	9.760	121.375
14	144.81	194.958	151.629	43.329	—	(1.468)	41.861	9.595	130.970
15	150.90	209.970	162.438	47.532	—	(1.468)	46.064	9.425	140.395
16	157.23	226.138	173.995	52.143	—	(1.468)	50.675	9.258	149.653
17	163.84	243.550	186.350	57.200	3.533	(1.468)	59.265	9.666	159.319
18	170.72	262.303	199.554	62.749	3.533	(1.468)	64.814	9.437	168.756
19	177.89	282.501	213.666	68.835	3.533	(1.468)	70.900	9.217	177.973
20	185.36	304.253	228.741	75.512	3.533	(1.468)	77.577	9.007	186.980
21	193.14	327.681	241.780	85.901	3.533	—	89.434	9.274	196.254
22	201.26	352.912	258.976	93.936	3.533	—	97.469	9.026	205.280
23	209.71	380.087	297.336	102.751	3.533	—	106.284	8.779	214.059
24	218.52	409.353	296.932	112.421	3.533	—	115.954	8.556	222.615
25	227.70	440.873	317.845	123.028	3.533	—	126.561	8.340	230.955
26	237.26	474.821	340.156	134.665	21.688	—	156.353	9.194	240.149

productivity is also a function of higher metallurgical recoveries in a flotation plant fed with clean, unoxidized ores during Year 12, compared with the recoveries from mine-stained and oxidized ores in Year 3.

Economic swings don't change the facts

Since the figures for production and sales and for the price of the mineral commodity are based on a statistical survey of past performance and a reasonable projection of the future, the average production and sales figures are valid regardless of business cycles. Also, the figures point up the desirability of timing plant construction to enable entry into the market shortly after a business trough is reached. Proper timing will take advantage of entrance into the market when demand is not only rising back to its pre-trough high but also climbing to a new high.

Year 1 is the year of completion of construction, plant break-in, and debugging. Year 3 sees the break-even point reached on a net profit basis. (Year 3 is also the time to start annual appropriations to a sinking fund to extinguish long-term debt. Such appropriations are shown as deductions from cash flow.) During Year 4, net

Table 2—Effect of a 5% royalty on current value
(expressed in index numbers)

Year	Sales (from Table 1)	Cost of 5% royalty before tax	Cost of 5% royalty after tax of 24.5%	Cash flow From Table 1, after royalty deduction	Cash flow For the year, discounted at 12%	Running total of DCF
1	0	0	0	0	0	0
2	45.098	2.255	1.703	(1.195)	(1.195)	(1.195)
3	58.812	2.941	2.220	1.359	1.083	(0.112)
4	77.298	3.865	2.918	13.111	9.332	9.220
5	100.000	5.000	3.775	18.637	11.843	21.063
6	107.700	5.385	4.066	20.173	11.446	32.509
7	115.993	5.800	4.378	21.864	11.076	43.585
8	124.924	6.246	4.716	23.725	10.731	54.316
9	134.544	6.727	5.079	25.774	10.410	64.726
10	144.903	7.245	5.470	22.981	8.287	73.013
11	156.061	7.803	5.891	25.463	8.199	81.212
12	168.078	8.404	6.345	28.192	8.105	89.317
13	181.020	9.051	6.834	31.196	8.008	97.325
14	194.958	9.748	7.360	34.501	7.908	105.233
15	209.970	10.499	7.927	38.137	7.803	113.036
16	226.138	11.307	8.537	42.138	7.699	120.735
17	243.550	12.178	9.194	50.071	8.167	128.902
18	262.303	13.115	9.902	54.912	7.995	136.897
19	282.501	14.125	10.664	60.236	7.831	144.728
20	304.253	15.213	11.486	66.091	7.673	152.401
21	327.681	16.384	12.206	77.228	8.009	160.410
22	352.912	17.646	13.322	84.147	7.792	168.202
23	380.087	19.004	14.348	91.936	7.594	175.796
24	409.353	20.468	15.453	100.501	7.417	183.213
25	440.873	22.044	16.643	109.918	7.244	190.457
26	474.821	23.741	17.924	138.429	8.140	198.597

profit reflects the tax loss carryover due to net loss sustained in Year 2. In Year 5, the initially designed levels of production and sales are reached, represented by index 100 for tonnage and index 100 for sales.

The initial plant capacity is designed for five-day operation. A shift to seven days will achieve a 30% gain in production. However, from Year 9 through Year 16, all depreciation cash flow is reinvested in additional equipment to increase production. As a result, depreciation at index 5.047 is no longer added to cash flow during Years 9 through 16. Depreciation at a reduced index of 3.533 is added to cash flow for the Years 17 through 26 to extinguish the new capital costs incurred during Years 9 through 16.

Starting at Year 21, net profit is increased by index 3.064, reflecting the end of annual interest costs on the long term indebtedness that was extinguished by the sinking fund during Year 20. Year 26 brings not only an addition of index 3.533 to cash flow because of depreciation, but also an additional credit (index 18.155) to cash flow due to the liquidation during the last year of product inventories, operating and maintenance supplies, salvage value, and accounts receivable.

In discounting cash flow at 12% to calculate current

value, standard conservative business practice was followed. After 10 years of stable and profitable operations, a number of risk factors are removed. After 10 years, the owners can often count on an additional 25 years of operation because the required ore reserves are already in place or can be acquired.

For this reason, owners who decide to sell a mining property can reasonably claim that future profits should be discounted at some rate less punishing than the standard 12%, to reflect the much smaller impact of the risk factor. A maximum 10% or minimum 8% discount rate is suggested, depending on the economic and technologic factors that apply at the time.

The same line of reasoning applies at the end of Year 26, when the mining business is to be liquidated. Calculations of profits beyond 26 years were not made because the 12% discount rate makes the profit contribution irrelevant. A more likely scenario, however, would show the mining company entering an additional period of profitability after Year 26, through delineation of new ore reserves or acquisition of new property. With risks substantially reduced, the evaluation of the property would be based on a suggested 8% to 10% discount on cash flow, rather than 12%.

Corporation can act as source of capital

The method of analysis indicated in Table 1 can be used to evaluate mineral projects proposed by a corporation's various operating divisions or subsidiaries. The only difference is that the parent corporation becomes the source of capital. There is no equity-and-debt capitalization. Rigorous financial management requires that the operating divisions or units must pay for the use of capital at the current rate of return, provide for the return of capital to the parent company, and earn a return on capital commensurate with the risk.

The standard conservative business practice of discounting cash flow at 12% provides, although inadequately, for monetary erosion due to inflation. In fact, the 12% discount rate has not reflected the 6% to 11% inflation rates of the past three years. An inflation rate of 3-4% over the next five to 10 years is very possible, and such fluctuations will somewhat discredit the 12% discount rate.

The case of third-party ownership

The effect of royalties was not considered in compiling Table 1. Rather, the ownership of the montelisite property was assumed to be in the hands of the mining company promoters. In financing the new operating company, the promoters retained a controlling share in the equity of the new venture in return for their expenses in acquiring control of the mineral deposit and in making the necessary geological, engineering, marketing, and financial studies.

Under normal circumstances, the mineral deposit would be owned by a third party. In this case, the promoters could not undertake costly exploration, development, and feasibility studies without assurance that the mineral deposit would be available for lease or purchase on reasonable terms.

Two avenues are open to promoters to secure control of the mineral deposit. The first is an option to purchase the property outright at a predetermined price. This course is more often followed by an established company with adequate financial and technical resources. The second alternative is to negotiate a lease of the property, with royalty clauses.

There are no rules that govern the level of royalties; however, it is difficult to envision a royalty rate less than 5%.

Gauging the effect of royalty on profit

The effect of a 5% royalty is demonstrated in Table 2, which can be used to gauge the effect of royalty on profit, the level of royalty payout consistent with risk and reward to the promoters, and the selling price that might be considered by the property owners. The figures demonstrate that a royalty of 5% causes a return of 82.7% of the total discounted cash flow to the mining company and 17.3% to the deposit's owners. Only a consideration of capital investment, level of profits, and rate of return can determine whether the mining company can afford to pay that level of royalty. The ratio 82.7 to 17.3, of and by itself, is totally meaningless.

Table 2 can also be used as a guideline for the buying price of the mineral property. Table 1 places the current value of the discounted cash flow, without consideration of royalties, at index 240.149. Table 2 shows this figure reduced to index 198.597 because of royalty payments. The difference, index 41.552, can be considered by both buyer and seller as a useful base point in negotiating a buying price for the mineral deposit by the mining company or entrepreneurs.

Finally, in the event that the mineral property is owned by the promoters who are to organize and manage the mining company, the figures in Table 2 are a useful guide in negotiating equity participation in the mining company to be formed. □

About the author

James E. Castle was graduated from Massachusetts Institute of Technology in 1935 with a B.S. degree in mining engineering, and he received a masters degree in metallurgical engineering from the Colorado School of Mines in 1943. In the past 25 years, he held the positions of division manager for Foote Mineral Co. at Kings Mountain, N.C.; general manager for the Industrial Minerals Div. of International Minerals and Chemical Corp.; and vice president of Commercialores Inc., Clover, S.C. Since 1972, he has served as a consulting mining engineer based in York, S.C.

Delaying debt during early development: a new approach to mine financing

Tomec Ulatowski, assistant vice president, Bank of America
Edward S. Frohling, president, and **F. Milton Lewis,** consultant, Mountain States Mineral Enterprises Inc.

THE MINING INDUSTRY has undergone many fundamental structural changes in recent years that have dramatically increased its reliance on debt to fund its expanding fixed asset base. Capital savings, or retained earnings, together with provisions for depreciation, have become insufficient to cover the costs of adding new production capacity and maintaining current production levels. This situation has been caused primarily by spiraling capital and operating costs that have not been offset by sufficiently higher commodities prices; a significant depletion of easily accessible, rich, metallurgically uncomplicated mineral deposits; political interference domestically and abroad; and the high costs of meeting strict environmental standards.

The deficiency in the internally generated cash flow of the mining industry has been covered mostly by new borrowings, which, in turn, have exacerbated the leverage problem and raised the level of risk for creditors of, and investors in, the industry.

In new grassroots mining projects, the role of debt is becoming even more important. In fact, the implementation of many mining projects now depends to a large extent on their ability to attract required amounts of credit. This ability is obviously a function of the credit strength of a new mining venture vis-a-vis the general availability of loan funds in capital markets.

Credit viability, however, is substantially affected by the tenor, grace, and repayment periods of the potential loans. The longer the credit and the lower the contemplated leverage, the better the cash flow for debt coverage. Unfortunately, the only major source of long term credits is institutional investors such as pension funds or insurance companies. Because their credit criteria are quite stringent, only a few mining projects can satisfy their requirements. For all practical purposes, the mining industry must rely primarily on medium term credit provided by commercial banks and government-supported financial institutions such as export-import banks.

We suggest an approach for extending the period for repayment of borrowed capital on new mining projects by up to 50% without changing the overall tenor of the loans. By delaying formal credit commitments and by financing initial construction costs entirely with equity funds, it is possible not only to substantially increase cash flow for debt repayment during the critical initial years of operations but also to improve the economic return to the project sponsors.

In today's credit market, sponsors of new projects cannot reasonably count on commercial bank loans to exceed eight years from the time of first commitment to the date of final repayment. Loans to overseas projects are, in most instances, even shorter in duration. If a two- to four-year construction period is needed, then the period for debt amortization becomes very brief indeed. It is not surprising, therefore, that some potentially viable mining projects that have high leverage characteristics fail to pass the cash flow credit standards set by lenders.

For large projects, loans are increasingly made on the so-called "off-balance-sheet" basis, often with limited recourse to the sponsoring mining companies. However, the parent company's liability to the lender usually extends until the project is completed and operating

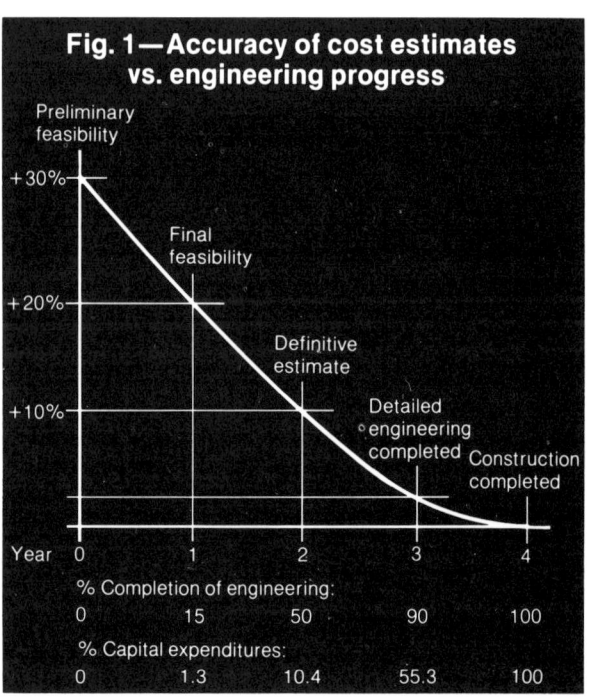

Fig. 1—Accuracy of cost estimates vs. engineering progress

according to predetermined output levels and cost efficiency criteria. Such liability amounts to something very close to a loan guarantee during the construction and startup phase of a project.

For example, sponsors of the Selebi-Pikwe nickel project in Botswana must continue to support it, principally because of such an obligation. Although production started in 1974, technical problems still affect the operation, and the completion guarantee has not been satisfied.

Similarly, lenders are protected in case of capital cost overruns—and in recent years, some major projects have been faced with costs substantially higher than originally estimated. The Tenke-Fungurume project in Zaire, based on an orebody that contains 6.0% copper and 0.4% cobalt, was projected to cost about $500 million. Recently, all work was halted, equipment orders were canceled, and the entire project staff disbanded because the project cost had escalated to more than $900 million. At that capital cost, the project was considered not feasible. The Cuajone mine of Southern Peru Copper Corp. is another example. At the outset, in 1970, the capital cost of the project was estimated at $335 million. That cost has since escalated to $730 million.

How to reduce the lender's risk

There are a number of ways by which to reduce critical risk areas of a mining project from a lender's point of view. If implemented, such practices should improve the overall financeability of new projects.

After a potential orebody has been discovered, standard practice in the industry is to estimate reserves and then prepare a preliminary feasibility study as a basis for obtaining financing, on the theory that further expenditures without firm funding commitments would not be justified. However, we do not necessarily recommend procuring loan funds at this stage in development.

Instead, very serious consideration should be given to deferring formal credit commitments as long as possible. The cost of additional detailed studies and engineering should be borne by the sponsors until a definitive estimate is completed. If the project is not viable, the cost to the sponsors is virtually the same whether or not loans have been made, as such loans must in any case be repaid by the sponsors under the terms of the completion guarantee. By deferring loan commitments, the periods of loan amortization can be extended by one to two years, for a considerable improvement in debt coverage, a higher return on equity, and an increase in confidence regarding the projected capital cost estimate.

A hypothetical case

Hypothetical development of a typical porphyry copper mine is examined here to illustrate the concepts previously outlined.

The first phase of the hypothetical venture is proving of the orebody. Preliminary drilling indicates that the deposit may contain more than 300 million tons of 0.6% copper, and that open-pit mining would be applicable. Rough estimates are made of the tonnage of overburden to be prestripped and the waste-to-ore ratios during the mining operation. Drill core samples are used for mineralogical examinations and laboratory tests.

It is determined that the large deposit could be extracted at a mining rate of 40,000 tpd, with a copper production rate of 70,000 tpy and a mine life of more than 20 years. Four years would be a reasonable schedule for bringing the project on stream after a

Table 1—Breakdown of project cost by six-month periods
(thousands of 1977 dollars)

	\-0*	0–½	½–1	1–1½	1½–2	2–2½	2½–3	3–3½	3½–4	Totals	Percent of total project cost
Mine											
Exploration appraisal	550									550	0.2
Drilling and mine planning		825	825							1,650	0.5
Removing overburden and stripping						3,500	3,500	3,500	3,500	14,000	4.8
Procurement of equipment					2,800	5,000	7,000	8,000	11,000	33,800	11.2
Subtotals, mine	550	825	825		2,800	8,500	10,500	11,500	14,500	50,000	16.7
Surface plants											
Engineering and home office	50	600	1,200	2,000	2,400	3,000	2,000	1,000	250	12,500	4.2
Field construction				5,000	15,000	50,000	60,000	62,500	45,000	237,500	79.1
Subtotals, plants	50	600	1,200	7,000	17,400	53,000	62,000	63,500	45,250	250,000	83.3
Six-month totals	600	1,425	2,025	7,000	20,200	61,500	72,500	75,000	59,750	300,000	100.0
Cumulative totals	600*	2,025	4,050	11,050	31,250	92,750	165,250	240,250	300,000		

* Includes all costs prior to presentation of preliminary feasibility study. Note: The cost of land acquisition and environmental impact, general administrative costs, and capitalized interest charges are not considered here.

preliminary feasibility study has been accepted.

Before preparing the preliminary feasibility report, it is necessary to lay out plot plans, including flowsheets, to estimate the order of magnitude of capital and operating costs and to calculate the possible rate of return. The capital cost estimate should be accurate within 30% (Fig. 1). It is assumed that such calculations and estimates indicate that the project is viable. Thus, a preliminary feasibility report is prepared, recommending that development proceed.

After the preliminary feasibility study has been approved by the sponsors, work should begin promptly to produce a final feasibility study that has an accuracy of 20% (Fig. 1), for completion during the first year. The study includes: 1) exhaustive surface geological examinations and mapping of the immediate area; 2) extensive drilling to establish grade and geometry of the deposit, retaining all core rejects for process metallurgical development; 3) development of the economic pit limit and mining sequence and establishment of a preliminary cutoff; 4) calculation of ore reserves; 5) establishment of the most likely extraction rate—in this case, 40,000 tpd; 6) selection of mine equipment; 7) evaluation of the economics of contracting overburden removal vs. removal by the sponsor; 8) preparation of capital and operating cost estimates for the mining operation; 9) determination of the metallurgical, chemical, and physical properties of the ore; 10) testing of ore hardness to permit sizing of comminution equipment; 11) testing to establish the concentrator flowsheet and recovery and grade of concentrate; 12) production schedule for concentrator and smelter; 13) equipment lists for concentrator, smelter, and sulphuric acid plant; 14) general description of site and facilities; 15) subsoil investigation; 16) location and dimension of site facilities; 17) plot plan; 18) preliminary general arrangement drawings; 19) preliminary sizes and types of construction; 20) preliminary structural design; 21) foundation sketches; 22) architectural criteria; 23) utilities, steam, water, and power requirements; 24) preliminary process piping and instruments; 25) preliminary motor lists; 26) substation designs and specifications; 27) capital cost estimates for mine and surface plants; 28) operating costs for mining, concentrating, smelter, and general functions; and 29) financial analysis of the project.

During the first year, while these analyses are under way, it is assumed that the project continues to be viable. At the beginning of the second year, the engineering contractor should assign a number of engineers to the project. About 50% of the total engineering effort should be expended to produce a capital cost estimate that will be accurate within 10% of the final costs (Fig. 1).

To avoid delays in the construction schedule, items for which delivery will require a long time are ordered six to eight months before completing the definitive estimate. Usually, terms for cancellations are negotiated to protect the sponsor if the project is disbanded after the definitive estimate is prepared. However, it is most unusual for a project to be terminated at such a late date.

It is assumed that the project continues to be attractive upon completion of the definitive estimate and that the sponsors promptly authorize development of the mine and construction of surface facilities.

After that, two more years are required to get the operation into full production. Concurrent with the start of construction, removal of overburden begins, with completion timed to coincide with the scheduled date for completion of construction. To defer large, early expenditures for earth moving equipment, overburden is removed by a stripping contractor.

The estimated expenditures for the various stages of the hypothetical project are shown by time periods in Table 1, and the percent of the total cost expended by years is indicated in Table 2. Fig. 1 shows the accuracy of capital cost estimates in relation to the amounts of incurred capital expenditures and the degree of completion of total engineering.

With this schedule, less than 2% of the total cost of the project will be spent in the first year, before completion of the final feasibility study, and only about 10% of the total cost will be spent in the first two years—to the point when the definitive estimate is completed. At that point, the accuracy of capital costs should be within 10%. The production and operating cost schedules should also be quite accurate. Thus, the relia-

Table 2—Project costs as percentages of total, by years

	Year 0 Preliminary feasibility presented	Year 1 Final feasibility completed	Year 2 Definitive estimate completed	Year 3 Detailed engineering completed	Year 4 Construction completed
Mine					
Exploration appraisal	0.18%				
Drilling and mine planning		0.5%			
Removing overburden and stripping				2.4%	2.4%
Procurement of equipment			0.9%	4.0%	6.3%
Surface plants					
Engineering and home office expense	0.02%	0.6%	1.5%	1.7%	0.4%
Field construction			6.7%	36.7%	35.7%
Totals	0.2%*	1.1%	9.1%	44.8%	44.8%
Cumulative totals	0.2%	1.3%	10.4%	55.2%	100.0%

*Expenses before presenting preliminary feasibility study include geological appraisal of region; 200-ft grid drilling to confirm anomaly; estimating tons, grade, and geometry; order-of-magnitude estimates of capital and operating costs; and preparation of preliminary feasibility study.

Table 3—Production parameters

Tons ore mined per operating day	40,000
Tons waste removed per operating day	60,000
Operating days per year	357
Tons ore mined per year	14,280,000
Tons waste removed per year	21,420,000
Tons, ore plus waste, per year	35,700,000
Ore grade, percent copper	0.60
Percent recovered: ore to copper	81.7
Pounds copper produced per ton ore	9.8
Tons copper produced per year	70,000

Table 4—Operating cost

	Cost per ton of ore	Cost per year	Cost per lb of copper
Direct			
Mining[1]	$0.804	$11,480,000	$0.082
Concentrating[2]	1.304	18,620,000	0.133
Smelting, freight, and refining	2.157	30,800,000	0.220
General[3]	0.784	11,200,000	0.080
Subtotals	$5.049	$72,100,000	$0.515
Indirect			
(non-operating)[4]	0.441	6,300,000	0.045
Totals	$5.490	$78,400,000	$0.560

1) Mining costs include removing waste material, mining and transporting ore to primary crusher, and reserves set aside for future mine development. 2) Milling costs include crushing, grinding, concentrating, and de-watering concentrates and tailings; tailings disposal; process water; delivering concentrate to smelter; and reserves for developing future tailings storage. 3) General costs include local administration expenses, local taxes, FICA cost, and insurance. 4) General nonoperating expenses include expense from sales, exploration, research, and administration allocated from the headquarters.

bility of the project will have been established before the beginning of large expenditures.

How lenders may view loan postponements

With the above analysis in mind, how would lenders evaluate postponement of formal credit commitments? Table 5 provides a summary of net cash flow statements for different leverage structures, assuming also three separate debt repayment schedules. The cash flows were developed using the production and operating cost schedules in Tables 3 and 4. Leverage for the hypothetical project (i.e., the ratio of total debt to equity) was varied at 75:25, 50:50, and 25:75. It was assumed that the overall tenor of the loans could not exceed eight years from the time of commitment to the date of final repayment. The grace period, or the timing of loan drawdown, was varied at four years, three years, and two years prior to the scheduled commencement of production. Repayment of loans was to be made in equal semiannual installments over the first four, five, and six years of operations, respectively. In total, our findings are based on nine separate cash flow simulations.

Table 5—Cash flows for various leverage structures and debt schedules
(million US dollars)

Leverage structure, debt/equity	Eight-year debt, grace/repay	Year 1	Year 2	Year 3	Year 4	Year 5	Year 6	Each subsequent year
25:75	4:4	19.44	20.44	21.39	22.36	41.84	41.84	41.84
25:75	3:5	23.14	23.92	24.70	25.48	26.26	41.84	41.84
25:75	2:6	25.61	26.25	26.91	27.55	28.21	28.85	41.84
50:50	4:4	−2.97	−1.02	0.93	2.88	41.84	41.84	41.84
50:50	3:5	4.43	5.99	7.55	9.11	10.67	41.84	41.84
50:50	2:6	9.37	10.67	11.97	13.27	14.57	15.87	41.84
75:25	4:4	−25.38	−22.47	−19.53	−16.60	41.84	41.84	41.84
75:25	3:5	−14.27	−11.93	−9.59	−7.25	−4.91	41.84	41.84
75:25	2:6	−6.87	−4.92	−2.97	−1.02	0.93	2.88	41.84

* These cash flows (equivalent to accounting cash flow less loan principal repayments) were used to develop the data in Tables 1, 2, and 4. Assumptions: copper price of 85¢; depreciation expense of $30 million annually; tax rate of 48%; interest rate of 10% annually.

Table 6—Cash flow/debt coverage ratio

Leverage structure, debt/equity	Eight-year debt, grace/repay	Year 1	Year 2	Year 3	Year 4	Year 5	Year 6
25:75	4:4	1.75	1.85	1.97	2.11	—	—
25:75	3:5	2.05	2.16	2.23	2.44	2.63	—
25:75	2:6	2.30	2.42	2.56	2.73	2.92	3.15
50:50	4:4	0.94	0.98	1.02	1.07	—	—
50:50	3:5	1.10	1.14	1.20	1.26	1.33	—
50:50	2:6	1.24	1.29	1.35	1.42	1.50	1.59
75:25	4:4	0.67	0.69	0.71	0.73	—	—
75:25	3:5	0.78	0.81	0.83	0.86	0.89	—
75:25	2:6	0.88	0.91	0.94	0.98	1.02	1.07

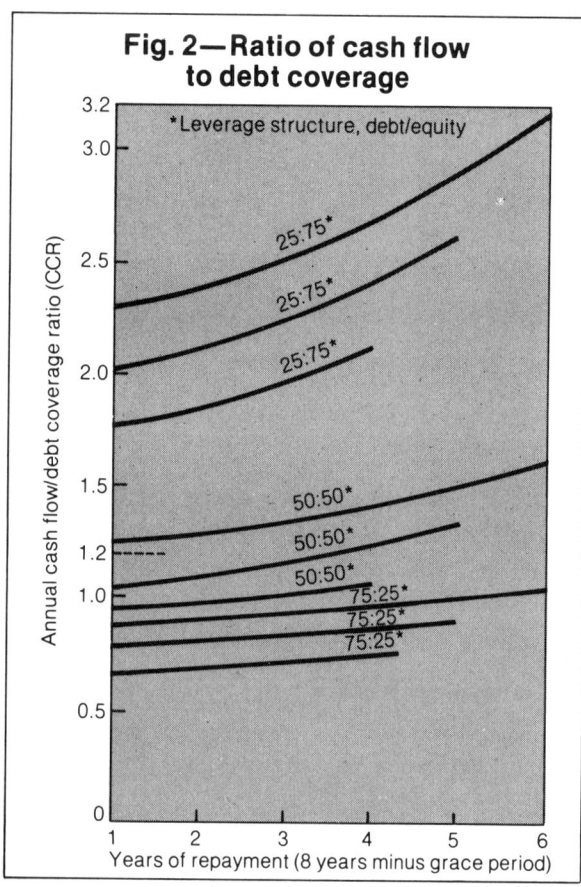

Fig. 2—Ratio of cash flow to debt coverage

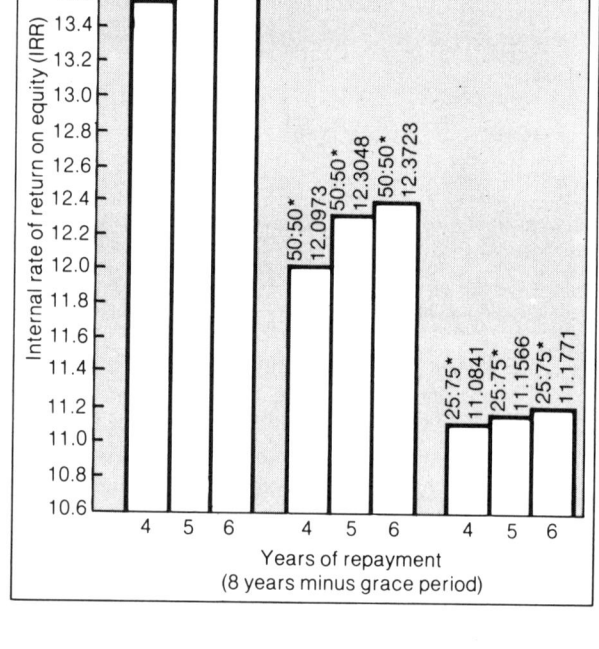

Fig. 3—Internal rate of return on equity

The ratio of annual cash flow to debt coverage is considered here to be one of the most important credit criteria. It is defined as:

$$CCR = \frac{NI + D + I - CE}{P + I}$$

where CCR = ratio of cash flow to debt coverage, NI = income, D = depreciation and other noncash charges, I = interest expense, CE = capital expenditure during years of operation, and P = principal debt repayments.

When the annual CCR falls below 1.00, cash flow generation is insufficient to meet the scheduled debt payments. In practice, a projected cash flow/debt coverage ratio of less than 1.20 (Fig. 2) would probably be unacceptable to most lenders, given conservative assumptions of all project variables and of prices.

Table 6 and Fig. 2 display the results of simulations for the CCR. All variables except debt and interest charges remain constant. Within a given leverage structure, a dramatic improvement in the CCR is produced simply by shortening the grace period and extending repayment by the corresponding amount of time. With a leverage characteristic of 50% debt and 50% equity, the hypothetical project could not be financed with grace and repayment periods of four years each because the projected CCR range, from 0.94 to 1.07, would be inadequate. Deferring the loan commitment to the end of the second year of construction and stretching the repayment period by two years produces CCRs in the range of 1.24 to 1.59, which would make the project significantly more attractive to lenders.

Loan postponement: the sponsors' viewpoint

The above analyses of cash flows from a lender's point of view have to be contrasted with the perspective of the sponsors: namely, does early funding of the project expenditures with equity money result in a reduction of the rate of return on equity? Table 7 and Fig. 3 show test results. Cash flows available to sponsors (accounting cash flow less principal loan repayments) was discounted on different equity bases over a period of 20 years. Perhaps surprisingly, internal rate of return (IRR) on

Table 7—Internal rate of return on equity

Leverage structure, debt/equity	Eight-year debt, grace/repay	IRR on equity, %
25:75	4:4	11.0841
25:75	3:5	11.1566
25:75	2:6	11.1771
50:50	4:4	12.0973
50:50	3:5	12.3048
50:50	2:6	12.3723
75:25	4:4	13.5714
75:25	3:5	14.0713
75:25	2:6	14.2347

About the authors

Tomek Ulatowski is an assistant vice president of the Bank of America in the project financing group of its World Banking Div. in San Francisco. His responsibilities include arranging financing for complex natural resources ventures and advising private companies on capital structuring and funding arrangements.

Edward S. Frohling is president of Mountain States Mineral Enterprises Inc., of Tucson, a company serving the mining industry worldwide as consultant in engineering design, mining and metallurgical technology, geology, exploration, and development. In the past, he has served as research engineer and chief plant metallurgist for Climax Molybdenum, mill superintendent for St. Lawrence Fluorspar, sales manager for Western Knapp Engineering Co., and sales vice president for Parsons-Jurden Corp.

F. Milton Lewis is an internationally known mining and metallurgical engineer. For the past six years, he has been a consultant to Mountain States Mineral Enterprises. For many years previously, he served as assistant to the general manager of the Copperhill, Tenn., operations of Cities Service.

---

equity increases, instead of decreasing, despite heavier equity outlays in the early phases of construction. In the case of a 75% debt and 25% equity leverage structure, the IRR rises from 13.5% to 14.23% when the only changes are an extension of the repayment schedule from four years to six years and the sponsors' assumption of 100% of the project costs in the first two years of construction.

Analysis of changes in the cash flow/debt coverage ratio (Fig. 2) and return on equity as a result of different leverage structures (Fig. 3) is also interesting. As anticipated, higher leverage produces a higher internal rate of return, but the difference is not as pronounced as one might expect. For instance, comparing a test run of 75:25 debt-to-equity structure with a test run of 25:75, with a schedule of four years' grace and four years for repayment of debt, the IRR on equity in the first case, in absolute terms, is only 2.49% higher (Table 7). The effect on the average annual cash flow/debt coverage ratio, however, is more significant, increasing from 0.70 in the first simulation to 1.92 in the second.

There is another important reason for project sponsors to finance directly the early development costs. As shown in Fig. 1, the accuracy of the capital cost estimate rises disproportionately faster than incurred expenditures. For example, payout of the initial 10.4% of the project cost gives the sponsors, as well as the lenders, a fairly comfortable final capital cost margin of plus 10%, while at the time of preliminary feasibility, this margin is as much as plus 30%. An increase in the level of confidence in the projected capital cost estimate, and the reliability of the project in general, considerably enhances its appeal to potential lenders.

It is our observation that sponsors of many mining ventures may not devote enough time to financing questions. The industry has reached the point where financing costs often exceed total operating costs per unit of output in new operations. It is essential that internal as well as external constraints confronting the sponsors be well recognized in the early planning phases of project development. Positive alternatives for capital structuring must be developed to prevent unnecessary delays at a later stage.

We believe that the basic findings presented in this article are valid for most projects. Each mining venture has distinct characteristics, which may require different approaches. However, sponsors must always view new project developments not only in the context of the company's capital allocation problems but also in terms of financeability of the mining ventures. □

Major slope failures occurred at this southwestern US copper mine in October 1970, after nearly a year of minor problems with slope instability. Pit sections several hundred feet long, consisting of several benches, were displaced.

How to cut risk of slope failure in designing optimum pit slopes

Dr. Ben L. Seegmiller, principal, Seegmiller Associates, Salt Lake City

THE PROFITABILITY OF AN OPEN-PIT OPERATION depends to a large extent on use of the steepest pit slopes possible—provided they do not fail during the life of the mine. Optimum pit slopes can be designed by using rock mechanics technology. Such technology includes gathering and analyzing pertinent data prior to pit design; rigorous application of rock mechanics principles during the design process; remedial actions to improve slope stability; and monitoring slopes during the life of the mine. To ignore rock mechanics technology in pit design is to place the entire mining enterprise in jeopardy.

Disruption of mining operations and safety hazards caused by slope instability can be severe. A classic case in point is the major slope failure[3] that occurred at a southwestern US copper mining operation in 1970-71. Minor slope stability problems first became apparent as early as 1969 but were limited to zones immediately adjacent to major faults. The stability problems initially amounted to no more than a nuisance, but in time, the unstable zones became larger, causing greater disruption of production and threatening safety. By late 1971, major failure had occurred, at a severe cost in production.

Mining at or near the slide toe had continued throughout the period of slope failure. This caused continued slope instability, which occurred on adversely dipping, weak geologic discontinuities.

The original plan for this mine called for bringing the overall pit slope to 37.5°. This plan would have resulted in exposing a major orebody at depth. Mining began with the backslope as planned, but slope failures that occurred after mining less than 100 vertical ft of bedrock forced the mine operators to lessen the backslope angle, in the hope that the failing rock mass would stabilize. However, stabilization did not take place, and as mining continued, the backslope angle was further reduced. When mining in the area of failure was completed, the overall slope had been reduced to approximately 27°. Mining had been successful in removing only a small portion of the orebody, at a high stripping ratio.

The case of this southwestern mine is not unique. Mining operations are disrupted and safety problems are caused by slope instability in numerous other mines throughout the world. In South America, a major slope failure halted all pit operations when sections of the mainline rail haulage system were destroyed. For more than three years, a giant iron mine in Australia has been hampered by safety hazards and mining interruptions caused by slope failure extending over 1 mi. In 1975, an operation

Continued instability at the copper pit caused failure of virtually the entire slope by mid-1971, and the slope was in continuous movement. By late 1971, the failure affected more than 500 vertical feet of rock and 100 vertical feet of alluvium.

in the western US suffered one of the few fatalities ever recorded in an open-pit copper mine as the result of slope failure.

Many mining companies have experienced damage to fixed structures located near the pit rim or inside the pit; many crushing facilities in such locations have been disabled by slope instability.

What can be done to stabilize slopes?

Fortunately, the study of failing rock masses, especially in open pits, has received much attention from experts over the past 10 years. Remedial action, including dewatering,[2] slope modification, and artificial stabilization,[4,5,6] is available to the mine operator. Safety hazards and disruptive effects of failure can be minimized. The safety aspects of slope instability have been greatly improved through the use of displacement monitoring techniques. (See E/MJ, June 1976, p 189, and September 1976, p 104.) Not only has monitoring and recording equipment been improved, but better techniques[7] have been developed to interpret data on instability.

Prevention of slope instability—a most important goal—may be achieved if optimum slope angles are determined when the mine is still in the planning stage. Using rock mechanics technology, planners can determine a sound engineering choice for optimum bench profiles and overall slope angles by using the following procedures:

- Begin an initial assessment of the important stability parameters as soon as it is apparent that a future open pit will be a reality.
- Start a detailed stability study as soon as possible after completion of the initial assessment.
- Collect as much stability data as possible during exploration and/or development drilling.

Such stability data will be concerned with factors of geologic discontinuities and discontinuity shear strengths, as well as with groundwater and seismic forces that may come into play. Potential modes of failure will be analyzed. Probability of failure, required safety factors, and the recommendation of optimum slope angles will be developed. All potential methods for improving stability and for taking remedial action in appropriate areas will be reviewed. A monitoring system will be programmed for the life of the pit. The payoffs of such stability studies have previously been discussed by engineers.[1,2] The emphasis is now on achieving practical stability results as defined by

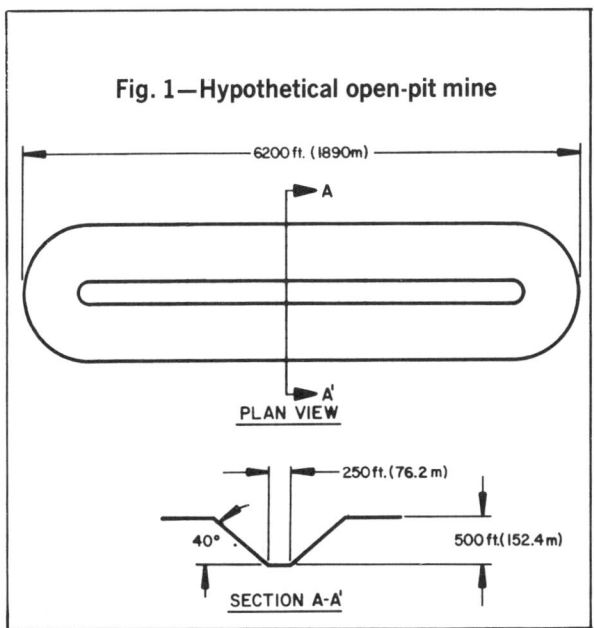

Fig. 1—Hypothetical open-pit mine

safety and economic considerations—as opposed to simply achieving stability.

The payoff in stripping requirements

An increase or decrease in slope angle in a moderate-sized to large open pit will significantly alter stripping requirements. Consider the open-pit plan and section shown in Fig. 1. The hypothetical pit is 6,200 ft in length from crest to crest, the width of the bottom floor is 250 ft from toe to toe, the vertical depth is 500 ft, the overall slope angle is 40°, and the unit weight of material is 165 lb per cu ft. If the slope angle could be increased safely to 45°, stripping would be reduced by approximately 25 million tons. Conversely, if the slope had originally been laid out at 45° and slope instability factors subsequently forced a reduction in slope angle to 40°, the increased stripping of 25 million tons required to maintain stability would significantly alter operations.

Fig. 2 graphically points up the significant changes in stripping required by small changes in slope angles. Such changes strongly affect the long term profitability of a mining operation, emphasizing the need for determining optimum slope angles during the planning stage.

Allow for variations in pit slope design

Some parts of a pit will generally have better stability factors than others; therefore, some parts of the pit slopes can be designed for steeper angles. Slope failure can be prevented by flattening slope angles or by other remedial actions in those parts of pit where stability factors are adverse. To achieve improved slopes, the desired mining plans must be closely studied, data affecting stability must be collected and analyzed, and a sound engineering approach implemented for operations.

Collecting stability data: prerequisite for design

The purpose of collecting geologic discontinuity data on faults, joints, and bedding planes is to determine the possible modes, sizes, and locations of potential slope failures.

The most important features governing the stability of a pit slope are planes of weakness. To design optimum slope angles, the location and orientation of planes of weakness must be known. Methods of obtaining discontinuity data include on-site surface mapping and oriented borehole core logging. Where rock outcrops are available, surface mapping may provide important data on the occurrence and orientation of faults, dikes, bedding planes, and joint sets. Surface mapping has the advantage of providing information on the continuity and the planarity of the discontinuities. However, such data may not be truly representative of the important structures at depth. Additional discontinuity data should be obtained from borehole core by orienting the core during drilling.

Several methods[8] of orienting core are available. (One orienting device is shown in an accompanying photo.) Borehole core is commonly collected to investigate, sample, and delineate orebodies. It is simple and inexpensive to extend the use of the core to rock mechanics studies. The core gives a reasonably good indication of the unweathered conditions that will prevail in a future slope at depth. The discontinuities may be obtained virtually intact with infilling materials if drilling systems utilize split tube core barrels. Where loose, decomposed overburden or dense plant growth covers a deposit, oriented core may provide the only means for determining discontinuity orientations. Where both surface outcrop mapping and core

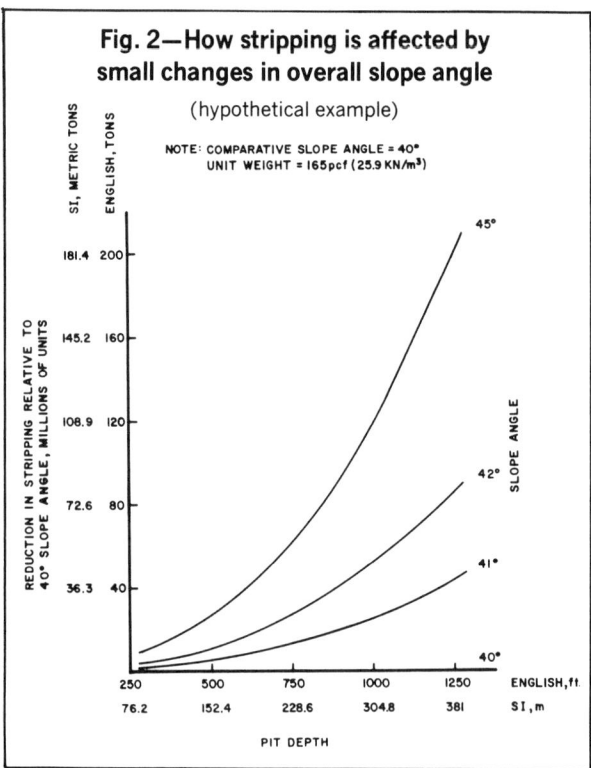

Fig. 2—How stripping is affected by small changes in overall slope angle
(hypothetical example)

NOTE: COMPARATIVE SLOPE ANGLE = 40°
UNIT WEIGHT = 165pcf (25.9 KN/m³)

logging can be performed, each method can be used to substantiate the findings provided by the other.

Discontinuity data should, at the least, include information on discontinuity types and locations, orientations, type of filling, thickness, hardness, relative roughness, spacing, and—if applicable—planarity and continuity.

How to predict discontinuity shear strength

The possibility of displacement along a certain discontinuity in a pit slope does not imply that such displacement is highly probable. Mechanical characteristics of rock materials determine how they will react to given stress concentrations. Stress concentrations increase as pit slopes become higher and steeper. To design optimum pit slopes for a future open pit, it is necessary to determine the amount of stress that its rock discontinuities will withstand. The reaction of a rock discontinuity to stress can be reasonably predicted if its shear strength parameters (sliding angle of friction and cohesion) are known. If the reaction has been determined, the likelihood of displacement can be ascertained.

The parameters of discontinuity shear strength can be determined by a direct shear test. The method involves selecting specific discontinuity samples (borehole core generally makes an ideal sample) and testing them with a direct shear apparatus. (See photo.) The direct shear apparatus allows the resistance to shearing along the discontinuity to be determined under loads similar to those expected in the future open-pit slope. Resistance to shearing is a function of the magnitude of the loads or normal forces that are applied to the discontinuity. In a simplified manner, the strength of a dry rock discontinuity can be represented by the equation:

$$S = F_N \tan \phi + CA$$

where

S = discontinuity strength (resistance to failure)

The Craelius Core Orientator provides the drill core orientation needed for collection of discontinuity data.

F_N = normal force across discontinuity
Tan ϕ = tangent of the angle of sliding friction
C = cohesional resistance on discontinuity
A = area of discontinuity

From the equation, it is evident that higher normal loads (i.e., higher values of F_N) result in higher discontinuity strength S. At very deep positions in a pit slope, the value of S will be higher for constant values of ϕ and C. Unfortunately, it is also true that at greater depths in a pit slope, there are greater shear forces—the forces that create unstable slopes. From a series of direct shear tests, the characteristic shear strength parameters, ϕ and C, of a particular discontinuity may be determined. This information, when combined with other stability data, serves to determine the optimum slope angles for a future open pit.

Adverse effects of groundwater on rock strength

While geologic discontinuities are the single most important factor in slope stability, the presence of and conditions created by groundwater are certainly a close second. The major adverse effect of groundwater is to reduce the shear strength of the rock discontinuities. In analytical terms, the major effect may be exemplified by rewriting the equation for the shear strength of a dry discontinuity, to allow for presence of groundwater:

$$S = (F_N - U) \text{Tan } \phi + CA$$

where
U = water uplift force normal to the discontinuity

The groundwater causes an uplifting or unweighting of the normal load across a discontinuity, thereby reducing the discontinuity's shear strength. The uplifting force U is a function of the density and head of the water at the point in question on the discontinuity.

A further effect of groundwater may be horizontal thrust. If an open tension crack exists in the slope, and surface runoff or groundwater flow fills the crack, a horizontal force will be exerted. The horizontal thrust, which also is a function of water density and head, will act in such a manner as to induce slope failure. In both uplift and horizontal thrust, remember that groundwater head or pressure—not groundwater flow—causes a reduction in the shear strength.

Methods of determining how much groundwater pressure may exist in the slopes of a future open-pit mine include analysis of the overall groundwater environment and direct measurement. Analysis of the overall groundwater environment may include studies of the sources of groundwater and the permeability of the rock mass. Such studies may become quite complex, but reasonable estimates of the significant factors can usually provide data sufficient for stability analysis. Because pit slopes vary widely in their hydrologic environments, detailed hydrology studies may be more important for the design of one open-pit mine than for another.

Direct measurement of groundwater pressures is essential during the process of collecting data on slope stability. The most convenient method of directly measuring groundwater pressures is placement of piezometers in boreholes located in the zones of interest. A piezometer can be an open hole or observation well, or it may be a sophisticated instrument placed at a specific location in a borehole. Open-hole piezometers are sufficient for relatively high permeabilities, but may be entirely inadequate for situations of low permeability.

When a stability study for a future open-pit mine is undertaken, there may be reasonable doubt as to the relative permeability of the rock mass. For this reason, the use of more sophisticated piezometers, such as the air-actuated variety, is recommended. (See photo.) They should be in-

Direct shear testing machine for borehole core provides good data on discontinuity shear strength.

stalled no later than the time when final orebody delineation holes are bored, for two reasons. First, when a costly borehole is completed, piezometer installation is simple, and such multiple use of exploratory boreholes yields major cost savings. Second, early installation of a piezometer permits a history of groundwater pressure changes to be recorded for study.

Because most groundwater systems exhibit a seasonal variation, a record over a period of at least one year can prove beneficial in predicting potential pressures during the wettest months of the year. Direct measurement of the rainfall and its correlation to changes in groundwater pressure will not only help deduce maximum potential pressure, but will also help determine seasonal periods when remedial action must be taken to prevent surface runoff from flowing into tension cracks.

While the effect of groundwater on slope stability cannot be overstated for any mine, the effects of seismic forces also are important for mines located in zones of high seismic activity. Collection of historic records on earthquake occurrence, intensity, and duration may provide adequate input data. The design of optimum pit slopes should take into account seismic factors if such factors have a moderate to high probability of occurrence.

Using stability analysis in open-pit design

Procedures for stability analysis are series of steps, the first of which is division of the potential pit into zones. The geometry may be different for each zone. However, the general slope geometry—especially the strike of the slope—within a given zone should be approximately constant. If the stability data (discontinuities, shear strength, ground water, etc.) change substantially within a given zone, the zone should be subdivided into smaller zones of similar characteristics. Analyzing a series of zones with specific common characteristics is easier than analyzing an entire pit replete with complex variables.

The second step in stability analysis is assembly of all discontinuity data for a particular zone, followed by failure mode analysis. Such analysis yields the possible modes of failure for the zone: circular, planar, wedge, and/or toppling. Analysis should include determination of the probability of failure, and the safety factor in the event of failure. Sensitivity analysis of stability variables can help establish the best procedures for remedial action. Finally, recommendations are made for bench profiles and overall slope angles for each zone of the open pit.

Piezometer readout unit in the field measures pressure of groundwater—often a significant factor in slope stability.

Recommended bench profiles and overall slope angles*
(hypothetical example)

	Individual bench profiles				Overall slope	
Zone	Alternating widths	Height	Bench angle	Width of Sloped portion	Maximum height	Slope angle
I	4 & 10 m	15 m	59°	9 m	141 m	45.1°
II	4 & 10 m	15 m	59°	9 m	182 m	44.7°
III	4 & 10 m	15 m	59°	9 m	182 m	44.7°
IV	4 & 8 m	15 m	65°	7 m	156 m	51.3°
V	4 & 10 m	15 m	75°	4 m	152 m	56.2°
VI	4 & 8 m	15 m	65°	7 m	186 m	50.9°
VII	10 & 10 m	15 m	75°	4 m	268 m	48.2°**
VIII	4 & 10 m	15 m	56°	9 m	298 m	44.1°**
IX	3 & 7 m	15 m	59°	9 m	130 m	49.4°
X	4 & 8 m	15 m	65°	7 m	168 m	51.1°
XI	4 & 8 m	15 m	75°	4 m	125 m	57.5°
XII	4 & 8 m	15 m	75°	4 m	156 m	58.9°

*Based on a minimum safety factor of 1.2 and a probability of failure of 10% or less.
**Must effectively dewater this zone or additionally reduce slope angle at least 6°.

The circular failure mode, or failure by rotational shear, is generally confined to soils or soft rock materials such as near-surface overburden. When such materials are encountered, standard circular analysis techniques should be used. While planar failure and wedge failure can occur in a variety of materials, they are commonly associated with hard rock slopes. Both planar and wedge failure mode analyses can be accomplished using stereographic projection techniques,[9] a method that traces the geologic discontinuity sets and the pit slope onto a stereographic projection overlay. Discontinuities and discontinuity intersections that undercut pit slope (i.e., dip at lesser angles) are presumed to be possible planar failure and wedge failure modes, respectively.

Further stability analyses are necessary for shear strength, groundwater conditions, and seismic forces, which can contribute to all possible failure modes. Discontinuities or discontinuity intersections that do not undercut a slope are not considered to be failure modes, and no further analyses of these modes are necessary.

Toppling failures commonly occur where columnar blocks of rock are created by several sets of discontinuities, particularly joints. When the weight vector of a particular columnar block no longer passes through the base of the block, toppling can occur. Most toppling failures are only a cleanup problem along benches and do not affect major overall slopes.

A stability analysis should be made whenever a particular mode of failure is considered possible. In essence, stability analysis determines the ratios of shearing strength to shearing force existing in a particular slope zone. The magnitude of the shearing strength is a function of the shear strength parameters, groundwater pressures, and seismic forces acting on the potential failure plane. The shearing force is primarily a function of gravity but may be increased by groundwater pressures and seismic forces. From the shearing strength-force ratios, a safety factor against failure and/or a probability of failure can be determined.

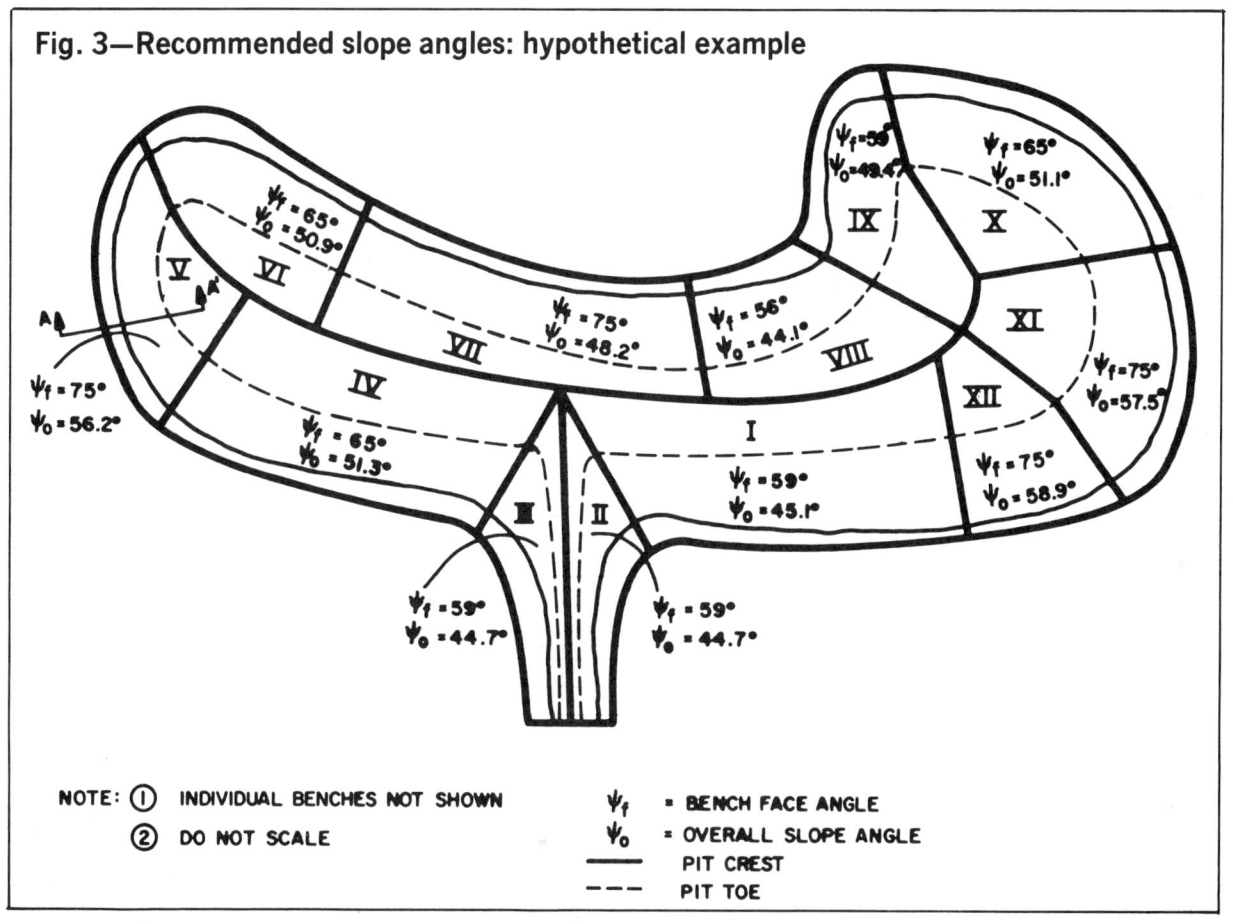

Fig. 3—Recommended slope angles: hypothetical example

A sensitivity analysis can be conducted to determine the effects of remedial action techniques—changing the strike of the pit slope, the slope angle, adding artificial stabilization to the slope, and dewatering the slope. The most important variables are determined from such a sensitivity analysis. Possible modification of these variables can be attempted to achieve slopes that conform to established safety requirements. As an example, a safety factor between 1.2 and 1.3 and/or a probability of failure of less than 10% may be required. Bench profiles and overall slope angles can then be recommended for each zone analyzed for the pit. Presumably, these recommended slopes are the optimum slopes—from a stability standpoint—available for initial pit planning and mining.

The recommendations can conveniently be presented in table form, in plan, and in section. Such forms of recommendations for a hypothetical example are shown in the accompanying table and in Fig. 3 and Fig. 4, respectively.

How remedial actions can improve slope stability

The specific purpose of any remedial action is to improve slope stability and minimize potential safety hazards. Remedial measures include rubble cleanup, acknowledgement of critical zones, dewatering, blast control, artificial stabilization, and displacement monitoring.

While loose rubble generally amounts to no more than a nuisance, it can present critical safety hazards that can be minimized by cleaning the rubble from loose, raveling benches. However, access to such benches with cleanup equipment is often a problem during mining operations. Use of bench profiles with alternating bench widths may offer a solution (Fig. 4). Such alternating bench widths allow a much wider bench every 98.4 ft, to which long term access could more likely be maintained. Periodic cleanup along benches, together with a 3- to 6-ft berm along the outer edge of the bench, may prevent most rock falls.

Monitoring zones of potential slope failure is the ongoing response to previous work. Stability and sensitivity analyses allow in-depth investigation of potentially critical slope zones, pinpointing where special attention should be directed while mining is in progress. These zones should be inspected periodically for tension cracks and other signs of instability.

Groundwater is one stability factor over which some control can usually be exerted during mining. Dewatering will almost always pay for itself as a low cost remedy to improve slope stability—specifically, when sensitivity analyses have indicated that either a particular slope must be dewatered or its slope angle must be reduced by 5° or more.

Blast control techniques such as presplitting and smooth wall blasting may preserve the natural strength of near-surface discontinuities. As most blast control techniques are expensive and limited in effectiveness, cost vs. anticipated results should receive close consideration before any large blast control program is put into effect. Judicious use in specific zones may be one approach.

Artificial stabilization techniques have proved to be effective in improving slope stability under the right conditions.[6] Such techniques, including the use of cable anchors, can represent a sizable investment, and a thorough study should be conducted before committing a mining operation to large scale artificial stabilization projects. Small scale projects—those which might be directed at improving slope stability in the vicinity of an in-pit crusher—may prove very favorable economically. Specific recommendations for the use of artificial support systems can be part of the total rock mechanics approach to maintaining slope stability.

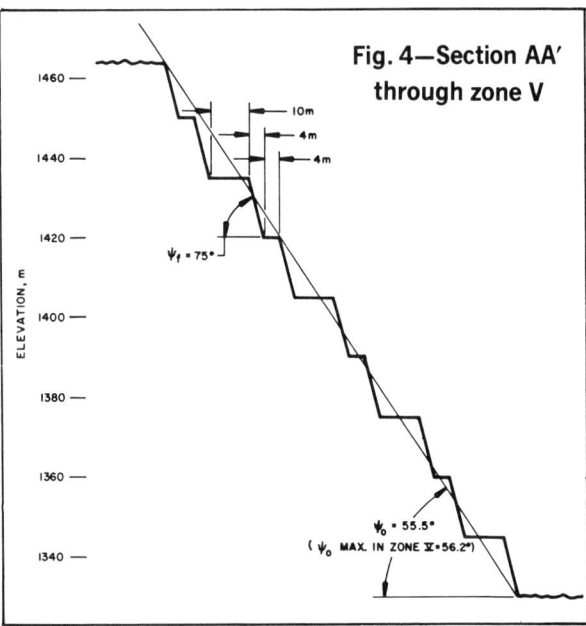

Fig. 4—Section AA' through zone V

A displacement monitoring plan, with implementation procedures spelled out in detail, should be part of the overall approach to achieving slope stability. Optimum slope angles may necessarily include some relatively steep slopes, which should be monitored along with the more sensitive zones to anticipate and prevent safety hazards. Displacement monitoring can serve as a tool for determining, in advance, the best time for undertaking appropriate adjustments or actions.

Rock mechanics studies should start early

To achieve optimum pit slopes at the lowest possible cost, rock mechanics studies should begin as soon as practicable, preferably during exploration and/or development drilling. Combining the collection of stability data with the collection of data for ore delineation is the surest way to minimize costs of rock mechanics studies. The core can be oriented to obtain discontinuity data; selected pieces of core can be used for direct shear tests; and the borehole can be used for emplacement of a piezometer. Obtaining such stability data during ore delineation drilling in no way interferes with the appraisal of the economic geology. In fact, it broadens the knowledge about the prospective pit. □

References

1) Stewart, R. M., and B. L. Seegmiller, "Requirements for Stability in Open Pit Mining," *Geotechnical Practice for Stability in Open Pit Mining*, AIME-SME, New York, 1972, pp 1-7.
2) Seegmiller, Ben L., "Slope Stability Research: Its Payoff in Mining," MINING CONGRESS JOURNAL, Vol. 59, No. 7, July 1973, pp 32-39.
3) Seegmiller, Ben L., "Rock Stability Analysis at Twin Buttes," *Proceedings of the 13th Symposium on Rock Mechanics* (University of Illinois at Urbana), ASCE, New York, 1972, pp 511-536.
4) Seegmiller, Ben L., "Artificial Stabilization of a Pit Slope at Twin Buttes, Arizona," MINING ENGINEERING, Vol. 26, No. 12, Dec. 1974, pp 29-34.
5) Coates, D. F., and R. Sage, "Rock Anchors in Mining," CANMET, Mines Branch, TB181, Nov. 1973, p 50.
6) Seegmiller, Ben L., "Cable Bolts Stabilize Pit Slopes, Steepen Walls to Strip Less Waste," WORLD MINING, Vol. 28, No. 7, July 1975, pp 36-41.
7) Seegmiller, Ben L., "Time-Dependent Output from In-Situ Measurements: Its Meaning with Respect to Stability," Presymposium Seminar, 9th Canadian Rock Mechanics Symposium, Ecole Polytechnique, Montreal, Que., Dec. 1974.
8) Seegmiller, Ben. L., "Site Characterization Using Oriented Borehole Core," *Proceedings of the 17th Symposium on Rock Mechanics*, University of Utah, Snowbird, Utah, August 25-27, 1976.
9) Goodman, R. E., *Methods of Geological Engineering*, West, San Francisco, 1976, p 472.

Electronic distance measuring instruments bounce laser, infrared, or microwave beams off reflectors and back to the instrument, where distance is calculated electronically. Above is a Geodimeter 710 electronic angle and distance instrument.

Pit slope displacement monitoring: an aid to open-pit mine operation

Allan M. R. MacRae, MacRae Rock Mechanics

SLOPE FAILURES EXACT A LARGE, UNPREDICTABLE SUM from the open-pit mining industry every year, and fatalities and large-scale equipment damage are not the only forms of loss. Direct cost for removal of slide material is considerable, and indirects associated with rescheduling and lost production are significant over the long term.

The measurement of small-scale slope displacements enables a trained engineer to predict future failure and permits the application of remedial measures before failure occurs. Because appropriate slope displacement monitoring systems provide mine operators with effective, low cost insurance against expensive accidents, such systems should be considered for implementation in all operating open-pit mines—not just those that have current stability problems.

This article describes existing slope displacement monitoring systems and some new developments, including information on system accuracy, range, applicability, and cost, based on the author's past projects. Advantages and disadvantages of the systems are discussed, and suggestions are made for future improvements in this field.

Requirements of a monitoring system

Gradual movements of several inches to several feet occur before ultimate failure of slopes in rock and in most soils. A monitoring system that is accurate to ½-1 in. is usually adequate for measurement of slope displacements. Monitoring systems with limited ranges are undesirable, since movements of several tens of feet have frequently been recorded before final failure.

Open-pit mining environments are some of the most hostile locations for sensitive measuring instruments. Blast fly rock, falling rock, heavy equipment operation, and corrosive ground water contribute to a high attrition rate for all permanently mounted instrumentation. Obviously, a large number of low cost installations providing redundancy of readings at the outset are more likely to give meaningful long term results than a lesser number of high cost installations. It is advantageous to use measuring systems in which the major instrumentation is portable and can be stored away from the open pit.

The nature of monitoring problems is distinctive in open-pit mining. Slopes are frequently designed with lower safety factors and with less engineering analysis than corresponding civil engineering works for highway or railway cuts in mountainous terrain. The quality of scaling is usually inferior, and the repeated aggravation of slope stability caused by nearby blasting and excavation continues throughout the life of the mine.

There are some factors, however, that work to a mine operator's advantage. Because the general public is ex-

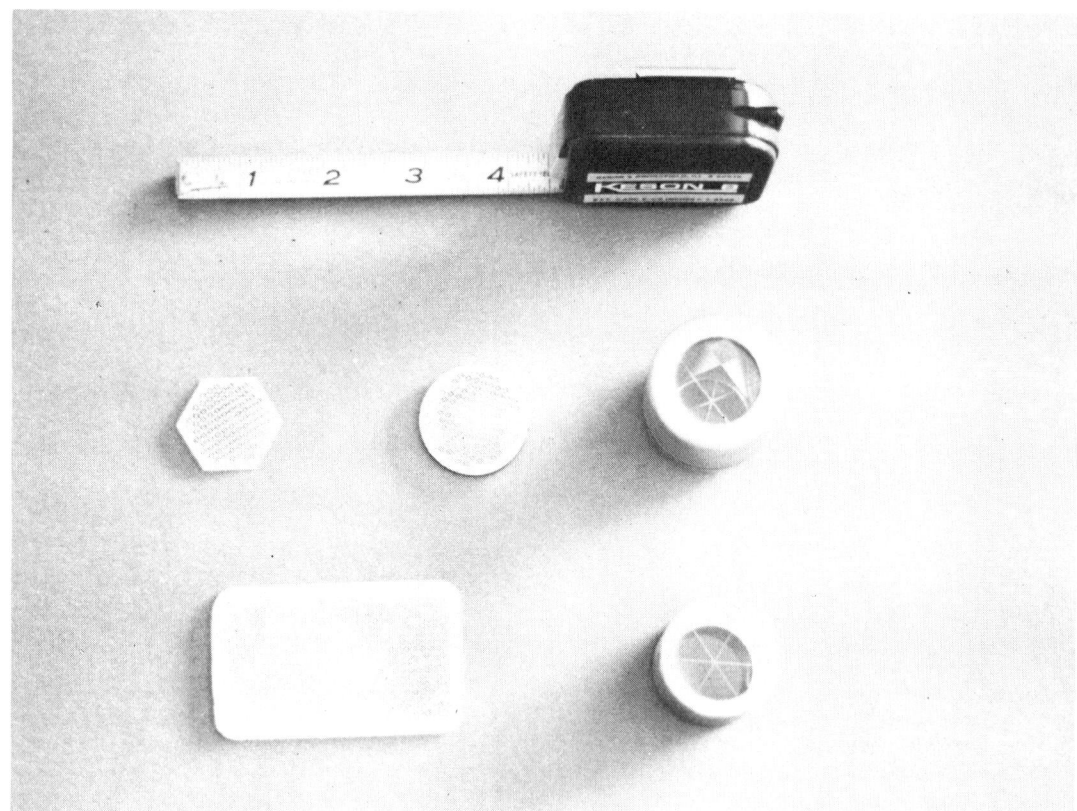

EDM retroreflectors are available in a variety of materials and sizes. The three on the left are plastic, and those on the right are MacRae 1-in. hollow and 1-in. solid glass. Reflector size and quality sharply affect instrument range.

cluded from a mine area, work can continue for limited periods in close proximity to unstable slopes if the ground movement is continuously monitored. At other times, such areas can be cordoned off until failure takes place or stability is restored. Some slope failures can be tolerated, provided they are predicted and properly dealt with in advance.

Monitoring is divided into two categories: detection and measurement. Many measuring systems are available, some much better than others, but none is well suited to initial detection of movement, especially of a small unstable zone located in a large surface of open-pit slope. Initial movement is usually detected by other methods, such as visual inspection, and monitoring is employed on a local scale to measure the degree of instability of the moving rock mass. However, by the time large visible surface cracks are noticed, it may be too late for remedial action. Improved detection systems are urgently needed.

No system is now available for the measurement of movement over continuous large areas of slope, and the monitoring of a finite number of sample points is the best available alternative. However, failure that takes place between sample points will not be detected by the monitoring system, and even small-scale rock falls can cause fatalities and sizable equipment losses. As better monitoring methods are developed, the use of overall slope monitoring systems will become more practical—a great benefit to the open-pit mining industry.

Extensometers, inclinometers, and deflectometers

Extensometers measure change in length between two or more reference points. The simplest are surface-mounted pins measured with a micrometer or tape. Extensometers may also be installed in boreholes to measure movements at depth. Inclinometers, which measure change in inclination, also are available in surface and borehole configurations. Borehole inclinometers and other deflectometers determine the offset of a hole perpendicular to its direction. Accuracies of all these instruments are generally in the range of hundredths or thousandths of an inch.

These units have major practical disadvantages. Either access to the monitoring area is required to take readings, which is often difficult or dangerous, or the units must be equipped with remote readout capability. Such capability is expensive and is susceptible to damage in the hostile working environment. Borehole units are often destroyed by the onset of movement, which causes shearing of the hole long before final failure takes place. The high cost of drilling makes even the simplest borehole instrument a sizable investment, especially since the nonrecoverable expenditure yields displacement results for a very limited area of slope. Application of this type of instrument is valid in certain specific cases, but large expenditures are seldom if ever practical.

How conventional surveying methods work

Conventional surveying systems make use of targets permanently mounted on the slope, with periodic measurement of the target coordinates using high-accuracy optical surveying equipment. Any change in target coordinates greater than system accuracy is attributed to ground movement.

Conventional surveying instruments such as levels and theodolites provide mine operators with what may seem to be an inexpensive monitoring system using available equipment. However, most open-pit mines do not have instruments of sufficient precision on hand, and expenditure

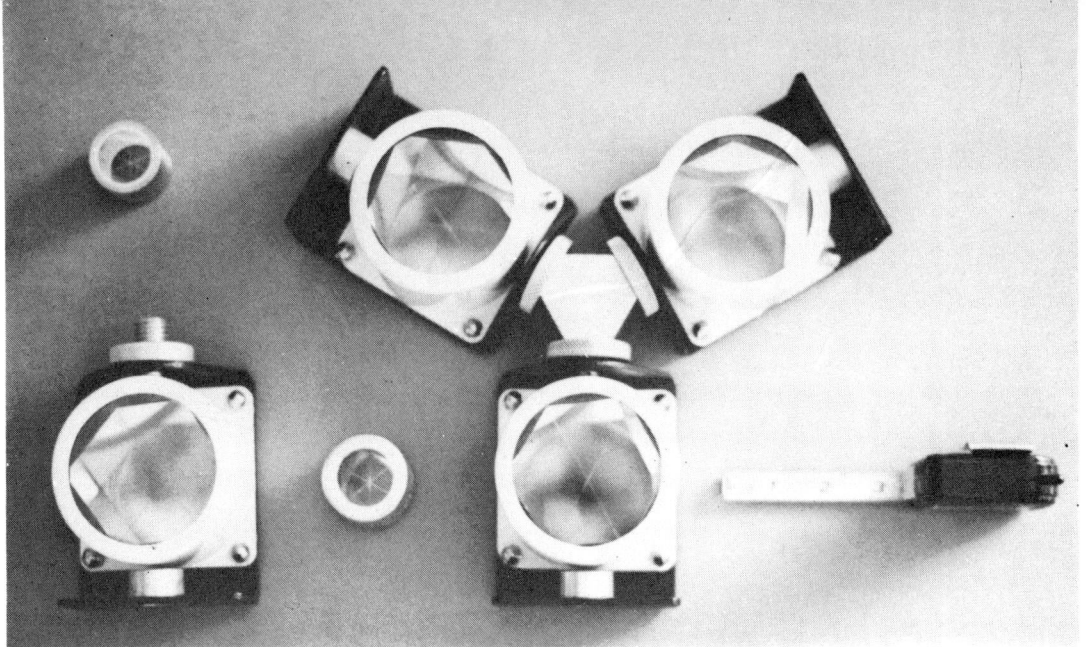

MacRae glass EDM reflectors: (left) 2½-in. hollow single; (right) 2½-in. hollow triple configurations.

of $3,000 to $4,000 would be required for purchase of a typical one-second direct-reading theodolite.

Leveling requires access to measuring points and is relatively inflexible in the typical open-pit because instrument stations and targets must have nearly equal elevations. Triangulation does not necessitate access but does require highly skilled surveyors and is exceedingly slow. (Expert surveyors from the Geodetic Survey of Canada worked for three days to measure 30 points using a Kern DKM-2A instrument in a program supervised by the author. Accuracy was approximately 0.4 in. in 1,000 ft.)

Results of triangulation give the three-dimensional component of movement. Leveling gives only the vertical component, which is adequate in some cases, provided the direction of slope failure is properly anticipated. Similar results can be obtained from a remote location by measuring vertical angles with a theodolite. This alternative is superior to leveling in that access to the targets is not required and instrument location is more flexible.

Electronic distance measurement surveying

Electronic distance measurement (EDM) surveying instruments function by bouncing a modulated beam off a retrodirective reflector and back into the instrument, where the distance is electronically calculated. The instruments, which use laser, infrared, and microwave beams, are available in a wide range of accuracies, maximum attainable distances, degrees of automation, and cost. To meet most monitoring requirements a number of fully automatic instruments are available, having a maximum range of 1 mi using a single 2½-in.-dia reflector, with accuracies of ±0.2 in. plus 1 ppm, priced at about $6,000 to $8,000. Such accuracy corresponds to a system accuracy of 0.6 to 1.0 in., irrespective of distance, within typical open-pit dimensions. Increased accuracy is currently available only with reduced automation or at greatly increased capital cost.

When access to the monitored area is safe for personnel and when labor cost is not prohibitive, a single reflector may be carried from point to point by the instrument operator's assistant. Alternatively, the reflectors can be permanently mounted on the slope face, which is faster, requires only one operator, and does not necessitate access to the unstable area. The cost of a standard 2½-in.-dia reflector is about $250; however, such a large number of measuring points dictates an investment of thousands of dollars in reflectors, many of which will be destroyed in the course of mining. Several alternatives are available.

In one installation (since copied elsewhere), the author used low cost plastic reflectors and a longer-range laser instrument, the Ranger III. It has a rated range of 8 mi using several standard 2½-in. glass reflectors and costs about $11,000. A foil-backed Stimsonite reflector was selected after testing about 10 different types, and it performed with accuracy equal to the standard prism but at greatly reduced range. Readings were obtained at 1,200 ft maximum with clean plastic reflectors and 600 ft with dust-covered reflectors. While this distance was adequate for the specific project, it is too limited for most larger pits, and the strong laser is a slight hazard to eyesight.

The author subsequently designed a high quality, 1-in.-dia glass reflector costing $60-70—roughly one-quarter the price of conventional units. Results using laser and infrared instruments have so far been very favorable—maximum range is only slightly reduced and the consistency of multiple readings is improved. Available since late 1975, such instruments have been used on six projects to date.

Currently, testing is being carried out on a 2½-in.-dia "hollow" reflector that costs about $135. Initial results indicate that it outperforms conventional 2½-in. units at extended ranges. A 5-in. unit of similar design is also being investigated.

The periodic measurement of the distance from a stable instrument station to a reflector gives the component of movement of the reflector in line with the station. If no other measurements are taken to provide the remaining components, the direction of ground movement must be correctly anticipated at the outset and the instrument station must be located accordingly, or failure could occur without being detected.

The three-dimensional direction of movement can be

> **About the author:** Allan MacRae was graduated from Queen's University, Kingston, with a B. Sc. in mining engineering in 1971. He has worked on a wide variety of projects in mining and civil engineering, concentrating on rock slope engineering and artificial slope stabilization. He has been self-employed since 1974. Information in this article was drawn from correspondence and engineering reports written by the author over the past several years and from his current research on slope displacement monitoring systems.

A Ranger III EDM instrument gives a digital readout for distance in a pit slope monitoring project.

measured by trilateration—measuring the distance to the target from three known instrument locations—but this procedure is slow and impractical. Either the reflectors must be turned manually to face approximately the three lines of measurement, or three reflectors must be permanently mounted.

A better method for three-dimensional monitoring is measurement of the distance and the vertical and horizontal angles to the target from the instrument station. The location of the instrument station is quite flexible using this method, and since only a few stations are required to monitor an entire open pit, it is feasible to provide temperature-controlled enclosures for instruments and operators. Greater instrument accuracy and improved operator efficiency make temperature control worthwhile. Instruments combining electronic angle and distance measuring capabilities are available. However, because of their high cost and questionable reliability, a better choice is conventional angle measurement, combined with a standard EDM unit. Some EDM units mount on the barrel of a theodolite and could save time by halving instrument pointing.

It is the author's opinion that EDM monitoring offers the greatest practical advantages at the lowest cost of all methods currently available, and that future advances in instruments and reflectors will further enhance its effectiveness.

Photogrammetric monitoring

In photogrammetry, stereo pairs of photographs are taken at known locations and orientations and are analyzed to provide the coordinates of selected points contained in both photographs. To obtain the accuracy suitable for monitoring purposes, permanent targets must be mounted on the slope for all points selected for measurement and for control points, which are precisely located by conventional surveying at the time the photos are taken. The positions of the selected and control points are measured in the photographs using a stereocomparitor. Their coordinates are calculated by geometric formulas and then revised using a regression analysis based on the known location of the control points. The regression analysis improves the accuracy of the coordinates from roughly 6 in. per 1,000 ft to ½-1 in. per 1,000 ft.

The equipment requirements are a terrestrial photogrammetric camera, a stereocomparitor, conventional surveying equipment, and a computer terminal. The purchase price would likely exceed $30,000, and only a trained photogrammetrist can produce satisfactory results. It is unlikely that contracted photo interpretation performed away from the site would be able to produce results fast enough. In one case investigated by the author, the best turn-around time estimate from a contractor located close to both the mine site and the necessary data reduction facilities was two weeks between taking of photos and production of results. Costs were significantly higher than for other methods. These constraints severely limit the application of photogrammetric monitoring at this time.

Sequential photographic monitoring

The author is currently developing a system that compares two photographs taken at different times with the same orientation. A simple viewing technique causes areas of the slope that have moved between photos to stand out from stable areas—providing for the first time a practical method of detecting movement over large areas of slope. In many cases, no targets will be required, and a continuous monitoring system, as opposed to a finite number of sample points, will be possible. Targets may be used if desired, however, and existing EDM reflectors or nonreflective types of targets are both suitable. Anticipated accuracy should be 1 in. per 1,000 ft. Because measurement of movement is made in the plane of the photograph, this technique would work well in conjunction with a single component EDM system. The high cost and slow turn-around time for photogrammetry are eliminated, and same-day results are expected. This technique, now in the laboratory and field testing stage, should be ready for field use within the year.

Wider use anticipated for slope monitoring

The monitoring of slope displacements to detect and predict failure is gaining acceptance in the mining industry. Its application is now limited primarily to localized monitoring in pits with established stability problems. The relatively low cost of implementing a monitoring system, the large savings to be derived from reduced accident rates, and the potential for improved operating efficiency make such a system an asset to any mine. The continued improvement of current systems, along with new developments that facilitate early detection of potential failures, will lead to routine use of overall pit slope stability monitoring in mines of the future. □

Select berm width to contain local failures

Dennis C. Martin and **Douglas R. Piteau,** D. R. Piteau Associates Ltd.

STABILITY ANALYSES for open pit slope design must consider the possibility of the failure of individual benches as well as the failure of the overall slope. In many cases, the probability of overall slope failure along major faults or weak zones may prove to be small, while the design of individual benches against excessive failure may be the controlling factor for design of the overall slope. Small failures can cause major disruptions to pit operations and can limit accessibility. A graphical method for design of individual benches to control small failures is described here.

Considerations for basic slope design

In rock slopes, instability occurs as a result of failure along structural discontinuities, such as bedding planes, joints, geological contacts, and faults. Instability seldom occurs in homogeneous material unless the rock is weathered or soft.

The most important single factor in stability analyses and design of rock slopes is the determination and evaluation of the orientation, geometry, and spatial distribution of discontinuities in the slopes. This process should be followed by evaluation of possible alternative angles of the proposed pit slopes relative to the orientation of the discontinuities.

Slope control may be accomplished by designing the slope so that no failure can occur or by excavating the pit under controlled conditions, with the slope designed for adequate access, while minor failures are caught on berms and removed as needed. The first solution is usually too conservative to be economical. The second solution requires a thorough consideration of slope geometry.

Parameters that govern the geometry of a slope are bench height H, berm width l, and bench face angle β. (See Fig. 1.) Normally, these parameters are determined by the strength and nature of the material of the slope, the size and type of equipment to be used, and mining regulations. Bench height should provide a safe working slope. For a given slope, higher benches permit wider berms.

In general, berms should be designed wide enough to entrap falling debris and provide access for cleanup.

Inclined bench faces reduce the likelihood of high stresses near bench crests and minimize tension cracks and overhangs. Problems of rockfall are thus reduced, and the safety of the slope is increased.

Slope and failure geometry are related

The volume of material in a bench failure is inversely proportional to either the dip of a plane failure or the plunge of a wedge failure. The volume varies with bench height. The shallower the dip or plunge of a failure, the greater the volume of material involved. Calculation of

Benches at this mine in British Columbia were designed to contain the wedge failures predicted by stability analysis.

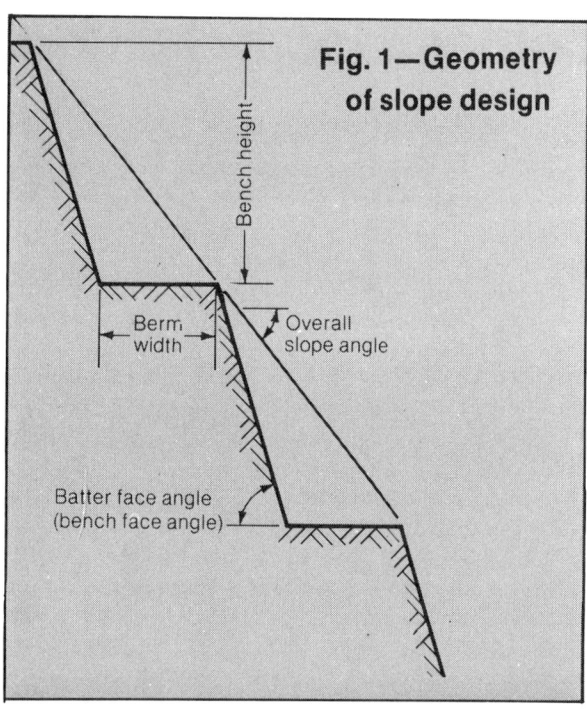

Fig. 1—Geometry of slope design

the cross-sectional area of a potential bench failure provides an estimate of the volume of failed material per unit width of berm.

For plane failures, the slumped material on the berm is assumed to form a uniform debris slope with a triangular cross section. Slumped material from a wedge failure is assumed to form an approximately conical debris slope. This slope extends outward across the berm along the projection of the line of intersection. It is assumed that the maximum extent of slumped material from a wedge failure will occur along the projection of the line of intersection and will have a triangular cross section—similar to that of a plane failure—of unit width along the line of intersection. Therefore, calculation of the cross-sectional area of a wedge failure along the line of intersection provides an estimate of the maximum volume of material, per unit width, that could slump onto the berm.

The vertical cross-sectional area A of a failure taken parallel to the direction of dip of the failure plane—or parallel to the line of intersection of a wedge failure—is calculated in Fig. 2 using the formula:

$$A = \frac{H^2}{2}\left(\frac{1}{\tan \beta_\omega} - \frac{1}{\tan \beta}\right) \qquad 1)$$

Fig. 2—Elements of bench design

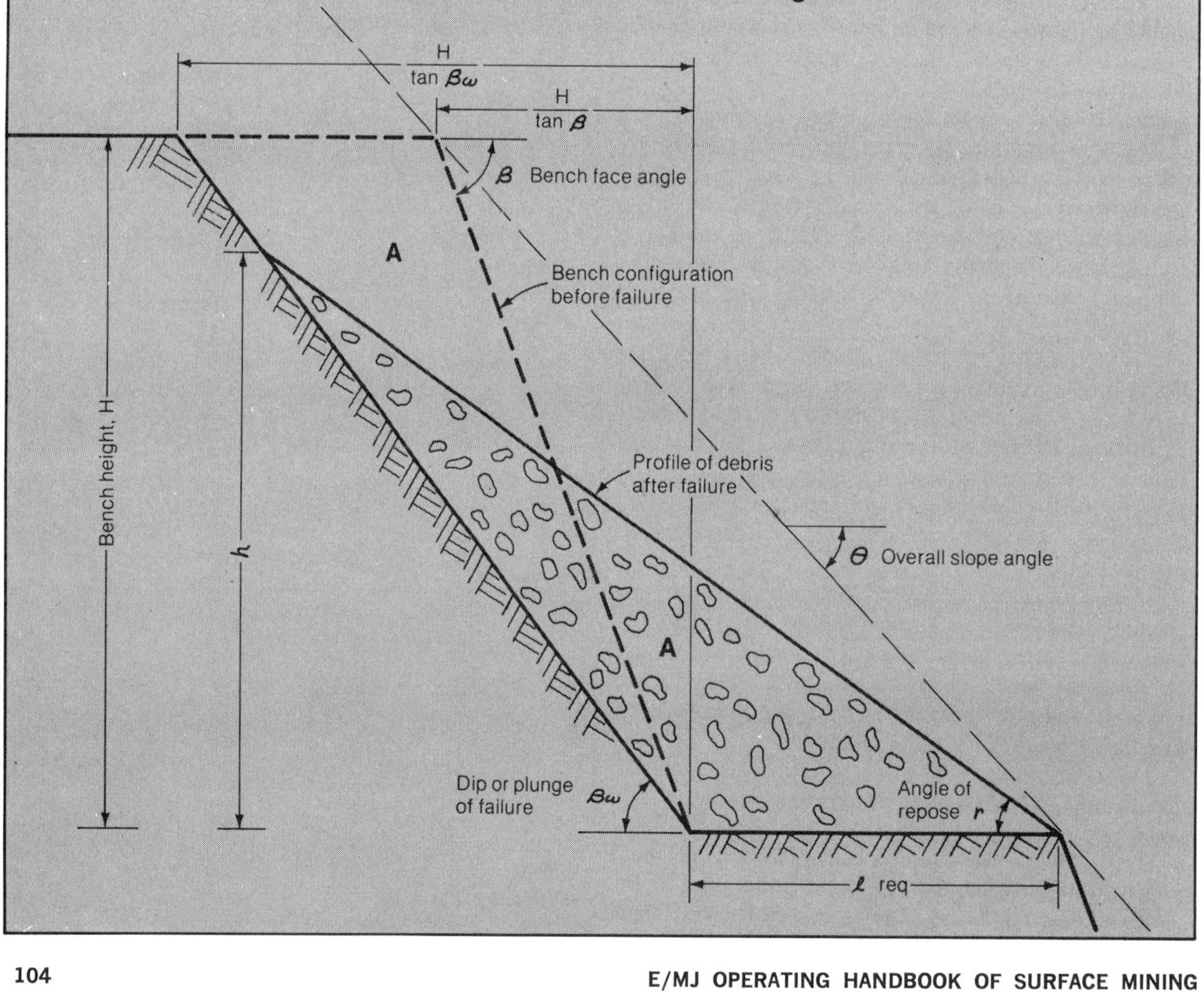

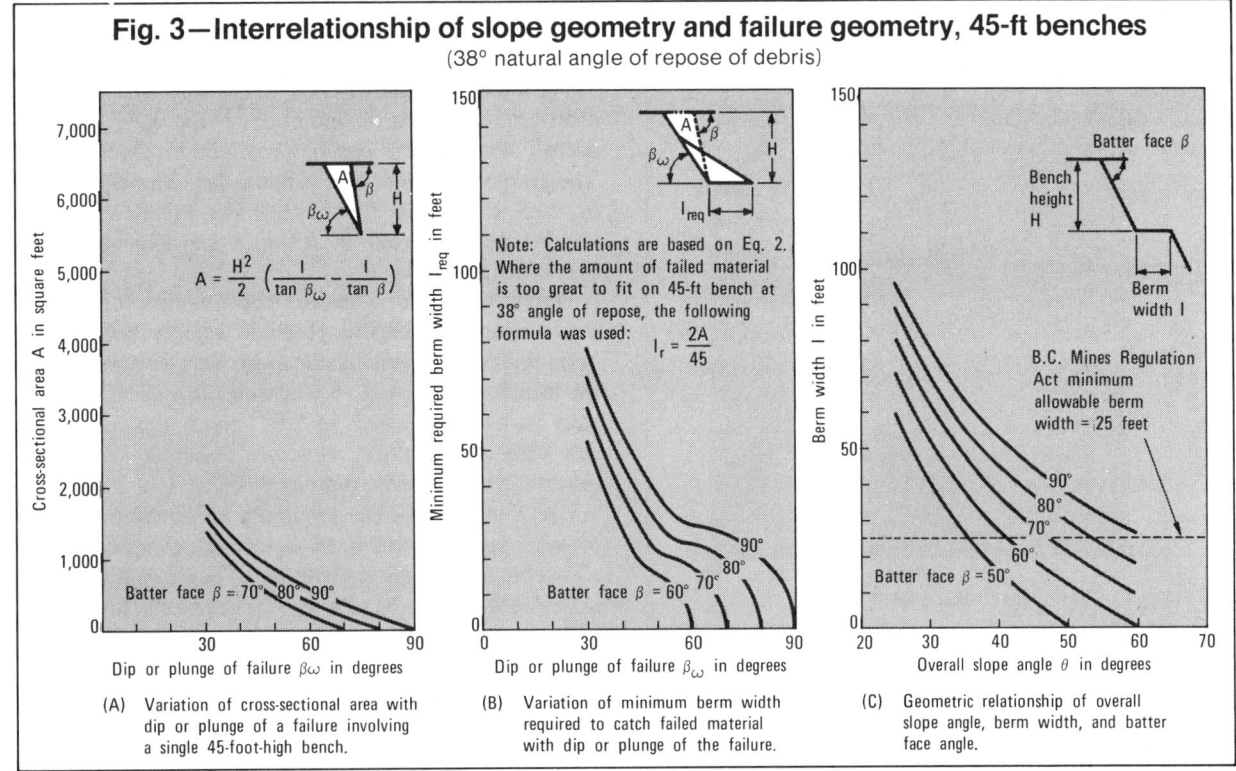

Fig. 3—Interrelationship of slope geometry and failure geometry, 45-ft benches
(38° natural angle of repose of debris)

(A) Variation of cross-sectional area with dip or plunge of a failure involving a single 45-foot-high bench.

(B) Variation of minimum berm width required to catch failed material with dip or plunge of the failure.

(C) Geometric relationship of overall slope angle, berm width, and batter face angle.

where H = bench height, β = bench face angle, and β_ω = the dip or plunge of the failure.

Cross-sectional area of a potential bench failure is used to calculate the minimum berm width l_{req} required to catch all failed material (Fig. 2). It is assumed that the failed material comes to rest at its natural angle of repose r, usually 35° to 40°. The formula used for calculation of the minimum berm width, from trigonometric relationships, is:

$$l_{req} = \sqrt{\frac{2A}{\sin r \cos r + \frac{(\sin r)^2}{\tan(\beta_\omega - r)}}} \qquad 2)$$

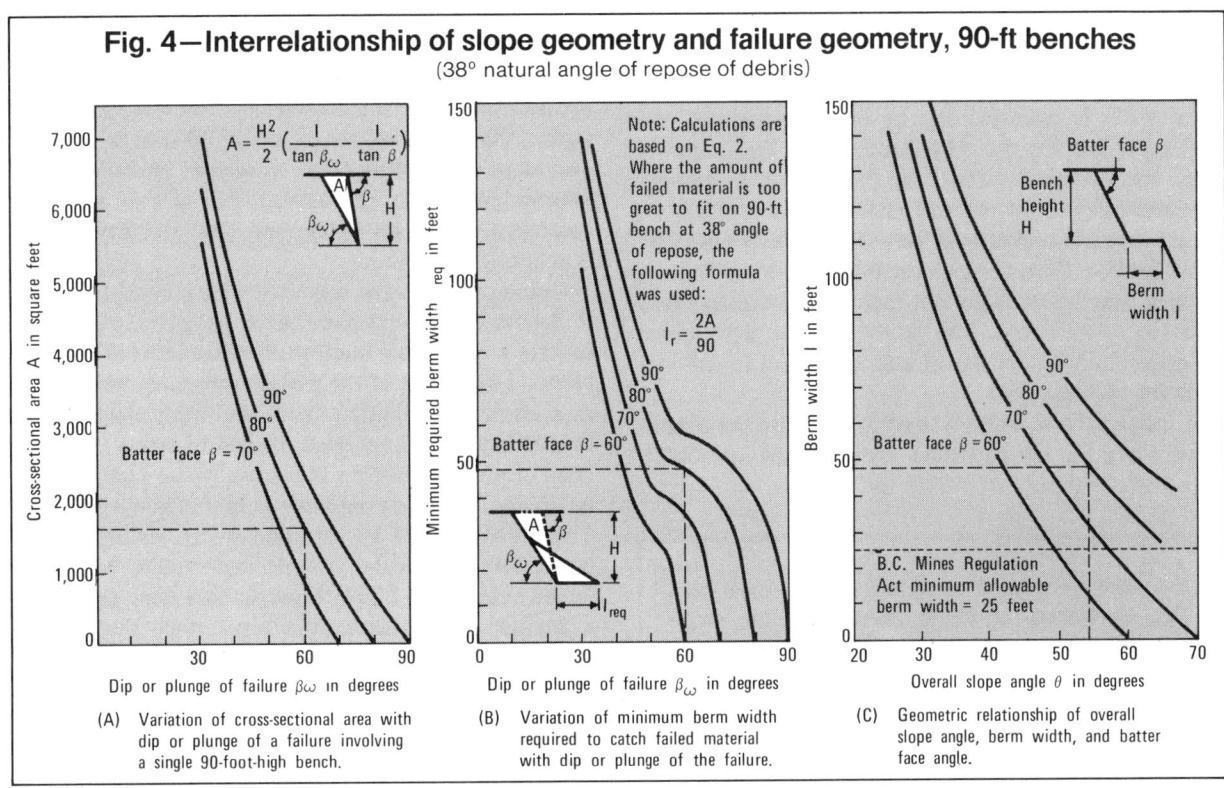

Fig. 4—Interrelationship of slope geometry and failure geometry, 90-ft benches
(38° natural angle of repose of debris)

(A) Variation of cross-sectional area with dip or plunge of a failure involving a single 90-foot-high bench.

(B) Variation of minimum berm width required to catch failed material with dip or plunge of the failure.

(C) Geometric relationship of overall slope angle, berm width, and batter face angle.

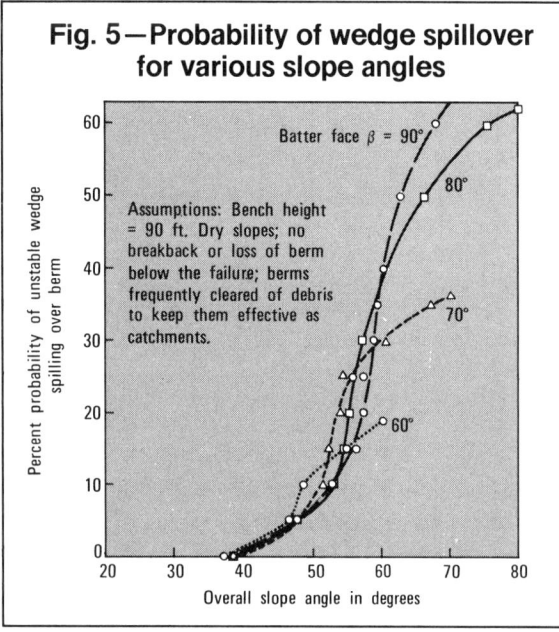

Fig. 5—Probability of wedge spillover for various slope angles

Assumptions: Bench height = 90 ft. Dry slopes; no breakback or loss of berm below the failure; berms frequently cleared of debris to keep them effective as catchments.

In cases where the amount of failed material is geometrically too large to be completely caught on the berm (for a particular bench height), it is assumed that the slump angle is less than r. The required berm width is then calculated on the assumption that a simple triangle of slumped material extends from the crest of the bench. In this case, the minimum berm width is calculated as:

$$l_{\text{req}} = \frac{2A}{H} \qquad 3)$$

The bulking (swell) factor—an increase in the volume of material during failure—is not considered. Bulking is a complex factor related to rock type, fracture intensity, and the mechanism of rock failure. Bulking can increase volume by as much as 50%. For conditions where Eq. 2 applies (e.g., steeply dipping failures), the minimum berm width is increased only by the square root of the bulking factor. On the other hand, where Eq. 3 applies (e.g., for shallow failures), the relationship is directly proportional, and the required minimum berm width can be 1.5 times the minimum berm width determined by that equation. Depending on the type and size of failure, bulking may be an important factor to be incorporated into the calculations. The factor can be determined experimentally by comparing unit weights of in-situ and of failed rock material.

Minimum berm width is used to calculate the overall slope angle for the particular bench height and bench face angle that are assumed in the analysis.

Acknowledgement: The technique described here was developed in conjunction with pit slope stability analyses and design work at the mines of Cyprus Anvil Mining Corp. and Cassiar Asbestos Corp. The authors wish to thank personnel of the two mines for their assistance.

Graphs of bench and failure geometry

For a particular bench height, the interrelationship of cross-sectional area A, minimum berm width l_{req}, and overall slope angle θ can be presented on three graphs. The graphs show the various bench face angles and dips, or plunges of the failure β_ω. The relationships for benches 45 ft high and 90 ft high are graphed in Figs. 3 and 4, respectively.

Design graphs for a specific bench height can be used to determine the size of a potential failure, including the berm width and overall slope angle necessary to contain the bench failure. Fig. 4 illustrates a typical example with 90-ft-high benches and 80° bench face angles. In this case, the geologic structure indicated that plane failures could develop, dipping at 60°.

Fig. 4 shows that the minimum berm width required to catch such failures is 48 ft, and the resulting overall allowable slope angle is about 54°. The amount of failure that would have to be cleaned up is approximately 1,600 cu ft per ft width of the failure (Fig. 4a). If the number and size of failures per unit length of bench can be estimated, the total amount of cleanup of failed material can be calculated.

The accompanying graphs assume that minimal backbreak of the bench crests will develop. Proper control of blasting and inclined bench faces will reduce backbreak. Where access is required along berms, berm width should be increased to permit equipment passage past failures. Where discontinuities are large and involve more than one bench, the overall slope angle may have to be flattened.

Graphical analysis applied to B.C. mine

The application of the analytical technique described here proved extremely useful at a mine in northern British Columbia. At this mine, analysis was made of the upper 700-ft-high section of an 1,100-ft-high hangingwall slope of argillitic rock. Numerous potential wedge failures, formed by the combination of two joint sets, controlled slope geometry and the stability of the benches. (See photo.)

Graphical technique was used with probability theory to determine the optimum bench geometry required to contain a reasonable number of wedge failures upon the berms. The plunge of the wedges varied mathematically as a normal distribution about the mean plunge value. Probability techniques were applied to assess the likelihood of unstable wedges occurring whose plunge would be greater than that determined by probability criteria. The probability of an unstable wedge spilling over a berm, for a particular overall slope angle, was determined as shown in Fig. 5. Mine management was then in a position to evaluate alternative slope designs.

A more complete discussion of the technique described here is presented in "Slope Stability Analysis and Design Based on Probability Techniques at Cassiar Mine," a 1976 CIM Bulletin by D. R. Piteau and D. C. Martin. ☐

Open-pit engineering takes quantum leap

THE TECHNOLOGY OF OPEN-PIT ENGINEERING is now highly refined, using rock mechanics for slope stability studies, and computers for design, economic analysis, and studies of operations performance. These breakthroughs have been accompanied by significant changes in the functions of mining engineers and in engineering equipment. Comparing modern survey instrumentation with that of little more than a decade ago is much like comparing spacecraft with World War I Spads. Computer hardware and software for today's mine programming is far removed from the data banks of 10 years ago. Sophisticated electronic equipment used to determine rock slope stability around pit peripheries is the product of the latest scientific achievements in many fields, including miniaturization. All these innovations are rooted in economics: the need to profitably exploit larger, lower grade surface deposits in an era of rising costs and expectations.

The day of the vernier is over

The growth of rock mechanics studies as a branch of mine operations has significantly altered the work requirements of mine survey departments and has impelled (along with changing needs in construction and tunneling) the development of complex survey instrumentation. Increasingly sophisticated equipment requires greater skill but also removes much of the drudgery from surveying and associated computations.

Optical-scale theodolites and, for more precise measurements, optical-micrometer theodolites have consigned the oldtime vernier theodolite to the dust heap. Optical-scale instruments are direct-reading to 1 min of arc, while optical-micrometer instruments read directly to a single second. The Wild T16D is an example of the former; the Kern DKM2A and the Wild T2 are examples of the latter. The Wild T16D provides an automatic index, excellent damping, and visual indication for proper leveling. The instrument can easily be estimated to 6 sec.

Wild Heerbrugg's T2 theodolite (1-sec reading) has automatic index, combines with EDM, gyroscope, and laser equipment.

The Wild Heerbrugg DI3S is an automatic survey system with a built-in computer for electromagnetic distance measurement (EDM). Features include sighting to 1,000 m with one prism and up to 2,000 m with nine prisms, and a keyboard for entering vertical and horizontal angles. Slope distance is displayed every 2 sec. The system can calculate and display horizontal distance, differences in coordinates, and differences in height. The DI3S combines with the T1, T16, and T2 theodolites and has an accuracy of ±5mm + 5ppm.

The AGA Geodimeter 700 is said to be the equivalent of a single-second theodolite for angular measurement. It is also equipped with an internal calculator to reduce slope distances to horizontal.

For extreme accuracy of ±0.2mm + 1 ppm and a range of 3 km, Kern offers the ME3000 Mekometer. Such precise instrumentation is often required in preliminary monitoring of open-pit slope movement and for checking surface strain induced by underground excavations.[1]

Modern theodolites also incorporate automatic collimation, or vertical circle indexing. Precision on single-second optical-micrometer theodolites is claimed to be ±3 sec. Vertical angle measurements may be made quickly and precisely, and trigonometric leveling is a practical alternative to conventional leveling.

For precision in azimuth determination, gyrotheodolites are becoming a common tool. The Wild GAK-1 reportedly has an accuracy better than ±25 sec of arc.

Automatic levels replace spirit levels

A wide range of automatic levels now on the market employ some form of pendulus compensator. Liquid compensators are most practical because they lack moving parts.

Geodetic automatic levels include the Zeiss Ni002, which is designed to reverse the compensator, thereby preventing residual tilting errors and eliminating the need for matched backsites and foresites. The instrument offers the highly precise measuring ability needed for certain rock mechanics readings. The Zeiss Ni007 is said to be suitable for leveling under dusty conditions because it has an integral parallel plate micrometer and sealed optics. When used with matched invar staves, it is said to produce a mean square error of ±0.5 mm, over 1 km two-way leveling.

Optical-scale and optical-micrometer theodolites, gyrotheodolites, automatic levels, and EDM instruments provide a profusion of instruments. One expert foresees three classes for future use: "Firstly, short-range instruments which may be attached neatly to a theodolite and used where accuracies of ±5 mm are satisfactory. Secondly, a high-precision short-to-medium range integrated system which may be used completely automatically for precise monitoring work, and perhaps electronic tacheometry. Thirdly, there is a requirement for high-precision instruments capable of measuring long ranges. These instruments should be interchangeable with theodolites and would be used for geodetic work."[1]

Laser alignment for surveying

A number of laser devices are now available for projecting a line to a target. The laser-theodolite, used in general survey work and mine surveys, has a built-in filter for eye protection. The GL01 from Wild-Heerbrugg is a low-cost laser beam attachment that focuses a bright red reference line some 100 m in bright sunlight and 400 m under more obscure conditions and at night. The attachment interchanges with a standard theodolite eyepiece and has a telescope magnification of 28x. The attachment operates from a 12-v battery and will fit T1A, T16, and T2 theodolites.

The AccuSweep 710 laser aligning, leveling, and locating system, from Constructors Supply, of Santa Fe Springs, Calif., projects a laser beam that is detected by a companion piece. The instrument projects a level beam through a 360° rotating prism. When the beam strikes the sensor, light-emitting diodes indicate high, low, and on-center locations. The beam operates at 500 ft in brilliant sunshine, reportedly with an accuracy of ⅛ in., and is most useful for construction.

Equipment for monitoring slope stability

In a recent, comprehensive paper[2] detailing the use of slope stability monitoring systems, Iain Weir-Jones noted that open-pit systems have two functions: the "maintenance of safe working conditions . . . and the provision of slope design and redesign which will permit the more economical operation of the pit." Weir-Jones categorizes three phases of instability encountered at open-pits, which require displacement sensors of varying characteristics and capabilities:

- Phase 1 sensors measure displacements of fractions of an inch or portions of a minute of arc. Widely spaced and manually read, such instruments provide a broad overview of pit crest behavior.

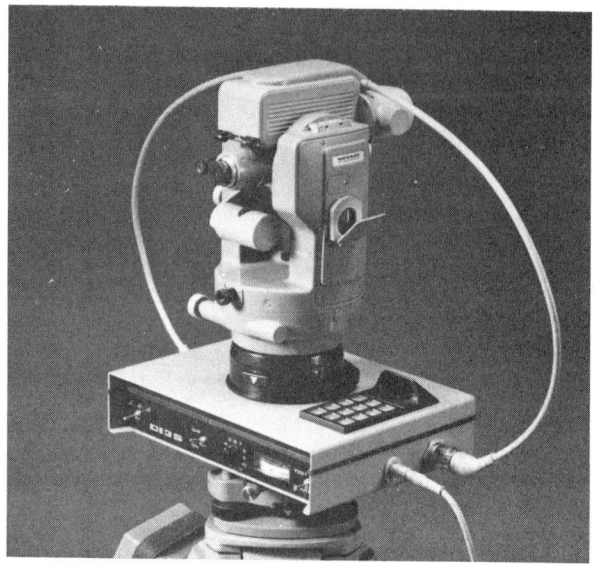

Wild DI3S Distomat is a reducing infrared distancer with 2,000-m range and fully automatic measurement.

- Phase 2 sensors measure displacements from fractions of an inch or minute of arc to several inches or minutes of arc, in conjunction with a telemetry and data acquisition system. The sensors should be concentrated in areas of known potential instability where the rock mass is beginning to undergo Phase 2 displacements.
- Phase 3 sensors measure displacements on the order of tens of inches or arcs of several degrees. Whenever possible, some of the sensors in the most active areas of failure should be continuously monitored using a telemetry

Applicability and approximate cost of various measuring systems

Measurement category	Function	Sensor category	Type of sensor	Reading system	Reading frequency	Acquisition telemetry	Capital costs, 1975	Annual operating costs, 1975
Phase 1	Locate areas of potential instability	Displacement; piezometric	Geodetic surveying tiltmeters: inclinometers, piezometers	Manual	Intermittent	Not necessary	$10,000 for complete pit coverage	$10,000 average pit, normal condition
Phase 2	Monitoring development of initial instability	Displacement; piezometers, load cells	Tacheometers, tiltmeters; inclinometers, strain bays, geophones, piezometers, load cells	Remote if sensor suitable; otherwise manual	Continuous if sensor suitable	Very desirable on all suitable sensors	$8,000 each location; savings for multiple locations and sharing telemetry systems	Depends on complexity and volume of data; $3,000 less for multi locations
Phase 3	Monitoring development of gross slope failure	Displacement; piezometers, load cells	Tiltmeters, surveying geodetic tacheometers: geophones, surface strain bays, piezometers, load cells	Remote if sensors suitable; operator safety must be considered	Continuous if sensor suitable; otherwise at frequent intervals (daily)	Essential on at least portion of system	$6,000 each location; may be savings for multiple locations	Depends on conditions and rate of failure; $5,000 each location
Auxiliary services	Examination of nondefinitive stability parameters in specific areas (SARN microseismic change of stress)	Subaudible rock noise; microseismic stress change	Geophones, acoustic detectors, borehole deformation gauges	Remote if possible; otherwise manual	Totally dependent upon situation	Desirable, but depends upon situation	Depends entirely upon situation	Depends entirely upon prevailing conditions

and data acquisition system. (The accompanying table provides more detail on the three phases.)

The three monitoring systems would normally be developed sequentially, as necessitated by the different phenomena associated with the three failure phases.[2]

In its simplest form, the Phase 1 system should incorporate precise surveying systems, portable tiltmeters, pneumatically operated piezometers, and possibly subaudible rock noise (SARN) sensors. A basic system must cover an entire proposed pit area. Because of the need to precisely and accurately detect minute Phase 1 displacements, surveying techniques and instruments should be capable of measuring displacements to ±0.25 in. both horizontally and vertically when sighting distances are 1,500 ft. This requires a tacheometer capability of at least ±0.25 in. and an angular accuracy of better than ±3 sec of arc in both horizontal and vertical planes. An instrument such as the AGA Geodimeter No. 710, a combination electronic theodolite and laser tacheometer, is one possibility.

Angular accuracies of ±10 sec of arc should be provided by portable tiltmeters, and piezometric measurements should be made to register to ±1.0 psi. Null-balance pneumatic pore pressure sensors will achieve this accuracy.

Annual operating cost for a Phase 1 program ranges between $20,000 and $30,000, with an additional capital cost of $20,000 to $30,000 for equipment, hardware, and installation. The expenditures appear paltry when the potential benefits of such a system are examined. However, the system is useless unless installed, operated, and maintained by skilled personnel. The data must be used promptly and intelligently.

A Phase 2 measuring system would be installed if data from the Phase 1 system suggest potential instability. The Phase 2 system should be tied to remote data acquisition and telemetry equipment. Geodetic leveling might be employed during initial development of a failure. The Phase 2 system must:

- Provide early warning of the development of a potential slope failure identified by the Phase 1 system.
- Provide data for estimating the time of possible slope failure.
- Provide data to assess the practicability of providing stabilization for the incipient failure.
- Provide data for evaluating effectiveness of a slope drainage system and/or support system.

A Phase 3 system should be installed at a pit when slope failure is well advanced. Because of the hazards involved, remote-reading capability is needed. The system's equipment is exposed to partial, if not entire, destruction.

Until site personnel have developed expertise in the analysis and use of data from the various instruments, management would be well-advised to employ outside technicians and engineers before attempting to design, purchase, and install slope monitoring systems. However, no open-pit management can afford not to review the potential savings inherent in such systems—savings in life, property, and the reduction of costly, unnecessary stripping of waste.

Computer use in pit planning and design

Within the last decade, the use of computers to design and plan large scale open pits has become standard. The ability of computers to store vast and diverse bits of information and to use these bits to rapidly iterate a variety of programmed operations has made computerization necessary for modern pit design and for operations planning and economic analysis.

A representative example of such computer use is the Lamco joint venture company's design of an open-pit iron mine in the Nimba Range of northeastern Liberia.[3] Production is approximately 13 million tpy of weathered hematite ore. A computerized "Ore Reserve Project" developed a reserve model in which ore and surrounding waste were divided into blocks. Input data for the blocks included assay data, geological and structural data, and variables for costs, prices, and potential slope angles. Initial methods were defined to arrive at design of the optimum pit, or pits, depending on changes in variables. The system was set up to provide a stripping model, production schedules for various rates of return, and methods to calculate net present value and discounted cash flow yield. In essence, the program directions were used to provide for both the establishment of ultimate slope angles and the economical evaluation of various pit layouts. Pits "at various slope angles were studied with regard to probabilities of slope failure and how these [failures] would affect costs and possibly create production losses. The risk levels that were accepted varied within the pit."[3]

The computerized pit planning system provided information on mineable ore reserves, the mining plan, equipment and investment, and a tabulation of the net present value during the lifetime of the particular mine pit.

Files internal to the system included geological and topographical data, rock data, hardness factors, structural geology, and equipment capability, availability, longevity, and costs. The computer output was composed of modules relating to specific calculations of volume, mineable ore reserves, production schedules, stripping schedules, equipment, investment plans, and cash flow. The system satisfies management's need for fast and comprehensive information on the effects of changing variables.

Computer simulates open-pit mining

Among the many computer programs developed to assist in design, equipment selection, and operation of open pit mines is the Wabco (Westinghouse Air Brake Co.) simulation program. According to company spokesmen, the program uses "the computer to simulate the thousands of events that take place simultaneously in the pit."[4] The program is offered as a free customer service, or on a fee plan without obligations. To use the program, mine operators must furnish a considerable amount of specific information about shovels, trucks, roads, dumps, crushers, and miscellaneous data on breakdowns, refueling, and other operating factors.

Shovel information includes loading cycles, spotting time (single or double), and material characteristics. Truck variables include empty and loaded vehicle weight, efficiencies, and shovel assignments. Dump and crusher variables include dump positions and turn-and-dump times. The haulage profile description provides detailed information on grades, slope lengths, curves, segment descriptions, speed conditions, no-pass zones, and traffic patterns. The end result of the program is a systematic, logical, and efficient production system. □

References

1) St. John, C. M., "Mine Surveying Developments in Europe," MINING MAGAZINE, September 1974, p 181.
2) Weir-Jones, Iain, and Bumala, Thomas G., "The Design of Slope Stability Monitoring Systems," Fall Meeting, AIME-SME, Salt Lake City, Utah, September 1975.
3) Jansson, Berne, and Werner, Hans, "Design of an Open Pit Mine at Nimba Range, Lamco, Liberia," 13th International Symposium on the Application of Computers and Mathematics for Decision-Making in the Mineral Industries, Technical University, Clausthal-Zellerfeld, West Germany, October 1975.
4) Butler, J. M., and Fouts, R. K., "Optimizing Open Pit Mining with Computer Simulation," MINING CONGRESS JOURNAL, March 1975, p 32.

Choose the right vertical wet pit sump pump

With the broad variety of pump designs and the wide range of construction materials offered today, users in the mining and metals industry can zero in on the pumps best suited to specific needs.

Leonard H. Sence, manager of marketing, Allis-Chalmers Industrial Pump Div.

THE NEW AND EXPANDING GENERATION of vertical pumps for submerged operation in a pit or sump covers an impressive range of head capacity and severe service conditions. The pumps are widely used in many applications, from influent handling to pumping effluent and waste materials, both indoors and outdoors in a great number of mining and metals processing plants.

The pumps described in this article are industrial types specifically designed for process fluids, slurries, clear and corrosive liquids, liquids with solids in suspension, two-phase liquids, and many more critical services in handling solids and liquids. The pump designs of the mid-1970s are far superior to their predecessors; they are more versatile and flexible in application and are available with a wider choice of design options, including wet end materials. They incorporate the newest design and engineering concepts in hydraulics, mechanics, and metallurgy to provide more reliable operation and lower overall maintenance.

New design concepts include standard components

The general vertical wet pit sump pump classification discussed in this article includes two basic types: centrifugal and vertical turbine. These newly designed pumps are pre-engineered and use modular construction and standard components. This means lower costs, more reliable performance, better deliveries, and consistent availability of renewal parts. Centrifugal pumps are adapted and modified versions of proven horizontal designs. Vertical turbine pumps are standard designs modified for handling abrasive or corrosive materials—applications for which standard designs are not inherently suited.

Some manufacturers design and build special vertical wet pit pumps, but use standardized components—to the benefit of both the builder and user. One advantage is in stocking spare parts. In the past, a separate set of spare parts had to be stocked for some wet pit designs. If a plant had a number of pumps in operation, including some horizontal and some vertical wet pit designs, the parts problem was further complicated. With modular designs and standard components, all major wearing parts are now identical for comparable horizontal and vertical designs in a given size, so parts stocking is simplified, costs are lowered dramatically, and deliveries are greatly improved.

"Wetted ends" (the suction end of the assembly is submerged) are made of castings. Other parts of the pumps, including mechanical or support members, may use castings or fabrications, whichever type is best suited to the task. By working closely with manufacturers, the purchaser can match pump materials properly to particular duty conditions in a way that was not previously possible.

Vertical wet pit sump pumps are suitable for almost any application in which other types are used—and often to better advantage. The following list of applications, while not complete and comprehensive, is typical for this pump design:

Coal preparation
Mineral fiber slurry handling
Steel mill scale handling
Ash sluicing
Aggregate handling
Mine dewatering and drainage
Taconite slurry handling and washing
Processed ore handling and washing
Reclaiming floor plant washings and other waste
Sludge handling
River water supply services
Air pollution control systems (scrubbers)
Mill discharge and tailings disposal
Leaching services
Scale pit dewatering
General plant waste disposal services
Pumping two-phase liquids (liquids with entrained air)

Obviously, not all vertical wet pit sump pumps are suited to all these services. Some designs are best utilized in corrosive applications or in liquids with smaller solids in suspension, while other designs can handle larger solids and highly abrasive materials. As with horizontal pump designs, selection of a vertical wet pit sump pump depends on the requirements of the particular application. The technical field representatives of pump manufacturers should be requested to assist users in the selection procedure. Some general and specific selection parameters are discussed here.

Advantages of using vertical wet pit sump pumps

The vertical wet pit sump pump has several inherent advantages, and many engineers in the mining and metals industries are carefully evaluating the economics of wet pit designs in comparison with the other configurations available.

■ Valuable space is saved, as the wet pit sump pumps can be installed in a plant where there is no room for a horizontal or vertical dry pit design. Vertical wet pit designs offer additional pumping capacity, while taking up very little, if any, usable floor space.

■ Total installation costs are generally lower, with barge or platform mounting used in many cases. Expensive excavation, concrete retaining walls, heavy foundations, and complex piping arrangements aren't usually required. The natural slope of the terrain provides a ready-made sump area in many instances, further reducing preparation and installation costs.

- Expensive priming equipment and valves are not needed, as the pump impeller is submerged directly in the liquid to be pumped. In many wet pit designs, a standard suction bell may be bolted to the suction flange to create better intake conditions. Suction strainers may also be provided. Certain designs do not need fresh water, such as might be required for stuffing box lubrication. This is particularly helpful where fresh water is not readily available.
- There is no problem in aligning pump and driver, which is done automatically by the design of the pump. There is also less piping to align, and aligning it is simpler.
- Routine maintenance requirements should be substantially reduced when all factors in the system are properly considered. There's no need for periodic packing or stuffing box adjustment with most designs. Additionally, since most designs do not use anti-friction bearings in the pump, periodic greasing or lubrication is not required.
- Vibration and critical speeds are easily determined with today's advanced technology, overcoming one potential problem in wet pit vertical types. For years, pump manufacturers have been plagued by long, tedious methods for calculating shaft system critical speeds to avoid vibration. This was a particular problem for long vertical designs where the pump has an extended column, is suspended from a baseplate or floor, and is equipped with a heavy motor mounted right at the top of the unit. Now, computers are used most effectively to calculate the critical frequency of a shaft system and to compare it with the pump operating speed. This procedure makes it possible to determine that the pump is running at a speed far enough removed from the critical frequency to avoid damaging the pump or foundation by excessive vibration. Although the critical speed analysis for long vertical pumps is more complex (because the entire system must be analyzed), computers are effective in selecting and checking pump designs. One additional factor that may be considered is the rigidity added to the unit by properly supporting pump discharge piping. In some cases, a base elbow supported in the sump adds substantial rigidity at the pump casing and significantly raises the pump critical speed.

Specific pump types

The variety of vertical wet pit sump pumps available—representative of the pump industry in general—is shown in Figs. 1-6. Table 1 compares characteristics and applications of typical vertical wet pit sump pumps.

Centrifugal single stage, open impeller. The pump illustrated in Fig. 1 uses ANSI Standard B73-1974 pump end components, which are available in the full range of machinable metals. The pressurized column design is standard on all sizes. A clean source of external liquid (usually water) is introduced into the top bearings at a pressure 15-20 psi above pump suction pressure. Bearings may be either cutless rubber or Teflon material. A lip seal arrangement pressurizes the column and prevents contaminating pumped liquid from entering the column. Column pipe is supplied in 1-ft increments from 2 ft to 20 ft; lengths longer than 20 ft can be specially engineered. The number of bearings furnished depends on column lengths.

In the cast pump casing, the discharge nozzle is located on the center-line of the suction nozzle. Discharge piping (with elbow) extends from the nozzle flange through the hole provided in the pump mounting plate. A combination rear cover and column adapter encloses the back side of the casing.

The cast impeller is a fully open, contoured vane type that provides for high operating efficiencies and low NPSH requirements. Open impellers of this type are also best suited to liquids with pulpy and crystalline solids. Impellers are designed to balance hydraulic thrust loads, and the pressure balance vanes on the rear of the impeller keep solids from collecting behind the impeller. Impeller axial operating clearances are preset and are easily maintained for the full life of the pump through a simple, external adjustment on the standard adjustable coupling. The pump mounting plate and motor support are fabricated steel. The pump is driven by a NEMA VP-HP standard vertical solid shaft, normal thrust, "P" flange motor which is directly coupled to the pump. These pumps have a minimum submergence level of 8 in. (all sizes).

Centrifugal single stage, open impeller close-coupled. The pump shown in Fig. 2 also uses ANSI Standard B73-1974 pump end components, available in a broad range of machinable metals. In the close-coupled design, the pump hydraulic components are assembled onto an extended motor shaft. The pump is supported by a fabricated steel mounting plate, and the pump itself is located immediately below this plate. An extended suction pipe, with suction strainer mounted at the extreme end, is furnished up to a maximum length of 72 in. (less pump length). The pump runs continuously and primes itself as the sump level rises to the eye of the impeller. An air vent in the discharge nozzle assures positive priming. The compact design eliminates the need for intermediate steady or support bearings in the pumped liquid. However, clear, clean liquid must be injected into the pump stuffing box (located above the mounting plate), to lubricate the packing and eliminate air buildup. A number of different stuffing box arrangements, including a variety of mechanical seals, are offered. The impeller clearance is adjusted from the motor end.

Centrifugal single stage, open impeller for corrosives and pulpy solids (Fig. 3). Pumps of this design are available in large capacities (100 to 11,000 gpm) to handle a variety of process and waste materials. Pump wet ends are offered in nearly any machinable metal. The fully-open, non-clog-type cast impeller has excellent capabilities for passing solids, chips, and splinters without clogging or air binding. The casing has a tangential discharge nozzle for CCW rotation only when viewing top (driver) end of unit. An adjustable wear plate, which provides compensation for up to ½ in. of wear, is optional with this design.

The pressurized pipe column requires a small quantity of fresh flushing water at about 40 psi. Flushing water flows downward from the top of the column to lubricate the lower bearings and fill the column. This action tends to flush the sump's slurry, which does get behind the impeller, back into the sump. Other features are similar to those of the smaller capacity pumps.

Special shear-lift force open impeller for larger solids and two phase liquids. The special impeller in Fig. 4 is a modification for the pump shown in Fig. 3. The "Shearpeller" (an A-C trademark) is a true non-clog impeller that uses both shear and lift forces to handle a variety of difficult pumping applications. Specially shaped radial vanes are narrow near the inlet to accept anything that enters the suction. At the outside of the Shearpeller, the vanes widen to substantially fill the chamber and provide positive pumping action. Vane spacing and its relationship with the casing provide unobstructed passages from the suction to the pump discharge. Essentially anything that can enter the pump can be passed through the vanes. The clearance between the vanes and casing wear plate can be adjusted

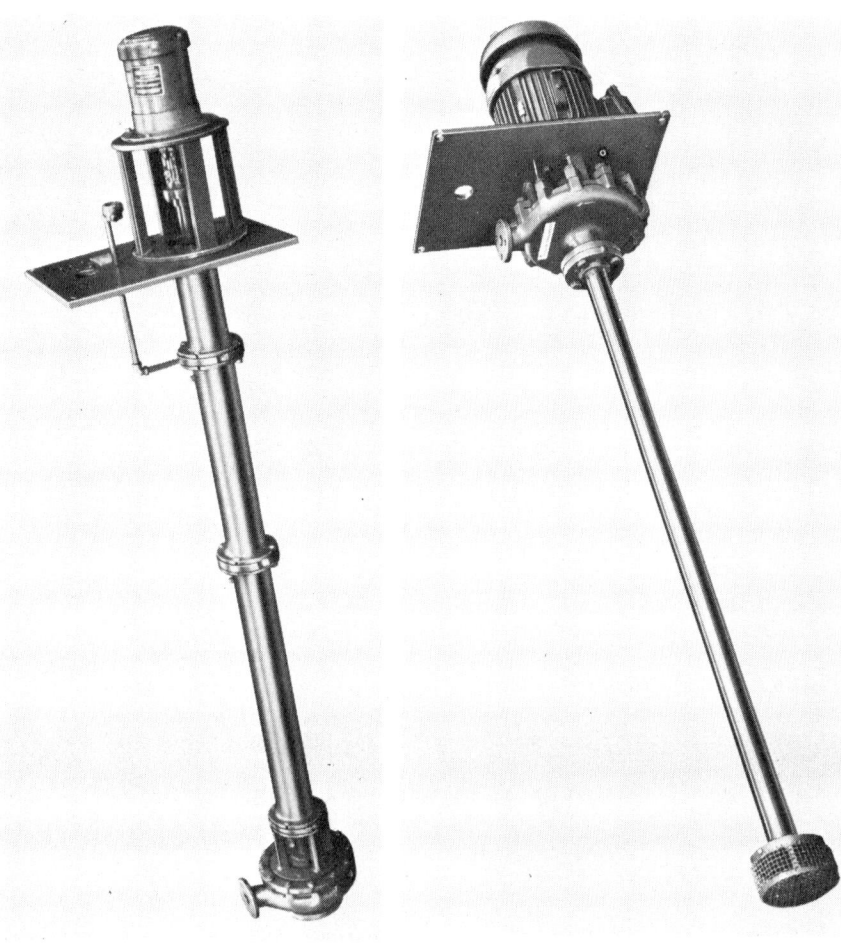
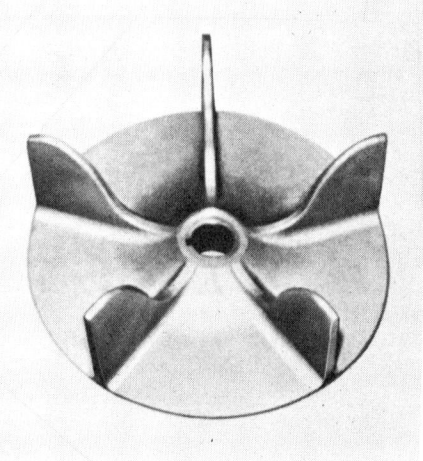
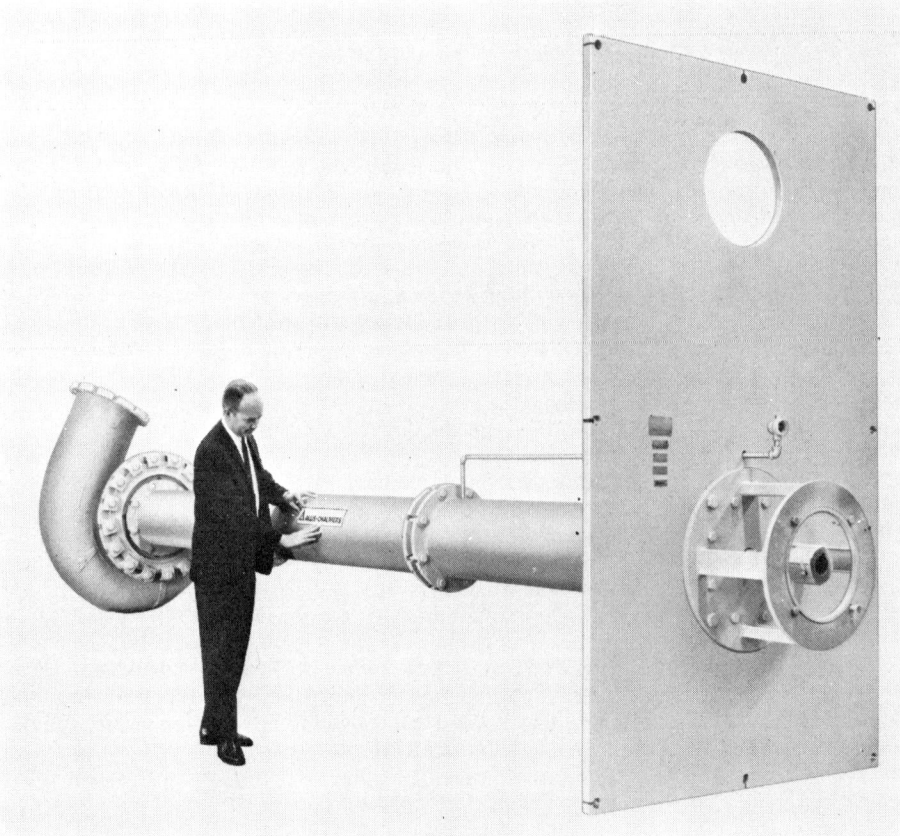

Fig. 4 (above)—'Shearpeller': special shear-lift force open impeller for single stage vertical sump pump to handle larger solids, two-phase liquids. (Allis-Chalmers PWX-V, available with either five or six vanes.)

Fig. 1 (far left)—Single stage, open impeller, vertical sump pump. (Allis-Chalmers CSO-V, V-100.)

Fig. 2 (near left)—Single stage, open impeller, close-coupled vertical sump pump with extended suction pipe and suction strainer. (Allis-Chalmers CSO-V, V-160.)

Fig. 3—Single stage, open impeller, vertical sump pump for corrosives and pulpy solids. (Allis-Chalmers PWO-V.)

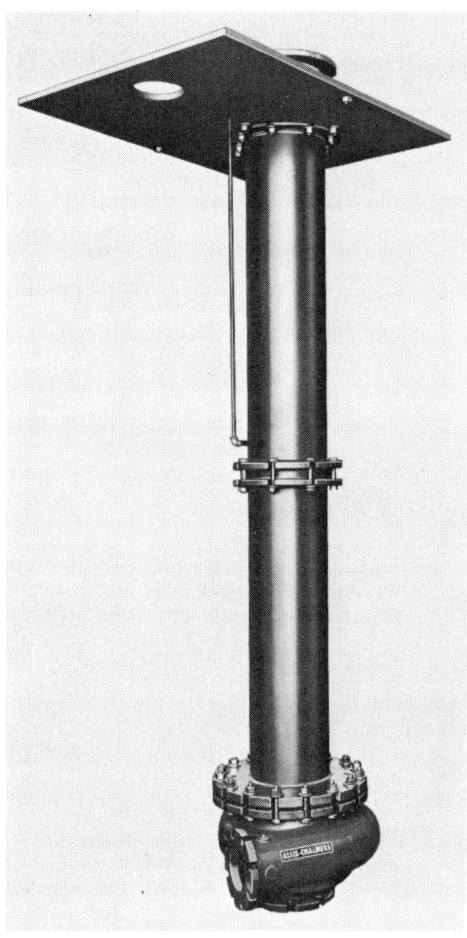

Fig. 6—Vertical turbine pump for single and/or multiple stages, with enclosed or open impellers and medium or high capacity bowl assemblies. (Allis-Chalmers type VT.)

Fig. 5—Single stage, enclosed impeller, vertical sump pump for coarse, abrasive solids. (Allis-Chalmers CWV.)

to the particular application.

Pumps with Shearpeller-type impellers have been used to solve a great number of difficult slurry handling problems. For example, long lengths of stringy, fibrous material can be put through a pump by adjusting clearance between the front face of the casing and the vanes. Pumps with Shearpellers can handle almost any type of solid (hard or soft), many slurries containing fragile crystalline solids, and even corrosive materials. They have also been successfully applied on frothy liquids with a gas or vapor content of up to 20% by volume, which is approximately seven times the amount of air, gas, or vapor that can be handled by a conventional centrifugal pump.

Shearpeller impellers are available in Ni-Hard for abrasive service, and in stainless steel for corrosive applications. Where additional head is required, Shearpeller-equipped pumps offer higher than normal heads at given impeller diameters and operating speeds. Operating efficiencies are closely comparable with those of other solids-handling centrifugal impellers and higher than for most "non-clog" designs. Another advantage is the ease with which a pump with standard open impeller can be converted in the field to use the Shearpeller, by ordering the few necessary conversion parts.

Centrifugal single stage, enclosed impeller for coarse, abrasive solids. The pump in Fig. 5 is very similar in design to the unit in Fig. 3 except that it uses an enclosed impeller and special hard metals to handle slurries with abrasive solids (⅛ to 1 in.) in suspension. To handle abrasives, major pump parts must have good wear-resisting qualities. In the Fig. 5 pump, the standard casing material is "Allisite" iron (an A-C trademark), an alloy with 350-450 Brinell hardness. Impellers and suction wear plates are made of Ni-Hard, a high-nickel alloy iron with Brinell hardness of 550-650. Optional construction in all-Ni-Hard metal is available for applications with 30% solids by weight. Other mechanical aspects are similar or identical to those of pumps shown in Figs. 1 and 3.

Vertical turbine pump, suitable for single and/or multiple stages, enclosed or open impellers, medium or high capacity bowl assemblies (Fig. 6). While vertical turbine pumps are best suited for clear, clean, non-corrosive liquids, they can be modified for corrosive/abrasive service. They would be selected over other types of pumps if higher pressures had to be developed.

For example, mechanically modified vertical turbine pumps have been found acceptable in some types of scale pit service. In this case, the bearings are of prime consideration. A vertical turbine pump modified for this type of abrasive service must have a source of clear, cool bearing flushing water available at 15 to 25 lb above the scale pit pump discharge pressure.

The flushing water is introduced into the tube that encloses the shafting and bearings, as well as the tail bearing of the pump, where it is led to the individual stages of the bowl bearings. This arrangement generally requires approximately 10 gpm per pump for operation. The flushing water runs continually through the pump so that there is always a liquid coming from the bearing to prevent foreign abrasive substances from entering and damaging any of the bearings. Contrary to popular opinion, clear water is an excellent lubricant for this type of (bronze) bearing.

Table 1—Guide to vertical wet pit sump pumps and their process applications*

Pump types	Representative number and range of sizes**	Normal capacity ranges	Heads to:	Standard temperature ranges	Normal working pressures to:	Typical applications
Single stage, open impeller, vertical wet pit design	Thirteen— 1½ x 1 x 6 through 6 x 4 x 13	10-15 gpm to 1,800 gpm max.	700 ft at 3,500 rpm; 240 ft at 1,750 rpm	+32°F to +212°F max.	375 psi with steel or steel alloys	Acid pits, waste sumps, overflow sumps, light sludge handling, tailings handling
Closed-coupled single stage, open impeller, vertical design for shallow sumps	Thirteen— 1½ x 1 x 6 through 6 x 4 x 13	10-15 gpm to 1,800 gpm max.	700 ft at 3,500 rpm; 240 ft at 1,750 rpm	-40°F to +250°F max.	375 psi with steel or steel alloys	Shallow waste sumps, ore washing, tailings handling
Single stage, open impeller, vertical wet pit design for soft solids, or corrosive/erosive services	Thirteen— 4 x 3 x 11½ through 16 x 4 x 21	100 gpm to 12,000 gpm max.	325 ft at 1,750 rpm; 210 ft at 1,160 rpm; 125 ft at 860 rpm	+32°F to +212°F max.	440 psi with steel or steel alloys	Acid sewer pit slurry, industrial waste waters, river water supply
Single stage, special radial vane open impeller, vertical wet pit design for large solids and two-phase liquids	Six— 4 x 3 x 11½ through 10 x 8 x 17	100 gpm to 5,000 gpm max.	260 ft at 1,750 rpm; 125 ft at 1,160 rpm; 70 ft at 860 rpm	+32°F to +212°F max.	440 psi with steel or steel alloys	Acid sewer pit slurry, industrial waste waters, river water supply, log bark chip sumps
Single stage, enclosed impeller vertical wet pit design for abrasive services	Eleven— 4 x 3 x 11½ through 16 x 14 x 21	100 gpm to 11,000 gpm	300 ft at 1,750 rpm; 215 ft at 1,160 rpm; 115 ft at 860 rpm	+32°F to +212°F max.	316 psi with Allisite or Ni-Hard	Slag pit, flood control, plant washdown, mill waste pits, scale handling, processed ore handling and washing
Vertical turbine open and enclosed impellers	Ten—5-in. through 24-in. bowls	70 gpm to 14,000 gpm max.	1,000 ft	160°F	500 psi with steel or steel alloys	Scale handling, cooling tower, raw water intake, mine dewatering, copper mine leaching

*This should not be considered a complete list of applications, but only as typical.
**Sizes indicate suction x discharge openings x nominal maximum diameter impeller.

Chrome alloy cast iron has been found to be the best material for impellers and bowls for abrasive service. Mild steel is selected for the column as well as the shaft enclosing tube, and either steel or cast iron for the discharge head. All bearings are usually constructed of high-leaded bronze (SAE 660 or equal). Line shafting of AISI 416 stainless steel or equal is recommended. Open type impellers are best for this service, and can be furnished in most vertical turbine pump designs.

Vertical turbine pumps in stainless steel construction are performing successfully in copper mine leaching. The 304 or 316 stainless steels are generally used, but other alloys may be suitable, depending on the type of corrosive to be pumped. CF 87 alloy has proved very successful in leaching service, handling such corrosives as copper sulphate, nitric acid, sulphuric acid, and sulphuric acid solutions of sodium dichromate.

Selection parameters for construction materials

A complete list of the liquids and slurries handled by vertical wet pit sump pumps, matched to the specific construction materials commonly recommended, can be found in the published Standards of the Hydraulic Institute, as well as in the catalogs and other publications of most pump manufacturers. Table 2 provides basic information on commonly used ferrous alloy casting materials for vertical wet pit sump pumps, along with some basic

Setting lengths	Materials of construction				
	Casing, casing cover, and impeller	Column pipe	Column bearings	Stuffing box	Motors used
From 2 ft min. to 20 ft max. in 1-ft increments	All pump wetted parts available in many machinable metals, stocked in cast iron, nodular iron, CF8M, CN7N, and Illium PD.	Avail. in either carbon or No. 316 stainless	Choice of fluted cutless rubber or Teflon	Not applicable	NEMA VP-HP standard design, solid shaft "P" flange vertical
6 ft max.	Same as above	Same as above	Not applicable	Choice of packing or variety of mechanical seals	NEMA "C" flange vertical with special extended shaft, adjustable bearing
Generally limited to 25-30 ft. Have been built with 40- to 50-ft settings. May be built with longer settings for special services	All pump wetted parts available in any machinable metal. Stocked in several metals.	Avail. in either carbon or No. 316 stainless	Choice of fluted cutless rubber or Teflon	Not applicable	NEMA VP-HP standard design, solid shaft "P" flange vertical
Same as above	Same as above except for impeller, which is available in CF8M and AISI 431 stainless.	Same as above	Same as above	Not applicable	NEMA VP-HP standard design, solid shaft "P" flange vertical
From 5 ft 0 in. to 25 ft max.	Casing available in Allisite or Ni-Hard; casing cover in Ni-Hard; impeller in AISI 431 stainless. (Also available in other hardened alloys such as 174PH.)	Steel	Fluted cutless rubber	Not applicable	NEMA VP-HP standard design, "P" flange vertical solid or hollow shaft
Settings normally to 50 ft.	Bowls available in CF8, CF8M; impeller in bronze, CF8, CF8M.	Carbon steel or CF8, CF8M	Cutless rubber, bronze, Teflon	Choice of packing or mechanical seals	Vertical solid shaft or hollow shaft

physical strength analyses and applications data. This information can be used as a general guide to materials selection.

A number of important factors must be considered in selecting the best and most economical material for a particular application:

Corrosion resistance. The liquid or slurry to be pumped should be carefully defined and described. Be sure to include the pH value of the liquid (a quantitative representation of the relative acidity or alkalinity). A solution having a pH of 7.0 is neutral, with pH values above 7.0 indicating alkalinity, and values below 7.0 indicating acidity. Since the pH value is expressed in a logarithmic scale, keep in mind that changes in pH represent more than a direct linear change. For example, a solution having a pH of 5.0 is 10 times as acid as one having a pH value of 6.0.

Electrochemical action. When two dissimilar metals are used in close proximity in a pump handling a liquid that is an electrolyte, severe corrosion may be caused by the galvanic cell action between the two metals. Where known, this should be avoided.

Abrasiveness of suspended solids. Wear resistance may be a key factor in selecting both the specific grade of alloy casting and the hardness to be attained. Size and concentration of solids must be accurately identified, and other physical characteristics of the solids defined.

Table 2—Guide to selection of casting materials for vertical wet pit sump pumps

Material	Similar to:	Tensile strength (psi)	Yield strength (psi)	Brinell Hardness Maximum	Machinability (based on AISI B-1112 = 100)	Weldability	Characteristics and typical applications
20% Chrome steel	ASTM A296 Grade CB 30 AISI 442	65,000	30,000	130-170	40	Poor	Corrosion resistant and heat resistant. Contains 22% to 30% nickel. Resistant to nitric acid, alkalies, organic chemicals, and oxidizing atmospheres.
28% Chrome steel	ASTM A296 Grade CC 50 AISI 446	55,000	–	241 max.	55	Poor	Suitable for handling oxidizing solutions such as high concentrations of nitric acid. Corrosion resistant and heat resistant. Resistant to dilute sulphuric acid in mine waters.
Allisite	A-48-62 Class 48	45,000	–	350-450	Not normally machined after heat treatment	Poor	A high strength, abrasion resistant iron alloy which contains 0.5% molybdenum and 1% each of either nickel or copper. Used on chemical pulps and slurries, dredge water, sump water, zinc tailings, dolomite, bauxite, and other solutions with suspended abrasive solids.
Ni-Hard No. 1	ASTM E 71-52 Class A-2	40-50,000	–	550-650	Not normally machinable	Poor	A harder, high strength iron alloy which contains 1.4-3.5% chrome, 3.0-3.6% carbon, 4.0-4.75% nickel, and 0.4-0.7% each of manganese and silicon.
17/4 PH (solution annealed condition H1150)	No ASTM available	180,000	150,000	310	50	Good	Precipitation hardenability of stainless steel castings of 17-4PH is based on the allotropic transformation of austenite to martensite, plus secondary strengthening through the precipitation of a copper complex. Used where some corrosion resistance plus high levels of strength and hardness are required.
CD4MCU (solution annealed)	No ASTM available	100,000-115,000	80,000-90,000	250-270	50	Good	An outstanding high strength, corrosion-resistant alloy developed for the ACI by Ohio State University. Relies on a duplex austenitic-ferritic structure plus a precipitation hardening reaction for its high strength. Shows high corrosion resistance to mineral acids over a wide range of temperature and concentration. Also shows resistance to oxidizing gases.
AISI No. 304 stainless (18-8 austenitic steel, low carbon)	ASTM A296 Grade CF8	70,000	30,000	150-190	50	Good	Has superior corrosion resistance when compared with straight chromium stainless steels. Most widely used corrosion resistant casting alloy.

Material	Similar to:	Materials analysis				Weldability	Characteristics and typical applications
		Tensile strength (psi)	Yield strength (psi)	Brinell Hardness Maximum	Machinability (Based on AISI B-112 = 100)		
AISI No. 304L stainless	ASTM A296 Grade CF8	70,000	30,000	150-190	50	Good	Same as CF-8 except low carbon content gives better weldability.
AISI No. 316 stainless 18-8 molybdenum austenitic steel)	ASTM A296 Grade CF8M	78,000	38,000	160-200	45	Good	Similar to CF8 except with 2-3% moly added to increase resistance to pitting, particularly by chlorides. Will also handle sulphuric acid.
AISI No. 316L stainless	ASTM A296 Grade CF3M	83,000	40,000	160-200	45	Good	Same as CF8M except low carbon content gives better weldability.
AISI Carpenter No. 20 stainless (high alloy)	ASTM 296 Grade CN7M	62,500	25,000	125-170	50	Good	Corrosion resistant special casting 28% nickel, 20% chromium, 2.5% moly, 2.5% copper. Addition of moly enables this alloy to handle hot sulphuric acid dependent on concentration and temperature. For extremely corrosive service, it is superior to CF8M (AISI No. 316 stainless).
Illium "PD" (solution annealed)	No ASTM available	95,000-105,000	65,000-80,000	201-217	45	Good	Developed to meet the need for a copper-free, hardenable alloy with good corrosion resistance. Has both high strength and high ductility. Shows excellent resistance to boiling nitric acid. Superior in corrosion resistance to CF8M on many reducing and oxidizing mineral acids.
Illium "W"	No ASTM Available	70,000	55,000	180	Poor	Good	Same as Hastelloy "C" below; resists corrosion of wet chlorine gas, hypochlorite, and chlorine dioxide. Resistant to halogens with oxidizing salts.
Hastelloy "C" (nickel-base alloy)	ASTM 494	72,000	46,000	180	Poor	Good	Contains 15.5% chrome, 16% moly, 4% tungsten, 4% iron, balance nickel. Suitable for hydrochloric acid and solutions containing free chlorine. Excellent corrosion resistance to hot dilute sulphuric, nitric, phosphoric, and organic acids.

Typical installation of four enclosed-impeller-type sump pumps in a scale pit. Maintenance requirements are minimal.

Pumping temperature. Cast iron loses tensile strength and becomes quite brittle at low temperatures. When service temperature is lowered, toughness tends to decrease, even in alloy steel parts. Remember, too, that the pH of a given solution varies somewhat with temperature changes, decreasing rather rapidly up to 300°F and remaining fairly constant above that. For example, a solution with a pH of 8.5 at 70°F will have a pH of about 7.0 at 300°F, and a 6.8 pH at 500°F.

Head (or head per stage). Since they affect both impeller peripheral velocity and liquid velocities in the water passages, heads must be calculated carefully.

Operating or developed pressure. If higher pressures are encountered, either through operation at higher than optimum design speeds or because of an abnormally high suction pressure, then either the pump design may have to be modified to obtain greater strength, or a stronger metal alloy must be selected. Pumps operating in series also must be watched carefully.

Structural suitability. The alloy selected must be suited to the structural features of the particular pump. The shape or configuration of specific castings may not lend themselves to certain alloys because of pouring problems, uneven cooling, etc.

Load factor. It would obviously be quite uneconomical to select a metal to give the longest possible life when the pump installation is temporary. A standard alloy lowest-cost pump might be used for temporary service where corrosion or erosion would wear out the pump in a relatively short period of time, since the pump life would still exceed its time in service. The same reasoning applies to installations where the pump is operated only infrequently and where idle periods do not contribute to disintegration of the metals.

Other economic factors. Plain common sense dictates that the choice of metals for a severe-service pump be based on considerations of optimum economic life. Materials should be chosen in a combination to ensure that the initial cost plus the cost of possible replacement parts yields the lowest overall total investment during the expected life of the equipment. In many cases, the materials chosen may be neither the cheapest nor the most expensive available. Conversely, where outstanding reliability is required, the very best materials must be employed, even if a pump is to be operated only once a year.

(While Table 2 provides a comprehensive comparison of various materials commonly used in vertical wet pit sump pumps, the pumps described here are not necessarily limited to the alloys included in the table.)

It is clear that each pump application must be evaluated on its own merits and requirements—for both the pump itself and the materials of construction. Similarities of function and design, of course, provide valuable clues to best selection. Where questions arise in selecting the right cast alloy and design to do the job, keep in mind that most pump suppliers have a well trained staff of specialists who can assist the user or the consulting engineer. □

High efficiency motors cut energy costs

A NEW LINE OF HIGH EFFICIENCY, high power factor electric motors designed to use substantially less electricity has been developed by the Century Electric Div. of Gould Inc. A typical industrial motor user (300-500 motors) could, after payback, save as much as $10,000 annually by switching to these motors, Gould claims, and payback for the higher initial cost of the units should take less than two years for all models. Available in 10 different models ranging from 1 to 25 hp, the motors are designed for a minimum power factor rating of 85%, and may allow the user to avoid paying a power factor penalty to the utility company.

Although the new motors have the same NEMA frame diameters as current Gould models, numerous modifications have been made to increase unit efficiency and power factor. Stator and rotor cores have been lengthened, the air gap has been reduced, winding material has been added to the rotor and stator, the slot configuration has been altered, and core steel with improved core loss properties has been added. Reduction of the air gap directly reduces the amount of current needed to magnetize the core, while the addition of copper and aluminum to the magnetic core reduces the flux density and core resistance, further reducing current requirements and increasing motor efficiency. Leakage resistance has also been minimized by optimizing the geometry of the stator and rotor slots, Gould reports.

Increased motor prices resulting from these modifications are more than justified by the energy saved in motor operation, according to Gould. For example, payback of the price premium for a 3-hp drip-proof motor of the new design is less than one year at an energy cost level of 2-3¢ per kwh and an in-service time of 4,000 hr annually. After payback, the same unit will save approximately $100 in the next 20,000 hr of operation, according to the manufacturer's calculations. Since higher-horsepower motors normally have higher efficiencies and better power factors initially, payback of the price premium will be proportionally slower at the same energy cost; however, even the 25-hp unit has a payback of less than two years at today's energy costs.

All of the new motors are four pole/three phase, available in both drip-proof and totally enclosed, fan-cooled designs. Besides the energy savings, a number of other benefits are claimed for the units. Magnetic noise is considerably reduced because of the lower magnetic density in the motor cores. The motors also run cooler (as much as 10°C cooler in some instances) because they have fewer current losses to dissipate. Cooler operation extends insulation life and allows use of smaller, quieter ventilation fans. In addition, sensitivity to line voltage variations is much reduced. Although voltage fluctuation itself does not have a large effect on motor efficiency, it can have a sizable effect on power factor.

Although it might be hoped that motors greater than 25 hp would be produced in the new design, Gould representatives note that 90% of all motors used in industry are in the 1- to 25-hp range, and high-hp motors already have fairly good efficiency and power factors. As for the future of the new models, H. S. Burker, director of marketing for Century Electric, says, "Skyrocketing electricity costs and possible future shortages virtually dictate evolution of high efficiency and high power factor motors. As energy costs continue to escalate in coming years, the value of energy-saving motors will be further reinforced."

For more information about high efficiency motors, write to Ray Jokerst, Gould Inc., Century Electric Div., 1831 Chestnut St., St. Louis, Mo. 63166.

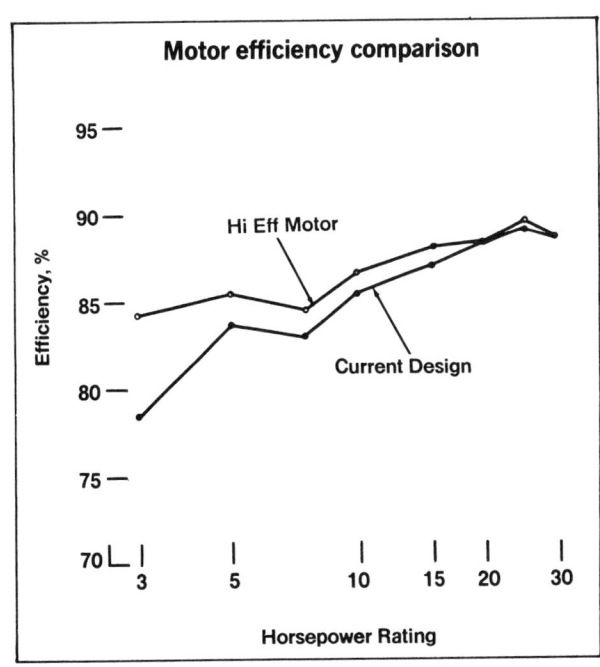

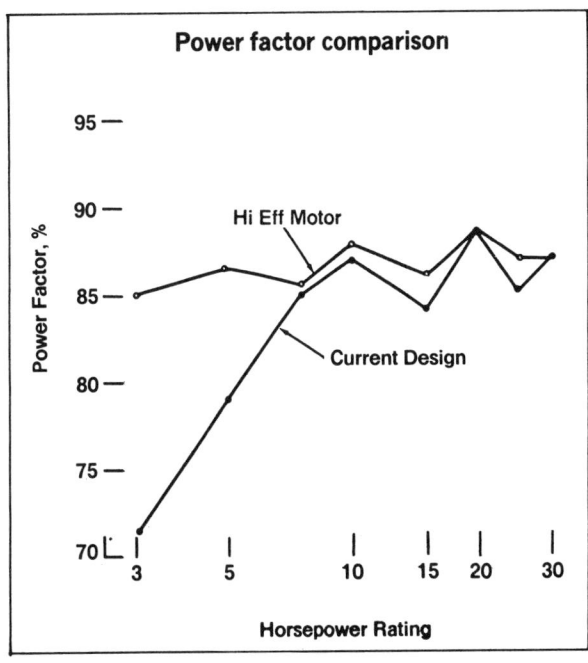

Nomographs simplify cable tramway design

THE CALCULATION OF DESIGN FACTORS FOR CABLEWAYS, once a complex and time-consuming task, has now been simplified through the use of two nomographs. Created by Adam Zanker, an engineer in Israel, the nomographs are said to permit the calculation of all desired variables in a matter of seconds.

Cableways are aerial hoisting and conveying devices using suspended steel cable or wire rope for tracks. The loads are suspended from carriages and are moved either by gravity or by power. Average loads for cableways employed in earth and coal transport are from 1 to 5 tons; for rock quarries, 5 to 20 tons; and for concrete, 12 to 50 tons.

The maximum clear span for cableways is 2,000 to 3,000 ft, while the usual spans range from 300 to 1,500 ft. A safety factor of at least 4 is advised for track cables, and the allowable deflection of track cables with their maximum gross loads at midspan is usually taken as 5½% to 6% of the span.[1]

The main relationships between all the factors influencing the design of a cableway are described by the following equations:[2]

$$h = [(wL + P)L] / 2H$$

$$P = (2hH - wL^2) / L$$

$$P = (8hH - wS^2) / 2S$$

$$H = [(wL + P)L] / 2h$$

where:
S = span between supports, in ft
L = ½ the span, in ft
w = weight of rope, in lb per ft
P = total concentrated load on rope, in lb
h = maximum deflection of rope, in ft
H = horizontal tension in rope, in lb

Table 1—Relationships between rope diameter and other properties

Rope diameter (inches)	Approximate weight (lb per ft)	Approximate breaking strength (tons)
¼	0.09-0.10	2-3
½	0.36-0.45	7-12
1	1.45-1.80	30-45
1½	3.20-4.00	70-100
2	6.20-7.20	120-170
2½	9.50-11.20	190-270
3	13.50-14.50	280-400
3½	18.00-20.00	380-500

Source: Baumeister, Theodore, ed., *Standard Handbook for Mechanical Engineers*, 7th ed., McGraw-Hill Book Co., 1967, Chapter 8. (Data abridged and rounded.)

Table 2—Range of each nomograph

Variable	Part 1	Part 2
w (lb per ft)	0-2.5	0-20
S (ft)	200-2,000	400-3,000
P (lb)	0-20,000	0-200,000
H (lb)	0-140,000	0-600,000
h (ft)	0-200	0-300

Using these equations, it is possible to calculate the expected deflection of cable when the load, span, and tension are known; the maximum allowable load (P) for a given span, tension, and an assumed deflection; the recommended span for other data known or assumed; and the necessary tension of the rope for other data known or assumed.

The process of designing cableways also requires data on the relationship between the cable (rope) diameter, its weight per linear foot, and its breaking strength. Particular attention should be paid to the rope's design safety factor (usually 4, but for a very good rope it may be 3). Table 1 shows the relationships of rope diameter, weight, and approximate breaking strength.

The two nomographs speed up calculation of design factors—generally a long, tedious process when using the above formulas and table. The method of using the nomographs is the same for both; they differ in their range only. Because the nomograph covering the full range of variables (Part 2) is very inaccurate in the low-values range, the additional nomograph is needed. Table 2 summarizes the range covered by each nomograph.

The method of employing either nomograph depends on the variable desired. There are four possible cases:

Case I—P, H, w, and S are known; h is desired.

1) Find the intersection point of the curves of known values S and P on the grid. Interpolate if necessary. Call this point A.

2) Connect point A with a straightedge to the known value w on the appropriate scale, and extend this line up to its intersection with the REFERENCE LINE. Mark this point B.

3) Connect point B with a straightedge to the known value of H on the appropriate scale. Read the value h on the intersection of the straightedge with the oblique h scale.

Case II—P, w, S, and h are known; H is desired.

Steps 1 and 2 are identical to the first two steps in Case I.

3) Connect point B with a straightedge to the known value h on the oblique scale, and extend this line up to the intersection with the H scale. Read the H value on this intersection.

Case III—S, h, H, and w are known; P is desired.

1) Connect with a straightedge the known values h and H on the appropriate scales, and extend this line up to the intersection with the REFERENCE LINE. Mark this point B.

2) Connect point B with a straightedge to the known value w on the appropriate scale. Mark point A as the intersection of the straightedge with the known S-value curve.

3) Find the appropriate P curve that intersects point A, interpolating if necessary. Read the value of this P curve on the P scale.

Case IV—P, H, h, and w are known; S is desired.

Step 1 is identical to the first step in Case III.

2) Connect point B with a straightedge to the known value w on the appropriate scale. Mark point A as the intersection of the straightedge with the known P-value curve.

3) Find the appropriate S curve that intersects point A,

Part 1

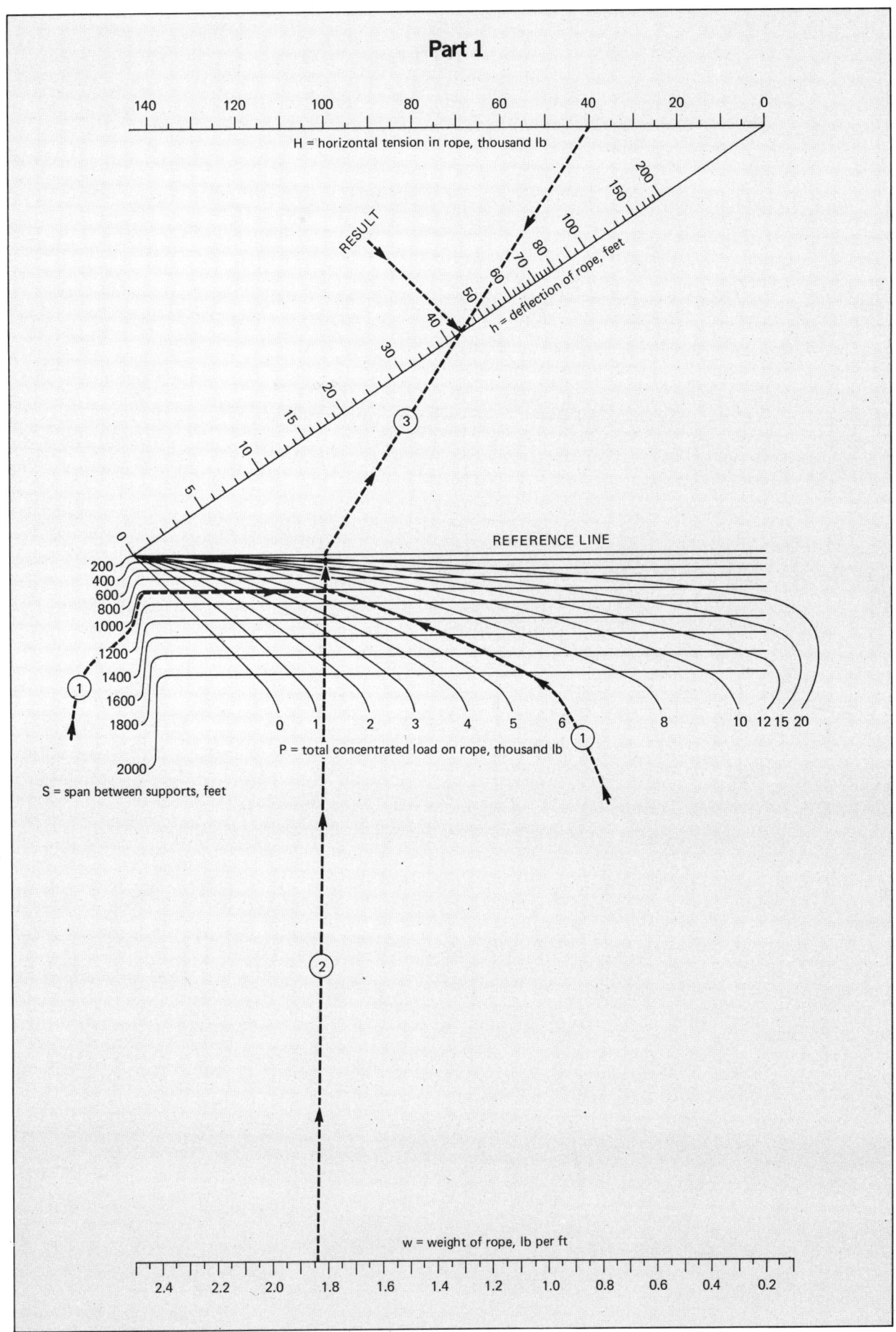

Part 2

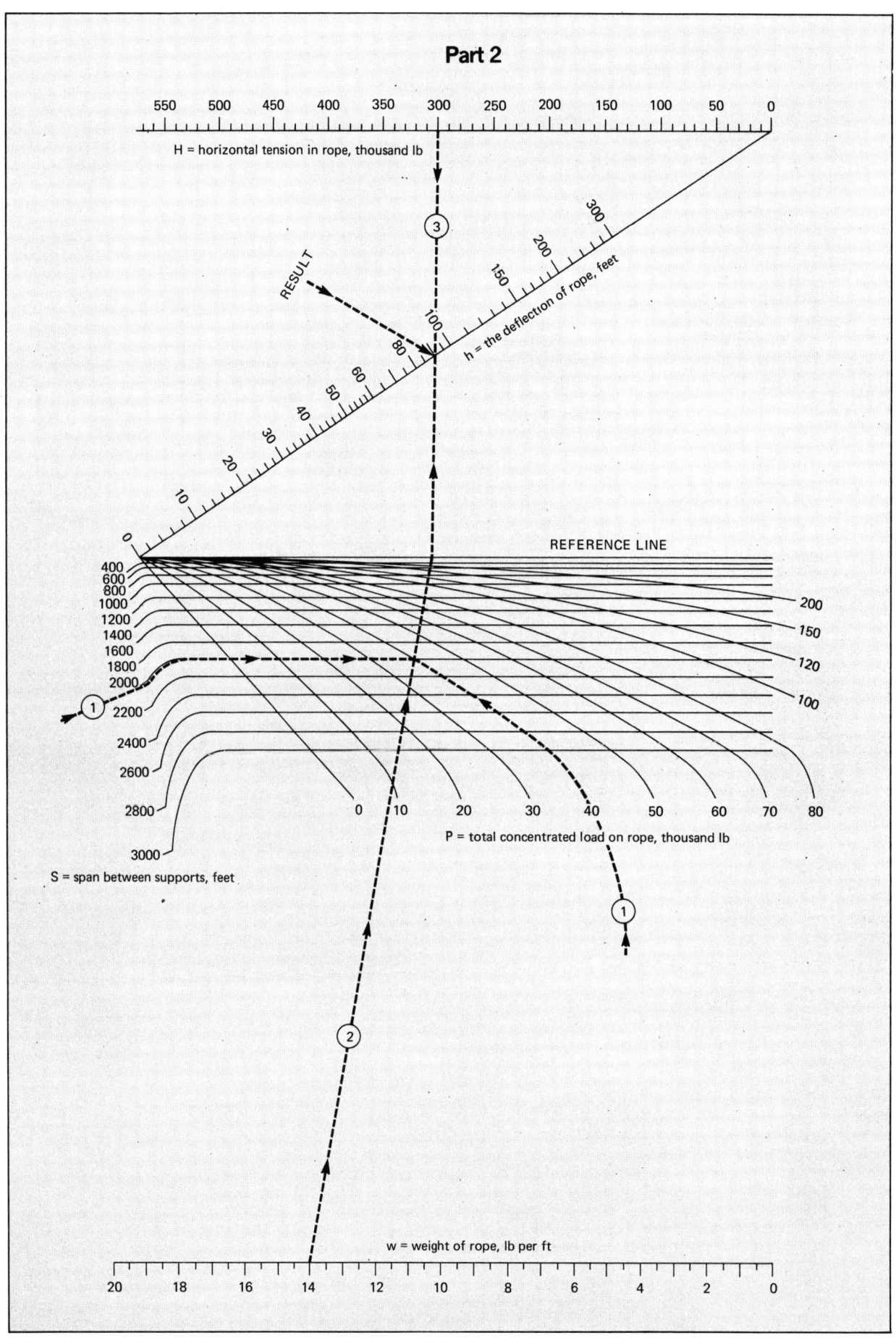

interpolating if necessary. This curve gives the desired S value.

Two examples will illustrate the use of the nomographs:

Example 1—Low range nomograph (Part 1).
- Given that $S = 1,000$ ft, $w = 1.84$ lb per ft, $P = 6,000$ lb, and $H = 40,000$ lb, find the value of h.
- To solve, use Case I method (the steps and values are indicated on the nomograph by dotted lines). $h = 43.5$ ft.

Example 2—High range nomograph (Part 2).
- Given that $S = 2,000$ ft, $w = 14$ lb per ft, $P = 40,000$ lb, and $H = 300,000$ lb, find the value of h.
- To solve, again use Case I method (steps are indicated by dotted lines). $h = 90.0$ ft. □

References
1) Baumeister, Theodore, ed., *Standard Handbook for Mechanical Engineers*, 7th edition, McGraw-Hill Book Co., 1967, Chapter 10.
2) ibid.

New survey instrument displays readings on both sides

A NEW ELECTRONIC DEVICE to measure distance and angles combines a distance meter, electronic digital theodolite, and microprocessor in a single package.

Introduced by Hewlett-Packard Co., the new HP 3820A "Electronic Total Station" is priced at $17,750. Hewlett-Packard says the unit will:

- Automatically measure horizontal, vertical, and slope distances to 5 km (3.1 mi) while correcting for earth curvature, refraction, and atmospheric conditions.

- Electronically measure horizontal and zenith angles to 1 sec, while automatically compensating for instrument mislevel.

- Send data to an optional external data collector for later processing, or directly to a calculator or computer.

- Track (continuously update) any of the quantities it measures or computes.

- Compute and display relative direction (clockwise angle from the previous to the current direction).

The 3820A is designed for applications such as land, construction, and control surveys, as well as precise traversing, photo control, trigonometric leveling, structural monitoring, and land slip studies. Typical mining applications include volumetric control of ore and waste excavations, earth movement or slope failure monitoring, and regional topographic surveys. One copper company has used the instrument to help solve a railroad relocation problem.

The 3820A automatically computes and displays information in the form and units most useful to the operator.

Three developments are said to make the 3820A one of the most advanced devices on the market: 1) a "lasing" diode, a solid state device that gives long range and high accuracy with extremely low power consumption; 2) an electronic level sensor, which makes the instrument the first of its kind able to compensate both horizontal and vertical angles for instrument mislevel; and 3) a highly sophisticated electronic circle interpolation technique, combined with a microprocessor, which allows the 3820A to display electronically horizontal and vertical angles.

The instrument has a 30x telescope; measurements are displayed in feet or meters, degrees or grads. Two-speed tangent screws provide fast sighting. The 3820A features electronic aim for sighting under poor conditions, and it has illuminated crosshairs for night work, plus an automatic self-test. The unit makes continuous distance measurements, keeping a running total of the mean and variance of the readings. If variance remains within specifications, the mean is displayed. □

Nomograph for in-situ uranium leaching

William C. Larson, geologist
Twin Cities Mining Research Center,
US Bureau of Mines

THIS NOMOGRAPH provides a fast, convenient method for estimating production at an in-situ uranium leaching operation. It has been designed to permit quick calculation of the recovery rate of uranium oxide (lb per year) for various mill throughput rates (gpm) and pregnant solution strengths (ppm U_3O_8), or vice versa. Each of the variables is expressed in the units of measure commonly used in the uranium industry. Using known or estimated values for any two of the variables, the third value can be read from the graph with the aid of a straightedge. For example, if a mill is designed to handle a throughput rate of 1,000 gpm and the average pregnant solution strength to the mill is 70 ppm U_3O_8, then annual production will be about 300,000 lb. The nomograph assumes 365 days per year of operation and 100% recovery in the mill's ion exchange systems.

The nomograph sheds some light on the sensitivity of production to changes in uranium concentration in pregnant feed obtained by in-situ leaching. For example, a 1,000-gpm operation averaging 100-ppm pregnant solution strength could produce about 439,000 lb per year of U_3O_8; however, if pregnant solution grade varies by ±10%, production could range from a low of 395,000 lb per year to a high of about 483,000 lb per year, illustrating the importance of optimizing the strength of pregnant solution. □

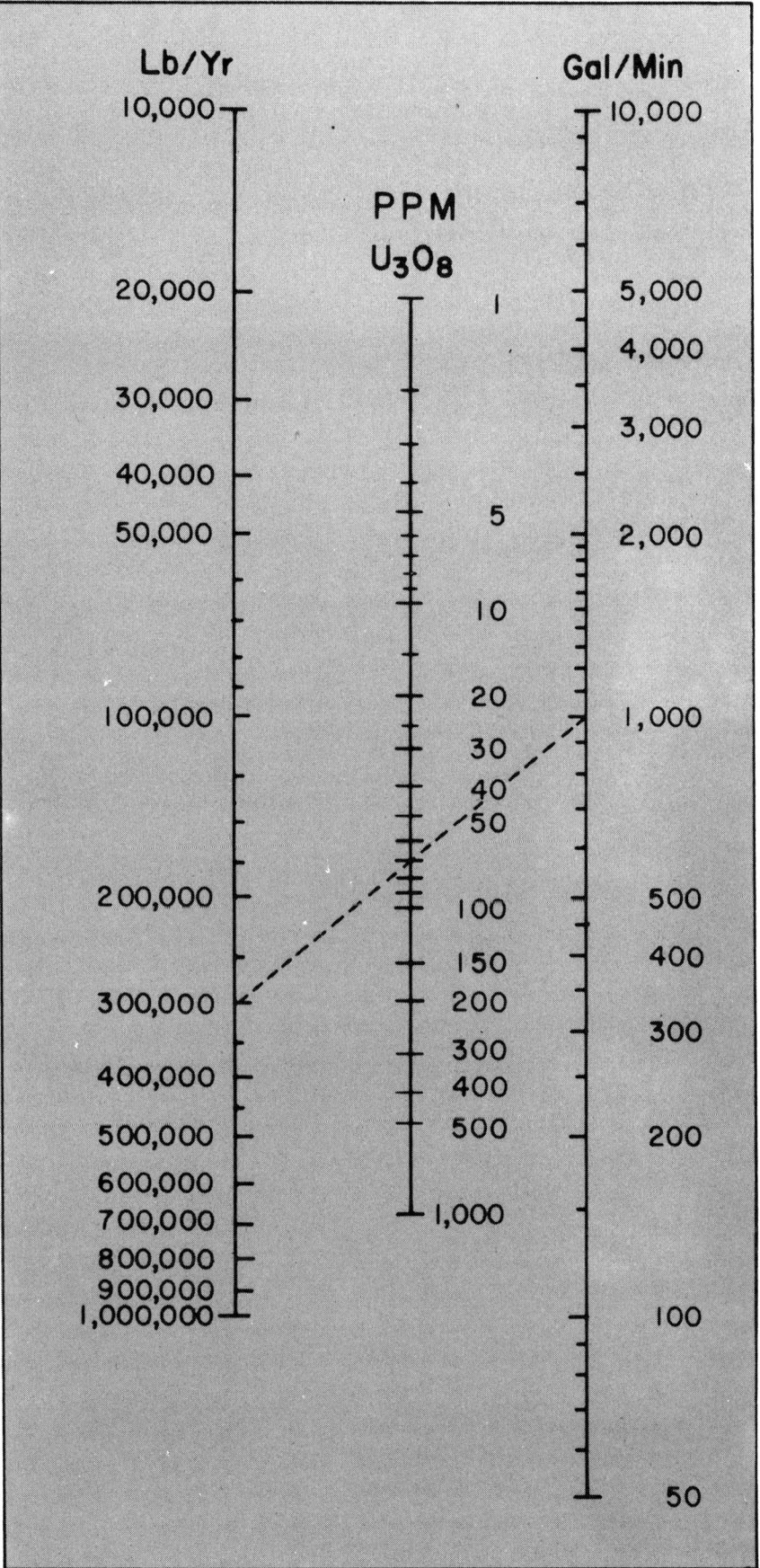

Water slurry properties

F. Caplan, P.E., Oakland, Calif.

THOSE WORKING WITH WATER SLURRIES are interested in the solids specific gravity (S), the percent solids by weight (W), the specific gravity of the slurry mixture (M), and the percent solids by volume (V). The relationships are shown on the nomograph here, prepared by F. Caplan, a professional engineer, of Oakland, Calif. If any two properties are known, the other two are fixed. The nomograph gives a rapid simultaneous solution to the equations. Example: What are M and V if $S = 2.5$ and $W = 62.5\%$? Align the S and W values and read $M = 1.60$ and $V = 40.0\%$. □

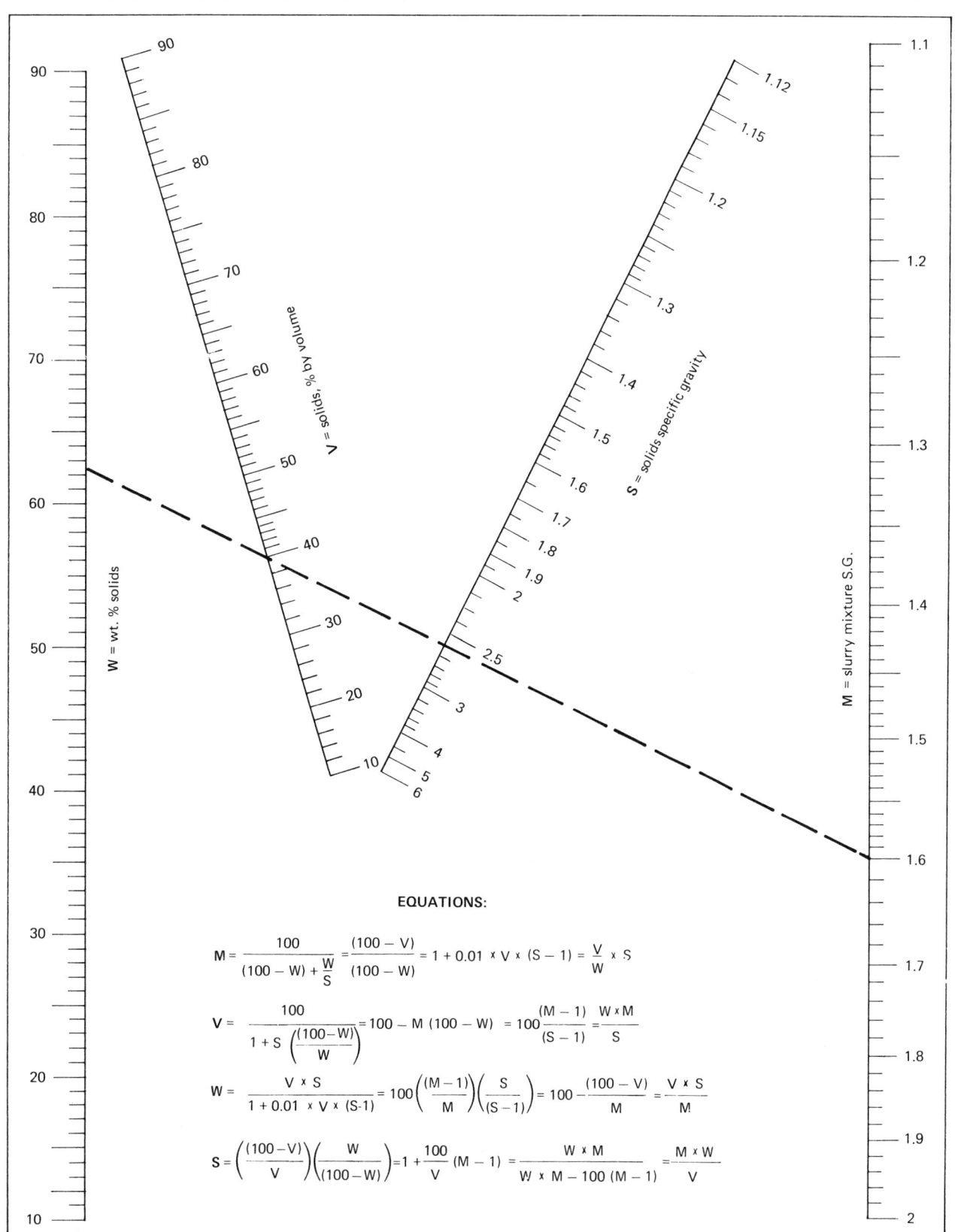

EQUATIONS:

$$M = \frac{100}{(100-W) + \frac{W}{S}} = \frac{(100-V)}{(100-W)} = 1 + 0.01 \times V \times (S-1) = \frac{V}{W} \times S$$

$$V = \frac{100}{1 + S\left(\frac{100-W}{W}\right)} = 100 - M(100-W) = 100\frac{(M-1)}{(S-1)} = \frac{W \times M}{S}$$

$$W = \frac{V \times S}{1 + 0.01 \times V \times (S-1)} = 100\left(\frac{(M-1)}{M}\right)\left(\frac{S}{(S-1)}\right) = 100 - \frac{(100-V)}{M} = \frac{V \times S}{M}$$

$$S = \left(\frac{(100-V)}{V}\right)\left(\frac{W}{(100-W)}\right) = 1 + \frac{100}{V}(M-1) = \frac{W \times M}{W \times M - 100(M-1)} = \frac{M \times W}{V}$$

Environmental impacts focus attention on waste handling

ENACTMENT OF A WIDE VARIETY of environmental controls during the past several years has wrought significant changes in the handling of mill tailings and mine and mill effluents. Environmental engineers have joined the staffs of many mine and mill operations, and the arrows pointing "to waste" at the corners of mill flowsheets have drawn much attention.

An International Tailing Symposium was sponsored by WORLD MINING in Tucson, Ariz., in late 1972, drawing registrants from 21 countries. Harris H. Burke, manager of soil engineering for Bechtel Inc., outlined the "Structural Characteristics Resulting from Construction Methods" for tailings dams, emphasizing that the separation of tailings into a coarse and a fine fraction and use of the coarse fraction in dam construction enhance the structural properties of dams.[35]

While the physical properties of tailing materials are quite variable, Burke said, milling processes often produce tailings that are excellent material for dam construction. (Exceptions include the black mud residues from cryolite recovery and the clay fines washed out of coal.) However, the hydraulic transportation and deposition processes generally used in moving tailings to storage ponds may leave a loose, saturated mass subject to liquefaction, especially under the dynamic stress conditions generated during an earthquake. Of less importance, but still a major factor, may be continued heavy blasting in a nearby open-pit mine.

Use of only coarse tailings fractions in dam construction and compaction of dam materials after emplacement increase dam stability. In addition, provision for adequate internal drainage, thus ensuring low seepage lines, can enhance dam strengths.

The two most common means for separating coarse tailings fractions are natural sedimentation of flat beaches or tailings ponds or mechanical separation by cyclones.

Designing safe tailings structures

Safe maximum embankment height and associated slope, along with the physical controls to be placed on the movement of water associated with a tailings structure, are among the basic questions to be addressed in designing safe tailings systems, USBM mining research engineer Dan Kealy said in a 1973 MINING CONGRESS JOURNAL report. Some answers to these questions are available in USBM publications.[36,37]

Some form of instrumentation should be used for monitoring the status and safety of every embankment at various time intervals, Kealy stated, especially tailings embankments that are under continual construction. Piezometers and slope indicators are the only instruments needed.

Rate of tailing deposition (annual rise) is important because it affects the phreatic surface (elevation of the "water table" within the tailings structure) and the pore water pressure. A large annual rise causes a high phreatic surface and therefore a high pore pressure. Higher embankments are more susceptible to failure; a rising dam that is safe now may be in a failure condition in five years.

Abandonment is another design criteria. In preparation for abandonment:

1) Tailings structures must be capable of handling 50-to 100-year storm conditions without adverse effect.

2) Decant systems must provide access to internal drainage for inspection monitoring and for potential leach operation. (The decant system is the key to design for abandonment.)

3) Consideration must be given to embankment geometry and esthetics relative to surrounding natural terrain.

4) Maintenance-free structures are desirable.

5) Exploration drilling prior to construction is a must to avoid construction over an unknown orebody that might require subsequent removal of the dam.

Reclamation at Climax, Urad, and Henderson

Most active mining operations in the US conduct ongoing tailings and waste dump reclamation programs. At its Climax mine near Leadville, Colo., Amax Inc. began tailings revegetation research in 1965. Subsequent development of the company's reclamation program was described by Amax environmental control engineer Larry F. Brown at the 1975 AMC convention in San Francisco.[38]

Amax's three molybdenum mines—Climax, Urad, and Henderson—operate at elevations ranging from 10,300 to 11,300 ft above sea level. Winters are severe, and growing seasons are very short. Native grass seeds are not commercially available, so much of Amax's research has been directed at finding commercially available seed species adaptable to its harsh operating environment.

At Climax, most of the tailings area is still being used for tailings deposition; however, overburden from an open-pit mine started up in 1973 is being used to reclaim a tailings area no longer in use. At Henderson, which will produce its first concentrate in 1976, reclamation will be easier than at Climax because extensive environmental planning has been part of the development of the mine.

Urad shut down at the end of 1974 after seven years of production, and a comprehensive reclamation program is under way. Two tailings areas covering about 125 acres pose the major reclamation problem, and three major waste products are being used to accomplish the job: mine-development rock from Henderson, sewage sludge from Denver, and wood chips from a nearby sawmill. Test plots begun in 1974 indicated that the most economical and beneficial tailings area treatment would be an initial application of 20 tons per acre of both sewage and wood chips, followed two or three years later by 10 tons per acre of sewage. Even with this application of 50 tons per acre of organics, inorganic fertilization will be necessary.

The revegetation process will follow these steps: cover with development rock, build up hills to break the flat contour; haul in and stockpile sewage and wood chips; spread P_2O_5 fertilizer and wood chips; rip wood chips and fertilizer into the surface with a dozer; spread sewage sludge; scatter dead timber on the surface; plant trees (both transplants and seedlings); seed with grass; irrigate (first year only); replant failures; and follow up with inorganic fertilizers.

The Urad reclamation project is expected to cost about $8 million. It will be essentially complete by 1982 but will require annual inorganic fertilization through 1996. By that time, a soil mature enough to support vegetation without additional fertilization should develop.

Complying with effluent guidelines

The Environmental Protection Agency has promulgated a number of mill and tailings pond effluent guidelines, with phase 1 deadlines coming due July 1, 1977. Dr. David E. Hyatt, manager of analytical services at the Colorado School of Mines Research Institute, reviewed these guidelines in some detail and examined available technologies and costs of application in a paper presented at the Western Mining Conference in Denver early in 1976.[39]

The first stage at which to consider technology bearing on the quality of final mill effluent is the mill processing circuit, Hyatt observed. He suggested the following steps in handling internal mill water to improve effluent quality:

1) Beneficiation processes in some cases can be designed so that process streams containing reagents such as cyanide, ammonia, and organic solvents are separated from tailings streams. The reagent-bearing streams can be recycled or treated to decompose the pollutants.

2) Reagents can in some cases be selected on the basis of recoverability and decomposability, as well as for their primary processing functions.

3) Tailings thickeners are now almost a necessity to obtain maximum clarification from ponds.

4) In instances where waste heat and excess water coexist in a mill, waste streams may be treated by segregation and selective evaporation to reduce their volume. If weather conditions are favorable, evaporative ponds may be feasible for controlling impurity bleed streams.

5) Physical modification of processing modules or of waste water handling systems to enhance aeration, solids-liquids contact, and exposure to ultraviolet radiation may promote the removal of some pollutants. Complexed cyanide ion, free cyanide ion, ammonia, oxidizable organic and metallic species, sulphide ion, and other waste water constituents are potentially influenced by this type of design modification.

6) Control of ore constituents or accessory minerals entering the mill may be practical to eliminate or sharply reduce particular pollutant levels in the mill waste streams. In most instances, however, the geology of the ore deposit will make this option impractical.

Hyatt also suggested that tailings ponds be sited in areas of limited or controllable runoff from natural water courses, because once such water enters the tailings system, it is subject to effluent regulations.

The large surface area of most ponds is conducive to evaporative loss of water and may either assist or aggravate plant water balance. In the southwestern US, evaporation rates may exceed 4 gpm per acre of surface.

Chemical treatment of waste water entering the pond may include oxidation, sorption, precipitation of soluble species, microbial degradation, and a variety of other potentially useful phenomena. Oxidation of cyanide, sulphide, ferrous iron, and other soluble species may render them less toxic or less soluble. Sorption of soluble metals on tailings, native soils, or on precipitation complexes of metals may provide an excellent opportunity to remove such soluble species as zinc (II), arsenic (III), cadmium (II), copper (II), and others. Precipitation of hydrous oxides or hydroxides of many transition metals may require a rather prolonged time, as more stable, soluble complexes are degraded and insoluble forms begin to predominate. Lime precipitation is perhaps the most common approach to metal hydroxide formation and, given adequate time and control of pH levels achieved, it may be satisfactory in many cases. Complexes of metals with cyanide and ammonia, however, are especially prone to stabilization and solubilization in caustic solution and may require special treatment. Microbial assimilation of such species as cyanide, sulphide, iron, copper, and zinc has been utilized at various levels from laboratory to full scale plant operation. Tailoring the environment of some or all of the tailings pond to accommodate beneficial organisms may prove highly successful in some instances.

Hyatt listed ion exchange, reverse osmosis, ultrafiltration, electrodialysis, electrooxidation and electroreduction, chemical oxidation and reduction, and activated carbon sorption systems among those available for treating pond effluent. While such systems are usually expensive to construct and operate, they may be justified by requirements to produce drinking-quality water.

"In the final analysis," Hyatt said, "we are forced to consider water as a real raw material in the ore dressing process. We may either use and reuse this water, or we may use it once and pass it on to the next user. In the first case, the quality demands placed on the water are largely of our own definition. In the latter case, 'the next user' is generally spoken for by regulatory agencies and our effluent quality is set by criteria outside the mill flowsheet. Under these conditions, the desirability of zero discharge and water recycle becomes appealing and plant design and operation to achieve this goal appears highly recommended." □

Copper mine wastes: good potential as medium for growing livestock forage

A. D. Day, K. L. Ludeke, G. O. Amaugo, and T. C. Tucker

WITH IMPROVED CULTURAL PRACTICES, barley grown on copper mine wastes may produce high yields of quality forage for livestock feed in the southwest US and similar areas elsewhere in the world. This conclusion was reached after two years of joint research conducted by the University of Arizona and Cyprus Pima Mining Co., Tucson, Ariz. The studies compared the growth and the fiber, protein, and amino acid contents of barley forage grown on four soil materials in copper mine wastes. The four soil materials were tailings, tailings-overburden, overburden, and desert soil.

The experiment was designed to be analyzed statistically. Replications of plantings were arranged horizontally along tailings slopes containing each type of soil material to insure an adequate sample of each soil treatment. A smooth, loose seedbed was prepared on a 1.5:1 tailings berm slope in each soil material using a "sidewinder" and "sheepfoot roller." (The sidewinder is a long, rotating roller with 20-cm, spike-like teeth used to break up the surface crust on soil materials in copper mine waste.) Approximately 13 cm of irrigation water was sprinkled over the area prior to planting. Twenty-nine kg per hectare of elemental nitrogen was supplied in pre-planting irrigation.

Arivat barley was broadcast planted by hand at the rate of 112 kg per hectare in December of each year. Immediately after planting, 11,200 kg per hectare of barley straw was applied to the experimental area. Following the straw application, 19 kg per hectare of elemental nitrogen was applied in 6 cm of irrigation water. Additional irrigation, fertilizer application, and other cultural practices were carried out as suggested by Arizona publications for barley pasture forage. (Cultural practices include proper application of fertilizer, weed control, irrigation, and soil tillage.)

Plant-less tailings slopes are susceptible to erosion by wind and water, causing pollution of the environment.

In March, the forage was harvested at the jointing stage of growth by hand-sickle cutting about 3 cm above soil level. Plant height, tillers per unit area, and forage yield were recorded at harvest time. The oven-dried plant materials were ground with a Wiley mill having a No. IEC 80559 screen (six holes per cm in each direction). The following data were obtained from the ground samples: 1) total fiber content, according to a technique described by Van Soest and Wine; 2) total protein, using the micro-Kjeldahl method for total nitrogen determination; and 3) amino acid content, by two-directional paper chromatography as described by Klein and Klein. The data were analyzed using the recommended standard analysis of variance, and arithmetic means were compared using Student-Newman-Keul's test as described by Steel and Torrie.

Plants grew tallest in desert soil

The experiments revealed that the average plant height of barley forage was greatest when grown in desert soil and least when grown in tailings soil material—a predictable outcome resulting from the sterile condition of the tailings soil. Barley plants grown in overburden and tailings-overburden were shorter than those grown in desert soil but taller than those grown in pure tailings.

Barley plant tillers per unit area were highest for barley forage grown in desert soil and lowest in tailings soil material. Plants grown in overburden had more tillers per unit area than plants produced in tailings-overburden or pure tailings.

Green forage and oven-dry forage yields were highest for barley grown in desert soil and lowest in pure tailings. Barley grown in pure overburden produced more pasture forage than crops grown in a mixture of tailings and overburden.

The relative differences in plant growth and forage yield for barley grown in the four soil materials was an indication of the relative amounts of plant nutrients (primarily nitrogen and phosphorus) in the four soil materials. Desert soil was highest in fertility, followed by overburden, tailings-overburden, and tailings, in decreasing order. Relatively high yields of pasture forage were obtained from barley grown in desert soil.

Barley forage grown in desert, overburden, or tailings soil materials contained similar amounts of total fiber—a higher fiber content than forage produced in a mixture of tailings and overburden. Barley pasture forage grown in desert, overburden, or tailings soil materials contained similar amounts of total protein but less protein than forage produced in a mixture of tailings and overburden.

As total fiber content decreases and total protein content increases, the nutritional value of livestock feed increases. Since fiber content and protein content are measures of feed value, barley forage grown in a mixture of tailings and overburden had a higher relative feed value than forage produced in desert, overburden, or tailings soil materials.

Barley pasture forage grown in desert, overburden, tail-

The authors: A. D. Day is an agronomist in the Department of Plant Sciences, University of Arizona, Tucson, Ariz.; K. L. Ludeke—agronomist, Cyprus Pima Mining Co., Tucson, Ariz.; G. O. Amaugo—graduate student, Department of Plant Sciences, University of Arizona; and T. C. Tucker—soil scientist, Department of Soils, Water, and Engineering, University of Arizona.

ings-overburden, or tailings soil materials contained similar amounts of the amino acids alanine, cystine, glutamic acid, methionine, and phenylalanine. However, forage grown in a mixture of tailings and overburden contained more aspartic acid than forage produced in pure tailings. Differences in amino acid concentrations in barley forage grown in the four soil materials may be partially explained by possible differences in the availability of nutrients to barley plants in the soil materials studied. Nutrients necessary for amino acid synthesis may have been more available to plants grown in desert and tailings-overburden soil materials than they were to plants grown in overburden or pure tailings. Methionine and phenylalanine, two essential amino acids for animal growth, were present in barley forage grown on copper mine wastes, and their concentrations were highest in forage produced in desert and tailings-overburden soil materials.

Phenylalanine is needed for the formation of its hydroxy compound, tyrosine. Phenylalanine and tyrosine are the sole precursors of the hormones thyroxine and adrenalin. Methionine, which is essential for growth of livestock, provides the sulphur necessary for cystine synthesis. Glutamic acid can serve as a substitute for arginine in livestock diets, and it can provide the amino group necessary for the synthesis of nonessential amino acids. Cystine concentration was highest in forage grown in desert and tailings-overburden soil materials. Cystine partially satisfies the need for methionine in animal diets. Traces of other amino acids found in barley pasture forage grown in copper mine wastes included glycine, lysine, serine, and threonine.

Desert, tailings-overburden soils: best potential

Relatively high variability was observed in fiber, protein, and amino acid data obtained from the two-year experiments. This variability may be partially explained by the fact that overburden, tailings-overburden, and tailings are very heterogeneous soil materials which vary greatly in fertility from one location to another. The occurrence of two essential amino acids, methionine and phenylalanine, and high concentrations of other amino acids in forage produced in desert and tailings-overburden soil materials indicates that these soil materials may have potential in growing forage for animal feed.

Forage yields from barley grown in overburden, tailings-overburden, and tailings were too low to justify the commercial production of this crop in such soil materials without special cultural practices to increase the soils' level of plant nutrients, content of organic matter, and capacity to hold moisture. □

References

1) Amburgey, L. A., "Fertilizer Recommendations for Arizona," Arizona Coop. Ext. Ser.
2) *Methods of Analysis*, 8th ed., Association of Official Agricultural Chemists, Washington, D.C.

Barley was grown on tailings berms at Cyprus Pima in experiments to produce livestock forage and prevent pollution.

Barley forage grew tallest in desert soil, with most tillers per unit area. Green and oven-dry forage yields were also highest from barley grown in desert soil. Forage grown in tailings-overburden mixture had highest relative feed value.

Georgia kaolin ranges from very sandy clay to clay that is essentially pure. Most mined kaolin is more than 90% kaolinite, with sand-sized quartz as the principal impurity. Shown here is Thiele Kaolin's Avant mine.

Georgia kaolin producers are reclaiming an acre of land for each acre mined

Lane White, Managing editor

THE KAOLIN MINES of Georgia produced 4.3 million tons in 1976, 75% of the total US output of kaolin. The nearly flat-lying deposits are generally 10 to 40 ft thick, but thickness ranges up to 60 ft. Mining at overburden-to-ore ratios of about 4:1—and as high as 10:1 in some cases—the Georgia producers use a variety of surface mining equipment. Draglines and scrapers are used for overburden removal; bulldozers, draglines, and front-end loaders for mining; and rear-dump trucks and slurry pipelines for ore transport.

In recent years, the kaolin mines of Georgia have operated under a law passed in 1968, during Lester Maddox's term as governor, requiring reclamation of an acre of land for every acre that is mined. Reclamation is now progressing at an even faster pace, as companies work to restore some mined-out areas where kaolin extraction was completed prior to passage of the law.

Reclamation costs currently run about $500 per acre, Paul F. Thiele, president of Thiele Kaolin at Sandersville, Ga., said during an E/MJ visit to the district. The kaolin producers express pride in the many acres of mined land that have been reseeded with grass and pine trees or returned to productive agricultural or recreational use. American Industrial Clay, a subsidiary of Georgia Kaolin, has created a 10-acre lake and stocked it with bream and bass at a recreation site on reclaimed land near Deepstep, Ga., and mine manager T.Y. Harrington reports a record catch of a 9-lb 3-oz bass. A second small pond has been stocked with channel catfish.

Other companies producing kaolin at Georgia mines include Anglo-American Clays Corp., Cyprus Industrial Minerals Co., Engelhard Minerals and Chemicals Corp., Evans Clay Co., Freeport Kaolin Co., J. M. Huber Corp., and Champion Papers Div. of Champion International Corp.

Colonial settlers discovered the Georgia kaolin deposits in the 1700s and mined them to some extent prior to the discovery of extensive kaolin deposits in Cornwall, England, in 1768, according to Haydn H. Murray in "Clay" (Monograph Series No. 38 of the Association of Pulp and Paper Industries). Mining lapsed until 1876, when Riverside Mills began operations in Richmond County. Since that time, mining has been conducted continuously in the kaolin districts, which extend in a belt along the inner edge of the

Reclamation is now a matter of course after final extraction of kaolin from Georgia mining operations, with land returned to recreational or agricultural uses. (All photos accompanying this article were made by Little Studio, Sandersville, Ga.)

Atlantic Coastal Plain, from Aiken, S.C., 150 miles to Macon, Ga.

Though many geologists from throughout the world have studied the Georgia and South Carolina kaolins, they are still not well understood. "Virtually all who have investigated the deposits agree that they have been transported. Areas of disagreement center about explanations of how such very large, fine-grained white clays could have been formed in environments in which most sediments being deposited consisted of sand having a higher iron content than the clay. Furthermore, an adequate explanation of origin of the deposits must account for the fact that some deposits are finer grained than others, some contain abundant accordion-like booklets and some do not, gibbsite is present in some deposits and not in others, and there are lignitic or organic rech layers in some deposits," Murray states.

The paper industry, which uses kaolin in paper coatings, is the largest consumer of kaolin; the key physical properties of the white mineral are its brightness and viscosity. The theoretical structural formula is $(OH)_8Si_4Al_4O_{10}$, and the theoretical composition is 46.54% SiO_2, 39.5% Al_2O_3, and 13.96% H_2O. The Georgia kaolins generally contain 85% to 95% kaolinite, with impurities being mainly quartz, muscovite, biotite, smectite, ilmenite, anatase, rutile, leucoxene, goethite, and traces of zircon, tourmaline, kyanite, and graphite.

Brightness and viscosity vary markedly, both vertically and horizontally within the kaolin deposits, requiring extensive core drilling prior to mining. Thiele Kaolin conducts pioneer drilling on 600-ft centers using a drill rig mounted on a three-tired Tryco chassis that rides on over-sized flotation-type tires. The grid is reduced to 100-ft centers before overburden removal if a deposit appears to have commercial potential, to establish a mine map and mining pattern that will produce a marketable kaolin mix.

Shovels or draglines mine the kaolin deposits, loading either into trucks for transport to a processing plant or stationary blunger or into portable blungers located in the pit. At the American Industrial Clay's mines near Deepstep, a 1-yd-capacity dragline loads directly into a blunger, as a bulldozer provides assistance in working the clay orebody. At Thiele Kaolin's Avant operation, a 6-yd B-E dragline mines kaolin and builds stockpiles that are loaded into rear-dump trucks by front-end loaders for transport to a stationary blunger.

The blungers separate kaolin into small particles and mix it with water and a dispersing chemical, usually a sodium polyphosphate or sodium silicate, to form a clay-water slurry. The percentage of solids in the blunger is usually between 30% and 40% but may rise to 50%.

The clay-water slurry is pumped from the blunger to hydroseparators and screens that remove plus 325-mesh material. After degritting, the kaolin slurry is collected in large storage tanks and pumped to a processing plant, in some cases several miles away. In 1976, Freeport Kaolin started up a 24-mi pipeline between its new Scott mining complex near Sandersville and its main processing plant at Gordon. The 10-in.-dia high-pressure pipeline (maximum 1,200 psi) delivers 500 to 1,500 gpm of kaolin slurry. A single Wilson Snyder piston pump,

This complex of kaolin processing and consuming facilities near Sandersville, Ga., includes operations of Thiele Kaolin Co. (center and lower left), Anglo-American Clays Corp. (upper left), and Burgess Pigment Co. (right, above railroad tracks).

with a second unit as standby, services the entire pipeline length. Use of piston pumps having a high mechanical efficiency of 85%—against 50-60% for centrifugal pumps—has extended the range of possibilities for kaolin slurry transport.

At processing plants, the first step in wet processing is separation of coarse and fine fractions in continuous centrifuges, which raise the minus 2-micron fraction from 60% to 80% (and possibly as much as 95%) of the total in the fine fraction. The coarse fraction is used as filler in paper, plastics, paint, and adhesives, while the fine fractions are used in paper coatings, high gloss paints, inks, special ceramics, and rubber. Further steps to produce suitable product grades may include flotation, delamination, selective flocculation, leaching, surface treatment, or magnetic separation.

Introduction of large magnetic filters to the kaolin industry since 1973 has broadened the range of processing possibilities. The filters can be used to upgrade a medium grade kaolin product to a premium grade product, to clean up the coarse fraction separated by centrifuging, or to process low quality material that would otherwise be uneconomic to mine. Processing costs for the filters range from 50¢ to about $2.00 per ton, and at one plant, the filters reduce anatase, a major discolorant, from 1.7% to less than 1% of the product. (Development of magnetic filters for the kaolin industry is described in AIME preprint 76-H-7 by J. Iannicelli, president and technical director of Aquafine Corp., which markets the machines.)

Final processing steps include dewatering by filtration, drying (usually in spray dryers), bagging, and loading. □

A kaolin exploration rig mounted on a three-tired Tryco chassis probes Georgia clays in search of mineable deposits.

Parade of scrapers climbs a steep grade to reach fill material for use in Homestake's Grizzly Gulch dam.

Homestake nears completion of project to impound tailings and recycle water

HOMESTAKE MINING CO.'S EFFLUENT CONTROL PROJECT in the Black Hills near Lead, S. Dak., is almost finished. The $10 million construction job includes a tailings impoundment area in Grizzly Gulch, two slurry pipelines from the processing plant to the impoundment area, a decant line, a recycled water reservoir, two 125-ft-dia and one 50-ft-dia thickeners, an enlarged sand storage dam, and a tailings pump house and substructure. The Grizzly Gulch project will eliminate discharge of tailings from the Homestake processing plant into Gold Run creek.

Homestake had contemplated various types of tailings impoundment areas for a period of 15 years and, prior to approval of the Grizzly Gulch project, had conducted studies of possible disposal systems in conjunction with EPA and the Lead-Deadwood Sanitary District. Approval of the Grizzly Gulch project was obtained from EPA and the South Dakota Department of Environmental Protection in 1975. The site was selected for its

A portable crushing and screening plant set up near the Grizzly Gulch impoundment dam prepares crushed rock for various phases of the job, including 100,000 cu yd of minus ¾-in. material for use in the chimney drain.

The Grizzly Gulch dam will rise 235 ft above its 1,000-ft-thick base, to a crest elevation of 5,350 ft.

natural topography and remoteness from population centers.

Dames & Moore designed the impoundment area, pipeline, and pumping system, and Summit-Delzer—a joint venture of two South Dakota contractors—has the contract for construction of the tailings impoundment area, a pipeline road leading to it, and all clearing and stripping of the impoundment area.

The construction contract was signed in May 1976, and in July, after clearing and grubbing operations were substantially completed, scrapers began to strip slopes of up to 45°. Homestake had originally planned to use mine wastes for fill at the impoundment site, but Summit-Delzer recommended stripping of material from the slopes at Grizzly Gulch, at a substantial cost savings to Homestake. By November 1976, 18 scrapers were moving 25,000 to 30,000 cu yd per day.

To build the impoundment, the contractor is moving 2 million cu yd of material, virtually all of it weathered schist. The primary movers are wheel tractors-scrapers, push-loaded by Caterpillar D8 and D9 dozers. The equipment fleet includes two Cat 657, four 651B, three 651, four 641, three 637, and two TS-24 scrapers. Seven D9s push-load the scrapers, and 12 D8s work on clearing, pioneering, and pushing. Most of the push tractors have single-shank rippers to tear loose the granite schist.

Other equipment at the dam construction site includes two Cat 834 compactors for working on the fill and three water wagons to aid compaction and keep down dust on haul roads. Eight Cat motor graders are used for haul road maintenance, and Cat 988, 980B, and 950 wheel loaders handle various materials at the site. Two 35-ton and two 25-ton Euclid trucks are available for haulage.

At one time during construction, scrapers were traveling 1,500 ft from cut to fill, loading at the top of a nearly 2:1 slope, and then descending to the flat portion of the road. The scrapers spread the material for fill at the dam site and returned to the cut via another 1,500-ft road having a 35% grade, cycling in 6 to 8 min. The crew worked six 10-hr shifts per week.

When completed, the Grizzly Gulch impoundment will span a 1,200-ft canyon, rising 235 ft high from a 1,000-ft-thick base to a 20-ft crest.

"So far as we know, this is the only tailings dam of its type anywhere," according to Dames & Moore senior engineer, Mark Carrigan, "The dam makes use of materials that are all within its immediate vicinity."

The impoundment dam is not constructed entirely of weathered schist. At the core of the dam is a 60-ft-thick section of clay to retard seepage, and behind the clay, a 2-ft thickness of sand prevents penetration of the clay into an adjacent 8-ft-thick section of minus ¾-in. gravel drain material, which allows any seepage through the clay to flow downward into a thick gravel blanket. Seepage flows to a downstream collection ditch and is

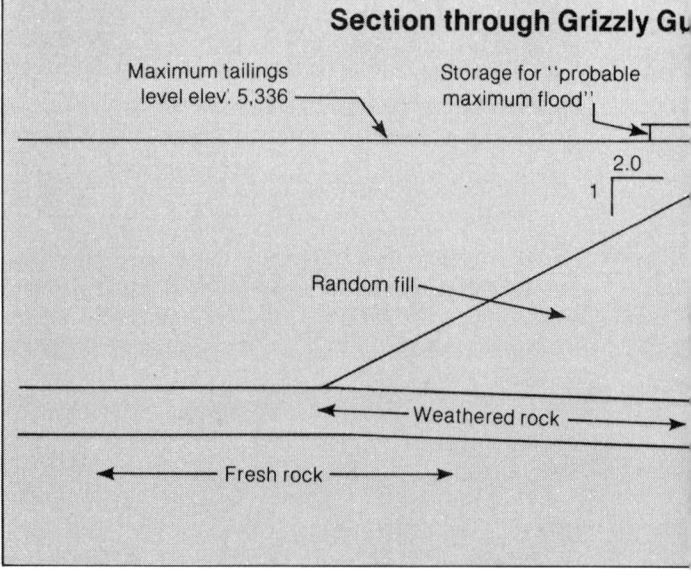

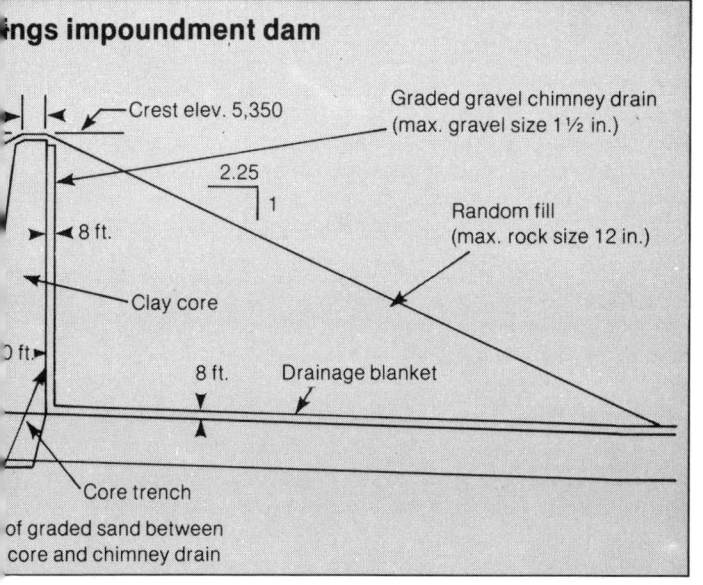

tailings impoundment dam

- Crest elev. 5,350
- Graded gravel chimney drain (max. gravel size 1½ in.)
- 2.25 / 1
- 8 ft.
- Random fill (max. rock size 12 in.)
- Clay core
- 8 ft. Drainage blanket
- Core trench
- of graded sand between core and chimney drain

then pumped back to the impoundment area, preventing contamination of downstream water. The remainder of the fill is minus 6-in. schist. (See diagram.)

The primary crusher on the property is a 30 x 40-in. Pioneer jaw type, and there are also two Telsmith cones at the site: a 4-ft standard and a 4-ft shorthead. Two 5 x 6-ft Cedarapids screening plants size the material. A 72-81 loader charges the plant. Five Chicago Pneumatic track drills and two rotary drills are in use on the project, along with two Chicago Pneumatic and two Ingersoll-Rand compressors.

The crushing plant operates two 10-hr shifts per day, producing 150 tph.

A logging company cleared the 270-acre area of ponderosa pine, spruce, aspen, and birch trees, and Summit-Delzer's fleet of dozers removed the remaining vegetation and stumps. The terrain has an average slope of 33%, and the maximum difference in elevation of the area is 400 ft. The west side canal spillway ranges up to a 42% grade.

Summit-Delzer also constructed a 1½-mi road to the dam from the tailings pump station. The pipelines will follow this road.

Two rubber-lined 8-in. pipelines will run from the tailings pump station to the dam, one to carry tailings and an identical line as a reserve. A third line will return water from the impoundment area to a new concrete reservoir for recycling to the mill.

Should power fail, automatic valves will open to dump tailings into two emergency bypass boreholes that will conduct them to the 1,100-ft level in the mine for emergency storage.

Homestake ore is crushed and classified as sands (plus 200 mesh) and fines (minus 200 mesh). After processing, about 60% of the sands are returned to the mine as backfill for Homestake's cut-and-fill stopes. Dry cement is added to the sand slurry for the top 6 in. of each lift to provide mine crews a solid floor on which to work.

Homestake now uses about 5 million gpd of water, and when the Grizzly Gulch project is complete, about 4 million gpd will be recycled. A 2.35-million-gal reservoir will receive decant water from the impoundment area. A slimes thickener system, a sand-dam enlargement to handle surges from sand processing, and a sand-dam overflow thickener also are being built.

A water treatment plant will remove heavy metals and small traces of cyanide from the water.

Eight Allen-Sherman-Hoff centrifugal pumps will pump tailings to the impoundment area for discharge at multiple points near the upstream face of the impoundment dam. Solids will settle, and a floating barge will pump surface water back to the 2.35-million-gal reservoir.

The initial impoundment is designed to hold eight years of Homestake tailings, after which 50-ft lifts will be added, eventually sufficient to contain 50 years of the mine's tailings output. When the area is finally filled, Homestake will build diversion canals to divert upstream water around the impoundment, and the area will be reseeded. □

How nomogram simplifies power factor evaluation

WHEN A LARGE ELECTRIC MOTOR is to be added to a system that already has a low power factor, it may be desirable to select a synchronous motor or an induction motor, or to install capacitors. By using the power factor improvement nomogram developed by electrical engineer Glenn Stangland, of St. Petersburg, Fla., it is possible to predict what the final power factor will be after installation, or to determine what the power factor rating of the added motor should be in order to adjust the final power factor to a desired value.

Today's energy problems and the penalty clauses for poor power factor require that plant engineers consider carefully the impact of adding power capacity. The Stangland nomogram provides a simpler method for evaluating power factors than the reactive kva method or the complex number method.

For each load (original and added) two of the following four variables must be known: kilowatts (kw), kilovolt-amperes (kva), reactive kilovolt-amperes (kvar), and power factor (PF). Any two variables will establish a single point on the chart, from which the other two variables may also be read.

What will be the new power factor of your plant when you add another motor? Here's how to use the nomogram to find out:

Example 1

Assume that a plant carries 790 kw at 1,000 kva. In the Plant Quadrant of the nomogram, mark point A where a vertical line from 7.9 on the Original Load kw scale intersects 10 on the Load kva circle. The synchronous motor to be added is rated 0.8 PF and 250 kw. In the Synchronous Motor Quadrant, mark point B where a vertical line from 2.5 on the Added Load kw scale intersects the 0.8 PF radial line.

To find the final power factor of the plant, draw the dashed line from A to B; then draw another line through the bullseye, parallel to A-B. Where this line intersects the perimeter, read the final PF—in this case, it is 0.92 lagging in the Plant Quadrant.

How can you determine what the power factor of the added load must be in order to raise the total plant PF to a desired value? Like this:

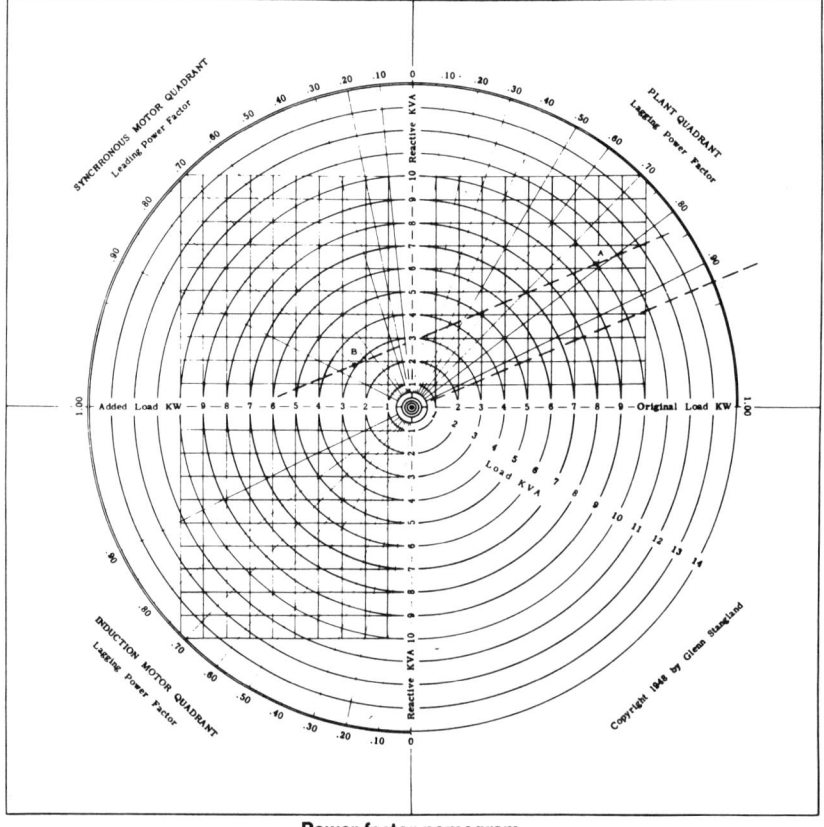

Power factor nomogram

Example 2

Assume that a plant carries the same 790 kw at 1,000 kva. Establish point A in the Plant Quadrant using the same procedure as before. The final desired power factor of the plant is to be 0.92. In the Plant Quadrant, draw a line through the bullseye intersecting the perimeter at 0.92 PF.

To find the necessary PF of a 250-kw synchronous motor, draw a line parallel to the first line through point A. Mark point B where this line intersects a vertical line from 2.5 on the Added Load kw scale in the Synchronous Motor Quadrant. Then draw a radial line through point B.

Where the radial line intersects the perimeter, read 0.8 PF leading as the required power factor rating of the new motor.

Note that each point established on the chart has four values. For point A, the kw is 7.9 (790), the kva is 10 (1,000), the kvar is 6.15 (615), and a radial line through A indicates a PF of 0.79 (lagging). Likewise, for point B, the kw is 2.5 (250), the kva is 3.1 (310), the kvar is 1.9 (190), and a radial line through B indicates a PF of 0.8 (leading).

A few short rules will guide the use of the nomogram in determining values for other loads:

- When the added load has a lagging power factor, work in the Induction Motor Quadrant.
- When the added load is a capacitor, work along the upper Reactive kva scale.
- When the added load is pure resistance, work along the left-hand kw scale.

Stangland's nomogram is not a new idea—having been copyrighted in 1948—but energy consciousness is making many old ideas timely today. □

Chapter 4
Drilling and Blasting

Blasthole drilling economics: a look at the costs behind the costs	138
Tank-mounted rock drill	141
International mining exhibition	142
Rotary drills dominate in open pits	143
Drilling trends: improved accuracy and mobility	147
New bit concepts get tryouts at Sandia Labs	149
Joy demonstrates 'maxi' and 'mini' high-energy impactors	151
Explosives: their classification and characteristics	152
The chemistry and physics of explosives	157
Explosives: the mechanics of detonation	167
Commercial applications of explosives	169
How to select an explosive or blasting agent for a specific job	172
Aluminum additives impart energy and sensitivity to many explosives	184
Keeping the lid on flyrock in open pit blasting	187

Blasthole drilling economics: a look at the costs behind the costs

Byron Chitwood, product manager, and **N. E. Norman,** vice president, Reed Tool Co.

BLASTHOLE DRILLING ECONOMICS are similar to the economics of other mining operations in that many costs involved are not readily apparent to the average employee working with blasthole drills, bits, and maintenance. To arrive at the true cost per hour and the subsequent cost per foot, all of the less obvious expenses should be applied for the drill and resultant blastholes. This study analyzes the costs associated with blasthole drilling, using specific examples.

During the past decade, rotary drilling of blastholes has proven the most economical method of excavating rock. Continuous improvement of drills, drilling tools, and procedures in drilling and blasting have held excavation costs to a level favorably below the general worldwide inflation of other mining costs. The drilling of larger diameter holes faster has been made possible by introducing larger and more powerful drills capable of applying higher down pressures and torques.

The end of the trend is not in sight. If products now in the planning stages reach the market (and there is every reason to believe they will), the day may not be far off when the mining industry will see 24-in. blastholes being drilled at production speeds. Over the last 10 years, the diameter of a blasthole, the down pressure on the bit, the wear on the rock bit and drill pipe, and the total drilling cost have all steadily increased. Thus, it is vitally important today to understand and evaluate the total economics of drilling.

Owning and operating a drill

The determination of true blasthole cost must take into account the following factors: cost of owning the drill, cost of operating the drill, cost of blasthole bits used, footage obtained with the bit, and number of hours drilled. To aid in understanding these costs, a breakdown of each category is in order.

The cost of owning the drill includes: 1) amortization and depreciation, 2) interest on borrowed money, and 3) taxes and insurance. Existing machinery must be paid for over a period of time that normally equals the life of the machine. Drills are usually depreciated in a period ranging from three to eight years. For the examples here, interest is calculated at 8% per year on the average investment represented by the drill. Taxes and insurance also must be added to the cost of owning the drill.

Let's take a look at a few examples of the costs discussed so far. The approximate prices for four Bucyrus-Erie blasthole drills are as follows:

40R—$350,000
45R—$500,000
60R—$715,000
61R—$795,000

Using an 8-year straight-line depreciation, the depreciation cost per year is:

40R—$43,750
45R—$62,500
60R—$89,375
61R—$99,375

Assuming an average interest rate on borrowed capital of 8% per year, the interest cost per year for each drill is:

40R—$26,875
45R—$31,250
60R—$44,687
61R—$49,687

Using a combined tax and insurance percentage of 8.25%, the tax-insurance burden for each drill is:

40R—$28,875
45R—$41,250
60R—$58,988
61R—$65,587

The totals of the latter three contributors to the cost of owning a drill are:

40R—$99,500
45R—$135,000
60R—$193,050
61R—$214,650

These are **direct costs**, whether the drill is operated continuously or intermittently.

The cost of operating the drill includes power, repair and maintenance, direct and indirect labor, and related equipment costs, including warehousing.

Power is the cost of fuel or electricity used to operate the drill.

Repair and maintenance includes repairs due to breakdown and also those for preventive maintenance.

Direct and indirect labor includes labor for operating the drill, such as the driller and helpers, plus a percentage of management costs and support help, such as mechanics and their facilities.

Related equipment is a fairly broad category of costs that includes drillpipe (cost of new stems, repairs and replacement of worn pipe); stabilizers (new units plus repairs to those worn or damaged); and recorders (new costs plus service charges, rentals, etc.). Warehousing and storage also are part of the broad category of related costs.

The following analysis of operating expenses uses three basic assumptions that are typical of drill rig operations: 18 shifts per week, 85% drill availability, and 20% moving time—equal to 4,900 hr of operation per year.

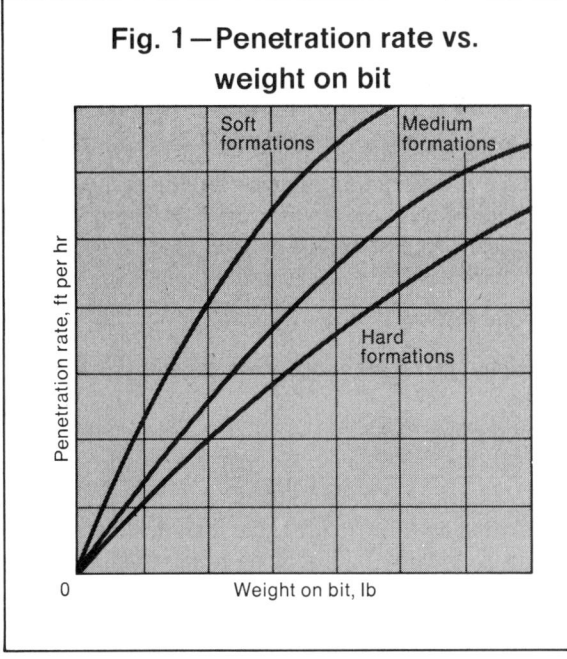

Fig. 1—Penetration rate vs. weight on bit

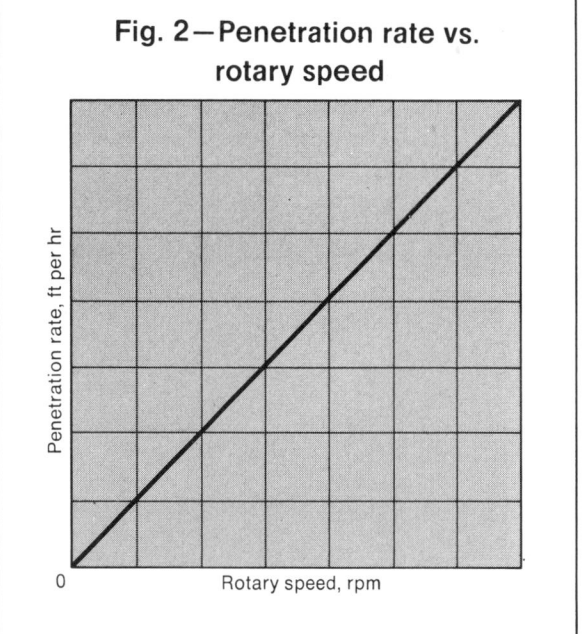

Fig. 2—Penetration rate vs. rotary speed

The estimated power cost per hour for each drill is:
- 40R—$4.05
- 45R—$4.80
- 60R—$5.60
- 61R—$6.90

Repair costs per hour are estimated to be:
- 40R—$30.00
- 45R—$34.50
- 60R—$39.75
- 61R—$45.75

Hourly direct and indirect labor costs are estimated at:
- 40R—$34.50
- 45R—$34.50
- 60R—$34.50
- 61R—$34.50

Related equipment costs per hour are calculated to be:
- 40R—$3.90
- 45R—$5.15
- 60R—$5.55
- 61R—$8.25

Using the costs of owning the drill stated previously, projected over 4,900 operating hours per year, the direct cost per hour is:
- 40R—$20.30
- 45R—$27.55
- 60R—$39.40
- 61R—$43.80

The sum of the direct costs and the operating costs is the **total drill cost** per hour:
- 40R—$92.75
- 45R—$106.50
- 60R—$124.80
- 61R—$139.20

Obviously, the hourly cost of operating a drill, when all costs are considered, is quite significant. The role of the drill foreman, engineer, and other employees associated with blasthole drilling is to gain maximum footage at the least cost, or to obtain the lowest drilling cost per foot. This goal must be achieved without sacrificing other good mining practices, such as proper blasthole spacing, hole size, and depth; the most economical powder utilization; and optimum fragmentation.

Controllable operating variables

In addition to the costs related to the drill itself, many other controllable variables have a dramatic impact on the total economics of drilling. In evaluating and controlling these variables, three factors must be considered: blasthole bit costs, amount of footage drilled, and operating hours.

To realize maximum benefits, changes in some of the variables must be accompanied by changes in others. For instance, if greater penetration rate is to be achieved by increasing weight, then more bailing air may be required to clean the bottom of the hole and flush cuttings efficiently. The variables and their relationships to drilling rates are as follows:

Weight on bit. Increasing the weight on the bit almost always increases the penetration rate (Fig. 1). However, a point is reached where the cone teeth are completely buried, and penetration rate does not increase in proportion to additional weight. Also, bit bearing life may be shortened, teeth may fail, and machine maintenance will probably increase. Of course, weight can be increased only up to that percentage of the weight of the drill that can be safely applied.

Rotary speed. Penetration rate rises with rising rotary speed (Fig. 2). As with increased weight, rotary speed is governed by upper economical and practical limits. Rotary speed and weight are the two variables most easily controlled by the driller, and they can be almost

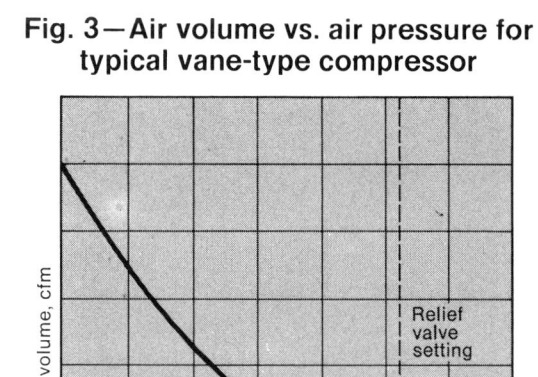

Fig. 3—Air volume vs. air pressure for typical vane-type compressor

infinitely varied up to the mechanical limits of the drill.

Air pressure and volume. The air compressor is selected at the time of drill purchase and is usually replaced only after years of service. The compressor in Fig. 3 has a maximum input horsepower and output pressure, and volumetric ratings at various rpm's. Since rpm and maximum input horsepower of a compressor are fixed, the volume (cfm) can be varied only by varying the pressure (psi). The air volume and pressure can be varied by changing the jet nozzles in the bit. The volume of air circulated must be sufficient to clean cuttings off the bottom and bail them from the hole efficiently. Also, air pressure must be adequate to cool the bearings of the bit. Optimum air pressure and volume can be achieved only through practical testing in a mine. Pressure and volume should be tested periodically to ensure maximum operating efficiency of the compressor.

Operator capability. This factor alone has considerable influence on overall drilling costs. An experienced drill operator watches variables such as weight on bit, air pressure, excessive torquing of the bit, reduced penetration rate due to dulling of the bit, and all the other factors that influence drilling performance. An operator's efficiency increases through training and experience. Personnel at certain mines report that the use of drill recorders actually increases driller efficiency. Such records are produced in the form of charts, which allow inexperienced drillers to study and practice the methods of the more experienced.

Formation. The type of rock to be drilled greatly influences drilling speed, bit life, and all other operating variables. Heavier or wet cuttings require more circulating air. Harder ones require more drilling weight for a given size bit to maintain efficient penetration. Tungsten carbide bits are almost always required for harder formations. Also, with good drilling practices and well maintained drills and equipment, the use of soft-formation tungsten carbide bits may prove very economical.

Calculating the total drilling cost

All the factors discussed up to this point must be considered in calculating the true drilling cost per foot. Calculation of this cost requires the following data: drill cost per hour, bit cost, bit life in hours, and bit life in feet drilled. Expressed as a mathematical equation:

$$\text{Total drilling cost} = \frac{\text{Drill cost}}{\text{Foot}} + \frac{\text{Bit cost}}{\text{Foot}}$$

This equation is expanded to indicate bit life and footage:

$$\text{Total drilling cost} = \frac{(\text{Drill cost per hr} \times \text{Bit life}) + \text{Bit cost}}{\text{Footage drilled}}$$

As indicated by this equation, the total drilling cost per foot can be greatly influenced by penetration rate (i.e., footage drilled per bit divided by bit life in hours). Since total cost per foot is inversely proportional to penetration rate, an increased penetration rate will greatly reduce the cost per foot, provided direct bit cost per foot is not greatly different.

As an example, the following calculation of the total drilling cost for a BE-60R compares a high ROP insert bit (M-62) with a tooth-type bit (M-34):

	M-34	M-62
Bit type	12¼-in.	12¼-in.
No. of bits used	6	2
Total bit cost	$5,088	$6,236
Total bit hours	149	118
Total footage	15,000 ft	15,000 ft
Drill cost per hr	$124.80	$124.80

Total cost per foot, M-34 =
$$\frac{\$124.80 \times 149 + \$5,088}{15,000 \text{ ft}}$$
$$= \$1.58 \text{ per ft}$$

Total cost per foot, M-62 =
$$\frac{\$124.80 \times 118 + \$6,236}{15,000 \text{ ft}}$$
$$= \$1.40 \text{ per ft}$$

The savings realized in operating the M-62 bits with the greater penetration rates are calculated as follows:

Savings = Cost per ft difference × Total footage
= ($1.58 − $1.40) × 15,000
= $2,700

In conclusion, to arrive at the true drilling cost per foot, all drill operating costs must be known. These costs greatly influence drilling economics. Initial bit cost or straight bit cost per foot should not be used as the ultimate criterion in drilling blastholes. □

References

1) "Rotary Blast Hole Bits—The Necessary Trend, Or Good Economy Is Not A Bit Cheaper" by J. B. Slack, annual meeting, Arizona Section of AIME, Dec. 7, 1970, Tucson, Ariz.
2) "The Influence of Stabilizers on Rock Bits in Rotary Blast Hole Drilling" by Roy N. Moore, Reed Tool Co. Technical Bulletin, October 1, 1975.

Tank-mounted rock drill

A NEW DRILLBOOM-COMPRESSOR PACKAGE being put through its paces at Kaiser Steel Corp.'s Eagle Mountain open-pit iron mine is attaining great productivity gains in secondary drilling and high bottom work. At the same time, the high-speed, track-mounted rock drill is winning high marks for its mobility, versatility, and its 95%-plus availability. The wide-tracked package is the "Pak-Trak" rig, manufactured by Ingersoll-Rand Equipment Corp. using standard production components. The M-41 torsion bar suspension system and parts are currently produced by leading makers of tracked vehicles.

In the first nine months of use, two yellow-and-black Pak-Traks have tripled Kaiser's secondary and high bottom drilling productivity, replacing two drills that had required two operators each, and two one-man rigs. The units thus permitted four workers to be transferred to other tasks, and secondary and high bottom drilling, which used to require one shift seven days a week, has been trimmed to five days per week of one-shift work without any reduction in the work accomplished.

Since July 1975, Kaiser's two Pak-Traks have been making fast work of boulders, ridges, and uneven spots in the pit floor left after primary blasting and ore removal. Drilling at roughly 2 fpm in very hard dolomite (precise drilling rate records are not kept for secondary drilling as they are for primary blastholes), each Pak-Trak finishes an average of 120 secondary blastholes per shift, for an average of 5 min per hole. The drills formerly used achieved approximately 50 holes per shift, an average of 12 min per hole. For secondary work, Kaiser is drilling 1⅞-in. holes, using 1¼-in.-dia Ingersoll-Rand "Spiral" drill steel in 12-ft lengths. For high bottom and pioneer road work, Kaiser uses 3½-in. bits. Bit rotation on the Pak-Trak is 150 rpm.

On the drill package, a high-production Ingersoll-Rand VL-140 valveless drifter powers the drilling cycle, working at the end of a 19.5-ft Model LHBER "Hydra-Boom." The combined horizontal reach of boom and drifter column is 41 ft, with capability for overhead drilling to 24.5 ft. The unit can also drill to 10 ft below grade, and the 100% boom swing cycle to 50° adds still more flexibility to the Pak-Trak's "mountain goat" mobility and drilling reach in craggy rock piles and rough terrain.

Angle or presplit holes are readily handled by the Pak-Trak. Kaiser's unit is a twin-engine model, with a Detroit 6V-53N diesel coupled to a three-speed, cycling-type, powershift transmission for the carrier, and a Detroit 6V-71N diesel to power the air compressor and hydraulics. An Ingersoll-Rand "Super Spiro-Flo" compressor provides 750 cfm of air at 125 psig.

After finishing work at one pit section, the Pak-Trak rig moves quickly to another jobsite with the drillboom in the vertical position without losing the drill steel. This saves time in setting up at the next location. The vehicle can move at speeds to 20 mph, can climb grades to 30°, and rides side grades to 37°. These capabilities have proven highly useful at Eagle Mountain, where Kaiser is working three iron ore pits—two of them separated by 6 mi.

The units at Eagle Mountain have a 30-ft turning radius and weigh in at 47,000 lb. The cycling powershift transmission works through a torque converter drive, which permits downshifting without declutching the carrier drive train. Triple brake systems and cushioned tracks reflect the design philosophy behind the unit and help to explain its very low maintenance requirements, I-R spokesmen say. On the drifter, only the shankpiece has needed replacement since July 1975. The original hammer is still functioning well.

Fuel consumption in the first year at Eagle Mountain has averaged about 10 gal per hr of operation, or 80 gal per shift. Ingersoll-Rand Model 150-BMP air starters on both engines contribute to this fuel economy and reportedly permit instant restarting regardless of the temperature. With two 250-gal tanks (one of which is readily converted for water), the Pak-Trak is said to be uniquely suited for remote operation in severe climatic conditions.

The operator's cab is positioned left-forward, giving the operator a clear view of the drill bit in below-grade drilling, such as ditch and ravine work. In the cab, sound reduction and roll-over protection design are augmented with tinted glass to ward off the desert sun and with air conditioning/heating systems. Ground clearance is 18 in., and the carrier's entire bottom is protected by 1-in. steel plate; ⅝-in. plates cover the sides and rear.

Kaiser supervisors at Eagle Mountain believe that the Pak-Trak is one of the most significant and successful new mining equipment items they have tested and accepted in their 28 years of mining there. With its proven versatility, high production rate, and various configurations, the unit is now moving into other applications in pioneer road building, pipeline construction work, and related jobs, according to Ingersoll-Rand. □

Looking perfectly at home in this 'mountain goat' posture, the 'Pak-Trak' traverses rough terrain to tackle secondary drilling.

International Mining Exhibition

RECORD ATTENDANCE and a dazzling variety of equipment marked the "Bergbau 76" International Mining Exhibition in Dusseldorf, May 22-29. The show and concurrent Ninth World Mining Congress attracted 101,500 visitors to Dusseldorf's sprawling, modern show grounds near the Rhine River. The 15-acre facility housed 500 exhibitors, 198 of them from countries other than Germany.

Great Britain led the foreign contingent with 57 exhibitors, most of whom were grouped in an area sponsored by the Department of Trade and the Association of British Mining Equipment Exporters. Other national contingents included 26 exhibitors from France, 26 from Sweden, and 18 from the US. A number of reasons were offered for the relatively small number of US exhibitors; one observer commented that strong demand for mining equipment in the US, especially in the coal industry, may have dissuaded some companies from exhibiting. Also, shipping equipment to the fair would be expensive for exhibitors who did not have a guaranteed buyer.

Orenstein & Koppel Aktiengesellschaft, a 100-year-old German company which gained early experience in bulk mining at the lignite open pits in central Europe, exhibited its new hydraulic mining shovel, the Model RH 75, with a 10-cu-m bucket, and a new wheel loader with a 4.2-cu-m bucket. O&K's large bucket wheel excavators were represented by photos. The company noted that these machines have found their way into a variety of surface mining applications, including bauxite mines in Surinam and Guyana (see photo), a phosphate deposit in Senegal, a manganese mine in the southern Soviet Union, diamond mines in West Africa, and the tar sands of Alberta.

New all-hydraulic rock drills were featured by a number of manufacturers. Commenting on pneumatic vs. hydraulic drills, Ingersoll-Rand president Thomas A. Holmes noted that comparisons are difficult because of differences in the power sources and the method of reticulating power to the operating faces. Pipelines distribute compressed air underground to pneumatic drill jumbos, usually from a large central compressor on the surface. Hydraulic drills usually carry their own hydraulic pumps, and electric cables supply operating power directly to each drill mounting.

Ingersoll-Rand's experience indicates that the price of hydraulic drills is about double that of air drills; however, power requirements for hydraulics are cut in half and performance is up 25%, for improved efficiency. The hydraulics produce more than 2½ times the performance per input horsepower of air drills, a very important factor in the current energy market, Holmes noted.

Ingersoll-Rand exhibited several newly developed machines, some of which have not yet been introduced to the European market. Included in the exhibit were a Damco D-6000 single-pass rotary blasthole drill, a self-contained "Uniboom" hydraulic drifter, and an all-hydraulic two-boom articulated 96 RMH "Rampmaster" jumbo.

Ingersoll-Rand also announced that it is developing one of the world's largest raise borers, the RBM-211. The unit will be capable of boring shafts up to 20 ft in diameter and 1,000 ft deep. The first model is now being built.

Gardner-Denver took the occasion of the Dusseldorf show to announce that it is launching a central parts distribution facility for Europe. The new center, near Brussels, will operate in cooperation with Gardner-Denver's worldwide parts distribution center near Dallas. Gardner-Denver's announced goal is to provide 95% parts availability and 24-hr emergency service anywhere in Europe or the Middle East. Gardner-Denver displayed its RD 16B blasthole drilling rig and its two-boom diesel "Minibore" jumbo.

Linden-Alimak AB, of Sweden, presented its new hydraulic rock drill in Dusseldorf. The drill, which is mounted on Alimak hydraulic jumbos, weighs about 100 kg and is designed for drilling with 1-in. drill steel. The percussion mechanism has only two moving parts—the piston and the slide—and the location of the slide (around the front part of the piston) provides the shortest possible oil flow route, Linden-Alimak states. The frequency of the drill is fixed at 3,400 blows per minute, while the rate of rotation is variable from 0 to 230 rpm.

Test drilling with the new Alimak unit at the Udden mine produced a penetration rate of up to 1.9 m per min using 35-mm integral steel, according to the manufacturer, and energy consumption was only one-fifth the energy required for pneumatic drilling. The noise level at a distance of 1 m from the machine averages at least 10 dBA lower than for a corresponding pneumatic machine.

Atlas-Copco also emphasized hydraulic drills at the Dusseldorf show, and a company spokesman expressed the opinion that the time is ripe for introducing hydraulic energy to rock drilling. While Atlas-Copco is not convinced that hydraulics are the only answer to a mine operator's problems, such drills do use less energy and create a better working environment, he said. The hydraulics are also very flexible, being adaptable to greatly differing rock conditions and hole sizes.

However, Atlas-Copco also spoke in support of pneumatic rock drills, noting that new models are more efficient, quieter, and produce less fog than earlier machines. Compressed-air drills are generally more rugged and less sensitive than hydraulics, he said, and they are less subject to problems arising from impurities in the system. They also require less qualified service.

Numerous jobs besides drilling in a mine require compressed air: reinforcement and grouting work, machine maintenance and service, pumping and drainage, and transport and loading, the Atlas-Copco spokesman noted. Thus, Atlas Copco is "not about to abandon compressed air."

Atlas Copco introduced its new crawler-mounted "Rotamec" 2200 rotary and in-the-hole drill at the Dusseldorf exhibition. The new model is the largest in a series that will ultimately comprise four models—two to be truck mounted and two to be crawler mounted. All will feature hydraulic power operation, including power supplied to the top drive rotation head.

The crawler-mounted Rotamec 2200 is a completely self-contained, medium-heavy rig designed for blasthole drilling on benches of varying height and rock hardness. Nominal hole size is from 4 to 9⅞ in. in sedimentary formations and about 7⅞ in. in crystalline formations such as granite. Two PRH 700 compressors deliver a total of 1,360 cfm of air at a pressure of 152 psi. Two Detroit Diesel engines develop 338 hp each at 2,100 rpm, providing power to compressors at one end and to main hydraulic pumps at the other.

The top drive rotation head features spur gear reduction

with a ratio of 18:1. It is powered by hydraulic motors of tandem design. Characteristic torque/rpm figures are: 8,500 ft-lb at 17 rpm, 9,300 ft-lb at 38 rpm and 4,150 ft-lb at 89 rpm. Pulldown is effected by two hydraulic cylinders on a roller chain, and maximum pull is 49,000 lb. The feed length is 30 ft, and drill tubes are pulled with the rotation head. Rapid hoisting speed is 130 ft per min. Slow hoisting speed is 10 ft per min. Pulling capacity is 28,200 lb.

The two-door cab of the Rotamec 2200 is soundproofed, heated, pressurized, and air-conditioned. All controls and instruments are housed in the cab, including oil filter indicator, emergency shutdown oil pressure gauge, and low oil pressure safety shutdown control.

The Joy Manufacturing Co. exhibit at Dusseldorf featured the company's new RRT 60 rotary drill, a rubber-tired unit that carries a 20- or 25-ft hydraulically positioned drill mast. The drill is driven by the carrier engine through a heavy duty transmission and heavy duty right-angle drive to a heavy duty floating drill head. Down pressure is transmitted and drill pipe is extracted through use of hydraulic cylinders and chain drive. A single drill pipe "make-and-break" system is incorporated in the unit.

The RRT 60 offers maximum portability, according to Joy, and it can negotiate reasonable gradients safely and quickly with the mast up. For steeper and rougher terrain or for longer distances, the mast is designed for quick breakover to maintain a lower center of gravity.

Hole size for the RRT 60 ranges from 172 to 273 mm and bit pressure is 27,300 kg.

Other Joy products in the exhibit included continuous miners, dust collectors, slurry pumps, and a skid-mounted Joy 22 SHD diamond core drill from South Africa. The heavy duty core drill can reach depths of 4,000 ft and features direct drive and four-speed transmission through an NW hydraulic swivelhead that can handle any size rod·up to NX wireline or PK rod. It is also fitted with a planetary type hoisting drum.

The Joy RRT 60 rotary drill is an integral, self-propelled, rubber-tired unit equipped with single tandem front axles and dual rear axles. The acoustically controlled cab is fitted with safety glass throughout. All controls are easily accessible.

Rotary drills dominate in open pits

THE ORE GRADES OF THE WORLD'S SURFACE DEPOSITS are declining while demand for mined products is on the upswing. The combination of increased demand, lower grade ores, and higher production costs requires faster, more efficient production methods. Pressure is keenly felt by drilling departments of all mines, which must keep ahead—or everything halts.

The superior efficiency of rotary blasthole drilling over other drilling methods has led to its primacy in almost all major open pits over the past decade. In taconites, holes up to 17 in. in diameter are now drilled to 65 ft in a single pass. Drills with pull-down forces of 130,000 lb and automated control of major functions are now common. These large diameter rigs are capable of penetration rates between 30 ft and 50 ft per hr in the hardest formations.

Cost of a rotary drill rig—depending on size and options—can top $500,000. Three manufacturers offering automated controls with varying degrees of sophistication are Bucyrus-Erie, Gardner-Denver, and Marion Power Shovel Co. All of the automated systems may be switched to manual control.

Gardner-Denver markets seven rotary blasthole drilling

The Gardner-Denver GD-80 rotary blasthole drill features rotary table drive for drilling holes up to 12¼ in. in diameter.

rigs, including the GD-80, GD-120, and GD-130. The numerals refer to pull-down power, in thousands of pounds. Optional programmed drilling control is available for all rigs. Interestingly, the Model GD-80 features a rotary table drive. The GD-80 can drill 9- to 12¼-in.-dia holes, while the GD-130—the largest rotary unit on the market—drills 17½-in.-dia holes up to 66 ft in a single pass. Gardner-Denver also offers a 350-hp, 1,940-cfm rotary screw compressor for use with the larger drills.

Gardner-Denver's automated programmed drilling package permits pull-down force to be limited to a preset maximum. A parallel system for manual control of pull-down force is standard. The automated control package includes two power module cards and three function module cards. Six additional plug-in options cover the functions of rotary motor speed, vibration allowance, main air pressure, feed rate, hydraulic pump motor loads, and provision for isolating the cycle for collaring. Selection of specific options should be based on specific drilling conditions and the skills of operating and maintenance personnel.

According to Tom Brunt, superintendent of maintenance for the Northwest Ore Div. of Jones and Laughlin Steel Corp.,[1] rotary table drive (as used on the GD-80) will "ultimately replace the top drive in many operations" because of its distinct advantages, which include reduced vibration of the mast, shorter time for hole collaring, and reduced wear on the drill steel. The kelly wear appears to be minimal. In purchasing the GD-80, J&L specified an oversized compressor because "increased air volume was considered desirable in trying to handle the heavy ore cuttings." Quick removal of cuttings from the hole is necessary for efficient drilling. Otherwise, energy is lost through unnecessary attrition in grinding the cuttings—prematurely wearing out the bit edges.

Bucyrus-Erie's new 60-R/61-R Series III drills can bore holes up to 17½ in. in diameter and to 65 ft in a single pass. Pull-down power ranges up to 110,000 lb. The new mast was recognized as the outstanding engineering achievement in industrial equipment for 1973 by the American Iron & Steel Institute. The mast, made of rectangular steel tubes and a welded steel skin, has more than 100 times the torsional strength of conventional latticework masts. The construction is said to provide smoother drill cycles and require less repair and maintenance. All four corners of the mast are reinforced with welded plate, forming a rigid U-section design.

The drill features an automatic pull-down chain equalizer and self-adjusting rotary head slide shoes. The rotary head moves on slides faced with Teflon, which reduces friction. Control options include preset collaring depth (after which increased rotary speed is allowed), automatic hoist of the drill bit after desired hole depth is achieved, and automatic water control. Standard controls on the master board regulate rotary speed and penetration rate.

With a standard 50-ft single-pass system, the mast can be tilted 30° from vertical for angle-hole drilling. An optional 60-ft or 65-ft single-pass mast permits drilling to 15° from vertical. Optional compressors include the 19-L water-cooled model, rated at 1,765 cfm free air at 40 psi.

Marion Power Shovel Co.'s M-4 and M-5 blasthole rigs can drill 12½- or 15-in.-dia holes to 55 ft in a single pass. They incorporate independently controlled hydraulic-powered crawlers for maximum maneuverability. Each crawler has its own independent propel motor, interchangeable with the hoist pull-down motor. The propel motor uses a double disc brake, set by internal springs and released by an air tube, for positive holding on steep slopes.

Marion offers a simplified automatic control system covering only down-pressure, bailing air pressure, and rotary torque. The drill operator or foreman need only set the dials on the operator control panel to the desired limits for each variable. Settings should be based on rock conditions, bit wear, and desired production rate. An experienced operator can change set points while the drill is working, to accommodate changing conditions. These controls are seen as a natural extension—rather than a replacement—of operator skills.

All three drill manufacturers—Gardner-Denver, Bucyrus-Erie, and Marion—believe that automatic controls reduce maintenance and repair and increase machine availability, thus reducing overall cost per ton of material drilled. The degree of acceptance of automation will depend on the simplicity of maintenance of the solid state hardware.

The Ingersoll-Rand DM-6 rig drills holes up to 10⅝ in. in diameter and offers a 1,110-cfm compressor. The heavier DM-7 drills holes to 12¼ in. and has a compressor rated at 1,420 cfm. Both drills deliver 90,000 lb of pull-down power and 8,750 ft-lb of torque, and can travel on slopes up to 30%. Diesel or electric drive is offered. A pressure-balanced feed control automatically adjusts down-pressure from 0 to 90,000 lb, depending on rock drillability. Rotation is infinitely variable from 0 to 100 rpm, with full torque at all speeds.

Ingersoll-Rand also manufactures a group of smaller blasthole drills, including the single-pass, rotary-table "Damco Deepholer." Three models are available, for single-pass drilling of holes 2¾ in. to 7⅞ in. in diameter, 40

Joy's Robbins RR-11-E rotary electric drill has 80,000-lb bit pressure and will drill 12¼-in.-dia holes.

to 60 ft deep. The mechanical-drive rotary table delivers engine torque directly to the kelly bar—forward for drilling, reverse for bit removal. The tower is constructed of welded steel tube with an open-front design. Because rotation is applied at the base, the tower is not subject to torque forces. The mast is raised and lowered by two hydraulic cylinders actuated from the driller's cab. Screw compressor sizes range from 250 cfm for the small model to 450 cfm for the largest drill.

LeRoi introduces all-hydraulic drill

An all-hydraulic crawler drill, Model LHD155, is manufactured by LeRoi Div. of Dresser Industries. The drifter delivers up to 2,000 blows per min. Hydraulic drills generally have penetration rates at least 50% faster than comparable air-drills, and because there is no exhaust, they operate at reduced noise levels. A smaller compressor (175 cfm) is used for removing cuttings, and the standard 12-ft steels can be expected to last longer due to the smooth hydraulic operation. The LeRoi rig's rotation motor operates between 0 and 150 rpm and delivers 350 lb of torque. The drill uses a 1¾-in. four-spline chuck with a 9/16-in. blow tube for 1½-in. or 1¾-in. drill steels. Power for the hydraulic systems is provided by a four-cylinder Deutz air-cooled diesel engine of 59 bhp.

Atlas Copco and AGA Geotronics of Sweden manufacture the DIT 70 instrument to reduce the margin of error and the time required for setup when drilling inclined blastholes. The DIT 70 is mounted on the feed beam of the crawler drill and its pointer is set for the desired hole inclination. The feed beam is then aligned from the operator's position, and an air bubble is centered within the instrument before drilling begins. Maximum deviation from the desired angle is said to be 0.2%, and the device can be used for all angle drilling between 0 and 45°.

Rotary bits are redesigned

Bits for rotary blasthole drilling have improved steadily over the past decade. Quartzites and taconites, once the province of down-the-hole drilling and jet piercing, are now amenable to rotary drilling. Improvements include changes in the metallurgy of the tungsten-carbide buttons, use of larger numbers of smaller inserts, specially shaped inserts, two-tier bits, larger bit bearings, and solid lubricants for bearing thrust faces. The benefits are increased penetration rates, more uniform drill speeds, less gauge wear, and longer life for drill steel and bits. Another development is the use of stabilizers on the bit to maintain alignment during collaring of holes; the payoff is improved back-reaming and better bearing and cutter structure loading during drilling.

With drilling speed increased by modifications of rotary drills and bits, greater bailing air volume is often required to remove cuttings—especially in heavier rocks and ores. High-volume, high-energy air systems not only speed up cuttings removal, but also cool the bits and lengthen bit life.

The Energy Research and Development Administration is developing four new drill bit systems to increase cutting rates and reduce overall drilling time and costs. The four systems, apparently designed mainly for deep-hole drilling, may also provide some fall-out technology applicable to bench-hole blasting. Two of ERDA's drill bits are designed to increase penetration rates and bit life; one chips rock with high voltage sparks, and the other fires minute projectiles into the rock in advance of a regular roller bit. The other two systems are designed to reduce the number of bit changes. In one system, a roller-cone bit is folded and removed as another bit is cycled into place from a magazine containing 10 to 12 new bits. In the other system, the cutting surfaces are on a chain that is advanced as needed to bring new cutting surfaces into position. The latter two systems are obviously geared to avoid pulling pipe in very deep holes, where such bit changes waste time and money.

Ingersoll-Rand's DM-6/7 drills holes to 12½-in.-dia, has variable pull-down from 0 to 90,000 lb, and compressor to 1,420 cfm.

Marion's M-4 rotary rig drills holes 12¼ in. in diameter, to 55 ft in a single pass. Bit load ranges up to 105,000 lb.

The Bucyrus-Erie 60-R will drill 12¾-in.-dia holes up to 65 ft in a single pass, with bit loading up to 125,000 lb.

Core drilling of large diameter bulk samples

Bulk metallurgical sampling by large diameter diamond core drilling to depths between 1,000 and 2,000 ft was carried out in the early 1970s in Queensland, Australia.[2] Intairdril (Aust.) Pty. Ltd., with the assistance of Eastman Directional Drilling (Aust.) Pty. Ltd., cored an 8-in.-dia hole to a depth of 1,450 ft at the Lady Loretta lead-zinc deposit, 72 mi north northwest of Mt. Isa, Queensland, and subsequently whipstocked four additional 8-in. core holes off the original hole below 800-ft depth.

Intairdril used an Ideco DIR-550 self-propelled rig powered by a 12-V71 GMC engine. The unit had a 102-ft double derrick rated at 212,000 lb net hook capacity with eight lines strung. The rig was equipped with an Ideco Model SHS-175 17½-in. rotary table and 9-ft-high, 150-ton substructure. Four Gardner-Denver WEN 860-cfm compressors, one Gardner-Denver RXE booster, and a unit for foam injection were used to provide air and foam as the circulating medium. Drill string was 4½ in. in diameter, with 5¾-in.-dia tool joints. The drill collar string consisted of one 10-in. collar weighing 8,500 lb, four 8-in. collars weighing 4,713 lb each, and twenty 6¾-in. collars weighing 3,228 lb each, for a total drill collar weight of 91,912 lb. Drill string weight was 16.6 lb per ft.

The 17.2-ft-long, 10-in.-dia core barrel was manufactured by Bourne Bros. Drilling Equipment Pty. Ltd. in Brisbane, Queensland. The swivel-mounted inner barrel was equipped with a threaded, tapered, core catcher retainer sub. Two types of core catchers were used. The first design was 2 in. wide, with built-in carbide inserts. Subsequently, the catchers were enlarged to a 4-in. width to withstand the heavy pull required to break the cores. The barrel was stabilized at the top with a carbide stabilizer and at the bottom with diamond reamers. Diamond core heads were used throughout the program. The diamond heads, manufactured by Triefus Industries (W.A.) Co., of Sydney, Australia, were of two types: a step-faced bit set with 120 AAA carats and a flat-faced crown head bit set with 115 AAA carats. All core heads were 10¼-in. OD, and all were face discharge. Three step-face heads, ten flat-face heads, and five reaming shells were used.

After the first hole was completed, it was decided that whipstocking (wedging) the vertical hole some 800 ft below ground surface was more economical than drilling and casing five separate holes from the surface. An Eastman single-shot survey was run to determine the wedge orientation.

A total of 77,000 lb of ore sample was obtained from the 1,540 ft of coring in the five holes. A total of 2,076 ft of 12¼-in. open hole, 1,540 ft of 8-in. coring, 1,129 ft of reaming from 10 in. to 12¼ in., and 420 ft of reaming from 12¼ in. to 17½ in. were completed in 110 days. Drill rate for 12¼-in. open hole averaged 4.47 ft per hr (including rig service, tripping in and out of holes, and unloading accumulated water) at a cost of $A35.00 per ft. Using the same cost parameters and diamond bits, 8-in. coring averaged 1 ft per hr at a cost of $A10.00 per ft. Diamond bit costs averaged $A8.96 per ft. Average length of 141 coring runs was 10.9 ft. Actual penetration rate while coring averaged 1.64 ft per hr. □

References

1) Brunt, Thomas B., "Unique Improvement in Medium Size Rotary Drilling," AIME meeting, Minnesota Section, Duluth, Minn., January 1974.
2) Rennie, C. C., and Miller, B. D., "Large Diameter Coring Bulk-Samples Ore at Australia Find," E/MJ, May 1974, p 85.

Drilling trends: improved accuracy and mobility

MOBILITY, OR THE LACK OF IT, has been the most costly and time consuming aspect of exploration diamond drilling. According to a worldwide diamond drilling survey conducted by US consultants Dames & Moore,[1] one of the most pressing needs in drilling is to make the equipment lighter and more portable. In Canada, where much of the exploration is carried out in inaccessible terrain, a prime requirement is for core drills that can be moved quickly and inexpensively from one area to another.

The Dames & Moore survey also indicated a clear need for improvements in bit design, core orientation techniques, and drilling fluids. Some of the more noteworthy advances in recent years have been made in these areas.

A lightweight, self-propelled diamond drill has been designed in joint work by Canada's Department of Energy, Mines and Resources and other organizations.[2] The design uses a standard diamond drill mounted on a lightweight chassis that is easily assembled and disassembled. It proved feasible to drive this chassis with the drill motor by designing a chain drive to connect the power takeoff on the drill transmission to the drive axle on the undercarriage. The specifications for the undercarriage included minimal weight and the ability to be dismantled and packed into a Twin-Otter aircraft. Conversion to diesel and/or liquid petroleum gas power was also considered.

Another drilling modification is the "Hydra-Wink," said to be "Canada's newest exploration drill."[3] The unit, 2 ft wide and 7 ft 8 in. long, can be transported by small plane or helicopter without being dismantled. It can be used for surface or underground drilling, with interchangeable gasoline, diesel, electric, or air power packs. The drill is said to be adaptable to augering, wireline coring, and soil sampling, among other applications. In addition, where a conventional drill rig would be able to drill 2 ft without rechucking, the Hydra-Wink can drill 5 ft without rechucking.

J. K. Smit and Sons has introduced a portable hydraulic core drill,[4] the JKS 300, which drills to 1,000 ft and weighs only 1,000 lb. This drill, too, can be transported by light plane or helicopter and assembled on-site by two men. According to Smit, the drill "bridges the gap" between large helicopter-portable drills, which are often impractical, and lightweight portable drills, which give low output in terms of footage below a certain depth.

A self-contained, mobile, boom-mounted underground exploration drill, for which drilling rates have "exceeded expectations," is a recent product of Boyles Bros. of Salt Lake City, Utah. The unit is mounted on a maneuverable, self-propelled buggy with a diesel-hydraulic power plant.

A new truck-mounted rotary diamond coring drill introduced by Canadian Longyear is said to be a new concept in drilling services. One of the main features of the Model 44 drill is its ability to tricone to substantial depths in sedimentary strata. Faster penetration at lower cost with triconing was reportedly achieved during a recent drill program in Canada's Maritime Provinces.

The drill, mounted on the deck of a dual-axle tandem Mack truck, is equipped with a 30-ft-pull vertical mast, double-lined hoisting cable, and mast-mounted hydraulic wireline hoist. The rig can be quickly converted to a standard coring drill.

Slim-hole drilling tested for geothermal exploration

In the US, Battelle's Pacific Northwest Laboratories in Richland, Wash., are evaluating a "slim-hole" drilling concept that could significantly reduce the cost of geothermal exploration.[5] The program, funded by the US Energy Research and Development Administration (ERDA), includes drilling on the China Lake Naval Weapons Center at Coso Hot Springs, Calif. This locale was selected jointly by ERDA and the US Geological Survey as a promising source of geothermal energy.

Two wells, each 4 in. in diameter and about 5,000 ft deep, will be drilled to evaluate the area's geothermal potential and to determine the effectiveness of the process for locating underground hot rock and hot water deposits. Four to six more wells will be drilled if the initial wells are successful.

The cost of the slim-hole operation is about one-quarter the amount for past geothermal drilling. Earlier geothermal studies used large rigs designed for oil drilling.

Reverse circulation drilling

Dual-tube drilling systems use reverse circulation for adverse drilling conditions. Drilco Industrial Div. of Smith International Inc. is one of the pioneers of such systems, which offer advantages in the areas of critical sampling, lost circulation zones, economical circulation volumes, and large diameter drilling. One common application is in slim-hole mineral exploration.

In reverse circulation drilling, drilling fluid and cuttings return up through an inner tube having a smooth inner diameter. Fluid returns to the borehole annulus by gravity flow, moving down the annular space around the drill pipe. The hydrostatic pressure of the water column causes water under pressure to sweep the face of the bit, picking up cuttings. The fluid and cuttings re-enter the inner tube through the drill bit circulation openings. Fluid level is kept close to ground level to prevent caving of the hole and to maintain flow across the bit. Erosion of the borehole wall is minimal because velocity in the annular space is low. The pressure of the water outside the drill pipe supports the borehole wall.

New all-hydraulic diamond sampling drill from Mobile Drilling—the B-53 Explorer—has a rated capacity of 150 ft.

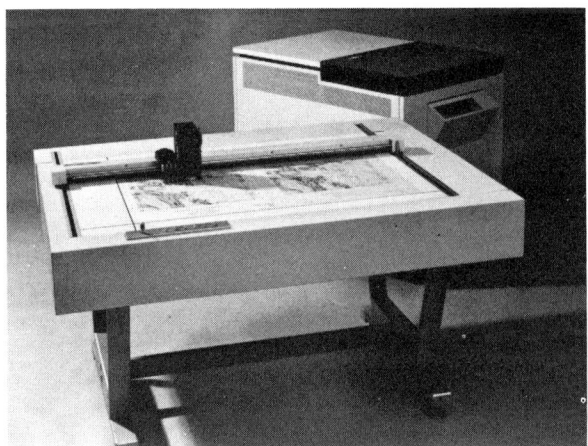

A flatbed plotter, the Model 430/101 from Broomall Industries, is used in high speed plotting of digital graphic data.

A common application of Drilco's "DuoTube" systems is recovery of chip samples for mineral evaluation. Chip samples from drag, roller, or hammer bits are carried to the surface through the inner tube, preventing sample contamination from formations above the point of drilling. In many projects, such chip samples have eliminated the need for coring. If cores are required, several types of units available allow the core to be pumped to the surface through the inner tube.

New tools measure borehole inclinations

Despite numerous improvements in all types of drilling equipment, it is still impossible to guarantee the straightness of a drillhole. To interpret geophysical measurements by drillhole and to properly map orebodies, borehole inclinations must be accurately measured.

One system to aid in measuring the inclination of boreholes has been developed by Atlas Copco and Aga Geotronics. The unit, mounted on the drill feed beam, is set to a desired inclination by adjusting a pointer and by centering an air bubble in the instrument tube. The error factor is reportedly less than 0.2%.

Atlas Copco also markets a more sophisticated instrument. This inclination measurement system consists of two pendulums mounted at right angles to each other and a direction indicator that measures the relation to magnetic north.

Another instrument to record the inclination of boreholes has been made available by Geolograph of Oklahoma City, Okla. The E-C inclinometer provides accurate pictures at one point or several different points of a hole during the same run. In wireline core drilling, the instrument is lowered in a protective case to the desired depth and kept there for 1½ to 2 min. The unit records automatically when it comes to rest. After recording, the inclinometer is raised from the hole. The angle of inclination is instantly available.

For the first time, J. K. Smit reports, an engineer can make a drillhole dip determination from the acid etch tube by direct reading, without conversion tables or capillary curve. Smit's "Bon Goniometer," incorporating all the requirements for determining true dip of the drillhole, can accommodate EX or EXT and AX or AXT sizes of etch tubes and will read etch·angles over the full range from horizontal to vertical.

The "Reflex-Fotobar" camera system, marketed by

Drilco's 'DuoTube' air-lift drilling system

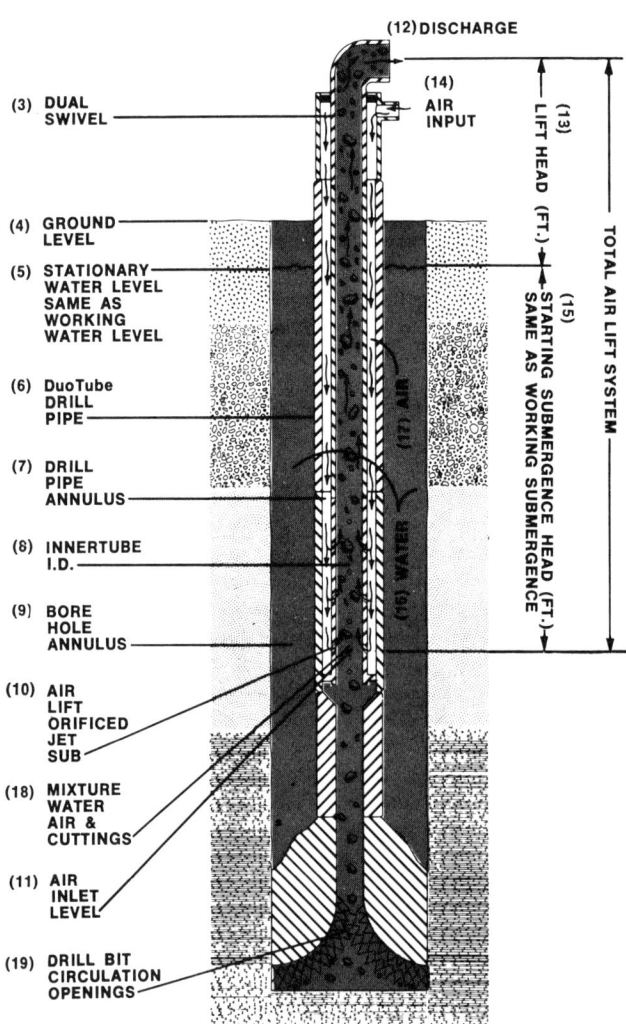

Atlas Copco and introduced two years ago, offers several advantages, including adaptability to hole diameters as low as 46 mm. The unit needs no orientation rods and may be lowered by cable or on the standard rod string. Furthermore, the unit is said to be completely undisturbed by magnetic zones or by casing. It may also be used inside wireline drill rods with an accuracy of measurement independent of time and direction. Since no gyroscope is used, no drift correction is necessary.

The Reflex-Fotobar probe consists of four 3-m rod sections screwed together. One section holds a miniature camera using standard 16-mm black and white film. The normal cassette holds enough film to measure holes 450, 900, or 1,350 m deep, depending on accuracy requirements. An electric impulse system exposes one frame every 60 or 120 sec. □

References

1) "Diamond Drilling Research Survey," MINING JOURNAL, March 22, 1974.
2) Mackenzie, Angus G., "Design and Construction of a Lightweight Self-Propelled Diamond Drill," WESTERN MINER, February 1976, pp 20-21.
3) Wink, Fred, "Canada's Newest Exploration Drill," THE NORTHERN MINER, March 4, 1976, p 18.
4) "Mobile Diamond Drill is Used for Inaccessible Areas," THE NORTHERN MINER, July 3, 1975.
5) "A method for underground mining. . . ," E/MJ, February 1976, p 138.

New bit concepts get tryouts at Sandia Laboratories

FOUR NEW DRILL BITS designed to increase cutting rates and reduce costs are under development at the Energy Research and Development Administration's Sandia Laboratories in Albuquerque, N. Mex.

Two of the drills—one chips rock with high voltage spark discharges and the other fires small projectiles into the rock in advance of a regular roller bit—are designed to increase both penetration rates and downhole bit life.

The other two systems aim primarily at increasing bit life. One permits a roller-cone bit to be folded and removed as another bit is cycled into place from a magazine containing 10 to 12 new bits. The other system places cutting surfaces on a chain that is advanced to bring new cutting surfaces into position. If the bits are successful, they will have special significance for deep well drilling, where pulling pipe to replace dulled bits is both costly and time-consuming.

Since each of the new bits is compatible with present rotary drill rig platforms, existing rigs can be used in testing and ultimately in deploying the bits for commercial purposes, Sandia states.

Spark drill based on Russian technology

Sandia developers believe the spark drill—first conceived by Russian technologists—has the greatest potential

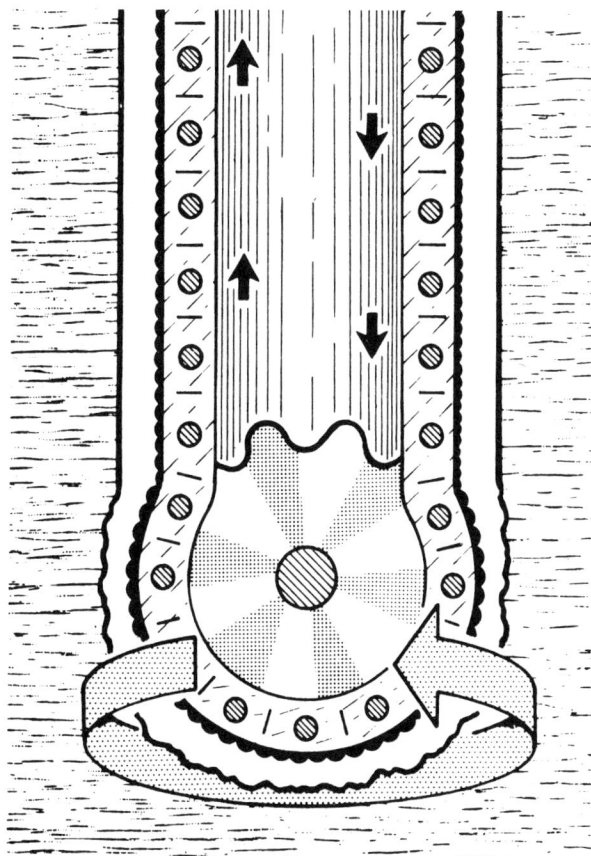

Continuous chain bit cutting surface is a long chain studded with tungsten carbide or diamond chips. When one cutting section wears out, a fresh one is exposed by rotating the chain.

of the four bits for ultimately improving drill performances. However, Sandia states, the spark drill's mode of operation is the most complex, and development problems are formidable. The design calls for generation of high voltage sparks between electrode gaps located on the bottom surface of the bit. Sparks are generated around the circumference of the bit to chip—or spall—the rock as the bit makes contact with the bottom of the hole.

The spark creates a high pressure shock wave in the drilling mud used in the drillhole. This wave is followed by stress release (formation of a bubble in the mud) and cavitation (collapse of the bubble). Sandia presently believes that bubble collapse produces a high pressure jet of fluid that further chips the rock.

The spark discharges are produced by a downhole electrical pulse generator that, in its final configuration, will discharge about 40 pulses per sec. The pulse generator will be energized through a cable from a conventional electrical generator at the surface.

So far, only low-energy lab models of the spark drill have been operated. For spark energies of 100 to 200 joules—equivalent to 1½ to 3 hp—shock pressures of 2,000 to 10,000 times atmospheric pressure have been measured. The jets produced by bubble collapse are thought to have produced even higher pressures.

In rock and concrete test blocks, the lab models have achieved drilling rates as high as 30 ft per hr, Sandia states. At the design objective of 150 hp, the bit may drill at rates of more than 100 ft per hr and offer the additional advantage of long downhole life. Sandia designers are aiming for a bit life of at least 100 hr.

The designers hope to have a bit ready for field testing in two years. Present work is concentrated on defining the spark-generated environment, understanding the mechanisms by which the spark fractures the rock, and defining a long-life bit design using computer simulations and lab testing.

Terra drill based on nuclear weapons research

The terra drill, which involves firing projectiles between the spacings in a standard tri-cone roller bit, utilizes the technology of high-speed earth penetration—terradynamics—which has evolved during Sandia's nuclear weapons development work over the past 15 years. The drill's performance is based on the principle that highly fractured rock can be drilled more rapidly than unfractured, homogeneous rock. Projectiles launched from a magazine located above the roller cones penetrate and weaken the rock ahead of the bit, which then pulverizes the fractured segments and cuts the hole to the proper diameter.

The projectile-firing assembly and the roller bit have not yet been combined into a single unit. In field tests, a gun-assembly capable of firing three projectiles simultaneously from barrels 120° apart was lowered into a hole, the projectiles fired, and the assembly raised from the hole and replaced by a tri-cone bit.

In these tests the penetration rate was about double that achieved when only the tri-cone bit was used. The tests were conducted in limestone, with modified rifle cartridges used to fire the projectiles into the stone at about 3,700 ft per sec. The projectiles penetrated about 3½ in.

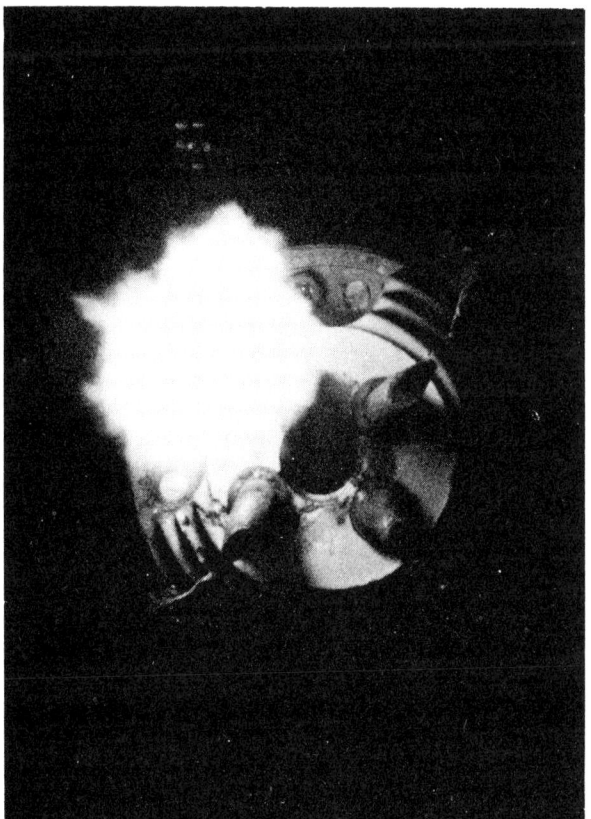

Spark generated across two electrodes of spark drill creates shock wave that chips rock as bit contacts bottom of hole.

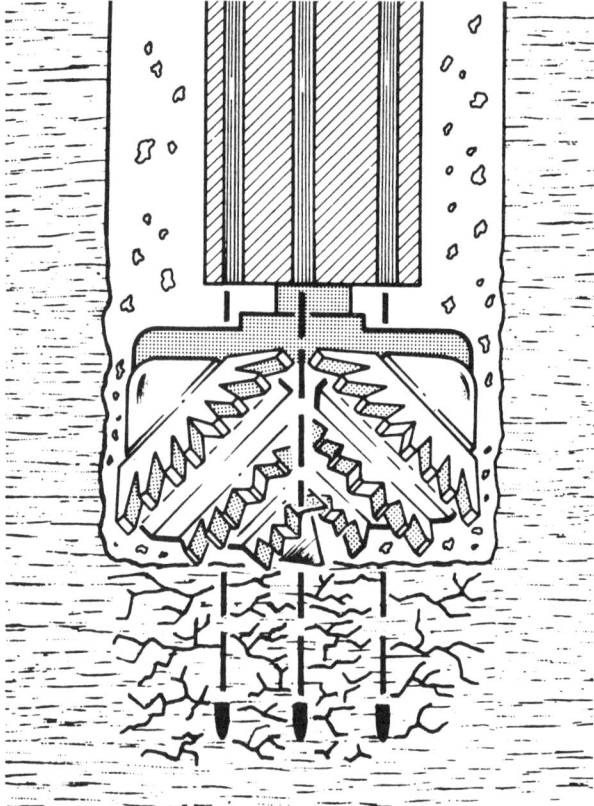

Terra drill launches small projectiles into rock ahead of bit, weakening the rock and increasing bit life and penetration rate.

According to Sandia, future development of the terra drill will focus on determining the synergistic effect, if any, of firing the projectile simultaneously, sizing and shaping the projectiles for optimum shattering of the rock, and developing cartridges that will float to the surface in the drilling mud.

Chain bit designed for 4¾-in. holes

The Sandia chain bit is under development for 4¾-in.-dia drilling but could be used to drill larger holes. The drill might find application in exploration, where bit, casing, and drill rig costs would be reduced, Sandia states. The chain bit cutting surface is located on the face of a continuous chain circulating between two sprockets—one at the bottom of the bit and another several feet distant at the top of the bit. The chain links are studded with tungsten carbide inserts or diamonds.

The hole is cut by the portion of the chain wrapped around the lower half of the bottom sprocket. As the bit is turned in the hole, the inserts scrape the bottom and sides of the hole, gradually deepening it. When the approximately 6-in.-long portion of the chain at the bottom of the hole becomes dull, another segment is cycled into place without removing the bit from the hole.

Sandia designers feel that the two sprockets can be located up to 10 ft apart, permitting use of a chain about 20 ft long. This would create about 40 separate cutting segments. Assuming that each of these bits is only half as efficient as a conventional diamond bit, the new system could still improve a bit life by 10-fold over conventional bits, the designers believe.

Major concerns for the designers at this point are whether the bit will drill a straight hole and whether it will penetrate at a rate competitive with conventional bits of the same diameter.

The bit is being designed in conjunction with Maurer Engineering Co., of Houston, and Christensen Diamond Bit Co., Salt Lake City. A working model will be ready for laboratory testing this summer, and a prototype should be ready for field tests in 1976.

Changeable bit avoids pulling drill stem

Sandia's changeable bit system would rotate a new roller bit into place at the bottom of the hole without having to pull the drill stem. Both new bits and dulled bits are stored in a magazine several feet above the bottom of the hole, and they are pulled into and out of the cutting position by a chain.

Sliding the new bit and the dulled bit past each other within the confines of the 7-in.-dia pipe is facilitated by hinging the gauge cutters (the portion of the bit that sizes the hole) so they can be folded slightly. Locks maintain the bit in a rigid position once it is on the bottom of the hole.

The major design problem is that the smaller cones required by the bit design will wear faster than the larger cones used in standard roller bits. However, if this rate of wear is only three or four times that of the larger bits, the new system could still be competitive, because up to 12 bits can be stored in the magazine.

Cutter heads for the new system, being designed and built by Reed Tool Co., of Houston, will be tested at a Reed facility. If the drilling rate tests are encouraging, a prototype system will be completed in fiscal 1976 (beginning July 1, 1975), and deep drilling field tests will be conducted in fiscal 1977. □

Breaking boulders in open pits and general utility duty at primary gyratory crushers have been natural applications for the Model 514 impact breaker (left). The Model 206 (top) works on the same principle but is smaller in size for use underground. Both models avoid metal-to-metal contact. The impactor is gaining acceptance for secondary breaking, but a longer range development goal is the evolution of a primary mining tool.

Joy demonstrates 'maxi' and 'mini' high-energy impactors

TWO HIGH-ENERGY IMPACT HAMMERS were demonstrated last month by Joy Manufacturing Co.'s Hard Rock Mining Div. at its new headquarters in metropolitan Denver, Colo.

The Model 514 "Hefti" delivers an impact of 20,000 ft-lb, which Joy says can break most boulders at the rate of about two blows per ton of rock—up to eight times the capability of typical impact hammers of equal weight. This unit has been designed with a pedestal mount for installation over gyratory crushers. Other special mounting adaptations have been designed for heavy-duty rubber-tired carriers for use in open pits and general demolition.

The Model 206 Hefti breaker packs 1,000 ft-lb of punch for a number of applications underground. This hammer is mounted on a special boom and track-type carrier designed by Joy, and it can travel through 4-ft x 6-ft-high passages. A prototype has been used successfully at finger raises on the grizzly level of a block caving operation.

A key feature of Joy's high-energy impactors is the "Fluid Tappet" operating principle. The tool point is attached to a striking bar that slides within a cylinder running the length of the hammer. Also in the cylinder is a free piston, which generates the impact energy by moving downward at high speed.

Between the piston and striking bar is a permanent pool of hydraulic fluid which, although incompressible, distributes the blow energy evenly to the striking bar. With no metal-to-metal contact, the piston face and striking bar retain their shape and strength indefinitely. Joy reports that operation is exceptionally quiet.

The propelling force for the Hefti piston is nitrogen gas at 1,200 psig, contained in a special chamber in the top of the hammer and the cylinder behind the piston. Hydraulic fluid pumped into the tappet area lifts the piston against the nitrogen pressure to the top of the cylinder. Sudden release of the fluid allows the piston to accelerate to maximum speed regardless of hammer attitude. The pressurized nitrogen also provides a cushion to prevent the striking bar from hitting the bottom of the cylinder.

Joy says the 514 Hefti is the most powerful boom-mounted impact breaker ever to be used successfully in mining and construction. Early prototypes have been used extensively in Canada and the US in many applications, including trenching in frozen earth, secondary breaking in pits, and demolition.

The simple controls for the 514 can be remotely located so that the operator has a safe and unobstructed view in breaking applications where the impact breaker is mounted over a gyratory crusher bowl. In addition to breaking oversized boulders, the hammer can be used to stir bridged rock in the bowl and to remove concaves when the crusher must be relined.

The 514 hammer, including the tool point, is less than 8 ft high and weighs 2,400 lb, excluding the boom mounting bracket.

The 206 Hefti has an outside turning radius of only 7 ft. It can reach more than 4 ft below grade to clear grizzlies and hangups. The smaller unit can be supplied with a diesel engine, Joy air motor, or electric motor. The maximum weight, with carrier and hammer, is 10,500 lb.

The 206 Hefti has undergone extensive field tests, and final production tooling is now being completed for delivery of initial orders in the next few months. Although only 40 in. high and 8 in. in diameter, the 350-lb hammer of the 206 delivers blows of 1,000 ft-lb at the rate of 200 per min.

Explosives: their classification and characteristics

J. J. Manon, chemical engineer

PERHAPS NO COMPOUNDS have been studied more thoroughly than explosives—sources from which tremendous energy can be quickly liberated under controlled and quasicontrolled conditions. With few exceptions, explosives are solids, liquids, or mixtures of solids and liquids. Upon explosion, the ingredients are rapidly transformed into other products (mostly gaseous), which occupy a much larger volume than the explosive in its original configuration. Furthermore, the explosive reaction generates considerable heat, which expands the gaseous products to such an extent that they exert enormous pressure on their surroundings.

Many factors, such as sensitivity, power, and shattering effect, must be considered in evaluating an explosive for a specific application. Equally important are the degree of toxicity of raw materials and intermediates that must be handled during production and use, hygroscopicity, water repellence, stability in storage, and cost of manufacture.

In general, military explosives differ from commercial explosives in having higher velocities of detonation, greater shattering effect, and less sensitivity.

Classification of explosives

As shown in Fig. 1, explosives are broadly classified as mechanical, chemical, or nuclear.

In mechanical explosions, inert materials are caused to vaporize very suddenly by the introduction of extremely hot matter. The "Cardox" device used in mining operations is a mechanical explosive. This device is a tube fitted with a rupture disk and filled with liquid carbon dioxide. When a heating element inside the tube is ignited, the carbon dioxide pressure increases, the disk ruptures, and the released gases expand within a borehole to shatter the lode.

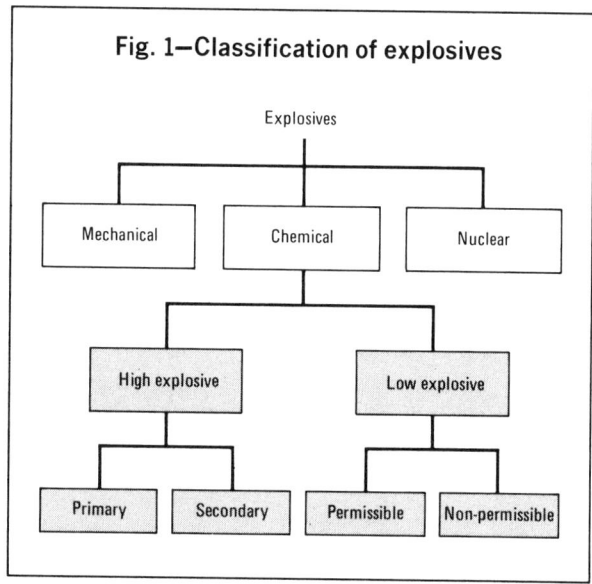

Fig. 1—Classification of explosives

Chemical explosives are of two main types: high and low. High explosives are characterized by very high rates of reaction (1 to 6 mi per sec) and high pressures (50,000 to 4 million psi). High explosives are subdivided into primary explosives, which are reliably detonated by spark, flame, and impact, and secondary explosives, which require a detonating wave of considerable magnitude for successful initiation.

Low (or deflagrating) explosives are characterized by much slower rates of reaction (a few inches or a few feet per second) and much lower pressures (up to 50,000 psi). For use in gaseous or dusty environments such as mines, even low explosives must pass certain tests before being placed on a "permissible" list. Permissibles are usually ammonium nitrate explosives, compounded to suit specific conditions.

Nuclear explosives consist of plutonium, uranium 235, or similar materials that are atomically active. The atomic reaction is controllable up to a critical level. However, once the critical level is exceeded, atomic decomposition is so rapid that an extremely destructive explosion occurs. Nuclear explosives are capable of producing on the order of 3.0×10^{15} ft-lb of work per pound, whereas trinitrotoluene (TNT), a chemical explosive, delivers about 8.4×10^4 ft-lb of work per pound.

Chemical groups common to explosives

On the basis of chemical composition, explosives can be further divided into:

- Inorganic compounds.
- Organic compounds, including nitric esters, nitro

Introducing the nonspecialist to explosives

Achievements in the science of explosives have been accelerated markedly by two major world wars and by the continuing world conflicts since the 1950s. During World War I, only a few explosives were available, together with some inferior substitutes necessitated by material shortages. Today, a broad range of explosives is produced for a wide variety of applications.

For the nonspecialist, who may find it difficult or time consuming to gain a basic understanding of the science and applications of today's explosives, the four-part review beginning in this issue of E/MJ will provide a good introduction. Part 1 discusses the fundamental facts that must be understood to appreciate 'how the energy of chemical explosives is stored, released, and applied. Future articles will examine the chemistry and physics of chemical explosives, the mechanics of detonation, and the range of commercial applications.

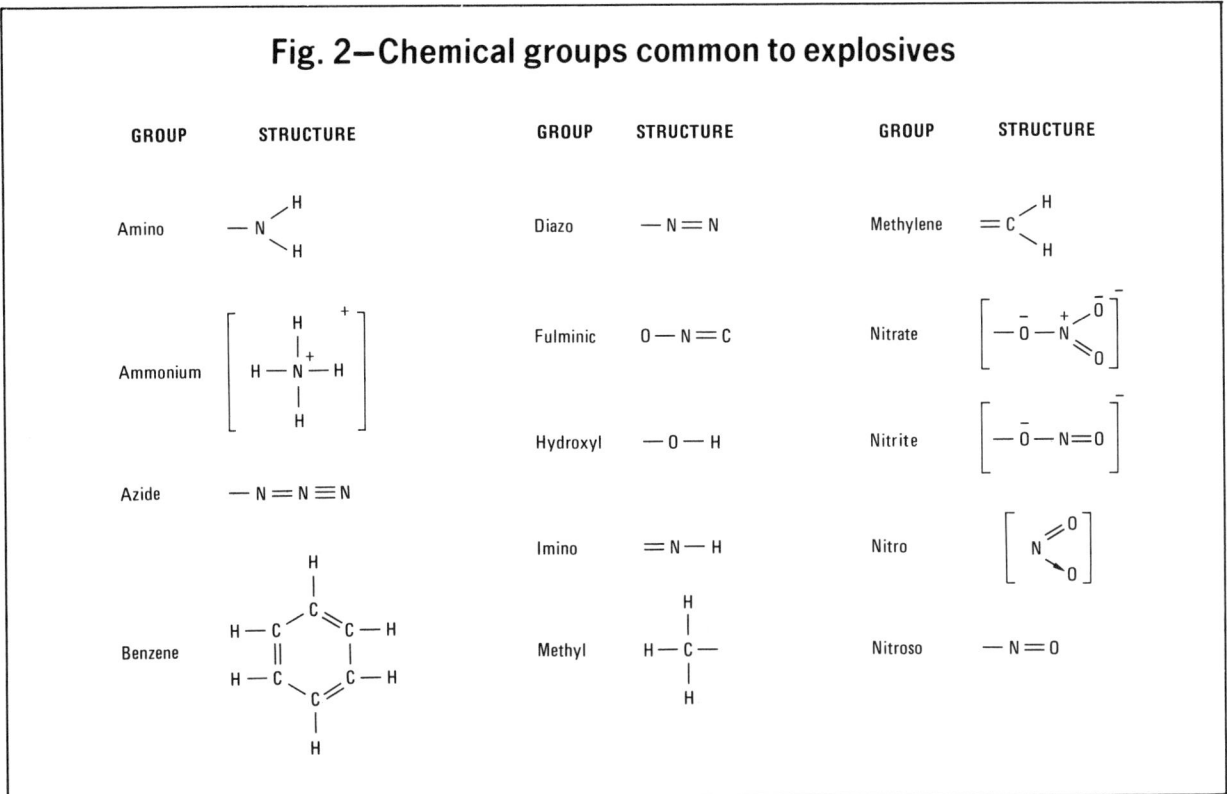

Fig. 2—Chemical groups common to explosives

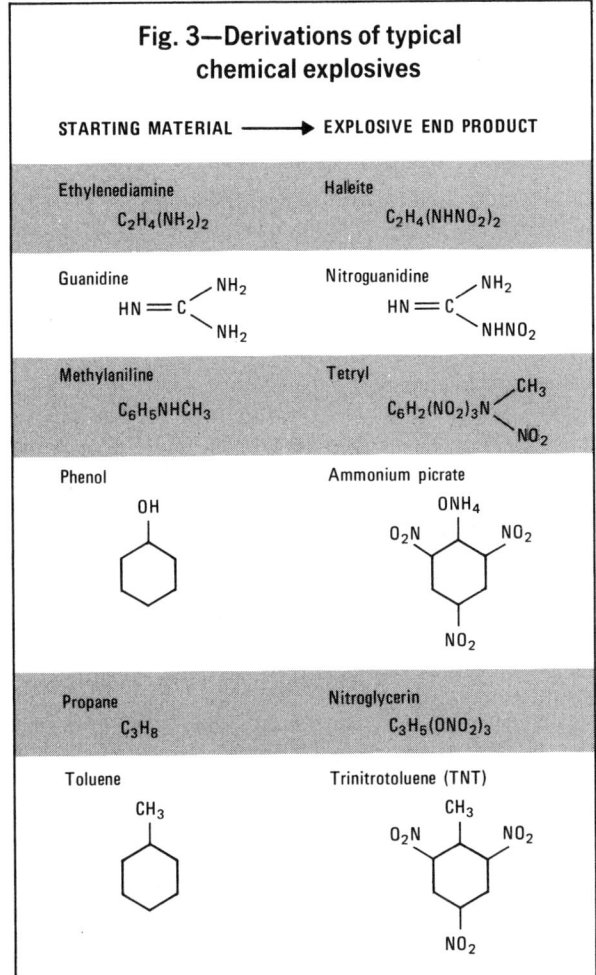

Fig. 3—Derivations of typical chemical explosives

compounds, nitramines, nitroso compounds, and metallic derivatives.

- Mixtures of oxidizable materials (fuels) and oxidizing agents that individually are not classified as explosives.

Certain groupings of atoms occur repeatedly in these compositions, and the compounds that are classified according to each grouping of atoms have reaction mechanisms with common characteristics. Fig. 2 shows the structures of the chemical groups that are of major interest in the study of explosives. Nitrogen is present in virtually all the groups. Thus, from a practical point of view, the chemistry of explosives is that of nitrogen compounds, although there are numerous chemical compounds and mixtures that have explosive properties but contain no nitrogen.

Most chemical explosives are related structurally to organic compounds of carbon, hydrogen, and generally nitrogen. To produce the typical explosive end products shown in Fig. 3, one or more hydrogen atoms of the starting materials have been replaced by chemical groups of the type listed in Fig. 2.

Characteristics of explosives

Explosives have individualized characteristics, each of which is uniquely important and must be evaluated to determine the potential usefulness of a specific explosive for a specific application. These characteristics include sensitivity, strength, power, brisance (shattering effect), stability, hygroscopicity, volatility, reactivity, and toxicity. There is a very close relationship between strength, power, and brisance.

Sensitivity is a measure of the impulse required to start an explosive reaction. Whether an explosive is sensitive or not depends not only upon its molecular makeup but also upon the crystal size, distortion, and treatment; the density of the explosive; the effects of moisture; and the temperature. High density, absorption of moisture, and coating of crystals with wax tend to reduce sensitivity. Changes in crystal size may either increase or decrease the sensitivity, depending on the amount of internal strain within or between crystals. Increased temperature and distortion of the crystalline structure invariably increase sensitivity.

Impact sensitivity. Explosion by impact is probably caused by the formation of "hot spots" within an explosive. Such hot spots are believed to be the result of adiabatic compression of small air or vapor bubbles trapped within the explosive, friction between grit and crystals of the explosive, or viscous heating of rapidly flowing explosive.

Upon impact, an entrapped gas bubble is severely compressed and highly heated. Furthermore, it is surrounded by explosive that is also under considerable pressure at the instant of impact. If the temperature of the gas and the pressure are high enough, explosion of the molecules adjacent to the gas is initiated, and the explosive wave propagates itself through the remainder of the explosive.

Among explosives, there are variations in the temperature required for explosion to occur, and therefore in the degree of compression and severity of impact required. In general, the sensitivity of an explosive to impact increases with temperature, and a molten explosive is much more sensitive than one that is hot but in the solid state. (See Table 1.)

Friction sensitivity. Like explosion by impact, the initiation of explosion by friction is attributed to the formation of hot spots. In frictional initiation, the first stage is usually a burning process. For a given frictional force, the incidence of hot spots is determined by the thermal conductivity of the sliding surfaces of the explosive and the foreign matter, such as grit. The melting point of the grit also is important, as it determines the highest frictional temperature that is attainable. If the melting point of the grit is low, an explosion cannot occur because the grit will lose its effectiveness before the temperature of detonation is reached.

Grit appears to have no initiating effect if its melting point is below 500°C and its hardness is below 3 on the Mohs' scale. Ordinarily, the most effective grit has a high melting point and a hardness value of 4 or more.

Heat sensitivity. Heat causes the decomposition of an explosive at a rate that varies with temperature. Almost all explosives have a critical temperature, below which the rate of decomposition is negligible. Furthermore, when an explosive is subjected to a high, but nonsustained, ambient temperature, an incubation period follows, during which the explosive absorbs heat without undergoing appreciable change. However, a sustained high ambient temperature has a marked effect on an explosive—causing the beginning of decomposition. Decomposition liberates heat, which, together with the high ambient temperature, accelerates the rate of decomposition of the remaining portion of the explosive. The avalanche effect is self-sustaining and, as the temperature approaches the critical temperature of the explosive, the rate of decomposition is dramatic. At the critical temperature, self-propagating detonation of the explosive occurs.

Spark sensitivity. To a degree, all known explosives are sensitive to both nonelectric and electric sparks. Nonelectric sparks, such as those from steel or burning wood, generally are more likely to initiate an explosion than the electric spark caused by the discharge of static electricity. Table 2 shows the sensitivity of specific explosives to electric sparks.

Detonating charge sensitivity. The sensitivity of an explosive to initiation by a detonating charge placed in direct contact with it varies according to the particle size, temperature, density, and physical state of the explosive. Equally important, the ability of a detonating charge to reliably detonate a specific explosive always depends on the characteristics of the detonating charge. Illustrating this point, Table 3 shows the relationship between minimum detonating charge and explosive for three typical detonating charges and 13 typical explosives.

An explosive may also be detonated by an explosive charge that is not in close proximity. This phenomenon, caused by transmission of a detonating wave through the air—not by the projection of burning embers or fragments—is known as "sympathetic detonation." When an explosive charge detonates, the detonating wave expands into the air, where it undergoes rapid decrease in velocity and pressure, to extinction. If the wave collides with an explosive at some distance before velocity and pressure have decreased appreciably, the explosive may be sympathetically detonated. The detonating wave, which travels at supersonic speed, is reflected upon impact with the explosive. Such reflections momentarily multiply the pressure in the detonating wave by a factor of two or more, depending upon the angle of impact. The detonating wave, in addition, exerts a directed blow, rather than a hydrostatic force. The directed blow produces a sudden intense force of momentary duration, far exceeding the effect of a gradually applied force of the same magnitude.

Strength. The strength of an explosive may be defined as its ability to displace the confining medium, or as the

Table 1—Effect of temperature on impact sensitivity

Temperature (°C)	Picatinny apparatus measurements (minimum height of a 2-kg weight causing explosion)		
	RDX	TNT	Ammonium nitrate
25	8 in.	14 in.	31 in.
75	–	–	28
80	–	7	–
90	8	3*	–
100	–	–	27
105	5	2*	–
150	–	–	27
175	–	–	12*

*Explosive in a molten state.

Table 2—Sensitivity of explosives to electric spark

Sensitive	Not appreciably sensitive
Ammonium picrate	Composition B
Black powder	Composition C-3
Diazodinitrophenol	PETN
Lead azide	RDX
Lead styphnate	TNT
Mercury fulminate	
Tetracene	
Tetryl	
Tetrytol	

Table 3—Sensitivity to explosive detonating charge

	Minimum detonating charge		
Explosive*	Lead azide	Mercury fulminate	Tetryl
Ammonium picrate	–	–	0.06 g
Composition A-3	0.25g	0.22g	–
Composition B	0.17	0.22	–
Composition C-3	–	–	0.08
Composition C-4	–	–	0.10
Haleite	0.13	0.21	–
Nitroguanidine	–	–	0.10
PETN	0.03	0.17	–
Picric acid	0.24	0.26	–
RDX	0.05	0.19	–
Tetryl	0.10	0.19	–
TNT	0.26	0.24	–
Torpex	–	0.18	–

*Condition of explosive: powdered 0.040-g sample pressed in blasting cap shell under pressure of 3,000 psi.

amount of energy released by the explosion. Strength is synonymous with work.

The constituent atoms and their arrangement determine the potential energy of an explosive. The degree of rearrangement, the rate of decomposition, and the quantity of gaseous products liberated determine the amount of work done by the explosive. The strongest explosives release their potential energy almost instantaneously, yielding a profusion of gas molecules.

Power. The strict definition of power is the rate of doing work. For an explosive, power depends on both strength and detonating velocity—the amount of energy released and the speed of release. In general terms, "power" is often used to indicate the effectiveness of detonation of an explosive, such as its potential to penetrate or shatter. Table 4 compares the effectiveness and detonating velocities of typical commercial and military explosives.

Brisance (from the French, meaning "to break"). Brisance, a unique characteristic of explosives, is the extremely disruptive shattering effect resulting from almost-instantaneous decomposition. Although there is no precise definition, the brisance of an explosive is universally accepted as being proportional to the product of its load density, reaction zone pressure, and detonating velocity.

Although it is difficult to predict accurately the brisance of an explosive, its cause is fairly well understood. Explosive decomposition proceeds as a self-sustaining wave, traveling at high velocity, which is enveloped by extreme pressures (on the order of 2×10^6 psi). On contact with contiguous material, the wave delivers momentary shocks of terrific intensity, which induce the shattering effect.

Stability. The very fact that a chemical compound undergoes extremely rapid decomposition when heated indicates an instability in its structure. While no precise explanation has been developed, it is generally recognized that groups common to explosives, such as the nitrate, nitro, nitrozo, diazo, and azide groups, are intrinsically in a condition of internal strain. Increased strain through heating or other external stimuli causes a sudden disruption of the molecules, leading to an explosive reaction.

Hygroscopicity (the characteristic of readily absorbing and retaining moisture). Negligible hygroscopicity is essential for acceptance of an explosive and outweighs all other characteristics—no matter how desirable—in the final determination of suitability for either commercial or military applications.

The absorption of moisture by an explosive affects not only its sensitivity but also its stability. Moisture is a most undesirable impurity because it promotes various detrimental changes:

- Cooling—the absorption of heat when moisture is vaporized, thus lowering the temperature of reaction.
- Discontinuity/decomposition—a hydrolytic reaction induced by moisture that produces free nitric and nitrous acids.
- Corrosion—interaction of the products of hydrolytic reaction with the explosive container.

Volatility. For commercial and military acceptance, it is important that an explosive exhibit low volatility—being only slightly vaporizable at the temperatures encountered in loading, handling, and storage. High volatility can cause loss by evaporation, undesirable development of pressure in explosive containers, and separation of the constituents of explosive mixtures.

Reactivity (external rather than internal). Since most explosives are loaded in contact with metal, coated metal, plastic, or wood, they must be as nonreactive with these materials as possible. Reactivity of an explosive, particularly in the presence of moisture, may produce metallic salts more sensitive to initiation than the explosive itself. In addition, reactivity causes deterioration of the explosive, with consequent loss of power or sensitivity, and invariably results in the liberation of gaseous products that produce undesirable pressure buildup.

Toxicity. Explosives cause varying degrees of toxicity when inhaled, ingested, or absorbed through the skin. The inhalation of vapors of the nitrated glycols, such as nitroglycerin, often causes severe headaches, and the ingestion of the dusts or vapors of nitro compounds has in some cases proven fatal.

The effects of skin contact with explosives vary considerably among individuals, ranging from simple skin discoloration to dermatitis, depending on the extent of contact. Most severe is the absorption of explosive ingredients through the skin, which invariably leads to incapacitating headaches, followed by unconsciousness, and ultimately acute or fatal systemic poisoning.

Relationships among explosive characteristics

Predicting the behavior of an explosive demands an appreciation of the interplay of its strength, detonating veloc-

---

About the author

J. J. Manon specializes in standardization of ordnance-related equipment and materials for the Sea Systems Command of the US Navy. Formerly vice president for ordnance/safety at John I. Thompson & Co. and vice president for ordnance programs at Potomac Research Inc., he has participated for over 18 years in research and development to refine both conventional and nuclear explosives and explosive ordnance. He holds a B.S. degree in chemical engineering from Catholic University of America.

ity, power, and brisance. When considering an explosive for a specific application, such factors as safety and cost are obviously important. But for effectiveness alone, the governing factor is an explosive's velocity of detonation.

Generally speaking, given two explosives of equal strength, the one that detonates at the higher velocity will be not only more powerful but also more brisant. It will be more powerful because of the increased speed with which the energy is delivered. It will be more brisant because of the intensity of the shock delivered.

If two given explosives are of equal detonating velocity, the stronger explosive will be more powerful because more energy is delivered in the same amount of time, and it will be more brisant because there is more force behind the shock.

The power of an explosive should not in any way be confused with its energy—the amount of work that the explosive is capable of doing. An explosive with greater strength that detonates at a relatively low velocity may actually be less powerful than an explosive of somewhat lesser strength that detonates at a relatively high velocity. Power and brisance can also be increased by increasing the velocity of detonation while slightly reducing the strength—power being thus increased by the more rapid transformation of energy, and brisance by the intensification of the shock produced. Conversely, if the velocity of detonation is slightly reduced, it is still possible to enhance both power and brisance by increasing the strength of the explosive. In this case, power and brisance are increased by the explosive force, in spite of the fact that it takes more time to release the energy and deliver the shock.

Power is of prime concern when evaluating the practicality of an explosive for military applications, with strength and detonating velocity being the major tradeoffs for achieving the desired power. However, brisance is emphasized in evaluating an explosive for suitability in quarrying, construction, mining, and similar commercial applications. To obtain the desired degree of brisance, whether for shattering or crushing effect, judicious tradeoffs are necessary, not only between strength and detonating velocity but also between such variables as reaction pressure

Table 4—Effectiveness and detonating velocity of typical explosives

Explosive	Primary use	Load density (g per cc)	Effectiveness (TNT = unity)	Detonating velocity (ft per sec)
Ammonium nitrate	Commercial	–	0.42	11,000
Blasting gelatin	Commercial	–	0.90	20,000
Composition C-2	Military	1.57	1.34	26,000
Composition C-3, C-4	Military	1.59	1.30	26,000
Nitramon	Commercial	–	–	20,000
RDX	Military	1.65	1.50	25,000
Tetryl	Military	1.55	1.26	23,000
Tetrytol	Military	1.60	1.20	23,000
TNT	Military	1.57	1.00	21,000
60% gelatin dynamite	Commercial	1.34	0.76	16,000
50% gelatin dynamite	Commercial	–	0.47	9,000
40% gelatin dynamite	Commercial	–	0.42	8,000
60% straight dynamite	Commercial	1.22	0.83	19,000
40% straight dynamite	Commercial	–	0.65	15,000

Straight dynamite contains nitroglycerin as the only explosive ingredient. The percent strength of a straight dynamite is the percentage by weight of nitroglycerin content.
Gelatin dynamite contains as an explosive base a jelly made by dissolving nitrocotton in nitroglycerin. A series of grades of gelatin dynamites are manufactured in strengths from 20% to 90%. The nitrocotton and nitroglycerin are the only explosive ingredients.
Blasting gelatin is 100% gelatin dynamite, composed of approximately 91% nitroglycerin, 8% nitrocotton, and 1% calcium carbonate.

and load density.

To achieve the rather select characteristic of brisance, formulations of black powder, ammonium nitrate, and straight and gelatin dynamites were developed, but they provided a limited choice for commercial operations. Today, however, extensive research and development has advanced the state of the art to the point where the user is able to specify explosives that meet very exacting brisance requirements. □

The chemistry and physics of explosives

J. J. Manon, chemical engineer

AN EXPLOSION IS A SERIES OF REACTIONS, highly exothermic in their summation, in which the starting material decomposes and then recombines to form the products of the explosion. Although there may appear to be little difference between a chemical formulation that is explosive and one that is nonexplosive, the presence of certain elements and molecular arrangements is the clue—as they invariably result in a compound or mixture that has explosive characteristics.

A case in point is the element nitrogen, an integral component of nearly all explosives and one of fundamental importance. Nitrogen, so stable as a gas in air, behaves in a contrary manner by being somewhat unmanageable when combined with other elements. It combines with difficulty and, even when combined, it is normally bonded loosely, causing it to be unstable and therefore very active chemically. More often than not, nitrogen bonds are easily ruptured, usually with violent suddenness and the release of considerable energy.

Also present in almost all explosives is oxygen or oxidizable elements that are easily but loosely bonded. Oxygen is usually combined in explosophore groups having low thermodynamic stability, such as nitrate ($-ONO_2$), nitro ($-NO_2$), nitramine ($-NH \cdot NO_2$), chlorate ($-ClO_3$), perchlorate ($-ClO_4$), and fulminic ($-ONC$). The oxygen joined in an explosophore group breaks away readily to combine with elements such as carbon, hydrogen, and sulphur, or with itself, thus achieving a union of much greater stability.

The nitrates and perchlorates are usually combined with sulphur, carbon, or other easily oxidizable materials in explosive formulations. TNT, which contains three nitro groups, has both the oxygen and combustibles in the same molecule. Some explosives, such as nitroglycerin, contain more than enough oxygen for complete combustion, whereas others, such as TNT, are deficient in oxygen, and the resulting incomplete combustion during an explosion produces a black smoke. To correct oxygen deficiency, ammonium nitrate, which has an excess of oxygen, is often mixed with explosives.

Azide ($-N=N\equiv N$) and acetylide ($-C\equiv C-$) are explosophore groups that contain no oxygen. The multiple bonding of these groups clearly identifies them as being unstable and readily inclined to convert to a more stable configuration.

Metallic elements—the most common being mercury and lead—also are constituents of some explosives. Such elements act as the nucleus in the formation of loosely bonded inorganic explosive configurations. Explosives consisting of metallic elements are generally extremely sensitive and very powerful.

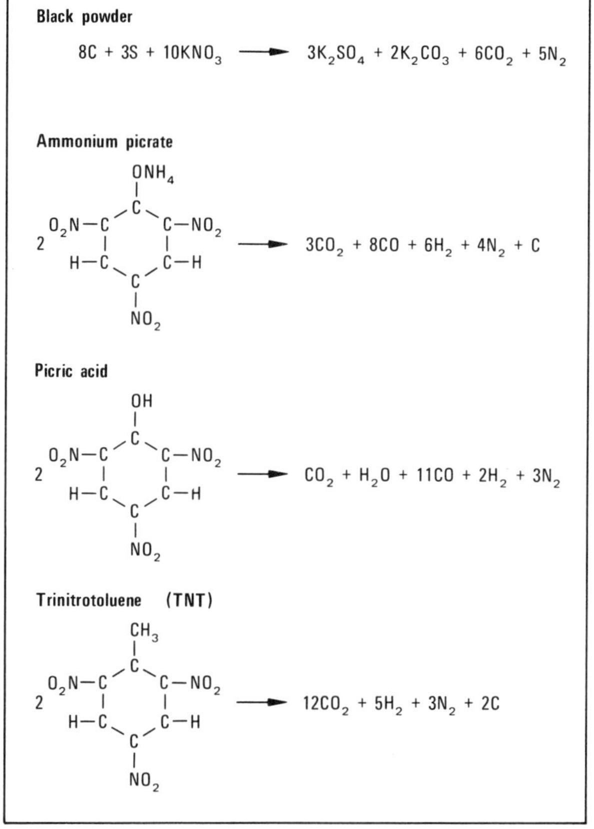

Analyzing the behavior of explosives

Some idea of why chemical explosives behave as they do can be gained from an examination of the idealized equations shown in Fig. 1 for the explosions of black powder, ammonium picrate, picric acid, and TNT.

In each of these typical explosives, there is an unstable union of nitrogen and oxygen in configurations that are inclined to convert to a more stable union when heat is applied. Upon molecular decomposition of the explosive, nitrogen and oxygen break away—nitrogen reuniting in these instances with itself, and oxygen combining with carbon, hydrogen, and sulphur. (The decompositions are actually more complicated than indicated by the idealized equations, and the composition of the gaseous products varies with changes in the temperature and pressure of the explosion.)

The chemical compositions of nitroglycerin, TNT, mercury fulminate, and lead azide indicate other aspects of the predictable behavior of explosives. (See Fig. 2.)

Each molecule of nitroglycerin and of TNT contains both the oxidizing element (nitrogen attached to oxygen) and the reducing element (carbon and hydrogen). From the equations in Fig. 1, it is evident that nitrogen would be more stable if linked with itself, and oxygen more stable if linked with carbon or hydrogen. Consequently, both nitroglycerin and TNT are unstable.

However, nitroglycerin is more unstable than TNT, for several reasons. In nitroglycerin, which is not struc-

Fig. 1—Idealized equations for reactions of selected explosives

Black powder

$$8C + 3S + 10KNO_3 \longrightarrow 3K_2SO_4 + 2K_2CO_3 + 6CO_2 + 5N_2$$

Ammonium picrate

$$2 \begin{array}{c} ONH_4 \\ O_2N-C{\cdots}C-NO_2 \\ H-C{\cdots}C-H \\ NO_2 \end{array} \longrightarrow 3CO_2 + 8CO + 6H_2 + 4N_2 + C$$

Picric acid

$$2 \begin{array}{c} OH \\ O_2N-C{\cdots}C-NO_2 \\ H-C{\cdots}C-H \\ NO_2 \end{array} \longrightarrow CO_2 + H_2O + 11CO + 2H_2 + 3N_2$$

Trinitrotoluene (TNT)

$$2 \begin{array}{c} CH_3 \\ O_2N-C{\cdots}C-NO_2 \\ H-C{\cdots}C-H \\ NO_2 \end{array} \longrightarrow 12CO_2 + 5H_2 + 3N_2 + 2C$$

turally a nitro compound, the nitrate groups are actually a combination of

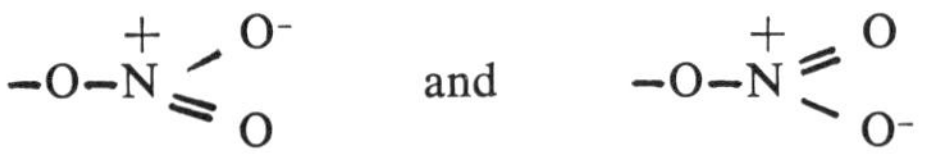

$$-O-\overset{+}{N}\overset{O^-}{\underset{O}{=}} \quad \text{and} \quad -O-\overset{+}{N}\overset{O}{\underset{O^-}{=}}$$

owing to resonance involving these two electronic forms, and each form contributes to the high degree of reactivity associated with nitroglycerin. In addition, the nitrogen in nitroglycerin is linked only with oxygen, whereas the nitrogen in TNT is linked with both carbon and oxygen, making it somewhat less reactive. Furthermore, the majority of the carbon atoms in TNT are joined in a ring configuration, which holds apart the reaction-prone bonds of the $-NO_2$ groups. In nitroglycerin, the $-NO_2$ groups are closer together, and the bonding lends itself to rupture and to ease of molecular interaction. Thus, nitroglycerin is so unstable that it often explodes unexpectedly or if jarred only slightly.

Although TNT rapidly releases considerable energy and gaseous products when detonated, because of its structure it does not rupture as easily as nitroglycerin, and molecular interaction is somewhat more difficult, making TNT safer to handle. In addition, TNT is more stable than explosives such as nitroglycerin because it does not undergo hydrolysis. During exposure to air, hydrolysis may occur in nitroglycerin, producing free nitric acid—a major cause of spontaneous combustion.

The structures of mercury fulminate and lead azide (Fig. 2) are extremely reactive configurations, and these explosives display severe molecular instability and high explosibility. In mercury fulminate, not only is the O-N bond easily ruptured, but the mercury atom is only loosely joined to oxygen. In lead azide, the nitrogen atoms are almost joined together, and they are in weak union with lead, a metal of low activity. Consequently, both mercury fulminate and lead azide are very unstable and extremely sensitive inorganic-type explosives.

In summary, unstable nitrogen and certain other elements, such as oxygen, carbon, hydrogen, and sometimes certain metals, are essential constituents of most explosives. However, the factors that contribute most significantly to the sensitivity, strength, and other characteristics of an explosive are the quantity of essential elements present, the spatial arrangement of the explosophore groups, and the nature of the bonding by which the elements and groups are united within each molecule.

Fig. 2—Chemical compositions of typical explosives

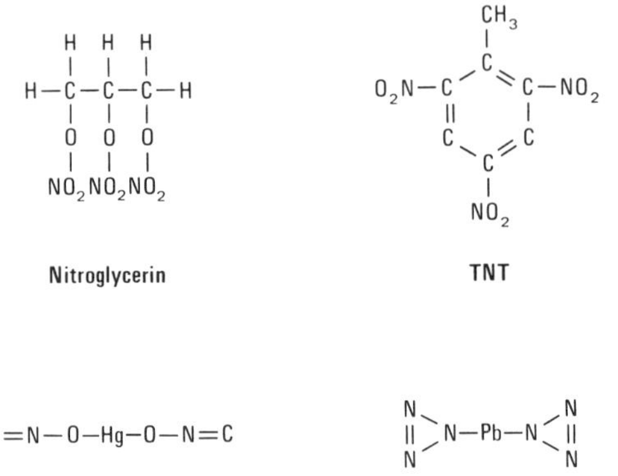

Table 1—Explosion properties of typical commercial and military explosives

Explosive	Density[a] (g/cc)	Mols gas per kg	Heat of (kcal/g)	Explosion Temperature[b] (°K)	Pressure[b] (atm)
TNT	1.59	30.5	1.12	3,420	75,000
Amatol 50/50[c]	1.55	33.7	0.95	3,020	70,000
PETN	1.60	33.7	1.41	4,540	11,200
RDX	1.60	33.1	1.43	4,500	109,000
Nitroglycerin	1.60	32.6	1.42	4,780	115,000
Tetryl	1.60	32.3	1.01	3,650	87,000
60% straight dynamite	1.32	31.1	0.99	3,690	54,000
40% straight dynamite	1.40	27.3	0.93	3,300	50,000

a) Density of original explosive.
b) Explosive state corresponding to products of detonation in static equilibrium with the volume of the original explosive.
c) Amatol 50/50 is a mixture of 50% by weight ammonium nitrate and 50% by weight TNT.

Thermochemistry of explosives

The thermochemistry of explosives concerns changes in internal energy, principally in the form of heat. The energy stored in an explosive is a form of potential energy (latent or static). The release of potential energy transforms it into kinetic, or mechanical, energy. The energy released by an explosion and changed thermodynamically into heat through the process of detonation is of prime concern here.

The law of conservation of energy states that in any isolated system, the total amount of energy is constant, although the form may change. Expressed mathematically,

Potential energy + Kinetic energy = Constant

Not all energy supplied can be converted into useful work, since a certain portion of it is always expended to overcome resistance:

Total energy supplied =
Work accomplished − Energy lost by resistance

Two alternative methods may be used to calculate energy changes: use of known chemical and physical laws, or analysis of end results or products. For explosions, the latter method is somewhat unreliable because the final products that may be conveniently analyzed are rarely those present at the instant of maximum temperature and pressure. Thus, it is most often necessary to rely on theoretical calculations based on known chemical laws to predict important properties of explosives, such as those listed in Table 1.

Heat of explosion

An explosion may occur either unconfined in the open

Table 2—Heats of formation and molecular weights of explosives and explosion products

Substance	H_f, kcal/mole at 25°C	M
Ammonium nitrate	—87.4	80
Ammonium picrate	94.0	246
Carbon	0.0	12
Carbon dioxide	94.0	44
Carbon monoxide	26.4	28
Hydrogen	0.0	2
Lead azide	—112.0	291.3
Mercury fulminate	—65.4	284.6
Nitrogen	0.0	28
Nitroglycerin	82.7	227
TNT	13.0	227
Water	57.8(g) 68.4(l)	18

air, where the pressure is atmospheric and constant, or in a confined chamber, where the volume is constant. In both cases, the same amount of energy is liberated by the reaction, but an unconfined explosion expends a certain amount of energy in pushing back the surrounding air. In a confined explosion, all of the heat released is available as useful energy.

When an explosion takes place at constant pressure, with the only work done being that of expansion or compression, the first law of thermodynamics states that:

$$Q = -\Delta(U + pV) \qquad 1)$$

where Q = heat released by the explosion
U = internal energy of the explosive
p = pressure
V = volume

Since the combination of properties $U + pV$ is referred to as the heat content or enthalpy H, then:

$$Q = -\Delta H \qquad 2)$$

Thus, when the only work is that of expansion against the prevailing pressure, the heat of explosion is equivalent to the change in enthalpy, which decreases when heat is given off or lost.

To predict the heat of an explosion, the known heats of formation of the explosive and the products of the explosion (Table 2) are used to compute ΔH, according to the following equation:

$$-\Delta H_{p(explosion)} = H_{p(products)} - H_{p(explosive)} \qquad 3)$$

As a specific example, apply the equation to nitroglycerin. The chemical reaction representing the explosion of nitroglycerin may be expressed as:

$$4[C_3H_5(NO_3)_3] \rightarrow 12CO_2 + 10H_2O\,(g) + 6N_2 + O_2 \qquad 4)$$

Accordingly, for nitroglycerin, ΔH_p is readily calculated for atmospheric conditions as follows:

$$-\Delta H_p = 12(94.0) + 10(57.8) - 4(82.7)$$
$$= 1{,}475 \text{ kcal per 4 g-mole}$$
$$= 368.8 \text{ kcal per g-mole at 25°C}$$

This calculation of the quantity of heat released at constant pressure assumes that the products of the explosion are reduced to atmospheric pressure and to a temperature of 25°C. Furthermore, in this calculation, the heat of formation of water is taken as that for water in the gaseous state. At atmospheric pressure and at 25°C, water is a liquid. However, at the moment of maximum pressure and temperature during the explosion of nitroglycerin, the products are gaseous. Assumptions such as these in the sample calculation account in part for the variations between explosion data that are calculated and data obtained experimentally.

Oxygen balance

With few exceptions, principally nitroglycerin and ammonium nitrate, explosives are oxygen-deficient—they do not contain enough oxygen to convert each atom of carbon and hydrogen present in the explosive molecule to carbon dioxide and water. Ordinarily, an explosive does not utilize atmospheric oxygen during the detonation process. Thus, the heat generated by explosion of an oxygen-deficient explosive is less than would be generated if enough oxygen were available to ensure complete oxidation.

For example, 80/20 amatol, which contains enough oxygen for complete oxidation, detonates according to the reaction:

$$21NH_4NO_3 + 2CH_3C_6H_2(NO_2)_3 \rightarrow 14CO_2 + 47H_2O + 24N_2 \qquad 5)$$

The heat of explosion for this reaction is approximately 1,000 cal per g of original explosive measured under conditions of 0°C and atmospheric pressure.

For 60/40 amatol, which contains only about 75% of the oxygen required for complete oxidation, the reaction is:

$$17NH_4NO_3 + 4CH_3C_6H_2(NO_2)_3 \rightarrow 17CO + 11CO_2 + 36H_2O + 8H_2 + 23N_2 \qquad 6)$$

Under the same conditions (0°C and atmospheric pressure), the heat of explosion of 60/40 amatol is only on the order of 880 cal per g. Thus, it is evident that a lack of oxygen results in a decrease in the heat of explosion.

The ratio of oxygen present to the amount of oxygen required for complete oxidation is used to define the oxygen balance of an explosive. Oxygen balance is expressed as a final percentage that is equal to the difference between 100% and the calculated percentage (oxygen present ÷ oxygen required). In the case of a shortage of oxygen, the final percentage is given a negative sign. Thus, an explosive having perfect oxygen balance to yield carbon dioxide and water has zero balance, an explosive lacking sufficient integral oxygen has a negative balance, and an explosive containing excess oxygen has a positive balance. The sensitivity, strength, power, and brisance of most explosives increase with increasing oxygen balance, reaching a maximum at the zero balance point.

As an example, consider TNT. While an idealized reaction is shown in Fig. 1, the explosion of TNT is more accurately represented as:

$$2CH_3C_6H_2(NO_2)_3 \rightarrow$$
$$12CO + 2CH_4 + H_2 + 3N_2 \qquad 7)$$

From this reaction, it is evident that 3 moles of O_2 are available for each mole of TNT. However, for 14 atoms of carbon, 14 moles of O_2 are required for complete conversion to CO_2; and for 10 atoms of hydrogen, 2.5 moles of O_2 are required for complete conversion to H_2O. Thus, 16.5 moles of O_2 are required to achieve zero oxygen balance for 2 moles of TNT, or 8.25 moles of O_2 per mole of TNT. Hence, there is an oxygen shortage of $8.25 - 3.00 = 5.25$ moles of O_2 per mole of TNT. Therefore, the oxygen balance for this reaction is negative and is calculated as follows:

$$100\% - \left(\frac{3.00}{8.25} \times 100\right) = 63.6\%, \text{ expressed as } -63.6\%$$

The addition of aluminum to an explosive mixture can increase both the heat and blast effect of the explosive. The aluminum is not oxidized appreciably in the detonation process, but oxidation occurs at the completion of detonation, as external oxygen reaches the aluminum. The energy released by this somewhat delayed reaction contributes markedly to the effectiveness of the aluminized explosive.

For example, carbon and oxygen commonly react in an explosion as follows:

$$C + O_2 \rightarrow CO_2 \qquad 8)$$

This reaction produces 94 kcal per g-mole at 25°C. However, with the addition of powdered aluminum (a more powerful reducing agent than carbon at the temperatures prevailing during an explosion), the reaction takes the following course:

$$C + 2O_2 + 2Al \rightarrow CO + Al_2O_3 \qquad 9)$$

The calculated heat produced by this reaction is approximately 425 kcal per g-mole, representing an increase of about 450% in the heat of reaction through the addition of aluminum.

Volume of explosion

In the explosion of nitroglycerin represented in Eq. 4, it is evident that 4 g-moles of nitroglycerin produce in the gaseous state 12, 10, 6, and 1 g-moles, respectively, of carbon dioxide, water, nitrogen, and oxygen. In other words, the explosion of 1 g-mole of nitroglycerin generates $29/4 = 7.25$ g-moles of gaseous products at 0°C and atmospheric pressure.

Since 1 g-mole of any gas at 0°C and atmospheric pressure occupies 22.4 liters, the total volume of the products of the explosion equals:

7.25 g-moles × 22.4 liters per g-mole = 162.4 liters

An increase in temperature to 15°C results in a corresponding increase in the molecular volume of the products of the explosion. The law of Gay-Lussac states that at constant pressure, an ideal gas expands 1/273 of its volume at 0°C for each degree of rise in temperature. From this law, the volume of explosion increases by a factor 288°K/273°K, to 171.3 liters at 15°C for each gram-mole of nitroglycerin available, assuming that the explosive reaction proceeds to completeness as indicated by Eq. 4.

The volume of explosion is commonly expressed in terms of moles of gas per kilogram of explosive, obtained by the relationship:

$$\frac{n_p \times 1,000}{n_e \times M_e}$$

where n_p = moles of gaseous products
n_e = moles of explosive
M_e = molecular weight of explosive

Accordingly, the number of moles of gas per kilogram of nitroglycerin equals:

$$\frac{7.25 \times 1,000}{1.0 \times 227} = 31.9$$

This value is in close agreement with the value given in Table 1 for the explosion of nitroglycerin.

Minimum energy available

A transition of energy, in the forms of work and heat, occurs immediately upon explosion in the open air, as the gaseous products of the explosion quickly expand until their combined pressures are reduced to the prevailing atmospheric pressure. During the explosion of nitroglycerin, the molecular volume increases more than 700% while the resisting pressure remains constant at 1 atm. An explosion under constant resisting pressure is referred to as a constant-pressure expansion.

The quantity of work that can be done by the gaseous products of an explosion when the pressure remains constant at 1 atm is the minimum energy available. The differential equation for this work of expansion w_e is:

$$dw_e = F dl \qquad 10)$$

where F = magnitude of the force
dl = element of distance through which the force is applied

Since pressure is force per unit area, the force F equals the pressure p multiplied by the surface area A of the envelope enclosing the gaseous products. Thus:

$$dw_e = pA dl \qquad 11)$$

However, the surface area A of the envelope multiplied by the element of distance dl traveled by the surface area as the gases expand is equal to the element of volume change of the gaseous products dV. Therefore, since p is constant:

$$\int_{w_{e1}}^{w_{e2}} dw_e = p \int_{V_1}^{V_2} dV \qquad 12)$$

or
$$w_e = p(V_2 - V_1) \qquad 13)$$

where w_e = work of expansion
p = pressure (resisting, 1 atm)
V_1 = volume of explosive
V_2 = volume of gaseous products of explosion

Because the volume of the explosive V_1 is negligible compared with the volume of the gaseous products V_2, the amount of work w_e available from 1 g-mole of nitroglycerin is calculated as follows:

$$w_e = p(V_2)$$
$$= 1 \text{ atm} \times 171.3 \text{ liters} = 171.3 \text{ liter-atm}$$

Converting liter-atmospheres to more conventional terms gives:

$$w_e = 171.3 \text{ liter-atm} \times 0.03531 \text{ cu ft per liter}$$
$$= 6.0 \text{ cu ft-atm}$$

A cubic foot-atmosphere is a measurement of energy, equivalent to 2,116 ft-lb. Therefore:

$$w_e = 6.0 \text{ cu ft-atm} \times 2,116 = 12,696 \text{ ft-lb}$$

This quantity of work is considered the minimum energy available, since the only work accomplished by the expanding gases is to push back the resisting atmosphere to make room for the increased volume.

Temperature of explosion

It is important to determine the maximum temperature to which the products of an explosion will be raised by the heat generated. The products of an explosion are essentially a mixture of gases, each of which has its own specific heat. If the explosion proceeds without loss or gain of heat and if all products of the reaction remain together, the products will assume a definite temperature.

Several methods have been developed for calculating the maximum temperature of an explosion. The most exact method requires solving five simultaneous equations conforming with the hydrodynamic theory of detonation. This method is used in scientific research, but for most applications, satisfactory approximations can be obtained by using the more direct method of calculation described as follows.

The temperature of explosion depends upon the quantity of heat generated, the volume of gaseous products of the explosion, and the heat capacities of the reactants and the products of the explosion. Moreover, the internal energy U and enthalpy H of an ideal gas are dependent only on temperature and are independent of pressure, and changes in pressure have a negligible effect on the internal energy content and enthalpies of solids and liquids. Accordingly, for an explosion that begins and ends with all materials at the same temperature, the following relationship applies for the enthalpies:

$$\Delta H = \Sigma H'_p - H_E \qquad 14)$$

where H_E = enthalpy of the explosive undergoing detonation, relative to the reference state for standard heat of reaction.
$\Sigma H'_p$ = sum of enthalpies of all products of the explosion, referred to the form of the chemical combination in which they entered the reaction at the standard reference condition.

For a given explosive, each product of the explosion has an enthalpy at $T_1°K$, which is by definition equal to the standard heat of reaction. It therefore follows that:

$$H'_p = H_p + \Delta H_{T1} \qquad 15)$$

where H_p = enthalpy of products of explosion, referred to its standard state at $T°K$.
ΔH_{T1} = standard heat of reaction at $T_1°K$.

Combining Eqs. 14 and 15 gives:

$$\Delta H = \Sigma H_p + \Sigma \Delta H_{T1} - H_E \qquad 16)$$

In an adiabatic reaction, the enthalpy change ΔH is zero. Thus, the enthalpy of the explosive must equal the sum of the standard heat of reaction and the total enthalpy of all the products, or

$$H_E = \Sigma \Delta H_{T1} + \Sigma H_p \qquad 17)$$

The temperature of the products which corresponds to this total enthalpy is calculated mathematically by expressing the enthalpy of the products as a function of their temperature.

Referred to a temperature $T°K$, the enthalpy H of n moles of any explosive is expressed by:

$$H = n \int_{T_1}^{T_2} c_p \, dT + n\lambda \qquad 18)$$

where c_p = molal heat capacity in calories per gram-mole, °K.
λ = sum of molal latent enthalpy changes in heating from T_1 to $T_2°K$.

Assuming negligible heat changes (that is, no changes in phase of products), then $n\lambda = 0$; and expressing c_p as a quadratic function of temperature ($c_p = a + bT + cT^2$), Eq. 18 becomes:

$$H = n \int_{T_1}^{T_2} (a + bT + cT^2) \, dT \qquad 19)$$

which on integration expands to:

$$H = n[a(T_2 - T_1) + \tfrac{1}{2}b(T_2^2 - T_1^2) + \tfrac{1}{3}c(T_2^3 - T_1^3)] \qquad 20)$$

To calculate the temperature of explosion T_2, the enthalpy of each product of the explosion must be obtained in the form of Eq. 20, and added together to represent ΣH_p in Eq. 17. This equation must then be solved for T_2. The method described here may be used to calculate the temperature of any explosion. As an example, the box on pp. 66 and 67 illustrates the calculation of the temperature of explosion of nitroglycerin. From the calculations and solutions presented for nitroglycerin,

and $\quad T_2 = 5,000°K$ for the cubic equation,
$\quad T_2 = 3,340°K$ for the quadratic equation.

These rather involved calculations can be accomplished more easily and more accurately if the temperature has been approximated or is known within reasonable limits. In this case, an alternative method of calculation assumes the final temperature T_2 and then uses the corresponding values of mean heat capacities.

For example, let it be assumed that the temperature of explosion of nitroglycerin is above 3,000°K, based on the graphical solutions of the cubic and quadratic equations shown in Fig. 3. From the data of Justi and Lüder, the mean molal heat capacities of the gaseous products in calories per gram-mole at 3,273°K are:

$$CO_2 = 13.55 \quad N_2 = 8.27$$
$$H_2O = 11.25 \quad O_2 = 8.77$$

Since from Eq. 19,

$$H = \text{mean } c_p (T_2 - T_1) \quad \quad 21)$$

it follows that

$$\Sigma H_p = \left[\frac{12}{4}(13.55) + \frac{10}{4}(11.25)\right.$$
$$\left. + \frac{6}{4}(8.27) + \frac{1}{4}(8.77)\right](T_2 - 298)$$

which reduces to
$$\Sigma H_p = 83.38 T_2 - 24{,}847$$

Substituting this value of ΣH_p in Eq. 17 gives:

$$83.38 T_2 - 24{,}847 = 368{,}800$$
or $\quad 83.38 T_2 = 393{,}647$

Solving this equation,
$$T_2 = 4{,}721°K$$

Although the temperature of explosion T_2 calculated by the mean c_p method is an approximation only of the maximum temperature that could be expected from the explosion of nitroglycerin, it is in close agreement with the temperature of explosion of nitroglycerin shown in Table 1. The deviation is only slightly more than 1%, principally because experimental values of heat capacities, rather than the empirical equations, were used by Justi and Lüder in deriving the mean values, and mean heat capacities do not vary greatly with temperature.

Pressure of explosion

The simple kinetic theory for the pressure-volume-temperature relation is represented by the equation:

$$pV = nRT \quad \quad 22)$$

where p = pressure
V = volume
n = moles of gas
R = gas constant
T = absolute temperature

This ideal-gas law permits satisfactory calculations of pressure-volume-temperature relationships at low pressures where the volume per mole v is relatively large and the distance between molecules is appreciable. However, under conditions of small molal volumes, corresponding to high pressures, the errors in assuming ideal-gas behavior may be unacceptable.

Examples of deviations from the simple kinetic theory are shown in Table 3. From the data in the table, it is obvious that the pV relation at constant temperature is not itself constant. Deviations from ideality are attributed to the electrical attractive forces between the molecules and the incompressibility of the molecules as compared with the gas as a whole. The molecular attractive force increases any pressure effect and thus tends to decrease volume, while the incompressibility of mole-

Table 3—Pressure-volume relationship per mole of gas at 0°C

Pressure (atm)	Hydrogen V	pV	Oxygen V	pV	Carbon dioxide V	pV
1	22.428	22.43	22.393	22.39	22.262	22.26
100	0.2386	23.86	0.2075	20.75	0.04450	4.45
400	0.07163	28.65	0.05887	23.55	0.04051	16.21
800	0.04392	35.13	0.04207	33.66	0.03779	30.23
1,000	0.03837	38.37	0.03886	38.86	0.03687	36.87

cules tends to decrease the pressure effect. As a result, real gases are more compressible than a perfect gas at low pressures and less compressible at high pressures. At some intermediate pressure, the two effects counterbalance, and the behavior of the gas follows Eq. 22 over a small range of pressure.

Several hundred equations of state have been proposed to express the pVT relationship of gases, but most are applicable only to a single gas over a limited range of temperatures and pressures. All equations of state that relate the pressure, volume, and temperature of a gas contain arbitrary constants. These constants, which are different for each substance, are attempts to correct for deviations from ideality. Four typical equations of state are:

van der Waals

$$\left(p + \frac{a}{v^2}\right)(v-b) = RT \quad \quad 23)$$

Dieterici

$$p = \left(\frac{RT}{v-b'}\right)e^{-a'/RTv} \quad \quad 24)$$

Beattie-Bridgman $\quad \quad 25)$

$$pv^2 = RT\left[v + B_0\left(1-\frac{b}{v}\right)\right]\left[1-\frac{c}{vT^3}\right] - A_0\left(1-\frac{a}{v}\right)$$

Benedict-Webb-Rubin

$$p = RTd + \left(B_0 RT - A_0 - \frac{C_0}{T^2}\right)d^2 + (bRT - a)d^3$$
$$+ a\alpha d^6 + cd^3 \frac{(1+\gamma d^2)}{T^2} e^{-\gamma d^2} \quad \quad 26)$$

In these equations, only R is constant for all gases. The values a, b, c, A_0, B_0, C_0, α, and γ must be determined or have been derived from experimental data and reported in the literature. The more constants an equation contains, the more accurately it will represent the data over a wide range of conditions. The lengthy equations of state are quite accurate and are used in scientific research. For engineering calculations, the van der Waals equation gives satisfactory results and provides the basis for an elementary understanding of the reasons for departure of gases from ideal behavior.

In the derivation of the simple kinetic theory, each molecule is considered to have an available free space, in which it may move about and which is assumed to be equal to the total volume occupied by the gas. This assumption is not correct except for conditions under which the volume of the molecules themselves is negligible as compared with the total volume occupied by

them. Actually, in each mole of gas there is a space or volume $(v - b)$ available for free motion, somewhat less than the total volume. The correction b by which the available volume per mole differs from the total volume per mole is dependent on the volume actually represented by the number of molecules themselves. It is this available volume that must be used in a more rigorous derivation of the kinetic theory pertaining to gases.

Another factor neglected in the simple kinetic theory treatment of a gas is the attraction existing between molecules, known as the van der Waals forces. These forces tend to draw the molecules together and diminish the pressure exerted to a point below the value corresponding to ideal behavior. It may be demonstrated from the kinetic theory that this reduction is inversely proportional to the square of the molal volume; that is, a/v^2.

Thus, the idealized equation of state $p = \dfrac{RT}{v}$

is corrected to become $p = \left(\dfrac{RT}{v-b}\right) - \dfrac{a}{v^2}$

Calculation of the temperature of explosion for nitroglycerin by using

In the explosion of nitroglycerin represented by Eq. 4, it is assumed that detonation is complete. Thus, H_E in Eq. 17 for nitroglycerin has no significance, $H_E = 0$, since standard heats of reactions are included in the summation of Eq. 17 only for products resulting from reactions taking place in the explosion and to the extent that the products are formed in the explosion. Thus, Eq. 17 for the explosion of nitroglycerin reduces to:

$$\Sigma H_p = -\Sigma \Delta H_{T1}$$

where $-\Sigma \Delta H_{T1}$ at $298°K = 368,800$ cal per g-mole (previously calculated as $-\Delta H_p$ for heat of explosion).

To solve for the temperature of the products of the explosion, ΣH_p is obtained as a function of temperature by means of Eq. 20, as follows: (Note: The empirical equations shown here for molal heat capacities of gases represent the value of heat capacities at any temperature. The constants used in these equations were established by Bryant, Justi, and Lüder.)

For CO_2:

$$c_p = 6.85 + 8.533 \times 10^{-3}T - 2.475 \times 10^{-6}T^2$$

and $H_{(CO_2)} = \dfrac{12}{4}\left[6.85(T_2 - 298) + \dfrac{8.533}{2} \times 10^{-3}(T_2^2 - 298^2) - \dfrac{2.475}{3} \times 10^{-6}(T_2^3 - 298^3)\right]$

$= 20.55 T_2 + 12.79 \times 10^{-3} T_2^2 - 2.48 \times 10^{-6} T_2^3 - 7,197$

For H_2O:

$$c_p = 6.89 + 3.283 \times 10^{-3}T - 0.343 \times 10^{-6}T^2$$

and $H_{(H_2O)} = \dfrac{10}{4}\left[6.89(T_2 - 298) + \dfrac{3.283}{2} \times 10^{-3}(T_2^2 - 298^2) - \dfrac{0.343}{3} \times 10^{-6}(T_2^3 - 298^3)\right]$

$= 17.22 T_2 - 4.10 \times 10^{-3} T_2^2 - 0.29 \times 10^{-6} T_2^3 - 5,420$

For N_2:

$$c_p = 6.30 + 1.819 \times 10^{-3}T - 0.345 \times 10^{-6}T^2$$

and $H_{(N_2)} = \dfrac{6}{4}\left[6.30(T_2 - 298) + \dfrac{1.819}{2} \times 10^{-3}(T_2^2 - 298^2) - \dfrac{0.345}{3} \times 10^{-6}(T_2^3 - 298^3)\right]$

$= 9.45 T_2 + 1.36 \times 10^{-3} T_2^2 - 0.17 \times 10^{-6} T_2^3 - 2,932$

For O_2:

$$c_p = 6.13 + 2.99 \times 10^{-3}T - 0.806 \times 10^{-6}T^2$$

and $H_{(O_2)} = \dfrac{1}{4}\left[6.13(T_2 - 298) + \dfrac{2.99}{2} \times 10^{-3}(T_2^2 - 298^2) - \dfrac{0.806}{3} \times 10^{-6}(T_2^3 - 298^3)\right]$

$= 1.53 T_2 + 0.37 \times 10^{-3} T_2^2 - 0.07 \times 10^{-6} T_2^3 - 487$

Adding these equations,

$\Sigma H_p = 48.75 T_2 + 18.62 \times 10^{-3} T_2^2 - 3.01 \times 10^{-6} T_2^3 - 16,036$

Then, equating ΣH_p to $-\Sigma \Delta H_{T1}$,

$48.75 T_2 + 18.62 \times 10^{-3} T_2^2 - 3.01 \times 10^{-6} T_2^3 - 16,036 = 368,800$

or $48.75 T_2 + 18.62 \times 10^{-3} T_2^2 - 3.01 \times 10^{-6} T_2^3 = 384,836$

This equation is best solved graphically by substituting values of T in the equation:

where $v = \dfrac{V}{n}$

The corrected equation of state is of course Eq. 23, the equation of van der Waals, which represents the general form of the pressure-volume relationship of a gas, even when compressed to the region of liquefaction. The constants a and b characteristic of each gas in the products of an explosion are termed the van der Waals constants.

Although van der Waals' equation is an improvement over the ideal-gas law, its results represent only a fair approximation where molal volumes are small. However, under conditions of small molal volumes corresponding to high pressures, the error in assuming ideal-gas behavior may approach 500%.

If the temperature of explosion, the volume, and the constants a and b are known, the pressure of explosion developed in a closed chamber can be calculated readily with a reasonable degree of accuracy by means of the van der Waals equation. The following example applies the equation to the explosion of nitroglycerin as represented by Eq. 4.

the empirical equation $c_p = a + bT + cT^2$

Table 4—Values of y vs. T_2

$y = 48.75 T_2 + 18.62 \times 10^{-3} T_2^2 - 3.01 \times 10^{-6} T_2^3 - 384{,}836$

When T_2 equals	y equals
−4,800°K.	+153,049
−4,500	+ 58,355
−4,400	− 25,604
−4,000	− 99,076
−3,000	−282,086
−2,000	−383,670
−1,000	−385,866
0	−384,836
1,000	−347,466
2,000	−237,036
3,000	−152,426
3,900	− 90,051
4,000	− 84,756
4,500	− 62,927
4,800	− 54,713
5,000	− 52,086
5,500	− 54,519
6,000	− 72,366

$y = 48.75 T_2 + 18.62 \times 10^{-3} T_2^2 - 384{,}990$

When T_2 equals	y equals
−6,000°K.	− 6,870
−5,000	−162,990
−4,000	−281,820
−3,000	−363,510
−2,000	−407,910
−1,000	−415,120
0	−384,990
1,000	−317,620
2,000	−213,110
3,000	− 71,310
3,500	+ 13,750
4,000	+107,730

Fig. 3—Solutions of cubic and quadratic equations for T_2

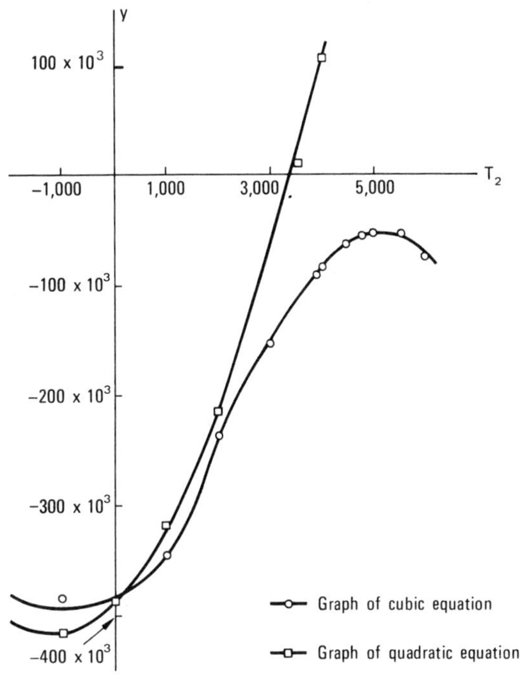

$y = 48.75T_2 + 18.62 \times 10^{-3} T_2^2 - 3.01 \times 10^{-6} T_2^3 - 384{,}836$

Values of y vs. T_2 are provided in Table 4.

Solving graphically gives the results shown in Fig. 3. The graph approaches the T_2-axis in the region of $T_2 = 5{,}000°K$, which represents an approximate solution for the temperature of explosion.

The temperature of explosion can be estimated with considerably less accuracy by disregarding the quantity $\tfrac{1}{3} c(T_2^3 - T_1^3)$ in Eq. 20. The resulting quadratic equation in T_2 in this case becomes:

$48.75 T_2 + 18.62 \times 10^{-3} T_2^2 - 16{,}190 = 368{,}800$
or $48.75 T_2 + 18.62 \times 10^{-3} T_2^2 = 384{,}990$

Solving this equation graphically as shown in Fig. 3 gives:

$$T_2 = 3{,}340°K$$

From the data of the International Critical Tables, the van der Waals constants for CO_2, H_2O, N_2, and O_2 are as follows:

$$a = \text{atm}\left(\frac{cc}{\text{g-mole}}\right)^2 \quad b = \frac{cc}{\text{g-mole}}$$

	a	b
CO_2	3.60×10^6	42.8
H_2O	5.48×10^6	30.6
N_2	1.347×10^6	38.6
O_2	1.36×10^6	31.9

Averaging these values gives:

$$a = 3.7 \times 10^6 \text{ atm}\left(\frac{cc}{\text{g-mole}}\right)^2$$
$$b = 37.4 \frac{cc}{\text{g-mole}}$$

Then, assuming the volume V to be 1 liter (1,000 cc) for this example, accepting $T = 4,721°K$ as previously calculated, and rewriting Eq. 23 in the form

$$pv = RT + bp - \frac{a}{v} + \frac{ab}{v^2}$$

it follows that:

$$v = \frac{V}{n} = \frac{1,000 \text{ cc}}{7.25 \text{ g-mole}} = 137.9 \frac{cc}{\text{g-mole}}$$

and $p\left(137.9 \frac{cc}{\text{g-mole}}\right) =$

$$82.06 \frac{(cc)(\text{atm})}{(\text{g-mole})(°K)} \times 4,721°K + \left(37.4 \frac{cc}{\text{g-mole}}\right)p$$

$$- \frac{3.7 \times 10^6 \text{ atm}\left(\frac{cc}{\text{g-mole}}\right)^2}{137.9 \frac{cc}{\text{g-mole}}}$$

$$+ \frac{3.7 \times 10^6 \text{ atm}\left(\frac{cc}{\text{g-mole}}\right)^2 \times 37.4 \frac{cc}{\text{g-mole}}}{\left(137.9 \frac{cc}{\text{g-mole}}\right)^2}$$

Solving this expression for p gives:

$$p = 3,658.5 \text{ atm, or } 53,780 \text{ psi}$$

This relatively simple calculation shows that a further decrease in volume is accompanied by a large increase in pressure. For example, from the graph shown in Fig. 4, the pressure at $V = 295$ cc ($v = 40.7$) is 115,165 atm. Conversely, as the volume increases, the pressure diminishes in the following manner:

V, cc	$v, \frac{cc}{\text{g-mole}}$	p, atm
10,000	1,379.3	286.7
100,000	13,793	28.1
1,000,000	137,931	2.8

The preceding calculation of the pressure of explosion by means of the van der Waals equation shows the order of magnitude of the pressures developed as the result of an explosion. Though accurate enough for the nonspecialist, the example involves a somewhat rudimentary attempt at adjusting for real gas behavior since

Fig. 4—Pressure-volume relationship for the explosion of nitroglycerin

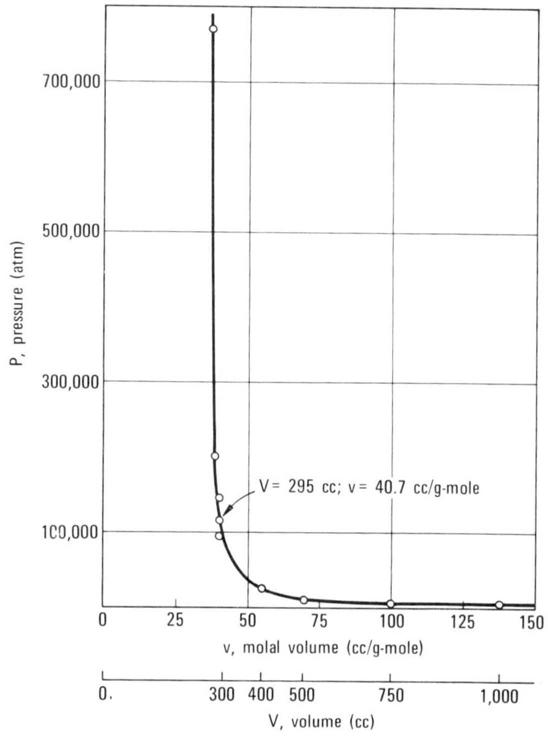

it is based upon the characteristic behavior of perfect gases, only grossly corrected. The actual gaseous products of an explosion have little in common with the concept of perfect gases.

Furthermore, many explosives generate appreciable quantities of solid or liquid substances as products of the reaction. For example:
- TNT produces free carbon.
- Aluminized explosives generate, among other products, Al_2O_3.
- Explosives containing sodium nitrate produce Na_2O and Na_2CO_3 and, if sulphur is present (frequently the case), Na_2SO_4, Na_2SO_3, and Na_2S.

A correction for the space occupied by the solid and liquid products of an explosion must be applied to the equation of state if a high degree of precision in the calculated pressure is required. Because of such considerations, an accurate determination of the pressure of explosion generally involves an extremely complex calculation. □

Mining and quarrying utilize the brisance of explosives—the extreme shattering effect produced by the supersonic speed of detonation.

Explosives: the mechanics of detonation

J. J. Manon, chemical engineer

DETONATION OF AN EXPLOSIVE is an exothermic reaction that occurs almost instantaneously, as an unstable molecular arrangement reverts to a more stable state. Detonation occurs only when the molecules of the explosive are supplied with enough energy—usually in the form of a shock—to set up within each molecule forces that exceed the attractive forces between its atoms. As the molecules come apart and the atoms rearrange to form new molecules, energy is released in the form of a pressure wave of high temperature. The released energy disrupts adjacent molecules in the material through which it passes, and the process continues until all the molecules have been disrupted. The extreme heat that develops causes atomic oxidation to take place, thus greatly increasing the molecular volume of the products of the reaction.

Detonation propagates with such rapidity that the rate of advance of the reaction into the unreacted material exceeds the velocity of sound in the unreacted material. The exceedingly transient nature of the detonation reaction makes it difficult to obtain repeatable results during experiments, even when the mechanics of detonation are investigated under laboratory conditions.

Detonation vs. deflagration

The rate of advance of the detonation reaction distinguishes it from deflagration. Although often resembling a detonation, deflagration is actually only the very rapid combustion of a material with self-contained oxygen. Under most conditions, the deflagration reaction advances into the unreacted material at less than the velocity of sound in the unreacted material. Unlike detonation, deflagration is always accompanied by flame, sparks, and the spattering of burning particles.

A low explosive is defined as a material that, when initiated in the accepted manner, deflagrates or burns rather

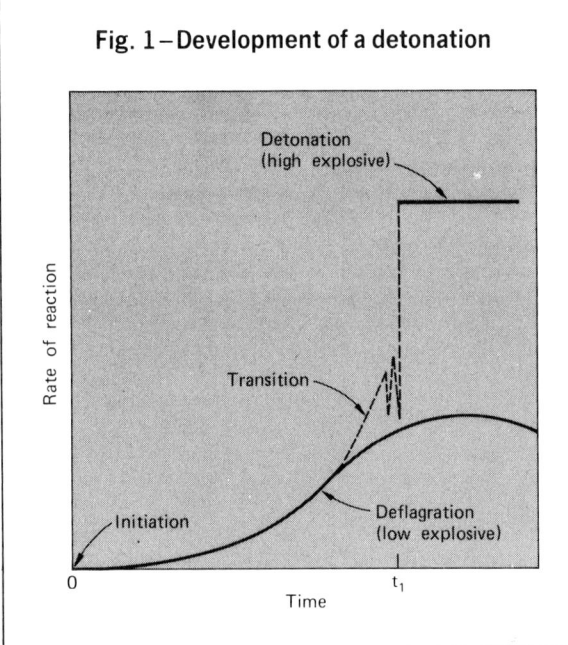

Fig. 1 – Development of a detonation

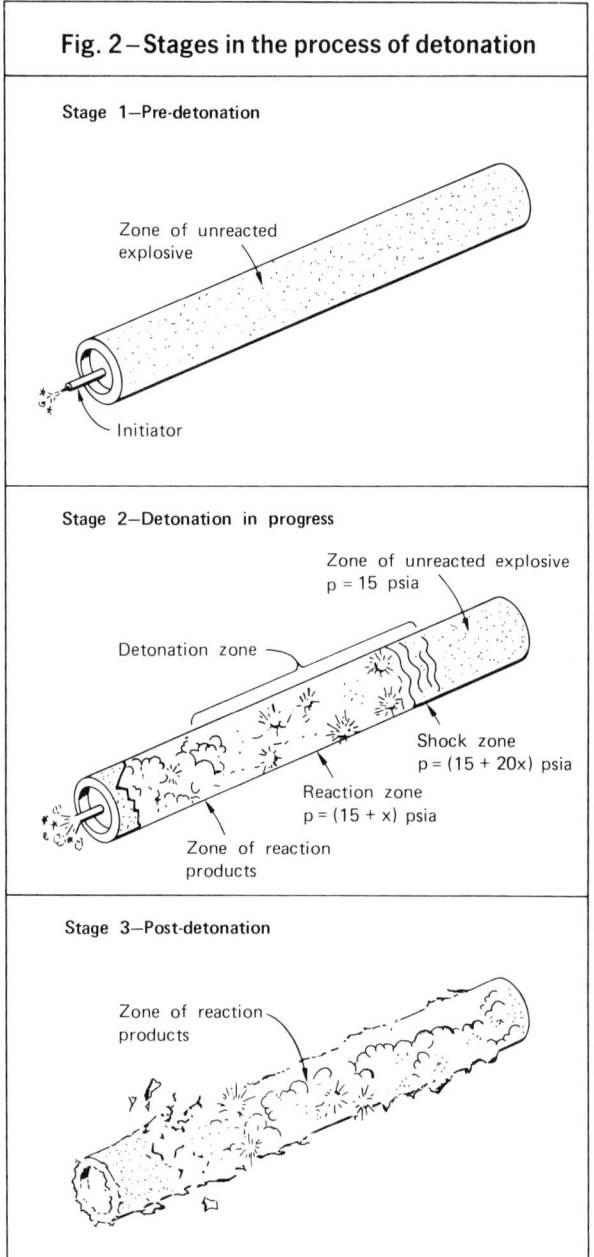

Fig. 2 – Stages in the process of detonation

than detonating. A high explosive, when initiated in the accepted manner, detonates rather than deflagrating or burning.

Whether a material reacts as a high explosive or a low explosive depends on the manner in which it is initiated and confined. For example, when initiated in the accepted manner, a solid propellant behaves as a low explosive. However, the same propellant may detonate if initiated by intense shock, such as that produced by a small caliber, high velocity projectile. Conversely, under certain conditions, a high explosive such as TNT can be ignited and will burn without detonating.

Detonation velocity

The rate of advance of the detonation reaction is termed the detonation velocity. Stable detonation velocity is a rate of advance that remains constant and continues without diminution through the unreacted material. When the detonation velocity of an explosive is equal to or greater than the stable detonation velocity, the reaction is termed a high-order detonation. When the rate of advance is less than the stable detonation velocity, the reaction is a low-order detonation.

The process of detonation

The development of detonation in an explosive is shown graphically in Fig. 1. The reaction starts as a slow combustion, then quickly builds up through the stage of deflagration, and finally undergoes a sudden transition to detonation. Low (deflagrating) explosives do not normally undergo the transition to detonation.

The process of a typical detonation is illustrated in Fig. 2. After the initiator functions, a detonation zone (in which the chemical reaction takes place) travels through the column of the explosive. The detonation zone includes the reaction zone and a narrow shock zone. Behind the reaction zone are the reaction products, and in front of the shock zone is the unreacted explosive in its original state. Little or no chemical reaction occurs in the shock zone, but because of the supersonic advance of the reaction zone into the unreacted explosive, the shock zone precedes it through the unreacted explosive. In the shock zone, the peak pressure may be as much as 20 times the peak pressure in the reaction zone. At or near the front of the shock zone, the high temperature to which the explosive is raised by compression initiates chemical reaction of the unreacted explosive.* This process propagates through the explosive until all unreacted explosive has been converted to reaction products.

In a detonation, the reaction products flow with high velocity (but at less velocity than that of the detonation zone) toward the unreacted explosive. In a deflagration, the reaction products may flow in a direction away from the unreacted explosive. □

---

*As each individual molecule of an explosive undergoes ordinary thermal reaction starting with a low initial temperature, there is a lag effect (induction period) that depends exponentially on the reciprocal of the initial absolute temperature. With an initial temperature of approximately 1,000°K, the induction period is on the order of 10^{-5} sec. With high initial temperature, it appears that the final 75% of the reaction requires only about 10^{-11} sec.

Commercial applications of explosives

J. J. Manon, chemical engineer

WHILE NUCLEAR EXPLOSIVES command worldwide attention because of their extraordinary capabilities, a wide variety of lesser-known chemical explosives is used in daily production throughout industry—with good results and little notoriety. Such applications of explosives are highly diversified. General commercial uses are outlined here.

Mining and quarrying. Explosives are used in each of the four basic operations: prospecting, exploration, development, and production. However, production consumes the largest quantity, to blast ore loose and to fragment it for easier handling.

Construction (excavating, clearing land, shearing steel, felling timber, and removing old walls and foundations). Related applications of explosives include highway and railroad tunneling, ditching, trenching, digging post holes, and breaking heavy machinery into scrap.

Seismic prospecting for natural gas and oil. Commercial explosives are used extensively for such work. The sudden shock caused by an explosion, often detonated on the surface, sends out vibrations that radiate into the ground in all directions. When the vibrations return to the surface, they are picked up by recording instruments that provide basic data for selection of the most promising drill sites.

Well shooting. Explosives are used to fracture oil-, gas-, and water-bearing formations to initiate the flow and to increase ultimate recovery. In addition, shooting is frequently successful in increasing water input during "water flooding" to flush out residual oil in a depleted field.

Underwater salvage and harbor-channel clearance. Explosives have proven very practical in clearing sunken vessels or other obstacles from inland waters, channels, and offshore waters. Explosives are used also to disperse sandbars, to deepen shallow harbor bottoms, and to widen narrow, filled-in channels.

The use of explosives under water has many advantages: speed, economy of labor and materials, and the elimination of elaborate, specialized floating equipment. However, underwater work with explosives requires more care and experience than similar work on land because visibility and other environmental conditions for drilling, loading, and firing are often less than favorable. Also, the effects of an explosion are quite different under water than in air.

Forming (use of the rapidly generated gas pressure of an explosion to form metal parts). Gas pressure and rate of deformation—important factors in metal forming—can be controlled by careful selection of the type and amount of explosive. Direct forming is usually done in a device in which the explosive has been preloaded to

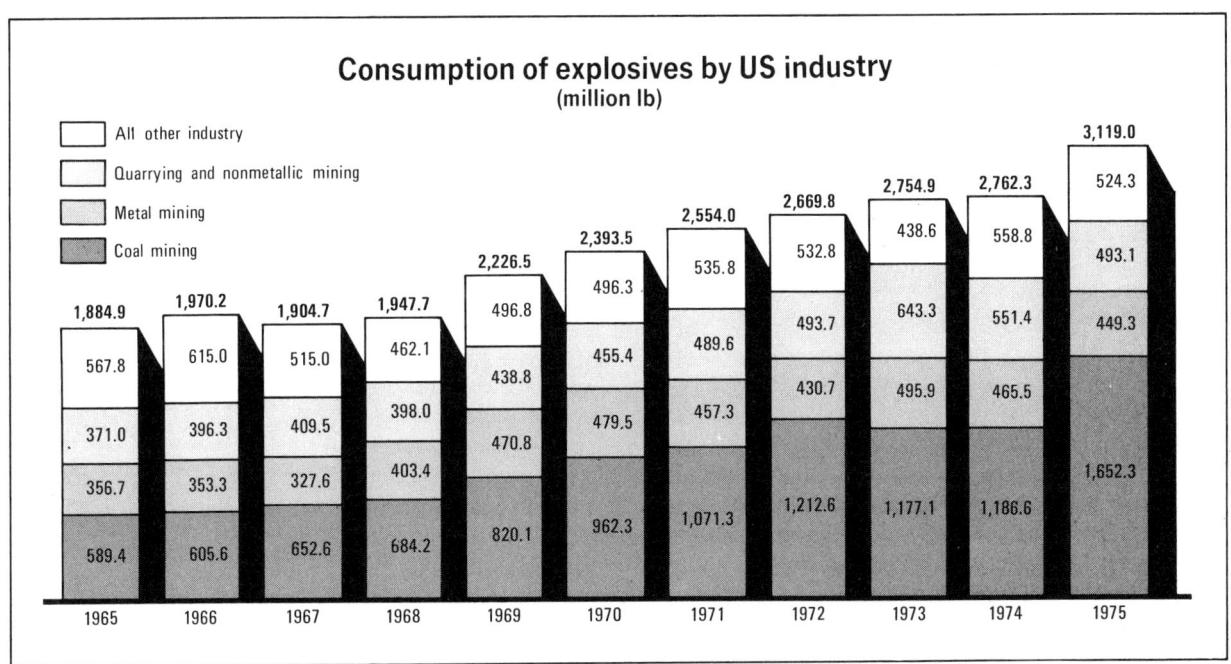

Military use of explosives

Chemical explosives are used in large quantities, for a variety of purposes, in conventional ordnance employed both defensively and offensively. Ordnance end products that contain chemical explosives include bombs, depth charges, hand and rifle grenades, guided missiles, land and naval mines, projectiles, rockets, small arms ammunition, and torpedoes.

Obviously, the state of world affairs dictates the production level of chemical explosives for military applications. Not so obvious is the fact that, to maximize production, the availability of raw materials strictly governs the types of military explosives selected for use. There will be no variation of this policy as long as conflicts are waged with conventional rather than nuclear weapons.

The expanding techniques of modern warfare have led to more specialized demands for explosives, which will continue even though the current emphasis is on defensive rather than offensive stockpiling. The trend in the US—more pronounced abroad—is to develop mixtures of known explosives with other materials to satisfy the more general military requirements. Explosives of this "binary" type include Alumatol, DBX, HBX, H6, Torpex, and Tritonal, which were developed for military use. In some cases, however, future military demand will reach a degree of sophistication that will require the development of entirely new explosives.

---

produce a given pressure in a given volume. The explosive is detonated in a chamber fitted onto dies. Gas pressure escaping from the chamber comes into contact with the metal work piece, bulging it outward to the shape of the dies.

The pressure generated by an explosive in metal forming may reach 7 million psi, compared with only 400,000 psi achieved by large hydraulic presses. Unlike such presses, which weigh as much as 10,000 tons, explosive forming equipment is small, simple, and comparatively inexpensive. Another advantage of explosive forming is increased strength of certain metals—up to 30% stronger than hydraulic pressings of the same metals. Furthermore, explosives can be used to form brittle metals, which resist conventional techniques, and loss of metal is prevented, in contrast to forming techniques that require a final machining operation.

Fastening. Rivets with explosive-filled shanks are set into metal by a special riveting iron that heats the rivet head, detonating the explosive charge in the shank. The resulting explosion causes the shank to expand throughout its length, forming a tight joint between two or more pieces of metal.

Bonding. Explosive processes are now capable of metallurgically bonding dissimilar metals and alloys without heat or intermediates. The resulting bonds are reported to be uniform in composition, with good fabricability. Theoretically, any two metals or alloys in wrought form that have sufficient ductility and impact strength can be joined. The explosive bonding process is a batch-type operation that takes place in a matter of microseconds. The process can be used to bond metals in a wide range of thickness combinations, and there is no limitation on the maximum thickness of the backing metal. Plate areas up to 140 sq ft have been explosively bonded.

Engraving. Several methods have been developed for engraving metals by explosives. In one method, a bas-relief carved at one end of a slab of explosive is placed in contact with a metal plate. Detonation of the explosive transfers the design onto the plate. Another method interposes a stencil between a plane surface of explosive and a metal plate. The explosive force is readily transmitted through the open parts of the stencil to the metal plate but is retarded by the solid portion of the stencil, producing a very accurate design.

Punching. Tools containing captive pistons and a punch can be actuated by a small explosive charge to punch holes quickly in high strength metals without leaving cracks or burrs on the surface.

Releasing. Bolts and slotted nuts can be remotely released by actuation of an explosive charge in the shank of the bolt, which ruptures the slotted nut and separates the parts. Typical applications include jettisoning wing tanks and separating rocket components and missile sustainers and boosters.

Testing. Explosive test methods are relatively simple and generally do not require complicated or expensive equipment such as large structural test models. Explosives are now used to test welded steel structures under water, as well as to study the internal structure of steel ingots. An explosive charge splits an ingot lengthwise, permitting observation of the primary structure. Crack initiation and crack propagation characteristics also are evaluated by explosive testing. The test piece is usually placed over a die and exposed to the controlled detonation force of an explosive charge suspended in air over the test piece. More than 25% of the total area of the test piece is unsupported and is bulged by the gas pressure of the explosion; the remainder of the test piece is effectively clamped to the die by the gas pressure of the explosion and remains flat over the supported area.

Another explosive test is used to evaluate the resistance of a steel plate to fracture under combined stresses and high rates of strain. The test is performed by the static detonation of a controlled explosive charge in direct contact with the specimen being tested.

Commercial consumption of explosives

In the US, there are about 20,000 commercial consumers of chemical explosives. Of these, approximately 1,000 use more than 100,000 lb annually, and about 8,000 consume more than 20,000 lb per year.

US consumption of explosives for commercial applications during 1975 increased 12.9% over that of 1974, to slightly more than 3.1 billion lb, according to the US Bureau of Mines. The coal mining industry (53.0% of total consumption) accounted for all of the increase. (See bar graph.) Six states—Kentucky, Pennsylvania, Alabama, West Virginia, Ohio, and Virginia—accounted for 52.4% of the total US consumption of commercial explosives.

The increase in US consumption reflects the sustained growth in use of blasting agents, predominantly ammonium nitrate. In the US, ammonium nitrate has been an important ingredient of explosives, particularly the permissibles, since the early 1960s. Explosives containing large percentages of ammonium nitrate have low explosion temperatures, and formulations of ammonium nitrate have achieved properties that approach the ideal blasting action of black powder.

(In mining, stripping, and quarrying, where maximum fragmentation is desirable, the low sustained pressure, or heaving action, of black powder is ideal. However, the hot, durable flame of black powder and its high degree of sensitivity to initiation are treacherous in manufacture, handling, and disposal. Consequently, black powder has declined in commercial importance, with production dropping steadily from the all-time high of 277 million lb in 1917 to 1.2 million lb in 1962. Since then, production has decreased to about 1 million lb annually.)

Continued growth is projected

Fighting the economic recession, certain US companies were recently able to stay in the black only because of strong explosives demand. The steady uptrend in commercial use of chemical explosives in the US is illustrated by consumption data for 10-year intervals:

Year	Million lb
1932	230
1942	500
1952	790
1962	1,310
1972	2,670
1975	3,119

Even though advances in technology have made chemical explosives more efficient, demand for this versatile, relatively inexpensive source of energy continues to grow. Per capita demand for explosives in the US has risen steadily with the rising standard of living. Because the richer energy and minerals deposits of the US have been markedly depleted over the years, consistently larger quantities of explosives will be required merely to maintain current production levels of coal, oil, natural gas, and minerals. Increases in production of energy and minerals will further expand the demand for chemical explosives—conservatively projected to exceed 4 billion lb per year by 1982. □

References

Bichel, C. E. *New Methods of Testing Explosives*, trans. Axel Larsen. London: Charles Griffin & Co., 1905.
Blatt, A. H. *Compilation of Data on Organic Explosives*. Department of Commerce, Office of Scientific Research and Development, Report 2014, February 1944.
Bowden, F. P., and A. D. Yoffe. *Initiation and Growth of Explosion in Liquids and Solids*. Cambridge: Cambridge University Press, 1952.
Cole, R. H. *Underwater Explosions*. Princeton: Princeton University Press, 1948.
Cook, M. A. *The Science of High Explosives*. New York: Reinhold Publishing Corp., 1958.
Davis, T. L. *The Chemistry of Powder and Explosives*. New York: Wiley & Sons, 1943.
Department of the Army. *Military Explosives*. Technical Manual 9-1910, April 1955.
Department of the Army, Ordnance Technical Intelligence Agency, Ordnance Liaison Group. *Encyclopedia of Explosives*. Durham, N.C., 1960.
Department of the Navy, Office of Naval Research, Underwater Explosion Research. *The Shock Wave* (Vol. I). *The Gas Globe* (Vol. II). *The Damage Process* (Vol. III). A compendium of British and American reports, 1950.
Department of the Navy, Naval Sea Systems Command. *Ammunition and Explosives Ashore*. Ordnance Publication 5, Vol. 1, Rev. 4, October 1974.
E. I. Dupont de Nemours & Co. Inc. *Blasters' Handbook*, 15th edition. Wilmington, Del., 1968.
Federoff, B. T., et al. *Encyclopedia of Explosives and Related Items*. Picatinny Arsenal, Dover, N.J., 1960-1975.
Fraenkel, K. H. *Manual on Rock Blasting*. Stockholm, Sweden, 1953.
Gilman, H., ed. *Organic Chemistry, An Advanced Treatise*, Vol. IV. (Ch. 10, "Chemistry of Explosives," pp 951-1000, by G. F. Wright.) New York: Wiley & Sons, 1953.

Little, A. D., Inc., punch card recording of data on explosives. (Final report to Picatinny Arsenal, Dover, N.J.) *Physical and Explosive Properties of Compounds and Mixtures* (Vol. I). *Compound Identification and Abbreviations and Trivial Names* (Vol. III). *Index to Compounds, Mixtures, References, and Microfilm* (Vol. IV). December 1961.
McAdams, R., and R. Westwater. *Mining Explosives*. Edinburgh, Scotland: Oliver and Boyd, 1958.
McGill, R. *Explosives, Propellants and Pyrotechnic Safety, Covering Laboratory, Pilot Plant, and Production Operations*. US Naval Ordnance Laboratory Technical Report 61-138, February 1962.
Meyer, M. *The Science of Explosives*. New York: Thomas Y. Crowell Co., 1943.
Naoum, P. *Nitroglycerin and Nitroglycerin Explosives*. Baltimore: Williams & Wilkins, 1928.
Nauckhoff, S., and O. Bergstrom. *Nitroglycerin and Dynamite*. Stockholm, Sweden, 1959.
Orlova, Y. Y. *The Chemistry and Technology of High Explosives*; three parts: *Nitro Compounds; Nitroamines; Nitric Esters*. Moscow, 1960. (Wright Patterson Air Force Base translation MCL-844/1&2, June 1961.)
Pearson, J. "Metal Working with Explosives," *Journal of Metals*, September 1960.
Robinson, C. S. *Explosions, Their Anatomy and Destructiveness*. New York: McGraw-Hill, 1944.
Sheffield, O. E. *Effects of Materials on the Properties of Explosives*. Picatinny Arsenal Technical Report 1783, November 1950.
Taylor, J., and P. F. Gay. *British Coal Mining Explosives*. London: George Newnes Ltd., 1958.
US Bureau of Mines, *Mineral Industry Surveys*. "Explosives," annual report.
Zeldovich, I. B., and A. S. Kompaneets. *Theory of Detonation*. New York: Academic Press, 1960. (Russian edition published in Moscow, 1955.)

How to select an explosive or blasting agent for a specific job

J. J. Manon, chemical engineer

THE WIDE VARIETY OF EXPLOSIVES on the market may seem bewildering to a nonspecialist. The selection of one explosive or blasting agent out of the many available must be based on an understanding of the basic properties of explosives, the general types of explosives and blasting agents that have been developed, the meaning of various government and industry classifications, the conditions at the jobsite, and the specific results desired from an explosion.

General characteristics of explosives (velocity of detonation, sensitivity, strength, etc.) were discussed in Part 1 of this series (E/MJ, October 1976, p 81). For a nonspecialist interested in learning how to match an explosive or blasting agent to the job at hand, more details on general characteristics are necessary, along with information on other properties, such as fume characteristics and freezing resistance.

Strength. The standard of comparison for strength of an explosive or blasting agent is usually straight dynamite. The strength of straight dynamite is stated as a percentage, approximately equal to its nitroglycerin content, by weight. A 50% straight dynamite, for example, contains approximately 50% nitroglycerin. The stated percent strength of any other type of explosive product indicates that it will perform as much work as straight dynamite of equal percent strength, on a weight-to-weight basis. For example, a cartridge of 40% ammonia dynamite is equal in strength to an equal weight of 40% straight dynamite although 40% ammonia dynamite contains much less than 40% nitroglycerin.

However, the blasting power developed by different strengths is not in direct proportion to the specified strengths. A 60% straight dynamite is not three times as strong as a 20% straight dynamite. There is no such simple relationship because the content of nitroglycerin in straight dynamite (on which the percent strength is based) is not the only energy-producing ingredient. Energy gained by increasing the nitroglycerin content is partially offset by a decrease in the energy contributed by the other ingredients. Thus, a 60% straight dynamite is only about 1½ times as strong as a 20% straight dynamite.

Strength is not a measure of effectiveness, which depends also on properties such as density and velocity of detonation.

Density is commonly expressed either in grams per cubic centimeter or in terms of the cartridge count—the number of 1¼ x 8-in. cartridges contained in a 50-lb case. In hardrock mining or for removal of heavy burden, a high density explosive or blasting agent is needed to provide sufficient energy for good breakage. To obtain better distribution of the force of an explosion, a low density explosive or blasting agent is often used in conjunction with one of high density. For light burdens or soft rock and ore, an explosive product of lower density will be effective and, of course, appreciably cheaper.

While the selection of an explosive or blasting agent to do a specific job cannot be based primarily upon its density, differences in density do correspond to differences in the velocity of detonation.

Velocity of detonation is the rate at which explosive energy is applied. For a given density, each explosive or blasting agent has a characteristic maximum velocity of detonation. The higher the velocity of detonation, the greater the brisance (shattering or fragmentation effect). To produce a heaving effect rather than shattering, lower velocity is more suitable. In general, hard materials require high velocity explosive products to produce good breakage; for soft materials, low velocity gives good results.

The method of determining the velocity of detonation is not entirely standardized. In testing, some manufacturers initiate the product to be tested with higher strength explosives having greater velocities. Also, the method of confining the charge of explosive or blasting agent during testing varies from paper tubing to steel pipe. All detonating velocities vary widely with diameter, degree of confinement, loading (packing) density or cartridge count, and method of initiation. Velocities of detonation can be modified also by increasing or decreasing the grain size of the ingredients of an explosive product. The customary procedure is to determine the velocity of detonation of 1¼ x 8-in. cartridge samples, but cartridges 1½ x 8 in. or larger are sometimes used.

Sensitivity is the relative ease of detonation. Explosives and blasting agents are at opposite ends of the sensitivity range. Among explosives, straight dynamites are more sensitive than other types because of their high nitroglycerin content. At the low end of the sensitivity range are certain water gel explosives and blasting agents, which are so insensitive that detonation requires good confinement and a high energy primer or priming system.

There is no direct relationship between sensitivity and

strength; however, as a general rule, the higher the strength, the higher the degree of sensitivity.

Fume characteristics. Some of the gases formed by detonation are relatively harmless, but others, referred to as fumes, are extremely poisonous. An explosive product with good fume characteristics liberates only a small amount of fumes when detonated.

The character of fumes depends largely on the ratio of carbonaceous ingredients to the salts that furnish oxygen for combustion. For example, if available oxygen in an explosive composition is insufficient for complete oxidation, carbon monoxide is produced; an overbalance of oxygen produces nitrogen oxides upon detonation. The production of fumes depends also on the completeness of detonation. An explosive or blasting agent with good fume characteristics may low-order detonate and produce excessive fumes if it is improperly primed or if it has deteriorated because of poor storage, improper handling, or absorption of water.

Fumes are especially hazardous in underground work. For open work, explosive products of greater strength—which are normally deficient in oxygen to a limited extent and thus have the more undesirable fume characteristics—may be used safely.

No explosive or blasting agent may be approved by the US Bureau of Mines as permissible for coal mine use if, upon detonation, it generates more than 2.50 cu ft of poisonous gases per pound of explosive or blasting agent. USBM fume class A includes permissibles that generate less than 1.25 cu ft per lb; for fume class B, the range is 1.25 to 2.50 cu ft per lb. Fume classifications for nonpermissible explosives, adopted by the Institute of Makers of Explosives, are based on the number of cubic feet of poisonous gases produced by a 1¼ x 8-in. cartridge when detonated by the USBM method. The classes are: No. 1—less than 0.16 cu ft; No. 2—0.16 to 0.33 cu ft; No. 3—0.33 to 0.67 cu ft.

Water resistance. If an explosive product is susceptible to penetration by water, its efficiency may be impaired under wet work conditions. After prolonged exposure, it may be desensitized to the point that it will detonate improperly or not at all. When water is encountered in blasting, an explosive or blasting agent with relatively good water resistance may be satisfactory if the blast is to be fired soon after loading; otherwise, a water-resistant type must be used.

Gelatin dynamites and most water gels have very good water resistance. Good resistance is characteristic of some of the high density, high strength dynamites and nitrostarch explosives. However, low density ammonia dynamites, ammonium nitrate-fuel oil blasting agents, and granular permissibles have little or no water resistance because they contain ammonium nitrate, which is hygroscopic, or because of their more open and porous composition.

Freezing resistance makes blasting possible in cold weather without the hazardous process of thawing an explosive product. The tendency of nitroglycerin to freeze at some temperatures encountered in storage and use prompted the partial substitution of antifreeze materials, such as nitrated diglycerin or the glycols. All gelatin dynamites and any granular explosive or blasting agent containing ammonium nitrate may stiffen appreciably in cold weather—an indication that freezing may have occurred.

Freezing also reduces the effectiveness of certain explosive products, especially the nitroglycerin-based dynamites. While freezing is not of as much concern

---

Three explosive ingredients: the 'nitros'

The common names of three ingredients of explosive formulations—nitroglycerin, nitrocellulose, and nitrostarch—are misnomers. Strict use of the term nitro is reserved for compounds in which the nitrogen atom of the $-NO_2$ group is attached directly to a carbon atom, as in TNT. (See E/MJ, December 1976, p 60.) In nitroglycerin, nitrocellulose, and nitrostarch, the $-NO_2$ group is attached to oxygen, and the three are, in fact, nitric esters (nitrates) of glycerol, cellulose, and starch, respectively. For this reason, they are often referred to in the literature as glycerol trinitrate, cellulose nitrate, and starch nitrate.

Nitroglycerin, the basis for modern commercial explosives, may be considered the first high explosive found suitable for practical application. For most purposes, it cannot be used alone because of its high degree of sensitivity to shock and friction and its tendency to detonate unexpectedly. However, nitroglycerin is used extensively in dynamite formulations. An objectionable characteristic of nitroglycerin-based explosives is the severe and persistent headaches caused by the absorption of nitroglycerin into the blood through the skin and as vapors inhaled into the lungs.

Nitrocellulose is not a compound but a mixture. Current practice is to designate nitrocellulose by percent nitrogen rather than by chemical terms. Commercial names for common types of nitrocellulose (also called nitrocotton) are: pyroxylin (collodion cotton), 11.2-12.2% nitrogen; pyrocotton (pyrocellulose), 12.6% nitrogen; and guncotton, 13.0% nitrogen and greater.

Nitrocellulose is of great value in explosive formulations because its rate of explosion or combustion may be regulated—unlike that of nitroglycerin, which detonates rather than burning smoothly. The brisance of nitrocellulose is directly comparable to that of TNT, and the velocity of detonation of guncotton is greater than that of TNT.

Nitrostarch, like nitrocellulose, is a mixture of various esters. From a chemical viewpoint, nitrostarch may be considered another form of nitrocellulose. Its nitrogen contents are comparable to those of the various types of nitrocellulose, and its thermochemical characteristics are similar to those of nitrocellulose.

Nitrostarch is the main explosive ingredient in some commercial explosives, in place of nitroglycerin. Such explosives are typically nonfreezing, unlike nitroglycerin explosives, and they do not undergo leakage or produce severe headaches.

The properties of ammonium nitrate

Ammonium nitrate (NH_4NO_3) has steadily increased in importance as an ingredient of explosives and blasting agents. Although it is relatively inactive and is considered a nonexplosive ingredient, ammonium nitrate can be sensitized, for example, by mixing with a carbonaceous fuel in proportions of about 94:6 by weight. Such a mixture detonates according to the following general reaction:

$$3NH_4NO_3 + (CH_2\cdot) \longrightarrow 7H_2O + CO_2 + 3N_2$$

In addition to low cost, one of the principal advantages of an ammonium nitrate formulation is its low temperature of explosion. Ammonium nitrate also decomposes readily and leaves no solid residue—making it suitable for use in gassy and dusty environments. However, its hygroscopicity is a drawback.

By varying the particle size of ammonium nitrate, it is possible to control the velocity of detonation. In general, fine particles produce very fast products of high shattering power, while coarse particles yield products much lower in velocity and brisance. Thus, different ammonium nitrate products are used both in hard rock, for fragmentation, and in soft materials, where heaving is desired. (An ammonium nitrate explosive or blasting agent often delivers a shattering effect greater than expected, which is ascribed to the large volume of gases produced.)

---

with water gels and similar products, the recommended procedure is to allow them to reach the minimum priming temperature before initiation is attempted.

Ground temperatures in the continental US average 40°F or higher, with 55°F closer to the average in many areas. The usual recommended minimum priming temperature is thus 40°F. However, several explosives now offer improved initiation at low temperatures, and a number of blasting agents deliver rated performance at both high and low temperatures.

Packaging. In virtually all instances where packaging is consumed in a blast, it must be considered a part of the explosive product because it contributes to the total gases resulting from detonation. The quantity and type of packaging consumed have an important effect on the amount of fumes produced.

Among the types of packaging, a variety of cartridge sizes and styles are available, including:

- Standard wrappers, perforated for ready expansion when firmly tamped in the blasthole, with plastic tubing for water proofing.
- Standard wrappers dipped in paraffin for extra water resistance.
- Shells that may be assembled quickly into a series of charges.
- Spiral-wound tubes that do not require special containers for rail or truck shipment.

The freer-flowing explosives and blasting agents, both metallized and nonmetallized, are supplied in multiwall paper bags, lined burlap bags, and plastic bags. Several are available also in coiled tubing and in continuous lengths to further simplify loading and priming. Slurry-type explosives and blasting agents are available in bulk, for delivery by tank trucks.

Method of initiation

Most cap-sensitive explosives are usually fired electrically, for reasons of economy. In areas where electrical storms are common, premature detonation of electric blasting caps is a serious hazard. In such cases, cap-sensitive explosives are often primed with detonating cord for added safety. (Detonating cord consists of an explosive core covered by suitable reinforced textiles, plastics, and finishes. The types of detonating cord in general use have a core of PETN.) To avoid premature detonation, blasts are initiated by detonating cord also in the vicinity of generating stations, transmission lines, radio transmitters, and radar towers.

Special primers have been developed to help bring non-cap-sensitive explosives and blasting agents to maximum steady-state velocity of detonation as quickly as possible. Various types of primers are available to meet specific requirements for safety, energy output, size, and cost. Typically, primers are cap-sensitive explosive formulations with high strength and high velocity of detonation.

The efficiency of certain blasting agents can be increased by the use of a booster-primer system. The booster furnishes substantial quantities of additional heat and enhances the performance of blasting agents. Boosters are generally not cap-sensitive, and high strength dynamites or other high velocity primers are required for reliable booster initiation.

Classification of explosives for shipment

To help meet regulations adopted for the shipment of explosives, the US Department of Transportation has established the following classifications:

Class A—explosives that represent a detonating hazard or other hazard of maximum explosion. Included in this class are dynamite, nitroglycerin, nitrostarch, and black powder. Sensitivity to blasting cap initiation is one criterion for the classification of explosives. An explosive that is sensitive to a No. 8 test cap normally receives a Class A rating.

Class B—explosives that represent principally a fire hazard, such as propellant types and certain powders. (Although ammonium nitrate possesses explosive characteristics under certain conditions, it is not included in either Class A or Class B. Ammonium nitrate is classified as an oxidizing material, for which special shipping regulations apply. Ammonium nitrate is not flammable at normal temperatures. However, in fires involving large quantities of ammonium nitrate, it becomes an explosion hazard.)

Class C—certain types of manufactured articles and assemblies that contain restricted quantities of Class A or Class B explosives, or both.

Types of explosive formulations

Alfred Nobel invented and gave the name dynamite to mixtures of nitroglycerin and kieselguhr, a porous, chemically inert substance. Kieselguhr absorbed nitroglycerin, resulting in an explosive that was much safer than nitroglycerin alone. Since then, the complexity, adaptability, and number of dynamite compositions has been increased by the addition of special purpose ingredients and the substitution of various carbonaceous fuels for kieselguhr. Today, dynamite compositions are precisely formulated for specific blasting operations.

Straight dynamite. Partial substitution of sodium nitrate for nitroglycerin and complete substitution of a carbonaceous (combustible) absorbent for kieselguhr produces an "active-dope" composition that is the basis for straight dynamites. In this type of dynamite, nitroglycerin is the only material that, by itself, is explosive.

Straight dynamites are basically stronger than the original Nobel dynamites. Other characteristics:
- High detonation velocities.
- Low detonation temperatures.
- Good water resistance in general—better in the higher strengths. (The lower strengths are desensitized by water but may be used under wet conditions if fired shortly after loading.)
- Very high flammability and a tendency to form salts with metals.
- High degree of sensitivity to shock, friction, and initiation, especially in the higher strengths.
- Objectionable fumes; not recommended for use underground or in confined spaces.

For general blasting, straight dynamites have largely been replaced by cheaper formulations such as ammonia dynamites and ammonia-gelatin dynamites. The higher strength straight dynamites, containing 50% nitroglycerin or more, are used for ditching and under water.

Ammonia dynamite—a formulation in which ammonium nitrate replaces part of the nitroglycerin and sodium nitrate content of straight dynamite. Ammonia dynamites are actually ammonium nitrate explosives in which nitroglycerin is used to sensitize ammonium nitrate to detonation. Ammonia dynamites provide the same blasting strength as most straight dynamites but contain only about two-fifths as much nitroglycerin. They are thus less costly but not quite equal in brisance. Ammonia dynamites have great heaving effect and low velocity of detonation, are hygroscopic, and are desensitized by water. They are preferable for dry blasting of soft rock.

Gelatin dynamite—formulated by including nitrocellulose in the composition of straight dynamites. The explosive base of most gelatin dynamites is a jelly made by dissolving nitrocellulose in nitroglycerin. These explosives have a high density and are virtually waterproof. Fume characteristics are good to excellent in the lower strengths but poor in the higher strengths. Gelatin dynamites are adapted to all varieties of wet work. When confined, they develop high velocity of detonation, with great shattering effect, making them preferable for blasting of hard, dense rock and ore in tunnel driving and in both underground and open-pit mining.

Ammonia-gelatin dynamite—a formulation in which ammonium nitrate replaces a portion of the nitroglycerin in gelatin dynamite. These semigelatinous explosives are equal in most respects to gelatin dynamites except for a somewhat lower velocity of detonation and slightly less resistance to water. However, certain ammonia-gelatin dynamites can be used under wet conditions, including some underwater work, if there is no prolonged exposure to water. Fume characteristics are generally good in all strengths. For many uses, an ammonia-gelatin dynamite can replace a gelatin dynamite, at a lower cost. Ammonia-gelatin dynamites are particularly well suited for outside construction work.

Semigelatin dynamite—a "hybrid" formulation with properties between those of gelatin dynamite and gran-

---

Abbreviations and terminology used throughout table on following pages

A	ammonia	Ex	explosive	NR	not recommended
al	aluminized	ff	free-flowing	NS	nitrostarch
AN	ammonium nitrate	Gel	gelatin(ous)	o	oil
ANFO	ammonium nitrate-fuel oil	Gr	granular	p	pigmented
av	average	hd	high density	pum	pumpable
—b	based	he	high energy	—s	sensitized
CIL	Canadian Industries Ltd.	HEx	high explosive	sf	specially formulated
dm	dry mix	HR	hard rock	S-G	semigelatin
Dy	dynamite	HV	high velocity	Sigma value	An indicator of the adaptability of an explosive to break rock and of the energy requirements for breakage. (Determined on the basis of independent research.)
ESC	Energy Sciences and Consultants Inc. (ESC acquired the explosives business of Dow Chemical Co. on Sept. 1, 1976.)	hyc	hydrocarbon		
		i	inhibited		
		ld	low density		
		LEx	low explosive		
		Liq Ex	liquid explosive		
		LV	low velocity		
ESN	Shock energy at center of charge on weight basis, Kcal per g.	m	metal(lized)	sl	slurry
		md	medium density	sp&c	specially processed and cast
		me	medium energy	SR	soft rock
ESNV	Shock energy at center of charge on volume basis, Kcal per g.	NA	not available	St	straight
		NCN	nitro-carbo-nitrate	WG	water gel
		NG	nitroglycerin		
ET	Explosive Technology	NH	no headache		

A guide to characteristics and typical applications of specific explosives and blasting agents

(Numbers in parentheses refer to footnotes)

Explosive or blasting agent	Manufacturer	Type	Permissible	Explosive class	Fume class	Non-cap-sensitive	% NG by weight	Velocity of detonation (fps)	Density, g per cc	Cartridge count*	Bag	Bulk	Cartridge	Cartridge (stick)	Cartridge (tube)	Cartridge (tubing)	Other	Open	Underground	Underwater	Dry	Relatively dry	Moderately wet	Wet	Blasting (general)	Excavation	Mining	Quarrying	Other	Coal	Metal	Ore	Overburden	Rock (soft to med.)	Rock (med. to hard)	Rock (hard)	Bottom load	H'vy load, hard form.	Presplit & contour	Other
Aluvite 1	Du Pont	NCN (al)			**	●	0	12,000-15,000	1.05		●					●		●			●				●									●					
Aluvite 2	Du Pont	NCN (al)			**	●	0	12,000-15,000	1.10-1.12		●					●		●			●				●									●					
Aluvite 3	Du Pont	NCN (al)			**	●	0	12,000-15,000	1.12-1.15		●					●		●			●				●									●					
Ammodyte	Atlas	A Dy		A				9,200-11,000										●								●	●	●							●				
Amogel 1	Apache	S-G Dy		A				14,100		110				●				●				●					●	●			●				●				
Amogel 2	Apache	S-G Dy		A				13,500		115				●				●				●					●	●			●				●				
Amogel 3	Apache	S-G Dy		A				12,800		120				●				●				●					●	●			●				●				
Amogel 4	Apache	S-G Dy		A				11,500		130			●					●				●					●	●			●				●				
Amogel 5	Apache	S-G Dy		A				10,500		140			●					●				●					●	●			●				●				
Amogel B	Apache	S-G Dy (hd)		A		●		10,000		95								●					●	●			●												
Amogel C	Apache	S-G Dy		A		●		11,000		97								●					●	●			●												
Amogel D	Apache	S-G Dy (hd)		A		●		12,000		100								●					●	●	●		●												
ANFO-HD	Du Pont	NCN (ANFO)				●	0	12,000-15,000	1.05		●							●			●	●				●	●	●							●				
ANOIL CVO	Trojan	NCN (ANFO)				●	0	10,000	0.74		●							●			●	●				●	●												
ANOIL Extra	Trojan	NCN (ANFO)				●	0	13,800	1.15						●				●			●			●		●	●											
ANOIL FR	Trojan	NCN (ANFO)				●	0	10,000	0.77						●				●			●			●		●	●											
ANOIL HD	Trojan	NCN (ANFO)				●	0	11,100	0.87										●			●			●		●	●											
ANOIL LD	Trojan	NCN (ANFO)				●	0	9,500	0.40										●			●			●		●	●											
Atlas 6-B	Atlas	WG Ex	●				0	11,500±1,700		145					●							●	●	●	●						●								
Atlas 6-F	Atlas	WG Ex	●				0	12,500±1,900		134					●							●	●	●	●						●								
Bag Powder, 5-70%	Trojan	NS-s Ex (ff)					0	NA			●							●			●				●											●			
Black Powder	GOEX	L Ex		A			0	13,100																															
Carbagel	Apache	NCN, WG (hyc-s)				●	0	11,480,0%M	1.20	185	●							●				●	●	●			●	●			●	●							
Carbagel 2	Apache	NCN, WG (m-s)				●	0	13,000,2%M	1.20	164	●							●				●	●	●			●	●			●	●							
Carbagel 5	Apache	NCN, WG (m-s)				●	0	13,000,5%M	1.20	199	●							●				●	●	●			●	●			●	●							
Carbagel 10	Apache	NCN, WG (m-s)				●	0	13,000,10%M	1.25	157	●							●				●	●	●			●	●			●	●							
Carbagel 15	Apache	NCN, WG (m-s)				●	0	12,000,15%M	1.25	175	●							●				●	●	●			●	●			●	●							
Carbaglo P	Apache	NCN (p)			1	●	0	8,000-15,000		136	●							●				●	●	●			●	●					●						
Carbamite P	Apache	NCN (o-s)			1	●	0	8,000-15,000	0.80	147	●							●				●	●	●			●	●					●						
Carbamite PB	Apache	NCN (i)			1	●	0	8,000-15,000		183	●							●				●	●	●			●	●					●						
Coalite BP	Atlas	Gr Ex	●				0	5,900±900		185				●				●			●	●					●			●									
Coalite 5P	Atlas	Gr Ex	●				0	6,900±1,000		164				●				●			●	●					●			●									
Coalite 5R	Atlas	Gr Ex	●				0	6,600±1,000		199				●				●			●	●					●			●									
Coalite 5U	Atlas	Gr Ex	●				0	8,900±1,300		157				●				●			●	●					●			●									
Coalite 5Y	Atlas	Gr Ex	●				0	6,600±1,000		175				●				●			●	●					●			●									
Coalite 5LR	Atlas	Gr Ex	●				0	9,200±1,400		136				●				●			●	●					●			●									
Coalite 5MR	Atlas	Gr Ex	●				0	7,500±1,100		147				●				●			●	●					●			●									
Coalite 5SR	Atlas	Gr Ex	●				0	6,900±1,000		183				●				●			●	●					●			●									
Coalite 8S	Atlas	Gr Ex	●				0	7,900±1,200		121				●				●			●	●					●			●									
Collier C	Hercules	Gr Ex	●				0	9,800±1,500		158				●				●			●	●					●			●									
C-X-L-ite	CIL	Dy						16,000		96			●												●							●				●			
Dellex 3	Dow/ESC	NCN, AN (m)	(1)			●	0	Sigma values: SR—NR, HR 1.19	1.13		●	●		●				●			●				●											●			

176   E/MJ OPERATING HANDBOOK OF SURFACE MINING

Product	Mfr	Type		Velocity	Sigma values: SR 1.34, HR 1.22	Page
Dellex 6	Dow/ESC	NCN, AN (m)	0			
Ditching Dynamite	CIL	St Dy	~50	17,500	1.13	
Ditching Dynamite	Hercules	St Dy	~50	17,400		
Ditching Dynamite	Hercules	St Dy	~60	19,000		
Drivex	Du Pont	WG Ex	0	17,300	1.25	
Dynagel	Apache	WG Ex (m)	1	14,500	1.15	
EL-844	Du Pont	WG Ex	0	12,300–12,630	1.13	
Extra Dynamites	Atlas	A-Dy		7,000–10,000		
Gas Well Gelatin	Hercules	Gel Dy		NA		
Gelamite D	Hercules	S-G Dy		17,700		
Gelamite 1 thru 5	Hercules	S-G Dy		9,850–12,500		
Gelamite IX thru 5D	Hercules	S-G Dy		9,850–12,500		
Gelatin Extra	Hercules	A-Gel Dy		18,000		
Gelatin Extra	Hercules	A-Gel Dy		21,300		
Gelatin Extra	Hercules	A-Gel Dy		23,000		
Gelatin 20	Apache	Gel Dy		11,400		87
Gelatin 25	Apache	Gel Dy		11,500		88
Gelatin 30	Apache	Gel Dy		13,500		90
Gelatin 35	Apache	Gel Dy		14,800		92
Gelatin 40	Apache	Gel Dy		15,700		94
Gelatin 50	Apache	Gel Dy		17,400		97
Gelatin 60	Apache	Gel Dy		19,700		98
Gelatin 75	Apache	Gel Dy		20,700		101
Gelatin 80	Apache	Gel Dy		21,700		102
Gelatin 90	Apache	Gel Dy		22,300		104
Gelatin 100	Apache	Gel Dy		23,600		106
Gel-Coalite Z	Atlas	Gel Ex		18,400 ± 2,800		100
Gel-Coalite 3	Atlas	Gel Ex		10,500 ± 1,600		124
Gelodyn No. 1	Atlas	S-G Dy		14,000		
Gelodyn No. 3	Atlas	S-G Dy		15,000		
Giant Gelatins	Atlas	Gel Dy		10,500–21,000		
GO Blast 2000	GOEX	NCN (ANFO)	0	10,500		
GO Blast 6000	GOEX	WG Ex	0	18,000		
GOEX-4	GOEX	Liq Ex (2)		19,500		
Hercogel A	Hercules	Gel Ex		17,100 ± 2,600		103
Hercol	Hercules	A Dy		6,550		
Hercol 2	Hercules	A Dy		10,500		
Hercol 4	Hercules	A Dy		9,500		
Hercol 6	Hercules	A Dy		8,850		
Hercomite B	Hercules	A Dy		6,550		
Hercomite 2 thru 7	Hercules	A Dy		7,850–11,500		
Hercomite 2A thru 7A	Hercules	A Dy		6,400–8,200		
Hercomite 2X thru 7X	Hercules	A Dy		7,850–11,500		
Hercomite 2XA thru 7XA (3)	Hercules	A Dy		6,400–8,200		
Hercules Gelatin	Hercules	Gel Dy		18,000		
HI-5-2, 5 lb	Tracex	HEx (TNT sp&c)	0	22,689 ± 658		
HI-6, 6 oz	Tracex	HEx (TNT sp&c)	0	22,689 ± 658		
HI-8, 8 oz	Tracex	HEx (TNT sp&c)	0	22,689 ± 658		
HI-12, 12 oz	Tracex	HEx (TNT sp&c)	0	22,689 ± 658		
HI-16, 1 lb	Tracex	HEx (TNT sp&c)	0	22,689 ± 658		
High Pressure Gelatin	Hercules	Gel Dy		19,700		
H.P. 226	Hercules	Gr Ex		6,200 ± 900		199
H.P. 299	Hercules	Gel Ex		16,400 ± 2,500		96
Hydratol S	Trojan	NCN	0	8,500	1.50	
Hydratol SA	Trojan	NCN (al)	0	9,600	1.50	

*Number of 1 1/4-in. x 8-in. cartridges in a 50-lb case. **Formulation should yield fumes substantially equivalent to fumes of dynamites rated Fume Class 1. (1) Approved as a permissible in Canada. (2) Available premixed or in two nonexplosive components. (3) Minimum fume work in blasting.

E/MJ OPERATING HANDBOOK OF SURFACE MINING

Explosive or blasting agent	Manufacturer	Type	Permissible	Explosive class	Fume class	Non-cap-sensitive	% NG by weight	Velocity of detonation (fps)	Density, g per cc	Cartridge count*	Bag	Bulk	Cartridge	Cartridge (stick)	Cartridge (tube)	Cartridge (tubing)	Other	Open	Underground	Underwater	Dry	Relatively dry	Moderately wet	Wet	Blasting (general)	Excavation	Mining	Quarrying	Other	Coal	Metal	Ore	Overburden	Rock (soft to med.)	Rock (med. to hard)	Rock (hard)	Bottom load	H'vy load, hard form.	Presplit & contour	Other
Independent A	Independent	Gr Ex	●					7,500±1,100		160				●				●	●		●	●					●			●										
Independent D	Independent	Gr Ex	●					6,200±900		171				●				●	●		●	●					●			●										
Independent E	Independent	Gr Ex	●					7,500±1,100		125				●				●	●		●	●					●			●										
Independent F	Independent	Gr Ex	●					7,900±1,200		169				●				●	●		●	●					●			●										
Independent H	Independent	Gr Ex	●					6,900±1,000		182				●				●	●		●	●					●			●										
Independent K	Independent	Gr Ex	●					9,500±1,400		137				●				●	●		●	●					●			●										
Independent Gel-N	Independent	Gel Ex	●					14,100±2,100		105				●				●	●		●	●					●			●										
Iremite 40	Ireco	S-G Dy		A				11,000						●				●			●	●	●			●	●	●					●	●						
Iremite 60	Ireco	S-G Dy		A				11,500						●				●			●	●	●			●	●	●					●	●						
Iremite 80	Ireco	S-G Dy		A				12,500						●				●			●	●	●	●		●	●	●					●	●						
Jetcord	ET	HEx (4)		A	**		0	10,000-30,000	(6)								●	●	●	●	●	●							●											●
Keotron Slurry	Keotron	Ex (sl)					0	NA	1.00-1.04								●	●	●		●	●	●							●										
Keotron Slurry	Keotron	NCN (sl)				●	0	NA	1.00-1.04								●	●	●		●	●	●							●										
MS-80-10	Dow/ESC	NCN (AN, alsl)				●	0	Sigma values: SR 1.27, HR 1.35, ESN 0.572, ESNV 0.629	1.20		●	●						●			●	●	●			●	●	●					●	●	●	●				
MS-80-15	Dow/ESC	NCN (AN, alsl)				●	0	Sigma values: SR 1.36, HR 1.45, ESN 0.667, ESNV 0.746	1.20		●	●				●		●			●	●	●			●	●	●					●	●	●	●				
MS-80-20	Dow/ESC	NCN (AN, alsl)				●	0	Sigma values: SR—NR, HR 1.55, ESN 0.672, ESNV 0.743	1.20		●	●				●		●			●	●	●			●	●	●					●	●	●	●				
MS-80-25	Dow/ESC	NCN (AN, alsl)				●	0	Sigma values: SR—NR, HR 1.65, ESN 0.716, ESNV 0.833	1.20		●	●				●		●	●		●	●	●				●	●					●	●	●	●				
Nilite 303	Du Pont	NCN (ANFO)				●	0	9,300	0.80-0.98		●	●						●			●				●															
NS-PD (5)	Trojan	NS Ex					0	12,000	1.15									●			●	●			●															
Oil Well Explosive	Hercules	Gel Dy		A				NA	1.33				●				●	●			●	●	●	●			●	●	●											
Pourvex Extra	Du Pont	WG Ex		B		●	0	16,000	1.33		●	●						●			●	●	●	●		●	●	●						●	●	●				
Power-Gel	Hercules	A-Gel Dy		A				16,500						●				●	●		●	●	●				●	●						●	●	●				
Quarry Dynamite 1	Apache	Gr Dy (ff)		A				6,200	0.91		●							●			●	●						●												
Quarry Dynamite 2	Apache	Gr Dy (ff)		A				5,900	0.90		●							●			●	●						●												
Quarry Dynamite 3	Apache	Gr Dy (ff)		A				5,600	0.91		●							●			●	●						●												
Quarry Dynamite 4	Apache	Gr Dy (ff)		A				5,300	0.93		●							●			●	●						●												
Quarry Dynamite 5	Apache	Gr Dy (ff)		A				4,900	0.95		●							●			●	●						●												
Quarry Dynamite 6	Apache	Gr Dy (ff)		A				4,900	1.04		●							●			●	●	●					●												
Quarry Dynamite 7	Apache	Gr Dy (ff)		A				3,600	1.10		●							●			●	●	●					●								●	●			
Red-D-Gel B	Austin	Gel Ex	●					16,100±2,400		107				●				●	●		●	●	●				●	●		●					●					
Red Diamond No. 2	Austin	A Dy	●					5,900±900		169				●				●	●		●	●	●				●	●		●					●					

Product	Manufacturer	Type		Velocity	Density	Strength	Fume*																										
Red Diamond No. 4	Austin	A Dy	•	8,200±1,200		121						•	•																				
Red Diamond No. 4-B	Austin	A Dy	•	8,500±1,300		113						•	•																				
Red Diamond No. 5	Austin	A Dy	•	6,600±1,000		142						•	•																				
Red Diamond No. 6	Austin	A Dy	•	10,200±1,500		133						•	•																				
Red Diamond No. 9-B	Austin	A Dy	•	6,200±900		170						•	•																				
Red Diamond No. 9-C	Austin	A Dy	•	7,200±1,100		156						•	•																				
Red Diamond No. 10-A	Austin	A Dy	•	6,900±1,000		182						•	•																				
Red Diamond No. 11	Austin	A Dy	•	5,900±900		218						•	•																				
Red Diamond No. 12	Austin	A Dy	•	11,500±1,700		119						•	•																				
Red HA	Hercules	Gr Ex	•	8,200±1,200		115						•	•																				
Red HB	Hercules	Gr Ex	•	11,200±1,700		140						•	•																				
Red HC	Hercules	Gr Ex	•	5,600±800		141						•	•																				
Red HD	Hercules	Gel Dy	•	5,900±900		155						•	•																				
Red HF	Hercules	Gr Ex	•	6,600±1,000		177						•	•																				
Red HL	Hercules	Gr Ex	•	6,200±900		189						•	•																				
Seismic Gelatin Grade 2	Trojan	S-G Ex		16,500	1.50																												
Seismic Gelatin Grade 2	Trojan	NG-s Ex		18,000	1.60																												
Seismic HV Gelatin 60%	Trojan	Gel Dy (sf)		20,000	1.50																												
Seismograph Amogel 60%	Apache	S-G Dy	A	NA																													
Seismograph HV Gelatin 60%	Apache	Gel Dy	A	NA																													
Seismograph Pattern Dynamite	Apache	A Dy	A	NA																													
Seismograph Special Gelatin 60%	Apache	S-G Dy	A																														
Special Bag Dynamite	Apache	A Dy (ff)	A	6,200	0.91																												
Special Bag HD (formerly LDX-705)	Apache	A Dy (sf)	A	6,200	1.01																												
Special Bag NH	Apache	AN Ex		6,200	0.98		0																										
Special Dynamite A	Apache	A Dy	A	10,200		115																											
Special Dynamite B	Apache	A Dy	A	10,200		120																											
Special Dynamite C	Apache	A Dy	A	9,800		128																											
Special Dynamite D	Apache	A Dy	A	9,500		135																											
Special Dynamite E	Apache	A Dy	A	9,700		142																											
Special Dynamite F	Apache	A Dy	A	9,200		152																											
Special Dynamite G	Apache	A Dy	A	8,900		162																											
Special Dynamite H	Apache	A Dy	A	8,500		172																											
Special Dynamite AL	Apache	A Dy (LV)	A	8,200		115																											
Special Dynamite BL	Apache	A Dy (LV)	A	7,880		120																											
Special Dynamite CL	Apache	A Dy (LV)	A	7,540		128																											
Special Dynamite DL	Apache	A Dy (LV)	A	6,880		135																											
Special Dynamite EL	Apache	A Dy (LV)	A	6,230		142																											
Special Dynamite FL	Apache	A Dy (LV)	A	6,060		152																											
Special Dynamite GL	Apache	A Dy (LV)	A	5,900		162																											
Special Gelatin 30	Apache	A-Gel Dy	A	13,100		90																											
Special Gelatin 35	Apache	A-Gel Dy	A	13,800		92																											
Special Gelatin 40	Apache	A-Gel Dy	A	14,400		94																											
Special Gelatin 50	Apache	A-Gel Dy	A	16,100		98																											
Special Gelatin 60	Apache	A-Gel Dy	A	17,400		101																											
Special Gelatin 75	Apache	A-Gel Dy	A	18,000		103																											
Special Gelatin 80	Apache	A-Gel Dy	A	18,700		104																											
Special Gelatin 90	Apache	A-Gel Dy	A	19,700		106																											
Standard 40%	Trojan	NS Ex		11,800		110	0																										
Standard 50%	Trojan	NS Ex		12,200		112	0																										
Standard 60%	Trojan	NS Ex		12,600		116	0																										

*Number of 1 1/4-in. x 8-in. cartridges in a 50-lb case. **Formulation should yield fumes substantially equivalent to fumes of dynamites rated Fume Class 1. (4) Explosive coreload: DIPAM, HNS, PETN, or RDX. (5) Used with low coreload detonating cord in blasting areas where static electricity or extraneous current is a hazard. (6) Available in numerous metal sheaths, explosive cores, and loadings per foot.

E/MJ OPERATING HANDBOOK OF SURFACE MINING

Explosive or blasting agent	Manufacturer	Type	Permissible	Explosive class	Fume class	Non-cap-sensitive	% NG by weight	Velocity of detonation (fps)	Density, g per cc	Cartridge count*	Packaging						Type of work			Conditions				General				Applications										
											Bag	Bulk	Cartridge	Cartridge (stick)	Cartridge (tube)	Cartridge (tubing)	Other	Open	Underground	Underwater	Dry	Relatively dry	Moderately wet	Wet	Blasting (general)	Excavation	Mining	Quarrying	Other	Coal	Metal	Ore	Overburden	Rock (soft to med.)	Rock (med. to hard)	Rock (hard)	Bottom load	H'vy load, hard form.	Presplit & contour	Other
Standard 70%	Trojan	NS Ex					0	13,300		119				•				•	•		•				•															•
Standard Dynamite 15	Apache	A Dy		A			~15	7,200		108				•				•			•				•				•											•
Standard Dynamite 20	Apache	A Dy		A			~20	7,800		108	•			•				•			•				•			•	•					•						•
Standard Dynamite 25	Apache	A Dy		A			~25	7,800		108	•			•				•			•				•			•	•					•						•
Standard Dynamite 30	Apache	A Dy		A			~30	7,900		108	•			•				•			•				•			•	•					•						•
Standard Dynamite 35	Apache	A Dy		A			~35	8,200		108	•			•				•			•				•			•	•					•						•
Standard Dynamite 40	Apache	A Dy		A			~40	8,900		108	•			•				•			•				•			•	•					•						•
Standard Dynamite 50	Apache	A Dy		A			~50	9,500		108	•			•				•			•				•			•	•					•						•
Standard Dynamite 60	Apache	A Dy		A			~60	11,200		108	•			•				•			•				•			•	•											•
Standard Dynamite 60	Apache	A Dy		A				12,800		110	•			•				•			•				•			•	•											•
Straight Dynamite 15	Apache	St Dy		A			~15	8,200		104				•				•			•				•				•											•
Straight Dynamite 20	Apache	St Dy		A			~20	8,900		104				•				•			•				•				•											•
Straight Dynamite 25	Apache	St Dy		A			~25	9,800		104				•				•			•				•				•											•
Straight Dynamite 30	Apache	St Dy		A			~30	11,200		104				•				•			•				•				•											•
Straight Dynamite 35	Apache	St Dy		A			~35	12,500		104				•				•			•				•				•											•
Straight Dynamite 40	Apache	St Dy		A			~40	13,800		104				•				•			•				•				•											•
Straight Dynamite 45	Apache	St Dy		A			~45	15,090		104				•				•			•				•				•											•
Straight Dynamite 50	Apache	St Dy		A			~50	16,400		108				•				•			•				•				•											•
Straight Dynamite 60	Apache	St Dy		A			~60	18,000		110				•				•		•	•				•				•											•
Stumping Explosive	Trojan	NS-s Ex		A				9,500	1.28	110				•				•	•		•				•				•											
Super B (7)	Trojan	A Dy (ld)	•	A				9,500	1.15	118-124	•			•				•	•		•						•			•										
Super D (7)	Trojan	A Dy (ld)	•	A				9,000	1.12	128-134				•				•	•		•						•			•										
Super E (7)	Trojan	A Dy (ld)	•	A				8,500	1.00	138-145				•				•	•		•						•			•										
Super F (7)	Trojan	A Dy (ld)	•	A				8,000	0.95	148-155				•				•	•		•						•			•										
Super G (7)	Trojan	A Dy (ld)	•	A				7,500	0.93	158-166				•				•	•		•						•			•										
Super H (7)	Trojan	A Dy (ld)	•	A				7,000	0.83	168-176				•				•	•		•						•			•										
Super 2A	Trojan	Gr Dy		A				7,500	0.88	160				•				•			•						•			•										
Super 3A	Trojan	Gr Dy		A				7,500	0.95	150				•				•			•						•			•										
Super 4	Trojan	Gr Dy		A				9,100	1.05	130				•				•			•						•			•										
Super 5	Trojan	Gr Dy		A				9,500	1.18	118				•				•			•	•					•			•										
Super 8	Trojan	Gr Dy		A				6,800	1.00	176				•				•				•					•			•										
Super 9	Trojan	Gr Dy		A				6,600	0.70	201				•				•				•					•			•										
Super 13A	Trojan	Gr Dy		A				6,900		150				•				•				•					•			•										
Super 14	Trojan	Gr Dy		A				9,200		134				•				•				•					•			•										
Super 15	Trojan	Gr Dy		A				9,500		120				•				•				•					•			•										
Super 23A	Trojan	Gr Dy		A				7,500		160				•				•				•					•			•										
Super 24	Trojan	Gr Dy		A				7,500		125				•				•				•					•			•										
Super 25	Trojan	Gr Dy		A				9,500		137				•				•				•					•			•			•	•					
Super Gel A	Trojan	Gel Dy		A				15,000	1.15	100				•				•	•		•	•	•	•	•		•			•					•				
Super Gel B	Trojan	Gel Dy		A				11,000	1.42	125				•				•	•		•	•	•	•	•		•			•					•				
Super Gel D-1	Trojan	Gel Dy		A				16,400		106				•				•	•		•	•	•	•	•		•			•				•	•				
Super Gel D-2	Trojan	Gel Dy		A				11,200		119				•				•	•		•	•		•	•		•			•					•				
Super Gel I-1	Trojan	Gel Dy		A				14,100		105				○				•	•		•	•		•	•		•			•					•				

Product	Manufacturer	Type			Detonation velocity	Density	
Temprel 3	Dow/ESC	NCN (AN, md-m)		0	Sigma values: SR 1.19, HR 1.10	0.95	
Temprel 6	Dow/ESC	NCN (AN, md-m)		0		0.95	
Temprel 9	Dow/ESC	NCN (AN, md-m)		0	Sigma values: SR 1.44, HR 1.32	0.95	
Temprel 12	Dow/ESC	NCN (AN, md-m)		0	Sigma values: SR 1.36, HR 1.50	0.95	
Temprel 15	Dow/ESC	NCN (AN, md-m)		0	Sigma values: SR 1.70, HR 1.65	0.95	
Tovan Extra	Du Pont	WG Ex (ff)	B	0	Sigma values: SR 1.80, HR 1.80	1.15	
Tovex 100	Du Pont	WG Ex	A	0	16,500	1.10	
Tovex 200	Du Pont	WG Ex (al)	A	0	12,700, dia. 1 in.	1.10	
Tovex 210 (8)	Du Pont	WG Ex (al)	A	0	13,090, dia. 1 in.	1.10	
Tovex 300	Du Pont	WG Ex (md-me)	A	0	13,090, dia. 1 in.	1.02	125
Tovex 310 (formerly EL-837)	Du Pont	WG Ex (ld-me)	A	0	11,500, dia. 1¼ in.	NA	162
Tovex 500	Du Pont	WG Ex (md-me)	A	0	11,810, dia. 1¼ in.	1.23	
Tovex 650	Du Pont	WG Ex (hd-he)	A	0	14,100, dia. 2 in.	1.35	
Tovex 700	Du Pont	WG Ex (md-me)	A	0	14,750, dia. 2 in.	1.20	
Tovex 800 (8)	Du Pont	WG Ex (md-he)	A	0	15,750, dia. 2 in.	1.20	
Tovex Extra	Du Pont	WG Ex	B	0	15,750, dia. 2 in.	1.33	
Tovex S	Du Pont	WG Ex	A	0	18,700	1.38	
Tovex T-1	Du Pont	WG Ex	A	0	15,700, dia. 2½ in.	(9)	
Tovite	Du Pont	NCN	**	0	22,310	1.12	
Trojamite A	Trojan	NS Ex			12,000-15,000 (max.)		125
Trojamite B	Trojan	NS Ex			10,000		140
Trojamite C	Trojan	NS Ex			9,500		160
Trojel EZ Por	Trojan	WG Ex (TNT-s)		0	9,000	1.46	
Trojel Slurry	Trojan	WG Ex (NS-b)		0	16,500, dia. 5 in.	1.40	
Tromax 45	Trojan	NCN (NS-b)		0	20,000+	1.31	
Tromax 55	Trojan	NCN (NS-b)		0	12,000	1.47	
Tromax 65	Trojan	NCN (NS-b)		0	14,500	1.49	
Tromax 75	Trojan	NCN (NS-b)		0	15,000	1.56	
Tromax 85	Trojan	NCN (NS-b)		0	18,500	1.60	
Tromax 95	Trojan	NCN (NS-b)		0	19,500	1.66	
Tru Cut A	Trojan	NG-s Ex			20,500	(9)	
Tru Cut B	Trojan	NG-s Ex			15,000	(9)	
Tru Cut C	Trojan	NG-s Ex			14,000	(9)	
Tru Cut D	Trojan	NG-s Ex			14,000	(9)	
Tru Cut E	Trojan	NG-s Ex			9,000	(9)	
Tru Cut F	Trojan	NS-s Ex			9,000	(9)	
40 WR	Trojan	NS-s Ex			11,800	1.25	117
50 WR	Trojan	NS-s Ex			12,200	1.20	120
60 WR	Trojan	NS-s Ex			12,600	1.12	122
70 WR	Trojan	NS-s Ex			13,300	1.10	125

*Number of 1 1/4-in. x 8-in. cartridges in a 50-lb case. **Formulation should yield fumes substantially equivalent to fumes of dynamites rated Fume Class 1. (7) Cartridge sizes: 7/8-in. through 2 1/2-in. diameter in 8-in. lengths, and 1-in. through 2 1/2-in. diameter in 12-in. or 16-in. lengths. (8) Low temperature initiation. (9) Density, in pounds of explosive per foot: Tovex T-1, 0.25; Tru Cut A, 0.80; Tru Cut B, 0.55; Tru Cut C, 0.45; Tru Cut D, 0.30; Tru Cut E, 0.25; Tru Cut F, 0.20.

E/MJ OPERATING HANDBOOK OF SURFACE MINING

Representative compositions of typical dynamites

Composition % by weight	Typical 40% strength dynamites			
	Straight	Gelatin	Ammonia-gelatin	Ammonia
Nitroglycerin	39.0	32.0	26.2	16.5
Sodium nitrate	45.5	51.8	49.6	37.5
Carbonaceous fuel	13.8	11.2	8.0	9.2
Sulphur	0	2.2	5.6	3.6
Antiacid	0.8	1.2	0.8	1.1
Moisture	0.9	0.9	1.4	0.7
Ammonium nitrate	0	0	8.0	31.4
Nitrocellulose	0	0.7	0.4	0
Totals	100.0	100.0	100.0	100.0

ular dynamite (which contains no nitrocellulose, has relatively low density, and is susceptible to the action of water). Semigelatin types combine the economy of ammonia dynamites with the water resistance and cohesiveness of ammonia-gelatin types. Semigelatin dynamites are good general purpose explosives that cost less than comparable gelatin dynamites and that offer good fume characteristics, fair to very good water resistance, moderately high velocity of detonation, and a degree of suitability for use underground.

Blasting gelatin—customarily formulated by colloiding 88-92% nitroglycerin with 8-12% nitrocellulose having a nitrogen content of 12%. Blasting gelatins are considered waterproof and have the highest velocity of detonation among commercial explosives commonly in use. They are adapted mainly to deep-well shooting, deep-water blasting, and cutting or blasting steel. They have occasionally been used underground for blasting exceptionally hard materials. Because of high nitroglycerin content, fume characteristics are poor.

Nitrostarch explosive—a formulation in which nitroglycerin is replaced entirely by nitrostarch, eliminating certain objectionable characteristics. Nitrostarch explosives contain no liquid sensitizers, do not produce headaches, cannot freeze, and do not exude or leak during storage. Various formulations are available, in strengths comparable to dynamites, and nitrostarch explosives are adaptable for all types of blasting work normally assigned to dynamites.

Water gel explosive—generally ammonium nitrate-based, containing no nitroglycerin, with a water content of 10-30%. These explosives have a gel-like consistency and may contain any one of a wide variety of explosive sensitizers, such as TNT, as well as varying amounts of inorganic salts, fuels, and thickening agents.

For many years, water gel explosives in non-cap-sensitive formulations have been widely used, except in underground coal mines. More recently, cap-sensitive formulations of water gels have been developed and approved by the US Bureau of Mines as permissible for coal mine use—a significant development because water gels are much safer to store, transport, handle, and use than nitroglycerin-based permissible explosives.

Another notable achievement is the development of water gel explosives of low-water formulation. The removal of 1% of water from a water gel formulation has the same effect as the increase in energy derived from the addition of approximately 1% aluminum. The low-water-formula water gel explosives are ammonium nitrate-based but are specially sensitized by monomethylamine nitrate.

Water gel explosives are suitable for wet and dry work in mining, quarrying, and construction, and some are ideally suited for underwater work.

Permissible—an explosive formulated especially for use in coal mines, where the presence of flammable gases and dust makes other explosives hazardous. When initiated, all explosives produce a flame that varies in volume, duration, and temperature. Permissible formulations produce a flame of small volume, short duration, and low temperature to minimize the likelihood of igniting gas or dust. Classification as a permissible explosive requires testing and approval by the US Bureau of Mines.

Types of commercial blasting agents

The distinction between explosives and blasting agents is chiefly their relative safety in handling and use. Explosives are generally cap-sensitive, whereas blasting agents are not. Blasting agents contain no nitroglycerin and cannot be detonated by a standard No. 8 blasting cap, which makes them the safest materials available for blasting purposes. (Certain water gels, although non-cap-sensitive, are nevertheless classified as explosives. Although such gels contain no nitroglycerin, they are not strictly blasting agents because they contain other ingredients classified as explosives.)

The blasting agents reviewed here are classified by the US Department of Transportation as nitro-carbo-nitrates (NCNs), which are considered oxidizing materials rather than explosives. An NCN normally requires a cap-sensitive primer or primer-booster to ensure detonation. Some NCNs are canned to ensure water resistance, but coupling (transfer of energy through the surrounding air space) is generally poor for canned types, and application is limited to work such as coyote tunneling (openings of small dimensions) and marine offshore seismic exploration. Other NCNs are cartridged to compete against various types and strengths of dynamites. Much better coupling is achieved by free-flowing NCNs, such as mixtures of ammonium nitrate and fuel oil (ANFO), slurries, and water gels.

In addition to safety, NCNs also offer appreciable savings, and they do not freeze or produce headaches. Blasting agents have now virtually replaced explosives for loading coyote tunnel blasts. With the increasing availability of a wide variety of blasting agents, many open-pit mine and quarry operations also have discontinued the use of cartridged nitroglycerin explosives except for special applications, and many underground mining operations are gradually following this practice.

ANFO—generally a nonwaterproof, free-flowing mixture containing mainly coarse ammonium nitrate and a small percentage of fuel oil as a sensitizer, in formulations of varying packed densities. The total rock breakage cost of ANFO is about one-quarter to one-third that of nitroglycerin-based explosives. However, the economies of ANFO mixtures are somewhat offset by certain undesirable characteristics:

- The loss of fuel oil by evaporation and migration can result in generation of hazardous quantities of fumes at the time of use, even if recommended procedures are followed.

- There is a potential hazard of exothermic reaction between prilled ANFO mixtures and sulphide ores under hot ground conditions. To counter this, ANFO mixtures have been developed containing an inhibitor that raises by a significant amount the incipient reaction temperature. The inhibitor reportedly has no significant effect on performance.

- ANFO mixtures are not cap-sensitive and must be well confined and heavily primed to obtain full efficiency.

ANFO mixtures are suitable when only a moderate degree of blasting action is required—as in coal stripping, open-pit mining of iron ore, and blasting of stratified limestone, sandstone, and shale.

Metallized dry and slurry NCNs—formulations of ammonium nitrate and varying amounts of metal particles, which provide tremendous chemical energy. Dry mixes are basically metallized ANFOs, whereas slurries consist of a combustible fuel as a sensitizer, mixed with granular ammonium nitrate (and sometimes sodium nitrate) and dispersed with an aqueous solution of ammonium nitrate of up to 20% water, producing a somewhat soupy mixture. In use, a thickening agent or catalyst is added to the mixture to form a gel for water resistance.

Metallized blasting agents contain no high explosive sensitizers, and the slurry types, especially, have a high degree of water resistance. Even at extremely low temperatures, these blasting agents retain high performance in initiation and propagation. The energy developed results in increased heat of explosion and extended high pressure. For this reason, metallized slurries are a logical choice for blasting extremely hard rock, such as taconite, especially under wet conditions. For medium-to-hard rock under relatively dry conditions, metallized dry mixes may be preferable because they offer significant reduction in costs. To counter the effect of water on dry mixes, increase pressure, and improve fragmentation, slurry boosting—intermittent charging of slurries with dry mixes—is sometimes used.

Wet explosive-based NCNs. Despite their explosive base, these blasting agents are not cap-sensitive and are therefore safer than conventional nitroglycerin-sensitized explosives. Insensitivity is so great that a primer-booster system is the only reliable method of initiation. Explosive-sensitized blasting agents are specially formulated to compete against specific strengths of more expensive dynamites (ammonia, gelatin, and ammonia-gelatin). Rated high in strength, velocity of detonation, density, and water resistance, these blasting agents produce high breakage and fragmentation and are extremely well suited for blasting tougher ores and rock formations under the most adverse conditions.

Water gel NCNs (metallized and nonmetallized). Nonmetallized formulations are sensitized with hydrocarbons and contain no high explosives. Both types have high strength, relatively high velocity of detonation, high density, and good water resistance, and they require high-energy priming. Water gel blasting agents are adapted for use in large diameter blastholes where water makes the use of dry ammonium nitrate blasting agents impractical or when high density is needed for blasting very hard materials. These blasting agents fill all voids in a blasthole, for good coupling effect, and the amount that can be loaded into a given hole is greater than for a lower density dry blasting agent.

Getting down to specifics

To help the nonspecialist select an explosive for a specific application, general information and comparative data are provided here in tabular form for more than 250 explosives and blasting agents that are commercially available. The information was compiled from various sources, including industry publications, the published reports of specialized R&D work, and agencies of the US government. The table is a unique guide to evaluating various explosive products that may be used, under specific conditions, to achieve a desired result.

The table does not include every available product, and no attempt has been made to list every possible application nor to anticipate all variations that may be encountered in use. The specific applications listed are those related to mining. All recommendations for type of work and conditions of use refer to the product as supplied, without special preparations for loading and firing. The numerical values for density, velocity of detonation, and other properties presented in the table are approximate averages, subject to variations.

For detailed information on a specific explosive or blasting agent, the manufacturer should be consulted. Most manufacturers are quite willing to offer advice based on field experience, and many will design and formulate products for special applications, such as welding, bonding, cladding, and forming. □

Acknowledgement

The author expresses appreciation for the aid of the following individuals and companies in providing data for this article: H. E. Bean, Apache Powder Co.; T. P. Dowling, Trojan Div., IMC Chemical Group Inc.; R. W. Eigell, US Naval Explosive Ordnance Disposal Facility; L. Galligher, Keotron Inc.; C. H. Grant, Energy Sciences and Consultants Inc.; D. Gregory, Institute of Makers of Explosives; W. L. Johannes, Explosive Technology; D. Levey, GOEX Inc.; D. D. Porter, Du Pont Co.; and P. D. Whiting, Trace X Chemical.

Aluminum additives impart energy and sensitivity to many explosives

Charles N. Mason and **Wayne C. Montgomery,** Aluminum Co. of America

THE DOMESTIC EXPLOSIVES INDUSTRY has grown at an annual rate of 8% over the past eight years—spurred largely by a 50% increase in demand for slurries. Over 311 million lb of slurry explosives were produced in 1975, most of them containing aluminum. Aluminum additives—granules, atomized particles, coated powders, and flake powders—are widely used in manufacturing explosives.

The addition of aluminum to explosives was patented at the turn of the century.[1] After World War I, aluminum prices had declined sufficiently to permit the metal to be included in some formulations of commercial dynamite explosives.[2] In 1957, Cook and others noted the potential for aluminized explosives.[3] The vast market that was then developing in mining, excavation, and construction required a variety of explosives, and the day of commercial dynamites was waning. In the early 1960s, the development of ammonium nitrate-based slurries was most significant, as explosives manufacturers experimented with a variety of aluminum powder additives. Aluminum powder and granules were used to increase the strength of explosives and as a fuel in the production of a blast. Aluminum flake powder was added to increase sensitivity of the mix to the initiation of detonation.[4] Of major importance in this trend toward increased use of aluminum was the demonstration by Van Dolah and others that slurry explosives sensitized by aluminum flake powder could be formulated to pass the safety requirements for use in underground coal mines.[5]

Aluminum a most valuable ingredient of water gels

Aluminum was added to water gels, or slurries, early in the development of these explosives. In discussing the history of slurries and the use of aluminum in 1969, Robinson[6] pointed out:

"In an aluminum-sensitized water gel, the aluminum oxidizer mixture must be subjected to a very high temperature to initiate a rapid reaction. This condition exists within the tiny air bubbles adhering to the surface of the aluminum when the bubbles are compressed adiabatically. Three factors are necessary for the successful operation of this hot-spot mechanism: the aluminum must be preserved from oxidation until the explosion; the more air bubbles of a suitable size (10^{-2} to 10^{-4} mm), the more initiation points there will be; and the bubbles must be in contact with the aluminum. After initiation, the reaction proceeds by an aluminum-surface-controlled, grain-controlled, grain-burning mechanism.

"Although aluminum is certainly one of the most valuable water gel ingredients, different grades of aluminum differ greatly in the way they behave in these explosives. Pigment grade (flake) aluminum, if properly protected from oxidation and not wetted completely, can sensitize an ammonium nitrate-fuel oil combination in a water gel without being present in sufficient quantity to affect the strength of the explosive. The sensitivity of these flake aluminum gels is greatly affected by temperature, and the aluminum content required to maintain sensitivity is approximately a linear function of the temperature. When warm, these products are among the most sensitive gels available."

Accumulated work has demonstrated that aluminum performs two functions in formulations of slurry explosives. The first function is the addition of energy, resulting from aluminum's high heat of combustion (13,400 Btu per lb). Second, aluminum acts as a sensitizer—a major factor in underground blasting, where aluminum has made small diameter boreholes susceptible to the advantages of slurry blasting. Recently, it was shown that as little as 2% aluminum flake powder, with a surface area greater than 2 sq m per gm, will sensitize 1-in.-dia slurries to initiation with a No. 6 blasting cap.[7,8]

The US Bureau of Mines[9] reports that use of slurry explosives in 1974 reached an all-time high of 293 million lb—close to a 30% increase in consumption in two years. The use of granulated aluminum, both atomized primary metal and scrap, has accelerated.

AN/FO plus aluminum gives a more powerful blast

Paralleling the development of slurries has been the increased use of aluminum additions to AN/FO. A report in 1968[10] described the added effectiveness of AN/FO blasts when aluminum granules, in 5% to 30% concentration, were added to the mixture. Lansdale discussed the economic advantages of using aluminized AN/FO in situations where manufacture of slurry blasting agents is economically unsound.[11] Cook took exception to these conclusions,[12] and all cases must be decided on the relative

Table 1—Effect of aluminum on AN/FO strength

Aluminum metal content (%)	Density (g/cc)	Relative wt. strength	Relative bulk strength
0	0.83	100	100
2.5	0.85	110	110
5.0	0.86	118	120
7.5	0.87	125	127
10.0	0.88	133	138
12.5	0.89	139	147
15.0	0.90	146	155

Table 2—Relative strength of aluminized AN/FO and metallized slurries

Explosive	Density (g/cc)	Wt. strength	Bulk strength
AN/FO 97/3	0.85	100	1.0
AN/FO/AL 87/3/10	0.93	124	1.36
AN/FO/AL 84/3/13	0.95	131	1.46
AN/FO/AL 82/3/15	0.96	135	1.53
Metallized Slurry			
1% Al, 14% H2O	1.25	86	1.26
7% Al, 14% H2O	1.30	100	1.53
10% Al, 14% H2O	1.35	106	1.68

Fig. 1—AN-based aluminized blasting agents, slurries, and slurry explosives

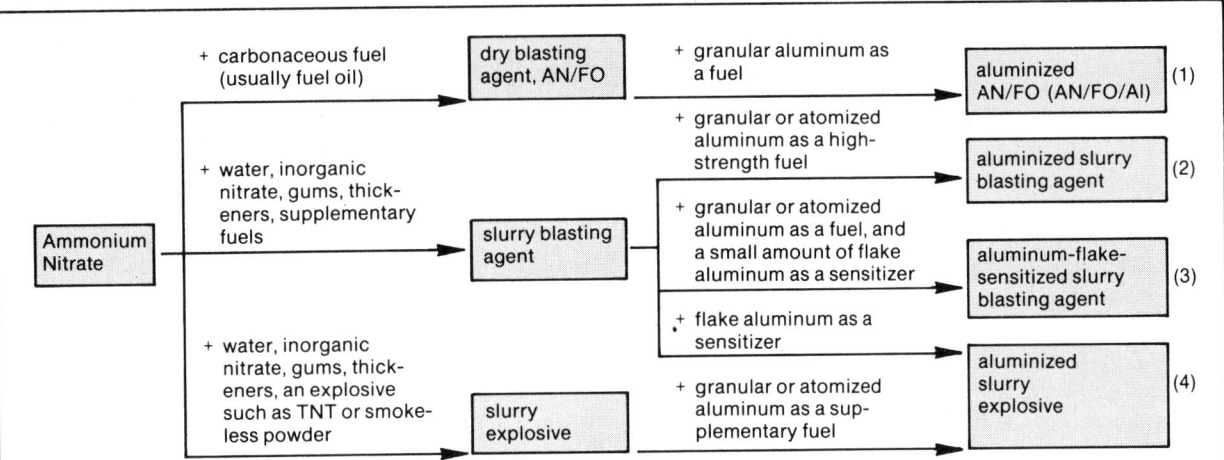

(1) The simplest product—a dry blasting agent—is formed by adding a fuel—usually fuel oil—to ammonium nitrate. The strength of these dry blasting agents is readily improved by adding the concentrated energy supplied by granular aluminum.

(2,3) Because AN is soluble in water, unprotected AN/FO cannot be used in water-filled boreholes. The next class of blasting agents—slurry blasting agents or water gels—is made water-resistant by adding gums and thickeners. Depending on whether aluminum is added to these slurry blasting agents simply as a fuel or as a fuel and sensitizer, they are termed aluminized or aluminum-flake-sensitized slurry blasting agents.

(4) If enough aluminum flake sensitizer is added to a slurry blasting agent, the resulting product is a cap-sensitive aluminized slurry explosive. (Such formulations are used in the new, small-diameter explosives.) Granular or atomized aluminum may be added as a supplementary fuel to a flake-sensitized slurry explosive to increase strength. In either case, the resulting product is cap-sensitive and must be classified as an explosive rather than a blasting agent.

Table 3—Typical properties of 'Aluminite' aluminum powders

Grade No.	Particle size range (%)	Coating (%)	Surface area (m^2/g)	Stability gas evolution (ml H_2)
Granules				
1600	Minus 8 mesh to 100 mesh	None	0.1	2
1601	Minus 8 mesh to 200 mesh	None	0.1	2
Atomized powders				
1620	Minus 30 mesh to 25-50% minus 325	None	0.15	10-14
1622	Minus 30 mesh to 10% minus 325	None	0.15	10-14
Coated atomized				
1620A	Minus 30 mesh to 25-50% minus 325	2	0.15	Less than 1
1641A	Minus 200 mesh to 85% minus 325	2	0.25	Less than 2
Nondusting atomized[1]				
1620G	Minus 30 mesh to 25-50% minus 325	0.25	0.15	Less than 1
1641G	Minus 200 mesh with 85% minus 325	1.75	0.25	2-3
Regular flake powders				
1650	94% minus 325	2	3-4	Less than 1
1662	99.5% minus 325	2.5	5-6	Less than 1
1670	99.95% minus 325	3	8-9	Less than 1
Dedusted flake powders[2,3]				
1651	94% minus 325	2.5	3-4	Less than 1
1663	99.5% minus 325	3.0	5-6	Less than 1

1) See reference 20. 2) See references 22 and 23. 3) Properties before dedusting treatment.

merits of blasting efficiency and capital investment.

Morrey claimed that the energy of AN/FO mixtures can be substantially improved by the addition of aluminum granules sufficient to provide oxygen balance.[13] Assigning standard AN/FO mixtures a value of 100, he arrived at the figures shown in Table 1. (Lang and Farreau noted that 1 lb of slurry explosive containing 10% aluminum has a weight strength of 117 units, providing 17% more energy than 1 lb of AN/FO.[15])

The Marcona open-pit copper mine in Peru was the site of a recent large scale application of aluminized AN/FO blasting.[25] Aluminized AN/FO is often effectively used as toe loads. Grant[16] and Woolsey[17] have reported on the effectiveness of aluminized slurry boosters in increasing the blasting performance of AN/FO. Tuttle[18] has reported that in many blasting situations, aluminized booster initiations were effective in improving blasting performance, while Condon and Snodgrass[19] found aluminized dry primers to be superior to all others tried.

Aluminum products tailored for explosives

During the development phase of slurry explosives manufacture, numerous types of aluminum, including scrap products, were tried as additives to the mix. As demand for slurry products progressed, it was feared that the supply of scrap aluminum would be insufficient, and several primary aluminum producers began production of aluminum particles for explosives. (The use of aluminum in AN-based blasting agents, dry and slurry, and in slurry explosives is summarized in Fig. 1.)

In 1969, Aluminum Co. of America began to develop aluminum powders with specific properties tailored for use in slurry explosives. Coatings were developed to protect the powders and prevent Al-water reaction.[20] (One potential problem, particularly with scrap products, was the possibility of aluminum developing spontaneous reaction with water in the slurry—and release of hydrogen gas during storage.) In addition to coatings, an experimental method was developed to test the water stability of aluminum powders for use in slurry explosives.[21]

Alcoa has now developed products in four distinct classes for use in the explosives industry: granules, atomized aluminum, coated atomized powders (including non-dusting grades 1620 G and 1641 G), and leafing grade high-surface-area flake powders specifically tailored for sensitization of slurry explosives formulations.

A serious deterrent to the use of aluminum flake powder has been the danger of dust explosions. To overcome this problem, Alcoa recently adapted[22] the Harshaw process[23] of dedusting fine powders. In the process, 0.2% Teflon is added to aluminum powder to markedly reduce dustiness and substantially reduce the hazard of a dust explosion.

The types of aluminum powders developed for the explosives industry are summarized in Table 3; typical applications are shown in Table 4. □

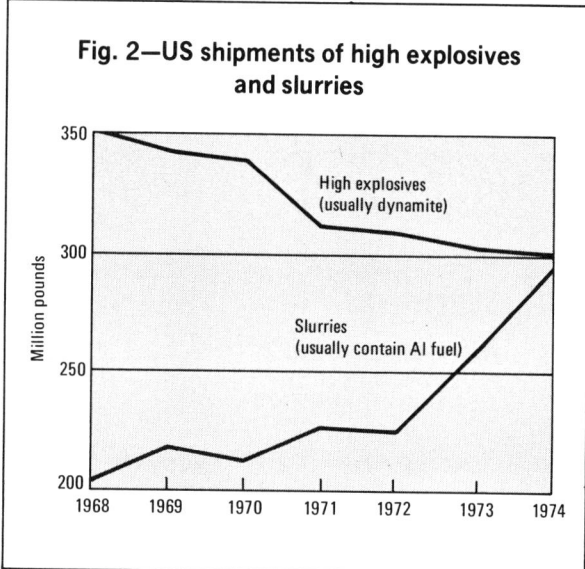

Fig. 2—US shipments of high explosives and slurries

References

1) Roth, G., German Patent 172,327 (1900).
2) Federoff, B. T., *Encyclopedia of Explosives and Related Items*, Vol. 1, Picatinny Arsenal, Dover, N.J., 1960, pp 148-150.
3) Cook, M. A., A. S. Fuller, R. T. Keyes, W. P. Partridge, and W. O. Ursenbock, "Aluminized Explosives," J. PHYSICAL CHEMISTRY, Vol. 61, 1957, pp 189-196.
4) Cook, M. A., "The Science of Industrial Explosives," Ireco Chemicals, Salt Lake City, Utah, 1974, p 18.
5) Van Dolah, R. W., C. M. Mason, and D. R. Forshey, "Development of Slurry Explosives for Use in Potentially Flammable Atmospheres," US Bureau of Mines Report of Investigations 7195, 1968, p 9.
6) Robinson, R. V., "Water Gel Explosives—Three Generations," CANADIAN MINING AND METALLURGICAL BULLETIN, Vol. 62, Dec. 1969, pp 1317-1325.
7) Hay, J. E., R. W. Watson, and R. W. van Dolah, "Development of Water Gel Permissible Explosives," 15th International Conference on Safety in Mining Research, Karlovy Vary, Czechoslovakia, 1973, p 10.
8) Clay, R. B., L. L. Udy, and D. T. Bailey, US Patent 3,367,805, February 6, 1968.
9) US Bureau of Mines Mineral Industry Surveys, "Apparent Consumption of Industrial Explosives and Blasting Agents in the US," June 18, 1975.
10) MINING MAGAZINE, 1968.
11) Lansdale, J. R., "How Dry Mix Explosives Can Shave Costs," E/MJ, July 1971, p 77.
12) Cook, M. A., "How Dry Mix Explosives Can Increase Costs Even in Dry Holes," E/MJ, September 1971, pp 140-141.
13) Morrey, W. B. "Explosives Products Blasting in Canadian Mines," United Nations Inter-Regional Seminar on the Application of Advanced Mining Technology, Ottawa, Canada, May 21-June 3, 1973, pp 47.
14) Bauer, A., "Current Drilling and Blasting Practices in Open Pit Mines," MINING CONGRESS JOURNAL, March 1972, pp 20-27.
15) Lang, L. C., and R. F. Farreau "A Modern Approach to Open Pit Blast Design and Analysis," 74th Annual General Meeting, CIM, Ottawa, April 1972, p 24.
16) Grant, C. H., "Metallized Slurry Boosting: What It Is and How It Works," COAL AGE, April 1966.
17) Woolsey, C. C., "How Enos Reduces Costs by Metallized Slurry Boosting," COAL AGE, April 1966.
18) Tuttle, C. E., "Using Aluminum Booster Initiation," MINING CONGRESS JOURNAL, September 1967, pp 41-45.
19) Condon, J. L. and J. J. Snodgrass, "Effects of Primer Type and Bore Hole Diameter on ANFO Detonation Velocities," MINING CONGRESS JOURNAL, June 1974, pp 146-152.
20) Kondis, T. J., and R. Rolles, US Patent 3,781,177, December 25, 1973.
21) Details of this test may be obtained from Alcoa.
22) US Patent Pending (Alcoa).
23) Vogt, J. W., S. Russel, and J. E. Owen, US Patents 3,838,064, September 24, 1974, and 3,838,092, September 24, 1974.
24) Watson, R. W., and J. Ribovich, "Recent Developments in Permissible Explosives in the US," International Meeting of the Directors of Mine Safety Research, Washington, D.C., September 22-26, 1975, p 14.
25) Morrell, W. L., C. Brave Renteria, P. M. Tinoco Soto, and B. Diaz Cornejo, "How Marcona Uses Carefully Controlled Blasting Techniques", WORLD MINING, September 1975, pp 46-49.

Table 4—Typical applications of 'Aluminite' powders

End Use \ Grade	Granular		Atomized		Coated Atomized				Flake				
	1600	1601	1620	1622	1620A	1620G	1641A	1641G	1650	1651 (dedusted)	1662	1663 (dedusted)	1670
Small-Diameter Slurry Explosives			X	X	X	X	X	X	X	X	X	X	X
Bulk Slurry Blasting Agents	X	X	X	X	X	X	X	X	X	X	X	X	X
Packaged Slurry Blasting Agents					X	X	X	X	X	X	X	X	X
Metallized AN/FO	X	X											
Primers/Boosters			X	X	X	X	X	X	X	X	X	X	X
Fixed Explosives							X	X	X	X	X	X	X

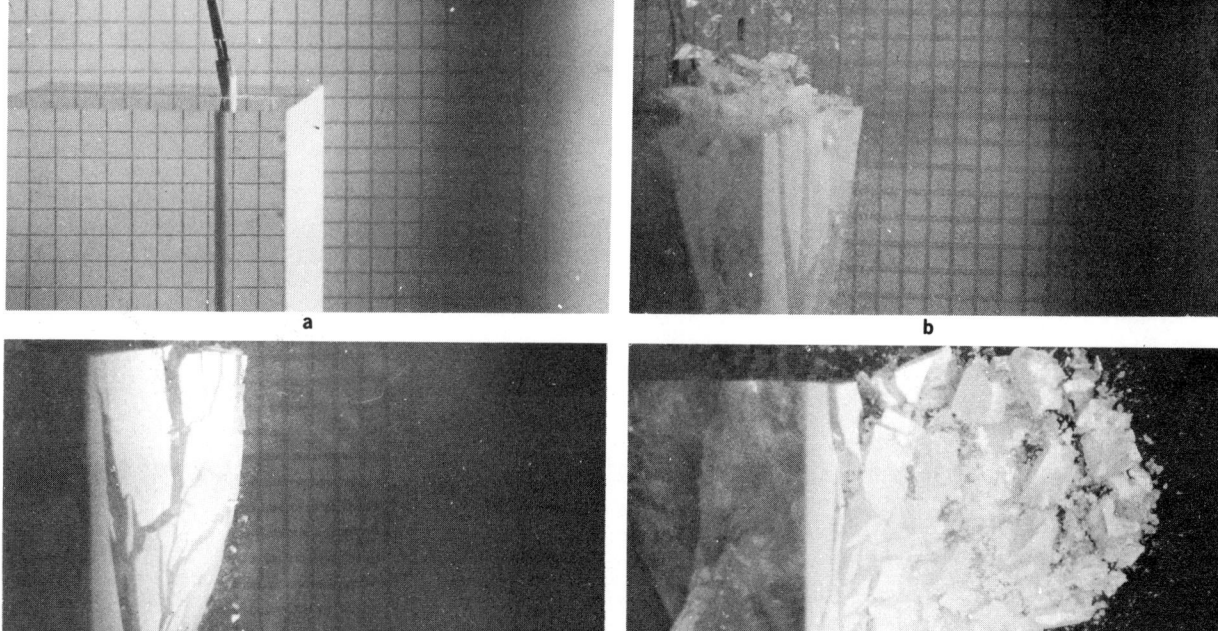

Fig. 1—Borehole in bench blasting with bottom charge, column charge, and unloaded hole. Diameter—0.100 m; rock constant—0.40; W-strength, bottom—0.95; W-strength, column—0.80; hole inclination—0.30 mm; angular deviation—0.02 mm; collaring deviation—0.10 m; degree of pack, bottom—1,200 kg per cu m; degree of pack, column—800 kg per cu m; burden—3.59 m; deviation, bottom—0.35 m; hole depth—13.88 m; bottom charge per m—9.42 kg; column charge per m—5.28 kg; bottom charge—55.36 kg; column charge—21.93 kg; spacing—4.48 m; average boulder size—1.10 m.

Fig. 2—Plexiglas blocks 100 × 60 × 60 mm. Hole is drilled with 15-mm burden from the longer side. (a) before shot; (b) 2.0-mm hole, 210 μsec after initiation; (c) 2.8-mm hole, 210 μsec after initiation; (d) 4.0-mm hole, 210 μsec after initiation.

Keeping the lid on flyrock in open-pit blasting

N. Lundborg, A. Persson, A. Ladegaard-Pedersen,* and R. Holmberg, Swedish Detonic Research Foundation

DANGER AND DAMAGE FROM FLYROCK in rock blasting has been a serious problem since blasting was introduced a hundred years ago. Not only have men been killed and injured, but buildings, equipment, and materials have also been destroyed or damaged. These hazards are greatest in urban settings. However, as the explosive impact intensifies because of the increasing size of borehole diameters, the problem also becomes a serious one in more remote areas. For instance, flyrock has been known to travel 1 km or more from the blast site at open-pit mines.

Investigation of the risks from various types of blasting, as a first step in defining the danger zones surrounding blasting areas, has been undertaken by the Swedish Detonic Research Foundation, where researchers separate blasting into two categories—bench blasting and crater blasting—to facilitate such an investigation.

As a prelude to the investigation, interviews were conducted with 25 personnel from various agencies and companies. The general consensus was that the most dangerous situation is shallow blasting with large boreholes (a low ratio between bench height and borehole diameter), generally termed crater blasting.

*Ladegaard-Pedersen is presently with the Mechanical Engineering Department, University of Maryland, College Park, Md., in the US.

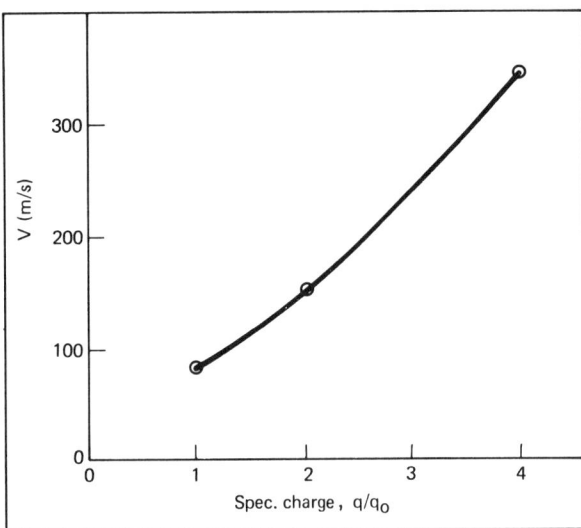

Fig. 3—Particle velocity of Plexiglas according to Fig. 2, vs. specific charge.

Minimizing flyrock in bench blasting

A borehole in a common bench blasting situation is represented in Fig. 1, with the bottom charge and the column charge indicated. An uncharged length of this borehole equal to the burden, or about 40 times the diameter of the borehole, is recommended. If this precaution is taken, there will be little chance of a crater blast causing flyrocks at the top end of the borehole.

Very important in determining the burden velocity is the specific charge used (the amount of explosive per cubic meter of rock to be loosened). An increase in the specific charge results in a higher burden velocity, as well as a smaller average fragment size. This is seen in Fig. 2, which shows the results of scale model blasts in Plexiglas obtained with high speed photography. All of the models shown were Plexiglas blocks 100 x 60 x 60 mm with a 15-mm burden. The holes were drilled in the 60 x 100-mm face in the center of the 60-mm dimension. Fig. 2a was photographed before the test began; Fig 2b was photographed 210 μsec after detonation of a 2-mm-dia borehole; Figs. 2c and 2d, also photographed after 210 μsec, represent results obtained from boreholes 2.8 mm and 4.0 mm in diameter, respectively.

A plot of the burden velocity of the Plexiglas material vs. the relative specific charge is shown in Fig. 3. The velocity of the Plexiglas material is rather high compared with the ordinary burden velocity in rock, which is 5-20 m per sec.

A. Ladegaard-Pedersen and A. Persson have conducted a series of bench blast tests with a single hole in rock boulders. The borehole diameter was 1 in. and high-speed photography was used to study the movement of the rock fragments. The experimental arrangement is shown in Fig. 4. After each shot, the distance from the shot hole and the angles of the flyrocks were determined.

A typical flyrock scatter pattern is shown in Fig. 5, with the borehole at the origin. In particular, note the position

Acknowledgement

The authors would like to express their thanks to the Swedish National Board of Occupational Safety and Health for support given to this project, and to Vasterbottens Grusforadlings AB and LKAB for actively taking part in the project.

Fig. 4—Arrangement at bench blasting.

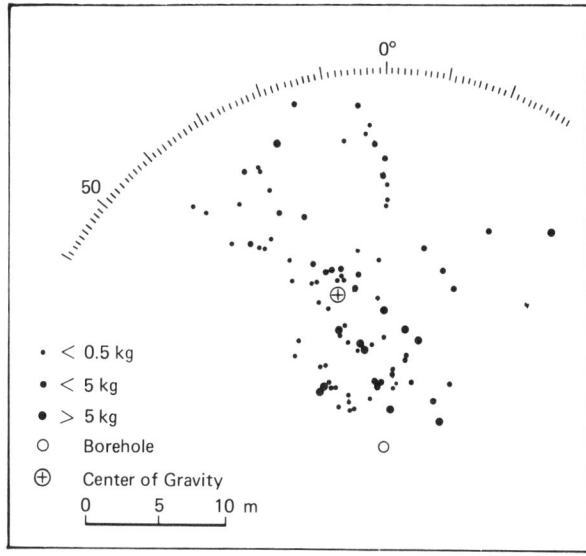

Fig. 5—Throw and scatter from blast according to Fig. 4.

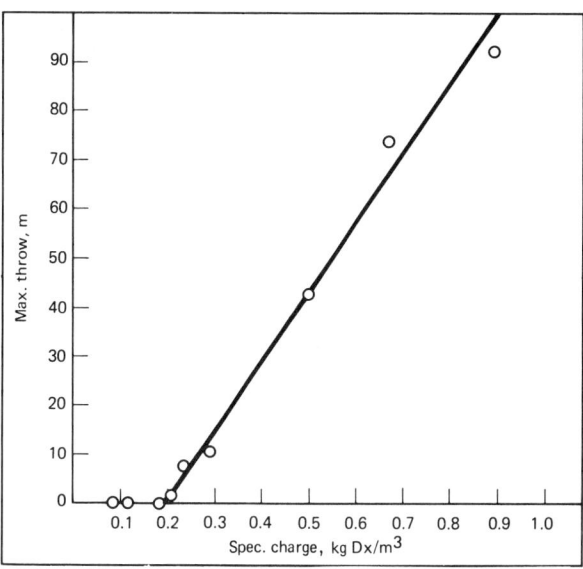

Fig. 6—Maximum throw at bench blasting vs. specific charge.

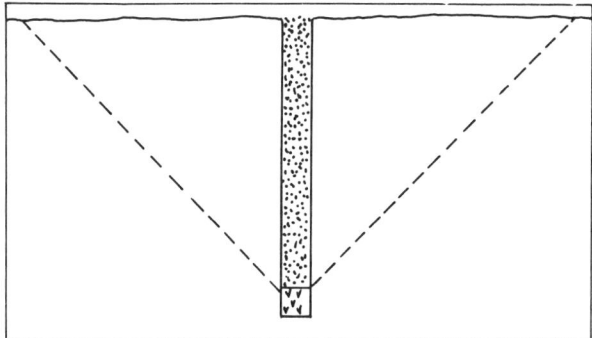

Fig. 7—The geometry of crater blasting.

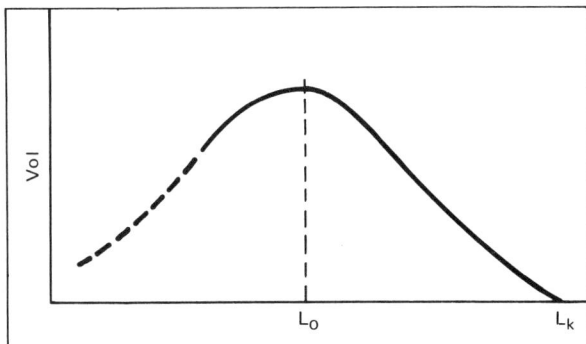

Fig. 8—Volume removed by a charge at different depths.

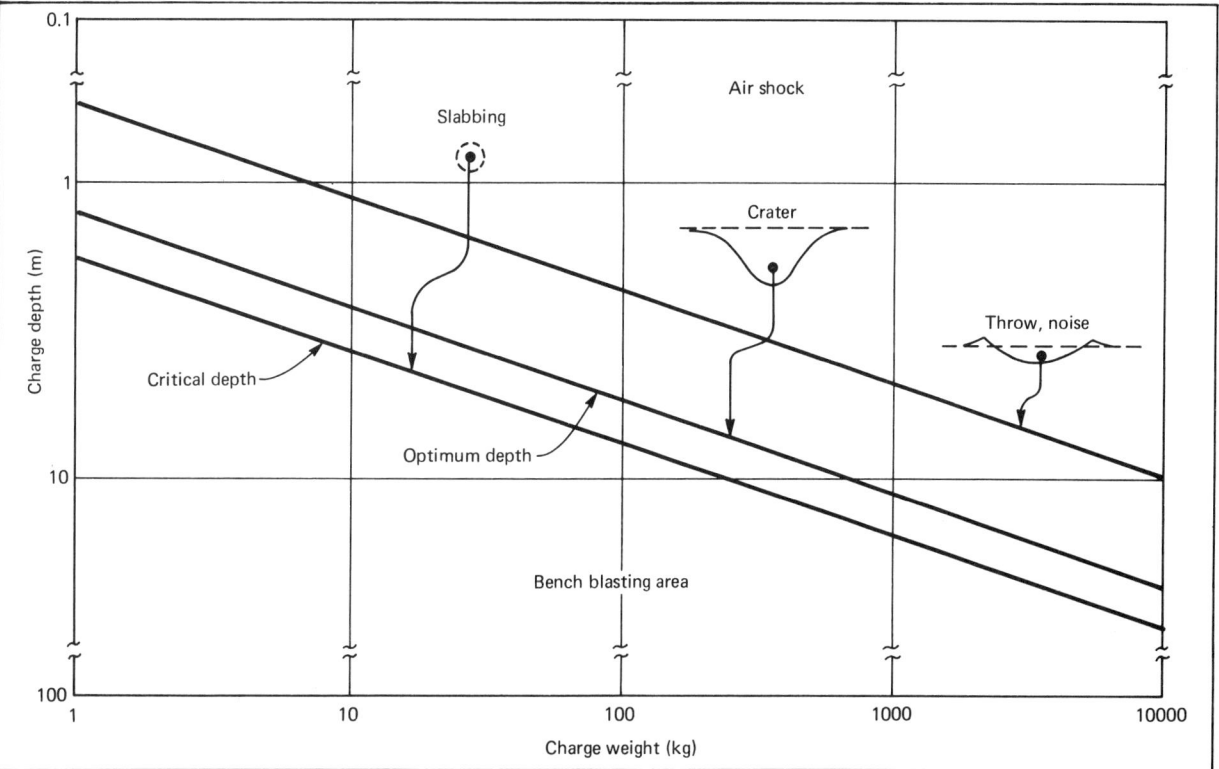

Fig. 9—Charge depth vs. charge weight at different parameters.

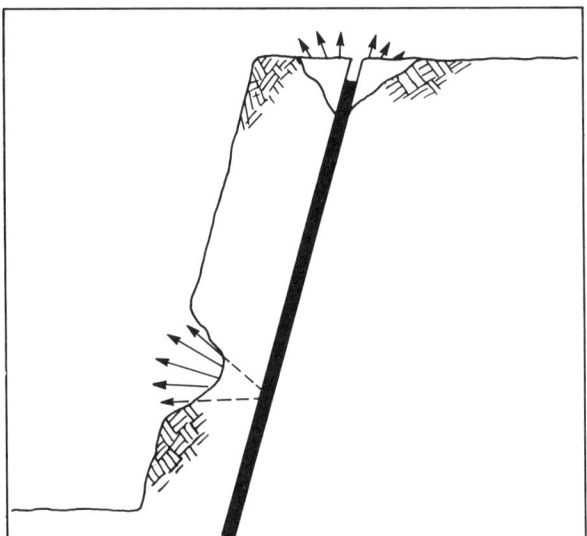

Fig. 10—Crater effects in bench blasting.

of the center of gravity of the flyrocks and the positions of the individual flyrocks.

The maximum throw as determined in these tests is plotted vs. the specific charge in Fig. 6. As the graph indicates, it is possible to avoid flyrock if the charge is smaller than a critical size (in this case 0.2 kg per cu m). However, it will hardly ever be possible to determine this critical charge size, as there will always be differences in rock strengths, variations in burden, faults in the rock, and other factors that cannot be predicted. Therefore, the specific charge will be increased beyond the critical charge size to avoid missed rounds.

Flyrock in crater blasting

The type of blasting called crater blasting is depicted in Fig. 7. Although the charge in the hole is assumed to be a point charge, it has, in reality, a length of up to 6 borehole diameters.

The crater volume for different charge depths at constant weight is given in Fig. 8. L_o is the optimum depth and L_k is the critical depth. For depths greater than L_k, the blasting is considered to be bench blasting. Fig. 9 shows the charge depth vs. the charge weight. Various transition lines are indicated, such as critical depth (where doming begins), the optimum depth (where the crater volume is at maximum), and the shallow depth (where most of the energy goes into the air in the form of shock effects).

In most open-pit mining, the current trend is to use large borehole diameters (7 to 10 in.) and a bench height of 10 to 15 m. These conditions result in maximum burdens (V) of 7 to 10 m, where the hole spacing $E = 1.25\ V$. In ordinary bench blasting, the unloaded hole length is equal to the maximum burden, which is about 40 times the borehole diameter.

In blasting situations where the ratio between the hole depth and the hole diameter is low, it is not possible from an economic point of view to keep the unloaded hole length equal to the burden, since this would cause unsatisfactory fragmentation, raising the costs because of the need for secondary blasting. This is unfortunate, since a charge placed too near a free surface results in flyrock throw from the upper end of the borehole. In granite, under no circumstances should the distance from the charge to the free surface be less than 50% of the maximum burden if the cratering effect is to be suppressed. Most of the flyrock comes from the surface, but it is also possible to obtain crater effects from the front of a round if the burden is reduced because of inhomogeneities.

Examples of crater effects in bench blasting are depicted in Fig. 10. A blasted round which utilized boreholes with 7½-in. diameters is shown in Fig. 11. The ratio between unloaded hole length and hole diameter was 10. The lower limit to avoid crater effects is 20 to 30, while the recommended value is 40. Fig. 12 depicts crater effects obtained in granite with fully loaded 1-in. boreholes. It should be noted that top-initiated holes give greater crater depths, as

Fig. 11—Blasting round with 10-m bench height and 41 7½-in. holes containing 16 kg of slurry explosives. (a) 0.05 sec after firing; (b) 0.75 sec after firing; (c) 4.05 sec after firing.

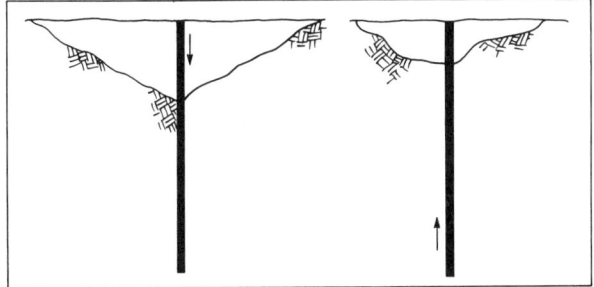

Fig. 12—Crater effects in fully loaded 1-in. boreholes with top and bottom initiation, respectively.

well as greater removed volumes.

While crater blasting is sometimes used in shaft sinking, it is used mostly in benching at operations isolated from urban areas, where flyrock can be tolerated. To avoid flyrock and still get good fragmentation, it is necessary that the length of the unloaded part of the hole be deeper than the critical depth. The critical depth depends on the type of explosive used, the hole diameter, and the rock type. Experiments in Plexiglas also show that the crater depth is greater and the crack lengths are shorter if the charge is top-initiated.

Flyrock velocity vs. borehole diameter

A number of boulders of different size surrounding a spherical charge are shown in Fig. 13. The impulse density (i) from a spherical charge may be written

$$\int p dt = i \sim \frac{Q}{R} \qquad (1)$$

where p is the pressure, Q the charge, and R the distance from the charge. For a constant value of the scaled distance $r = R/Q^{1/3}$, we get

$$i \sim Q^{1/3} \sim d \qquad (2)$$

where d is the charge diameter.

Equation 2 shows that the impulse density is proportional to the charge diameter when r is constant.

It may easily be shown that this also holds true for a cylindrical charge.

The force (F) on the boulders is proportional to the impulse density and the projected area of the boulders, that is,

$$F \sim i\phi^2 \qquad (3)$$

where ϕ is the mean diameter of the boulders.

The total impulse of a boulder now is

$$I = \frac{\pi \phi^2}{4} i \qquad (4)$$

It is well known that the impulse may also be written

$$I = mv \qquad (5)$$

where m is the mass and v the velocity of a body. This yields

$$\frac{\pi \phi^2 i}{4} = \frac{4\pi}{3} \rho \frac{\phi^3}{8} v \qquad (6)$$

where ρ is the density of the rock, or

$$i = \frac{2}{3} \phi \rho v \qquad (7)$$

and from Equation 2,

$$d = c\phi\rho v \qquad (8)$$

where c is a constant.

To determine the constant c, measurements of $\phi\rho v$ were made for different d-values. This procedure obtained the relationship

$$\frac{\phi\rho v}{2,600} = 10 d \qquad (9)$$

where ρ is the density of the rock in kg per cu m, ϕ the diameter in meters, v the velocity in meters per sec, and d the borehole diameter in inches. The average density of granite is 2,600 kg per cu m. Equation 9 is shown in Fig. 14.

Measuring flyrock velocity, maximum throw

To investigate the validity of Equation 9 and to determine the factor of proportionality, several blasted rounds were photographed and the flyrock velocities measured. In a number of these rounds, the maximum throw and the diameter of the stones, including the furthest, were also measured. From these values were calculated the velocities, assuming initial throw angles of 45° as giving a maximum throw. These values are also shown in Fig. 14. The many low values are due to the fact that the initial throw angles of these stones were not 45°. The approximate upper limit of the $\phi\rho v$ values obtained is given by Equation 9.

Calculating the throw

As demonstrated above, it is known that $\phi\rho v$ is a function of d. As the density of the rock is known, a value of ρ may be chosen which yields a given velocity v. Utilizing a computer, maximum throw can then be calculated as a

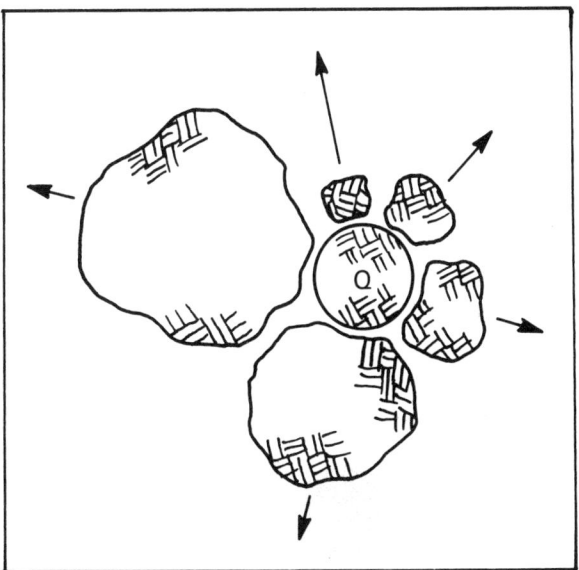

Fig. 13—Spherical charge (Q), surrounded by stones of varying size.

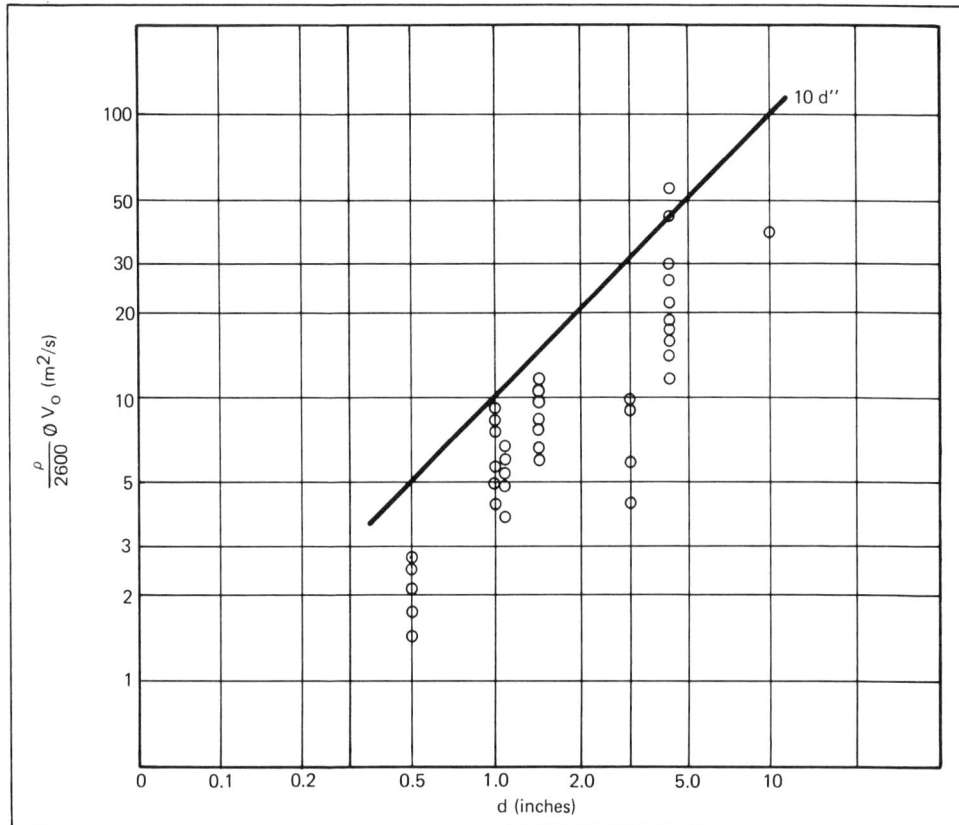

Fig. 14—$\frac{\rho}{2,600} \phi v$ vs. borehole diameter.

function of stone diameter with d as a parameter. The results are given in Fig. 15. From the calculations, the maximum throw is

$$L_{max} = 260 \, d^{2/3} \quad (10)$$

The diameter of these stones is

$$\phi = 0.1 \, d^{2/3} \quad (11)$$

where ϕ is in meters and d in inches.

Fig. 15 and Equations 10 and 11 indicate that some boulders are thrown quite far. For example, with 10-in. boreholes the maximum throw is about 1,300 m, with the stone diameter at 0.5 m. This means that very large areas must be evacuated to avoid accidents.

People must be protected against flyrock, no matter what the cost. Since the enclosed area is great, the probability of hitting a single spot is small, but this cannot be used as an excuse not to protect people in the area of blasting. An alternative may be to reduce the throw. It has been found that bench blasting always gives a shorter throw than crater blasting. It can be shown that the same dependence of throw on hole diameter that was found for crater blasting can be used to give the maximum throw for bench blasting. For example, for a specific charge of 0.5 kg per cu m (see Fig. 6),

$$L_{max} = 40 \, d$$

Compared with Equation 10, the throw is smaller by a factor of approximately 6. Thus, one way to reduce throw is to avoid crater effects. Another approach is to cover the rounds, but in practice it is recommended that the weight of the cover should be equal to the weight of the round blasted, which photographed impossible for large rounds. ☐

References

1) Eriksson, B., and Ladegaard-Pedersen, A., "Flyrock in Blasting I, Interviews," Swedish Detonic Research Foundation, Report DS 1971:32, 1971 (in Swedish).
2) Ladegaard-Pedersen, A., and Persson, P., "Flyrock in Blasting II, Experimental Investigation," Swedish Detonic Research Foundation, Report DS 1973:13, 1973 (in Swedish).
3) Ladegaard-Pedersen, A., "The Dependence of Charge Geometry on Flyrock Caused by Crater Effects in Bench Blasting," Swedish Detonic Research Foundation, Report DS 1973:38, 1973 (in Swedish).
4) Lundborg, N., "Calculation of Maximum Throw in Rock Blasting," Swedish Detonic Research Foundation, Report DS 1973:4, 1973 (in Swedish).
5) Lundborg, N., "The Hazards of Flyrock in Rock Blasting," Swedish Rock Blasting Committee, Stockholm, 1974 (in Swedish).

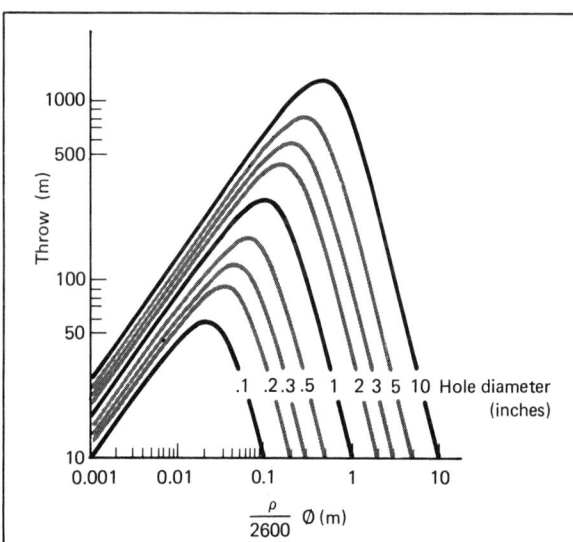

Fig. 15—Calculated maximum throw vs. boulder size and borehole diameter as a parameter.

Chapter 5
Materials Handling and Transport

Ongoing evolution in dredge design pays off for world's placer miners	194
Many improvements in shovels and draglines	202
How to maximize efficiency of excavators in high altitude environment	207
Cat rolls out world's largest crawler tractor	212
New conveyor drive with feedback circuit: soft starts for loaded mine belts	213
Pena Colorada development includes 30-mi slurry pipeline	215
Polybutylene: for piping corrosive slurries	216
Trucks are key transport at most open pit mines	216
Open pit conveyors offer potential savings	221
Marconaflo strips silt and pumps new life into Caland	222
New rail corridor developed for Minas Gerais iron ore	225
Iron ore transport—Great Lakes are major artery for North American trade	226

Tin is mined on Bolivian Altiplano with a 14-cu-ft bucket-line dredge capable of 102-ft digging depth. (Photo credit: Estalsa.)

Ongoing evolution in dredge design pays off for world's placer miners

placer deposit. A mass of gravel, sand, or similar material resulting from the crumbling and erosion of solid rocks and containing particles or nuggets of gold, platinum, tin, or other valuable minerals that have been derived from rocks or veins.

—*Dictionary of Mining, Mineral, and Related Terms*
US Bureau of Mines

PLACER MINING, especially for recovery of gold, platinum, and tin, is done by the most modern methods as well as the most primitive techniques. Mining methods include ground sluicing, panning, scraping, excavation by draglines, gravel pump mining, and dredging. In wet excavation, nothing has been devised to equal the capabilities of the dredge, in either mining or public works projects. Dredging is cost-effective, reliable, and capable of mining large volumes of material, although operating costs may reach $90,000 per month per dredge. (As a measure of the changes that have taken place, the average *revenue* of the 124 dredges operating in the US in 1912 was $90,500 per dredge per year.)

There have been few radical changes in dredge design since the early years of dredging, when the most important improvements were close-connected bucket-lines, stackers with rubber belts, and spuds to hold the dredge in place. Since that time, however, there has been constant improvement in the design of drive and control mechanisms, composition of wear parts, jig recovery systems, electric controls, and structural design.

What is dredging?

Dredging is defined as the underwater excavation of a placer deposit by floating equipment. Operations include excavation; transportation from the pond bottom to the concentration plant; concentration and recovery of heavy minerals for further treatment; and return of the tailings to the excavation behind the dredge.

> **Editor's note:** A short course on placer exploration and mining was held in Reno, Nev., on Oct. 25-30, 1976. The meeting was sponsored by the Mackay School of Mines of the University of Nevada. This article is a summary of the mining-oriented papers presented at the short course.

A typical dredging system for mineral sands may consist of a dredge delivering material through a floating pipeline to a screen and surge bin, located on a floating pontoon attached to the concentrator or plant. A feed pump delivers material at controlled density to the floating plant. Most plants now operate on automatic controls. Tailings are pumped through a stacking system—also, in some cases, on an independent pontoon—for disposal behind the plant. Power is brought to the plant and concentrates are pumped ashore in lines supported by pontoons. There are many variations on this general flow scheme.

Dredges offer a unique set of advantages. They are the only self-contained, high capacity, mobile units capable of mining, recovering minerals, and disposing of tailings in a continuous operation. Other advantages:

- Economy of operation even when water must be transported from some distance or from deep wells.

- A high order of digging availability. The hydraulic dredge, on a three-shift basis, averages 500 hr pumping time per month, or 16.7 hr per day; bucket-line dredges average 600 hr per month.

- Capability of digging tougher and more difficult ground than can be dug economically by bucket wheel, dragline, or shovel.

What minerals are dredged?

Placer minerals mined by dredging include:

Cassiterite. More dredges are used in tin mining—over 100 machines—than are used anywhere else in mining. The majority of these dredges are of the bucket-line type, with bucket capacities ranging from 3 to 24 cu ft, and are equipped with a preconcentration plant on board. A small percentage of tin dredges are suction cutterhead units, one of them specially designed to operate offshore in a swell. The maximum depth for suction dredges is technically limited to about 50 m, but relatively new bucket wheel hydraulic dredges can be fitted with a pump on the ladder, enabling them to reach far greater depths.

Gold. Usually mined with a bucket-line dredge having a concentration plant.

Heavy mineral sands (rutile, ilmenite, zircon, monazite, garnet, etc.). Suction cutterhead dredges predominate, pumping into a separate preconcentration plant that floats in the dredge pond. Such plants consist of spiral cones, pinched sluices, etc. Developments in beneficiation, including the use of jigs with circulating loads of oversize, may reduce the physical size of the plant needed for primary concentration.

Magnetite. Dredging is done by a suction cutterhead type with a pipeline feeding an onshore separation plant. Preconcentration on board by jigging with a circulating load of oversize may be feasible. An offshore operation is under consideration, using wave- or swell-compensated dredge with on-board magnetic separation plant and a trailing hopper.

Phosphate. Dry excavation methods of mining have traditionally been used. However, some operations are

Dismountable 3-cu-ft bucket-line dredge, used by Koba Tin for its mining operations on Bangka Island, Indonesia, features a jigging system, spuds, ladder-mounted hydraulic bucket-drive, and hydraulic ladder hoist rams. (Photo credit: IHC Holland.)

using suction cutterhead dredges for stripping overburden or mining the ore itself. These dredges pump phosphate-bearing rock to a stationary concentrator.

The bucket-line is very efficient

The lowest-cost dredging method for placer deposits is the bucket-line or bucket-ladder dredge. The bucket-line excavates and elevates material by means of steel buckets up to 24-cu-ft in capacity on a continuous chain, washing and concentrating the values in a continuous process. Materials that are excavated in the front of the dredge by buckets are discharged at the rear after concentration and recovery of metals. Thus, the pond or paddock in which the dredge floats advances as the ground is mined.

Conventional bucket-line dredges have high cutting or digging force and can handle most types of material, including some large boulders. Disadvantages are that bucket-line dredges are difficult to relocate, high in first cost (particularly for deep digging), and expensive to maintain. The capital cost of a bucket-line dredge may be 50% greater than the cost of a suction dredge of equal capacity. However, the power requirement is less for bucket-line dredges than for suction cutterhead dredges and far less than for gravel pump mining, both of which transport solids by pumping.

Bucket-line dredges are massive enough to dig all but the hardest bottoms. Boulders as large as the buckets are rolled aside by the digging action, but boulders much larger than the bucket size restrict the dredge's operation.

Malaysia's bucket-line tin dredges

Since all of Malaysia's tin mining dredges are bucket-line units, that nation has been a pace-setter in bucket-line developments. A few of Malaysia's more noteworthy contributions: twin trommels (screens) with a stripping chute between them; bigger buckets; longer digging ladders; tailings pumps (with or without hydrocyclones); circular jigs; mechanical distributors; and numerous improvements and refinements of nearly all dredge components for inland operations.

A development cited as particularly significant by Norman Cleaveland, dredge consultant, is that during the past decade, some of Malaysia's deep-digging dredges—to 150 ft below pond level—have abandoned the use of bow lines as a support for the lower end of the ladder. This would indicate, he says, that designs of both ladders and hulls "are far more robust than during past years, when it was accepted that the bow lines at the lower ladder point were an essential protection for both ladder and hull."

The ability of recently designed ladders and hulls to withstand such high stresses, Cleaveland says, opens up "at least two attractive possibilities for expanding the scope of mining dredges." One possibility is to increase digging depth without increasing ladder depth; the other is to increase the ability of a dredge to handle boulders previously considered too large and too numerous.

Greater digging depth

The possibility of increasing digging depth is based on the assumption that recently designed ladders would be substantially strengthened if supported at the lower ladder point by the bow lines. Such support should make it possible to lower the top tumbler to 20 ft above the deck and thus add 30 ft or more to the digging depth of the largest dredges. "Of course," Cleaveland adds, "it would then be necessary to re-elevate the dredged material to the treatment plant by secondary and lighter bucket elevators."

One of the largest dredges afloat, Conzinc Riotinto's *Sri Timah*—a 24-cu-ft bucket-line—is mining tin in Malaysia.

Cleaveland notes that the problem of boulders was given careful study in 1954 by an international dredge mining consulting firm, Thurman & Wright. Their theoretical solution called for use of a dragline with a boulder rake, working from the dredge face, to deposit boulders far enough back into the pond to clear the bucket-line catenary. Bow lines posed a major problem, and frequent shifts of the shore anchors were considered to prevent both the boulder rake and the boulders from fouling the bow lines, which, in accordance with standard practice, would have a connection with the ladder point.

"Since it now seems practicable to avoid connections of bow lines with the ladder point," Cleaveland says, "the Thurman & Wright solution to the boulder problem becomes increasingly attractive. By taking the bow lines from the deck to shore anchors and by avoiding connections with the ladder point, these lines could be kept well clear of the boulder rake and the boulders dumped back into the pond."

Bucket-line has its limits

There are practical limits on the size of dredge buckets, the depth and width of the dredging area, and the overall size of the dredge itself, says Patrick H. O'Neill, senior vice president of Rosario Resources. Where ground is shallow, the digging ladder is short and a small narrow hull with tapering bow is necessary to dig the corners, so smaller buckets must be used due to weight limitations.

In easily dug ground, O'Neill says, large buckets can be used, but larger buckets and greater depths require larger and heavier equipment, which in turn dictates a larger hull with less maneuverability.

Difficult dredging conditions, such as hard, uneven bedrock, large boulders, or cemented gravel, require oversize drive units and extra strength throughout the dredge. This reduces the bucket capacity for a given weight of dredge and size of hull.

World's largest dredge

Some of the largest dredging machines are used to mine Malaysian tin. In 1970, construction of the world's largest tin mining dredge was commissioned by a Malaysian company, for mining a large, low grade tin deposit. The dredge has some features unique to Southeast Asia. Among them:

■ An all-welded pontoon instead of riveted construction—unusual for this type of dredge. The design resulted in a substantial weight savings.

■ A novel support gantry for the long overburden and tailings chutes, which also reduced weight and cost.

■ An ore separating and concentrating plant equipped with large capacity circular jigs, fitted with an asymmetric sawtooth pulsator drive developed by IHC Holland. This feature greatly simplifies the feed splitter arrangement, reducing the space requirements and improving the efficiency of the treatment plant.

Jigs changed the course of dredging history. This 25-ft-dia circular unit has 12 hydraulically actuated hutch cones.

■ A four-wheel hydraulic drive on the revolving screens instead of the conventional two-wheel or single-wheel electric drive. Some experienced dredge operators prefer a simple chain drive for the main trommel because it greatly reduces the wear on the supporting rollers, the surfaces of which can then be lubricated.

The experience gained with the operation of this dredge, and similar dredges built subsequently, has spurred studies of a number of problems in the design of still larger dredges. Some of the problem areas:

■ The bucket chain is subjected to much abrasion and wear, boosting the operating costs. Mining consultant Cleaveland has designed a bucket chain to protect the connecting pins and their bushes from the adverse effects of sand, thus prolonging service life. A prototype of the new design is being tested in a laboratory and at one of the technical universities in Holland.

■ On larger dredges, the capacity to beneficiate must be greatly increased. Larger capacity can be achieved by changes in design of the revolving screens that feed the jigs and by use of high capacity screens for primary ore concentration. This approach simplifies the distribution problem and reduces the danger of seriously overloading some of the jigs, causing loss of valuable minerals.

■ Water pumps and jet nozzles in the main trommel, used to disintegrate and slurry dredged material, draw high power requirements. Therefore, a system of pumps and nozzles has been developed that is very flexible in performance, requires minimal power, and permits the continuation of mining in case of failure of one of the components.

■ Gravity affects flow of dredged spoil through the ore separation plant in most alluvial mining operations. Gravity also affects the tailings disposal system, which usually uses open chutes or launders. As dredging capacity increases, tailings must be deposited farther from the dredging face to avoid recirculating the tailings into the dredging process. The longer chutes and higher starting point that are required dictate a higher dredge and a longer ladder.

One proposed means of transporting the tailings a sufficient distance from the stern of the dredge, Cleaveland says, is to use conveyor belts, which are reliable, relatively low in cost, and low in power consumption. However, the jig tailings must then be dewatered before they can be put on the conveyor belt.

Jig design holds key to more capacity

A breakthrough in jig design has been reported that promises to provide adequate treatment capacity for bucket-line dredges of far greater size than any now operating, including suction cutterhead dredges. The jig simultaneously increases mining capacity and economizes on headroom and floor space, offering savings in weight and power.

Pacific Tin Consolidated built and operated a series of these circular jigs for tin dredges in Malaysia that are fed at the center and discharged at the periphery. The most distinctive feature of the jigs is a skimming device that contours the jig bed surface and prevents both pyramiding and channeling of the pulp, thus assuring a reasonably uniform 'jigging' action over the entire jig bed. The skimmers act somewhat like the wipers on a flotation cell. The circular shape of the bed results in deceleration of the pulp as it moves toward the periphery. Deceleration facilitates concentration of the heavier particles and, combined with the action of the skimmers on the lighter fraction, substantially increases the capacity per unit of jig bed area.

The first of the jigs was 5-ft-dia, but the size was gradually increased to 25-ft-dia, with a capacity of approximately 300 cu yd per hr. Much larger jigs of this type appear entirely feasible, for treatment of 3,000 cu yd or more per hr.

This type of jig is being used also for recovery of diamonds in Brazil, in a joint venture of Pacific Tin Consolidated, Guggenheim Brothers, and Dragagem de Ouro SA, a Brazilian firm.

Cutterhead dredges mine mineral sands

A suction cutterhead dredge has a cutter of curved steel blades that rotate at the end of a ladder below the dredge pond. The cutter is designed to scoop sand toward the pump section as it slowly rotates, and to exclude gravel of a size too large for the pump being used.

Pulp transported to the concentrator by a pump and floating pipeline has a density of about 20% to 30%. Early indications are that these figures will be exceeded with bucket wheel dredges and submerged pumps. Power requirements for transport to the plant are greater than for bucket-line dredges, but far less than for gravel pump mining.

Suction cutterhead dredges and plants operate over the range of 100 to 1,250 cu yd per hr. Larger capacities are possible. A 100-cu-yd-per-hr plant weighs about 150 tons; a 1,250-cu-yd plant, 1,700 tons—about one-half the weight of a bucket-line dredge of comparable capacity.

Suction cutterhead dredges are used in large scale mining of heavy mineral sands deposits, primarily in Australia, New Zealand, and the US. The mined material is screened and undersize is transported hydraulically to a wet gravity plant that may or may not be built on the same barge. The concentrate from this plant is then dried and upgraded by dry separation.

Waipipi uses twin dredging system

The original suction cutterhead dredge employed by Waipipi Iron Sands Ltd. of New Zealand was designed to produce more than 1,800 tph in spoil; however, the cohesive nature of the material mined, along with other factors, limited its ability to excavate and transport more than about 1,500 tph. For this reason, a second dredge of similar capacity was recently built to permit the plant to achieve and eventually surpass its full design capacity of 323 dry ltph.

Waipipi operates the two dredges as independent units, each working half the operating face of the pond. Even though the working face is divided into two almost equal sections, dredging is stepped in such a way that the lead machine works some 100 m forward of the trailing machine. This procedure avoids interference between the two dredges, especially their winch ropes. The two dredges deliver slurry to a common surge bin.

Waipipi employs a five-wire dredging system: a headline to keep the cutterhead in contact with the working face; two bow winches to traverse the dredge back and forth across the face; and two stern winches that react against the headline to keep the dredge positioned and aligned. The ladder, with a depth capability of 28 ft below the water line, is raised and lowered by using two 80-ton-capacity hydraulic rams.

Although the second dredge has been operating for only a short time, many of the expected advantages have already materialized:

■ Because the combined dredge feed can exceed plant capacity, higher recovery is possible when one dredge operates at maximum output while the second reworks the pond bottom to clean up the cutter throwback.

■ Grade variances to the plant are minimized by the blending effect of a two-dredge operation.

■ Short shutdowns of the concentrator for moving the dredge anchor positions, minor operational problems, and maintenance and lubrication checks are reduced or eliminated by coordinated dredging.

■ Major repairs can be done without completely shutting down the mine facility.

However, there are also some problems with the new dredging scheme:

- Current mine planning requires the dredges and plant to negotiate periodically a turn through 180°. This will be the most difficult maneuver attempted to date, with some loss expected in operating time and production rates.

- Installation of winches on the floating pipeline is being considered, to counteract the strong influences of wind and weather.

- Two dredges can deliver a pulp volume exceeding the capacity of the trommel and surge bin, even when the actual tonnage of solids is at the appropriate level. It is thus necessary to maintain a pulp velocity of about 18 ft per sec in the floating lines, which dictates the volume that must be handled on the screening barge.

Bucket wheel dredge: a modern mining tool

The recent development of an underwater bucket wheel cutter and submerged pump, both mounted at or near the end of the ladder, will considerably extend the depth of mining below water level. An increase in mining depth will remove some of the chief limitations of suction cutterhead dredges.

One of the limits is the inability to effectively mine heavy minerals, including gold. The bucket wheel recovers much more material than the basket cutter. Not all the material excavated by a basket cutter is transported through the slurry system; some is dislodged, manipulated, and to some extent classified as the heavy, desirable fractions settle out and remain behind. The bucket wheel has a degree of force feed, channeling excavated material into the interior of the wheel, where it is quickly drawn up the suction line.

With the bucket wheel, says Thomas N. Turner of Ellicott Machine Corp., there is no overdigging, resulting in a savings in horsepower. Also, the concentration of cutting force on a much smaller cutting edge allows the bucket wheel to dig efficiently much harder material and, in either swing direction, allows the force to reach 2,000 to 3,000 psi.

Other advantages of the bucket wheel cited by Turner include the ability of the cutter to clean up a horizontal or inclined stratum of ore. Since many placer ores are alluvial deposits, the cleanup capability of the bucket wheel is a major advantage over the conventional cutter, which overdigs, mixing ore with the under- or overburden. Also, with a spud carriage, the bucket wheel dredge is reported to achieve 75% or greater efficiency.

New dredge designs

New dredge designs have recently been patented for both bucket-line and suction dredges. These designs enable such dredges to operate economically in deeper water at greater capacities. New designs provide for:

- Mining depths of at least 300 ft below the water surface for suction dredges and approximately 200 ft

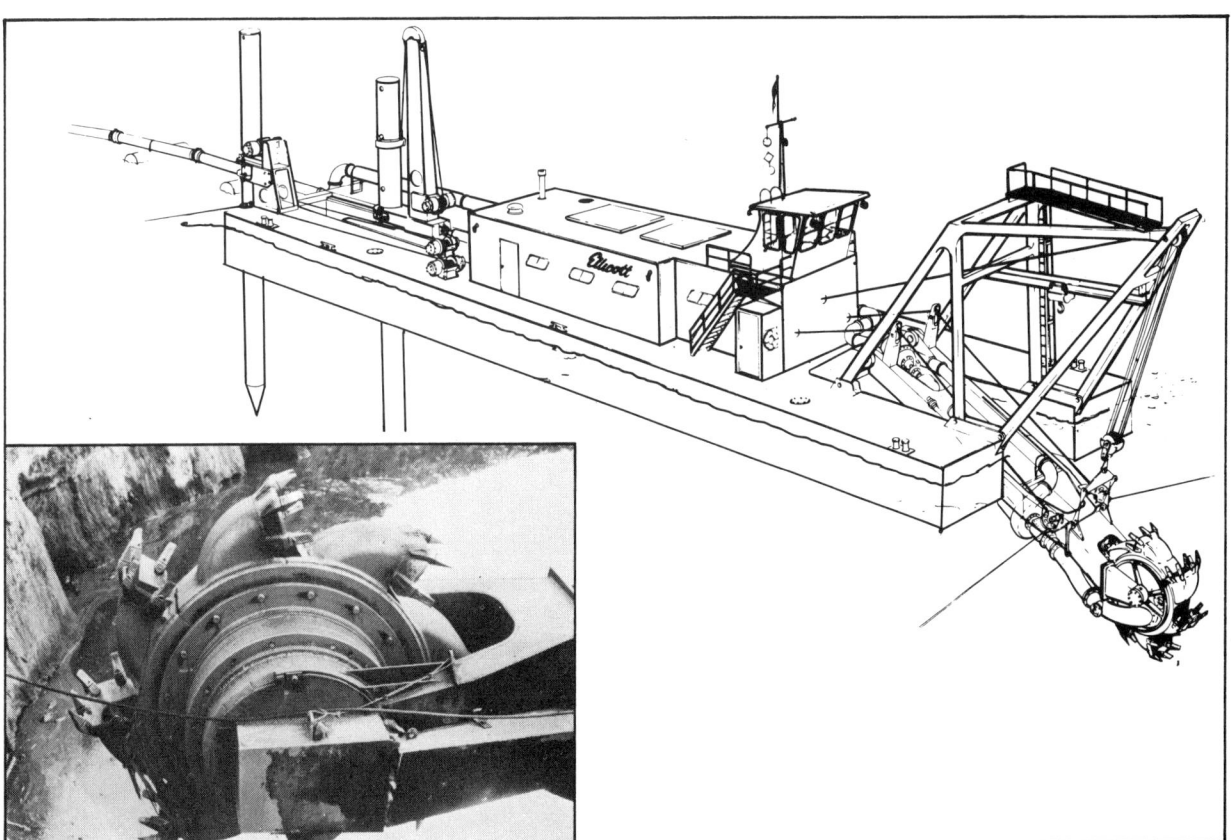

Bucket wheel dredge—Ellicott's Model WE87—is rated at 1,000 tph, with 50-ft digging depth. The unit includes a hydraulically driven rotating bucket wheel (see inset) with 100-hp drive unit and roller bearing-supported reduction gear.

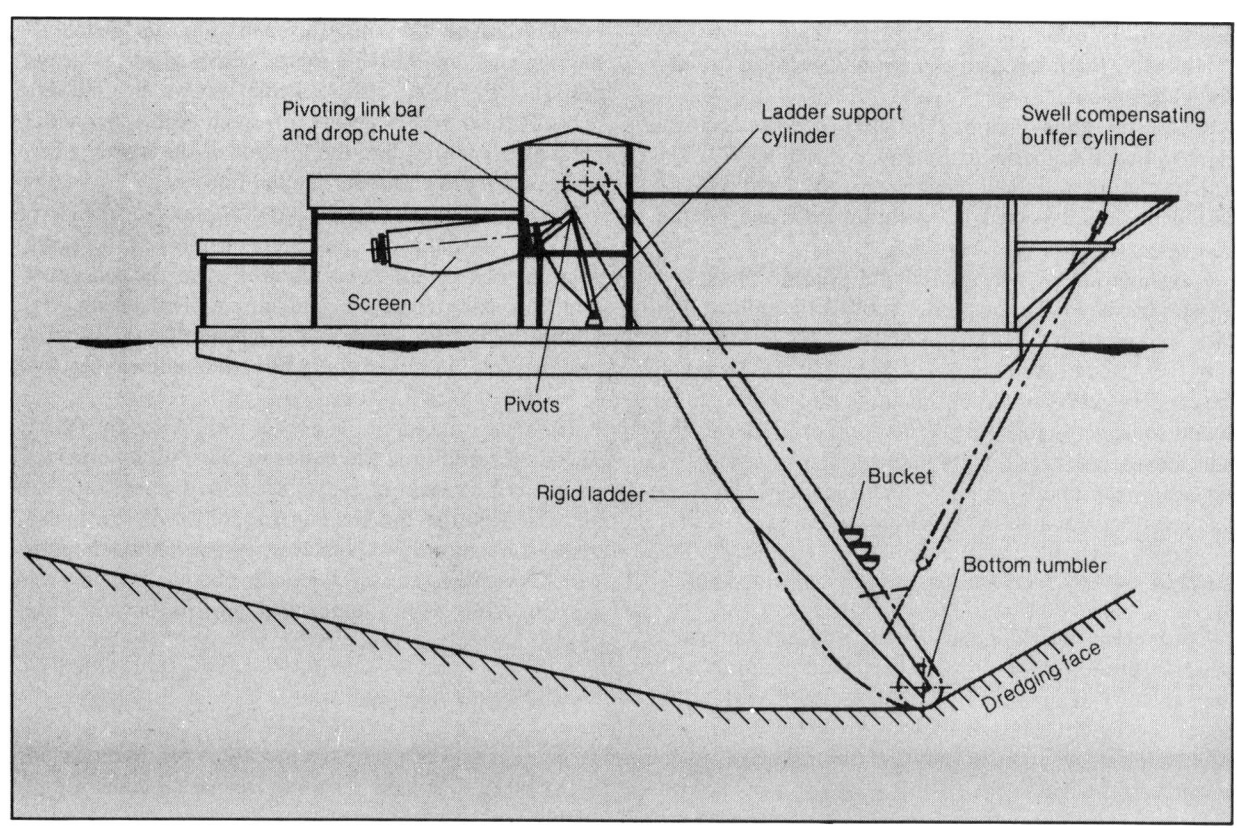

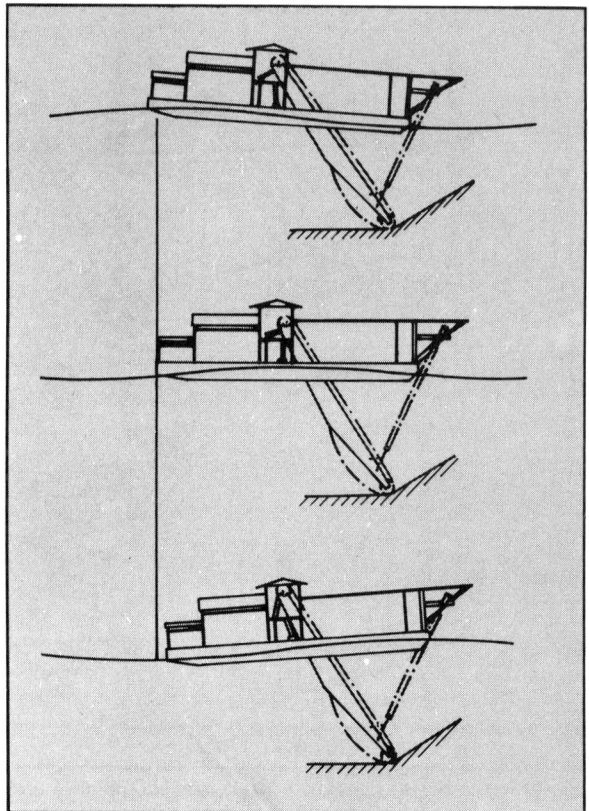

A new design for an offshore tin mining dredge by IHC Holland (above and below) is based on a flexible ladder support system. The dredge, using a bucket-line, is suitable for coastal waters.

below the surface for bucket-line dredges.
- Continuous optimum production under sea wave and swell conditions.
- Substantially lower ratios of dredge displacement weight to production capacity than with conventional dredges.
- Increased efficiency and production.
- Economical increases in the digging depth of conventional dredges through relatively minor structural and mechanical alterations.
- Installation of sea swell compensating systems on conventional one-piece ladder dredges.
- Larger buckets and/or higher bucket speeds.

Offshore dredges

As land-based resources have become scarcer, more attention has been given to mining marine placer deposits on the sea floor. One of the firms focusing on these deposits is IHC Holland, which has completed design of an offshore tin mining dredge suitable for working Indonesia's coastal waters. Water depth there is not great enough to warrant the development of a new, completely submerged mining tool, says a company spokesman. Moreover, the required mining capacity and the relatively thin layers of alluvial deposits ruled out economical design of a walking platform.

IHC's design was therefore based on a floating pontoon. Since the deposit is consolidated and requires mechanical excavation, a conventional bucket-line was chosen as the digging tool. However, weather conditions during part of the year would cause considerable movement of the surface pontoon, making normal dredging impossible. Thus, flexible connections were provided between the pontoon and the bucket ladder. The flexible connections will enable the bottom end of the ladder to remain in contact with the dredging face independent of pontoon movement.

The upper end of the ladder is connected to the pontoon by a hinged beam, while weight is supported by a pair of hydraulic cylinders connected to air pressure vessels and acting as springs. The forward, lower end of the ladder is suspended by the conventional hoisting tackle from a pivoting yoke, in turn supported by similar hydropneumatic springs.

The supporting springs are carefully chosen to minimize change in bottom tumbler position while the pontoon moves in a horizontal and vertical direction with the waves. The system has been optimized with the aid of computer programs, and the resulting dredge has been subjected to model tests in a wind and wave tank.

The flexible suspension of the bucket-line requires that the chain drive motors and their gear reducers be installed on the ladder itself. This arrangement permitted IHC to connect the drop-chute—which receives material dumped by the buckets—in such a way that clearance between bucket chain and chute is minimal, irrespective of the ladder angle. The loss of dredged spoil by spillage through the chain and the chute has been virtually eliminated in tests.

Continuous dragline concept

The Cleaveland-O'Neill-Guntert Continuous Dragline, according to one source, will be in a class by itself—exceeding the present limits of digging capacity offshore, digging depth, and wave toleration. The continuous dragline design, the source says, stresses simplicity while retaining most of the advantages of a bucket-line dredge. The design, however, has yet to be perfected and tested.

Wave toleration will be determined by the hull and treatment plant—not by the digging equipment. A catenary is the simplest and most effective method of compensating for wave action. Digging depths at least double those of conventional dredges seem probable. Potential digging capacity covers the entire range of fully developed land-based dragline buckets—up to 250 cu yd per bucket. Dual suspension of the buckets improves stability, loading, and load retention.

Power requirements will depend on the material excavated, but experience with one continuous dragline designed by Ronald Guntert indicates that only 1 hp is needed for 1 to 3 cu yd per hr of material handled. Since the buckets on a continuous dragline are nearly in balance, the power applied will be focused almost exclusively on the working face and in hoisting solids. Solids will be delivered to the treatment plant in dewatered form, at a relatively uniform rate.

The power required for conventional draglines—about 12,500 lb of line pull per cubic yard of bucket capacity—provides a safe estimate of the power needed for the digging equipment on a continuous dragline.

To date, designs have incorporated the power and transmission units of Caterpillar tractors. These units reportedly provide good flexibility in speed control, coupled with load-seeking characteristics and overload protection, which assures both maximum capacity and safety.

Applying Marconaflo to mining placers

A nondredging offshoot of Marconaflo technology with potential applications in placer mining is being adapted to slurry uranium ores and then pump them to the surface through a borehole.

The scheme calls for a series of six self-contained mining units to be positioned through holes drilled into the ore. An oscillating Marconajet would direct a high pressure jet stream of water into the orebody, producing a slurry. The slurry would be pumped to the surface and on to a collection tank from which it would be transferred to processing. A high pressure water pump would deliver return water from processing back to the Marconajet. Tailings would be returned to a backfill unit for redepositing in the mined-out cavities.

According to a Marcona Corp. spokesman, tests showed that even in ore as consolidated as that of the Powder River Basin of Wyoming, mining rates as high as 35 tph could be achieved at radial distances out to 25 ft. Requirements included the proper combination of water pressures, an additive such as Separan, and certain nozzle design refinements.

In a followup program, begun during late summer in the original Powder River Basin test hole, water pressure was varied from 500 psi to 1,500 psi, with and without the addition of sand. Resulting slurry densities pumped to the surface varied from 5% to 30% by weight. The orebody was cut to a distance of more than 20 ft from the drillhole, and over 300 dry tons of material was recovered. Additional test programs are under way. □

References

Note: All papers listed here were presented at the Placer Exploration and Mining Short Course, University of Nevada, Reno, Oct. 25-29, 1976.
1) Breeding, William H., "The Evaluation of Placer Deposits."
2) O'Neill, Patrick H., "Placer Mining with Bucket Ladder Dredges."
3) Lord, John F., "Placer Mining Evaluation, Methods and Applications."
4) Kastelic, William R., "Dredging Operations in Alaska."
5) Wein, V. S., "Dredge Mining Iron Sands in New Zealand."
6) Cleaveland, Norman, "Dirt, Diamonds, and Gold Dust."
7) Griffiths, S. J., "Mining of Australian Mineral Sands."
8) Le Neve, W., "Mine-Stripping with the Cutter-Suction Dredge."
9) Newey, C. O., "Placer Mining: Notes on Applicability of Methods."
10) Ziegler, R. B., "Dredge Mining Methods and Equipment for the Exploitation of Alluvial Mineral Deposits."
11) Turner, Thomas N., "The Bucket Wheel Hydraulic Dredge: the Modern Mining Tool."
12) Cleaveland, Norman, "More Proposed Improvements for Placer Dredges."
13) McKay, Cameron E., "Comparative Characteristics of Hydraulic and Bucket-Ladder Dredges."
14) Miscovich, John A., "Hydraulic Placer Mining Methods with the Intelligiant."
15) Sims, W. Norman, "Marconaflo System Design Elements."
16) Wolff, Ernest N., "Small Scale Placer Mining Methods in Alaska."
17) Harris, Jack, "Placer Mining—What Options?"
18) Cleaveland, Norman, "The Continuous Dragline Dredge—a Concept."
19) McKay, Cameron E., "Some New Concepts in Dredge Design."

Many improvements in shovels and draglines

CHANGES TO UPGRADE THE POWER AND EFFICIENCY of excavating shovels are wide-ranging, from 200-yd stripping mammoths to the latest in electric drives for hardrock excavators.

The modern electric shovel is massive, strong, and efficient, providing round-the-clock production with 90% to 95% availability over long years of service. Such shovels have no competition in bank excavation of hard rock, where tough digging conditions are part of the game.

In 1974, E/MJ conducted a market survey among hardrock mining operations, 50% of which moved more than 5 million tpy of ore and waste. The operators listed Bucyrus-Erie, P & H, and Marion as the source of 90% of their shovels. Only 40% of the shovels were over 6 cu yd in size, and only 14% were larger than 12 cu yd. Significantly, more than half of the respondents planned to purchase shovels larger than 12 cu yd and they favored electric shovels by nearly four to one. The development of large 12-yd to 25-yd electric shovels for hardrock mining is the most significant advance in shovels for this decade. Most open-pit hardrock mining in the near future will likely be accomplished with shovels in this size range.

'Electrotorque' uses solid state technology

The P & H 2800, the largest hardrock shovel, uses the unique "Electrotorque" control system, a totally static solid state electronic system that converts ac to dc without rotating machinery.

In 1945, Harnischfeger (P & H) applied an eddy-current "Magnetorque" coupling to the transmission and control of shovel power. Two Magnetorque units can be applied to a single shaft, offering considerably lower inertia than a single coupling having an equivalent capacity. For shovels up to 15 cu yd, this lower inertia provides rapid response during acceleration, deceleration, and reversal of the direction of rotation.

To meet demands for larger capacity electric shovels, P & H developed the Model 2800, rated at 22 to 40 cu yd. However, because it isn't advantageous to multiply the number of Magnetorque units on shovels of 20 yd or larger, P & H sought a new system, incorporating the latest advances in solid state electronics. The result was Electrotorque, "an adjustable speed, static, stepless control and ac power conversion for application to specifically tailored, low-inertia dc motors."[1] This breakthrough utilizes such recent technological advances as high capacity thyristors and electronic circuits, which provide high responsiveness and close correspondence between static and dynamic characteristics. Torque overload is eliminated, reducing abuse of shovel mechanical power transmissions and the shovel structure. Less mechanical maintenance is required, and shovel availability is greater.

Electrotorque provides fully adjustable and automatic conversion or inversion of electrical energy. Thus, both conversion of ac to dc during "motoring" and inversion of dc to ac during regeneration achieve previously unattainable efficiencies. The system provides a speed control range of greater than 50 to 1, and performance is superior to previous regenerative electrical drives, Harnischfeger states.

While providing good performance, reliability, and reduced maintenance, Electrotorque also eliminates such rotating machinery as the large ac motor and the dc crowd/propel and swing generators. The system components are mounted in pullout drawers for easy maintenance, and an indicator tray facilitates troubleshooting. If a fault occurs, indicator tray pilot lights indicate the source of the problem, and the troublesome tray can be quickly replaced.

The Electrotorque system provides both rectification and control. "It rectifies three-phase ac power into dc power, controls this dc power automatically with precision, and then applies it to dc shunt-wound motors. Static solid-state precision control of both armature and field supply to the motor provides smooth, stepless operation through the most rugged load digging cycle. Eliminating ac drive motors and dc generators greatly increases shovel efficiency and reduces maintenance and downtime costs."[1]

P & H is developing an addition to the system that would automatically correct power factor. Power-factor-corrected shovels would tend to raise a mine's average power factor. The modification would consist of a bank of fixed capacitors as well as additional capacitor banks to be electronically switched into or out of the system by a "Hall Effect" transducer.

The Model 2800 also features a new crowd design, including a powerband connection between motor and crowd transmission. The powerband is a group of V-belts with a common back, which prevents the V-belts from overturning when subjected to sudden shock loading.

The third advanced design incorporated in the Model 2800 is in the propel system—long a high-maintenance item. Several basic problems were solved by taking the propel system off the shovel deck and placing it as close to the final drives as possible, on the back of the carbody.

The new design consists of a propel motor base and a three-reduction spur gear transmission bolted to the back of the carbody. Each crawler frame has a V-type, spring-set, air-released brake and an air-shifted steering jaw clutch. All gears in the propel drive run in oil. The motor and transmission can be easily removed for repairs. The

Bucyrus-Erie's top-sized shovel is the 295-B, shown here loading coal with a 31-cu-yd bucket. Rock bucket is 21 cu yd.

Bucyrus-Erie's 1500-W swings a 70-yd bucket. The 285-ft triangular boom is made of tubular steel; pressure system detects cracks.

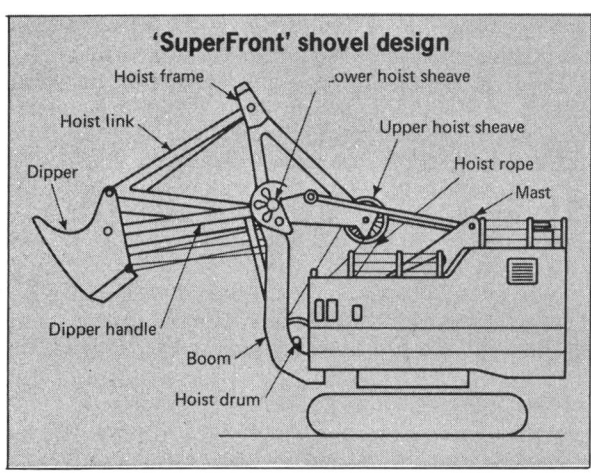

Marion's SuperFront design provides powerful cutting force, especially in the toe of the bank, and gives clean, level mine floor.

advantages of the propel system were readily apparent, and P & H has applied the system to the 1900 and 2100 series of shovels as well. When one propel transmission was returned to Milwaukee after 20,000 hr of operation, the gears, bearings, and shafts were still in good condition.

'SuperFront' shovel digs straight into the toe

Marion Power Shovel Co. redesigned the front end of its hardrock mining shovel, producing the radical "Super-Front." The shovel digs straight into the toe of a bank, as opposed to the crowd-hoist arc motion of conventional shovels. Initially, the new design is being offered on the 21-cu-yd model 194M-HR-1 and the 26-cu-yd 203 M-HR-1R. A prototype machine, operating in a Minnesota taconite mine, apparently achieved significant productivity gains in comparison with conventional equipment. Marion engineers claim that the superior performance of the SuperFront lies in its ability to make a flat pass, to "slice" rather than "rake" the dipper teeth through the bank—concentrating the digging force in the toe area.

The SuperFront design drastically changes the arrangement of boom and handle, although the machine has the same operating ranges as a conventional shovel. The front end is lighter, more efficient, and stronger, with hydraulic crowd and a controlled pitch motion. The boom is really a stiff leg, about which the hoist frame structure rotates to produce concentrated hoist and crowd motion.

The SuperFront is equipped with a variable pitch dipper that enables the operator to maintain it at a constant angle relative to the mine floor. The operator can make a long, flat pass, leaving the mine floor clean and level. Marion engineers say that the three controlled motions of hoist, crowd, and dipper pitch contribute to a substantially increased cutting force, greater dipper capacity for the same machine weight, a better fill factor, and a faster digging cycle.

At the start of the cycle, the operator selects the position of the pitch. When the dipper reaches its optimum point in the toe of the bank, the operator releases the pitch, which permits the dipper to rotate upward until halted by the

The Marion 8750 dragline giant is characteristic of machines used not only for stripping and mining, but also for reclamation.

dipper's mechanical stops. As the dipper begins its upward movement, it generates a breakout force exceeding 250,000 lb, achieving superior fill. This characteristic gives the SuperFront a special advantage over shovels in mines where low banks are the standard, Marion states. The variable-pitch dipper also reduces spillage and improves loading because it can be positioned in a more vertical attitude at the dump point.

The arrangement of the SuperFront moves the machine's center of gravity closer to the center of rotation. This arrangement reduces the power needed to swing the machine and reduces loading on the swing gears.

In the redesign, only two forces—tension and compression—are present in the truss structure members. The bending and torsion present in conventionally designed shovels are eliminated. Repositioning the hoist rope and all hydraulics away from the digging face should reduce damage to these components. The SuperFront design also eliminates the sliding joints of the conventional dipper handle movement through the yoke block area.

The Bucyrus-Erie hardrock mining shovels

Bucyrus-Erie's line of mining shovels ranges from the Model 155-B, with a standard 9-cu-yd dipper, to the 295-B, with a standard dipper of 21 cu yd. The shovels feature Ward Leonard drive, simplified static control and specially designed dippers. Modular design permits shovel components to be removed as units for maintenance. Other features include a lower works propel and low-inertia, disc-type air clutches for propel. All dipper sticks are tubular. For shovels to be used in hot climates and/or high altitudes, oversize blowers and a high-altitude filtering and ventilating package are available. Cold weather options include low temperature air hoses and low temperature grease for electrical equipment, heated lube cabinets, an insulated machinery house equipped with heaters, a heavy handle, and alloy-steel take-up axle. The operator's cab is designed for the environment.

Environment affects electric shovel efficiency

Altitude, temperature, and aridity-humidity factors have serious effects on the efficiency and the longevity of an electric shovel. According to one authority,[2] "If no action is taken to compensate for an altitude increase, standard electrical excavation apparatus will be derated by 0.4% to 1% for each 10% increase (330 ft) above the standardized 'high altitude' elevation of 3,300 ft. The derating factor, however, is not the same for all types and designs of excavators. Furthermore, these rule-of-thumb derating factors are based on maintaining the same temperature rise of the excavating unit over the 'standard' ambient temperature, which is assumed to remain unchanged." High-altitude, rarefied atmosphere reduces dissipation of heat, critical gradients for corona and spark-over, and capacity of the air compressor. The low humidity that is characteristic of high altitudes "can have an adverse effect on the formation of a proper and durable film on the commutators."

The solution to these problems is to specify properly sized blowers on the machine for ventilation and to use high-altitude, low-humidity brushes. The shovel purchaser should specify to the manufacturer the altitude and ambient temperature at which the machine will operate. The main heat losses that must be dissipated into the ventilating air are electrical losses. Air blowers and air filtration equipment can then be sized and the specifications passed on to the electrical vendor. As an example, air at 8,000 ft has only three-quarters the density it has at sea level. Compensation is necessary for efficiency.

Draglines booms: bigger and better

Walking draglines are more versatile than ever before. Long booms (360 ft plus) and a host of design changes, inspection methods, and new materials are being incorporated in the final product. Bucyrus-Erie, Marion, Page, Northwest, Manitowoc, and Clark Equipment's Lima Div. are among the major manufacturers of draglines, which

The P & H Model 2800 design incorporates the advanced-technology 'Electrotorque' static generator system, without moving parts.

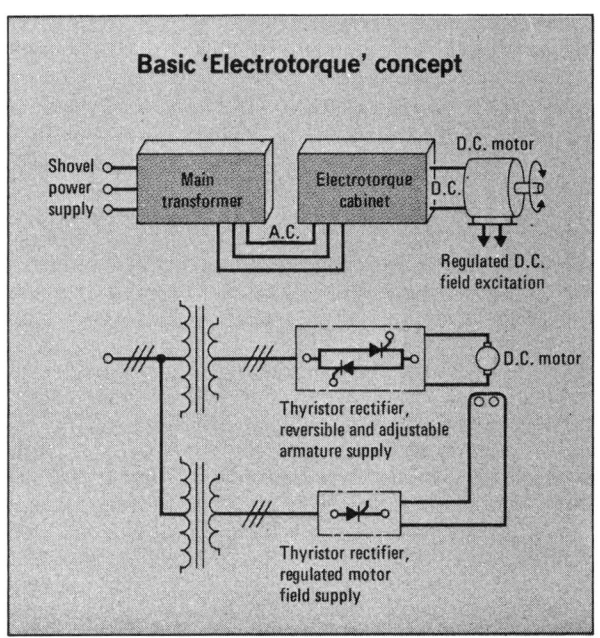

range in capacity from little more than a yard to stripping giants with buckets exceeding 200 yd. The machines can move material at 10¢ to 20¢ per bank cubic yard (owning and operating costs), and are used not only for stripping and mining but also in the reclamation of mined land, where their long reach proves most effective. All draglines are built to cycle through a 90° arc in less than a minute and should provide a productivity slightly over 250,000 bench cubic yards per year per cubic yard of bucket capacity.

The long reach of a dragline is its outstanding characteristic. "A dragline with 360 ft of boom and—more important—340 ft of dumping radius can cut and spoil 130 to 140 ft of overburden without rehandling."[3]

In an interesting application at The Anaconda Co.'s open-pit copper mine at Butte, Mont., a Bucyrus-Erie 480-W dragline was scheduled to spend several years working on the eastward expansion of the Berkeley pit.[4] The expansion was to move through a large area of wet, sandy, unconsolidated overburden up to 150 ft thick. The 480-W, with a 175-ft boom and 18-cu-yd bucket, was used to reach down and remove the overburden to two benches. Aside from this exotic application in hardrock copper mining, however, the dragline is the mainstay for much stripping and reclamation work and in some mining sectors—notably the Florida phosphate pebble industry—it is the mainstay of production.

The long boom and other dragline improvements

Bucyrus-Erie, a leader in the manufacture of draglines, has long been in the forefront of boom design, and a recent paper[5] by its chief structures engineer is instructive. In summary, the paper states that long booms are being designed and fabricated with confidence using "today's materials, analytical methodology, fabrication technology, and engineering expertise. And the current 360 ft in length [of booms] is by no means a limit; present structural technology can easily accommodate 400 ft and more."

Bucyrus-Erie has developed a standard of six load sets and nine distinct combinations of those basic loads to design booms. Increases in operating radius and bucket size have not been accompanied by a longer cycle time, which is still typically under 1 min. Using simulation, the company was able to confirm that the final stresses were very close to those predicted by the standard load set.

All booms are designed to meet allowable stresses specified in the AISC structure code, and boom welds conform to the American Welding Society structural welding code. The formulas are used to check every member of the boom for every load condition. Because Bucyrus-Erie booms are built of circular tubes, Section 10 of the AWS code is applicable. While none of the codes includes consideration of stress relief, all chord welds in the factory and the field are stress relieved. Each member of the boom is checked for buckling under all load cases and for fatigue at four points at each end.

The boom design procedures are based on a finite element analysis of the entire front end of the machine. The structures are analyzed using either EASE (a proprietary CDC program), or NASTRAN, the NASA Structural Analyzer developed for the space program. In either case, Bucyrus-Erie obtains deflections, forces, and stresses in each member of the boom and mast for each of the standard loads. When testing was done to verify the accuracy of the analytical techniques and mathematical modeling, test results generally differed by less than 10% from the analytical results, and on the conservative side. Test results provided a mass of data, which were first analyzed by Bucyrus-Erie engineers to confirm that all extreme points fell within the design parameters.

All boom members are thick-walled cylinders. ASTM A-618 steel is used for chord material and Grade B API-5LX material is used for the lacings. A-618 is used primarily in 16-in.-OD tubes. Although weight savings made aluminum attractive for booms, the welding difficulties, cost, and poor fatigue performance precluded its use.

The tubular shape of boom members not only offers an efficient cross section, but also permits use of a chord pressurization system for early detection of cracks. The main chords are filled with pressurized nitrogen. If a crack appears, the pressure drops and a gauge in the cab warns the operator to shut down. Chords are sealed off in four separate sections to speed pinpointing of the fault.

As the result of a computer optimization study, Bucyrus-Erie has standardized chord OD and lacing patterns, eliminated cluster lacing welds, lowered the percentage of boom weight devoted to lacings, and changed the geometry of the dragline front end. Most significant in draglines of less than 100-cu-yd capacity is the increase in boom length. Bucyrus-Erie engineers determined that they could take weight out of the boom by lengthening the mast. Furthermore, within limits, the mast weight goes up less than the boom weight goes down. "The key is opening up the angle between the main suspension ropes and the boom at the tip."[5] Further study showed that while machines of less than 100-cu-yd capacity were best equipped with a single triangular boom, larger machines should be designed with twin triangular booms for a further savings in total boom weight.

Along with advances in boom design and construction, improvements in dragline design over the past decade also include:

- Use of higher quality steels, metallurgy, and better welds, combined with superior sonic and X-ray testing, checks by magnafluxing, and Brinell hardness tests.
- Radial base design for improved distribution of loads and custom sizing for the specific job.
- More dependable walking systems using improved lubrication, shaft and journal design, antifriction bearings, and outboard propel bearings (for lower stresses).
- Modular drive systems with standardized components.
- Customized automatic centralized lubrication.
- Improved tub design through changes in bottom plate thickness, vertical bulkhead thickness, and spacing; use of Nylatron sleeves and washers in the roller circle and improved antifriction bearings on the center journal.
- Cam-and-slide walking mechanism for large draglines.
- Ball joints for boom-point sheave and walking-shoe connections.
- Improved field erection procedures, including machining and boring to overcome minute manufacturing errors.
- Customized design for temperature conditions at the operating site (specialty steels, insulation, oversize blowers, air conditioning, sun shields, etc.). □

References

1) Cherones, W. J., "New Trends in Shovel Mining," ASIA MINING, May 1975, p 57.
2) Ivy, J. G., "How to Maximize Efficiency of Excavators in High Altitude Mining Environments," E/MJ, April 1976, p 90.
3) Johnson, Tegner C., "How Design Improvements Boost Walking Draglines' Productivity," MINING ENGINEERING, October 1974, p 46.
4) "Draglines in the US and Sahara," MINING MAGAZINE, March 1974, p 213.
5) Wheeler, O. E., "Long Boom Design Considerations," AIME Annual Meeting, Las Vegas, Nev., Feb. 22-26, 1976.

Mining shovels like this Marion 151-M (a diesel-electric) are digging ores around the world at altitudes as great as 11,000 ft.

How to maximize efficiency of excavators in high altitude mining environments

J. G. Ivy, supervisor of electrical engineering, Marion Power Shovel Co.

"High altitude" mining conditions are defined by NEMA, IEEE, and ANSI* to apply for all electrical equipment of the type used on excavators designed to meet nameplate ratings (including temperature rise) at an elevation of 3,300 ft. The 3,300-ft altitude was chosen because it is equivalent to the "even" metric height of 1,000 m.

Altitude is critical to operation of electrical mining equipment. For example, if no action is taken to compensate for an altitude increase, standard electrical excavation apparatus will be derated by 0.4% to 1% for each 10% increase (330 ft) above the standardized "high altitude" elevation of 3,300 ft. The derating factor, however, is not the same for all types and designs of excavators. Furthermore, these "rule of thumb" derating factors are based on maintaining the same temperature rise of the excavating unit over the "standard" ambient temperature, which is assumed to remain unchanged.

The main obstacles to successful operation

Equipment derating is a recognition of the reduced ability of rarefied atmosphere to carry off heat and cool an apparatus. This problem must be solved to achieve successful shovel operation at high altitudes.

Other problems at high elevation are reduction of critical gradients for corona and spark-over roughly in proportion to the density of the air, reduced capacity in the air compressor (which is a system support component of almost every excavator), and less effective commutation.

The following guidelines will help to assure full-capacity operation above the 3,300-ft level for new machines and for used machines that are relocated to high altitudes.

---
*National Electrical Manufacturers Association, Institute of Electrical and Electronics Engineers, and American National Standards Institute.

Buyer is responsible for machine specifications

The equipment user must accurately specify to his vendors the operating conditions for new machines, including both altitude and ambient temperature, at the time an equipment bid is solicited. Standard ambient temperature for electrical equipment is 40°C (104°F), which is relatively warm. In many instances, the climate of a high altitude mine is significantly cooler than standard.

Machine insulation responds only to total temperature variations in a given environment. The division of total temperature between "rise" (from no load) and "ambient" is immaterial.

If cost control is important, the equipment buyer must not overspecify. The ambient temperature specified to the vendor need not be the highest temperature on record. An evaluation of regional ambient temperatures has been compiled by the American Society of Heating, Refrigerating and Air Conditioning Engineers (ASHRAE) from US Weather Bureau data. The ASHRAE handbook lists temperatures that are, on average, exceeded by 1%, 2½%, and 5% of all hours of the summer season. It would be safe to use the plus 1% temperatures in specifying equipment. Selected reference temperatures are included in Table 1 for some locations having altitudes above 3,300 ft.

Operation of equipment at *modest* increases above rated ambient temperature for *limited* periods reduces life expectancy but does not usually produce immediate catastrophic equipment failure. Insulation aging is a slow chemical process accelerated by heat. Such aging goes on at normal rated operating temperatures at a pace that gives long life—10, 20, or even 30 years. Operation at elevated temperatures cuts this life in half for each increase of 8-10°C. In other words, if a machine is forced to operate at a temperature averaging 8° above normal for 4 hr on a given afternoon, it ages about 8 hr during that 4-hr period. The machine may still have a long and useful life provided such operation does not happen too often.

Steps to ensure long life for new excavators

What actions are taken by an excavator vendor and its suppliers, the electrical vendors, in response to a high altitude spec in a bid request? What studies are made and what changes are likely to be required to ensure the most efficient utilization of electrical excavation equipment?

The first step is a check of the excavator house ventilating system for capacity, keeping in mind that the ventilation system is sized to dissipate total losses inside the house with a reasonable rise in air temperature. When air flow is sufficient for heat dissipation, house back pressure will take care of itself. Furthermore, the main heat losses that must be dissipated into the ventilating air are the electrical losses. Mechanical equipment is not 100% efficient, but a much greater proportion of the mechanical heat losses are conducted into the frame and dissipated through it, with minimal assistance from the vent air.

In adapting the ventilation system to high altitudes, pulley ratios may have to be changed to speed up belted fans. Fan-driving motor horsepower may have to be increased. In extreme cases, more fans may be required. Most machines use some form of air filtration equipment, which must be sized for the increased air flow.

The altitude-ambient temperature specification is also passed along to the electrical vendor. The dc mill motors used in excavators have Class H insulation, the highest temperature rating among all classes of insulation in common usage. Hence, the use of higher capacity blowers is the usual solution to the altitude problem for such motors.

Table 1—Elevations and ambient temperatures at selected locations

	Elevation (ft)	Maximum temperature (°F)*		
		1%	2½%	5%
Arizona				
Flagstaff	6,993	84	82	80
Fort Huachuca	4,664	95	93	91
Prescott	5,014	96	94	91
Winslow	4,880	97	95	92
Colorado				
Colorado Springs	6,173	90	88	86
Denver	5,283	92	90	89
Grand Junction	4,849	96	94	92
La Jonta	4,188	97	95	93
Pueblo	4,639	96	94	92
Trinidad	5,746	93	91	89
Idaho				
Idaho Falls	4,730	91	88	85
Pocatello	4,444	94	91	88
Twin Falls	4,148	96	94	91
Montana				
Billings	3,567	94	91	88
Butte	5,526	86	83	80
Livingston	4,653	91	88	85
Nevada				
Ely	6,257	90	88	86
Reno	4,404	95	92	90
Tonopah	5,426	95	92	90
New Mexico				
Almagardo	4,070	100	98	96
Albuquerque	5,310	96	94	92
Farmington	5,495	95	93	91
Santa Fe	7,045	90	88	85
Utah				
Cedar City	5,613	94	91	89
Milford	5,028	97	94	91
Salt Lake City	4,220	97	94	92
Wyoming				
Casper	5,319	92	90	87
Cheyenne	6,126	89	86	83
Laramie	7,266	82	80	77
Rock Springs	6,741	86	84	82
Sheridan	3,942	95	92	89

Source: ASHRAE.
*Column headings indicate, on average, the percentages of summer hours during which the stated temperatures are exceeded.

Certain vendors supply some sizes of mill motors with oversize blowers as standard equipment. For example, to facilitate standardized manufacture, the electrical vendor may use a motor-blower combination that can be operated at either 50 or 60 Hz. At the 50-Hz speed, the blower will cool the mill motor properly for standard altitude and ambient temperature. At the higher 60-Hz speed, the blower will move about 20% more air, making it suitable for an altitude above 3,300 ft or for above-normal ambient temperature. This practice is not uniform for all motor sizes from any of the electrical vendors and is not uniform among equipment vendors.

The situation for dc generators is different than that for motors. The generators are self-ventilated, being cooled by the air circulated by the inherent fan action of the arma-

Dispersing heat to cool excavators at high altitude is one problem that must be solved for successful shovel operation.

ture. The generator insulation is usually Class B or F, or possibly a mixture of the two. Furthermore, the thermal loading of the generator may not fully use the allowable temperature rise for the insulation. Therefore, each application should be studied individually. The price increase, if any, will be for upgrading the insulation temperature rating class.

As is the case with dc motors, the policies of the two largest generator suppliers in the US are not identical.

The situation for motor generator (MG) set driving motors is similar to that for dc generators. If changes are necessary because of altitude or high ambient temperature, they are made in the class of insulation. MG set driving motors are chosen on the basis of the maximum torque required. When the torque requirement is satisfied, the motor will, from a thermal loading standpoint, nearly always be oversize.

The voltage class of the MG set driving motor insulation is also checked against the altitude spec. One electrical vendor uses this general rule: on machines of 4,160 v and above, insulation voltage class is raised one level when the altitude is over 5,500 ft, and two voltage levels when the altitude is above 9,900 ft. This rule is approximate and does not apply to all vendors.

The margins for standard high voltage wiring insulation and collector ring insulation are usually great enough to make special design unnecessary up to an altitude of 10,000 ft and possibly higher.

Air compressor capacity is rarely a problem in new machines, which usually use multistage compressors. The compression ratio of the initial stage is relatively low, and output is affected little by elevation. Also, air compressors are sized to make continuous operation unnecessary, and the effects of high altitude are easily offset by a small increase in compressor operating time.

High-altitude, low-humidity brushes may be required. In many cases, the high altitude environment is also one of low humidity, which can have an adverse effect on the formation of a proper and durable film on the commutators. In this case, high altitude brushes are included in the initial complement when the machines are shipped.

Equipment performance characterized by 'fan laws'

The performance requirements for new excavators also apply when adapting used machines for high altitude operation. However, since the alteration of the unit—or at least the planning to determine feasibility—is likely to be a do-it-yourself procedure, additional information is useful.

The fundamental premise of the ventilation heat-dissipation calculations is that for equal temperature increases, the weight of air that must be pumped through the excavator house and through the motors is the same at high altitude as at low altitude. But since the air is less dense at higher elevations, more volume is pumped—meaning greater resistance to flow, higher fan pressure, and higher horsepower.

One statistic easy to remember is that at 8,000 ft, air has only about three-quarters the density it has at sea level; hence, four-thirds the volume of air is required to produce the same cooling. The density of air at various altitudes is shown in Table 2.

The fans that produce the house ventilation are either centrifugal or propeller-type. The motor blowers are always the centrifugal type. Performance of these devices can be characterized by a few simple relationships (fan laws):

For conditions of constant air density and variable speed,

1) Fan volume varies directly with fan speed.
2) Fan pressure varies with the square of fan speed.
3) Fan horsepower varies with the cube of fan speed.

For conditions of variable air density and constant speed,

4) Fan volume is independent of density.
5) Fan pressure varies directly with density.
6) Fan horsepower varies directly with density.

7) The back pressure produced by the aerodynamic load varies as the square of the volume and directly with

Table 2—Air density ratios at various altitudes and air temperatures

Altitude (ft)	Density ratios		
	-20°F	70°F	100°F
0	1.204	1.000*	0.946
3,300	1.07	0.886	0.839
4,000	1.04	0.864	0.818
5,000	1.00	0.832	0.787
6,000	0.965	0.801	0.758
7,000	0.930	0.772	0.730
8,000	0.895	0.743	0.703
9,000	0.860	0.714	0.676
10,000	0.828	0.688	0.651

*"Standard air" for the fan industry is air at sea level, 29.92 in. of mercury barometric pressure, and 70°F. It has a density of 0.075 lb per cu ft.

air density.

As one illustration, suppose that a machine that has been operating satisfactorily in southern Illinois at a few hundred feet above sea level is being considered for duty in a western coal field at an elevation of 8,000 ft. (For simplification, the difference in ambient temperature will be ignored in this example.)

The air density at 8,000 ft is about three-quarters of the air density in Illinois. To pump the same weight of air through the machine, the fans must handle four-thirds the volume of air. The pressure at the output of the fan must rise to $(4/3)^2$ the present pressure.

Fan Law No. 1 (volume varies directly with speed) dictates that the fan speed must be increased by one-third. If the fan is driven by a V-belt, the speed change can be accomplished with a change in pulley ratio. The impeller must be mechanically suitable for the higher speed. Suitability can be checked through the supplier or possibly by using a fan catalog. If the fan is directly connected, a new fan or an additional fan, if it is part of a group, will likely be required. Sometimes, propeller fans may be adapted to a higher altitude by purchasing a propeller having a different pitch and/or more blades.

Fan pressure rises to $(4/3)^2$ the original pressure because of the increase in speed, but this higher pressure is reduced to three-quarters of the value at the higher speed by the lower density (Law No. 5). The net result of these two effects is that the fan output pressure rises by the ratio 4:3. This is precisely the way the aerodynamic load reacts (Law No. 7); therefore, the problem of matching the fan to the load may be disregarded, at least for reasonable departures from the old operating conditions.

The fan thus runs at four-thirds speed to pump four-thirds the volume of air, which has a density of three-quarters normal. Fan Law No. 3 states that horsepower increases in the ratio of $(4/3)^3$, but Fan Law No. 6 states that horsepower (for a given speed) changes as density, which is three-quarters normal. The net result is that the required horsepower will increase in the ratio of $(4/3)^2$ or 178% of the low altitude horsepower.

Table 2 gives density ratios for three temperatures: $-20°F$, $70°F$, and $100°F$. The density variation over this temperature range is about 20%. A rigorous calculation of fan speed and horsepower would use the ratios of lower density for the higher temperature to calculate speed and the ratios of higher density at lower temperature to check horsepower. This procedure would ensure adequate ventilation on hot days and proper horsepower for operation in cold weather.

If fan speed is to be increased by changing pulley ratios, there is a possibility that the same motor can be used at higher altitudes. It is suggested that the motor load be estimated from electrical input measurements under the low altitude conditions to determine what horsepower is actually used. While the fan in the example would probably not be sufficiently over-motored to allow continued use of the same motor at the higher altitude, the use of the same motor might be possible when the change in altitude is less drastic.

The foregoing example purposely neglected the probable difference in maximum ambient temperature between the mine in southern Illinois and the mine in the West. If it is desired to take advantage of this difference, a convenient rule of thumb is that each change of $1°F$ is equal to 250 ft in elevation. This rule is not precise but is conservative and convenient. An accurate calculation would require data on the rise of air temperature through each electrical machine—information that is often not readily available.

Table 3—Correcting factors for determining actual compressor capacity at various altitudes

(based on 7% cylinder clearance)

Altitude (ft)	Gauge pressure (psi)					
	25	40	60	80	100	125
0	1.0	1.0	1.0	1.0	1.0	1.0
2,000	0.992	0.987	0.984	0.977	0.972	0.962
4,000	0.982	0.974	0.963	0.953	0.942	0.923
6,000	0.972	0.961	0.945	0.928	0.908	*
8,000	0.962	0.945	0.925	0.900	0.873	*
10,000	0.951	0.931	0.902	0.872	0.840	*
12,000	0.938	0.914	0.878	0.839	*	*

How to use the table: For a single stage compressor, multiply the sea level capacity by the correction factor to obtain actual capacity at the altitude and discharge pressure desired. For a multistage compressor, the factor that applies to the lowest pressure stage determines output.

Source: *Compressed Air Data Handbook*, Ingersoll-Rand.
*With 7% clearance, the compression ratio is 14.3. At these altitudes, the output will be quite small.

Air filtration equipment

Many machines are equipped for filtration of ventilating air. At higher flows, the pressure drop of the filters rises in accordance with the fan laws stated previously. The cleaning efficiency of centrifugal filters will rise, but probably only slightly, at higher cfm rates. The cleaning efficiency of impingement-type filters may be reduced. If the air flow change is large, it would be wise to consult the filter supplier or a filter catalog.

The ability of a used MG set to operate at a higher elevation should be checked by the excavator builder and the electrical supplier. When the problem is referred to them, specify that only their best judgment is desired—not a guarantee of performance. For an old machine, the warranty responsibility of the electrical vendor has long since expired. If asked to accept this risk a second time—for no additional compensation—the vendor is likely to give the operator a very conservative judgment.

If the new application is marginal, but only slightly so, air-in, air-out temperature measurements can be useful. The type of digging required of an excavator may not necessarily load all motions to the nameplate horsepower. If possible, measurements of load demands should be made at the excavator's new location. This will preclude making the fix (the alterations to adapt it to a new altitude) during the move.

If MG set heating is a problem, it may help to:

- Direct more house ventilating air to the MG set through revised arrangement of baffles and/or exhaust louvers.
- Remove any covers that restrict ventilation; enlarge openings if practical.
- Add some supplemental fans blowing directly on the hot generators.
- Rewind with higher temperature insulation.

The loss of capacity to be expected of an air compressor at increasing altitude is shown in Table 3. If compressors are multistage, chances are there will be no problem.

Experimentation may also be required to determine the brush grade for best commutation at the new location. If in doubt, the operator must assume that high altitude brushes will be needed. □

New shovel targeted at improving economics of overburden removal

A LARGE ELECTRIC STRIPPING SHOVEL MOUNTED ON TWO crawlers is being developed at Harnischfeger Corp. in Milwaukee. The new Model 5700 stripping shovel has 90-ft booms and a 60-ft dipper handle carrying a 25-cu-yd dipper. In time, a short-coupled version of the machine will be offered, carrying a 40- to 50-cu-yd dipper for heavy duty digging. The extended working range of the shovel is expected to improve the economics of stripping operations, Harnischfeger states.

The new shovel will feature a "Power Band" crowd drive, joystick controls, bogie-mounted lower rollers, independent propel for each track, "Electrotorque" static power conversion, and fully automatic lubrication—all to be sold as standard equipment.

Crowd drive is achieved through a drive belt of multiple V's having a common back to prevent belt turnover under shock loads and quick reversal. The completely enclosed belt will be easily tensioned for lasting adjustment, according to Harnischfeger. Crowd transmission gearing will run in an oil-tight gear case welded integrally with the boom. The high-alloy-steel splined shipper shaft will ride on sleeve bearings.

Harnischfeger's Electrotorque controls will convert incoming ac power to dc without rotating machinery and will supply and regulate power to shovel drive motors without any rotating electrical equipment. Heart of the system is the thyristor, which makes the conversion from ac to dc.

Digging cycles will be fast, smooth, and less tiring, Harnischfeger claims, because the reliable, light-touch, fast-response solid state control will facilitate coordination of all shovel operations. Hoist, swing, crowd, and dipper trip will be joystick controlled, while brakes for hoist/crowd, swing, and propel will be pushbutton activated.

The centralized, completely automatic lubrication system will furnish vital moving parts with a timed, measured supply of oil or lubricant—a feature that is expected to extend service life of major components and greatly reduce maintenance time and costs. Two separate timing arrangements are incorporated, adjustable to individual pit requirements.

The 72-in. crawler shoes will have an extra-heavy roller section, and the 16 heavy-duty forged steel rollers will be bogie-mounted for smooth travel, maximum stability, and long life. Rugged crawler frames will be mounted on a full-length shear ledge to absorb and resist jolting, twisting, and abrasion.

In the steering system, two propel motors will drive independent propel transmissions to provide differential motor speed to each track for simultaneous steer and propel.

The heavy duty carbody will be made of quenched and tempered high-strength, low-alloy steel welded automatically to assure uniform strength.

Fast response dc motors with heavy duty blowers will power four swing transmissions, and a spring-set, air-released brake will be mounted on each motor shaft. The spur-type swing gears will be force lubricated.

Permanently lubricated tapered rollers riding on heavy-forged track will comprise the roller circle. □

The 90-ft boom of the Model 5700, constructed of quenched and tempered high strength steel, will be welded into a solid-bond, multiple-box girder unit for structural strength without excess weight. The straddle-mounted, 60-ft dipper handle will be simple and sturdy, with dipper sticks widely spaced to hold the dipper squarely in the bank, Harnischfeger states.

Cat rolls out the world's largest crawler tractor

A RADICALLY NEW CRAWLER TRACTOR—much larger and more productive than is now offered—will be manufactured by Caterpillar Tractor Co. in the first quarter of 1978. The 700-hp D10, a new design, is said to be at least 50% more productive than the D9 tractor, the company's next largest model. The D10 machine will be used mainly for dozing, ripping, and push-loading in large-scale mining and mine reclamation.

In tests conducted at a uranium mine, one D10 push-loaded 505 scrapers in one shift. The previous high of 480 scrapers loaded was set by two D9 tractors, with a greater total horsepower, working in tandem.

The most obvious physical difference from other crawler tractors is the elevation of the drive sprockets above the track roller frames of the D10. Since the drive sprockets are not used to help support the D10, components are protected from shock loads. A resilient new undercarriage design cushions the ride and increases the traction.

The D10 is powered by the 700-fwhp D348 engine, a 60° V-12, with double-overhead camshafts, turbocharging and aftercooling for high horsepower, excellent low-speed response, and good lugging ability.

Extra weight was necessary to allow the machine to apply its horsepower effectively. The case and main frame are a heavy-duty welded structure consisting of a cross member at the front to assure rigidity, fabricated box section side members, and a high strength steel casting for the drive case at the rear. All gear centers are self-contained in the power train modules. The D10 power train sits low in the frame—a low center of gravity providing good stability.

Further productivity gains are achieved also by mounting the tools as close as possible to the machine. For the bulldozer blade, a simple tag link arrangement for lateral stability was invented. This device replaces the sliding center ball and diagonal braces in the company's present tractor designs. The tag link allows the dozer blade to be located closer to the D10, which gives the operator a better view of his blade load and improves the machine balance, dozing control, and maneuverability. More direct down pressure is applied to the blade because the lift cylinder attaches at a more nearly vertical angle.

The D10 ripper can penetrate and rip rock of high seismic velocities. The ripper is attached directly to the main frame by 4-in.-dia pins, enabling ripper loads to be transmitted directly to the tractor main frame and eliminating the problems of bolted joints on an otherwise conventionally mounted machine.

Modular design of major components offers faster, more efficient servicing of the machine in the field and facilitates repair and replacement of components. The D10 has six power train modules—engine, torque divider, bevel and pinion gear, transmission, steering clutches and brakes, and final drives. Each can be replaced quickly in the field. Removal of final drives, for example, takes only about 2 man-hours. The complete transmission and bevel gear module can be removed as a package in about 2.5 man-hours.

There are only 13 grease fittings on the whole D10 machine—one on the dozer tilt brace and 12 on the ripper—reducing the time and expense of lubrication. One SAE 30 oil is used for the engine, transmission, steering clutches, brakes, and final drives—simplifying maintenance and lube inventories and eliminating the cost of a special gear lubricant in the final drives.

For more information, write to Caterpillar Tractor Co., c/o Grover Halter, 100 NE Adams, Peoria, Ill. 61629. □

Weighing more than 90 tons, the D10 measures 15 ft tall and is 31 ft long with the bulldozer and ripper installed.

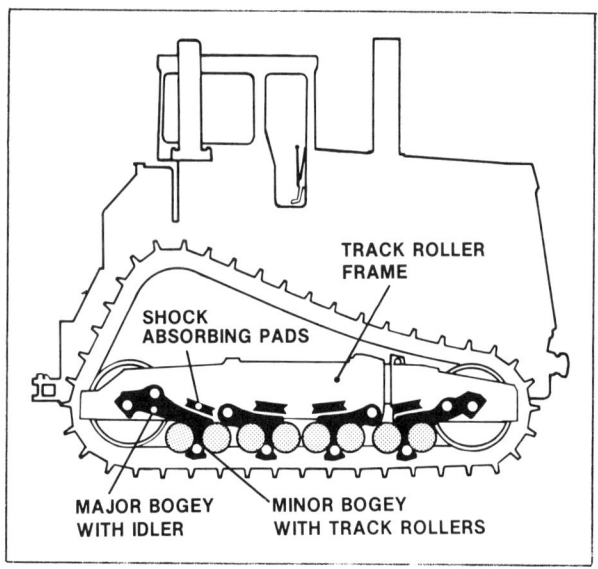

Oscillating major and minor bogeys are attached to the track roller frame, with travel limited by rubber pads.

New conveyor drive with feedback circuit: soft starts for loaded mine belts

A NEW CONVEYOR BELT DRIVE SYSTEM that provides "soft start ups" through controlled acceleration has been developed by Synchrotorque, a division of Philadelphia Gear Corp. The "Synchrodrive" variable speed drive uses a set of oil-immersed clutch discs that are squeezed together at precise pressures through a feedback system to impart smooth acceleration to both heavily loaded and completely empty conveyors. Without a speed and acceleration control system that modulates motor output, conveyors can easily be overstrained, resulting in damaged lacing or belt snapping, the manufacturer points out.

The new drive can also be coupled easily to a set of flywheels to provide coasting capabilities, thus preventing possible belt damage when a conveyor is stopped quickly by a power failure or an emergency. In addition, the Synchrodrive's controller is substantially smaller than typical rheostat controllers, and the motor used with the drive is less complex than standard motors.

"A conventional way to start heavily loaded conveyors is to use a wound-rotor motor, typically controlled by a liquid rheostat," says John Liu, manager of Synchrotorque. "Such rheostats occupy at least a 5-ft square, and are 4 to 5 ft high. This is approximately 100 times the cubic space that a Synchrodrive controller takes. A wound-rotor motor is also considerably more complex than the simple squirrel-cage motor used with a Synchrodrive—it has slip rings, while the squirrel-cage does not." Liu also states that a Synchrodrive is lower in initial cost than other drives, and its controller makes starting procedures fully automatic. "In wound-rotor installations, the operator usually has to cut in various resistors to pick up the belt speed, and this can create a problem because of the human element," Liu says.

How the Synchrodrive works

The key component in a Synchrodrive unit is its "disc pack"—two sets of discs interspersed with each other (see simplified schematic). One set is attached to the input (driven by the motor), and the other is attached to the output (coupled to the load). Both disc sets ride on splines so that they can be shifted axially and clamped together to transmit torque from the input to the output.

The torque, however, is *not* transmitted by contact friction between the two sets of discs, as is the case with a friction clutch. Instead, oil is continuously passed between the surfaces of the discs, which are grooved and contain oil pockets. It is these oil films that actually transmit the torque when combined with the hydraulically-supplied clamping force that squeezes the disc sets together.

An increase in the clamping force increases the oil film's resistance to shear, thus raising the output speed. This "hydroviscous" principle is used in Synchrodrives to produce controlled variable output speed in motors with capacities up to 20,000 hp running at 3,600 rpm.

To control drive output, the operator initially sets the desired speed setpoint and acceleration time, after which the process is automatic when the controller is turned on. The Synchrodrive uses an electric-hydraulic control system that responds to the command signal linearly through a

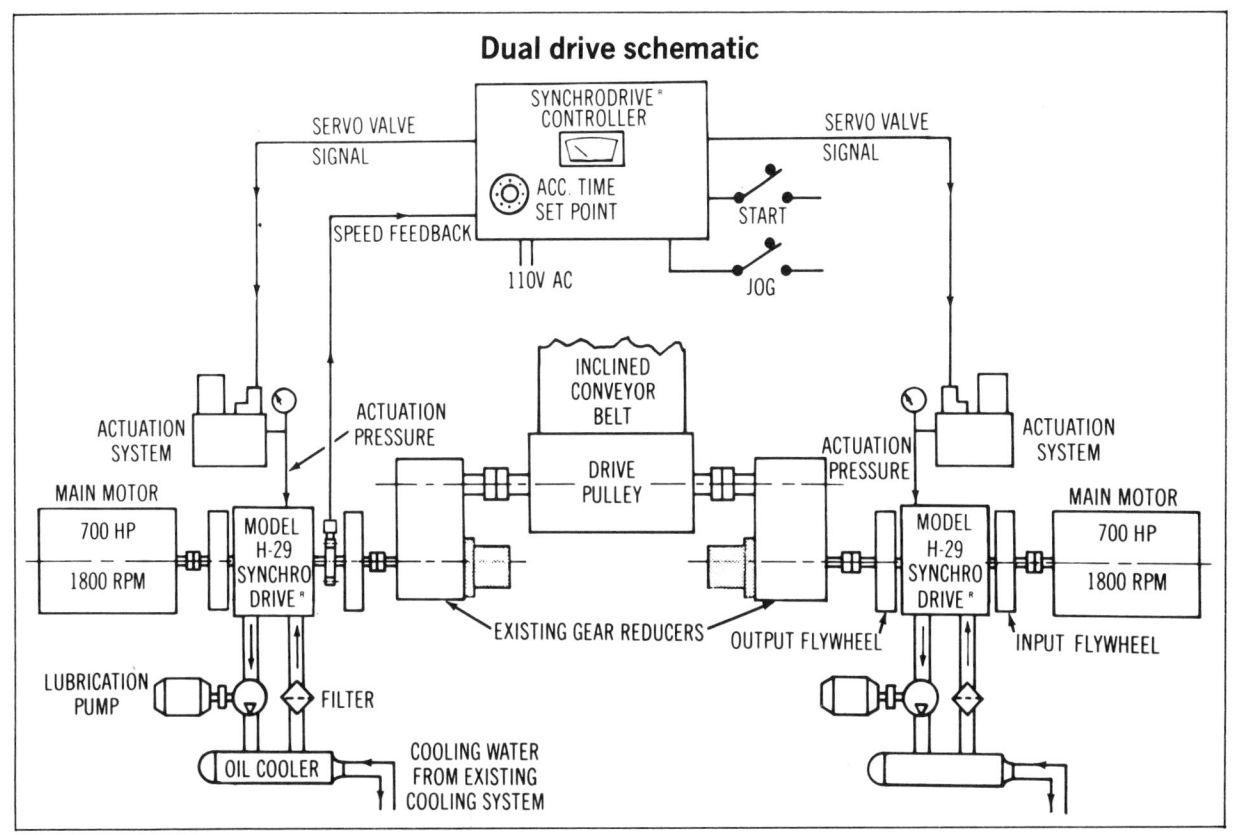

Dual drive schematic

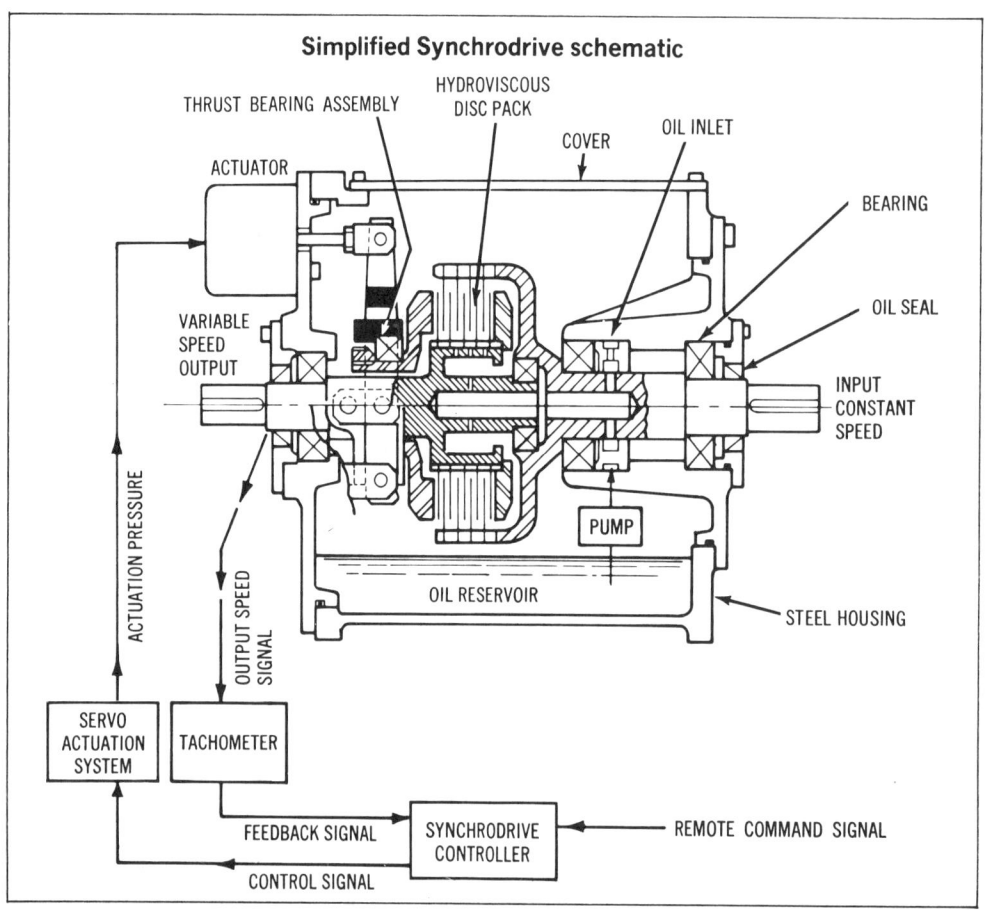

Simplified Synchrodrive schematic

speed feedback mechanism. A comparator circuit in the controller measures the difference between the setpoint and the actual output speed, then feeds back an error signal to a high-gain amplifier.

The amplifier output energizes a servo valve, which in turn establishes a proportional hydraulic actuation pressure. This pressure operates the clamping piston that varies the force on the disc pack. As the driven load increases or decreases in speed, the speed feedback signal goes through the loop, then stabilizes at the set point.

This modulation may seem to be a lengthy process, but the response time is actually extremely fast. Full torque modulation usually occurs within 50 milliseconds, even for units in the 10,000- to 20,000-hp range. There is, of course, slippage between the driving and driven discs when a Synchrodrive is producing a reduced output speed; however, there is no metal-to-metal contact during the slippage because of the oil film, and wear is negligible.

The servo control system is available in both a simple, highly responsive, hydropneumatic version and an electronic version. The latter includes an electronic box using either dc or digital-tachometer feedback signals.

Two Synchrodrives were recently installed on a conveyor system used to haul copper ore from a large mine to a crushing station. Each drive is coupled to a 700-hp motor on either side of the head pulley, and drives the belt through gear reducers (see dual drive schematic). The Synchrodrives at this installation are designed to lock up automatically in the event of a power failure—the clamping mechanism locks all the discs solidly together so that the input rotates with the output on a one-to-one basis. If such a lockup occurs, a flywheel coupled to the drive output will keep the conveyor going for about 100 ft, to avoid an abrupt stop that might overstrain the belt. □

Synchrodrives, coupled to a loader, are set up on a testing stand, where their ability to control acceleration is checked.

Pena Colorada development includes 30-mi slurry pipeline

Pena Colorada is investing $52 million in the first stage of its project, which includes development of the mine, a 2.5 million-mtpy magnetic separation plant, and a 4,545-mtpd pellet plant (1.5 million mtpy based on 330 days per year operating time). Concentrates will be transported in slurry form through an 8-in.-dia steel pipe to the pellet plant, located about 30 mi from the mine site, on the coast near the port of Manzanillo. Production startup was scheduled for fourth-quarter 1974.

The deposits, located on a mountain top at an elevation of 3,000-3,600 ft, consist of ore with virtually no overburden. The mine is being exploited via conventional open-pit methods, including rotary and track drilling, and truck haulage of ore.

Average ore grade at Pena Colorada is about 47%, but may vary from 20% to 30% in places. The ore, mostly magnetite, with some hematite near the surface, will be blended to achieve the desired grade of concentrates (67-68%) for the pellet plant. Ore-to-waste ratio is about 1:0.05.

Lurgi Chemie und Huttentechnik GmbH designed the precrushing, milling, concentrating, filtering, and pelletizing plants. Coarse ore, up to 32 in. in diameter, is crushed to a maximum size of 10 in. by an Allis-Chalmers gyratory crusher, then ground to 1 mm via autogenous grinding.

In the event that Pena Colorada decides to use a grinding medium in the future, the medium may be hematite from the mine. This would serve a dual purpose, since the company could also recover the 4% magnetite contained in the hematite.

Pulp discharged from the mill is collected in a sump, where repulping water is added to make a solids content of about 40%. Two slurry pumps, double-stage machines designed to operate concurrently, move material to a pump distributor which sends it to four magnetic separators.

Preconcentrate (iron content of about 60%) is mixed with the discharge from the ball mill, classified by two cyclone groups (coarse material is fed to the ball mill), then distributed to eight finisher magnetic separators. These units are double stage and designed for countercurrent operation. The final concentrate is sent on to a 200-ft-dia Dorr Oliver cable torque thickener where solids content is increased to about 50-60% by weight at minus 325 mesh—suitable for pipeline transmission.

Tailings slurry from the primary and secondary magnetic separators goes to a primary tailings thickener for elimination of coarse tailings, then to a large secondary thickener, which also takes overflow from the concentrate thickener.

Since there is a drop in elevation of more than 3,200 ft over the 30-mi length of the Bechtel-designed pipeline, the slurry moves by gravity flow. The only pump is positioned in a testing loop, where it controls the condition of the slurry. Normex SA, of Monterrey, was responsible for construction of the pipeline.

At the agglomerator on the coast, slurry is filtered through Eimco disk filters, mixed with bentonite in a Loedige-type mixer, and fed to the balling units. Three 25-ft-dia pelletizing disks are employed.

Green pellets are heat-hardened in a Lurgi traveling grate system which is oil fired. Pellets of 67-68% iron will then be shipped by rail to the various partners. □

'**Big red rock,**' the literal translation of Pena Colorada, where proven reserves of 107 million mt averaging 47% iron will be mined. Ore, mostly magnetite, with virtually no overburden, will be blended to achieve a 67-68% concentrate for the pellet plant.

Polybutylene: for piping corrosive slurries

USING POLYBUTYLENE PIPE to transport gypsum slurry is paying off at Mobil Chemical Co.'s diammonium phosphate plant at Depue, Ill. The plastic material, for which basic technology was originated by Mobil, has been developed and commercialized by Witco Chemical Corp. Witco recently installed a ½-mi pipeline made of polybutylene resin to transport abrasive, corrosive gypsum slurry to settling ponds at Mobil's Depue plant. Plant capacity for pumping slurry and process water has increased from 7,000 to 9,500 gpm, and interior walls of the polybutylene pipe remain smooth, with minimum scale buildup, according to plant production manager, Dave Thomas.

In addition to resisting severe chemical attack, polybutylene is also resistant to stress cracking, creep under load, and widely varying weather conditions, according to Witco, making the material suitable for large-diameter pipe designs. Its coilability and light weight are also attractive, Witco notes.

The pipeline at the Mobil plant is 14-in.-OD with 1-in. wall thickness, installed in 52-ft sections, each section weighing 600 lb. The sections were joined by butting the ends together and fusing them with portable electric buttwelding equipment. The pipe now lies in a shallow trench, uncovered, with the only support being on the pipe bridge from the plant to the slope behind it.

Witco, now completing a 50 million-lb polybutylene

Polybutylene pipe in 52-ft sections is installed without covering and is supported only at entrance to Mobil plant.

manufacturing plant at Taft, La., expects to take and maintain the lead in commercialization of this material using the company's marketing know-how and Witco-Mobil technology. Witco is currently producing polybutylene at a semi-works facility in Beaumont, Tex.

Trucks are key transport at most open-pit mines

OPEN-PIT TRANSPORT OF ORE AND WASTE is handled largely by truck haulage, and this single item often represents one-half of all mining costs. The rapid inflation of equipment and parts costs, combined with the tripling of fuel prices, has forced open-pit operators to pinpoint areas for cost savings in fuel consumption, tire wear, and engine performance. Operators now periodically review the advisability of changing truck haulage systems or replacing sections of the haul with other transport modes, such as conveyors or slurry pumping.

For many, if not most mines, truck haulage remains the only practical method of transport. These mines may have short hauls, numerous working faces, great depths, or ore blending requirements that demand truck haulage. However, high fuel prices, shortages, extensive and frequent maintenance, high tire costs, and high labor requirements for trucks are prompting operators to search for more eco-

nomical forms of transport—even if limited to one section of the total transport profile. This search could slow the trend of the past several decades toward ever-increasing truck haulage capacities.

The 35-ton to 85-ton trucks offer the simplicity of two axles, commonly mechanically driven from the rear axle. Exceptions are Mack, which offers three-axle tandem drive, and International, which offers a two-axle, all-wheel-drive truck. Trucks in this size range are powered by diesel engines with power-shift transmissions and torque converters. Fluid torque retarder braking systems are incorporated in most models.

The break-even point for the electric wheel drive is above the 85-ton level, unless 85-ton trucks are to be used in a deep pit with excessive grades (+12%). Unit Rig's Model M-85 is the smallest electric wheel drive.

For trucks up to 85- or 100-ton capacity, high speed die-

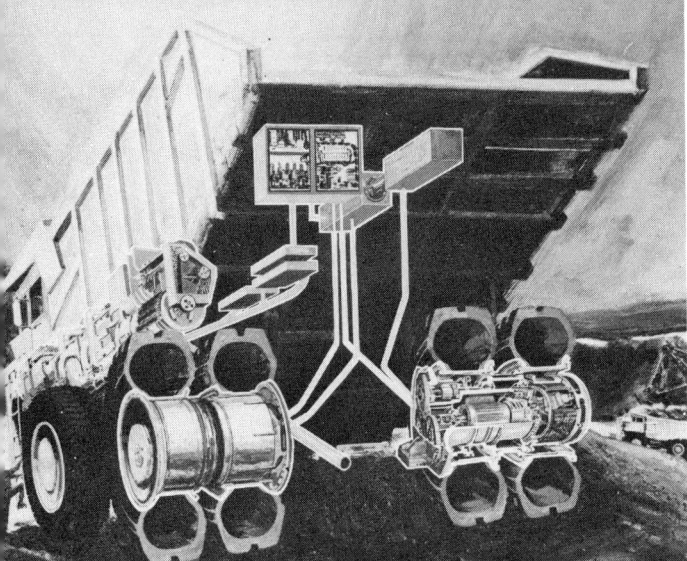

More than 2,700 vehicles at over 120 open-pit mines worldwide use General Electric's motorized wheel drive system, introduced in 1963. This technological breakthrough opened the way for giant haulage trucks of more than 100-ton capacity.

sel engines manufactured by General Motors' Detroit Diesel Allison Div., Caterpillar Tractor Co., and Cummins Engine Co. lead the field. Detroit Diesel manufactures the only two-cycle engine. Proponents of the two-cycle engine point to the lower first cost and superior acceleration. Those in favor of the four-cycle engine, including Caterpillar and Cummins, cite lower fuel consumption at less than peak loads. Furthermore, use of four cycles reduces engine heat buildup and overall maintenance. Four-cycle engines also operate efficiently on lower grade fuels.

Detroit Diesel high speed engines range from 475 hp to 1,600 hp, Caterpillar engines from 425 hp to 1,200 hp, and Cummins engines from 335 to 1,600 hp. Most engines are turbocharged and either aftercooled or intercooled.

Fully automatic power-shift transmissions are standard in all trucks up to 100-ton capacity. The transmission generally consists of a torque converter and hydraulic, clutch-operated planetary gear sets that can be shifted up or down at proper speed under full power. The final drive is reached through mechanical linkages through the drive shaft to differential and final-drive planetary sun gears. The alternative of manual transmission with torque converter is used only at operations where the haulage road profile requires few shifts in gear. Major manufacturers of transmissions include Allison (GM), Clark Equipment Co., Twin Disc Inc., and Fuller Co. In addition, both International Harvester and Caterpillar manufacture transmissions for their own trucks.

Some of the recent points of concern in designing rear-dump trucks with capacities between 35 and 85 tons are covered in an article by R. D. Pugh,[1] manager of sales engineering for Euclid Inc., subsidiary of White Motor Corp. Design parameters for the new Euclid R-50 included an overall guideline of simplicity, with remote-mount transmission, load height not to exceed 11½ ft, soft suspension, improved cab visibility, low net weight, ⅓:⅔ weight distribution over front and rear axles, easy accessibility for servicing major components, strong braking and retarding capability, improved maneuverability, and stronger body. The melding of these objectives was not a simple matter, and in some cases adjustments had to be made between conflicting solutions. Significantly, tandem axles, twin engines, and similar compromises were avoided because "today's technology offers power trains of proven reliability."

The design criteria were largely met. Stiffeners were used to increase the strength of side panels and floor. Loading height criteria were met by using space between frame rails and rubber discs improved suspension. A short 165-in. wheel base allowed for a lighter, more durable frame. Maximum retarder horsepower was increased from 705 to 900, and total braking force was improved to 37.4% of the total gross vehicle weight. Many of these improvements grew out of experience with previous models and the proposals of fleet owners.

Capacities now range up to 350 tons

There are few points of comparison between trucks under 100-ton capacity and those over this mark—now up to 350 tons with the introduction of the Terex 33-19 off-highway rear-dump hauler. A prototype of the 33-19 has been operating at Kaiser Steel's Eagle Mountain iron mine in California since January 1975. Low speed diesel engines, the motorized wheel, and giant tires are the salient characteristics of the giant haulers, which cost up to $1 million apiece.

With such a large capital investment, these trucks tend to be designed for specific applications at the purchaser's mine. Computer programs provide the mine designer/purchaser with the best potential combination of haul profile, truck fleet, and loaders. (A thorough discussion of off-highway mine trucks is provided in a series of articles by Alan Burton.[2])

Simplicity is emphasized in all the latest designs for giant rear-dump trucks. The Euclid R-170, with a wheel base of 18½ ft, has a low center of gravity and a loading height of only 17 ft 5 in. All major components are easily accessible. The power-train module (engine, alternator, blower, fan, and radiator) rolls out as a unit for ease in servicing. The braking system includes air/oil front brakes and discs in the rear; both front and rear are dual systems, and there is an extra inboard disc on each wheel motor for emergency braking. The truck's suspension system utilizes energy-absorbing, compressible fluid ride struts.

The 350-ton Terex 33-19 is the largest off-highway rear-dump truck in the world. It is likely to remain the largest for some time to come. Total tonnage when fully loaded is over 600 tons. The power source is a 3,300-hp GM diesel locomotive engine driving an electric alternator that powers four electric traction motors mounted within the truck's rear wheels. The 33-19 is over 25 ft wide, is 67 ft long, and travels on ten 40.00-57 tires with a nominal load-carrying capacity of 111,120 lb per tire at 70 psi and 30 mph. The truck features automatic rear-axle steering. To provide the

Euclid's R-170 was introduced in 1975. Loading height of the 170-ton truck is 17 ft 5 in. Cab location allows good vision.

E/MJ surveys open-pit trucks

In 1974, E/MJ conducted a market survey of off-highway haulage truck usage at metal and nonmetallic mining properties in the US and Canada. Altogether, 704 metal and nonmetallic mining locations in the US and Canada were contacted by a mail questionnaire, and 158 usable questionnaires were returned, representing a response of 22.4%. Of the total usable replies, 65 were from open-pit operations producing more than 1 million tpy of ore, and of these, nearly 50% produced 25,000 tpd (all material moved) or less, while 20% moved more than 100,000 tpd of ore and waste.

The operators reported a total of 1,561 trucks in the field, 68% of them manufactured by Unit Rig, Wabco, and Euclid. The other manufacturers listed, in order of usage, were K. W. Dart, Caterpillar, Terex, Mack, and International Harvester.

Of the trucks, 22.4% had a payload of 45 tons or less, 66.2% fell in the 45- to 100-ton range, 17% were in the 100- to 150-ton range, and only 5.4% had capacities over 150 tons. At the time of the survey, only 11% of the trucks were less than one year old, more than 50% were over four years old, and 14% were more than 10 years old.

Some 90% of the trucks were two-axle, and over 97% were rear-dump. Trucks with heated bodies were reported by 44% of US and 88% of the Canadian respondents. Fully 70% of the operations used body liners/bars in the trucks.

At the mining operations, average haul lengths were relatively short: 45% were less than 2 mi, while some 37% were between 2 and 4 mi. Slope length for the haul was less than ½ mi for 33% of the operations, ½ to 1 mi for 40%, and 1 to 2 mi for 16%. For grades against the load, 36% ranged between 8% and 9%, while 26% of the grades were 10% or greater.

As for physical availability, the fleets showed 21% of the trucks available 60% to 69% of the time, 35% of the trucks available 70% to 79% of the time, and nearly 37% of the trucks available over 80% of the time. Truck downtime for tire problems accounted for less than 9% of total downtime, but tire repair, maintenance, and replacement represented 28% of all maintenance costs for the trucks. Downtime for engine repairs represented 17% of total downtime, but engine repair costs represented only 18% of maintenance costs. "Other" items were responsible for over 70% of total truck downtime and over 50% of repair and maintenance costs.

Average hourly operating costs (maintenance, tires, and fuel, but excluding labor) for 50% of the operations was $10 to $20, while 13% reported $20 to $25, and 18% reported costs exceeding $25. Costs have undoubtedly risen drastically, particularly for fuel, since the questionnaire was posed.

Engines preferred by the respondents, in order of favor, were GMC/Detroit Diesel, Caterpillar, and Cummins. Major complaints registered by the operators related to the cost and availability of spare parts and components, the complexities of design and construction, unavailability of technical services when needed, and a lack of uniformity of spares, even for the same model truck. Other complaints related to tire wear, braking systems, and interference with operator vision. In general, there was a desire for more sturdily built chassis and more reliable hydraulic systems.

---

rear axles with freedom of movement in the horizontal plane, there is a fixed bolster center for each rear axle in which a preloaded sphere can move up and down.

The steering angle at the rear axles is 5° (10° included between axles), and steering is "initiated by the amount and direction to which the front axle has been turned. The point at which the front axle initiates the rear steering mode is independently adjustable for RH and LH turns and can be tailored to mine operating conditions."[3]

The engine is a GM EMD 16-645-E4 driving an EMD AR 10-D14 alternator with built-in three-phase, full-wave rectification. The complete power plant and its accessories are enclosed in a hood that is pressurized with filtered air. The hood design allows for individual engine cylinder and liner replacement in all 16 positions. The complete engine and alternator can also be removed.

Electric wheels drive largest rigs

Unit Rig's Lectra Haul trucks pioneered use of diesel engines with electrically driven wheels, and the company has reaped the benefits by becoming the largest manufacturer in the field. More Lectra Hauls are used than all other makes combined, within its competitive range.

Recently, a driverless truck equipped with automatic control has been developed by Unit Rig. Programmed control covers steering, direction, truck separation, speed, braking, and stopping functions, including automatic stop in case of equipment malfunction. The driverless trucks will automatically track a guidewire with an accuracy of ±6 in. on a straightaway and ±18 in. on a curve. These trucks will start automatically in the direction commanded by a logic system in the master control unit, which instructs the truck to accelerate and maintain any one of seven discrete speed levels preprogrammed to match the haulage profile. Speed levels are adjustable to varying road conditions.

The master control unit commands dynamic retarding and/or friction braking to match the haul road profile and to bring the truck to a smooth stop without sliding. The control system also monitors oil pressure, water temperature, tire pressure, and other functions.

Wabco's 170-ton-capacity Haulpak truck is powered by a Detroit Diesel 16V-149TI engine at 1,600 hp. The drive system includes General Electric 776 motorized wheels and the GTA-15 alternator. The electric control system was improved by incorporating a Model FL114 excitation panel, which prevents momentary bogging of the engine and improves fuel economy by relating maximum fuel injection to the engine speed.

The Wabco power module is a removable unit consisting of engine, alternator, exciter, blower, and radiator. Brakes are air over oil—and, of course, dynamic retarding.

The electric wheel was the technological breakthrough that permitted the advent of trucks of 100-ton capacity and bigger—by eliminating the need for "expensive, complicated, and heavy mechanical transmissions, and permitting the traction drive motor to be mechanically independent of the prime mover."[2] Another benefit of the motorized wheel is dynamic braking; the traction drive motors are reversed to generators and the energy created is dissipated in heat.

The heart of the electric system combines a dc series motor with the appropriate mechanical hardware to supply propulsion and retarding power to the vehicle. The design uses the motor magnet frame as the wheel axle. Full engine horsepower is translated into effective rimpull. Power is supplied to the drive wheels through sun-geared planetaries, driven by the independent electric motors, generally mounted within the wheels. The commutator and brushes are located on the outboard end of the wheel rim for ready inspection. GE produces two basic motorized wheels, GE-772 and GE-776, which are combined with either an alternator or generator and control. In addition, GE has introduced a plug-in motor version of the GE-772 wheel—the GE-773 motor, which is used on front-end loaders and the large 210-ton-capacity trucks. The company offers a computer program to estimate such factors as operating temperatures on the various segments of a mine haulage road.

While GE dominates the electric wheel market, competition comes from Unit Rig, Wabco, and Westinghouse. Unit Rig's electric wheel, the W-100, uses a plug-in electric motor made by Reliance Electric Co. to power Lectra Hauls up to 200 tons. Wabco manufactures a wheel system for use on its trucks, although both Unit Rig and Wabco also offer GE electrical systems. The Wabco 150 CW features an all-Westinghouse drive system.

Pros and cons of the big haulers

The last few years have seen the advent of 200-ton-capacity trucks—and larger. However, there are reservations as to whether the trend to ever-larger trucks will continue. Certain adverse factors may limit truck sizes. The large, slow diesels used on the giant trucks (about 900 rpm) are heavy and costly. High fuel costs have eliminated the gas turbine from consideration. Large trucks reduce operating labor costs, but tire costs are phenomenal. Capital investment for a 200-ton truck is likely to be more than three times the price of a 100-ton truck. Large truck dimensions adversely affect pit haul road sizes as well as the size of prime loaders and service facilities. Downtime of the giant trucks is extraordinarily costly in terms of wasted capital and lost production.

On the positive side, the giant trucks tend to offer productivity increases that exceed capacity multiples. Queuing time at loading and dumping points is reduced. Use of giant trucks reduces the needed number of operating and repair personnel—which may be of vital significance in reducing labor and infrastructure expenses at remote mining areas. The Unit Rig driverless truck may make an important contribution to future mining operations in remote areas.

The pros and cons of giant trucks obviously require serious consideration before making a decision to purchase. When extremely long, steep grades are needed for pit haul roads, use of trolley assist from a fixed overhead line deserves consideration. Problems associated with trolley assist include additional heavy equipment on the trucks, careful road maintenance, and extra investment. However, if fuel prices are high and cheap hydroelectric (or other) power is available, trolley assist may be quite valuable.

Tire costs: a problem area

Most mine operators believe that the operating life and characteristics of truck tires are unsatisfactory. Tire costs range from 25% to 40% of total mine operating costs. The giant truck tires can cost more than $10,000 each, and tire prices have recently been rising at a rate of 15% to 20% annually. Because of their size, the giant tires require special effort and investment in transport, storage, and handling.

The condition of mine haulage roads, tire selection, and maintenance are three areas in which operations personnel can improve efficiency. Until recently, most mining operations were conducted with cursory attention to mine road grades, radii of major curves, and grader cleanup of spills along the route and at loading and dumping points. Now, many mine roads are designed and constructed to the standards for public highways, with prime attention to road loadings and the quality of road building materials. Maintenance also conforms to exacting standards. A recent trend toward utilizing the services of a tire engineer at mine operations is paying off in cost reductions. Daily attention to tire pressures, minor damages, haul road conditions, and standardized preventive maintenance is worth the cost.

Nothing is more important than selecting the right tire in the first place. The process requires knowledge of the vehicle and tire service conditions, including data on the haulage profile. Haulage profile data should include the tire loads for loaded and return trips, the ambient temperature of the site, the various speeds and distances of the haul, and potential hazards to the tire from road fill, spills, etc. The industry provides two ratings—the Tire and Rim Association rating and the ton-mile-per-hour rating—which should be used in tire selection. In all cases, it pays to consult experts of the various tire manufacturers.

Sometimes, conditions that support the selection of a particular tire type require further thought. Bias-ply tires offer good resistance to heat buildup (the major cause of tire failure) but are quite sensitive to damage from cuts and abrasion. The steel cords in radials tend to help dissipate heat, but radials require a firm suspension system and close attention to tire pressures. The soft sidewall of radial tires causes vehicles to tend to yaw on cornering.

Regardless of overload, 90 psi is considered to be the maximum inflation pressure for tires on off-highway haulage trucks. As pressure fluctuates with heat, work, and minor leakage, tire pressure should be checked daily. ☐

References

1) Pugh, R. Dell, "Design Problems on Rear Dump Haulers," MINING MAGAZINE, July 1975, p 27.
2) Burton, Alan K., "Off-Highway Trucks in the Mining Industry," MINING ENGINEERING, August 1975, p 28.
3) Felix, Gerald L., "Development of a 350-ton Haulage Truck," MINING CONGRESS JOURNAL, March 1976, p 52.

The Terex 33-19 hauler, designed for a payload of 350 tons, is powered by a GM EMD 16-645-E4 engine with 3,000 flywheel hp.

Death is a blind spot

Around noontime on a day in February 1975 at an open-pit mine in the West, the operator of a giant haulage truck, waiting in position for loading, called the dispatcher to report that the truck wasn't running. An hour and a half later, the driver finally got the truck started and drove off.

Meanwhile, the truck foreman had been told to pick up the driver of the disabled truck. The foreman drove his pickup into the loading area and parked in front of the haulage truck that he found waiting there. However, this haulage truck was not the previously disabled vehicle, and the driver was unaware that the foreman had pulled up in front. The driver proceeded to make the turn to begin moving into loading position. As he moved forward, it felt as if his truck had struck a rock. He stopped the truck and got out to investigate, finding the mangled remains of the pickup. It took two hours to remove the foreman's body.

In 1973, haulage truck accidents at metal and nonmetal mines caused 24 fatalities and 643 disabling injuries. The major contributory cause of the accidents was found to be poor visibility.

The wheels of a 150-ton rear-dump truck are taller than a man. From the cab, rear vision is totally obstructed. A mirror off the right side window affords limited vision rearward and partially blocks visibility to the right.

A study by MESA's Health and Safety Analysis Center in Denver charted the blind spots around a 150-ton vehicle. Looking to the right through the side window from the operator's seat, the driver could not see a 6-ft-tall figure within 50 ft of the vehicle. To the left, the figure was blanked out within 10 ft. Cab posts, vent windows, door posts, exhaust stacks, air cleaners, oil baths, and other equipment obscured the range of vision.

After analyzing haulage truck accidents, HSAC encouraged truck manufacturers to redesign and modify trucks and cabs to improve vision to the side and front.

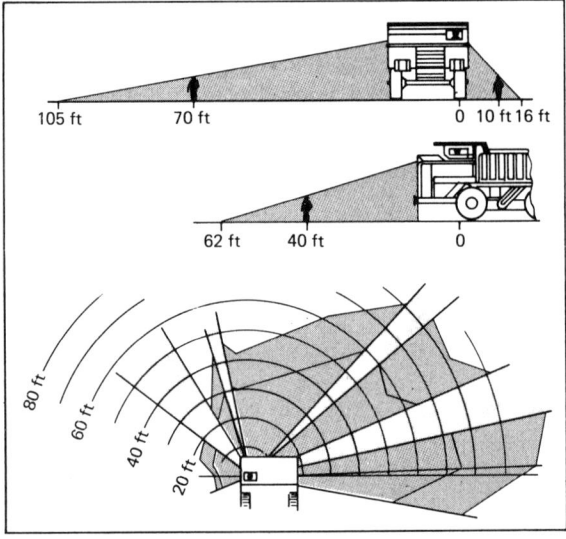

Vision limitations from cab of 150-ton rear-dump hauler: (top) front and side limits; (bottom) blind spots in field of vision. (Source: MESA.)

Manufacturers recognize the problem and are making modifications.

The HSAC study concluded that other action was also needed to improve safety, including: 1) training truck operators and other mine personnel to be aware of visibility hazards of large equipment, 2) developing and enforcing strict maintenance and driver training programs, and 3) enforcing safety and equipment maintenance standards.

As illustrated by the specific accident described here, special caution is needed at loading and dumping areas. Parking areas should be designated. Contact by radio or other means should precede the entry of smaller vehicles into loading and dumping areas. □

Open-pit conveyors offer potential savings

THE EXTRAORDINARY COSTS OF TRUCK HAULAGE, combined with the specter of fuel shortages, suggest that the next major advance for open-pit mining will be the use of large scale, portable or semiportable crushers in the pit, combined with belt conveying of ore and waste. Large scale conveying is not new—having been practiced for years at several metal mines, including the giant Twin Buttes, Ariz., copper mine—but it has not yet emerged as a principal means of ore and/or waste transport.

A number of manufacturers produce mobile crushers, including Krupp, Fives-Lille Cail, Iowa Manufacturing Co., and Kennedy Van Saun Corp. Generally, such crushers have a maximum capacity of less than 1,000 tph and accept boulders not more than 1 m in breadth. Jaw crushers and hammermills are most often used. Traveling mechanisms include tires, crawlers, walking pads, or track wheels for rail mounting. Future developments seem likely to favor heavy duty, high capacity crushers that are semiportable. Such crushers, moved infrequently from one station to another as pits are deepened, would be used as primary crushers to provide material sized for large scale belt-conveying from the pit.

The longest belt conveyor system for moving ore is now operating at the Bu Craa phosphate mines in the former Spanish Sahara. The system consists of 11 individual conveyors, totaling 100 km in length. The belts convey 2,000 mtph of phosphate rock from the mines to the Atlantic seaboard. The conveyor is 1 m wide and travels at 4.5 m per sec. The system is automated, with control signals transmitted through a high-tension line running parallel to the conveyor.

The Twin Buttes operation in Pima County, Ariz., a partnership of Anaconda and Amax, uses an alluvium handling system consisting of two 60-in. conveyors, each of which can move 8,000 tph.[1] The pit-to-surface "C" conveyor exits the pit at 25% grade. The "D" conveyor rises at 11.5% grade to a truck load-out bin. The conveyors will be extended to the maximum length possible for 5,000 hp each—totaling approximately 6,200 ft long. A new 60-in. "E" conveyor will be added to the end of the D conveyor. The E belt will be both shiftable and extendable. It will be extended 20 times in increments of 256 ft and will be moved 25 times in its expected 10-year life span. The Twin Buttes pit also employs a few miles of conveyors to move crushed ore from the two primary crushers in the pit to stockpiles or to a secondary crusher.

New belt drive uses radial tires

A single-flight conveyor system may now be extended for unlimited distances by use of intermediate drive units, which position radial tires on the flanged edges of the conveyor belt to provide driving force. The intermediate drive system was designed and developed jointly by B. F. Goodrich and Continental Conveyor Co.

The system is to be used at Brewster Phosphates' Lonesome mine in Florida, where a 2½-mi conveyor installation will be driven by twelve 200-hp intermediate drive modules. (See E/MJ, May 1976, p 79.) Each module will use twelve 7.50 R-16 Goodrich radial steel truck tires. Four tires, two per side, will be positioned above the belt's top strand to exert a downward force on the belt edges. Four additional tires will be placed immediately below the top tires and between the top and bottom belt strands. These four center tires will provide the drive for the belt. Finally, four tires will be positioned directly below the belt's bottom strand to exert pressure to hold the strand firmly against the drive tires. Both the top and bottom belt strands are effectively sandwiched between pressure tires and drive tires.

The 54-in.-wide, 30,000-ft-long belt will be constructed with tension-bearing brass-plated cables, each 3/16 in. in diameter. Nylon breaker plies, placed above and below the cables, absorb impact and shock at loading points. The belt's top and bottom covers are oil-resistant.

The belt, traveling at 885 fpm, will move 4,000 tph of phosphate-bearing matrix on the top strand, while returning waste sands at 1,800 tph on the bottom strand. The innovative system thus provides simultaneous two-way transport of ore and waste.

The intermediate drive concept is said to "eliminate to a great degree the need for multiflight conveyor systems and costly material transfer points." The system reduces weight requirement for conveyor structures, hardware, and belts. Engineers at Brewster Phosphates believe that the total system will consume only 10% of the electrical power required for a slurry pipeline, the company's previous transport method. □

Reference

1) St. John, C. R., and Kronke, J. W., "Use of Belt Conveyors in Open Pit Mining," MINING CONGRESS JOURNAL, April 1975, p 56.

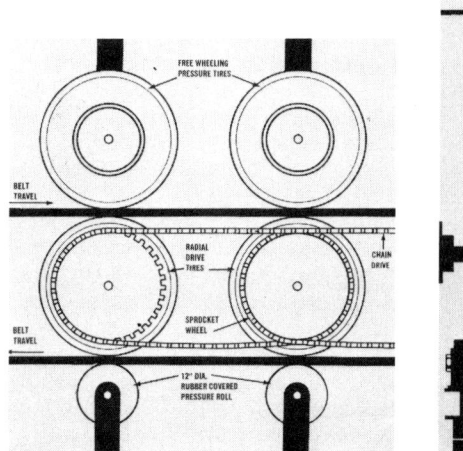
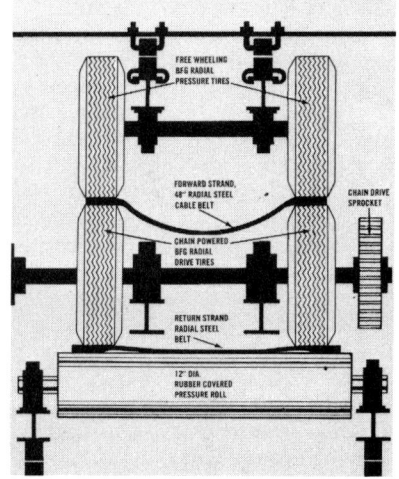

'Revolutionary' may be the word for the intermediate drive conveyor system developed jointly by B. F. Goodrich and Continental Conveyor Co. The system allows single-flight conveyors to be used over unlimited distances, with significant savings in costs of structure and power. Side and end views here show one application of the concept.

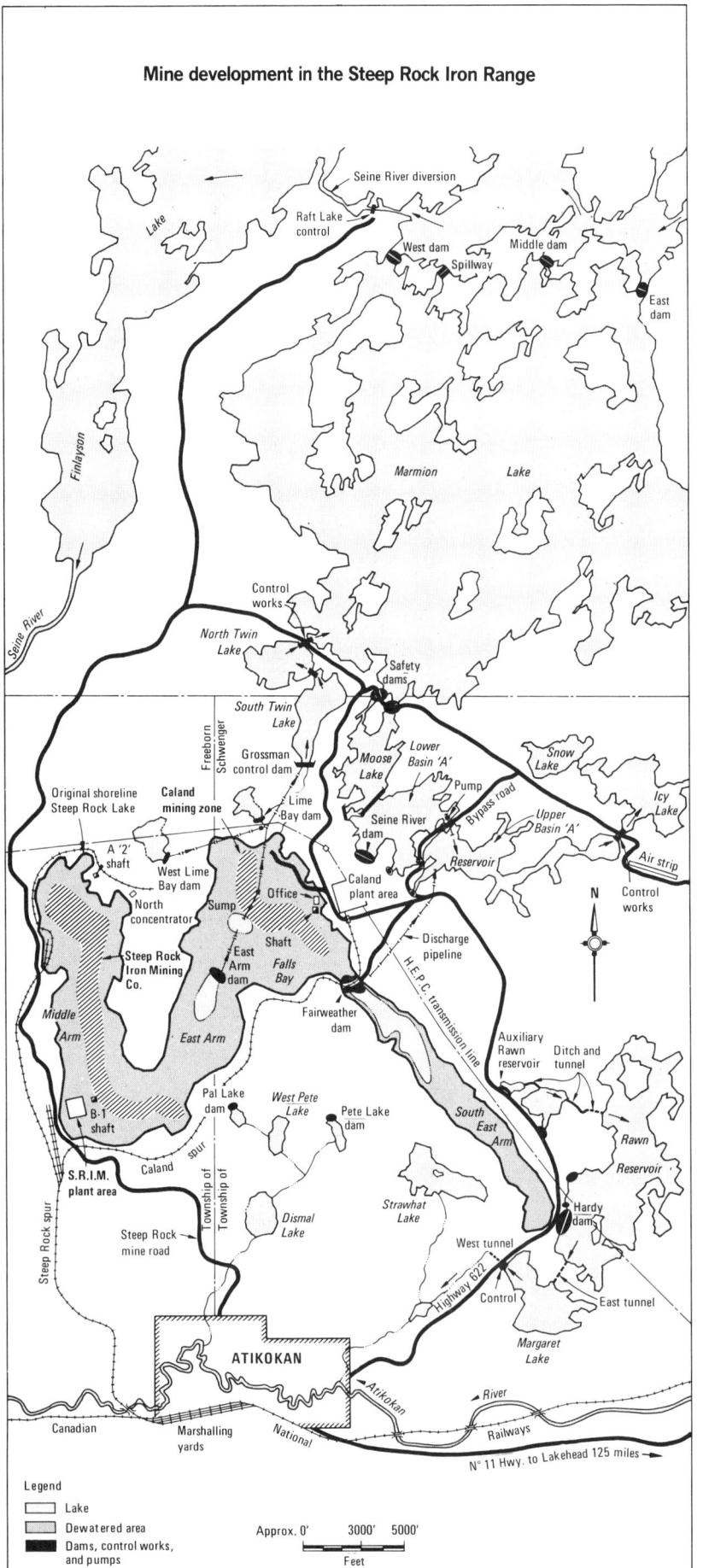

Mine development in the Steep Rock Iron Range

From left to right: 1) Map of Steep Rock Iron Range shows relationship of ore deposits of Caland Ore Co. and Steep Rock Iron Mines to former lake system, which was pumped out and dredged to expose the ore for mining. Note the numerous dams installed for rearrangement of natural drainage and for water control. 2) Caland generalized pit plan shows approximate geometry of redeposited silt, which must be moved by hydraulic mining to extend the pit. 3) Marconaflo slurry reclaim of hangingwall silt is shown in detail.

Marconaflo strips

Stan Dayton, Editor in chief

A MINI-HYDRAULIC SLURRY MINING PROGRAM is scheduled to strip 265,000 cu yd of redeposited silt from Caland Ore Co. Ltd.'s open pit on the Steep Rock Iron Range near Atikokan, Ont. This program is a microcosm of an earlier project at the site—one of the largest preproduction dredging and water diversion projects in mining and construction history—but it will help buy Caland, an Inland Steel Co. subsidiary, at least a three-year lease on mining life.

During the 1950s, Caland and neighboring Steep Rock Iron Mines Ltd. mobilized an inland flotilla of cutterhead suction dredges to drain a lake system while pumping and disposing of 283 million cu yd of silt overlying the goethite-hematite-limonitic orebodies of the Steep Rock district. This event—which took place in a then-remote locale in Canada—still ranks as one of the monumental engineering achievements of all time. Caland's effort alone required the removal of 162 million cu yd of lake bottom material plus extensive damming, diking, and diversion of the drainage pattern within a 25-sq-mi area.

The principals in the 1976 scenario are a tandem set of Marconaflo units— a Dynajet 1000 capsule and a caisson

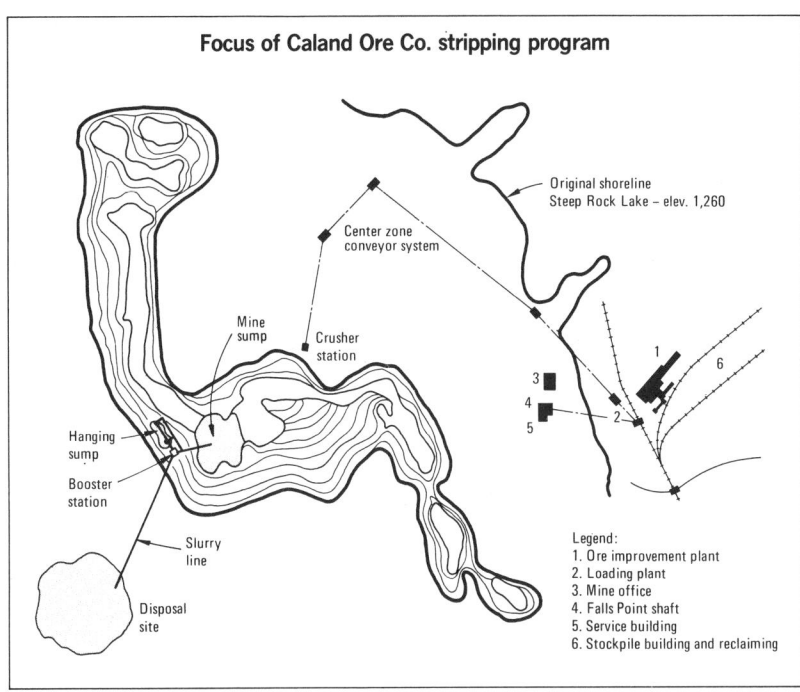

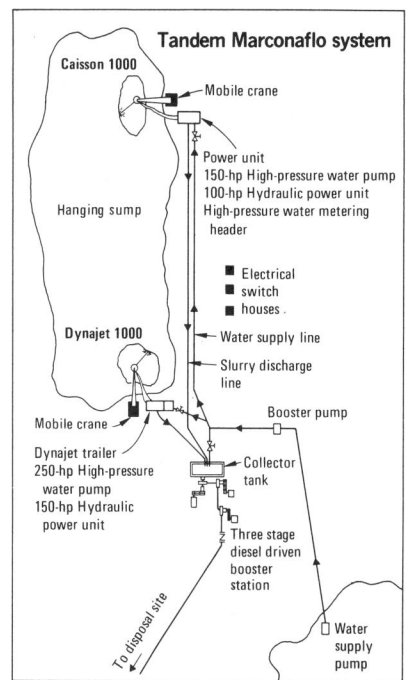

silt and pumps new life into Caland

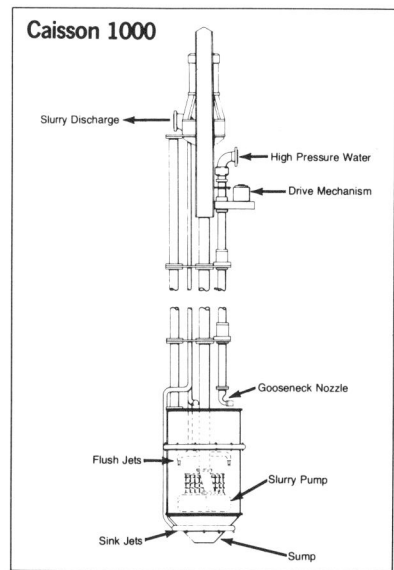

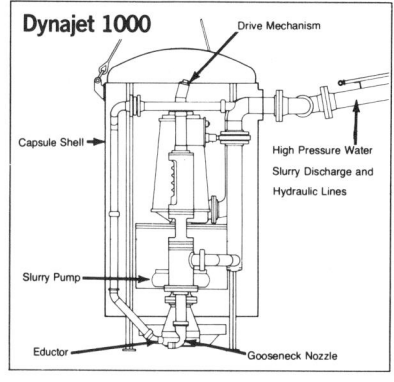

1000 jet that Atikokan contractor Bruce Davidson leased for the job. The work is coordinated by project supervisors Alex Mattichuk, of Caland, and Lester Huffman, of Marconaflo. For Marconaflo, the Caland effort marks the first use of its slurry repulp and reclaim system at an open-pit mine—a new addition to a growing list of actual and conceptual slurry handling applications.

The problem: expanding the pit

Caland was scheduled to discontinue mining at the end of this year, while continuing to operate its pellet plant on accumulated stockpiles through 1978. During a recent evaluation of the Inland Steel ore position, it was decided to extend the mining program through the 1979 shipping season and to continue pelletizing through 1981 at current rates—about 2.5 million ltpy of wet crude ore, from which about 1.25 million ltpy of 2-in. x 3/16-in. lump and 1 million ltpy of pellets are recovered.

Substantial resources of iron remain in the Caland pits. The deposits in the Steep Rock district have never been bottomed by boreholes, but Caland ore bears the twin burdens of an Ontario mining tax and a royalty payable to Steep Rock Iron Mines under the terms of a 99-year lease negotiated in 1953. In addition, the maturing pits operate with a stripping ratio of about 4:1 (cu yd to lt). As a result, the Caland mines are nearing the economic limits of open-pit mining.

During the original stripping program, a 1,500-ft-long x 300-ft section of silty lake bottom in the East arm of the former Steep Rock Lake was dredged and terraced on the hangingwall side of the deposits. Before this silt slope could be trap-rocked, erosional forces began washing clay and sandy silt down-slope. Caland built a landfill dike to contain the erosion in a hangingwall sump, which had maximum dimensions of 600 ft in length x 300 ft in width. The greatest depth is 50 ft. The pit perimeter for the extended mining program will include the dike.

Enter Marconaflo

For safety reasons, it is obviously necessary to remove the accumulated sedimentary wash in the sump. The material consists of layered clay and fine sand in a loosely compacted, high-moisture environment. Attempts to reclaim the sump product using Caland's conventional spread of trucks, electric shovels, front-end loaders, and other earthmoving machines resulted in little but problems and delays.

The choice of the Marconaflo slurry system over dredging for removal of the redeposited silt was based on the

Clockwise from upper left: Dynajet 1000 (left foreground) and caisson 1000 Marconaflo units slurry and reclaim redeposited silt from hangingwall sump. Slurry is delivered through 3,000 ft of pipeline, against a head of 330 ft, to a disposal area in the former East Arm of Steep Rock Lake.

flexibility of the system in the confined Caland operating area, lower water requirements, and estimated dredging costs significantly higher than the approximately $500,000 contract negotiated with B. R. Davidson Construction Ltd. It was estimated that a dredging system would have required handling about five times as much water volume.

The heart of any Marconaflo system is a patented gooseneck nozzle that jets high pressure water. The nozzle rotates in a circular arc in unconsolidated "dry" material of variable moisture content, undercutting the solids and causing them to collapse into the jet stream, producing a slurry of reasonably high density.

The Marconaflo Dynajet 1000 and caisson units are shown here schematically. Each is suspended from a crane at the jobsite and linked with hydraulic power packages by means of umbilicals that include electric cables or hydraulic drive systems. Both units consist of a self-contained jet-rotating mechanism, high pressure water line, one or more Marconajet gooseneck nozzles, a sump, and a slurry pump.

The caisson unit contains, in addition, a set of vertical sinking jets which allow it to bury its sump in unconsolidated solids. The caisson on lease for the Caland project is equipped with a single gooseneck nozzle that jets water through an arc of approximately 135° although the unit can be furnished with two nozzles, each arcing close to 180°. The capsule (Dynajet 1000) is housed in a casing approximately 5½ ft in diameter. It contains two goosenecks with an action arc close to 360°.

Both systems are furnished with mobile hydraulic power plants mounted on-highway trailers and other supportive elements. The project equipment deployed at Caland includes: a Dynajet 1000; a caisson 1000; two mobile cranes; three ASH booster slurry pumps driven by Cat 343 diesels; one slurry collection tank; 3,000 ft of Spiralweld 16-in. slurry discharge pipe sections joined with Victaulic couplings; roughly 320 ft of 10-in. high pressure water line; two high pressure water pumps rated for 900 gpm at 300 psi; one make-up water system with booster pump; two hydraulic power units; and one electrical switch house.

The Marconaflo cycle starts at the 432-ft level in the Caland mine sump. The iron ore company delivers high pressure water to the leased Marcona jet equipment, perched on the 670-ft level, by means of a 200-hp primary pump station and a 65-hp booster station. The two slurry units operate at opposite ends of the semidried hangingwall silt sump, pumping repulped slurry at about 43% solids to the surge collection tank.

Here, a float-controlled switch governs the three diesel-powered ASH pumps that deliver the slurry through 3,000 ft of pipeline against a head of 330 ft. The slurry is discharged at an elevation of about 970 ft in a large landfill containment in the middle arm of the former Steep Rock Lake. Preliminary grab samples of artificially slurried solids from the hangingwall sump exhibited extremely poor settling characteristics in lab tests. Yet the low velocity slurry actually discharged at the end of the Caland pipeline, which falls to a delta area, produces a visually crystal-clear ponding of the water beyond the sharp delta boundary—a fact that puzzles Caland planners, who now feel that they built a containment area somewhat larger than necessary.

The two Marconaflo units are equipped with 1,400-gpm slurry pumps, although each is nominally rated as a 1,000-gpm unit. The slurry booster pump station has a rating of 3,500 gpm. At a solids content of 40% by weight, the system is rated at 375 dry stph (188 dry stph from both the caisson and the Dynajet); at 33% solids, the total capability is estimated at 300 dry stph.

Contractor Bruce Davidson began 24-hr operation starting June 1. By July 5, it was estimated that a total of 150,000 cu yd of material had been excavated from the hangingwall sump. System availability was about 50% during the first 20 days and 75% from June 22 to July 5.

Both leased units are next destined for a project at Iron Ore Co. of Canada. Also figuring in Marconaflo's future are conceptual plans and considerable pilot testing of the use of the Marconajet principle in the mining of uranium and oil sands, and in the development of a system for hydrometallurgical treatment of copper and uranium. □

New rail corridor developed for Minas Gerais iron ore

Ernest McCrary, chief, McGraw-Hill World News Bureau, Buenos Aires

A LIMITING FACTOR for any mining or smelting project in Brazil is transportation availability, since a large part of the country's vast interior still lacks basic infrastructure. Much of the burden of moving ore and metals to local industrial centers and export outlets falls on the national railway system, operated by the government's Rede Ferroviaria Federal SA (RFFSA). During 1974, RFFSA handled 18.4 billion metric ton-kilometers of traffic, with iron ore accounting for almost half the total.

To cope with the needs of Brazilian iron ore and steel expansion plans, RFFSA is undertaking a 1975-79 program to increase rail facilities. Among the most ambitious projects is construction of the "Railway of Steel," an 834-km line that will link the iron ore-producing region of Belo Horizonte with the Volta Redonda steel mill complex and the Sao Paulo industrial center. The electrified line will be Brazil's most modern one, with a maximum grade of 1%, a wide gauge (1.6 m), and a minimum curve radius of 900 m.

Contracts with 21 Brazilian companies were signed in March 1975 for construction of the first sector, a 400-km stretch from Belo Horizonte to Volta Redonda via Itutinga. The line is slated to begin operations by 1978, although some industry sources think 1980 is a more realistic target. First tenders for equipment, about 30% of which will be imported, should be called before the end of 1975.

Total cost of the project is estimated by the government at $1.1 billion. By contrast, industry sources estimate the cost at $2.5 billion. The line will haul primarily iron ore and pellets, steel products, scrap iron, cement, and some other mineral and agricultural products. Hauling capacity will begin at 511,000 mtpy, eventually reaching 28.2 million mtpy.

Other projects to be undertaken in RFFSA's rail expansion program include:
- Upgrading the existing 10,800 km of track.
- Construction of 3,800 km of high quality lines and spurs.
- Widening of 3,200 km of line.
- Adding 298 locomotives, 20,000 cars, and other rolling stock.

(Continued on p 145)

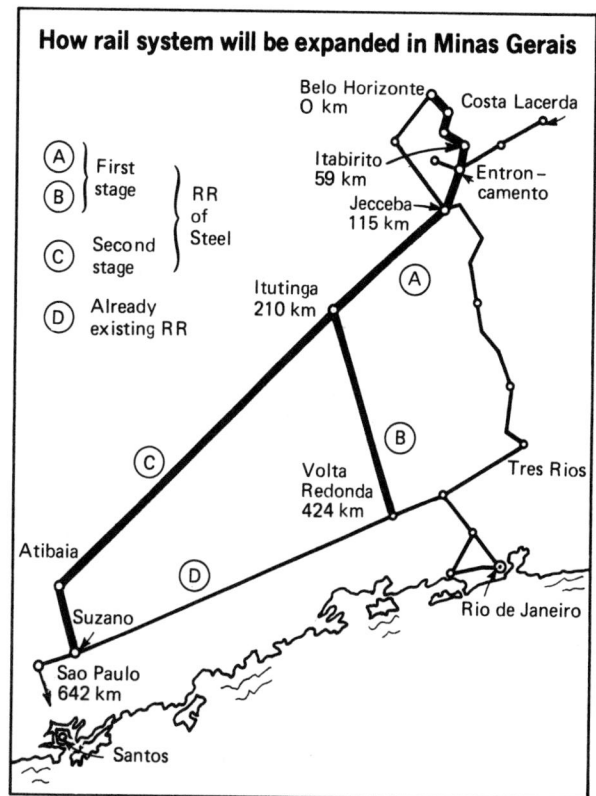

Great Lakes-St. Lawrence Seaway Navigation Season Extension (1972-73 winter activities)

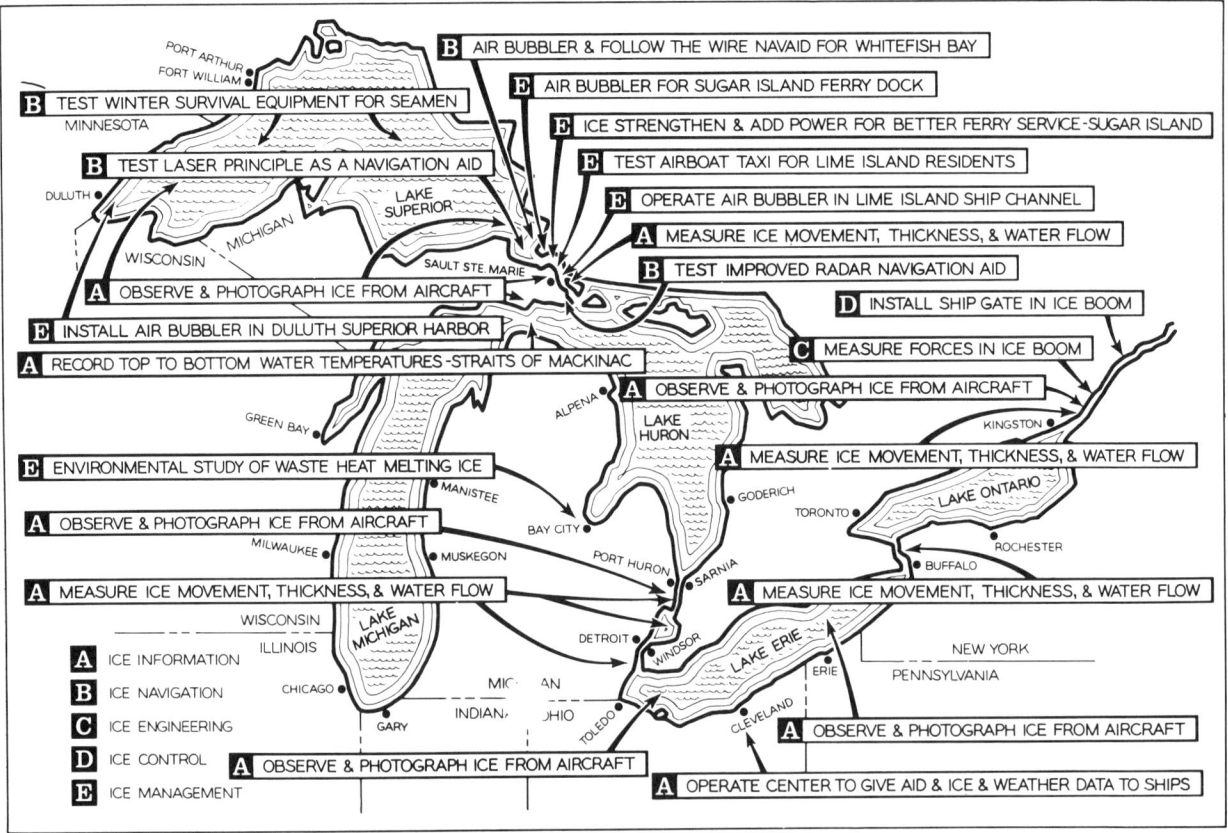

Iron ore transport—Great Lakes are the major artery for North American trade

NORTH AMERICAN IRON ORE CONSUMPTION in 1973 totaled 146.9 million lt, of which 95 million lt (almost 65%) was shipped to and from ports on the Great Lakes and the St. Lawrence River. With an ore production of 141.9 million lt averaging 60.8% Fe, the continent was very nearly self-sufficient in iron ore supply.

The production breakdown last year was 90.8 million lt averaging 60.58% Fe in the US, 48.0 million lt averaging 61.75% Fe in Canada, and 3.1 million lt averaging 59.0% Fe in Mexico. Exports totaled 16.7 million lt, principally from Canada, and imports supplied 21.7 million lt, primarily to the US.

US demand for iron ore is projected to rise to 211 million ltpy by the year 2000. Canada will require 34 million ltpy, and Mexico will be consuming 13 million ltpy. Production by the year 2000 is projected at 125 million ltpy in the US, 110 million ltpy in Canada, and 13 million ltpy in Mexico. A projected net 10 million ltpy will be imported.

By the year 2000, it is forecast that no less than 164 million ltpy of iron ore will be moving through the Great Lakes-St. Lawrence transport system. Additional tonnages to be shipped will include 34 million ltpy to northeast US ports; 15 million ltpy to Gulf Coast ports; and internal traffic of 25 million ltpy in the US, 7 million ltpy in Canada, and 13 million ltpy in Mexico.

Plans to increase the ore handling potential of the Great Lakes-St. Lawrence system are already underway at official US, Canadian, and user agencies. Key to the program is an extension of the navigation season, complemented by increases in vessel capacity, new vessel construction, and new onshore storage facilities such as those of the Pittsburgh & Conneaut Dock Co. and the Bethlehem Steel complex at Burns Harbor, Ind.

The basic objective of the Great Lakes-St. Lawrence Seaway Navigation Season Extension program, which has been in effect since December 1971, is a 12-month shipping season, as compared with a seven- to eight-month season in 1959 and a nine- to 10-month season in 1973. The program was originally launched under a US Congressional authorization of $6.5 million, which has been supplemented with an additional $3 million and an extension to December 1976.

Vessel modification by installation of self-unloading equipment and by lengthening of existing ships has been a significant factor in raising overall ore carrying capacity. A 96-ft mid-section added to Interlake Steamship's *John Sherwin* increased its capacity by 5,300 lt to 30,500 lt, and two of five such extensions in 1973 added 120-ft mid-sections to the *Armco* and the *Reserve* to increase their capacities from 20,700 lt to 26,500 lt.

Typical of new "super" self-unloading lake ore carriers are the 55,000-lt *S. J. Cort* and *Roger Blough*, which were commissioned in 1973. Comparable in capacity is the 52,000-lt *Presque Isle* of Litton-Great Lakes Corp., a modified 1,000-ft self-unloading tug-barge. The largest lake carrier now on the boards is a 59,000-lt, 1,000-ft-long vessel with a planned beam of 105 ft. According to the 1973 annual report of the Lake Carriers Association, two 770-ft, one 800-ft, and seven 1,000-ft vessels were on order in 1974.

Pittsburgh & Conneaut Dock Co.'s 10,000-ltph ship unloading capability at Conneaut, Ohio, is coupled with a rail loading system that is independent of ship arrivals, to eliminate unloading delays. Winter storage at the port alleviates stockpiling problems at the steel mills, and ore blending at the port delivers a directly chargeable cargo to the mills. Present storage capacity is 3.2 million lt of various ores, coal, stone, and other bulk materials. Reclaiming from stockpiles is by means of two bucketwheels, each with a capacity of 5,000 ltph. Rail loadout capacity is 40,000 lt in 12 hr, with all types and sizes of cars loaded with pre-set weights.

Welland Canal is key to future ore movement

If there is a single serious potential bottleneck to future iron ore movements between the Great Lakes and the St. Lawrence, it is the Welland Canal, which has a history of problems. Constructed in 1932 as a wholly Canadian effort, the canal provides a bypass around Niagara Falls and is the sole navigational link between Lake Ontario and Lake Erie. Eight locks on the 28-mi canal provide a lift of 326 ft—with one-half of the lift encountered in the 2,400-mi seaway from the Atlantic to the head of Lake Superior.

Meandering through the center of the city of Welland, with numerous bridges for pedestrian and vehicular traffic and old structures that block the line of sight, the canal is an extremely cumbersome passage. Construction of an 8.3-mi section to bypass the southern end of the canal has cut ½ hr from the 13- to 14-hr trip and has eliminated some six bridges, but in spite of these improvements the superstructure of one vessel struck a pedestrian bridge in the summer of 1974 and closed the canal for 14 days.

Recent studies by the US Army Corps of Engineers indicate that the Welland Canal will reach its capacity by 1990. The All-American Canal Project proposes construction by the US of a canal to supplement the Welland system, with costs projected in 1972 at $2 billion. However, based on past performance, 10 years might be required for implementation, once detailed plans have been completed.

The Welland Canal is a vital link for North American iron ore movement—providing passage for almost 20% of supply in 1973. If the canal is to adequately serve the iron ore trade in the future, prompt and decisive action is required to improve the system.

From mine to port, rails are dominant

Virtually all of the 146.9 million lt of North American iron ore consumption in 1973, regardless of origin, was moved by rail from mine to port. For the most part, the rail systems that move iron ore are captively owned by the mine operators, directly or by participation in the principal corporate entity. Typical of this type of operation are two Labrador Trough railways—the Quebec, North Shore & Labrador Railway (QNS&L) and La Compagnie De Chemin De Fer Cartier, owned and operated by the Iron Ore Co. of Canada and Quebec Cartier Mining Co. These railroads transported 26 million lt and 10 million lt of iron ore, pellets, and concentrates, respectively, in 1973. With the Mt. Wright mine startup scheduled for 1975, the QCM system will be required to handle no less than 25 million lt.

The construction and operations of the QNS&L are typical of this type of heavy service. Starting at tidewater at Sept-Iles, Que., on the St. Lawrence, the 356-mi railway terminates at Schefferville. Maximum elevation is 2,066 ft at Mile 150 and averages 1,700 ft for the balance of the line. The ruling grade is 0.4% southbound and 1.35% northbound. Speeds are 30 mph loaded and 40 mph unloaded. Maximum curvature is 8°, and 40% of the total mileage is on curved track. Tunnels located at two points in the system are 2,200 ft and 1,050 ft long. A total of 34 sidings are all equipped with power operated switches.

The main track is laid with 132-lb rail, with 14-in. and 18-in. tie plates on 8-ft and 8-ft 6-in. treated ties, and tie replacement by 9-ft ties. The track structure is supported by rock ballast on a subgrade 24 ft wide.

Paralleling the track is a 23,000-v power line extending the full length of the railway. It provides power for the signal locations, communications, and lighting of camps and tunnels, as well as for a landline carrier and physical communications circuits related to the microwave system which services the entire area of operations.

As for rolling stock requirements, the QNS&L is now using 83 General Motors diesel locomotives (23 1,750-hp GP-9s and 61 3,000-hp SD-40s), 3,429 ore cars, and 1,100 miscellaneous cars for passengers, special freight, and maintenance service.

The key to economy of operations and maximum utilization of equipment and trackage is the unit train concept—a unit consisting of a large number of cars with a common cargo which move to a common delivery point. In the case of the QNS&L, a typical unit train consists of 260 cars loaded to a maximum of 100 lt each. In 1973, the system handled 26 million lt of ore, pellets, and concen-

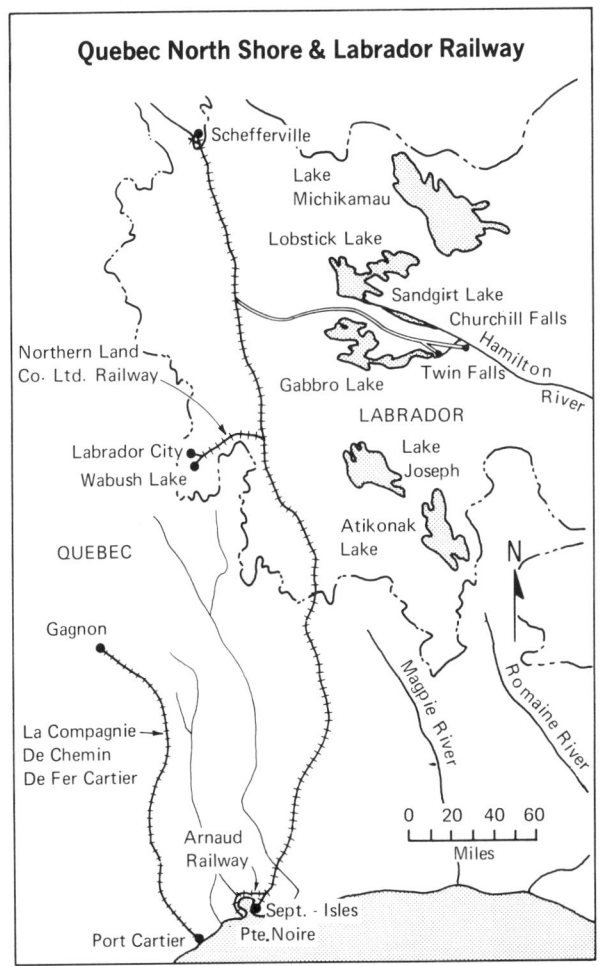

trates with a turnaround time of 25-35 hr, exclusive of loading. Average speed for all ore trains, loaded and empty, was 20 mph, as compared with the US-Canadian average of 55 mi per day.

Railway automation as practiced in North America appears to be confined to accounting, box car inventory, and train makeup at major marshalling yards. However, QNS&L operations feature a considerable degree of automation at the Carol Lake facility, and such practices might find wider application in future North American iron ore movements.

A totally electric and completely automated railway facility at Carol Lake moves no less than 20 million ltpy a distance of approximately 5½-7½ mi. Using strategically dug hoppers with surge capacities of 2,500, 18,000, and 60,000 lt, and keeping the haul from the working face to the hopper or ore pass to a maximum of 13,000 ft, trains are programmed to start, stop, inch, dump at the two crushers, and return the cars to loading pockets.

Rolling stock at Carol Lake consists of four diesel-electric GP 9 locomotives and 65 side-dump ore cars of 100-ton capacity, operated on a unit basis with 15 to 20 cars per movement. The automatic apparatus is keyed to a system designed by General Railway Signal Co. that provides for separate controls over each segment of track and is actuated by the position of the train on the track.

The trains operate at 30 mph on the single-track main line, 15 mph on the side track and passing sidings, and 7½ mph near the crusher and loading pockets. Loading speed is ⅛ to ⅜ mph and dumping speed is 0 to 2 mph.

At the loading end, the operator takes over remote control of the train at a point 100 ft from his station; after the train is brought under the apron feeders, the system returns to automatic. At the dumping end, the operator takes over remote control after the train stops 300 ft from the building. When the train is ready for dumping, it is positioned by the operator and automatic controls then take over. The sequence of operations can be broken at any time.

In rail services at Carol Lake, the needs of the mining operation are obviously dominant, uncomplicated by rail union and other labor regulations. Nevertheless, wider use of such systems is dictated if requirements in the transport sector of North American iron ore industry are to be met more efficiently by the year 2000.

Internal railing of ore is minimal in North America

Internal railway movements of North American iron ore are minimal, accounting for only slightly more than 10 million lt out of a total of 146.9 million lt consumed.

US and Mexican rail transport of ore appear to be similar, with the major portion typified by the Pilot Knob-Meramec movements to Granite City Steel; Atlantic City-Cedar City to Provo; Lone Star Steel; La Perla to Altos Hornos and to HyL at Monterrey; and the standard unit train operations to Conneaut and the Pittsburgh District via the Bessemer & Lake Erie Railroad.

By the year 2000, internal North American rail transport of iron ore is forecast to increase from the present 10 million lt to 45 million lt—25 million lt in the US, 7 million lt in Canada, and 13 million lt in Mexico.

The present US railway system, and the planned program to alleviate the east-west and north-south congestion corridors, appear to be adequate to meet the forecast needs for internal movement of iron ore. Since the greatest activity will continue to be in the Midwest and West, where there is no significant congestion at present, no delays are foreseen.

Canadian internal requirements are comparatively small, and since consuming centers will continue to be concentrated on the Great Lakes and the St. Lawrence, all anticipated needs can easily be met.

Mexico's railway system, which has five separate lines under federal control, faces a significant challenge if the projected fourfold increase in ore movement is to be attained. The La Perla and Jalisco operations presently supply the bulk of ore to operations at Alto Hornos, Monterrey, and Puebla. The Michoacan orebody in the vicinity of Las Truchas will not impose any additional burden on the railway system, since pipeline transport is planned. However, transportation problems are posed by other iron ore deposits presently working, developing, or to be developed—such as Cerro de Mercado in Durango, Pena Colorada in Colima, and the Baja California and Sonora deposits. Problems may arise not only because of the tonnages involved, but also because of technical factors in the bed, rail, grade, and maintenance. Prevailing technical and physical factors could preclude the use of sizable unit train operations.

Pipelining needs to prove its economics

The single most intriguing technological proposal for iron ore transport is slurry pipeline systems—which offer possibilities as wide as the imagination. However, in spite of obvious advantages, independent assessments have proved established transportation modes to be competitive. Moreover, slurry systems, such as Marconaflo, preclude the use of the facilities for other applications.

An in-depth evaluation of the possibility of pipelining 10 million ltpy of Mesabi Range taconite concentrates to the Chicago area was published by the US Bureau of Mines in 1971. The study indicated a slight advantage for pipelining. However, when taking into account the handling costs for moving slurry to the furnaces, either a direct economic tradeoff was indicated, or pipelining proved to be a few cents per ton more expensive than rail-vessel transport.

However, economic and application limitations encountered to date for pipeline systems should not preclude consideration of slurry transport of iron ore. Many in-plant applications are technically and economically justifiable, and movement of tailings over short distances by pipeline is well established.

A total system concept of pipelining may also be viable for certain individual operations, such as the 4 million-ltpy system now under study for moving concentrate from the Lake St. Joseph operations of Steep Rock Iron Mines to Ignace, Ont., where the concentrates will be pelletized.

However, a survey of numerous authorities indicates a current consensus that the established transport system is generally more competitive than pipelining.

Inland waterways: minimal factor in ore transport

Despite availability of a 25,000-mi transportation network of navigable inland waters, only 3.9 million lt of iron ore was transported by this means in 1972—less than 2% of the total ore consumed in North America. Of the total iron ore movement by inland waterways of the US, 75% of the traffic was on the Black Warrior, Warrior and Tombighbee River System—the principal artery for moving imported ore from South America into the Birminghan District.

The largest single factor limiting the use of inland waterways is that more than 70% of US iron and steel capacity, and an even larger percentage of all North American capacity, has ready access to deep water ports. □

Chapter 6
Maintenance

Open pit maintenance backstops rising production demands	230
Troubleshooting the rotary compressor	236
Pointers on selection, use, and maintenance of hose	240
Reuseable pipe insulation saves energy and speeds up installation and maintenance	242
New anaerobic adhesive technology helps keep mine and plant equipment running	244
The dollars and sense of selecting wear materials	248
Diverse uses win an expanding market for rubber in mining	254
Rebuilding worn mine car wheels	259
New load sensing system keeps ore trucks well filled	260
Wire rope fittings	260
New choker hitch adjustment table for wire rope slings	263
Simulator helps train fire fighters	264
New device protects mine vehicles from fire	265
Wet suppression system controls dust problems at Inspiration	266

The main shop at Pinto Valley (foreground) is centrally located to minimize travel to concentrator, mill, and mine.

Open-pit maintenance backstops rising production demands

Dan Jackson, Western Editor

As MINING EQUIPMENT increases in size, putting greater production responsibilities on each operating unit, pressure increases for maintenance organizations to keep equipment operating at high percentages of availability. Mine management must assemble a task force of skilled technicians, properly position them in an efficient organization, provide efficient facilities, and coordinate activities through an exacting reporting and record system.

Open-pit maintenance must follow a regular system of inspections that leads to controlled procedures. Equipment parts must be replaced on predetermined schedules, before failures occur. Purchasing and warehousing systems must be organized to provide the right parts at the right time and in sufficient quantities to achieve optimum equipment availability. Two specific requirements for maintenance managers are use of the best management practices and good engineering judgment.

In preparing this report on maintenance, E/MJ visited two Arizona copper operations—Cities Service Co.'s Pinto Valley mine at Miami, which has been operating for about two years, and Inspiration Consolidated Copper Corp., also at Miami, which has been in production for many years. Despite the difference in ages of these operations, basic procedures do not vary greatly. To avoid repetition, this report emphasizes the newer Pinto Valley operation and some of its innovations.

At the Inspiration pit, which has been producing since 1947, continual improvement of maintenance practices is emphasized, and the mine maintenance department has been reorganized to meet the demands of larger and more sophisticated equipment.

Servicing about 70 major mining units and 80 service vehicles and automobiles that contribute to production of more than 70,000 tpd of ore and waste, the Inspiration maintenance department makes use of 25 forms for reports and records. Based on the historical data accumulated, the department has computerized its maintenance cost accounting. The company plans to expand the computer program to include preventive maintenance planning and scheduling. The computer is currently being used in planning equipment replacement schedules.

In recent years, Inspiration has also taken on the task of rebuilding major components in-house. Richard Trusty, mine maintenance superintendent, said, "The program is reaping cost savings. For example, the last big engine overhaul done by an outside firm cost $21,000. We did a similar job for $12,000."

If any factor can be singled out as being most important for a successful maintenance operation, Trusty added, it is a management philosophy of people involvement—"getting all of the people involved in the maintenance program to feel that they individually are an important and integral part of the program."

Cities Service: an exercise in modern maintenance

CONFRONTED WITH the challenge of establishing a maintenance organization from the ground up at its new Pinto Valley mining operation, management of Cities Service Co.'s Miami Copper Operation first organized a team from members of its mine and maintenance departments to visit and study several ongoing mining operations, as a basis for incorporating proven methods into Cities Service's operations. Among the objectives set for the Pinto Valley maintenance program:

- Take advantage of the accomplishments and failures of other mines operating under similar circumstances.
- Choose a shop location that works smoothly and efficiently with the mine layout and then establish the physical requirements for shops and warehouses.
- Organize a flexible operation that takes advantage of potential labor saving techniques and that encourages efficient work practices.
- Provide opportunity for maintenance personnel to review and make recommendations for selection and design of new equipment and facilities.
- During the preproduction period, establish a formal training program for all new personnel.
- Establish a planning and scheduling group to control major and preventive maintenance work.

Having accomplished these objectives, Cities Service then established its successful maintenance organization. Crawford E. Chiasson, manager of engineering and maintenance services, notes that work practices set during the preproduction period were continued and that flexibility of the labor force was emphasized. These factors, combined with modern facilities and an effective preventive maintenance program, enable Cities Service to maintain the new Pinto Valley operation with only 20% more maintenance personnel than were required at its previous Copper Cities operation, although Pinto Valley has more than three times the production capacity of Copper Cities.

Average equipment availability at Pinto Valley in 1976 exceeded 75% for the 150-ton and 170-ton haulage trucks, 82% for the shovels, and 79% for the drills, Chiasson said.

Preproduction maintenance

Pinto Valley mine development required removal of 60 million tons of overburden to reach the orebody. For this work and for the erection of mining equipment, management decided to use its own work force to give mining and maintenance personnel preproduction experience. Substantial cost savings also were realized.

Preproduction maintenance work was based on a flexible-crew concept, with crews reporting directly to the mine coordinator. Work assignment flexibility allowed efficient use of all maintenance personnel. Each person performed whatever work he or she was qualified to do, an approach that proved especially helpful during the assembly of major equipment—shovels, drills, and haulage trucks. Specialty work—electrical and welding—was performed by those with special skills.

A new concept in maintenance organization

In contrast to most open-pit maintenance organizations, Cities Service maintenance personnel all report directly to the maintenance department, rather than some reporting directly to mining and processing operations. This practice reduces the required number of personnel.

Crews are assigned to mine and processing areas strictly on the basis of need. For regular work, some personnel are assigned to specific areas on a permanent basis. Maintenance foremen also are assigned on a permanent basis, and they direct activities of all crafts in their areas. Assigned personnel handle minor emergencies to prevent disruption of scheduled work.

When additional work is scheduled, labor is drawn from the general shops for temporary assignment. The extra workers report to the permanently assigned foreman, regardless of their craft. General craft shop foremen are called on only when their expertise is required. The system reduces the need for moving general shop foremen and personnel from one area to another.

All crafts workers are identified by trade and assigned to craft shops or work areas. Each crafts worker performs his own rigging, operates whatever mobile equipment is required to do the work, and is unrestricted in the use of tools or other machinery of the craft. Qualifications are the only limiting factor.

Pinto Valley organizes repair crews according to a

Pinto Valley schedules regular haulage truck inspections after 40, 100, 240 and 500 hr of operation.

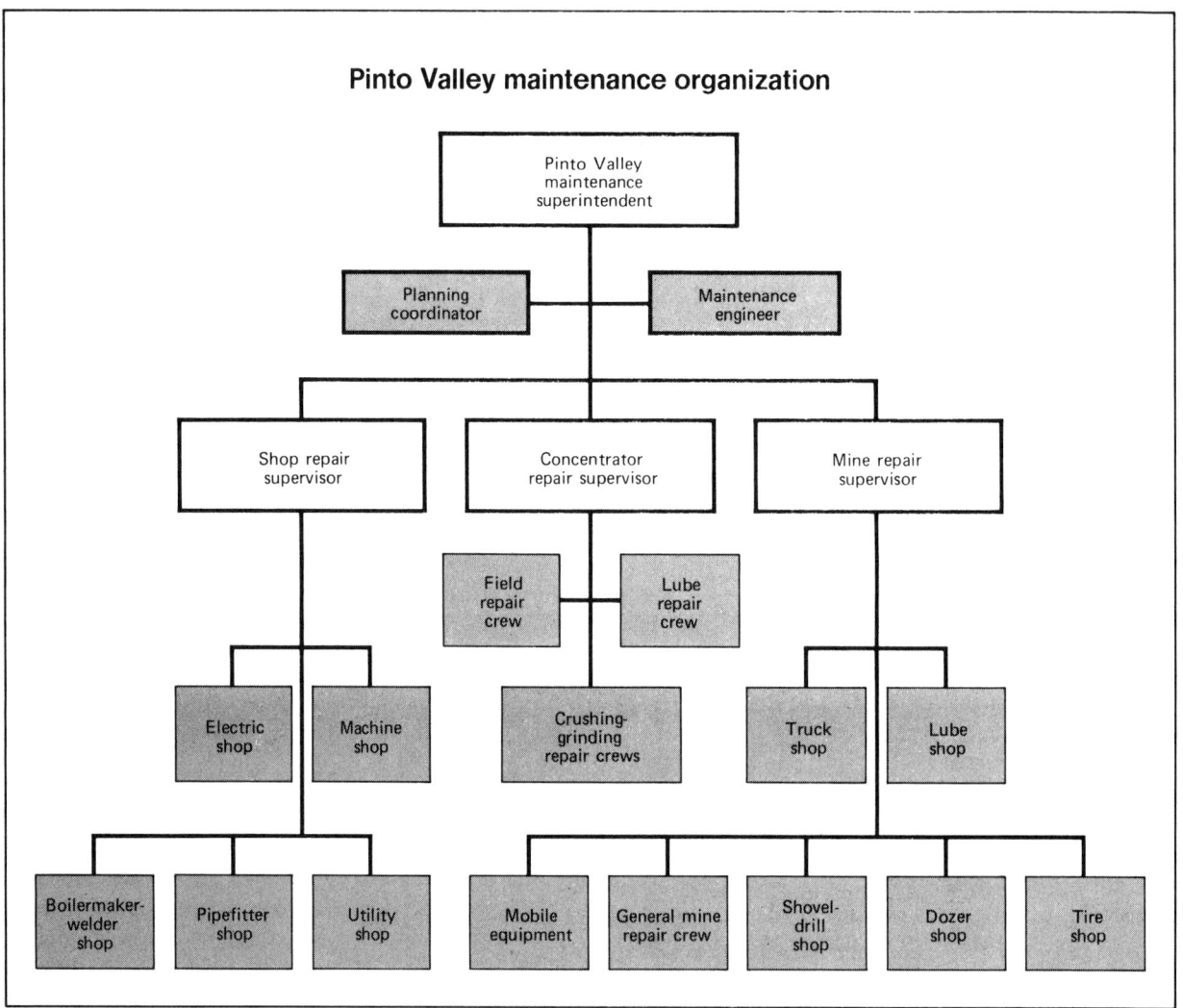

Pinto Valley maintenance organization

flexible concept that calls for crafts workers within a crew to assist each other in performing work, often eliminating the need to call in special skills of other workers.

Flexibility in labor assignment also allows management to move crafts workers from a regularly assigned area to a high priority job elsewhere on the property. Depending on the type of repairs in progress, the reassigned worker may or may not work in his usual craft line. As soon as such a job is done or personnel requirements are reduced, the crafts workers return to their regular assignments.

A craftsman can be promoted to a specialist if he becomes "exceptional" in his craft or "outstanding" in two or more crafts. Cities Service provides a continuing training program in a broad range of skills.

The Pinto Valley organization also includes a maintenance engineer and a planning coordinator. The maintenance engineer provides technical assistance in all facets of maintenance and repairs, efficiency studies, preventive maintenance, and warehouse stocking programs. The planning coordinator satisfies the urgent need for greater efficiency in utilization of costly manpower and equipment.

Representatives of top management, operations, and maintenance meet weekly to establish a priority schedule for major maintenance work to be performed during the coming week. Man-hour and cost records provide information for improved planning and scheduling of future maintenance work.

Modern shops improve maintenance quality

Maintenance facilities at Pinto Valley include a main shop having 75,000 sq ft of work area, a 35,000-sq-ft warehouse, a 15,000-sq-ft mine shop for tire maintenance and lubrication, and an additional 26,000-sq-ft covered storage area for housing large, slow-moving inventory.

The main shop consists of three 72 x 340-ft bays equipped with 10-ton and 20-ton overhead traveling cranes. Main shop areas include a machine shop, electrical shop, haulage truck shop, boilermaker-welder shop, shovel-drill shop, and pipe shop.

The mine tire and lubrication shop is close to the open-pit operation to minimize haulage truck downtime. The facility provides areas for preventive maintenance, lubrication, and tire maintenance for all mining vehicles.

Pinto Valley, major mining equipment

Drills: Four Marion M-4s.
Shovels: Two P&H 2100 BL (15 yd), three P&H 2300 (20 yd).
Front-end loaders: One Dart D-600 (12 yd).
Haulage: 15 150-ton and five 170-ton Wabco trucks.
Ancillary equipment: Two Caterpillar 769B water trucks and one 50-ton Wabco converted to a water truck; Cat bulldozers—seven D9, one D8, two D7, and one D6; three Michigan 280 rubber-tired dozers; eight van buses for transporting workers to the mine area; four Caterpillar motor graders; one 75-ton American crane plus various 5- to 30-ton hydraulic cranes; various forklift trucks; about 150 small trucks and automobiles.

Pass-through bays are provided for the haulage trucks and 150 smaller vehicles. Dozer and drill maintenance also is performed at this shop.

The main warehouse, attached to the main shop, is designed for receiving, stocking, and central disbursement. Parts are delivered directly to the work areas by a warehouse clerk. Warehouse and shop aisles are wide enough to deliver larger stock by forklifts.

Preventive maintenance is key to availability

More than 60 major equipment items, along with more than 150 service trucks and automobiles, are under the direct care of the Pinto Valley maintenance department. An exacting reporting and record system makes it possible for the maintenance department to include all units in the preventive maintenance program.

All haulage trucks are inspected at the beginning of each shift by the operator, using a prepared checklist. Additional scheduled inspections are made after 40, 100, 240, and 500 hr of operation. These inspections are generally performed in the mine lubrication shop by the lube service crew.

Daily hour-meter readings and 24-hr tachograph charts are used in scheduling inspections. Detailed records of all inspections and of the life of all component repairs and/or replacements are kept to allow prediction of average component life for future preventive maintenance scheduling.

Truck-bed liner thickness is measured periodically with ultrasonic thickness gauges to project approximate replacement dates. Most wear takes place near the lip of the bed. Wear strips are now installed in this area, extending bed-liner life by as much as 1,500 hr. Placed 4 to 6 in. apart, the wear strips create a tumbling action of the ore instead of the normal sliding action, which causes excessive wear.

Haulage truck oil is changed during scheduled preventive maintenance inspections. Oil is drained at 7 gpm by a suction system, and new oil is added at the rate of 10 gpm by a pressurized system. A complete oil change can be done in about 10 min. All off-highway units are equipped with dry-break (valved) couplers at drainage and fill points, minimizing downtime and eliminating contamination.

Oil samples taken during each change are forwarded to a consulting laboratory for spectrographic analysis. Abnormal results are reported to Pinto Valley for immediate action. This procedure identifies fuel oil contamination, indicates the extent of water leaks by chrome inhibitor content, and warns of component wear by metal traces.

To increase truck availability, gravity feed fueling systems having a 90- to 95-gpm flow rate are located alongside haul roads, where drivers can refuel their own equipment. The system also eliminates contamination and reduces spillage through the use of dry-break connections and automatic shutoff.

Shovels receive a daily walk-around visual inspection by the mine repair crew, which also performs scheduled electrical and lubrication preventive maintenance. Dippers require more maintenance than any other shovel component; however, excessive wear has been slowed by lining sides and bottoms with discarded dozer cutting blades spaced 4 in. apart. Dipper teeth also wear rapidly. Several types are continually being tested to determine which design or material provides the best results.

Wire rope cable life is another maintenance concern. Overall average life is about 70 shifts—900,000 tons of muck for the P&H 2100 and 1 million tons for the P&H 2300. Detailed cable records allow replacement prior to actual failure. With proper training and planning and the use of a hair-pin wound cable that allows stringing of both ends at the same time, a cable can be changed in less than 2 hr on the P&H 2100 shovel and in less than 4 hr on P&H 2300 shovel.

CITIES SERVICE COMPANY
PINTO VALLEY OPERATIONS

FIFTY (50) HOUR PREVENTATIVE MAINTENANCE INSPECTION REPORT
WABCO ORE HAULAGE TRUCKS

EQUIPMENT NO.:   DATE: HR. METER RDG.:

✓ CHECK IF O.K.   X — ADJUSTMENT   O — REPAIRS NEEDED

I. *CAB, INSTRUMENTS, AND GAUGES:*

1. CHECK OPERATIONS OF INSTRUMENTS AND GAUGES. _____
2. CHECK CONDITION OF CAB, SEATS, & GLASSES. _____
   A. Use emergency kill switch to shut engine down. _____

II. *UPPER DECK:*

1. RADIATOR —
   A. Check coolant level.
   B. Check for coolant leaks.
2. GREASE RESERVOIR —— AUTOMATIC LUBE SYSTEM:
   A. Fill reservoir until grease seeps from weep hole. _____
   NOTE: Record the amount of grease added.
   B. Visually check for grease build-up & lube system leakage, wipe off any excess grease and oil. _____
   C. Check system for proper timing and injector system. _____
3. AIR TANK —
   A. Drain moisture from the tank. _____
4. BRAKE POWER CLUSTERS —
   A. Check fluid level of all (4) power clusters on deck area. _____

III. *ENGINE COMPARTMENT:*

1. FAN AND SHROUD —
   A. Visually check condition of fan blades & shroud. _____
   B. Check for proper belt condition and operation. _____
2. AIR STARTER LUBRICANTS —
   A. Fill to proper oil level. _____
3. TURBOCHARGERS —
   A. Visually check oil and/or air leaks. _____
   B. Check condition of hoses and clamps. _____
4. FUEL FILTER AND STRAINER —
   A. Drain condensation from filter & strainer. _____
5. BATTERY —
   A. Check condition of terminals and cables. _____
   B. Fill to proper level with distilled water. _____
6. CRANKCASE —
   A. Check oil to assure an accurate reading. Allow a few minutes for oil to drain back into case before checking. _____
   B. Fill to proper level with MIL-2104B 30 WT. oil. _____

IV. *WHEELS AND FRAME:*

1. HYDRAULIC RESERVOIR —
   A. Check oil level at top sight glass with ore body down and engine shut off. If necessary fill to proper level with Series 3 10 WT. oil. _____
   B. Visually check for oil and air leaks. _____
2. FRAME AND ORE BED —
   A. Visually check for cracks or broken welds. (record on proper forms) _____
3. FUEL TANK —
   A. Check for fuel leakage.
   B. Fill tank to maximum capacity and record. _____
4. WHEELS —
   A. Visually check wheel mounting bolts for missing or loose bolts. _____
5. TIRES —   1.   2.   3A.   3B.   4A.   4B.
   A. Check and record condition of tires. ☐ ☐ ☐ ☐ ☐ ☐
   B. Check inflation pressure of each tire. (If necessary, inflate to proper pressure & record)
   1.___ 2.___ 3A.___ 3B.___ 4A.___ 4B.___
6. HYDRAIR SUSPENSIONS —
   A. Visually check piston extension on each suspension.
   B. Check for excessive oil leaks.
   C. Check condition of suspension skirt. _____
7. HYDRAULIC PUMP DRIVE SHAFT —
   A. Using a hand gun, lubricate each zerk fitting with one or two pumps of grease. _____
8. DRIVE BELTS:
   A. Check exciter blower and battery alternator v-belts for proper adjustment and tension. _____

V. *FINAL DRIVE HOUSING:*

1. MOTORIZED WHEEL GEAR CASE —
   A. Check oil level at sump inside final drive housing.
   NOTE: To assure an accurate reading permit a few minutes (Min. 20 minutes) for oil to drain into the case before checking. _____
2. BRAKE FLUID RESERVOIRS —
   A. Check for leakage. _____
   B. Check fluid level at glass indicator — If needed fill with Hydraulic Brake Fluid. _____
3. AIR RESERVOIRS —
   A. Drain condensation from brake apply tanks. _____

SIGNATURE OF MECHANICS PERFORMING ABOVE INSPECTION: _____

PARTS REMOVED/INSTALLED INFORMATION			
QTY	PARTS DESCRIPTION	PARTS NO.	SER. NO. (IF APPLICABLE)

Two lubrication trucks service most equipment at the job site. One truck has 12 metered service systems, including treated water, diesel fuel, gasoline, grease, air, oil suction, solvent, and five oil-holding compartments. Total carrying capacity is about 1,800 gal. The other truck has three systems for servicing the P&H shovels, a 3,000-lb bulk grease container, a 200-gal open-gear composition, a compressed-air tank, and pressurized pumping equipment. Shovel-grease bins are filled during the lunch hour to increase lube truck availability.

At most open-pit operations, lubrication servicemen are not qualified or permitted to make minor repairs. At Pinto Valley, lube servicemen are qualified and paid as heavy duty mechanics, and they make minor adjustments or repairs as required during preventive maintenance inspections or during lubrication. As a result, haulage trucks return to the main shop less often for repairs.

Electricians at the mine lubrication shop perform scheduled preventive maintenance inspections and repairs while trucks are in the lubrication bay. Servicemen and electricians assist each other, to reduce haulage truck downtime.

Tires are by far the largest single item among maintenance costs. They receive great care and attention to keep costs down as much as possible. Tread depth of all tires in use is measured each week, plotted, and graphed. This information is used to calculate costs per ton, per mile, and per hour. The same information pinpoints the proper time to rotate tires or turn them around to promote even wear and realize full tire life. A Haltec large-bore inflating-deflating system, used on all 36.00 x 51 tires, has reduced downtime 65% for deflating and 85% for inflating.

A Hyster 250E lift truck provides a safe and efficient handling method for the larger haulage truck tires. It can handle 10,800 lb, rotate 18° to either side of center, rotate holding pads 90°, side shift 10 in. to either side, tilt 15° forward and backward, and wrestle an alligator with one hand tied behind its back. Clamp openings range from 60 to 144 in. The truck can be used also for removal of the front tire and spindle assembly and for dismounting and remounting front suspensions by installing a special holder on the unit.

A Uni-press P-100 heavy duty tire changing machine, consisting of a 100-ton ram, mounting and demounting shoes, and hydraulic adapters, handles tires of 33- to 51-in. rim diameters. Changing a 36.00 x 51 tire takes about 30 min. Tires ranging from 9.00 x 20 through 10.00 x 22 can be changed in less than 10 min by a Royal 931A truck tire changer, eliminating the strenuous and time consuming job of breaking the bead with double jack hammers.

Record keeping plays a key role in optimum preventive maintenance scheduling. Pinto Valley, with 60 major mining units and 150 service vehicles to maintain, has kept the number of its inspection forms to about 30. The mine's preventive maintenance program is not yet computerized, but the planning and scheduling department has set up a system of records that can be converted to a data bank when sufficient data become available. ☐

Troubleshooting the rotary compressor

Leonard Basaj, engineer, Compressor Div., Allis-Chalmers Corp.

USERS OF ROTARY COMPRESSORS, drill rigs, or other air-operated equipment occasionally call upon our company to send out a field engineer to troubleshoot and settle disputes about performance of the equipment. Such a field trip is expensive, involving not only the engineer's time, travel, and living expenses, but also costs for shipment, installation, and removal of test equipment. In many cases, such a costly trip could have been avoided if operating personnel had been sufficiently aware of the details of compressor construction and operation and of basic principles, terms, and definitions involved in compressing air. Major factors affecting compressor air delivery efficiencies include engine speed, site elevation of the compressor, air temperature at intake, filter cleanliness, and valves, piping, and air leakage in the system.

Rotary sliding vane compressors are well suited for drill rig service because of simplicity of construction, which facilitates servicing. Major components are a horizontal cast-iron cylinder and cylinder heads with roller bearings supporting an eccentrically mounted rotor (Figs. 1 and 2). The crescent-shaped space between the rotor and cylinder is generally divided into separate cells by eight radially sliding vanes. Air enters the cylinder through the inlet ports and, as the rotor revolves, each cell in turn is cut off from the inlet port at a point where cell volume is at its maximum. Air volume in each cell is reduced to a minimum as the rotor-vane assembly rotates toward the discharge port-opening—compressing the air within the cell. At the bottom of the cylinder, the rotor curvature clearance approaches within a few thousandths of an inch of the cylinder bore, so the compressed air is displaced into the discharge piping no matter what the pressure level is at that point—an important characteristic of positive-displacement compressors. Overcompression or undercompression within the cylinder normally has a negligible effect on discharge temperature of the air or horsepower requirements of the compressor.

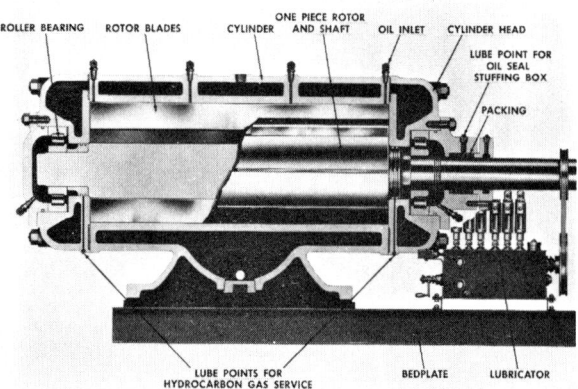

Fig. 1—Section through a rotary compressor.

The rotor sliding vanes are made of asbestos cloth and phenolic resin laminate. At present, these are the most suitable materials readily available. Vane material must have a low density and coefficient of friction, together with high strength and temperature resistance, and the material must be non-abrasive to the rotor slots and cylinder bore. Vane material and lubricating oil characteristics set permissible discharge air temperature limits near 350°F. Above this temperature, the vanes turn brittle and frayed, and the laminations separate at the rubbing edge, while the oil becomes carbonized and varnished. Plastics and lubricants that can tolerate higher temperatures are available, but they lack other desirable qualities. Those materials permitting higher operating temperatures while coming close to satisfactory physical requirements are too costly. Since the asbestos-resin vane material has a tendency to absorb moisture, swelling occurs in humid climates when the compressor is not operated for several weeks. Swelling must be prevented to avoid binding of the vanes.

Bearings are cylindrical roller type, NJ-400 series, designed for the highest load-carrying capacity within the dimensional frame. Each rotor has two bearings with separable inner races to facilitate removal of the cylinder heads as the inner race is shrunk on the shaft. The bearings have special internal clearances on the order of C4 to C5. Such clearance is necessary to shrink-fit the inner race on the shaft and to accommodate cooling of the outer race by the water jacket in the cylinder head while in operation.

A shaft seal or stuffing box is located where the shaft emerges from the cylinder head. A stuffing box with semi-metallic packing is used for service on drill rigs because of more severe service. Split-piston ring-type seals are located on each end of the shaft, immediately adjacent to the end faces of the rotor. The seals prevent air leakage from the high-pressure discharge side along the ends of the rotor into the bearing cavity and from there to the low-pressure inlet side.

Proper rotor clearance is of prime importance. The cylinder heads are dowelled to the cylinder to permanently position and locate the rotor through the roller bearings, coming as close as possible to the bottom of the cylinder bore and cylinder heads without making contact. It is most

Fig. 2—End view of rotary compressor; cylinder head removed.

important that such clearances be maintained after repair or dismantling of the compressor or replacement of parts. (The required "bottom," "end," and "net rotor float" clearances are stamped on the compressor nameplate.)

Clearances—particularly the bottom clearance—affect the **volumetric efficiency** of the compressor. Volumetric efficiency is expressed as the ratio of the air (cfm) actually taken into the compressor (measured at inlet temperature and pressure) to the internal volume (cfm) available for handling the air. The difference between these two volumes is the leakage through the clearances back to the inlet side of the compressor. The ratio shows the reduction in cfm between maximum possible ingested air and actually ingested air. The leakage is in turn proportional to the pressure differential across the compressor. Hence, the rating curve (Fig. 3) declines with increasing discharge pressure. The rating curve is not theoretical but represents the manufacturer's average shop-test performance on numerous, similar machines. The curve shows the volume of air aspirated, compressed, and delivered on the discharge side at a specified discharge pressure; however, this volume is always expressed at the compressor inlet conditions.

Pressure ratio is a dimensionless ratio of discharge pressure (absolute) to inlet pressure (absolute). The back leakage, and therefore the slope of the rating curve, is a function of the pressure ratio. The rating curve assumes a certain atmospheric inlet pressure, usually 14.4 psi absolute (the average atmospheric pressure in the midwestern US) and 60°F. For practical reasons, the rating curve is plotted against the discharge gauge pressure, but the discharge pressure scale is also proportional to the pressure ratio. Therefore, whenever the inlet pressure is other than 14.4 psia, an "equivalent discharge pressure" must be calculated to properly read and use the rating curve. For example, if a compressor operates at a location 4,000 ft above sea level where the barometric pressure is only 12.7 psia—with negligible pressure drop across the intake filter—and is discharging at 40 psi gauge, the pressure ratio is:

$$(12.7 + 40.0)/12.7 = 4.15$$

If the inlet were 14.4 psia, the equivalent discharge pressure for this pressure ratio would be:

$$14.4 \times 4.15 - 14.4$$

This is equivalent to:
$$14.4(4.15 - 1.0) = 14.4(3.15) = 45.4 \text{ psig}$$

Therefore, the compressor rating curve should be entered at 45.4 psig to find the compressor capacity rating for this example, because at this point the curve represents the pressure ratio and hence the volumetric efficiency. The capacity would always be expressed in cfm at inlet temperature and pressure, because only this volume divided by the compressor displacement gives an idea of volumetric efficiency.

If there is a need to know the air volume at the compressor discharge, the inlet volume may be recalculated to any other set of temperature and pressure conditions (point of use, sea level, etc.), remembering that the volume is inversely proportional to the absolute pressure (gauge pressure + barometric pressure) and directly proportional to absolute temperature (°F + 460).

Compressor capacity is equal to theoretical displacement minus the amount of internal leakage. Within the rotary compressor, the only leak path is through the clearances under and around the ends of the rotor. The clearances are fixed and do not change in time. The rotor vanes do not wear on their ends but only on the rubbing edge

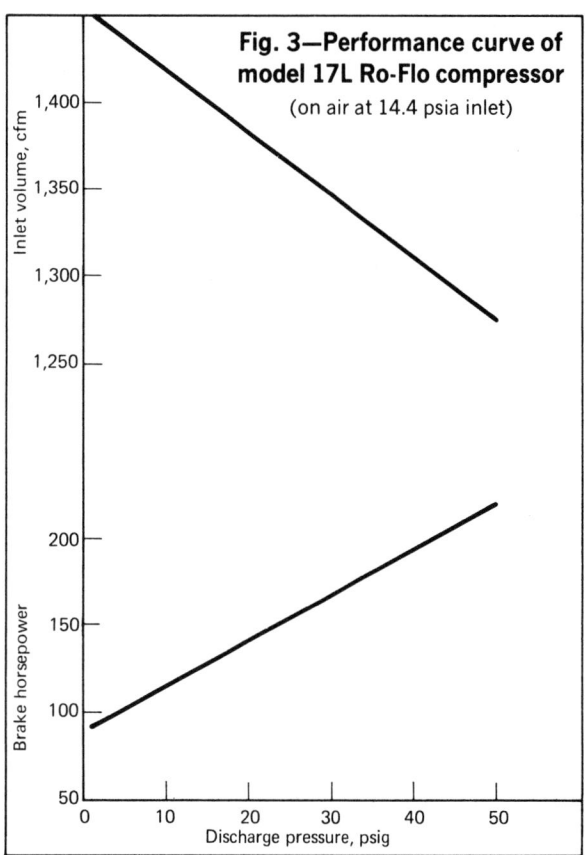

Fig. 3—Performance curve of model 17L Ro-Flo compressor
(on air at 14.4 psia inlet)

and the sides. The wear on the rubbing edge cannot affect the compressor capacity because the centrifugal force—several hundred pounds per vane—maintains a steady, positive contact between the vane and the cylinder bore. A case of severe wear of the cylinder bore, resulting in an increase of bottom clearance, would compensate for increased leakage by increasing displacement of the then-larger cylinder bore diameter. Therefore, it can be concluded that a rotary sliding vane compressor does not lose or change its capacity with age.

Possible causes of air loss and compressor problems

The quantity of air delivered to the point of usage is generally less than that discharged by the compressor because of external losses within the air distribution system,

Fig. 4—Data for shape of a test nozzle

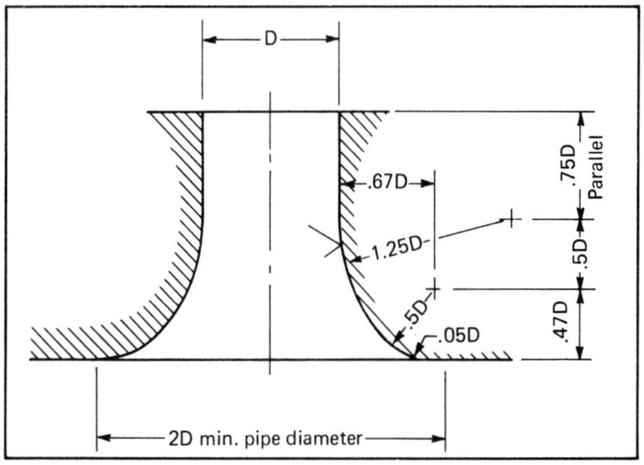

Troubleshooting guide for rotary compressors

Factor affecting compressor capacity	Effect	How much capacity affected acfm	scfm or lb/min.	Action required to remedy
1. Pressure ratio	Internal leakage through rotor clearances is proportional to pressure ratio.	Determines the slope of the performance curve.		None.
2. Elevation above sea level or low barometric pressure	Pressure ratio for the same gauge discharge pressure is increased.	Capacity reduced to that corresponding to a higher discharge pressure.	Directly proportional to inlet pressure.	Compressor speed may be increased to gain more air volume by increasing engine speed or changing sheave diameters.
3. Low compressor rotational speed.	Air volume delivered is directly proportional to speed for small deviations from standard.	In proportion to speed.		Check speed with tachometer. Correct engine speed, belt slippage, if necessary.
4. Excessive rotor clearances.	Clearances greater than those shown on the nameplate increase internal back leakage and discharge temperature.	1% capacity loss per 0.002-in. increase in bottom clearance or 0.008-in. increase of rotor float up to 150% of nameplate clearances. Above that, loss of capacity is more abrupt.		For proper operation, compressor must be reassembled with nameplate clearances.
5. High inlet temperature	Higher inlet air temperature produces higher discharge temperature for same discharge pressure; hence hotter rotor preheats inlet air and reduces its density.	Approximately 1% capacity reduction per 10°F above 100°F.		Relocate air intake if practical. To reduce excessive discharge temperature, small amounts of water may be injected into the cylinder.
6. Dirty intake filter	Lowers the inlet pressure.	Capacity reduced to that corresponding to a higher discharge pressure.	Directly proportional to inlet pressure.	Service the filter regularly, install pressure drop indicator, install prefiltering element.
7. Leaks in the shaft seal	Volume of air delivered is reduced by the amount of leakage through packing.	Usually less than 1%.	Usually less than 1%.	Tighten packing gland. Add or replace packing rings.
8. High cooling water temperature	Air discharge temperature is increased by 6°F for each 10°F increase in cooling water outlet temperature above 110°F. Capacity is thus affected, as in 5.	Approximately 1% up to 140°F.		Maintain cooling system's best efficiency. Check radiator for external and internal blockage, scale; pump and fan speed, etc.
9. Leaks in discharge piping	Volume of air delivered to bit is reduced by the amount of leakage.	By the amount lost.		Tighten leaky joints.
10. Loss into formation	Compressed air escapes from bottom of hole through cracks in formation to atmosphere or fills cavities.	Undetermined.	Undetermined.	None (sporadic occurrence). Water injection helps (see 12).
11. Orifices in drill bit	When smaller orifices are used in the bit to increase air pressure, more air is diverted for cooling cone bearings, less air blows through jets to pick-up chips and prevent regrinding. Bailing velocity not affected.	Undetermined. (Also, see 1.)		Operate at lowest practical pressure.
12. Water injection into discharge piping for dust control, etc.	Part of the water evaporates, increasing volume and discharge pressure. Intake air volume is reduced due to higher discharge temperature and pressure, but the volume of vapor compensates.	Approximately 2%, but offset by added vapor.		None.

Fig. 5—Setup for field test of compressor

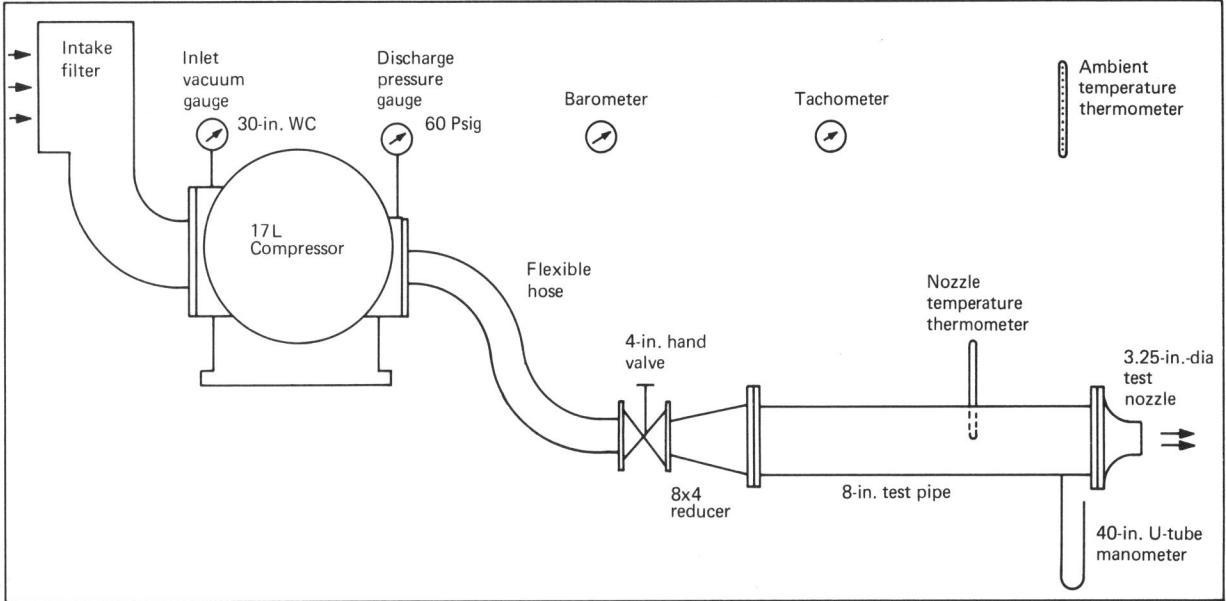

such as leaks in discharge piping, valves, joints, and other hardware. The intake filter will produce excessive pressure drop if it is dirty, and while the compressor's inlet volume does not change, air will enter the compressor at a lower inlet pressure. Therefore, the compressor is ingesting a lesser cfm of free air. Only at zero pressure drop across the intake filter is the inlet volume equal to cfm free air. We have already mentioned the effect of elevation on inlet pressure, hence cfm of free air. It should be carefully noted that compressor capacity changes in direct proportion to the speed of the drive engine, with a specific cfm of intake air for each specific rpm. Losses of bailing air at the drill bit may be caused by the bit end encountering cracks or voids in the rock formation being drilled. The accompanying table is a checklist for troubleshooting air losses.

Setting up to field test the rotary compressor

Whether at the factory or in the field, testing of compressors must be done in accordance with rules and procedures established by such recognized standards as the ASME Performance Test Codes for Compressors and Vacuum Pumps. Prime requirements include use of a properly shaped test nozzle (Fig. 4) arranged in an established length of pipe to insure laminar air flow through the nozzle, together with the necessary instruments (properly calibrated and connected) to insure valid temperature and pressure readings. The test equipment may be connected to the inlet flange or the discharge flange of the compressor or installed within the piping on either side (Fig. 5). The purpose of the test nozzle is to provide a calibrated flow channel (venturi), properly shaped to insure laminar flow, having a predictable and repetitive efficiency (discharge coefficient), and providing a measurable pressure drop in the flow stream. The volume of air may be calculated when the nozzle cross section area and the pressure drop are known. Orifices are not recognized as accurate flow-measuring devices because their discharge coefficients can vary from 0.60 to 0.90, while the nozzle discharge coefficients range from 0.97 to 0.995. An orifice can be calibrated for a given test setup, but another means of flow measurement is needed.

Determining needed air pressure and volume

The volume and pressure of air required for rotary drilling are determined by designers of drill rigs and tool bits. Aside from the manufacturers' literature, few references are available. The Compressed Air and Gas Institute's *Compressed Air and Gas Handbook* contains a section on rotary drilling that features a chart for selecting the air volume required with a given drill pipe and hole size for a desired bailing velocity (Fig. 6). The air requirement is expressed in cfm of free air. The pressure is determined by the size of orifices used in the drill bit, usually falling in the range of 20-50 psig. Low pressure is favored over high pressure because with low pressure, the power demand for the compressor is less and the discharge temperature and leakage loss are lower, while slightly more air is delivered from the compressor. Furthermore, a pressure that is too high causes rock chips to sandblast the tool cones into a prematurely worn condition. □

Fig. 6—Chart for determining bailing air velocity

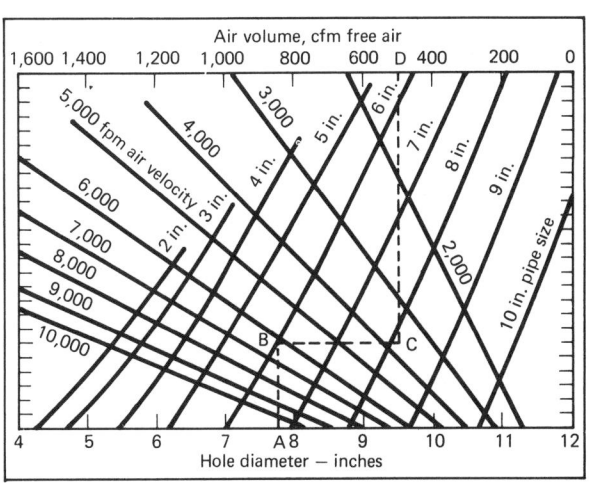

The tube of this hose has been softened and swollen by repeated, excessive exposure to oils or chemicals.

Pointers on the selection, use, and maintenance of hose

EVERY OPERATOR WANTS INCREASED AVAILABILITY of equipment, as well as lower operating costs. Failure of an inexpensive component, such as hose, can cause expensive downtime of major equipment in the mine and mill. Experts at Gates Rubber Co., Denver, Colo.—world's largest maker of rubber hose—offer the following suggestions for selection, use, and maintenance of hose to improve equipment reliability.

Selecting the right hose for the particular job

Select a hose with an interior diameter (ID) large enough to minimize pressure loss. The length of hose should provide for some slack. Remember that hydraulic hose can elongate up to 2% and contract some 4% of its total length when in use.

Determine the maximum operating pressure to which the hose will be subjected and order a hose of that rated working pressure. Never subject a hose to pressures higher than its designed pressure rating. Failure of the hose can cause injury and property damage. The most common cause of failure in hydraulic hoses is use of the wrong hose to perform a specific job.

When ordering hose, specify the type of equipment on which it will be used. Note the location of the hose on the equipment, and if the hose will be bent, determine the size of the bend radius along the inside of every curve. Select a hose for the needed bending radius, and never use it at a reduced radius.

Hose selection must take into account the chemical and physical properties of the material to be conveyed by the hose. Air lines that convey some oil must have a tube that is resistant to oil, or the ID will swell, restricting flow and increasing pressure. When ordering hydraulic hose, notify the hose manufacturer of the brand name and number of the fluid to be carried. The manufacturer should also be informed whether the hose is to be used for suction and/or pressure flow and whether the flow will be of a steady or a pulsating nature.

Order hose that is resistant to any deleterious conditions in the specific, external work environment at the jobsite. Temperature, weathering, and chemicals to which the hose will be subjected will determine the proper cover stock. Again, the normal, external stresses of movement, bending, etc., require selection of a stock that will minimize their effects.

Proper selection of fittings and couplings is most important. Portable crimp machines are available to produce factory-type assemblies with permanent couplings at the user's work site. This can be a distinct advantage at remote locations as a means of reducing parts inventories. Reusable, screw-on couplings are available for many types of heavy machinery. For permanent couplings, substitution of one manufacturer's product for another is poor policy, because they may not correctly match. Reusable couplings are generally interchangeable.

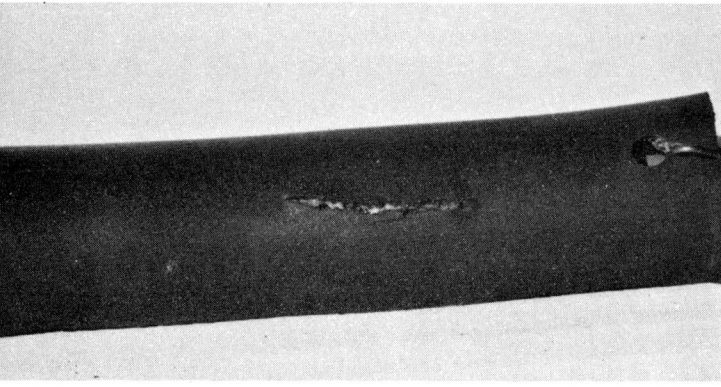

Hose cover and carcass were ruptured by excessive pressure.

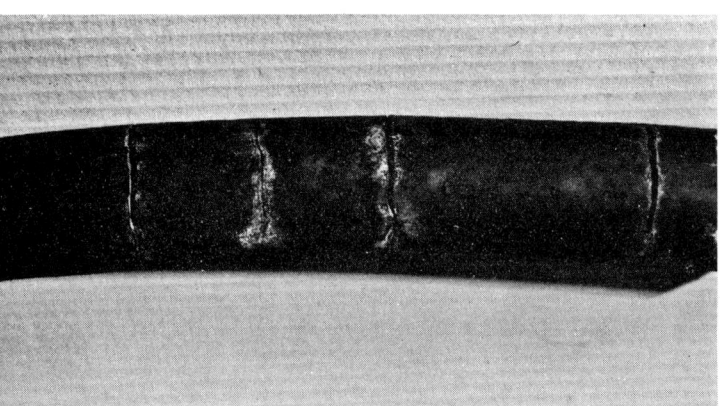

High ambient temperature hardened and cracked this cover.

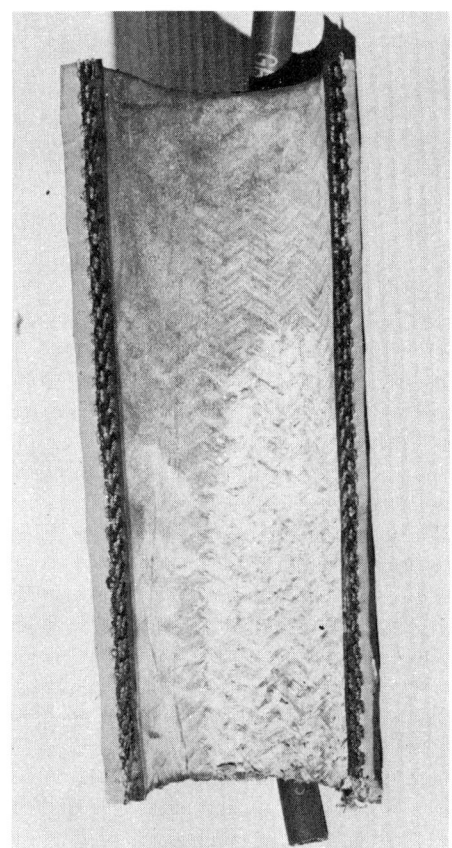

A sharp bend in this hose directed the abrasive it was carrying against one small area. The result: an eroded tube.

Guides for installing and using hose

Hose not in use should be stored in a relatively cool building and not subjected to direct sunlight, heating, or steam pipes. Keep hose on a flat surface, preferably within its original container. Properly stored, hose should have a minimum shelf life of five years.

When installing hose, be sure it is properly routed. Failure to route hydraulic hose properly and failure to observe the manufacturer's recommended minimum bend radii create undue stresses at the couplings and are a major cause of premature hydraulic hose failure. Permitting sharp bends in other types of hose causes the material to impinge on the tube stock at that point, resulting in localized wear and early failure.

In attaching hydraulic hose, never twist the hose. Use proper adapters and hold the coupling end in a fixed position when tightening the mating fitting to the port or another outlet. Always allow reasonable slack and make sure that the hose doesn't vibrate against other equipment. If it does, reroute it or give it protective cover. When aligning fittings, never use excessive force or push enlarged ends over pipe. Proper design facilitates assembly. Further guidelines:

- Never lift long lengths of hose in the middle while leaving ends hanging. Use dollies or a crane and give support over the entire length by slinging every 8 to 10 ft.
- Never hang hose vertically without adequate support.
- Avoid exposing a hose to temperatures above or below its designed temperature range.
- Don't gouge, kink, drag, or subject hose to excessive bending or pull hose near an angle next to a coupling.
- Never permit hose carcass to be exposed to corrosive fluids to which it is not resistant. Keep chemical hose ends clear of acids unless the ends are capped.
- Never subject hose to pressures—including surges—beyond the rated working pressure.
- Don't locate hoses where they are subject to crushing by traffic or damage by falling objects.

Hose inspection and maintenance

Set up a 30-day inspection system for hoses, but immediately inspect any hose subjected to unusual abuse. The hose to be inspected should be cleared of all matter and laid full length in a clean, dry area. Inspect the exterior for signs of blistering, cuts, and abrasion. If the reinforcement is exposed, or the outer cover is loose, the hose should be replaced. Be certain that all couplings are secure, and check the hose for soft spots adjacent to the couplings. If soft spots are present, the hose should be replaced.

Frequent or premature hose failures in a hydraulic system may be the symptom of malfunctions elsewhere. A regular inspection of all hydraulic equipment should be part of any maintenance program.

When installing new hydraulic hoses, make sure they are long enough to prevent sharp flexure. Hydraulic fluid leaking around couplings requires immediate attention. When using air lines, check the oil pots to make sure they are not feeding excessive amounts of oil to the hose.

Hoses should be rotated 90° periodically and switched end for end to achieve longer life. When not in service for extended periods, small diameter hoses should be coiled and placed out of harm's way, while larger hoses should be removed from the work area, cleaned, and stored. □

Reusable pipe insulation saves energy and speeds up installation and maintenance

AS PART OF AN ENERGY CONSERVATION PROGRAM at its Newgulf Frasch sulphur mine, Texasgulf Inc. is converting from use of a thin, low-density, blanket-type pipe insulation to a thick, high-density, molded fiber glass insulation. In doing so, the company has improved the thermal efficiency of its operation and has lowered the annual cost of insulation because the new insulation is reusable. Single-piece construction has also helped reduce installation cost, since the new insulation is applied 33% faster than the previous blanket type.

At the Newgulf installation, elemental sulphur is mined using the basic hot water injection methods of the Frasch process. Huge amounts of superheated water and piping are required for the process—up to 12 million gpd of water and 150 mi of piping. Temperature control is critical to keep the liquid sulphur from "freezing up" in the system. These demands require an efficient pipe insulation that can also be reused, because the piping is moved frequently from well to well.

According to Texasgulf's insulation supervisor, August Svatek, the company previously used a "one-time" fiber glass blanket wrap covered by a metal jacket. When lines were moved, the insulation wrap and jacket were thrown away, and the lines were rewrapped—a costly procedure. Furthermore, the thin blanket was not very efficient in saving energy. When the cost of producing energy from natural gas escalated dramatically, Texasgulf initiated an energy conservation program.

Insulation methods were among the first ways Texasgulf examined to conserve energy. After a thorough investigation of available insulations and their relative efficiencies, "850° Snap-On Fiber Glass Pipe Insulation" was selected as meeting not only the requirements for improved efficiency but also the reusage criterion.

Manufactured by CertainTeed Corp. of Valley Forge, Pa., 850 Snap-On insulation is supplied in cylindrical sections having an integral hinge that spreads open to receive the pipe and then snaps closed after the insulation is in place. Its high density and molded construction offer durability that the previous blanket insulation system lacked. In addition, 850 insulation has a low k-factor of 0.29 at 200° mean temperature, providing better thermal efficiency compared with the blanket's k-factor of 0.39 on a 1-in. to 1-in. basis.

All of the 850 insulation used at Newgulf is 4 in. in diameter and 1½ in. thick. "A 2-in. thickness was initially considered," Svatek states, "because we were relating it to values of 2 in. of calcium silicate insulation, which was also being examined. The thermal performance of the fiber glass was better than calcium silicate,

Even after three usages, this section of 850 insulation has retained its shape and its ease of installation.

however, and we found we could get virtually the same peformance with 1½ in. of 850 insulation as we could with 2 in. of calcium silicate. Thus, the decision to utilize 1½-in. fiber glass was made, since we were obtaining added insulation for essentially the same cost."

The energy savings of the new insulation were apparent almost immediately. "The first uses were on the steam lines," Svatek notes, "and we could quickly see the results because we didn't lose the same amout of steam pressure during cold or inclement weather as we did before. We knew the new insulation was working and that it was already becoming a definite factor in reducing energy needs."

The 850 Snap-On insulation is now being phased into the entire Texasgulf insulation program, and eventually all Frasch piping will be insulated with the material. Each time a Frasch line is moved and the old blanket-type insulation is removed, the new insulation is applied in its place. The application procedure is basically a three-step operation: first, a section of insulation is snapped around the pipe, then a 0.006-gauge corrugated aluminum jacket is wrapped around the insulation for weather protection, and finally, an aluminum wire is used to hold the jacket firmly in place. Aluminum is used for both jacket and banding to resist the corrosive atmosphere.

Since the introduction of 850 insulation, the ease, speed, and cost of application have improved greatly. "Installation is much faster than with either the blanket insulation or calcium silicate," Svatek says. "With the blanket insulation, a crew would average about 700 to 800 linear ft of pipe per day. With the 850 pipe insulation, the same crew averages about 1,000 ft per day, an increase of nearly 33%, or in terms of production, 200-300 ft per day per crew. The figures compared to calcium silicate are even higher."

No saws or special tools are required to cut the 850 insulation, making the fabrication of elbows and other types of fittings quick and easy. For example, notches to fit over couplings can be sectioned out of the insulation's interior using only a knife.

Svatek also notes that 850 insulation is less subject to damage. "Calcium silicate is a much more brittle material and tends to break during shipment, storage, and handling. Moreover, we usually cannot salvage calcium silicate insulation when we have to move Frasch lines." Svatek adds, "Reusage was probably one of the most important factors leading to 850's use at Texasgulf. The blanket type of insulation, for example, has no resiliency at all in terms of physical abuse. It was simply too thin and too light, whereas the 850 insulation is firmer, thicker, and denser, to resist impact damage."

The insulation crews also prefer the 850 insulation because it does not stick to the pipe. By contrast, crews had to pry or cut off blanket insulation that stuck, which could not be reused. Because it has considerably higher density and does not fluff away as did the blanket, the 850 fiber glass can be removed very easily. A majority of the new insulation can thus be salvaged for reuse on new lines.

The average reusage rate of CertainTeed insulation is still unknown, but so far, at least one line is coverd with insulation that was used three times previously. The insulation on numerous other lines is in its third application, and scores of lines carry insulation that has been used at least once before.

Svatek believes that he'll be able to obtain easily at least three usages from each section of 850 insulation, and he plans to utilize each section until reuse is no longer possible. "The only factors that will reduce the reusage rate are the degree of abuse the insulation must undergo, which is usually dependent on its location within the facility, and how the insulation is handled by the crews. Insulation that is removed and applied with care, for example, will obviously have a longer productive life."

The initial cost of the 850 insulation is higher than for the blanket insulation, but because of the reusage factor, the life-cycle cost of the molded insulation is far less expensive. "It is simply cheaper to use over the long run," Svatek states. "Plus, we are lowering our energy costs because of the added thermal performance."

The CertainTeed insulation is functioning so well that it is also being used at Texasgulf's year-old Comanche Creek facility near Fort Stockton, Tex. Not only are the 4-in. Frasch lines at this facility insulated with the 850 product, but the 6-in., 8-in., and 12-in. Frasch piping as well. Svatek notes that the Fort Stockton facility, in fact, used the new insulation prior to Newgulf. "Fort Stockton received the first shipments," he says, "because it was a new installation under construction at the time and proper insulation was a critical priority in order to conserve energy from the outset. At Newgulf, on the other hand, we are essentially retrofitting. In both cases, however, the same means—insulation—are being utilized to meet the same end—conservation." □

The fiber glass blanket previously used deteriorated quickly under physical abuse and inclement weather.

Locking flywheel bolts with anaerobic adhesive prevents them from loosening during operations and provides a seal against oil leaks.

New anaerobic adhesive technology helps keep mine and plant equipment running

James Claflin, market manager, industrial MRO, Loctite Corp.

THE MONEY-SAVING ADVANTAGES of anaerobic adhesives as maintenance materials have been quickly recognized. A variety of management-mandated programs are now in progress to educate maintenance and repair personnel about the technology, using films, literature, seminars, and traveling classrooms.

Polymer hardens when deprived of oxygen

"Anaerobic" adhesives contain a unique polymer that is kept in a liquid state by access to oxygen. When deprived of oxygen, it hardens without shrinking. The liquid material may be injected between closely fitted metal parts, where it fills all voids, depriving itself of air. The hardened resin is molded against the microscopic roughness of the interfacing parts, preventing the parts from moving until they are deliberately sheared by the force of a tool. Parts that have been properly joined by oxygen-sensitive polymers have virtually complete resistance to loosening by vibration, but the parts can be readily disassembled with the use of tools.

Oxygen-sensitive polymers were laboratory curiosities until implications of their usefulness attracted the attention of the late Dr. Vernon Krieble, then head of the Department of Chemistry at Trinity College, Hartford, Conn.

After retirement from the university, Dr. Krieble founded what is now Loctite Corp. in Newington, Conn., to manufacture and market the polymers. Krieble had learned how to control anaerobic polymers, using inhibitors to produce a range of curing speeds, developing viscosity ranges adaptable to various clearances, and developing a range of shear strengths (mild for soft metals). The materials must be packaged in oxygen-permeable plastics.

Engineers quickly accept Krieble's strange resins

One of the first companies to use the new resins was the neighboring Branford Vibrator Co. of Branford, Conn. The firm, which manufactured ore car shakeout vibrators, could not keep the machines from vibrating themselves loose. Even double-nutting or welding connections didn't work. The company turned to anaerobics for thread-locking and when they proved successful, Branford simplified designs and offered "no-shake-loose" guarantees to buyers.

Another neighboring firm, a construction company, required frequent refitting of new 9-in. bearings for a rock crusher. Refittings were accomplished by weld buildup of metal and machining. Krieble's young company proved that use of anaerobics would prevent spin-out, and metallizing and machining could be largely eliminated.

Preventive maintenance techniques using anaerobic polymers were also pioneered by manufacturers of mining equipment. Caterpillar was quick to recommend anaerobics for locking troublesome track bolts on the company's tractors. International Harvester was first to apply anaerobics as a gasketing material, using them to seal differential flanges on off-road "Pay" haulers. These huge trucks placed great torque on differential housings, and conventional gaskets were frequently torn, causing loss of fluids. Changeover to anaerobic gasketing solved the problem. Bolts could be torqued to specifications, and the metal-to-metal contact between flange faces increased the resistance to shifting.

The use of anaerobic thread-locking, fluid-sealing, and retaining adhesives on mining equipment should increase equipment availability and save maintenance dollars. All the forces that can destroy machinery act within the mining environment, including severe impact, vibration, extended stress, corrosion, and extremes in temperature. Furthermore, the need for equipment to run continuously, the isolation from suppliers of spare parts, and the necessity of stocking backup parts and equipment militate for an aggressive program of preventive maintenance that uses materials such as anaerobic adhesives. Mining conditions attack mechanical devices at their weakest interfaces: thread fasteners, threaded connections in fluid lines, flanged joints in piping and machinery, and closely fitted assemblies typical of shaft- or housing-mounted parts (bearings, bushings, sleeves, gears, and other parts).

How to lock threaded fasteners

Several anaerobic adhesives have been designed specifically for locking threaded fasteners, with various combinations of viscosity, shear strength, and cure speed to make them suitable for different tasks. All anaerobics provide high breakloose torque and high prevailing torque during removal.

- High-strength, high-viscosity adhesives such as Loctite 271 firmly anchor large studs or cap screws that are seldom disassembled.
- Medium-strength, medium-viscosity Loctite 242 adhesive is used to lock nuts, bolts, and other parts that are frequently disassembled for repair.
- High-strength, low-viscosity adhesives such as Loctite 601 hold closely fitting joints between bearings in housings.

Of the countless threaded fasteners used in mining equipment, some are more susceptible than others to loosening by vibration. At its Kidd Creek operations in Timmins, Ont., Texasgulf Canada Ltd. uses anaerobic adhesives for:

- Locking base pad bolts, cap bolts in the rotary head, and hydraulic column mounting bolts on a Robbins Model 61 raise boring machine.
- Locking the hydraulic cylinder rod nuts on "Scooptram" dump cylinders.
- Locking motor mount studs in the block of a 10-cylinder Deutz diesel engine on a Wagner ST8 Scooptram.
- Setting rocker arm adjustment nuts on the Deutz engine to salvage used tappet arm ESNA nuts and to lock and seal flywheel bolts.
- Holding fasteners that had previously worn into softer metal castings and die castings.

Anaerobics seal fluid-handling systems

Mine operators are well aware of the serious conse-

Sealing hydraulic fittings with anaerobic compound avoids the problem of locating a leak among 700 joints.

quences of hydraulic fittings that leak: equipment damage, production interruptions, costly downtime, loss of expensive fluids, and the hazards of flammable fluids that escape.

Two anaerobic materials have been carefully engineered to seal the threaded connections and flanged joints of fluid-handling systems. "Pipe Sealant with Teflon" (PS/T) is used on threads, and "Gasket Eliminator 504" on flanges. PS/T is Teflon-filled to provide lubricity and slow curing, while 504 is a gel that clings to any surface.

PS/T has proven such an effective adhesive that General Motors' truck plant at Pontiac, Mich., has eliminated the use of some 50 other sealants, standardizing PS/T for all truck fittings in systems that handle air, oil, coolants, and hydraulics.

PS/T seals parts instantly, but the assembled components can be aligned during the 24-hr curing period of the adhesive. Once curing is accomplished, the fittings are locked against loosening by vibration but are easily disassembled when required. PS/T effectively seals parts against contaminants and is not subject to attack by corrosives, including synthetic or hydrocarbon fluids.

In the past, Scooptrams and jumbos at the Kidd Creek mine chronically leaked hydraulic oil from the hundreds of fittings on each machine. The use of PS/T has drastically reduced leakage.

Use of anaerobics for flange sealing is a significant departure from conventional methods of gasketing. Traditional methods squeeze compressible materials between mating parts having surface imperfections. Such soft gaskets—made of cork, paper, felt, and composition materials—"take a set," resulting in loss of bolt tension. Inadequate bolt tension and vibration of the flange faces abrade and tear the soft gasket material, and leakage then follows.

When the anaerobic Gasket Eliminator 504 is applied to mating surfaces, it provides a metal-to-metal fit after flange bolts are tightened. Because the sealant does not take a set, there is no loss of bolt tension. The gel-like material is applied to mating surfaces from a tube or caulking gun, filling all surface imperfections. Once the material has cured, it locks the mated parts against lateral shifting. Pressure resistance beyond 5,000 psi can be achieved. When required, the flanges can easily be separated by wedging, and the mated surfaces easily cleaned. The use of 504—a "gasket in a tube" that can be carried in each mechanic's toolbox—makes it unnecessary to stock extensive inventories of gaskets. The material is good for sealing all covers, access ports, and other flanges where clearances do not exceed 0.030 in.

Gasket Eliminator 504 has been used to seal oil cooler adapters, retarder valve covers, transmission casing halves, planetary gear covers, and all types of pumps and gear reducers. PS/T is used to seal hydraulic fittings on continuous miners, loaders, trucks, jumbo drills, roof bolters, and rotary drills.

Anaerobics retain fitted parts

Force fitting is a traditional assembly technique for holding bearings in housings or for mounting pulleys, fans, rotors, and other shaft-mounted components. A variety of other assembly methods are also used for shaft-mounted parts, including keys, tapered shafts, knurls, splines, set screws, pins, and split hubs. All these techniques require costly machining.

Anaerobic adhesives can be substituted for many of these assembly techniques. Anaerobics can be used to fit parts with a clearance on the diameters of up to 0.005 in. and a surface finish no finer than 63 RMS. Alternately, adhesives can be incorporated into press-fit procedures for additional holding force. In this case, the material acts as a lubricant during pressing. Railroad overhaul shops use anaerobic adhesives in press fitting wheels to axles.

Anaerobic retaining compounds can prevent bearing spin-out or seizing on heavy-duty mining equipment. The tight metal-to-metal fit provided by anaerobics seals the joint against corrosive liquids and prevents fretting, galling, and resultant bearing seizure. When bearings must be replaced, use of anaerobics makes it unnecessary to metallize or remachine the hubs or housings up to size.

To facilitate the assembly of large-scale parts, Rhein-Braunkohlewerke AG used an anaerobic adhesive to fill a clearance of 0.004 in. between the 27-in. roller bearing and shaft of a 7,600-ton strip mining excavator. Pressing such a bearing on the shaft would have required a large work force and major equipment. Anaerobic assembly was done by hand, without a jig press. The anaerobic seal has greater push-out resistance than a press fit.

Anaerobic adhesives have been used to retain fitted parts on wheel bearings for heavy-duty trucks, power-steering pump bearings, diesel engine cylinder liners, and bushings and sleeves on all types of equipment.

Fast-bonding adhesives for maintenance

Cyanoacrylates are high-strength, easy-to-use adhesives

Mechanic restores front wheel bearing fit to 120-ton truck without metallizing or remachining. Anaerobic retaining compound is applied to clean shaft, and bearing is slipped onto shaft. After 20 min curing period, the assembly is complete.

Large 27-in. bearing on a 7,600-ton stripping excavator is securely mounted using a high-strength anaerobic adhesive.

that permanently bond parts within seconds. These materials require a close fit and airborne moisture for curing. The bond is established by a few seconds of firm manual pressure, without using clamps. Cyanoacrylates—one-part, clear liquids with a potential tensile strength up to 5,000 psi—are effective on smooth, nonporous surfaces with clearances not exceeding 0.003 in. They bond metal, vinyl, rubber, ceramics, and most plastics and are commonly used for repairing loose soundproofing material and loose mounting rubber and for remounting all types of trim. Because of their unique ability to bond rubber instantly, cyanoacrylates are used for making O-rings from cord stock. Kits on the market contain a variety of cord stock sizes, adhesive, and accessories. This repair method saves time and money—especially when shaft-mounted parts need not be disassembled to build an O-ring around the shaft.

Epoxy adhesives are well known for their strength and ability to fill gaps. The parts to be joined must usually be clamped together after application of the epoxy to allow an extended curing period. Epoxies are suited for bonding or patching rough parts such as broken castings or for strengthening riveted sheet metal assemblies. They work well on almost any material, including wood, glass, ceramics, and metal.

Anerobics seal pores in castings and welds

Anaerobic adhesives have been developed for sealing pores in welds and castings to prevent seepage. Low viscosity is required to penetrate microscopic pores. Parts can be soaked in sealant, or sealant can be painted on the surfaces. After penetrating the open pores by capillary action, the adhesive self-hardens, providing the seal. To assure that the parts to be joined are free of oil or other liquids, steam cleaning, solvent cleaning, or baking may be required.

How to use adhesives effectively

The cardinal rule for effective use of adhesives is cleanliness. However, when anaerobic adhesives must be used on extremely dirty, oily, or cold surfaces, primers will maximize curing effectiveness. While newer versions of the adhesives will cure on oily parts, priming guarantees full bond strength. Apply only the amount of adhesive needed; excessive adhesive migrates from the joint.

Because many mechanics tend to be unsure about adhesive strength, they use versions stronger than required—creating unnecessary problems when the parts must be disassembled. Parts that are excessively bonded can be separated by heating to 450°F.

The curing speed of adhesives varies, ranging from minutes to several hours. If stress is placed on an adhesive bond before curing is complete, the bond will be destroyed. The curing process is speeded up by heat and retarded by cold temperatures. Anaerobics should not be used if the ambient temperature exceeds 350°F.

Because gap-filling ability varies among anaerobic adhesives, the size of the gap to be filled should be considered in selecting the proper adhesive for the job. □

References

1) Kennedy, B. and Claflin, J., "Heavy Duty Adhesives," HEAVY DUTY EQUIPMENT MAINTENANCE, September 1975, pp 45-49.
2) "'Anaerobic' Adhesives: Versatile for Railroads," PROGRESSIVE RAILROADING, September 1975, pp 103-105.
3) Batson, R. I. and Tokarski, J. G., "Keeping Fasteners Tight," MACHINE DESIGN, September 18, 1975, pp 86-89.
4) Cross, R. and Shea, E., "Automotive Gaskets Out of a Tube," COMMERCIAL CAR JOURNAL, June 1975, pp 88-91.
5) "Guide to Tolerances and Finishes," Aerospace Div., Martin-Marietta, Orlando, Fla.
6) Irving, R., "Adhesives Assist Fasteners in the Vibration Battle," IRON AGE, July 21, 1975, pp 33-35.
7) "Anaerobic Adhesives . . . On the Road to High Reliability," AUTOMOTIVE INDUSTRIES, November 1972, pp 52-55.
8) Nystrom, R. G., "Cut Labor Costs and Downtime with Adhesive Bonded O-rings Made on the Jobsite," PLANT ENGINEERING, March 7, 1974, pp 226-227.

The dollars and sense of selecting wear materials

Richard A. Thomas, Assistant editor

AT A TIME WHEN THE GROWING COMPLEXITY of process technology and the dictates of a pinched economy create many questions and few answers, a fresh look at structural materials used in minerals processing can be helpful. This review highlights consumable materials that are significant factors in plant operating costs on a month-to-month (or in some cases day-to-day) basis.

Cost/wear ratios, downtime, material availability, and a host of other factors influencing material usage demand particular attention when viewed against the backdrop of inflation, the need for increased efficiency in existing processes, and the dearth of standardized, accepted "how to" guides for materials assessment and selection. Materials designed for "sacrificial wear" through mechanical abrasion or chemical corrosion are especially important in this context.

The greatest wear logically comes in the comminuting phase of processing, when ores are mechanically reduced in size by primary and secondary crushing and by grinding in various types of mills. The material properties of greatest concern are abrasion resistance (influenced strongly by carbon content in ferrous materials) and toughness (a measure of resistance to impact). Complications arise from the almost inversely proportional relationship between the two properties. Materials with higher carbon volumes, such as white irons, have greater abrasion resistance, but they are more brittle and thus more subject to fracture than low-carbon materials such as steels. Likewise, martensitic (heat treated) structures generally have greater hardness and compressive strength than austenitic (as-cast) structures, but they are more subject to spalling and breakage.

The engineer must determine the optimum combination of these and other properties for each service—a job sometimes made difficult by variations in experts' opinions on the "best" material for a particular need. There are also substantial differences between laboratory data reported for a given material and that material's performance in a commercial scale operation.

Last year's Amax-sponsored Symposium on Materials for the Mining Industry, held on July 30 and 31 at Vail, Colo., aired numerous opinions about the relative merits of several standard alloys and pointed up the gaps in objective evaluation caused by non-standardized testing and reporting. Data here were taken in part from the symposium preprints, which are now available through Climax Molybdenum Co.

The demands of crushing service

Although low- and medium-alloy steels and several specialty alloyed irons have enjoyed some popularity gains in crushing service, high-alloy (10-18%) austenitic manganese steels continue to predominate, especially where severe crushing is required (Table 1). Toughness is frequently a must for mantles, bowl liners, segmental concaves in gyratory and cone crushers, and the movable and stationary plates of jaw crushers. A high degree of fracture toughness, coupled with adequate abrasion resistance, gouging resistance, and moderate cost, make austenitic Mn steels popular where repeated and severe impact occurs.

Hardenability (not to be confused with hardness) is another property that establishes the 100-year-old dominance of austenitic Mn steels (often called Hadfield steels). Under repeated impact, these steels tend to work-harden, with plastic deformation of the microstructure. Hardness increases of 300 HB and more can be achieved by work-hardening. Although several other alloying elements besides manganese—including Mo, Cr, Si, and Ni—can change the hardenability of steels, manganese is still the most potent (Fig. 1). Although carbon very strongly influences the maximum hardness of a given steel, it has only a minimal effect on hardenability.

As with all other structural materials, Mn steel does have drawbacks. Although its abrasion and gouging resistance are adequate, they are not great. Molybdenum and/or chromium are often added in 1-3% amounts to improve the abrasion resistance of Mn steel. Hardfacing of the ore-contacting surfaces with weld material is frequently necessary, especially when the ores processed are highly abrasive. (Taconites and high-silica ores are good examples.) Mn steel also lacks machinability and has a generally lower yield strength.

Wear scars form on the Mn steel mantle of a gyratory crusher.

Photo credit: Amax Inc.

Table 1—Typical compositions of cast austenitic manganese steels

	Percentages				
	Mn	C	Cr	Mo	Other
Standard grade	12.0-14.0	1.0-1.4	—	—	—
Chromium alloyed	12.0-14.0	1.0-1.4	1.5-2.5	—	—
1% Mo alloyed	12.0-15.0	0.8-1.3	—	0.8-1.2	—
2% Mo alloyed	12.0-15.0	1.0-1.5	—	1.8-2.2	—
1% Mo lean alloy[1]	5.0-7.0	1.1-1.4	—	0.8-1.2	—
High yield strength[2]	12.0-15.0	0.4-0.7	2.0-4.0	1.8-2.2	2.0-4.0 Ni 0.5-1.0 V
Machinable[3]	18.0-20.0	0.3-0.6	—	—	2.0-4.0 Ni 0.2-0.4 Bi

1) US Patent No. 3,113,861.
2) US Patent No. 3,057,838.
3) US Patent No. 3,010,823.

Fig. 1—Relative effects of common alloying elements on hardenability of steel castings

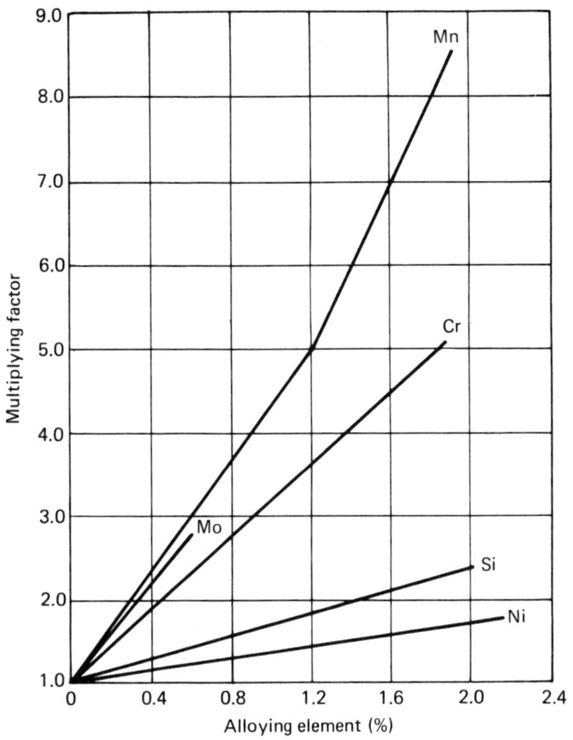

A relatively new trend is the use of "lean manganese" steels in crushing service. Some of the extreme toughness in Hadfield 12-13% Mn steels is being sacrificed for improved abrasion resistance by reduction of the manganese content to 5-7%. This reduction still allows the high degree of toughness characteristic of Mn steels.

If crushing severity is mild (small particle size and/or favorable ore friability characteristics), a less tough material with greater abrasion resistance can be used. Oil-quenched low-alloy steels and alloyed cast irons appear suitable under certain well defined operating conditions.

Availability is a critical factor in material selection. Orders for Mn castings have recently been backlogged because of the shortfall in foundry capacity, and customers are being advised to plan for longer lead time when ordering manganese alloy crushing equipment. Average lead time for new crushers has already stretched out from 7½ months to 18 months over the last year. A general awareness of the difficulty in obtaining replacement parts for processing and mining equipment is dictating an increase in the use of hard facing alloys to prolong the life of components in wear service.

Milling service—a very different animal

The milling stages of comminution commonly use a much wider variety of materials. There are three major divisions of candidate materials for mill liners: 1) ferrous alloys, both cast and wrought, 2) rubber and other elastomers, and 3) ceramics and natural stone materials. Although the elastomers are gaining popularity, particularly in double stage and fine grinding operations, ferrous alloys are still the principal lining materials in ball, rod, and autogenous mills. Ceramic liners are now largely restricted to the cement and pigment industries.

While toughness is the keynote in crushing service, abrasion resistance is the most important factor in milling operations. Large-grained martensitic structures provide much greater hardness and low-stress abrasion resistance than smaller-grained austenitic or pearlitic structures. Abrasion resistance is also a function of carbon volume percentage. Higher-carbon steels and white irons (more than 2% C) are generally more abrasion resistant—and less tough—than low-carbon steels. Martensitic Cr-Mo white irons, which incorporate chromium carbides (Cr_7C_3 type) in a martensitic matrix, are now billed as the most abrasion resistant materials commonly used.

While abrasion resistance is primary, toughness in mill liners is also important. Impact in mills is a function of service conditions (mill speed, bell diameter, interior lift contour, etc.) that may be varied as necessary; however, spalling and breakage continue to occur, even in the most expensive liners. One trend in liner upkeep is use of liner plates with fewer bolt holes, speeding up removal and replacement.

Cost factors in mill lining have a high priority because

Table 2—Typical costs of materials used for mill linings*

Material	Cost per lb	Installation cost per lb[1]	Installed cost per lb	Relative weight of complete lining	Relative installed cost of lining[4]	Toughness rating[5]
Martensitic Cr-Mo white iron	$0.38	$0.04	$0.42	100	42	6
Martensitic Ni-Cr white iron	0.30	0.04	0.34	100	34	7
Martensitic Cr-Mo steel	0.36	0.04	0.40	100	40	5
Austenitic 6Mn-1Mo steel	0.32	0.04	0.36	100	36	3
Austenitic 12Mn steel	0.30	0.04	0.34	100	34	2
Pearlitic Cr-Mo steel	0.28	0.04	0.32	100	32	4
Pearlitic white iron	0.22	0.04	0.26	100	26	8
Rubber	1.17	0.10	1.27	23[2]	29	1
Ceramic	0.37	0.18	0.55	44[3]	24	9

* Costs and weights are based on averaged data from several large milling operations in the western US in December 1973.
1) Installation cost includes cost of bolts plus labor, except for rubber, where bolt cost is included in cost per lb, and for ceramic, where cement was used in place of bolts.
2) Relative weight of rubber lining includes weight of bolts and metal reinforcement.
3) Ceramic assumed to have same lining volume as the ferrous materials.
4) Relative installed cost of lining does not include cost of lost production during shutdown for relining.
5) Highest order of toughness = 1, and lowest = 9.

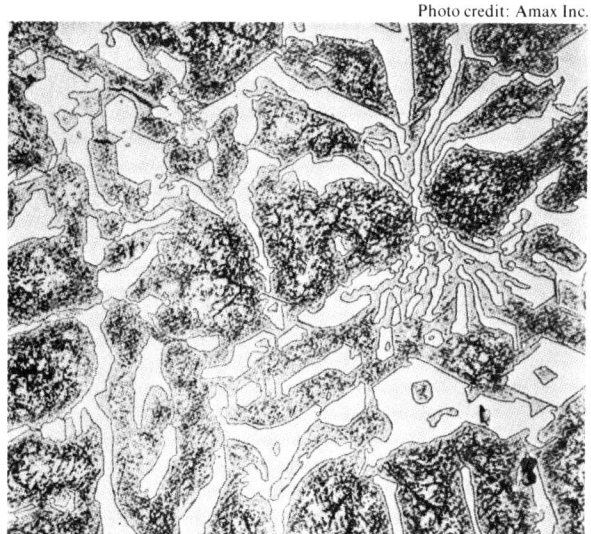

Typical microstructure of a mill liner made of martensitic Cr-Mo white iron. The section shows Cr_7C_8-type carbides in a martensitic matrix. Magnification is 500 x.

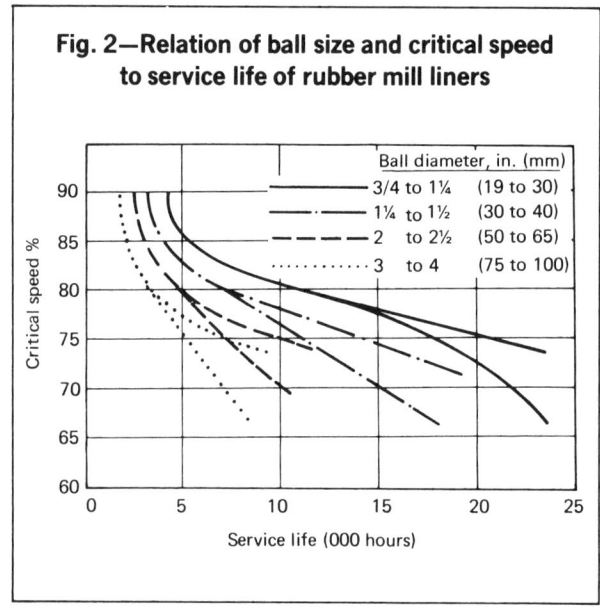

Fig. 2—Relation of ball size and critical speed to service life of rubber mill liners

of the increasing necessity to process lower grade ores. Most of these ores contain high percentages of silica and other abrasive gangues that increase liner wear. *Total* cost of a given lining differs substantially from its *installed* cost. Total cost includes costs of the material, the installation, and the shutdown time for relining, which in turn is measured in terms of lost production. Although the value of lost production varies considerably from mill to mill, it can account for more than 50% of the installed cost. However, the installed cost is traditionally considered the major cost factor in liner selection, and it has risen rapidly over the last 30 years.

It cannot be overemphasized that today's technology has not produced a singular "best" mill liner. Widely varying mill and ore conditions, plus fluctuations in the availability and price of materials, make it unlikely that any material will merit such a designation in the near future.

Although literally hundreds of ferrous materials have been tested as mill liners since the 1930s, only a few have survived to dominate in milling service (Table 2):

Martensitic Cr-Mo white irons. These are the most abrasion resistant of the popular materials; unhappily, they are also highest in cost per pound. Tungsten carbides are even harder, but their first cost makes them prohibitively expensive in most applications. Cr-Mo white iron liners are surprisingly resistant to spalling and breakage, although some high-impact mills will cause them to break. They are enjoying increased use in the taconite industry, where abrasion levels are very high. Chromium improves abrasion resistance of the iron, while molybdenum fosters formation of the martensitic matrix and increases the amount of carbon that may be used.

Martensitic Ni-Cr white irons. Frequently known as "Ni-Hard" irons, these materials exhibit good-to-excellent abrasion resistance, frequently coupled with marginal toughness. Although nickel acts much like manganese on the transformation of steel, recurrent spalling and breakage has largely restricted chill-cast Ni-Hards to medium- and low-impact ball mills, and to rod mills where a high pulp level sufficiently cushions impact.

Martensitic Cr-Mo steels. Low alloying costs and the potential for a variety of applications are promoting quite rapid growth in this group. A number of recently developed wrought and cast compositions capable of full hardening by air quenching may replace conventional oil-quenched types. Good-to-excellent hardness and relatively good toughness, especially in the medium-carbon range, will provide substantial competition for the white irons in the future. These steels are already being used in high-impact service where Cr-Mo irons and Ni-Hards are not feasible.

Austenitic Mn steels. These very tough steels, once the "workhorses" of milling, are falling into disuse because of their lower abrasion resistance. The 12% Mn steels so popular in crushing have been largely displaced by the harder 6% "lean" steels developed in 1959, which in turn are being displaced by martensitic irons and steels. An additional problem with austenitic Mn steels is the plastic deformation that accompanies work-hardening. Material flow and volume expansion make liner removal difficult and sometimes cause bolt breakage.

Pearlitic steels and irons. Pearlitic (lamellar) materials offer comparatively low first cost and good accessibility—they are easily castable by most foundries. Pearlitic "Chrome-Moly" steels, favored over pearlitic white irons and high-carbon unalloyed steels, are popular in high-impact service as liners, clamp and lifter bars, and grates. Several engineers and metallurgists project trends away from pearlitic materials because of the availability of more wear-resistant martensitic substances and the recent tendency toward narrowing of the cost differences between various candidate materials.

This narrowing of the range of installed costs, due to increasing labor and liner production rates, has created a trend toward selection of the more expensive longer-wearing liners. For mill liners, total cost considerations are becoming more important than installed cost.

Pro's and con's of nonferrous liners

Rubber and other elastomers offer several advantages over ferrous alloys under certain conditions. Since their advent in grinding back in 1921, elastomers have undergone significant technological development and have become considerably more popular, especially in the fine grinding mills. Light weight, noise-dampening properties, high resistance to impact, and lower installed cost compared with an equal volume of ferrous lining make elasto-

Table 3—Corrosion effects on common plastics

Material	Acids Weak	Acids Strong	Alkalies Weak	Alkalies Strong	Organic solvents	Water absorption (% per 24 hr)	Oxygen and ozone	Ionizing radiation	Temperature resistance (°C) High	Low
Fluorocarbons	Inert	Inert	Inert	Inert	Inert	0.0	Inert	P	550	G-275
Polyethylene (low density)	R	A-O	R	R	G	0.15	A	F	140	G-80
Polyethylene (high density)	R	A-O	R	R	G	0.1	A	G	160	G-100
Polypropylene	R	A-O	R	R	R	Less than 0.01	A	G	300	P
Polyvinyl chloride (rigid)	R	R	R	R	A	0.10	R	P	150	P
Polystyrene	R	A-O	R	R	A	0.04	SA	G	160	P
Nylon	G	A	R	R	R	1.5	SA	F	300	G-70

Note: R = resistant, A = attacked, SA = slight attack, A-O = attacked by oxidizing acids, G = good, F = fair, P = poor.

mers popular where mill feed is relatively free of highly abrasive materials that tend to cut into the lining.

Notable restrictions on the use of elastomers include their working temperature and the critical mill speed. For the most part, working temperatures for rubber linings are restricted to a maximum of approximately 200°F. In addition, manufacturers report a strong link between mill speed and rubber's service-life expectancy. Rubber liners are reported to be suitable only when critical speed is below roughly 75% of maximum speed, making them inappropriate for many primary grinding mills (Fig. 2).

Because ceramics and natural stone ("Silex") liners have exceedingly low toughness, they are restricted to fine grinding plants, where impact and spalling are reduced by low critical speeds and high pulp densities. Advantages claimed for these materials include excellent resistance to heat and chemical attack, light weight, and relatively low installed cost. Ceramic bricks containing 85% alumina have largely supplanted other materials in this group because of their greater abrasion resistance.

Corrosion can be a big problem

Corrosion, simply defined as erosion by chemical rather than mechanical means, is a very significant factor in the selection of many wear materials. This is especially true in hydrometallurgical processes, where slurry-contacting and reagent-contacting surfaces are subjected to highly reactive environmental conditions, such as pH extremes and high temperatures. Abrasion and corrosion often act together in these environments: microspalling induced by slurry particles can remove the protective surface films of some ferrous materials (such as stainless steels), accelerating corrosion of the less resistant material underneath the films.

Proper design is of high priority in corrosion control, frequently taking precedence over material characteristics. A well designed piping system that uses cheaper, less corrosion-resistant material will sometimes outlast by many times a poorly designed system made of highly corrosion-resistant materials. Fig. 3 illustrates selected examples of design influences on corrosion.

The scope of materials for corrosion service is far too broad to be presented in any detail here. However, the following discussion of broad categories may help to improve upon the frequent "guesses" in material selection.

According to IRON AGE, corrosion experts in the high-alloy castings field agree that the five alloys shown in Fig. 4 can handle about 90% of the conditions encountered in the chemical processing industry. Mild steel has been included only for comparative purposes. (Detailed property data and design considerations for the alloys are available from the Steel Founders Society of America, Rocky River, Ohio.)

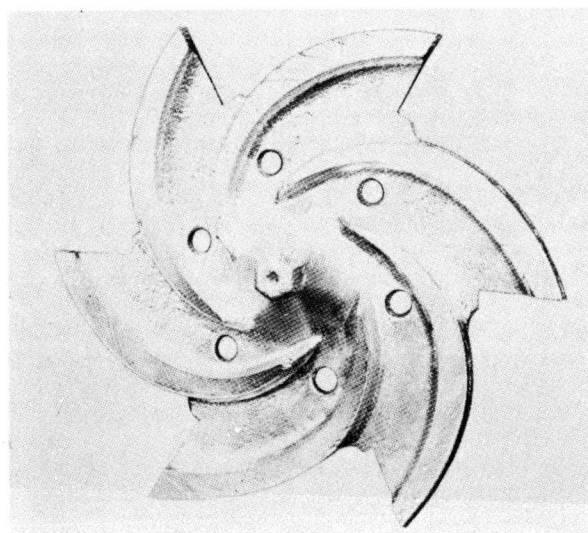

Photo credit: Amax Inc.

Incorrect selection of materials can quickly sabotage system performance. These two pump impellers, made of different alloys, were in caustic slurry service for the same time span.

Stainless steel use in the processing industry is both popular and growing. Numerous applications of AISI stainless steel in copper recovery operations, as well as details on the types and chemistry of corrosion, are presented in E/MJ, May 1975, p 117.

Two categories of nonmetallics are very widely used for corrosion protection in mineral processing: natural and synthetic rubbers, and plastics. (Many other nonmetallic materials are candidates for corrosion service, such as acid brick, ceramics, glass, wood, and concrete, and the economics of a particular application is the final criterion for selection.) A major disadvantage of rubber appears to be its inability to resist the high abrasion levels that often accompany corrosion. A common mistake, made because of "metals-oriented" thinking, is the use of harder rubber for erosion-corrosion environments. Soft rubbers are reported to be best for abrasion resistance. Rubber is frequently used to line pipes, tanks, and centrifugal slurry pumps, and has been considered a standard material in corrosion service for many years.

Industry use of plastics has increased tremendously over the last 20 years, but certain drawbacks still keep plastics from overtaking the ferrous materials. The main disadvantage of plastics is their price, which may be three to 175 times that of mild steel per pound. In addition, certain heat limitations generally restrict the maximum service temperatures of plastics to well below the service temperatures of metals (Table 3). Polyvinyl chloride (PVC), probably the most common industrial plastic, has a maximum service temperature only slightly above the boiling point of water.

Fluorocarbon plastics, such as "Teflon" and "Kel F," have much higher service temperatures and are highly corrosion resistant (inert), but their price substantially limits their use; however, TFE components are widely used in corrosion-resistant valves, and as linings for some pipes, expansion joints, and heat exchangers. Other common industrial plastics include high-density polyethylenes, polypropylene, and recently, polybutylene (see E/MJ, April 1975, p 108).

Corrosion-resisting materials for transporting ore slurries in pipelines have merited much research, with considerable data generated in recent years. Short-distance piping systems provide in-plant transportation for liquid/solid mixtures in such common operations as filtration, pulp handling, sludge transport, and tailings disposal, while long-distance slurry systems, though fewer in number, transport numerous materials as far as 270 mi. The economics of such systems could be seriously affected by erosion-corrosion problems, since even a pinhole (resulting, say, from pitting corrosion) in such a line could be enlarged catastrophically in minutes by the outflow of high-pressure, abrasive slurry.

Tests have shown that two factors very strongly influence slurry pipeline corrosion: slurry linear velocity, and slurry concentration (percentage solids). In general, increases in either factor will sharply increase the corrosion rate through disruption of surface films that normally hinder the diffusion of oxygen to corrodible surfaces. (In certain cases, the material transported will form a protective scale on the inside pipe wall; however, this scale normally requires periodic "pigging" to prevent excess buildup that could clog the line.) Slurry abrasiveness is also obviously important. More abrasive materials, such as iron, induce corrosion faster than less abrasive materials, such as coal. The role of proper design should be re-emphasized here, since factors like particle settling velocity and slurry turbulence influence the effectiveness of even short lengths of slurry piping. For example, vertical piping

Fig. 3—Typical design considerations for wear resistance

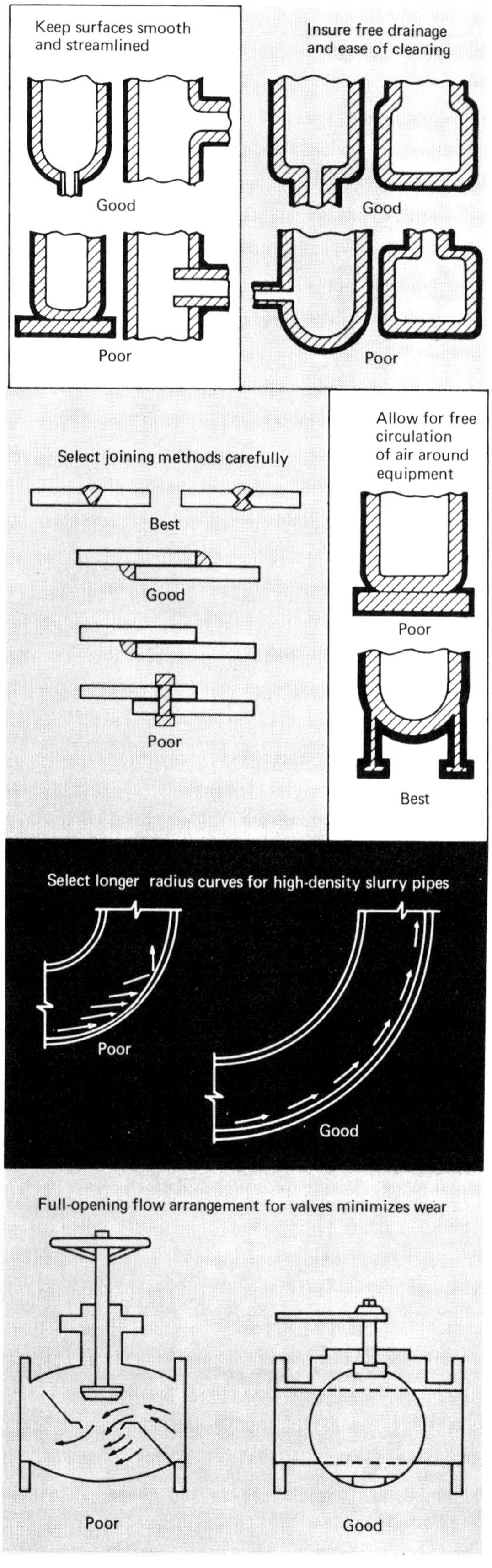

Fig. 4—Alloy selection charts for chemical processing industry

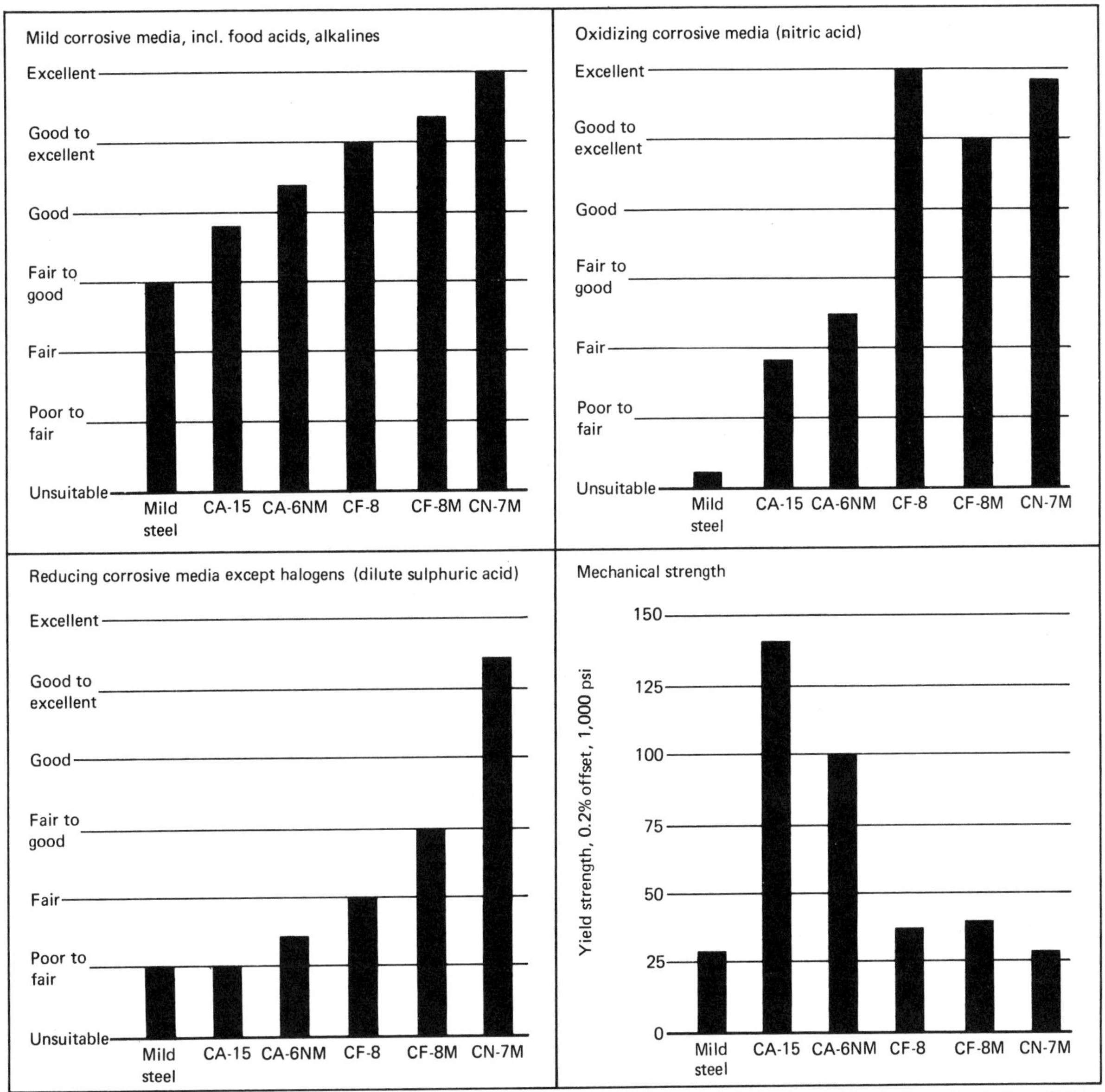

If corrosion resistance is primary, select alloys with high ratings in the medium to be encountered. Then consult the last chart to determine those alloys having sufficient mechanical strength. If mechanical strength is primary, reverse the procedure, starting with the required strength. Alloys shown are: Mild steel, annealed; CA-15, annealed at 1500° F; CA-6NM, air cooled from above 1750° F, tempered at 1100-1150° F; CF-8, CF-8M and CN-7M, solution annealed at 2000° F.

is often less subject to corrosion than horizontal piping, since solids are not deposited as readily on pipe walls.

Corrosion in scrubbers, resulting from high-velocity, hot corrosive gas streams, often represents another costly maintenance problem in processing plants. Although stainless steel alloys are reportedly preferred for handling corrosive gases, they may be readily attacked in the more severe gas-liquid environments. Where the risk of steel alloy construction is unacceptable, brick linings frequently substitute. Acid brick, carbon brick, or silicon carbide brick is used to partially or completely line the scrubber interior, supported by an outer carbon steel structure.

Wear-resistant materials have numerous other applications in mineral processing. Leach tanks, classifying screens, mill discharge grates, grizzlies, loading buckets, and other ore- and slurry-contacting equipment are all subject to erosion and/or corrosion. Even excluding all nonmetallics, global use of steel in wear applications is conservatively estimated at 3 million tpy. "Calloy," a recently developed alloy reported by its originators to be "the best compromise between . . . manganese steels and . . . the cast iron alloys" is good evidence that wear materials are the subject of active research in the industrial sector. □

References

1) "Symposium: Materials for the Mining Industry," Climax Molybdenum Co., 1975.
2) Anon., "Proper Use of Materials Reduces Scrubber Corrosion," IRON AGE, Sept. 30, 1974, pp 54-55.
3) Wilson, C. L., and J. A. Oates, Corrosion and the Maintenance Engineer, Hart Publishing Co. Inc., 1968.
4) Fontana, M. G., and N. D. Greene, Corrosion Engineering, McGraw-Hill Book Co., 1967.
5) Aude, T. C., and others, "Slurry Piping Systems: Trends, Design Methods, Guidelines," CHEMICAL ENGINEERING, June 28, 1971, pp 74-90.
6) Postlethwaite, John, and others, "Erosion-Corrosion in Slurry Pipelines," CORROSION, Vol. 30, August 1974, pp 285-290.
7) Kopecki, E. S., "Stainless Steel: Effective Corrosion Control for Copper Recovery Operations," E/MJ, Vol. 176, May 1975, pp 117-121.

Diverse uses win an expanding market for rubber in mining

Richard A. Thomas, Associate editor

ONE OF MINING'S FASTEST GROWING consumable and fabrication materials, rubber is finally claiming a prominent place among the major industrial products for abrasion- and corrosion-resistant applications. The mining industries now use more rubber products than any other industry. About 14.7 million lb went into conveyor belts alone last year, while 10 million lb went into mining cable.[1] Use of rubber for wear applications in mining and aggregate processing will soon be entering its third decade, while corrosion-resistant applications of rubber go back even further. Some rubbers and rubber products are so widely used that their nonchemical names have become generic—among them "Adiprene," "Hypalon," "SBR," "Neoprene," and "EPDM."

Where does all the rubber go? Uses in mining and processing are almost too numerous to mention (Fig. 1): linings for primary, secondary, and tertiary ball, rod, autogenous, and semiautogenous mills; flat and V-belting; scalping and dewatering screens; linings for truck boxes, pumps, pipes, bins, hoppers, feeders, launders, flotation cells, troughs, skips, and washing drums; classifier shoes; scraper blades; skirtboards; cone crusher feed plates; hose and cable covering—and the list goes on.

Health-related uses for rubber also are increasing as the government, inspired by a newly environment-conscious public, continues to place a higher priority on worker health and safety. A miner's gear can include rubber in earmuffs and plugs, masks and respirators, and rubberized clothing. Rubber also is used extensively to cut noise levels at the source (mills, fans, compressors, etc.) using antivibration mountings, and to control dust-producing operations through sealing systems.

Rubber scores high in versatility

A review of rubber's properties quickly shows why it can be used in so many applications. Rubber is resistant to most chemicals used in mineral processing (except mineral oils, for which concentration should not exceed 1.5 kg per ton material[2]). It has a low specific gravity, weighing about one-seventh as much as steel. It does not rust, and is easy to work; rubber components may often be cut to size with a knife. It can stand up almost indefinitely against vertical impact, as long as the force involved does not distort it beyond its elastic limit. Low temperatures are practically harmless to rubber, although rubber compounds tend to stiffen.

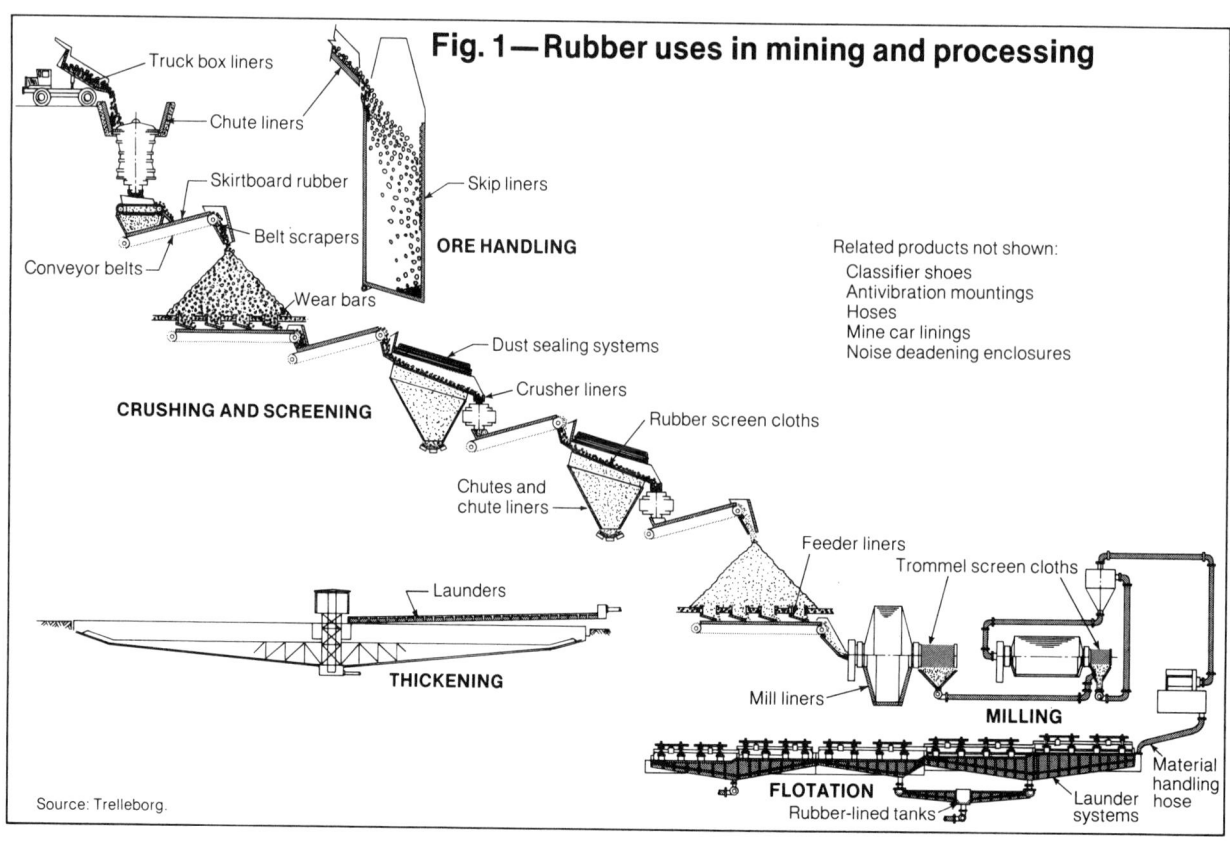

Fig. 1—Rubber uses in mining and processing

Source: Trelleborg.

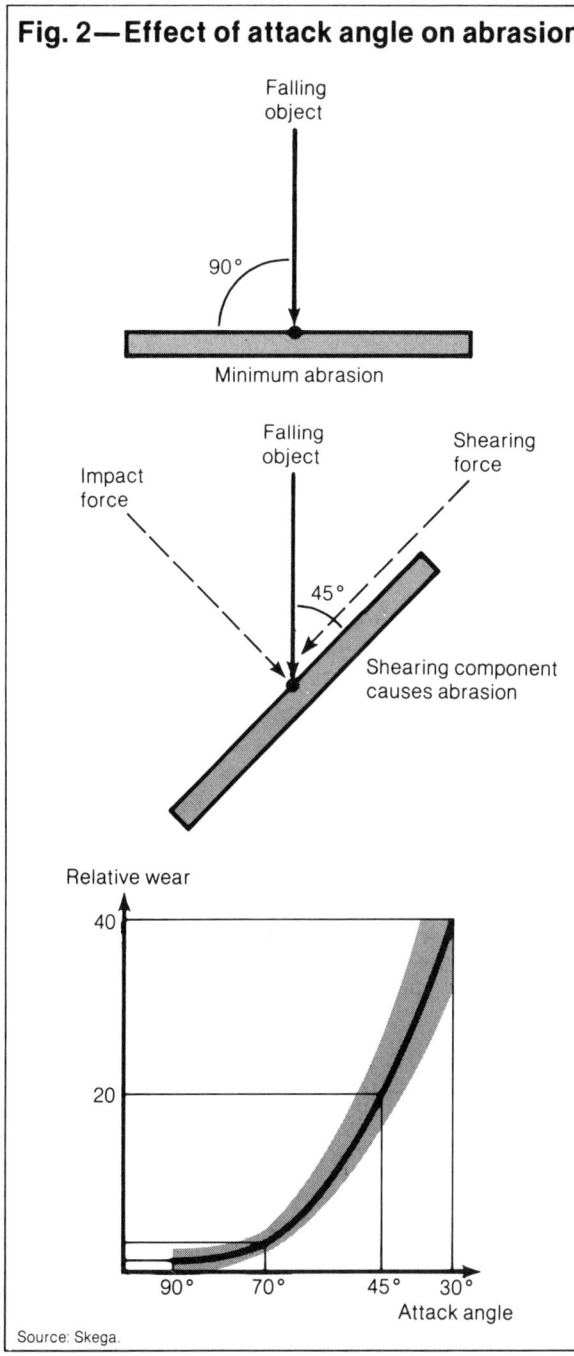

Fig. 2—Effect of attack angle on abrasion

rise to abrasion. With a perpendicular impact angle, rubber wear is minimum, especially at velocities under 20 fps (drop heights under 9-12 ft).[3] When material velocity exceeds the critical speed that can be withstood by rubber, there is not sufficient time to absorb impact energy. Instead, the instantaneous surface tension created exceeds the critical value, no "sideways" floating of rubber occurs, and the rubber is cut.

In most applications, the wear process is complex, resulting from both impact and shear forces. The rate of wear for rubber, a primary function of particle size and velocity, then becomes especially sensitive to angle of impact. Most abrasion damage is done by the shearing force whose vector is parallel to the rubber's impact surface—particularly at impact angles under 30° (Fig. 2).

Trelleborg Rubber Co. divides the major wear mechanisms affecting rubber into three categories:[4] "sliding," which occurs in launders, classifier shoes, tertiary mills, belt scrapers, spiral concentrators, and flotation cells; "impinging" (thrown particles), occurring in screen decks, chutes, deflector plates, secondary grinding mills, feeders, and hoppers; and "impacting" wear, which is seen predominantly in truck boxes, mine cars, primary and autogenous mills, and scalping screens. Trelleborg emphasizes that an insufficient thickness of rubber in impacting service results in crushed rubber in static applications and melted rubber in dynamic applications.

Rubber vs. metal liners: no clearcut choice

Although in the past rubber has not been used extensively in grinding mills in the US, domestic markets for rubber mill liners are growing. Rubber liners are used to a greater extent in Europe, particularly in the Scandinavian countries. Use of rubber as a mill liner was first tried in 1921, when several patent applications were filed, but rubber grades and processing techniques could not effectively utilize these patents at the time.[5] Rubber liners were reintroduced, with greater success, in the early 1950s.

By the early '60s, rubber was being used in discharge grates and autogenous mills and was well on its way toward being accepted in an application once dominated by Mn steel, Cr-Mo steel, Ni-Hard, and stone. Today, rubber liners are used for all common mill types, helping to grind materials as abrasive as taconite, copper ore, and silicates in autogenous mills up to 28 ft in diameter and rod mills up to 8 ft in diameter (with 4-in.-dia rods).[4] Even self-sorting spiral linings have been introduced, primarily for use in the cement industry.

Natural rubber, with its impressive elastic and noise-dampening qualities, has certain notable limitations, including incompatibility with high heat levels, oil, ozone, and sunlight (a real problem in conveyors); however, by proper compounding, these qualities, as well as impact and abrasion resistance, may be controlled. Hardness can be adjusted to make bowling balls or surgical gloves, heat resistance to 400°F can be achieved, and oil-mildew-ozone-acid resistant rubber compounds are on the market.

Unlike rigid wear materials, rubber does not resist abrasion by offering high hardness. Instead, it elastically deforms and elastically absorbs the energy of impinging particles. In contrast, steel deforms plastically, giving

The major advantage cited for rubber liners is low weight, which saves trunnions, bearings, and power and makes installation faster and easier. This in turn means less downtime and expensive labor. Time required to line a mill with rubber is only one-quarter to one-third that for steel,[2] and in most cases one man can handle a rubber liner plate. (The heaviest rubber lifter bar weighs about 250 lb, requiring three men.) Another advantage is rubber's beneficial effect on the operating noise level of most mills (Fig. 3).

Opinions are mixed on rubber liner economy as compared with steel's economy, probably because of consumers' very varied experiences with the material. Depending on the application, the lifetime of rubber liners can exceed by several times the life of Mn steel. However, rubber liners can also be wholly inappropriate in some applications. Factors of special importance are local availability and price of high-quality steel castings, downtime (often overlooked in calculating grinding economy), and scrap value. According to Skega AB, the cost of rubber liners is now of the same magnitude as that of steel linings.[6]

"If a rubber lining is correctly designed, it will normally give at least the same capacity as any other liner," Skega states.[2] Physical factors to be considered when selecting rubber as a mill lining include mill speed and diameter; grinding medium; size, texture, and hardness of feed (Fig. 4); and spacing and height of lifter bars. Changes in any given factor will change the angle of incidence between charge and liner, potentially increasing wear. Rubber liner wear normally increases with an increase in mill peripheral speed, especially when combined with large feed size (½ to 1½ in.). In secondary grinding with lifters, speed below 77% of critical speed is said to give the best economy. "Wave-type" liners are inappropriate because they permit too much sliding, causing low-angle abrasion.

Because the surface pressure from an autogenous charge is lower than from a steel ball charge, it has been found advantageous to line primary autogenous mills with rubber.[2] However, manufacturers suggest caution when grinding very coarse feed, recommending that mill speed not exceed 70% of critical. Standard rubber liners are limited to a ceiling temperature of about 155-190°F, and they wear more rapidly in the presence of mineral oils and some chemicals.

Rubber screens cut downtime and noise

Screening is another phase of processing, once completely dominated by steel, where rubber technology is now making sizable inroads. All-rubber screen cloths were developed in the '50s as an improvement over rubber-clad steel screens and punched plates. During the last two years, all-rubber screens have found increasing favor because their maintenance costs are lower than for wire cloth and because rubber has superior environmental qualities. Screening machines in sizes up to 8 x 20 ft are now operating successfully with all-rubber cloth in light to heavy applications.[7]

Rubber screens are available for both dewatering and primary scalping. Because scalping screens require greater strength, many are still reinforced with steel cable using advance bonding and molding techniques. Some screens are a lamination of two different kinds of rubber having differing characteristics—one rubber for support, the other for flexibility. Aperture selections include round, square, tapered (for reduced blinding),

Photo credit: Goodyear Tire & Rubber Co.

These rubber pump linings, in the process of being trimmed with an ordinary knife, will stand up to the abrasive slurries encountered in hardrock mining far better than metals.

"hourglass," and other shapes in convenient dimensions.

Rubber's major advantage over steel screens is greater lifespan, usually five to eight times longer than that of wire cloth. The price of all-rubber screen cloth is also about five to eight times that of wire cloth, but savings come from drastic reductions in downtime for repeatedly changing panels. The total cost of changing screen panels is the most expensive and time-consuming maintenance procedure for screening. Rubber screens are installed in virtually the same way as wire (small additional support is sometimes required), but less often.

Other advantages of rubber screening include reduced "blinding" or clogging and a noise level reduction of up

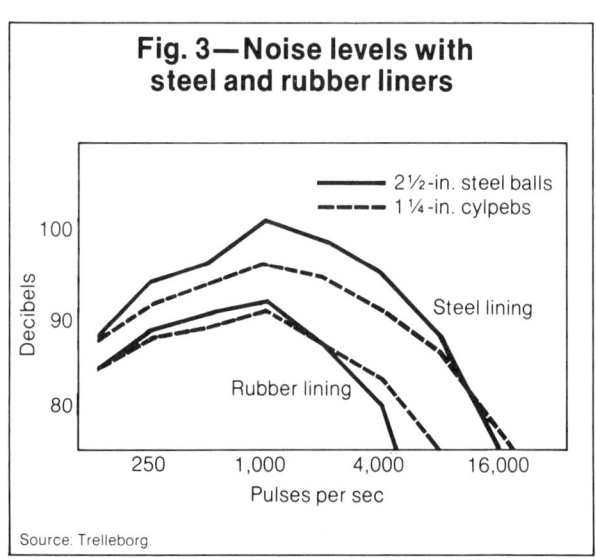

Fig. 3—Noise levels with steel and rubber liners

Source: Trelleborg.

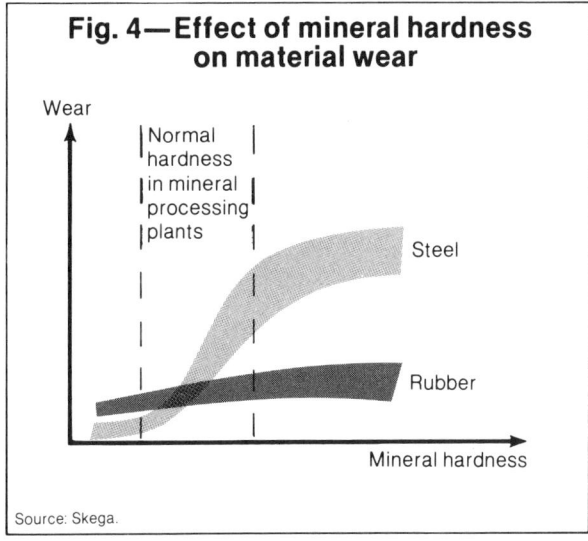

Fig. 4—Effect of mineral hardness on material wear

Source: Skega.

to 15 dB. Rubber screens also increase the life of the screening unit itself by reducing metal shock and minimizing metal fatigue.

One disadvantage of all-rubber cloth is that it has approximately 6% less open area than wire cloth; however, the "live bouncing" effect of rubber and reduced clogging, combined with proper selection of aperture size, may overcome this drawback. Generally, larger deck angles of repose call for larger hole sizes in relation to required product size. Also, obviously, higher tonnages require thicker rubber. The most common thicknesses used in copper screening applications are ⅝ to ¾ in.

Conveyor belts and V-belts on the rise

Rubber conveyors and V-belts have long been two of rubber producers' less flashy, more stable markets. Most producers have been making rubber-covered conveyor belts since the beginning of this century. V-belts are the most common drive in the mining/processing industry, finding application in motors, compressors, mills, crushers, agitators, conveyors, hoists, and pump systems.

In the last few years, conveyor and V-belting have both been enjoying an upswing. The Rubber Manufacturers Association (RMA) reports that flat belt sales have doubled in the last five years, and sales are expected to hit $380 million per year by 1980.[8] V-belts have grown at an 8% annual rate during the last five years. Part of this growth is attributed to increased activity in coal mining and other responses to the energy crisis. The coal industry is by far the biggest consumer of conveyor belting.

"After 75 years of playing around with conveyor belts, people have finally come to realize that this is the best way to handle bulk materials. It is the most economical and most efficient," claims Uniroyal's George Greener, by way of explaining the current growth pattern in belting.[8] The efficiency he speaks of is improving as the general trend toward automation, mechanization, and size scale-up forces industry to demand constant improvements in belt size and quality. A single belt will now carry as much as 16,000 tph. Such large belts are most often reinforced by textile materials or metal, and belt manufacturers are utilizing the latest synthetic rubbers for increased environmental and heat resistance. (Ordinary belts are damaged at temperatures above 150°F as the rubber loses adhesion and oxidizes.) More engineering attention is also being paid to mechanisms of material deposition on belts—probably the single most important factor affecting belt service life.

Other wear-resistant applications

The recent high cost of steel and difficulties in getting deliveries have prompted many an engineer to try rubber elements (often urethane) in wear applications, as substitutes for T-1, Chrome-Moly, Ni-Hard, and the like. Rubber is being substituted successfully as wear plates; in hopper, bin, and chute linings; in hydrocyclone separators; for pump interiors and impellers; and just about anywhere that falling ore and abrasive slurries are encountered. Du Pont estimates the use of rubber in these categories to be about 1.2 million lb yearly.

Of the newer applications, rubber truck box liners are rapidly gaining acceptance. Such liners are easy to install with T-bolts or welded studs, and they reportedly outwear metal liners by several times, reducing downtime for box repair. They are lighter in construction than metal, thus reducing tire cutting, and their elasticity during loading reduces chassis shock; needless to say, driver acceptance is good. Rubber also reduces material sticking at colder temperatures because it is a poorer conductor than steel.

Perhaps the biggest rubber-lined truck today is a 200-ton "Lectra-Haul" at Kaiser Resources in Canada. Such linings have been wearing well over periods of years at taconite, limestone, and copper installations.[9] As with screens, the initial expense for these liners is higher than for steel, but the cost figured over the life of the rubber lining is quite competitive.

The major disadvantage of these liners is their volume. For a 45-cu-yd end-dump truck, a rubber liner occupies 91 cu ft, vs. 19 cu ft for a steel liner—representing a 4.5-ton payload loss.[3] The problem can be overcome by designing new boxes to compensate, rubber manufacturers say—easier said than done, though obviously more feasible at newly developing installations.

Rubber hose for mining and processing applications is currently in an upward trend that matches the industry trend toward hydraulic equipment. The US Department of Commerce predicts that the hose industry will experience an above-average growth rate through 1985, and rubber hose is expected to maintain its dominance over plastic hose because it still outperforms plastic in high and low temperature ranges. Over the next year, a major factor in hose use will be its growing replacement of rigid metal piping for handling materials less expensively, according to RUBBER WORLD.

In processing, rubber-lined pumps have been proven superior to hard alloys for handling fine slurries.

According to one rule of thumb, ¼- to ⅜-in. particle size is the upper limit for standard rubber-lined pump parts. Practical operation curves for rubber-lined pumps have been developed by some pump manufacturers. They are usually based on pressure-molded, rubber-covered impellers, which operate with considerably less performance loss throughout their service life, according to A-S-H Pump engineers.

Although the industry uses rubber primarily for wear applications, nonwear applications are also on the increase. Synthetic rubber sheeting is used to line tailings ponds, settling ponds, and potable water reservoirs in many mining operations. Advanced dust sealing systems using rubber are available for conveyors, feeders, screens, and crushers. In line with today's environmental consciousness, rubber antivibration mountings are now provided for many processing machines to minimize structure-borne noise.

Trends in research

Rubber, like steel, plastic, or ceramic materials, cannot be considered the most suitable material for all wear applications; it is not a panacea. However, conversion to rubber elements in mining, milling, and concentrating operations is on the increase in the US, and rubber manufacturers promise continued improvements in compounding and design that will expand rubber's range of applications over the next few years. The Swedish rubber industry, in particular, has a heavy investment in research, and continues to develop technology that contributes strongly to mining industry achievements.

Ongoing rubber-related research in mining has made the following advances:

- A-S-H Pump (Envirotech Corp.) has put to use technology gained in the application of rubber mill liners to design a new breed of slurry pump.[10] The new design utilizes a rule-of-thumb stating that when the lining thickness is doubled, the "cut-through" value of a section increases five to eight times, depending on the compound used. A-S-H recently completed a prototype program, resulting in a new line of pumps with thick rubber linings and several design features said to control velocities better in critical wear areas.

- B. F. Goodrich and Continental Conveyor Co. have jointly developed the "Intermediate Drive" conveyor system for long distances.[11] It uses a specially designed steel cable-reinforced belt and employs a unique turn-over system for movement of material on both forward and return strands of the belt.

Acknowledgement: The author wishes to thank representatives of Du Pont, Trelleborg Gummifabriks, A-S-H Pump, Skega AB, Goodyear, B. F. Goodrich, and Uniroyal for their assistance in collecting data for this article.

Photo credit: Trelleborg Rubber Co.

Rubber linings for truck boxes can outwear metal liners by several times if properly designed. They also offer attractive shock-absorbing properties. The drawback is their volume.

- Du Pont neoprene rubber will be the basis for construction of the new "Serpentine" coal mine belt developed jointly by Joy Mfg. Co. and B. F. Goodrich.[8] The belt is capable of carrying loads around right-angle corners.

- The Malaysian Rubber Producers' Association has devised a rubber-based sealant for ventilation control in mines.[12] The sealant takes the form of rubberized gypsum plaster and may be sprayed or troweled.

Whether rubber will someday become the dominant wear material remains open to speculation. However, all indications are that rubber will play an important role in the economics of tomorrow's mining property. □

References

1) Personal communication with Public Affairs Dept., E. I. du Pont de Nemours & Co., Wilmington, Del.
2) "Skega-Lining for Grinding Mills," Ref. 13-02-01-75, Skega AB, Ersmark, Sweden.
3) "Skega Heavy-Duty Wear Components," Ref. 13-02-93-73, Skega AB.
4) "How to Reduce Wear, Noise, and Dust in the Mines," Trelleborgs Gummifabriks AB, Trelleborg, Sweden.
5) "Description and Application of Rubber Mill Liners in Grinding Mills," Trelleborgs Gummifabriks AB.
6) Jonsson, Jan, "Wear Resistant Rubber Performance in Primary Autogenous Mills," Skega AB.
7) "Application of All-Rubber Screen Cloth to American Mining," Trelleborgs Gummifabriks AB.
8) "Hose and Belting; Today and Tomorrow," Rubber World, June 1976.
9) Wallace, Dan, "Wear Resistant Rubber Performance as Truck Box Liners," A-S-H Pump (Envirotech Corp.), Paoli, Pa.
10) Horne, C. A., "Slurry Pumping Practice," A-S-H Pump (Envirotech Corp.).
11) News release, The B F. Goodrich Co., Akron, Ohio, Aug. 20, 1975.
12) Brevan, A. R., and T. D. Pendle, "Flexible Natural Rubber Based Sealant for Ventilation Control in Mining," Malaysian Rubber Producers' Research Association.

Rebuilding worn mine car wheels

CLIMAX MOLYBDENUM CO. is saving a substantial amount at its Climax, Colo., mine by salvaging 1,300 worn steel mine car wheels each year. The tread and flange areas of wheels are rebuilt with hardsurface alloy, and the cost of a rebuilt wheel is about two-thirds that of a new wheel.

The Climax mine, averaging 47,000 tpd of molybdenite ore production, has about 30 mi of underground track. Nineteen trains carrying 220 tons each are in constant use to shuttle ore to the crusher, while nine smaller trains carry supplies, mine personnel, and equipment. In all, 2,500 wheels are in constant use at the mine. Metal-to-metal wear and impact from both the loading and side-dumping operations cause rapid wheel wear, usually most severe on the outside of the tread surface. (At times, this surface is worn down as much as 1½ in.)

Climax ships 100 to 150 worn wheels each month to Hardsurfacing Specialties Inc. in Denver, Colo. Hardsurfacing Specialties rebuilds the wheels with Haynes "Sta-Mang" tube wire by the submerged-arc welding method, then machines them and ships them back at the rate of 25 per week. Sta-Mang is an iron-base alloy containing 13% chromium, 15% manganese, and smaller amounts of molybdenum and nickel.

Before rebuilding, the wheels are wire-brushed to remove any adhering rust or dirt. Then they are faced using 7/64-in. tube rod. The worn area is built up in 1/8-in. layers using a welding head traveling at 14 in. per min. The tread area is built back to size and checked by a profile gauge, and an additional 3/32 in. of alloy is then added for the finishing stock.

Two Hobart automatic welders with horizontal spindle positioners are used for rebuilding the treads, where most wear occurs. A third machine builds up the flange area. Welding current is maintained at about 300 amps and 27 v dc, reverse polarity. An average of 45 lb of rod is applied to each wheel.

Hardsurfacing Specialties selected Sta-Mang alloy because it is machinable—as deposited, it is a relatively soft 19 on the Rockwell C scale. A 20-in.-dia wheel faced with Sta-Mang can be finish-machined in about 25 min with tungsten carbide tools on a vertical boring mill. Once the wheel is in service, the pounding action of loading and dumping at the mine work-hardens the facing material to a maximum hardness of Rockwell C-46. The result is a tough, wear-resistant wheel surface.

For Climax, hardsurfacing is not only less expensive than buying new wheels but also makes wheels more readily available. The delivery time for new wheels was six to eight months when the hardsurfacing program was started about a year ago. Rebuilding also keeps more than 5 tons of valuable alloy steel off the scrap pile each week. □

The flange area is rebuilt with a separate automatic welder.

Wheels are machined on a vertical boring mill after facing.

New load sensing system keeps ore trucks well filled

A NEW ELECTRIC WEIGHING SYSTEM that allows ore haulage trucks to be filled to maximum capacity before they leave a loading area has been introduced by Martin-Decker Co. of Santa Ana, Calif. The system is accurate and rugged, and it helps operators keep loads within weight limits prescribed by manufacturers' warranties for truck tire wear, braking dynamics, and structural wear, Martin-Decker says.

The basic system consists of four load sensing pins, connecting cables, and an easy-to-read panel that houses three colored lights. The panel is mounted on the truck deck. The pins—fabricated from high-strength steel with bonded strain gauges mounted inside—are interchangeable with the original, standard pivot and upper hoist pins furnished by truck manufacturers. The pins remain accurate under rugged conditions during hauling and dumping, according to the manufacturer.

The "Truck Load Indicator" is activated when the truck operator raises the truck bed off its bumper pads. Weight information is relayed to the light panel located outside the cab, in view of the shovel operator. A green light indicates that the system is operating; an amber light means that one more dipper load will fill the truck bed; a red light indicates that the truck is fully loaded.

Operating from a standard 12/24-v dc battery, the system works independently of the truck's other equipment. Options include recorders, tape and card printers, and a dash-mounted digital panel meter.

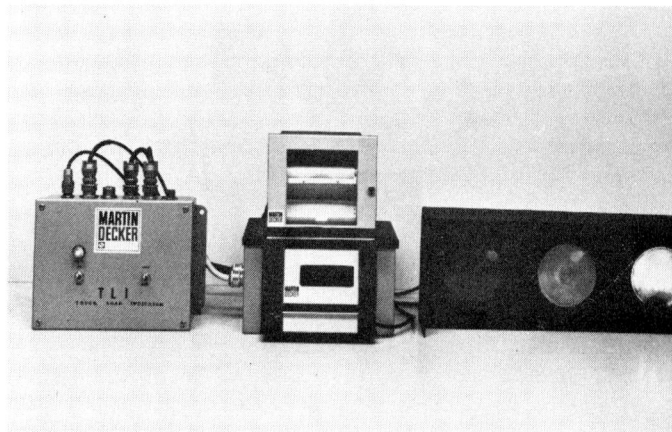

The 'Truck Load Indicator' consists of a control box (left), recorder, digital display meter, light panel, and sensing pins.

Wire rope fittings

WIRE ROPE END ATTACHMENTS may be as important as the wire rope to which they are fastened in doing a lifting or pulling job. Wire rope users should thus have a good working knowledge of the types of attachments available and an understanding of how they affect ultimate rope serviceability.

There are numerous types of end attachments, and just as one of the many available types of wire rope will give maximum performance for any given set of conditions, so one type of end attachment will perform best on any given job. There is no "universal" attachment that is best for all conditions.

Some attachments, though they may be the only ones available for use under certain conditions, can reduce a wire rope's efficiency by 50%. If an end rope attachment alone is the predominant factor in a system, rope breaking strength must first be reduced by the efficiency loss for that end attachment before a design factor is applied for the rope. This is also true for slings and holding assemblies such as boom pendants. Some approximate efficiencies for the most widely used wire rope end attachments are listed in Table 1.

Because the lowest efficiency value in a wire rope system is the proper starting point for applying a design factor, other factors affecting efficiency, such as reeving, may offset efficiency loss at the rope end attachment. The reeving of a crane hoist line, for example, may be only 85% efficient, while the rope end attachment may be 95% efficient. In such a case, rope with 100-ton breaking strength

Table 1—Approximate efficiencies for most widely used wire rope end attachments

	IWRC	FC
Hand-tucked splices	80-90%	80-90%
Mechanical splices	90-95%	90-92.5%
Swaged steel fittings	95-100%	90-95%
Spelter sockets*	100%	100%
Wire rope clips**	80%	80%
Wedge sockets	75-90%	75-90%

*Spelter sockets in smaller rope sizes (usually less than 7/16 in.) may not always develop 100% efficiency, and are not recommended by some rope manufacturers.
**When properly applied and maintained per clip manufacturer's recommendations.

would have usable strength of 85 tons, to which the design factor for the system would be applied.

Types of rope end attachments

There are only two ways to attach something to a wire rope (or vice versa): forming a loop in the rope or attaching a fitting to the rope. Loops are made either by splicing the rope to itself—hand-tucked or mechanical splices—or by use of clips, clamps, or wedges. The efficiency of the loop varies according to the type of splice or attachment and according to rope diameter. These limitations must be observed (Table 2).

Fittings secured directly to wire rope can be applied by cold forming (swaging) of the metal in the fittings; by pouring a liquid material such as molten zinc or epoxy, which bonds to wires that have been "broomed out" in a cone-shaped socket; or by a wedging arrangement.

The two basic types of loop splices in common usage are the hand-tucked splice and the mechanical Flemish eye splice secured with a compressed metal sleeve. A third common loop is formed by securing the turned-back end of the wire rope to the long end with a compressed metal sleeve.

Hand-tucked splices should be left unserved to allow the splice to be inspected, and they should never be used if the rope may rotate and cause tucked strands to pull out.

The use of a Flemish eye splice without a sleeve or with a damaged sleeve, however, can be very dangerous, because it can slip out under vibrating loads and is greatly affected by the diameter of the pin, etc.

Poured and swaged attachments

From the standpoint of strength alone, poured attachments made of molten zinc (commonly called spelter sockets) are among the most efficient, delivering 100% of rope breaking strength. However, because "brooming" impairs the symmetry of the rope and the rigidity of the attachment acts as a sudden arrestor for vibration waves along the wires of a rope, progressive deterioration of wires can occur where the wires enter the socket. Wire fatigue failure in the wire rope usually occurs first at this point.

Poured zinc sockets must not be confused with the babbitted sockets that are often poured in the field. Many babbitt metals do not adhere to wires as well as zinc does, and these sockets have been shown under test to pull out at values as low as 50% of rope breaking strength.

Where spelter sockets are subject to constant vibration, frequent inspection is essential, and the appearance of more than one broken wire in a rope at its entry to the spelter socket is usually sufficient to rule out further use. Sometimes wires break inside the rope or inside the socket, making detection difficult. Poured sockets usually are not attached in the field because of the elaborate, closely controlled procedures required.

On an efficiency par with poured zinc attachments are adequately designed fittings applied to a wire rope by cold forming of a metal in matched dies under high pressure. Commonly called swaging, this method delivers from 95% to 100% efficiency, depending on wire rope diameter and construction. Fittings applied by rotary swaging are just as efficient, and this method is often used when close tolerances or threaded studs are desired.

Swaged end attachments are available in a variety of shapes. Most common are those that match the pin sizes and general configuration of open and closed spelter sockets and are usually interchangeable with them. Swaged end attachments can also be obtained in the form

(A)

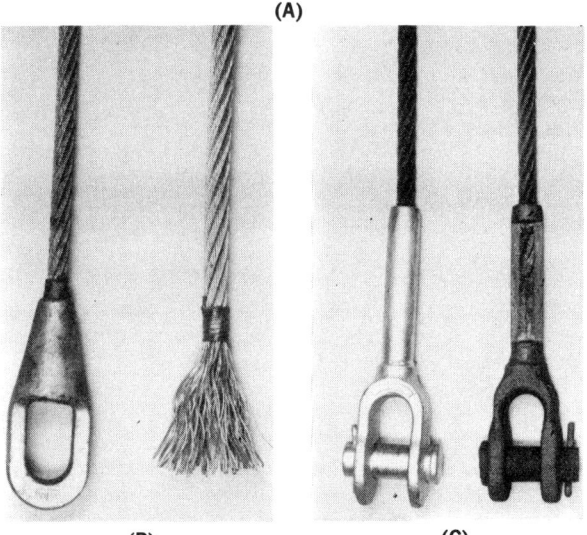

(B) (C)

(D)

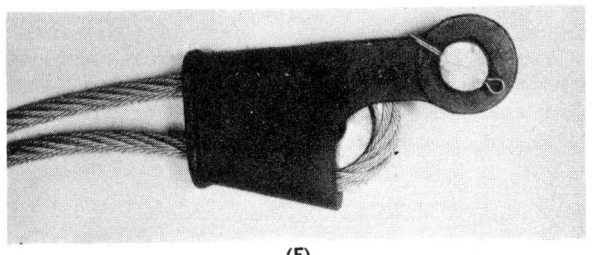

(E)

The wide variety of available wire rope fittings includes: (A) splices, with the mechanical splice loop at the left yielding higher efficiency than the hand-tucked splice at the right; (B) zinc-poured fixtures that deliver 100% of rope strength but subject wires in the rope to metal fatigue caused primarily by the rigidity of the attachment; (C) attachments secured to the rope end by cold forming; (D) clips and clamps, which must always be applied as shown to secure the cut end to the live end of the rope; and (E) wedge sockets, which are easy to install but less efficient than most other wire rope fittings.

Table 2—Approximate efficiency for loops as percentage of nominal rope strength

Rope diameter		Hand-spliced loops (6x19 and 6x37 fiber core and IWRC improved plow steel grade*)	Mechanical splice loops (all 6x19 and 6x37 class ropes)		
In.	Mm.		Improved plow steel and extra-improved plow steel		Stainless steel IWRC
			Fiber core	IWRC	
1/4	6.5	90%	92.5%	95%	95%
5/16	8	89	92.5	95	95
3/8	9.5	88	92.5	95	95
7/16	11	87	92.5	95	95
1/2	13	86	92.5	95	95
9/16	14.5	85	92.5	95	95
5/8	16	84	92.5	95	95
3/4	19	82	92.5	95	95
7/8	22	80	92.5	95	95
1	26	80	92.5	95	95
1 1/8	29	80	92.5	95	95
1 1/4	32				
1 7/8	48	80	90	92.5	—
2 and larger	51 and larger	80	—	90	—

*For stainless steel, reduce values shown by 10.

of hooks, ring eyes, threaded bolts, etc. Special designs of almost any shape can be machined at the end of the shank that is swaged onto the end of the rope.

Swaged fittings are far more resistant than poured zinc fittings to wire fatigue at the point where the rope enters the socket. Impact loading tests at one company showed resistance to fatigue failure seven times greater for swaged fittings than for poured zinc sockets.

With swaged fittings, too, frequent inspections for broken wires should be made, and the appearance of more than one broken wire normally mandates removal from service.

Clamps, clips, and wedges

Clips are usually of the U-bolt-and-saddle type, while clamps are usually paired steel forgings with grooves to match the rope diameter and three or four bolts to provide compression. With either system, the rope is subjected to a certain amount of crushing, although somewhat less so with clamps. With both, there is a tendency for the rope to slip through the fittings after it has been reduced in diameter by the first few loadings, and nuts must be retorqued to the fittings manufacturer's specifications after initial loadings.

It is imperative that clips and clamps are installed precisely as specified and in the numbers and sizes approved by the manufacturer of the fittings. Clips must always attach the short or "cut" end of a wire rope to the "live" or long end, and all clips must be applied in the same direction, with the saddle on the "live" side and with the same torquing on all clips.

Although considerably less efficient than socketed and swaged attachments, clips and clamps are very convenient to install in the field and therefore quite popular. Efficiency is sacrificed for convenience.

Wedge-type sockets rival clips in ease of field installation. With such fittings, the rope is secured to the end attachment by passing it around a grooved, wedged-shaped piece of steel and pulling down under load into the "bowl" of the fixture. Such fittings are widely used, especially on excavating equipment, because they can be readily installed and removed in the field.

Wedge-type sockets are not 100% efficient in transferring rope breaking strength; however, ropes on which they are used are usually subject to more or less rapid deterioration from abuse and abrasion, so the weakest point in the system develops at some point along the rope other than the attachment. For this reason, such attachments are popular in construction and mining applications.

The low efficiency of wedges is primarily due to the way the rope bends sharply around the wedge and to the distortion of the wedging action. A new rope will fail at the point of wedging when loaded to destruction. The firm gripping action of the attachment also abruptly stops vibration in the rope, resulting in progressive fatigue failure of wires at the socket. However, the problem is not considered to be as severe as with poured sockets.

In-line wedge fittings also can be attached in the field. In this type, the rope is passed up through the small end of a fitting having an internal tapered cone similar to that of a spelter socket. The strands are then spread apart, and a tapered plug is placed under them. When the final end attachment—such as a clevis, hook, or eye—is screwed back onto the tapered cone section, the plug is forced between the strands and a wedging action results. Again, efficiencies with these fittings vary, depending on the amount of distortion and the correctness of attachment.

Thimbles prolong rope life

When a rope end is looped, a metal thimble should be installed in the loop whenever possible. Thimbles are available in a variety of styles and materials. The thimble prevents a rope from being crushed and from being bent at a diameter smaller than the rope manufacturer's recommendation. The grooving, therefore, must be the proper size for the rope diameter.

While the most common methods of attaching fittings to the ends of wire rope have been discussed briefly here, it should be noted that an infinite variety of fittings and combinations of fittings is available. Standard catalog items include open and closed sockets (both poured and swaged), hooks, eyes, clevises, shackles, threaded studs, straight buttons, and turnbuckles.

OSHA regulations now specifically prohibit use of tied knots except for certain cable-controlled scraper applications. Wire rope was simply not designed to be distorted in such a manner.

Which attachment is best? All are serviceable, and each is suited for certain applications. All factors of a specific application should be carefully considered before making a selection. □

Editor's note: This article was prepared and distributed through the cooperation of the Wire Rope Producers Committee of the American Iron and Steel Institute. The author is William H. Myers, chief engineer, Paulsen Wire Rope Corp. He has been active in AISI, the Wire Rope Technical Board, and the Wire Association for many years and now serves on many committees, including metrication, breaking weights and strengths, slings, ferrous management, and papers.

New choker hitch adjustment table for wire rope slings

A CHOKER HITCH CAN SOMETIMES REDUCE by 50% the actual breaking strength of wire rope in a sling body, according to new research sponsored by the Wire Rope Technical Board. The board has developed a table for adjusting the rated capacity of wire rope slings to cope with problems imposed by a choker hitch. The table can be particularly useful where chokers are used by riggers to "roll" or maneuver loads at the start of a lift.

A choker hitch is a contact sling hitch in which the sling passes entirely around the load. Under most circumstances, a choker will form an angle of approximately 135° with the lifting or pulling leg of a sling. For this angle, the rated capacity tables currently in use for slings are appropriate. However, when a choke is drawn down tight against a load, or when a side pull is exerted that results in an angle less than 135°, an adjustment must be made to compensate for a further reduction in the sling's rated capacity. To put it simply: as the angle of choke decreases, there is a corresponding loss in sling efficiency.

It is significant that choker hitch tables now in use throughout the industry base these sling capacities on 75% of the rated capacity of a sling in a vertical pull. The new information indicates that catalogue rope strength is a more significant factor in calculating the effect of extreme choke angles than was previously believed to be the case.

Slings pulled to destruction to develop data

Investigation into the relationship between choke angle and sling efficiency was undertaken by varying the angle and pulling slings to destruction. Under test conditions, failure almost invariably occurred at the point of choke rather than in the splice, which normally had been the assumed point of failure.

Analyses were run separately for fiber core (FC) and independent wire rope core (IWRC) ropes, and two different equations were developed. At smaller angles, where crushing is a major factor in rope failure, FC ropes were found to be significantly less efficient than IWRC ropes. This disparity seems logical, since FC ropes are known to have less crush resistance than IWRC ropes.

A single equation for both rope types was then developed to calculate the change in efficiency for various choke angles. This equation was used to determine sling rated capacity reductions, as shown in the accompanying table, for representative choke angles smaller than 135°.

It must be remembered that these data were developed from new ropes pulled once to their failing point. Actual efficiency of a used sling can be expected to differ from the predictions in the table because a sling is literally "consumed" during its useful life. (This is why a "design factor" is included in calculations for sling rated capacities.)

It should also be pointed out that data was derived only from those tests where sling failure was at the point of choke. In a few cases during the testing program, slings failed at contact points with sharp edges on the load. When edge protection is not used, choker hitch efficiency is obviously meaningless if the edge is sharp enough to cause failure at this point rather than at the point of choke.

Tabular statistical material on the test results and efficiency lines plotted from this data may be obtained by writing to Fred W. Donecker, New Haven Works, US Steel Corp., New Haven Conn. □

Choker hitch rated capacity adjustment

(for wire rope slings in choker hitch when angle of choke is less than 135°)

Angle of choke	% of sling's normal rated capacity*
121-135°	.95
91-120°	.82
61-90°	.71
31-60°	.60
0-30°	.48

* For IWRC and FC wire ropes.

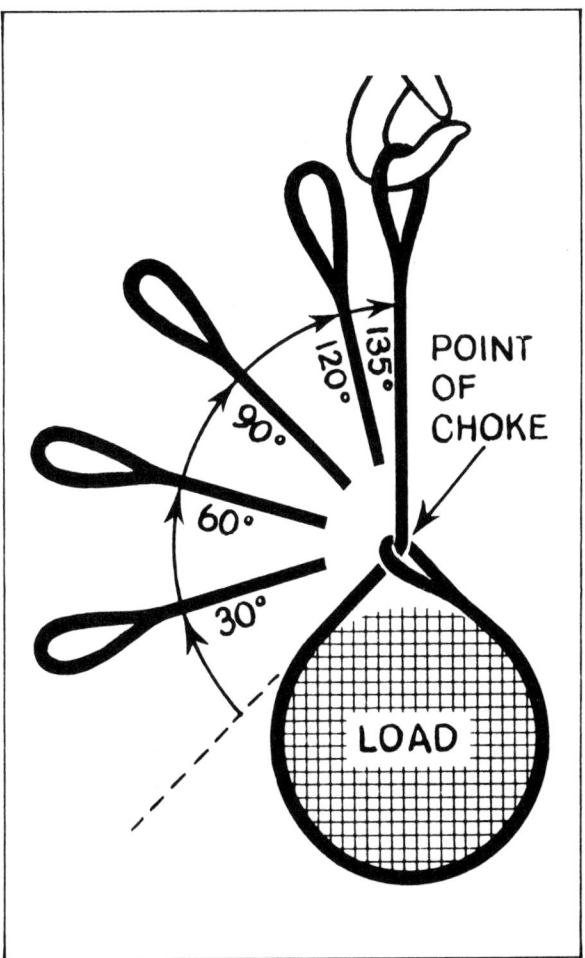

As the angle of choke decreases from its average of about 135° there is a corresponding loss of sling efficiency.

Simulator helps train fire fighters

THE ANSUL CO., a leader in fire protection equipment and fire control education, unveiled a new fire fighter's training device at the recent annual meeting of the National Fire Protection Association in Washington, D.C. The patented "Dynamic Fire Simulator and Trainer," a computer-controlled device, creates imitation fires that are in many ways difficult to distinguish from the real thing. The simulator employs movie images that look and sound like fire, it throws out intense heat, and it reacts like a real fire to extinguishing techniques. If the trainee attacks the simulated fire correctly, it goes out; if not, it reflashes like a real fire.

The fire simulator is housed in a 40-ft-long mobile classroom van that will accommodate up to 20 trainees at a time. The van may be used to train as many as 80 employees a day, according to Ansul representatives. The 2-hr training course, which includes lecture, reading material, training film, and practice with the simulator, averages $18-25 per person trained. (Longer courses are available.)

Besides the capacity to train such a large number of people so quickly, two additional advantages are cited for the simulator in contrast with traditional fire training mechanisms: It does not waste costly fuel, and it does not pollute the air with smoke and noxious fumes.

In operation, the simulator uses 16-mm special effects movie film projected onto a rear projection screen. Two projectors are used—one showing the fire, the other showing a superimposed image of the object or area being burned. Five radiant heaters mounted above and in front of the screen simulate the heat of the fire, while continuous loop audio cassettes reproduce the sound of the fire behind the screen.

The "fire" reacts to a trainee's extinguishing technique through three electromechanical devices: a pressure-sensitive screen using load cells behind the screen surface, an optical shutter, and a process minicomputer. The amount of pressure on the screen from the escaping extinguishing agent—an inert "clean agent" gas—indicates the distance of the extinguisher nozzle from the screen and the point of impact. The shutter mechanism, consisting of a series of tiny doors that operate independently, is positioned in the "out-of-focus" plane of the fire's projected image. If the fire is properly extinguished, the doors close in the appropriate order, and the fire, heat, and sound fade away.

The entire sequence is coordinated and controlled by the computer, which has been programmed with information about the correct way to attack a given fire. The computer closes down the entire shutter mechanism only if the right combination of pressure, timing, and sweeping distance is sensed on the screen. For example, stopping one type of fire requires a rapid side-to-side sweeping of the extinguisher at the base of the fire, with a predetermined overlap on each side. If a trainee aims at the center of the flame or fails to sweep in a broad enough arc, the screen will darken momentarily in the "extinguished" area, then reflash as soon as the extinguisher is turned off or runs dry. The computer also monitors the way the trainee pressurizes and actuates the extinguisher. If the trainee performs incorrectly, no inert gas is released. Twin exhaust fans at the screen base expel all discharged gases used in training.

Packaged training programs for the simulator are programmed for the following common fires: flammable liquid spill, flammable liquid in depth (for example, pan fire), gravity-fed flammable liquid, and impinging pressure jet (such as a broken propane line).

Ansul notes that it has received inquiries about the fire simulator from several major mining and manufacturing companies, and it envisions a fleet of training vans traveling here and abroad in the future. For more information, write to The Ansul Co., International Headquarters, Marinette, Wis. 54143. □

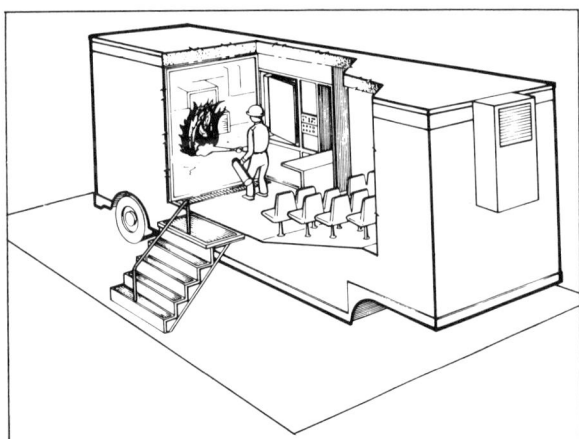

Classroom setup in van allows one trainee to practice while others look on. Extinguishing agent is discharged directly onto the pressure-sensitive training screen.

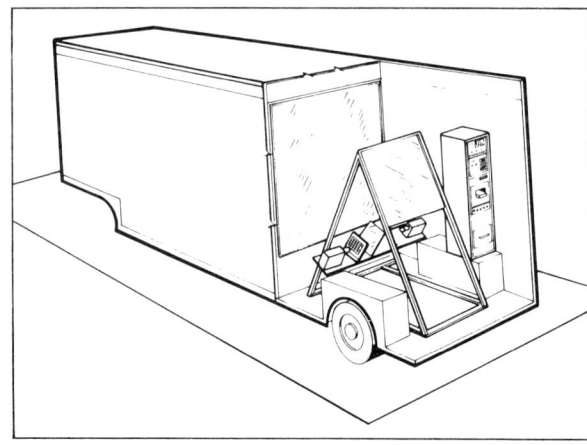

The heart of the fire simulator is behind the rear projection screen. Images from two projectors are combined by a series of mirrors and are cast through a grid shutter onto the screen.

New device protects mine vehicles from fire

THE ANSUL CO. of Marinette, Wis., highly regarded for its products to detect and suppress fires, has come up with a useful, nonelectrical fire detection and actuation device that is especially applicable to mine vehicles. Mine operators, who have seen the costs of giant haulers rise astronomically in the past decade, should find the device to be of particular interest.

Automatically activated fire suppression systems on mine vehicles are subjected to a degree of vibration and abuse that can compromise their reliability. On the other hand, manual release systems to put out fires have often proved to be impractical, either because a fire drives the operator out before he is able to pull the release lever or because the fire is detected too late.

By contrast, Ansul's SCAD (self-contained actuation and detection) pneumatic devices have proved to be reliable in the most abusive environments, according to the manufacturer. They have only four components and are adaptable to any vehicle. Their great advantage is that they need no outside power source.

The four components of a SCAD device are pressurized tubing, an actuation device at one end of the tube, a pressure makeup device at the other end, and a warning module that lights up when pressure in the tubing falls below a certain range. The tubing, which is effective over a wide range of lengths, is looped around the areas of the vehicle where fires may start. If a fire breaks out, the tubing bursts at 355°F, relieving pressure inside the device and activating the fire suppression system. The pressure makeup device performs a maintenance function, replacing pressure within the tubing as required.

The SCAD device was tested over 18 months on several types of vehicles. One test was run on a 150-ton-capacity rear-dump truck operating over rough roads in an open-pit mine. The tubing was looped around the upper edge of the engine compartment above the exhaust manifolds and turbo chargers and through the torque converter area above a nest of hydraulic lines. The tubing was attached to hydraulic lines and frame members by electricians' slip-cable ties. The temperature extremes during the test period were $-40°F$ and $+90°F$. The SCAD device worked perfectly, even though subjected to the radiant heat of the exhaust manifold and engine block, as well as considerable abrasion and impact against frame members. At the end of the test period, the device showed no significant indication of wear, nor did false discharges occur.

SCAD's three unique advantages are that it needs no outside power source to operate, it can operate at temperature extremes, and it can be completely tested and recycled in 3 min. The SCAD warning light for pressure drop does require electricity, but it serves only a maintenance function. Electrical failure caused by a fire does not affect the ability of the SCAD device to activate a fire suppression system. □

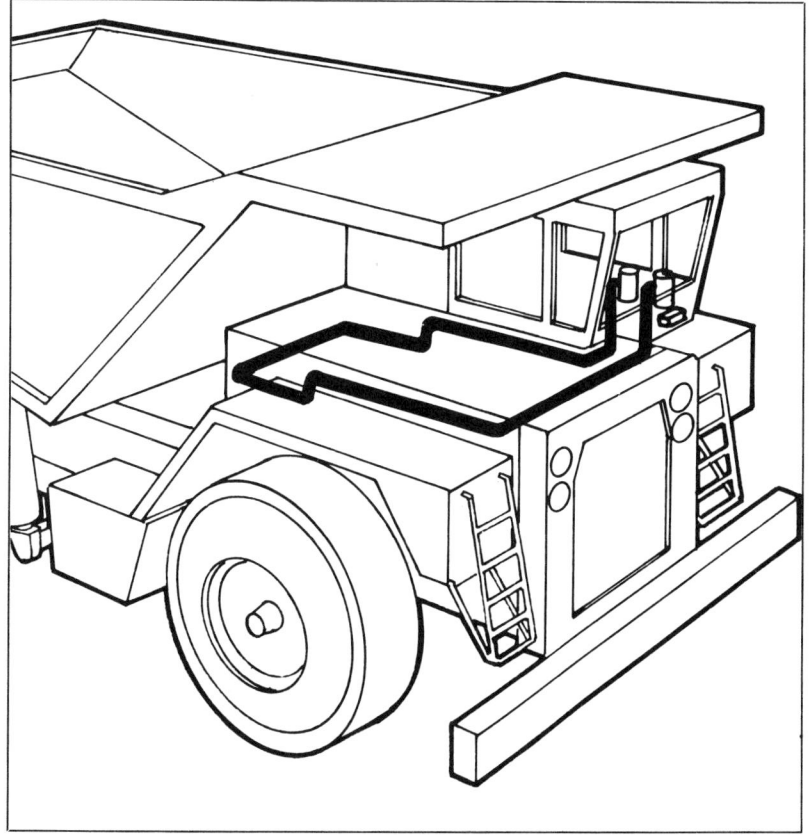

The SCAD system is easily mounted on vehicles such as off-highway dump trucks, LHDs, and front-end loaders. For dump trucks, the area of greatest fire hazard includes the engine, turbocharger, and torque converter behind the engine. Points at which a fire might be ignited include the turbocharger, exhaust manifold, brakes, electric wiring, and overheated bearings. A break in the hydraulic lines or fuel lines that run through this area of the truck could spray combustible fluid onto one or more of these ignition sources.

To protect against such fires, SCAD detection tubing should be laid around the upper perimeter of the engine compartment, extending back to encompass the area of the torque converter and transmission.

Wet suppression system controls dust problem at Inspiration

DUST GENERATED DURING TRANSPORTATION and comminution of ore frequently creates maintenance problems, reduces visibility, and poses a potential health hazard to personnel. To correct these problems and comply with government regulations, Inspiration Consolidated of Inspiration, Ariz., installed a "Chem-Jet" dust control system designed by Johnson-March Corp.

The system suppresses dust at several locations along the processing route by wetting the ore with a mixture of "Compound MR" and water in a 1:1,000 ratio. A proportioner continuously and automatically mixes the MR concentrate with water at the set ratio, while spray headers coat the ore at points of greatest dust generation. Actuators under the ore conveyor belts permit the flow of dilute solution to the headers only when the belts are loaded and moving. This system, in conjunction with a series of dust collectors at strategic points, reportedly provides a satisfactory level of dust control throughout the crushing, screening, and handling sections of the plant.

The wet suppression system treats ore nine separate times using a cumulative total of about 1½ gal of dilute solution per ton of ore. Ore is sprayed at the truck dump; at the heads and discharge ends of the primary, secondary, and tertiary crushers; and at various conveyor transfer points. One of the most important advantages of the system is the carryover of dust control from operation to operation, Johnson-March says.

While some residual dust is inevitable, Inspiration plant operators report a major improvement with the Chem-Jet system. Without the system, the areas around all three crushing and screening stages become so enveloped in dust within a few minutes that operators cannot even see the areas they are responsible for controlling. Although the Chem-Jet system does not solve *all* of Inspiration's dust problems, it has greatly improved working conditions, has met the code requirements, and has been found to work satisfactorily under almost all plant conditions.

Occasional cold weather "freezes" occurring three or four times in the last few years have put the system out of commission. On those few occasions when solution-carrying lines were not drained in expectation of a freeze, service was temporarily disrupted until the lines were thawed out. The designers point out that such drainage should be undertaken when necessary to avoid system downtime. Inspiration engineers considered a heat tracing system to prevent freezing, but they concluded that the small inconvenience accompanying such infrequent temperature conditions does not justify the expense of additional equipment.

Normal maintenance expenses for the dust suppression system are reportedly minimal, but a few preventive measures are important. Water of suitable quality must be used to dilute the MR concentrate, and suitable filtering must be provided prior to feeding water to the proportioner. (Filtration is particularly important if there is an appreciable concentration of solids in the water, as is often the case with surface water in mines.) Chem-Jet spray nozzles need to be cleaned and checked periodically. Screens in each of the nozzles trap foreign objects that might be large enough to block the nozzle heads. Checking and cleaning at six-month intervals is normally satisfactory unless the water contains unusually high amounts of silt.

When these maintenance steps are followed, Johnson-March assures that the system will provide continuing, effective dust control. □

Proportioner at the primary crusher automatically dilutes Compound MR to 1 part per 1,000 parts water.

Spray header mounted above crusher treats ore as it falls, a technique that provides maximum surface coverage.

Chapter 7
Copper Ore

Copper: the birth of modern mass mining of low grade ore	268
Open-pit copper mining in Arizona	272
Pinto Valley's deep, low-grade pit: success through good planning	284
Montana's giant Berkeley pit girds for another 22 years	287
Construction is well along at Aznalcollar	290
Rio Tinto Patino mines in northwest Spain	292
Panama: A major mine takes shape at Cerro Colorado	294

Copper: the birth of modern mass mining of low grade ore

US PORPHYRY COPPER DEPOSITS provided the birthplace of modern mass mining of low grade ores. The concept of achieving important economies through large scale operations was developed by a pair of young engineers, Daniel C. Jackling and Robert C. Gemmell. In 1899 they outlined a bold plan to mine and mill indicated reserves of some 12 million tons of 2% copper ore from Bingham Canyon, Utah, at a rate of 2,000 tpd—a figure that staggered the imagination in those days, when a 500-tpd mill was considered huge.

Today that mine, now owned by Kennecott Copper Corp., regularly produces 108,000 tpd of ore. On a single day (October 13, 1974), the mine broke all production records by loading and hauling a combined 504,167 tons of ore and waste. It is now the largest open-pit mine on earth—the evolutionary product of human ingenuity and modern equipment.

Last year US copper production was mainly concentrated in the hands of 18 companies, which operated 15 primary smelters. Mine production originated at some 39 locations, accounting for close to 96% of domestic output. Over 50% of the nation's copper ore is mined in Arizona.

Most US copper is extracted from benched open-pit mines, which use 8- to 20-cu-yd electric shovels and diesel, electric-wheel-driven haulers with payload capacities of 50 to 170 tons. The ore is broken by shooting multiple rows of blastholes drilled by rotary rigs that bore hole diameters of 9 to 17 in. Supporting equipment includes bulldozers, rubber-tired and tracked front-end loaders, water wagons and motor graders.

Underground mining of US copper is dominated by two producers: Magma Copper Co.'s San Manuel unit and Copper Range Co.'s White Pine mine. San Manuel, at roughly a 60,000-tpd mining rate, is a contender for the world's largest underground mine. A block caving mining system and railroad haulage of ore to production shafts is used at this Arizona mine. The 25,000-tpd White Pine mine is based on a room-and-pillar extraction scheme for the flat-lying mining beds. In addition to these two operations, significant amounts of underground copper ore are mined at Magma's unit at Superior, Ariz., and at UV Industries' mine at Bayard, N. Mex. These four mines were joined this year by underground output from the Lakeshore unit near Casa Grande, Ariz.—a jointly owned venture of Hecla Mining Co. and El Paso Natural Gas, with Hecla serving as the operational manager.

An open-pit-oriented industry

The US copper industry in 1973 surface-mined 286 million tons of ore and 757 million tons of waste. The underground sector extracted 34.9 million tons of ore and 1.3 million tons of waste in 1973. While surface mines account for about 80% of domestic copper yield, it is likely that underground mines will slowly assume a somewhat larger share of the production load in the future. This trend, barely perceptible now, is suggested by the current pattern of exploration for copper in the US. Much of the search is centered on deep-seated deposits.

Competitively, the US position in copper is strong in terms of reserves, engineering talent, transportation, sales to home grown markets, and relative capital formation ability.

Conversely, no significant new copper mining districts have been developed to a productive stage since crews of United Geophysical Co. discovered ore within a magnetic anomaly in the Pima mining district of Arizona in 1950—now the site of Cyprus Pima Mining Co.'s 60,000-tpd open-pit mine and concentrator.

In addition, the competitive edge of US copper has been blunted by the rapidly rising costs of environmental controls. It is estimated that 20-25% of the capital costs of integrated copper producers are currently being siphoned off by pollution abatement requirements, and smelter operating costs have increased by 4¢ to 8¢ per lb of recovered blister copper, according to some sources.

The impact of environmental expenditures has fallen heavily on integrated companies with smelters, which must meet rigid emission and effluent standards. This burden, however, is also shared by nonintegrated producers of con-

Vat leaching at Inspiration is first step in recovery of copper from oxide ores as well as mixed oxide-sulphide ores.

All ore is surface-mined at Inspiration, using equipment such as this 10-yd P&H shovel and 75-ton Dart off-highway hauler.

World's largest mine, located at Bingham Canyon, is operated by Utah Copper Div. of Kennecott. A shaft site and development work on a potential copper deposit below the perimeter of the pit is scheduled for completion in 1981.

centrates and precipitates, which toll or sell their output to smelting companies. Toll and sales arrangements are taking a larger bite from custom processed concentrates, resulting in a smaller net smelter return.

The cost of mining

In 1973 the US Bureau of Mines conducted an economic appraisal of the domestic copper industry, based on the 1970 values of investment and operating costs. The summary of bureau-estimated open-pit operating costs ranged from $0.394 per ton of ore mined at a 30,000-tpd operation to $0.303 per ton for a 100,000-tpd mine. Investment in open-pit equipment, shops, and facilities ranged from $119 per daily ton of capacity to $172.

In spite of dramatic improvement in surface mining equipment, recent productivity figures for domestic copper mining have revealed troubling trends. S. D. Michaelson, formerly chief mining engineer of Kennecott's Metal Mining Div., analyzed the three major unit operations in open-pit copper mining this way: Blasthole drill productivity has been improving at a reasonably satisfactory rate—averaging about 4.2% a year for the period 1965 through 1973. This about matched the rates of cost inflation during that time span. The improvement was attributed mainly to better and heavier equipment and improved drill bits. Electric mining shovels in the copper industry showed the biggest gain in productivity: a 5.7% annual increase, due primarily to larger bucket capacities.

Even though trucks are getting larger and showing greater availability, the truck productivity increase at US copper open pits over the 1965 to 1973 period was only about 2.8%. The comparatively low improvement rate was explained by the fact that haulage distances are growing longer and the average lift traversed by trucks is increasing. This is an inescapable fact of life at most open-pit copper mines, which led Michaelson to the conclusion that new and more productive methods are needed for moving ore and overburden.

Combining all trends of the unit operations involved in open-pit copper, plus those for maintenance, staff, and miscellaneous functions, Michaelson found that open-pit copper mine productivity was increasing at average rate of only 2.6% a year. This level is well below the 1965 to 1973 inflationary rate and distressingly short of matching the inflation of 1974 and 1975. Michaelson said that productivity trends for total maintenance and staff functions varied from essentially flat to declining.

It seems logical that the unit operation trends will continue over the near term, and it seems unrealistic to expect significant open-pit productivity gains to stem solely from larger and better equipment used within the designs of current mining plans. On a more positive note, open-pit mining costs account for only about 10% to 12% of the cost of producing copper.

Underground mining of copper is expensive. In the USBM study of the domestic copper industry, the operating costs of a typical 6,000-tpd cut-and-fill copper mine were estimated at $6.996 per ton of material mined (1970 basis). The hypothetical operating cost of a 25,000-tpd room-and-pillar mine was pegged at $3.25 per ton of material mined, and the cost for a 30,000-tpd mine using block caving was estimated at $2.455 per ton of ore.

Capital investment was established at $2,160 per daily ton of capacity for the cut-and-fill mine; $630 per daily ton for the room-and-pillar mine; and $840 for the producing unit based on block caving.

Theoretically, an underground cut-and-fill mine would need an ore grade of 10% to 12% copper to achieve costs per pound of copper equivalent to those of an open pit mining 0.6% copper. Similarly, a room-and-pillar mine would need 5% to 6% ore and a block cave mine, 4% copper. Such mines, if they exist at all, are indeed rare.

At Magma's San Manuel block cave mine in Arizona, for example, ore grade is about 0.7% copper. At White Pine (room and pillar), mill feed is about 1% copper, and Magma's cut-and-fill mine at Superior, Ariz., produces an approximate 4.5% copper ore. Per pound of recoverable copper, underground mass mining is four to six times as costly as open pit ore operations, and selective mining by cut and fill is more than twice as costly as open-pit mining if the USBM data are realistic.

If a case is made for worrisome productivity trends in open pits, the case is even stronger for underground mining of copper in the US. This is particularly disturbing because it is expected that a growing amount of the nation's copper needs will have to come from underground sources.

Needed: at least $1 copper for new investment

USBM estimated the 1970 capital cost of a 152,000-tpy copper smelter at $42 million. The operating cost of such a plant amounted to $0.04 per lb of copper or $0.064 per lb of metal when allowing for a 12% rate of return on investment, using a discounted cash flow (DFC) calculation, and providing for Federal tax at 50% of gross profits. This estimate was established for a plant in which a portion of the concentrate was charged directly to the converters, where it was combined with matte produced from a reverberatory furnace.

The capital cost of a 300,000-tpy copper refinery, using 1970 values, was $57 million. The operating cost was calculated to be $0.031 per lb of copper after taking generous credits for the sale of spent 60° Baume sulphuric acid at $26.21 per ton, $0.46 per lb for nickel sulphate, and $0.67 per lb for copper oxide. After allowing a 12% return on investment using DFC and allowing for Federal taxation at 50% of gross profits, the refining cost amounted to $0.048 per lb of copper (1970 basis).

In summary, refined primary copper could be produced from US open-pit sources for about $0.25 to $0.35 per lb in 1970. Underground copper from high-tonnage, bulk mining systems could be recovered at costs of $0.38 to $0.45 per lb of refined metal. Today, a price of about $0.75 a lb is required to support the recovery of refined copper from open pits. A price of $1.00 to $1.50 is necessary to prompt new investment in US copper development projects.

The cost of energy is a new dimension that must be considered in copper operations. A recent USBM study indicated a 1973 energy cost of $0.0483 for the production of a pound of refined copper in the US. It is likely that the 1973 costs have since escalated some 50% to 100% at producer locations.

Even though energy costs are thought to represent less than 10% of current production costs, energy input must be considered in assessing the economic limits of mining. The amount of energy required for mining and beneficiation of copper ore varies inversely with the grade of ore mined.

Thus, technocrats who hold that improving technology will create ore reserves from submarginal resources have a new restraining factor to deal with. If the grade of copper ore drops from 0.6% to 0.2%, the energy input would likely triple for mining and milling copper through the concentrate stage.

Earl Cook, writing in the February 20, 1976 issue of SCIENCE, suggested that there may be a geochemical barrier to recovery at about 0.1% copper, which is about 16 times the geochemical background. Below 0.1%, some investigators say that most of the copper is in solid solution in common silicate minerals and is not amenable to selective physical or chemical extraction.

It is true that technology has created ore reserves from worthless rock, but the energy input-metal output relationship imposes new finite mining limits that need new breakthroughs, as does the apparent geochemical limitation. Cook also points out that most copper porphyries exhibit rather sharp geochemical boundaries. Such a condition would also place finite limits on the extension of reserves surrounding known deposits, even if technology gives industry the ability to mine 0.1% copper.

The natural US environment for copper

The US copper industry is predominantly based on production from porphyry deposits, as well as the closely related vein and replacement type of orebodies. Porphyry deposits are large, relatively low grade occurrences of disseminated mineralization genetically associated with intrusions of felsic igneous rocks.

A typical porphyry deposit is oval in plan and pipelike in vertical section. It may have horizontal dimensions of 4,000 x 8,000 ft and contain 800 million tons or more of 0.6% copper, with smaller amounts of molybdenum (0.01% to 0.15%). Studies suggest that 70% of such an orebody lies in the intrusion and 30% in the surrounding country rock. Such deposits are characteristic of production centers at Ajo, Morenci, and Miami in Arizona, for example, or at Santa Rita, N. Mex.

Vein, pipe, and replacement deposits are usually associated with porphyry intrusions, but they occur as localized concentrations within favorable, reactive host rocks. Vein deposits form when ore minerals are deposited in faults and fractures by metal-rich solutions given off by a crystallizing magmatic intrusive. Veins are tabular in form and are found in attitudes varying from near-horizontal to near-vertical. Much of the Butte, Mont., production previously came from underground mining of such deposits, although operations are now based on open-pit mining of disseminated and vein "fingerlet" ores of low grade. The Bisbee and Magma underground operations in Arizona are also sites of vein deposits.

Replacement deposits are formed near igneous contacts with reactive host rocks. The hosts may be limestone, dolomite, calcareous sandstones, or even diabase sills as at Ray, Ariz. These deposits tend to be tabular and may be concordant with bedding. The grade may be high, but as a rule these orebodies are now mined from open pits centered on large, low grade bodies and are generally regarded as part of the porphyry orebody. The Mission and Pima mines in Arizona are typical of such deposits. The distinction between replacement deposits and the classic porphyry deposits is blurred and largely academic. For example, open-pit mining of Bingham Canyon porphyry ore steadily encroaches on chalcopyrite replacement bodies in limestone to the west.

In general, the resources of copper in vein, pipe, and replacement deposits are small in comparison with the porphyry deposits.

According to a US Geological Survey report, the grade of 38 US and Mexican porphyry coppers averages about 0.59% copper contained in an average deposit of 815 million mt. This compares with 21 known copper porphyries in Canada, where the average deposit is 245 million mt of 0.49% copper; 20 South American porphyries which average 773 million mt of 0.99% copper; and 24 southwest Pacific porphyries containing an average 203 million mt of 0.53% copper.

Beyond the porphyries

Strata-bound deposits are another relatively important source of copper, possibly accounting for one-quarter of the world's resources. In the US, the most important example of this type of deposit is the Precambrian Nonesuch shale of the Upper Peninsula of Michigna and northern Wisconsin. Here, the copper occurs primarily as chalcocite in silttones, shales, sandstones. Such deposits are the scene of White Pine Mining Co. operations.

Elsewhere in the US, strata-bound Precambrian copper deposits occur in the Belt Supergroup in western Montana and adjacent parts of the Idaho panhandle. Copper sulphides persist as disseminations in the Revett formation. While this area has no commercial copper production, the district is being explored.

The Nacimiento copper operation near Cuba, N. Mex., an Earth Resources unit, is situated on a deposit typical of the red sandstone stratas of late Paleozoic or early Mesozoic age.

Copper is also found in massive sulphide deposits in volcanic rocks. The prime example of an active mine based on such a deposit is the Bruce operation of Cyprus Mining Co. near Bagdad, Ariz.

Two magmatic segregate deposits of the US hold interesting concentrations of copper and nickel: the Duluth Gabbro, south of the eastern end of the Mesabi Iron Range in Minnesota, and the Stillwater area, southwest of Billings, Mont. The Stillwater area hosted some chromite production in the past and the magmatic segregate is also the scene of current exploration for platinum by Johns Manville.

The Duluth Gabbro has received the most intensive investigation for the feasibility of commercial production of copper-nickel sulphides. However, both this area and the Stillwater complex are considered too low in grade for development under current pricing conditions.

Native copper ores of the Keweenaw Peninsula in Michigan contain elemental copper in amygdaloidal volcanic flows and conglomerate beds. This district produced a considerable tonnage of copper in times past but is now inactive. The area, however, is being reinvestigated for commercial production possibilities by a group including Homestake Mining Co.

In summary, the copper resources of the US are extensive and not in short supply. The US Geological Survey has estimated US reserves at 90 million tons of copper, equivalent to about 20% of the agency's estimated total world reserve of 450 million tons.

There is no immediate shortage of copper resources on the domestic scene, but the production potential of the future is threatened by reduced rates of exploration and discovery. In large part, the slowdown reflects the industry struggle with environmental problems, productivity, inflation rates, cash flow liquidity, and public and legislator apathy—if not outright antibusiness sentiments. □

More than 1 billion tons of material has been mined from Phelps Dodge's Morenci pit since the beginning of World War II.

Open-pit copper mining in Arizona

Richard Hoppe, Senior editor

ARIZONA'S 50-ODD OPEN PITS mine 159 million tpy of ore and 447 million tpy of waste. Excluding coal, sand and gravel, stone, and water, the state's production represents 26% of all US surface mineral mining. Arizona's closest rival is Florida, where 325 million tpy is mined, principally from phosphate fields.

Arizona ranks first in copper mining, producing 54% of all US ores. Utah is a far distant second, at 14%. Copper ore, like iron, is recovered principally from open pits, which produce 90% of all US copper ore. For this surface mining issue, E/MJ in March visited six of Arizona's open-pit copper mines: Morenci, Metcalf, Ray, Sacaton, Sierrita, and Cyprus Pima. The pits have varied methods of operation and production rates. All are valiantly attempting to achieve efficient, economic operations in the face of a multitude of problems, created largely outside the boundaries of their management. The chief bogies are energy costs, for both fuel and electricity, the continued pace of inflation, and the specter of scarce water among contending users. The only relief for the mine operators appears to lie in applying materials handling methods that consume the least energy and are least respondent to inflationary pressures. Sierrita's use of in-pit crushing and conveyor haulage is one example. As for the water supply problem, no solution will provide continued massive use for all the parties in contention—mining, agriculture, and urban. Certain sectors will be hurt.

Trucks continue to be the number one movers of material in copper pits. Most mines seem to have settled on a maximum size around 170-ton capacity. Larger capacities require excavators, roads, and investments larger than present management considers practicable. Electric shovels have gradually increased in size to 20 cu

Mine locations: 1) Morenci; 2) Metcalf; 3) Ray; 4) Sacaton; 5) Cyprus Pima; 6) Sierrita.

yd. It is unlikely that hardrock shovels will exceed this size significantly in the next decade or two.

Future discoveries of orebodies in Arizona are likely to prove difficult. The basin-range structure of much of the state means that most orebodies have been covered with postmineral valley fill of transported, not residual, material. Seven of 10 discoveries made since 1960 were completely covered. Sacaton is probably one of the last discoveries to be initiated by surface exploration; the find was the result of district-wide geologic mapping of features that are considered classic for porphyry copper deposits. Future discoveries will generally require sophisticated exploration techniques combined with extensive deep core drilling. □

All-railroad haulage at Morenci conserves energy

MORENCI'S OPEN-PIT RAIL HAULAGE SYSTEM may appear somewhat outdated in an era of giant haulage trucks, but it is nevertheless an efficient, profitable operation. Considering the rising costs of diesel fuel, rail haulage may again be a worthwhile consideration for many large open pits. At Morenci, over 150,000 tpd of ore and waste is hauled by railroad to the ore crusher and waste dumps. The average one-way haul to the crusher is 3.4 mi; to the waste dumps, 5.8 mi. Such distances, from mining benches out of the pit to the point of discharge, would be exceedingly costly for truck haulage.

Morenci was located as a placer gold deposit in 1870 and as a copper deposit two years later. The first copper discoveries were surface outcrops of oxidized veins. Underground mining continued for decades. The open pit, started at the beginning of World War II, appears to have a reasonably long future. Even at this late date, operations in several sections of the open pit are excavating timber used in the old underground workings. Churn and diamond drilling continue to provide new data on the orebody.

Geologically, the Morenci-Metcalf district is a structural high, cropping out as a window in an Eocene to Miocene volcanic field. The Precambrian granitic basement is overlain by a 3,000-ft sequence of Paleozoic and Cretaceous sediments. Late Cretaceous-early Tertiary Laramide intrusives penetrated the sediments as stocks, plugs, dikes, and sills. Major veins and structural orientations of N20°-40°E and major Basin and Range faulting N30°-60°W are present. The Laramide intrusive complex, with its typical porphyry copper alteration-mineralization sequence, spans a time from 62 million to 49 million years ago.

The orebody, roughly circular, is somewhat elongated in a N40°E direction with the long axis 3 mi long. Vertically, the deposit is bowl-shaped. In the western portion, the Morenci orebody dips 11° to 17° easterly, while in the eastern portion, the Metcalf orebody dips 15° to 19° southwesterly. The supergene blanket comprising the orebody is 1,000 ft thick near the center of the deposit.

Mineralization consists of a supergene-enriched hypogene system of disseminated micro-veinlet and vein pyrite, chalcopyrite, and bornite, with moderate amounts of molybdenite occurring in quartz veins and as fracture coatings. Supergene enrichment, concentrated in the phyllic zone, consists of chalcocite and minor covellite almost completely replacing bornite and chalcopyrite, and partially replacing pyrite. Local oxidation products in the upper reaches of the mine benches consist of chrysocolla, azurite, brochantite, and cuprite.

Overburden consists of low grade leached capping in intrusive and locally sedimentary limestone and shale rocks. Precambrian granite is the dominant country rock, while Laramide monzonite porphyry hosts 75% of the supergene ore.

Railroad equipment has 90% availability

Benches are 50 ft high and up to 150 ft wide along the top of the pit (165 ft crest to crest). An average shovel cut along a bench is 45 ft wide, with rail track shifted after each cut. The overall working slope of the pit is 3 to 1; final slopes will be 1.3 to 1.

Unit trains at Morenci are typically made up of either seven or 11 80-ton cars; larger trains make favorable-grade hauls.

Morenci pit factsheet

Owned by: Phelps Dodge Corp.
Location: North of town of Morenci (Route 666), Greenlee County, Arizona.
Production (1976 average): 63,840 tpd ore grading 0.80% Cu; 95,480 tpd waste.
Startup: 1942, after four years of pre-stripping.

Major mining equipment

Drills (rotary): One 7-in., nine 12¼-in., one 13¾-in., one 15-in.
Shovels (electric): Six 6-cu-yd, one 7-cu-yd, five 9-cu-yd, three 12-cu-yd, three 15-cu-yd.
Haulage: Diesel-electric locomotives—four 1,200-hp, 20 1,750-hp, 10 2,000-hp; side-dump cars—300 40- and 42-cu-yd.
Ancillary equipment: Two track maintainers, one ballast regulator, two spot tampers, 10 track shifters, 12 tracked dozers, four rubber-tired dozers, one 150-ton locomotive crane, two 80-ton cranes, three 40-ton cranes, four 4-cu-yd rubber-tired front-end loaders, six motor graders.

The highest and the lowest active bench elevations are now 4,950 ft and 4,200 ft, respectively. The final pit bottom is scheduled for elevation 3,350, a long time away, which will leave a pit 8,000 ft in diameter and 2,200 ft deep.

Blastholes are drilled 12¼-in.-dia to 15-in.-dia on 33-ft to 45-ft centers in single rows. The smaller diameter drill averages 320 ft per shift; the larger, 470 ft. Average drill bit life is 3,500 ft. As the drills are electric-powered, considerable cable movement about the pit is required.

After blastholes are drilled, cuttings are sampled and sent to the laboratory for assay determinations. Assay results are the basis for flagging sections of each bench face as either ore, leach-dump material, or waste.

Morenci's blast fragmentation is quite good, particularly in view of the mine's overall powder factor: 4.9 tons of material broken per lb of explosives. ANFO is loaded into dry blastholes, while gels are used in the wet ones.

Flexibility in the daily selection of loading points is somewhat hampered in any track mining scheme, but this problem is mitigated at Morenci by the extreme size of the pit—containing over 30 mi of active bench track. Maintenance and shifting of track is a major part of pit operations.

Track panels, including those with switch points, are made up in 39-ft sections outside the pit and transported to the benches on flatcars. A self-propelled, rail-mounted 80-ton crane is used to unload the panels and place them ahead of the crane. The panels are bolt-connected by the field crew, and the crane and flatcar move ahead, laying new track ahead of the crane. Alternately, old track in good condition is merely shifted after the cut of the shovel along the bench. Track panels are made of wooden ties and 90-lb rail. Permanent track is made of 133-lb rail. About 10% of the mine track is replaced each year, in addition to installation of new track as the pit is expanded and deepened. Permanent track inside and outside the pit is ballasted with smelter slag; active track is not ballasted.

Railroad gradients within the pit are designed to a maximum 3% adverse haul and 4% favorable haul. Most track outside the pit, leading to the concentrator and dumps, is level. As only one locomotive is used for each train, the number of cars per train is limited to either seven or 11, depending on whether it is assigned to an adverse or favorable haul gradient.

All Morenci railroad cars are side-dump, 80-ton-capacity units. Haul cycle time averages 2 hr or more, but the railroad system is profitable because of the availability of the equipment—90% or better—and the

Blastholes are truck-loaded at Morenci. Overall powder factor is 4.9 tons per lb—extraordinarily light for track mining.

Track extensions and replacements are 39-ft panels, brought to the face on flatcars and offloaded by rail-mounted crane.

relatively inexpensive operating costs of a railroad system for long hauls.

Waste material is hauled to the south, beyond the concentrator, and distributed on two different levels along the edge of an expanding waste hill. As each section of the dump becomes filled by new material building up from the toe of the dump to the crest, the edge of the dump is releveled by a dozer, and the dump track is shifted out to the new crest.

A total of 2,900 people work for the Morenci branch of Phelps Dodge, a figure that includes personnel for both the Morenci and Metcalf mines, the concentrators and smelter, and such peripheral activities as limestone quarrying for feed to the smelter. Currently, operations are scheduled three shifts a day, with 11 days of work followed by three days of shutdown at both mines. ☐

Downhill truck mining at Metcalf

PHELPS DODGE STARTED MINING the Metcalf open pit in 1975 to exploit the northeastern portion of the Morenci orebody. Its favorable location permits much of the orebody to be mined by high side-hill cuts, with a downhill haul route for the ore trucks. Metcalf is located on the eastern side of a valley—the western side of a mountain chain—some 2 mi north of the Morenci pit. The Metcalf crusher is at the western edge of the pit, at elevation 4,500 ft, and is connected to the Metcalf concentrator (near the Morenci concentrator) by a 5-mi railroad line.

Waste haul is level; ore moves downhill

The planned final dimensions of the Metcalf pit, to be reached far in the future, are roughly 5,000 ft x 7,000 ft in plan view and 2,300 ft vertically.

Ore is currently mined along the eastern slopes of the side hill at elevations 5,300 to 5,500 and near the western edge at elevations 4,600 to 4,800—close to the primary crusher and switchyard. As mining progresses, ore will come from benches as high as elevation 5,750 along the eastern slopes, and waste above it will be cut back from as high as 6,300 ft. Currently, the one-way haul for ore trucks is a little over 2 mi downhill. Waste hauls average 1 mi one way, on essentially level grades.

This makes material transport, now 38,000 tpd of ore and 70,000 tpd of waste, a relatively easy operation. Haul roads are 100 ft wide, with ramps between levels set at a 10% grade. Final pit slopes will be 1.33:1, identical to Morenci's. The current bench height is 50 ft and widths are 100 ft or more.

Shovel productivity is high

Blastholes are drilled 12¼-in.-dia, 65 ft deep, in single or multiple rows on 33-ft centers. The burden distance is also 33 ft, measured from the toe of the bench. The drills, unlike those at Morenci, are diesel-powered, and they average 425 ft per shift. Bit life ranges around 9,000 ft, or three times that at Morenci. Morenci uses a combination of steel and tungsten-carbide bits, while Metcalf drills with tungsten-carbide bits almost exclusively. The south wall of the Morenci pit is composed of tough-to-drill metasediments.

Morenci and Metcalf blasting practices are essentially identical. Spacing is the major factor accounting for the difference in powder factors: 4.9 tons per lb at Morenci, vs. 3.7 tons per lb at Metcalf.

The blastholes are loaded with ANFO from a truck to a height of 25 to 30 ft. Two down-lines of detonating cord are placed in each hole. To each cord is attached a

Metcalf pit factsheet

Owned by: Phelps Dodge Corp.
Location: 2 mi northeast of Morenci pit.
Production (1976 average): 37,880 tpd ore grading 0.86% Cu; 69,520 tpd waste.
Startup: 1975, after five years of prestripping.

Major mining equipment
Drills: Four 12¼-in. rotary.
Shovels: Five 15-cu-yd electric, plus one 10-cu-yd rubber-tired front-end loader.
Haulage: 25 100-ton-capacity rear-dump trucks.
Ancillary equipment: Five tracked dozers, five rubber-tired dozers, four motor graders, two water trucks, one 80-ton crane.

3-lb cast primer, one located at the hole bottom, the other 15 ft from the bottom, at the toe elevation.

Blasting is normally done at noon or quitting time, shooting anywhere from 15 to 60 holes initiated by a No. 6 cap attached to the surface detonating cord and a stretch of safety fuse. When wet holes are encountered, slurried gel is used in place of ANFO. The gel is brought to the face in 50-lb bags and is hand-loaded.

Any secondary drilling and blasting is done with a 1⅞-in.-dia, single-boom drill and 60% gel sticks. Productivity of the Metcalf 15-cu-yd shovels is 15,000 tons per shift, compared with 8,800 tons per shift for identical shovel units at Morenci. Obviously, less waiting time for loading is the big advantage for Metcalf. Also, as a general rule for open pits, the newer the pit, the higher the productivity—even when using similarly sized equipment. Phelps Dodge management attributes the difference in shovel productivity to the following: Rail shovels must swing nearly 180°, vs. 90° for truck shovel operations; the truck body target is relatively easier to load; and, perhaps most important, availability of haulage units is better at the shovel. One could debate whether a 180° swing is needed for railroad mining, but if the angle were reduced, a larger number of track shifts would be needed.

As at Morenci, long term mine planning for Metcalf is based upon results of churn and diamond drilling, while control over daily mining benches is the result of analysis of blasthole cutting samples. The ore trucked to the crusher, a 60-in. gyratory, is reduced to a nominal minus

Metcalf benches are side-hill cuts into orebody. Virtually all ore at the new mine is located above the primary crusher.

8-in. size and conveyed to a 32,000-ton-capacity stockpile. Unit trains of 20 cars, each of 100-ton capacity, are loaded from a tunnel beneath the stockpile through pneumatically operated drop gates. The locomotive operator positions the bottom-dump cars under the gates for loading, then drives to the Metcalf concentrator. □

Ore quality control is focus of mining at Ray

THE RAY OREBODY WAS DISCOVERED shortly after the Civil War and was originally mined underground. Benches in the center of the pit, those containing the best sulphide values, daily uncover sections of old timbered mine workings.

The land around Ray—high peaked mountains and steep valleys—is starkly beautiful. Towering rocks have been eroded to tormented shapes. The Ray orebody occurs in older Precambrian schist and granite and in younger Precambrian diabase and Apache Group rocks. The copper and molybdenum mineralization in the vein and disseminated porphyry deposit is associated in time with the Laramide Granite Mountain Porphyry intrusion. In plan view, the orebody is a rough oval, 12,000 x 8,000 ft. Hypogene copper mineralization is largely confined to tabular diabase sills. Most overburden is post-mineral Tertiary conglomerates and rhyodacite tuffs.

Ray is not a true porphyry

At current mining rates, the Ray orebody should last another 70 years. When completed, the excavation will be 12,000 ft x 8,000 ft in plan and 1,500 ft deep. Working benches are 40 ft high, of variable width, and the active pit slopes range from 26° to 37°, depending on the soundness of rock zones and the distribution of fractures and planes of weakness. Haul roads, generally limited to 8% grades, are 80 ft wide, divided by a 5-ft pile of crushed rock.

The geology and location of the mine create two major operating problems for management: economic disposal of waste material and control of the quality of ore sent to the concentrator.

Because Ray is located between tightly parallel mountains, space for waste disposal is limited. Even with careful planning, distances for spoil disposal grow longer as uphill hauls to the north and south of the pit are extended.

The topography at Ray also required driving a 16-ft-dia concrete-lined tunnel 18,300 ft long to divert Mineral Creek away from the open pit. The diversion work included construction of an arch dam to control and meter water through the tunnel. The system, designed on the basis of 100-year flood data, provides for a runoff of 33,000 sec-ft coursing from Devils Canyon and Mineral Creek in the north. All the water diverted by the dam and tunnel reenters the original Mineral Creek channel south of the mine and flows into the Gila River 3 mi beyond.

While the water diversion system has long been completed and the location of waste disposal dumps is decided upon years in advance, the control of ore grade and quality sent to the concentrator is a continuing problem. Mining control requires both long and short range forecasting and daily control at the operating benches.

Ray is not a true porphyry deposit, which is usually described as a massive, low grade orebody of consistent zoning of mineralization. At Ray, the mineralization is jumbled; both rock and ore change quickly in character and quality. Because consistency is not the rule over any reasonable distance, ore control is the result of a number of interrelated programs. A great deal of sampling, analysis, and decision making is required before individual sections of mine benches are color-flagged as sulphide or silicate ore or as waste.

Computerized pit diagram

Ray uses three separate sampling programs: long range and deep diamond drilling, mid-range rotary drilling of 200-ft-deep holes on 100-ft centers, and sampling of blasthole cuttings. Each year 10,000 to 20,000 ft of long range drilling and 12,000 to 18,000 ft of mid-range drilling results are added to the computerized block diagram of the pit. The computer output permits prediction of problem areas and selection of the best of a variety of tactics to overcome them. The goal of programming is to develop the most economic mining schedule, eliminating as much as possible any surprises.

The assay results of sampled blasthole cuttings can be posted within 24 hr of sampling. Sampling results normally include information on the percentages of total

Dumps for waste from Ray mine are planned years in advance, as space for waste disposal is limited by mountain slopes.

Ray pit factsheet

Owned by: Kennecott Copper Corp.
Location: South of Superior on state route 177, Mineral Creek mining district, Ray, Arizona.
Production: 45,000 tpd ore grading 0.8% sulphide Cu and 0.9% silicate Cu over a five-day week; 90,000 tpd waste over a seven-day week.
Startup: 1911 as underground mine; 1952 as an open pit, after four years of prestripping.

Major mining equipment
Drills (rotary): Five Bucyrus-Erie 40R (9-in. bits), two Bucyrus-Erie 60R (9⅞-in. bits).
Shovels (electric): Two Marion 4161 6-cu-yd, three P&H 1600 7-cu-yd, three Marion 191M 15-cu-yd, one P&H 2100 15-cu-yd, one P&H 2800 25-cu-yd (just erected).
Haulage: 12 85-ton Dart trucks (inactive on present schedule), four 100-ton Darts, 33 120-ton Wabco trucks.
Ancillary equipment: Three Cat 16 graders, two Cat 14 graders, one Cat 814 rubber-tired dozer (all for road maintenance), plus nine rubber-tired dozers, two D9 dozers, six D8 dozers, three TD25 dozers, one HD21 dozer.

copper and nonsulphide copper, together with estimated concentrate grade and probable recovery factor. Each section of the sampled bench face is then color-flagged as silicate ore, sulphide ore, or waste. The cutoff grade for ore is currently 0.4% Cu. Ray now mines 45,000 tpd of ore—30,000 tpd of sulphide and 15,000 tpd of silicate.

Along with regular operating personnel, Ray employs quality control technicians in the field on all production shifts. They are there to advise pit supervisors on all questions concerning the quality of ore sent to the crushers. In cases where further refinements of mill head blending is needed, a front-end loader is assigned to dig and load a specific section of bench.

Production is now concentrated in three pit areas: the west pit, the central area (mostly sulphides), and the eastern slope (mostly silicates). Silicate ore is vat-leached at Ray, while sulphide ore is crushed outside the pit, then moved 20 mi by rail to the concentrator at Hayden. Currently, most sulphide ores are chalcocite with minor chalcopyrite. The sulphides contain molybdenum and traces of gold and silver, recovered in downstream processing. Silicate ore is principally chrysocolla, averaging 0.9% Cu. Waste is removed both from the perimeter of the pit and from the deeper benches, as inclusions between sections of ore.

The pit is now 800 ft deep, and one-way haulage distances to the sulphide ore crusher, the silicate ore crusher, and the waste dumps average 5,000 ft, 7,500 ft, and 9,500 ft, respectively. The waste haul is adverse all the way. An average of 25 trucks work every shift, fed by five shovels—two in ore and three in waste. Availability of shovels, trucks, and the 12-cu-yd loader is figured at 75%, 75%, and 55%, respectively.

Seven drill shifts per day are needed for blastholes. A 40R averages 350 ft per shift; a 60R, 500 ft per shift. Bit life averages 3,000 ft, with a wide range of 1,500 ft to 9,000 ft. Blastholes are drilled and blasted in single rows, on 18- or 24-ft centers, 45 ft deep.

Dry holes are loaded with Carbamite (prepackaged and oiled ammonium nitrate prills). About 12 50-lb bags are slit and hand-loaded into each hole, providing for 15 to 18 ft of top stemming with drill cuttings. The explosive column is detonated by a 1-lb Atlas Kinepak booster attached to the detonating cord downline, 2 ft from the bottom of the column. If more than one row is blasted at a time, 9-ms and 17-ms delays are used between the rows. Wet blastholes are pumped dry and a plastic liner is inserted before charging. Holes that can't be pumped dry are loaded with explosive gels and detonated with one Kinepak for every 50 lb of gel.

About 900 operating personnel are employed at Ray, including maintenance and supervisory staff. The operating costs for mining (excluding depreciation) break down as follows: truck haulage (including tire costs) 52%, haul road maintenance 11%, loading 21%, drilling 6%, blasting 7%, and waste dump maintenance 3%. Tire life for the Wabco trucks is 5,000 hr, and life of the Detroit Diesel or Cummins engines is over 8,000 hr between major overhauls. □

Pit crushers and conveyors move Sierrita ore and waste

SIERRITA'S IN-THE-PIT CONVEYOR SYSTEMS now move 250,000 tpd of material, including 92,000 tpd of ore, out of the pit to the waste dumps and the concentrator. Using 42 120-ton to 170-ton trucks each shift, the new system has reduced ore haulage truck requirements from 24 to 14 units per shift, has cut overall energy consumption per ton moved, and should pay back the capital investment in something over six years. The conveyor systems are also less likely to be affected by inflationary pressures.

The Sierrita pit is an extension of Duval's older Esperanza orebody, 1½ mi away. Sierrita's reserves are stated at 450 million tons of 0.47% copper. The large amounts of molybdenum in the ore make the mine economic; 60,000 lb of moly metal is contained in each day's concentrate production. The Sierrita pit has made Duval the second largest moly producer in the world.

Sierrita's concentrator, started up in 1970, has been expanded from a capacity of 60,000 tpd to 92,000 tpd, a massive plant by any standard. The Esperanza pit sends another 16,000 tpd to its own concentrator.

Currently, Sierrita is 750 ft deep and about 5,000 ft x 6,000 ft in lateral extent. The benches are 50 ft high. When exhausted, the mine's final slopes will be 45°. Haulage roads are designed for an overall slope of 8%, with ramps set at 10% grade. The roads are divided by a 5- to 6-ft windrow of crushed rock with a double-lane, 70-ft-wide uphill ramp and a single, 35-ft-wide downhill lane. The rock divider will stop any runaway truck.

Long range mine planning is based on a continuing program of deep-hole diamond drilling—as much as 2,000 ft deep. Day-to-day operations depend on the laboratory analysis of samples from blasthole drilling. Much of the waste now removed comes from ore-bearing benches far from the periphery of the pit. Because of the high tonnage of waste at deeper pit levels, management decided to convert the in-pit ore crushing and conveyor system for use in waste disposal and to erect a new ore crusher-conveyor system deeper in the pit.

Coping with rising fuel costs

Coming on stream this year, Duval's truck-crusher-conveyor systems for both waste and ore within the

In-the-pit crushing and conveying of both ore and waste at Sierrita mine is probably an idea whose time has finally come.

Sierrita pit factsheet

Owned by: Duval Sierrita Corp., a wholly owned subsidiary of Pennzoil Co.
Location: 20 mi southwest of Tucson, Ariz.
Production: 92,000 tpd ore grading 0.35% Cu and 0.035% Mo, with minor amounts of Ag; approximately 164,000 tpd waste.
Startup: 1970, after two years of prestripping 125 million tons of waste. Original capital investment was $195 million.

Major mining equipment
Drills (rotary): Four Bucyrus-Erie 45Rs, four B-E 60Rs.
Shovels (electric): 10 P&H 2100s, 15-cu-yd capacity.
Haulage: 15 120-ton Dart trucks and the following Wabco trucks: 23 120-ton units, 22 150-ton to 170-ton units, one 250-ton Model 3200 test unit.
Ancillary: Six Cat 14 graders, 12 track dozers, seven rubber-tired dozers, six water trucks, and four front-end loaders.

Sierrita pit represent an idea whose time has arrived. Despite a decade of serious consideration of conveyors by many open-pit operators, surprisingly few have chosen this route. Now, with the specter of spiraling energy costs and inflation, many pit operators may take another look at conveyors. Sierrita's performance will likely be studied for years to come.

Sierrita's top and bottom elevations are now at 4,100 ft and 3,350 ft. Until this year, all ore from the benches was trucked to two 60 x 89 AC gyratory crushers at 3,950 ft and then conveyed to the mill. All waste was trucked beyond the pit periphery and dumped. The new system uses the former ore crusher station for crushing waste. The new ore crusher station is located deeper in the pit, at elevation 3,600 ft.

The new system required relocation of equipment and the purchase of two new crushers, new conveyors and belt, a movable stacker, and ancillary facilities. The capital investment was $32 million. Management figures the changeover will reduce truck fleet requirements by 25% and pay for itself in six to eight years. Further moves of the crushers and conveyors are envisioned as the pit deepens.

Both sets of crushers are identical, but settings for waste are at 8½ in., while ore is crushed to a nominal 6 in. Beneath both sets of crushers are 84-in.-wide Nico pan feeders, equipped with Nuclear leveling devices. Material is kept 5 ft deep over the pans to prevent damage from impact.

Both conveyor systems were designed by Mountain States Engineering. The five ore belts, four of them new, are 60 in. wide. They travel 16,000 ft to the concentrator, both up and down slopes. Maximum grade is 16°, and belt capacity is 6,500 tph. About 75% of the Goodyear steel-cable belt has a strength of 3,150 lb per inch of width (piw). Top idlers are spaced on 5-ft centers, with return idlers every 20 ft. Power to the system is supplied by nine 1,250-hp GE wound-rotor motors.

The 8,000-ft-long, 8,000-tph waste conveyor system has four separate belts, including a movable stacker belt. The belts, 72-in. wide, are set to a maximum 13°. Belt strength for the Goodyear steel-cable belt is equally divided between 3,150 piw and 1,000 piw. Power for the belts, through the stacker, is supplied by four 1,500-hp GE wound-rotor motors and four 500-hp Westinghouse wound-rotor motors. The stacker belt is skid-mounted on 115-lb rails so that it can be moved readily by a dozer. The crawler-mounted stacker was designed and built by Thomas Systems of Fort Worth, Tex. A crew at the mine is assigned to splicing and vulcanizing belts. This is an arduous, time-consuming task, but Sierrita's crew can join a section in less than one day.

Six 15-cu-yd shovels and 42 120-ton to 170-ton trucks operate each shift to move more than 250,000 tpd of ore and waste. Normally, five blasthole drills are employed on each shift. Blastholes are drilled either 9⅞-in.-dia or 12¼-in.-dia, 60 ft deep. The drills average between 45 and 50 ft per hr. Holes are spaced on 24-ft and 27-ft centers in multiple rows. Holes are stemmed for about 50% of their length, and the bottom column is loaded with ANFO. About 70% of the wet holes encountered are dewatered, sleeved with plastic lining, and loaded with ANFO. Where this is impractical, slurry is used. The bottom 10 ft of the ANFO column consists of aluminized ANFO. Priming is done with two 1-lb aluminized slurry boosters, shaped like sausages and attached to the down cord—one 5 ft from the bottom and the other at 15 ft. The overall powder factor for blasting is a respectable 0.25 lb per ton. □

Large truck fleet at Cyprus Pima makes long, steep hauls

THE PIMA OREBODY, of which Cyprus Mines Corp. is the majority owner, was the first major southwestern copper deposit discovered by purely geophysical means. The geophysical anomaly was registered in 1950 by United Geophysical, and the discovery was followed by diamond drilling. The first or second hole in the flat desert land hit high grade copper mineralization over a considerable interval.

The orebody initially appeared to be a section some 200 ft wide, plunging at 45° and thinning out at a flattening dip about 600 ft from the surface. It looked like a deposit of some 10 million tons containing about 1.75% Cu. Now, with the acumen of hindsight, it is apparent that Pima and properties discovered later—Mission, Eisenhower, Palo Verde, and San Xavier—are one massive deposit of low grade copper with considerable waste material interspersed between ore zones. Reserves remaining at Pima alone are estimated to exceed 150 million tons of 0.5% Cu. If the No. 1 concentrator were moved, another 100 million tons probably could be added. Obviously, the 1950 discovery probed only the tip of an iceberg. Perhaps the lessons of the Pima discovery, hidden by considerable cover, can be applied for future discoveries.

The Pima ore consists of multiple flat-lying and irregular masses of mineralized rock dipping southeast. The ore zone is as much as 1 mi. wide and is 1,500 ft thick. The several deposits are in a complexly fractured and altered plate of Mesozoic clastics, Paleozoic carbonates, and monzonite, resting on a basement granite.

The sulphides were deposited from hydrothermal solutions in open fractures. Finely disseminated grains also are present, probably from diffusion-replacement. The entire orebody was buried by compound sand, gravel, and conglomerate, with bedrock outcrops occurring on two sides of the Pima pit.

Production at Pima has grown from 3,000 tpd of mill feed in 1957 to the present two-mill throughput of 56,000 tpd. Capital investment for the mine and plant expansions, in four stages, totaled more than $70 million. Some 940 hourly and salaried personnel are employed in mine and mill operations—237 at the mine alone. Maintenance crews work 21 shifts a week, and mine personnel work 20 shifts a week. Concentrates are shipped by rail to the Phelps Dodge smelter at Douglas and to the Magma smelter at San Manuel.

The Pima pit is designed for the following working dimensions and final dimensions: bench heights, 40 ft and 80 ft; bench widths, 50 ft and 40 ft; pit slopes, 27° and 39°; haul road widths, 120 ft and 100 ft. The final pit will measure 1.25 mi wide, 1.3 mi long, and at least

More than 75 electric-wheel haulage trucks make up the fleet at Cyprus Pima. Truck capacity ranges from 100 to 170 tons.

Pima pit factsheet

Owned by: Cyprus Mines Corp. 50.01%, Union Oil 25%, Utah International 24.99%.
Location: 22 mi south of Tucson, Ariz.
Production: 56,000 tpd ore grading 0.48% Cu, 0.015% MoS_2, and minor Ag; approximately 100,000 tpd waste.
Startup: 1957, after two years of prestripping. Operation has undergone numerous expansions from original 3,000-tpd mill.

Major mining equipment

Drills (rotary): Two Bucyrus-Erie 45Rs, four B-E 60Rs.
Shovels: Four Marion 8-cu-yd, four Marion 15-cu-yd, three P&H 2300 20-cu-yd, two Dart 15-cu-yd loaders.
Haulage (rear-dump, electric-wheel trucks): 29 Unit Rig 100-ton, 15 Unit Rig 170-ton, 15 Wabco 150- and 170-ton, eight Euclid 170-ton, one Unit Rig 130-ton, 10 Wabco 100-ton, one Wabco 3200B 225-ton. (79 trucks total.)
Ancillary equipment: Two Cat 633C self-loading scrapers, four 10,000-gal water trucks, 12 track dozers, five rubber-tired dozers, two backhoes, three prill trucks.

1,400 ft deep. Currently, the pit is 1 mi wide; the surface is at elevation 3,300 ft, and the pit bottom is at elevation 2,310 ft. On the northern edge, the Pima pit adjoins Asarco's Mission pit, and the two operating companies have worked out an agreement for mutual waste and ore removal. Because of low copper prices, Cyprus Pima cut back stripping by 37% at the beginning of 1977. At some point, full scale stripping must resume if mining is to continue.

Pima has made a tremendous investment in its varied truck fleet. The hauls for both ore and waste are long and steep. The waste haul cycle time averages 35 min for a 33,000-ft round trip, up ramps averaging approximately 8% in grade. The ore haulage cycle time averages 28 min over a 28,000-ft round trip. The current schedule, with reduced stripping, assigns 29 170-ton capacity trucks to operate each shift. When normal and catch-up stripping is resumed, at least 45 170-ton units or their equivalents will be required. Management believes that for the Pima operation, the 170-ton-capacity truck is the ideal size. Truck haulage accounts for 53% of total operating costs. Holding down costs is a constant battle against ever-increasing pit depth, longer hauls, inflationary pressures, and higher priced fuel.

Blasthole drilling rigs average between 60 and 150 ft per hr, depending on the rock. Holes are drilled on 30-ft centers, 9⅞-in.-dia for alluvium. In rock, the pattern for 9-in. and 9⅞-in.-dia holes is generally 24 ft x 27 ft. For 12¼-in.-dia holes, the pattern is 31 ft x 31 ft. In alluvium, the ANFO factor is 0.5 lb per cu yd, while dry rock holes consume 0.7 lb per cu yd. Slurry is used in wet holes at 0.9 lb per cu yd. □

Sacaton works pit while preparing to go underground

SACATON STARTED OPEN-PIT STRIPPING in 1972 and this year began contract sinking of a 20-ft-dia shaft for a follow-up underground operation. The shaft will be sunk 2,000 ft over the next two years, then drifting will be done over a distance of ½ mi to the periphery of the underground ore, which is likely to be mined by block caving.

The discovery of Sacaton in 1961 was the direct result of Asarco's district-wide search for features common to porphyry copper deposits. The Sacaton outcrop was discovered and mapped by Asarco geologists as a small hill of granite cut by a monzonite porphyry dike and containing significant sericitic and argillic alteration. Both rock types contained traces of limonite derived from pyrite and the oxidized leaching of chalcocite.

This classic outcrop was considered a significant lead. A follow-up drilling program of 73,000 ft of holes on a wide-spaced grid outlined two potential ore zones. Evaluation of the data resulted in a temporary suspension of interest, which was rekindled five years later when copper prices improved. The final development program included 47,000 ft of additional drilling to provide data

Sacaton pit factsheet

Owned by: Asarco Inc.
Location: 6 mi northwest of Casa Grande, Pinal County, Arizona.
Production: 11,500 tpd of ore grading 0.76% Cu and 63,200 tpd of waste; three shifts per day, seven days per week.
Startup: May 1974, after two years of prestripping and a capital investment of $40 million.

Major mining equipment

Drills (rotary): Two Bucyrus-Erie 45Rs, one Robbins RRT-60.
Shovels: Three P&H 9-cu-yd electric shovels and two Michigan 475 loaders with 12-cu-yd buckets.
Haulage: 20 Wabco 85-ton Haulpaks, mechanical drive.
Ancillary: Two Cat 14 graders, two Cat 769B water trucks, one Euclid R-35 water truck (all for road maintenance); also two Cat D8 and one D9 dozers, one Cat 834 wheel tractor, one Cat 824 wheel tractor, one Terex S-24 scraper, one Amerind-McKissick ANFO truck.

for planning the project.

Two ore zones at Sacaton

The western open-pit orebody is roughly 1,200 ft in diameter and varies from 100 to 700 ft deep, overlain by 100 to 500 ft of leached capping.

The eastern orebody, about 600 ft x 1,200 ft in plan and 300 ft thick, lies at a depth of 1,500 ft. It will be mined by block caving after the open pit is exhausted. Sacaton's reserves were published in 1974 as approximately 47 million tons, with about two-thirds mineable by open pit and one-third underground.

Mineralization in the pit consists of supergene chalcocite and minor covellite. Hypogene mineralization is chalcopyrite. The sulphides occur as thin fracture fillings and disseminated grains. The main oxidized copper mineralization is chrysocolla, malachite, and brochantite. Pit overburden consists of weakly consolidated sand, silt, and conglomerate. The granite and monzonite porphyry country rock is intensely altered and generally well fractured. Sulphides, oxides, and waste occur in close proximity, requiring close control of blasthole sampling along the pit benches.

Haul roads kept hard and clean

The final Sacaton pit will be roughly 2,800 ft x 3,000 ft in plan and 1,000 ft deep. The deepest mining level is now 500 ft. Final pit slopes are designed 1 on 1 for rock and 1 on 1.25 for alluvium. Benches are 40 ft high, and haulage roads are designed on an 8% grade, 80 ft wide. The roads are kept hard and clean by two graders and one water truck working around the clock. Other equipment is assigned to road work as needed. Water for the roads comes from the small amount of pit drainage collected in a sump at the bottom of the pit. A small sump pump and switching arrangement allows the driver to fill the water truck.

Mine production is scheduled for 21 shifts a week, with a workforce of 116. The primary crusher is located 1 mi from the rim of the pit. Loading and hauling is scheduled to provide two shovel shifts per day in ore and four shovel shifts per day in waste. Cycle time for the trucks to the waste dumps is a 15-min round trip; for the ore trucks, a 22-min round trip. Sacaton management schedules waste disposal in two areas, with the longer haul assigned in cold weather when the greater distance does not create as much tire heat.

Drilling is done 17 shifts a week. Blastholes in waste are on a 23 x 25-ft pattern, while blastholes in ore are in staggered rows on an 18 x 21-ft pattern. Dry holes are loaded with ANFO, while slurry is used in all wet holes. All blastholes are drilled 50 ft deep, allowing for 10 ft of subgrade.

For dry holes, the normal blasthole column of ANFO is interrupted by one 25-lb bag of aluminized ANFO at 40 ft of depth—the bench level. The column is initiated by detonating cord attached to a 1-lb booster.

Slurry is used in all wet holes, hand-loaded from 50-lb bags and boosted by ¾-lb explosives for each two bags of slurry.

All downlines are 50-grain detonating cord; surface trunk lines are made up of 30-grain detonating cord. Blasts are set by a regular cap attached to safety fuse. Delays are used between rows of holes. Some 20 to 60 holes are shot at the end of the day shift. Overall powder factors are 0.75 lb per ton in ore and 0.60 lb per ton in waste. The heavy powder factor assures good fragmentation and relatively easy digging. □

Mine haul road (top right) leads to truck-dump primary crusher (center). Minus 8-in ore is sent to mill (foreground).

Pinto Valley's deep, low grade pit: success through good planning

IT WOULD HAVE BEEN OUT OF THE QUESTION 10 years ago to mine the low grade ore at Cities Service Co.'s Pinto Valley operation, 6 mi west of Miami, Ariz. However, the mine, based on a deep pit design, is a reality today. The pit, with a projected life span of 24 years, will ultimately measure 6,000 by 3,500 ft, with a final depth of 1,450 ft from the highest point on the backslope. It contains some 350 million tons of ore averaging 0.44% sulphide copper, small amounts of molybdenite, and over 500 million tons of waste.

The Pinto Valley mine and mill, completed ahead of schedule and at capital costs slightly below estimates, began production at its first division in June 1974 and at the second division in October. Design capacity of 40,000 tpd will recover more than 60,000 tpy of copper. Cities Service is continuing development of the underground Miami East ore deposit, where production is expected to begin in 1976. The new mines are boosting the copper production of Cities Service, whose previous operations in Arizona and Tennessee never topped the 50,000-tpy mark. The company's two previously active pits near Miami—Copper Cities and Diamond H—were exhausted and shut down in May 1975, although the leaching operations there will continue for several years. A solvent extraction, electrowinning plant to produce copper at the Miami and Pinto Valley leach operations is under construction and should be completed in mid-1976.

How Pinto Valley was discovered and developed

Mines in the Miami area have been exploited since the coming of the railroad in 1909. The Castle Dome orebody, developed during World War II by Miami Copper with the assistance of the US Defense Plant Corp., was worked for 10 years. During the 1950s, Cities Service acquired interests in the Copper Cities and Diamond H properties and, recognizing the need for further reserves when these two properties would be depleted, the company initiated exploration near the old Castle Dome workings during the early 1960s.

By 1969, 150 holes averaging 800 ft deep on a rectangular 400-ft grid pattern had been core drilled and assayed for copper on 5-ft intervals. Analyses and plotting of the drilling program had outlined a large, low grade porphyry copper deposit whose principal mineral, chalcopyrite, together with small amounts of molybdenite, occurred in small grains and veinlets throughout the rock mass. Major mineralization was found in an uplifted block of quartz monzonite porphyry bounded by faults on the east and west.

Cities Service hired a computer company to help analyze exploration data and establish the degree of reliability for interpolation of tonnages and grades. The study confirmed a high degree of reliability for the exploration drilling grid. Preliminary pit design included bench-by-bench tabulation of ore and waste grades and tonnages. Mining sequences were set up and analyzed to evaluate the most logical development scheme.

In December 1969, Parsons-Jurden Co. was hired to provide a comprehensive feasibility study and design engineering for a beneficiation plant. Fluor Utah Co. entered the picture in 1970 to assist Cities Service in designing a general mine plan, including layout of haulage roads and dump locations and a definition of equipment needs. Results of this work were turned over to Parsons-Jurden, which completed its study late in 1971. Meanwhile, orders for stripping and production shovels, trucks, and drills were placed in 1971—long before final approval of the project—to compensate for long delivery times.

Final approval for Pinto Valley came in May 1972, and the initial blast set off mine development on May 8. Some 2.25 million tons of initial stripping on top of Porphyry mountain was contracted to make working room for the larger operating equipment to be used for major preproduction stripping.

In August 1972, after the first 15-yd production shovel had been assembled, Cities Service began to strip over 450 ft off the top of the mountain—60 million tons of waste. As additional mining equipment was received, stripping rates accelerated to an average of 128,000 tpd in 1973, working five days a week. In parallel with preproduction stripping, plant site clearing and grading began on May 22, 1972, and erection of steel for the concentrator started in March of 1973. The transition to production mining in 1974 required only the additional operating personnel needed to go from a five-day work week to seven days. Total employment at the Pinto Valley operation is now about 100 management and 450 hourly workers.

Computer is used for economic mine planning

Long range and intermediate mine planning at Pinto Valley uses exploration drill data. The original block value computer model of the orebody was significantly revised in 1973 to incorporate a method of zone interpolation for metal values between drillholes along zones of mineralization, rather than horizontally, as in bench interpolation. The new system presumed that grade distribution was controlled by geologic features. Results of this interpolation, in three dimensions, were then translated to bench block values. The new system provides a better, more accurate estimate of grade distribution on individual benches and within specific mine areas, based on all experience so far.

Long range planning at Pinto Valley uses a computer program to determine the configuration of the "ultimate" economic pit. This configuration is a maximum truncated cone that uses the data of the block value matrix. By severely restricting economic input values, the program can be made to select a small "best" pit with the optimum combination of high-grade ore and low stripping ratio. The derived pit slopes and bottoms are then deleted from the topographic matrix and the program is repeated to find the subsequent best pit. In addition to the economic factors, variable input parameters include slope angles, bottom elevations, and minimum bottom radii.

After prestripping rates are adjusted between programmed mining phases, reserve estimates by bench for each phase are produced in an array that shows ore and waste tonnage and grade for each 0.02% copper cutoff grade. A second program analyzes this array by using cost and price input to show the economic consequences for each cutoff, allowing decisions on cutoff grade to be made using factors such as net revenue per ton and per year,
pounds of copper produced, production lifetime, and present value. Computations of present value must consider the impact of future mining, together with a synthesis of the several phases in mining out the entire orebody.

Day-to-day control of ore production at Pinto Valley is based on assays of blasthole drill cuttings derived from conventional lab work. An on-site X-ray analysis facility is under construction to handle the large number of daily assays. Cuttings samples will be dried, pulverized, briquetted, and placed 10 at a time in the computer-controlled analyzer, which will scan each sample and report the copper and molybdenum content on a teleprinter. Results will be posted on mine maps, to be used in determining which areas should be mined for mill ore, leach dump, or waste.

The identified areas are flagged in the field by survey crews, as a guide for foremen and shovel operators. At present, all material containing plus 0.34% sulphide copper is sent to the mill, material above 0.10% total copper is sent to the leach dumps, and the rest is wasted.

Big pit equipment requires close control

Except for certain old dump areas at Pinto Valley, all material must be drilled and blasted. Three Marion M-4 diesel-electric rotary drills use rotary cone bits to drill 12¼-in.-dia blastholes 55 ft deep, including 10 ft of subdrilling. Maximum bit loading is 105,000 lb, and the drilling rate averages 750 ft per shift. The drillhole layout depends on the rock encountered. The eastern sector of the pit is easier to drill and blast than the western sector, which has wide-spaced, near-vertical fracturing of the monzonite. Burdens range from 22 ft to 28 ft and spacings from 25 ft to 32 ft on a rectangular grid of two to six rows.

An ANFO-mix truck loads a hole in 3-4 min and some 60 holes are blasted daily. Minimum stemming using drill cuttings is 28 ft. Two Primacord downlines are lowered in each hole, each carrying a 1-lb cast primer, with the first primer located 3 ft from the bottom and the second one 9 ft from the bottom. The surface blasting hookup is by parallel rows of connecting Primacord, with 9-ms non-electric delays between rows. Whenever possible, blasts are made to a free face. In secondary blasting, which represents 1-2% of total blasting, the boulders are set out from the face and shot with stick powder. The overall powder factor for the mine was 0.60 lb per yard in 1974.

Shovel loading at Pinto Valley in 1974 averaged over 14,000 tons per shovel shift. The two 15-yd and two 20-yd electric shovels are backed up by a 12-cu-yd Dart front-end loader, which is also used to reclaim ore from stockpiles. The mine's eighteen 150-ton diesel-electric trucks averaged a one-way haul of 0.9 mi in 1974, carrying 20 to 25 loads per truck shift. Tire life averages 3,600 hr. The pit roads, not including berms, are 90 ft wide on straight sections and 100 ft wide on curves, with a maximum grade of 7%.

Plans call for dispatching haulage trucks individually to the various loading points by radio, with the dispatch station located on a ridge overlooking the mine. The Motorola "Modat" system will be installed, with a separate radio frequency dedicated to dispatching and an automatic status-signaling system using the same frequency. Dash-mounted push-button consoles in each shovel and haulage truck will allow the operator to signal the machine's status and phase in the haul cycle. The receiver at the dispatch station will automatically acknowledge the signal and record the equipment identification code, the time, and the date. Operating personnel intend to add equipment to the Modat system which they believe will aid dispatching and

The land dwarfs big, new hard-rock mining equipment: 15- and 20-yd P&H shovels, 150-ton Wabco trucks, and Marion rotary drills.

provide significant production data to improve loading and haulage efficiency.

Maintenance and stores: heart of the system

Large-scale, equipment-intensive mining—the key to exploitation of low-grade deposits—requires standardization of equipment and efficient repair and maintenance procedures planned in advance and carried out by knowledgeable personnel. Unless these well known precepts are applied consistently, operations will be plagued with continual breakdowns, production losses, low worker morale and, ultimately, failure to achieve the profit goal.

Pinto Valley's maintenance department is directly responsible for all maintenance and repair of mine and mill equipment and facilities. A 90,000-sq-ft central workshop provides general repair and maintenance, and a smaller mine shop is located near the final pit perimeter. The central workshop has three 72 x 340-ft bays. The high truck shop bay has two 20-ton traveling overhead cranes, while the other bays each have four 10-ton traveling cranes covering all shop areas. Offices, tool room, warehouse issuing, and sanitary facilities are at the center of the shop, with additional office and storage space on the second and third levels of the center section. Main work areas are the truck shop, the machine shop, electrical shop, shovel-drill shop, boilermaker shop, welding shop, pipefitting and utility shops, and the mobile-equipment dispatch area.

The mine shop carries out scheduled lubrication, tire inspection, and preventive maintenance for haulage trucks, as well as minor repairs to mine equipment and maintenance of all dozers. Pass-through bays are provided for the 150-ton trucks, and oil changes on the haul units take place concurrently with PM inspection. Oil samples are forwarded to a consulting laboratory for spectrographic and particle-count analysis, and the mine is informed immediately by telephone if the analysis shows any serious abnormality. Tire PM gets careful attention, including checks on inflation pressure, tread wear, and damages. The results are graphed for use in tire cost comparisons and tire rotation and replacement.

Field repair crews, permanently assigned to specific areas within the mine and mill, handle regular maintenance and minor, local emergency repairs. When additional field workmen are needed, they are called from the shops and assigned to the local field foreman. The shop craft foremen are sent to the field only when a situation demands their particular knowledge.

All PM is systematized, with haul units inspected after each 40, 100, 240, 500, 1,000, 2,000, and 3,000 hr, in accordance with detailed inspection recommendations for each interval. Daily hourmeter and 24-hr tachograph charts are used for scheduling inspections. Records of all inspections, repairs, and replacements for each unit help to pinpoint problem areas and predict component life for replacement scheduling and ordering of parts.

Controlled ordering and storage of supplies, wear parts, and replacement parts are equally important to a proper maintenance system. Pinto Valley's main warehouse, located behind the main workshop, has 35,000 sq ft of covered storage and is used for centralized receiving, stocking, and disbursement of fast-moving material. Aisle space in the work-shops permits forklift delivery of large materials and parts. When an item is needed, the shop foreman, or journeyman, notifies the warehouse issue clerk by intercom, and the item is delivered within minutes to the worksite. The same principle is applied in supplying field crews. During plant construction, the contractor was instructed to put up a permanent building for his temporary use; after construction the building was converted to 26,000 sq ft of covered storage for large and slow-moving items.

Reporting directly to the maintenance superintendent are the supervisors of the concentrator, mine, and shop repair; a planning coordinator; and a maintenance engineer. The latter two are responsible for planning, scheduling, and updating PM; for providing technical assistance in problem areas; and for improving overall equipment efficiency and reducing overall costs. At a weekly meeting, management, production, and maintenance representatives systematically review the problems, decide on solutions, and establish a priority list of activities to improve the total operation. □

At the heart of the Berkeley mining operation are 15-cu-yd electric shovels working in concert with 100-, 150-, and 170-ton off-highway haulers. The pit boasts a fair-sized fleet of 89 electric-wheel trucks, with an average availability of 72%.

Montana's giant Berkeley pit girds for another 22 years

Richard A. Thomas, Associate editor

ANACONDA'S BERKELEY PIT, nestled in the Rockies at the northeast edge of Butte, Mont., was at one time the largest-tonnage surface operation in the US using truck haulage. Still a giant that has merely been outstripped by other giants, Berkeley in November 1975 passed the 1-billion-ton mark for material moved. The pit has a projected life span of another 22 years—seven within the present pit parameters and 15 after an expansion east— and will ultimately cover twice its current 693 surface acres, although three-fifths of the final pit will be backfilled by the time mining ceases.

The orebody, which originally contained 285 million tons of ore averaging 0.71% Cu, is one of several in the Butte area. Deep-vein mining of copper ore was active in Butte until November 1975, when low copper prices made Anaconda's underground operations unprofitable. The region to the west of the pit, plus much of the ground under uptown Butte, is riddled with idle underground mine workings, and the pit intersects numerous old shafts. A few of these workings are being maintained to facilitate reopening of the underground mines in the future, should it become economically feasible.

The Berkeley orebody occurs in quartz monzonite of the Boulder batholith, a late Cretaceous to early Tertiary intrusive cut by quartz porphyry dikes trending east-west. The orebody is elongated along its east-west axis and measures approximately 10,000 x 5,000 ft horizontally. The ore block, now mined to a depth of 1,600 ft, will ultimately be mined down to 2,000 ft.

Mineralization is primarily copper sulphides, occurring in a steeply dipping network of fissure veins a few inches to several feet in width and averaging 0.62% Cu. Closely spaced jointing provides extensively mineralized wall rock, along with intervein ribs of lower grade mineralization. Primary minerals are chalcocite, enargite, bornite, and chalcopyrite in a gangue of pyrite and quartz. Accessory metals include silver (found in the upper part of the oreblock) associated with zinc.

An important blanket of secondary chalcocite coating pyrite and copper sulphides was formed over the orebody

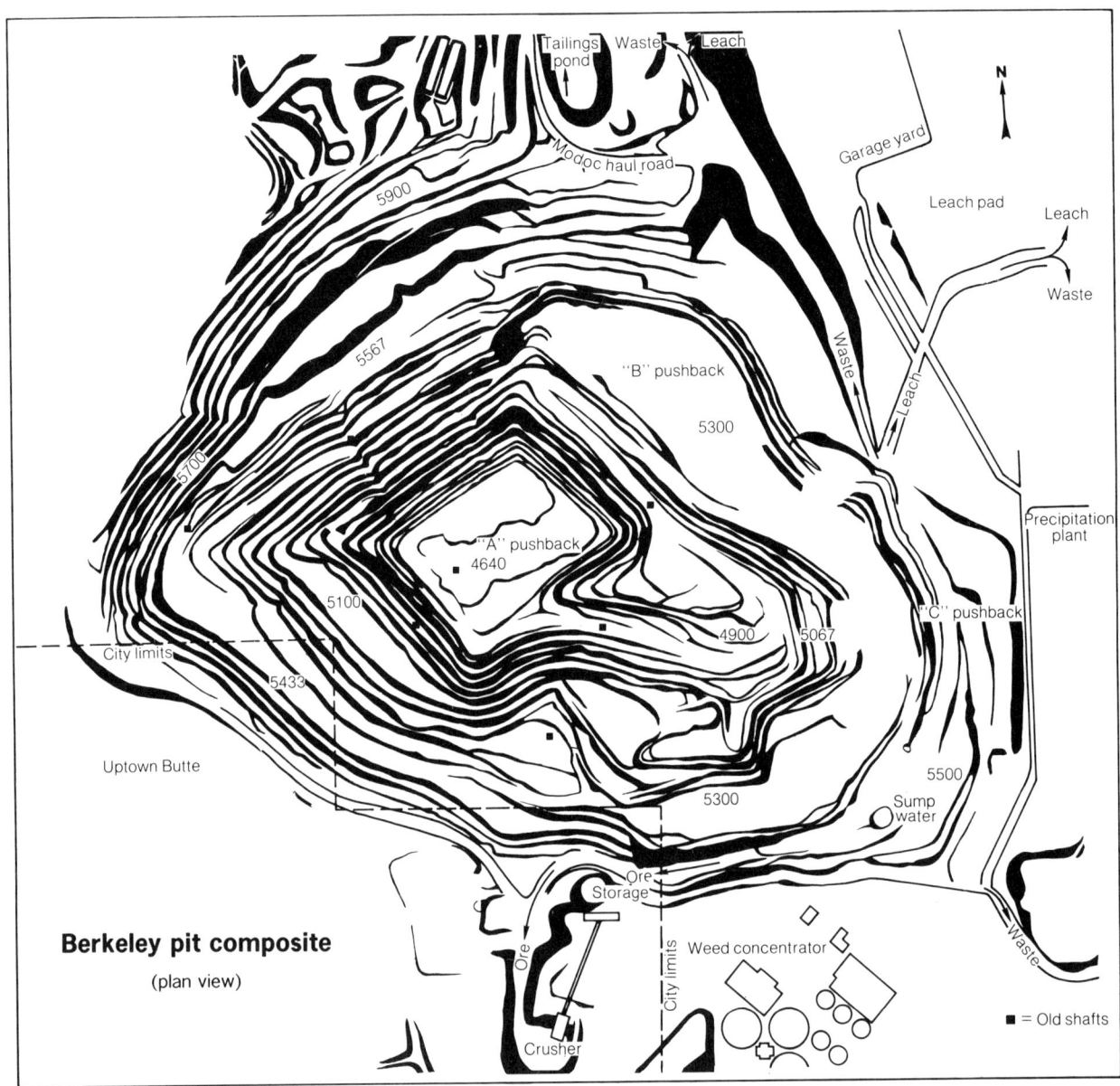

Berkeley pit composite
(plan view)

Berkeley pit factsheet

Owned by: The Anaconda Co.
Location: Butte, Mont.
Production: 46,000 tpd ore grading 0.65% Cu, with small amounts of gold and silver. Ore cutoff is 0.30% Cu, with waste rock grading 0-0.09% Cu and leach dump rock grading 0.10-0.29% Cu. Stripping ratio is 2.75:1, and total tonnage moved per day is 190,000-195,000 tons.
Startup: 1955, following churn and diamond drilling.

Major mining equipment

Drills (rotary): Eight Bucyrus-Erie 45Rs.
Shovels: Three P&H 2100 (15 yd), three P&H 2100 BL (15 yd), two B-E 280 (15 yd), one B-E 270 (13 yd), plus one B-E 20-yd dragline.
Front-end loaders: Three Cat 930, two Cat 992, two Hough 400C.
Haulage: 68 100-ton Unit Rigs trucks, nine 150-ton Wabco trucks, 12 170-ton Unit Rigs.
Ancillary equipment: Two Cat 16G Road Patrols, four Cat 16 Road Patrols, four Cat D-8K dozers, two Cat D-9G dozers, 12 Cat D-8H dozers, two Fiat Allis 21C dozers.

---

as a result of surface erosion. The zone was formed by supergene enrichment, resulting in a totally leached bedrock cap 75-150 ft thick, beneath which the copper content exceeds 1% in many locations. The western portion of the orebody is leached bedrock at grass roots, while the eastern portion is overlain by up to 400 ft of alluvium.

Ore-bearing rock is generally moderately hard (under 4,000 psi shear) in the secondary enrichment zone to very hard (15,000 psi) in the fresh monzonite of the back slopes. Surface oxidized rock is generally soft (under 2,000 psi). The alluvium is unconsolidated and water-filled in some places. Anaconda uses a Bucyrus-Erie 18-cu-yd dragline to excavate this material. The unit can stand high on drained alluvium while loading the wet alluvium below grade, and it exerts less bearing pressure than an electric shovel would.

The pit has an average slope of 41°, with a range from 31° in soft material to 45° in hard rock. The excavation plan has resulted in 31 levels. Benches 40 ft high and 120-350 ft wide are alternated with safety berms emplaced to break the continuity of otherwise long slopes and to control sloughing. The safety berms are of alternate 10- and 30-ft widths, with an additional 60-ft-wide berm at intervals of 240 vertical feet. Needless to say, the pit's major engineering problem is control of sloughing and slope failure. A rock mechanics firm was recently contracted to study the slope stability problems encountered at the Berkeley.

Three pushbacks (pit widening efforts) are in progress at the mine: "A" pushback, near completion, has progressed to the pit bottom; "B" pushback is evident as an extra-wide bench on the 5,300 level; and "C" pushback, on the northeastern edge of the mine around the 5,500 level, has just started. In years to come, plans call for Berkeley to expand east and possibly link up with the Continental East pit in the foothills southeast of the Berkeley pit. The 17,000-tpd Continental East is a fairly new pit, having started up in 1973. It is currently dormant.

Berkeley's mining cycle starts with drilling of 9⅞-in.-dia blastholes using Bucyrus-Erie 45R rotary drills. Five of the Berkeley's eight 45R drills are usually in service at a total fleet availability of 70% on a three-shift, five-day week. Steel-tooth rotary bits are used most often; tungsten carbide button bits are used where required by ground conditions. Drilling averages 450 ft per shift and is slowest in the quartz porphyry dikes. Production holes are drilled to 46 ft—6 ft below the bench height. Development and secondary drilling is done with three Ingersoll-Rand T-4 truck-mounted rigs, one of which uses reverse circulation.

Blasting patterns are multirow; rectangular six-row patterns of 21 x 21 ft or 25 x 25 ft are most common. The finishing row on any bench is a single-row shot of 18- to 21-ft spacing and 12- to 15-ft burden to improve slope conditions. Berkeley uses ANFO as its blasting medium, made at a 36-tph on-site nitrate mixing plant. Holes are primed with 1-lb boosters placed 2 ft from the hole bottom, and charges are stemmed with a minimum 18 ft of cuttings. Delays of 17 millisec between holes and 5 millisec between rows are used. The powder factor varies from 0.35 to 0.95 lb per cu yd of material.

Broken material is excavated mainly by electric shovels, which load into trucks. Anaconda uses a fleet of 89 electric-wheel off-highway haulers at Berkeley. Haulage distances average about 3 mi up maximum 7% grades. The 25 mi of haul roads are maintained using motor graders in combination with the dozer fleet. Haul roads, a minimum 90 ft in width, spiral up 600 vertical ft from the pit bottom, then go into a switchback system to reduce the grade over the remaining distance to the pit edge.

Depending on the copper grade, rock is hauled to the leach pads, to waste dumps north and southeast of the pit, or to the primary crushing complex directly south.

The underground crushing installation incorporates dual vibrating grizzly feeders feeding a 60 x 89-in. Traylor gyratory. Throughput averages 4,000 tph during two shifts, six days a week. The crusher processes 75% of the daily run, reducing ore to minus 6 in. Wood-picking belts ahead of the crusher permit the removal of old timber once used to support Butte's deep mine workings.

Crushed ore moves by conveyor to coarse ore storage bins, then to secondary crushing in the Weed concentrator's three Symons 7-ft Standards, which deliver a minus 1¼-in. product. Grinding is done by six Marcy 9 x 12-ft rod mills and 12 ball mills that have been rubber-lined and converted from semiautogenous mills. Krebs 20-in. cyclones separate the ball mill discharge into sands (30% plus 65 mesh) and slimes fractions that are processed in two flotation circuits.

In both circuits, ore is subjected to bulk, cleaner, and scavenger flotation to float copper and attendant silver and gold values. The sands circuit has a middlings thickener and a regrind ball mill in closed circuit with a cyclone. Final concentrates, averaging 25% Cu at 80% recovery, are shipped via rail to the company smelter in Anaconda, Mont.

Tailings are thickened in three 325-ft thickeners, then pumped 3 mi uphill to the tailings pond north of the pit. Pumping such a distance requires three pumphouses (one main and two boosters) with a total of 22 pumps. Water decanted and recirculated from the tailings pond makes up about 95% of the plant's total process water; the rest is piped from Georgetown Lake and Silver Lake, 30 mi away. Power for mine and plant is drawn from the Montana Power Co.

Like any large operation, Berkeley has some problems. Next on the list after the engineering problems of slope control come social problems. Workers at Berkeley are represented by 17 unions, including Teamsters, operating engineers, ironworkers, painters, and builders. Also pressing is an ongoing "discussion" with the Hillcrest community concerning the environmental conditions and location of the south dump—currently ¼ mi from the nearest Hillcrest property line. A related concern is the typically large expense of environmental protection, particularly water pollution control and in-plant dust control. More than $10 million has been spent for environmental controls at the Berkeley complex since 1971. Other ever-present problems include the rigorous Montana reclamation laws, which the head of environmental engineering says are "probably more stringent than anything the Federal government will develop," and the public road that cuts across one truck haulage path, causing a loss of efficiency.

The near future holds numerous beneficial projects for Berkeley. Plant engineers expect to reduce the amount of makeup water drawn from Silver Lake by implementing plans for more efficient reclamation; the new "Nonel" nonelectric blast ignition system is being tested; the concentrator is scheduled to accept delivery of an Outokumpu "Courier 300" on-stream analyzer in May; and an emissions control R&D program is focusing on engine throttle delay control and driver education. □

Dam built to divert the Agrio River away from its course across the Aznalcollar pit will also store process plant water.

Construction is well along at Aznalcollar

Lane White, Managing editor

THE LARGEST OPEN-PIT metal mining operation in Europe is taking shape northwest of Sevilla, in southwestern Spain. Andaluza de Piritas SA (Apirsa), a subsidiary of Banco Central, is developing the $130 million project at Aznalcollar to produce 2 million tpy of ore from each of two distinct orebodies—a 45-million-ton mass of complex pyrites grading 0.44% Cu, 1.74% Pb, 3.33% Zn, 67 g Ag per ton, and 1 g Au per ton; and a 35-million-ton mass of pyroclastic ore overlying the pyrite orebody that grades 0.58% Cu, 0.40% Zn, and 10 g of silver per ton.

Dragados y Construcciones, another Banco Central subsidiary, has the contract for major construction, including prestripping of 44 million tons of overburden and construction of a 46-m-high dam and 1,750-m-long x 4.2-m-dia diversion tunnel to change the course of the Agrio River, which flows across the Aznalcollar pit site. Waste removal after startup will total 10 million tpy. As of late 1976, 23.3 million tons had been stripped.

Wright Engineers, of Vancouver, has the contract for plant design. Startup is scheduled in 1979 for production of 15,778 mtpy of Cu, 21,043 mtpy of Pb, 50,382 mtpy of Zn, and 80 mtpy of silver contained in concentrates.

A 2-tph pilot plant has operated at the Aznalcollar mine site since November 1974 to establish basic parameters for design of the crushing, milling, and flotation plants. Plans are also being considered for heap leaching an additional 20 million tons of low grade (minus 0.3% Cu) pyroclastic copper ores.

Apirsa will concentrate the Aznalcollar ores in two separate flotation circuits—one for pyrites and one for pyroclasts—and tailings from the two circuits will be impounded separately. Pyrite tailings will represent a substantial potential resource, containing 600,000 tpy of sulphur and 700,000 tpy of iron. Studies are now in progress to find economic uses for these materials.

The Aznalcollar project is proceeding under the direction of Jose Luis Penche, general manager of Apirsa, and project superintendent Dr. Juan Contreras Fernandez.

Aznalcollar mined since antiquity

The deposits in the Aznalcollar area have been known since prehistory and were mined during the Roman era,

Stripping is proceeding at the rate of 1.4 million tpm, and a mining plan has been drawn up for an ultimate pit 1,500 m long x 700 m wide x 300 m deep. Material to be removed during the life of the mine will total 234 million tons of waste, 43 million tons of pyrites, and 30 million tons of pyroclasts, for an ore-to-waste ratio of 1:3.2.

Basic engineering for Aznalcollar processing facilities is well advanced, and site preparation for the plant began in October 1976. Major equipment has been ordered, including primary, secondary, and tertiary crushers, ore storage bins, rod and ball mills, and flotation cells.

Factors in electing to mine by open pit

During the course of its feasibility study for developing the Aznalcollar deposits, Apirsa gave consideration to both open-pit and underground mining. Among other considerations, an open pit was chosen because it will allow almost 100% recovery with very little dilution. An estimated 30% of the deposit would be lost in underground mining. Another key factor: Open pit mining permits much closer control of feed to the concentrator, an important advantage in view of the two distinct orebodies being mined.

Current planning calls for use of two 12-in.-dia rotary drills and additional 7.5-in.-dia rotary drills, 15-cu-yd electric shovels, a 7-cu-yd and a 12-cu-yd front-end loader, and 24 85-ton mechanical-drive trucks as the major pit equipment. Mechanical drives were selected because service facilities for electrical drives are not readily available. Mine management is considering adding 120-ton-capacity trucks to future operations. Auxiliary equipment will include bulldozers, wheeled tractors, graders, water trucks, repair trucks, lube trucks, fire trucks, etc.

Three stages of crushing will reduce Aznalcollar ores to 12 mm. For milling pyrite ores, Apirsa will install a rod mill and four ball mills, each 4 m dia x 6 m long; for the pyroclasts, a rod mill of the same dimensions and a 4.5-m-dia x 6.6-m-long ball mill will be used. Both flotation circuits will include regrind mills. The Aznalcollar pyrites require very fine grinding to liberate copper, zinc, lead, silver, and gold minerals, with an ultimate reduction of 98% minus 400 mesh (80% minus 18 microns and 32-35% minus 5 microns). The pyroclasts are reduced to 80% minus 180-200 mesh for the bulk rougher float.

At the Aznalcollar pilot plant, reagents in the pyrite circuit are SO_2, lime, amyl xanthate, and Aeroflot 238 for copper; lime, $ZnSO_4$, NaCN, and amyl xanthate for lead; and lime, $CuSO_4$, and amyl xanthate for zinc. In the pyroclastic circuit, Na_2SO_3 is added in grinding, and a bulk rougher float is made with amyl xanthate and lime. Reagents used in the subsequent copper and zinc circuits are essentially the same as in the pyrite circuit.

On-stream X-ray analysis and computer automation will be integral to plant design.

Production is anticipated at 24,333 mtpy of copper concentrates, 42,086 mtpy of lead concentrates, and 92,981 mtpy of zinc concentrates from pyrite ores.

Preproduction stripping will total 44 million tons.

from which old mine workings and slag piles still remain. In 1876, Sevilla Sulphur Copper Co. began working underground mines that reached a depth of 200 m in the eastern end of the deposit, penetrating the pyrite mass. Banco Central, Spain's second largest bank, acquired the mineral rights to the area in 1960 and formed Apirsa, which operated small scale mines at the extreme eastern end of the property from 1960 until the end of 1970.

In 1969, the company decided to explore the deposits at depth and test their possible extension to both the east and the west. Core drilling from July 1969 to February 1972 totaled 21,500 m in 105 holes and established the existence of a large mass of complex pyrites overlain by another mass of copper-bearing pyroclast. Each of these distinct zones of mineralization is about 40 m thick. The pyrite zone is 1,400 m long, and the pyroclast zone is 1,000 m long. The deposit has been drilled to a depth of about 300 m below surface. Drill hole data and a computer were used to calculate reserves, grades, and grade distribution in 15 x 15 x 10-m blocks.

Laboratory testing to define the flotation characteristics of the ores was done at facilities in Spain, West Germany, and Canada, and to complement these studies Apirsa erected the 2-tph semi-industrial pilot plant at the mine site. In April 1975, King Don Juan Carlos I officially inaugurated construction of the Aznalcollar project, signaling the start of most of the work.

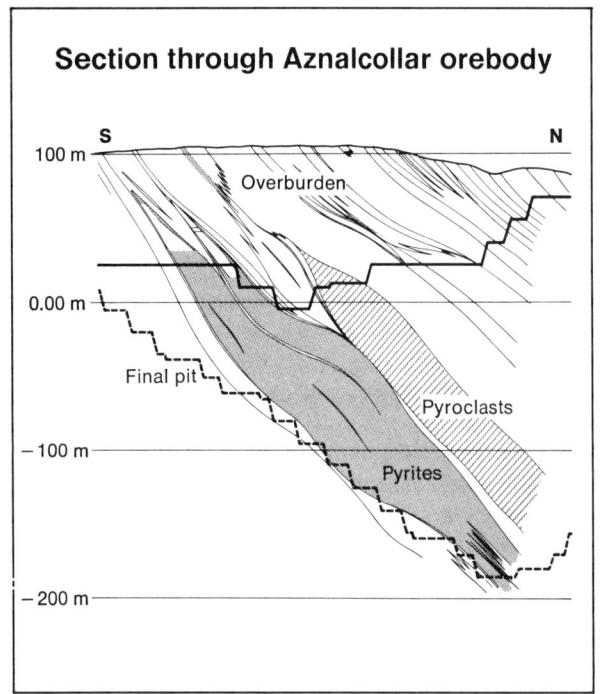

Section through Aznalcollar orebody

Pyroclast concentrates are expected to total 38,780 mtpy for copper and 7,783 mtpy for zinc. Copper concentrates will grade 25% Cu, lead concentrates 50% Pb, and zinc concentrates 50% Zn. Silver will be recovered in copper and lead concentrates.

Tailings dams will be constructed for separate impoundment of pyrite and pyroclast tailings, with total storage capacity anticipated at 27 million cu m. Overflow water from the tailings dams will be treated at a water purification plant and returned to the river.

Construction of the dam and tunnel system for diversion of the Agrio River was nearing completion in late 1976. The dam will back up a lake of about 40-million-cu-m capacity, which will provide water for Aznalcollar operations. A small dam downstream from the principal regulation dam will divert water into the diversion tunnel, which will have a capacity to carry 60 cu m per sec of water.

Construction is under way on most of the buildings needed to service the mine and plant: a shop for pit equipment, general maintenance shop, warehouse, tire storage, lube shop, service station, office facilities, change houses, and a kitchen and dining room.

Electrical supply will be drawn at 132 kv from a substation of Cia. Sevillana de Electricidad at Guillena. A substation at Aznalcollar will transform current to 15 kv and 6 kv.

When it goes into production, the Aznalcollar mine and plant will employ a workforce of about 2,000. □

Rio Tinto Patino mines in northwest Spain

RIO TINTO PATINO'S Grupo Minero Santiago mines copper ores from two open pits near the historic medieval pilgrims' shrine of Santiago de Compostela in northeastern Spain. Its reserves include a third orebody not far from its Arinteiro concentrator. Started up in mid-1975, the Arinteiro plant was expected to process 1.6 million mt of ore during the year ended June 1977, said Jose Luis Saura Roch, director of the group, when E/MJ visited the property in late 1976.

The Arinteiro orebody is now the main producer for the Santiago group, with minor production coming from the Fornas deposit. The Arinteiro orebody and the Bama orebody, which will be developed in the future, occur in the flanks of a regional anticline. Arinteiro is in the east flank and Bama in the west. Erosion has removed the crest of the anticline and created a valley between the two orebodies, which strike nearly north-south. The Arinteiro orebody dips 25° to the east between schist hangingwall and footwall rocks and has an average thickness of 25 m. The ore-bearing formation is metamorphic with amphybolite facies, and the copper mineralization is always associated with garnet, which represents about 20% of the orebody. The mineral suite includes chalcopyrite, pyrrhotite, pyrite, and ilmenite.

The Fornas orebody, which is about 30 km from the Arinteiro plant, is more massive and has a higher sulphur content than the Bama and Arinteiro orebodies.

Rio Tinto Patino started a mineral exploration program in the Santiago area in 1967, conducting geological, geophysical, and aerial surveys over an area of 1,300 sq km. The survey located more than 20 anomalies, which were investigated first by ground geophysics and geochemistry and finally by core drilling of about 17,000 m of hole from the surface.

Arinteiro equipment suite includes rotary and Airtrac drills, electric shovels, and trucks to haul both ore and waste.

As of May 1976, Rio Tinto Patino had established indicated reserves of 8.15 million mt grading 0.745% Cu at Arinteiro, 15.84 million tons grading 0.600% Cu at Bama, and 750,000 tons grading 1.02% Cu at Fornas. Average grade for all three deposits is about 0.66% Cu, and the total ore-to-waste ratio for the three pits is expected to be about 2:1. An additional 6.6 million tons are classified as probable reserves, and 30 million tons are classified as possible reserves.

Western-Knapp conducted the feasibility study for the project.

For overburden removal at Arinteiro, Rio Tinto Patino drills 9-in.-dia vertical holes on a 6.5 x 6.5-m pattern, using a Bucyrus-Erie 45-R rotary drill. Water in the overburden requires pumping of blastholes. Explosives are loaded in plastic bags.

In Arinteiro ore, Rio Tinto Patino uses three Gardner-Denver Airtracs drilling 3½-in.-dia holes inclined at 15° on a 2.7 x 2.7-m pattern. Benches are 10 m high, and blasting is done ANFO and dynamite. In the early stages of mining, fragmentation was a problem at Arinteiro Saura said. Results were improved by using more powder, drilling a closer pattern, and blasting four to five rows at a time; however, some secondary blasting is still required.

Loading equipment at Arinteiro includes a B-E 150-RB 6-cu-yd electric shovel, a B-E 110-RB 6-cu-yd electric shovel, and two Cat 988 front-end loaders. Cat 769 32-ton-capacity rear-dump trucks haul ore to the concentrator over an average distance of 600 m, and waste to dumps over an average distance of 800 m. Other equipment on the property includes a Cat D9, two Cat D8s, and a Cat 824 wheel dozer.

The Arinteiro plant processes ore through conventional crushing, grinding, flotation, thickening, filtration, drying, and tails distribution circuits. An Allis-Chalmers 42 x 65-in. jaw crusher reduces run-of-mine ore to minus 120 mm at a maximum capacity of 500 tph. A conveyor belt transfers the crusher product to a coarse ore stockpile. Variable-feed vibrating feeders extract ore from the stockpile to feed a 5½-ft Symons secondary cone crusher and a 7-ft Symons Shorthead tertiary crusher, which produces a minus 20-mm product for grinding. Crusher product feeds from a 6,500-ton live stockpile of fine ore to a closed circuit rod mill and ball mill in series, each followed by cyclones. Grinding circuit equipment includes a Koppers 3.8-m-dia x 4.9-m-long, 1,250-hp rod mill; a Koppers 4.7-m-dia x 5.5-m-long, 2,500-hp ball mill; two A-S-H open circuit cyclone pumps; and two batteries of three D26B Krebs cyclones.

Grinding produces a maximum 65-mesh, 60-65% minus 200-mesh, 30% solids pulp for feed to a 14-cell rougher circuit of 300-cu-ft Fagergren cells arranged in three groups of five, five, and four in series. The roughers recover 90-95% of the copper and 5% of the iron in the feed. (Iron sulphides are present in the feed in a ratio of about 5:1 to copper sulphides.) Regrinding reduces the rougher product to 90-95% minus 325 mesh, liberating the copper, and regrind pulp feeds to three cleaning stages, where the remaining iron and gangue

Coarse ore stockpile at Arinteiro has 3,000-ton live capacity.

are depressed. Overall copper recovery is 86% in a concentrate grading 21% copper. A 23-m-dia thickener, built on "stilts" to provide covered surge storage for thickener product under the thickener tank, dewaters the concentrate to 55-60% solids. An Eimco 10 x 14-ft drum filter further reduces moisture to 10-13%. A 1.2-m-dia rotary kiln makes a final moisture reduction to 8-9%.

The entire Arinteiro concentrator operation is housed efficiently and compactly in a single 120-m-long building. The control panel is equipped with automatic alarms to monitor process streams. All conveyor galleries and the coarse ore stockpile are enclosed to keep down dust.

Concentrates produced at Arinteiro are trucked to Villagarcia and then railed to Rio Tinto Patino's Huelva smelter, a total distance of 1,000 km. The mine and plant payroll at Arinteiro averages about 260. Fornas is mined by a contractor.

The climate at Arinteiro is damp, averaging more than 2 m of rainfall per year. The terrain is relatively gentle. These factors, together with a requirement that no plant effluent be discharged to the regional watershed, which drains a farming district that has been cultivated for centuries, governed the design of the Arinteiro tailings impoundment and water recycle system. Two large cresent-shaped dam stages will be built, the second atop the first. The first dam stage has been built to a height of 20 m, using mine waste and plant discharge. Construction materials include (from the downstream face to the upstream face): fresh and weathered rock, a filter of crushed rock, a layer of impervious clay, and an upstream surface of impervious clay combined with fresh rock. Tailings discharge to the ponding area through valves placed around the crest of the impoundment dam.

A central wall divides the ponding area—with half of the pond used as clear water storage while the other half accepts slimes. The height of the first impoundment dam will be increased by 25 m, in 3-m-high sections, as sufficient sands settle behind the dam to provide support for these structures. Seepage through the dam is collected, directed to a single sump, and pumped back to the dam. A fixed pumping station in the center of the ponding area recycles water to the concentrator process streams. □

PANAMA: A major mine takes shape at Cerro Colorado

IN ITS HISTORIC ROLE as a crossroads for world trade and transportation, Panama developed a more-than-passing acquaintance with the mining industry. For the early Spanish conquerors, the isthmus provided a route for the movement of Peruvian silver from the Pacific to the Caribbean coast for subsequent shipment to Europe. One observer, Father Thomas Gage, reported seeing 200 mules arrive at Portobello on the Caribbean coast one day in 1637, laden with nothing but wedges of silver. The mules were unloaded in the marketplace "so that there the heaps of silver wedges lay like heaps of stones in the street, without any fear or suspicion of being lost."

Later, in the mid-1800s, forty-niners from the east coast of the US, hell-bent for the gold fields of California, made Panama one of the more traveled routes to the the new El Dorado, and since the early 1900s, the Panama Canal has been an important transport route for all industry and the subject of much debate and some contention between Panama and the US. A new treaty governing the canal may be moving toward ratification and has attracted widespread attention. However, Panama's preparations to join the ranks of world copper producing nations have attracted little notice, even in the mining industry, although this latest entry into mining will also have substantial impact on the Panamanian economy. The canal treaty and Panamanian mining development are somewhat interrelated in that failure of the treaty to win approval in the US Senate, followed by a probable increase in tensions between the two countries, could affect the ability of mine developers to raise capital for Panamanian investment.

By the mid-1980s, Empresa de Cobre Cerro Colorado SA—owned 80% by the Panamanian government and 20% by Texasgulf—may be producing 190,000 tpy of blister copper from ore mined at the Cerro Colorado copper porphyry deposit in western Panama. Assuming a copper price of $1.00 per lb by that time, the project will generate $380 million in annual sales of copper alone for this nation of less than 2 million people. If other known, potentially commercial copper deposits are developed, mining will become an even greater factor in Panama's economy.

Codemin, the government company that holds the 80% Panamanian interest in the project, and Texasgulf are currently in the second year of a feasibility study to determine how the project will be developed, with Texasgulf supervising the study and Brown & Root Inc. and Seltrust Engineering Ltd. contracted to perform much of the work. The study is budgeted at about $19 million—no insubstantial figure in itself—and final costs of development including mine, concentrator, smelter, roads, port facilities, and phosphoric acid plant, are projected in the neighborhood of $1 billion.

Current planning is based on an open-pit mine to produce 33 million tpy of ore and 61 million tpy of waste, with a concentrator at the isolated mine site to produce 2,300 tpd of concentrates. Concentrates would move by slurry pipeline to a smelter (possibly equipped with an Outokumpu flash furnace) on the Pacific coast near the Pan American Highway, about 60 km east of the city of David. A phosphoric acid plant also is being studied, to use sulphuric acid produced from smelter

Field headquarters for the Texasgulf Panama feasibility study of the Cerro Colorado copper project are at Escopeta camp.

offgases. Texasgulf personnel reviewed the Cerro Colorado project for Panama's Chief of Government Omar Torrijos, President Demetrio Basilio Lakas, and a large delegation of other interested Panamanians from both inside and outside the government, in a presentation at the mine site in July 1977. Moving more than 100 people into and out of the isolated, mountainous area in a single day was in itself something of an undertaking.

The Cerro Colorado deposit—more than 1 billion tons of 0.6% copper—is located in precipitous mountains near the continental divide in Chiriqui province. The terrain and heavy rainfall will constitute the chief operating problems. Though only 30 km by air from the Pan American Highway, the Cerro Colorado project will require an investment of $65 million in roads alone to overcome the problems of terrain.

The deadline for completion of the feasibility study is May 1978, after which both parties will have 90 days to consider whether they want to proceed. The alternatives were detailed for E/MJ by Codemin technical director Jaime Roquebert:

- If both Panama and Texasgulf decide to go ahead with the project, the next step will be raising money for financing—not an insignificant problem for a $1 billion project.

- If each decides not to proceed at that time, the possibility of later development will be reconsidered annually for 20 years.

- If Panama decides to proceed and Texasgulf does not want to participate, Texasgulf will retire from its equity position and receive compensation, while retaining first option to continue as manager.

- If Texasgulf wants to proceed but Panama says no, development will be postponed until Panama elects to proceed. (Roquebert pointed out that this possibility is not likely; if the project looks sufficiently sound to attract Texasgulf's participation, then Panama—which has motives such as social and economic progress that favor development, in addition to the profit motive—should also find the project attractive.)

The Cerro Colorado contract

Texasgulf entered the bidding to participate in the development of Cerro Colorado—one of 16 companies to do so—after Panama failed to reach an agreement for development with Canadian Javelin, which had held an exploration concession for the deposit and which had conducted the drilling program that established its size and commercial importance. (See E/MJ, December 1972, for a report on Canadian Javelin's work.) Roquebert cited several obstacles that had prevented Panama from reaching an agreement with Canadian Javelin: First, the company has had financial difficulties; second, Panama questioned whether Canadian Javelin possessed the technological resources to pursue such a large project; and third, Panama wanted at least 51% of the ownership, as did Canadian Javelin.

Canadian Javelin was compensated with $5 million in cash and $18.6 million in Panamanian bonds. Panama then considered the possibility of developing Cerro Colorado on its own, but its lack of technological resources argued against that course, so it went looking for a partner.

Texasgulf was selected for a number of reasons, Roquebert said. Among them were management ability, as demonstrated by a relatively low ratio of employees to sales; partial ownership by the Canadian government, which, Panamanian officials felt, might make Tg more comfortable than other companies in working with the Panamanian government; the size of the company—large enough to offer a wide range of technology but not so large as to overpower a small country; and experience with fertilizer production, which may find practical application in the Cerro Colorado project.

Texasgulf may also have helped its case, Tg vice president-international Kenneth J. Kutz said, by asking Panamanian officials what they wanted in the contract, rather than laying down a lot of conditions.

The agreement that resulted, signed in February 1976, may be unique in being specifically designed to be short term if Panama so desires. Texasgulf will manage the project for 15 years for a fee based on both gross sales and profits. After 15 years, Panamanians trained by Texasgulf to operate the mine, concentrator, and smelter will manage the operations. After 20 years, Panama has the option to buy out Texasgulf's 20% share. Texasgulf will pay a 50% tax on profits and a 10% tax on dividends, so in effect it will receive only 9% of the profits.

The thinking that motivated the specific time frames of the Cerro Colorado contract arose partly from Panama's experience with the canal. "We had had experience with one contract in perpetuity," Roquebert said, "and we did not want to do that again." Though Panama has the option of acquiring the Tg share after 20 years, it is not bound to do so. It may elect to keep Tg as a partner and invest its funds in other economic development.

Empresa de Cobre Cerro Colorado is headed by a board of directors (five Panamanian and two Texasgulf), an executive committee (two Panamanian and three Texasgulf), and a general manager (Texasgulf).

Among the responsibilities of the board of directors are approval of budgets and production plans; approval of sales plans; approval of sales contracts of greater duration than one year; approval of pay and remuneration policies; approval of plans for expansion of greater than 15% of capacity or for introduction of new technology; approval of suppliers of material and equipment valued at more than $5 million; selection of design, engineering, and construction contractors; and designation of outside auditors.

At Texasgulf Panama, Enrique Ruiz-Williams is vice president and resident manager. Ruiz-Williams, who worked in Central America with Texasgulf exploration offices at the time that Canadian Javelin was developing data on the Cerro Colorado deposit, says: "I always did like that deposit." Now he has the opportunity to help turn it into a mine.

Texasgulf's responsibilities under its management contract include all exploration, evaluation, design, construction, and operation of the project.

Panama expects to negotiate somewhat similar contracts with Mitsui and its several partners, which have been drilling the Petaquilla copper porphyry deposit east of Cerro Colorado, and with Asarco, which has been investigating the Cerro Chorcha prospect to the west. At Petaquilla, the Japanese companies' exploration contract expired on September 4, giving them 90 days to offer a proposal for an exploitation contract. The deposit is reported to contain 200 million to 300 million tons of 0.7% copper ore, and the mining rate is projected at a possible 18,000 tpd.

Codemin is organized into three divisions: technical, legal, and social. Those working in the social division of the Cerro Colorado development are preparing the Guaymi Indians for the arrival of their new neighbor. The Guaymi live in small groups and engage in subsistence farming in the mountains surrounding Cerro Colorado. They have had very little exposure to modern civilization—much less to a large industrial enterprise—and Codemin is working to prepare them for this cultural shock. A radio program on the subject is presented regularly in the Guaymi language (Codemin passed out the radios needed to make such a program effective), and the first school was recently built in the district. There are about 25,000 Guaymi, with 7,000 in the Cerro Colorado area. The project payroll will total only 2,500 so it is not viewed as a solution for all Guaymi problems. However, some Guaymi will find employment in the mine.

Probing the Cerro Colorado orebody

The existence of copper mineralization in the region surrounding Cerro Colorado has been known since at least 1932, but it was not examined closely until Panama Canal Co. geologist Bob Stewart walked into the area early in 1957, at the request of Pablo Pinel and Jose Zarn, who had been prospecting in the area. Stewart, who is now employed by Codemin, wrote a report estimating that there could be at least 100 million tons of 0.5% copper at Cerro Colorado, and for several years he tried unsuccessfully to interest North American copper companies in the deposit.

Between 1965 and 1969, the United Nations assisted the Panamanian government in a number of mineral surveys in the Azuero area of west-central Panama, and the UN team discovered the Cerro Petaquilla copper porphyry—the first deposit to be established as a copper porphyry between those in Peru and those in Mexico. The Petaquilla discovery aroused new interest among producing companies in possible Panamanian mining development, and at that time Canadian Javelin obtained the exploration concession for Cerro Colorado. Javelin's operating subsidiary, Pavonia SA, drilled 42,000 m of core holes—91 deep holes and 72 short holes—and proved that Cerro Colorado is one of the largest, if not the largest, known undeveloped copper

Winding mine roads mark the Cerro Colorado development area, with the ridge of the Continental Divide as a backdrop.

deposits in the world. Principal rock types in the area are andesite, granodiorite, granodiorite porphyry, feldspar porphyry, and latite porphyry. The granodiorites intruded Cretaceous andesites.

During the year after Texasgulf started its feasibility study in July 1976, the company added to information available on the Cerro Colorado orebody by driving an adit 458 m into the orebody. The adit provided bulk samples for metallurgical testing, fresh rock for conducting rock mechanics tests, a site for monitoring water flow, and an opening from which previously drilled core holes could be backreamed to confirm grades. Texasgulf backreamed five holes to 12 in. in diameter, attaching a funnel and pipe to the bit to assure 100% recovery of the drill cuttings. (Core recovery on the project averaged about 85%.) The grades obtained from backreamed cuttings confirmed those obtained from the original core.

In addition, Texasgulf drilled 51 holes to obtain specific information: eight holes to determine the periphery of the deposit, two fill-in holes, three pit wall holes, seven hydrology holes, 12 overburden holes, 15 adit holes, and four limestone holes. Rainfall averages 4,000 mm per year at Cerro Colorado, and water flows from the pit are expected to be heavy, so hydrology studies were given special attention. The pit will be open to the south, allowing drainage by gravity, but consideration has been given to opening drainage galleries in the pit walls to help keep the mine dry.

The elevation of the mine site ranges up to a maximum of 1,500 m, and the concentrator will be at an elevation of about 800 m. Current planning calls for ore to be moved from the pit to the concentrator by conveyor belt, partly to avoid the problems created by truck haulage on steep, wet roads. Once loaded, gravity acting on the weight of the ore will be sufficient to move the belt, and this energy may be used also to generate electricity. Current planning anticipates use of 16-cu-m shovels loading 166-mt-capacity trucks in the pit. Consideration is also being given to placing the primary crusher in the pit.

(Mine planning for Cerro Colorado is proceeding in three stages, with each being a refinement of the previous one. Information presented in this article represents thinking during stage-two planning and is subject to change.)

Geologic studies during feasibility planning included surface mapping, making of cross sections, use of the computer at Texasgulf's Raleigh, N.C., offices to make conventional statistical and geostatistical evaluations of core assays, and a rock mechanics study conducted by Golder Associates of Seattle. The final geologic report was scheduled for October 1977.

Mine planning, undertaken by the Texasgulf special projects group at Timmins, Ont., currently envisions an ultimate pit 3 km long x 1 km deep.

Bench testing to establish the concentrator flowsheet has been done at Texasgulf's Golden, Colo., laboratory, while bulk samples were tested at the Colorado School of Mines Research Institute pilot plant. Grinding will reduce ore to 70% minus 200 mesh, and some consideration is being given to installing semiautogenous grinding mills. The primary mineralization in Cerro Colorado ores is chalcopyrite, which will be concentrated in a

Exploration adit intersected all but one of the major rock types in the Cerro Colorado orebody and provided bulk samples.

conventional flotation circuit.

Mine waste and concentrator tailings disposal present something of a problem in the precipitous terrain that surrounds the Cerro Colorado deposit. While sites for mine waste dumps have been located—some on the north slope of the continental divide—no nearby area would provide the long-term capacity needed for tailings impoundment. To solve this problem, Texasgulf is proposing a 42-km tailings slurry pipeline to a disposal site on the Pacific coastal plain, not far from the proposed smelter site. Planning is also in progress for a port at La Popa on the Pacific coast. The Pacific site was selected, rather than a Caribbean location, because much of the necessary infrastructure is in place there.

The Cerro Colorado project still has a wait of several years before it joins the world's active copper mines, but conversations with those working on the project reveal much confidence on their part that Cerro Colorado is firmly headed toward that goal.

Potential for additional development

Panama's copper deposits were late in attracting attention, probably because of rough terrain and heavy vegetation. Now that their commercial potential is established, Panama is looking for other potential resource development. Current projects include an examination of geothermal steam as a possible power source in the Panamanian west near Costa Rica and exploration for gold in the eastern province of Darien. Geologist Giorgio Recchi, of the government's natural resources research laboratory, is conducting a study of arsenic as a trace indicator of gold. The analytical facilities of the lab, under the direction of Dr. Anna de Cermelli, provide support for this field work. □

Chapter 8
Iron Ore

Iron ore: how producers tailor a product for iron making	300
Hibbing Taconite starts up phase 1 with notable mining and milling features	307
Minntac expanding to 18.5 million ltpy	308
Hanna's Whitney mine	310
Erie at Hoyt Lakes—a taconite pioneer	311
Reserve	312
Butler	313
National	314
Eagle Mountain moves 170,000 tpd of ore and waste	314
Utah's Iron Springs district is a major western resource	315
McKinley	316
Republic transfers primary crusher to pit	317
Lind-Greenway—mining two western Mesabi pits	318
Tilden	318
Empire expansion is second in decade	320
Inland profits by proximity to Jackson County Iron	321
Cliffs in Minnesota—Canisteo natural ores	321
MacIntyre mines ilmenite-magnetite ores	322
IOC—a study of logistics, based on varied resources	322
Steep Rock has the deepest open pits in Canada	324
Scully mine	325
Caland	326
Aguas Claras: programmed growth to 25 million tons of ore	328
Samarco: major new materials handling concepts for iron ore	332

Giant Minntac operation of US Steel is well along in an expansion program that will equip it with a capacity of about 18 million ltpy. At that rate, it will be the world's largest pelletizing operation and possibly the best-researched plant.

Iron ore: how producers tailor a product for iron making

THE NEW IRON AGE DAWNED IN AMERICA during the mid-1950s when a pair of concentrators and two new pelletizing facilities began producing premium blast furnace feed on a commercial scale from "worthless" taconite—a flinty 28% to 35% iron bearing formation associated with the rapidly depleting reserves of high grade, direct-shipping ores in the Mesabi Iron Range of Minnesota.

While concentration and agglomeration of low grade ores into an acceptable feedstock was then viewed as a means of extending US ore reserves, it was not fully appreciated what a profound impact the use of pellets would have on the steel industry. High quality pellets tailored for iron making have been credited with reducing both the flux and coke charge requirements by as much as 10% to 15% each. In addition, these innocuous little marbles have boosted blast furnace throughput dramatically—as much as 40% to 50%.

Taconite is a hard, banded, siliceous rock of very fine grain containing magnetite. The first technical challenge in its development was mining this material, which is so hard it rings when struck with a hammer. Next came the problem of crushing and grinding the ore to minus 200 to minus 325 mesh so that the tiny magnetite grains could be pinned to the drums of magnetic and electromagnetic separators and removed from the matrix of gangue in the slurry. Then the magnetic concentrate, consisting of tiny grains, had to be put back together again in strongly bonded particles having a ⅜-in. dimension.

The pellet had to be strong enough to withstand degradation and chipping during transit because this feedstock undergoes considerable materials handling abuse. En route to steelmaking centers, the pellets are repeatedly fed through bins, chutes, feeders, conveyors, bedded in stockpiles, and reclaimed during the trip from the mine to the blast furnace—a trip usually taking place by both rail and inland waterway shipping.

The size of pellets is important in iron making. They must be large enough to prevent them from being swept from the furnace burden as the blast of air is blown through the smelting charge, yet small enough and of sufficient porosity to permit gaseous reducing reactions to take place.

Commercialization of modern American taconite concentration and pelletizing techniques involved more than 30 years of research and investigation. In the US, this effort culminated in new installations that went into production at Reserve Mining Co. in Minnesota during 1955 at a rate of about 3.9 million ltpy—approximately one-third the present capacity. Soon after, Erie Mining Co. started a 7.5-million-ltpy plant. Both plants are located on the eastern end of the Mesabi Iron Range.

From this modest beginning, the American iron ore industry had grown to 66.55 million ltpy of installed pelletizing capacity at the end of 1975. Another 21.8 million ltpy of new pelletizing capacity is under construction and due to phase into production during the period 1976 through 1978. The technology spawned by the late E. W. Davis, widely known as "Mr. Taconite" in the US, along with his

Pellet technology vastly extended the reserves of US iron ore by making it possible to process ore once considered too low in grade to mine. Iron making economies were also realized. A pellet stockpile at a Hanna-managed operation is shown here.

associates at the former Mines Experiment Station at the University of Minnesota and others from industry, soon spilled into an international arena.

Exporting Minnesota technology

In the US, the development spread from the low grade magnetic ores of the Mesabi to the mixed hematitic-magnetic ores of Michigan, the magnetic ores of Missouri, and the mixed iron ores of the West. Virtually all US production utilizes magnetic concentration prior to pelletizing. In the case of ores containing a major or minor nonmagnetic fraction, spiral concentrators, heavy media separators, and/or flotation assist in upgrading unrecovered iron values from the magnetic concentration circuit.

Abroad, the principle of concentration and agglomeration has been applied to many types of low grade ores, including calcined iron oxides produced from pyritic feeds. Pelletizing is of great importance even in the vast high grade iron ore districts of Brazil and Australia. In such areas, this unit operation is producing suitable blast furnace feed from the rising mountains of high grade iron ore fines that are unavoidably created during crushing to specification size ranges.

During the evolution of US iron ore from an industry based largely on direct shipping of washed and classified natural ores to one founded mainly on producing pellets from low grade ores, many vexing problems had to be solved. For example, taconite ores of the Mesabi were too hard for churn drilling—a primary means of putting down blastholes when Reserve and Erie were in the planning stage.

As a result, the two pioneer operations turned to jet piercing of blastholes, a method developed by Union Carbide, which used a rotary lance that burned a mixture of liquid fuel and oxygen. Such rigs bored blastholes by means of thermal shock imparted to the rock, which caused chips and fragments to spall from the formations drilled. Later on, rotary drilling achieved a high degree of sophistication, and with the development of improved rotary bits and machines, this method of blasthole drilling has supplanted many of the jet piercing units. Thus, unconventional, fill-in technology bridged a gap in a more conventional unit operation in mining.

Beyond the tough problems of mining, iron ore processing sparked wide study of crushing and grinding systems, giving rise to such evaluative yardsticks as the Bond Work Index and Blaine Tube analysis. The former is a measure of energy input and work output, the latter an empirical definition of the specific surface area created as particles are reduced in size.

Structure of the US iron ore industry

Last year, iron ore was produced by 35 companies which operated 66 mines and 44 concentration plants, according to the US Bureau of Mines. These companies were equipped with pelletizing facilities at 21 locations. In addition, two new pellet plants were under construction in Minnesota, and expansions were underway at three existing Minnesota operations. The US production suite included 60 surface mines and six underground mines in 1975. Three mines also recovered byproduct iron ore, but such sources normally account for only about 1% of domestic production.

About 96% of total US ore shipments originated from open-pit mines, and about 94% of all crude ore received some kind of concentration before shipment. Pelletized

The many faces of iron ore are revealed in this and opposite photo. Above, a 1966 view shows Kaiser Steel's Eagle Mountain operation, which started the westward march of pelletizing technology. The plant is located in southern California.

material, ranging in grade from 61% to 66% iron and 2.6% to 8.75% SiO_2, made up 72% of all American iron ore products shipped to the steel industry.

Minnesota, by far the leading producer, last year furnished 69% of the domestic output. Michigan had a 13% share of the 1975 ore shipments. The remaining production is scattered in some 18 states. The production of shippable grades of ore last year amounted to 82 million lt, about 9.4% of total world shipments of 875 million lt. In the US, the level of 1975 shipments required mining an estimated 218 million lt of crude ore. On the average, US producers must mine and dispose of at least 1 lt of waste for every long ton of ore mined. Most of these operations must mine a little over 3 lt of crude ore to produce 1 lt of finished pellets.

The major proportion of the underground feed for the industrial iron ore stream originates at the Pilot Knob operation of Hanna Mining Co. and the Meramec operation of St. Joe Minerals Corp. and Bethlehem Steel Co. in Missouri; the Grace mine of Bethlehem in Pennsylvania; the Cleveland Cliffs Mather unit in Michigan; and CF&I's Sunrise mine in Wyoming.

Ownership of US iron ore companies is divided between two categories. Some of the producers are captive units of individual or jointly ventured steel companies. Others are merchant iron ore producers, such as Cleveland Cliffs Iron Mining Co., Hanna Mining Co., or Oglebay Norton Co. Pickands Mather, a prominent merchant producer, is now a subsidiary of Moore McCormack—a marine shipping concern. Most of the steel companies, however, have substantial capital investment in the facilities of merchant producers and are committed under long term contracts to take varying shares of the output of the merchant companies.

The US is in a reasonably strong iron ore position in terms of productive capacity, ore reserves, and competitive ability. The chief worry is rooted in steel, where the forward investment needs of $2.5 billion per year for a 30% expansion over the next 10 years are outrunning the cash flow generated by the industry. US demand for iron ore is projected by the Bureau of Mines to grow at an annual rate of 1.5%—about 30% of the growth rate projected abroad. Traditionally, the US has imported 20% to 30% of its iron ore requirements. During the 1970s, the chief foreign sources have been Canada (48%), Venezuela (31%), Brazil (8%), Liberia (6%), and other nations (7%).

The taconite profile

Most US ore is benched from open-pit mines by blasting vertical, or occasionally slanted, drillholes of 15-in. to 17¼-in. diameter. Typical crude ore grades for a concentrator-pelletizer installation range from 22% to 36% iron.

Great attention is paid to drilling patterns and blasting techniques because most engineers consider explosives an

Mining, milling, and waste disposal are integrated into a single system at Utah International's Iron Springs unit in Utah. Here, an 8-yd dragline is supplying feed for an impressive dry, alluvial concentrator mounted on crawler treads.

inexpensive source of energy, while crushing and grinding iron ore to a size from which the iron-bearing mineral grains can be recovered is highly energy-intensive. Large amounts of steel are also consumed at the wearing faces of mining shovels, truck bodies, chutes, feeders, and crushing and grinding equipment—up to 10 lb for every long ton mined at some taconite mines. Thus, within reasonable limits, mine managers strive for a fragmentation size that will minimize the amount of work required for crushing.

Electric shovels and off-highway haulers at American iron ore mines are big and growing bigger. Because iron ore has a higher specific gravity than copper ore, producers have been a shade slower in trying super-size excavator and haulage components. In fact, it has been normal to equip electric shovels with buckets a cubic yard or two less in capacity than the model rating for other ores. Off-highway diesel-electric haulers of 100-ton to 170-ton capacity are a common feature of iron ore mines. The giant Terex 350-ton prototype truck has undergone trials at Kaiser Steel Corp.'s Eagle Mountain iron ore mine in southern California.

Iron ore producers have been quick to try new and heavier drilling equipment because of the tough blasthole problems they face. As a rule, Minnesota and Michigan iron ore mines tend to operate on a seasonal basis—concentrating on stripping and waste removal in the winter and crude ore production in the warm weather months. However, this work routine was once more pronounced than it is today. With the use of bubblers, photographic observation of ice movements, and more sophisticated monitoring of weather conditions, the shipping season on the Great Lakes is beginning to approach 12 months.

Iron resources of the US

The iron content of the earth's crust has been calculated at slightly over 5%. Part of the iron has been concentrated by geologic forces into deposits within many rock types. Of the many commercial deposits, the three most productive types have been sedimentary hematitic deposits of primary ore enriched by weathering processes; hematite and magnetite deposits of complex origin in metamorphic rocks; and replacement and vein deposits.

The US Geological Survey has estimated US iron reserves at 9 billion mt and identified iron resources (including reserves) at 101 billion mt. The term "reserve" is applied to an identified deposit from which minerals can be extracted at a profit using existing technology. Resources may or may not be evaluated as to extent and grade and may or may not be commercially recoverable within existing technology and economic conditions.

The USGS reserve and resource figures are a slight modification of a United Nations iron ore survey published in 1969. The UN placed US reserves at about 10.5 billion lt with a recoverable iron content of 2 billion st. The UN survey also listed 96.3 billion lt of potential US ore and resources of 106.8 billion lt.

While US reserves amount to only about 4% of the world total, they are sufficient to supply 100 years of production at recent shipping rates.

The iron formations of the Lake Superior district consist of chemically precipitated iron oxide, carbonates of iron, silicate and sulphide facies, thinly banded and interlayered with chert and other materials. Thicknesses range from 15 m to 300 m. The southwesterly trending beds of the Mesabi Iron Range dip to the southeast. The eastern portion of the formation has been metamorphosed and is the major source of taconite. Magnetite is the major iron mineral in taconite.

The Michigan jaspilite ores also consist of metamorphosed sediments, but specular hematite is the dominant ore mineral. Meramec at Pea Ridge, Mo., is an example of a massive magnetite-hematite deposit in igneous rock, as is Hanna's Pilot Knob operation. Magnetite, however, is the dominant mineral at Pilot Knob.

US Steel's Atlantic City operation is based on large bedded deposits of the Lake Superior type. Kaiser Steel's Eagle Mountain, Calif., deposits are centered on magnetite bodies in metamorphosed dolomites. CF&I's Sunrise mine in Wyoming is based on a red earthy hematite of Precambrian age. J&L Steel Corp.'s Benson mine in New York develops an elongate tabular mass of magnetite.

Alabama has the largest reserves and resources of iron ore outside Minnesota. Major ore formations occur in the Birmingham area and the Russville district in the northeastern part of the state. □

North American Iron Ore Producers

Name of operation/location	%	Ownership (managing partner in bold)	Start up	Mine	Drills	Haulage (ore)	Ore & waste (ltpd)	Ore: waste ratio	Ore mined (ltpd)	Ore grade (ave. %)	Ore minerals
United States											
Arcturus mine, Marble, Minn.	100	U.S. Steel	na	op	rotary	truck, conv	na	na	na	na	hem
Black River Falls mine, Black River Falls, Wisc.	100	Inland Steel	1969	op	rotary	truck	20,000	1:1.7	9,000	33	mag
Butler Taconite, Nashwauk, Minn.	37.5 / 37.5 / 25	Inland Steel / **Hanna Mining** / Wheeling Steel	1967	op	rotary	truck	38,000	1:1.5	22,800	21.8	mag
Canisteo mine, Coleraine, Minn.	87.2 / 12.8	Mesaba-Cliffs / National Steel / **Cleveland Cliffs**	1933	op	rotary	truck	na	na	29,450	38.10	goe, hem
Cedar City mine, Cedar City, Utah	100	Utah International	1946	op	rotary	truck	10,000 st	na	6,000 st	39.8	mag, hem
Comstock mine, Cedar City, Utah	100	CF&I Steel	1953	op	rotary	truck, conv	15,600 nt	1:2.33	4,700 nt	51.92	hem, mag
Coons Pacific[1], Eveleth, Minn.	100	Coons Pacific	1950	—	—	—	—	—	—	—	hem
Eagle Mountain mine, Eagle Mountain, Calif.	100	Kaiser Steel	1948	op	rotary down-h	truck	170,000	1:4.7	30,000	34	hem mag
Empire Iron Mining Co., Ishpeming, Mich.	40 / 25 / 20 / 15	Inland Steel / McLouth Steel / **Cleveland-Cliffs** / International Harvester	1964	op	rotary	truck	86,000	na	45,000	33	mag
Erie Mining Co., Hoyt Lakes, Minn.	45 / 35 / 10 / 10	Bethlehem Steel / Youngstown S & T / Steel Co. of Canada / Interlake / **Pickands Mather**	1957	op	rotary	truck, jet rail	145,000	1.6:1	90,000	32	mag
Eveleth Expansion Co., Eveleth, Minn.	40 / 23.5 / 20.5 / 16	Armco Steel / Steel Co. of Canada / **Oglebay Norton** / Dofasco	1976	op	rotary, jet	truck	na	na	na	na	mag
Eveleth Taconite Co., Eveleth, Minn.	85 / 15	Ford Motor / **Oglebay Norton**	1965	op	jet, rotary	truck rail	24,000	1:0.43	17,000	23.5	mag

Name of operation/location	%	Ownership (managing partner in bold)	Start up	Mine	Drills	Haulage (ore)	Ore & waste (ltpd)	Ore: waste ratio	Ore mined (ltpd)	Ore grade (ave. %)	Ore minerals
Gross-Nelson mine Eveleth, Minn.	100	Rhude & Fryberger	1966	op	down-h	truck	8,000	3:1	6,000	48	hem
Groveland mine Randville, Mich.	100	Hanna Mining	1959	op	rotary	truck	31,500	1:0.65	14,250	35	hem, mag
Hill Annex mine Calumet, Minn.	100	Jones & Laughlin	1917	op	rotary, down-h	truck, conv	21,000	na	20,000	36.55	goe, hem, lim
Hull-Rust mine Hibbing, Minn.	100	Rhude & Fryberger	1965	op	down-h	truck	8,000	3:1	4,000	58	hem
Jackson County Iron Co. Black River Falls, Wisc.	100	Inland Steel	1969	op	rotary	truck	21,000	1:1.8	7,500	36	mag
Lind-Greenway mine Grand Rapids, Minn.	100	Jones & Laughlin	1953	op	rotary, down-h	truck	20,500	1:2.42	20,000	30	goe, hem, lim
Lone Star Steel Co. Lone Star, Tex.	100	Northwest Industries	1947	op	rotary	truck	na	2.6:1	na	26.68	lim, sid
Luck Mining Co. Silver City, N.M.	100	Private	1938	op	rotary	truck	730	4:1	180	43	hem
MacIntyre Development Tahawus, N.Y.	100	N L Industries	1942	op	rotary	truck	21,600	na	5,000	28	mag
McKinley mine McKinley, Minn.	100	Jones & Laughlin	1968	op	rotary down-h	truck	30,000	1:2.5	17,000	56.5	goe, hem, lim
Minntac Plant Mt. Iron, Minn.	100	U S Steel	1967	op	rotary	truck, rail	175,000	2.5:1	110,000	22	mag
National Steel Pellet Plant Keewatin, Minn.	85 15	National Steel **Hanna Mining**	1967	op	rotary	truck, conv	40,800	1:1.43	24,000	31	mag
Nevada-Barth Corp. Carlin, Nev.	100	Nevada-Barth	1960	op	perc	truck	1,200	1:1	1,200	60	hem, mag
Pioneer Pellet Plant Ishpeming, Mich.	32.25 20.00 20.00 15.25 12.50	Republic Steel Bethlehem Steel McLouth Steel **Cleveland-Cliffs** Sharon Steel	1965	—	—	—	—	—	—	—	hem, mar
Plummer mine Coleraine, Minn.	100	U.S. Steel	na	op	rotary	truck, conv	na	na	na	na	hem
Republic mine Ishpeming, Mich.	46.50 31.00 12.50 10.00	Jones & Laughlin **Cleveland-Cliffs** Wheeling-Pittsburgh International Harvester	1956	op	rotary, jet	truck	57,200	na	24,200	36	hem, mag
Neville mine Chisholm, Minn.	100	Pittsburgh Pacific*	1974	op	rotary	truck	na	3.75:1	8,650	na	hem
New York Division Star Lake, N.Y.	100	Jones & Laughlin[2]	1944	bp	rotary	truck	15,600	1:0.15	9,600	23.2	mag, mar
Rana mine Kinney, Minn.	100	Rhude & Freyberger	1974	op	down-h	truck	7,000	3:1	3,600	58	hem
Reserve Mining Co. Silver Bay, Minn.	50 50	Republic Steel Armco Steel	1955	op	jet	truck	130,000	1.89:1	85,000	24	mag
Rouchleau group Virginia, Minn.	100	U.S. Steel	1943	op	rotary	truck, rail	na	na	na	na	hem, lim
Sherman mine Chisholm, Minn.	100	U.S. Steel	1948	op	rotary	truck, rail	na	na	na	na	hem, lim
Stephens mine Aurora, Minn.	100	U.S. Steel	1957	op	rotary	truck	na	na	na	na	na
Tilden Mining Co. Ishpeming, Mich.	30 27 20 10 8 5	Algoma Steel Jones & Laughlin **Cleveland-Cliffs** Stelco Coal Wheeling-Pittsburgh Sharon Steel	1974	op	rotary	truck	46,800	na	36,800	36	hem
U S Pipe & Foundry Co. Russellville, Ala.	100	Jim Walter Corp.	1954	op	rotary	truck	1,500	1.9:1	700	48	goe
Whitney mine Hibbing, Minn.	85 15	National Steel **Hanna Mining**	1973	op	rotary	truck, conv	44,100	3:1	20,300	na	goe, hem
Wyoming mine Virginia, Minn.	100	Pittsburgh Pacific*	1960	op	rotary	truck	na	2.5:1	3,200	na	hem

Name of operation/location	%	Ownership (managing partner in bold)	Start up	Mine	Drills	Haulage (ore)	Ore & waste (ltpd)	Ore: waste ratio	Ore mined (ltpd)	Ore grade (ave. %)	Ore minerals
Canada											
Adams mine, Kirkland Lake, Ont.	100	Dofasco	1966	op	rotary	truck	18,800	na	12,250	19.5	mag
Caland Ore Co., Atikokan, Ont.	100	Inland Steel	1960	op	rotary	truck	25,000	1:2.5	14,000	55	goe, hem
Griffith mine, Red Lake, Ont.	100	Steel Co. of Canada **Pickands Mather**	1968	op	rotary	truck	31,000	1.4:1	14,500	24	mag
Hilton mines, Shawville, Que.	50 / 25 / 25	Steel Co. of Canada / Jones & Laughlin / **Pickands Mather**	1957	op	rotary	truck	9,500	9.5:1	8,500	34	mag
Iron Ore Co. of Canada—Carol Lake project, Labrador City, Nfld.	26 / 19 / 18 / 10 / 6 / 6 / 6 / 5 / 5	**Hanna Mining** / Bethlehem Steel / National Steel / Hollinger Mines / Youngstown S & T / Republic Steel / Armco Steel / Wheeling Pittsburgh / Labrador Mining & Exploration	1962	op	rotary	truck, rail	150,000	1:0.2	125,000	38.5	hem, mag
Iron Ore Co. of Canada—Schefferville		(see above)	1954	op	rotary	truck	104,800	1:2.8	37,000	52	hem, mag
Iron Ore Co. of Canada—Seven Islands		(see above)	1954	—	—	—	—	—	—	—	hem, mag
Marmoraton Mining Co., Marmora, Ont.	100	Bethlehem Steel	1955	op	down-h	truck	16,000	3:1	4,000	28	mag
National Steel Corp of Canada, Capreol, Ont.	100	National Steel **Hanna Mining**	1957	op	rotary	truck	6,644	1:0.25	5,395	26.5	mag
Quebec Cartier Mining, Port Cartier, Que.	100	U S Steel	1959	op	rotary	truck	53,000	na	48,000	34.2	hem
Quebec Iron and Titanium Corp., Sorel, Que.	66.66 / 33.33	Kennecott Copper / New Jersey Zinc	1949	op	perc	truck	na	1:0.8	3,000,000 (year)	86	ilm
Sherman mine, Temagami, Ont.	90 / 10	Dofasco / Tetapaga Mining **Cliffs of Canada**	1968	op	rotary	truck	30,600	na	12,400	23	mag
Steep Rock Iron Mines, Atikokan, Ont.	100	Steep Rock Iron Mines	1944	op	rotary	truck	na	1:3.5	na	59	goe, hem, lim
Wabush mines, Wabush, Lab.-Que.	25.6 / 16.4 / 15.6 / 10.2 / 10.2 / 10.2 / 6.6 / 5.2	Steel Co. of Canada / Dofasco / Youngstown S & T / Inland Steel / Interlake / Wheeling Pittsburgh / Finsider / **Pickands Mather**	1965	op	rotary	truck	68,000	3:1	50,000	36	goe, mag
Westfrob Mines, Tasu, B.C.	100	Falconbridge Nickel	1967	op	rotary, perc	truck, rail	10,200	1:1.14	4,800	47.5	mag
Mexico											
Cerro de Mercado mine, Durango, Mex.	100	Fundidora de Monterrey S.A.	na	op	rotary	truck	8,000 mt	1:1	4,000 mt	na	hem, mag
Hercules mine, Hercules, Coahuila	100	Fundidora de Monterrey S.A.	1971	op	rotary	truck	6,000 mt	na	3,000 mt	60	hem, mag
La Perla Minas de Fierro, La Perla, Chihuahua	100	Altos Hornos de Mexico S.A.	1958	op	rotary	truck	10,800	na	7,500 mt	48	hem, mag
La Perla Minas de Fierro, Camargo, Chihuahua	100	Altos Hornos de Mexico S.A.	1937	op	rotary	truck	na	na	8,000 mt	45-55	hem
Las Encinas S.A., Pihuamo, Jalisco	100	Hylsa Steel Group	1955	op	rotary, track	truck, aerial tram	16,000	1:2.2	6,000 mt	60	mag, hem
Las Truchas Lazaro Cardenas, Michoacan	100	Siderurgica Lazaro Cardenas-Las Truchas S.A.	1976	op	na	truck	48,000	1:4	8,000 mt	55	mag
Peña Colorada, Colima, Mexico	47.62 / 27.14 / 15.72 / 4.76 / 4.76	Altos Hornos / Hylsa Steel Group / Tubos de Acero / Fundidora / Government	1974	op	rotary, track	truck	na	1:0.05	9,600 mt	43	mag, hem

The largest trucks now operating on the Mesabi Range have 117-cu-yd boxes and are powered by 1,600-hp diesel engines.

Hibbing Taconite starts up Phase I with notable mining and milling features

Robert Sisselman, Associate editor

HIBBING TACONITE CO., one of the Mesabi Range's newest entries, came on line late in 1976 at an initial design capacity of 5.4 million ltpy of pellets. An ongoing construction program, to be completed by 1979, will increase capacity to 8.1 million ltpy of pellets. Total cost of the project is expected to exceed $300 million. Some of the project's key features:

- Open-pit mining equipment that is among the most formidable in use on the Iron Range—most notably 170-ton ore haulage trucks and electric shovels equipped with 16-cu-yd dippers.
- Single-stage, closed circuit crushing.
- Single-stage, closed circuit grinding in 36-ft-dia, fully autogenous mills.
- Traveling grate pelletizing systems fitted with external combustion chambers that can be switched from residual fuel oil to direct firing of coal for indurating pellets. (Plant modifications and the addition of coal handling facilities will be required to utilize coal.)

Rotary drilling is employed

Hibbing Taconite (Hibtac) mines deposits in the lower cherty member of the Biwabik iron formation, which dips 3° to 5° southeast and strikes east-west. Blastholes are drilled by five rotary drills; two additional units will be purchased for the expanded production level. Six of the seven drills will be capable of drilling 55-ft-deep holes, and the seventh will drill to 66 ft in depth.

In the initial mining area, development will proceed on 50-ft benches, with a daily mining rate of about 75,000 tons, including 50,000 to 55,000 tons of crude ore. The ratio of total material to product now approximates 5:1. Drilling places 12¼-in. and 15-in. holes on spacings varying from 24 x 24 ft in development cuts to 36 x 36 ft.

Shock subs used to help absorb some of the vibrations during drilling are reportedly proving effective. Results to date indicate an increase of up to 50% in bit life.

An average Hibtac blast produces 400,000 to 500,000 tons of ore, using a combination of ANFO and slurry. Drillholes are top-loaded with ANFO and the remainder with slurry. A 45-ton crane equipped with a drop ball accomplishes secondary breakage.

Trucks are among largest on Mesabi

Hibtac employs one of the largest fleets of haulage trucks on the Mesabi Range. In the initial mining operation, 13 170-ton trucks are being used. When the project reaches full size, the total will be 19 units. Trucks have 117-cu-yd boxes and motorized wheel units and are

Blasthole patterns are drilled by five rotary, semiautomatic, 250,000-lb drills equipped with 12¼-in. and 15-in. tungsten carbide button bits.

Hibbing Taconite factsheet

Owned by: Bethlehem Steel (78.33%), Pickands Mather (15%), and Stelco (6.67%).
Location: 5 mi north of Hibbing, Minn.
Production: Initially 5.4 million ltpy of pellets; 8.1 million ltpy in 1979, after expansion.
Startup. Late 1976.

Major mining equipment
Drills (rotary): Five Ingersoll-Rand, 12¼-in. and 15-in. bits.
Shovels (electric): Five P&H 16-cu-yd.
Haulage: 14 Wabco 170-ton trucks.

Additions for expansion
Drills (rotary): Two, 12¼-in. and 15-in. bits.
Shovels (electric): Two P&H.
Haulage: Six 170-ton trucks.

---

powered by 16-cylinder, 1,600-hp diesel engines. Tires are 36:00 x 51 and are 10 ft in diameter.

The five electric shovels used to load ore are equipped with 16-cu-yd dippers. The shovels have a working weight of 1,395,000 lb. Two additional shovels will be put into operation for completion of the project.

Haulage distance from pit to crusher averages 7,000 ft over haul roads that are a minimum of 100 ft wide, with grades designed to a maximum of 5%.

In the mine services building, eight bays on one side and seven on the other accommodate trucks, tractors, graders, loaders, and other mobile mining equipment. Maintenance of drills and shovels is done in the mine.

Auxiliary pit equipment includes 10 crawler tractors, five rubber-tired tractors, three 10-cu-yd front-end loaders, one 5-cu-yd front-end loader, two 8,500-gal water tank trucks, and three motor graders.

The mine operates 20 shifts per week, with one down shift on Wednesdays for maintenance. □

Minntac expanding to 18.5 million ltpy

NORTH AMERICA'S BIGGEST iron ore operation, the Minntac complex of US Steel on Minnesota's Mesabi Range, will boast a rated capacity of 18.5 million ltpy of pellets when its Step III expansion is completed, early in 1978. The complex currently produces about 12.5 million ltpy of pellets. Late in 1977, testing of the new facilities will begin, and the concentrator and agglomerator additions will come on line during 1978.

The process of expansion has boosted materials handled at Minntac to a total of 90 million tons for 1977, which includes about 40 million tons of crude ore. To prepare for Step III mining, surface and waste rock was stripped to the east and west of the main pits, while development work was done downdip at 10° to the south-southeast. The mine now stretches about 38,000 ft along strike and is about 1 mi wide downdip in some areas.

During Step II, Minntac mined about 170,000 ltpd of crude ore. In the transition stage, ore is being mined at the rate of 240,000 ltpd. After completion of Step III, the rate will rise to an average of 350,000 ltpd. Step III output will be about 60 million tpy of ore to 60 million tpy of waste; Step II ore-to-waste ratio was 0.8:1.

Rotary drilling on 40-ft benches

Minntac is mining 40-ft-high benches. Seven rotary drills are scheduled for 120 drill shifts per week at current production levels. To maximize the use of lower cost ANFO, 12-in. and 15-in. blastholes are dewatered by a submersible pump when possible; otherwise, the holes are charged with pumped slurries. Plastic sleeves are used in all holes. Blasts are limited to five holes in

Minntac factsheet

Owned by: US Steel Corp.
Location: Mountain Iron, Minn.
Production: 12.5 million ltpy of pellets; 18.5 million ltpy after expansion (1978).
Startup: 1967.

Major mining equipment
Drills (rotary): 12-in. and 15-in.
Shovels (electric): 22 12-yd units.
Haulage: 120-ton trucks; 50-cu-yd railcars, with 10 cars per train driven by diesel locomotives.
Auxiliary equipment: Bulldozers, graders, wheel-type loaders, sprinkler trucks.

width, fired on a 45° echelon hookup with millisecond delay connectors to minimize ground vibration and air shock. Shots are fired only in favorable weather, and a typical blast breaks about 750,000 lt.

Ore loading to rail haulage is continuous, on a schedule of 20 shifts per week. Eight or nine shovels are usually employed in taconite, and about 20 to 21 shovel positions are kept open in plant feed. Unit trains are made up of nine to 15 cars—50-cu-yd side-dumps or 40-cu-yd cars side-boarded to 50-cu-yd capacity. Twenty-two trains haul ore to the crusher. The locomotives are 1,200- and 1,500-hp diesel-electric and can be remotely controlled by an operator equipped with a radio backpack for positioning at loading and discharging points.

In a major change, Minntac will modify the present mining scheme, which uses shovels in the pit to load ore directly into railcars. Ore is then trammed by rail an average distance of 3 mi to the crusher. As the mine develops, however, there will be some areas where rails cannot be positioned because of adverse grades and the excessive stripping that would be required. In those areas of the pit, Minntac will become a combination truck-and-rail operation. Crude ore will be loaded by shovel into trucks that will, in turn, dump onto stockpiles for reloading into railcars. Eventually, Minntac hopes to build an interface where crude ore can be unloaded directly from truck to railcar, using either a vibrating feeder or some other type of loading pocket. In 1978, 3 million tons will be mined by a combination of truck and rail—a small but growing part of the expanding production.

Computer programming of daily shovel positions is a big help in maintaining a uniform, blended feed for the plant. Pertinent information, including magnetic iron and silica content, is collected from a standard diamond drill grid of 300 x 200 ft, filled in as necessary by additional drillholes and sampling of blasthole cuttings.

With the exception of the 6½-yd shovels, which have been eliminated in favor of 12-yd machines, Minntac is staying with the pit equipment sizes it has been using since 1969. Twelve 12-yd shovels were added recently, bringing the total shovel fleet to 22. Also purchased were 14 new locomotives. The current fleet of stripping cars, which are used also at the company's natural ore operations in northern Minnesota, are being replaced as necessary. The mine also uses 100-ton trucks, of which 19 additional units were purchased in 1976.

Processing additions the most visible

The most obvious change at Minntac is the construction under way for the Step III expansion at the concentrating and agglomerating sites. Two 60 x 110-in. Traylor gyratory coarse crushers and a fine crusher building will be added, along with a new maintenance building to service trucks and other mobile pit equipment.

At the concentrator, six new rod mills and 12 ball mills are being installed, along with 10-ft-long cobber, rougher, and finisher magnetic drum separators. Fifteen 2,400-ton concrete storage bins for crushed ore have been added.

At the agglomerator, construction includes installation of two 21-ft-dia x 130-ft-long grate kilns. The kilns will start operating early next year, using direct coal firing. The five grate kiln lines now in operation at Minntac will be converted to coal firing as rapidly as redesign and restructuring can be accomplished. Coal handling facilities now being constructed at the plant site will be completed at the same time as the agglomerating facilities. Coal will be unloaded from vessels at Duluth docks for rail transfer to Minntac. □

Hanna's Whitney mine

Natural ores from the new Whitney mine near Hibbing, Minn., began entering the raw materials flow of the nearby Pierce concentrator in 1974, and by 1975 the new mine is expected to be accounting for almost all of the concentrator's raw materials feed. The Hanna-managed operation—ownership is 15% Hanna and 85% National Steel—is physically an extension of a portion of the eastern end of the huge Hull-Rust pit. The location on the pit rim, of course, affects all aspects of the Whitney mining operation.

Now 3¼ mi long, a mile wide, and 535 ft deep, the Hull-Rust has shipped more than 687 million gross tons of ore since first production in 1895. However, current production is only a small fraction of that during World War II years, when the mine supplied a quarter of US iron ore output.

During 1974, Whitney ores will produce about 700,000 tons of concentrates, with production expected to rise to 1.6 million tpy in succeeding years. The versatile Pierce concentrator—incorporating a variety of screening, washing, spiral, cyclone, and heavy media processes—will produce an additional 300,000 tons of concentrates this year from lean ore drawn from old mine stockpiles and another 300,000 tons from the nearly depleted Pierce Group mines.

Stripping for the Whitney mine began late in 1973, and during the first year, 4.2 million yd of overburden and 1.5 million yd of waste rock were removed. Future stripping requirements will run at about 2.5 million yd of surface material and 1 million yd of rock, according to Leo Kruez, superintendent.

In mid-1974, when E/MJ visited the property, the first layers of ore were being mined and dumped into the adjacent pit for reloading into trucks and haulage to the Pierce screening and primary crushing plant on the Hull-Rust pit

The versatile Pierce concentrator combines screening, washing, spirals, cyclones, and heavy media concentration methods.

floor. Mine planning calls for a haul road to be cut to the pit floor from the mining level to eliminate the double handling. The haul to the crusher is about ¾ mi, and after crushing, a 48-in.-wide conveyor system carries the ore ¾ mi to the concentration plant on the surface.

Concentrate will average about 53% Fe and 9.1% Si.

Major pit equipment includes three rotary blasthole drills, 12 shovels ranging in size from 2- to 11-yd capacity, and eight 75-ton, ten 50-ton, and nine 34-ton haulage trucks. The 75-ton trucks are used primarily in stripping operations. The Whitney expects to move eventually to an all 75-ton-capacity fleet, but Kruez echoed a common complaint in the mining industry last summer when he said, "New equipment is hard to get—and you can get gold quicker than you can get parts. The parts shortages are the worst they have been in 30 years."

Drilling in Whitney ore—primarily hematite—is described as easy, and some ore can be dug without blasting.

The Whitney utilizes four 10-yd front-end wheel loaders in a variety of functions, mainly for loading out concentrate, but also as backup for the shovels in loading crude.

Explosives are ANFO prills.

In the Hull-Rust pit, ore is first screened at 5½ in., with undersize conveyed to the surface wash plant and oversize either hauled to a rock dump or passed through a jaw crusher—depending on the nature of the ore—and then conveyed to the surface.

The Pierce plant produces a concentrate mix of about 70% fines and 30% coarse. Some concentrate, mostly fines, is shipped by rail direct to Granite City, Ill., and the remainder is railed to Great Lakes ports for transshipment to Midwest steel mills. ☐

Ore from the Whitney mine (foreground) is hauled by truck on Hull-Rust pit floor haul road to crusher located below Pierce concentrator (visible on pit rim in background). A conveyor moves crushed ore from pit to surface.

Erie at Hoyt Lakes—a taconite pioneer

A 10.3 million-tpy producer of taconite pellets, Erie Mining Co. moves 50 million tpy of combined ore and waste at extensive operations near Hoyt Lakes, Minn., on the eastern end of the Mesabi Range. Working six active mining areas, electric shovels load out ore into 90-ton-capacity railcars for haulage to the concentrator, or into 85- to 100-ton rear-dump trucks for intermediate haulage to rail loading facilities. Major processing steps include crushing through gyratory and cone crushers, rod and ball milling, magnetic separation, thickening, filtering, and pelletizing through balling drums and shaft furnaces.

A pioneer in taconite processing, Erie started up at its present plant in 1957 at 7.5 million annual tons of capacity. An expansion to 10.3 million tpy was completed in 1967. Erie processing design was based on experience gained at a 200,000-tpy preliminary plant that came into production in mid-1948—the first commercial-sized taconite plant. Pickands Mather & Co. manages Erie, and ownership is held 45% by Bethlehem Steel Corp., 35% by Lykes-Youngstown Corp., and 10% each by Interlake Inc. and The Steel Co. of Canada Ltd.

Erie taconites occur primarily in the upper and lower cherty members of the Biwabik iron formation and average 31% total Fe and about 22.5% magnetic Fe. Crude ore is mined at a rate of 30 million tpy.

Overburden varies in thickness from zero to 70 ft, averages 25 ft, and is composed of glacial till, large boulders, muskeg, sand, and gravel.

Active Erie mining areas—numbered 1, 2, 3, 6, 8, and 9— extend from area 8, about 20 mi east of the crusher, to area 9, about 6.6 mi to the west. In areas 1, 2, and 3, ore is loaded directly from the bank into railcars, and in areas 6, 8, and 9, ore is loaded into trucks, hauled to loading pockets, and fed into rail cars through vibrating feeders. Ore shovels range in size from 8- to 13-cu-yd capacity.

In stripping, shovels up to 16-yd capacity load into 85-ton and 100-ton rear-dump trucks. Front-end wheel loaders ranging up to 10-cu-yd capacity perform cleanup chores in mining areas and at loading pockets.

Diesel electric locomotives of 1,800 and 2,000 hp are used on the crusher haul, pulling nine or 17 cars on maximum grades of 2%. Trains are remotely controlled by a single operator wearing a belt-mounted control unit. Operators maintain radio contact with a central traffic control unit, and all communications on the system are taped.

Erie drills blastholes with rotary and jet piercer equipment, the jet piercers being used in the harder ores. Blasting for shovel-to-train loading is predominantly on long open faces, and for shovel-to-truck loading on shorter but wider patterns. Spacing has varied from 30 x 30 ft in some of the ores at the western end of the operations to 18 x 27 ft in the harder eastern ores. Bench heights average 35 ft.

Low density prills are generally used in dry holes, and slurries are the blasting agent in wet holes. A skull-cracker handles all secondary breaking.

Erie pellets, averaging 65% Fe, are shipped by a company-managed, 72-mi mainline railroad to Taconite Harbor for transfer to Great Lakes ore carriers.

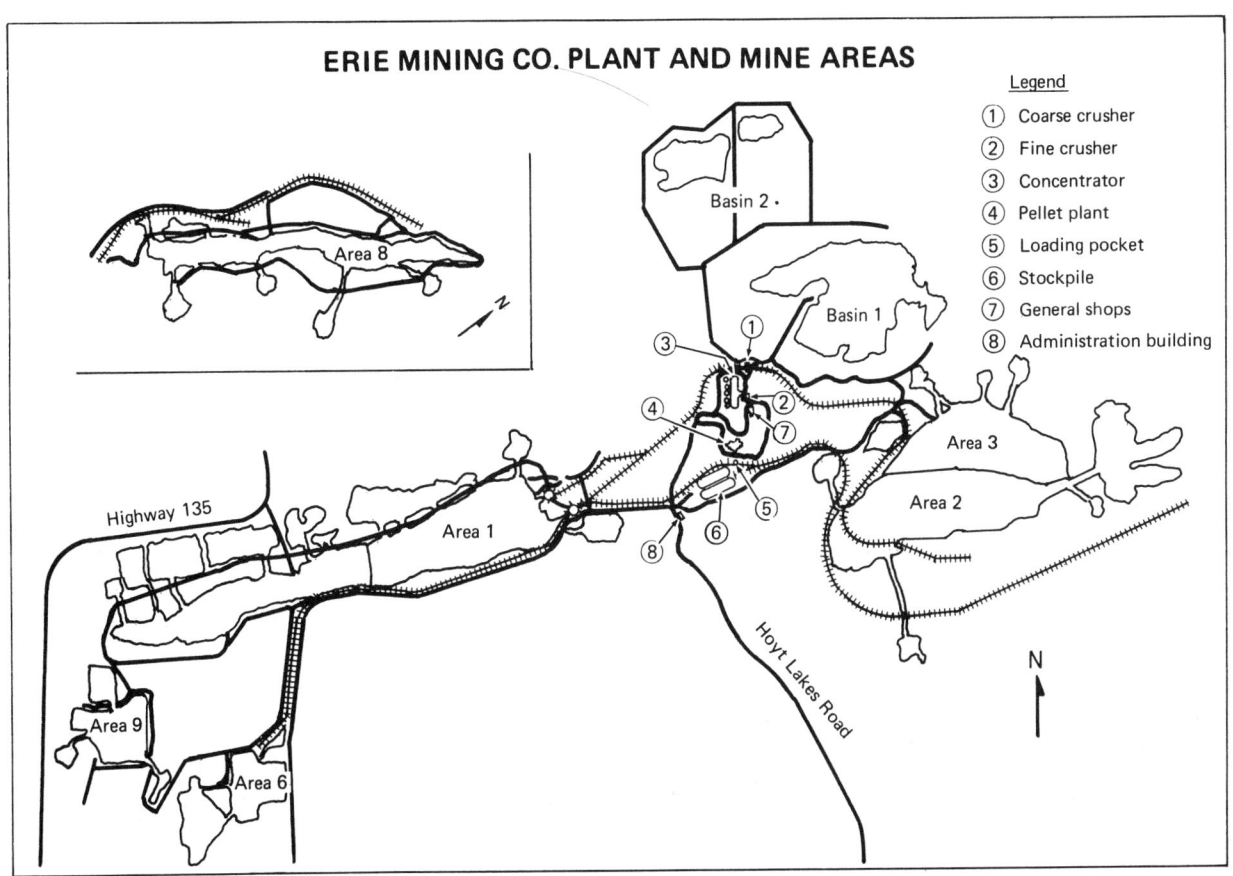

Reserve

Reserve Mining Co.'s 10.8 million-ltpy taconite operation was the world's first large-scale pellet producer, and by any standards represents a significant benchmark in mining history.

Reserve went into production on a more modest scale in August 1955, with a rated capacity of 3.75 million ltpy, following a $190 million construction project that began in 1951. By 1960 a continuing program of adding or enlarging facilities had hiked Reserve's capacity to 6 million ltpy, and in the same year a major $120 million expansion was launched. This expansion brought production to the 9.6 million-ltpy level in 1964. Two years later the current capacity was reached, after a $25-million expansion and improvement campaign.

The $350 million investment tab is likely to grow substantially if a land-based alternative tailing disposal plan—estimated by Reserve at $242.6 million—is accepted by state, local, and federal authorities as well as environmental groups. This would put capital investment in the operation at $53.50 per ltpy of capacity, higher than the oft-quoted rule-of-thumb figure of $30 to $35 per annual lt of capacity that prevailed a few years ago.

Reserve really is the culmination of a lifetime devoted to processing technology by "Mr. Taconite"—the late E. W. Davis, once director of the University of Minnesota's Mines Experiment Station (now known as the Minerals Resources Research Center). In honor of his work, the Reserve board of directors named the Silver Bay, Minn., concentrating and pelletizing facilities the E. W. Davis Works.

Owned equally by Republic Steel Corp. and Armco Steel Corp., Reserve constitutes a massive materials handling operation. The open pit, at Babbitt, stretches about 9 mi long and 1 mi wide, and the E. W. Davis Works is 47 mi away on the shore of Lake Superior, where a lake shipping terminal is located. Linking the two operating divisions—Babbitt and Silver Bay—is a double-tracked company-owned railroad, equipped with centralized traffic control, which annually handles over 1.4 billion ton-miles of crude taconite.

Located near the eastern end of the Mesabi, Reserve's orebody is about 140 ft deep at its thickest point. It averages about 23.5% magnetic iron. To say that this rock is hard and abrasive is an understatement—it even looks hard and mean in its blasted state. For example, the 100-lb dipper teeth on the 12-cu-yd shovels are worn down to about 25 lb in eight shifts. It is estimated that 2.4 lb of steel is consumed for every gross ton mined.

The mine is operating with 35-ft benches in three levels of taconite. Exploration drilling on a 250-ft grid delineates the ore and provides grade control information. This data is supplemented by bank sampling and fill-in diamond drilling if needed. The equipment suite includes ten 11-cu-yd shovels in ore and four 12-cu-yd shovels in waste. In addition, the Babbitt Div. is equipped with two 10-cu-yd and five 5-cu-yd front-end loaders.

Reserve panorama shows rail car dumper, fine crushing plant, concentrator, pelletizing plant, and ship loading facilities. The two boat loaders at Silver Bay have a capacity of 3,800 ltph. Pellets are discharged to the holds by movable booms.

The hauler fleet is composed of 43 90-ton, articulated side-dump units, and another 38 rear-dump trucks sized from 50 tons to 150 tons in capacity.

Ore, rock waste, and overburden removal scheduled for 1974 include: 31 million lt of taconite; 13 million cu yd of rock; and 1 million cu yd of overburden—largely glacial till. To meet the concentrator's daily appetite for 85,000 lt of ore, Reserve normally schedules 110 shovel shifts and 15 front-end loader shifts in ore during a 20-shift week.

Reserve uses 11 jet-piercing and one rotary drill for blasthole work, with the rotary used largely in waste rock. The jet piercers have a three-port burner at the bottom of a 55-ft rotating drill stem. Fed a mixture of fuel oil and oxygen, the burners direct a flame which reaches 4,400°F against the taconite, causing it to spall-off from the thermal shock. The burner is water cooled and the coolant flashes into steam when it contacts hot taconite. The expanding steam flushes the spalled chips from the hole as it rushes up to the collar of the hole.

Hole diameter is somewhat variable due to differing rock characteristics, but averages about 9 in. The bottom 4 ft of the blasthole, driven to a 38-ft depth, is chambered to 14 in.

The chamber and lower portion of the hole are loaded with an ANFO-based slurry from pumper trucks. The upper portion is loaded with prilled ANFO if dry, or with slurry if the hole is wet. The holes are connected diagonally with Primacord fuse with 5- to 17-millisecond delay connectors between the rows.

Blasted ore is delivered an average 1.9 mi to one of two crushing installations by the side-dump trucks. They are dumped by the crusher operator, who uses a remote-controlled hoist and grapple to engage a dump bar at the side of the trailer box.

The concentrator produces a 65% iron concentrate for the balling and pelletizing lines at Silver Bay. Reserve has two 8 x 218-ft and six 6 x 168-ft traveling grate furnaces. The finished product is an 11/32-in. pellet of 60.7% iron and 8.7% silica. □

Butler

Originally designed to produce pellets at a nominal rate of 2 million ltpy, Butler Taconite, on the western side of the Mesabi Iron Range, has pushed its capacity to 2.6 million ltpy through a number of improvements since operations started up in April 1967. Butler has always produced a very clean, high-specification pellet at 65.5% iron and 4.5% silica, and the operation is believed capable of producing a product containing only 2-3% silica if warranted by demand from steelmakers. Along with National Steel, Butler pioneered semi-autogenous grinding in Minnesota iron ore.

Owned by The Hanna Mining Co., Inland Steel Co., and Wheeling Steel Corp., Butler is managed by Hanna, and in design is a near carbon copy of the nearby National Steel Pellet Plant, another Hanna-managed operation. Butler, near Nashwauk, Minn., is developed in the old Patrick Group of natural ore mines, which were exhausted of conventional direct-shipping grade red ores years ago. Advancing technology in mining, processing, and steelmaking has converted the once-useless magnetic taconite underlying the natural ores to a valuable resource.

The taconite at Butler is carried mainly in the Lower Cherty member of the Biwabik Formation, which dips to the southeast at about 6° to 7°. The ore is about 180 ft thick and averages about 32% total iron, 22% magnetic iron, and yields a product weight recovery of about 32%. Surface-mined in 40-ft benches by a conventional shovel and truck system, Butler ore is coarse crushed to minus 5½ in. and delivered by a 54-in. x 2,820-ft conveyor through a lift of 303 ft to an A-frame storage barn having a capacity of 135,000 lt.

Butler is geared to produce 8,317,000 ltpy of crude ore. To reach this goal, it must also remove about 1.6 million cu yd of rock waste and 1.6 million cu yd of surface overburden—sand, gravel, till, and tree stumps. The mine operates 10 shifts a week in ore and 11 shifts a week on stripping. Normally, two shovels per shift are needed in ore for blending purposes. Two shovels are also positioned in waste each shift.

The excavator fleet includes five 11-cu-yd electric shovels. Additional support equipment consists of a 6-cu-yd shovel; a 3-cu-yd backhoe used at the crusher for nipping; a 3-cu-yd dragline employed on a dike project; and a 7-cu-yd dragline used on a diversion ditch. Two 5-cu-yd wheel loaders are available—one in the pit and one at the plant.

The haulage fleet is composed of eleven 100-ton diesel-electric, rear-dump trucks and one 85-ton diesel-electric of the same make.

For cleanup at shovel positions and roadway maintenance, Butler uses three rubber-tired bulldozers, five tracked bulldozers, two graders, and water wagons mounted on 34-ton truck bodies.

Mining is taking place in two pits. Pit 1 furnishes about 75% of the crude and Pit 5 now supplies about 25% of plant needs. Four rotary drills handle the blasthole work. The 40-ft benches are drilled 5 ft below grade, and the final pit walls are shaped to a berm at every second lift to provide a 0.875:1 final slope.

The rotary drills utilize patterns of 32 x 32 ft for 15-in.-dia holes and 28 x 28 ft for 12¼-in.-dia holes in ore. Expanded spacings of 12¼-in.-dia holes are used in waste. Penetration rates of 43-44 ft per hr are now being realized in both hole sizes in ore. Bit life during the first half of 1974 was about 2,500 ft in the 12¼-in. holes and about 1,400 ft for the 15-in. holes. Drilling utilizes water flushing for dust suppression, with the attendant problems of sky-rocketing prices and shortages of anti-freeze additives during winter months.

Blasting practice at Butler is the subject of continual study. Currently, the energy in explosives is considered one of the cheapest sources of power and one way to attack reductions in truck, shovel, and crusher steel wear while working toward increased throughput in the primary mills. The 15-in. holes are bottom loaded with 600 lb of slurry, followed by 1,350 lb of ANFO in the next 22 ft of column. Drill cuttings are used as stemming for the top 18 ft or so of the borehole. This charge is primed twice—once in the slurry and another in the ANFO. Detonating lines are tied with 9- and 17-millisecond delays.

The 12¼-in. holes are similarly loaded—500 lb of slurry in the bottom, 950 lb of ANFO in the next 22 ft, and stemming to the collar in the next 18 ft. Shots of 75 to 100 holes are included in a typical blast, and when possible these are detonated behind a 30-ft buffer zone of broken ore. At any given period, mine planners at Butler attempt to keep about 1 million lt of broken ore in the pit for loading.

Mechanical availability of haulers at Butler is described as very good at 80%, based on hours operated divided by hours operated plus repair time. □

National

National, which is managed by Hanna, is a near twin of the neighboring Butler Taconite Project. Located on the western side of the Mesabi, National ore is carried in the Lower Cherty member of the Biwabik Formation. The company mines a magnetic taconite of about 32% iron in a somewhat thinner horizon than the 180-ft-thick bed mined by Butler.

National is developed on 35-ft benches in the old Section 18, Russel, and Stevenson mines, which many years ago were exhausted of natural ores. As pointed out by a company spokesman, National is a classic example of the need for a reasoned approach to surface mine reclamation. Had the exhausted natural ore mines been restored to their original contours, they would not be producing pellet feed today, not to speak of supporting the planned expansion—events brought about by advancing technology and the demand for more steel. As it was, the old mining area only had to be dewatered and the walls scaled here and there to make them safe when it was determined that the remaining resources were needed and could be profitably produced.

The mining program

The mining department annually handles about 2 million cu yd of surface material, 750,000 cu yd of waste rock, and 8,750,000 lt of ore in meeting current production requirements (the figures cited vary from year to year). Mining in ore is scheduled on a weekly basis of 10 shifts, while stripping is spread over 11 shifts per week. To satisfy production goals, three shovels are normally positioned in ore and two in stripping each shift. Daily ore output of 37,000 lt (on a five-day, two-shift basis) meets weekly concentrator demand at a rate of 26,400 ltpd.

The mining machinery inventory at National includes four shovels in the 12-cu-yd to 14-cu-yd range; two shovels sized at 8 and 11 cu yd; and a 6½-cu-yd shovel. These shovels are all electrically powered. A 2½-cu-yd diesel shovel and three 6-cu-yd wheel loaders supplement the excavator fleet. The haulage team is composed of ten 100-ton units (all diesel-electrics) and five older 34-ton rear dumps. Other support equipment includes three track-type and three wheel-type bulldozers and three water wagons mounted on 34-ton truck bodies.

Three large rotary drills handle blasthole requirements. The National mining plan is based on 35-ft benches driven to a final pit wall slope of 0.5:1. When the mine re-entered production as a taconite supplier, the blastholes were 9⅞-in.-dia on a 22 x 22-ft pattern. Since then, hole diameters and spacings have increased substantially in the never-ending quest for improved efficiency. Today most blastholes are 15-in.-dia on a 35 x 35-ft spacing in ore and 38 x 38-ft centers in rock. The company is now taking a close look at 17½-in. drill bits; this would necessitate a change in drill steel from 13-in. to 16-in.-dia, however.

Drill and blast practice is under continual review at National. The current tendency is to blast a little finer by pulling in the spacing a bit to see if economics can be achieved in crusher mantle and liner wear. During the first half of 1974, National was realizing a bit life of 1,714 ft, compared with a 1973 average of 1,565 ft.

Virtually all blasting is now done with ANFO delivered in the hole from pumper trucks. All holes are lined with a polyethylene sock. The ANFO is primed top and bottom with 1-lb boosters. Drill hole cuttings are used for stemming the explosive charge to the collar. This practice, however, is also under re-evaluation. Anti-freeze in a ratio of about 1,500 gal to 6,000 gal of water has been used during the winter to keep the drill cuttings from freezing. Because the price of anti-freeze has nearly quintupled in the past year (from 76¢ to $3.55 per gal), there has been increasing discussion of turning to dry drilling and hauling in stemming from other sources.

Recent powder factors achieved at National are 0.51 lb of explosive per ton ore and 0.85 lb of explosive per cu yd in rock waste. Shots involving up to 100 holes are fired only when meteorological conditions are favorable, to reduce noise and vibration to a minimum. Engineers check conditions at local weather reporting centers and at the weather station at International Falls, some 100 mi to the north. Test shots are fired to test for localized inversion.

To meet the requirements involved in the expansion program, the mining department has placed orders for four new shovels, two rotary drills, and fourteen 100-ton trucks. In addition, a second gyratory will be installed in the pit, matching the current primary crusher, a 60-in. gyratory housed in a concrete-lined silo extending 90 ft below ground level. Trucks dump directly into the crusher bowl, and ore is crushed to minus 5½ in. Crusher capacity is now about 3,000 ltph.

A 54-in. x 2,735-ft-long steel-core belt conveyor system delivers crushed ore through a lift of 273½ ft at 600 ft per min, discharging it to a crude ore stockpile located under an A-frame storage shed. Total capacity under the shed is 144,000 lt, and stored ore is reclaimed by six underground conveyors which feed the six parallel semi-autogenous dry grinding lines.

Hardened pellets at National are conveyed to a surge pile serving a semi-automatic unit train loadout system. These trains are made up into 200-car units hauled by four 1,500-hp diesel electric locomotives. The unit trains are shared with National's neighbor—Butler Taconite—on alternate days. During loadout at each plant, the trains are inched under a small surge bin. Made up of 70-ton cars, the loaded train averages about 14,000 lt of pellets which are hauled to a lake terminal at Superior, Wis. □

Eagle Mountain moves 170,000 tpd of ore and waste

Kaiser Steel Corp.'s Eagle Mountain mine, at Eagle Mountain, Calif., will produce about 3.8 million tons of pellets and concentrates in 1974, working three open pits that require massive overburden removal. Current production of 30,000 tpd of ore is accompanied by movement of 140,000 tpd of waste, for a combined materials handling operation rated at 170,000 tpd.

The Eagle Mountain orebody dips at 45° to 55°, with

The East pit of the Eagle Mountain mine has been in production continuously since 1948 and is now 1,100 ft deep.

A 17-cu-yd shovel recently added to the Eagle Mountain equipment roster loads out 100- and 150-ton-capacity trucks.

magnetite being the primary ore. Near the surface, ores have been oxidized to hematite. The chief gangue element is pyrite in the magnetite and gypsum in the hematite. Country rock is hard—usually quartz monzonite or quartzite. In quartzite, which is brittle, 12¼-in.-dia down-the-hole drills drill 60-ft holes on a 32-ft spacing. Production drilling equipment for both ore and waste includes three 12¼-in.-dia and two 9⅞-in.-dia units. Other drilling equipment includes a truck-mounted pioneering drill and drills for secondary blasting.

Loading equipment includes a Marion 192-M 17-cu-yd shovel, added to the Eagle Mountain equipment list this year. The other electric shovels are five 12-cu-yd, two 8-cu-yd, two 6-cu-yd, and one 4½-cu-yd Bucyrus-Eries. Mine-to-plant haulage is accomplished with eight new 150-ton-capacity Terex units and 48 100-ton Kenworth Darts.

Ore from the three Eagle Mountain pits—the East pit, the Central pit, and the Black Eagle or West pit—is blended to obtain an average grade of 34% for processing. Three crushing stages reduce the ore to 1 in., and dry magnetic separation sorts out a coarse 55% Fe concentrate for direct blast furnace feed. Hematite is concentrated by heavy media separation, and fines are separated by jigging and wet magnetic separation for sinter plant feed.

Magnetite pellet plant feed passes a fourth crusher stage and three stages of magnetic separation and grinding. Pellet capacity at Eagle Mountain's Dravo traveling grate plant, started up in 1965, is 2.6 million st. Pellet grade is 62.2% Fe.

Reserves at Eagle Mountain, which has been producing since 1948, total about 400 million st, measured and indicated, and the mine has a future life of 25 to 30 years as an open pit. Depending on the economics of future production, the mine could eventually be converted to an underground operation. (Such a move would be necessary if all reserves are to be tapped.)

All Eagle Mountain production is shipped to the Fontana, Calif., works of Kaiser Steel, about 160 mi away. The sinter plant is located at Fontana, and annual capacity at Fontana is 3.4 million stpy of ingot. □

Utah's Iron Springs district is a major western resource

The Iron Springs Mining District in southwestern Utah, some 15 mi west of Cedar City, is one of the largest iron ore producing areas in the Rocky Mountains, with ore shipments from the district averaging 2.5 million tpy. Producing companies include US Steel, with an output of 500,000 tpy at the Desert Mound mine; CF&I, producing 1 million tpy at the Comstock mine; and Utah International, producing about 1 million tpy of combined tonnage from several open pits. About half of the ore produced is shipped to US Steel's Geneva plant and the other half to the Minnequa Works of CF&I.

Iron ore was first discovered in the district in 1847 but it was not until 1922 that the first profitable mining venture was initiated.

In 1942, the Reconstruction Finance Corp. contracted the construction of a completely integrated steel mill near Provo, Utah, with US Steel as operating agent (US Steel purchased the mill after World War II). Also motivated by war requirements, CF&I retained Utah Construction Co.—now Utah International (UI)—to develop and operate one of its properties near Iron Springs.

From 1923 to 1973, the Iron Springs district produced some 88 million tons of iron ore. The largest percentage of this total was produced from 1942 to 1973. Reserves are presently estimated to be more than 300 million tons.

Deposits in the Iron Springs district are clustered along the margins of three intrusions of quartz monzonite porphyry. They are oval in plan, 3 to 5 mi in diameter, and

Alluvium processing plant designed by Utah International personnel is a one-of-a-kind "dry-land dredge." It processes alluvial iron-bearing gravel that could not be processed economically by conventional mining and concentrating methods.

are aligned in a northeast direction. Jurassic, Cretaceous, and Tertiary sedimentary strata and Tertiary volcanic rocks flank the intrusions. Margins of two intrusions are complexly folded and faulted.

Principal iron ore minerals are hematite and magnetite. Only magnetite is mined in the district. Ore occurs as contact metasomatic-hydrothermal replacements and breccia fillings mainly in Jurassic limestone, but also in younger strata and porphyry. Small fissure veins of magnetite occur in all three porphyry intrusions.

All mines in the district are open pits, up to 500 ft deep, with the largest pit being about 2,500 ft in diameter. Active properties include one pit operated by US Steel and five operated by UI, plus one pit operated for CF&I.

The bulk of production is direct-shipping ore. Generally, the grade ranges from 45% to 68% iron, with the average between 50% and 55%. Preparation prior to shipping involves crushing, screening, and blending. Three crushing and screening plants are in use by the various companies, and a beneficiation mill was installed by UI in 1961 to process low-grade ore ranging from 20% to 45%.

Two products—open-hearth and blast-furnace feed—are shipped from the district via the Union Pacific Railroad.

There are only minor variations in mining methods and equipment at the seven active operations, since ore deposits are similar in character and call for standard mining practices. One ore deposit is being mined by two companies. Pits are designed with sloping walls 60° to 65° and 25-ft safety benches for each 75 to 100 ft of depth. Lifts vary from 25 ft at the UI pits to 37½ ft at the US Steel pit.

Bench heights are chosen to permit selective mining while maintaining production rates.

Material in the various pits is loaded into trucks by electric- or diesel-powered shovels equipped with 2½- to 6½-cu-yd dippers.

Haulage fleets consist of trucks ranging in size from 32 to 75 tons. Distances from mines to plants vary from ½ mi to 12 mi. CF&I's haulage distance, for example, is ½ mi, US Steel's 6 mi, and UI's longest haulage distance is 12 mi. Grades are maintained at about 5%.

UI is the only company in the district with beneficiation facilities for processing low-grade ore. Its mill installation not only permits processing low-grade ore that previously was stockpiled, but has also made possible the shipment of a better product. Crushed ore is sized and passed over a magnetic separator, and the reject and undersize is recrushed and sent to the mill feed-pile. The plus 1¼-in. product goes to the open-hearth stockpiles for shipment. Mill feed is scrubbed and screened to 3/16 in. The coarse fraction (minus 1¼ plus 3/16 in.) is concentrated with belt magnetic cobbers. Fines are pumped to drum-type wet magnetic separators for concentration.

During 1963, UI designed and had built a one-of-a-kind plant—a "dry-land dredge." Weighing in at 550 tons, the track-mounted unit is capable of moving under its own power. Alluvium material, received from a converted 6-cu-yd dragline, is screened and then passed over magnetic cobbers. Two products are recovered in the plant: a coarse high-grade ore and a fine low-grade material which is further processed at the mill. □

McKinley

Producing 2.4 million tons of concentrate from an annual mine production of 3.5 million tons of crude ore, J&L's McKinley mine is described as a good example of a high grade, channel-type ore deposit typical of the east-central Mesabi Range. The orebody occurs on the east limb of an anticline-syncline structure roughly transverse to the strike of the Biwabik iron formation and contains high grade blue-black hematite, yellow limonite-goethite, and "painty" hematite ores. Beneficiation is accomplished by screening, washing, and classification to make a coarse and fine concentrate averaging 60.0% Fe, 6.60% SiO_2, 0.032% P, 0.59% Al_2O_3, 0.58% Mn, and 5.88% moisture.

The McKinley pit is mined using down-the-hole rotary drills, electric loading shovels, and rear-dump haulage trucks. A noteworthy production application of a prototype piece of mining equipment has been underway on the property since July 1973, when McKinley introduced the first model of Gardner-Denver's rotary table drive blasthole drill into its production cycle. The rotary table drive is described as "a unique improvement" by Thomas B. Brunt, superintendent of maintenance for J&L's Northwest Ore Div. Vibration levels on the machine are much lower than on a top drive machine, and since the mast is not subjected to torsional stress, maintenance costs are low. Because of its larger air capacity, the drill achieves a 60% greater penetration rate using 11-in. bits than a previously used machine with 9-in. bits, and the greater diameter permits increased hole spacing, with a resulting 46% increase in tonnage per foot drilled.

Holes are currently drilled 35 ft deep on a 30 x 30-ft pattern. Explosives are all wet-hole powder—ANFO bagged in polyethylene.

Five- and 6-yd shovels load a fleet of nine 75-ton and eleven 40- to 50-ton trucks, usually with two shovels in ore and one in waste. Four 85-ton trucks were scheduled to be added to the truck fleet in October 1974. Introduction of a tailgate on one of the haulers has proved useful in preventing spillage of the wet, sometimes sloppy, silt-clay overburden. Haul roads grade a minimum 8%.

Pit water drains into a lower sump and a main sump, with two pumps in the lower sump capable of pumping 3,000 and 5,000 gpm to the main sump, and two pumps in the main sump capable of pumping at 1,000 and 2,500 gpm. Water is pumped to a settling pond, and either used in the McKinley wash plant or pumped to a secondary clarification pond for final settling before discharge.

Primary ore is dumped into a 170-ton pocket and is then scalped at 5 in. on a 6 x 12-ft screen. Major processing equipment includes washing screens, spiral classifiers, a 5-

The ore haul from the McKinley pit is handled by 40-, 50-, and 75-ton trucks over a distance averaging about 4,500 ft.

ft cone crusher, and 60 five-turn spirals. Fines, shipped at minus ¼ in., are dewatered by a drum filter and a Linatex-Derrick dewatering screen. Fines account for approximately 65% of the McKinley production.

Republic transfers primary crusher to pit

A major tunneling and construction project at Cleveland-Cliffs' Republic mine will result in installation of a 54-in. Traylor primary crusher within the pit footwall, about 500 ft below the elevation of the present surface crushing plant. To provide a means of ore transfer from the pit crusher to the surface, an 11-ft x 15-ft tunnel is under construction to serve as a conveyor galley. Sloped at 13°, the tunnel is being driven with trackless mining equipment and in mid-1974 was being worked on two faces, from the surface and from a 300-ft access adit in the wall of the Republic pit.

Based on a tightly folded and steeply dipping iron ore deposit, the Republic hematite ores provide 8.1 million ltpy of concentrator feed, with concentrates subsequently pelletized at both the Republic and the Humboldt pellet plants. (The Republic-Humboldt operation is located about 15 air miles west of the Empire-Tilden reserves of Cleveland-Cliffs, with the Humboldt plant being 6 mi north of Republic. After the Humboldt mine was exhausted in 1970, the plant was converted to pelletizing of Republic concentrates.) Combined production from Republic mine ores is 3.5 million ltpy of pellets.

Jones & Laughlin, Wheeling-Pittsburgh, International Harvester, and Cleveland-Cliffs are the owners of the Marquette Iron Mining Co. Started up in 1956, the Republic mine of Marquette Iron currently holds reserves mineable by open-pit methods for an estimated 15 years of additional production.

Until recently, drilling of blastholes was done by jet piercers, but two rotaries drilling 12¼-in. holes have now been added—intended primarily for stripping, but presently being used for crude ore production also. Electric shovels load out ore into trucks ranging from 65- to 105-ton capacity, with 75-ton units being standard.

Folding and uplifting of the synclinal Republic deposit has left one limb of the syncline with a near-vertical dip and very competent metadiabase at the footwall contact. Republic is leaving this contact as a vertical highwall, and to prevent loose rock fall, is dressing it with 10-ft and 12-ft rolls of cyclone fencing held in place by rock bolts.

Cleveland-Cliffs, which emphasizes environmental controls at all of its operations, takes particular pride in reclamation work at the exhausted Humboldt mining operations. A planting program initiated seven years ago has produced a good growth of grass and trees on the tailings basin just three years after the mine shutdown, and the site now can count wildlife that includes deer, fox, hawk, killdeer and migrating geese. The Humboldt pit has been filled by natural water inflow and will become a lake.

Lind-Greenway—mining two western Mesabi pits

North of Grand Rapids, at the far western end of the Mesabi Range, J&L's Lind-Greenway mine extracts 20,000 tpd of crude ore grading about 30% Fe and processes it by washing, screening, heavy media, and jig concentration methods into about 970,000 tpy of 58½% Fe, 9% Si concentrates.

The Lind-Greenway mine works two pits on a single orebody split by the south-flowing Prairie River—the Lind pit east of the river and the Greenway pit to the west.

Working three shifts per day and mining soft hematite-limonite-goethite ores, Lind-Greenway achieves about 30% recovery by weight of mined crude. All ore requires drilling and blasting, with 6½-in. holes drilled 30 ft deep on an 18 x 18-ft square pattern. Two down-the-hole drills, two 6-cu-yd-capacity electric shovels and a fleet of twelve 40- and 50-ton haulage trucks constitute the major pit equipment. Explosives are polyethylene bagged ANFO.

Auxiliary equipment comprises two wheel-loaders having 9- and 6-cu-yd-capacities, a 2½-cu-yd-capacity diesel shovel, two tractors, and two graders.

The two pits require pumping at a combined rate of 1 billion gal per year. Water from the Lind pit flows south to the abandoned pit of the Jessie mine, which serves as a settling basin. Overflow from the Jessie pit flows to the Prairie River. Water from the Greenway pit is pumped to tailings basins to the northwest of the mine, and after settling is transferred by a siphon system to Prairie Lake.

The Lind-Greenway plant at the north end of the Greenway pit receives ore at a truck dumping pocket, feeding a double deck scalping screen that splits ore at 4 and 6 in. Reversible conveyors permit transfer of both plus 4-in. and plus 6-in. material to a rock reject pocket or to further screening and crushing, depending on the quality of oversize material.

Double deck screening at 1¼ in. and ¼ in. produces a plus 1¼-in. fraction that reports to two cone crushers, a plus ¼-in. minus 1¼-in. fraction that is processed in the heavy media section, and a minus ¼-in. fraction that reports to the jig section.

Heavy media feed is split by screening at ½ in. to create feed for a coarse and a fine heavy media section. In both sections, an 84-in. Akins separatory vessel and ferrosilicon media effect the iron concentration. Typical operating gravity is 3.10 in the coarse and 2.90 in the fine section.

Lind-Greenway concentrates report to fine and coarse concentrate pockets and are loaded out into rail cars for shipment. Coarse concentrates account for about 70% of the operation's production.

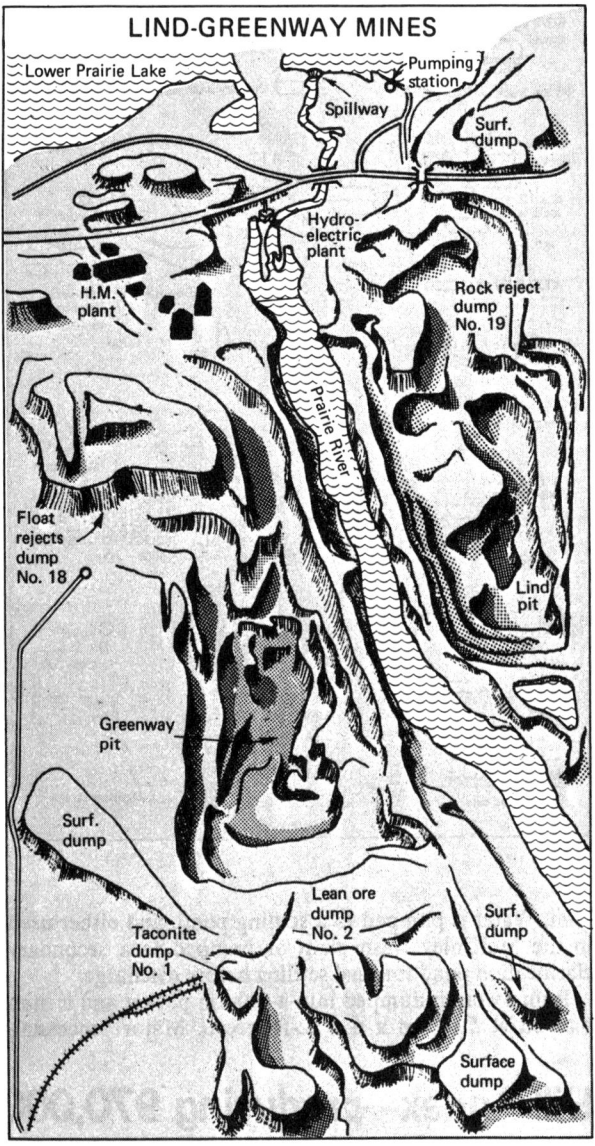

Tilden

Algoma Steel Corp. Ltd., Jones & Laughlin Steel Corp., The Steel Co. of Canada Ltd., Wheeling-Pittsburgh Steel Corp., Sharon Steel Corp., and The Cleveland-Cliffs Iron Co. are the participants in Tilden Mining Co.

Cleveland-Cliffs has owned the fine-grained martite-hematite Tilden deposit since 1865, but the ore had resisted economic processing because of the fine grain size (grinding to 85% minus 25 microns is required to liberate the mineral). Furthermore, slimes developed in fine grinding interfered with the various flotation systems tested.

When the US Bureau of Mines developed a selective flocculation process which appeared to have application to the treatment of some ore types, Cleveland-Cliffs entered into a cooperative program with the USBM in an effort to apply this system to Tilden ores. The selective flocculation technique proved to be successful in eliminating slimes which are detrimental to flotation, with a minimum of iron losses in the slime fraction. In this process, the iron minerals are selectively flocculated with a prepared starch product, while the siliceous slimes are dispersed with sodium silicate. A thickener-type vessel is used to make the separation between the flocculated iron mineral and the dis-

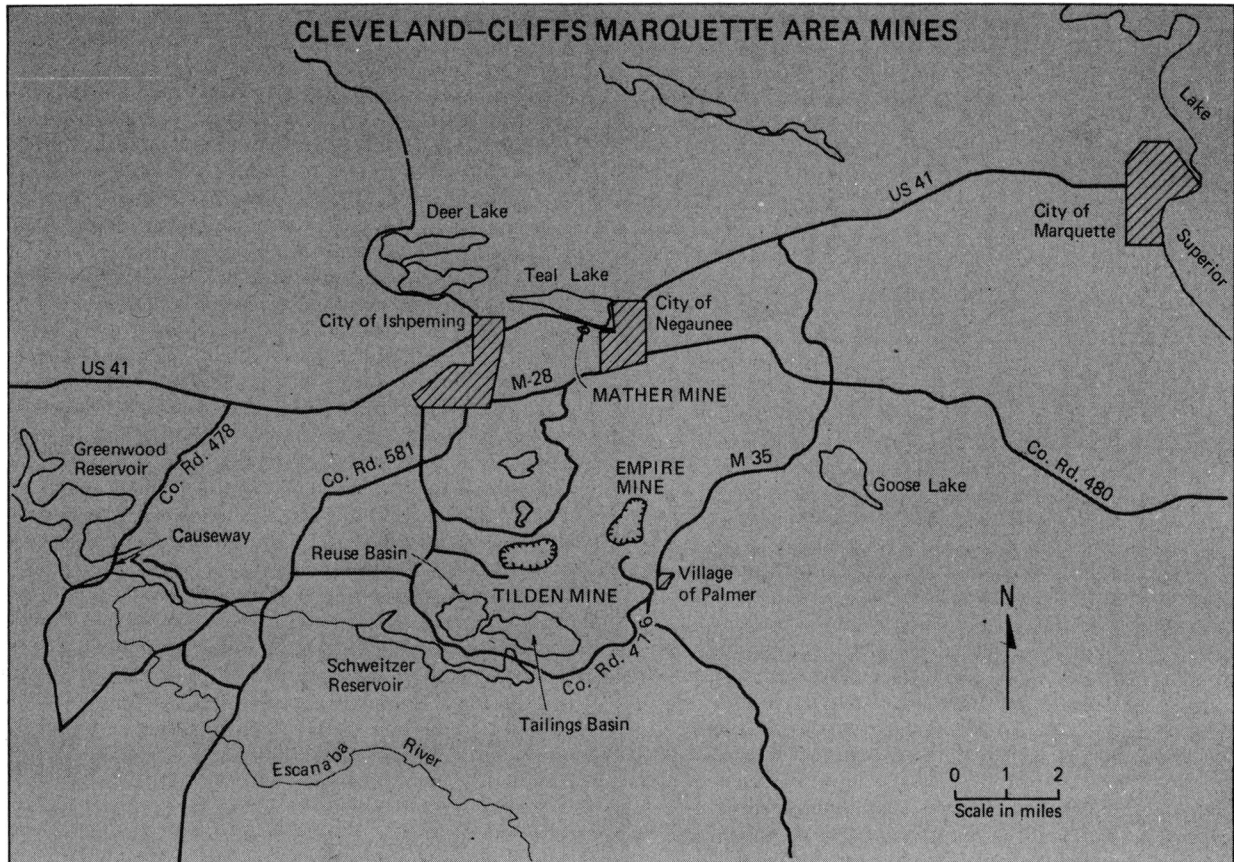

persed gangue. In the work by USBM, the desliming stage was followed by an anionic flotation system for final upgrading of concentrates.

Cleveland-Cliffs developed a two-stage autogenous grinding system for liberating the martite-hematite from a siliceous gangue, followed by selective flocculation and a multistage cationic silica flotation circuit which produced the final concentrate. At present, the process requires careful control of water quality and reagent additions, to keep total water hardness in the 40-50 ppm range and the flocculation pH at about 10.5 to 11.0.

The color of thickener overflow indicates whether the flocculation process is working properly. With proper selective flocculation and silica dispersion, thickener overflow is reddish—about the same color as tomato soup. If iron mineral is not flocculating, the overflow tends toward a dark color.

About one-third of the silica present in the ore is removed in the selective flocculation thickener, and the remainder is removed by flotation. A lime addition to the thickener overflow clears the water in the recycle pond and sets up a softening reaction for the re-use water.

Thickener underflow is drawn off at about 50% solids, and the silica float is accomplished in 500-cu-ft flotation machines. Flotation concentrate averages 65% Fe from ores grading about 37% Fe.

Preparation of the Tilden ores for the flocculation-flotation concentration includes single stage crushing in a 60-in. gyratory unit, and grinding through six lines, each having a 27-ft-dia. x 14½-ft autogenous mill followed by two pebble mills, 15½ x 30 ft. Caustic soda and sodium silicate are fed into the primary autogenous mills. The starch solution is fed to conditioners ahead of the selective flocculation thickener and the flotation cells. Amine is fed directly into the flotation cells.

Screening after autogenous grinding produces a minus 3-in. plus 1¼-in. fraction that is used as grinding media in the pebble mills. A minus 1¼-in. plus ½-in. fraction reports to an intermediate crusher, along with excess pebbles. This crushed product is returned to the primary mills. Minus 2-mm material reports directly to the pebble mills, which are operated in closed circuit with 15-in. cyclones.

Filtration following flotation is characterized by live steam injection to the enclosed filter discs. The steam heats the filter cake and entrained water, thus serving to reduce the moisture content of the filter cake to a suitable level for balling.

Mining to meet requirements of autogenous mills

The Tilden mine is based on more than a billion tons of crude ore reserves. The ore varies in iron content and in grindability. The orebody, dipping northerly at 30° to 40°, has been folded and there are accompanying joints and fractures. Blasting must achieve proper chunk availability for the mill feed, and crude ore blending is required to achieve a feed uniform in size and chemical content.

Blastholes are now being drilled at 12¼-in.-dia, but provision has been made to move up to 15-in. holes. Three drills and five 10-yd-capacity electric shovels were on the property when E/MJ visited it in July. The truck fleet comprised 15 75-ton haulers.

Maintenance bays in the Tilden shops have been built large enough to accommodate 200-ton haulers, and in the future larger capacity trucks may be required. For the present, the smaller trucks are an aid to blending. Five shovels were being used last summer—three in ore and two in waste.

Bench height is 45 ft, and haul roads are 100 ft wide at maximum grades of 8%. The 2,800-ft ore haul to the concentrator is presently downhill, which will be the case for another six years at present mining rates.

The ultimate pit will be 9,000 ft long, 4,500 ft wide, and 1,200 ft deep.

Greenwood Reservoir, built by Cleveland-Cliffs, will supply makeup water for the Tilden plant. The reservoir is open to the public for boating, hunting, and fishing, and fox, porcupine, mink and raccoon find a home along the 26-mi shoreline.

Makeup water for the Tilden plant will originate from the Greenwood Reservoir, a 1,400-acre lake built by Cleveland-Cliffs 7 mi southwest of Ishpeming on the Middle Branch of the Escanaba River. The water draw will be 5,000 gpm for processing that requires 86,000 gpm—an effective 94% recycle.

A source of pride for Cleveland-Cliffs, the lake's 25-mi shoreline and 13 islands are a very scenic recreation area. The shoreline was surveyed prior to flooding, and all trees below the final water elevation were cut and grubbed, giving the effect of a natural body of water. □

Empire expansion is second in decade

Just a couple of miles east of the Tilden Project, Cleveland-Cliffs' Empire Mine and pellet plant has been in production since late 1963, producing 64.65% Fe, 6.50% SiO_2 (dry analysis) pellets from low grade magnetic ores. Started up at a rated capacity of 1.2 million ltpy and expanded to 3.5 million ltpy in 1967, Empire was putting the finishing touches on its second major expansion—to 5.3 million ltpy—when E/MJ visited the property in mid-1974. Inland Steel Co., McLouth Steel Corp., International Harvester Co., and Cleveland-Cliffs are the owners of Empire Iron Mining Co.

To process increased ore output from the Empire pit, five grinding lines were added to the concentration plant, bringing the total to 21, with the new equipment being similar to but larger than the primary autogenous mills and pebble mills of the earlier lines. At the pellet plant, an Allis-Chalmers grate-kiln line similar to that installed at the time of the first expansion will contribute 1.8 million ltpy to Empire pellet production.

The Empire orebody, with reserves measured at about 812 million lt of crude ore, is mined by conventional rotary drill, electric shovel, and rear dump haulage truck methods. Because of variability in crude ore grade, grindability, and mineralogical composition, accurate blending is required to achieve optimum mill feed.

The orebody dips 38° to the northwest. From the footwall to the hangingwall, magnetic ores are present, successively, in a lean carbonate horizon, a rich silicate horizon, a rich carbonate horizon, and a lean carbonate horizon. Grade mined for the concentrator averages just over 33% Fe, and weight recovery in the concentrator is 35.9% to natural concentrates. The orebody is intersected by dikes normal to the strike and several major faults. Extensive sampling of blasthole cuttings provides data for blending.

Blasthole drills—two B-E 60Rs and a 61R—drill 12¼-in. holes 50 feet deep on 30-ft centers. Bench height is 45 ft. Multiple delays minimize flyrock, and all blasts are monitored with a seismograph. Blasting is conducted with either ANFO or slurry. About 60% of the blastholes are wet.

Loading equipment on the property includes seven shovels ranging in capacity from 6 yd to 11 yd.

A haulage fleet of 17 85-ton and eight 100-ton capacity trucks moves ore over permanent haul roads that are maintained at grades of 6% to 7%. (Temporary roads may grade up to 12%.) Primary crushing in a 60-in. gyratory reduces the ore to about 9 in.

The Empire expansion, along with the neighboring new Tilden Project, adds substantial impact to the Cleveland-Cliffs production. It is notable that these projects are drawing on reserves within a relatively compact area a few miles south of Ishpeming, Mich. Expertise gained in developing these projects, and the processing refinements that made them possible, can be expected to prove valuable background for future Cleveland-Cliffs development on the Marquette Range. □

Inland profits by proximity to Jackson County Iron

Among the smaller taconite operations which have been developed recently, the Jackson County Iron Co. open-pit mine and pellet plant at Black River Falls, Wis., came onstream in December 1969 at a rated capacity of 750,000 tpy of high grade 65% Fe pellets. Seven days after startup, the concentrator at the plant engineered and built by Dravo Corp. achieved its designed 24-hr feed rate, and eight days after its startup, the pellet plant produced at its design rate over a continuous 24-hr period. The wholly owned Inland Steel operation has produced consistently at levels above rated capacity ever since, and in 1973 chalked up a pellet output of 955,000 tons. Production in 1974 is again expected to exceed 900,000 tons.

The efficient Jackson County Iron Processing plant has all of its major equipment under one roof—three crushing stages, rod and ball mills, cyclones, magnetic separators, balling discs, and a 10-ft-wide by 105-ft-long Dravo-Lurgi traveling grate indurating machine. A central automated control room monitors all processing steps.

An active replanting program on mine waste rock dumps, which are terraced and covered with the originally stripped soil, has achieved remarkable success with a hybrid poplar tree and is a point of particular pride for Jackson County Iron superintendent Lemoyne Olson. The poplars—a crossbreed of an eastern cottonwood and an eastern black poplar—were planted on the first waste pile slopes in 1971. When E/MJ visited the property in the summer of 1974, the earliest plantings of the hybrid poplar had reached a height of about 20 ft and were expected to exceed 30 ft five years after planting, and stand as high as 50 ft after 10 years.

Jackson County Iron mining operations move about 7.2 million tpy of material to produce 2.6 million tpy of crude.

Wisconsin's only iron mine

The iron deposits on which Jackson County Iron is based were first reported in 1839, but low grades blocked large-scale commercial production until the present facility was brought onstream. The mine is the only operating iron ore producer in Wisconsin and is relatively isolated from the major iron producing districts of the upper Midwest in Minnesota and the upper peninsula of Michigan.

The iron formation of which the Jackson County deposits are a part is traceable for several miles across west-central Wisconsin, about 50 mi southeast of Eau Claire. The pit now being mined is in the largest of several deposits rated as potential ore sources, and its reserves are sufficient for 15 years at current operating rates. The other deposits could provide an additional five years of feed for the concentrator, Olson said.

The Jackson County ores occur in a general environment of steeply dipping, metamorphosed Pre-Cambrian rock overlain by flat-lying Paleozoic sandstones. The resistant iron orebodies outcrop as small hills on a generally low-relief landscape.

The orebody now being mined dips at about 65° and has two major zones of interior waste rock interbedded with three 90- to 100-ft-thick taconite beds. The interior waste accounts in part for the high overburden-to-ore ratio at the mine. Ores grade from 20% to 48% Fe, and recovery by weight in the pit is about 36.5%.

The small size of the pit precludes blending as the ore is mined, and in a departure from most taconite operations, Jackson County Iron blends its ore in outside piles, after third stage crushing and ahead of the rod mill.

Major pit equipment includes one B-E R60 rotary drill, three B-E 6-yd shovels, and two 85-ton Wabco, six 75-ton Dart, and four 27-ton Euclid haulage trucks. Two 12-cu-yd front-end loaders supplement the shovels. Other equipment includes two rubber-tired dozers, two crawlers, and two graders. A dropball is used five shifts per week as a secondary ore breaker.

Blastholes drilled to 12½-in. diameter and 40-ft depth are usually wet and require pumping. Slurry is loaded in holes that cannot be dewatered. Other holes are bottom-loaded with slurry and then loaded with ANFO in a plastic sock. Blasthole patterns are 22 x 22 ft in ore and range from 26 x 26 ft to 19 x 19 ft in waste, depending on hardness. Bench height is 35 ft. Water flows into the pit at about 1,500 gpm.

Waste is dumped on nearby waste piles, and in addition to the poplars mentioned above, plantings on waste have included legumes and grasses. Advice on the planting program came from a number of sources, including the University of Wisconsin, the US Agriculture Department, the Forestry Department, and the Soil Conservation Service.

Production is shipped daily to Inland's Indiana Harbor Works in 25- to 30-car trains and unloaded directly into blast furnaces. The cycle for the 100-ton cars is completed in three days, and because of its all-rail shipping, Jackson County Iron is able to ship year round—an important factor in the economics of Inland Steel's only wholly-owned US pelletizing operation. □

Cliffs in Minnesota—Canisteo natural ores

The Canisteo mine—which may be described as a typical westend Mesabi Range, low-grade property—shipped 1.1 million tons of concentrated natural iron ores in 1973. A similar level of production is anticipated for 1974. Canisteo is held jointly by Jones & Laughlin Steel, Cyclops Corp., Wheeling-Pittsburgh Steel, National Steel, and Cleveland-Cliffs (manager), and is operated by Mesaba-Cliffs Mining Co. Crude ores grading about 40% Fe are mined at several locations on the floor of the large Canisteo pit, which first began producing in 1905. A full range of concentrating equipment in the Canisteo plant upgrades the ore to 56% Fe and 9.50% SiO_2, natural analysis. With the split at ¼ in., ore is shipped as 54% coarse and 46% fines.

Major pit equipment includes two electric rotary drills that drill 9-in. blastholes, 29 34-ton haulage trucks, two 65-ton haulage trucks, and seven electric loading shovels with capacities ranging from 5 to 8 cu yd.

Heavy water inflow into the pit requires pumping by two turbine and two horizontal pumps, each rated at 500 hp. Makeup water for the concentrator is drawn entirely from the pit and averages 1,600 gpm. Pumping for dewatering in the pit is used as a means of leveling out the Canisteo operation's power draw, with pumps operated at full capacity when shovels shut down for lunch, or when part of the plant equipment is down, for example. □

MacIntyre mines ilmenite-magnetite ores

A principal world source of titanium dioxide (ilmenite), MacIntyre Development of NL Industries Inc., in Tahawus, N.Y., is also responsible for mining and marketing associated deposits of magnetite.

The ilmenite-magnetite orebody, averaging 28% iron, has a northeast-southwest strike 6,000 ft long and a northwest dip of 30-45°. The ore zones themselves are composed of lenticular veins and masses of closely associated magnetite and ilmenite, which are separated by gabbroic and anorthositic waste zones.

The South Extension pit, which opened in 1961, is the present site of mining activity. Mine benches are spaced at 44-ft vertical intervals, with a 50-ft-wide permanent bench left at every third bench. Haulage roads are built at 12% maximum grades.

Primary blastholes are drilled using two methods: a 10-in. rotary drill operating on a 25-ft spacing; and a 6½-in. down-the-hole drill, with holes on an 18-ft-sq pattern. Both drills have a bit life of 2,500 to 3,000 ft, using tungsten carbide button bits.

Blastholes are loaded with aluminized slurry which is pumped into the hole by truck and stemmed with 16 ft of drill cuttings. Blasts consist, for the most part, of two or three rows of holes with five to 10 holes per row. On the average, 2¼ tons of rock are broken per pound of explosive. Oversize, resulting from primary blasting, is broken by a rubber-tired mobile crane using a 10,000-lb forged steel billet as a drop ball.

Three electric shovels, with 6-cu-yd buckets, load ore for the crusher and waste for the dumps into 85-ton haulage trucks. Each truck has a 1,000-hp diesel engine directly coupled to a generator which supplies power to the two electric wheel motors. Haul roads, dumps, and areas around the shovels are kept clean by bulldozers and graders. □

IOC—a study in logistics, based on varied resources

With varied resources of limonitic, goethitic, magnetic, and hematitic iron ores, and with reserves measuring in the billions of tons, The Iron Ore Co. of Canada (IOC) is a study in logistics. Its operations embody selective mining, blending, and complex scheduling of equipment, process plants, transportation, and personnel. In 1974 the company produced more than 25 million lt of iron ore, concentrates, and pellets and accounted for almost 40% of the iron ore shipped out of Canada.

IOC is owned by Hanna Mining Co., Hollinger Consolidated Mines Ltd., Labrador Mining & Exploration Co. Ltd., and six US steel companies: Armco, Republic, Bethlehem, National, Pittsburgh-Wheeling, and Youngstown Sheet & Tube.

Major logistical support for IOC operations in the Labrador Trough is provided by the Quebec North Shore & Labrador Railway, a common carrier, running 360 mi from the shores of the St Lawrence River to Schefferville—the northernmost point of IOC operations. (See special section on transportation.)

Schefferville: focus on selective mining

In the Schefferville area, the rocks of the Labrador Trough are water-laid sediments that were folded and faulted into mountain ranges and subsequently eroded to low ridges, leaving beds of iron ore exposed at the surface as long sinuous bands surrounded and separated by other rocks. In this environment, more than 40 economic deposits are scattered along a northwest-trending strip, 5 to 10 mi wide and 60 mi long. The deposits range in size from 1 million tons to 50 millions tons. Reserves are estimated to exceed 400 millions tons of direct-shipping and beneficiative open-pit ore. The operations straddle the boundary of Quebec and Newfoundland-Labrador, with 60% of the reserves in Quebec.

The principal iron minerals in the ore are limonite, geothite, martite, and hematite, in color variations from yellow to brown, red, and blue-black. Ore classifications are: non-Bessemer—55% Fe natural and less than 10% silica (dry basis); manganiferous—more than 50% Fe and more than 3.5% Mn; and crude plant feed—50% natural Fe and 14% silica (natural analysis) for beneficiation at Sept-Iles. Moisture content ranges from 8% to 10%.

Working with the variations in iron content (40-67%) and gangue materials (silica of 2.2-30%, and manganese of 0.08-11.7%) demands dexterity backed up by continual sampling and analysis. Beginning with initial exploration drilling, sampling and analysis follow each step of the entire operation until the ore is blended to final grade at Sept-Iles.

Open-pit mining begins with the stripping of overburden and waste rock during the winter, accompanied by installation of railway spurs and roads. Mining is carried out in 38-ft benches drilled and blasted to 42 ft. Electric Bucyrus-Erie 50-R rotaries drill 9⅞- to 10⅝-in. holes in 21- to 25-ft square patterns. Approximately 0.8 lb of ANFO per ton is detonated on a multirow basis. A high water table necessitates the use of slurried explosives, consisting of ammonium nitrate, pelletized TNT, and water. The product, "Hydromex," was developed by IOC, Ireco, and Canadian Industries Ltd. Blasting technique is especially important because of the unusually wide variation in rock hardness and the intermittent presence of permafrost.

With seven pits in operation at one time, mining practice centers on a combination of equipment best suited to the specific needs of the particular pit. A typical setup is two electric shovels, one in ore and the other stripping, to load two to six trucks; one or two tractors; a rotary drill; and a screening-crushing plant. The 11 electric shovels are of various sizes. Haulage is handled by a fleet of 34 120-ton trucks—29 Lectra-Hauls and five K-W Darts. Tractors, graders, and front-end loaders are Caterpillars.

The high water table makes dewatering mandatory in all pits.

The crushing plant location puts it not more than 4,000

ft from the working face. Waste haulage is kept to a maximum of 1 mi. A good portion of the waste contains 30-40% Fe and is stockpiled for future use. Pit operations are maintained around the clock, with mining confined to a season of 180-230 days, depending on the weather.

When needed, preliminary blending is done at the pit. Ore is then delivered to a crushing and screening plant, where a combination of jaw and single roll crushers deliver a 6- to 8-in. product to a Hazemag impact crusher, which reduces it to 2 in. The crushed ore is loaded into rail cars, and after sampling and analysis, unit trains transport it to Sept-Iles for blending and loading aboard vessels.

Power for the Knob Lake operations and the town of Schefferville is supplied by a captive hydroelectric plant at Menihek, 30 mi to the south.

Like all other Labrador Trough operations, IOC maintains extensive training facilities to alleviate the critical labor shortage that characterizes all northern regions. IOC now has a staff of 10 instructors supervising 225 personnel in training. Programs are geared to apprenticeship training for journeyman certification, involving 4,000 hr of instruction over a four-year period. An 11th grade education is required to qualify for this program. In the present equipment operators' program, 100 pupils are signed up for 1,000 hr of class and field instruction. Due to the bilingual nature of the operation, both French and English are taught. In 1974, $250,000 was budgeted at Schefferville for training.

Carol Lake operations—large and innovative

Located wholly within Newfoundland-Labrador, near the west shore of Wabush Lake and 120 mi southwest of Schefferville, Carol Lake operations are large. In 1973, Carol Lake mined 30 million lt of crude ore to produce 13 million lt of concentrates and 9 million lt of pellets.

The Carol Lake deposits are located in hills rising 500 to 1,000 ft above adjacent lakes, with little or no overburden. The deposits are principally specularite and magnetite averaging 38.4% Fe, with reserves estimated at more than 2 billion lt of open-pit ore.

Open-pit operations are based on 45- and 65-ft benches. Three Bucyrus-Erie 50-R and nine 60-R electric rotaries and one Gardner-Denver 120 are used to drill 10-in.-dia holes. The type of explosives varies, depending on rock hardness, but is usually aluminized slurry in 22- or 33-ft square patterns. For soft materials, ANFO and T3 with no aluminum are used. A single blast may break from 350,000 lt to as much as 700,000 lt.

Thirteen electric shovels of various makes, with 10-cu-yd dippers, load the ore for transport to ore passes by 44 diesel electric trucks—fifteen 130-ton Lectra-Hauls, twelve 160-ton Terexes, and seventeen 120-ton Wabcos.

IOC's Labrador Trough terminus at Sept-Iles handled 22 million lt of product in 1973. Concentrator and pellet plant (lower left) have a capacity of 6 million ltpy of pellets, produced via the grate-kiln process.

As with all IOC operations in remote areas, the Carol Lake facility is self-sufficient, equipped with a 53,000-sq-ft warehouse, 70,000 sq ft of maintenance floor area, a centralized heating plant, and a reliable source of power from Churchill Falls. Twin Falls, an IOC-built hydroelectric generating facility now owned by Hydro-Quebec, has been on a caretaker basis since July 1974.

IOC headquarters at Sept-Iles is responsible for overall administration, QNS&L Railway operations and administration, and the Sept-Iles terminals, including shipping, stockpiling, and beneficiation and pelletizing of Knob Lake ores.

Complex materials handling at Sept-Iles

It is estimated that in 1974 more than 22 million lt of direct-shipping ore, concentrates, and pellets will be processed by IOC through the Sept-Iles terminal. The orchestration of the various elements of this massive materials movement is a symphony of coordination, involving mining, blending, beneficiating, pelletizing at two locations, loading, transporting, and shipping on a global basis.

Direct-shipping and plant-feed ores account for the largest category of movements within the terminal. Ore cars arriving from Schefferville are individually weighed by a double electronic scale at the rate of one every 15 sec. The cars are separated according to grade in a 12-track classification yard with a capacity of 900 cars. Sidearm pushers take the cars onto a single-track barney lead.

Ore blending is accomplished in the shiploading system by bringing cars in proper sequence on the lead from the 12 classification tracks. The cars are then pushed into a tandem rotary dumper where ore passes through a grizzly to divert into roll crushers any oversize, such as frozen chunks from the stockpile. The product is then fed onto two 72-in. conveyors for transfer to two 60-in. belts leading to 300-lt mixing bins. From the bins, the ore is fed to the conveyor system of the loading docks. The original dock, with two 60-in. conveyors, can load directly into a vessel's hold through two traveling shiploaders at the rate of 4,000 ltph each. A new loading pier is equipped with two 72-in., 7,500-ltph conveyors.

The original loading and mooring dock will accommodate up to 105,000-lt vessels with a draft of 38 ft at low tide. Expanded facilities adjacent to the original dock can handle vessels as large as 250,000 lt with draft of 60 ft.

Stockpiling of ore from Knob Lake can be carried out by diverting ore from the dumper to two 48-in. conveyor systems. The ore is dumped by two 60-ft-high self-propelled stackers covering a pile area of 120 x 5,000 ft on each side of each conveyor. Stockpile capacity exceeds 6 million lt. Reclaiming from stockpile is handled by 6-cu-yd shovels and front-end loaders. The reclaimed ore is fed into the processing system after sampling and analysis.

To meet moisture specifications and to facilitate handling, certain Knob Lake ores must be dried. The 13½ x 110-ft oil-fired rotary dryer has a nominal capacity of 300 ltph.

Carol Lake concentrates are handled similarly at Sept-Iles, with stockpiling in a different area.

Stockpile capacity for pellets is substantial at Sept-Iles—up to 4 million lt of inventory.

The Ore Movements Div. is responsible for coordinating activities at Sept-Iles. Ore Control plans and coordinates all movements to meet scheduled deliveries. Marine Services handles the total waterborne function, from tugs to pilots, mooring, servicing, and acting as an agent for foreign general cargo ships and tankers if requested. Chemical Laboratory is responsible for quality control analyses and special duties in monitoring water, air, and other environmental factors.

IOC operations in the Laborador Trough are well suited for expansion, should the demand increase for quality ores, concentrates, and pellets. The IOC assets included defined reserves totaling billions of tons and a logistical support system second to none in capacity, quality, and operating knowhow under the most trying of climatic conditions, along with an *esprit de corps* rarely found in such a large staff. If there is a single element that is precarious, it is trained personnel. But here again, IOC is on top of the problem with an aggressive training program at all operating locations and a recruiting campaign to spark the interest of young people just starting their careers. □

Steep Rock has the deepest open pits in Canada

Steep Rock Iron Mines Ltd., Canada's only independent iron ore producer, supplies 1.45 million ltpy of 62.5% iron oxide pellets to Algoma Steel Corp. and Detroit Steel Corp. from operations centered at Atikokan, Ont. The company was originally organized to develop direct-shipping crude and wash or gravity-concentrated ores from reserves containing goethite and hematite in a ratio of about 5:1. The first shipment was made in 1944.

Since that time, the character of its operations has changed considerably, but Steep Rock Iron remains one of the more resourceful and imaginative companies on the Canadian mining scene. In the late 1930s and early 1940s, the company defined a major iron ore district—the Steep Rock Range—containing a number of orebodies lying under a wilderness lake system. The deposits were under 70 to 300 ft of water and were covered by silt ranging from a few feet to 300 ft thick. Steep Rock devised a way to rearrange the topography and drainage system, then started to dewater the lakes over the ore zones, pumping the water into newly created natural reservoirs.

The company then launched one of the most massive preproduction stripping projects in mining history—comparable in scale to the earth moving required for the Panama Canal—to uncover additional orebodies. Under a lease and royalty arrangement negotiated in 1949, neighboring Caland Ore Co., an Inland Steel Co. subsidiary, joined the effort to develop an orebody on the eastern side of the Steep Rock Range. Together, Caland and Steep Rock Iron stripped some 283 million yd to prepare orebodies for production. In all, five orebodies have been identified. None have been bottomed by drillholes, but the open pits are maturing in the Steep Rock district.

In Steep Rock Iron Mines' future is the potential Sanjo Metals project, based on large magnetite reserves at Lake St. Joseph, some 180 mi north of Atikokan. The Lake St. Joseph deposits are under consideration for open-pit development, in a plan that envisions the production of 4.0 million ltpy of 70% iron superconcentrate, all indurated to oxide pellets, and some further reduced to metallized pellets or sponge iron.

At Steep Rock, four orebodies have been mined—one by underground and open-pit methods, and the other three by open pit only. All operations are now centered on open-pit mining at the Hogarth mine. The Hogarth will carry pelletizing operations into 1978, and redesign of the North Roberts pit can add another four or five years of life. Beyond that, there is plenty of productive potential, but realization is dependent upon emerging technology and market and economic factors. The relatively high grades of the Steep Rock ores put these deposits in a good position to take advantage of technical breakthroughs in underground extraction.

Steep Rock Iron is mining two types of ore, each having a variety of metallurgical characteristics. Direct ore includes material grading more than 54% Fe, which can be fed directly to the pellet plant. Crude ore, grading 40% to 54% iron, is beneficiated by scrubbing, washing, jigging, and spiral concentration to a 59% concentrate for the pellet plant. The concentrator is operated on a seasonal basis during warmer weather months.

The Hogarth open-pit mine is equipped with three Bucyrus Erie 40-R and one 45-R rotary drill. The excavator fleet consists of three P&H 1900 electric shovels equipped with 9-, 10-, and 11-yd buckets, a 6-yd P&H 1600 electric, a 7-yd Lima dragline, and two P&H 1400 4½-yd electric shovels. Nineteen 100-ton Lectra Haul trucks make up the haulage fleet, with two 50-ton Caterpillar trucks used around the pellet plant and for odd jobs in the pit.

The Hogarth is scheduled to go to 1,100 ft in depth—the same depth to which the South Roberts pit was mined. This means long waste hauls. The 100-ton trucks are equipped with 1,000-hp GM engines, except for two units which have experimental Cat 1,200-hp diesels.

Rotaries bore 9⅞-in. blastholes on an 18 x 18 ft pattern or 7⅞-in. holes on a 14 x 14 ft spacing. Prilled ANFO is used in dry holes, while wet holes are loaded with a slurry blasting agent.

Steep Rock's 1.45 million-tpy-capacity pellet plant came on-stream in 1967 at a cost of $28 million. The stack is 300 ft high.

The iron-bearing formations dip steeply, and the ore zones are contained between a footwall carbonate and a hangingwall volcanic ash. The ore is made up of three stratigraphic members: the footwall paint member—highly variable in character and containing manganiferous waste, with iron values up to 55%; the goethite member, largely ore but containing waste bands; and the pyrite member, at the hangingwall between ore and the ash rock.

The paint rock is the least stable member. From past experience, the maximum slopes maintainable in the various rock types are: overburden 11½°; carbonate 58°, paint rock 37½°; ore 42½°; and ash rock 42½°. Engineers designing the pit make use of the steepest possible final slopes consistent with safety and failure considerations. Mine design is based on 37½-ft benches with 20-ft berms. Haul roads are 70 ft in width on grades up to 10%. □

Scully mine

The Scully mine of Wabush Mines is the largest single supplier of iron ore to the Canadian steel industry, mining 17 million ltpy of crude ore averaging 35% Fe and 43% silica to produce high grade concentrates and pellets of 66% Fe.

Wabush Mines is an unincorporated joint venture of Dominion Foundries and Steel Ltd., The Steel Co. of Canada Ltd., and Wabush Iron Co. Ltd. Wabush Iron Co. Ltd. is in turn owned by six companies: The Lykes-Youngstown Sheet and Tube Co., Inland Steel Co., Interlake Inc., Wheeling-Pittsburgh Steel Co., Finsider of Italy, and Pickands Mather & Co. Pickands Mather manages the project.

Ores from the Scully mine are quartz-specularite-magnetite schists. Reserves are modestly estimated at 400 million tons of concentrate by the company—compared with the 3 billion tons of crude ore projected by the Geological Survey of Canada. The mine is located about 30 mi west of Mile 224 on the Quebec North Shore and Labrador Railway, the principal transportation artery of the Labrador Trough, operated by the Iron Ore Co. of Canada.

The Scully mine, 2 mi from the town of Wabush, covers 5½ sq mi. Open-pit methods remove a very small amount of overburden, followed by the development of 40-ft benches. Four electric Bucyrus-Erie 60-Rs drill 12¼- and 9⅞-in.-dia blastholes in a single pass. Explosives are 85% ANFO, with the remainder aluminized ANFO for bottom loading. Slurry is used occasionally for bottom loading if required. It is routine to blast 250,000 to 350,000 lt per firing.

Loading at Scully is accomplished with seven 190-B Bucyrus-Erie 8-cu-yd electric shovels for ore and overburden. Some 17 million ltpy of ore is hauled by 14 diesel-electric trucks—one M100 Lectra Haul, nine Sicard 100-ton KW Darts, and four Terex 33-15 150-tonners. A variety of other equipment, including front-end loaders, dozers, and small trucks, is available for development and clean-up work.

Electric power is supplied from Twin Falls, a captive hydroelectric installation of approximately 300 Mw, constructed in association with other users.

Residential services for the Scully mine are provided by the town of Wabush and nearby Labrador City.

Concentrate is railed from the mine site at Wabush to the pellet plant at Pointe Noire, 200 mi to the south, on the north shore of the St. Lawrence. Company-owned rolling stock travels over tracks of three separate railways. Unit trains of 120 90-ton cars are handled by five Wabush Lake Railway locomotives from the mine to Ross Bay Junction. At Ross Bay, Q.N.S.&L. locomotives take over to deliver to the junction with Arnaud Railway near Sept-Iles, 24 rail miles from the pellet plant. Six Arnaud Railway locomotives owned by Wabush Mines complete the haulage to the concentrate bins, where the cars are bottom dumped automatically while the train travels over the bins at 2.5 mph.

Pointe Noire—main outlet for Scully production

Located on the north shore of the St. Lawrence, 18 mi west of Sept-Iles, Pointe Noire is the principal outlet for Scully mine production, in the form of pellets.

Scully mine concentrate is dry ground in nine ball mills: seven 13½ x 28 ft (3,000 hp), one 14½ x 33 ft (5,000 hp), and one 14½ x 34 ft (5,000 hp). The product, 63% minus 325 mesh, is balled following additions of bentonite and water in pug mills. Of the 18 balling drums, 15 are 10 x 31½ ft and three are 10 x 28 ft.

Induration is carried out on three lines using a 38-windbox Dravo-Lurgi grate system, 10 x 310 ft, having two drying, one preheating, and one firing stage. Induration temperature is 2,450°F, with cooling to 300°F, followed by screening to eliminate fines. Pellets are either stockpiled or shipped directly. Ground storage capacity is 2.5 million lt.

Pellets are loaded into vessels from a 1,600-ft-long dock, using two shiploaders rated at 4,000 ltph each. During 1973 some 6 million lt of pellets were handled by Pointe Noire. □

Caland

Now the largest iron ore operation in Ontario, Caland Ore Company Ltd., an Inland Steel Co. subsidiary, can surely claim its share of credits for opening the western portion of the province to mineral development.

Under a lease and royalty agreement with Steep Rock Iron Mines Ltd., Caland not only participated in one of the world's greatest pre-production mine stripping programs in history, but also dredged more mud than Steep Rock Iron to develop its reserves under the Steep Rock Lake system. Of the 283 million cu yd of material moved by the two companies, Caland dredged close to 162 million cu yd for disposal in the Marmion Lake system.

Shipping its first brown and red natural ore in 1960, Caland added further to its laurels in 1965. In that year, along with the Pioneer plant of Cleveland-Cliffs Iron Mining Co., Caland became one of the first two North American operations to process and pelletize natural iron ores.

The Caland ore zones are in a faulted segment of the Steep Rock Iron Range, offset about 3 mi by the Samuels fault from mines operated by Steep Rock Iron Mines on the western side of the range. Caland took an option on the area in 1949 and in 1953 signed a 99-year lease with Steep Rock Iron to develop and mine the ore under the Falls Bay portion of the Steep Rock Lake.

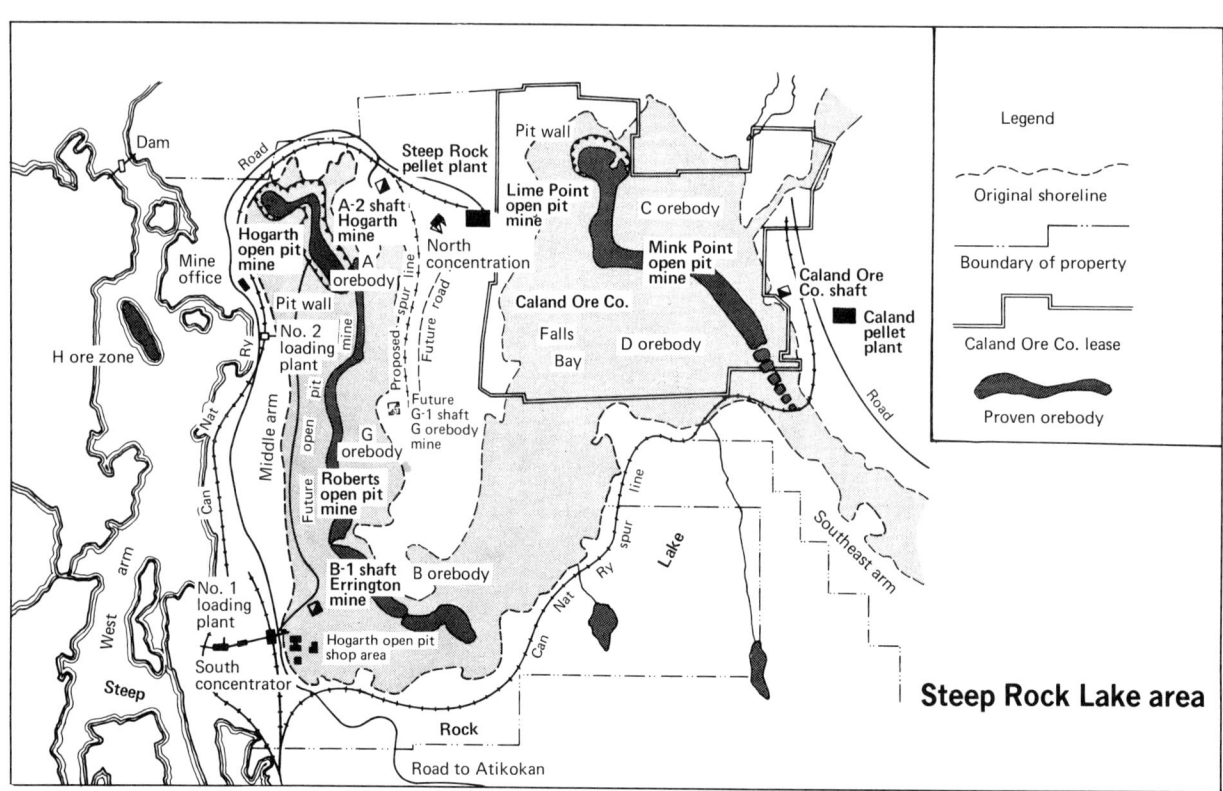

Steep Rock Lake area

In the seven-year period after the lease was signed, a series of massive civil engineering projects evolved. Construction Aggregates Corp. of Chicago (earlier employed on a similar program by Steep Rock Iron) won a contract from Caland for the removal of the estimated 160 million cu yd of silt underlying the lake, which was more than 100 ft deep in places. CAC assembled two 36-in. suction dredges at the site, along with pipelines, booster stations, and other shore facilities. Pumping started in 1955 and was completed at the end of September 1960, when 162 million cu yd of lake bottom material had been dredged.

Simultaneously with dredging, water control facilities were constructed to divert and pump run-off water from a 25-sq-mi drainage area surrounding the mine site. Engineering studies indicated that 60% of the run-off could be diverted to other watersheds by construction of dams and diversion tunnels. In the South East Arm area of the original Steep Rock Lake, run-off from an 11-sq-mi area was diverted into the Atikokan River watershed by construction of the Hardy Dam and three diversion tunnels. At the mouth of the South East Arm of Steep Rock Lake, the Fairweather Dam was constructed to impound run-off from an additional 3 sq mi. Both dams are earth-filled structures built on silt and clay foundations provided by the original lake bottom.

To the north of the mine site, the Grossman Dam was constructed to provide control over the amount of recharge water returned from Marmion Lake to the dredge pool. With completion of dredging, this dam now impounds run-off water from the North and South Twin Lakes catchment areas and diverts it northward to Marmion Lake.

In 1960, a complex pumping system was installed to handle run-off water from a 10-sq-mi drainage area where gravity drainage was not practical. This system, designed to handle the worst flood conditions that could be expected in a 20-year period, consists of five separate pumping locations with a total pumping capacity of 26,700 gpm. In all, 23 dams were constructed around the perimeter of the original lake.

To handle ore transportation from the pit, a three-flight conveyor system, 36 in. wide and over 5,000 ft long, was installed to serve the Lime Point mine—the first to go into production. This 5,000-ft system provided a lift of 480 ft and terminated at rail loading facilities. The lower end of the system was relocated in the winter of 1963-64 to bring it closer to actual mining operations. The revised system contains four flights, totaling 5,000 ft in length, with a lift of 680 ft.

The Falls Point shaft, an eight-compartment vertical opening sunk to 1,330 ft in footwall granite, was completed in 1958. Equipped with three friction hoists (two skip units and one cage hoist), this shaft system supported over 6,000 ft of lateral underground mine development. Although underground operations were deferred indefinitely in 1961, the shaft and skipways were used as part of a unique transportation system for handling surface ore from mines on the southeastern end of the holdings.

Open-pit mining began in 1959 in the Lime Point area at the north end. Since 1961, all Caland production has originated from open pits, and in 1971 the underground facilities were permanently abandoned.

The next chapter in Caland's history opened in 1962, when Inland researchers began examining the possibility of pelletizing its natural ores. Research culminated in 1965 with the opening of an ore improvement plant and a pelletizing installation. The ore improvement plant was designed to crush, dry, and screen 2.5 million ltpy of wet crude ore, producing 1.25 million tpy of lump-sized minus 2 in., plus 3/16-in. The minus 3/16-in. fines from this plant are ground, balled, and then indurated in a 1 million ltpy Dravo traveling grate.

The Caland ore structure is similar to that of Steep Rock Iron Mines, steeply tilted, and bounded on the footwall with paint rock (probably a weathered residual), up to 400 ft thick. The hangingwall consists of ash rock. With the possible exception of Lime Point, the ore zones are continuous and up to 480 ft wide.

The ore zones are mineralized with goethite and hematite in a ratio of about 5:1. They contain minor amounts of limonite, along with quartz and chert gangue. The goethite varies from hard, very fine grained, metallic bluish lump, to hard fragments less than 1-in.-dia within a matrix of earthy red hematite and brown goethite. The hematite is erratic in occurrence. The crude ore averages about 54% iron in its natural state and about 58.5% on a dry basis.

The Caland mines are nearing the economic limits for open pitting within the framework of the existing mine designs. It should be pointed out that these ores carry the twin burdens of the Ontario mining tax and a royalty payable to Steep Rock Iron. Nevertheless, more recent evaluation of the Caland ore position indicates promise of continuing operations past the originally announced deadlines for ceasing mining at the end of 1976 and pelletizing in 1978. There is a substantial tonnage remaining because these ores have not been bottomed.

The Caland excavator fleet consists of two Bucyrus Erie 150-B 6-yd machines and two P&H shovels—a 4½-yd model 1400 and a 6-yd model 1600. The haulers are nine Terex R-65s and three Wabco 75-ton Haulpaks. Three small Euclids (45 tons) are available for working around the plant stockpiles and for other miscellaneous duty. Two Bucyrus Erie 40-R rotaries and a Chicago Pneumatic 750C handle drilling.

This fleet is supplemented by two Cat D-8s, a Cat D-9, and two Cat 824s. A Hough H400B modified with an 8-yd bucket is used for cleanup at the pit. Two others are used at the plant. A Wabco 777 grader is employed on road maintenance. Roadways are designed for 80-ft widths on maximum grades of 10% for ore. Some waste hauls include sections up to 12%. Caland blasts dry holes with prilled ammonium nitrate loaded pneumatically from a truck. Wet holes are lined with plastic sleeves and shot with low energy slurries.

While Caland's primary function is to produce iron units, it handles as much water as ore and waste combined. Each year it pumps 2 billion to 3 billion gal of water from its pits—equivalent to 8 to 12.5 million tons. Water in the mine sumps is collected by barge-mounted pumps for delivery into a pumping system that empties it behind the Grossman Dam area. Working against an approximate head of 800 ft, the total installed capacity at the main and booster pumping stations is 15,000 gpm.

The natural ores, while softer, are more difficult to handle in some ways than the magnetic taconites. They are often wet and sticky, tending to plug at feed and transfer points. Early in the testing program, it was determined that wet grinding of the ore would produce excessive sliming. This factor accounts for the selection of dry screening and the center peripheral discharge, dry rod mills in the pellet plant. □

Aguas Claras: programmed growth to 25 million tons of ore

MINERACOES BRASILEIRAS REUNIDAS SA, now Brazil's second-ranking iron ore producer, anticipates reaching its planned 12-million-mtpy operating rate at Aguas Claras this year, after a restricted start caused by transportation difficulties.

Aguas Claras is located near the southern outskirts of Belo Horizonte. MBR has sunk $200 million into developing and equipping the mine and establishing a superport at Sepetiba Bay, some 602 railroad km south of the mine. Most of the output from these installations is committed under long term delivery contracts.

The MBR projects directly benefited from a $130 million program by the Brazilian government's Rede Ferroviaria Federal SA (RFFSA), for upgrading the Central Division rail line. Key elements of this vital support system included acquisition of new rolling stock, construction of sidings, and installation of two spur lines—one at the mine (22 km) and the other a 35-km shortcut around congested Rio de Janeiro.

MBR controls about 1.6 billion mt of ore reserves containing more than 64% iron at Aguas Claras and other mines in the Iron Ore Quadrangle—the most important of which are Matuca and Pico de Itabirito. Aguas Claras, however, is the launching pad that will put MBR into orbit. This new producer is designed for staged expansion, first to 15 million mtpy and then to 25 million mtpy. These levels are theoretically attainable within the next two years and the next seven years, respectively, assuming the market would support such an output.

Concurrently, MBR is studying the possibility of stepping up production at Matuca and Pico to 5 million mtpy each, and has run feasibility studies on a pelletizing plant of 3 million mtpy sited at the mine or port. Thus, there is a 30- to 35-million-mtpy future in MBR's view.

The Aguas Claras operation is based on a highly efficient open pit, requiring only minimal stripping, and a finely tuned crushing, sizing, and washing plant that splits out four products (see table and flowsheet). The plant, located on benched and filled slopes of the steep southeastern side of the Serra do Curral, is designed along clean, functional lines that funnel down to a set of four closely bunched, parallel product conveyors, which roughly follow an original slope contour.

These outhaul conveyors serve the stockpiles, which are grouped in line. Three stockpiles are built by individual radially slewing stackers. The fourth pile, for sinter feed, which constitutes about half the product tonnage, is bedded by a traveling stacker. Total product storage of 224,000 mt at the mine is limited to about a one-week production run because of topographical reasons. Even so, about 5 million cu yd of material was handled to site the plant and supporting facilities.

The size distribution of stockpiles at the mine is roughly as follows: 120,000 mt for sinter feed; 29,000 mt for coarse ore; 44,000 mt for natural pellets (peletore); and 31,000 mt for pellet feed (minus 100-mesh fines).

Strengthening a creaky roadbed

Aguas Claras got off to a flying start in July 1973 when the first rail carloads were dispatched to Sepetiba Bay. The port terminal, about 120 km west of Rio de Janeiro, was completed in November 1973. Late in the same month, the

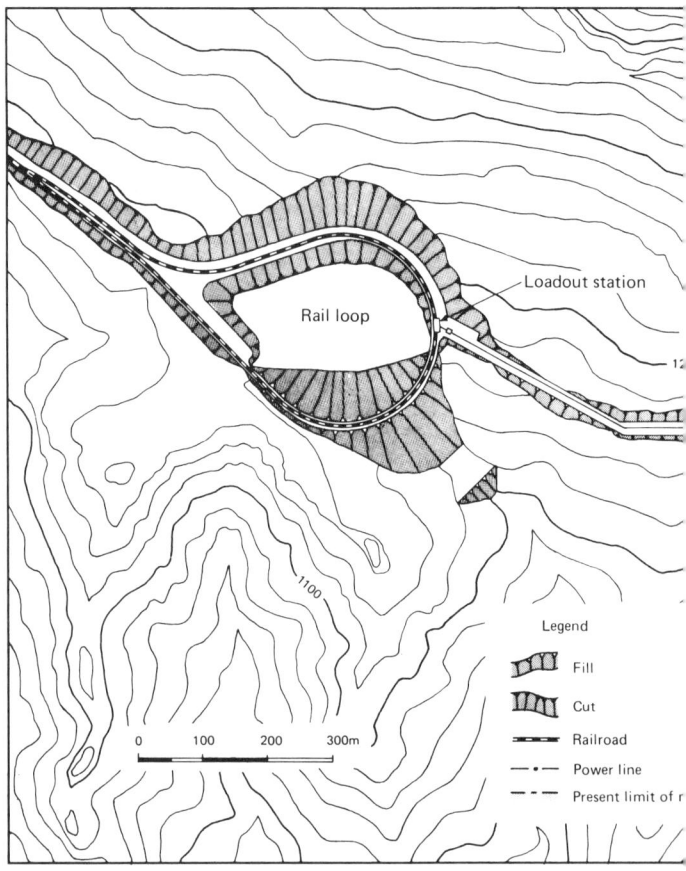

155,000-DWT *Honshun Maru* sailed for Japan with the first iron ore cargo produced by the project. The entire program had been completed on time and under budget. For the next year or so, however, operations were bottlenecked by a railroad bridge failure, and car loadings were limited by tonnage and by length of trains.

MBR had signed a long term contract with RFFSA to ship iron ore over the Central line in unit trains of up to 12,000 mt. This tonnage represented a 100% increase in the amount previously handled by the line. When the magnitude of the rail difficulties became apparent, RFFSA went

Major mining equipment at MBR

2	Bucyrus Erie 45R drills, 9⅞-in. holes
3	CP in-hole drills, 6½-in. holes
3	Atlas Copco wagondrills, 3½-in. holes
2	P&H 1900 shovels, 8 cu yd
3	P&H 1600 shovels, 6 cu yd
12	Lectrahaul M-100 trucks, 100 tons
15	Caterpillar trucks, 50 tons
3	Caterpillar 824 bulldozers
2	Caterpillar D-9 bulldozers
1	Komatsu 155A bulldozer
2	Komatsu 85A bulldozers
2	Caterpillar 992 front end loaders, 8 cu yd
1	Allis-Chalmers 645 front end loader
1	Wabco grader
3	Caterpillar 12E graders
1	P&H crane, 50 tons
1	Grove crane, 15 tons
2	Water trucks, 4,160 gal

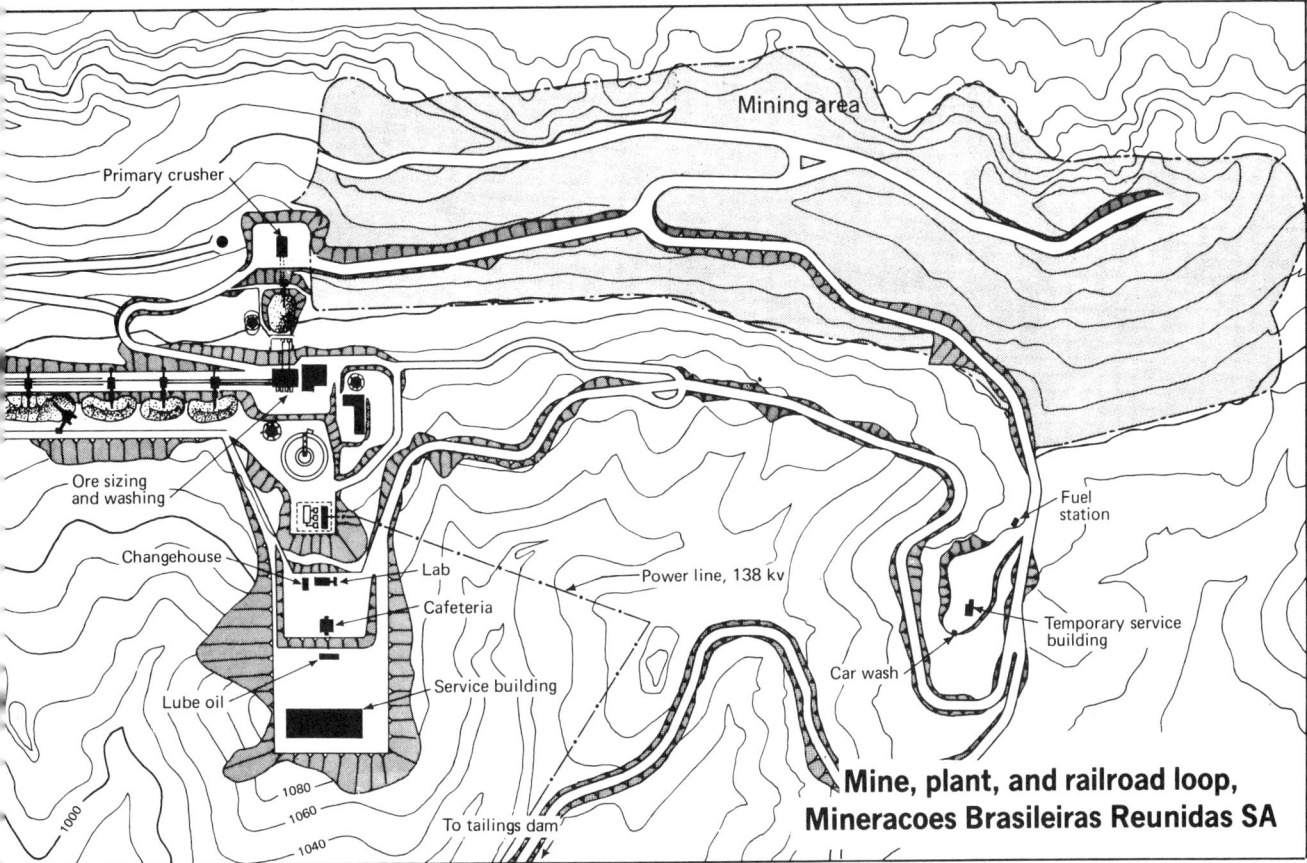

Mine, plant, and railroad loop, Mineracoes Brasileiras Reunidas SA

into action.

Through November 1974, 18 bridges were replaced or strengthened along the broad-gauge, 1.6-m Central line. Other improvements consisted of widening tunnels, increasing the length of sidings, reinforcing the roadbed, and upgrading the communications network. These steps were in addition to the original purchase of 80 locomotives and 1,340 ore cars and the construction of the spur lines at the mine and the Rio bypass. Since then further rolling stock has been ordered.

As a result, capacity car loadings have resumed, allowing MBR to gradually build stockpiles at Sepetiba Bay so that loading of large ore carriers can be handled more efficiently. At the end of June 1975, stockpiles at the port terminal exceeded 1.1 million mt, and rail shipments were pushing the 1.1-million-mtpm level, signaling the end of a difficult period. During 1974, MBR was only able to ship about 5.9 million mt originating from Aguas Claras.

Learning to live with high grade

Aguas Claras is one of the largest deposits controlled by MBR. It has eye-popping mineable open-pit reserves: 378 million mt of hematite ore with a dry grade of 68% iron, 0.051% phosphorus, 0.52% SiO_2, and 0.92% Al_2O_3. The ore, typical of the Iron Ore Quadrangle, is in a superficially enriched cap of the host itabirite. The orebody strikes northeast and dips to the southeast at 30° to 60°. In thickness, it ranges from 600 to 1,100 ft.

The deposit is well known, and development was more a matter of working out the geometry of the orebody rather than the geology. MBR is starting to probe the underlying itabirite to determine the extent and grade of this resource. For planning purposes, reserves have been grouped into 30,000 blocks of 50 x 50 x 13 m for establishment of benches and shovel positions for the various ore types—hard, soft, and mixed.

Designed for a 12-million-mtpy level, operations are geared for a two-shift, six-day week at the mine, and a three-shift, six-day work week at the plant. The mine is developed in 13-m benches with a stripping ratio of 0.21 cu m to 0.23 cu m per mt of ore. Putting the pit into production required removal of 3.1 million cu m of waste. Waste removal was designed to pioneer the roads and mining faces supporting a full scale production effort.

The mining fleet is listed in an accompanying table. The benches are shaped by blasting vertical holes 9⅞ in. in diameter, drilled with a pair of Bucyrus Erie 45-Rs, or 6½-in. holes drilled with three CP units. The patterns are variable, depending on hole size and ore type. Both ANFO and slurries have been used to shoot the holes, but most of the blasting is now concentrated on Du Pont-supplied ANFO augered to the hole from a truck.

Sizing products from crude ROM

The present haul from the mine is downhill on a 1-km minus 8% grade to the primary crusher. The 60 x 89-in. Allis-Chalmers gyratory (built by Kobe Steel) was deliberately oversized so that it could accept a 25-million-mtpy production rate—a long-run economy move. The relatively small increase in purchase cost for the larger unit will more than offset the expense of duplicating a smaller installation or adding capacity at a later time. The primary crusher provides two dumping positions for the 100-ton trucks in the present arrangement. The crusher can handle feed at a rate of 4,500 mtph or more, and it is now used with an open side setting of 8 in.

The plant was built by Bechtel of Brazil (Bechtel do Brasil Construcoes Ltda.) to a design worked out jointly by

Bechtel and Hanna Mining Co. Bechtel managed engineering, construction, and procurement.

Process water is recovered from the 75-m-dia tailing thickener overflow. Flocculant is added to the tailing thickener to produce a clear overflow; the underflow is pumped to a dammed tailing basin. The plant makes a 92% recovery of products from the feed, and personnel are now aiming for a 96% recovery.

Unit trains loaded on the move

Four stackers receive the sized products of the plant on separate 30-in. conveyor lines so that all sized ore can be deposited simultaneously in a linear arrangement of product piles. The layout will allow for future expansion. The one-week storage capacity of products destined for shipment is considered the minimum necessary for coordinating the mine, railroad, and marine terminal. A single Demag crawler-mounted bucket wheel (built by Hitachi of Japan) services all the product piles.

This unit reclaims ore at a capacity of 4,000 mtph, discharging feed from its tail conveyor to a traveling hopper over a 54-in. feeder belt. The feeder belt loads a 920-m, 54-in. conveyor line that terminates at an 800-mt surge bin at the loadout center on the mine track loop.

The surge hopper is drawn down by a 72-in. apron feeder, which empties the product to a 60-in. loadout belt equipped with an electronic weigh-scale. A short shuttle conveyor fed from the weighing belt deposits ore in cars. An empty train moves continuously at 400 m per hr under the system. The weigh-scale records the weight and sounds a shutdown alarm at a predetermined point. The official weight of the 95-mt-capacity cars is recorded on a track scale as the loaded train moves at 8.8 km per hr across the platform. The loadout system has a rated capacity of 4,000 mtph, although average train loading rates have been 3,000 mtph.

The MBR project at Aguas Claras was designed for unit trains of 100 or more 95-mt cars. During the period of transportation difficulties, the trains were coupled in 82- to 84-car units, and loading of the cars was reduced about 15%. The trains are powered by three to six General Electric diesel-electric locomotives of 2,500 hp, depending on the terrain and grades. The rolling stock inventory of 1,340 cars and 80 locomotives that RFFSA had initially acquired to provide service is scheduled for expansion by 250 new cars and another 40 locomotives.

Porto Sepetiba: the world's newest superport

The industrial installation for the port is situated on a

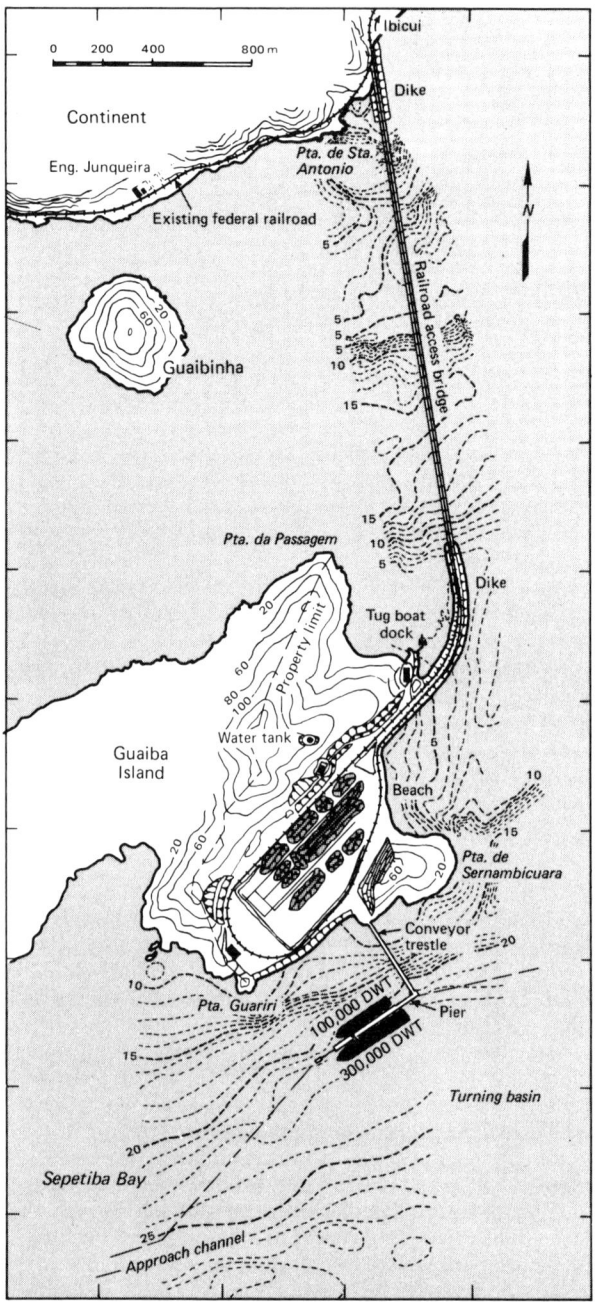

Background: how MBR is structured

Mineracoes Brasileiras Reunidas SA is 51% owned by the Brazilian holding company Empreendimentos Brasileiros de Mineracao SA (EBM), which is controlled by Caemi (Cia. Auxiliar de Empresas de Mineracao SA). Caemi, with headquarters in Rio, is a diversified Brazilian holding company with interests in mining, steel, meat, food, paper, plywood, and real estate. A subsidiary company, Caemi Internacional SA Comercio e Representacoes, engages in international trading in many of the world's major cities.

The remaining 49% ownership of MBR is vested in St. John d'el Rey Mining Co. Ltd., a closed-end, nondiversified investment company with principal offices in Cleveland, Ohio. MBR is the major asset of St. John d'el Rey, which is two-thirds owned by The Hanna Mining Co., also of Cleveland, Ohio.

MBR's largest producer is the new Aguas Claras mine, which was developed mainly to serve the export market. MBR holds a contract, signed in 1970, to export 105 million mt of ore to a group of Japanese companies over a 16-year period extending to 1988. Annual shipments to Japan will reach a level of 7 million mtpy. The remaining Aguas Claras production is sold abroad to steel producers in Europe, the US, and South America, the bulk of it under long term contracts.

MBR also controls two other iron ore mining operations in the Iron Ore Quadrangle of Brazil: the Pico and Matuca mines. Combined, these two operations shipped about 2.4 million mt of ore in 1974—about half for the domestic Brazilian steel industry and half for export. The export tonnage of Pico and Matuca fell short of the target because of rail transport limitations.

Aguas Claras mine is developed on 13-m benches after an initial 3.1-million-cu-m stripping program exposed the ore.

Iron ore output of MBR is marshalled in stockpiles at Sepetiba Bay, where 250,000-DWT vessels can be loaded at 7,000 mtph.

backfilled portion of Guaiba Island, masked from view of the mainland by natural island topography. Unit trains cross a 1,705-m trestle over salt water to reach the island. The trestle is supported on 31-m-long steel spans held by concrete-capped tubular steel piling. The stockpiles are located in an area of about 300,000 sq m, of which two-thirds was reclaimed from the sea during dredging of an offshore channel for inbound ore carriers. In all, about 2.5 million cu m of hydraulic fill was deposited from the 9-million-cu-m dredging project.

On the seaward side of Guaiba, a 390-m conveyor bridge ends at a doglegged pier where carriers up to 300,000 DWT can tie up. Smaller 120,000-DWT vessels can be loaded from the in-shore side of the pier.

Trains arriving at the port are uncoupled from the locomotives at the terminal, and coupled cars are then pushed through a single-barrel rotary dumper by a mechanical Barney system, one car at a time. When it is time to expand capacity, a second car dumper will be added in-line with the first, and the locking arms and cable arrangement of the car positioner will be modified to haul two cars at a time through the dumpers. The unloading rate is 4,000 mtph into a track hopper system served by pan feeders and a collector conveyor system. Storage capacity on the island is 1.7 million mt of ore and readily expandable.

MBR product specifications

Product	Size	Specification
Coarse	½ x 2 in.	Maximum 10% minus ½ in.
Natural pellet	¼ x 1 in.	Maximum 10% minus ¼ in.
Sinter feed	100 mesh x ¼ in.	Maximum 20% minus 100 mesh
Pellet feed	Minus 100 mesh	Approximately 70% minus 325 mesh

The stockpiles are built within the railroad turn-around loop. The 4,000-mtph collector conveyor system originating at the track hopper feeds a pair of bucket wheel stacker-reclaimers. These machines can reclaim stockpiled ore at 7,000 mtph. Output is delivered to a system of reversible belts that transfer ore to a 7,000-mtph conveyor leading to the shiploader. The ore is automatically sampled and weighed en route. Alternatively, the 4,000-mtph collector system at the track hopper can deliver ore directly to the 7,000-mtph belt system serving the shiploader. In this event, a bucket wheel reclaimer can be used to bring the shiploader up to capacity.

The shiploader, a slewing-boom type, has a travel distance of 250 m on the pier—a 450 x 22-m concrete structure mounted on tubular piling.

MBR's Sepetiba Bay terminal is also equipped with a pair of rail-mounted sizer-reclaimers. These units are self-fed mobile screening plants, each with a 1,000-mtph capacity. They are equipped to reclaim coarse (2 x ½) and natural pellet ore (1 x ¼) from stockpiles and resize these products prior to shiploading—eliminating fines generated during material handling at the mine and port. These unusually versatile machines not only help ensure quality control of the products, but they can also stockpile ore.

The access channel to the pier is 15 km wide and was dredged to a minimum depth of 22.5 m to permit passage by 250,000-DWT ore carriers. For the expansion program, additional dredging will deepen the channel to about 26 m and the sand will be used to enlarge the terminal.

Scheduled additions for the expansion include the second car dumper, duplication of the belt conveyor system, and enlargement of the stockpile area to store up to 5 million mt of ore. In addition, another shiploader and a new stacker-reclaimer will be installed.

Aguas Claras, Brazil's newest iron ore producer, is equipped with fine facilities that provide a solid base for future growth □

Samarco: major new materials handling concepts for iron ore

SAMARCO MINERACAO SA IS LAUNCHING what is easily the most imaginative iron ore project in Brazil—a $400 million program to develop a mine and concentrator in the Minas Gerais Iron Ore Quadrangle and a 5-million-mtpy pelletizer and port at Ponta Ubu in Espirito Santo State. Linking these facilities will be the world's largest slurry line. The 508-mm buried pipeline will initially deliver 7 million mtpy of finely ground concentrate recovered from 10 million mtpy of ore by cationic flotation.

Samarco is now owned 51% by SA Mineracao da Trindade (Samitri), Brazil's third largest iron ore producer, and 49% by Marcona International SA, a unit of US-based Marcona Corp.*

Scheduled for first production in April 1977, the boldly conceived Samarco project is unusual in many respects and will pioneer a number of Brazilian and world "firsts."

The mine, for example, will be designed around a conveyor collection system. Plans call for using shiftable conveyor belts on each of two 8-m benches. Paralleling the mining face, which will be driven from the hangingwall to the footwall, the bench conveyors will be fed from portable hoppers containing an integral tail conveyor. Soft itabirite and hematite will be dug by front-end loaders, assisted as necessary by bulldozers and rippers in tougher digging material. The loaders will then shuttle the ore to a pair of portable hoppers on each bench. As the upper bench reaches the mining limit, the equipment line will be leapfrogged over the second bench to start work on the third level.

The crude ROM will be delivered downhill over a 600-m-long regenerative conveyor to the concentrator. While such a system may seem revolutionary, the conditions of the Germano orebody are ideal for a radical development plan. This mining routine will greatly whittle down the size of the earthmover fleet needed for a more conventional development pattern. With 6.4-cu-m machines, Samarco planners point out that the output can be handled by only eight loader shifts per day—two loaders working two shifts per day on each bench, with a fifth standby machine. Stripping and waste removal needs at Germano are minimal since the waste-to-ore ratio is only 0.16:1. While some of the thin canga and laterite over the orebody might have to be shot, the minor tonnages involved, along with the small waste inclusions in the ore, can be easily be moved to dumps by a fleet of four 32-mt trucks.

---

*Since nationalization of its Peruvian iron mining assets (a major source of income), Marcona Corp. has been negotiating a possible sale of its interest in the Samarco project.

Mining schedule for Samarco ore

Item	Initial	Optimum	Future
Annual dry conc. production (000 mt)	7,000	8,000	12,000
Required annual dry ore production (000 mt)	10,000	11,429	17,143
Mine operating schedule (days)	360	360	360
Operating days per week	7	7	7
Operating shifts per week	14	14	20
Operating shifts per year	720	720	1,028
Effective operating hours per shift	6.67	6.67	6.67
Effective operating hours per year	4,802	4,802	6,857
Deduction for shifting mine conveyor (hours)	—132	—132	—192
Effective operating hours per year (net)	4,670	4,670	6,665
Mined ore to stockpile			
Dry mtph (100% availability)	2,181	2,447	2,572
Wet mtph (8% moisture)	2,327	2,660	2,795
Estimated system availability (%)	90	90	85
Design throughout, collecting conveyors (wet mtph)	2,585	2,955	3,288

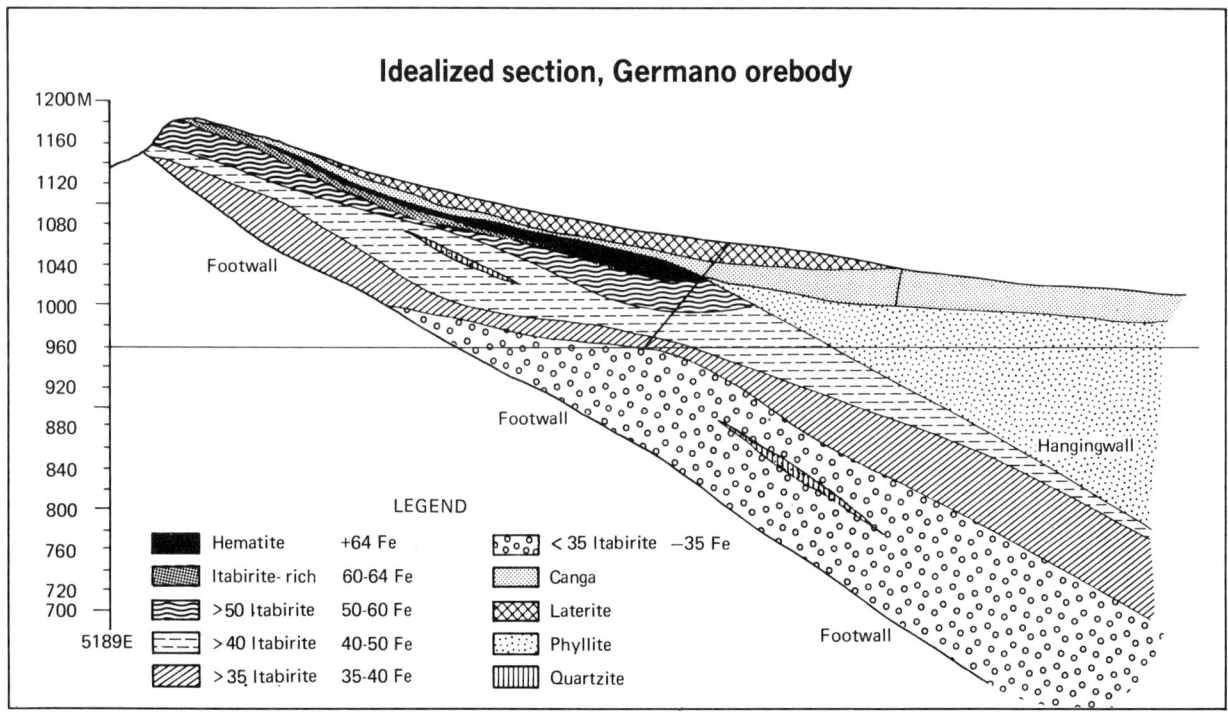

Germano mine and concentrator site

Samarco mining and crushing flowsheet

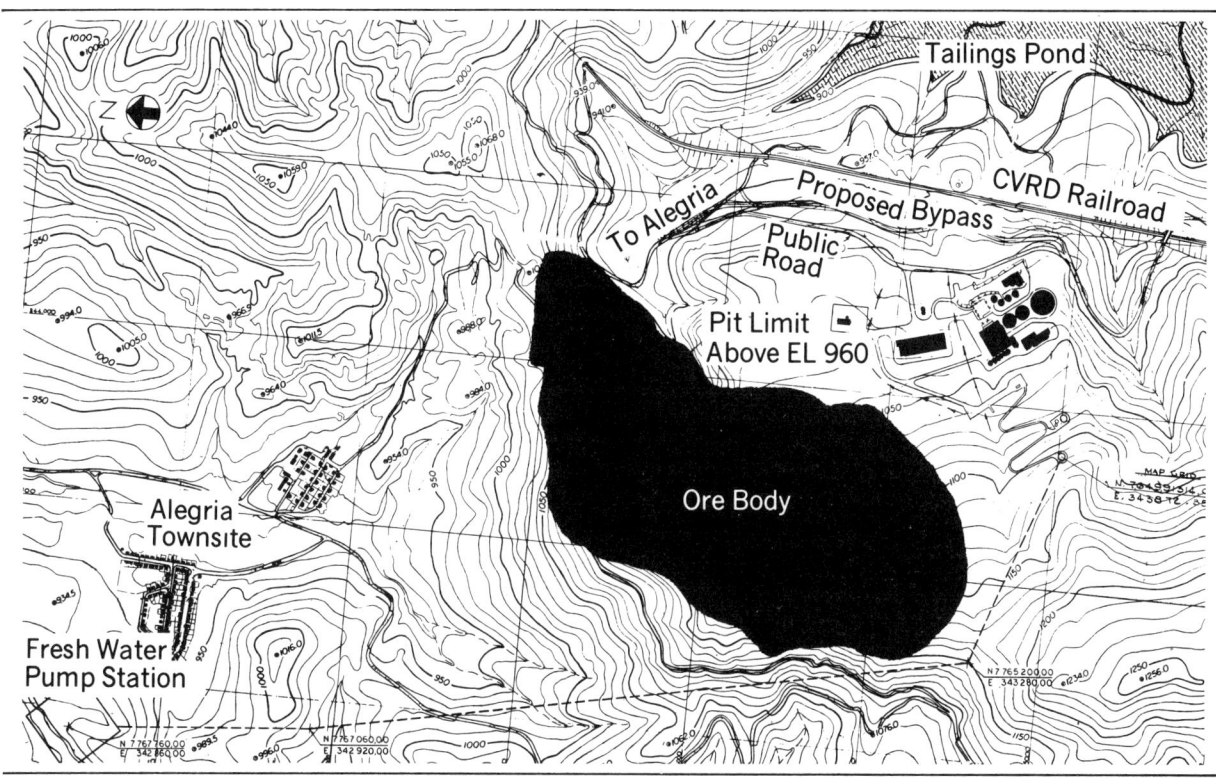

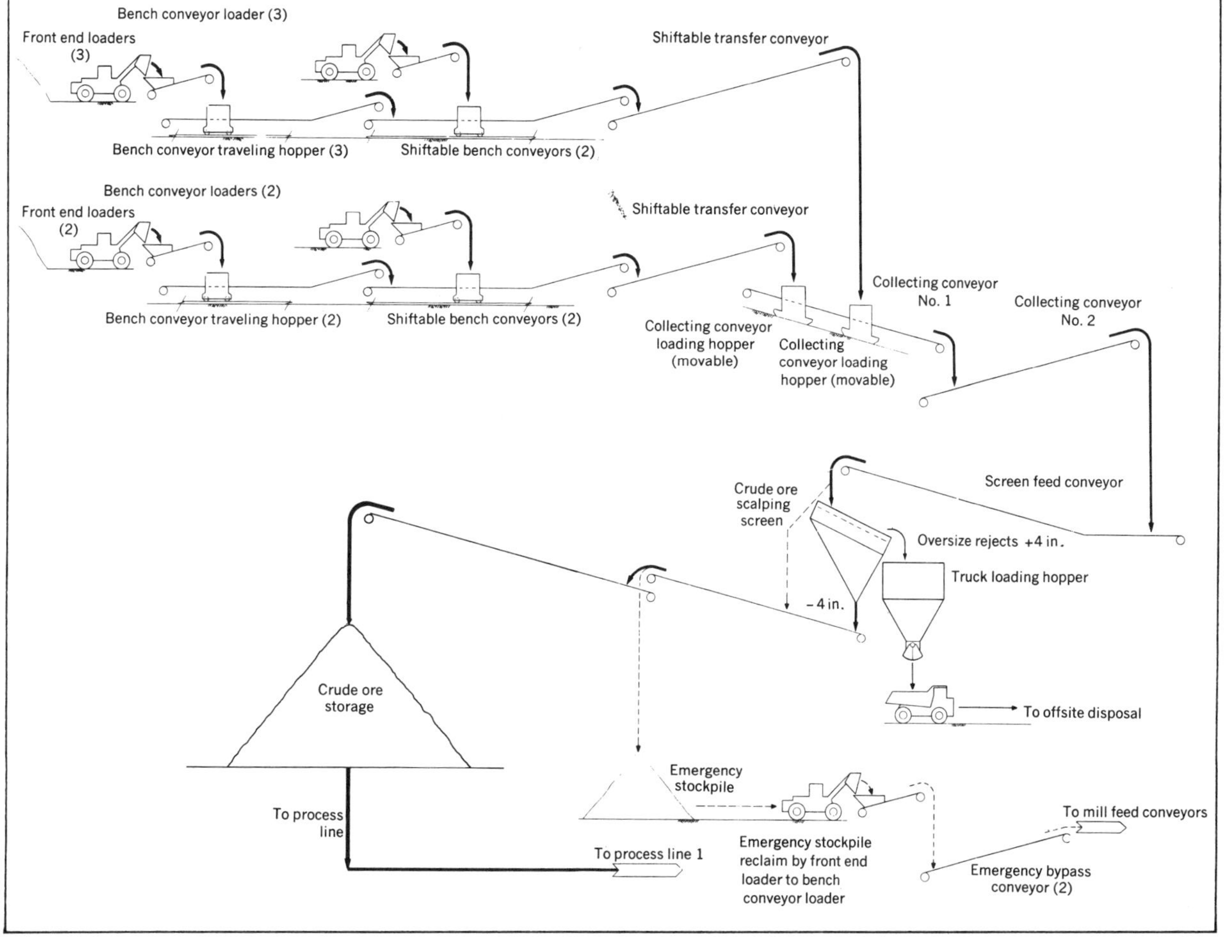

Germano ore a mix of hematite and itabirite

The Germano deposit is one of several orebodies in the Alegria complex. It is located about 5 km south of Samitri's Alegria mine, where current production of about 2.5 million mtpy is undergoing an expansion program. The Germano deposit is typical of the Iron Ore Quadrangle—superficially enriched hematite derived from the host itabirite and capped by a thin layer of weathered laterite and canga.

The deposit outcrops for about 1,000 m along the gentle easterly slope of a north-south ridge. The formation, within presently defined ore reserve limits, has an average width of 600 m and a surface area of about 0.75 m. It dips 30° to the east at a somewhat greater angle than the gently sloping surface. The hangingwall consists of weathered phyllite and quartzite. The footwall is of the same material, but little weathered. Eastern mining limits under the thickening hangingwall are yet to be fully established. It is possible that the itabirite formation thickens to the east, but it will probably prove to be less enriched and lower in grade.

The northern mining limit is defined by a footwall outcrop, and to the south the ore is pinched out by a progressively greater hangingwall.

The deposit has been explored to the 960-m level by close-order drillholes and galleries to establish a 15-year mining reserve of open-pit ore of 150 million mt grading 52% iron. Iron-rich canga, somewhat higher in phosphorus, has not been included in the mining reserve. From this material, it is estimated that 125 million mt of 67.5% concentrates will be recovered. Below the 960 level, there is a potential 239 million mt of 39% iron, which is to be uprated to the category of known or inferred by fill-in drilling on a grid system. This potential, grading about 39% iron, could yield another 125 million mt of concentrates.

The iron formation has been intensely folded and faulted, then deeply weathered. Alteration has disintegrated and softened the ore, leaving the iron ore formation somewhat porous. Drilled on a 100 x 200-m grid, the cores provided the most complete data about the deposit.

General testing procedures included: 1) examination, geological description, and splitting of cores; 2) sampling and chemical analysis of half the cores in 9-m to 12-m intervals for iron, phosphorus, LOI, and insolubles; 3) compositing of metallurgical test samples from the remaining cores, using iron grade and hydration as guides (these composites cover the entire ore section of each drill hole); and 4) beneficiation tests on the composites, with iron analyses of feed and product by various screen sizes for overall weight recovery and concentrate grade.

How mining is reduced to a transportation system

The ore within the 15-year mining plan is friable, and no drilling or blasting is contemplated once the canga and other waste has been removed. Using front-end loaders to feed the conveyors in ore, each bench will be driven to the limits of the footwall. As the excavation advances beyond a reasonable working range of the front-end loaders, a face conveyor will be moved in the direction of the advance.

Two face conveyors will be used in series on each of the two benches. Production from both benches will be transported by transfer conveyors to a common collecting belt feeding a system terminating at the crude ore stockpile. As mining progresses down the orebody, the transfer conveyors will be relocated. A second collecting belt will be added in the fifth year of operation, and the first collecting conveyor will then be relocated.

A simulated mine plan was developed by Samarco to determine incremental variations in crude ore tonnage and grade resulting from utilization of the bench conveyor system for the production of 7 million mtpy. The estimate covered 15½ years, including initial production at 80% of rated capacity during the last half of 1976. From 1977 through 1986, the average crude is expected to be 54% iron, and during the last five years it will be 50% iron. It is expected that within a year or two, accumulated operating experience will make it possible to produce 8.0 million dry mtpy of concentrate from mine ROM.

Because the crude ROM stockpile at the plant is not intended to do any significant amount of blending, the proper mix of ore must be obtained directly from the mine benches. The mining system will have considerable flexibility for blending because of the mobility and working range of the front-end loaders and the ease with which they can be positioned. At all costs, however, the upper bench cannot be allowed to block the progress of the lower bench. Maximum use of downtime is essential to move the conveyors. To facilitate this operation, one of the four bench conveyors can be prepositioned in advance when starting a new bench.

In normal operation, it is expected that the ore will run freely from mining faces and will not overhang at the face. Bulldozer capacity must be adequate to keep material moving and to assure that loaders can work up to capacity. On a 50-sec cycle and 75% job efficiency, it is estimated that each loader will produce about 865 mtph. Thus, for the 2,585-mtph ROM requirement, four machines should be able to handle the necessary excavation.

The loaders will dump ore into the receiving hoppers of the face conveyors. These portable units will be equipped with 1,524-mm-wide belts rated at 1,000 mtph with a variable speed drive. Five of the face conveyors will be installed and towed by tractors to appropriate locations. A portable grizzly will be positioned under the hopper tail conveyor to protect the bench conveyor belt.

All canga and most overlying phyllite must be drilled and blasted. Laterite and some weathered capping can probably be ripped. A sixth front-end loader will be assigned full-time to stripping. It will load 32-mt trucks. Handling of inter-ore waste will add only 6-7% to the capacity requirements of the five ore loaders.

For expansion, all or part of the mining fleet can be worked on a third shift. Few capital additions will be required, except possibly in maintenance facilities. □

Chapter 9
Bauxite

Sangaredi pit in Guinea carves up a rich deposit of solid bauxite 336
Sangaredi—an African plateau of bauxite 339
Surinam: 62 years of bauxite development 347
Guybau and Bermine: Digging deep for ore 359
Jamaica: government partnership and recent declines shape industry's profile 362
Trombetas: major bauxite reserves in search of a future 374
Reynolds is Haiti's only bauxite producer 377
Alcoa's Dominican bauxite mine uses solar drying 378

Sangaredi pit in Guinea carves up a rich deposit of solid bauxite

Richard Hoppe, Senior editor

THE SANGAREDI OPEN-PIT BAUXITE MINE, in northwest Guinea, west Africa, is isolated from centers of commerce and supply but profits from a number of remarkable advantages. The deposit is a solid plateau of bauxite, a total of 180 million tons grading 59% alumina (Jamaican bauxite grades less than 50%), with no overburden on the surface and no waste inclusions. The configuration of the orebody permits single-level railroad haulage along a mile-wide face, with a slight downgrade haul to the switchyard. The mine, operated by Cie. des Bauxite de Guinee (CBG), a consortium of aluminum producers and the Guinean government, began shipping ore in August 1973. It is now producing more than 7 million mtpy and is slated for 9 million mtpy by 1980. Sangaredi is the largest single bauxite mine in the world.

From the mine, ore is transported by rail to the plant at Kamsar, 137 km to the southwest. Located on the estuary of the Rio Nunez, 17 km from the Atlantic, the Kamsar plant crushes bauxite to minus 6 in. and dries it to a 5% moisture content before shipping.

The bauxite is shared among the corporate members of the consortium. The Republic of Guinea is paid taxes on bauxite production and on profits. Sangaredi's development also benefited the surrounding countryside. More than $400 million was spent to develop the mine, the port and plant, the railroad, two fairly large towns, and the myriad support facilities.

Western Guinea is covered by Ordovician, Silurian, and Devonian sedimentary rocks that were intruded by doloritic sills during the Triassic period. The dolorites appear to be the source of the huge amounts of bauxite found in the Boke region—perhaps more than a billion tons in all. But the Sangaredi deposit shows no contact with the dolorites, and it probably resulted from sedimentary transport.

The top of the Sangaredi deposit, at elevation 245 m, about 30 m above the surrounding countryside, is flat. The surface is slightly pocked and is covered with age-old detritus, bauxite pebbles, and rocks ranging up to boulders a foot or more in diameter. The terrain resembles photographs of the surface of the moon.

Development of railroad mining at Sangaredi required excavation of a box-cut along the southern periphery of the orebody.

Sangaredi's eastern and southern slopes are steep, while the northern and western flanks slope gently to the surrounding countryside of low hills and plateau.

Single-level mining by railroad

Mining Sangaredi is analogous to eating a two-layered cake, one layer at a time. The bottom of the upper layer is at elevation 229 m, 40 m above the Sangaredi switchyard. To open up the initial face, a box-cut was drilled, blasted, and excavated across the southern perimeter of the orebody. Tight drilling and small fragmentation of the ore was required for the box-cut because it was excavated with front-end loaders and 10-ton trucks. Once completed, the cut was graded and a drainage ditch was opened to the southern slope. Single-line, standard-gauge track was laid from the switchyard up a ramp of filled and compacted bauxite to the face. Active mine track is set on bauxite ballast prepared at a stone crushing and screening plant near the mine entrance. Track ties are steel. Track sections are made in advance, loaded onto flat cars, and slung into place by a mobile crane. The initial track dead-ended at the eastern end of the pit. Once sufficient cuts were advanced northward, it was possible to form a looped track. The loop speeds train movement to and from the shovels and, in case of derailments at the face, it will allow cars to move to the switchyard from either side of the derailment while

Setup and operation of Ingersoll-Rand rotary drills is simplified by the flat mine surface, which is free of overburden.

Blasting at Sangaredi uses ANFO and a cast primer attached to detonating cord.

Sangaredi pit factsheet

Owned by: Cie. des Bauxites de Guinee (CBG), a Delaware company owned 49% by the Republic of Guinea and 51% by Halco Mining Inc. Halco is a consortium of aluminum producers Alcoa, Alcan Aluminum, Pechiney, VAW, Martin Marietta, and Alumetal.
Location: Northwest Guinea, west Africa.
Production: 7 million mtpy of bauxite averaging 59% Al_2O_3; no waste stripping before or during operations.
Startup: August 1973, after $400 million capital investment, including $100 million for Guinean infrastructure.

Major mining equipment

Drills (rotary): Four Ingersoll-Rand DM4s and one T4, with 6¼-in.-dia bits.
Shovels: Three P&H 1900 9-cu-yd electric, plus three Cat 988 rubber-tired, front-end loaders.
Haulage: Mainline locos—seven GM SD-40 diesel-electric (3,000 hp); mine tramming locos—four GM SW-1001 diesel-electric (1,000 hp); 400-plus open-gondola Gregg ore cars, each carrying 75 mt.
Ancillary equipment: Two Cat 14 graders, two Cat D8 and two D9 track dozers, Pioneer ballast plant, 60-ton rubber-tired lowboy, numerous P&H mobile cranes.

Inspection of fragmentation from a blast confirms that an increase in the ratio of spacing to burden results in better shots.

repairs are underway. Good ballasting, proper drainage, accurate gauge settings, proper alignment, and good control of car loading by the shovel operator eliminate the causes of 90% of all derailments.

Two shovels load 21 shifts a week, at the rate of 650,000 mtpm. A third shovel is always on standby. A 1,000-hp diesel-electric loco pulls 20 to 25 cars in front of each shovel. The loaded train, with each car carrying 75 mt of bauxite, is switched back to the yard for makeup into trains of 80 to 90 cars bound for Kamsar.

As the shovels progress across the face, which is 12 to 15 m high, make-up track is installed on the graded ground behind the shovels. The 18-m-long track panels are standard gauge, made of 60-kg-per-m rail and steel ties. When a cut is completed, the "new" track is connected to the permanent entrance track and the "old" track is ready for the next phase of trackbuilding — a leapfrogging of one track over another. New supplies of track are used only for replacement of damaged sections or for extensions as the face progresses farther north.

All ballast for mine track is made of crushed bauxite, nominally 2 in. x ¾ in., prepared in a special crushing and screening plant located alongside the mine entrance. The ballast plant is fed by 10-ton dump trucks, which are loaded by Cat 988s in special sections of the pit. The rubber-tired loaders are also used to load special trains of selected bauxite that is calcined at Kamsar and sold as abrasive grade material to customers around the world. Presently, Sangaredi mines 120,000 mtpy of this scarce commodity.

In drilling and blasting, 6¼-in.-dia holes are drilled in multiple, staggered rows on a pattern of 3 m burden, 7 m spacing. The maximum is five or six rows, with 35-ms delays between rows. All holes are drilled 1 or 2 m below grade and stemmed 1 m from the surface. Both wet holes and dry holes are filled with ANFO, mixed to a weight ratio of 94.5:5.5. A polyethylene sleeve is used to protect ANFO in wet holes. The holes are top-primed with a 5-lb cast primer. With bottom priming, it was found that detonating cord caused deflagration of ANFO in some cases. In general, excellent, low cost fragmentation is achieved, partly because spacing exceeds burden by at least a ratio of 2:1. Closer spacing used in the past produced numerous boulders because radial cracking between holes occurred before the burden movement took place. Opening up the spacing not only improved the fragmentation but also reduced the powder factor — for sound technological reasons. □

Sangaredi—an African plateau of bauxite

Within 100 mi of Guinea's Atlantic coast, the world's largest, richest bauxite mine is operated under the aegis of the government and a consortium of the world's major aluminum producers. The open pit is a single-level railroad operation set to produce 9 million mtpy by 1980.

Richard W. Hoppe, Senior editor

FROM THE AIR, the Sangaredi bauxite deposit resembles an artist's palette. The southern half bulges wider than the north, and the flat surface is covered with age-old bauxite detritus, from pebbles to small boulders. Soil cover over the rubble is nonexistent. Yet in the rainy season, pale-green grass grows high over the terra-cotta surface, except for the mining cuts to the south. When the dry season arrives, the grass is scorched brown.

The plateau of Sangaredi rises 100 ft above rolling hills covered by scrub brush, thorn trees, and grass. The plateau is solid bauxite, up to 100 ft thick and roughly a mile wide in all directions. In 1973, reserves were more than 180 million tons, sufficient for operations into the final decade of the century. When Sangaredi is exhausted, nearby deposits will take its place. The Boke region, in which the mine is located, is host to more than a billion tons of scattered bauxite.

Bauxite bolsters the economy of a new nation

Guinea, under the lead of its long-time President, Sekou Toure, was the first nation to opt out of the former territory of French West Africa. The nation declared itself a republic in 1958 and has since followed

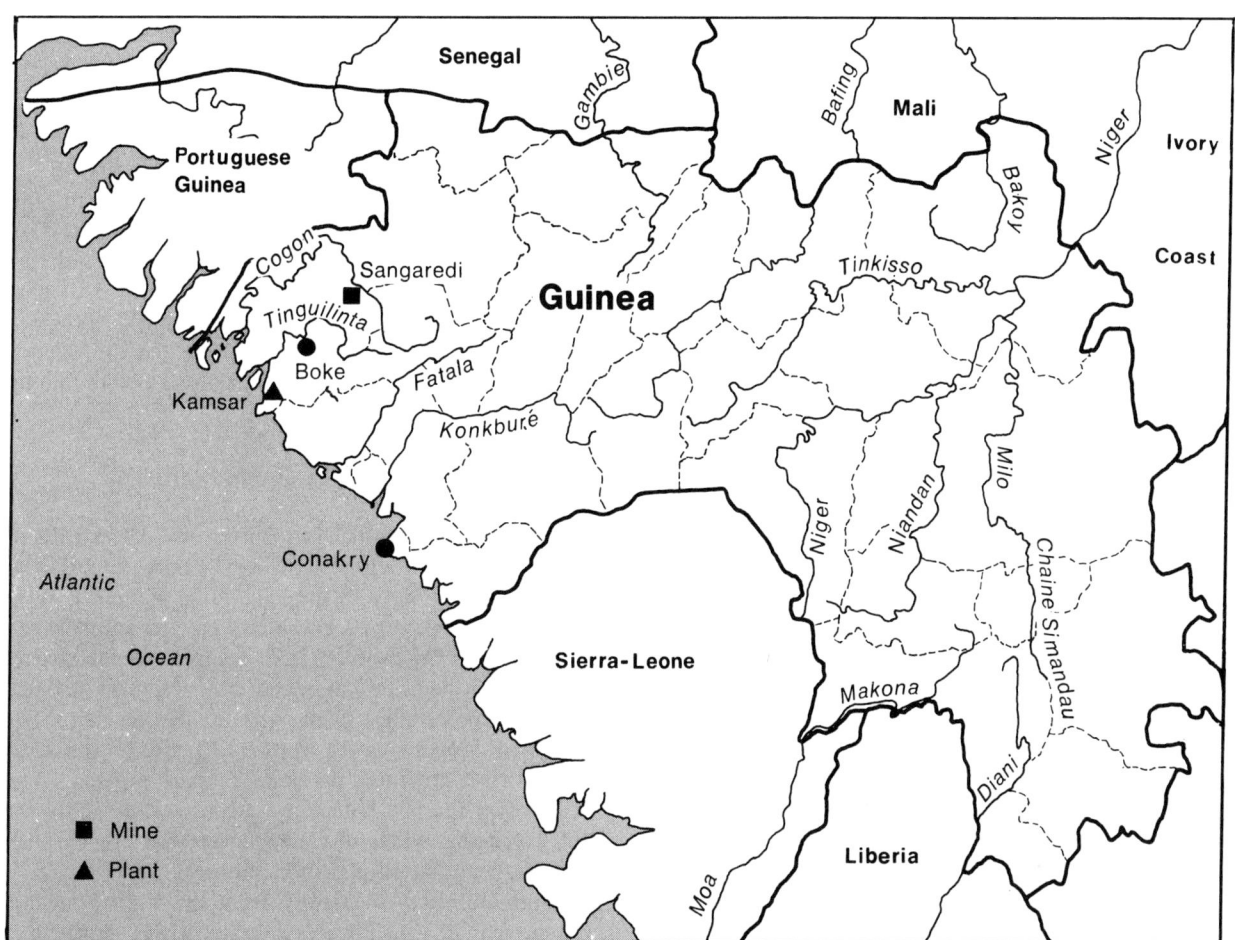

The single-level railroad mining operation started by opening a box cut at the southern end of the 100-ft-thick bauxite plateau.

its own brand of African socialism, largely ignoring the blandishments of both Soviet and Western politics. Guinea's pragmatism has attracted significant aid from the USSR, China, Cuba, and the Western world.

Guinea is located on the western bulge of Africa; its territory covers some 95,000 sq mi. Most of the 5 million inhabitants are still engaged in subsistence farming and animal husbandry. The nation has numerous tribes, each with distinctive cultures and languages. President Toure is attempting to bring cohesion to this polyglot society. Guinea's capital, the port city of Conakry, lies at the end of a peninsula that juts into the Atlantic and is reached by scheduled flights from several European and African cities.

Before the mine at Sangaredi opened in 1973, several relatively small bauxite pits operated in Guinea, on islands off the coast and in the interior. In addition to bauxite, Guinea has major iron ore reserves in the southeast, surrounding Mount Nimba, and some gold and diamonds are found in the country, but the main economic asset is the huge bauxite reserves.

The existence of bauxite in the Boke region has been known at least since the 1920s. At that time, a French subsidiary of Aluminum Co. of Canada was granted exploration rights for an area of 2,800 sq mi. Exploration appears to have been desultory until the 1950s. Drilling of the Sangaredi plateau began in January 1955 and was completed in 15 months. The drills cut chip samples on a 150- to 300-m grid covering the entire plateau. Drilling totaled 143 holes, to an average depth of 25 m, and the exploration team also dug two 12-ft-dia test pits.

The exploration work delineated more than 180 million mt of bauxite averaging 60% alumina (Al_2O_3). While some of the drillholes showed clay beneath the bauxite, a good percentage of the drillholes had stopped while still in bauxite. Clearly, the exploration program had hit on the largest, richest single bauxite deposit known in the world, but 17 years elapsed before mining began.

Sangaredi too big for a single company

After its successful find at Sangaredi, Alcan entered into a long term agreement for bauxite mining and alumina processing with the Federation of French West Africa. The company's subsidiary on the scene began construction of a railroad from Kamsar, at the coastal estuary, to a point 60 km inland, near the town of Boke, where a processing plant was to be located. The Sangaredi deposit lay a further 70 km to the east. Several river crossings, including a major five-span steel bridge over the Rio Nunez, were constructed before the anti-colonialist winds of change swept the French from Guinea, negating all plans for Sangaredi.

After Guinea's breakaway from the French colony, the agreement with Alcan's subsidiary was terminated.

The mainline track, 137 km from mine to plant, was welded in place. The 60-kg-per-m rail is supported by 1,700 sleepers per kilometer.

The new nation's leadership was determined that the country would own part of any future mining operation and a substantial portion of any supporting infrastructure, such as port and railroad facilities, as well as the major townsite. Alcan departed temporarily from the scene.

In 1963, negotiations for bauxite mining at Sangaredi were completed by the Guinean government and Halco Mining Co., at that time a wholly owned subsidiary of Harvey Aluminum Inc. As a result of the negotiations, Cie. des Bauxites de Guinee (CBG) was chartered in Delaware, owned 51% by Halco and 49% by the Republic of Guinea. The Guinean government then applied to the International Bank for Reconstruction and Development (better known as the World Bank) for a loan to capitalize the mining project's infrastructure—which the government would own outright.

Both the mining project and the supporting infrastructure were originally based on open-pit production of 1 million mtpy of bauxite. Even allowing for hindsight, this target was impractically low.

The World Bank allocated $1.7 million for technical studies related to the proposed infrastructure. The Agency for International Development (AID) also provided a $140,000 loan for Guinean franc expenses within that country. (Guinea's currency is used only within its borders.)

In 1965, President Toure established a public agency, Office d'Amenagement de Boke (OFAB), under the Minister of Economic Development. OFAB was charged with the planning, construction, and operation of the infrastructure of the mining project.

World Bank studies showed what should have been clear from the outset. A 1-million-mtpy mining rate was patently insufficient to pay back the huge capital investment needed; 6 million mtpy was a more realistic target. But this was more bauxite than Harvey could possibly use.

Harvey then approached several of the major aluminum producers, which had been waiting for some time for the other shoe to drop. The result of many meetings among the producers was a major reorganization of Halco, with final participation in the company distributed as follows:

Aluminum Co. of America (US)	27%
Alcan Aluminium Ltd. (Canada)	27%
Harvey Aluminum Inc.* (US)	20%
Cie. Pechiney and Ugine Kuhlmann (France)	10%
Vereinigte Aluminium Werke AG (Germany)	10%
Montecatini-Edison SPA (Italy)	6%

---

*Before production began at Sangaredi, a majority of the shares of Harvey Aluminum Inc. were sold to Martin-Marietta Corp., and Harvey was renamed Martin Marietta Aluminum.

A massive reinforced concrete structure 80 ft high houses the dual-car elevator system and feeders to the two hammermills.

Construction and operating data

Design hours: 1.1 million.
Construction hours: 33 million.
Employment during construction: 5,250 Guineans and 700 workers of other nationalities, including Americans, Belgians, British, Canadians, Dutchmen, Frenchmen, Italians, Pakistanis, and Yugoslavs.
Goods handled through Port Kamsar: 380,000 tons.
Equipment discharged at Port Kamsar: 36,000 tons.
Equipment erected: 29,000 tons.
Cement used: 115,000 cu m; 2 million concrete blocks were fabricated and 760 concrete piles built.
Volume dredged in river and on land: 4.8 million cu m.
Power installed: 30,000 kw.
Length of cable and piping: 650,000 m and 220,000 m, respectively.

Personnel for CBG: 1,900 Guineans and 175 others.
Production: 4 million dry metric tons per year of bauxite beginning in fiscal 1973, now 7.2 million, and rising to 9 million mtpy in 1980.
Transport (at 9 million mtpy): 250 to 300 ships per year and a railroad traffic density of six trains each day, 290 days per year.

The 20-year agreement calls for each of the partners to take bauxite in proportion to their participation in Halco. During the construction phase, the target for production was raised to 9 million mtpy, to be achieved five years after startup.

In December 1968, all major agreements among the partners and lending and insurance agencies were signed in Washington. Startup was set for mid-1972, with the first year's production scheduled at 4.7 million mt. Financing for the 6-million-mtpy project was estimated at $180 million, including $80 million for OFAB.

The World Bank extended to OFAB $64.5 million in foreign exchange credits for a 24-year period, including an initial grace period of five years. The loan carried an interest rate of 6.5%. AID was to provide OFAB as required with an additional amount, up to $21 million, for a local-currency loan to be paid back over 25 years at 2.5% interest. The AID money was to be used for costs internal to Guinea.

The CBG mining project was financed with funds from Halco and by loans arranged by Kuhn Loeb & Co. A five-year standby credit of $75 million was extended to Halco by a group of European, Canadian, and US banks, headed by Bank of America.

The Export-Import Bank provided CBG with a further $25 million in credit to purchase US exports of equipment and services. Other export credits were arranged in Germany, France, Belgium, and Yugoslavia. CBG and OFAB chose as prime engineering contractor for the project the Belgian firm Soc. de Traction et d'Electricite SA. Design and construction of the project were complex efforts, involving contractors and suppliers from many parts of Europe and the US. The project was completed a year later than originally scheduled, and regular shipping of bauxite began from the port of Kamsar in August 1973.

The final cost of the project was $400 million, including expenditures of more than $100 million for the OFAB infrastructure. The most significant factor in the escalation of project costs was the decision during construction to increase the scope of the project by 50%, to 9 million mtpy. Sangaredi also experienced the cost increases normal to most international projects, caused by inflation, currency changes, strikes, delays, and the host of problems inherent in developing any project in such relative isolation.

Railroad mining in the Sangaredi pit

The configuration and location of the orebody, a solid plateau of bauxite approximately 100 ft thick and 1 sq mi in area, make track mining the most economic approach. Mining the orebody is like eating a cake, one layer at a time. Because the orebody has no overburden or waste inclusions, the cake-eating analogy is especially appropriate.

The bottom of the first cut, at elevation 229 m, slightly above the Sangaredi switchyard, required a ramp of filled material for access to the mine. A box cut was drilled, blasted, and excavated across the southern

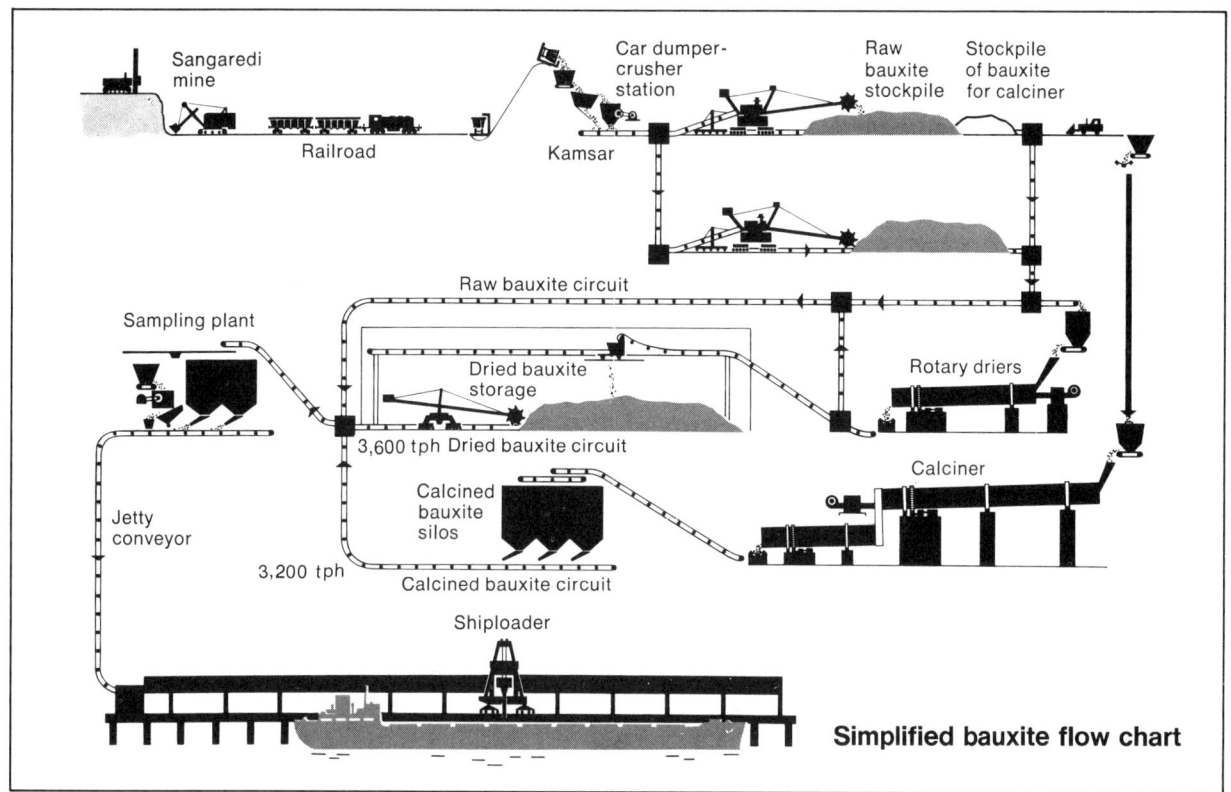

Simplified bauxite flow chart

periphery of the plateau to open up the first face. Track was laid in the cut, and mining of the northern face then began. (For a more detailed description of track mining at Sangaredi, see E/MJ, June, p 138.)

In the pit, bauxite is drilled, blasted, and loaded from the 40-ft-high face into 75-ton railroad cars. Maintaining the track and moving it is the biggest support job in the mine. (As at most mines in developing countries, the most difficult problems at Sangaredi are the proper operation and maintenance of increasingly complicated machinery, manpower training, and storage of adequate parts and supplies. Solving these problems will contribute more to profitable operations than the technological advances of the past several decades.)

Five Ingersoll Rand DM4 and T4 6¼-in.-dia rotary drills are available for blastholes, but only three are used on a single drilling shift. The holes are drilled in staggered rows parallel to the face. A 40- to 60-ft-wide blasted buffer zone is kept between the pit face and subsequent blasts to prevent rock throw from damaging mine track.

The drilling schedule is 46,000 m per month. Burden between rows is 3 m, and spacing between holes in the row is 7 m. The 6¼-in.-dia holes are drilled 1 m below track grade.

After the holes are checked, they are loaded from an ANFO truck. The mixture of 94.5% AN and 5.5% fuel oil is metered in the truck mixing bin while the auger system delivers the mix to each hole.

In the dry season, a Primacord line is hung one-third of the distance down the hole. At the end of the hanging Primacord is a 5-lb cast PETN primer. ANFO is then filled to within 1 m of the collar, and the Primacord is fastened to the E-cord trunk line. The hole is then stemmed with drill cuttings.

In the rainy season or in wet holes, a polyethylene sleeve is lowered into the hole before charging. In this case, three cast PETN primers of 3 lb each are evenly distributed down the Primacord for the full length of the hole.

The trunklines are connected in parallel rows, each row separated by a nonelectric 35-ms delay. The final lines are hooked to a regular blasting cap, connected to a length of safety fuse. A maximum of five or six rows is shot for each blast.

A yard loco pulls 20 to 25 ore cars around the loop in front of each shovel. Loading is done by two P&H 1900 electric shovels on each shift, with a third shovel as standby. After the cars are loaded, they are hauled to the switchyard and made up into trains of 85 cars for the 80-mi haul to the plant at Kamsar. Ore is loaded on 21 shifts a week. The production schedule calls for loading 650,000 tons of bauxite each month.

As the shovels progress along the face, panels of made-up track are installed on the leveled ground behind them. When the cut has been completed, the new track is connected to the loop and the old track is ready for the next phase of track building.

Ballast for the mine track is bauxite that has been crushed and sized in a plant alongside the mine. The plant is fed by 10-ton trucks, loaded by Cat 988s, from a specially blasted section in the face. The front-end loaders are also used to fill some ore cars with selected bauxite to be calcined at the plant. Halco ships 60,000 tpy of calcined abrasive grade bauxite to customers throughout the world.

Bauxite is crushed, dried before shipping

At Kamsar, bauxite is unloaded, crushed, dried, stockpiled, and shipped, using equipment of extraordinary size. The huge Kamsar plant, encompassing 150 acres, was constructed at a cost of $200 million. Plant foundations alone cost more than $10 million.

When ore trains from Sangaredi arrive at Kamsar switchyard, cars are placed on two tracks that feed the car dumping system. The dual system incorporates two rail-mounted charger units that position each car for hoisting. Each car is raised 50 ft to a car dump station. The car is then rotated 120° and the bauxite falls into one of two large hoppers. Each hopper bottom is a traveling apron feeder, which conveys the bauxite to a 1,000-tph hammermill. The emptied car is returned to the ground, automatically placed upon a car-traverser, and shifted to the "empties" track.

Crushing is done above ground because of the extremely poor soil conditions at the plant site. Each crusher is capable of reducing bauxite chunks of 4 x 5 x 6 ft to minus 4-in. particles in a single pass. The combined 2,000-tph crusher output is conveyed to a 700,000-mt-capacity open stockpile. More than 3 km of conveyors are used within the plant, excluding the loading dock. Most of the belt is 1,600 mm wide. The conveyor system is intricate and flexible, allowing bauxite from the crusher to be sent directly to stockpiles, to the driers, or to the shipping dock. Two 2,000-tph bucket wheels are located alongside the open stockpile area for storing and reclaiming raw bauxite.

Bauxite sent to the rotary dryers has a moisture content of 8% to 15%. To meet shipping requirements, moisture content must be close to 5%. Less than 5% moisture causes dusting problems at the unloading ports, while bauxite having more than 6% moisture tends to be quite sticky, creating handling problems.

Bauxite from stockpiles or crushers is conveyed to the dryers through three 200-ton-capacity transfer hoppers located at the firing end of the dryer building. The three rotary dryers are 15 ft in diameter and 160 ft long.

Ore from the bins is fed into each dryer at rates of 375 to 600 tph, depending on the moisture content of the feed. Elaborate controls are needed to assure a proper balance of feed and drying gases. The dryers burn preheated Bunker C fuel, fired at 2,300°F in a refractory-lined combustion chamber. Alongside the dryers, a rotary kiln, 9.5 ft in diameter and 300 ft long, is used to calcine a separate bauxite feed.

A series of cyclones and electrostatic precipitators removes 98% of the dust from the gases before they pass the induced draft fan and up a common stack.

Bauxite from the dryers is conveyed to a covered storage building, which can hold more than 160,000 tons. Material from covered storage is reclaimed with a 4,250-tph rail-mounted bucket wheel inside the building. Between the covered storage building and the dock is a

---

Rail connection between mine and plant

The railroad, which is single-line and standard gauge (1.435 m), runs approximately 142 km between switchyards at the Kamsar plant and the Sangaredi mine. Crushed dolorite quarry rock—at 1,410 liters per m—was used as ballast over the laterite or rock sub-base. Rails are standard U.I.C. quality B, weighing 60.34 kg per m, laid on 1,700 metal ties per kilometer. Track was laid in 18-m lengths and butt-joined using aluminothermic welding. Sliding expansion joints are located at both ends of bridges. Gradients were generally held at a maximum +0.5% from mine to port and +1.5% from port to mine. Near the mine, it was necessary to increase the grade to 2.0% for 2 km toward the switchyard. More than half the mainline has curved track, but the radius of curves was held to a minimum of 300 m near the mine connection and 500 m elsewhere.

The single-line operations made necessary the construction of two intermediate passing sections. One section has two tracks of 1,700 and 1,610 m long, and the other section has three tracks—1,700, 1,610, and 1,520 m.

The line has four passenger stations and is equipped with electric light signaling to indicate occupied track circuits. Communication is by radio and hand-carried train orders. The mainline traverses 24 water crossings, varying from large, steel truss bridges to concrete beam bridges and Armco culverts.

Traffic consists of five round-trip ore trains per day. Passenger trains run four times per week.

The entire mainline track is controlled by OFAB, with CBG traffic having priority. Major OFAB rolling stock includes three GM Type BB 1,500-hp diesel-electric locos and 26 freight cars. Track maintenance equipment includes an automatic track leveling/ballast-tamping machine and a 50-ton wrecking crane. Major CBG rolling stock consists of seven GM Type CC 3,000-hp diesel-electric locos for mainline service, four Type BB 1,000-hp diesel-electric locos for mine and yard service, 400 Gregg 75-ton-capacity open gondola ore cars, and 11 freight cars.

Fourteen Canadians employed by CANAC, the consulting wing of the Canadian National Railroad, work on the site as consultants and instructors for operation and maintenance of the railway facilities at Sangaredi.

Port facilities at Kamsar

The port at Kamsar is located on the left bank of the Rio Nunez estuary, 17 km northeast of the open Atlantic. It was designed to handle 300 ships carrying bauxite each year, plus fuel and supply ships, with minimum dredging to maintain the channel. Berthing maneuvers are relatively easy.

The upper 10 km of the channel, together with the turning basin, waiting berth, and dock area, was dredged during construction. Ships of 32-ft draft can enter and depart on the half-rising tide. The channel is 120 m wide and marked with 21 buoys. Seven approach buoys are located outside, in the open sea.

The ore loading quay, connected to land by a jetty, is a reinforced concrete slab, 50 cm thick, 260 m long, and 18 m wide. It carries a conveyor and rail-mounted traveling shiploader weighing 320 tons. The quay is supported on prestressed 2-m-dia concrete piles sunk into firm ground. Twelve separate tubular piles serve as fenders. The shiploader has a free travel of 165 m and a maximum loading rate of 4,250 tph.

The approach jetty, 1,536 m long, is topped with a 5-m-wide concrete slab. The slab is supported by 128 spans of 12 m each, constructed of crossbeams and longitudinal beams on concrete piles, varying in diameter from 80 to 200 cm. The deck carries the conveyor belt system, pipes for water and fuel, and a road for trucks of up to 15-ton capacity.

Shallow-draft supply ships use an old quay located in the inner harbor, which was constructed by the Alcan subsidiary in the late 1950s. This dock, used for discharge of supplies during construction at Sangaredi, is equipped with a railroad spur and diesel electric derrick with a lift capacity of 125 tons at 7.65-m radius.

Harbor equipment includes a coastal tug, two motor barges, and two pilot boats. All facilities except the shiploader, conveyor system, and pipelines are owned by OFAB.

---

sampling building, where complex automatic devices cut the stream of bauxite conveyed to ships to provide a representative sample of the cargo. Samples are analyzed at Kamsar and at the final destination.

Mining project required building two towns

Because Kamsar is relatively isolated from sources of supply, the operation must be highly self-sufficient. The rotating stores inventory totals $12 million, including fuels, explosives, spare parts, and other supplies. Major rebuilds and overhauls must be done on site. The Kamsar shop reprofiles railroad car wheels and rebuilds crusher hammers.

Kamsar and Sangaredi, 140 km apart, both required extensive building of support facilities, being little more than points on a map before the project began. CBG constructed more than 300 housing units at Sangaredi, and OFAB and CBG constructed over 650 units at Kamsar. Expansion of this housing is now under way.

Sangaredi's power is supplied by three 3,000-hp supercharged diesel engines connected to three 2,500-kva generators. Main voltage is 6 kv, and there is an emergency power source of 175 kva. Kamsar's power plant uses six 6,000-hp supercharged, dual fuel diesel engines running on No. 6 fuel. The engines drive 5,000-kva, 6-kv generator units. A 375-hp emergency unit drives a 330-kva, 380-v generator.

Fresh water for the Kamsar town and plant is taken from the Tinguilinta River, above tidal influence near the town of Boke. The water is treated and piped at 160 cu m per hr. Sangaredi uses treated water from the Kogon River east of the mine, supplied at the rate of 60 cu m per hr.

Both towns have reasonable amenities, including schools, stores, warehouses, and fire and sanitation facilities. Communication is by telephone and radio-telex. Sangaredi has a four-bed dispensary and equipment for emergency diagnoses and operations. Kamsar's 60-bed hospital has more sophisticated equipment.

At Kamsar, the workshop provides 9,600 sq m of interior floor space for major repairs and overhaul of electrical and mechanical equipment. At Sangaredi, maintenance of mine equipment is done in smaller shops.

Both Kamsar and Sangaredi are accessible from Conakry by a plane to Boke followed by an hour's drive, or by a grueling 8- to 10-hr drive over rough roads. CBG and OFAB operate a six-passenger Piper aircraft and a 65-passenger coastal vessel between Conakry and Kamsar. CBG's offices are in Kamsar and Conakry, while Halco is headquartered in Pittsburgh, Pa.

By 1980, Sangaredi is scheduled to be producing more than 9 million tpy of bauxite. Two other operations produce bauxite within Guinea—Friguia and OBK. Friguia, a partnership between the state, Alusuisse, Pechiney, VAW, and Noranda, produces 700,000 tpy of alumina from operations 70 km northeast of Conakry. OBK is owned entirely by the state and is operated by Guineans and technical assistants from the Soviet Union. The OBK operation produces about 2.5 million tpy of bauxite, with 90% going to the USSR and the remaining 10% available to be sold by Guinea on the open market.

Chief among potential new mines is the Ayekoye deposit north of Sangaredi, which might be opened up in the 1980s, backed by Mideast oil money. Present discussions center on engineering studies by Alusuisse for producing 8 million tpy of combined bauxite and alumina. Rumors of several new mines persist in the capital; it is evident that Guinea represents a major power among bauxite producers. □

Between the crusher station and dryers, two 2,000-tph Fives Lille-Cail bucket wheels stockpile and reclaim ore.

The construction phase: Skeleton of feeder building for rotary dryers and completed dust collection system (center right).

SURINAM: 62 years of bauxite development

IT WAS THE QUEST FOR GOLD that inspired the early explorers and colonialists of Surinam. But this particular brand of yellow fever flagged after more than 200 years of search and sporadic production, giving way in 1915 to emphasis on bauxite, which lacked the romance of gold but was more important industrially.

Today Surinam is synonymous with bauxite. Two companies—Suriname Aluminum Co. and NV Billiton Maatschappij Suriname—enjoy a special relationship with the nation, a former Dutch colony that gained independence in November 1975. Under an agreement of protocol, the Netherlands will continue to supply aid for 10 to 15 years and will forgive past debts, and the two nations will cooperate in the field of development. Surinam has long been an associate member of the European Common Market.

Suralco first to plunge into Surinam

Suralco, an Alcoa subsidiary, and Billiton are the dominant companies on the local scene. They may be joined in the future by a third producer, NV Grassalco, a state-owned company that plans a mining-refining project in the western part of the nation.

Suralco established its presence in 1915 on the thinly capped bauxite hills near Moengo, on the eastern side of Surinam's coastal plain, and made its first shipment of bauxite in 1922. In the hot, humid, and physically debilitating conditions, the struggle to put Moengo into production is a story that would fill chapters. In 1938, Suralco began developing buried bauxite in the swampy terrain near Paranam, about 35 km south of Paramaribo, Surinam's capital. The first ore from Paranam was shipped in 1941. Since that time, Suralco has industrialized Paranam with crushing, drying, and supercalcining facilities. In 1965, it opened the first unit of a 1-million-mtpy alumina refinery and the first potline of a 60,000-mtpy smelter.

Today, Suralco produces metal-grade, abrasive-grade, and refinery-grade bauxite for the export market, as well as metal-grade feed for internal refining and smelting. Mine production sites are Moengo and Lelydorp. The Suralco refinery and smelter were tied to development of the Brokopondo hydroelectric project on the Suriname River, approximately 110 km south of Paramaribo.

Under a unique joint venture agreement signed in 1958, the Surinam government and Suralco began to lend substance to a scheme by hydropower expert Professor W. J. Van Blommestein to harness the flow of the Suriname River (now measured as a dam runoff of 510 cu m per sec—18,000 cu ft per sec—at best efficiency). The Afobaka dam, completed in 1964, consists of two flanking earthfill structures joined by a concrete midsection that houses the power plant and spillway. The dam spans 1,913 m (6,275 ft). Equipped with six 42,000-metric-hp turbines, the generating capacity of Afobaka is 180,000 kw at 13.8 kv. The dam, 177 ft high from the spillway foundation to the deck, impounds a reservoir of 1,560 sq km (600 sq mi).

The government underwrote the cost of preliminary

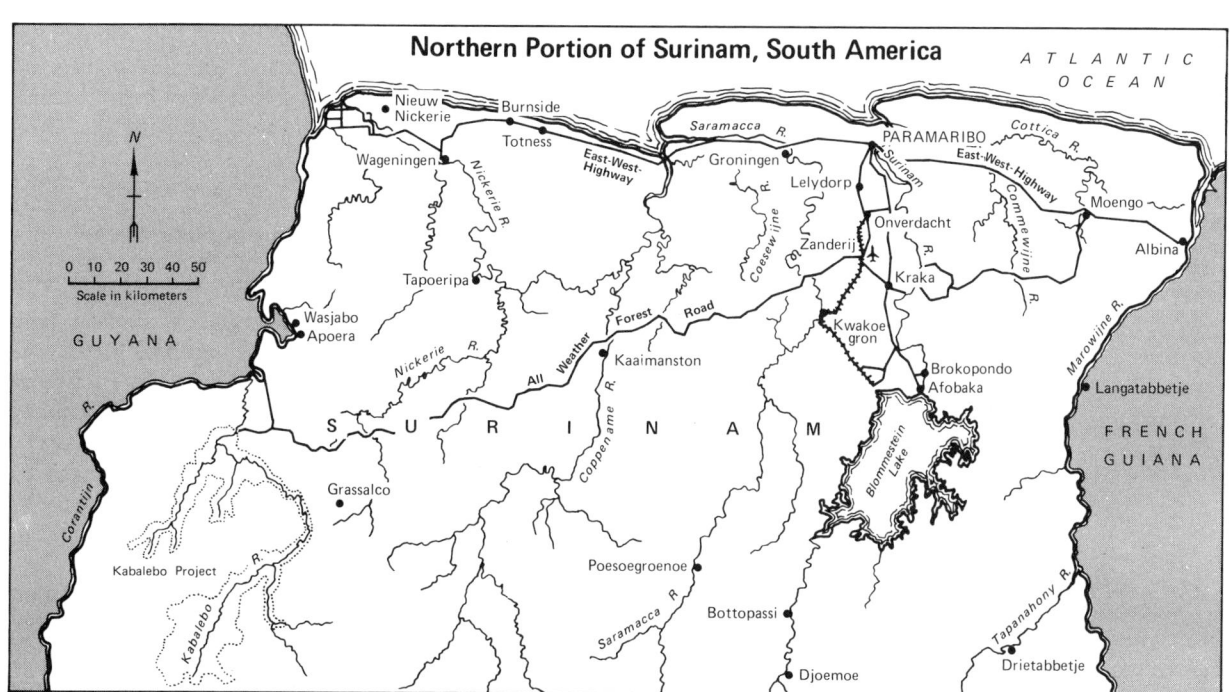

Northern Portion of Surinam, South America

Digging wheels strip upper overburden at Billiton after hydraulic dredging of 14.9 million yd of swampy muck to 7 m.

Suralco uses a slurry transport system to dispose of difficult swampy cover. This photo shows pumps on Slurrifier.

engineering and provided the necessary plots of land, water, and roads. It also accepted the task of transmigrating more than 5,000 Bush Negroes and their possessions from the impoundment area.

Suralco took on responsibilities for financing and construction of the project, maintenance and operation of the dam and powerhouse, and installation of a high-voltage line from Afobaka to Paranam. In addition, the company committed itself to the construction of refining and smelting facilities as part of the 1958 Brokopondo pact. At the end of the 75-year agreement, the dam and power plant will revert to the state.

Billiton enters the scene

Billiton's involvement in Surinam began in 1939 with an exploration program that encountered the frustrations common to mineral search in the tropics. Billiton ultimately discovered bauxite on an old plantation, Onverdacht, the surface of which was below sea level. Onverdacht is 10 km south of Suralco's Lelydorp mining site in the Paranam district. The geologic and mining environments at Onverdacht and at Lelydorp are similar. Onverdacht bauxite dips gently to the south under overburden that thickens and becomes wetter and more difficult to handle as the mining front progresses down dip.

Billiton has a mining capacity of 3.0 million mtpy. About 40% of the Suralco refinery capacity is reserved for Billiton, which toll-refines a portion of its mine output into alumina. Billiton is equipped also with crushing, drying, and calcining facilities on the Suriname River at Smalkalden. Its plans for a refinery were shelved when Suralco entered into the 1958 Brokopondo agreement with the government of Surinam, which called for Suralco to install refining and smelting facilities by 1976.

Because it was more economic to build one large plant than two small ones, Billiton contracted with Suralco for a share of capacity in return for a matching share of financing. As a result, Suralco's refinery came on line with a larger capacity and years ahead of the 1976 deadline.

Grassalco: the new face in bauxite

Grassalco is alive, well, and building a railroad. The group is studying the development of plateau-type bauxite remnants in the Bakhuis Range near the Corantijn River, which borders Guyana on the western side of Surinam. Here, Grassalco has identified 50 million mt of mineable bauxite grading at least 42% available Al_2O_3. This zone has been drilled on a 50 x 50-m grid. About 20 km to the south, another group of deposits with a 50-million-ton potential has been drilled on a 100- to 200-m grid.

The Grassalco project is an outgrowth of Operation Grasshopper—a nationwide ground-air geologic mapping and mineral reconnaissance mission sponsored by Surinam in the period 1959 through 1964. As part of the

Secondary stripping of lower overburden at Billiton, using draglines, follows primary digging-wheel cuts in upper overburden.

program, Aero Service (now a division of Litton Industries) flew a 66,000-mi, low-level, magnetometer-scintillation counter survey using a DC 3. This survey revealed a magnetic high in the Bakhuis region, leading to the discovery of extensive bauxite deposits.

A Surinam subsidiary of Reynolds Aluminum Co. acquired a concession in the Bakhuis area in 1971. Grassalco and Reynolds arranged a joint venture project, and Reynolds agreed to build a 200,000-mtpy refinery, expandable to 400,000 mtpy, contingent upon identifying 50 million mt of bauxite having a 42% available Al_2O_3 content within 6 airline km of the planned rail loading terminal. Grassalco bought out Reynolds' interest in 1975 for approximately $3 million.

It has been decided to locate the refinery at Apoera on the Corantijn River. Prefeasibility studies were completed a few months ago for a 575,000-mtpy refinery, to be built with the consultation of Alcoa. Billiton supplied consulting services for the mine feasibility study and the final design of mining, which was completed a year ago. Final refinery feasibility has not yet been decided. At a cutoff grade of 38% available Al_2O_3, deposits at the mining site nearest the rail terminal average 5.5 m in thickness.

In the meantime, Morrison Knudsen started construction of a 71-km standard-gauge railroad from the river terminal at Apoera in April 1976. Specifications for the line include a gauge of 1,435 mm, rails of UIC 54, maximum axle leading of 27.5 mt, normal mainline radius of curves of 500 m, maximum grades of 0.5% against the load and 1.7% against the empty train, and minimum radius of curves in the yard of 120 m.

A word about plate tectonics

The basements of Surinam and of Guyana, French Guiana, southeastern Venezuela, and a huge section of Brazil north of the Amazon occupy the Guyana Precambrian shield. Surinam is on the northern edge of the shield. Laterite deposits have been formed in the environment of platform cover. Such chemically residual deposits as bauxites, low-grade iron ores, manganese ores, and float of chromite, emery, and canga derived from itabirite have been identified.

Two types of bauxite are distinguished: the partly buried deposits of the coastal plain, typified by Suralco's Lelydorp and Billiton's Onverdacht, and the plateau type of the hinterland, such as Moengo and Bakhuis. The bauxite deposits of the coastal plain were formed as a result of weathering and decomposition of arkosic and subarkosic sediments. Those of the hinterland were formed mainly by bauxitization of basic rocks of the basement. The main ore mineral is gibbsite. It is thought that bauxitization of the coastal plain and the plateau deposits took place during the early Tertiary on a peneplain. The buried deposits have been subjected to continued tropical weathering. During this process, the alumina of bauxite starts to recombine with silica to form kaolinite. Also, percolating solutions attack the

Mini-stripping of shallow cover on plateau bauxite remnants, using Poclain ⅜-yd backhoes, is typical of Suralco's Moengo mines.

iron-rich capping, leaching much of the iron.

Surinam contains a number of gold and diamond placer deposits. The gold placers occur in alluvial creek and colluvial sediments derived from the Precambrian basement. The alluvial placers are generally transported not much further than 2,000 m from primary mineralization. Diamond placers occur in alluvial and eluvial gravels in the northeastern part of the country. More recently, diamonds have been found in the creek gravels in the mid-southern portion of the nation, near the Brazilian border. Cassiterite and columbite-tantalite placers noted in the northeastern part of the country are thought to be related to pegmatites of the area. The pegmatites themselves occupy a broad east-west band 20 km in width, which extends into French Guiana. Tin, beryllium, niobium, and tantalum mineralization has been noted in these deposits.

Among other mineralization in Surinam, primary gold is associated with quartz veins and altered pyrite-bearing wall rock. Chalcopyrite is generally associated with metamorphosed basic intrusives and volcanics. Chalcopyrite has also been found in quartz veins and granite, together with bornite, digenite, and brochantite, at Wedeboh Soela along the Saramacca River.

Bornite and chalcopyrite are found in a contact zone between granulite facies metasediments and metadolerite near the Upper Nickerie River in the Bakhuis Mountains. Recently relatively strong geochemical zinc anomalies were found in the northeast-dipping nose of the granulite facies rock structure of the Bakhuis Mountains. Pentlandite and molybdenite occurrences also have been reported.

The business climate

Surinam may well be one of the most colorful nations of the Caribbean basin. Populated by Creoles, Hindustanis, Bush Negroes (descendants of the early slaves), Javanese, Amerindians, Dutch, Lebanese, Jews, and Chinese, it is possibly the most racially mixed society on either side of Singapore. Guyana to the west may be a close second in racial diversity.

The atmosphere of Surinam is peaceful, benign, and serene. The country is development-oriented, raw materials-oriented, and export-oriented, and its people are colorful and straightforward in dealings.

The prime emphasis for the plan of independence is development, focused in six areas: 1) Greater Paramaribo, which is viewed as an administrative and commercial center with growth possibilities in service activities; 2) Moengo-Albina-Patamacca, where the emphasis will be on bauxite, forestry, agriculture, and cattle raising; 3) Apoera-Kabelebo-Adampada, where bauxite mining and a new refining center are planned, along with iron ore mining, oil palm plantations, and forestry industries; 4) the Brokopondo area, which offers possibilities for gold mining, lateritic iron ore, agriculture, and tropical and oil palm plantations; 5) the Tibiti-Coppename area, for bauxite and gold extraction, horticulture, cattle raising, and forestry; and 6) the Nieuw Nickerie-Wageningen-Cornie area, where rice is grown by the largest mechanized rice company in the world.

Surinam welcomes foreign investment and is committed to a program of growth. □

Suralco

BAUXITE MINING at Suralco requires both mini and maxi stripping programs. The 3- to 5-m-thick bauxite layers in the hills of the Moengo concession occur in slightly elevated table-land below a thin layer of earth and an iron-rich laterite capping. The total overburden is generally 1 ft or less.

As the plateau remnants are heavily forested, the stripping problem is one of clearing the vegetation and removing the overburden, using bulldozers and two ⅜-yd Poclain hydraulic backhoes, one of which is equipped with a hydraulic impactor. The iron-rich capping overlies an irregular surface of mineable bauxite. The crustal cap is removed carefully because it makes an excellent surface dressing for the mine roadways at both Moengo and Lelydorp.

Compared with the difficult stripping program at Lelydorp, overburden removal at Moengo almost takes on the appearance of mining with a spoon.

At Lelydorp, the stripping ratio is now over 5:1. To cope with this problem, Suralco is now using the largest walking dragline in South America—a Bucyrus-Erie 1350W, having a 40-yd bucket—teamed with a Bucyrus-Erie 480W 10-yd dragline and a Slurrifier. The Slurrifier is a skid-mounted barge containing four Intelligiant hydraulic monitors and two series of three high-pressure pumps. One pump set is used as a booster on the freshwater supply line for the monitors; the other pump set serves as the first of four booster stations on the 21,600-ft slurry line.

Geometry of deposit and mine orientation

Of the three bauxite deposits that have been defined at Lelydorp, Lelydorp 1 has not yet been opened. Mining is concentrated at Lelydorp 2, while Lelydorp 3W contains the freshwater sump for the slurry transportation system.

The bauxite deposit at Lelydorp 2 dips to the northeast under thickening cover. The overburden consists of an upper horizon of saturated sands and silt, about 40 ft thick in the southwest and thinning to about 20 ft in the northeast. The lower overburden, which contains hard clay intermixed with river sands and silt, is about 20 ft thick on the southwest side and thickens on the northeast to about 80-100 ft.

The stripping and mining panels are oriented southwest-northeast. The bauxite zone, 15 to 18 ft thick, is underlain by kaolin clay and is sandwiched top and bottom by a 1-ft layer of high-grade pebble. The average thickness of the overburden is about 80 ft. The maximum depth of the bauxite is about 70 ft below sea level.

A dragline walkway is established on the southwest boundary of the mining zone, at right angles to the panels. From the walkway, 150-ft-wide finger ramps are driven 600 ft into the mining zone. The upper overburden near this perimeter is excavated by draglines. The mine haul road accesses the exposed bauxite level from the southeast, opposite the midpoint of the highwall. The cut at this point is about 3,800 ft wide—2,000 ft on the northeast side of the haul road and 1,800 ft on the southwest side. The hard clay of the lower overburden forms a parting and dragline bearing surface between the upper and lower highwalls. As it is excavated, this material is used to dike the pit for protection against the annual rainfalls of 80 to 100 in.

Lelydorp 2, which produced its first ore in August 1969, may now be considered to be approaching middle age. It was phased in as production phased out at Onoribo mine west of Paranam, where a suction dredge and a B-E 480W 10-yd dragline handled stripping. The deeper Lelydorp 2 mine required a larger excavator—the 1350W unit.

The 1350W weighs 2,300 tons and is equipped with a 285-ft triangular boom angled 32° above horizontal. The boom provides a 200-ft reach, a 200-ft cast, and a maximum 150 ft of spoil build above horizontal. The excavator is fed from a 13.8-kv high-tension cable. Dig, swing, hoist, dump, and walking are powered by a range of 14 440-v dc motors. It took two years to assemble the machine on site. In the early development, the machine was immobilized at times by the marshiness of the terrain and by its own weight. It has also suffered occasionally from a broken leg on one of its walking shoes. But the 1350W is the least expensive, most efficient earthmover at Lelydorp—as the primary excavator, it accounts for about 80% of the total stripping tonnage.

B-E 5-yd dragline excavates blasted bauxite at Lelydorp. It may stack ore for wheel loaders or load trucks directly.

Major components of Suralco's mining fleet at Moengo

 2 Koehring 1066C hydraulic backhoes, 3.5-cu-yd buckets
 5 Caterpillar 988 wheel loaders
 2 Caterpillar D9 bulldozers
 7 Caterpillar D8 and 1 D7 bulldozers
10 Caterpillar 769B haul trucks, 35-st capacity
 2 Poclain hydraulic LC 80 backhoes, 3/8 cu yd (crawler mounted)
 1 Poclain hydraulic LY 80 backhoe, 3/8 cu yd (wheel mounted)
 5 Mobile auger drills mounted on D-4 dozer chassis
 1 Motor grader
   Caterpillar 824 wheel dozers
 3 General Electric 50-st diesel-electric locomotives
 4 General Electric 35-st locomotives (for switching)
150 side-dump mine cars, 20-st capacity

At the outset, it was known that the 1350W could not cope with the thicker sections of overburden and would require assistance from an alternative earthmoving system. The feasibility of a bucket wheel excavator or a dredge was investigated. The BWE was ruled out by delivery time and the type of materials to be handled. The dredge system was ruled out because it would have produced material that couldn't be contained in the mined-out area, requiring an enlarged impoundment area—bigger than the 1,200-acre pond required by the Slurrifier.

It was decided finally to couple the Slurrifier system to dragline excavation. The Slurrifier, a hydraulic earth-moving fortress mounted on skids, was built in Florida for Suralco and put into operation in April 1974. The four hydraulic guns are remotely controlled from an operator's cab and are programmable through various arcs of sweep as determined by localized excavating conditions. Fresh water from the Lelydorp 3W sump is delivered by three Gould pumps at 2,000 gpm through a 20-in. spiral-weld pipeline. Three boosters on the skid-mounted barge feed water at 200 to 250 psi through 6-in. pipelines to the hydraulic guns.

Equipped with Intelligiants having 2½-in. nozzles, the four water cannons jet 45 tpm of water against the working surface, which may be either an upper highwall of loosely consolidated virgin material or material stacked by the 480W 10-yd dragline for the Slurrifier. The 20-in. slurry line is equipped with four booster stations, each consisting of Pettibone pumps driven by 1,000-hp engines. These units deliver the slurry, at 25-30% solids, 4 mi to a 1,200-acre disposal area safely beyond the identified mining areas. As the solids settle, clear water is decanted from the disposal area back to the sump at the Lelydorp 3W for reuse. Makeup water is drawn from drinking water reservoirs in the district.

Operating costs for the Slurrifier are about four times those of the 1350W dragline. As a result, stripping tactics are designed to optimize use of the walking dragline. The large dragline is capable of double-casting overburden at a cost competitive with the Slurrifier. Thus, the 1350W is the preferred stripping tool, and the Slurrifier works only in scheduled positions that exceed the double handling limitation. The 1350W normally back-casts into mined-out terrain, although it occasionally forward-casts saturated material that won't stack onto virgin ground ahead of the highwall.

The Slurrifier is used to cut and slurry soft upper overburden, or it is positioned to slurry piles built by the 480W. In combination with the 480W, the Slurrifier moves about 90,000 yd per month. Capable of stripping

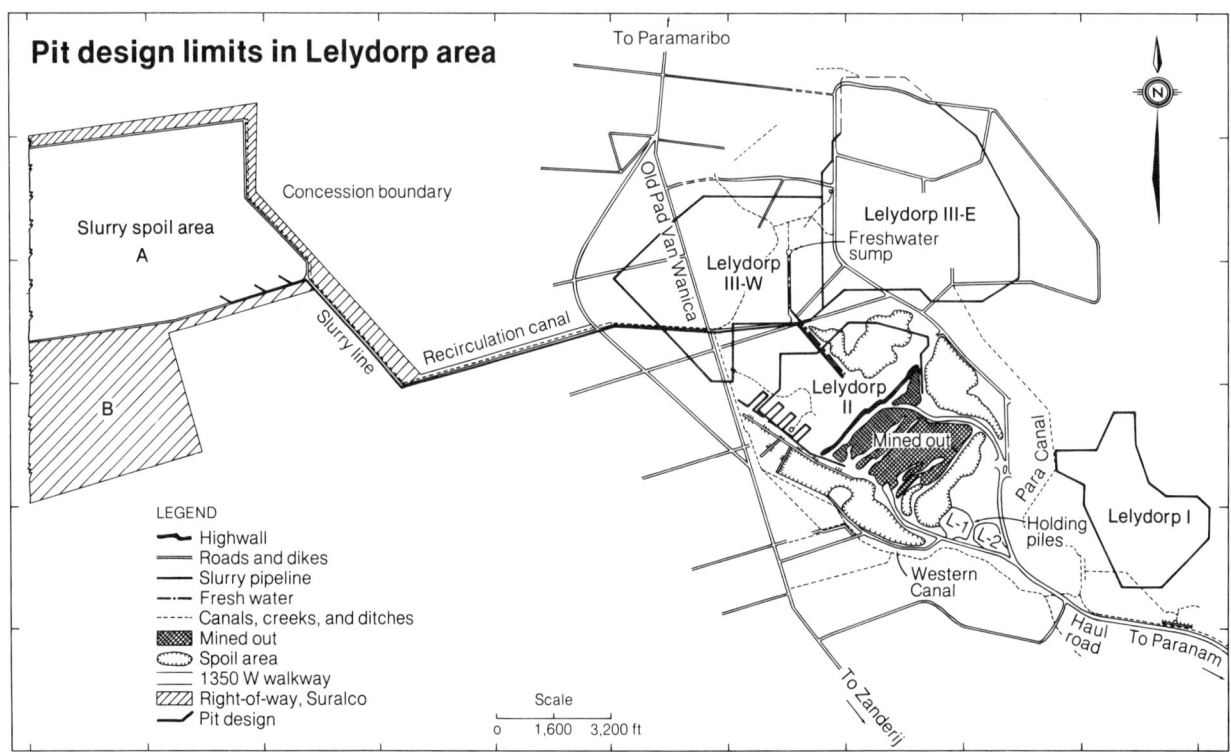

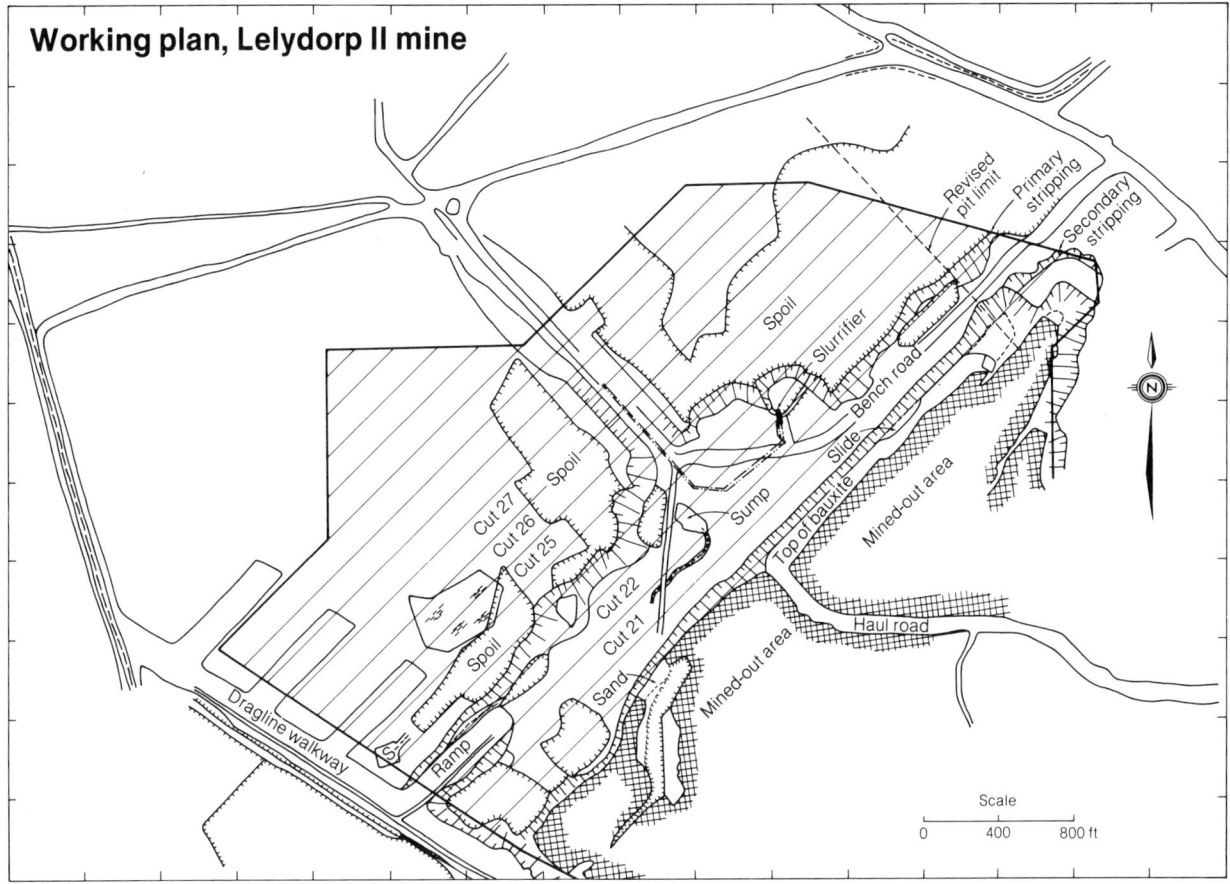
Working plan, Lelydorp II mine

about 350,000 yd per month, the Slurrifier is typically operated at about 200,000 yd per month.

Suralco personnel indicate that the system is successful. The Slurrifier doesn't move earth at the rate originally envisioned, but its rate is adequate as a complementary system.

How mining is organized at Lelydorp

Dilution of the ore is not much of a problem. The pit walls are sloped to a 1:6 angle of repose in the upper soft overburden, while the lower overburden is sloped at 1:1.5. The highwall slope is maintained at a 1:1 slope for maximum dragline reach. Some zones of the water-saturated material of the upper overburden won't stack, and the material flows to a nearly flat angle of repose—accounting for some of the forward-casting that is done. Also, the 1350W has occasionally been used to stack lower overburden on top to increase the upper highwall.

Operations are grouped into four departments: 1) mine preparation and haul-road maintenance and development, which occupies two work shifts per day; 2) the Slurrifier department; 3) the dragline department; and 4) the ore production department. Stripping is done three shifts a day, seven days a week. Mining is done three shifts a day, in a five-day week.

The mining fleet is composed of two B-E 5-yd draglines, of which one is usually in reserve. In addition, a loader handles dragline-stockpiled material. Of the 18 35-ton Euclid haul trucks, 11 are utilized in the mining cycle. The remaining seven trucks haul Moengo ore from dockside to the plant. Two Cat D8 ripper dozers work with the mining excavator.

The ore must be drilled and blasted. Blastholes are

Export shipments of all bauxite grades by Suralco
(metric tons)

Year	Moengo	Paranam	Totals
1976	585,723	312,460	898,183
1975	733,771	290,094	1,023,865
1974	1,610,863	474,324	2,085,187
1973	1,602,629	446,692	2,049,321
1972	1,524,317	372,692	1,897,009
1971	1,563,311	558,214	2,121,525
1970	1,677,382	584,248	2,261,630

Aluminum and alumina exports by Suralco
(metric tons)

Year	Alumina	Aluminum
1976	559,856	46,297
1975	646,797	26,430
1974	580,483	54,184
1973	705,116	54,195
1972	839,287	52,557
1971	723,171	47,395
1970	438,092	52,823

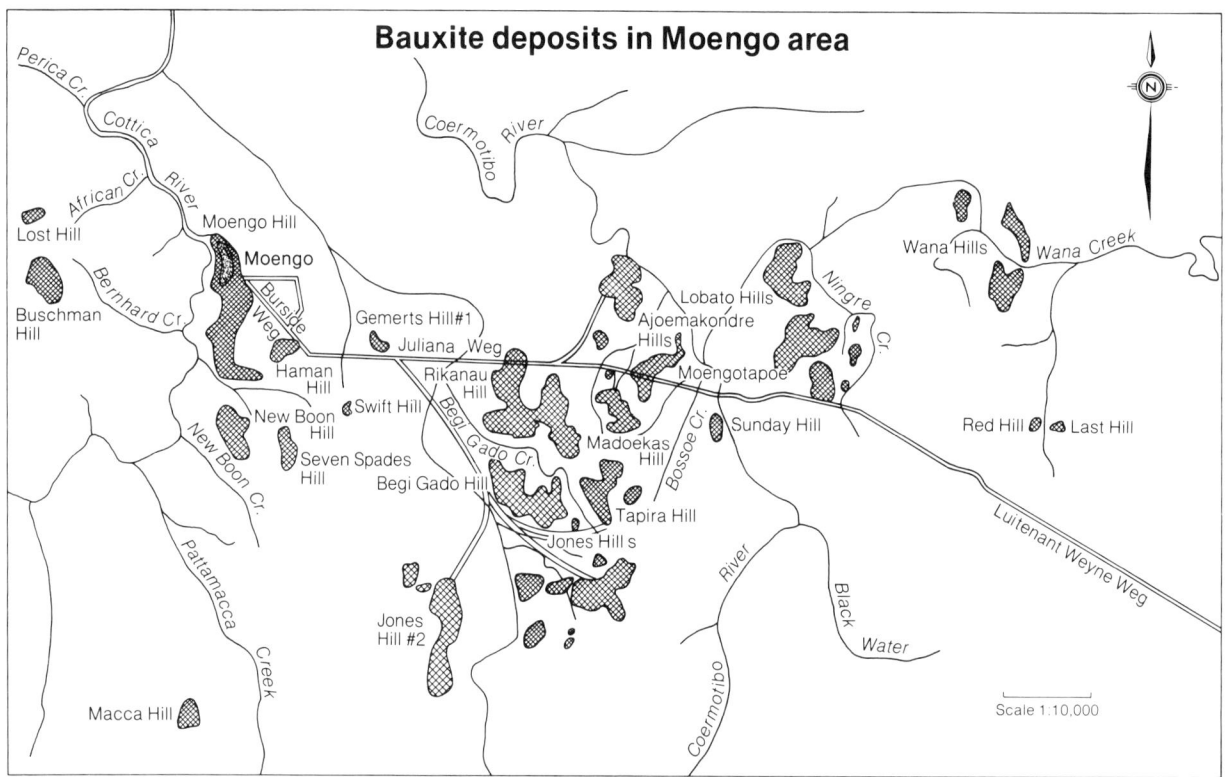

Bauxite deposits in Moengo area

drilled by two Mobile auger drills mounted on Cat D4s, which auger 4-in. holes to a depth of 8 to 10 ft. The spacing of the holes varies from 10 to 15 ft. The holes are loaded with bagged ANFO, which is primed with water gels. The stripping program establishes a 150-ft-wide cut of exposed ore along the highwall, and mining progresses in a 50-ft-wide strip along the spoil toe from the side wall to the haul road. Then, the entire width of the exposed seam is taken in the next pass.

Mining at Moengo

The extraction of bauxite at Moengo is complicated more by transportation and scheduling logistics than by problems of earthmoving. Ore production at one time was centered near the drying and calcining plant, on the bank of the deep but very narrow Cottica River. Bauxite was transported to the plant crusher by means of a narrow, 36-in.-gauge railroad.

The mining scene has now shifted several kilometers to the southeast, to the Begi Gado group, opened late in 1971; to Jones Hill, opened in October 1972; to Tapira Hill, opened in October 1974; and to Jones 1C, which is now under preparation for mining. Most of the production now comes from Tapira Hill and is hauled 15 km by rail to the plant in 20-mt side-dump cars. Such trains are composed of a maximum of 35 cars and a 50-st diesel-electric locomotive, which travels over 80-lb rail.

In a typical development, a rail spur from the main line is driven to a stockpile site at each of the mines. Stripping is primarily a clearing and cleaning operation to expose the ore. While the approach to development is dictated by local topography at the mine site, a central haul road is generally established on bauxite, and random mining panels are laid out using a herringbone roadway system on 400-ft centers.

All of the ore must be drilled and blasted. Mobile augers bore 4-in. holes, to a depth of 15 ft if necessary, in an approximate 10 x 12-ft pattern. Holes are loaded with bagged ANFO and Deta Prime. A typical shot may involve 200 holes.

The two Koehring 3.5-yd hydraulic backhoes are used for face-loading bauxite into the Cat 35-ton trucks. The five Cat 988 front-end units are used as loaders in the mine or on mine stockpile reclaim as necessary. The two D-9 bulldozers are often used to pile ore for the loaders.

Mining operations are grouped into three departments under the mine superintendent, who reports to the Moengo production manager. The departments are: supervision of ore production; development and preparation, which includes drilling and blasting; and ore transfer, which includes railcar loading and track maintenance. A mine engineering department reports directly to the production manager. The Moengo mining operations employ 205 hourly and weekly personnel, nine monthly personnel (foreman level), and four staff members. □

Skid-mounted Slurrifier has four programmed Intelligiants and is used as an auxiliary stripping unit at the Lelydorp mine.

Typical ore loading team at Moengo operations includes a Cat 988 loader working with a fleet of Cat 769B 35-ton trucks.

Billiton: A study in long-range dredging and bucket wheels

BILLITON'S STRIPPING PROGRAM for Onverdacht bauxite is very large in scope but quite different from the systems employed at neighboring Suralco. Billiton has long used bucket wheel excavators as major stripping tools. More recently, the company used a pair of suction dredges in a 14.9-million-yd prestripping campaign on swampy upper overburden. This tactic was designed to maximize the efficiency of the two digging wheels over a 10-year period.

Much of the stripping and all of the mining takes place below sea level, requiring super-coordination of excavation and large-scale dike building and pumping of the pit. Primary stripping is done by the BWEs. Secondary stripping follows, with Bucyrus-Erie 450W walking draglines equipped with 11-yd buckets.

The earthmovers strip a highwall extending some 5,700 ft from the east and west sidewalls of the mine. The stripping and mining panels advance from south to north to expose a 50-m-wide panel of bauxite, which is drilled and blasted for excavation by four Marion 111M draglines.

The mining program is geared to a production rate of 2.5 million to 3 million mtpy of bauxite. In its best year, Billiton produced 3.2 million mt of bauxite. The company produces some chemical-grade ore, but the largest share of output is refinery grade. Chemical-grade bauxite contains less than 1.5% Fe_2O_3 and preferably less than 4.5% silica. For refinery grade, the specifications tolerate more iron, typically 4.5% to 7% Fe_2O_3, and the required alumina content is 59%, of which 54% is considered available. SiO_2 averages about 4.8%, most of which is reactive silica.

Going to great depths for bauxite

The ore dips to the north in advance of the mining front. Up to 35 ft thick in the middle and thinning to 10 ft at the fringes, the ore at Billiton's Para mine arcs downward from the thicker midsection. The average depth of overburden is now more than 80 ft. The company classifies overburden according to its physical and digging characteristics, making three types, from top to bottom: 1) slime, mud, and clay having a 70% water content; 2) loose, white sand interbedded with clay; and 3) kaolinites interbedded with compacted sand.

The digging wheels at Billiton had experienced some difficulties in the swampy, upper sections of the overburden. On occasion, a digging wheel broke into a saturated mud zone, which would run to a nearly flat slope. Some of these slides were quite large, creating a subsidence zone several hundred feet in advance of the highwall. One run in the mid-1960s was so serious that it toppled a bucket wheel, damaging it beyond repair. The only item salvaged was the track chassis, which is now used on one of the belt wagons.

Such conditions have prompted a number of protective measures. Chief among them was the dredging program that started in 1973 and was completed in 1975, lessening the possibilities of slides and mud rushes. But other protective measures have been adopted as well, including detailed soil stability tests in advance of stripping. When approaching ground known to be dangerous, the digging wheel is positioned at a 45° angle to the face cut, and the belt wagons are never positioned directly behind the wheel, so that it can't back away from a slide. The depth of cut of the wheel is limited, to minimize exposure of the side of the wheel to a potential slide. When a slide occurs, the wheel is used to dig itself out if it isn't buried.

Soil stability testing is carried out on a 50-m grid by driving a resistance cone into the overburden. Resistance

O&K bucket wheel excavators at Billiton are equipped with 9.1-m wheels. Selected overburden is used for building mine dikes.

values (kg per sq cm) are plotted against depth and entered into a computer program. The computer prints out values along grid and block lines, determining block volumes scheduled for the digging wheels and the 450W draglines. The resistance values are classifiable as soft, medium, and hard, for scheduling of excavation equipment, determination of digging wheel and dragline working surfaces, and disposition of the spoil. The hard overburden stacks well and is used as dike building material.

Dredging and primary stripping

Two cutterhead suction dredges designed in Holland were shipped, dismantled, to Surinam, where they were reassembled at a site on the bank of the Para River, a tributary of the Suriname River. The area marked for dredging was pumped out, and the timber and vegetation were piled and burned. This zone and a slurry disposal site required the construction of protective dikes. An existing canal was extended from the site of dredge erection to the work site to allow the assembled units to be towed to the Para mine.

Each dredge had a total installed horsepower of 3,255. The suction pipelines were 0.75 m in diameter and the pumping pipeline was 0.65 m in diameter. The dredges worked south toward the mining pit, enlarging a pond that ultimately grew to a surface dimension of 1 x 2.2 km. As the pond was enlarged, the discharge line from the dredges to the disposal area stretched to more than 3,600 m. Slurry pipe floats and, eventually, a floating booster pump station were required on the pond section of the pipeline to lift the slurry over the dike. The dredges excavated an average depth of 7 m of overburden, gaining for the bucket wheels approximately 10 years of excavation free of the soft, saturated overburden. On completion of the dredging program, the units were disassembled and sold.

After prestripping, the next stage of mine development is bucket wheel cuts of approximately 14 m. One wheel works a highwall on the east side of the mine and the other a cut on the west side. The machines typically make two cuts each from a bench having a minimum width of 400 ft. The finishing cut may leave 7 to 9 m of overburden excavation remaining for the 450W draglines. The bucket wheel excavators work in tandem with belt wagons and long, 48-in.-wide conveyor systems. The belt wagons discharge spoil to a face conveyor, which moves material out of the pit to a sidewall roadway. The spoil is transferred to a belt traveling 90° south from the working face to mined-out country.

The spoil conveyor terminates at a stacking bridge, which works on top of a dikeway extending back into the mined-out zone. Spoil is deposited by the stacker for a team of Cat bulldozers and scrapers, which build the dike to a final slope of 1:3. Some of the softer material stacks at an angle of repose of about 1:50. The sand material will stand on a slope of 1:1.3. The stripping volume is now greater than can be maintained in the mined-out area, necessitating the construction of huge

The digging wheels are usually paired with two belt wagons, which feed conveyor system moving overburden out of the mine.

dikes across the pit from sidewall to sidewall.

The two LMG bucket wheel excavators were supplied by Orenstein & Koppel. One of the units was recently rebuilt, and the two digging wheels now have a combined working capacity of approximately 4 million mtpy at 70% utilization during scheduled working hours. Both machines are equipped with 9.1-m-dia wheels, each having 12 0.4-cu-m buckets. The two digging wheels vary somewhat in front and tail conveyor lengths, as well as in surface bearing pressures (see table). The belts on the digging wheels, belt wagons, and spoil conveyors are 48 in. in width, and they travel on 30° troughing idlers. Both digging wheels are of the cell-less type. Two belt wagons are typically placed behind each wheel to deliver spoil to the face conveyor.

Secondary stripping and mining

The B-E 450W draglines are fitted with low-angle 185-ft booms. They can cast material 165 ft into the mined-out area. The 450Ws work on a bucket wheel bench and take a cut about 50 m wide. The machines are capable of a stripping rate of 1.3 million to 1.5 million mtpy. Final cleaning of the top of the bauxite is done with bulldozers.

The ore is drilled on a somewhat variable pattern, but a typical spacing would require one hole for every 10 sq m of ore to be blasted. Seven hydraulic augers mounted on Fordson tractors are available for blasthole and sample drilling. A newer mechanical auger—a Portadrill

Bucket wheels used by Billiton for primary stripping

Name	Ba Gridi	Kapasi
Weight (mt)	800	770
Ground pressure (kg per sq cm)	0.97	1.21
Wheel diameter (m)	9.1	9.1
No. of buckets (400 l each)	12	12
Length of wheel conveyor (m)	30	20
Length of tail conveyor (m)	25	30
Bearing diameter (mm)	6,700	7,000
Supplier	Orenstein & Koppel	

Other major components of earthmover fleet

2 B-E walking draglines (11-yd buckets, 185-ft boom)
4 Marion crawler-mounted draglines (4.5-yd buckets, 90-ft booms)
10 Wabco Haulpak 50-st trucks
20 Cat bulldozers (Models D6, D7, and D8)
9 Scrapers
3 Cat wheel loaders (Models 950, 988, and 992)

Statistics of Para mine at Onverdacht

Avg. Al_2O_3 content	55.8%
Avg. grade with cutoff	
SiO_2	4.2%
Fe_2O_3	2.5%
Pit slope ratio	1:3

Secondary stripping and stacking of waste near toe of bauxite is handled by 11-yd B-E draglines having 185-ft-long booms.

built by Winter Weiss—also is used. The drills bore 4-in. blastholes, which are loaded with ANFO packed in plastic bags. Primer selection depends on the wetness of the holes. The shots are fired electrically, breaking multiple rows of holes. Typically, 40 holes are shot at a time. Blasting is done at 11:45 a.m. and 5:45 p.m. daily. Blasting of loaded holes must follow closely on the heels of drilling because the holes can close overnight.

Four Marion 111M draglines equipped with 90-ft booms and 4.5-yd buckets are used in the mining cycle. These excavators work with a fleet of 50-ton Wabco Haulpaks that are phasing out older 35-ton models. The haulers are equipped with aluminum rock boxes heated by exhaust gas to reduce sticking of ore to the truck bed at the unloading site. The trucks deliver the ore either to a new crushing plant and railroad load-out center near the northeastern part of the mine or to Suralco's Paranam refinery, about 9½ km from the mine. About 630,000 tpy of capacity at this 1-million-tpy plant is reserved for Billiton.

The mine is equipped with six skid-mounted, diesel-driven pumps, each having a capacity of about 10 cu m per min (1,580 gpm). The pumps handle inflow water and water draining from the overburden and bauxite formation. It is standard practice to dig three or four sumps at the base of the bauxite formation and the toe of the spoil to collect such drainage for discharge.

As mining progresses at Billiton, it is quite possible that another dredging program will be launched.

The new crushing plant is equipped with a double-toothed roll crusher. The Haulpak trucks usually dump directly into the crusher pocket. The crushed ore is delivered from the new rail load-out center to Smalkalden in trains of 125-ton capacity.

At the Smalkalden drying plant on the Suriname River, about 7 km from the Para mine, the cars are unloaded at dump pockets. Feeders and a conveyor system can either stockpile wet mine-run ore or convey this product directly to bins serving the two rotary kilns. The dryers reduce the moisture content of the ore to about 3% for shipment overseas. Smalkalden is equipped with two shiploaders for trimming ocean-going vessels of 16,000- to 23,000-ton carrying capacity.

Billiton, an important factor in the Surinam economy, may choose to enter the market for calcined refractory grade at some point in the future. The company has quality reserves to support such an operation. ☐

Guybau and Bermine: Digging deep for ore

THE MOST STRIKING ASPECT of bauxite mining in Guyana is the diversity of stripping plans and the mining depths required to recover the ore. Plant managers might take exception to this sweeping statement, in view of other achievements of the industry. They proudly point to the installation of the No. 14 kiln, an 11½-ft-dia x 314-ft-long calciner, which is the biggest in the bauxite world and which incorporates some locally generated design innovations.

It is a fact, however, that stripping ratios at both Guybau and Bermine are about 10:1. Guybau has seven active mines in the Linden area. Before installation of the new kiln, the production capacity of Guybau was roughly 900,000 dry ltpy of metal-grade bauxite, 650,000 ltpy of supercalcined refractory grade, and 300,000 dry ltpy of alumina. The No. 14 kiln puts supercalcining capacity at nearly 1 million ltpy. The company has the capability of mining nearly 5 million ltpy of bauxite. Guybau is the world's largest producer of refractory-grade bauxite.

Bermine is about a third the size of Guybau. Unlike Guybau's mines and plants, which are centralized, Bermine's operations are split between mining at Kwakwani and drying and calcining at Everton, 80 mi downstream on the Berbice River.

The production mix in Guyana
(000 long tons)

	1974	1975	1976
Guybau			
Alumina	310	293	247
Metal-grade bauxite	721	814	306
Dried refractory-grade bauxite	22	7	Nil
Calcined refractory-grade bauxite	686	690	664
Bermine			
Metal-grade bauxite	455	338	348
Chemical-grade bauxite	200	169	320
Calcined refractory-grade bauxite	52	86	66

South Arrowcane mine conveyor system transports spoil from digging wheels. Lower overburden is stacked by 11-yd draglines.

Kara Kara mine uses rail-car loading at the mining face, scrapers on upper overburden, and draglines on lower waste.

New East Montgomery mine is destined to become Guybau's biggest producer, but ore lies under 250 ft of cover.

Sand and clay mask the ore

The bauxite deposits at many of the mines are overlain by as much as 200 ft of overburden. At the new East Montgomery mine, the 35-ft-thick ore zone is buried under as much as 250 ft of cover. Guyanese bauxite is widely known for its low contents of iron and silica. Large ore sections at some of the mines contain less than 2% each of Fe_2O_3 and SiO_2. The alumina content is commonly 65%. One wag describes Guyanese bauxite as calcine grade with a few pockets of metal grade. It is necessary to add some iron-rich laterite to the refinery feed.

To generalize, the upper overburden consists of fine, white compacted sand up to 150 ft thick. Some of this sand is of glass quality. Below the sand is a layer of hard clay, 30 to 50 ft thick. The clay is tough to dig and may be water-saturated. Locally, the upper sandy formation may contain interbedded lenses of clay. The bauxite zones are 30 to 40 ft thick.

Tropical weathering and percolating ground water have produced a cap that contains as much as 20% silica. The cap, up to 1-6 ft thick, is not considered to be ore. The ore deposits are underlain by kaolin, and recovery of this resource is now receiving serious study. The kaolin, however, presents a very poor bearing surface for heavy equipment.

Primary stripping removes the upper sandy formation with interbedded clays. Stripping is usually done with bucket wheel excavators, although hydraulic monitors have been used occasionally to undercut and slump upper layers for collection and pumping to a settling basin.

Guybau has six digging wheels, the largest of which is capable of excavating 3,500 ltph. The BWEs work in sandy clay with belt wagons and conveyor systems. The sandy zones are ideal digging material for the wheels, and conveyor transportation of such material presents few problems. The interbedded clays are tougher to dig. At the face, this material looks compacted and dense. The wheels can dig the clays rapidly, but the moisture content is released by repeated vibrations of the bed on the conveyor belts. During heavy tropical rains, the material turns to slop on the belts. Even under more ideal conditions, the clays cause conveyor problems, building up on troughing and return idlers and sticking at transfer points.

Moving the next layer

Secondary stripping of the hard clay is usually done with draglines. The largest dragline on hand is a 28-yd Bucyrus-Erie 1300W walking machine having a 325-ft boom angled at about 32°. At the time of assembly, it was the longest dragline boom in the world on a Model 1300W. The tubular members of the boom contain compressed air for identification of cracks. A 23-yd Bucyrus-Erie 1260W dragline is now being erected, a nine-month process. The 28-yd machine was commissioned in May 1976 at the East Montgomery mine. The 23-yd machine is destined for service at the older but highly productive Kara Kara mine. Several B-E 480W

Typical specifications of specialty grades of Guyana product

	Guybau refractory	Bermine refractory	Bermine chemical
Al_2O_3, %	88.00	89.00	60.00
SiO_2, %	6.50	5.25	4.50
Fe_2O_3, %	2.00	2.00	1.00
TiO_2, %	3.25	3.50	2.70
LOI, %	0.25	0.25	30.50
Moisture, %	—	—	3.00

O&K bucket wheel excavators remove overburden at bauxite mines in Surinam and Guyana. In Surinam, the loam overburden contains much water. In Guyana, the overburden consists of solidified sands and clay. The Surinam machines can produce 22,000 bank cubic meters daily using a bucket wheel boom that has a 31-m reach and a digging height of 20 m. The largest of the machines in Guyana produce 33,000 bank meters per day, reach 26 m, and dig banks up to 20 m high.

draglines are in use, as well as 4-yd 88W units. The 4-yd machines are generally used in ore.

There are many variations on this general plan of primary and secondary stripping. For example, the Kara Kara mine employs a fleet of scrapers, including Cat 773 models and Terex TS 24 machines, to strip the sandy upper formations. The 11-yd draglines excavate the lower clay formations. Smaller draglines and power shovels dig blasted ore at the Kara Kara mine and load trains of up to 35 cars, each having a 15-lt capacity.

At Kara Kara, the company's biggest producer, the mining face is more than 3,000 ft long. Today it is the only mine in the company to employ direct rail loading at the face. This system, however, imposes a certain rigidity on production because it is almost impossible to blend various grades of ore. Kara Kara produces both refractory- and metal-grade ores. Lacking the advantages of an intervening set of stockpiles, ore quality control is a demanding task at Kara Kara.

The other mines use truck haulage to build stockpiles at rail loading sidings. Such stockpiled material is then reclaimed by front-end loaders, which dump into the railcars. The most distant mine in the Guybau production mix is Ituni, 37 mi southeast of Linden. Ituni ore is delivered to the Linden plant in trainloads of 100 cars.

The new East Montgomery mine is situated on 30 million lt of high-quality calcined refractory-grade ore. It has been designed for a production rate of 1 million to 2 million ltpy. At East Montgomery, scraper fleets removed the top 35 to 40 ft of overburden, and digging wheels then excavated two 40-ft cuts to the dragline bench. The new 28-yd dragline excavated the next 60 to 80 ft of overburden to reach the bauxite horizon, establishing an initial box cut. The dragline bench is 300 ft wide, and the cut over the top of the bauxite is 40 ft wide. The upper sands were sloped to a final 25°. The natural angle of repose of this material is about 30°. The mining plan calls for an initial box cut 4,000 ft in length, which will widen to as much as 5,000 ft as mining progresses. As designed, the final pit would cover an area of approximately 10,000 x 5,000 ft.

Since several mines are worked simultaneously, producing various grades of ore, the plant requires a large marshaling area with numerous switching options. Inbound trains are shunted to sidings until their cargo is scheduled for processing. □

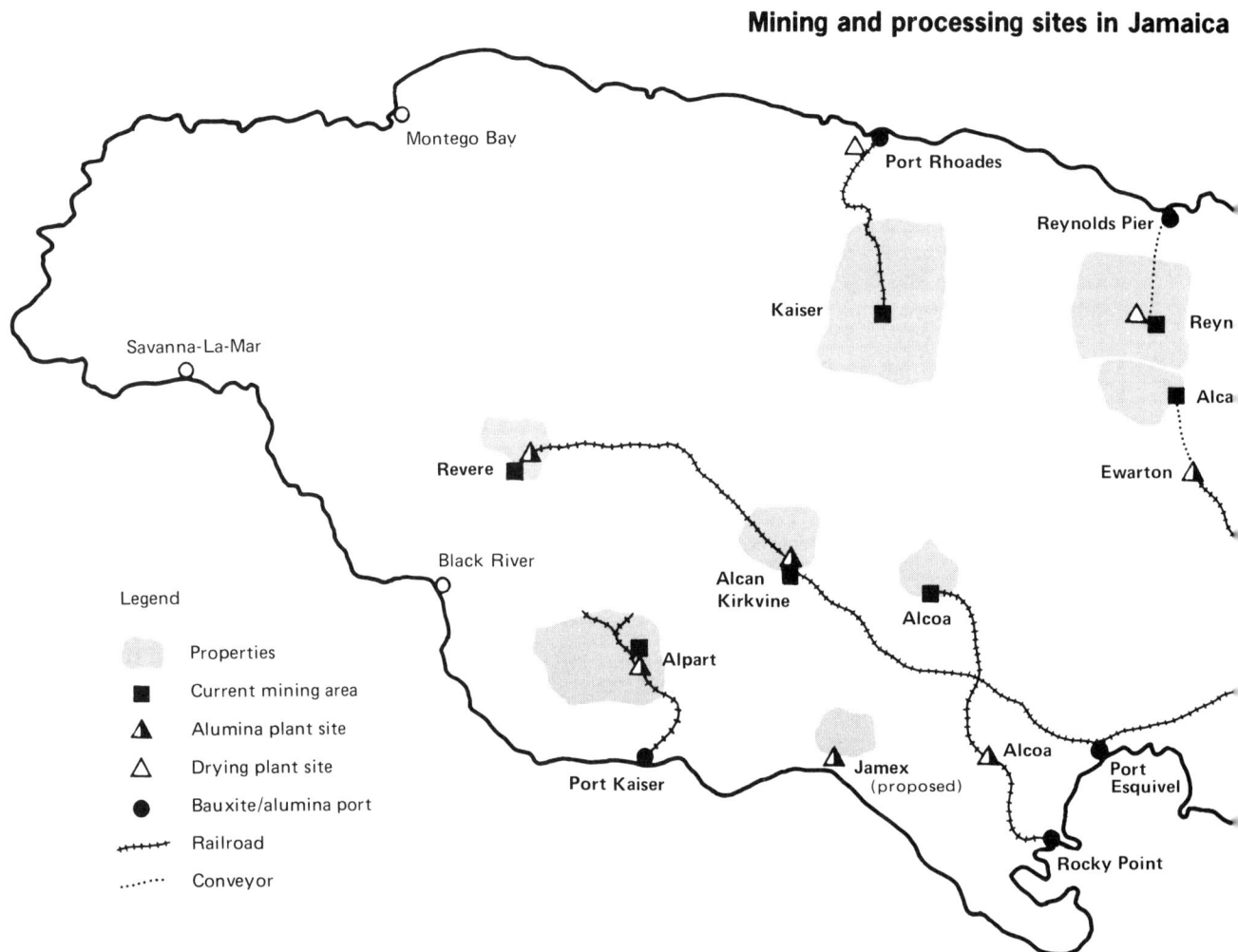

Mining and processing sites in Jamaica

JAMAICA: government partnerships and recent declines shape industry's profile

Richard A. Thomas, Associate editor

IN THE MINDS OF MOST AMERICANS, Jamaica will forever remain a small tropical resort island where fun and sun hold sway. The more urbane, politically conscious traveler or reader may see past the mangoes, sunsets, and rum punches to the country's current economic crisis—foreign exchange reserves more than $200 million in the red, 27% unemployment, fears of defaulting on the external debt, rising violence, and the like. However, surprisingly few see Jamaica as an industrial nation which, in the brief span of 20 years, has risen from an agricultural economy to the world's second largest producer of aluminum raw materials.

Mining of bauxite now ranks first in terms of export value for Jamaica, and shipments of bauxite and alumina account for about two-thirds of the country's export dollars. Most of the bauxite and about one-third of the alumina are slated for the US market, which obtains 40% of its supply from Jamaica. Five large companies—four US and one Canadian—currently mine Jamaican bauxite at an overall rate of 10 million to 15 million mtpy.

Operations are for the most part concentrated in the north- and south-central areas of the island. Roughly one-third of the "red gold" is refined into alumina in Bayer-process plants, with capacities ranging up to 1.3 million stpy. Recent government efforts to nationalize the "commanding heights" of the Jamaican economy have led to government-controlled mining partnerships with three operators—Alcoa, Kaiser, and Reynolds. Similar partnerships with Alpart (itself a three-way partnership) and Canadian-based Alcan seem likely in the future.

Operating companies are currently struggling on their way up from production declines of the last three years, the result of both external and internal problems. Externally, aluminum markets were soft over these years, and

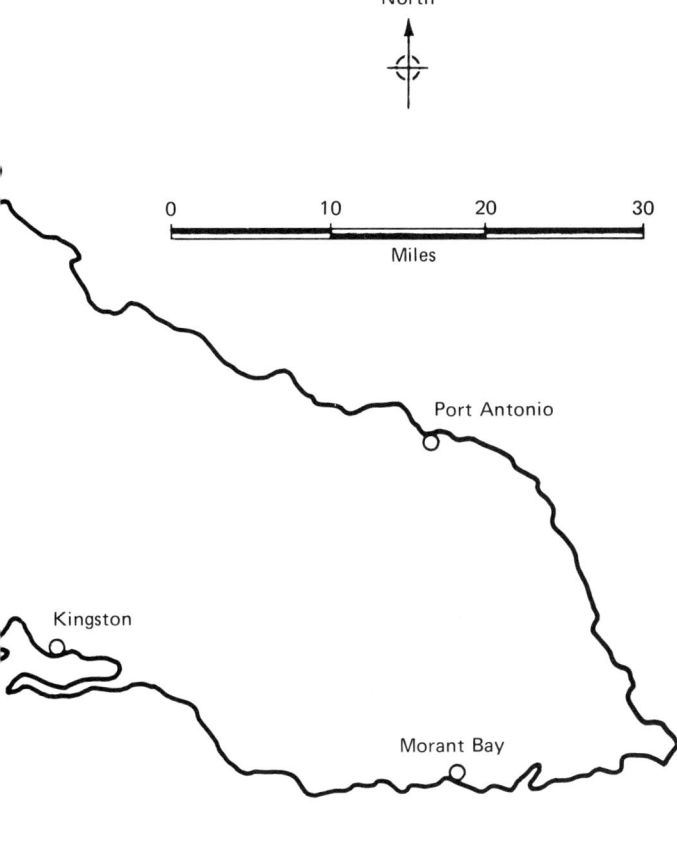

the US and world recessions placed many restrictions on company operating capacities and desires to expand. Internally, production declines were engendered by strikes at all the operating companies following the expiration of contracts with the National Workers Union in December 1975; by an accident that caused temporary shutdown at one operation; and—most significant— by government attempts to nationalize the industry, including the application in 1974 of a bauxite production levy that was five times the size of the previous tax.

Economists say the government's nationalization efforts, aimed not only at the bauxite industry but also at Jamaica's utilities, radio, and banking sectors, are scaring away foreign private investors. To this assertion, the government has officially replied:

"Foreign private capital is welcome in Jamaica and is assured of fair and consistent treatment, provided:
  a) the investment is consistent with national purposes;
  b) it operates in Jamaica on the basis of good corporate citizenship;
  c) so far as ownership is concerned, it is willing to enter into partnership with local private interests, the Government, or both, as may be required by the Government of Jamaica."

Mining methods of the operating companies vary only slightly: Reynolds uses shovels and draglines, whereas Alcan uses backhoes and draglines; Kaiser uses 42- and 50-ton trucks, while Alcoa uses 32- and 50-tonners; average pit depths differ somewhat, as do truck haul distances and blending practices. The substantial variations are found in the methods of long-distance ore haulage (conveyors, trains, aerial ropeways, etc.).

To differing degrees, all the operators must be flexible in dealing with Jamaica's most striking physical feature—the mountainous nature of its surface. Nearly half the island is more than 1,000 ft above sea level. Another common denominator is the fervor with which each company pursues its reclamation and restoration programs. Since 1952, when Reynolds made the first commercial shipment of bauxite from the island, Jamaica has maintained a stance that is almost unique in world mining history—placing emphasis on land rehabilitation at the *inception* of mining. Today, operators reclaim an average of 1¼ surface acres for each acre disturbed by mining.

While the mining companies have generally scraped a profit from their operations on the island, their presence has also been of substantial benefit to Jamaica. The multinationals have created more jobs and improved housing, boosted the GDP, provided a number of impressive vocational training centers, and have even contributed to the fertility of the arable land and the quality of the livestock. With deference paid to the production declines of the last three years, most Jamaicans, when asked, express optimism that the symbiosis will endure, to the continuing advantage of both participants.

An interview with JBI representatives

Since early 1976, dealings between the Jamaican government and the bauxite/alumina companies have been handled through the government's company, the Jamaican Bauxite Institute (JBI), which is responsible to the Minister of Mining and Natural Resources. The JBI's varied functions include:

- Preparation of briefs for the government negotiating team.
- Technological research into the economic mineralogy, chemical mineralogy, and processing of bauxite.
- Monitoring and evaluating trends in the aluminum market (yearly production levies are based on JBI recommendations).
- Allocation of reserve mining lands to companies, and planning of land use in conjunction with companies.

In a brief interview with Dr. Carlton Davis, acting executive director of the JBI, and the Hon. Patrick Rousseau, chairman of the board, E/MJ inquired first about the type and state of research in progress. "We are very concerned about maintaining the economic processability of our ore," explained Dr. Davis. "For that reason we have set up a research and development unit,

Factsheet, Jamaican bauxite and alumina operations

	Kaiser	Reynolds	Alpart	Alcoa
Ownership	51% Jamaican gov't. 49% Kaiser	51% Jamaican gov't. 49% Reynolds	36.5% Kaiser 36.5% Reynolds 27% Anaconda Co.	94% Alcoa 6% Jamaican gov't.
Facilities and location				
Mining	Water Valley	Lydford	Essex Valley	Breadnut Valley
Drying plant	Port Rhoades	Lydford		
Alumina plant			Nain	Halse Hall
Shipping port	Port Rhoades	Reynolds Pier	Port Kaiser	Rocky Point
Production	6 million dry stpy bauxite	2.5 million dry ltpy bauxite	1.3 million stpy alumina	550,000 stpy alumina
Ore grade	45%	42.5%	42%	42-45%
Mining method	Open-pit, multiple lift			
Average pit depth	40 ft	40 ft	12 ft	70-80 ft
Average haul	2 mi	2 mi	3½ mi	4 mi
Type of alumina plant	Drying only	Drying only	High-temperature Bayer	High/low-temperature Bayer
Major excavating equipment	4 P&H 1400DE shovels 3 BLH 2400B draglines	2 P&H 1500 shovels 3 Marion 111M shovels 2 Marion 111M draglines 1 Cat 992B loader	2 P&H shovels (6-yd) 2 Koehring backhoes (6-yd) 1 Manitowac dragline (6-yd)	1 Bucyrus Erie 88B shovel 2 P&H 955A shovels 1 Bucyrus Erie dragline (4.5-yd) 2 Cat 988 loaders
Major haulage equipment	8 KW Dart trucks (42-ton) 16 Euclid R50 trucks (50-ton)	21 Cat 769B trucks (40-ton) 1 Overland conveyor (1,000 tph)	18 Euclid R50 trucks (50-ton)	7 Wabco Haulpak trucks (50-ton) 7 Oshkosh trucks (32-ton) 2 Mack trucks (50-ton)

which is starting rather slowly." Research is currently concentrated in three areas, Dr. Davis said: 1) the problem of iron mineral transformation is being examined because different transformations strongly affect alumina settling characteristics; 2) methods for utilizing high-silica bauxite are being checked—particularly important in view of the fact that the legal maximum silica level for Jamaican bauxite is now 8%; and 3) all types of red mud disposal and/or utilization systems are being evaluated. "We are very aware of the limited land space of our island," Dr. Davis said.

Chairman Rousseau added, "We are also building a very strong economics unit, which so far has an excellent track record in predicting the average realized price for aluminum ingot." The JBI's predictions have been no more than tenths of a penny off the mark.

Asked about the future of bauxite mining in Jamaica, Rousseau said: "We are very bullish about the future of Jamaican aluminum, and aluminum in general. The last three years have been very bad for Jamaica—strikes, the Alcoa accident, production cuts, no expansions—but industry analysts expect that the US [Jamaica's main market] will become a net importer of aluminum in the next few years." Bauxite production was up 23% during first-half 1977 compared with the same period in 1976; alumina exports increased by 41.5% over the same time span. METALS WEEK editors report: "Jamaica's production rates reinforce the government's claim that its state-owned bauxite industry will earn J$200 million this year."

Rousseau elaborated, "We are looking in the long run to participate as much as possible in the various stages of the aluminum industry, particularly the later stages of development. We are looking very closely at the fabrication end of the business because we feel we must participate in the manufacture of the end product—there lies a part of the profit that we should be enjoying. We are giving some very serious thought to fabrication plants on the island."

Explaining the numerous recent contacts with governments of Caribbean and Middle East countries, Rousseau said, "We are trying to diversify our market because every time the US industry catches a cold, we get influenza. We want to get away from such a heavy—almost exclusive—dependence on US and Canadian markets." In this regard, Jamaica is known to have communicated with Mexico, Venezuela, Trinidad, Algeria, Guyana, Iran, Romania, and Iraq. A few of these contacts—notably Mexico, Venezuela, and Algeria—have made serious commitments for which provisional "letters of intent" have been traded.

"We are examining and are fairly close to a final decision stage on building a smelter in Mexico, in which Jamaica will participate," Dr. Davis said. "Final deci-

Alcan	
Kirkvine	Ewarton
100% Alcan	100% Alcan
Russell Place	Schwallenburgh
Mandeville	Ewarton
Port Esquivel	Port Esquivel
1,500 mtpd alumina	860 mtpd alumina
45%	43.8%
40 ft	30 ft
1.6 mi	1½-2½ mi
Low-temperature Bayer	Low-temperature Bayer
1 BLH 2400B dragline	1 BLH 2400B dragline
1 Cat 992 Loader	2 P&H 1055 draglines
1 Warner Swasey backhoe	2 Cat 988 loaders
8 Cat 773 trucks (50-ton)	12 Cat 769B (35-ton) 1 Aerial ropeway (420-tph)

smelter.

Jamex would be fed either through expansion of the government's newly acquired equity partnerships (agreements gave the government this option) or from the "Javamex" refinery, which the government plans for Jamaica. "Our aim is to build a refinery in South Manchester that will have a final size not less than 600,000 mtpy. Some foundation work has already started, and we hope to start actual construction sometime next year," Davis said. The refinery will be 51% Jamaican-owned, with the remaining interests held by Mexico and Venezuela. Mines surrounding the refinery will produce 1.5 million tpy using reserves consolidated from blocks previously owned by Kaiser, Alcoa, and Reynolds.

In addition to supplying the Jamex smelter, "We are now trying to finalize details of supplying alumina from our upcoming refinery to Algeria," Rousseau said. A memorandum of understanding to that effect has been signed by both countries.

Plans for Jamaica's participation in construction of a smelter in Trinidad were recently called off; the government of Trinidad and Tobago has decided to forego foreign involvement in the initial stages of smelter development. The project was slated to include Trinidad and Tobago, Jamaica, and Guyana, and was to be located on Trinidad to make use of the country's natural gas resources.

Bauxite geology

Jamaica's bauxite occurs exclusively as pocket and blanket deposits on the Karst surface of the Tertiary White Limestone group, a relatively pure limestone covering two-thirds of the island's mountainous surface. Deposits averaging 250,000 to 400,000 tons predominate, with most exhibiting surface areas of 5-12 acres

sion on whether to proceed will be made in the next three to four months." The project, called "Jamex," will center on construction of a 150,000-mtpy aluminum

Statistical profile of Jamaica

Area, sq km	10,962
Total midyear population (est.)	
1976	2,044,700
1980	2,169,700
Percentage of urban population, 1976	55.8
Avg. annual rate of growth of total population (percent), 1970-76	1.5
Gross domestic product (millions of 1973 dollars), 1975	2,186.7
Gross domestic product per capita (1973 dollars), 1975	1,085.8
Rates of annual growth (percent), 1960-75	
Total GDP	4.0
GDP per capita	2.5
Gross investment (millions of 1973 dollars), 1975	618.9
Trade (millions of dollars), 1975	
Exports	807.6
Imports	960.4
International reserves (millions of dollars), October 1976	67.8
External public debt (millions of dollars), Dec. 31, 1975	802.0
Exchange rate (units of the national currency per dollar)	
December 1975	0.91
October 1976	0.91
Percent change in consumer prices during 1976*	7.6
Central government tax revenue as a percentage of GDP, 1975	17.5
Percentage of total central government expenditures, 1975-76	
Education	16.2
Public health	6.9
Housing	3.0
Birth rate per 1,000 inhabitants, 1975	30.5
Mortality per 1,000 inhabitants, 1975	7.0
Infant mortality per 1,000 live births, 1975	26.3
Years of life expectancy at birth, 1970-75	70.2
Percentage of literacy, 1960	81.9

*To September. Source: "Economic and Social Progress in Latin America," 1976 report, Inter-American Development Bank.

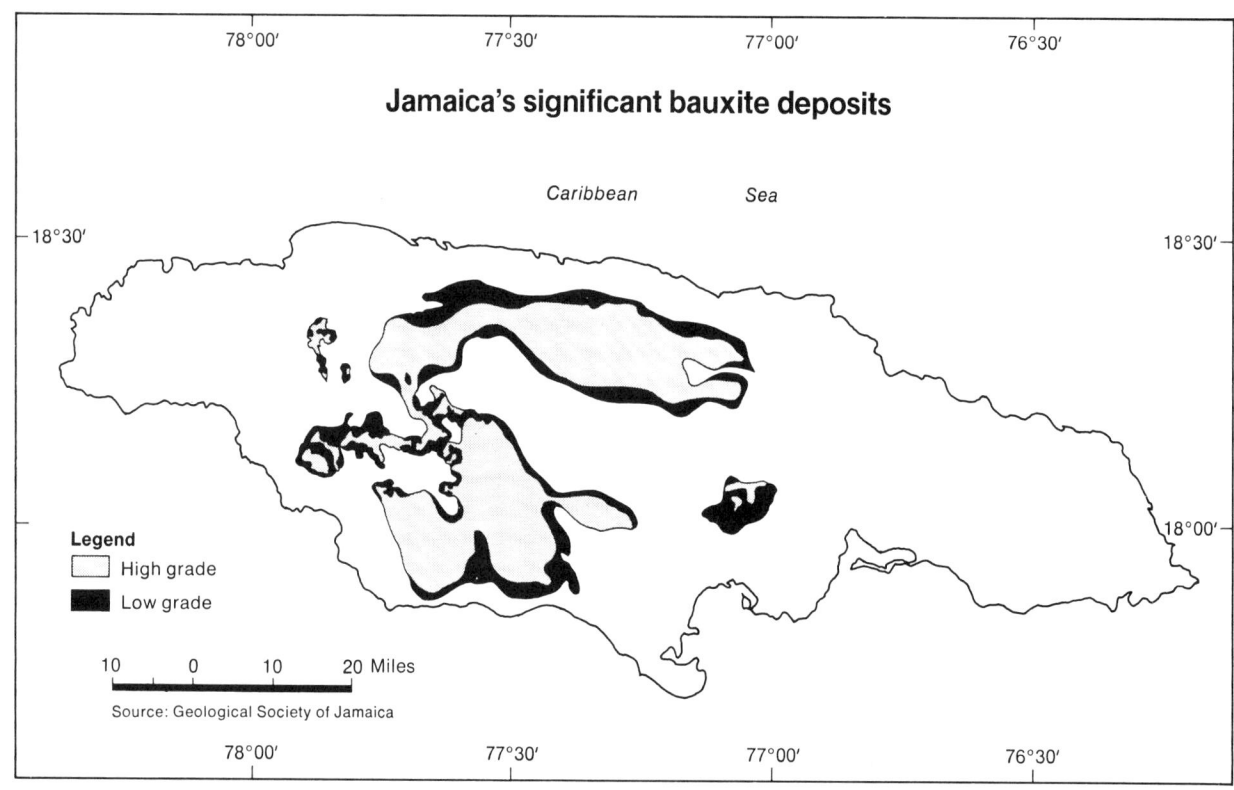

and depths of 25-40 ft under 1-2 ft of soil overburden. The actual ranges for these dimensions are considerably wider (deposits run from a few tons to more than 3 million tons), but the economics of mining puts a limit on exploitation in certain cases, especially in the low end of each range.

Jamaica's bauxite is mostly a dark, earthy red, with localized variations from off-white to yellow. It is generally soft and unconsolidated ("like pressed dirt"), it shows no internal structural characteristics, and it almost always makes a sharp, obvious contact with the underlying white limestone. Its age is probably pre-late Pleistocene; the limestone parent rock ranges from middle to late Miocene.

As a rule, Jamaican bauxite is quite permeable in situ, but when disturbed or compacted it loses this property. Interstitial and combined water content ranges from 17% to 25% of the total weight. The average grade mined is 45% "total available alumina" (50% actual total), with 1.5% reactive silica. Gangue minerals other than silica include iron (17-21%), titania (1.7-2.8%), phosphorus (average 0.5% P_2O_5), and managanese (average 0.3%). Total bauxite reserves are estimated at 2 billion tons, according to METALS WEEK. (Interestingly, the Jamaican government has established its own definition of "bauxite" under the mining regulations: Bauxite legally contains at least 47% alumina as measured by the standard difference method, and not more than 8% silica. Industry spokesmen sometimes joke that many of their orebodies are "not bauxite at all" because the grade is too low, or the silica too high.)

Although Jamaican bauxite did not gain economic significance as an ore of aluminum until the 1940s, its presence in Jamaica was noted as long ago as the 1820s. Two theories have since been advanced and widely accepted for the genesis and emplacement of these deposits. The earlier theory holds that the deposits were formed from the residues left after solution of the underlying limestone by groundwater. Such solution explains the Karst topography and the formation of Jamaica's central "Cockpit Country." The newer theory suggests a derivation of the bauxite from Cretaceous volcanic deposits underlying the limestone. Mechanisms have been demonstrated whereby eroded material from these volcanics might be transported into the limestone areas via cavern systems and Karst streams. Subsequent weathering of this alluvial material could conceivably produce the bauxite deposits.

There are drawbacks to full acceptance of either theory. The residual theory implies the erosion of an extremely large volume of limestone, and evidence for the existence of such a volume is incomplete. On the other hand, the volcanics and related alluvium are genetically more remotely related to the bauxite than are the limestones. The residual theory currently enjoys the greater support.

Bauxite is by far the most abundant economic mineral found on the island, but it is not the only one. Gypsum, mined by quarry methods, is used as a retarder for cement and as a plaster constituent. High grade silica sand is used for the manufacture of flint glass. Limestone, Jamaica's most abundant material, is used in road construction and as a Bayer-process additive. A good-quality marble is found in St. Thomas, and small deposits of copper, zinc, lead, and manganese occur in Portland, St. Andrew, and upper Clarendon Parish. □

Kaiser — Jamaica's largest bauxite producer

WATER VALLEY, set 15 mi inland from Discovery Bay on Jamaica's tourist-dotted north coast, is the mining scene of the newly christened Kaiser Jamaica Bauxite Co., one of the world's largest open-pit bauxite operations. Kaiser's theme, "In Partnership with Jamaica," is not just a public relations campaign—Kaiser Bauxite Co. was the second and largest of the island's bauxite operating companies to enter into a partnership with the Jamaican government. The partnership agreement, signed on February 2 this year, gave 51% ownership of the 6-million-tpy operation to the government, while insuring that Kaiser will have a 40-year bauxite supply based on current production levels. The agreement also set a fixed production levy for seven years.

Kaiser has been operating at its present north coast location (St. Ann Parish) since 1967; before that, Kaiser worked deposits in south-central Jamaica (St. Elizabeth Parish) and shipped dried ore from Port Kaiser on the south coast. Many of the former deposits in St. Elizabeth have been mined out and reclaimed, Kaiser having removed 43 million tons of bauxite during 1953-1967. The remaining deposits there, along with Port Kaiser, now belong to Alpart, in which Kaiser has a one-third interest.

In addition to inland mines, Kaiser operates the impressive Port Rhoades storage-drying-shipping facility in Discovery Bay Harbour, fed by railcars from the mine site. The facility, which opened in 1967 after extensive work to clear a deep-water channel, includes a 125,000-dry-ton closed storage dome, a McDowell-Wellman rotary car dumper, and three rotary kiln dryers for reducing bauxite's moisture content prior to shipment.

Kaiser's bauxite deposits, like those of other operating companies on the island, lie on or very close to the surface in bowl-shaped and elongated pocket-shaped depressions enclosed by Tertiary limestone. The surface area of most deposits ranges from ½ acre to several acres, and depths range from 15 to 100 ft, with a 40-ft average depth. Most of the bauxite is gibbsitic ($Al_2O_3 \cdot 3H_2O$), although boehmitic and diaspore (both monohydrate) forms also are found. Overburden averages 18 in. of topsoil.

Mining of deposits is preceded by a thorough program of prospecting and mapping, directed by the company's property management and mine engineering departments. Initially, deposits are drilled on an exploratory basis on 500-ft centers. Just prior to mining, all areas are redrilled on a 50 x 100-ft grid to outline pits and obtain grade estimates.

Kaiser's long-range mining plans call for subdivision of the government-designated mining area (see map) into "loadouts," each covering roughly 3 sq mi and requiring five or more years to mine. Mining began first in the Dry Harbour Mountain area of Tobolski (Loadout I), from which 30.6 million tons were recovered before the land was reclaimed. Mining is currently active in the Water Valley area (Loadout II), which will be expanded to include part of the Armadale (No. 4) block in 1978, bringing the active mining area to 4,500 acres. Mining of the expanded Loadout II is expected to conclude in 1983, after recovery of 54 million tons of ore. Operations will then shift to Nos. 3-5 in the Hyde Park area for recovery of another 54 million tons.

The entire mining area specified by the 40-year government lease (Blocks 1-11) covers 65.5 sq mi, and ownership of the surface rights to roughly half of this area has been consolidated. The other half is privately owned by numerous low-yield farmers, with whom Kaiser has had widely varying success in its efforts to purchase land. Blocks 12 and 13 are "reserve," and will

Mined lands look like this a few years after Kaiser initiates its rehabilitation program. So far, 2,100 acres have been reclaimed.

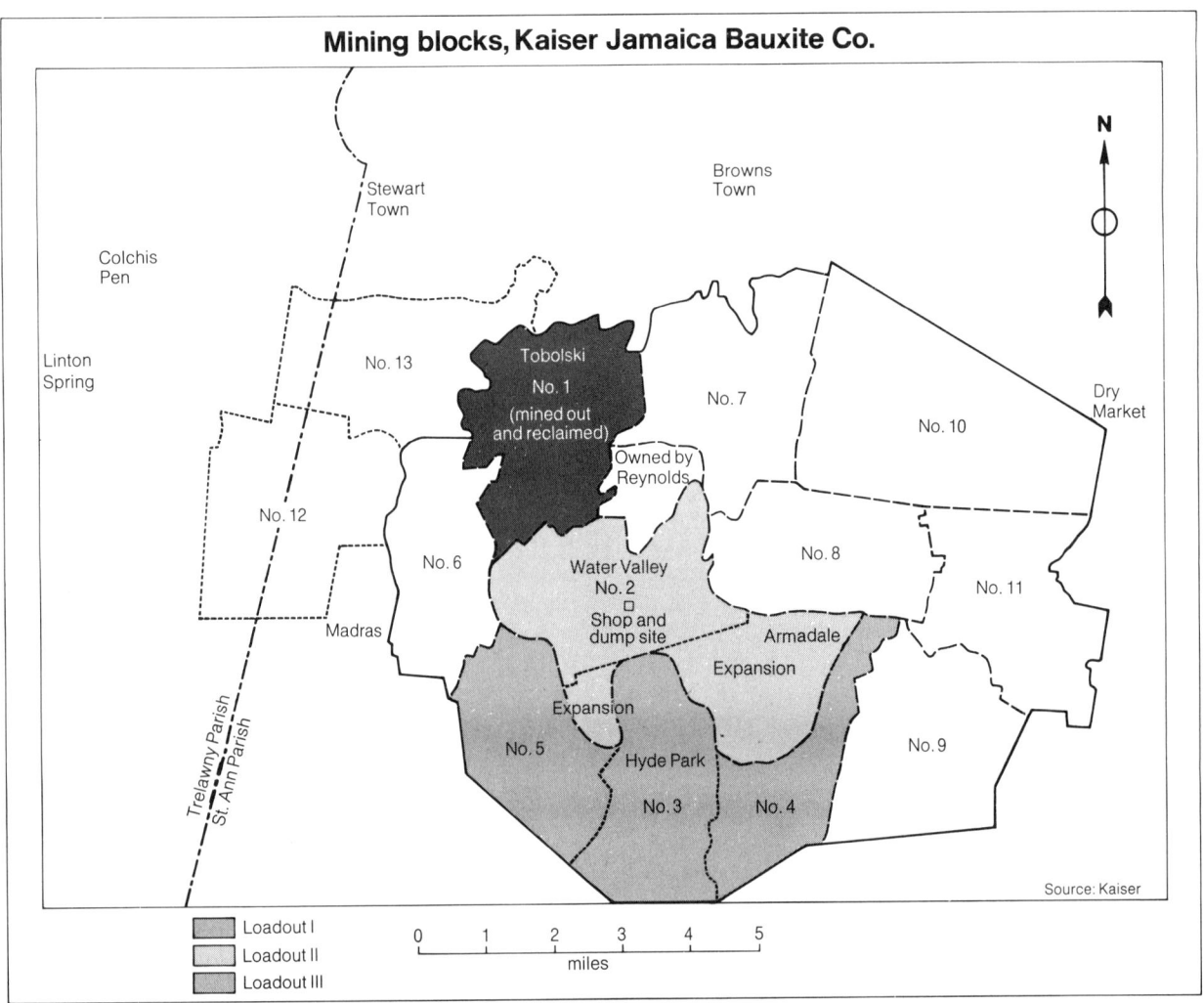

Mining blocks, Kaiser Jamaica Bauxite Co.

be mined only if they are needed to fulfill the 40-year mineral supply clause.

Mining is currently in progress in four pits, totaling 24,000 wet stpd. Before pits are mined, topsoil is stripped from the surface with Caterpillar D8 dozers and scrapers and stockpiled around the perimeter. Mining of the upper benches is carried out with four 600-tph P&H 1400DE shovels with 6-cu-yd buckets. The shovels, which take 20-ft vertical cuts into the pit face, work in concert with a fleet of 24 off-highway haulers. When the pits become too narrow or deep to be mined with the shovel-truck combination, Kaiser employs three Baldwin Lima 2400B draglines with 10-cu-yd buckets. The 435-tph-rated draglines sit above the pit bottom and load directly into trucks, which stand at the pit perimeter or on the downward-spiraling ramp.

Kaiser's hauling fleet, largest on the island, consists of 16 50-ton R50 Euclids and eight older 42-ton KW Darts. All units have specially designed aluminum bodies, and truck beds are heated by redirection of the exhaust to minimize sticking of the ore.

The average one-way haul to the railcar loading point in Water Valley is now 10,000 ft; however, near-term expansion plans will bring this figure to 13,000 ft. Loads are dumped over grizzlies into gondola cars or onto the surge pile adjacent to the loading ramp. The pile is maintained, in addition to the one at Port Rhoades, because haulage is frequently interrupted during the heavy rainfalls of Jamaica's two rainy seasons.

Ore is transported 15 mi in unit trains of 20 84-ton cars to the Port Rhoades complex, then unloaded by a Wellman automatic rotary car dumper that turns each car upside down, emptying its contents into a hopper. The hopper feeds conveyors that in turn feed a traveling stacker, which distributes bauxite evenly over a 350,000-ton wet stockpile. Dozers push this stockpile into hoppers that feed three dryers (totaling 1,000 tph of throughput), which drive off the interstitial, uncombined water from the bauxite, thereby reducing the shipping weight. The dryers—two 10 x 80-ft rotary and one 13 x 100-ft rotary—operate at 1,800°F to reduce the bauxite from 22% moisture, as mined, down to 16.5%. The dryers are all fired with Bunker C oil and are equipped with cyclones that discharge partially cleaned gases into Research Cottrell electrostatic precipitators for final dust removal.

Dryer products are transported in an enclosed conveyor system to the aluminum-covered storage dome, then to the pier, from which charter ships carry the ore to Kaiser's alumina plants in Gramercy and Baton Rouge, La. Dry ore production from the drying plant is 25,000 stpd.

While power for the mining area is drawn from the Jamaican Public Service Co., power for the shipping complex is supplied by Kaiser's 6,600-kw generator installation. Water is taken from the company's privately owned wells.

Overall, Kaiser runs an efficient, tidy operation in Water Valley, with few problems or surprises. When pressed, the Kaiser mine planning staff admits to difficulties caused by the hilly terrain, problems in acquiring surface rights, and some trouble with fog and the rainy season, which can cut production by 50%. (Water Valley recently experienced the heaviest rainfall since mining began there.) All these problems are experienced in some degree by the other bauxite and alumina companies of Jamaica.

Kaiser's reclamation and resettlement programs are noteworthy. In land rehabilitation, Kaiser exceeds government requirements, which stipulate that all lands mined must be returned to their original level of productivity as soon as possible after mining operations are completed. Kaiser not only restores the land to its original productivity but also increases the fertility of the soil by fertilization and scientific agricultural methods. Also, land "resculpting" by dozers often leaves more arable surface area than was originally present. More than 2,100 acres have already been rehabilitated through the company's program.

Kaiser's land and housing resettlement program, in effect since 1954, provides for the resettling of small holders from whom lands have been purchased, to prevent social and/or economic dislocation. To date, 14,500 acres and several hundred new houses have been provided for inhabitants through this program. Kaiser has also adopted the policy of leasing to reputable farmers all lands that come into its possession (except those required for mine-related use in the immediate future), and it has designed a number of production incentive schemes for its tenant farmers, including a small farm competition, farmer training seminars, and the land amortization program. □

Alpart

NEWEST OF THE ALUMINUM COMPANIES operating in Jamaica, the Alumina Partners of Jamaica (Alpart) in Essex Valley, St. Elizabeth Parish, can lay claim to uniqueness on more than one account—it is the only consortium of bauxite/alumina corporations on the island, and it operates Jamaica's biggest alumina plant, at one time the largest such plant in the world.

Alpart is the result of a partnership undertaken in 1966 by Kaiser Aluminum and Chemical Corp. (36.5%), Reynolds Metals Co. (36.5%), and The Anaconda Co. (27%), all of whom own Alpart through Jamaican subsidiaries—Kaiser Jamaica Corp., Reynolds Jamaica Alumina Ltd., and Anaconda Jamaica Inc., respectively. Back in 1969, the three parent companies pooled their knowhow to design and construct Alpart's 1.3-million-stpy plant on a 300-acre site in Nain, at a total cost of about $280 million.

The original managing partner of Alpart was Kaiser, but under the terms of the agreement, Reynolds assumed the managerial role on July 1, 1976. Not surprisingly, many of Alpart's holdings came from its parent companies. Current holdings include bauxite mining properties and agricultural lands (Alpart Farms Ltd.) surrounding the plant, totaling 33,000 acres; the Nain alumina plant; and Port Kaiser, Alpart's shipping facility on the south shore. Port Kaiser, originally a bauxite loading port for Kaiser during the '50s and '60s, was redesigned for alumina storage at Alpart's inception.

As of late October, there was no partnership agreement between Alpart and the Jamaican government, although one might reasonably be expected in the future. Negotiations are rumored to be taking place; however, the government's ban on press coverage of bauxite negotiations in progress relegates most reports on the topic to the level of speculation.

Bauxite mining at 10,000 wet stpd takes place in those areas of Essex Valley immediately surrounding the plant. Alpart engineers jokingly describe their ore as "the worst on the island." It has a total available alumina content of 42%, slightly lower than that of other operating companies, and it must be blended from three or four pits to balance the silica level, hematite/goethite ratio, and percentage of iron pisolites. The pisolites pose a problem because of their higher-than-average iron content, and the silica (reactive SiO_2^{--}) in the refining process tends to cause a loss of caustic soda and the formation of unwanted sodium aluminum silicates.

Alpart's bauxite deposits are relatively shallow, ranging from 5 to 50 ft deep and averaging 12 ft. In a few areas, the deposits coalesce into a blanket structure. Gibbsite predominates, although boehmite also is present; contacts with the Miocene limestone are sharp. High-silica topsoil overburden is stripped to a depth of 18 in. and stacked nearby prior to mining—S.O.P. for all the operating companies.

In rehabilitation of mined lands, Alpart's programs are comparable to those of the other four Jamaican bauxite producers. After mining, pits are contoured and topsoil is respread. Grass is then planted and periodically plowed back, with the objective of returning the land to at least its former productivity.

Ore is excavated with two P&H 6-cu-yd shovels (629 tph each) taking 12-ft vertical cuts; one Manitowac 6-cu-yd dragline (437 tph) for deeper pits; and two Koehring 6-cu-yd backhoes (408 tph each), which are used for pit cleanup because their maneuverability yields higher recoveries than the shovels or draglines, Alpart engineers say. The mine operates 15 shifts per week, recovering an average of 85% of the estimated in-place ore.

Haulage to the 75,000-ton wet ore stockpile adjacent to the plant is accomplished with Alpart's fleet of 18

Euclid R-50 rear-dump trucks. Each 50-ton unit has an exhaust-heated bed lined with polyurethane to minimize sticking. The average haul is 18,000 ft (minimum 25-min round trip), on haul roads 40-50 ft wide and maximum 10% grade.

Alpart has recently been capping its marl haul roads with calcium chloride to hold down dust. The hygroscopic nature of $CaCl_2$ minimizes the number of visits necessary from the road-watering trucks, but a drawback lies in obtaining the $CaCl_2$, which must be imported. "One of our biggest problems is logistics," says assistant plant manager Tony Dunn. "We have to import caustic, oil, starch, HCl—just about everything we use in the plant except bauxite comes through the port." Port Kaiser is 12 mi by rail from the plant site. One plant additive is not imported.

Alpart, like other Jamaican bauxite/alumina producers, has an extended list of nonmining interests. Alpart Farms conducts a varied agricultural operation that includes research into the use of local agricultural byproducts for livestock feed; cattle feedlots at Nain and Friendship; and a dairy farm in Pepper, St. Elizabeth. Alpart's land resettlement program insures that the sellers of land will receive equal or greater acreage elsewhere, including a new reinforced concrete-block house if the land sold has a house. Alpart currently has about 1,200 tenant farmers. Since the start of Project Land Lease in 1975, Alpart has handed over to the government 3,600 acres for a cooperative livestock farm. Among other activities, adult literacy and youth development programs are sponsored, and the Alpart Training School teaches basic industrial skills. □

Alcan—Bauxite pioneer

THE ONLY CANADIAN-BASED alumina producer on the island, Alcan Jamaica Ltd. is justly proud of both its pioneering role in the development of the industry in Jamaica, and its own operations, which include two bauxite mines and two alumina plants. Alcan's Kirkvine alumina refinery in Manchester Parish and its Ewarton Works in St. Catherine, together with the corresponding mining properties, represent an investment of J$206.2 million.

Alcan has been in Jamaica since 1942, when it explored the island's extensive bauxite deposits, acting as an agent for the Jamaican government. In 1943, it formed the subsidiary Jamaica Bauxites Ltd. (later to become Alcan Jamaica Ltd.) to acquire key properties in Manchester, St. Catherine, and St. Elizabeth. Nine years later, Alcan started up the Kirkvine Works, the first alumina refining plant in the Caribbean. The St. Elizabeth holdings were traded for northern Manchester properties in 1957, and the Ewarton Works was started up in 1959. By 1968, both plants were operating at 550,000 mtpy of alumina—30 times the capacity originally envisaged when Kirkvine was designed.

Over the last 10 years, Alcan has continued to acquire property to consolidate the fragmented ownership of deposits it partially controlled into mineable blocks. These efforts have not met with complete success, even in areas of small holdings where deposits must be acquired to assure the short-term future of mining operations at both plants. Alcan currently owns 51,200 acres of land, distributed as follows: 6,000 acres—industrial activities; 7,100 acres—Alcan farming; 25,500 acres—tenant farming; 12,600 acres—rocky hillside (unfarmable, being conserved for watershed control purposes). In addition to the land and plants, where rated capacity now totals 1.2 million stpy, Alcan has Port Esquivel, with 68,000 tons of storage capacity. Port Esquivel is on Jamaica's south shore, 32 mi by rail from each plant.

Open-pit bauxite mining operations at Kirkvine and Ewarton are basically similar to other mining operations on the island. At Kirkvine, pocket deposits average 40 ft deep but range up to 140 ft. Kirkvine mines 4,500 mtpd of wet ore averaging 45% available alumina with 1% silica. After topsoil stripping with Cat 631B tractor scrapers, excavation is done with one 7½-cu-yd BLH 2400B dragline, one Cat 992 10-cu-yd front-end loader, and one Warner-Swasey 4½-cu-yd backhoe. The dragline and front-end loader work in conjunction with Cat D9 dozers that rip and clean around the pit face. "We're getting away from the shovels most of the other operators use," says resources development manager R. E. Anderson. "They allow less flexibility within relatively small but deep orebodies and also contribute to the generation of excessive tramp limestone." Current extraction is 95% of the in-place ore.

When E/MJ visited Kirkvine Works, two pits were being mined in the Russell Place Block, which will be worked until 1978 for a total recovery of 9 million tons. Ore haulage to the central stockpile area or direct to the plant is done with eight Cat 773 50-ton trucks. Hauls average 1.6 mi on 50-ft-wide main haul roads with maximum 6% grade. Alcan uses only water on its roads to suppress dust, although it has tried both Bunker C and calcium chloride.

Ewarton's ore pockets, averaging 30 ft deep, are smaller and lower in grade than Kirkvine's, and the terrain is more rugged. Mining of ore with 43.8% available alumina and 1.8% silica is in progress in the Schwallenburgh area. After scraping a minimum 12 in. of topsoil, excavation is done by one 7½-cu-yd BLH 2400B dragline, two P&H 1055 4½-cu-yd draglines, and two Cat 988 6-cu-yd front-end loaders. All excavating equipment is supported by Cat D8 and D9 tractor dozers for cleanup and ripping of more consolidated ore.

Ore is hauled 1½-2½ mi to the Schwallenburgh loading station in 12 35-ton Cat 769B trucks and three 50-ton Cat 773 trucks. A 420-tph aerial ropeway system connects the loading station and the plant, which are separated by 4.3 mi and 1,100 vertical feet. □

Alcoa—The newcomer with progressive ideas

OLDEST AND LARGEST of the multinational aluminum companies, Alcoa was paradoxically the last to gain a foothold in the Jamaican bauxite industry. Alpart holds the title of "youngest" only by a technicality; its two operating parents—Kaiser and Reynolds—settled in Jamaica long before Alcoa came on the scene.

Alcoa Minerals of Jamaica, wholly owned subsidiary of Aluminum Co. of America, was formed in 1960 and acquired bauxite lands in the Clarendon Parish. Mining started in 1963, and in 1972 Alcoa placed on stream its Clarendon ("Halse Hall") alumina refinery, now rated at 550,000 stpy.

October 6, 1976 saw the signing of Alcoa's joint venture agreement with the Jamaican government, the first such agreement with an alumina producer. The agreement gave the government 6% of the company's total refining and mining assets on the island (most of Alcoa's capital investment is concentrated in the plant). In return, Alcoa now has a guaranteed 40-year bauxite supply and is subject to a 7½% fixed levy for eight years. Unlike the other operating partnerships, Alcoa did not wait for the Jamaican government to pass enabling legislation for the joint venture. Alcoa has already donned its new name, "Jamalco," and is propagating its use with the appropriate slogan, "We can't wait for tomorrow."

Alcoa's holdings include the 2,600-acre Halse Hall Estate with its alumina facilities; mining properties in the Breadnut Valley, Teak Pen, Pennants, and Mocho regions of Clarendon Parish; the Rocky Point shipping port and bauxite drying facility on the south shore; and several thousand leased acres of agricultural land in southern Manchester.

Mining is now in progress in the Breadnut Valley and Pennants properties at the rate of 1.3 million ltpy, and all bauxite ore is processed into alumina at the plant. (Before construction of the plant, and more recently when the plant was shut down by an explosion, Alcoa shipped kiln-dried bauxite from Rocky Point.) The original Teak Pen region is mined out, and rehabilitation efforts are meeting with success in this area. The Mocho region is still 90% unmined and will constitute the major source of Alcoa's newly won 40-year supply.

Alcoa's deposits are relatively deep, at 70-80 ft, with small surface areas. "We're Johnny-come-lately's in Jamaica, so we didn't get the best properties" says mine superintendent T. A. Cathey. Orebodies average 200,000 tons with 1% silica, and can range up to 115 ft deep with 4 acres of surface. Cathey also mentioned the "vast difference in bauxite compaction from pit to pit," necessitating mining flexibility. TAA of the ore ranges from 42% to 45% and is strongly dependent on whether the plant processes ore through high- or low-temperature digestion.

Before excavation, orebodies are drilled on 100-, 200-, or 400-ft centers for delineation. Soil overburden, typically 12-18 in. thick but up to 4 ft in gullies, is stripped and stockpiled with Cat D8 dozers. Excavation at 7,000 wet ltpd is done with one Bucyrus Erie 88B power shovel (5½ cu yd) taking a 20-ft cut; two P&H 955A shovels (2½ cu yd) taking 16-ft cuts; one B-E dragline (4½ cu yd), which will dig as far as 30 ft below grade; and two Cat 988 front-end loaders for flexibility. Cleanup and ripping support for the excavators and loaders is provided by six D8 dozers.

Alcoa gets an extraction ratio of 100% to 150% of the ore delineated, explained by the fact that the original grid work is wide and did not delineate all mineable ore. Also, a deposit no thicker than 4 ft will be mined if it is adjacent to a pit of some depth. A major influence on mine planning is the abundance of small surface plots (½-5 acres) still owned by area residents who refuse to sell, mine engineers say.

At the time of E/MJ's visit, four pits were on "active" status and two of them were being mined on a 15-shift-per-week basis. In some of the very deep pits, Alcoa periodically uses a local contractor with 10-cu-yd trucks. "We just don't have the equipment to clean the bottoms of some of them," Cathey explains.

Alcoa's haulage fleet consists of seven 50-ton Oshkosh trucks, seven Wabco Haulpaks, and two 50-ton Macks. Hauls to the railhead average 4 mi, on some of the finest roads in Jamaica. Alcoa haul roads have a maximum 10% grade with minimum 37-ft width and are covered by calcium chloride.

At the railhead, trucks dump onto grizzlies resting over railcars or onto a stockpile, which has a belt that feeds cars. Ore cars are hauled on Alcoa-owned track by Jamaica Railway Corp. engines 12 mi to the plant site near Hayes, or to the Rocky Point port if necessary.

Also notable are the company's training efforts. Alcoa established the Vere Industrial Training Center in cooperation with the Jamaican government in 1971. Aimed at training Jamaica's youth in a variety of industrial skills, the center has been used to educate both Alcoa employees and nonemployees and was recently given, complete with all equipment, to the government for program maintenance. □

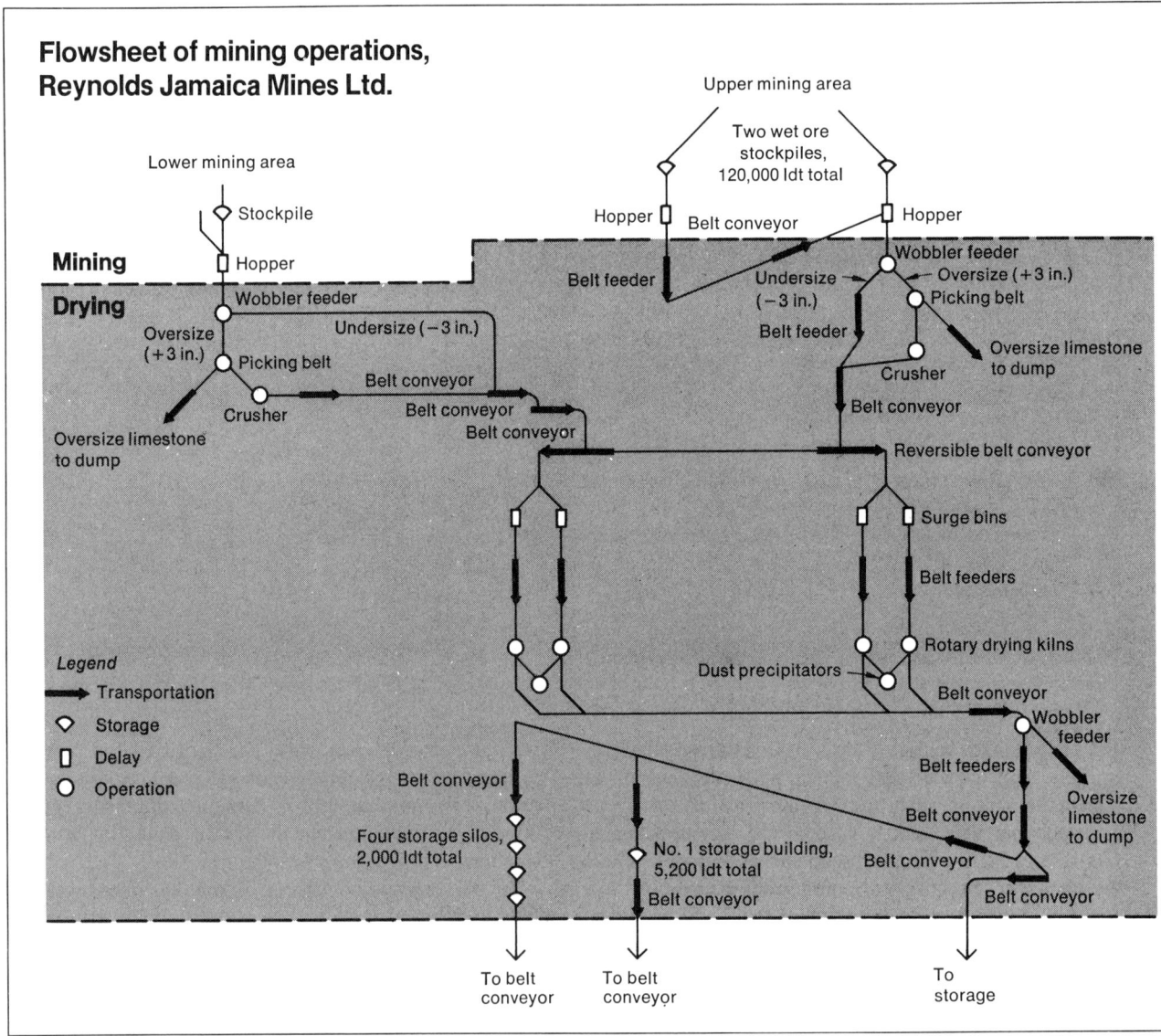

Flowsheet of mining operations, Reynolds Jamaica Mines Ltd.

Reynolds—Rounding the quarter-century mark

DESCRIBED BY THE JAMAICAN GOVERNMENT as the island's "first recognized bauxite producer" established under the Bauxite Industries Encouragement Law of 1950, Reynolds Jamaica Mines Ltd. has had two occasions to celebrate this year—a "25 years of operation" anniversary on June 22 and a partnership on March 31. Reynolds was the third operating company to sign a partnership agreement with the Jamaican government; the agreement created Jamaica Reynolds Bauxite Partners, with provisions similar to those of Kaiser's partnership agreement, including:

■ Government acquisition of 51% of Reynolds' mining assets, at book value.

■ Government acquisition of 100% of Reynolds' reserve lands and agricultural assets, totaling 65,000 acres.

■ A guaranteed supply of bauxite for 40 years, based on present capacity.

Reynolds' mining properties near Lydford, St. Ann Parish, about 7 mi south of Ocho Rios, are producing 2.5 million ldt per year of bauxite for shipment. Holdings include the mining properties and equipment; an on-site ore drying facility; a six-section, high-capacity, covered overland conveyor system running from the mine site to Ocho Rios; and a shipping facility—Reynolds Pier—in Ocho Rios. Reynolds also holds a 36.5% share in the Alpart alumina operation in Nain, along with co-owners Kaiser and Anaconda. Reynolds manages the Alpart facility as an entity separate from bauxite mining operations in Lydford. (See Alpart review.)

Reynolds' bauxite deposits are predictably similar to other Jamaican bauxite deposits. Reynolds geologists describe them as "basin deposits, mainly gibbsite, averaging 200,000 dry lt, generally located in depressions made by underlying limestone." Deposits are mined to depths of 20-100 ft—the average is 40 ft—after removing 18 in. of topsoil. There is wide variation in the quality of bauxite being mined, Reynolds engineers say;

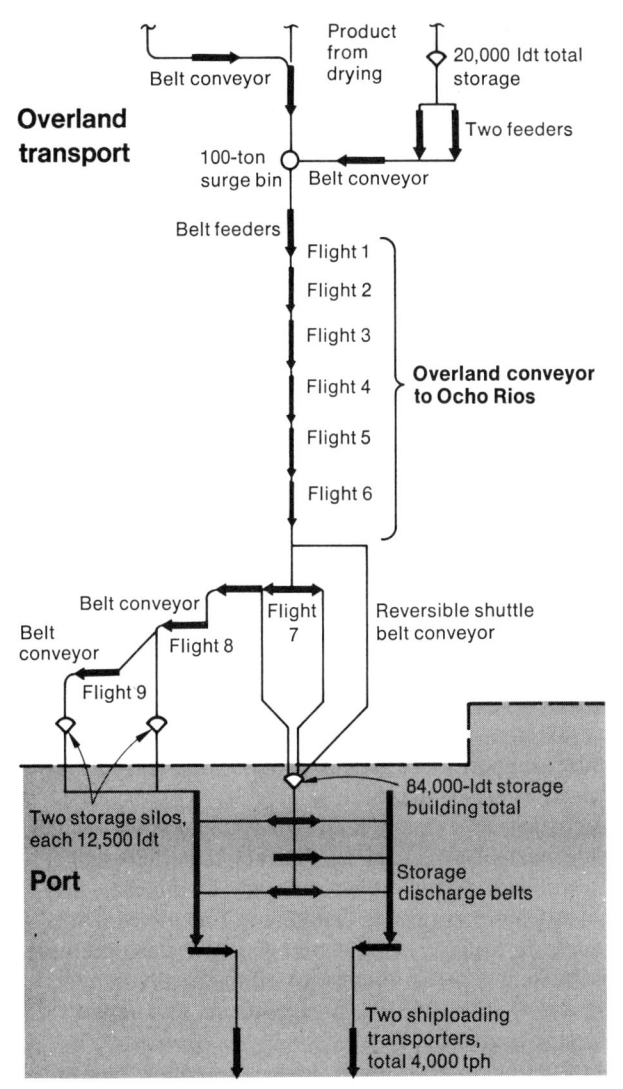

Overland transport

Product from drying — Belt conveyor
20,000 ldt total storage
Two feeders
100-ton surge bin
Belt conveyor
Belt feeders
Flight 1
Flight 2
Flight 3
Flight 4
Flight 5
Flight 6
Overland conveyor to Ocho Rios
Belt conveyor
Flight 8
Flight 9
Flight 7
Reversible shuttle belt conveyor
Two storage silos, each 12,500 ldt
84,000-ldt storage building total
Storage discharge belts
Port
Two shiploading transporters, total 4,000 tph

sump, and by stockpiling.)

Haulage to the wet ore stockpiles feeding the drying facility is done by a fleet of 21 shovel- and dragline-loaded Cat 769B dump trucks. Caterpillar rates these units at 35 tons, but Reynolds has fitted them with Atlas-made aluminum truck bodies, bringing their capacity to 40 wet st. The average haul is about 2 mi, on roads grading up to 5% against the load, but distances may go as high as 6 mi.

Stockpiled ore at the head of the drying facility is fed through hoppers onto wobbler feeders, which scalp off oversize (plus 3 in.) feed. Chunks of limestone gangue are removed from the wobbler oversize on picking belts, and the remaining plus 3-in. bauxite, accounting for less than 5% of total feed, is crushed in a Williams 200-hp hammermill before being recombined with the wobbler undersize. Conveyors with in-line surge bins deliver this minus 3-in. wet feed to the head of the dryer.

Reynolds currently runs all of its wet ore through a single 250-tph Standard Steel rotary dryer operating at 1,780°F. Installed in 1974, the 13- x 80-ft dryer has supplanted four previously used Traylor countercurrent-flow dryers. The new dryer, which features parallel heat flow and shorter retention time, is producing the equivalent of all four Traylors at approximately 60% of the fuel cost, according to plant personnel. The dryer reduces unbonded moisture from 22% to 15%; dust is reclaimed by cyclone collectors and water scrubbers.

Dried ore moves by belt to covered storage, then to a surge bin before traveling 6½ mi from the plant site to Reynolds pier via the 1,000-tph overland conveyor. Built in six sections to conform to the hilly terrain, the 42-in. conveyor belt is suspended from a prestressed concrete canopy. Before construction of the overland conveyor in 1967, Reynolds transported ore to the port by two aerial tramways.

Ore from the conveyor is stored at the port in three buildings totaling 62,000 tons and is then loaded onto ships headed for Corpus Christi, Tex. The port also receives general cargo for Reynolds and stores and ships sugar from the bulk installations owned by Northern Shippers Ltd.

Power for Reynolds operations is generated by a plant adjacent to the drying plant's main offices and maintenance area. Water is drawn from Reynolds' wells in Moneague Basin.

Reynolds, like the island's other operating companies, is justly proud of its restoration work. Reynolds has put a great deal of time and money into restoration—"We spend literally thousands on each acre we reclaim," says general manager Kirby Harrison. Reynolds reclaims and landscapes 1.25 acres for every acre it mines and uses 90% of the restored land for grazing pastures. "Pangola" is the main grass planted because of its ability to suppress weeds and withstand drought; "Paragrass" also has been tried, with some success. Reynolds has fully restored roughly 1,400 acres since 1953.

silica levels, an important factor in processing viability, range up to 5%. The ore's "maximum extractable alumina" (MEA) level averages about 42.5% by weight.

Production, at 10,000 wet ltpd, currently comes from four of six operating pits in what Reynolds calls the "lower" (western) mining area; the eastern, "upper" area is inactive. Before mining, pits are delineated by grid drilling with power drills, and soil overburden is stripped off and piled at the pit edge using 44-cu-yd Cat 657B tandem scrapers pushed by D9 tractor dozers.

Excavation is done primarily by 6-cu-yd shovels; Reynolds uses two P&H 1500s (6 cu yd) and three Marion 111Ms (4½ cu yd). Where possible, pits are taken in 12-ft vertical cuts and ramps are spiraled down. Deep pit cleanup is done with one of two Marion 111M draglines. Reynolds also mines with a Cat 992B 10-cu-yd front-end loader in concert with ripper-armed Cat dozers. Average recovery is 99% of the premining reserve estimate for a given ore pocket. Mining is scheduled for 10 shifts per week and is not "called on account of rain." (Reynolds handles the rainy season by sloping pit bottoms away from the cutting face to create a local

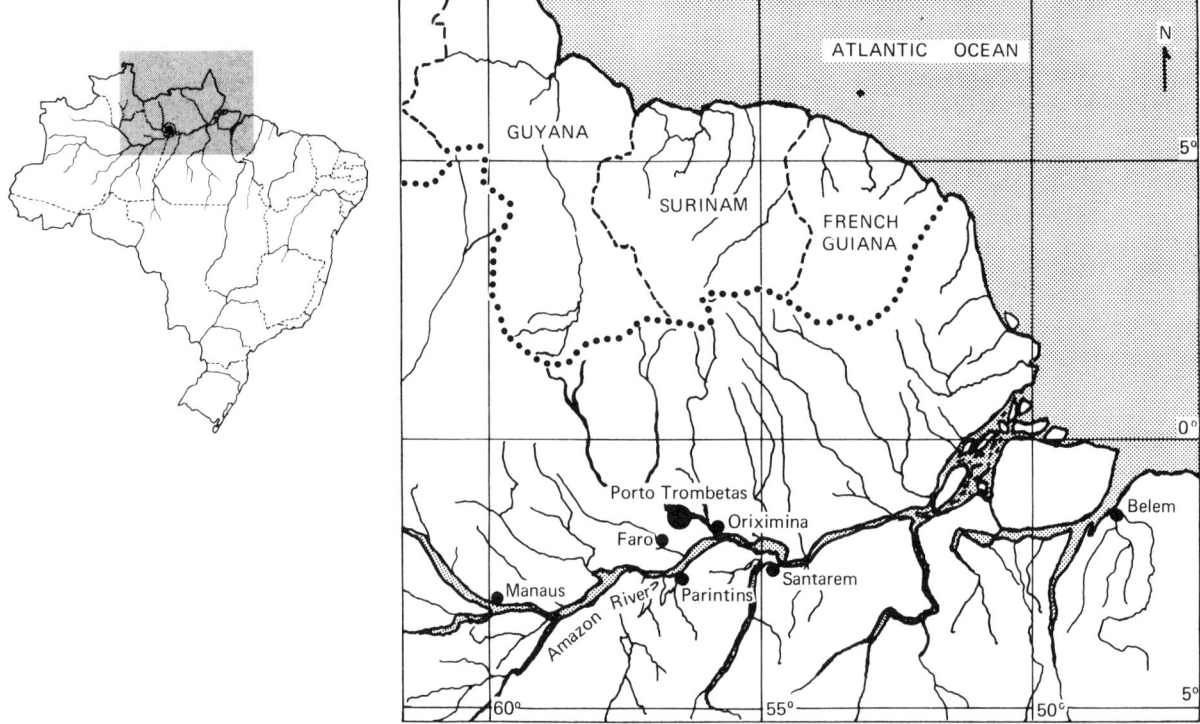

Trombetas: major bauxite reserves in search of a future

A $260 MILLION BAUXITE DEVELOPMENT plan by multinational Mineracao Rio do Norte SA envisions initial production of 3.35 million mtpy of washed ore, with staged expansions to 8 million mtpy and then 10 million mtpy.

The scene is about 120 km upstream on the Trombetas River from its junction with the Amazon in western Para State. Here, Rio do Norte will locate a deepwater port about 1,100 km west of the Atlantic Ocean, along with a planned community and bauxite washing operations. These facilities will serve a mining operation to be developed about 25 km to the south and linked to the port by rail.

The Trombetas project is sometimes referred to as one of the Big Three in the Amazon region. The other two are the Carajas iron ore project and the much discussed Albras (Aluminio do Brasil SA) alumina-aluminum project 40 km southwest of Belem, both of which would draw power from a planned hydroelectric plant at Tucurui on the Tocantins River in eastern Para State.

Rio do Norte is viewed as a possible future supplier of bauxite for Albras, but the Trombetas feasibility program is strictly shaped to serve international markets and is independent of the Albras project. It is estimated that Trombetas can be producing three to four years after the financial package is finalized and the nine companies now participating in Rio do Norte agree to proceed.

The Trombetas project has weathered some trying times. High quality bauxite was first discovered in the Trombetas area in 1966 following a determined exploration effort by Aluminium Co. of Canada geologists (see box for background of discovery). Alcan defined a 500-million-mt reserve of readily treatable ore in one mining horizon and had even started site work in 1971 on a 3-million-mtpy project for its own account.

Market conditions forced a postponement in 1972. Since then the project has been restructured, reorganized, and regrouped under Rio do Norte. While majority ownership is now in Brazilian hands, Alcan retains a 19% share.

In the meantime, the original 1971 capital cost estimate of $90 million for a 3-million-mtpy project inflated steadily to $117 million in 1972 and to $260 million early in 1975. The latest figure includes a built-in inflation allowance of 12% for 1975 and 10% for each year thereafter.

Good quality ore in a virgin area

Bauxite is found on flat-topped plateaus, remnants of an original peneplain, which lie some 70 m to 120 m above the surrounding country. These plateaus are highly dissected and vary in shape and size from a few hectares to several thousand hectares. A typical vertical section through a plateau in the concession area would show some 6.0 m of clay overburden overlying a 1-m bed of nodular bauxite. The nodular bauxite is separated from a 5-m bed of massive bauxite by a 1-m-thick layer of high-iron later-

Table 1—Average chemical analysis of Trombetas bauxite

	Nodular bauxite	Massive bauxite
LOI	27.9%	28.6%
SiO_2	7.1	4.8
Fe_2O_3	8.2	9.3
TiO_2	1.3	1.4
Al_2O_3	55.5	55.9
Reactive SiO_2	6.8	4.6
Available Al_2O_3*	47.1	49.9

*Gibsitic alumina extractable by low temperature digest.

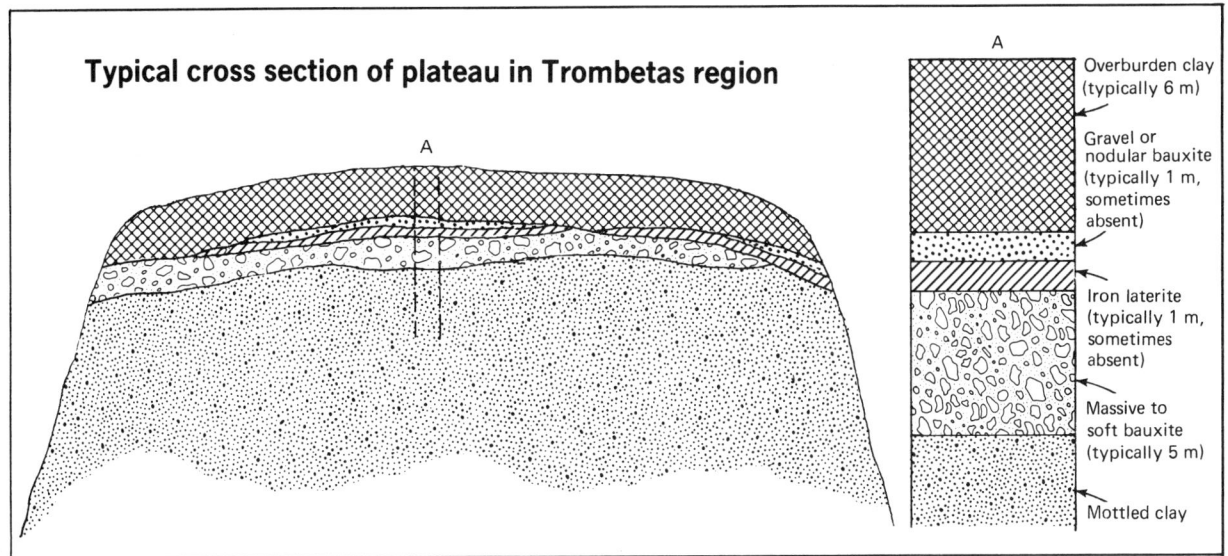

ite. The massive bauxite is underlain by mottled clay. The nodular bauxite and laterite beds are intermittent and absent in places.

The nodular material consists of hard bauxite nodules in a clay matrix, while the massive bauxite varies with depth from hard and dense to sugary and blocky material. Increasing amounts of clay are found toward the base of the bauxite bed. On a washed basis (after removal of minus 20-mesh fines), the average analysis for nodular and massive bauxite in the concession area is shown in Table 1.

Ore reserves in the Trombetas concession now total some 500 million mt of massive and 100 million mt of nodular bauxite on a washed and dried basis. Virtually all reserves are of the trihydrate type, with very little monohydrate content. The ore has good settling and filtration characteristics. As can be seen from Table 1, the nodular bauxite is poorer in quality than the massive bauxite. The latter is higher in available alumina and lower in reactive silica. The average recovery of product from crude bauxite is expected to be approximately 68% on a dry basis.

The game plan for Trombetas

After preliminary engineering studies had shown that a good port site was available on the south bank of the Trombetas River and that a railway was feasible from the port to the bauxite deposits about 25 km to the south, Alcan decided in June 1971 to sponsor a major bauxite project. The program was intended primarily to satisfy Alcan's own bauxite requirements, but also to produce a product for sale to others.

Alcan was well along with basic engineering to produce 3 million mtpy and had started preliminary site work when the international aluminum market entered a turbulent period in mid-1972. Alcan suspended work on the project because the change in the world market cut down its internal bauxite needs and seriously eroded its ability to interest other bauxite consuming partners. The hiatus was of concern not only to Alcan but to the Brazilian government as well.

Discussions were immediately launched to reactivate the project as soon as market conditions improved. As a result, an agreement was signed in December 1972 between Alcan and Brazilian government-controlled Cia. Vale do Rio Doce to undertake a joint feasibility study. This agreement also established the basic conditions under which the project would be started. Provision was made for minimum Brazilian ownership of 51% and for minimum participation by CVRD and Alcan of 21% and 19%, respectively.

On completion of the joint feasibility study in late 1973, a decision was made to reactivate the Trombetas project. Various international and Brazilian companies were contacted to ascertain their interest in participating in a multinational consortium. A direct outcome of these contacts was a shareholders' agreement, signed in Rio de Janeiro on June 11, 1974, establishing Rio do Norte's new organization, as shown in Table 2.

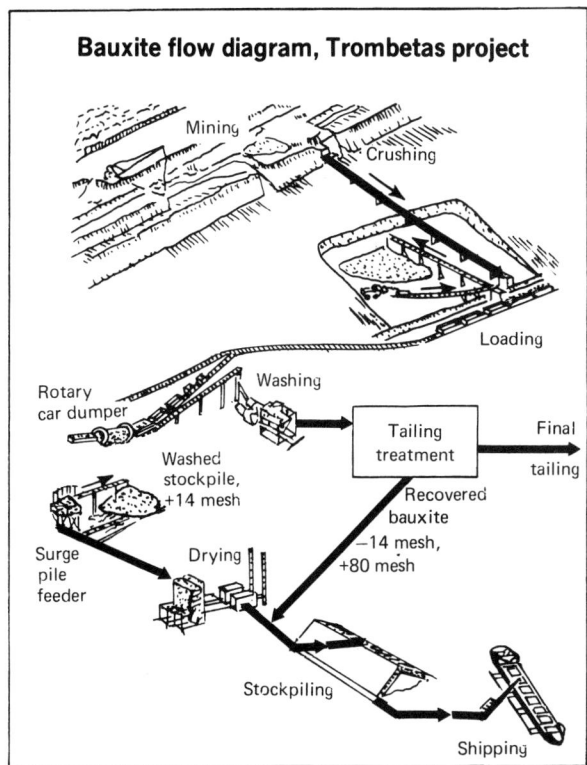

Total system plan shows bauxite flow from mining to the port and townsite, where the washing and drying plant will be sited.

The attack on development

A fine port site (Porto Trombetas) has been identified on the Trombetas River due north of the bauxite deposits. Here, the land along a 4-km stretch of the river is relatively flat and well drained, and the terrain to the ore deposits presents little difficulty in constructing a railroad.

Table 2—How ownership of Rio do Norte is divided

Cia. Vale do Rio Doce	41%
Alcan Aluminium Ltd.	19%
Cia. Brasileira de Aluminio	10%
A/S Aardal og Sunndal Verk	5%
Norsk Hydro AS	5%
Instituto Nacional de Industria	5%
Reynolds Aluminio do Brasil Ltda.	5%
Rio Tinto-Zinc do Brasil Ltda.	5%
Mineracao Rio Xingu SA	5%

Deep water access to the port is provided by the Trombetas and Amazon Rivers. A preliminary 1,000-m airstrip, slashed from the forest near the port site, is now in use.

The Trombetas area is virtually uninhabited. The nearest village, Oriximina, is 80 km downstream. Into this low-lying, dense jungle terrain, which is typical of the Amazon Basin, Rio do Norte must hack out a 20th century living design for 3,000 humans with full amenities, and a total supporting infrastructure for the bauxite mining, washing, and shipping operations. In short, another pocket of almost self-sufficient civilization will be created in the Amazon. The community will include sophisticated communication links with the outside world, a power plant, a hospital and full medical facilities, housing, shopping centers, entertainment facilities, water treatment plant, and sanitation and sewage treatment. It is also not inconceivable that an enterprising farmer or two will be subsidized to provide food stocks.

Despite a location about 1.5° south of the equator, the climate is not unpleasant. Temperatures vary from a daytime high of about 30°C to a nighttime low of about 20°C. Rainfall is seasonal and heavy at times from December to May. The average is about 2,000 mm annually.

Mining operations will start on the eastern edge of the Saraca Plateau, which lies some 25 km south of the port site. In the initial stage, two faces will be opened, one extending to the north and the other to the south from a midway point. Stripping of overburden will be carried out mainly by 18-cu-yd walking draglines, while smaller amounts will be removed by tractor-scraper. The exposed bauxite bed will be drilled and blasted. Mining will be done by 6½-cu-yd pull shovels working from the top of the massive bauxite bed. This material is expected to provide a far better equipment load-bearing surface than the underlying clay. The pull shovels will load 35-ton rear-dump trucks for hauling the crude ROM to the crushing plant to be located at the edge of the plateau.

It will be expensive to mine the lower grade nodular bauxite sandwiched in a thin, discontinuous bed between the overburden and laterite of the plateaus. Thus, it is not now planned to process this material in the first years of operation. Rio do Norte, however, hopes to develop a cost-efficient mining and recovery system for this resource as the project matures. □

Dragline stripping system will expose bauxite mine faces for extraction by means of pull shovels after they are drilled and blasted. A road cut normal to the advance of dragline casting will provide a midway entry into the bauxite mining area.

Reynolds is Haiti's only bauxite producer

BAUXITE RANKS SECOND only to coffee exports among Haiti's foreign exchange earners. The country's only bauxite mine is owned and operated by Reynolds Haitian Mines, a subsidiary of Reynolds Metals Co. The mine is located near the village of Miragoane on the coast overlooking the Gulf of Gonave, about a 2-hr drive east of Port-au-Prince. Reynolds began exploration of the Haitian deposits as far back as 1944, finally starting to mine the ore in 1956 and to ship it in 1957. Shipments are processed at the company's alumina plant in Corpus Christi, Tex.

Many challenges confront Reynolds Haitian Mines, including one of the world's steepest haul grades and difficulty in obtaining equipment parts due to the remoteness of the mine.

Mining without drilling and blasting

Reynolds mines residual lateritic pockets of bauxite on an eroded limestone surface of Miocene age. Shallow pockets of ore vary from 3 to 10 ft thick; deeper ore is 9 to 40 ft thick. Along with 50% alumina, Reynolds' ore averages 3% silica and 21% iron. Conventional combinations of shovels with trucks and front-end loaders with trucks are used to mine the ore. Topsoil, which varies from 6 to 12 in., is removed by bulldozers and stockpiled for resurfacing prior to reclamation.

Ore is mined on two daily shifts, five days per week, using one of two mining systems, depending on ore thickness. In shallow bauxite, two front-end loaders—one 6-yd Cat 988 and one 10-yd Cat 992—load into 35-ton rear-dump trucks. Reynolds maintains a fleet of 16 Cat trucks, of which 12 to 13 are used per shift and three to four are on standby. Deep ore is mined with two 4-yd Marion 111 diesel shovels, one of which is always on standby.

The trucks have been specially fitted with heated aluminum bodies. The aluminum bodies are durable enough because the ore is not highly abrasive and contains few large lumps except for an occasional limestone boulder.

The sharp drop in elevation from the mine (at 3,000 ft) to the drying plant (at sea level) over a distance of only 10 mi makes for one of the steepest haul grades in the world. Grade is a maximum of 12% over short stretches but averages closer to 9%. Haul roads range in width from 40 to 46 ft.

A further challenge to Reynolds is the asphalt used to surface about 13 km of the haul road, which becomes extremely slippery when wet. Haul trucks stop abruptly at the first sign of precipitation, resuming work only after the rain has subsided and the road dries.

As a result of the steep grade, a special braking system has been fitted on all trucks. Management is also testing radial ply tires on trucks as replacements for bias ply. Tires used are 18.00 x 25 in.

Additional mobile equipment includes two Cat G319 85-hp graders used for road maintenance and seven Cat dozers—one D4, two D7s, and four D8s—for such duties as scraping off topsoil, picking lean ore, or feeding the dryers.

Drying plant will get a new ore feed system

Bauxite at 25% moisture is dumped at the wet ore stockpile prior to drying. In the current feed system, dozers push ore from stockpile through 10-in. grizzlies over two 85-ton hoppers. Material is fed to two belts that in turn feed two Koppers Hardinge dryers, 8 ft 7¾ in. in diameter x 70 ft long. Dryers run on Bunker C oil.

Ore is fed to each dryer at the rate of 75 tph to reduce moisture to 15%. A vibratory screen removes oversize limestone and bauxite, the latter tending to ball up in the dryers. If excessive bauxite comes off the screen, it must be recycled to the dryers. The limestone rocks are collected by truck two or three times a shift and are sent to a waste dump.

A new feed system is planned, to be patterned after that used at Reynolds Jamaica Mines (see separate article). Ore will be fed directly from stockpile or dumped into the single 100-ton hopper. Beneath the hopper will be installed a specially modified wobbler (movable-bar) feeder equipped with self-cleaning bars. Undersize at minus 3 in. will go directly to the dryers.

Oversize will pass from the wobbler feeder onto a picking belt, from which oversize limestone will be removed by hand. The balance of material—the bauxite lumps—will fall into a hammermill crusher with a 2-in. setting and will be returned to the hopper.

Bauxite shipped to alumina plant in Texas

A 24-in. belt conveys dry product to the covered ore storage building, designed to hold 79,000 ldt, of which 20,000 ldt are live. Beneath the building, chutes draw bauxite onto a 48-in. conveyor to a transfer house and on to the pier-head building via a second 48-in. belt. Ore is transferred onto a third 48-in. belt and dumped at 1,800 to 2,000 ldt per hr through a telescoping spout and into the holds of Reynolds ships. Product is shipped twice monthly to alumina plants in Corpus Christi, Tex. Shipments range from 15,000 to 30,000 ldt.

Power is supplied to the plant, staff housing, and hospital at Paillant, and to the town of Miragoane by three 625-kva diesel generators. Electricity is transmitted to the plant and Miragoane at 4,160 v. The plant steps down power to 480 v, mainly for dryer motors and conveyors.

Fuel is imported. A 40,000-bbl tank is used to store Bunker C oil for the dryers; a second 40,000-bbl tank stores No. 2 diesel oil for trucks and the power plant. Water is no major problem, since the process is a dry one. Three wells drilled by Reynolds, one of which is 800 ft deep, can supply water for all plant and personal needs.

The remoteness of Reynolds Haitian Mines demands a

Shallow deposits are mined by a combination of front-end loader and truck at the rate of 2,500 ltpd, on 10 weekly shifts.

Each truck is specially fitted with a heated Atlas aluminum body to increase the carrying capacity to 40 tons.

larger-than-normal inventory of equipment parts. The maintenance buildings provide two work bays for servicing trucks; two bays for small vehicles; a repair shop with four bays for big trucks; two bays for tractors; machine shop; welding shop; and an engine and transmission rebuild shop. Small running repairs are made at the mine. Some supplies come from Port-au-Prince, while others arrive by air and sea—very often in the same ships that leave filled with dried ore.

Reynolds Haitian is continually training qualified people for skilled jobs, especially as equipment operators and in repair and maintenance functions. In addition to conducting on-the-job training, the company pays for successful completion of relevant courses.

Reynolds has rapport with government

In 1976, Reynolds paid $9.5 million in direct levies and taxes to the Haitian government. However, a new agreement that became effective January 1977 for a five-year period includes a new formula for computing taxes. Reynolds' contract provides for a proportional tax and a severance tax. The proportional tax is based on the tonnage of bauxite exported. The severance tax is comprised of a number of elements, the main one being a tax rate of 7.5% of the average realized price of primary aluminum.

The current five-year contract may be extended for an additional five years. □

Alcoa's Dominican bauxite mine uses solar drying

THE ONLY BAUXITE MINED in the Dominican Republic comes from a district that may be more familiar to naturalists and readers of NATIONAL GEOGRAPHIC than to mining engineers. In the Bahoruco Mountains of Pedernales province, in the southwest portion of the country, scientists have been marveling over varieties of squirrels and frogs found nowhere else on earth. Not far away, on the coast, Alcoa is approaching its 20th year of shipping bauxite mined in the mountains.

Cabo Rojo means "Red Cape." Named by Spanish seamen who noticed the pink limestones reflecting a reddish glow in the late afternoon sun, Cabo Rojo serves as both headquarters and shipping port for Alcoa. The Red Cape boasts more than rare and exotic reptiles such as *Eleuthero Dactylus Alcoae* (a newly discovered species of frog). The facility utilizes one of the world's longest mining haul roads. Also, solar drying facilities on the shipping dock are used instead of drying kilns mainly because the desert climate along the coast keeps the ore moderately dry. It almost never rains at Cabo Rojo.

Production of bauxite in 1977 is projected at 625,000 mt, a slight increase over the 516,000 mt mined in 1976, but far less than the all-time high of 1.2 million mt reached in 1974. The steady decline in production has been attributed both to market conditions and to a shift of Alcoa production to Guinea, Africa.

A new bauxite agreement signed on May 2, 1977, for a one-year period, gives the Dominican Republic an extraction tax of $15.84 per dry mt (based on Alcoa's average sale price of aluminum) plus a royalty of 55¢— for a total of $16.39 per dry mt. This effectively honors the Dominican government's desire to tie the bauxite royalty to the world market price for aluminum.

Alcoa's 8,784-hectare concession includes the mining areas of Las Mercedes and Aceitillar, at elevations of 1,200 ft and 4,200 to 5,000 ft, respectively. In addition to currently outlined reserves of 14 million mt, the concession also contains 14 million mt of marginal, high-silica bauxite that may be amenable to exploitation at some future time.

Operations at Cabo Rojo started up in 1958, although exploration had been conducted in the area by Alcoa as early as the 1940s. Ore is produced at the rate of 2,500 mtpd. The ore contains the equivalent of 1,000 mtpd in alumina, averaging 38-43% Al_2O_3 in the form of gibbsite or low-temperature-digestor (LTD) ore and 35-38% boehmite, or high-temperature-digestor (HTD) ore.

A typical lateritic profile

The bauxite deposits are of possible Tertiary age and were probably derived from the residue left after solution of the underlying Eocene and Oligocene limestones. The deposits are not overlain by sedimentary strata, since they have never been submerged. Due to crustal disturbances, the topography of the deposits is very irregular, with limestone pinnacles protruding into the bauxite.

Most of the bauxite occurs as elongated or circular pockets, funnel-shaped in profile and ranging from 20 to 50 ft or more in depth. One deposit is as deep as 270 ft. The very large deposits occur more or less as a continuous blanket completely covering the projecting ridges, pinnacles, and knots of limestone. Las Mercedes is one example. The individual deposits vary in size from very small pockets to large basins over 2 sq km. Las Mercedes, the biggest deposit in Alcoa's concession, is a maximum of 1 mi long and ½ mi wide.

The ore itself is finely divided, earthy material of moderate hardness but needs no drilling or blasting. The overburden is mostly a thin layer of topsoil and is not generally removed prior to mining. The country rock consists of Oligocene limestones.

Haul distance is one of mining's longest

Mining is conducted on 12-ft lifts via conventional shovel-truck methods. Auger drilling on 50-ft centers is made to isolate LTD and HTD ores. When mining is completed at Las Mercedes, the pit will ultimately be 1,400 ft wide, 2,200 ft long, and 60 to 72 ft deep. Diesel-powered shovels excavate at the rate of 318 cu yd per hr. Cycle time in loading is 2 min; availability of shovels and trucks is 43.8%. Three trucks and one shovel are always on standby.

Trucks haul ore a distance of 13 mi from the lower mines of Las Mercedes to the dock. Round-trip cycle time is 1 hr 20 min. Haul-road grades vary from zero to a maximum 6.975%. The haulage distance from the upper mines of Aceitillar to Cabo Rojo on the coast is among the longest in the world—24 mi. The maximum grade is 9%. Haul-road width for both upper and lower mines is uniformly 33 ft.

Major exploration and mining equipment consists of one Mobile B30H5 drill for mine sampling, one Bucyrus-Erie 54B 1½-cu-yd shovel, and one 88B 4½-cu-yd shovel. Main haulage equipment is comprised of six 35-ton KW-Dart D3230 tandem ore haulers; three 38-ton KW-Dart D3230 end-dump trucks; and four 45-ton Mack M-43SX trucks.

Equipment for the limestone quarry includes 1 Ingersoll-Rand Crawlair CM350 and four Mack 30-ton IRSW dump trucks. Road maintenance uses one Caterpillar 950 2½-yd wheel loader; one Cat 12F grader; one Hystar C-350 roller; and one Littleford asphalt tank and trailer.

Additional equipment consists of one Hough 120 Payloader, rated at 6 cu yd, for shiploading of limestone; one Lorrain 30-ton crane; one Cat 12 G grader for road and mine floor maintenance; two Cat D9 tractors; one Cat D9G; four Cat D8Hs; and two Cat D8Ks. In

Round-trip cycle time ranges up to 2½ hr for trucks making the trip from the upper mines at Aceitillar.

Limestone pinnacles intrude up to 25 ft into the bauxite.

addition, a fleet of Ford pick-up trucks with fully automatic transmissions is used by Alcoa staff.

Alcoa employs a work force of 315, including those assigned to the quarrying operation. The mine operates two shifts per day, five days a week. The maintenance department at Cabo Rojo also works 10 weekly shifts. The power plant personnel work three daily shifts, seven days per week. Production, in tons per manshift at the mine, is 104.167, excluding rock quarry personnel; at the maintenance, quarry, and shiploading facilities, the figure is 8.591. The overall average is 7.937 tpd per man.

Each truckload of bauxite brought to dockside is sampled and analyzed. During shiploading, samples are taken every 10 min from the conveyor. Separate stockpiles are maintained for LTD and HTD ores, of which only one type is shipped out at a time. Stockpiles are spread out somewhat for solar drying, which lowers the moisture content from about 15% to 10%.

Three dozers push ore into two sets of two 50-ton hoppers each, which feed two Syntron vibratory feeders positioned over two 48-in.-wide, 590-ft-long conveyor belts. Each Syntron feeder is bottom-heated by four 60-kw transformers to prevent ore from sticking—one of the world's few bottom-heated systems. A boom conveyor 48 in. wide x 213 ft long positioned over the ship's hold drops bauxite at 1,500 tph. Each ship, which can transport up to 33,000 mt, takes on bauxite twice monthly and crushed limestone once a month. The limestone, destined for Surinam, is used in the Bayer process as a replenishing agent for caustic soda. Up to 15,000 mt of limestone are shipped each month.

Maintenance and parts—a critical aspect

The maintenance facilities at Cabo Rojo are adjacent to the administration building. Six work bays accommodate old and new Mack and Dart trucks and all the tractors. Routine maintenance of shovels is done in the field; shovels recalled from the mines at higher elevations would require as much as one week to reach the maintenance facilities at Cabo Rojo.

Because of the remote location, obtaining parts can be a problem. However, Alcoa keeps a well-stocked inventory, including truck engine blocks. Heavy-duty equipment and most parts are either trucked or shipped in, although some machinery is transported by light plane. Aircraft are chartered by Alcoa also to carry as many as 18 staff members from Santo Domingo to Cabo Rojo on Mondays and back again on Fridays. Trucks from Santo Domingo travel the single road over a distance of 350 km in 6 to 7 hr. Heavy equipment comes by ship, usually from Florida. Air transport is used to bring in perishable goods such as locally purchased meat, butter, and milk, as well as urgently needed parts.

Most of the laborers and equipment operators live in modern company housing in nearby Pedernales, a town of 10,000. A few live in barracks at the plant site. Supervisors and most of the foremen live in a staff building and trailers at Cabo Rojo.

Power and water use is minimal

Power is supplied by three 350-kw Caterpillar turbocharged generators and one 860-kw unit at Cabo Rojo. Electricity is used mostly for conveying bauxite and for the bottom heaters of feeders. At night, power output drops to only 90 kw, most of it for personal use.

Water is used mainly for washing down equipment and for personal use, since Alcoa's is a dry process. The water is obtained from the main 320-ft-deep well in the foothills of the Bahoruco Mountains, at an elevation of 318 ft. A submerged 7½-hp electric pump draws water at the rate of 60 gpm, allowing it to flow by gravity a distance of 11 km to a 100,000-gal storage tank at Cabo Rojo. Daily consumption is limited to about 50,000 gal, as excessive pumping can result in contamination from salt water. □

Maintenance facilities handle old and new trucks, but shovels and large wheel loaders must be serviced outside.

Chapter 10
Phosphates

Phosphates are vital to agriculture—and Florida mines for one-third the world 382
Lee Creek may share link with Kidd Creek as the two Texasgulf
    units gear for expansions 393

Phosphates are vital to agriculture —and Florida mines for one-third the world

'We may be able to substitute nuclear power for coal power, and plastics for wood, and yeast for meat, and friendship for isolation—but for phosphorus there is neither substitute nor replacement.'—Isaac Asimov

Richard W. Hoppe, Senior editor

ON A NIGHT FLIGHT over the flatland of central Florida, just past the sparkling lights of Lakeland, a cluster of what appear to be huge fireflies can be seen swinging slowly back and forth along the ground below. These apparitions—dozens of huge draglines, all in a radius of 20 mi—continuously feed the largest phosphate rock operation in the world.

Florida's Bone Valley Formation produces more than 75% of US output of marketable phosphate rock and some 30% of the world total. More than 85% of phosphate rock production is used for fertilizer. There is no substitute for phosphorus in agriculture. Because of the world's rapid population expansion, all soils under cultivation require the replenishment of nitrogen, phosphorus, and potassium. Without such replenishment, harvests are doomed. The successes, shortcomings, problems, and solutions of the nine major companies making up the central Florida phosphate industry have serious implications for both the US and the world.

Until 1973, profitability in production of phosphate rock was a sometimes thing. Then the specter of a worldwide phosphate rock shortage was perceived in late 1973, and Morocco—producing some 7% of the world total—raised the ante in a big way. Moroccan 72% BPL product sold for $10-11 per ton in July.1972. By January 1974 the price had escalated to $40 per ton, and by January 1975 it was coasting along at $65 per ton. Phosphate rock producers and exporters in Florida followed suit in raising prices, but to lower levels because of long term contracts and other factors.

Buyer resistance in 1975 put a damper on the spiraling price increases and resulted in significant reductions in late 1975 and early 1976. Current quotations for 72% BPL phosphate rock are about $41 per ton in Tampa, Fla., and $46 per ton in Morocco (the latter price subject to discounting on quantity and other factors). Whatever the short term outcome of this price bouncing, the long term effect should be greater production at reasonable profits and an increased perception of the industry's importance.

Investment in central Florida's phosphate industry is about $3 billion, contributing $1.5 billion annually to Florida's economy and providing direct and indirect employment for more than 60,000 people. Tampa, Florida's major port, ranks fourth in the nation in value of annual tonnage exported and ninth nationally in volume handled. Fully 95% of Tampa's outbound cargo is related to phosphate rock.

Current production of phosphate rock from the Bone Valley Formation runs to 38 million tpy, equal to Florida's entire output between 1889, when production began, and the outbreak of World War II. In 1929-1930, significant technological breakthroughs were achieved, including the introduction of electrically driven draglines to mine overburden and matrix, high pressure water guns to provide a slurry for the new dredge-type pumps, and—most important of all—introduction of flotation for recovering fine material that had previously been discarded after washing. The new systems increased "reserves," reduced waste, and required large capital investments. Operations became concentrated in companies that not only mined and beneficiated phosphate rock but also manufactured the end products required by domestic and foreign agriculture.

Surge tank at Brewster's Haynsworth mine permits the matrix slurry from the two dragline wells to be fed to a common main. The tank's "head" determines how booster pumps down the line will be operated, permitting a steadier feed rate.

Brewster workers install an in-the-line blind end in matrix pipeline to protect booster pumps from shock. Lateral carries matrix.

Dams built to impound clay and phosphatic slimes will no longer be required if new reclamation methods succeed. Slimes at 2% to 6% solids are now sent to impoundment dams, where they settle to only about 15% solids after many years.

Moving 38 million tpy

A typical phosphate mining operation consists of one or more 40-yd draglines excavating a cut 325 ft wide and 40 ft deep over a length of 2,000 to 4,000 ft. Except during the initial box-cut, when overburden is cast on virgin ground, the dragline casts overburden into mined-out sections. About 25 ft of sand and clay overburden is removed to uncover 15 ft of matrix. The dragline casts matrix at the rate of 1,500 yd per hr into a well that is excavated on unmined ground. Wells are approximately 10 ft deep, 60 ft wide, and 100-120 ft long. A steel grizzly with vertical bars spaced 6 to 9 in. apart separates the well into two sections.

The dragline casts matrix along the edge of the upper half of the well, creating a surge pile. Three high pressure water guns—typically "Intelli-giants" or Universals with 3-in.-dia. nozzles—jet water at 175-200 psi into the matrix, breaking it into a slurry that slumps into the well and passes through the grizzly to the lower well. A centrifugal dredge-type pump with an 18- to 20-in.-dia suction pipe submerged 6 ft into the lower well removes slurry at 35-40% solids and pumps it to the matrix pipeline leading to the plant.

In advancing a cut, a dragline normally moves in steps of 150-175 ft, each requiring well set-ups along the route.

Because the matrix bed may vary in content and thickness, careful planning—based on accurate data—is required to maintain the efficiencies of the total operation. One factor commonly used in mine planning is the "matrix ratio," defined as the number of cubic yards of matrix required to produce 1 ton of final phosphate rock product. A matrix ratio of 3:1 requires a dragline production rate of 1,200 yd per hr to feed a plant producing 400 tph of product. Another element in mine planning is the total yards of material mined (overburden plus matrix) per ton of product.

The mining of phosphate pebble is analogous to sand and gravel operations. Before mining begins, land must be cleared—removing pine trees, stumps, and other vegetation—and sometimes drained. Mine planning includes design of pit cuts, location of waste disposal ponds, design of dams and spillways, and selection of methods to reclaim all lands for later use. The mine planner also considers the location of gravity-flow ditches and sumps and lays out pumping stations and pipelines for matrix and reclaim water. Electric power, water, and pipe must follow the moves of the draglines. Operations must not pollute local water supplies. Because water economy is of paramount importance, the industry is recycling 85-95% of all water used in mining, transport, washing, flotation, and acid production. Water is the life blood of the industry.

Pumping of matrix slurry (normally over a distance of 2-6 mi and in one case 10 mi) is the standard method of transporting matrix from pit to plant. Factors that have favored slurry transport include the excellent pumping char-

> **Editor's note:** This report on mining and reclamation in central Florida's phosphate operations is based on an E/MJ field trip in early February 1976.

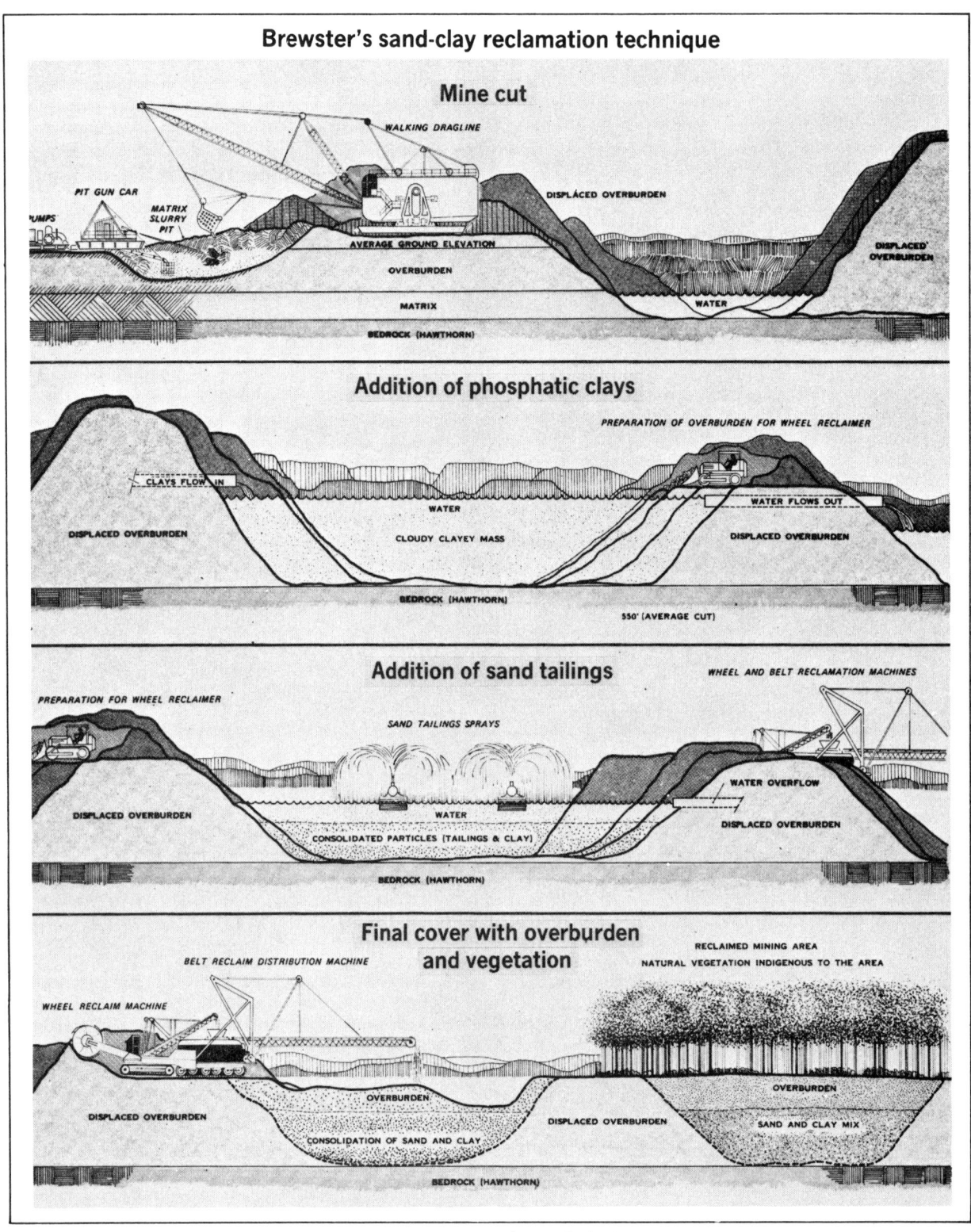

Brewster's new technique for slimes disposal has good potential for land reclamation and quick water reuse. Sand-clay reclamation method releases water trapped in slow-settling slimes. After the material consolidates, overburden is spread and seeded.

acteristics of the matrix, a level terrain, wet beneficiation processes, continuous flow, and a competitive cost advantage over other methods. However, the last factor may no longer apply.

Centrifugal dredge-type well and booster pumps are used. Suppliers include Georgia Iron Works, Pettibone, A-S-H, Thomas, and most recently Warman. Lift (booster) stations are located 3,500 ft apart along the slurry lines. Pump suction and discharge sections are 16-20 in. in diameter, and impellers are 44-48 in. in diameter. Pump motors range from 800 to 1,500 hp. Some motors are constant-speed with fluid drive and reducer. Others are wound-rotor with variable speed drive.

Pumping systems are designed to accommodate the

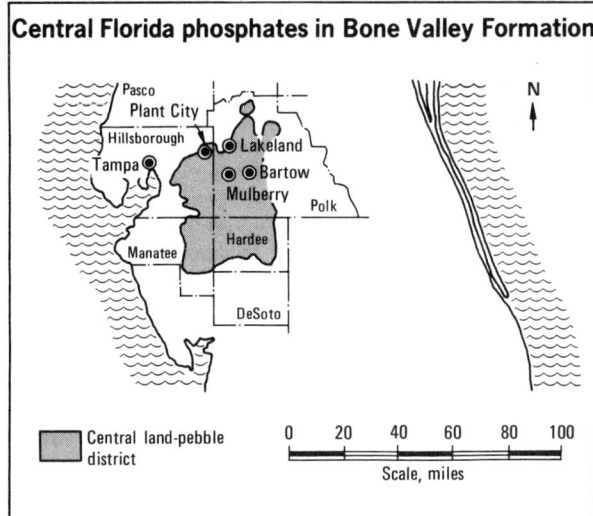

Central Florida phosphates in Bone Valley Formation

heaviest work loads anticipated, loads created by a high pebble-to-feed ratio in the matrix. These ratios, together with pipeline distances and plant production requirements, determine specifications for pumps and pipe. The largest pump in the district is a Georgia Iron Works 20 x 20 LSA 48 used to move a high pebble-to-feed matrix.

Matrix slurry is pumped above critical velocity, generally at 15-18 fps. The pump impeller must impart to the slurry sufficient velocity to avoid settling and plugging of matrix between pump stations. However, use of a velocity significantly above the critical level wastes energy. Critical velocity is a function of slurry density—around 40% solids by weight.

To achieve continuously a 40% solids intake of slurry at the well pump is an impossible task, but an experienced pump operator will come close to the mark by keeping an eye on the water level of the well, the pump ammeter, and the vacuum gauge. These indicators give him an idea of conditions at the intake. International Minerals & Chemical is now completing installation of meters to record flow and density on all of the company's lines. These records are expected to be useful in pinpointing problem areas. Another company uses a 3-in.-dia water line installed along the suction pipe to impart further slurrying action at the intake and has also welded a cutter bar within the well pump's suction side-liner. The bar breaks up large material and protects the volute.

Normal pump productive time is 85%, including downtime during the 2- to 4-hr dragline moves that occur every two to four days. All downtime is used for equipment maintenance. (All mines in central Florida operate 20 to 21 shifts per week.) Major inspections of pumps are made every four to six weeks. Pump shell life is about 2,000 hr, and shells are rebuilt every nine months. Booster pump impellers last 3,000 to 5,000 hr, and well pump impellers somewhat less. Metals for the pump case, impeller, and side-liners are generally Ni-Hard, chrome alloy cast iron, or manganese steel.

Matrix pipelines are 16 to 20 in. in diameter. Pipe is abrasion-resistant, spiral-weld steel. The price of pipe has tripled since 1972. Pipelines are rotated 90° or 120° every six to nine months. Life of matrix pipe normally ranges between 18 and 27 months. Clay slimes in the slurry act to retard pipe wear.

Water used by the high pressure water guns and conveyed in the matrix slurry is reclaimed from sand tailings and slimes ponds. Decanted water flows through spillways into excavated sumps. Sump pump stations consist of a 4,160-v substation, associated switch gear, and a bank of deep-well vertical turbine pumps—typically Peerless 600-hp pumps, each rated at 4,000 gpm and 200 psi. Intermediate booster pump stations to the mine well may use Hazleton horizontal-centrifugal pumps.

Inflation prompts design review

Reacting to massive cost increases for power, pipe, and parts (up about 300% in little more than three years), along with supply problems, many companies have decided to review the design of matrix conveying systems. Several companies have revised their systems or plan to do so.

At Agrico's Saddle Creek mine, a satellite washer is in-

Florida phosphate industry terminology

Phosphate rock is a commercial term for rock containing phosphate materials of sufficient grade and composition to permit their use, before or after beneficiation, in manufacturing commercial phosphate products. Over 85% of phosphate rock mined is used in fertilizers. Phosphate rock is marketed according to its content of *BPL* (bone phosphate of lime), expressed as a percentage. BPL is tricalcium phosphate, $Ca_3(PO_4)_2$. Mining data generally refer to BPL content. Chemical analyses for acid production and byproducts indicate percentages of P_2O_5 (phosphorus pentoxide). Because 1% BPL = 0.458% P_2O_5, phosphate rock of 70% BPL contains 32.04% P_2O_5.

Matrix, a synonym for ore, is the term used in Florida to define material mined for profit. The matrix is a loose conglomerate in the Bone Valley Formation that contains 20-25% phosphate rock, 30-40% clays (slimes), and 35-50% silica sands. It is often water-laden. The matrix varies in thickness from 5 to 30 ft and is overlain by sandy clay. Beneath the matrix lies Hawthorne limestone bedrock or bedclay.

Pebble generally refers to hard phosphatic nodules (minus ½ in. x 14 mesh) retrieved from washing plants. "Fine pebbles" are nominally 14 x 20 mesh.

Feed is a nominal 14 x 150-mesh material sent to flotation plants. Flotation concentrates grade 66-75% BPL. Both pebble and concentrate are marketed as phosphate rock or further treated in chemical plants for the manufacture of fertilizer products. Fertilizers include:

- Regular *superphosphate* (approximately 18% P_2O_5).
- *TSP* (triple superphosphate, approximately 44% P_2O_5).
- *DAP* (diammonium phosphate, approximately 18% N, 44% P_2O_5).
- *Urea-ammonium phosphate*, with a relatively higher nitrogen content than DAP and a relatively high P_2O_5 content.
- *Complete fertilizer*, described by three numbers (such as 8-10-12) that state the percentages by weight of water-soluble nitrogen, phosphoric acid, and available potash (N-P-K).

For prospecting and exploration, 1-mi-sq sections are divided into 40-, 10-, and 2.5-acre blocks. Prospect holes are usually drilled one per 40-acre block. Land can be purchased on information from programs in which one hole per 10 acres is drilled. This crew is using a 1250 Failing drill rig to core 4-in.-dia holes. Drilling normally ranges 30-80 ft deep to the Hawthorne limestone formation. For mine planning and production, holes are centered in each 2.5-acre block—closer if anomalies show up. The cores are analyzed for P_2O_5, oxides of iron and alumina, and percentages of pebble and feed in the matrix.

stalled between the mine and plant. The satellite station includes a hammer mill and cyclones that reduce matrix to minus 1½ in. Partially deslimed matrix is reslurried and pumped to the main plant. The permanent satellite station is located 1 mi from dragline operations and 5 mi from the main plant. As mining moves farther away, distance from mine well to satellite will increase to 5 mi.

In a radical departure from convention, a 14,500-ft-long, 54-in.-wide, steel cable conveyor system will transport deslimed matrix at 65% solids from the mine area to the wash plant at Brewster's new Lonesome mine. Matrix slurry from the mine will be pumped to a nearby bank of cyclones and associated equipment. Deslimed, plus 150-mesh material will be dewatered to 65% solids, placed on the conveyor belt, and transported to the main plant. Sand tails from the flotation plant will feed onto the bottom belt (reverse direction) and move back to the mine over the same system. A transfer conveyor will direct the sand tails to a slurry tank.

Sand tails and slimes will be pumped from this location to the disposal ponds. Reclamation will proceed as ponds are filled and drained.

Brewster's belt system—supplied by Continental Conveyor & Equipment Co. of Winfield, Ala.—will be powered by rubber-tired drive modules located at intermediate points, with electric motors driving steel-belted radial tires in contact with the belt edge. Engineers at Brewster believe that advantages of this system will include reduced belt tension, fewer idlers, smaller terminal structure, and simplified take-ups. They expect the system to consume only 10% of the electric power required by an equivalent pipeline. Savings are also anticipated in capital replacement and repair and maintenance.

Capacity may top 55 million tpy in early '80s

The nine major companies mining phosphate rock within the Bone Valley Formation are clustered about the town of Mulberry in Polk County, the "phosphate capital of the world." These nine companies will produce close to 40 million tons of phosphate rock in 1976. If current plans jell, the nine will be joined by another half-dozen primary producers (mine operators) before the end of 1980. If all the expansion programs and new mines currently projected are brought on stream, Bone Valley capacity will exceed 55 million tpy of phosphate rock by the early 1980s.

Agrico Chemical Co., a subsidiary of the Williams Companies, is one of the world's largest fertilizer manufac-

---

Geology of central Florida phosphate

Phosphorus—from the Greek word meaning "I bear light"—has its origins in the mineral apatite, which is widely distributed in igneous rocks but is seldom found in masses of sufficient size for mining. More than 80% of phosphate rock production comes from secondary deposits of marine phosphorite, such as those of the Bone Valley Formation. Leaching of primary apatite carries phosphate minerals—adsorbed on iron or aluminum hydroxides or clays, in particulate or dissolved organic compounds, or in solutions—into the oceans, which are nearly saturated with phosphate. However, the phosphate content of the oceans is not uniform. Deep cold waters contain up to 0.3 ppm of PO_4, while warmer, near-surface waters contain as little as 0.01 ppm. Because the solubility of phosphate in upwelling water is lowered by changes in temperature and pH, phosphate may be precipitated by organic or inorganic processes. Phosphorites, along with shale, chert, and limestone, are depositional products that change in composition as the result of physical, chemical, and biological processes.

The marine phosphorite deposits of central Florida occur in a roughly horseshoe-shaped zone, 40 mi wide and 60 mi long, called the Bone Valley Formation, which is a product of submarine reworking of a phosphate-rich residuum. Leaching and weathering further upgraded the deposits.

A perfect "ringer" for the "horseshoe" would hit the peg at the town of Mulberry. The top of the shoe runs slightly north of Lakeland, and the legs extend into Hardee and Manatee Counties in the south. Fossilized remains of prehistoric marine animals, which are regularly found in the formation, gave rise to the name—Bone Valley Formation. "Valley" is a misnomer, as the location was once a coastal lagoon and is now flat.

Phosphatic land pebble is recovered from the lower part of the Bone Valley Formation (Pliocene age) and from the upper part of the underlying Hawthorne For-

turers. The company produced about 6 million tons of phosphate rock in 1975 and marketed about 50% of the total. The new Fort Green mine-plant came on stream in 1975. Modernization of the plants at Payne Creek and Saddle Creek has been completed. In 1975, Agrico bought from Stauffer Chemical Co. additional reserve lands adjacent to Agrico's previous holdings.

In an atypical arrangement at both Fort Green and Payne Creek, two independent main matrix lines feed two separate halves of a washer plant. Each matrix line is loaded from a separate dragline. Commingling of matrix feed occurs only beyond the wash plant.

Agrico owns more than 50 mi of internal railroad, and it recently completed construction of a new phosphate rock loading terminal at Tampa. The company produces a full line of fertilizers, phosphate rock, TSP, DAP, and granulated urea, plus silicofluorides.

Borden Chemicals' Smith-Douglas Div. has been mining and processing phosphate rock since 1908. The Teneroc mine, currently producing less than 1 million tpy of phosphate rock, is due to be replaced in 1978 by the new Big Four mine in Hillsborough County. The new mine is said to have been planned for 1.25 million tpy of product, all to be used internally in fertilizer manufacture.

Brewster Phosphates (American Cyanamid 75%, Kerr-McGee 25%) was formed in 1971 as a consolidation venture. Its new Lonesome mine, to open late in 1976 or early in 1977, will add 2.8 million tpy of phosphate rock capacity, at a cost of more than $75 million, excluding the land (18,300 acres). Overburden on the Lonesome property averages 25.5 ft and matrix 11.5 ft. Phosphate rock product is expected to grade about 70-71% BPL. Brewster operates acid and fertilizer plants in Louisiana. The company appears progressive and innovative, as exemplified in its new method of controlling slimes disposal, its water reclamation system, and the decision to go ahead with a double-duty conveyor system for handling matrix from the mine and tailings from the plant.

Gardinier Inc. is a wholly owned subsidiary of SOPAG, a French consortium of Gardinier SA and fertilizer cooperatives. The Gardinier mine, including reserves and plants, was purchased from Cities Service Co. in 1973. Gardinier produces 2 million tpy of phosphate rock from reserves sufficient to last about 20 years.

W. R. Grace & Co., with more than 80,000 acres of reserve lands, recently began two expansion projects for production of phosphate rock and acid fertilizers. The new Hookers Prairie mine, designed for 2.8 million tpy of phosphate rock, may come on stream in late 1976. The mine will employ a 67-cu-yd Bucyrus Erie dragline, the largest in the district. Product from Hookers Prairie will be shipped by railroad to Grace's chemical plant at Ridgewood (Bartow). The Ridgewood plant produces sulphuric acid, phosacid, DAP, and NP fertilizers. The sulphuric acid plant was recently replaced by a new installation.

In 1977, two additional sulphuric acid plants and a large phosacid plant will be added to the Ridgewood complex, doubling capacity of phosphoric acid. Expansion of the chemical complex is a joint venture with USS Agri-Chem. Grace now markets some 30% of its phosphate rock production. In 1980, the company plans to replace the Bonny Lake mine with the Four Corners mine, to be opened in Hillsborough-Manatee Counties. Production is scheduled at 3 million tpy.

International Minerals & Chemical Corp. (IMC) is the giant in phosphate rock production at 11 million tpy—nearly 10% of the entire world output. Some 50% of the company's production is exported. Locally, IMC supplies CF Industries and Royster Co. IMC bought about 2,500 acres of reserve land from Royster in 1973.

IMC recently completed construction of a $110 million phosphate chemical fertilizer complex near the Polk-Hillsborough county line. The plant is slated to produce 600,000 tons of phosacid in its first year. The company also has extensive shipping facilities at Port Sutton.

Around Lakeland, IMC is engaged in cattle grazing, citrus farming, operating nurseries, and developing an 800-acre planned community.

Mobil Oil Corp. operates two mines in Polk County, producing between 4 and 5 million tpy of phosphate rock. Mobil's reserves, estimated to exceed 40 million tons, are in Polk and Hardee Counties. A new operation may be de-

---

mation (Miocene age). The matrix ranges in thickness from 1 to 35 ft and is overlain by 10 to 50 ft of sand and clay. Ground water is close to the surface. Beneath the matrix is the solid or weathered phosphatic-bearing Hawthorne limestone.

Phosphate pebbles are hard, generally white, gray, tan, brown, or black, sized ½ in. to 20 mesh, and have a BPL content of 55-70%. Matrix normally grades 25-35% BPL in place. Some 90% of the matrix is recovered in mining, and about 95% of the pebble is recovered from wash plants. Feed is nominally 14 x 150 mesh, with only about 70% of its BPL values presently recovered in flotation. Flotation product ranges from 68% to 75% BPL.

In the central Florida mining district, generally high-BPL-grade material with a pebble-to-feed ratio of 1:1 is found along the upper periphery of the "horseshoe." Splitting the horseshoe north-south is the Lakeland-Bartow Ridge, a zone containing medium-BPL-grade material with a pebble-to-feed ratio that can reach 3:1. The southern part of the deposit, extending into Hardee and Manatee Counties, contains matrix of much lower grade: pebble of 55-68% BPL and feed heads of 12-20% BPL, with a low ratio of pebble-to-feed that, when mined, will send increased percentages of the matrix to flotation mills.

Throughout the district, there are variations in matrix thickness and quality, pebble-to-feed ratios, slimes settling rates, and chemical qualities of plant water. Such variations have a distinct effect on recovery.

The US Bureau of Mines in 1973 reported 1.2 billion tons of recoverable reserves in the district. Present operations, centered around Mulberry, will inevitably be extended south. Given present technology, known reserves, and projected production rates, the Bone Valley is likely to be depleted within 30 years. Other prospects will be developed by then. Phosphate operations in central Florida are important to both the local and national economies. The estimated 1.2 billion tons of phosphate rock reserves in the area are also said to contain 150,000 tons of recoverable U_3O_8. The Florida reserves also represent the largest known source of fluorine in the US, containing an average of 3-4% fluorine. Both U_3O_8 and fluorine are now being recovered from acid plants and sold as commercial byproducts of phosphate production.

Brewster's twin 45-cu-yd draglines alternately strip and mine matrix. Matrix pipelines merge to feed plant. (Matrix is dark horizon.)

Bucyrus-Erie 1260 fills bucket at USS Agri-Chem's Rockland mine, then casts 40 cu yd of matrix to a mine well, where high pressure water guns form a slurry.

Remote-controlled water guns, normally two or three, are installed on a pit car. Each gun jets 3,000-4,000 gpm at 175-200 psi into matrix.

Nine producers mine phosphate rock in Bone Valley Formation

	Mine	Annual production (tpy x 10⁶)	Average grade of product (% BPL*)	Year mine opened	Year mine projected to close	Draglines	Daily production of matrix (tons)	Flotation feed heads (% BPL)	Pit width (ft)	Pit depth (ft)	Average thickness of matrix (ft)
Agrico	Payne Creek	3.0	68	1965	NA	9 Bucyrus-Erie	NA	23	250-325	30-70	12
	Saddle Creek	1.5	72	NA	1983	for three mines,	NA	31	250	60	7
	Fort Green	3.0	68	1975	NA	sized 18-42 yd	NA	18	325	70	12
Borden	Teneroc	1.0	NA	1950	1978	3 Bucyrus-Erie (7, 10, and 20 yd)	NA	NA	200-350	20-40	5-15
Brewster	Haynsworth	3.0	70	1967	1990	2 Page (45 yd)	36,000	30	550	36	12
	Lonesome	2.8	70	1976	1996	2 Page (45 yd)	30,000	30	550	36	12
Gardinier	US Phosphoric Products	1.8	67	1967	1996	3 Bucyrus-Erie (8, 40, and 42 yd)	24,000	25	330	40	20
W. R. Grace	Bonny Lake	2.3	68	1945	1980	2 Bucyrus-Erie (21 and 42 yd)	25,000	23	200-350	45-60	5-25
	Hookers Prairie	2.8	68	1977	1994	1 Bucyrus-Erie (67 yd)	30,000	22	NA	40	19
IMC	Clear Springs	2.5	72	1969	1985	1 Marion (20 yd) 1 Bucyrus-Erie (40 yd)	25,000	32	275	48	20
	Kingsford	4.5	68	1966	1995	1 Marion (45 yd) 2 Page (45 yd)	43,000	22	275	48	20
	Noralyn/ Phosphoria	5.0	69	1949/ 1974	1990	4 Bucyrus-Erie (20, 25, 30, 35 yd)	45,000	26	275	40	18
Mobil	Fort Meade	3.0	NA	1967	1990	2 Bucyrus-Erie (20 and 38 yd)	NA	NA	300	35	15
	Nichols	1.5	NA	1972	1990	1 Bucyrus-Erie (40 yd)	NA	NA	300	35	15
Swift	Silver City	2.0	68	1964	1983	1 Page (45 yd)	22,000	24	300	30	15
	Watson	1.0	73	1937	1990	1 Bucyrus-Erie (14 yd) 1 Page (30 yd)	14,000	32	250-350	65	15
USS Agri-Chem	Rockland	2.0	68	1968	1986	2 Bucyrus-Erie (35 and 40 yd)	36,000	24	350-550	35-50	15-20

NA—not available. * BPL—bone phosphate of lime.

veloped after 1979 to replace the Fort Meade mine.

Swift Agricultural Chemicals Corp., part of the conglomerate Esmark (with interests in petroleum, meat, food lines, and insurance), has been operating since 1900. Swift mines phosphate rock at Silver City and Watson and owns reserves in Manatee County, which will probably be developed in the early 1980s as Silver City is depleted.

USS Agri-Chemicals, a division of US Steel, is the managing agent for the Rockland mine-plant, a joint venture with Freeport Chemical Co. The 2 million tpy of phosphate rock product is split 50-50 by the owners. USS is said to own independently more than 30 million tons of reserves in Polk, Hardee, and Manatee Counties.

In addition to the nine active producers, several new mining ventures are being developed or discussed by other companies in the district.

Beker Industries Corp. has purchased reserve land in Manatee County from Union Oil and Pittsburgh Plate Glass, estimated to contain about 60 million tons of product. A mine may open in 1978 to produce 3 million tpy of phosphate rock. The company has been granted approval of its documentation of environmental impact and may be the first in the district—in present times—to use a dredge for removing overburden and matrix.

CF Industries Inc. has purchased 19,000 acres of land in Hardee County estimated to contain 50 million tons of product. A 2.5-million-tpy mine may be opened in 1978.

First Mississippi Chemical is said to be looking for a partner in developing a 3-million-tpy mine in Hardee County, based on 60 million tons of reserves.

Phillips Petroleum Co., which owns reserve lands in Manatee County, has reportedly been negotiating with Farmlands Industries for a joint venture mining operation to produce 3 to 4 million tpy sometime in the 1980s. Reserves are said to be about 60 million tons.

TA Minerals (Transammonia Inc.) will begin mine and plant production this year. The Polk County operation is slated to produce 400,000 tpy from virgin land and from old IMC tailings.

Southern Recovery Co. will open the first tertiary recovery plant in the history of the Florida phosphate industry. Dagus Engineers and Envirobasic Corp., of Tampa, were selected to supply advanced design and equipment for the recovery and restoration system. Output is expected to be 75,000 to 100,000 tpy of 77% BPL product.

Other companies are conducting or planning scavenger operations based on secondary or tertiary tailing material. Many old tailing deposits (the residue from days of "high-grading" impelled by economics) can now be turned into profits.

Mining phosphate is not all beer and skittles

Several problems, varying in seriousness, afflict the phosphate rock and fertilizer industry of central Florida. Chief among these problems appear to be:
- An inadequately experienced, somewhat unstable group of younger workers.
- The proliferation of regulatory agencies.
- Environmental problems, particularly in water use and slimes disposal.

For many good reasons, including rapid expansion, a large number of workers at phosphate mines and plants are young and inexperienced. A substantial minority of these workers are uninterested in the work and are prone to job-hopping. One company stated that its annual turnover rate is 30%, in spite of (or in some cases because of) on-the-job training programs to improve skills. Approximately 50% of the company's dragline operators have less than a year of operating experience. Other companies note that maintenance work and particularly work in wash and flotation plants is considered boring by many of the young—even in positions at the foreman level.

Workers' lack of interest and skills adversely affects all phases of operations (preventive maintenance, repairs, and operation and control of reasonably sophisticated equipment) necessary to keep plant throughput at design capabilities. However, this problem does not affect the entire industry. Some operations appear to be running well, with many of the younger workers well motivated and no less productive than the old-timers. In general, the larger companies appear to have the more serious problems.

As for regulatory agencies, what the phosphate rock industry now requires is regulation based upon well defined objectives and recognition of the trade-offs inherent in each decision. The activities of regulatory agencies now overlap, and the number of agency personnel is phenomenal. The result is confusion, wasted time, wasted effort, voluminous paper work, and fuzzy or conflicting rules.

Three to five years may elapse between a company's decision to mine at a specific location and the approval for mining. In the interim, millions of dollars are spent, and the cost estimates of the original proposal escalate. The process leading to approval to mine begins with a Development of Regional Impact (DRI) application, a massive document prepared by the mining company that details proposed construction, mining, and plant operations. The DRI includes much other information, such as an inventory of all plants, trees, animals, insects, reptiles, and birds on the property. The study details the impact of proposed mining on housing, roads, water resources, air quality, etc. The DRI is reviewed by local, regional, and state bodies. If the DRI is approved, the company may then apply for mining permits from the regulatory agencies.

A W. R. Grace & Co. directory of public officials responsible for review and/or approval of a DRI application lists 29 commissions or departments and 100 public officials—an absurdly high number.

After approval of a DRI, each mining operation is subject to regulation by Federal agencies, including the Environmental Protection Agency (EPA), Occupational Safety and Health Administration (OSHA), Mining Enforcement and Safety Administration (MESA), and US Geological Survey (USGS).

In addition, phosphate operations in Polk and Hillsborough Counties are subject to the authority of the following state, county, and district agencies and regulations:
- Florida Department of Natural Resources

The 'Mud-Cat,' a small, handy suction dredge, is used by USS-Agri-Chem for various clean-up jobs. The dredge has an auger feed and can work to 15 ft below the water line. It is being readied for clean-up of muck and debris from a return-water ditch.

- County Protective Development Regulation
- County Lime Rock Mining Ordinance
- County Zoning Ordinance
- County Building Code
- County Health Department
- County Environmental Protection Act
- Southwest Florida Water Management District
- Florida Department of Environmental Regulation

As mining progresses into other counties, similar ordinances, codes, regulations, and confusion will be encountered. The cost of such confusion is borne not only by the phosphate rock producers but also by the general public. The phosphate producers ask not for an end to regulation but for an end to their Tower of Babel.

The phosphate industry uses a lot of water. Approximately 10,000 gal are needed to produce each ton of phosphate rock product. Producers recycle and reuse 85-95% of their process water. Even so, remaining requirements for makeup water are prodigious, and exhaustive studies and efforts are in progress to reduce the use of makeup water. The two major targets are natural replenishment of ground water and reduction of the time during which vast quantities of water are tied up in slimes ponds.

IMC recharges aquifer with near-surface water

Makeup water for the phosphate industry is supplied from deep wells that tap the Floridan Aquifer several hundred feet below the Hawthorne limestone. Over the years, there has been a gradual decline of the aquifer—the main source of ground water in the area. Around IMC's Kingsford mine and in the overburden, a "perched" water table is separated from the Floridan Aquifer by a series of impermeable beds.

IMC, in cooperation with the Southwest Florida Water Management District, the Florida Department of Pollution Control, and the USGS, has developed a system of recharge wells—a gravity-flow system that is replenishing the Floridan Aquifer from the perched table through the impermeable beds. Recharge well casing has screens located opposite the water-bearing sands in the overburden. Water moves by gravity into the well, drops to the limestone sequence, and finds its way into the Floridan Aquifer through cracks, crevices, and caverns. By lowering the water table in the shallow surface aquifer, less rainwater and surface water is lost to runoff, evaporation, and transpiration, and infiltration of rainwater is increased—a further source for recharge.

More than 50 recharge wells are now in use, each averaging 200 gpm of flow. The project also includes 60 observation wells and 20 surface monitoring stations. A study of the chemical and bacteriological character of the recharge water showed it to be of better quality than water in the Floridan Aquifer. Should water in the shallow aquifer ever develop detrimental properties, the recharge wells will be plugged.

Slimes disposal: a tough problem

For over 40 years, the bane of the industry has been the problem of disposal of clay slimes—all material in the matrix smaller than 150 mesh. Clay slimes are not presently susceptible to flotation recovery—even though they carry as much as 30% of the phosphate values contained in the matrix. Inability to dewater is the most salient, consistent characteristic of these slimes and the root of all the water problems the industry faces.

The following figures illustrate the magnitude of the problem. In 1972 it was estimated that 1.5 billion tons of phosphate slimes were stored behind dams and about 4.5 billion tons of water were locked up with the slimes—the result of 40 years of flotation tailings disposal. Mile upon mile of 40-ft-high dams contain the slimes. Each acre-foot of mined matrix requires a minimum 1½-acre-ft volume for slimes disposal; the dams provide storage for the excess. The heavy cost of the slimes disposal includes dam construction, monitoring, and maintenance; liability; loss of water; loss of real estate; and problems of public relations.

In 1975 the phosphate industry spent over $30 million in research and development for pollution abatement and water conservation. Over the past decade, more than $200 million has been spent for such purposes. A large proportion of this money went toward licking the slimes problem. More than a dozen programs, many assisted by the USBM, have been carried out, but as late as September 1975 it was reported that "no method has been proved to be technically feasible at the field scale and economically acceptable."

That statement now appears in need of revision, because three methods currently under study—one a full field-scale program—appear to offer practical results. The minimum acceptable goal is to raise slimes ponds quickly to 40% solids. This will eliminate the need for dams, provide rapid recycling of water, reduce makeup water needs, and allow reclaimed land to be used productively.

For many good reasons, phosphate producers want the land reclamation program to be a success. Land itself is worth over $1,000 an acre. Reclamation underway or completed over the past 10 years affects 30,000 acres. Reclaimed land will be used for pasture, farming, homesites, pine forestry, recreation, and wildlife.

Analysis of 15 representative slimes samples from different producers indicated that physical, chemical, and mineralogical compositions vary from location to location. Most plants discharge slimes at 2-6% solids content. One significant factor affecting early settling rates is the percentage of the clay mineral attapulgite in the slimes. For example, a sample from the Noralyn mine of IMC, which had 1,270 counts per sec of attapulgite, had settled to only 5.7% solids in 30 days. A Brewster mine sample showed only 30 counts per sec of attapulgite and registered 11%

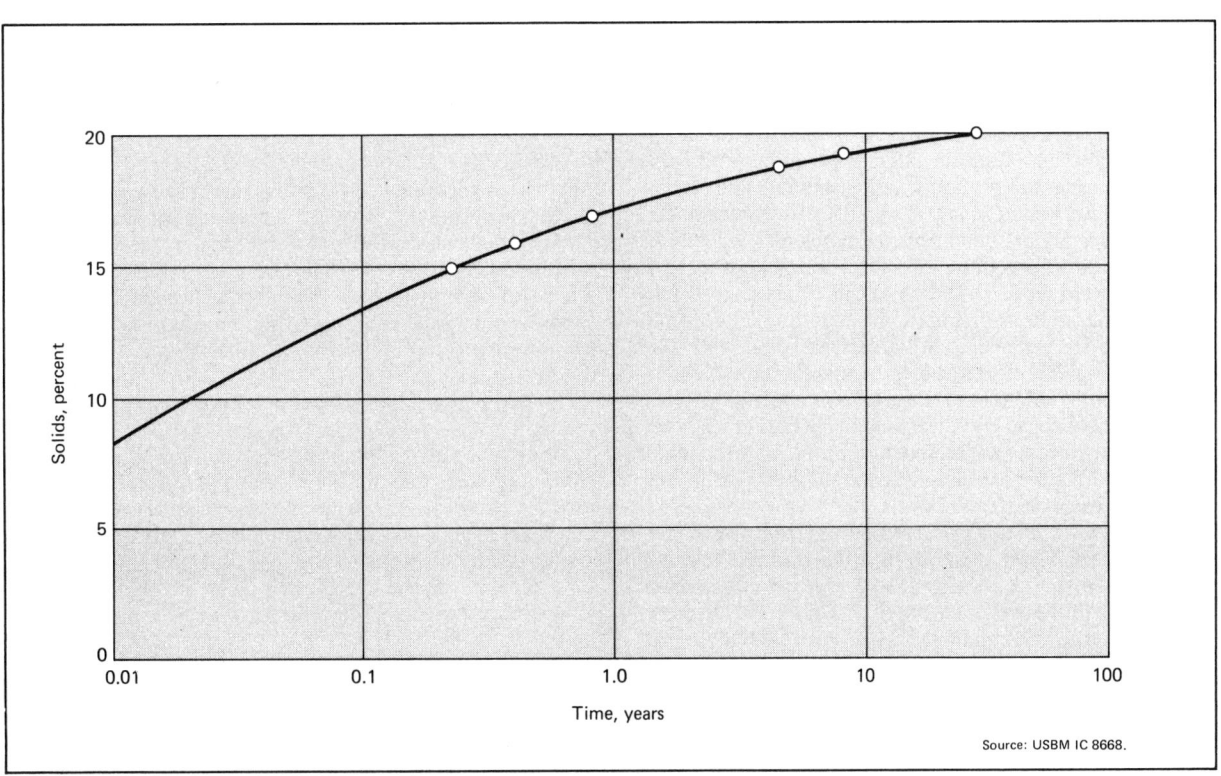

The settling rate of phosphate clay slimes approaches a limit above 15% solids.

solids in 30 days. A sample from Agrico's Saddle Creek mine showed no detectable attapulgite, and after 30 days this sample registered 16% solids. Clearly, the presence or absence of this mineral profoundly affects the early recovery of decant water from the ponds. Settling is hindered by clay minerals with colloid-like properties in slimes. (Most slimes are approximately 80% minus 20 micron, although some contain 70% material finer than 1 micron.)

As the particles in suspension thicken to plus 15% solids, the time required to increase the solids density rises logarithmically, reaching what appears to be a limiting pulp density. This is why ponds, after decades, still remain unsettled. A breakthrough is needed to rapidly increase the recovery of water once 15% solids has been achieved.

Three new slimes disposal systems look good

At Brewster, a 500-acre, full-scale test is nearing completion. Engineers began depositing slimes in the test area in March 1975, and when the project is completed in June 1976, the area will contain slimes removed from 3.3 million tons of product mined over 1¼ years. The system being tested to treat the slimes appears to be a big success, and Brewster is adapting its entire mining operations to accommodate the method.

Laboratory tests have shown that when fine grain sands were sprinkled over clay slimes that had consolidated to 12% solids, the sands penetrated and mixed with the clays, liberating water and producing a thick sand-clay mixture of about 45% solids. Field tests by Brewster on a 20-acre site duplicated the laboratory results. The 500-acre site was then chosen for the definitive test.

Within the 500 acres, mine cuts 36 ft deep, 550 ft wide at the centerline of the windrows, and 2,600 to 3,200 ft long were left after mining. Clay slimes at 2-6% solids were introduced into the sections and allowed to settle to 12% solids over a period of weeks. Then sand sprayers on pontoons sprayed tailings sand over the water covering the clay slimes. The procedure is said to increase total solids of the mixture in the ponds to 40-45%. After the pontoons are removed and the decant water is drained off, a 1,500-tph Mechanical Excavator bucket-wheel stacker will spread windrow overburden on top of the sand-slime material. The area will then be seeded with grass and ready for use. Brewster claims to have no further need of dams.

In a second program, at Swift's Silver City mine, a common-line mixing of sand and clay slimes is being pumped and discharged to a disposal area. If immediate segregation of the mix can be prevented, Swift believes that results similar to Brewster's may be obtained, obviously at reduced effort. Swift claims that this system provides clear water at a spillway located ½ mi from the mix discharge. Previously, all-slimes discharge created mud at the spillway 8 hr after discharge. Swift engineers have checked the bottoms of some test areas two to three years after filling, and claim to have found 40% solids.

The third method, under evaluation by USS Agri-Chem and the Florida Phosphate Council, uses alternating layers of tailings sand and clay slimes. If small scale tests give positive results, the system will be applied to mined-out cuts 300 ft wide and 2,500 ft long.

The phosphate industry has been able to solve the problem of air-borne emissions; help formulate earthen dam building regulations; is reducing particulate emissions, as well as sulphur dioxide and ammonia emissions; and has reduced water-borne phosphorus and nitrogen emissions by over 90%. It now appears to be on the path to control of its slimes disposal problem. □

The phosphate industry has spent millions to develop a system for the rapid dewatering of slimes ponds. One method under study distributes alternating layers of tailing sands and slimes. The weight of the tailings sands squeezes the slimes, releasing water and increasing the solids content from 15% to over 40%. This test model is being readied by USS Agri-Chem in cooperation with the Florida Phosphate Council. If the test succeeds, the system will be introduced into uniformly mined-out cuts, 300 ft wide and 2,500 ft long.

Bibliography

1) Blakey, Arch Frederic, *The Florida Phosphate Industry*, Harvard University Press, Cambridge, Mass., 1973.
2) Stowasser, W. F., "Phosphate Rock," *Mineral Facts and Problems*, 1975 ed., US Bureau of Mines.
3) Ross, Richard C., "Uranium Recovery from Phosphoric Acid Nears Reality as a Commercial Uranium Source," E/MJ, December 1975, p 80.
4) Beall, John V., and Merritt, Paul C., "Phosphate and Potash Minerals to Feed the World," MINING ENGINEERING, October 1966, p 76.
5) "The Florida Phosphate Slimes Problem," USBM IC 8668, 1975.
6) Barr, James A., "Phosphate Rock," *Industrial Minerals and Rocks*, AIME, 1960.
7) Catheart, James B., and Gulbrandsen, R. A., "Phosphate Deposits," USGS Professional Paper 820, 1973.
8) "Phosphates Feed the World—How to Utilize Low Grade Deposits," WORLD MINING, November 1975, p 51.
9) Moudgil, Brij M., and Bunch, John P., "Mined Land Reclamation by the Florida Phosphate Industry," SME Fall Meeting, Salt Lake City, 1975.
10) Wang, Kung Lee, Barry, W., and Powell, Andrew F., "Economic Significance of the Florida Phosphate Industry," USBM IC 8653, 1974.
11) Lamont, W. E., McLendon, J. T., and Clements, L. W. Jr., "Characterization Studies of Florida Phosphate Slimes," USBM RI 8089, 1975.

'Super Dragon,' which cost $8.5 million, is the largest portable dredge built by Ellicott Machine Corp. of Baltimore.

Lee Creek may share link with Kidd Creek as the two Texasgulf units gear for expansions

Innovative dredge stripping of phosphate overburden at Lee Creek . . . More underground ore, a new mill, a new Mitsubishi smelter at Kidd Creek . . . And, in between, a possible link-up to produce phosphoric acid.

Robert Sisselman, Associate editor

AS PART OF A LONG RANGE PLAN to expand phosphate mining and processing facilities at Lee Creek, N.C., Texasgulf Inc. has more than doubled its mining output, from just over 2 million tpy to 5 million tpy. Toward this end, the company has purchased a Marion 8050 50-cu-yd dragline to operate in tandem with its Bucyrus Erie 2550 72-cu-yd dragline, plus a dredge that is unique to phosphate mining in the US.

The new mining scheme is only one facet of Texasgulf's expansion plans, which call for eventual production of 1 million tpy of 100% P_2O_5 by about 1980. Lee Creek currently supplies 7-8% of all phosphoric acid consumed in the US.

Texasgulf's track record of expansion is impressive. In 1973, the company spent $23 million at Lee Creek, part of it for construction of a third acid train—a 50% increase in capacity for 100% P_2O_5. The acid train consists of one sulphuric acid producing unit and one phosphoric acid producing unit, which together turn out 170,000 tpy of 100% P_2O_5. In 1975, $53 million went into expansion, including installation of a fourth acid train and accompanying superphosphoric acid facilities, plus another fertilizer manufacturing unit, two new calciners, and the dredge and draglines. This expansion boosted production to 680,000 tpy of 100% P_2O_5. A fifth and a sixth train are slated to come on stream by 1980 to lift capacity to 1 million tpy.

Dredging overburden: an economic reality

Texasgulf's is the only phosphate operation in the US that employs a dredge—used at Lee Creek not to mine but to prestrip the first 40 ft of overburden. Only one other firm—Beker Industries, in Florida—is planning a dredging operation. Back in 1964-1965, during the mine's development stages, Texasgulf dug its first test pit with a dredge, removing about 1 million yd over a period of several

Dredge cutter head is hydraulically driven. The dredge itself is 136 ft long and 36 ft wide, with a bare weight of 485,000 lb and a digging depth of 50 ft.

In Lee Creek slurry pit, ore is pumped at 1,250 tph solids through 18-in.-dia pipeline to the concentrator. Pumping distance varies from 10,000 to 14,000 ft.

months. The dredge did double duty, stripping the overburden and mining the ore, but the economics proved unfavorable.

The new mining method has advantages. The dredge performs solely as an earthmoving machine, removing between 12 million and 15 million cu yd of overburden annually, and permits increased recovery of ore. Lee Creek was losing "a good 10% ore the old way," observed general manager James R. Paden, "and now we should recover that fraction."

The main reason why dredges have not been used to date at any of Florida's phosphate operations is that overburden in Florida is much shallower—30 to 35 ft vs. 80 ft in North Carolina—and may be prestripped and back-cast solely by draglines without any threat of contaminating the ore.

The original Lee Creek mining plans called for stripping all overburden with draglines, back-casting the waste rock into the mine area to reach the 40 ft of ore.

The principal drawback with this procedure, said Paden, was that "the reach of the dragline and the angle of the spoil pile was such that the spoil tended to slough into the orebody, causing a loss of ore." Dredging offers some secondary benefits. The space left between the toe of the spoil pile and the bottom of the ore can be ditched for removal of excess water.

Since the development data for Lee Creek did not indicate a potential problem with the original mining plan when the facility came on stream in 1967, the operation was faced with headaches from the very outset.

When management recognized the need to increase mining capacity above that produced via the original mining method using a single Bucyrus Erie 72-yd dragline, it was decided to seek an alternative method that would strip a portion of the overburden and remove it entirely from the ore pile.

Three possible mining systems were considered: 1) a truck and shovel operation—which posed an expensive problem in disposing of waste; 2) a bucket-wheel operation, in which a specified quantity of material would be prestripped and belt-conveyed to another location; and 3) prestripping of the orebody using a dredge.

Dredging would cut the first 40 ft of overburden, pump the slurry to a mined-out area, and allow it to settle out. The water would later be pumped from the mining section, generally a 200-acre plot, and the remaining overburden would be dried out for one year. Draglines would be moved into position to finish the stripping. In this manner, Texasgulf would dragline-strip 40 ft and back-cast it into the mined-out area. The spoil pile height would be decreased and there would be no dilution of the ore.

Texasgulf chose the "Super Dragon" dredge, Ellicott Model 38000, which operates on 3,500 hp and transports overburden in the form of slurry over distances of 5,000 to 10,000 ft, depending on the position of the dredge. The Super Dragon is equipped with a 30-in. pump and an 8-ft cutter head. The all-electric unit was shipped to Lee Creek on rail cars in 1975 and assembled in about two months.

Additional equipment may be ordered if the fertilizer market maintains its 4% annual growth rate, and all indications are that it will do so. Even now, Texasgulf is seriously considering expanding mining from the current 5 million tpy to 10 million tpy, to keep pace with US and world demand for fertilizers to feed a growing number of hungry people. □

Chapter 11
Uranium

Rapid building program puts RMEC into production of U_3O_8
   in Powder River Basin 396
Wyoming uranium miners set sights on higher production 400
In-situ leaching opens new uranium reserves in Texas 405
Developers eye Texas potential for in-situ leaching 413

Rapid building program puts RMEC into production of U_3O_8 in Powder River Basin

Dan Jackson, Western editor

ROCKY MOUNTAIN ENERGY CO. dedicated its 1,000-tpd Bear Creek uranium mine-mill complex north of Douglas, Wyo., on September 22—only 16 months after the start of construction in May 1976. The Bear Creek operation—among the first to start up as a direct result of higher uranium prices—is an outgrowth of a six-year, $24 million joint exploration venture with Mono Power Co., a subsidiary of Southern California Edison Co. Rocky Mountain Energy Co. (RMEC), a subsidiary of Union Pacific Corp., is the operating partner in the joint venture.

A contractor began stripping at Bear Creek in August 1976, and mine production of ore started in June 1977 at an initial rate of 900 tpd (27,500 tpm). Current plans call for increasing production to 1,400 tpd of ore before yearend and maintaining that rate until 1990. About 600,000 tons of U_3O_8 will be produced annually.

More than 5 million cu yd of overburden was removed to reach ore in the Carson No. 1 pit, the first of seven open pits that will be developed on the current reserves. (See map.) Overburden removal is underway at the Hardy No. 1 and Dilts pits. Total recoverable reserves in the seven orebodies are estimated at 3 million tons, with about half the total in the Hardy-Hornbuckle deposit. Grades average 0.15% U_3O_8. Exploration drilling continues in the Bear Creek area, which encompasses Federal, state, and private lands.

Erratic ore zones influence mine practice

RMEC started its stripping operation by hiring a contractor—the fastest way to get the mine into production. The 5 million cu yd stripped from the Carson No. 1 pit was removed in a nine-month period. The Dilts pit also is being stripped by a contractor, but RMEC itself is handling stripping at Hardy No. 1, using a shovel-truck combination. The contractor operates a fleet of Caterpillar scraper-loaders.

Topsoil is stored for future use in reclamation; overburden, at the rate of about 667,500 cu yd per month, is stored in waste dumps located away from drainage to minimize erosion. The low-profile dumps are located also to extend ridgelines of existing hills. After mining, pits will be backfilled with overburden and contoured to blend with the natural topography of the area. Overburden dumps will be graded, covered with topsoil, and revegetated with native plants or other suitable shrubs and grasses.

About 10% of the overburden is lightly blasted to increase loading efficiency, with blasting done during daylight hours only. An exploration drill equipped with a 6¾-in. drag bit is currently used for blasthole drilling.

The RMEC mining plan has been developed to minimize the number of overburden disposal sites. Mined-out pits will be backfilled with overburden from future pits.

The 1,000-tpd Bear Creek mill, about 70 mi northeast of Casper, Wyo., was designed for compactness and for a generally aesthetic blending with the surrounding landscape. The maximum mine-to-mill ore haul will be 6 mi.

Generalized section through an area of Bear Creek ore

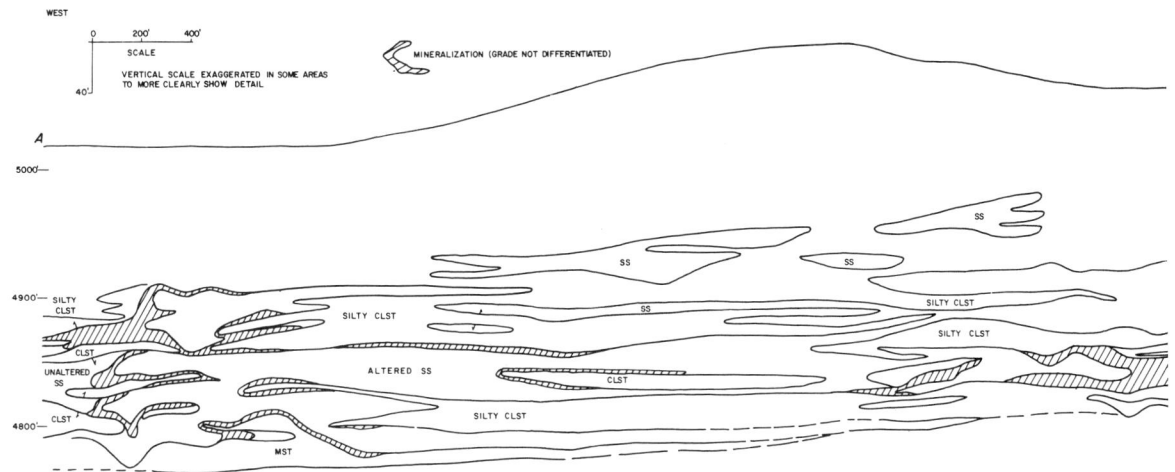

Uranium in the Powder River Basin

The Powder River Basin, in which the Bear Creek uranium deposits occur, is a large structural and physiographic basin in northeastern Wyoming. Except on the north, structural highlands completely surround the basin: the Black Hills uplift to the east, the Hartville uplift and Larmie Mountains to the south and southwest, and the Bighorn Mountains uplift to the west. Structurally, the basin is a north-northwesterly-trending asymmetric syncline, the west flank being steeper than the east.

In the deepest part of the basin, about 18,000 ft of sedimentary rocks, ranging from Cambrian to Oligocene in age, overlie the crystalline basement.

The Bear Creek project is located about 9 mi east of the basement axis, and the Eocene Wasatch formation dominates the project landscape, except where it is overlain by alluvium in stream valleys. The virtually flat-lying strata of the Wasatch have sand in thick lenses of coarse- to fine-grained arkosic sandstone commonly interbedded with siltstone, carbonaceous shale, and coal. Thin beds of conglomerate occur locally. The siltstone and shale are only semiconsolidated, and the sandstone beds are generally friable. The formation is about 1,000 ft thick on the Bear Creek property, consisting of alternating claystone, siltstone, and sandstone of fluvial origin. The base of the lowermost sandstone that contains ore is about 700-800 ft above the base of the Wasatch formation.

The lithology of the rocks above the ore-bearing unit varies considerably throughout the project because of the interfingering of claystone, siltstone, and sandstone. The thickness of the overburden ranges from 100 ft to 270 ft as a result of an increase in surface elevation from north to south. The overburden is mostly claystone, with several discontinuous lenses of sandstone up to 20 ft thick. Throughout most of the area, claystone constitutes 60-90% of the total overburden and sandstone 10-40%.

Uranium has been mined in the Powder River Basin since the 1950s, initially from small shallow deposits in the Wasatch formation. Since the mid-1960s, when ore was discovered at depth, exploration by drilling, which still continues, has proved the existence of many large uranium deposits in the southern part of the basin. No precise data are available concerning total tonnage discovered to date, but there are at least 10 deposits containing more than 1 million tons of ore each. More than 90% of known ore reserves occur in the Fort Union and Wasatch formations, while a few deposits occur in the Lance and Fox Hills formations, of Cretaceous age.

The Wasatch and Fort Union deposits typically occur at a boundary between oxidized yellow and unoxidized gray sandstone in roll-front deposits. The boundaries of the deposits are generally very sinuous and occur at several stratigraphic horizons. Ore grade is not continuous along the boundaries of the roll-front but occurs in local concentrations connected by stretches of low grade mineralization.

Ore minerals are mainly uraninite and coffinite, but small quantities of a variety of secondary uranium-vanadium minerals may be present. In and near the ore zones are also concentrations of vanadium, selenium, arsenic, and iron sulphides.

The ore-bearing units range from 50 ft to 100 ft thick and consist of fine-, medium-, and coarse-grained sandstones that for the most part are poorly indurated, although well-indurated, calcite-cemented sandstone may be found in and near the ore.

Overburden over the seven Bear Creek orebodies varies from 100 to 270 ft thick, and highwall slopes are maintained at 47-52°.

The shovel-truck stripping operation stops a few feet above the anticipated ore zone, and scraper-loaders are moved in to complete the stripping to within ½ ft of the ore. As soon as radiation is detected, scraping stops, and the ore is drilled and sampled. After ore pockets have been delineated, the scrapers remove barren material from the pit. Occasionally, they are used also in fine-scraping the ore.

Once orebodies are defined, a mining fleet of front-end and hydraulic backhoe loaders moves in to remove ore. The front-end loaders mine the larger deposits, while the backhoes work the smaller deposits to reduce dilution. Single-shank ripper-dozers rip the ore prior to loading.

The Bear Creek uranium ore occurs in poorly consolidated sandstone that is typically coarse to fine-grained. Because of the extremely erratic nature of the mineralization, an ore control program has been in force since mining began, including use of instruments to locate ore, semiquantitative analysis of uranium content, and precise excavation to minimize dilution. Radiation-detecting instruments in use include hand-held geiger probes and a tower-mounted beta-gamma scanner.

Four quality-control technicians work with each loader, directing the loader operator and defining the orebody. One takes a bag sample, which the truck driver delivers to the beta-gamma operator. While the truck is en route to the mill, the sample is tested, and the driver is directed to the proper unloading pad.

Ore trucks haul out of the pit on an 8%, 60-ft-wide road. Haulage distance throughout the life of the mine will vary from less than 1 mi to a maximum of 6 mi.

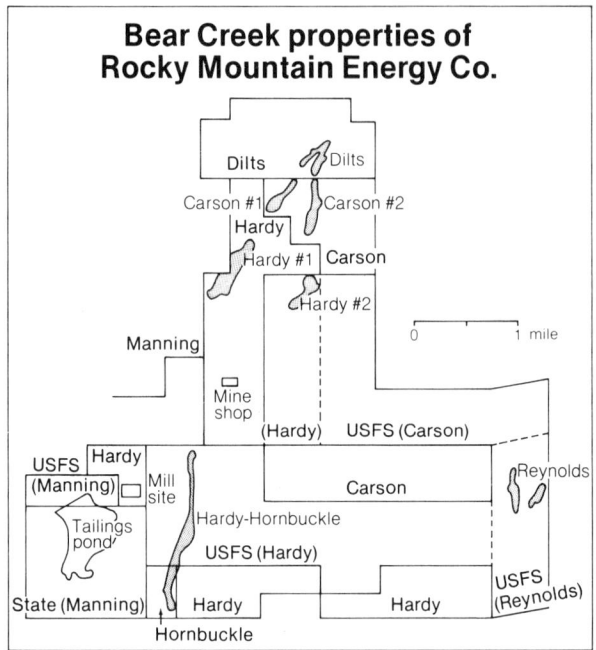

Quality control technicians using geiger probes direct the ore-loading operation of a backhoe in a Bear Creek uranium pit.

Three ore stockpiles—high grade, mill run, and low grade—are maintained at the mill site.

Most of the Bear Creek ore is located below the local water table. Using backhoes, Bear Creek miners dig 12-ft-deep trenches around orebodies for drainage to a collection sump. Water is pumped out of the pit, treated with barium chloride, and clarified in a settling pond. Flows from the various pits are expected to range between 600 and 2,000 gpm, with an average of about 1,000 gpm. Some of this water is used for dust control, and the remainder is discharged into existing drainageways. Several downstream ranches make use of it for irrigation.

Reclamation follows mining

Throughout the projected 15-year life of the project, Bear Creek will disturb about 2,000 acres and will reclaim the same amount. Reclamation is already part of the mining operation, with the goal of returning land to use for livestock grazing and as a wildlife habitat. Natural drainage patterns will be re-established, and where irrigation is feasible, the land will be contoured to provide a gently sloping surface, permitting use of circular irrigation systems. Topsoil will be spread over reclaimed areas after reducing slopes to acceptable limits. Contour furrows will be established at the slope toe to trap sediment. Haulage roads compacted by heavy equipment will be ripped prior to contouring.

Current plans call for developing two freshwater lakes on the property when mining is completed, for livestock and wildlife needs and as a potential source of irrigation.

Seed mixtures to be applied to reclaimed areas were chosen on the basis of soil and overburden studies, baseline vegetation studies, and discussions with the Soil Conservation Service. The mixtures consist of western wheatgrass, thickspike wheatgrass, green needlegrass,

Bear Creek mining equipment

Shovel: one P&H 2100BL, 17-cu-yd capacity.
Trucks: eight Wabco electric-wheel 120Cs, 120 tons; six Wabco diesel 35Cs, 35 tons.
Scrapers: four Caterpillar 633Bs, self-loading.
Motor graders: two Caterpillar 16Gs.
Dozers: three Caterpillar D9Hs; one Caterpillar rubber-tired 824B.
Backhoes: one Caterpillar 245; one Northwest 55DH.
Water truck: one Wabco 75-ton truck with 11,000-gal Klein tank.
Front-end loader: one Fiat-Allis 945B.

and sweetclover—a composition that may be changed as experience is gained.

Tailings dam creates a 150-acre impoundment

No aspect of uranium mining and milling is a more environmentally sensitive issue than the disposal of tailings. The tailings management program for Bear Creek was selected to solve environmental problems in a practical way. Early studies pointed out major problems in blowing dust, seepage, radon emanation, and dam stability. The disposal site was investigated in detail to assess the ways in which these problems could be solved. A full-height dam was built to ensure stability and minimize the potential for blowing dust. The disposal area overlies a clay deposit, which was tested to determine potential for seepage, and some pervious areas were covered by additional clay and compacted. The problem of radon emanation is solved by covering the dried tailings with mine overburden, a portion of which is natural clay.

The dam is about 50 ft high and 1,700 ft long. The upstream slope is 2½:1 and the downstream slope 3:1. The natural materials used for construction were compacted to provide a stable, impervious structure. A chimney and toe drain ensure long-term stability. Following deposition of the tailings, mine overburden will be placed on the dry portions of the beach, covered with topsoil, and revegetated.

Environmental monitoring

Three high volume air samplers have been installed on the Bear Creek property at sites selected by the Wyoming Department of Environmental Control. The samplers are maintained and operated in conformity with a sampling schedule set by the US Environmental Protection Agency. Meteorological information is recorded continuously, and the data is computer-processed to provide input to predictive models.

Bear Creek has also established a radiological monitoring program.

At full production, the Bear Creek mine-mill complex will employ about 250 people, with an annual payroll of $4 million. The operation is expected to produce more than $8 million in state and county taxes during the life of the project.

The rapid expansion of the natural resources industry in the Powder River Basin has brought the social pressures that go with an expanding population. RMEC has sought to reduce its impact on the communities near its operations by guaranteeing the purchase of housing to stimulate construction. □

Wyoming uranium miners set sights on higher production

Lane White, Managing editor

IS ANOTHER URANIUM BOOM IN THE MAKING? Some uranium producers think so. Some people who aren't involved in uranium production—but would like to be—think so too.

Since Westinghouse announced in September that fulfilling its contracts to supply uranium to some 20 utilities would be "commercially impracticable," uranium prices have skyrocketed. By mid-November, one uranium producer was reportedly asking $40 per lb of U_3O_8 for a new contract. Most existing contracts, some with several years to run, are pegged around $10 per lb.

In September, when producers were considering pleasurably the prevailing talk of $20-per-lb U_3O_8, E/MJ toured Wyoming uranium country, visited the state's seven uranium mills, and talked with a number of people in the uranium industry. Their mood ranged from cautiously to thoroughly (perhaps even wildly) optimistic. Pessimism had been banished to other, more recession-prone sectors of the US. The uranium producers, having anticipated the coming strong demand, already had a number of new and expansion projects under way and others on the drawing board.

However, there are good grounds for caution in assessing the future of the uranium industry. Stiff environmental regulations make it increasingly time-consuming and expensive to license new milling capacity. Labor is in short supply. No important new uranium district has been discovered in the US in 20 years. Utility companies are stretching out construction schedules for new nuclear reactors. Anti-nuclear groups are active in a number of states and could block some reactor construction. In June 1976, California voters will go to the polls to determine the fate of a possibly precedent-setting initiative: it places almost impossible qualifications on continued nuclear development, and it could lead to a phase-out of nuclear power in the state.

The above factors will slow nuclear reactor construction in the US and, consequently, growth of uranium demand.

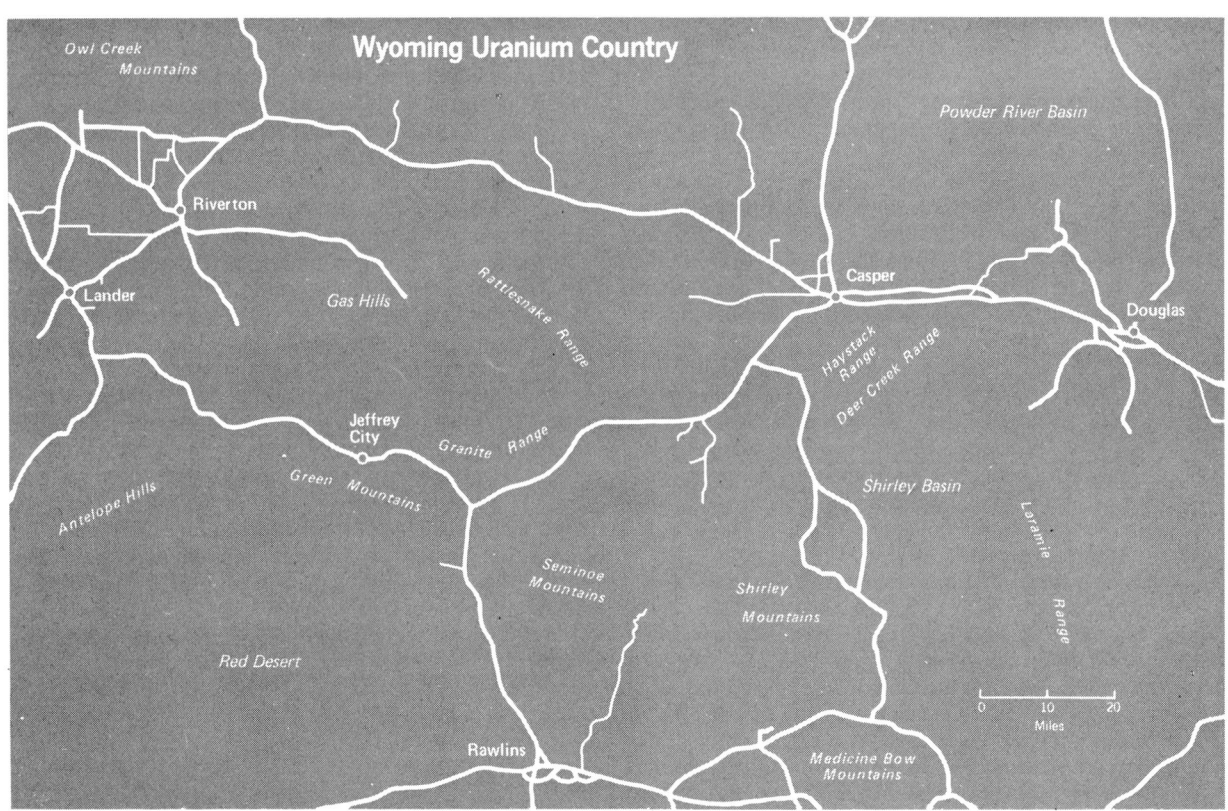

However, one of the uranium industry's thorough-going optimists might reply that these obstacles do not negate the fundamental strength of the uranium market: 56 nuclear reactors are now generating electricity in the US, 65 reactors under construction will come on stream over the next 10 years or so, and more than 100 additional reactors have been ordered, or announced but not yet ordered. Demand for uranium to fuel these reactors will double sometime in the next 10 years. Some government projections even foresee this doubling taking place within five years. Such projections are cited by the uranium industry's most optimistic participants as they head for the Wyoming hills to stake claims, put down exploration drillholes, and turn over land.

More than 11 million ft of uranium exploration drilling was done in Wyoming in 1974—half of all uranium exploration drilling in the US. (New Mexico followed with 4.9 million ft, Texas with 3 million ft, Colorado with 815,000 ft, Montana with 757,000, and other states with a total of 1.6 million.) Some 40 companies report drilling activity to the Energy Research and Development Administration's Region 3 office in Casper, and Harlen Holen of that office suggests that Wyoming in 1975 will again account for half of US uranium drilling.

About 70% of the Wyoming drilling has focused on the Powder River Basin in the northeastern part of the state. Other areas of interest include the Shirley Basin, the Gas Hills, and the Red Desert south of Crooks Gap.

The Red Desert is well known for low grade uranium mineralization, and higher prices might make mining commercially feasible in the district. John S. Wold's Wold Nuclear Co. has been one of the big plungers in the current Wyoming uranium land play by assembling a large block of Red Desert acreage that includes land purchased from Amax Uranium.

The bulk of Wyoming uranium drilling has been done in areas of known uranium mineralization, with a minimum of frontier-type drilling, Holen said. ERDA is conducting a number of aerial and ground surveys throughout the US to seek out large potential areas of uranium mineralization that could be examined more closely by private industry.

One particularly interesting aspect of the Wyoming uranium scene is the variety of companies involved in mining, drilling, and servicing uranium properties—companies ranging in size from Exxon to small drilling contractors who work out of an office in the kitchen. Among the utility companies, the Tennessee Valley Authority, which maintains an office in Casper, has won the special regard of the uranium industry for a willingness to invest exploration dollars as part of a program to secure sources of nuclear fuel supply.

(Because E/MJ was unable to cover completely every sector of Wyoming uranium, the exploration end of the business—with its diversity of interests—was of necessity short-changed. For more extensive coverage, see the June 19, 1975 annual mining issue of the RIVERTON RANGER. The Wyoming Mining Association office in Casper, under the direction of executive secretary Bill Budd, is also a good source of information.)

Expansion programs in progress at Wyoming uranium mills will boost production capacity from 9,000 tpd to 11,500 tpd over the next few years. (New Mexico is the leading uranium producing state, with 13,000 tpd of capacity at three mills.) At least three companies are considering construction of new milling capacity in the Powder River Basin, and additional yellowcake may be produced from the several solution mining research projects now under way on Wyoming uranium ores.

Utah International modifies to mine lower grades

With 4.2 million lb of annual concentrate capacity at its mines and mills in the Gas Hills and Shirley Basin, Utah International Inc. is Wyoming's largest uranium producer. Recent activity at both locations has centered on mill-modification studies to assess the feasibility of handling increased throughputs of lower grade ores and on expansion of mining and overburden removal fleets to move larger tonnages. The company is also considering plans for future increases in production, including a new pit development. The Utah International exploration office in Riverton conducts exploration programs ranging over the seven-state area of Wyoming, Montana, Idaho, Washington, Oregon, North Dakota, and South Dakota.

Low grade Lucky Mc ores are also now being tolled at the nearby 950-tpd Federal-American Partners mill.

While higher uranium prices have accelerated Utah International's planning and development, the company's vice president for metal mining operations, Charles K. McArthur, notes that higher prices have not been immediately reflected in Utah's revenues. Existing lower priced commitments will take the bulk of the company's 1975 uranium production. Only in future years will Utah have significant production no longer committed to the lower priced sales arrangement, and the company is hopeful that sharply higher prices and improved results can then be obtained.

The Lucky Mc stripping fleet now stands at 24 Cat 657B tandem-powered, push-pull scrapers assisted by four Cat 633 elevating scrapers, along with a P&H 2100 BL shovel and seven Unit Rig M-100 rear-dump trucks. Mining equipment includes a fleet of 2½-yd backhoes and 25-ton trucks.

In the Lucky Mc push-pull stripping operation, the trailing machine push-loads the lead scraper. When the first scraper is loaded, the operator of the trailing machine engages a hook-and-bail mechanism, and the lead scraper pulls the second through the loading cycle. The two machines then make independent runs to the fill area. Up to 1,900 flywheel horsepower is available during the two-scraper loading operation, and loading time averages about 0.8 min per unit in dead loading material.

Topsoil is stockpiled for later use in reclamation, and sandstone and shale overburden is disposed of in backfilling previously mined pits or at surface waste dumps. In a procedure that is duplicated with minor modification at most Wyoming uranium open-pit mines, ore pockets are identified with Geiger counters, and elevating scrapers then meticulously remove waste in the immediate area of the ore. At Lucky Mc, Cat 245 or Poclain HC300 backhoes load the ore into Mack rear-dump trucks. The ore is assayed at a probe tower by X-ray analysis for uranium content and then taken to blending piles near the mine. Front-end loaders reclaim the blended ore and load it into 35-ton trucks for the haul of up to 7 mi to milling facilities.

The Lucky Mc reclamation and reseeding program is restoring disturbed areas as soon as possible after overburden disposal is completed, if no future utilization of the area is anticipated, according to mine manager Lee Nugent. A weather station set up in May 1975 is helping to monitor environmental control. Rainfall on the semiarid central Wyoming sagebrush steppe averages about 9 in. per year. Pubescent wheat, crested wheat, western wheat grass, and yellow clover have been successfully seeded in reclaiming disturbed acreage.

Modification of the Lucky Mc mill is being studied, under the direction of mill superintendent Glenn Dooley. The objectives include an expansion in grinding capacity,

A backhoe loads out ore in one of Utah International's Lucky Mc pits. Gas Hills uranium occurs in coarse-grained, conglomeratic arkoses of the early Eocene upper Wind River formation. Roll-type orebodies, produced by passage of uranium-bearing solutions, occur mostly along the margins of altered tongues of conglomeratic sand, requiring careful separation of ore and waste.

addition of leach agitation capacity, and expansion of the CCD thickening and wash circuit. (Leaching at Lucky Mc is followed by uranium extraction in a moving bed resin circuit and solution upgrading in a solvent extraction circuit). A 20-40% increase in tonnage throughput is anticipated from the mill modifications, which will make feasible treatment of lower grade ores. Throughput will rise from about 1,200 tpd to about 1,600 tpd. Increased crusher throughput will be handled by adding crusher shifts.

At Utah International's Shirley Basin operations, the key mill modification to date has been addition of a cyclone wash circuit in parallel with a previously existing CCD wash circuit. After a sand-slime split in the first cyclone in the circuit, sands are washed through five successive cyclones in series, and slimes report to the CCD circuit. Installation of the cyclone circuit allowed ore throughput to increase at the Shirley Basin mill from 1,200 tpd to 1,800 tpd, mine manager Jack Russell said.

The Shirley Basin ore is milled through an autogenous mill with no preliminary crushing. There is not a conveyor in the plant. Static bed resin columns extract uranium following leaching.

Utah International has been mining its Shirley Basin property since 1960, with production coming from underground operations during 1960-1963. Solution mining maintained production from 1963 through 1970. The mill was completed in 1971, and mining was converted to open-pit methods. Present mining takes place in a single open pit; however, other mineralized areas near the plant will also be extracted eventually by open-pit methods. Overburden removal and mining equipment and methods are similar to those in use at Lucky Mc.

Utah International is backfilling the Shirley Basin mine about as fast as land is disturbed, and reclamation of disposal areas is proceeding. About 100 acres were seeded this fall, Russell said, and experience indicates that growth is just as good following fall planting as after spring planting. Moreover, fall planting avoids the problem of coping with muddy spring ground.

The Shirley Basin mine has worked with a number of agencies, including the High Plains Research Project of the University of Wyoming, to develop its reclamation procedures.

Heap leaching highlights Union Carbide operation

Union Carbide's Gas Hills mining and milling operations have responded to stronger uranium demand by stepping up mine production and mill throughput and by successfully trying a large-scale heap leaching experiment on ores grading as low as 0.03% uranium. Based on success of the heap leaching project at Gas Hills, the technique is being applied on a still larger scale at Union Carbide's Maybell property in northwestern Colorado.

Mill feed through the Union Carbide Gas Hills mill will rise to 450,000 tons in 1975 from 390,000 tons in 1974 and is targeted for another increase to about 500,000 tons in 1976. Overburden removal for new mine development will jump to about 12 million in 1976 from about 9 million in 1975. The mill throughput increase was achieved by increasing the mill speed, increasing the sizing on the cyclones, and adding ion exchange capacity, Union Carbide superintendent Jim Massey said.

The Union Carbide heap leaching operation is performed on a single 250,000-ton pile of run-of-mine ore. The pile rests on a base measuring about 600 x 400 ft and

Heap leaching has proven a viable method of processing low grade uranium ores at Union Carbide's Gas Hills mine. The ore pile—stacked, leveled, and divided by dikes into 14 pond areas—was leached over a period of three years, from 1973 to 1975.

sloping slightly to one side to permit drainage. Ore is stacked and leveled, and the flat surface of the pile is divided by small dikes into 14 ponds to facilitate control of leaching solutions. Leaching can only be done in the spring and summer and must be stopped with the arrival of freezing temperatures in the fall.

Leaching takes place in a two-step cycle, with ponds sprayed first with a leaching acid and then washed with tailings liquor. The liquids percolate through the ore pile and drain through perforations in drainage tile located over the base. Pregnant solution is processed through resin-in-pulp and solvent extraction circuits.

Leaching was done in three separate years, with four of the 14 ponds sprayed for the first year, another four for the second year, and a final six to finish the pile in 1975. Maximum production from the Gas Hills leaching project is expected to be about 40,000 lb per year, Massey said. The Maybell project in Colorado may produce as much as 100,000 lb per year.

Most current mine production comes from a pit near the Union Carbide mill in the east Gas Hills. In the west Gas Hills, overburden is being stripped from three pits in preparation for mining next year. Major equipment includes push-loaded scrapers, self-loading scrapers, a 6½-yd front-end loader, and 35-ton rear-dump trucks. A beta-gamma scanner provides grade control at the pit.

Major equipment in the Union Carbide mill includes a jaw crusher and an open-circuited rod mill that grinds to minus 28 mesh.

Petrotomics rebuilds mill for 1978 startup

The 1,500-tpd Shirley Basin uranium mill of the Petrotomics Co.—now owned 67% by Getty Oil Co. and 33% by Skelly Oil Co.—has been shut down since late 1974, but after a thorough renovation, it will be back in production in early 1978. Mine development for a nearby Petrotomics open-pit mine will proceed as mill renovation moves ahead, with mine startup planned at 1,000 tpd. Mill capacity above 1,000 tpd will be available for processing ore from other mines, according to Petrotomics superintendent, Chuck Wolff.

First on stream at 500 tpd in 1962 and subsequently expanded to 1,000 tpd in 1968 and 1,500 tpd in 1970, the Petrotomics mill features crushing grinding through a rod mill, acid leaching, CCD washing, solvent extraction, and yellowcake precipitation with ammonia. Mill renovation includes a major modernization of the dust collection system around the crusher and in the final product area.

Stripping at the new Petrotomics mine was scheduled to start early in 1976; however, a small complement of stripping equipment, including scrapers, was at work during the fall of 1975. Overburden from early stripping was used as fill for a new shop. Ore at the new pit ranges from 150 to 400 ft below surface. For future stripping, a truck-and-shovel system is under consideration, backed up by front-end loaders. Mining equipment in the pit will include backhoes and front-end loaders.

Long life is anticipated for the renovated Petrotomics

A truck-and-shovel stripping program will remove 40 million yd of overburden from Exxon No. 2 pit. Waste will be used to backfill the No. 1 pit, now nearly mined out. All topsoil is removed by scrapers and stockpiled for use in revegetation.

operation, Wolff said, based on the favorable new economics of rising uranium prices. The mill shutdown in 1974 followed a suspension of mining at Getty properties in 1973 and a subsequent cessation of mining on Kerr-McGee properties in the Shirley Basin. Kerr-McGee's previous 50% interest in the Petrotomics mill was purchased by Getty Oil and Skelly Oil in April 1975.

Exxon boosting output at Highland operations

Started up in 1972 at a capacity of 2,000 tpd, Exxon's Highland uranium mine and mill, 45 mi northwest of Douglas in the Powder River Basin, has Nuclear Regulatory Commission approval for expansion to 2,850 tpd, and further expansion to 3,000 or 3,200 tpd is anticipated. When its new Buffalo underground mine comes on stream in 1977, Highland's mines will be producing uranium by four different methods: open-pit mining, which accounts for most of present Highland mill feed; in-situ solution mining; pit wall mining; and underground shaft mining.

Highland open-pit reserves extend a distance of about 2 mi southeast of the mine office and mill site. The No. 1 pit, at the southeast limit of the mining area, has been worked since 1972 and will be mined out in 1976. Stripping of the No. 2 pit, located between the mill and the No. 1 pit, is in progress and will require removal of 40 million yd of overburden from 40-ft benches (25 million yd were removed from the No. 1 pit.) No. 2 pit overburden will serve as backfill for the No. 1 pit, which Exxon will return to the original surface contour. Future plans call for development and mining of three more pits before ores accessible to open-pit mining are exhausted, Highland superintendent, Morris Worley, said. Highland processes ores grading as low as 0.05% uranium, and saves "anything with uranium in it" for future processing.

Exxon purchased two P&H 2100 BL 16-yd shovels and nine Lectra Haul M-100 rear-dump trucks in 1975. The new equipment is at work stripping the No. 2 Pit. Two Michigan 380 rubber-tired dozers, an articulated Cat 16-G motor grader, and a 15-yd Dart front-end loader are also newcomers to the Highland equipment list. Elevating scrapers are used for fine ore control in the pit, and four 2½-yd backhoes load out ore into 35-ton mechanical-drive trucks.

Exxon draws additional ore from two pit wall mines in the east wall of the No. 1 pit. US Energy Corp. is working one of the mines under contract at 2,500 tpm, and Exxon works the other at 1,000 tpm. The pit wall mine under Exxon supervision served as a test site for equipment to be used at the Buffalo underground shaft mine, including an Alpine F6A continuous miner and Eimco 912 1-yd LHD. Exxon is pushing to finish production at these pit wall operations, because backfilling has already begun in the east end of the No. 1 pit and will soon block the entrance adits.

The Highland ores occur at the top of the Fort Union formation—a Tertiary sequence of about 3,000 ft of interbedded shales and sandstones. Maximum economic depth for open-pit operations is about 500 ft. The topography rises as the mineralized horizon dips slightly to the north.

In-situ leaching opens new uranium reserves in Texas

This complex of pipes, valves, and wells—part of a less-than-3-acre pattern near George West, Tex.—does not look like a uranium mine. But since April it has been extracting U_3O_8 from sandstones at depths to 550 ft by in-situ leaching. The Atlantic Richfield-US Steel-Dalco joint venture may be only the first of several commercially scaled, in-situ leaching operations to successfully produce uranium concentrate from Texas ores.

Lane White, managing editor

A COMMERCIAL IN-SITU URANIUM LEACHING OPERATION that is quite probably the largest ever built started up in April, 10 mi southwest of George West, Tex. Producing from a pattern of 66 injection wells and 46 extraction wells occupying an area of less than 3 acres, the Clay West mine and plant are expected to reach design capacity of 250,000 lb per year of yellowcake by the end of the summer. By late May, results were sufficiently favorable to make the owners think seriously about an early expansion.

Built at a cost of $7 million by joint venturers Atlantic Richfield (50% owner and operator), Dalco (25%), and US Steel (25%), the Clay West mine may be only the first of several mines to extract U_3O_8 from a uranium province that stretches from north of Houston to Brownsville, at the southernmost tip of the state. Westinghouse subsidiary Wyoming Minerals is building a 250,000-lb-per-year plant near Bruni, with startup planned before the end of 1975, and Mobil Oil is setting up a pilot-scale plant in the same area. A number of other companies are reported to be actively interested in development of in-situ uranium leaching in Texas.

Fig. 1—Uranium extraction flowsheet, Clay West, Tex.

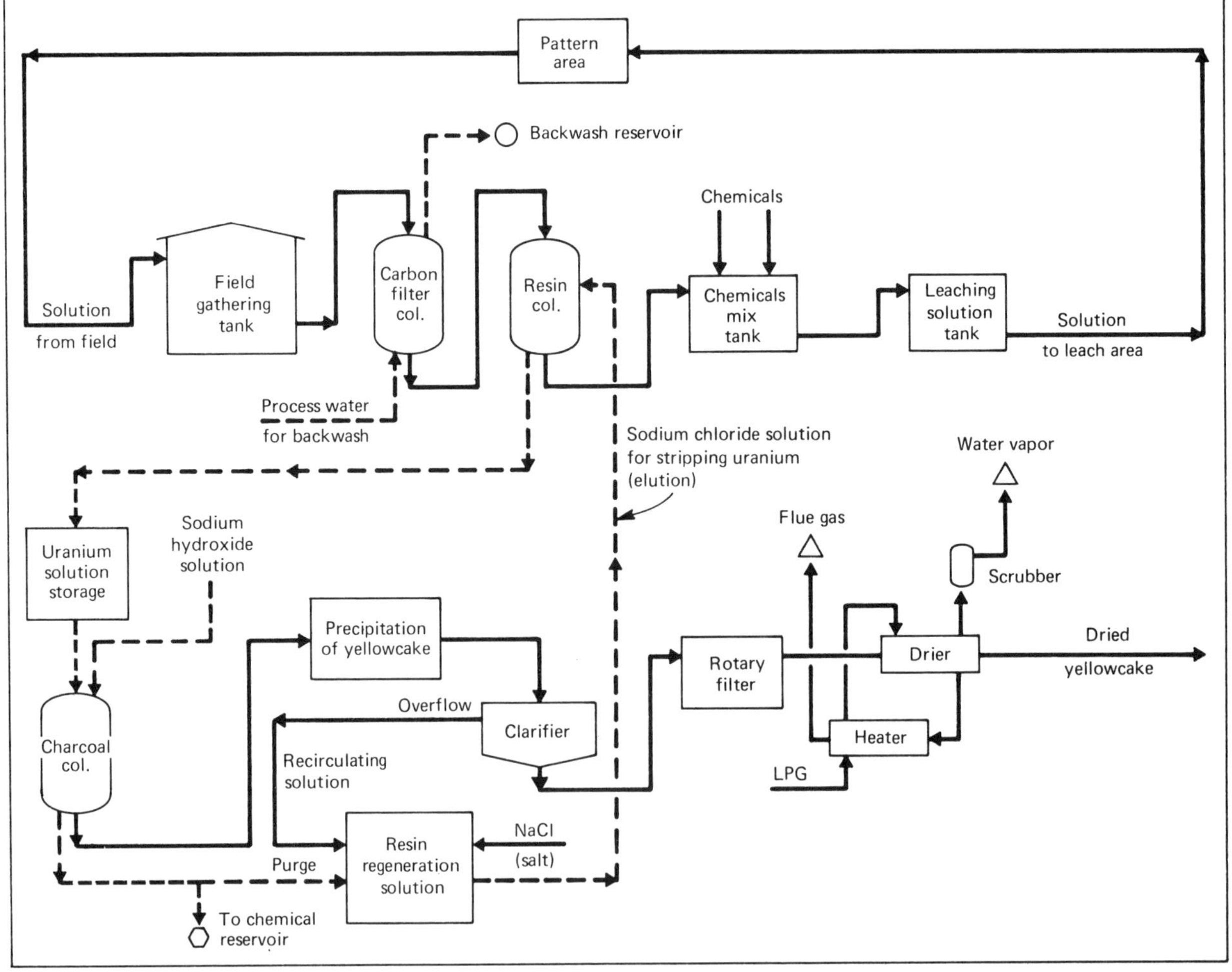

Chemicals mix tank in the Clay West plant area feeds leaching solution to a surge tank located at the in-situ mining pattern.

The Atlantic Richfield (Arco) Clay West operation will employ 45 people, supported by a staff of 12 at Arco uranium operations headquarters in Corpus Christi. Reserves are thought to be sufficient for at least 20 years' production, uranium operations manager Glen R. Davis said during E/MJ's visit to the property. The Arco-Dalco-US Steel partnership has access to 35-40 sections, and patterns of injection and production wells will eventually be operated up to 2 mi from the central processing plant.

The Clay West operation uses a proprietary alkaline leach solution developed during pilot testing by Dalco and US Steel. Solution is pumped into and out of uranium-bearing ore zones at equal rates to prevent loss of solution in the sandstone formation. The pregnant solution is collected at an 800-bbl field gathering tank and then pumped to the plant area. There the solution passes through one of six parallel trains, each consisting of a carbon column and an ion exchange column in series (Fig. 1). A commercial resin extracts U_3O_8 in the ion exchange column. Solution circulates through the leach pattern at 2,000 gpm.

New environmental control procedures were formulated by the Texas Water Quality Board to govern Clay West operations, as there was no precedent for the Arco request to pump a solution into and out of an aquifer. The company will be required to monitor the zones around producing patterns to assure that no leaching solution escapes the producing area, and when a pattern is exhausted, Arco

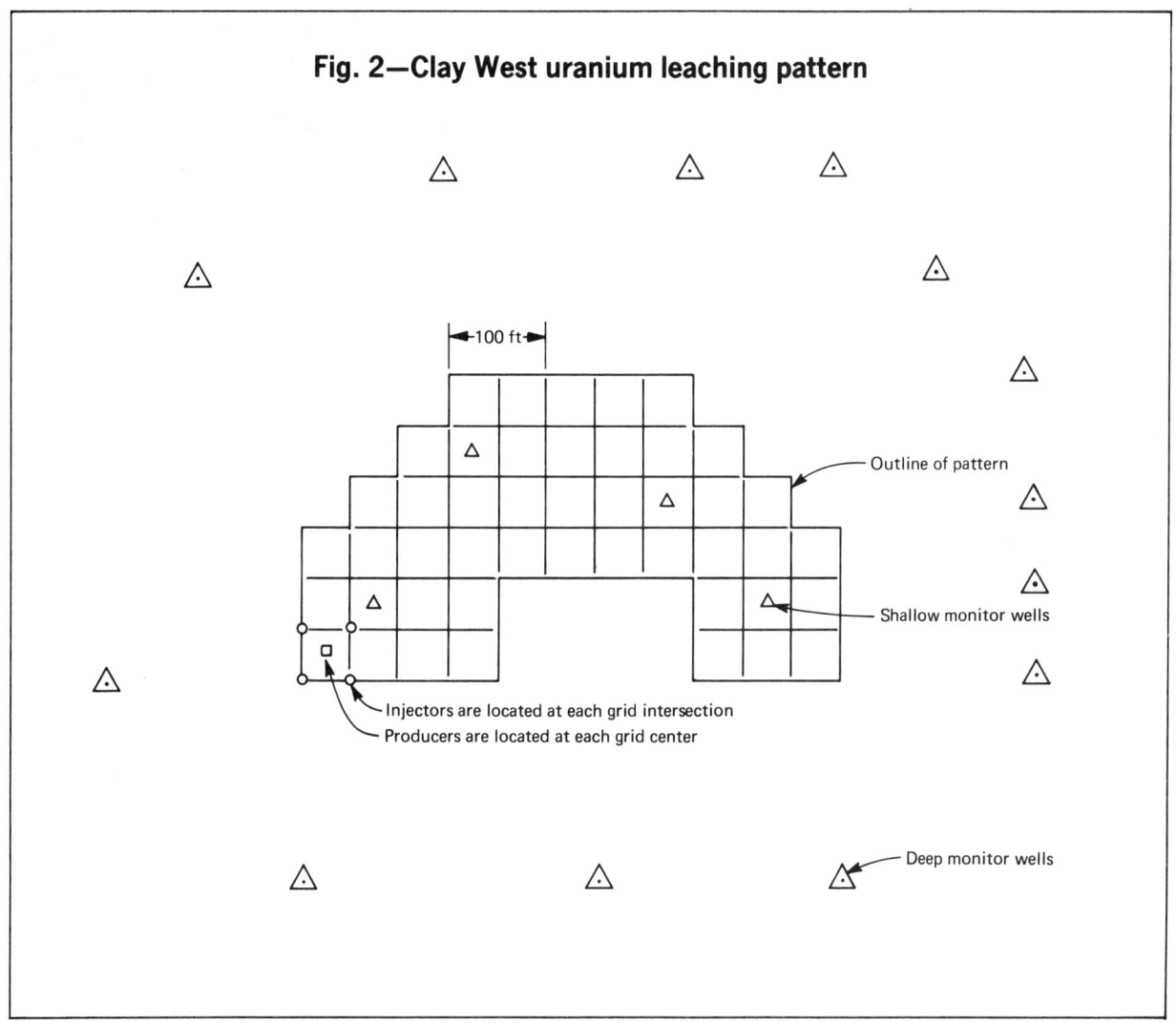

Fig. 2—Clay West uranium leaching pattern

must restore the aquifer to the chemical condition that prevailed prior to operation.

A deep disposal well will be used to dispose of solution pumped from the patterns during aquifer renovation.

Oakville sandstone is source horizon of U_3O_8

The Clay West mine extracts uranium from a maximum depth of 550 ft in the Miocene Oakville sandstone—about 350 ft of interbedded sands, silts, and bentonitic clays. The ore occurs in zones 10 to 60 ft thick and grades from a low 0.05% U_3O_8 to as high as 0.5%—the latter being uncommon. Regionally, rock formations dip toward the Gulf of Mexico at about 79 ft per mi.

The Oakville is underlain by Catahoula clays—about 2,100 ft of clays and thin beds of sand that have a higher-than-normal background count of U_3O_8. The U_3O_8 in the Catahoula is thought to derive from volcanic ash deposited during Catahoula time, according to Arco geologist Charles Trimble. Percolating ground waters dissolve the U_3O_8 and transport it to neighboring rocks, where, in the presence of H_2S derived from oil-bearing formations, the U_3O_8 precipitates, sometimes in commercial concentrations.

The Clay West mine taps the Oakville deposits through a pattern of production wells spaced at 50-ft intervals (Fig. 2). The 46 extraction wells are interspersed at regular intervals with a grid of injection wells and are surrounded by monitor wells.

The Oakville sandstone is a regional aquifer having a slow rate of flow—about 12 ft per year. Should the monitor wells detect leaching solution escaping from the production zone, the rate of production can be increased or the rate of injection decreased to pull the solution back.

A Midway drill of the type used for seismic blasthole drilling sinks the 4-in.-dia injection wells and the 6-in.-dia extraction wells (Fig. 3), the latter being larger to accommodate a submersible pump at the bottom of the well. Open screened sections of pipe in the ore zones permit production of leach solution with minimal extraction of entrained particulates.

Well piping, along with most other piping at the Clay West mine, is of PVC, to minimize corrosion and to keep corrosion products out of the system, Davis said. This protection will prevent plugging of injection wells and contamination of the yellowcake product. Two 12-in. mainline PVC pipes connect the plant and production areas.

The pregnant leach solution arrives at the processing plant carrying dissolved U_3O_8. It first passes through a carbon column, which removes any sand present in the solution, and then through an ion exchange column, which extracts the uranium. The carbon columns are backwashed periodically to remove trapped sand. A backwash reservoir provides clean water and acts as a settling pond. The water

View of the Clay West plant across one of two solution storage ponds: chemicals mix tank is shown at the right, storage and process facilities at center, and yellowcake processing building to the left.

is recirculated and evaporation losses are made up by water from a fresh water well.

A sodium chloride solution is used to extract U_3O_8 from the ion exchange column. The rich uranium-bearing solution (about 1% U_3O_8) passes through a charcoal column for removal of impurities, including molybdenum, and then reports to precipitation tanks, where yellowcake is precipitated with ammonia. Recovery of moly as a byproduct is a possibility in the future.

Chemical wastes from the plant are disposed of in reservoirs lined with highly resistant chlorinated polyethylene lining. The design of the reservoirs keeps net annual evaporation rate equal to the volume of chemical wastes generated each year. Reservoir capacity is sufficient to accommodate periods of high rainfall and low evaporation. During the first year of operation, a critical examination of waste streams is seeking opportunities for waste reduction.

After precipitation, yellowcake is allowed to settle in a clarifier, filtered, dried, and packed for shipping to the Allied Chemical uranium hexafluoride plant at Metropolis, Ill. The dryer, the only source of air emissions in the plant, is a screw-conveyor unit based on indirect heat transfer between a recirculating heated oil and yellowcake solids. The heat-transfer oil is heated externally in a unit fueled with liquefied petroleum gas. The quantity of flue gas from the dryer is insufficient to require a permit from the Texas Air Control Board.

One of the advantages of the dryer is minimal dust problems, because of the absence of air contact. For added protection, however, exhaust gases will be scrubbed by a two-stage water scrubber. The exhaust from this scrubber will be virtually dust-free, releasing only water vapor to the air.

The Clay West operation is not energy-intensive, as circulating solutions all flow at ambient temperatures. Power draw for the entire operation is about 1,500 kw from San Patricio Electric, a small co-op producer at Sinton, Tex. The major costs of operation are labor and chemicals.

Mine manager Walter Ely noted that creation of jobs at the Clay West mine has provided a welcome injection of

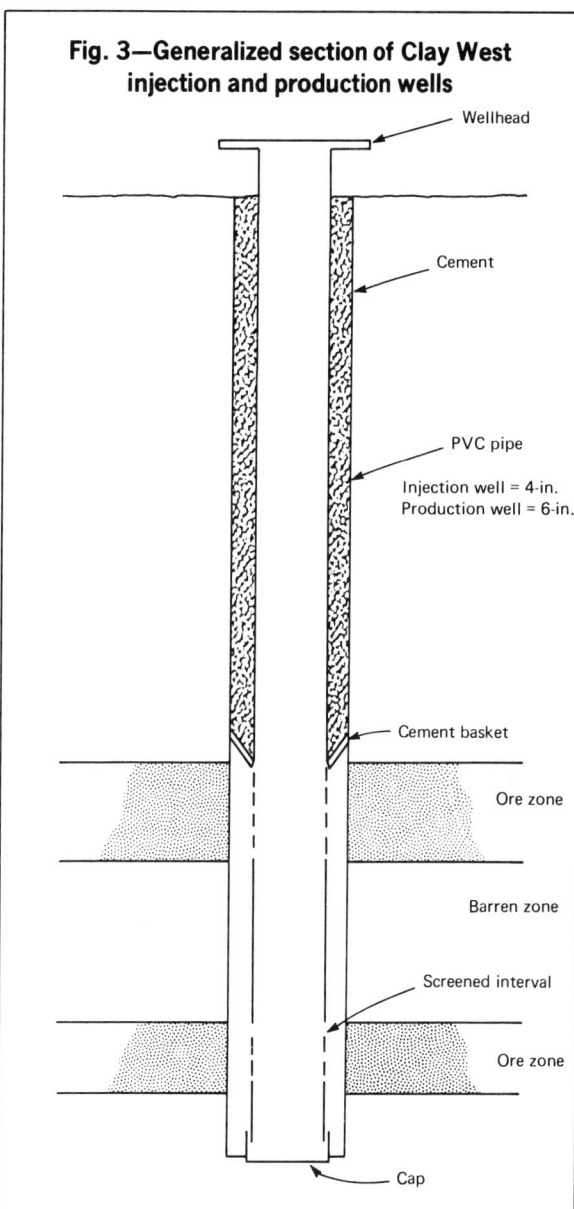

Fig. 3—Generalized section of Clay West injection and production wells

cash into the local economy. The mine is located in pleasant, rolling countryside that has produced well for farmers and ranchers but has provided few non-agricultural jobs. The Clay West mine offers an opportunity for some George West natives to secure long-term employment near home, and the $500,000 annual payroll will help support additional jobs in the George West community.

Arco has adopted a system of rotation for its employees that will regularly move each into a different job in various areas of mine and plant activity. The system is expected to create a more interesting work environment for the employees and more highly trained and valuable employees for Arco.

Controlling solution in the leaching zone

Waters present in the Clay West orebody are not now a source of potable water due to naturally-occurring high levels of radium. As noted above, the two primary environmental considerations will be to prevent contaminants from leaking out of the ore zone during leaching and to restore the water in the orebody after conclusion of leaching. During leaching, injection and production rates will be balanced, with each injection and production line equipped with direct-reading flow meters. A central instrument panel in the pattern area monitors the flow meters, and a daily check is made to balance total 24-hr production against total 24-hr injection.

All injection and producing wells in the leach area are cased and cemented to the surface, preventing upward migration of injected solutions behind the casing. Four shallow monitor wells drilled in the pattern area are sampled and analyzed routinely to determine whether the leach solution moves upward.

A detailed program of water well sampling was formulated by Arco in consultation with the Texas Water Quality Board, and all water wells within a 5-mi radius of the pattern were sampled and analyzed prior to production. During production, one-eighth of these wells will be examined every three months to detect any change in the

Six pairs of carbon column and ion exchange column tanks are the heart of the Clay West plant site. Building in the background houses offices and a well-equipped laboratory. Farm country beyond the building is typical of the George West area.

Clay West clarifier is a wood-stave thickener-type unit.

Rich eluate tank provides surge capacity ahead of charcoal column.

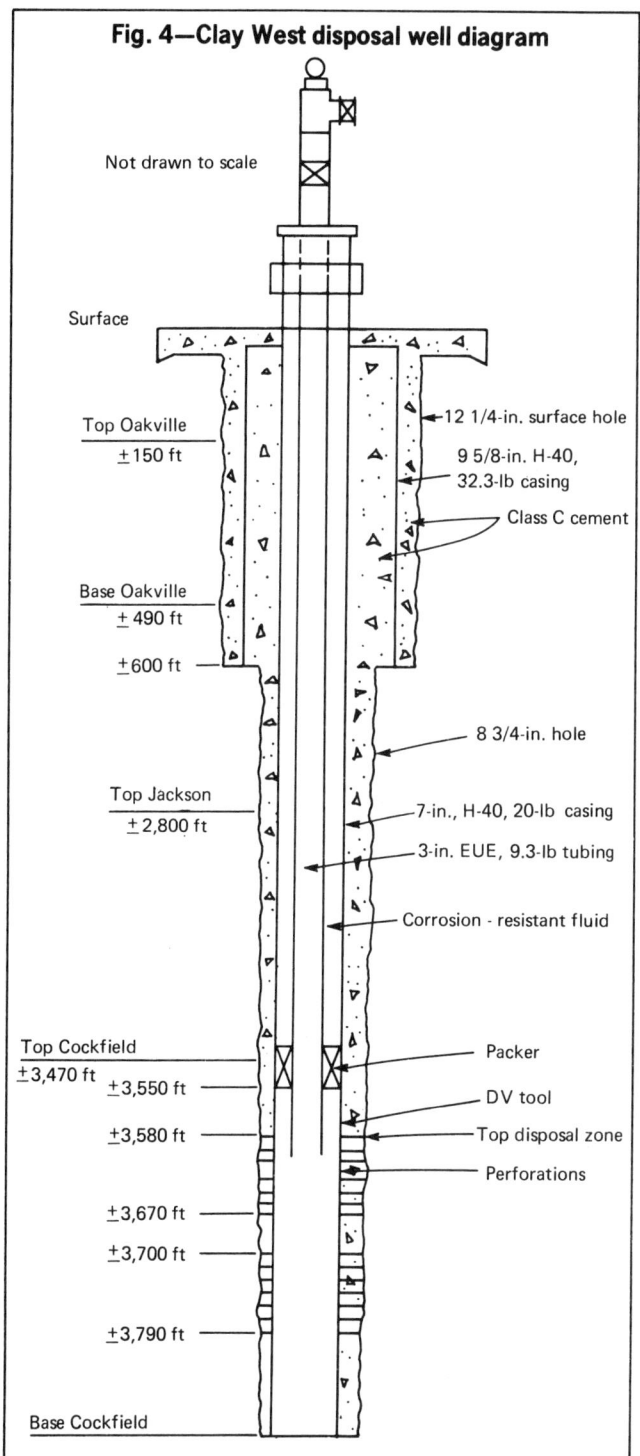

Fig. 4—Clay West disposal well diagram

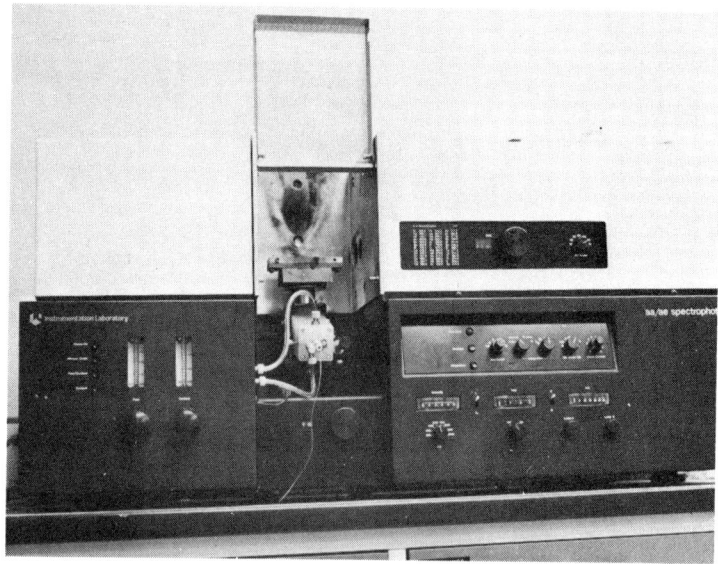

The Clay West laboratory is equipped with a spectrophotometer, a Technicon, and an atomic adsorption apparatus for analyzing the many samples required both for process solutions and for regional water sampling. Monitor wells in the leach area are sampled regularly to detect any migration of injected solutions. If migration occurs, the material balance of reservoir fluids can be controlled, resulting in a net flow of native water into the leaching area, preventing any migration outside the leach area.

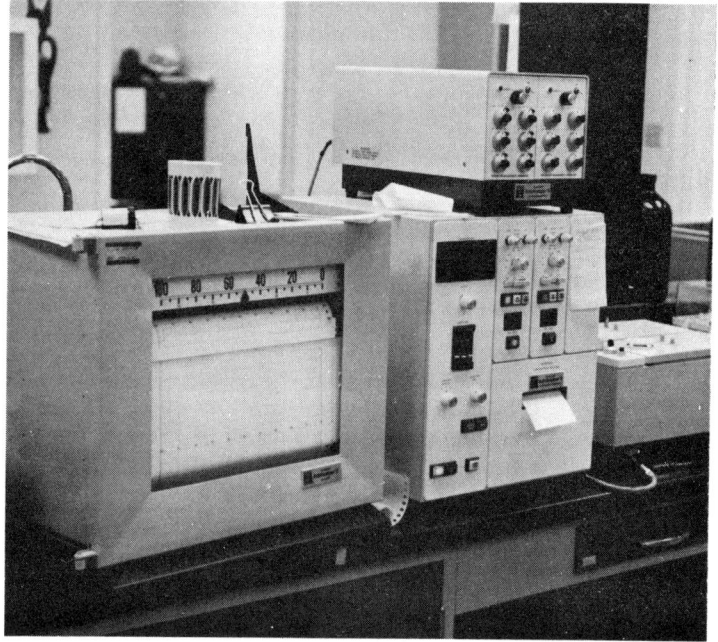

chemical analysis of the water. The wells will be analyzed for calcium, sodium, iron, molybdenum, bicarbonate, sulphate, chloride, nitrate, nitrite, ammonium, pH, and total dissolved solids (List A). The same wells will be analyzed for Gross Alpha and Gross Beta radiation. If Gross Alpha exceeds three picocuries per liter, a barium co-precipitation for radium 226 will be performed. If Gross Beta exceeds 50 picocuries per liter, a lead 210 determination will be performed. Every six months, the nearest six wells used for drinking water will be examined radiometrically and List A analyses will be run.

During development of the Clay West leach pattern, 28 operating wells were sampled and analyzed for List A ions. In addition, 10 of these wells were analyzed for radiation and heavy metals—magnesium, fluoride, arsenic, barium, boron, cadmium, copper, chromium, lead, manganese, mercury, nickel, selenium, silver, uranium, zinc, simple cyanide and P-alkalinity as $CaCO_3$, and total alkalinity as $CaCO_3$ (List B). As part of this program, some wells were sampled and analyzed as many as four times prior to operation.

To monitor surface drainage, Spring Creek is sampled

Clay West process building houses precipitation tanks, rotary filter, heater, dryer, and packaging and shipping facilities.

upstream of the Clay West plant site and downstream of the pattern area. The Nueces River, which provides drinking water for Corpus Christi, is sampled above and below its confluence with Spring Creek. Samples are analyzed radiometrically and chemically.

Arco also organized an in-house environmental task force to perform a baseline study of the Clay West environment prior to moving into the area. The task force included biologists, radiologists, chemical engineers, petroleum engineers, geologists, hydrologists, and zoologists. Among its subjects of study were fish, amphibia, birds, insects, bacteria, shrubs, grasses, roots, stems, soils, and streams.

The present plan for orebody restoration is to pump contaminated solutions out of the leached zone into a deep disposal well until ion concentrations are down to acceptable levels. Pilot tests conducted by Dalco and US Steel demonstrated that when injection is stopped but production maintained, there is a gradual decrease in ionic species in the produced solutions. These data are proprietary but were released on a confidential basis to the Texas Water Quality Board. Other alternatives to pumping the orebody will also be studied, and techniques for converting the aquifer back from an oxidized state to a reduced state are under investigation.

The Clay West disposal wells—two are planned—will be drilled to a total depth of 4,500 ft, down through the Cockfield sandstone of Upper Claiborne (Oligocene?) age. The

---

On a smaller scale, other mines have recovered U_3O_8 by in-situ leaching

While the new Clay West in-situ uranium leaching mine in Texas is the first of its type to produce on a commercial scale, limited quantities of uranium have been produced by other in-situ mines operating now or in the past. A number of these operations are described briefly in "Analysis of Non-coal Underground Mining Methods," prepared by Dravo Corp. for the US Bureau of Mines and published in 1974.

Mine water near Grants, N. Mex., was found to carry 2-10 ppm of dissolved uranium, the report states. The slightly basic water (7 to 8 pH) takes the uranium into solution as the tricarbonate ion, which is readily extracted by ion exchange. Oxidation of the insoluble tetravalent uranium to a soluble hexavalent uranium is accomplished by exposure to air and possibly by bacterial action. After passing through ion exchange, the water is returned to the mine and sprayed on drift and stope walls. It then drains back to a sump for return to the ion exchange columns. Production of 5,000 to 15,000 lb per month is dependent on the flow of water and the ground area being wetted.

The same procedure is used in the Elliot Lake district in Canada, the report states, except that an acid environment is generated by the oxidation of iron sulphides in the ore.

"The Pitch mine in Colorado was water leached by drilling injection wells from the surface into the abandoned and caved stoping areas," the Dravo report notes. "The water percolated through the old mine workings, collected in the main haulage tunnel, and passed through an ion exchange column. The stripped water was then returned to the injection wells. Later in the program, soda ash and bicarbonate were added to the leach solution to improve extraction. This operation is now closed, but has potential for producing additional uranium by in-situ leaching."

Utah Mining and Construction Co. (now Utah International) experimented with a series of injection wells, usually three, around a production well. Based on groundwater flow, the injection wells were drilled upstream from the production well. Tracer dyes were used to study solution flow between injection wells and the production well. After flow patterns were established, an acid leach solution was injected. Withdrawal rate was slightly more than the injection rate. The pregnant solution was passed through ion exchange columns for uranium extraction, and then it was rejected because it contained soluble gypsum that would blind the leach area if reused.

"The area under leach from each set of wells was very small," according to the Dravo report, "seldom larger than 25-ft dia. The project never produced more than 7,000 or 8,000 lb per month of U_3O_8, even with as many as five well systems operating. Leaching was discontinued in 1968, when the operation was converted to an open pit."

Exxon (Humble Oil) is experimenting with the same leach method in the Powder River Basin in Wyoming, the report states, except that a carbonate system is used, permitting recirculation of the leach solution.

"With the depletion of higher grade deposits of uranium," the report concludes, "much of the future production may depend on successful in-situ leach extraction. This is particularly important for small, isolated deposits of lower grade values that will not economically support conventional . . . extraction."

Cockfield is the proposed disposal zone.

During aquifer renovation following leaching, Arco expects to pump an estimated 150 gpm of slightly saline water from the leach pattern, with a probable maximum of 2,000 mg per liter total dissolved solids. This water will be pumped to the disposal well after most of the uranium has been removed. The native water in Cockfield sands is much more saline than the disposal stream.

The surface hole will be drilled 12½-in. dia and 600 ft deep, through the Oakville aquifer and into the underlying Catahoula clays. H-40, 32.3-lb pipe with a diameter of 9⅝ in. will be set as casing to 600 ft, and Class C cement circulated to the surface. An 8¾-in. hole will then be drilled to 4,500 ft. Upon completion of drilling, electrical and bulk density logs will be run in the hole.

Casing—7-in.-dia, 20-lb, H-40 pipe—will be set on the bottom and cemented in two stages. The first stage will bring cement to the top of the Cockfield sand, a depth of about 3,500 ft. Utilizing a D-V tool, sufficient additional cement will be pumped to circulate to the surface.

Injection intervals will be determined from electric and gamma-ray logs. Proposed intervals are from 3,580 ft to 3,670 ft and from 3,700 ft to 3,790 ft. The balance of the Cockfield sand between the depths of about 3,790 ft and 4,500 ft is considered a reserve for future disposal, if volumes or pressure gradients exceed present estimates.

When the ore zone of a leaching pattern has been restored, Arco will turn the surface back to normal use. The area will need reseeding, but reclamation in the usually understood sense will be unnecessary. The leaching operations will leave the surface essentially undisturbed. Within a few years after leaching stops, it may be difficult to identify a leach pattern area as ever having been different from the surrounding countryside. □

Developers eye Texas potential for in-situ uranium leaching

Emmy Crawford, McGraw-Hill World News, Houston

IN ADDITION TO the Arco-US Steel-Dalco plant now in production near George West, Tex., several other in-situ uranium leaching projects are in various stages of planning, design, and construction in south Texas.

The most advanced project belongs to Westinghouse's wholly owned subsidiary, Wyoming Minerals, which is building a 250,000-lb-per-year plant near Bruni, Tex., about 40 mi east of Laredo. While Wyoming Minerals has not revealed any details of its process, a source at the Texas Water Quality Board states that the operation will use a weak ammonia leach and a proprietary ion exchange extraction system.

Wyoming Minerals also plans a second commercial uranium in-situ leach plant near Ray Point, north of George West in Live Oak County. The Texas Water Quality Board has received an application for this operation, but as of early June, no date had been set for a hearing.

In Duval County, Union Carbide is considering a pilot-scale in-situ leach operation, but for it too, no hearing date had been set by early June.

(While not of direct interest to Texas uranium production, a Burlington Northern-Wyoming Minerals joint venture calls for Wyoming Minerals to conduct minerals exploration on 8.4 million acres of Burlington Northern railroad property in Oregon, Washington, Idaho, Wyoming, Montana, North Dakota, Minnesota and Wisconsin. The agreement, which includes gas, oil, and uranium as well as other minerals, will run five to eight years, and Wyoming Minerals will get up to 50% interest in discovered properties, depending on how much money it invests in the project. The joint venture company—called Bur-West—is headquartered in Billings, Mont.)

Mobil pilot plant is under construction

Southeast of Bruni, in Webb County, Tex., Mobil Oil Corp. is building a pilot plant to test the feasibility of a proprietary in-situ uranium leaching method. The plant is expected to start up around October 1 to leach U_3O_8 in place, at depths of 410 to 430 ft.

Present plans call for an initial 18-month test program, with an overlapping 15-month test at a nearby site if the first program is successful. The capacity of the pilot scale operation will not be determined until solution is actually put into the ground, and Mobil has no present timetable for commercial development.

The Mobil pilot operation will inject a leach solution into the uranium-bearing formation through 15 injection wells and extract it through seven production wells. The solution is identified as a dilute ammonium carbonate made by mixing gaseous ammonia and carbon dioxide with formation water treated with ordinary water softener. An unidentified oxidant is also added. Solution produced will be collected in a surge tank and then pumped to a holding tank at the recovery plant site, about 700 ft away.

A sand filter will remove suspended solids, and an ion exchange column will extract U_3O_8. The barren effluent from the ion exchange column will be pumped to a holding tank where an oxidant and leach chemicals are added, and the solution will be recycled to the injection wells.

Uranium will be extracted from the ion exchange resin by an unidentified chemical, and the U_3O_8-rich eluate will be pumped to a holding tank and then to a precipitation tank for uranium precipitation. Ammonia and carbon dioxide gases generated in the precipitation process will be vented to a 20-ft-high fume scrubber. Water spray in the scrubber will absorb the vapors, and the resulting solution will be recycled to the injection well stream.

Filters, ion exchange, and water softener tanks will be backwashed periodically and the water held in a 500-bbl tank. If backwash water is found to contain excess solid or radioactive material, it will be pumped to an evaporation pit.

A system of eight monitoring wells will determine if there is leakage of chemicals outside the planned injection production pattern. □

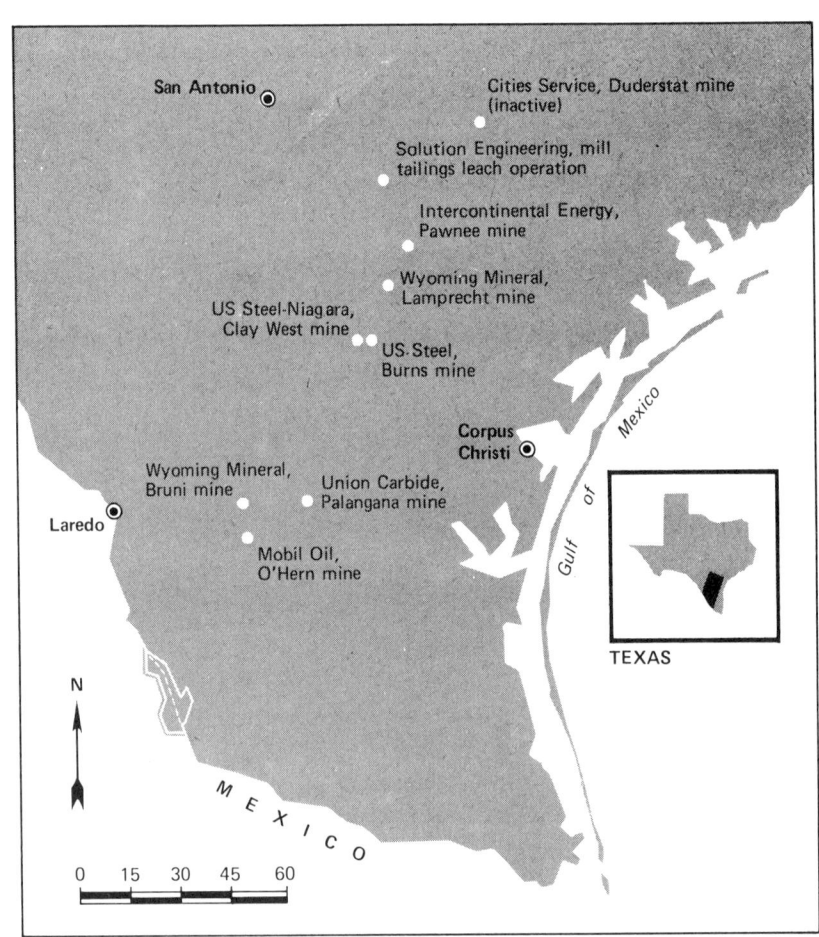

In-situ uranium operations in Texas

Company	Location	Capacity (lb per year U_3O_8)	Status
US Steel, Niagara Mohawk	George West	250,000	Expanding to 1 million lb per year.
US Steel	Burns Ranch	150,000	In production.
Wyoming Mineral	Bruni	100,000	Full production will be 250,000 lb per year.
Wyoming Mineral	Ray Point	500,000	Being developed.
Union Carbide	Duval County		Pilot testing.
International Energy	Pawnee mine	180,000	On stream.
International Energy	Ray Point	300,000	On stream in March 1978.
Solution Engineering	Alice	1 million lb total production	Recovery from tailings.

Chapter 12
Other Surface Mines

Placer mining's dwindling experts review vanishing technology	416
How Cortez Gold Mines heap leached low grade gold ores at two Nevada properties	419
Heap leaching will produce 85,000 oz/year of dore bullion for Smoky Mountain Mining	424
Mining the beach for diamonds at CDM	427
Kerr-McGee expands soda ash output nine-fold from Searls Lake brines	434
Brines are source for iodine, bromine, and other minerals	439
Petrosix: a Brazilian answer to oil shale technology	439
New McDermitt mine joint venture emerges as dominant force in US mercury production	442
Nevada barite output up sharply in '70s	444

Placer mining's dwindling experts review vanishing technology

PLACER EVALUATION AND EXPLORATION requires good judgment and practical experience—experience that is being lost through the rapid attrition of the world's placer mining experts. A number of these experts were featured speakers at the Placer Exploration and Mining Short Course sponsored by the Mackay School of Mines, University of Nevada, in Reno, October 25-29, 1976. The purpose of the course: to make younger engineers aware that placer technology is still viable and of value. The placer experts put special emphasis on placer sampling and evaluation.

The purpose of any mineral evaluation is to determine whether a deposit contains sufficient recoverable values to justify development. The evaluator, according to William H. Breeding, president of Placer Service Corp., New York, should perform initial sampling in the most promising areas.[1] If the results of that sampling program are negative, the evaluator can probably reject a project without further expense. If the results are positive, he can probably recommend a quantitative evaluation leading to an investment decision.

Breeding observed that tax and remittance laws of some countries are so severe that all but potential bonanza properties in those nations can be eliminated without further evaluation. "In the US," he said, "a mining investor may be satisified with a 15% return on his capital. In developing countries, higher rates of return, generally in excess of 20%, are required by most investors."

In countries where labor cost is low, channel sampling may proceed in open shafts 3 ft x 4 ft. Breeding has supervised sinking of shafts in placer deposits to depths exceeding 180 ft, using hand labor. However, he said, at depths of more than 50 ft, it is preferable to offset the shaft at intervals of 40 or 50 ft to limit the risk of accidents from falling material.

In channel-sampling shafts or on newly exposed banks, Breeding's experience indicates that recovery will often be better than results from drilling or from mining. One possible explanation: On long exposed faces, the heavier material dislodges during sampling and falls more readily than lighter material.

The size of the sampling channel can be varied according to the material sampled. With very coarse material, a large channel is preferred; with fine material, a smaller channel. Where labor costs are high and the equipment is available, Breeding believes that pits and trenches may be dug more quickly and cheaply with a hydraulic backhoe. The pits and trenches may then be channel-sampled.

Banka drill is among the most useful

Drilling equipment used in placer exploration includes the Banka drill, light power or airplane drills or small Cyclone drills, and churn drills.

The Banka drill, according to Breeding, is effective in countries with low-cost labor when coarse gravel is not present and depths are not great. Depths to 60 ft in ground that is not too "tight" can be drilled by a good crew at acceptable rates.

For placer exploration, especially in tin mining, the Conrad-Banka hand drill is considered to be the most accurate by many experts, including I. R. Alders of Conrad-Stork, Haarlem, Holland.[2] The Conrad-Banka, said Alders, may be disassembled to facilitate transport into remote areas.

One of the main interests of placer mining companies is tin, now being mined offshore. To find offshore tin fields, Alders noted, exploration drilling has until now been performed from the surface of the ocean. However, adverse weather conditions have always been a handicap. The decision to drill directly from the sea bottom is thus a logical step.

Alders noted that Conrad-Stork took that step by developing the "Geodoff" drilling concept. Geodoff, in operation since 1967, is a remote-controlled rig that can cover the continental shelf area to depths of 200 m and can work independently of the movements of the command ship. With Geodoff, Alders said, counterflush drilling, first developed by Conrad-Stork 40 years ago, is possible on the ocean bed. (See illustration.)

A double-walled drilling tube made of glass-fiber polyester and a cutting shoe of steel are used. Air is injected into the inner tube just above the cutting shoe, and seawater flows in spontaneously between the inner and the outer tube. The tube is connected with the exploration ship by a flexible hose through which the material flows up to the ship into a processing plant. Drilling depths of 15 to 20 m can be achieved with Geodoff. The main difference between Geodoff and the counterflush drilling devices used on land is that penetration is not performed by rotation but by vibration of the drillstring, together with a remote-controlled variable pulldown.

Churn drill: the old standby

The 6-in. churn drill with 7½-in. drill shoe has been the standard for placer work for the last 60 years, progressing from the early Keystone drills to the modern models of Bucyrus-Erie and other manufacturers. Churn

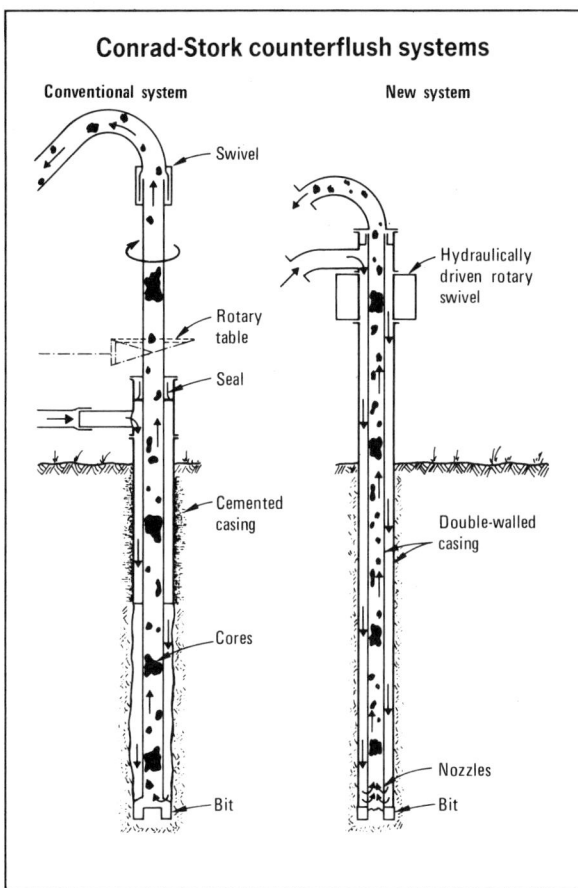

Conrad-Stork counterflush systems

drills are said to be capable of drilling to 400 ft and more, although progress at the greater depths is slow and costs are high. Costs can range from under $5 per ft to over $25, said Breeding.

According to Douglas B. Colp, consulting mining engineer in Fairbanks, Alaska, one reason why churn drilling evaluation has proven so successful in Alaska is that much of the placer ground is frozen.[3] Churn drilling of thawed and/or wet ground can produce a high R/E factor (correlation between estimated recovery and actual recovery); however, such drilling can also produce some very erratic results.

According to Colp, regardless of the placer drilling technique chosen to evaluate a potential gold-bearing gravel deposit, the weight of the gold from a particular sample interval must be directly related to the volume of core recovered from the same interval. In other words, if a drillhole increment or interval contains a larger core volume than is theoretically possible, the value of that increment must be downgraded. Conversely, if it contains too little core, its value may be raised. Colp said that most placer engineers base their adjusting procedures on either the ratio between theoretical and actual core rise or between theoretical and measured core volume.

In view of rapidly escalating costs, Colp noted, a less costly method of evaluation is required that will approximate the almost perfect R/E factor obtained in some areas by churn drilling.

More accurate results from frozen ground

Like Colp, William R. Kastelic, vice president of UV Industries, Salt Lake City, emphasized that drilling results in frozen ground have proven more accurate than those obtained in unfrozen ground.[4] A possible reason is that there is no tendency to force gold out of the drillhole under the casing or to produce a run-in of values.

Kastelic stated that the volume of holes drilled without casing can be computed with relative accuracy by repeatedly pouring a set amount of water (usually 5 gal) into a hole and then measuring the rise of water in the hole by means of a float connected to a tape measure. The measurements are made at limited intervals (usually 5 min) to assure that no water escapes from the hole.

Drilling of thawed ground employs the same equipment used for frozen ground, except that casing and drive shoe are required. Casing is usually 6 in. in diameter with a 7½-in. drive shoe having an inside bevel, although other sizes of casing and drive shoes have been used with success, Kastelic reported.

On sampling: a few 'don'ts' for evaluators

The lifting of restrictions on gold ownership by US citizens, coupled with a generally bullish attitude toward its long range value, has generated new interest in gold properties, including placers. According to John Wells, much of the field work stimulated by this new interest in gold has been assigned to personnel who may not appreciate that placers are more difficult to sample than lode deposits.[5] Also, few seem aware that drilling equipment and analytical procedures routinely used for hard rock sampling may yield completely misleading results when applied to placers. Among the procedures not recommended for placer sampling:

- Use of small diameter or uncased drillholes.

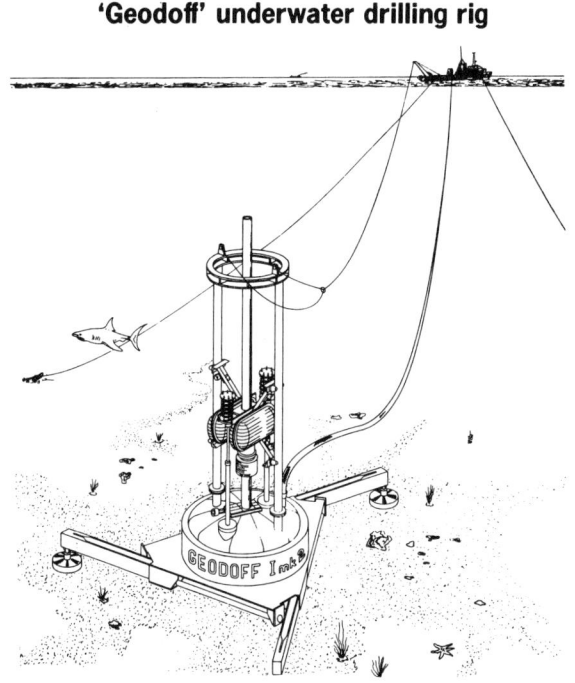

'Geodoff' underwater drilling rig

- Splitting of samples.
- Use of fire assay or atomic adsorption methods of analysis for determining the gold content of placer materials.

If uncased holes are used, Wells said, any caving or raveling will result in nonrepresentative samples. Despite this disadvantage, attempts are being made to sample and evaluate gold placers by means of uncased holes 5 in. or smaller in diameter, he said. These holes are generally drilled by rotary rigs or by equipment using double-walled drive pipe adapted for sample recovery by reverse circulation of air or water. In either case, some sloughing of the hole is inevitable.

There are exceptions for which small holes can be used. When evaluating beach-type deposits containing rutile, ilmenite, magnetite, or zircon, auger or jet drillholes 2 in. in diameter and smaller have been succesfully used. In such cases, Wells said, the fine-grained nature of the material, the relatively large amount of valuable mineral in the deposit, and its low unit value combine to eliminate some of the uncertainties normally associated with small diameter holes.

With few exceptions, however, the splitting of gold placer samples should be strictly avoided. Wells stressed that in a gold placer, the gold content is so small and its distribution is so uneven that any attempt to proportionately divide the sample by mechanical splitting or other means is likely to yield erratic results. However, when dealing with fine-sized placer materials having a low unit value, such as magnetite or ilmenite sands, substantial reduction of a bulk sample or concentrate by mixing and splitting is a common and generally accepted practice.

Valuations based on fire assays or on atomic adsorption analyses of placer material usually result in a substantial over-valuation of the ground. Wells defined fire assaying as a miniature smelting process that reports the total gold content of the assay sample, including gold locked in rock particles or in other forms not recoverable by placer methods. For this reason, he stressed that sample values for gold placers should not be determined by fire assay. Furthermore, no amount of mixing or careful division of a typical gravel sample can produce a 15-g or 30-g crucible charge representative of the bank-run material.*

In recent years, atomic adsorption methods of analysis have largely replaced fire assaying for routine gold determinations. The AA method, Wells said, will create the same problems as fire assaying.

Diamond evaluations use scout drilling

Unlike most placer deposits of gold and base metals, the value of a diamond deposit is not directly proportional to the amount of precious mineral contained within the ore because the value of a diamond depends considerably on its quality and tends to increase geometrically with increasing crystal size. Diamonds occur as individual crystals, not finely divided particles as in disseminated metal ores, making it impossible to assay for diamonds by taking relatively small samples.

According to K. E. S. Applin, of Selection Trust, Capetown Province, South Africa, detailed prospecting is commonly done in regions where diamond fields have been established, focusing on areas with geology and structure similar to the known fields and following present or paleo-drainages away from the fields.[6]

For efficiency in sampling, Applin emphasized, it is important first to scout-drill a deposit accurately. Although scout drilling at small diameters—4 in. to 6 in.—does not provide sufficient sample volumes for diamond evaluation, it does indicate where large diamond samples should be taken.

The main data obtained by scout drilling are the depths and nature of alluvium, the quality of the alluvial gravel, types of bedrock, probable extent of the deposit, and possible locations of richer areas within the deposit. Richer areas are usually associated with depressions in the general bedrock level, better development of basal gravels in terms of thickness and sorting, and larger heavy mineral concentrates, which can be determined by panning gravel samples obtained from the boreholes.

In tropical areas, conventional scout drilling is done by hand-operated Banka drill. In the arid zone of southern Africa, mechanized percussion drills are generally used. Both "traditional" methods are slow, Applin said. An improved method developed for scout drilling of waterlogged loose ground in Sierra Leone incorporates a hydraulically operated rotary drill rig mounted on a four-wheel tractor with large diameter wheels suited to swampy conditions. Drilling is done with 10-ft lengths of continuous spiral flight solid-stem augers of 6-in. diameter, which are socket- and pin-jointed.

An improved type of drilling for arid areas employs an air flush system, in which compressed air is fed down hollow drill rods to a rotary bit and the blown air carries cuttings up to the collar of the hole. A hydraulically operated drill rig similar to that used for continuous flight augering is suitable for this work, together with a 400-cfm compressor. In particularly hard formations, a down-the-hole pneumatic hammer drill can be substituted for the rotary bit. Although samples collected by air flushing consist largely of dust and chippings, the method produces enough large particles to enable a geologist to identify gravel, bedrock, and types of overburden. □

References

1) Breeding, William H., "The Evaluation of Placer Deposits," Placer Exploration and Mining Short Course, University of Nevada, Reno, October 25-29, 1976.
2) Alders, I. R., "Placer Exploration and Its Equipment," Placer Short Course, Reno, 1976.
3) Colp, Douglas B., "A Placer Gold Evaluation Technique Comparison between a Hammer and KLAM Drill," Placer Short Course, Reno, 1976.
4) Wells, John H., "Some Notes on Placer Sampling," Placer Short Course, Reno, 1976.
5) Kastelic, William R., "Drilling and Evaluating Alaskan Gold Placers," Placer Short Course, Reno, 1976.
6) Applin, K. E. S., "Exploration for Alluvial Diamond Deposits," Placer Short Course, Reno, 1976.

---

*The amount of sample used in a fire assay crucible charge is 14.583 g or 29.166 g (less common). These amounts represent ½ assay ton and 1 assay ton, respectively.

The Cortez Gold Acres mine produced feed for the company's conventional mill and low grade ore for heap leaching (background).

How Cortez Gold Mines heap-leached low grade gold ores at two Nevada properties

D. M. Duncan and T. J. Smolik*

FOR 7½ YEARS, Cortez Gold Mines has been successfully operating heap leaching circuits for low grade gold ores in conjunction with a conventional 2,300-tpd milling operation at its Nevada mine sites. A total of 10 million tons of ore has been processed—one-half by heap leaching. Additional ore in the district offers potential for continued production.

Early in the Cortez operation, management recognized that a substantial tonnage of subgrade ore would have to be removed during normal mine operation. In 1969, Cortez started work to develop technology for recovering the gold values in this ore. At the same time, the US Bureau of Mines Salt Lake Research Center was performing small scale heap leaching tests on a number of gold ores.[1] The technique appeared to be a logical choice for Cortez, and the company inaugurated pilot testing at that time. Commercial scale heap leaching of the oxidized limestone ore from the Cortez deposit began in 1971.

Early in 1973, when Cortez reserves were exhausted, properties at Gold Acres, 8 mi from the Cortez plant, were placed in production, extracting a fault breccia ore of ground-up limestone, chert, and shale with a high percentage of clays. Economics again dictated heap leaching of the low grade ore. (See cover photograph.) High grade ore was trucked to the Cortez plant for milling. A carbon recovery circuit was constructed at the Gold Acres site to process pregnant heap-leach liquor. The integrated heap leach and carbon recovery operation remained very profitable as long as Gold Acres was mined. Gold Acres leaching is reviewed in detail here, with a discussion of the similarities and differences of the distinct Cortez and Gold Acres leach circuits.

Mining similar at both sites

Because both the Cortez and Gold Acres ore zones were small, 15-ft benches were required to control ore grade. Blasthole drilling on a 12 x 12-ft pattern was accomplished with three rotary drills—two track-mounted and the third truck-mounted—drilling 6¾-in.-dia holes. A truck-mounted rig dispensed an ANFO mix into the blastholes, and primacord was used for shot detonation. A B-E 5-yd shovel and a B-E 3½-yd shovel were used for digging and loading. Three 988 Cat

---

*D. M. Duncan, formerly general manager of Cortez Gold Mines, is currently manager of the Pitch uranium project of Homestake Mining Co. T. J. Smolik, formerly mill superintendent at Cortez Gold mines, is now metallurgical development engineer in the uranium division of Homestake Mining Co.

loaders, four D8 Cat dozers, two motor graders, 12 35-ton Haulpak rear-dump trucks, two 110-ton Euclid bottom-dump haul trucks, and two water trucks completed the list of mine equipment. The machinery was used also to haul leach ore, prepare the leach sites, and haul materials for construction of leach pads.

A truck-mounted portable lab aided in grade control at the digging face. Analysis of grab samples could be obtained within minutes and proved to be an important supplement to conventional blasthole assays. Blasthole assays could be used to locate and flag ore zone locations, but the portable lab assays could pinpoint the ore, especially when blasting caused displacement.

Cortez mill cutoff grades varied with the gold price, haulage distance, and varying royalty agreements. The mill cutoff grade dropped as low as 0.040 oz per ton at Cortez and 0.050 oz per ton at Gold Acres, emphasizing the importance of good control of ore grade.

The portable lab included a hydraulic system to operate the crushing and grinding equipment, while a 7.5-kw generator supplied all electrical requirements. The lab truck also contained chemical dissolution facilities and a Model 1000 Varian Tectron atomic absorption (AA) unit. Grab sampling during shovel operations—with close cooperation between the shovel operators and the ore grade control technicians—permitted substantial tonnages of mill-grade ore to be salvaged instead of being diluted to leach-grade ore. At a leach cutoff grade of 0.015 oz per ton, the portable lab also allowed salvaging some leach ore that would otherwise have been wasted.

Leach ore was trucked in 35-ton Haulpaks directly from the pits to leach pads prepared on gently sloped valley terrain about 1 mi away. The terrain at the leach sites graded about 5%, which was considered optimum for adequate heap solution drainage without undue erosion. Preliminary preparation for the leach site included removal of vegetation, grading, and compaction of the base with a vibrating roller compactor. Impervious pad material was then hauled to the site with 110-ton bottom-dump trucks.

Leach pad construction

Pad materials were local clay-silt or slime tailings. The clay-silts used for pad construction were 60% minus 200 mesh and at 90% compaction produced permeabilities of about 0.05 in. per day. Slime tailings used were 80% minus 200 mesh and at 91% compaction produced permeabilities of 0.025 in. per day. Pad material was spread in thin, 2- to 3-in. layers, brought to the required moisture content, and then compacted with a Bros self-propelled, 78-bhp, 14,000-lb vibrating machine. Compaction control was maintained by on-site measurements with a Model A Campbell Pacific Portaprobe. Compaction of all pad materials was maintained above 90%. Successive layers were added and treated until a pad depth of about 15 in. was attained. Required pad thickness was a function of percolation rate and length of leach time.

After the pad was constructed, a 3- to 4-in. layer of coarse gravel was placed over the pad to prevent erosion by leach solution movement and to provide a porous medium through which the effluent solutions could move laterally under the heaps. The gravel also protected the pad from impact damage by large rocks cascading down the face of the heap during dumping. Occasionally, if insufficient gravel was placed, flooding occurred within the heap, causing poor leaching conditions and uncontrolled solution flow from heap faces. Leach solutions normally traversed the length of the heaps through the gravel and collected in a ditch at the front of the heap. The ditch, lined with 30-mil butyl rubber or Hypalon, directed the leach effluent to a central point, where it entered a steel or asbestos-cement pipe for gravity flow to the pregnant solution storage pond.

The ponding areas were constructed in the same manner as the leach pads, being lined with compacted tailings or local clay silts. The ponding areas were large enough to hold two or three days of heap drainage in case of plant operating problems or to retain runoff from a major rainfall. The Gold Acres facility required a pregnant solution storage of 1.6 million gal and a barren solution storage of 1.0 million gal.

Ore heaped 20 ft high at Gold Acres

After experimenting with various heap heights, including 10 ft, 20 ft, and 30 ft, an average height of 20 ft was established at Gold Acres. Ore was dumped in a single lift for the 20-ft heaps, and any area driven on by the trucks was thoroughly ripped before leach solutions were applied. A D8 Cat was used to push ore after truck dumping.

Heap base dimensions on the individual pads varied but were typically 350 ft wide x 450 ft long. With a top slope of 2½%, an average 20-ft heap contained about 170,000 tons of ore. A total of 2.2 million tons of ore was heap-leached at Gold Acres, while 2.8 million tons were heap-leached at the Cortez site.

A D8 Cat with an extended 30-in. ripper worked the tops of the heaps prior to leaching, and during the leaching cycle, the surfaces of the heaps were periodically ripped again to minimize ponding.

Placing additional lifts of ore on top of leached-out heaps was not satisfactory, producing low gold extractions from the Gold Acres ore.

The rocky, competent Cortez limestone ore was leached in both 20-ft and 30-ft lifts. Additional lifts placed over leached-out ore produced better gold extractions than at Gold Acres, but the extractions were not as good on the second lift of ore as on the first. Single 60-ft lifts of Cortez ore produced low gold extractions and were subsequently redistributed in lower lifts for further leaching.

Leach solutions were pumped from the carbon plant through 6-in. steel pipe to the heap surfaces. The 3-in. pumps used were equipped with 60-hp, 3,600-rpm motors. Piping to distribute solution over the heaps was Class 160, 3-in.-dia PVC, spaced 50 ft apart. Armstrong

Spraymatic plastic sprinklers with ⅛-in. nozzles, spaced on 50-ft centers, were used for applying leach solution. Solution flow to a typical heap was maintained at 300 gpm, for a solution application rate of 0.0025 gpm per sq ft. Normally, three areas were available for leaching, with the third area leached intermittently to maintain an average effluent flow of 550 gpm.

With an average yearly water evaporation loss of 30%, maintaining an effluent flow of 550 gpm required an average fresh water make-up of 235 gpm. However, the evaporation rate varied considerably with the seasons, and the peak fresh water requirement ran as high as 550 gpm. The fresh water at Gold Acres was of poor quality and caused severe scaling problems. A large barren pond was used to "condition" the water before introduction into the spraying system.

Sodium hydroxide (purchased at a 50% liquid concentration) was metered into the barren pond with fresh water and recycled barren solution. Dissolved solids in the hard water precipitated out in the pond, minimizing scaling problems. With the caustic addition, the pH of the leach solution was maintained at 10.5. Sodium cyanide stock solution (at 15% strength) and an S-35 Baroid water treatment chemical were metered and injected into the pump lines as the leach solution returned through the pumps to the leach heaps. The sodium cyanide concentration of the leach solution was maintained at 0.030%. Reagent consumption for Gold Acres ore averaged 0.45 lb NaCN and 0.41 lb NaOH per ton of ore.

Gold production from the heaps was monitored by sampling, assaying, and measuring each effluent flow. Truck counts during the leach haul and survey measurements of the heaps provided tonnage figures, and blasthole assays and portable lab assays were used to determine the grade of each heap. This information provided enough data to calculate gold recoveries on each heap.

Leach extraction and ore character varied, depending on the area mined. (Typical curves for extraction vs. time are shown in the accompanying graph, including the low leach extraction rate for a second 20-ft lift of ore placed above the original No. 2 heap.) The clayey Gold Acres ore averaged 50% extraction. By contrast, the "blocky" Cortez leach ore averaged 65% extraction.

Carbon adsorption recovery plant

A 75 x 40-ft pre-engineered building housed all spray and process pumps, reagent mixing and distribution facilities, carbon adsorption columns, pressure stripping facilities, carbon reactivation furnace, and all associated electrical instrumentation and controls. A location directly in front of the pregnant and barren storage ponds was chosen to facilitate solution transfer. A 24-ft eaves height was required for gravity flow through the five carbon adsorption columns, such flow requiring a 3-ft differential between columns. An 18,000-gal tank for caustic solution, a 6,000-gal fuel oil tank, and bulk storage for cyanide were located outside the building.

Gold-bearing pregnant solution was pumped through

Carbon adsorption columns at Gold Acres are 7 ft in diameter x 8 ft high; each holds 3,000 lb of activated carbon.

the carbon columns at a flow rate of 550 gpm. The tanks each held 3,000 lb of 12 x 30-mesh coconut shell activated carbon. An upward flow rate of 14.3 gpm per sq ft produced a carbon bed expansion of about 35%. As the pregnant solution passed through the carbon bed, the carbon absorbed the soluble gold cyanide complex. The tanks were arranged so that the pregnant solution flowed upward through the first and decanted and then flowed by gravity through each of the remaining carbon columns. A total of 48 solution ports or nozzles evenly spaced about a baffle plate near the bottom of each tank permitted even solution flow through the carbon. Each port had three openings or slots measuring ⅜ x ¾ in. and was constructed to prevent the carbon from dropping into the manifold chamber under the baffle plate. In the countercurrent system, high grade gold solutions contacted the most heavily loaded carbon. (See flowsheet.)

Carbon advanced hydraulically through 2-in. Schutte-Koerting eductors in a direction opposite the pregnant solution flow. High pressure water from the heap spray pumps was used as motive water through the eductors, at a flow rate of 40-50 gpm. About 1,500 lb of carbon (dry weight basis) was periodically advanced from each carbon column. Carbon removed from the No. 1 column was treated in the stripping circuit for gold recovery and then returned to the No. 5 carbon column. Solution overflow from the No. 5 column, depleted in gold values, was pumped to the barren storage pond for reagent make-up and subsequent recycle back to the heaps. The data for April 5, 1976 are typical of an operating day:

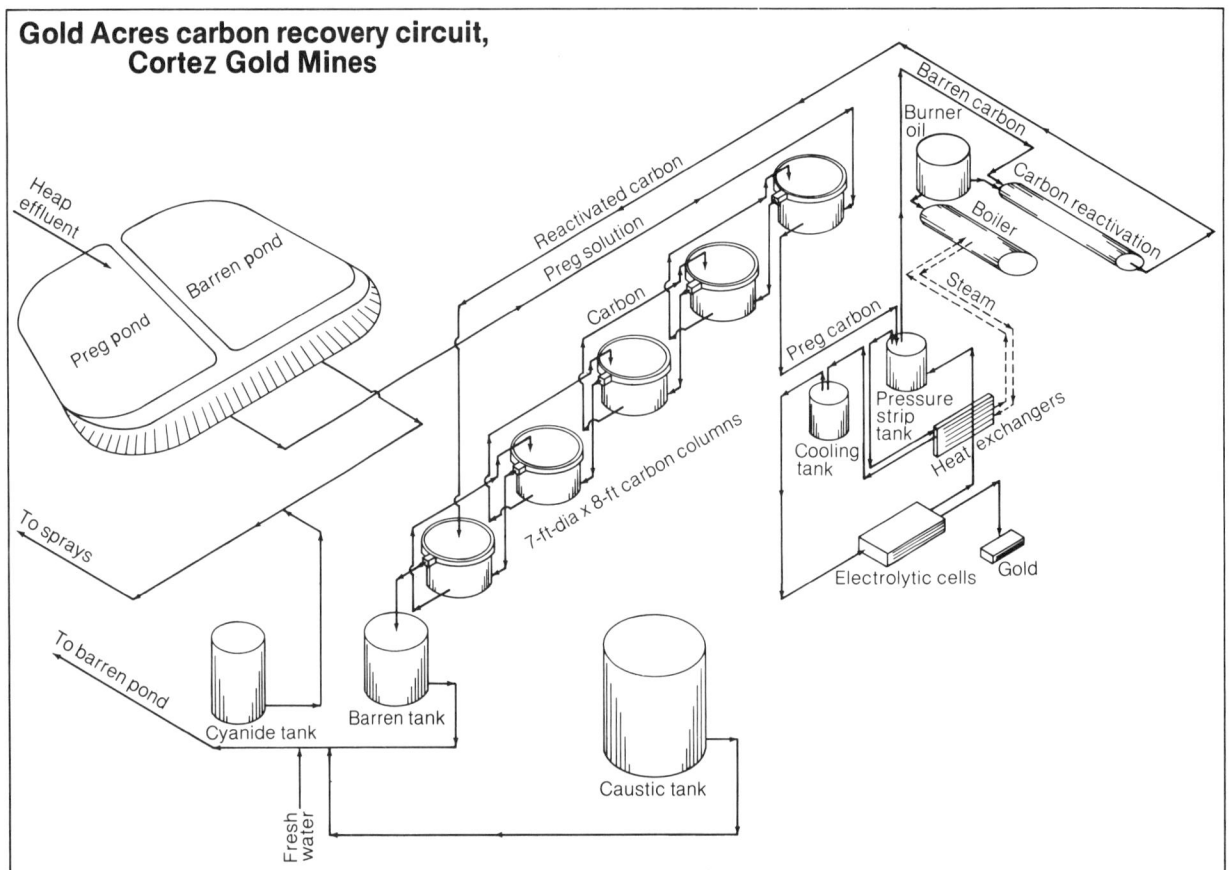

Gold Acres carbon recovery circuit, Cortez Gold Mines

- Operating time — 24 hr.
- Pregnant solution flow — 3,290 tons at 548 gpm.
- Pregnant solution assay — 0.021 oz per ton.
- Barren solution assay — 0.0005 oz per ton.
- Gold recovery from pregnant solution — 97.7%.

At the Cortez mill, where a zinc precipitation circuit was available when the mill was operating, the effluent solutions from Cortez heaps were combined with the mill pregnant solution for gold recovery in the Merrill-Crowe precipitation circuit. When the Cortez mill operation was curtailed, a small four-stage, 5-ft-dia carbon column circuit was installed for gold recovery and performed very satisfactorily. Pregnant carbon from the Cortez circuit was stripped and reactivated in the Gold Acres plant.

Carbon stripping in pressure vessels

There are various known methods of stripping gold-loaded activated carbon, among them atmospheric hot caustic stripping,[2] pressurized hot caustic stripping,[3] and methanol stripping.[4] Each method has merit, and the best approach is a matter of management preference. Atmospheric stripping is slow, typically taking around 48 hr for a carbon strip cycle. Pressure stripping reduces the cycle to 12-20 hr but requires pressurized vessels. Methanol stripping, which can further reduce the stripping time, operates at atmospheric pressures but increases the stripping cost.

Pressurized hot caustic stripping was used at the Gold Acres carbon plant. Between 1,200 and 1,700 lb (dry weight basis) of loaded carbon was introduced into a 42-in.-dia x 10-ft pressure vessel. A 1% sodium hydroxide solution was used for stripping, at a pressure of 60 psi and a temperature of 240°F. A 25-hp steam boiler supplied heat, with fin-tube heat exchangers external to the stripping vessel used to reclaim the heat and preheat incoming strip solution. All facilities were constructed of mild steel.

Stripping solution was pumped at 13 gpm into the bottom of the strip vessel, passed through the loaded carbon, and discharged from the top of the pressure vessel. After passing through the heat exchangers, the strip solution was cooled to 180°F, sent through the electrolytic cells for gold recovery, and then recycled back to the strip vessel. The carbon was usually stripped to 0.5-2.0 oz per ton of gold loading, then washed, reactivated, and recycled back to the carbon columns.

Gold was electrowon from the strip solutions in two rectangular electrolytic tanks, each measuring 3½ ft long x 3 ft wide x 3 ft deep. The electrolytic tanks were constructed of mild steel and lined with neoprene rubber. Anodes were made of perforated, electrolytic grade carbon, while cathodes were constructed of perforated ¼-in. polypropylene sheet and fabricated to hold 2 lb of carbon steel wool. The polypropylene sheet served as an insulating medium between anodes and cathodes. Each tank could hold six cathodes and seven anodes, although fewer cathodes and anodes were normally used, to reduce the quantity of steel wool that would have to be refined. The caustic solution used for carbon stripping served as electrolyte, with spent electrolyte recycled back to the pressure vessel to recover more gold from the loaded carbon. After stripping a batch of carbon, cathodes were removed from the tanks, and the plated steel wool was treated in the refinery for recovery of gold doré bullion.

A 200-amp rectifier was used in the gold electrowinning circuit. Cathodes were connected in parallel so that under normal operating conditions a potential of 2.5 v could generate 22.5 amps per cathode. In this batch electrowinning, gold values were taken to depletion, and the average current efficiency was low. (Data from a typical strip electrowinning log are shown in the accompanying table.)

After completion of the strip cycle, barren carbon was washed with fresh water and educted to the carbon reactivation circuit. A screw feeder delivered the dewatered carbon at a rate of 2.5 dry lb per min to a rotary-type, oil-fired reactivation furnace. The stainless steel tube through which the carbon passed measured 20 in. in diameter x 12 ft long. A temperature of 1,350°F was maintained in the stainless steel chamber during carbon reactivation. After the high temperature treatment, the carbon was quenched and educted back to the No. 5 carbon column for reuse.

Heap leaching: low cost operation

The integrated heap leaching and carbon recovery circuit for gold required a minimum of operating labor. One full-time worker and a part-time helper were required 8 hr per day, seven days per week, to take care of the leaching, carbon column, stripping, and reactivation circuits. The major costs of the operation were power, reagent requirements, pad preparation, and leach

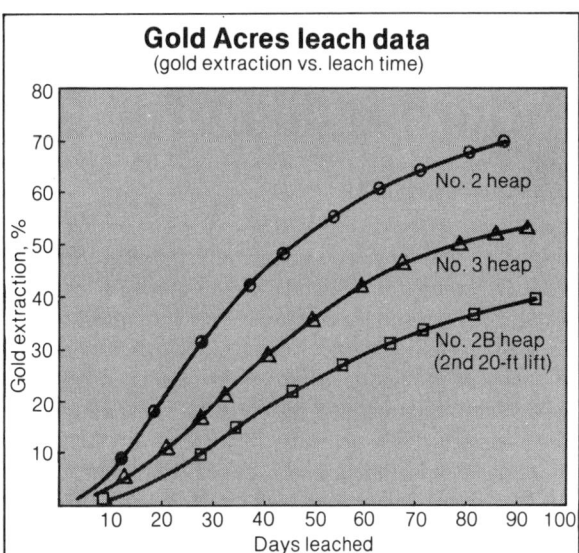

haulage. The carbon loss in the Gold Acres circuit was insignificant: an indicated carbon consumption of 0.0025 lb per ton of ore leached. Repair costs were moderate.

A leaching operation was viable as long as run-of-mine ore produced reasonable gold extractions. Crushing of the Cortez or Gold Acres leach ores could not be economically justified, precluding purchase of expensive crushing equipment and additional operating expense. With different ore grades and/or leaching characteristics, however, the effect of crushing on the rate of gold production and recovery should be evaluated.

With suitable topography and the availability of adequate soils or tailings, construction of a leach pad is relatively inexpensive. In other cases, soil sealers or more expensive permanent pads of concrete or asphalt may be considered.

The leaching characteristics of different ores have a dramatic effect on the economic viability of heap leaching. Percolation problems may be severe with one ore and moderate with another. Reagent consumption can vary drastically with varying percolation rates and varying content of sulphide mineralization in the ore. Each potential leach property must be tested and evaluated individually.

The presence of other metals, such as silver, copper, zinc, and mercury, in the pregnant solution can create special problems with carbon loading capacity and gold bullion quality. Under the right circumstances, however, the simplicity of operation and the low capital and operating costs make carbon adsorption-electrolytic recovery of gold economically superior to conventional zinc precipitation circuits. □

Typical strip-electrowinning log at Gold Acres

Date: March 14, 1976.
Carbon identification: CP-4V1.
Strip conditions: reagents—150 lb NaOH, 25 lb NaCN; flow—13 gpm = 2.5 bed volumes per hr; vessel pressure—65 psi; vessel temperature—235°F.
Electrolytic cell: nine cathodes used, 18 lb steel wool; 190 total amps at 2.5 v.

Time	Solution assays, oz per ton	
	Cell feed	Cell discharge
8:00 a.m. (start)	—	—
12:00 a.m. (at temp.)	24.7	18.7
3:00 p.m.	17.5	10.1
7:00 p.m.	5.4	1.0
11:00 p.m.	0.7	0.07
7:00 a.m., March 15	0.06	0.01

Off: carbon washed 1½ hr.

Strip time: 23 hr total. **Average current efficiency:** 30.3%.

Assay data:

Carbon	Doré bullion
Preg carbon (1,202 lb): 485.4 oz/ton	Weight: 333 oz
Barren carbon (1,202 lb): 0.4 oz/ton	Gold: 859.64 fine
Indicated gold in carbon: 291.5 oz	Silver: 119.58 fine
	Gold recovery: 286.3 oz.

References

1) Potter, G. M., "Recovering Gold from Stripping Waste and Ore by Percolation Cyanide Leaching," USBM TPR 20, December 1969.
2) Zadra, J. B., Engel, A. L., and Heinen, H. J., "Process for Recovering Gold and Silver from Activated Carbon by Leaching and Electrolysis," USBM RI 4843, 1952.
3) Ross, J. R., Salisbury, H. B., and Potter, G. M., "Pressure Stripping Gold from Activated Carbon," AIME annual meeting, Chicago, Ill., 1973.
4) Lindstrom, R. E., Peterson, D. G., and Heinen, H. J., "Extraction of Silver from Marginal Ores," AIME annual meeting, New York, N.Y. 1975.

Heap leaching will produce 85,000 oz/year of doré bullion for Smoky Valley Mining

Lane White, Managing editor

HIGH, dry, and sparsely populated, the Big Smoky Valley stretches for about 100 mi through central Nevada, between the high peaks of the Toquima Mountains of the east and the Toiyabe Mountains on the west—sites of the ghosts of numerous mining camps. At Round Mountain, about 55 mi north of Tonopah on the valley's eastern flank, gold was discovered in 1905, and production from underground mines continued until 1935. Placer operations produced intermittently through the late 1950s, and over the years an estimated total of $8 million in gold was mined in the district.

In 1977, Smoky Valley Mining Co. has revived gold production at Round Mountain, heap leaching low grade ores to produce 85,000 oz per year of doré bullion assaying 67% gold and 33% silver. The company, a subsidiary of Copper Range Co., employs about 100 people. Felmont Oil Corp. and Case-Pomeroy & Co. are partners in Smoky Valley Mining. The processing scheme includes open-pit mining, crushing to 100% minus ½ in., cyanide-lime trickle leaching, carbon adsorption and desorption, electrowinning, and refining.

Smoky Valley Mining works gold deposits in sections 19 and 30 T10N R44E in Nye County, on the western side of Round Mountain, an isolated hill of mineralized welded rhyolite tuff flanked by gold placer deposits of similar eroded materials. The property is remote from its major sources of supplies. Reno is about 240 mi to the northwest and Las Vegas is about 262 mi to the southeast by the shortest highway routes.

Climatic conditions are extreme in central Nevada. Summers are hot and dry, with temperatures on occasion exceeding 100°F, while winters are windy and cold, with temperatures dropping below zero. The work area elevation on the Smoky Valley Mining property ranges from 6,100 ft to 6,600 ft above sea level. Vegetation consists of sage and desert grasses. Precipitation averages 8 in. per year, and snowfall is minimal. Leaching activity is expected to proceed during 10 months of the year.

Water for Smoky Valley Mining operations is drawn from Jett Canyon in the Toiyabe Mountains and, during periods when Jett Canyon is dry, from wells in the valley bottom. In Jett Canyon, about 8.5 mi west of the plant site at an elevation about 760 ft above the plant, a small concrete stream diverter provides input for a 15-in.-dia water pipeline that first went into operation in 1915. The Smoky Valley Mining plant draws make-up water at the rate of about 400 gpm.

F. E. Girucky is general manager of the operation, D. E. Hayes is executive secretary, R. W. Frailey is assistant general manager, R. M. Jones is mine and maintenance manager, R. J. Leone is manager of ore quality control, R. H. Hattrap is manager of administra-

Each of five 400-ft-long x 250-ft-wide leaching pads holds about 40,000 tons of ore, stacked 10 ft high.

A control panel at the primary crusher monitors and controls ore flow from the crusher through to fine ore storage.

A **761-ft-long conveyor** advances ore from the primary crusher to the secondary crusher. The conveyor reaches a height of 52 ft 5 in. (left). Three vibratory feeders beneath the fine ore stockpile pull ore and feed it to a conveyor for transfer to a truck loading bin near the leach pads (below).

tive services, and L. G. Hayes is manager of technical services. At Smoky Valley Mining, operations are divided between two departments—mining and maintenance, and leaching and gold recovery—supported by three service departments: geology, engineering, and administrative services. Buildings on the plant site are six in number: administrative, change house, combination warehouse and plant maintenance shop; adsorption-desorption-refinery; reagent mixing complex; and laboratory. Equipment installations include primary, secondary, and tertiary crushers; surge-stockpile facilities; a truck loading bin; interconnecting conveyors; and permanent asphalt leach pads.

Mountain States Engineers was awarded the design and construction contract.

Mining 8,000 tpd at 1:1 stripping ratio

The Smoky Valley mining and maintenance crews work three shifts per day, seven days per week, providing plant-wide maintenance, stripping 8,000 tpd of waste, and moving 8,000 tpd of broken ore through a crushing and conveying system to a truck bin near the leaching pads.

The welded rhyolite tuff of Round Mountain probably dates to the Miocene, though the age has not been definitely established. Fracturing in the Tertiary permitted intrusion by hydrothermal solutions high in gold, silver, and other trace minerals. Gold-bearing pyrites formed first; oxidation of the pyrite then remobilized the gold. Grade control is difficult because it is difficult to make a visual distinction between ore and waste. Grade control is maintained through drill cuttings and photogeology, with best results gained on drillhole assays. Assaying has been aided by the installation of improved sample collecting devices on the Ingersoll-Rand blasthole drills. Ore at Smoky Valley averages 0.06 oz of gold per ton, and the current cutoff grade is 0.02 oz per ton.

Blastholes are drilled on a 17 x 19-ft pattern, using an Ingersoll-Rand T-4 drill to sink 6¾-in.-dia holes. They are blasted with ANFO, using 50 lb of aluminized ANFO containing 7% aluminum on the bottom. Kinepak primers and Nonel delays are used for detonation. A P&H shovel of 6-cu-yd dipper capacity loads out ore at a 35-ft bench. There are also three Cat 992 front-end loaders on the property, using slicks on the front and regular tires on the back. Other equipment includes nine Euclid R-50 trucks, one Terex 8250, and a Cat D9. The trucks make a short ore haul to an Allis-Chalmers 42 x 65-in. primary gyratory crusher having a design capacity of 550 tph. Primary crushing reduces the Smoky Valley ore to minus 7 in.

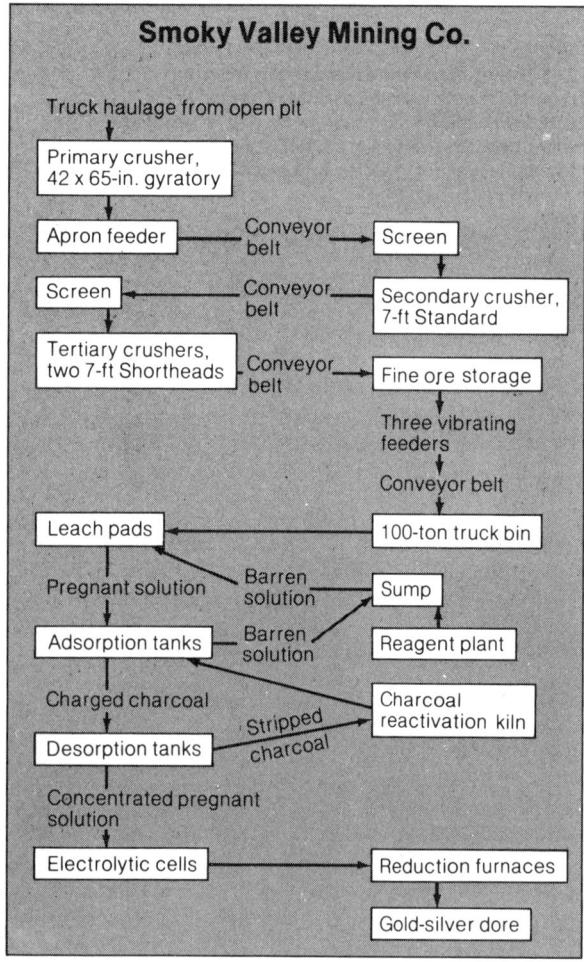

A Stephens-Adamson 42 x 20-in apron feeder draws ore from a 75-ton bin under the primary crusher and feeds it to a 36-in.-wide conveyor belt, which moves it 761 ft to the Symons 7-ft Standard secondary crusher for reduction to minus 2 in. Another 36-in. conveyor belt, 182 ft long, advances the ore to two 7-ft Symons Short Head tertiary crushers in parallel, which reduce the ore to 94% minus ⅜ in. x 1½ in. An 1,100-ft-long, 36-in.-wide conveyor belt then advances the material to a 30,000-ton fine ore stockpile that has a 9,000-ton live load. Three vibratory feeders beneath the stockpile pull ore and feed it at a normal capacity of 1,000 tph to a 1,200-ft-long, 36-in.-wide conveyor belt, which transfers it to a 100-ton truck loading bin located near the leach pads. The truck loading bin has automatic bin gates with a manual override and is equipped with a weightometer and a two-stage automatic sampler.

Rear-dump trucks draw ore from the ore bin and transfer it to the five leaching pads, which cover a total area 2,100 ft long x 282 ft wide. The individual pads, which are constructed of high grade asphalt 7 in. thick with a protective membrane 2 in. from the bottom, are separated by haulage roads.

Leach solution, with sodium cyanide added at about 1 lb per ton of ore, is sprinkled at about 400 gpm over each heap by Bagdad wigglers. The leach pads slope at about 3% to a common drainage trench on the western side of the pile. The normal leaching cycle is expected to be 27 days for leach solution sprinkling, two days for washing, and two or three days for drainage, for a total leach pad on-off cycle time of about 35 days. A lime addition maintains the leaching pH between 9.5 and 10.5.

Worthington turbine pumps are used for moving solution to the heaps and from the heaps to the refinery, with flow meters measuring the rate of flow both ways. A 2.5-million-gal solution storage pond provides capacity for holding all solutions in the event of a plant emergency and maximum rainfall, and a well below the leach pads monitors ground water to assure that no cyanide escapes the processing system.

Effluent from the heap leaching pads moves at 1,200 to 1,600 gpm through five countercurrent charcoal adsorption tanks in series. Gold and silver in the pregnant leaching solution precipitate onto activated 12 x 30 mesh coconut carbon, starting at the No. 1 tank. Each of the 8-ft-high x 12-ft-dia adsorption tanks holds about 7,000 lb of carbon.

Loaded carbon advances from the No. 1 tank to three desorption vessels, each of 1-ton capacity, in series, while barren solution from the No. 5 tank receives a sodium cyanide and lime addition and is returned as leaching solution to the asphalt leaching pad.

About 1 ton of gold-loaded charcoal is removed from the No. 1 adsorption tank each day at a chemical analysis of about 250 tr oz of gold per ton of charcoal, and a corresponding amount is advanced at each of the other tanks. Charcoal, treated in an Envirotech reactivation kiln following desorption, is added to the system at the No. 5 tank. Charcoal reactivation takes place under controlled heat (1,100°F) in the absence of air.

In the desorption circuit, caustic-cyanide solution at 190°F redissolves and strips gold and silver values from the loaded charcoal. The pressure vessels are heated by hot water jackets.

The adsorption-desorption system requires a make-up carbon addition of about 1 ton every 24 hr.

Pregnant solution from the desorption circuit flows through electrowinning cells in the refinery at Smoky Valley Mining. Metal values are electrowon from the solution at 60 amps and 2.5 v in three electrolytic cells in parallel, precipitating on steel wool cathodes. Cathodes are usually loaded to 100 oz of metal values per pound of steel wool before they are removed from the electrowinning cells. About 1,000 tr oz of gold and silver are removed from the cells at each reloading.

Barren caustic-cyanide solution returns from the electrolytic cells to the desorption circuit, where chemicals are added to restore it to the original concentration.

Loaded cathodes are smelted in one of three Lindberg crucible reduction furnaces, the steel is slagged off, and the doré metal is poured into bars for marketing.

Laboratory facilities at Smoky Valley Mining include atomic adsorption instruments and conventional wet lab and fire assaying equipment to serve exploration programs, mine planning, pit operations, grade control, leaching and processing control, and quantification of gold-silver in the product to be marketed. □

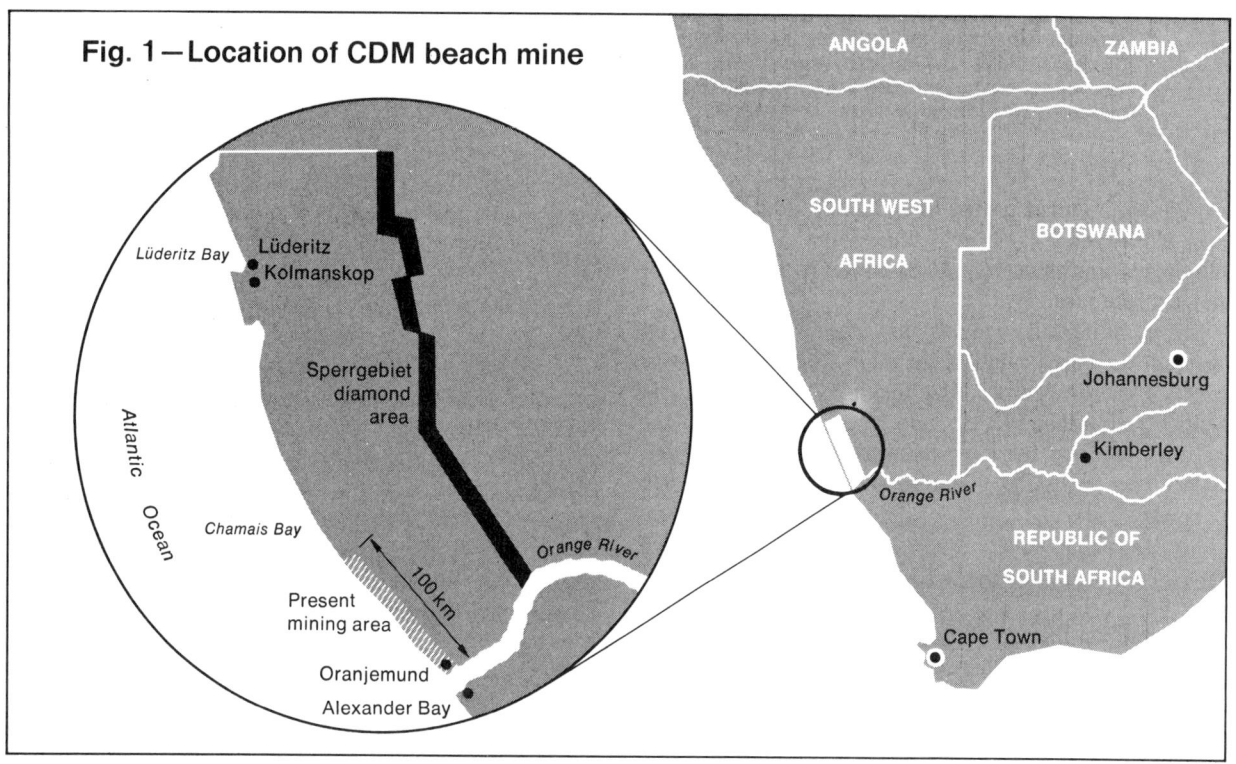

Fig. 1—Location of CDM beach mine

Mining the beach for diamonds at CDM

D. L. Hodgson, technical assistant, Consolidated Diamond Mines of South West Africa (Pty.) Ltd.

USING A VERSATILE FLEET OF EARTHMOVERS, Consolidated Diamond Mines of South West Africa Ltd. is conquering mountainous seas and exceptionally heavy tides to mine diamond gravels to 16 m below mean sea level on southern Africa's Atlantic coastal strip, just north of the Orange River.

While CDM has surface-mined marine terraces above high water in this area since 1920, the foreshore area (land west of and below the high-water mark) presented special challenges. Not until the 1960s was a system devised to sample the wet sands below high water; diamond sampling, even under ideal conditions, is a difficult, painstaking exercise requiring considerable expertise.

in the 1970s, CDM "bit the bullet" and launched commercial mining in the foreshore after successful test extraction campaigns. Today, the company deploys a 1,000-cu-m-per-hr bucket wheel excavator (BWE) and stacker, along with bowl scrapers, hydraulic backhoes, bulldozers, and off-highway haulers in a large earthmoving operation behind a sea wall constructed of stripped overburden. Exposed diamond gravels are mined on a progressively shrinking scale that ends when bedrock is swept clean by special work gangs.

The system allows CDM to mine 190 m to the seaward side of high water. In addition, an extension of the mining limits to 200 m seaward of the high-water mark now appears feasible at the Western block, where the BWE is in service. This strip is about 9 mi long and 0.6 mi wide.

The technical aspects of this offshore beach mining operation make it one of the most interesting in the world. CDM strips about 140,319 mtpd and generates about 40,000 cu m per month of diamond-bearing gravels for the plant. The grade of these gravels ranges from about 13.26 to 14.27 carats per 100 ft of terrace treated. Diamond production in 1975 amounted to 1,747,739 carats, or one carat per 25 mt of overburden stripped.

The mine is situated in an isolated desert environment on a coastline subject to heavy seas, especially during the winter (Fig. 1). The sea has a mean temperature of 11°C, producing a strong southerly wind in the day and misty conditions at night. Consequently, men and machinery are subjected to adverse working conditions, and any structure seaward of the high-water mark must be built to withstand heavy seas.

Throughout the mine, diamondiferous gravels are covered by varying depths of barren overburden sand. For many years, mining of the foreshore in the southern section of the mine was not viable because of the difficulties of sampling and the depths of overburden. In the late 1960s, Benoto drills, capable of handling the wet sand, were used for sampling in the area. Favorable results obtained from the drilling program prompted the start of experimental foreshore mining in 1970. The

The heart of CDM's operation is a giant bucket wheel excavator stretching the width of the mining area. This aerial profile (looking east) shows, from left to right, beach sand overburden being stripped, diamondiferous gravels, dozed windrows, and bedrock.

experimental mines proved to be feasible, and CDM has now established a beach mine face 820 m long, employing approximately $6.3 million of capital equipment at the face.

Diamondiferous gravels are found immediately beneath the beach sands at the mine. Part of the gravels directly overlie bedrock, but they are mainly found in gullies and potholes in the very irregular surface of the bedrock. Mining these gravels consists of three stages: overburden stripping, loading-hauling, and bedrock cleaning.

Stripping overburden with the BWE

Overburden depth at the mine varies from 5 to 25 m, with the deepest overburden occurring on the western side. Overburden-to-headfeed ratio is about 12:1; hence, to provide 40,000 cu m per month headfeed for the treatment plant, a minimum 0.5 million cu m of overburden must be moved each month.

The sand overlying the deposit is singularly free of coarse or heavy gravels and is ideally suited to transportation by high capacity earthmoving equipment. An O&K SH400 bucket wheel excavator was commissioned in June 1975. The track-mounted electro-hydraulic machine has a guaranteed output of 1,000 bank cu m per hr. The 6.4-m-dia bucket wheel is equipped with ten 0.4-cu-m buckets on its circumference. The unit works in conjunction with a 116-m-long conveyor bridge and a spreader. The spreader has a stacking range of 35 m, can work through 230°, and, like the conveyor bridge, is track-mounted. The conveyor bridge was designed to allow mining operations to take place beneath it.

The BWE cuts a face at 45° to the coastline (Fig. 2). This angle allows the spreader to stack against the sea wall, thus creating a seal of barren overburden sand behind the mine workings. It also allows the BWE to work as close to the sea wall as possible. (However, if the BWE works too close to the wall, wet conditions cause poor cutting results and movement is difficult.) In addition, cutting the face at right angles to the dominant gully direction facilitates mechanical cleaning with a Poclain excavator.

The BWE makes two horizontal cuts along the face to provide flatter angles for the conveyor bridge and to prevent slumping. If the mine face is stripped in one cut, slumping occurs because the maximum working height of the BWE is below the top of the overburden band. The BWE's cab directly faces the bank at a low elevation, making the driver vulnerable to sudden slumps.

The BWE starts at the east end of the face and works toward the western side. As it advances westward, the cable from an automatic feeder is placed in protective cradles that are painted white for high visibility at night.

The mining face direction is controlled by lines given by surveyors, and the BWE operators work up to pegs on these lines. The working elevation is checked regularly, using profiles to sight onto a fixed point on the unit. Three operators run the BWE. One controls the bucket wheel, one controls the receiving end of the conveyor bridge, and the third controls the spreader. One relief operator and a supervisor round out the crew.

The stacker works with a Caterpillar D9-S blade dozer, which establishes the pad on which the stacker moves. A D-65 Komatsu bulldozer dozes up the advancing toe of the embankment as required and levels the footwall for the tracks of the excavator and bridge.

The BWE works three 8-hr shifts six days a week, with 2 hr of maintenance per day performed by CDM's engineering department, which assigns a permanent fitter and electrician to the BWE. These men work a day shift but are on permanent standby. If possible, non-scheduled maintenance is done on Sunday, and every 480 hr the machine is given a major service of 10-12 hr.

Maintenance problems are made more difficult by the prevailing wind, which carries fine sand, and by the corrosive atmosphere. One modification to suit local conditions has been the installation of additional limit switches and warning sirens.

The availability of the BWE has not been as high as expected—a problem that will have to be solved if targets set for the unit are to be achieved. Running cost of the BWE is $173 per hr; at the present rate of

stripping, the cost per cubic meter moved is 18.2¢. Conventional stripping with scrapers costs between 23¢ and 29¢ per cu m, depending on the site conditions and the type of scraper used.

Stripping the box-cut: not any easy job

The section of the mine just east of the beach wall cannot be stripped using the BWE. Instead, a box-cut (Fig. 2) must be maintained ahead of the BWE face to prevent excessive seepage in the advance toe of the face, which would hamper the work of the BWE. The box-cut section is stripped with a fleet of conventional open-bowl Caterpillar 641 and 666 scrapers pushed by Caterpillar D9-C blade dozers.

Dimensions of the box-cut are roughly 100 x 150 m, with the direction of advance being parallel to the coastline. Overburden stripped from the box-cut is dumped on the sea wall for maintenance, requiring a high scraper cycle time of about 10 min. However, continual maintenance of the wall is necessary, and dumping space other than on the seaward side of the workings is limited.

Because of the height of the water table, stripping of the box-cut is not an easy process, requiring three separate stages of roughly 6 m each. Initial stripping is done until the water level is reached. A bank of wellpoints is then inserted to lower the phreatic zone and allow the box-cut to be stripped. The process of stripping and wellpoint placement continues down to the diamondiferous gravels. Even with three banks of wellpoints in operation, stripping of the last few meters is done under very wet conditions, with water seeping in from the landward side as well as from below the lowest bank of wellpoints.

Moving gravel to the plant

Loading and hauling of diamondiferous gravels take place continuously under the conveyor bridge of the BWE. For this operation and for subsequent bedrock cleaning, the following equipment is used (indicated capital and operating costs include both maintenance and amortization):

- Komatsu D56E bulldozer ($11.09 per hr).
- Poclain LC-80 hydraulic excavator ($8.07 per hr).
- Caterpillar 988 front-end loader ($15.48 per hr).
- Caterpillar 769B haul trucks ($14.47 per hr).

The diamondiferous gravel is trammed to the No. 4 treatment plant, a one-way distance of 2.5 km to the tipping bin. The beach mine face provides 40% of the headfeed to the No. 4 plant. Because the ore is fine and wet, diamondiferous gravels from the mine must be mixed with ore from the other mine faces in the No. 4 plant mining area to obtain optimum plant efficiencies.

Exposed diamondiferous gravels that lie above the bedrock peaks are dozed with the small Komatsu dozer into windrows parallel to the cutting face and about 30 m ahead of the advancing bedrock cleaning face. The majority of the gravels is excavated from gullies and

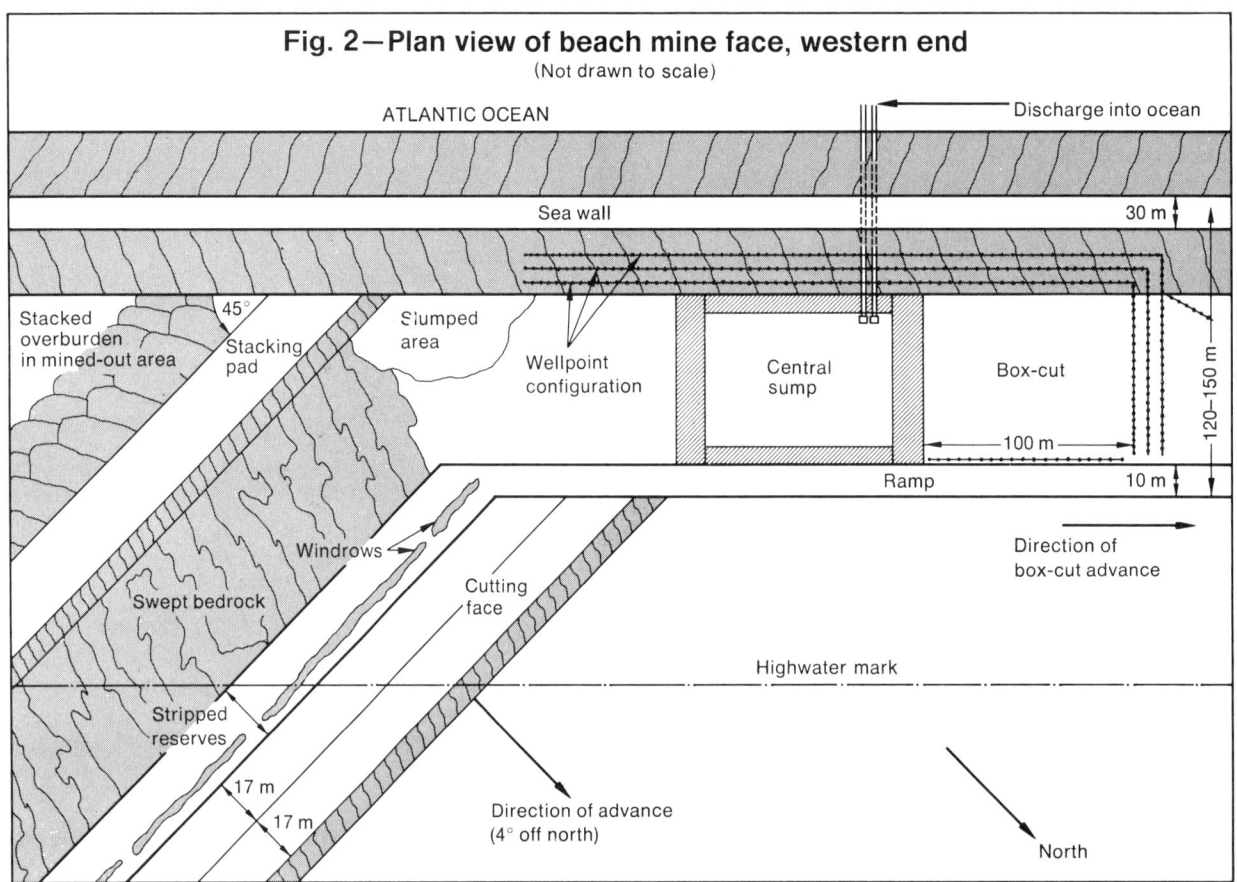

Fig. 2—Plan view of beach mine face, western end
(Not drawn to scale)

potholes and placed on the windrow side of the face by Poclain excavators. This material is then dozed up against the windrow; breaks are left in the windrow for entrance into the face and for supervision. The windrow is not allowed to build up to large dimensions because space is limited.

Loading of the windrow starts form the east and continues along the mine face. Haul trucks back up to the end of the windrow and load from the working face side of the windrow. This provides working space on the mine side of the windrow and ensures that any movement of the windrow will be away from the working face. The Cat 988 FEL and 769B truck used in this operation are well matched and have high availabilities—81.1% and 81.5%, respectively, for 1976. The 769Bs handle 91 cu m per hr for a 2-km one-way haul.

Bedrock is cleaned by hand

Bedrock cleaning is done by Poclain excavators and by gangs of 27 men plus one headman, who sweep the bedrock with hand-held brushes. Additional equipment used by the sweeping gang includes shovels, steel scrapers, chisels and hammers, and pavement breakers (plus compressors).

The track-mounted Poclain excavators are capable of removing 75 cu m per hr from gullies averaging 1.3 m in depth. The excavators use two interchangeable buckets: a narrow one and a much wider one designed for shallower or wider gullies and more uniform bedrock conditions. These units, working ahead of the bedrock cleaning gangs, operate through two 10-hr shifts. The machines are always operated in a full circle when discharging material, thus avoiding the stop-start stresses of major direction changes.

The excavators discharge material directly opposite the pickup point, which leaves maximum space for the cleaning gang to dump the material they generate and for the D65 dozer to maneuver in pushing excavated material onto the windrow.

When the bulk of the material has been removed, sweeping of the bedrock and scraping of the cracks and crevices begins, to recover diamonds washed onto the shore by wave action. Any gravels cemented together are broken up, either with hammers and chisels or with pavement breakers, depending on the degree of cementation. A swept-out area is broom-clean, with only waste schistose bedrock remaining. When sweeping is done in areas below the water table, water from the gullies being swept is continually pumped to sumps.

The sweeping method has proven to be the most effective in recovering all diamonds—winning out over hydraulicking and vacuuming. Total recovery of the diamonds, which are deposited in a random and unpredictable manner, is essential because the diamonds can be individually valued.

In July 1976, CDM's mining projects division took delivery of a Vactor-700 vacuum unit, which proved able to suction all loose material up to boulders of 150 mm dia during initial tests. It is now being modified to suit

The bedrock cleaning operation is quite thorough, as each diamond found can be individually valued. Sweeping by hand is necessary because machines have difficulty in negotiating the rough bedrock knobs. The sea wall is visible in the background.

local conditions. The Vactor-700 will not eliminate the sweeping gangs, as it cannot handle cemented material or all the unconformities in the bedrock, but it is reducing the manual labor. Its main advantage over previously discarded vacuum units is that it is modern, compact, and truck-mounted for maneuverability. Also under review is a mechanical brush system that could further assist the sweeping gangs.

Dewatering and maintaining the sea wall

The entire beach mining operation depends on the stability of the sea wall. Not only would all machinery be buried if the wall were breached, but the work necessary to reopen the mine face and the loss in revenue would be substantial. Because a theoretical study of the sea wall would be a long and involved process, an empirical approach has been adopted for its dimensions and maintenance.

The base of the sea wall is 20 m below mean sea level, while the top is 11.5 m above mean sea level, giving the wall a total height of 31.5 m (Fig. 3). The wall averages 30 m wide at the top, with a 38° angle of repose on the landward side. Ideally, the inside of the wall would be vertical, and there would be no inflow of water into the mine through the wall. Such conditions would allow bedrock sweeping to be done farther westward of the high-water mark, with recovery of additional diamonds. However, the permeability and natural angle of repose are far from the ideal because the material used for the sea wall is merely beach sand, with a small amount of rounded marine pebbles and boulders. Dewatering the mine for bedrock cleaning is the major mining problem; the dewatering program controls slumping and the angle of repose of the sea wall's inside face.

In dewatering the box-cut, stainless steel wellpoints are used (Fig. 2). Each wellpoint is 6 m long and consists of a 50-mm-dia riser pipe with a 75-mm-long section of reinforced stainless steel continuous mesh at the bottom. The base of each wellpoint has an 80-mm cutting edge with a ball valve. All wellpoints are water-jetted into position. The wellpoint section is attached by a 50-mm thread onto the riser pipes.

The wellpoints are connected by 50-mm flexible hoses to 150-mm suction header pipes and are spaced 0.75 m apart. Pumping is done by 50-hp vacuum pumps, with each pump servicing a bank of 72 wellpoints. Water is pumped into a central sump.

The single line of wellpoints on the inside of the ramp leading out from the sump area (Fig. 2) ensures access to the box-cut and sump area. The ramp is used to remove sweepings from the box-cut and for working on the pumps and wellpoints. Inflow of water from the landward side of the ramp and the bottom edge of the BWE face is a problem that can be solved only by a better understanding of the existing flow nets and greater pumping capacity for additional wellpoints.

The sea wall has 220 m of wellpoint coverage along the wall, plus some wellpoints at right angles to the wall. The total is roughly 1,200 operating wellpoints,

The sea wall, made of ordinary beach sand, demands constant maintenance to keep it in place and to keep operations behind it relatively dry. Wellpoints and pumps continuously dewater the wall, and sand washed away by erosion is regularly replaced.

suctioned by 15 vacuum pumps handling a total seepage of about 4,000 gpm. As the overburden face advances northward, a seal is made against the sea wall to the south using waste overburden sand. As the bedrock cleaning face also advances north, the need for wellpoint protection along the sea wall is progressively eliminated, and 100-m-long sections of wellpoints are withdrawn using a Galion 15-ton crane. After withdrawal, inflow from this area increases and minor slumping toward the sump occurs.

Water from the central sump is pumped by Flygt submersible pumps over the sea wall. At present, two 50-hp pumps are operating, along with four lines of two 25-hp pumps in tandem. To reduce the head on the pumps, the pipes pass through the wall about 5 m below the top of the wall. Positioning the discharge pipes as low as possible would be most efficient, but they must be sufficiently elevated to avoid damage by the high seas. Support of these pipes is a problem. Heavy spring tides break the supports and collapse the pipes onto the sea wall, resulting in discharge directly onto the bottom of the wall and increased erosion. Plans are in progress to pile drive supports into the bedrock on the seaward side.

The eastern portion of the mine face is dry, but halfway along the face toward the sea, the water table is intersected and the gullies must be pumped using 1-hp and 5-hp Flygt pumps before sweeping begins. The water is pumped into a small pipeline feeding a secondary sump at the bottom of the face, then to the central sump by a 25-hp pump.

Overall dewatering of the mine requires numerous continuously operating pumps spread over a relatively large area. Power is supplied by overhead cable at 6.6 kv onto the sea wall, where it is transformed to 550 v. On the wall, caravans house the switchgear for the vacuum and submersible pumps, plus four emergency generator sets in the event of a power failure.

Problems with the dewatering system

The availability of the vacuum pumps, which has been disappointing, is particularly troublesome because failure of a pump in the bottom bank of wellpoints requires immediate replacement. Otherwise, the pressure and volume of seepage water at the wall bottom will cause significant slumping in a few hours. Slumping causes problems of access to the wellpoints and pumps and reduces the sump capacity.

Blinding of wellpoints is another major problem. The No. 4 plant, just south of the mine face, has for years pumped its waste slimes into the sea. The slimes, deposited on the sea bed along the shore, are being encountered now that this area is being mined. Besides blinding wellpoints, the slimes adversely affect the seepage patterns. The wellpoints can draw some water through the slimes layer, but when a pump fails, seepage water collects along the slimes/sand interface and results in large outflows near the base of the wall.

At present, it is not possible to determine how much water is being drawn by each of the wellpoints, but CDM plans to introduce a transparent flexible connector hose from the wellpoints to the 150-mm-dia suction manifold.

In soft sand, removal of wellpoints is easy if they are lifted vertically using a Galion crane standing on gravel.

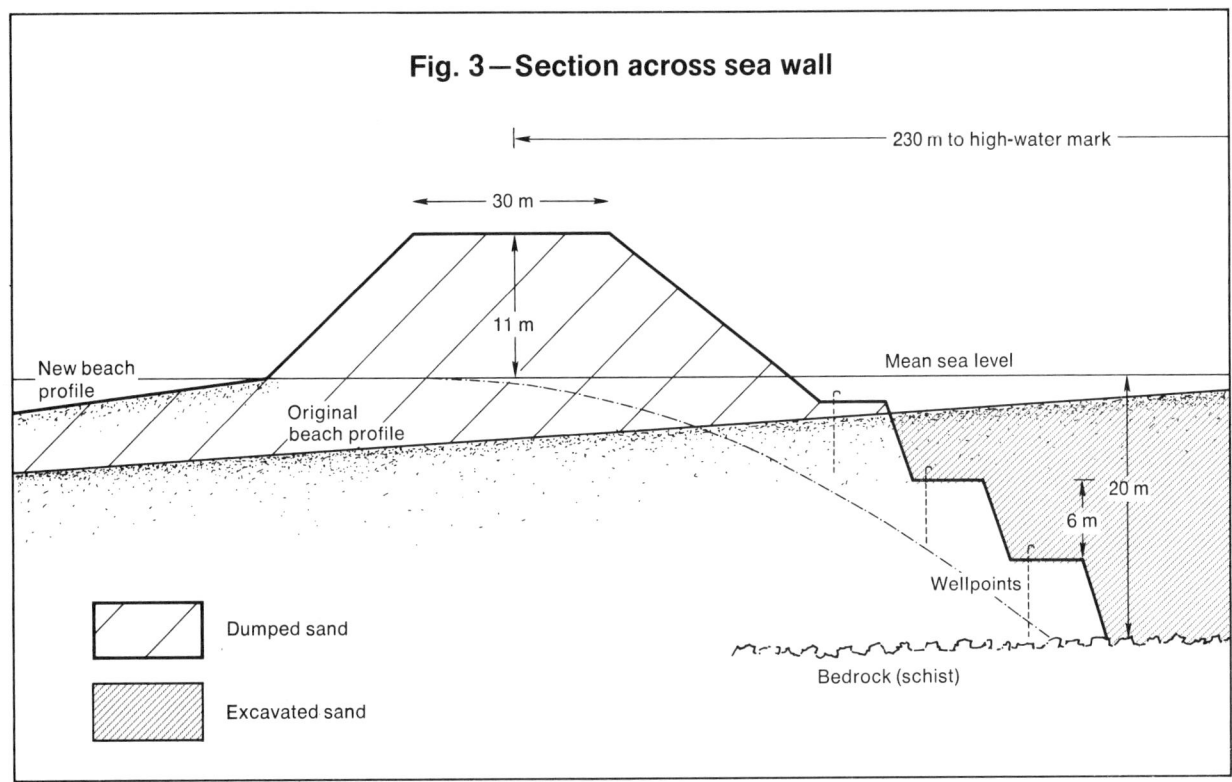

Fig. 3—Section across sea wall

However, associated with the slimes is an iron-silicate material that makes removal of the bottom bank of wellpoints difficult and results in damage to these wellpoints.

Because of the high incidence of vacuum pump breakdown, it is not feasible to wait until the lagging wellpoints are withdrawn before removing a defective pump. Unfortunately, pumps on the middle and top banks are inaccessible under the present system using the Galion crane. Removal would require a large crane operating from the top of the wall, or an access road at the level of the top bank of wellpoints. CDM will try the latter idea by inserting a temporary retaining barrier in the sea wall opposite the top bank of wellpoints.

The other major problem in dewatering is inflow of sand into the mining area. The collection of fine sand at the bottom of the wall and the abundance of water creates a type of "quicksand," especially south of the sump where the wellpoints have been withdrawn. In these areas, electric cables must be supported on top of barrels to prevent burial, and working conditions are difficult. A close watch on the operation is required to prevent burial of submersible pumps in slumped areas.

Coastal research is active

The CDM mine employs two full-time coastal engineers to research the design, stability, construction, and protection of the sea wall. During adverse sea conditions, the wall is subjected to considerable wave attack, which causes extensive erosion, especially on the newly constructed northerly portion of the wall. The sea bed profile opposite this section is generally deeper than the profile opposite a naturally occurring beach or an established part of the sea wall. The width of the surf zone is considerably narrower here, and the toe of the wall is well within the swash zone.

The wave climate at the mine is being measured to determine quantitatively the energy input to the system. Wave parameters are measured by a Waverider buoy and a subsurface current direction sensor. Offshore surveying of the sea bed is done from a ski boat using an echo sounder and conventional surveying techniques. A sled with a 9-m mast is towed through the surf and surveyed to determine the profile under the waves.

CDM envisions the use of groynes (wing dams) to assist construction of the sea wall. Groynes will trap sand ahead of the wall's advance to cause a buildup of the beach and the offshore profile. In a future area of operation, a series of mobile offshore breakwaters may be employed to protect the wall from severe wave attacks and cause a natural accretion of the littoral drift material. Such breakwaters would also eliminate rip currents in the region of the sea wall, which have in the past eroded a 10-m width of wall overnight.

CDM is now sweeping bedrock 190 m seaward of the high-water mark, and the center line of the sea wall is a further 40 m seaward—ample proof that the large scale beach mining concept works. The sea wall will continue to advance out to sea, and CDM plans to sweep bedrock 200 m seaward of the high-water mark in the future.

The efficiency and availability of the BWE are expected to improve as operators and engineering staff become more familiar with the unit. The target is movement of 0.5 million cu m a month using the BWE alone, thereby increasing diamond recovery. □

Kerr-McGee's operations at Trona: upper right—borax and potash complex; lower left—new soda ash plant, with power plant stack at extreme left, carbonators and crystallizers at mid-right, and rotary dryers and bleachers in foreground.

Kerr-McGee expands soda ash output nine-fold from Searles Lake brines

Gerald Parkinson, McGraw-Hill World News

A 1.3-MILLION-TPY SODA ASH PLANT—by far the largest ever built to produce soda ash by direct carbonation of natural brine—is scheduled to be put on stream by Kerr-McGee Chemical Corp. at Trona, Calif., in February 1978. The new plant will boost the company's net production of soda ash to 1.45 million tpy. Currently, Kerr-McGee makes 150,000 tpy at its Westend facility, about 3 mi from Trona. Both operations are located near the shore of Searles Lake, which is the company's source of brine.

A 55,000-tpy soda ash plant now operating at Trona will be shut down, and an adjacent plant that produces 90,000 tpy of soda ash and 260,000 tpy of salt cake is being converted to a 450,000-tpy salt cake operation. Kerr-McGee's new soda ash plant is adjacent to the existing operations at Trona, where triple-effect evaporators concentrate mineral-rich brine for the soda products plant and the main plant cycle, which makes borax and potash products.

The expansion will increase total output of all products at the Trona-Westend complex from 1.45 million tpy to 2.75 million tpy. Salt cake output will go from 480,000 to 650,000 tpy. Total cost of the expansion will be about $200 million.

Kerr-McGee is expanding soda ash production to help fill a supply gap caused by the closure of synthetic soda ash plants, which cannot economically meet new pollution control requirements. Only three synthetic plants are now operating in the US. (See E/MJ, March 1977, pp 141-142.) The new plant will help increase total capacity of natural soda ash plants in the US to 8.8 million tons, up from 7.3 million tons in 1976. Total plant capacity for both natural and synthetic soda ash will reach approximately 10.8 million tons by the end of 1977.

Characteristics of common Searles Lake minerals

Mineral	Composition	Color	Streak	Hardness	Luster	Taste	Specific gravity	Crystal form
Borax	$Na_2B_4O_7 \cdot 10H_2O$	Colorless to white	White	2 —2.5	Vitreous, resinous	Sweetly alkaline	1.715	Monoclinic; prismatic. Some faces striated.
Burkeite	$Na_2(CO_3)(SO_4)_2$	White, yellow, or gray	White	3.5	Vitreous to greasy	—	2.57	Orthorhombic. Commonly as irregular, warty masses.
Gaylussite	$Na_2Ca(CO_3)_2 \cdot 5H_2O$	Colorless, white or gray	White	2.5—3	Vitreous	—	1.99	Monoclinic; prismatic. Often elongated or a flattened wedge shape.
Glaserite	K_2SO_4	Amber, colorless, or white	White	—	Vitreous	—	2.7	Orthorhombic; dipyramidal.
Halite	$NaCl$	Colorless, white	White	2 —2.5	Vitreous	Saline	2.1—2.3	Isometric; cubic or octahedral.
Hanksite	$Na_{22}K(SO_4)_9(CO_3)_2Cl$	Amber, colorless	White	3 —3.5	Vitreous to dull	Saline	2.56	Hexagonal; dipyramidal.
Nahcolite	$NaHCO_3$	Colorless, white	White	2.5	Vitreous	—	2.2	Monoclinic; prismatic.
Northupite	$Na_3MgCl(CO_3)_2$	Colorless, yellow, or gray	White	3.5—4	Vitreous	—	2.4	Isometric; diploidal, octahedral.
Pirssonite	$Na_2Ca(CO_3)_2 \cdot 2H_2O$	Colorless, white	White	3 —3.5	Vitreous	—	2.36	Orthorhombic; rhombic, pyramidal.
Sulfohalite	$Na_6ClF(SO_4)_2$	Colorless, yellow, or gray	White	3.5	Vitreous to greasy	Weakly saline	2.5	Isometric; hexoctagonal.
Thenardite	Na_2SO_4	Colorless, white, or gray	White	2.5—3	Vitreous	Faintly saline	2.7	Orthorhombic; dipyramidal.
Trona	$Na_3H(CO_3)_2 \cdot 2H_2O$	Colorless, white	White	2.5—3	Vitreous, glistening	Alkaline	2.14	Monoclinic; prismatic. Often striated.
Tychite	$Na_6Mg_2(SO_4)(CO_3)_4$	White	White	3.5—4	Vitreous	—	2.6	Isometric; diploidal, octahedral.

About three-quarters of the new plant's production will be shipped through the Port of Long Beach, and three-quarters of the Long Beach shipments will go to eastern markets.

Innovations in processing

Production of soda ash by direct carbonation of brine is a process peculiar to the Searles Lake operations. Spokesmen for Kerr-McGee know of no similar plants elsewhere in the world. Most natural soda ash is produced by mining and milling trona; the area near Green River, Wyo., is the center of such production in the US.

In the direct carbonation process, carbon dioxide is added to brine to form sodium bicarbonate in a mother liquor that contains the remaining brine salts. The solution is cooled, causing sodium bicarbonate to crystallize. The crystals are then filtered out of the mother liquor and dried to drive off CO_2 and water, leaving sodium carbonate (soda ash).

The new plant operates on a much bigger scale than the older facilities and also incorporates a number of processing innovations, which greatly improve the efficiency. It is designed for a throughput of 10,000 gpm of brine. Kerr-McGee spent about $1.5 million to test new ideas in a pilot plant over a period of several years.

"We will produce 1.3 million tons of soda ash in the new plant, compared with 1 million tons of products in the present Trona plant, but with only about 25% of the number of pieces of equipment," says Morgan Locke, manager of western manufacturing operations.

Innovations at the new plant include:

- Carbonation in pressure vessels at about 13.5 psig, instead of the atmospheric pressure used in earlier plants. Pressurization improves carbonation.
- Use of fresh brine to cool and help crystallize sodium bicarbonate.
- Production of processing steam and electricity by a coal-fired, 64-Mw power plant. The present Trona-Westend plants use oil or gas for direct firing and electrical generation. When they were built, oil and gas were cheap and readily available. The power plant, believed to be the first in California to be coal-fired, must meet tough pollution control regulations. Out of the $200 million project cost, about $22 million went for pollution control equipment, and $16 million worth of the equipment is installed at the power plant.

However, a side benefit—and another innovation—is the recovery of carbon dioxide from flue gases, for use in the carbonation process. Recovery from flue gas is more economical than current methods of obtaining CO_2. The

Trona plant now operating buys CO_2 and also injects some flue gas directly into the carbonator, while the Westend plant obtains CO_2 by calcining limestone.

Searles Lake: a 'sandwich' of salt bodies

Brine for the new soda ash plant will be pumped from about 300 ft below the surface of Searles Lake. Drilling has indicated that this is the most favorable depth for obtaining brine with a sodium carbonate content of about 6.5% by weight, which is the basis of the plant design.

Searles Lake is a "dry" lake that consists of layers of massive salt bodies sandwiched between layers of mud. Kerr-McGee is currently working two of the salt bodies: the Upper Structure, which extends from the surface to a depth of 75-90 ft, and the Lower Structure, which extends from about 100 ft to 135 ft. Brine for the soda ash plant will be pumped from the next salt body in the sequence—the Mixed Layer, which extends from 200 ft to depths of more than 700 ft.

The lake surface consists of solid crystals of sodium chloride, with some borates and trona, extending to a depth of about 15 ft. The rest of the salt deposits are a mixture of solids and brine. The brine, which has a mineral content of roughly 35% by weight, percolates to the lake surface in places. Sodium chloride makes up about 16% of the brine, or just under half of the mineral content. Other common minerals in the lake include borax, burkeite (sodium sulphate and sodium carbonate), hanksite (sodium sulphate, sodium carbonate, and potassium chloride), glaserite, and trona.

Kerr-McGee owns about 4,500 acres at Searles Lake and leases about 15,000 acres from the US government. The entire Searles Lake deposit covers roughly 35-40 sq mi, and the company estimates that mineralization averages about 50 million tons per sq mi.

Pumping brine from wells

Mining is done by drilling a well and cementing a casing into the drillhole. Brine rises in the casing and is pumped out by shallow-well pumps. At the Trona complex, about 150 wells are in operation, and the brine from various wells is blended to provide the desired feed for each plant. Each group of wells is serviced by a pipeline gathering system. The liquid in the lake is replenished by recycling end liquors from the plants.

Kerr-McGee now operates about 1,000 acres of solar ponds to increase the concentration of certain brine components that have become diluted over the years. Sodium chloride and small amounts of other salts are precipitated in these ponds. The zone that will provide feed for the new soda ash plant contains extensive beds of nearly pure trona, filled with high-carbonate brines. These beds will be mined by injecting end liquor and water into the structure to dissolve the trona, creating a flow through the porous beds to the pumping wells. Deep-well pumps will deliver the solution to the brine line without need for evaporation.

About 30 10-in.-dia, high capacity wells will serve the plant. Peabody Floway deep-well turbine pumps of 400-gpm capacity will deliver brine to a 300-acre/ft collecting pond. From there, the feed will be pumped about 5 mi to the plant through a 24-in.-dia pipeline. Brine, pumped at 150 psi, will be received at the plant in a 1-million-gal storage tank. Brine temperature is about 80°F at the wellhead.

Carbonation and crystallization

After passing through heat exchangers, carbonation of brine will begin in an 80-ft-high precarbonation tower. Brine fed into the top of the tower will flow down over polyethylene saddles that fill about half the structure, increasing the surface area of the brine for better reaction with CO_2. The gas, pumped in from the bottom, will have been diluted by use in carbonation of previous charges of brine feed, but it will partially carbonate the fresh feed.

The carbonation section is equipped with three primary carbonators in parallel and a secondary carbonator. Each vessel is about 35 ft in diameter and 40 ft high and has an operating capacity of about 250,000 gal, or 80% of total volume.

Since CO_2 forms a corrosive mixture when combined with the brine, the interiors of all vessels are lined with glass-reinforced polyester, and pipes are made of reinforced plastic, stainless steel, or rubber-lined steel.

Carbonation with CO_2 gas will convert the sodium carbonate in the brine to sodium bicarbonate. Most of the gas will be supplied by recovery and recycle of CO_2 from the decomposition of sodium bicarbonate. Additional makeup CO_2, essentially pure, will be recovered from boiler flue gas by monoethanolamine extraction and supplied to the carbonation system. The sodium bicarbonate will be crystallized from the carbonated brine under controlled conditions to optimize the recovery of soda ash.

Processing starts in precarbonation tower, and brine then flows into four 35-ft-dia carbonation vessels (left). Soda ash product is stored underground, beneath A-frame.

"We have three distinct trains, with two units operating in parallel on each train," says Leonard A. Harris, who is responsible for manufacturing liaison for the new plant. "We will be able to shut down any one of them for maintenance and continue production on the other trains."

Water vapor and CO_2 will be removed from the sodium bicarbonate filter cake in steam-heated dryers. Water vapor will be condensed from the exhaust gases from the dryers, and CO_2 will be recycled to the brine carbonators.

The impure sodium carbonate (light ash) will go by bucket elevators from the three dryers to 150-ton-capacity surge bins, which will provide in-process storage. Each bin will feed a gas- or oil-fired rotary bleacher, operating at 850°F to burn off discoloring materials. The bleaching agent will be sodium nitrate.

Other impurities, such as sodium chloride and sodium sulphate, will be removed after the material has been recrystallized in a sodium carbonate monohydrate crystallizer. In this process, the light soda ash will be formed into larger, denser crystals.

A two-stage Bird centrifuge will take out all but 5% of the free moisture, and the remaining free and combined moisture will then be removed in a 450-psig rotary steam tube dryer. The crystals will be screened at 16 mesh. Lumps will be diverted to a roller mill for crushing. The final product will be anhydrous sodium carbonate with a density of about 62 lb per cu ft, compared with 40 lb per cu ft for the light ash prior to crystallizing. About 95% will be greater than 100 mesh.

Stansteel Corp. of Los Angeles, a subsidiary of Allis-Chalmers Corp., supplied 18 rotary dryers for the plant. The heaviest units are the six bicarbonate steam tube dryers, each of which weighs 325 tons and measures 12 ft in diameter by 100 ft long. These are the biggest steam tube dryers Stansteel has made to date. Stansteel also supplied the bleachers and monohydrate dryers. The bleachers are 13.5 ft in diameter and 100 ft long.

Underground storage for rail shipment

Kerr-McGee will store soda ash in a V-shaped, concrete-lined underground chamber that has an aboveground A-frame cover of corrugated steel. This method of storage is less expensive than conventional steel tanks, says Harris. The 10,000-ton-capacity warehouse will be slightly pressurized to keep out moisture.

A conveyor belt located in a tunnel under the warehouse will carry the product up a closed ramp to a 125-ton loadout bin atop a 120-ft tower. Six slide-gate valves and vibrating feeders will drop material through the warehouse floor onto the conveyor automatically, controlled by level-indicating instrumentation in the loadout bin. The bin will supply a shuttle conveyor that can feed two railcars at one spotting. The facility is designed for possible future conversion to unit train loading. Pullman-Torkelson Co., of Salt Lake City, designed and built the storage and loadout systems.

Ralph M. Parsons Co. is prime contractor for the rest of the project, including the power plant, which will use two 32-Mw General Electric single automatic extraction, noncondensing steam turbines. Steam for the turbines will be generated by two 600,000-lb-per-hr, 1,500-psig coal-fired boilers made by Combustion Engineering Inc. The tangential-fired boilers will use overfire air to maintain a lower flame temperature and thereby meet NO_x emission standards. Coal will come from New Mexico.

Electricity is, in fact, a coproduct with process steam. About 85-90% of the heat generated will be used for the process and only 10-15% for electricity. The power plant will supply 60 Mw to meet the electricity needs of both the soda ash plant and the existing Trona plant and will also provide some steam for the latter. Process steam will be extracted from the turbines at 450 psig. The 40-psig exhaust steam will be used mainly for the evaporators in the Trona main plant cycle.

Tight control of air pollution

Searles Lake is near the northern boundary of San Bernardino County, which makes it subject to the tough air pollution regulations of the South Coast Air Management Control District. Each boiler may release no more than 10 lb per hr of particulates, 200 lb per hr of sulphur as SO_2, or 140 lb per hr of NO_x.

Each boiler is equipped with an electrostatic precipitator rated at 98.5% efficiency and a sodium carbonate flue gas scrubber rated at 95%. The precipitators, made by Pollution Control Walther (now a division of Combustion Engineering), operate on the cold side of the

In building the coal-fired power plant, which will recover CO_2 from flue gases, $16 million was spent for pollution control.

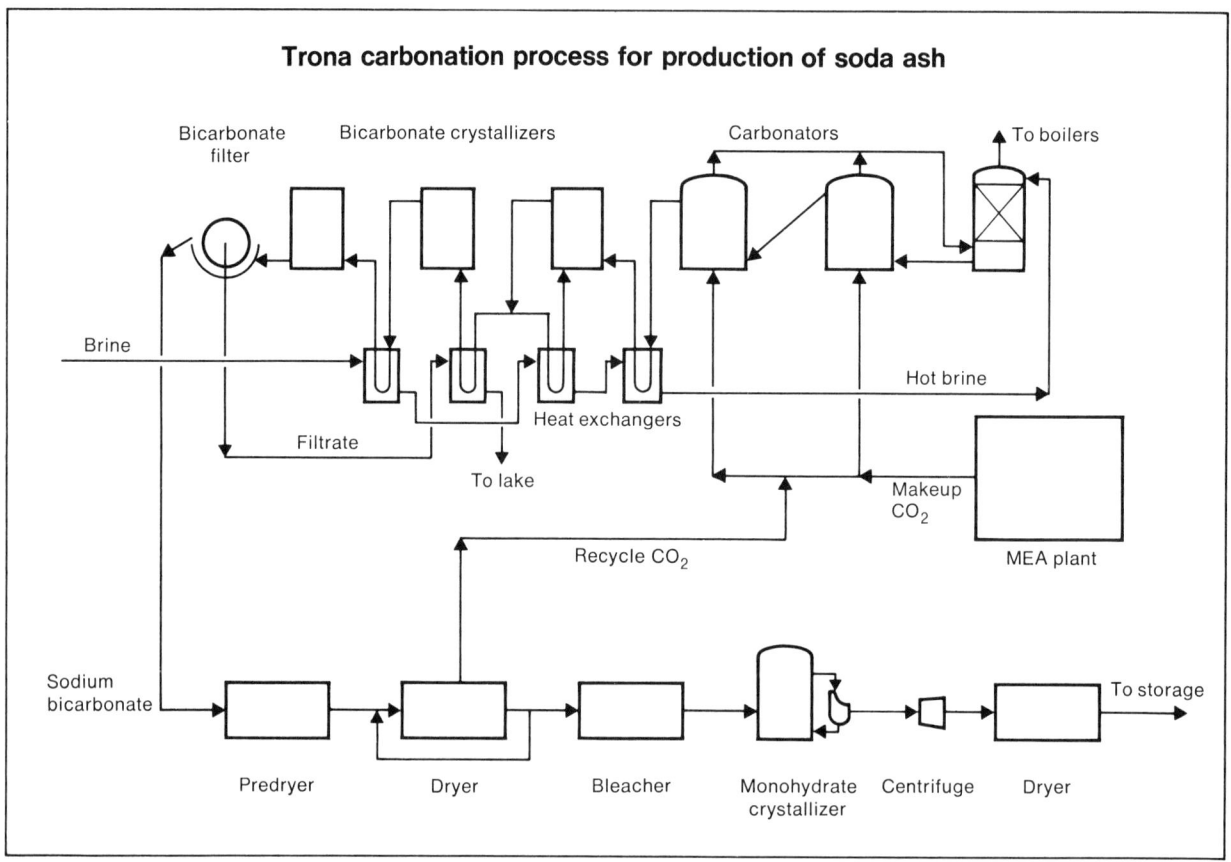

Trona carbonation process for production of soda ash

boiler air preheaters. Hot side precipitators could not guarantee compliance with pollution regulations, says Donald K. Higgins, chief of power/utilities liaison.

However, the 300°F temperature of the cold side makes it difficult to collect fly ash. The western coal that will be used has a sulphur content of only 0.7%, and particle ionization at 300°F will be insufficient for efficient collection of fly ash by the precipitators. Kerr-McGee will mix petroleum coke with the coal to raise the sulphur content to 1.5% and improve particle ionization and fly ash collection.

The two flue gas scrubbers, supplied by Combustion Equipment Associates of New York, will use end liquor from the soda ash plant to extract SO_2. The scrubbers are designed to operate in the sulphite/sulphate range. The scrubber liquor will be returned to the lake with the rest of the plant end liquor. Scrubbed flue gases will be processed through two monoethanolamine (MEA) plants for extraction of CO_2. Each plant will produce 300 tpd of CO_2—the main source of makeup CO_2 in the closed-cycle system. Liquid CO_2 will be stored for plant startup and for use in emergencies or for speeding up carbonation of a completely fresh brine charge.

Water conservation is an important feature of the entire Kerr-McGee operation. The Trona main plant cycle is a net producer of fresh water from brine, through its triple-effect evaporators. The water produced will be fed to the power plant boilers along with condensate from the dryers. Steam condensate is returned to the process in the closed-cycle system.

New sources have increased Kerr-McGee's total supply of brackish water to 10,000 gpm, of which 8,000 gpm will be used. The new plant will need only about 2,400 gpm for wash and cooling water (no makeup will normally be required for boiler feed water), plus about 546 gpm of fresh water for processing and pollution control. The monohydrate crystallizer is the biggest single user of fresh water.

"For the size of the plant, we probably make as much reuse of water as any major chemical plant in the world," says Lloyd Bailey, who will manage the new facility.

Two Foxboro Fox 210 data loggers—one for the process and one for the utility systems—will monitor about 700 points in each system. All controls are Foxboro Spec 200 electronic equipment. All plant motors will be operated from the control room via two-wire control systems.

The bulk of soda ash production will be shipped by rail to Long Beach, 200 mi away, where Kerr-McGee is building a dockside storage and shipping facility. The facility will have two 50,000-ton and three 15,000-ton silos. The Port of Long Beach will build a traveling shiploader for soda ash and other products and may add more silos in the future.

The converted 450,000-tpy salt cake (sodium sulphate) plant at the Trona facilities will use a new process to recover glauber salt from brine. A glauber crystallizer system will be added, but the existing filters and dryers will continue to be used. Parsons is also prime contractor for the salt cake plant, which is scheduled to go on stream about November 1978. □

Brines are source for iodine, bromine, and other minerals

US PRODUCTION OF BROMINE is believed adequate to meet projected domestic needs at least through the year 2000, but iodine demand greatly exceeds production. More than 90% of US iodine supply is imported, most of it from Japan. The US iodine supply-demand balance could be reversed if economic means were available to extract iodine from domestic oil well brines—which contain enough iodine as waste to supply double the world demand. Treatment of these brines to recover both iodine and other values, such as bromine, would produce a strategically valuable resource and at the same time alleviate disposal problems in petroleum production.

Some oil field brines in Oklahoma having high iodine levels (300-500 ppm) are now being developed as sources of iodine, but most oil well brines are too low in iodine content for economic recovery.

In one Oklahoma joint venture, Amoco will be responsible for field development and Houston Chemical Co. for operation and marketing at a plant scheduled for startup in second-half 1976. The plant will operate in a closed loop system, with the only two effluents being iodine and spent brine to be reinjected into the field to push fresh brine toward the producing wells. This approach will minimize air pollution in processing oil well brines.

Another Oklahoma venture, by Ethyl Corp., is not as advanced as the Amoco-Houston Chemical project.

The Oklahoma oil field brines contain even greater quantities of bromine than iodine, but the lower price of bromine—about one-half that of iodine—and the cost of added plant facilities for a dual process make dual recovery uneconomical at this time. Moreover, the oil well brines have only one-tenth the bromine content of natural brines in Arkansas.

Both Oklahoma ventures expect to use a standard oxidation-blow out procedure in which sulphuric acid, chlorine, and sodium nitrate are mixed with the brine.

Total Oklahoma iodine production is expected to be about 2 million lb per year, approximately one-third of US demand. Too great a domestic production of iodine could prompt the Japanese to lower their prices so that recovery from US oil well brines would no longer be economic. (Japanese production has leveled off recently because of problems with pollution and subsidence, but renewed growth is anticipated.) Recovery of iodine from brackish waters in Indonesia could also alter world supply.

US bromine supply in 1973 came from 10 plants in three states—Arkansas, Michigan, and California. Arkansas continues to be the leading supplier and is increasing its share of US production.

In California, bromine is extracted from Searles Lake brines, while in Arkansas and Michigan, bromine is separated from well brines. Bromine is usually separated from brines by using chlorine to oxidize bromide to bromine, removing the bromine with steam, and then, after condensation, separating the water and the bromine.

Searles Lake brines are also treated industrially to recover soda ash, salt cake, and borax. Tungsten is present in these brines in low concentrations but is not extracted commercially. The US Bureau of Mines has developed several ion-exchange resins that extract tungsten, but commercially available resins have proven ineffective. In laboratory testing, tungsten and coextracted boron are eluted from the resin with water for subsequent separation and recovery. Because process development is in its infancy, commercialization depends on continuing research and development. □

Petrosix: a Brazilian answer to oil shale technology

OIL-PINCHED BRAZIL is now in a decision-making period that could lead to the first commercial scale oil shale project in the Western Hemisphere. The recovery of petroleum products and other derivatives from widely occurring oil shale formations of Brazil has been studied since the late 1880s.

More recently, research and development efforts have focused on a 2,200-mtpd prototype mine and processing plant. Petrosix,* a unit of Brazil's state-controlled oil company, Petrobras,** staged a series of production runs in the prototype plant starting in 1972. These individual processing campaigns were shaped to determine design criteria, engineering parameters, operating conditions, and capital and operating costs for a venture based on the Irati shales of Parana State.

The prototype mine and plant, located at Sao Mateus do Sul, about 70 km southwest of Curitiba, has shown a consistent yield of 1,000 bbl of oil, 36,500 cu m of light gas (900 Btu per cu m), 17 mt of sulphur, and a theoretical 75 bbl of LPG from every 2,000 mt of shale. The kerogen content of the shale averaged 7.4% by weight. Petrosix finished its last production run on schedule in May 1975—an 82-day continuous performance at a test mine and plant that could qualify for an award in industrial design.

The prototype program has now arrived at the moment of truth. Engineering estimates have been prepared for a commercial scale 112,000-mtpd oil shale strip mine and retorting complex with an anticipated yield of 52,000 bbl of oil per day plus associated byproducts.

It is unlikely that Petrobras will reach a decision on the commercial plant until January 1976, but it is obvious the Petrosix group is doing its homework very well. In contrast to test plants in the US, which end with recovery of shale oil, a complete byproduct system (with the single exception of LPG recovery) was prototyped in a continuous circuit at the Sao Mateus do Sul module. The technical integrity of the process has been demonstrated, according to Petrosix personnel, and the financial and strategic aspects of a proposed full size plant are now undergoing review.

The prototype centers on a top-fed, 18-ft-dia vertical retort capable of contacting a moving bed of oil shale with externally heated recycle gas. Petrosix engineers say this technique avoids troublesome clinkering problems from a direct-fired combustion gas. The system is also harmonious with Brazilian national objectives because it promotes recovery of sorely needed byproducts.

Back in 1968, the cost of a commercial plant was estimated at about $240 million. Today, a more realistic estimate of the system, which would include a 560-km gas transmission line to Sao Paulo, is $500 million to $600 million. The tentative Petrosix estimate of 1968 was distributed: 31.2% for mining, 7.9% for solids handling, 38.8% for retorting, 11.7% for gas treating and sulphur recovery, and 10.4% for the gas transmission line. This split of costs has not changed much since 1968.

If Petrobras decides to proceed, Brazil will witness the development of its largest strip mine in a system designed for near-instantaneous reclamation. Spent shale will be hauled back to the mine for deposit between spoil piles built by an excavator fleet of large draglines that could include a pair of 105-cu-yd machines, two 60-cu-yd units, and two smaller 20-cu-yd excavators. Some of the overburden and all the shale beds must be blasted and loaded

---

*Petrosix is derived from SIX, an acronym for Superintendencia do Industrializacao do Xisto (a unit of Petrobras established to study oil shale recovery).
**Petrobras is an acronym for Petroleo Brasileiros SA.

Occurrences of oil shale in Brazil

1. Devonian Oil Shale of Para-Amazonas
   Outcrops: Banks of Amazon, Xingu, Tapajos, Trombeta, Curua, Paramari, and Urubu Rivers
2. Cretaceous Oil Shale of Maranhao
   Outcrops: Codo - Barra Da Corda - Serra da Desordem
3. Cretaceous Oil Shale of Ceara
   Outcrops: Crato
4. Cretaceous Oil Shale of Alagoas
   Outcrops: Riacho Doce - Caramagibe - Bica da Serra
5. Cretaceous Oil Shale of Bahia
   Outcrops: Marau
6. Tertiary Oil Shale of Sao Paulo
   Outcrops: Paraiba Valley
7. Oil Shale of Amapa
8. Permian Oil Shale of Irati Formation

Test oil shale strip mine made use of a 6-cu-yd dragline for stripping and power shovel loading of shale in rear-dump trucks.

by shovels. It is anticipated that large haulers will be used to deliver mine output to the plant and return retorted shale to the mine.

The plant will contain a battery of 16 or more scaled-up retorts, each with a complete set of equipment componentry for oil collection, gas recirculation, and external heating arrangements for recycle gas. All the necessary byproduct recovery systems would be positioned in the complex, including conventional recovery of LPG.

Is Brazil ready for Petrosix?

The development of the Petrosix process to the threshold of a commercial system comes at an auspicious time—a time when the exploitation of Brazil's large oil shale resources has become very important to the nation's fuel supply.

More than 80% of the country's 1974 petroleum requirements was supplied through imports, and these needs are expected to grow at about 8% per year. Paradoxically, Brazil has what may be the world's second-largest resources of pyrobituminous oil shale. The development of these resources could substantially lessen the nation's dependence on foreign sources for liquid and gas fuels, and could add to critically short sulphur supplies. Brazil's sulphur production is only a tiny fraction of current demand. This shortfall has to hurt in an economy heavily oriented to agriculture.

The oil shale process was conceived and developed by the engineers of Petrosix. At an early stage, Chicago-based Paul Weir Co. participated in a mining study, and the Denver consulting firm Cameron Engineers Inc. had a contract for a portion of the prototype plant, which terminated in 1972. Since then, Petrosix officials say the process has been modified and remodified several times in seeking Brazilian solutions to problems.

The Irati formation—Petrosix's target

Brazil's oil shales are found in many basins and are of differing age groups. The Petrosix project is sited in the Permian-age Irati formation, which extends from Sao Paulo State to the Uruguay border. Although the Irati beds generally have great lateral continuity, the oil shale does not remain at the same stratigraphic position within the formation from Rio Grande do Sul to Sao Paulo State. In southern Parana and Rio Grande do Sul, the Irati generally contains two distinct beds of oil shale separated by beds of shale and limestone. In Santa Catarina, Sao Paulo, and northern Parana, the oil shale beds are erratically distributed in a section of limestone and dolomite.

The target shales are dark brown and dark gray to black,

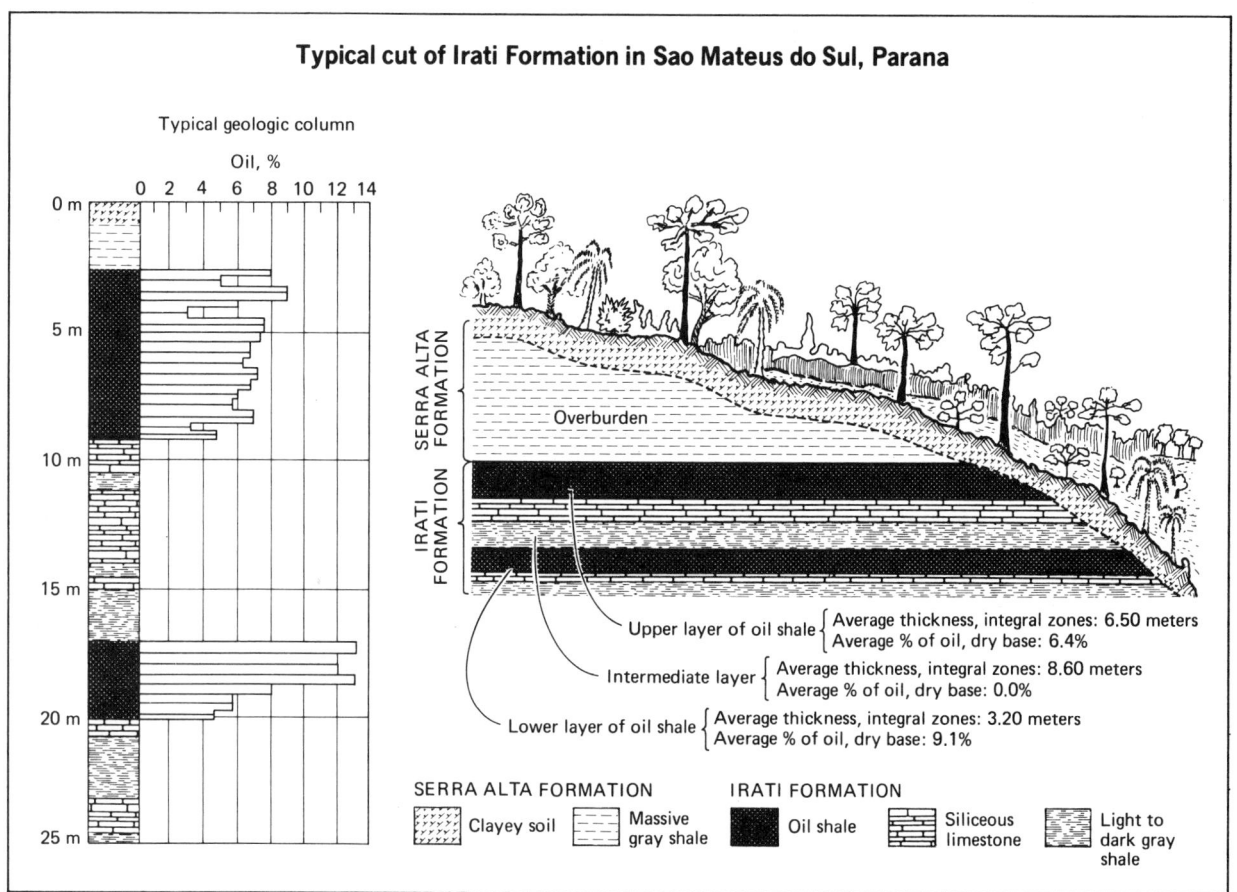

very fine grained, finely laminated and fissile. The kerogen content ranges from 2% to 14%. The density of the oil shale beds varies from 1.80 to 2.45, generally decreasing with an increasing oil content.

After reconnaissance and 400-m and 800-m grid drilling, three mining sites have been established—two in Rio Grande do Sul and one in Parana at Sao Mateus do Sul. The latter site is the one where initial commercial mining would take place. Here, the lower and upper oil shale beds average about 3.2 and 6.5 m in thickness, respectively. The average oil content is about 9.1% in the lower bed and 6.4% in the upper layer. The combined average is 7.4% oil content. Between the two beds is an 8.6-m zone of limestone and shale, barren of kerogen. Both oil shale beds are to be developed under the mining plan.

The Sao Mateus do Sul site covers a northwesterly-striking outcrop zone in a 20 x 4-m band. Company officials say the zone is well defined and that reserves are economically recoverable. The normal dip of beds in this area is about 1.5% to the southwest under a topography of rolling hills and gentle slopes. The 4-km width of the proposed mining zone is a directly related function of the downdip 30-m depth of overburden, which established the practical mining limits.

The reserves at this location are 600 million bbl of oil, 10 million mt of sulphur, 4.5 million mt of LPG, and 22 billion cu m of light combustible gas.

A need for coarse feed

Mining will be complicated to some extent by the need to mine two separate horizons while dealing with an intervening band of waste. The only other potential problem is the possibility of soft floors and equipment-bearing surfaces during heavy rains. The test mine was equipped with a 6-cu-yd dragline having a 50-m boom, three 1¼-cu-yd shovels, and 12 rear-dump haulers. Supporting this fleet were appropriate drills, bulldozers, front-end loaders, and graders.

The ore is crushed in two stages, with a single covered surge pile behind the primary and a pair of covered surge piles downstream from the secondary crushing and screening plant. Because the retort is a vertical gravity flow vessel, fines are not acceptable feed. Petrosix has successfully briquetted crusher plant undersize into approximately 1-in.-dia nodules for reentry to the retort feed stream.

Scrapers strip combined cinnabar-corderoite ore from McDermitt open pit with the aid of Cat dozers. The ore zone encompasses an area of about 135 acres. Design and development of the project was handled by Placer Amex, of San Francisco.

New McDermitt mine joint venture emerges as dominant force in US mercury production

Robert Sisselman, Associate editor

THE ONLY MAJOR MERCURY MINE in the US is newly on stream and tuning up to achieve a designed annual throughput of 20,000 flasks of prime virgin metal by the end of 1975. Production from the McDermitt mine in Humboldt County, Nev., should be ample to supply just under 50% of primary metal requirements of the US, which in 1974 imported 45,000 flasks and produced only 1,200. What's more, from open-pit mining through furnacing, production will comply with strict environmental and health guidelines established by state and Federal agencies.

McDermitt mine is located 11 mi southwest of the town of the same name and only a short distance from the Oregon-Nevada state line. The $9.7 million fully integrated facility is a joint venture of the US subsidiary of Canada's Placer Development Ltd.—Placer Amex Inc. (51%), and Sterling Mineral Venture (a joint venture of New Jersey Limited Partnerships). Placer will act as managing partner for the project.

Construction at McDermitt began in April 1974, with official dedication of the complex in June 1975. The mine is only half a mile from the former Cordero underground mercury mine, which began producing metal from cinnabar ore in 1941 and was among the nation's leading producers until its closure in 1970. There are but four or five remaining mercury producers in the US, all small and all producing prime virgin metal.

'Hot spots' not uncommon in lake bed ore

McDermitt's orebody contains an estimated 3 million tons of combined cinnabar and corderoite ore averaging 10 lb of mercury per ton. Based on current production plans, mine life will be 20 years. Although average grade is 10 lb mercury per ton (0.5%), grades mined in any one day may range up to 20 or 30 lb per ton. According to one mine spokesman, local "hot spots" are not uncommon in this type of mercury occurrence.

Mineralization occurs as very fine particle sizes thinly layered within montmorillonite clay lake beds, as discrete crystalline particles, and as a "smear" on the clay. The ore minerals, cinnabar (HgS) and corderoite ($Hg_3S_2Cl_2$), occur free, but require physical separation from the clay.

Corderoite was discovered on the project site by Placer

Amex geologists and identified at Stanford University by Dr. Eugene Foord with Dr. Pieter Berendson in 1973. The mineral, characterized by photosensitivity that turns it black in sunlight, was found adjacent to the Cordero holding, and Foord set about the laborious task of establishing its characteristics. The new mineral was subsequently named after the Cordero mine and approved by the International Mineralogical Association. Corderoite is essentially a chloride of cinnabar and had been synthesized in the laboratory, but this was the first time the mineral was found in nature.

The McDermitt orebody occurs in Miocene-age tuffaceous lake sediments within 200 ft of the surface and extends over an irregular area 2,200 ft x 2,500 ft. Because of its mode of deposition—occurring parallel to bedding in volcanic tuffs deposited in an aqueous environment—the ore is relatively flat lying. It does, however, dip slightly northward, increasing in depth as it follows the slope of the desert floor—but at a slightly steeper angle. Thickness averages about 20 ft but is extremely variable, depending on the source and location of penetrating solutions.

The deposit has been interpreted as cinnabar deposition in a tuffaceous lakebed environment. The mercury minerals are assumed to have entered the orebody as hot aqueous solutions—perhaps as hot springs deposits—although there are varying schools of thought on their genesis.

The question of how the corderoite was formed has engendered some debate: Is it a supergene alteration product of cinnabar formed by acidic chlorine-rich solutions, or is it a primary mineral that was deposited with the cinnabar? The latter theory appears questionable at this point.

The clay lake beds contain, and are underlain by, a good deal of colloidal, siliceous bedded material that has segregated and precipitated in the form of siliceous rock. This rock is of two varieties: one is referred to in non-technical terms as "opalite"; the other is chalcedony. The opalite, which occurs beneath the lake beds, is very dense and tough and is a good grinding media for the autogenous mill. However, the chalcedony, occurring as layers interstratified with the lake beds, is brittle, breaking down rapidly into sand.

Remoteness of mine leads to four-day work week

McDermitt ore, at 70% cinnabar and 30% corderoite, is being open-pit mined using scrapers and bulldozers for both stripping and mining. Ore is mined at a ratio of 1 ton ore to 4.7 tons waste. The eight-man mine workforce is on a four-day, 10-hr-per-day work week by mutual agreement. A. M. Laird, McDermitt's manager, explained, "We're so far away from a major city here that an employee is forced to take off a whole day just to go to the bank, to see a doctor, or to visit a government representative."

Mining will go through several stages over the life of the mine, with plans calling for removal of the highest-grade center portion of the orebody first. In the initial stage, waste has already been stripped down to ore.

Stripping at McDermitt is related to both ore production requirements and material requirements for the construction of the mine's four tailings dams. Since the tailings dams require clay and gravel in specified quantities, mining must move from one stripping area to another to achieve the proper ratios.

Mining at the rate of 3,000 tpd uses three Cat 631-C 30-yd scrapers pushed by one continuously operating Cat D8H dozer. McDermitt maintains two such dozers. The D8H also rips ahead of scrapers when required. Very

Overall pit equipment availability is about 95% at McDermitt.

rocky areas are broken with the D8H or by light blasting. Rocky material is then loaded with a 4-yd Cat 966 front-end loader into an 18-ton Mack hauler. Cycle time for waste is 15 min, for ore 7 min.

Drilling is currently minimal, owing to the nature of the ore. Management, however, is considering the use of drilling equipment to produce opalite feed for grinding media in the autogenous circuit. Some of this material has been blasted as encountered in the orebody—using a combination of ammonium nitrate and dynamite. The chalcedony inclusions, however, range in size from 2 in. to the size of a house. Opalite beds underlie the clay deposit. Until recently, most of the blasting has been done on the chalcedony inclusions in the clay ore zone.

Ore is hauled ¼ mi on the main 60-ft-wide haulage road to the mill stockpile, 1,000 to 2,000 tons in capacity. Waste is hauled 1.4 mi, 3% down grade, to the tailings ponds.

Maintenance of pit equipment is performed in a service building equipped with four bays, each 25 ft wide. The fourth bay is reserved for machine shop duties. In the rear of the building are a parts warehouse and an electrical repair shop.

Three Cat 30-yd scrapers operate in McDermitt's mine fleet.

Nevada barite output up sharply in '70s

Lane White, Managing editor

NEVADA BARITE MINES, most of which extract ore by surface mining of highly convoluted orebodies in hilly to mountainous terrain, have increased their production rapidly since 1971, when 192,000 tons were produced. Production in 1976 totaled 716,000 tons, somewhat lower than the peak of 761,000 tons attained in 1974. The number of mines in operation has risen from five in the early 1970s to about 15.

Most Nevada barite is marketed for use as a weighting agent in drilling mud and must meet a specific gravity specification of 4.2 or higher. Natural barite ($BaSO_4$) has a specific gravity of 4.5. Some ores meet the 4.2 spec as mined and require only grinding prior to shipment. Lower grade material is beneficiated by jigging, tabling, or flotation; however, the process of concentrating barite ore often begins at the mine face, where bulldozers may be used to sort high grade materials from waste. An experienced and knowledgeable bulldozer operator on this assignment can make an important contribution to economic mine and plant operation.

Many of the Nevada barite mines are located near the town of Battle Mountain, in the north-central portion of the state, and the deposits on which they are based have, in most cases, been known for years to local prospectors, promoters, and producers. However, most deposits are located far from the railroads that move finished product to market, and costs of transportation for the low priced commodity ruled out earlier production. In a paper, "The Nevada Barite Industry Today," presented at the February 1976 annual meeting of AIME, K. E. Laughery of NL Industries' Baroid Petroleum Services Div. credited local prospectors and producers for their perseverance and willingness to gamble in bringing new Nevada barite mines into production. Producing companies now active in the state include All Minerals Corp., Baroid Petroleum Services, Chromalloy American, Dresser Minerals, Eisenman Chemical Co., FMC Corp., IMCO Services, Milchem Inc., Milwhite Co., Tom Norris Inc., Old Soldier Mining Co., and Rocky Mountain Refractories-Zane Hunt Mining.

Nevada barite deposits are located on a 50- to 70-mi-wide belt trending north-northeast on the Antler orogenic belt in the central part of the state. In the northern Shoshone Range and elsewhere, bedded barite is nearly always associated closely with igneous dikes of varying composition. In an unpublished thesis, Milchem senior geologist A. Wallace Mitchell notes that the fractures occupied by the dikes are related to regional tectonic features and appear to be very significant in the localization of the bedded barite occurrences.

The barite usually forms in lens-shaped bodies, with thicknesses up to or greater than 100 ft and lengths and widths ranging up to several hundred feet. A series of lenses may occur along a strike of several hundred feet.

The geologic origin of the Nevada barite deposits is not firmly established; some features point to a sedimentary origin, while others indicate a hydrothermal origin. Sedimentary origin is indicated by apparently strata-bound features in which crosscutting relationships between barite and the host rock cannot be demonstrated. However, Wallace feels that structural and igneous relations argue more strongly for hydrothermal origin. Also, the time span of formations containing bedded barite ranges from Cambrian to Devonian—a considerable span for a specialized sedimentary environment.

Barite mine operators use a variety of equipment, including rotary and pneumatic drills, scrapers and dozers for overburden removal, front-end loaders and an occasional small power shovel, and rear-dump trucks. If ore is to be moved any distance, it is usually hauled in 35- to 40-ton-capacity belly-dump haulers.

Argenta mine feeds Milchem jig plant

Milchem Inc. is benching into a mountainside at an elevation of about 6,000 ft, 15 mi east of Battle Mountain, to supply feed to its jigging and grinding plant about four road miles to the north, at an elevation of 4,550 ft. The company became active in the Battle Mountain barite district in the early 1960s and started up its Bateman plant in 1968. The Argenta mine and plant now in operation started up in 1974. The mine property had been worked previously by small operators using a heavy media plant to upgrade the ore.

The Argenta ores occur in folded and contorted pods or lenses in the Devonian Slaven Chert, with generally dark gray to black barite in beds that usually range up to 1 ft thick, while interbedded chert ranges from 1 to 4 in.

At Milchem's Argenta mine near Battle Mountain, a front-end loader removes waste. Scrapers are also in common use for removal of overburden at Nevada barite mines.

thick. Overall ore thickness may exceed 100 ft but is very erratic.

Milchem currently operates at waste-to-ore ratios of up to 3:1, according to Richard L. Reyburn, manager of the company's Nevada operations. Two Terex 24-cu-yd capacity S24 scrapers and two Cat D8 dozers are used in the stripping operation. Gardner-Denver Airtracs are used to drill 4-in.-dia holes for blasting with ANFO. A dozer sorts ore and waste at the bench face, which is 20 ft high, and two Terex front-end loaders—a 5-yd 7271 and a 3½-yd 7251—load ore into bottom-dump ore haulers that are operated by a contract trucker. Milchem has two 40-ton-capacity Mack trucks on the property for waste removal.

The mine produced about 350,000 tpy of feed for the Argenta plant in 1976, with about 50% recovered as product.

A truck-mounted Ingersoll-Rand rotary drill equipped with Baker down-the-hole tools is used for establishing reserves, with 5½-in.-dia holes usually sunk as deep as 250 ft and occasionally to 500 ft.

At the Milchem plant, run-of-mine ore is reduced to minus ¾ in. through two stages of crushing, using a 24 x 36-in. jaw crusher and a cone crusher. Crushed ore advances to the jig plant, which is equipped with four three-cell Bendelari jigs. Jig product advances to two Eagle Iron Works spiral classifiers that produce a minus ¾-in., plus 100-mesh product for grinding through a Raymond mill. Jig overflow is screened at plus 14 mesh, with oversize moved to a cherts tailings pile. Undersize is cycloned with a cut at 100 mesh. This material reports to the spiral classifiers. Classifier tails are pumped to a tailings pond, and the pond water is recycled.

Baroid floats low grade Rossi ores

The Rossi mine of NL Industries' Baroid Petroleum Services Div. is operated under contract by Tom Norris, who hauls ore 30 mi over a private road to Baroid's flotation and grinding plant at Dunphy, about 25 mi east of Battle Mountain. Baroid now obtains the bulk of its ore from two low grade pits at the isolated Rossi site, but some stringers of high grade are still found in pits that were first mined as early as 1947. Baroid acquired the property in 1947 and started up the flotation plant in 1963. Hard winters limit mining operations to eight or nine months per year.

At the mine site, Norris is assembling a jig plant that will be used to process stockpiled low grade material accumulated during the selective mining of the high grade pits.

The two low grade pits now being mined are located on a hill, with one orebody 100-150 ft thick dipping toward the valley at about 65° along a strike length of 1,000 ft. A second, parallel orebody is located over the crest of the hill. The first of these orebodies is being extracted by benching into the hillside. Scrapers remove overburden and deposit it at the edge of the mined area, to be bulldozed over the hillside. The most recent bench taken was 20 ft high, with a 40- to 50-ft-high highwall at the back of the bench. A down-the-hole rotary drill is used for drilling blastholes, and front-end loaders load the ore haulers. Conventional highway-type rigs, each pulling two belly-dump trailers for a total load of 80 tons, transport ore to the plant at Dunphy.

At the plant, crude ore is crushed through a jaw crusher and a cone crusher. Material to be processed through the plant's 10-cell flotation circuit is ground through a 5-ft-dia x 10-ft ball mill. Flotation concentrate is dewatered by a disc filter and dried in a 5-ft-dia x 40-ft-long rotary dryer.

A Raymond mill reduces the flotation product and some direct grinding ores to 93% minus 325 mesh. Baroid operations superintendent, Terral G. Young, cites low power consumption and low media consumption as the motivating factors for use of Raymond mills in the final grinding of barite.

Baroid Petroleum Services, which produced 80,000 tons at the Rossi mine in 1976, sends its Nevada production to customers in the intermountain, West Coast, and Alaskan markets.

Dresser's Greystone mine is top US producer

The Dresser Minerals Div. of Dresser Industries Inc. moves about 1 million tpy of waste to produce 250,000 tpy of barite at its Greystone mine south of Battle Mountain—the largest single barite mine in the US and one of the largest in the world. About 60% of the Greystone's output is high grade, direct-grinding ore that is hauled by a contractor 36 mi to Dresser's grinding plant at Battle Mountain. Some of the high grade ore is shipped for final size reduction to Dresser grinding plants in Galveston and Brownsville, Tex., and New Orleans and Westlake, La.

The remainder of Greystone output is beneficiated at a jig plant at the mine site. This ore, which grades about 60% barite, is dumped to a trommel and crushed through primary and secondary crushers before advancing to the plant's four three-cell Bendelari jigs. Power for the plant is provided by diesel-powered generators.

The Greystone ores occur between two slices of a thrust fault zone in difficult terrain. Bulldozers equipped with rippers break down both overburden and ore, which are loaded into trucks by front-end loaders. Consideration is being given to adding scrapers for moving overburden. Blasting, which dilutes high grade materials, is not done.

Production at the Greystone mine during most of the past 20 years has depended primarily on locating and following high grade ore zones. Dresser now plans additional rotary drilling on the property to gain better information on the overall configuration of the orebody, as a basis for pit planning.

Greystone ore is currently extracted from five or six mine faces, none of which is more than a 1-mi haul from the jig plant. Mining equipment includes six Caterpillar D8 dozers, one 988 and three 966 front-end loaders, and one 30-ton-capacity and five 35-ton-capacity Wabco rear-dump trucks. □

General Index

Accidents
    MESA Health and Safety Analysis Center 220
    truck visibility 220
Acid handling 114
Adhesives, anaerobic technology 244–247
Aerial cameras 25
Aero service 63–65
Aeromagnetic studies 44–45
African bauxite 336–346
Agrico Chemical Co. 385
Aguas Claras Mine 328
AIPG 11
Air compressor capacity 209
Air density 210
Air filtration equipment 210
Air pollution 437
Airborne AFMAG 53
Airborne EM 53
Airtrace 48
AISC structure code 206
Alaska Mineral Resource Assessment Program 23
Alcan 370
Alcoa 184
Alcoa Minerals of Jamaica 371
Algoma Steel Corp. 318
All-American canal project 227
Allison transmissions 217
Alpha Nuclear Corp. 57
Altitude, effect on equipment 207
Alumina Partners of Jamaica (ALPART) 369
Amax, Inc. 126
Amazon 65
Amazon basin 62–65
American Welding Society 206
Anaconda Co. 2, 369
Anaerobic adhesives 244–247
Ancient stream channels 49
Annual cash flow 90
Anomalous leads 42
Ansul Co. 264, 265
Aquifer recharging 390
Arizona copper mining 272–286
Artificial stabilization 98
Asarco 282
A-S-H Pump (Envirotech Corp.) 258
ASHRAE 208
Atlantic Richfield Co. 406
Atlas Copco 142
Atomic absorption spectro-photometer 42
Atomic oxidation 167
Aznalcollar mine 6, 290–292

Banka drill 416
Barite 444–445
Barringer 54
Barringer Research 52
Bauxite, world's largest mine 339
Bauxite mining 336–380
Beach mining 427–433
Bearing maintenance 244–247
Beattie-Bridgman equation 162
Bechtel Corp. 215

Belt conveyors
    drive with feedback circuit 213–214
    in pit 221
Bench design 104
Benedict-Webb-Rubin equation 162
Berkeley Pit 2, 205, 287–289
NV Billiton Maatschappij 347
Bingham Canyon mine 2, 268
Biogeochemistry 47–48
Blasthole bit costs 139
Blasting 338
    charge depth vs. charge weight 189
    crater blasting 190
    flyrock control 187–192
Bone Valley Formation 382
Borden Chemicals 387
Borehole core 94
Boulder problems, dredging 197
Boulder rake 197
Boulder size 192
Box cut 429
Brazil 439
    project Radam 62–65
Brazilian bauxite 374–376
Brazilian exploration 66, 68–72
Brazilian iron ore 225
Brewster Phosphates 6
Brinell hardness tests 206
Bromine 439
Brown & Root Inc. 294
Bucket wheel excavators 348, 361
Bucket wheels 346, 356
Bu Craa Mine 221
Bucyrus Erie 143, 144, 146, 202–204
Bulk samples 72–74
Business cycles 83
Butler Taconite 313

Cable tramway 120–121
Caland mine 222–224
Caland Ore Co., Ltd. 326–327
Canadian Cordillera 51
Canadian Diamond Drillers Association 20
Canadian exploration 60
Canadian Javelin Ltd. 295
Canisteo mine 321
Cap sensitive explosives 174
Carol Lake 228, 323
Cash flows 89, 90
Cassiar Asbestos Corp. 106
Castle Dome mine 284
Caterpillar Tractor Co. 217
    D10 212
Cerro Colorado mine 294–297
Cities Service Co. 230, 284
Clam-drill system 79
Clark Equipment Co. 217
Clean Air Act 7
Cleveland-Cliffs Iron Co. 317
Climax mine 126
Climax Molybdenum Co. 259
Coastal Zone Management Act of 1972, 7
Coeur d'Alene 22
Colorado School of Mines 34

Commercial blasting agents 182
Compressed Air and Gas Institute 239
Compression ratio 209
Compressor performance 237
Compressors, ASME Performance Test Codes 239
Computer 76
    economic mine planning 285
    exploration data 284–285
Computers
    Maintenance cost accounting 230
    optimization study 206
    pit diagrams 277–278
Concealed deposits 21
Conrad-Stork system 417
Consolidated Diamond Mines 427
Consortiums 341
Continental Conveyor & Equipment Co. 6
Conveyor belts 6, 257, 334, 359
    intermediate drive 221
Copper
    investment costs 270
    upper Peninsula of Michigan 271
Copper economics 58
Copper mining 268–298
Copper production 268
COREMAP 43
Corrosion resistance 252
Cortez Gold Mines 419
Cost reductions 279–280
Craelius Core Orientor 95
Credit 86–91
Crone Geophysics 52
Current value 83
CRIB 43
Cuajone mine 87
Cummins Engine Co. 217
Cyanoacrylates 246
Cyprus Anvil Mining Corp. 106
Cyprus Pima mine 12, 281

Dam construction 134–135
Dames & Moore 134, 147
K. W. Dart, 218
Data storage and retrieval 43
Debt coverage 90
Deductive reasoning 27
Depreciation 84
Detection and measurement 100
Detroit Diesel 217
Dewatering 431–433
Diamond core heads 146
Diamond deposits 418
Diamond mining 427–433
Dieterici equation 162
Digital recording 56
Direct shear test machine 96
Discontinuity shear strength 94
Discounted cash flow 82
Dominican Republic bauxite 378–379
Dorr-Oliver 215
Dragline cycles 205
Dragline stripping 349, 376
Draglines 7, 204–206, 383, 388

boom design 205–206
dumping radius 205
Dredges 222, 393–394
   bucket-line 196
   bucket-wheel 199
   continuous dragline concept 201
   cutterhead 198
   design 194–201
   new designs 194–201
   twin system 198
   world's largest 197
Dredging
   digging depth 196
   minerals recovered 195
Dresser Minerals Div. 8, 445
Drilling
   borehole inclinations measurement 148
   air pressure and volume 140
   blasthole 138
   bulk samples 72–74
   bulk sampling 146
   core 146
   diamond 147
   economics 138–140
   ERDA research 149
   large-dia percussion 73
   rock formation 140
   rotary speed 139
   trends 147–148
   weight on bit 139
Drills
   bits 145
   placer exploration 416
   rotary 5, 143–145
   tank-mounted 141
Driverless truck 218
DuPont 258
Dunn Geoscience 10
Dust explosives 186
Dust problems, suppression 266

Eagle Mountain-Kaiser Steel 141
Eagle Mountain 302, 314–315
Eddy currents 52
Effluent guidelines 127
Eisenhower mine 281
Electric shovels 6, 202–206
   breakout force 204
   cold weather options 204
   'Electrotorque' 202
   environmental factors 204
   'Magnetorque' 202
   overburden removal 211
   Ward-Leonard drive 204
Electric wheel 218–219
Electrochemical action 115
Electromagnetics 52
Ellicott Machine Corp. 199
Elliot Geophysical Co. 44
Emissions control 289
Empire mine 320
Endangered Species Act of 1973, 7
Energy Supply and Environmental Co-ordination Act of 1974, 7
Engineering 107–109
Environment 390
   impact of expenditures 268
   regulations 7

waste handling 126
Environmental legislation 7
Environmental monitoring 399
Environmental Protection Agency (EPA) 127, 133
Equipment availability 231
Equipment evolution 5
ERDA 145
Erie Mining Co. 311
EROS Data Center 26–28, 39
Euclid Inc. 217
Europe's largest open pit, Aznalcollar 290
Excavators
   derating factors 207
   efficiency in high altitudes 207–211
   ventilating systems 208
Exploration
   bulk samples 72–74
   bulk sampling 78
   nuclear logging system 75–77
Exploration methods 18–20
Exploratory boreholes 96
Explosives 152–186
   aluminum additives 184–186
   AN properties 174
   charts of 176–181
   chemical groups 153
   chemistry & physics 157–166
   classification and characteristics 152–156
   classification for shipment 174
   commercial applications 169–171
   density 172
   detonating velocity 156
   dynamite compositions 182
   formulation types 175
   freezing resistance 173
   fume characteristics 173
   mechanics of detonation 167–168
   method of initiation 174
   NCN's metallized dry and slurry 183
   (nitro's) 173
   selection of 172–183
   sensitivity 153–154, 172
   strength 154, 172
   US industry consumption 169
   velocity of detonation 172
   water gels 183
   water resistance 173
Exxon 404

Fan laws 209
Fatalities and injuries 220
Feasibility study 88, 291
Federal Water Pollution Control Act 7
Fire protection 264–265
Fitted parts, adhesives 246
Fives-Lille Cail 221
Florida phosphates 205
Florida phosphate mining 382–392
Fluid handling systems, sealing 245
Fluor Utah Co. 285
Flux-gate magnetometer 44

Fragmentation 338
Frasch sulphur mine 242
Freeport Kaolin 131
Fuller Co. 217
Fume classes of explosives 173

Gamma-ray spectrometry 55
Gardinier Inc. 387
Gardner-Denver 142, 143, 144, 146
Gas Hills uranium 402
Gelatin dynamites 175
General Electric motorized wheel 218
General Railway Signal Co. 228
Generator insulation 209
Genetic links 37
Geobotany 47–48
Geochemical halos (HALOS) 22
Geochemistry 40–42
Geodetic survey of Canada 18, 101
Geology and geophysics 26
Geology
   computer systems 43
   uranium 397
Geologic discontinuities 92
Geology of bauxite 365
Geology of Central Florida phosphates 386
Geophysical Survey systems 52
Georgia Iron Works 384
Geostatistics 43
Geothermal steam 298
Geo-Western 52
Getty Oil Co. 403
Gold Ores 419–426
Goodrich, B. F. 6, 221
Goodyear Aerospace 62–65
Gould, Inc. 119
Government policy 58–61
Grace, W. R. & Co. 387
Gradiometers 45
Gravimeters 44
Great Lakes transport 226–228
Greystone mine 8
Groundwater 95
Guinea, West Africa 339
Guyana bauxite 359–361

Haitian bauxite 377–378
Halos 40
Hanna 310
Harnischfeger (P & H) 202–203
Haul roads 283
Haulage trucks 6
Heap leaching 403, 419–426
Heavy mineral sands 195
Helicopters 53
Hematite ore 316
Hewlett-Packard 123
Hibbing Taconite Co. 4, 307–309
High altitude, defined mining conditions 207
Homestake Mining Co. 133
Hose, selection, use and maintenance 240
Hoyt Lakes taconite 311
Hydraulic crowd 203
Hydrogeochemistry 46–48
Hydrothermal alteration 39

IHC Holland 200
Ilmenite-magnetite ore 322
Impactors 151
Impoundment dams 383
Induced polarization 51
Ingersoll-Rand 141, 142, 144
Injection wells 409
Inland waterways 228
In-pit crushing and conveying 272, 279–280
In-situ leaching 124, 405–414
Inspiration Consolidated Copper Corp. 230, 266
"Intelli-giants" 383
International Harvester 217
International Minerals & Chemical Corp. 387
International Mining Exhibition 142
Iodine 439
Iowa Manufacturing Co. 221
Iron ore 225, 226–228, 300–334
    Brazil 328–334
    chart of North American producers 304–306
    high grade 329
    resources of US 303–304
    structure of US industry 301–302
    Wisconsin's sole mine 321
Iron Ore Co. of Canada 322–324
Iron Springs 315–316

Jackson County Iron 321
Jamaican bauxite 362–73
Jig design 198
Johnson-March Corp. 266
Jones and Laughlin Steel Corp. 144, 317
Joy Manufacturing Co. 143, 145, 151

Kaiser Bauxite Co. 367
Kaiser Engineers 74
Kaiser Steel Corp. 6, 314–315
Kaolin mines, reclamation 130–132
Kelly bar 145
Kennecott Copper Corp.
Kennedy Van Saun 221
Kern 107
Kerr-McGee 434
Kidd Creek 393
Koehring 369
Krupp 221

Labor productivity 7
Lake brines 434–439
Lake Carriers Association 227
Land rehabilitation 367
Land withdrawals 8–9
Landsat 32–39
Laterites 379
Lee Creek 393–394
Le Roi Div., Dresser Industries 145
Lima Div., Clark Equipment 204
Limestone pinnacles 380
Lind-Greenway mines 318
Linden-Alimak AB 142
Limonite-goethite ores 316
Loan postponements 89–90
Loading and dumping time 219
Locktite Corp. 244

Locomotives 227, 228
Long hauls 379
Low-cost dredging 196
Low grade ore 268
Lubrication 235
Lucky Mc 401

Machine specifications 208
MacIntyre-Tahawas 322
Mack Trucks 218
Mackay School of Mines 194
Magmatic segregate deposits 271
Magnafluxing 206
Magnetic filters 132
Magnetometers 44–45
Maintenance 230–266
    adhesives 244–247
    organization 231–232
    preventative 233–235
    rotary compressors 236–239
Maintenance control 286
Maintenance and parts 380
Manitowoc draglines 204
Mapping 66–68
Major Florida phosphate producers 386–387
Marcona pit 185
Marconaflo 201, 222–224
Marine Protection, Research and Sanctuaries Act of 1972, 7
Marion Power Shovel 143, 144, 146, 203–204
Martin Marietta Corp. 33
Materials handling 332–334
Matrix 385
McDermitt mine 442–443
McKinley mine 316–317
Mercury mine 442
Mesabi range 4, 307
Metalog 75–77
Metallogenic relationships 36
Metallurgical sampling 146
Metcalf pit 3, 275–277
Mexico's railway system 228
Milchem Inc. 444
Military use of explosives 170
Minas Gerais 225
Mine car wheels, rebuilding 259
Mine development, Pena Colorada 215
Mine financing 86–91
Mine planning 284–286
Mine vehicles, fire protection 265
Minerals
    discovery rate 18
    distribution 10–11
Minerals exploration, government agencies role 61
Minerals Leasing Act of 1920, 9
Mining Law of 1872, 9
Minntac (USS) 300
Minntac operations 308–309
Mission pit, 12, 281
Mitsui 296
Mobile Drilling 147
Mobil Oil Corp. 387
Monetary erosion 85
Morenci pit 3, 272, 273–275
Morocco's phosphates 382
Motors, high efficiency 119
Mountain States Engineering 280
Multispectral Scanners (MSS) 25

NASTRAN (NASA Structural Analyzer) 206
National taconites 314
National Steel 310
Nationalism 58
Natural radioactivity 55
Nevada 419
Newmont Exploration Co. 54
Nonferrous liners 250
Noise Control Act of 1972, 7
North American iron ore consumption 226
Northwest draglines 204
Nuclear logging system 75–77
Nuclear Regulatory Commission 404

Oakville sandstone 407
Ocean Dumping Act 7
Oil companies 61
Oil-immersed clutches 213
Oil shales 439–441
Oils, spectrographic analysis 233
Open-pits list of major pits throughout the world 12–16
Operating costs 278
Ordinary leads 42
Ore control 398
Ore haulage 216–220
Ores 11
Overall slope angle 94

Pacific Tin Consolidated 198
Page draglines 204
Palo Verde mine 281
Panama 294–297
Pathfinders 41
Parsons-Jurden Co. 285
Pena Colorada 215
Permissibles 171
Perovskite 72
Petrotomics Inc. 403
Phelps Dodge Corp. 3
Phosphate mine cuts 384
Phosphate mining 382–394
    prices 382
    mining history 382
    terminology 385
Piezometer 96
Pima copper district 46
Pinto Valley Mine 230–235, 284–286
Piping slurries 216
Pipelines 131, 228
Pipes, fiber glass insulation 242
Pit crusher 317
Pit design 273–286
Pit dredging 352, 355
Pit operations, copper 273–298
Pit planning, computer use 109
Pit slope design 92–98
Pit slopes
    berm width design 103–106
    failure geometry 103
    monitoring 99–102
Placer Amex 442
Placer deposits 78, 194
Placer mining 194–201, 416–418
Polaris Resources Inc. 78
Polybutylene 216
Polymer 244
Porphyry deposits 270

Port facilities 345
Portable crushers 221
Portable spectrometers 56
Ports 330
Power factor 119, 136, 274
Pregnant solutions 124
Pressure ratio 237
Prestripping 290
Primary dispersion patterns 40
Primary and secondary stripping 357
Production data 4
Production trends 269–270
Project Birddog 28
Prospecting 21–24, 46–48
    Aeromagnetic studies 44
    airborne reconnaissance 52
    Alaska 23
    alphameter 57
    ancient stream channel 49
    biogeochemical guides 22
    Brazilian exploration 66–68, 69–72
    borehole logging 56
    computer use 32–39
    copper 58–61
    electromagnetics (EM) 52
    'Feverish' trees 24
    geochemistry 40–42
    Glossary for remote sensing 29–30
    ground pulse system 54
    hydrogeochemistry 46–48
    induced polarization 51
    minerals exploration costs 60
    oil companies 61
    photogeologic techniques 32–39
    Project Radam-Brazil 62–65
    radiometry 55
    radon exploration 57
    Reconnaissance aircraft 28
    remote sending 25–31
    satellite 32–39
    satellite studies 23
    satellites 25–31
    side-look radar 62
Prospecting and exploration for phosphate rock 386
Proton magnetometers 44
Pumps 384–385
    construction materials 114, 115
    vertical sump pumps 110–118

Queuing time 219

Railroad gradients 274
Railroad haulage 273–275
Railroad mining 340, 337, 369
Railroading 329–330
Railroads 225, 227–228
Ray mines 277–278
Reclamation 130–132, 367, 414
    Brewster's sand-clay technique 384
    Greenwood Reservoir 320
Reed Tool Co. 150
Regional structural analysis 38
Regulatory agencies 390
Reserve's taconites 312–313
Resources Conservation and Recovery Act of 1976, 7
Resource distribution 10
Resource management 11
Resource nationalism 58–61
Return-on-equity 90
Reynolds Haitian Mines 377–378
Reynolds Jamaica Mines Ltd. 372
Rio do Norte ownership 376
Rio Tinto Patino Mines 292–293
Rock discontinuities 94–96
Rock mechanics
    discontinuity shear strength 94
    geologic discontinuities 92
    groundwater effects 95
    monitoring slopes 99–102
    relating slope geometry and failure geometry 105
    pit slope design 92–98
    shear testing 96
Rocky Mountain Energy Co. 396
Rotary table drive 144
Royalty 85
Rubber
    properties 254–255
    vs. metal liners 255
    uses in mining 254–258
Russian drilling technology 149
Rotary compressors 236–239
    troubleshooting guide 238

Sacaton mine 282–289
Safe Drinking Water Act 7
St. Lawrence Seaway 226–228
Samarco 332–334
Sampling 417
San Xavier Mine 281
Sangaredi Mine 5, 336–346
Santiago, Spain 292
Scale model blasts 188
Scaling 99
Schefferville area 322
Scintrex 55
Scintrex MIP 52
Scrapers 7, 368, 442
Scully-Wabush Mines 325
Self-unloading vessels 226–228
Seismic prospecting 169
Selebi-Pikwe mine 87
Seltrust Engineering Ltd. 294
Sept-Iles transport 324
Sequential photographic monitoring 102
Shallow deposits 378
Shovel productivity 275–276
Side-looking airborne radar (SLAR) 25
Sierrita mine 279–280
Single-pass drilling 143
Slimes 383
Slimes disposal 391
Slope design 99–106
Slope failures 92–98
Slope stability
    monitoring 108
    remedial actions 98
Slope stabilization 93
Slurrifier system 352
Slurry pipelines 215, 216
Slurry system 222–224
Slurry transport 132, 348
Smit, J. K. & Sons 147
Smith International, Inc. 147
Smoky Valley Mining 424
Soda Ash 434–438

Sohio Petroleum Co. 50
Solar drying 378
Soils, soft rocks 97
Solid propellants 168
Sonic testing 206
Southwest Africa 427
Spain 290–293
Spectrophotometers 24
Stability analysis 96
Stainless steel 252
Stability data 92–95
Steel Founders Society of America 251
Steep Rock Iron Ore Mines, Ltd. 324
Stockpile reclaiming 227, 228
Stores 286
Straight dynamite 172
Straight-line depreciation 138
Stripping 94, 222–224, 350
Stripping overburden 428
'Superfront' 203
Superphosphate 385
Surface mining
    Europe's largest 6
    tonnages 2
Surinam 347–358
Suriname Aluminum Co. 347
Surveying
    electromagnetic distance measurement (EDM) 101, 102, 107
    extensometers, inclinometers, deflectors 100
    laser alignment 107–108
    theodolites 107
Swedish Detonic Research Foundation 187
Swell factor 106
Swift Agricultural Chemicals Corp. 389
Symposium on Materials for the Mining Industry 248
Synchrotorque Div. of Philadelphia Gear Corp. 213

Tachograph charts 233
Taconites 302–303
Tailings impoundment 133–135
Tailings structures 126
Temperature of explosion 164
Tenke-Fungurume project 87
Terradex Corp. 57
Texas uranium 405
Texasgulf, Inc. 242, 294, 393
Thermal patterns 50
Thermonic channel trace 49–50
Thiele Kaolin 130
Thomas Systems (Tex.) 280
Threaded fasteners, locking 245
Thyristors 202
Tilden mine 318–320
Tire and Rim Assoc. 219
Tires
    maintenance 235
    problem areas 219
    ratings 219
Total drilling cost 140
Toxic Substances Control Act 7
Trend in blasthole diameters 190
Trombetas project 374
Trona 438

Truck engines 217–219
Truck mining 275–283
Trucks 216–220
   design parameters 217
   E/MJ survey results 218
   mechanical device 216, 217
   35-85 ton capacity 216–217
   85-350 ton capacity 217–219
   pros and cons of large size 219
   tire costs 219
Tubular steel boom 203
Twin Buttes mine 221
Twin Disc Inc. 217

Ultrasonic thickness gauges 233
Union Carbide 402
Unit Rig 218
Uranium
   ancient channel search 49
   borehole logging 56
   leaching 124
   mining 396–414
   radiometry system 55
   search 46–48

USBM, economic appraisal of copper industry 269
US Dept. of Transportation 174
US Energy Corp. 404
USGS
   R & D group 21
   Survey report on porphyry coppers 271
US mines (metal), discovery and production rate 19
US Steel 406
USS Agri-Chemicals 389
Utah International 401

Valuation 82–85
Van der Waals equation 162
Variable pitch dipper 203
Volumetric efficiency 237

Wabco 218
Waste haulage 216–224
Waste pile design 128
Water, recycling 133–135
Water diversion 277

Water slurry properties 125
Wear materials 248–253
Wedge failures 103
Weighing system 260
Well shooting 169
Western-Knapp 293
Western Mining Conference of 1976, 127
Westinghouse computer system 109
Westinghouse uranium 413
Wheeling-Pittsburgh 317
Whitney Mine 310
Wild Heerbrugg 108
Wire rope
   fittings 260–262
   slings 263
Wire Rope Producers Committee 262
Wright Engineers 290
Wyoming uranium 400–404

X-ray testing 206

Zeiss 107

Authors Index

Albers, John P. 18
Amaugo, G. O. 128
Asimov, Isaac 382
Basaj, Leonard 236
Caplan, F. 125
Castle, James E. 82
Chender, Michael 58
Chitwood, Byron 138
Claflin, James 244
Crawford, Emmy 413
Day, D. 128
Dayton, Stan 222
Duncan, D. M. 419
Frohling, Edward S. 86
Hildebrand, R. A. 78
Hodgson, D. L. 427
Holmberg, R. 187
Hoppe, Richard 272, 336, 339, 382

Ivy, J. G. 207
Jackson, Dan 230, 396
Ladegaard-Pedersen, A. 187
Larson, William C. 124
Lewis, Milton F. 86
Ludeke, K. L. 128
Lundborg, N. 187
MacRae, Allan M. 99
Manon, J. J. 152, 157, 167, 169, 172
Martin, Dennis C. 103
Mason, Charles N. 184
McCrary, Ernest 225
Montgomery, Wayne C. 184
Nargolwalla, S. S. Dr. 75
Norman, N.E. 138
Parkinson, Gerald 434
Persson, A. 187

Piteau, Douglas R. 103
Seegmiller, Ben L. Dr. 92
Seigel, H. O. Dr. 75
Sence, Leonard H. 110
Sisselman, Robert 21, 32, 307, 393, 442
Smolik, T. J. 419
Stangland, Glenn 136
Thomas, Richard A. 248, 254, 287, 362
Thompson, James V. 72
Tucker, T. C. 128
Turner, William M. 49
Ulatowski, Tomec 86
Wayland, Thomas E. 25
Watson, David L. 72
White, Lane 130, 400, 405, 424, 444

References

The material in this book has been drawn from the following issues of *Engineering and Mining Journal*.

Page Numbers	E/MJ ISSUE
2-9	Jun 1977, 78-84
10-11	Oct 1975, 90-91
12-16	Jun 1977, 85-92
18-20	Jan 1977, 71-73
21-24	Jan 1977, 76-79
25-31	Jul 1976, 67-73
32-39	May 1975, 87-94
40-42	Jun 1976, 126-128
43-45	Jun 1976, 110-112
46-48	Jun 1976, 134-136
49-50	Jul 1976, 86-87
51-55	Jun 1976, 113-116, 118
55-57	Jun 1976, 118, 120, 122
58-61	Aug 1976, 77-80
62-71	Nov 1975, 165-174
72-74	Aug 1977, 80-82
75-77	Aug 1975, 101-103
78-80	Jul 1976, 76-78
82-85	Sep 1977, 138-141
86-91	May 1977, 65-70
92-98	Dec 1976, 53-59
99-102	Sep 1976, 104-107
103-106	Jun 1977, 161-164
107-109	Jun 1976, 188-191
110-118	Oct 1975, 92-100
119	Sep 1975, 132
120-123	Aug 1976, 74-76
123	Aug 1977, 109
124	Sep 1977, 159
125	Oct 1975, 106
126-127	Jun 1976, 236-237
128-129	Feb 1976, 90-91
130-132	Jan 1977, 154-156
133-135	Apr 1977, 83-85
136	May 1975, 127
138-140	Jun 1977, 168-170
141	Sep 1976, 139
142-143	Jul 1976, 88, 90
143-146	Jun 1976, 191-194
147-148	Jun 1976, 108-109
149-150	Jul 1975, 100-101
151	Aug 1977, 112
152-156	Oct 1976, 81-85
157-166	Dec 1976, 60-68
167-168	Jan 1977, 74-75
169-171	Feb 1977, 76-78
172-183	May 1977, 82-93
184-186	Jul 1976, 83-85
187-192	May 1975, 95-100
194-201	Jun 1977, 174-180, 184
202-206	Jun 1976, 195-199
207-210	Apr 1976, 90-93
211	Jan 1976, 126
212	Nov 1977, 208
213-214	Sep 1975, 130-131
215	Nov 1974, 159
216	Apr 1975, 108
216-221	Jun 1976, 199-206
222-224	Aug 1976, 86-88
225	Nov 1975, 128-H1
226-228	Dec 1974, 69-71
230-235	Jun 1977, 113-118
236-239	Aug 1975, 104-107
240-241	Dec 1975, 86-87
242-243	Feb 1977, 80-81
244-247	Apr 1976, 94-97
248-253	Jul 1975, 83-88
254-258	May 1977, 71-75
259	Aug 1977, 105
260	Oct 1976, 94
260-262	Oct 1976, 74-76
263	Nov 1975, 185
264	Jul 1977, 96
265	Dec 1977, 74
266	Aug 1975, 122
268-271	Jun 1976, 70-74
272-283	Jun 1977, 95-106
284-286	Jul 1975, 89-91
287-289	Jul 1977, 107-109
290-293	Jun 1977, 130-133
294-298	Nov 1977, 192-196
300-304	Jun 1976, 76-79, 81
304-306	Nov 1974, 100, 102, 104
307-309	Jun 1977, 122-123, 125-126
310-327	Nov 1974 Issue
	Dec 1974 Issue
328-334	Nov 1975, 120-128
336-338	Jun 1977, 138-140
339-346	Aug 1977, 83-90
347-350	Nov 1977, 75-78
351-358	Nov 1977, 87-96
359-361	Nov 1977, 71-74
	Jul 1976, 89
362-366	Nov 1977, 98-102
367-370	Nov 1977, 111-116
371	Nov 1977, 120-121
372-373	Nov 1977, 118-119
374-376	Nov 1975, 153-155
377-380	Nov 1977, 138-142
382-392	May 1976, 80-89
393-394	Sep 1976, 94-95
396-399	Oct 1977, 77-80
400-404	Dec 1975, 61-64, 67-68
405-413	Jul 1975, 73-81
413-414	Jul 1975, 81
	Jun 1977, 23
416-418	Feb 1977, 73-75
419-423	Jul 1977, 65-69
424-426	Jul 1977, 70-72
427-433	Jun 1977, 145-151
434-438	Oct 1977, 71-75
439	Jul 1975, 167
439-441	Nov 1975, 158-160
442-443	Dec 1975, 72-73
444-445	Jun 1977, 157-158